P9-EJJ-821

PORTLAND OR.

# THE JEWISH RELIGION

*For my grandson*
*Abraham Peter Jacobs*

# The
# Jewish Religion

## A COMPANION

Louis Jacobs

OXFORD UNIVERSITY PRESS

1995

Oxford University Press, Walton Street, Oxford OX2 6DP

Oxford   New York
Athens   Auckland   Bangkok   Bombay
Calcutta   Cape Town   Dar es Salaam   Delhi
Florence   Hong Kong   Istanbul   Karachi
Kuala Lumpur   Madras   Madrid   Melbourne
Mexico City   Nairobi   Paris   Singapore
Taipei   Tokyo   Toronto
and associated companies in
Berlin   Ibadan

Oxford is a trade mark of Oxford University Press

Published in the United States
by Oxford University Press Inc., New York

© Louis Jacobs 1995

All rights reserved. No part of this publication may be reproduced,
stored in a retrieval system, or transmitted, in any form or by any means,
without the prior permission in writing of Oxford University Press.
Within the UK, exceptions are allowed in respect of any fair dealing for the
purpose of research or private study, or criticism or review, as permitted
under the Copyright, Designs and Patents Act, 1988, or in the case of
reprographic reproduction in accordance with the terms of the licences
issued by the Copyright Licensing Agency. Enquiries concerning
reproduction outside these terms and in other countries should be
sent to the Rights Department, Oxford University Press,
at the address above

This book is sold subject to the condition that it shall not, by way
of trade or otherwise, be lent, re-sold, hired out or otherwise circulated
without the publisher's prior consent in any form of binding or cover
other than that in which it is published and without a similar condition
including this condition being imposed on the subsequent purchaser

British Library Cataloguing in Publication Data
Data available

Library of Congress Cataloging in Publication Data
The Jewish religion : a companion / Louis Jacobs.
Includes bibliographical references and index.
1. Judaism—Dictionaries.   2. Judaism—Essence, genius, nature.
I. Title.
   BM50.J28   1995   296'.03—dc20   95–3203
ISBN 0–19–826463–1

1 3 5 7 9 10 8 6 4 2

Typeset by Graphicraft Typesetters Ltd., Hong Kong
Printed in Great Britain
on acid-free paper by
The Bath Press, Bath

# Contents

# Introduction

The chief aim of this book is to help readers, Jewish and non-Jewish, to grasp more fully ideas and terms they encounter in works on the Jewish religion; hence the main Jewish beliefs, practices, and personalities are presented in dictionary form. Obviously, in a work of this kind, the selection of the topics to be examined depends on what the compiler considers to be most essential, an assessment that will not necessarily commend itself to all readers, some of whom may object to the inclusion of matters they consider to be of only peripheral interest and to the omission of those they feel to be significant. For all that, it is hoped that the book does succeed in elucidating the majority of Jewish religious concepts which the average reader is likely to come across in his or her reading. (This expression, a sop to political correctness, will be used only very sparingly. 'His', without the addition of 'or hers', is used in neither an exclusive nor a patronizing attitude towards women, but simply in order to avoid awkward circumlocution.) The numerous cross-references, marked by*, will be of help in pursuing particular topics through the book. Brief bibliographies are supplied at the end of each article except where either no special work is available on the subject in English or where the subject is adequately covered by articles in the standard encyclopaedias and other works of reference, a list of which is found at the end of the book. The bibliographies appended to the articles are chiefly provided for further reading and discussion and do not always express the same viewpoint as that presented in the article itself. An apology is perhaps necessary for referring to my own writings in the bibliographies and for using them as the basis for many of the articles. It seemed pointless to refrain from using my own work where relevant but the material in my other books has not simply been copied as it stands; it has been revised both to fit in with the scheme of this book and to enable me to rethink my views on occasion. Painful though it is for an author to admit his mistakes, the Talmudic Rabbis, referred to frequently in this book, praise acknowledgement of errors in the quest for truth.

Biblical quotations are either from the Authorized Version (AV) or from the Jewish Publication Society of America's translation (JPS) in modern English, The AV is used especially for verses familiar to the English reader, for example in Psalm 90: 10: 'The days of our years are threescore years and ten; and if by reason of strength they be fourscore years' (AV) rather than the banal: 'The span of our life is seventy years, or given the strength, eighty years' (JPS). But where the JPS is more accurate, this version is quoted. Where the context requires it, for example in Rabbinic understanding of a biblical verse, I have supplied a translation which differs from both the AV and the JPS. Hebrew and Aramaic expressions are given in transliteration but always translated into English. It has become conventional among Jewish authors, when referring to dates, to avoid the terms BC and AD with their Christian connotations, and to use, instead, as is done in this book, the terms BCE ('Before the Common Era') and CE ('the Common Era').

The book covers only the religious aspects of Judaism; the cultural aspects are considered only in their relation to the religious, although the two are really so interlinked that any attempt to separate them too categorically will certainly result in distortion. Each article in the book can stand as a unit on its own for purposes of reference or simply for browsing, but to tie everything together a brief account must now be given of the Jewish religion and the manner in which it is followed today.

## The Jewish Religion

The Jewish religion or Judaism, as it has been called from Hellenistic times, differs from its 'daughter religions', Christianity and Islam, in that it is centred on a people, the Jews, of whom, at the end of the twentieth century, there are around twelve million (no exact figures are available), residing mainly in the USA and Canada, the State of Israel, the former Soviet Union, South Africa, Australia and New Zealand, Great Britain and Ireland, France, and other European countries. The three basic concepts in Judaism, as formulated by the later Jewish mystics, are: God, the Torah, and Israel. Israel in this context refers to the Jewish people, known as the children of Israel, after the name given to the patriarch Jacob, as told in the biblical book of Genesis. (The name Israel for the State of Israel has, of course, a different connotation and was coined only when the State was established.) The Torah ('Teaching') is conceived of as God's revelation to the people of Israel. The name Torah applied in the first instance to the laws and teachings given to Moses on Mount Sinai but also embraces all the subsequent teachings of Judaism in which the original Torah receives its application. The latter is known as the Oral Torah because it originated in the laws and teachings believed to have been imparted to Moses 'verbally' and then elaborated on by the Jewish sages; the Talmudic literature is the great depository of the Oral Torah. Like the Talmudic sages, post-Talmudic authorities developed the teachings further, each in accordance with his own temperament and social background, while preserving the essential unity of the whole. The Torah, in its wider meaning, thus embraces the whole of authentic Jewish doctrine, both that which is seen as implied in the Pentateuch, the five books of Moses, and that which was added throughout the ages by way of commentary, elaboration, and application of the original doctrines. The Torah, for all the reverence in which it is treated, is never an object of worship in Judaism, but it is through the Torah that God conveys His will to the Jewish people, and through them to the whole of mankind. This, at any rate, is the traditional picture according to which human beings are passive recipients of the divine will as conveyed in the Torah, even though they do have a role to play in interpreting the Torah. Modern scholarship, biblical and post-biblical, has, however, succeeded in demonstrating, to the satisfaction of many contemporary Jews, that the static, traditional account has to yield to the notion of historical development, that the Torah did not simply drop down from heaven but is the result of the divine–human encounter through the ages. Yet modernists among Jews, though they accept that the traditional picture requires a considerable degree of revision in the light of critical research, still largely maintain that the tradition retains its force, since in its essentials the truth by which Jews are expected to live remains unaffected. Whether, for example, monotheism erupted spontaneously in ancient Israel, or whether, as many scholars have argued, a gradual development can be discerned from polytheism through henotheism to pure monotheism, does not obscure the fact that monotheism did eventually emerge as the fundamental idea upon which Judaism rests.

The same applies to the two other concepts, Jewish peoplehood in its special providential role, and the Torah as the revelation of God's will. It is certain that long before the Christian era these major themes had assumed a definite form which they have retained ever since. Judaism affirms that God, the Creator of the world and all that is in it, has chosen the Jewish people to live according to His will as revealed through the Torah and eventually to lead all men to His service.

## Judaism and Modernity

There is much truth in the observation by the pioneering historian, Leopold Zunz, that the Jewish Middle Ages lasted until the end of the eighteenth century, in that the currents of thought and life which followed the Renaissance and shattered the medieval picture largely passed by the Jews. Confined in the ghetto, European Jewry, constituting by far the largest segment of Jewry at the time, cultivated its own traditional way of life until the Western world and its culture was opened to Jews after the French Revolution and the subsequent Jewish Emancipation. Yet already in the second half of the eighteenth century, the Haskalah ('Enlighten-ment') movement had as its aim certainly not the disavowal of traditional Judaism but the encouragement of the new science and learning among the Jews, of an openness to Western ideas and norms that might result in a rationalist approach to the tradition, and a general widening of Jewish horizons. The Haskalah did not necessarily imply that Jewish observance should be abandoned. Many of its adherents, the Maskilim, were totally observant in their private lives. Nevertheless, the traditionalists were bitterly opposed to the Haskalah, fighting it with every means at their disposal. And the Maskilim were not content with the introduction of the new learning into the Jewish schools. The traditional method of Torah study, with its complete emphasis on the Talmud and the Codes of Jewish law and without any systematic approach to education, also came under attack. The Maskilim urged a return to the study of the Bible in its plain meaning, unencumbered, as they saw the ideal, by the older type of Rabbinic exegesis.

The Haskalah paved the way for the emergence of the Reform movement in early nineteenth-century Germany, a movement that posed the severest threat to the traditional way of Jewish life. It was in Germany, in the first instance, that the Jew who had recently emerged from the ghetto to take his place in Western society experienced the tension between the traditional way of life and the allure of the new ways. Some of the more intellectual and wealthy Jews were so enamoured of German culture that they cast off entirely what they considered to be the fetters of tradition, to become completely assimilated even to the extent of converting to Christianity. Early Reform in Germany was not a negative movement. On the contrary, it had the positive aim of stemming the tide of apostasy, declaring that Judaism still had the power of its truth to hold its adherents, if only some of the Jewish institutions were recast and the religion reformed so as to make less marked the differences between the Jew and his Gentile neighbours.

At first, the Reformers introduced comparatively minor changes in the liturgy. They removed some of the less inspiring prayers from the Prayer Book; introduced some new hymns in German; brought in an organ accompaniment to the prayers; and inculcated a greater sense of decorum in the Western style. Sermons in the vernacular were also introduced. The most far-reaching of the early reforms was the abolition of prayers for the restoration of the sacrificial system and for the return of the Jews to their ancient homeland, thus involving a complete reinterpretation of the Messianic hope. The supernatural elements in Messianism were disregarded, as were the more pronounced particularistic elements in the traditional faith. The Messianic vision, to which they were faithful, meant for the Reformers the emergence of a better world in which liberal ideals would triumph. The prophetic theme that Israel would become a light to the nations was understood by the Reformers not to refer to a Jewish people in the Holy Land, spreading from there the truth about God and His relationship to man, but rather to the mission of Israel among the nations of Western Europe who had themselves been influenced, through Christianity, by the Jewish values of peace, justice, and freedom. The Reformers understood Judaism as 'ethical monotheism', with its institutions not as divine laws but as human means of furthering this ideal until it became the religion of all mankind. From this viewpoint there followed the idea that the dietary laws, for example, had played an important role in assuring Jewish survival in the past but could now be a hindrance in that they frustrated social relations between Jews and Gentiles.

The polemics between the Orthodox, as the traditionalists came to be called, and the Reformers were fierce. The Orthodox treated Reform as rank heresy, as no more than a religion of convenience which, if followed, would lead Jews altogether out of Judaism. The Reformers retorted that, on the contrary, the danger to Jewish survival was occasioned by the Orthodox who, through their obscurantism, failed to see that the new challenges facing Judaism had to be faced consciously in the present as Judaism had faced, albeit unconsciously, similar challenges in the past. From Germany the Reform movement spread, becoming particularly active in the New World, where the most influential American Jews, led by German Reform Rabbis, adopted Reform wholeheartedly. Since World War II, however, in many Reform circles, a greater awareness of traditional values has become evident. Some Reform Rabbis have argued for a greater appreciation of the legal side of Judaism, the Halakhah, which, they maintain, possesses its own wisdom and insights.

The reaction to Reform by the Orthodox took two different forms. In the first, the Orthodox denied that the West had anything of real value to teach the Jews. Only in external matters of little ultimate consequence was the Jew obliged to conform to Western mores. Spiritual needs could be catered for entirely adequately by the rich tradition Jews had inherited. The Hasidic movement, which arose in Eastern Europe in the eighteenth century, went its own way, in any event, concerned solely with the joy of drawing nearer to God. The Mitnaggedim, the traditionalist opponents of Hasidism, also pursued their own path, establishing Yeshivot, schools of Talmudic learning, into which were introduced the ideals of the highly individualistic, moralistic Musar movement with its stress on self-improvement as the goal of Jewish life.

A different response to Reform was that of neo-Orthodoxy, founded by Samson Raphael Hirsch of Frankfurt (1808–88). Hirsch advocated total loyalty to the Torah in its traditional formulation, but recognized that the Jew can gain much from an appreciation of the values of Western civilization. For neo-Orthodoxy there was no need for the believing Jew either to opt out of Western culture, as the other traditionalists advocated, or to surrender any of the practices of the Torah, which, for neo-Orthodoxy, are divinely ordained and hence immutable. The neo-Orthodox were to be found occupying positions in the highest echelons of Western society—as university professors, physicians, bankers, artists, writers, musicians, scientists, and businessmen, no different in dress and in many of their ideas from their Gentile friends and neighbours yet staunchly and proudly adhering to the Orthodox way of life in all its details.

The emergence of Nazism in Germany and the Holocaust which followed led many of the erstwhile followers of Hirsch to become thoroughly disillusioned with the master's high regard for German culture. A significant number began to argue that Hirsch did not advocate neo-Orthodoxy as in any way an ideal but only as a means of halting the drift towards assimilation and Reform, in which, they claimed, it was in any event unsuccessful. Consequently, many of them preferred to embrace Hasidism or to enter the Yeshivah world with its basic indifference to the modern world and its values. The movement known as Modern Orthodoxy, however, in the USA, has an ideal not very different from that of Hirsch's neo-Orthodoxy.

A third religious movement, Conservative Judaism—particularly strong in the USA but with adherents in other parts of the world (in Israel and in England this form is known as the Masorti ('Traditional') movement)—seeks a balance between Orthodoxy and Reform, taking issue with Orthodoxy in its theory and with Reform in its practice. Conservative Judaism affirms the validity of the traditional observances, accepting the authority of the Halakhah, yet more open to change than Orthodoxy. Conservative Judaism maintains that historical investigation has exposed the inadequacies of Orthodox theory. The Torah, on this view, has now to be seen not as a single entity revealed by God at one time in its entirety, but as the product of the historical experiences of the Jewish people over the ages in their long quest for God. In the Conservative view, Jewish observances are binding on the Jew because they are the means by which he gives expression to his religious life. Divine inspiration is seen in a dynamic way; a human element is always present to understand and co-operate with the divine. On this view God did not only give the Torah *to* Israel but *through* Israel. Accordingly, the devout Jew can allow himself to be completely open on the question of origins; this is a matter of scholarship, not of faith. But it is not origins which matter for religion. What matters is the development of ideas and institutions so as to serve the Jewish quest for God. For instance, the Conservative Jew is not disturbed at the suggestion that the dietary laws may have had their origin in primitive taboos, nor that the Sabbath may have originated in ancient Babylon. The fact is that the dietary laws and the Sabbath have become powerful vehicles for Jewish survival and for the holy living that is the aim of such survival. An offshoot of Conservative Judaism in the USA is Reconstructionism which, as its name implies, seeks to structure afresh Jewish life so as to embrace other aspects of Judaism as well as the religious. In the expression of its founder, Mordecai Kaplan, Judaism is not only a religion but a religious civilization. Reconstructionism generally has a naturalistic view of religion itself in which God is not a Person but the 'power that makes for salvation'.

If, as mentioned earlier, Judaism is thought of as a triad, consisting of God, Torah, and Israel, then it can be said that contemporary Reform places the emphasis on God, Orthodoxy on the Torah, and Conservative Judaism on peoplehood, though all three movements affirm all three and it is largely a question of where the emphasis is to be placed.

Modern Zionism, as a secular, political movement, naturally places the emphasis on Jewish peoplehood. The Zionist movement has definite implications for the Jewish religion in its awareness of the tension between Judaism as a religion and Judaism as nationalism. In the early days of the movement it was opposed by many of the Orthodox both because of its interpretation of Judaism in nationalist terms and because it seemed to compromise the Messianic hope, traditionally seen as a matter of direct divine intervention rather than of human endeavour to secure the return of the Jews to Palestine by political means. Nevertheless, the Orthodox movement of Mizrachi believed in the possibility of a religious form of Zionism, with its slogan: 'The Land of Israel for the People of Israel in accordance with the Torah of Israel.'

The Reformers were also in opposition to Zionism because this movement seemed to be incompatible with the Reform idea of the mission of Israel among the nations, according to which the Jews in the Diaspora were not in 'exile' but fulfilling a divine purpose. On the other hand, some Reformers argued that for Reform to be true to its nature by acknowledging change in response to changing circumstances, a revision of the mission of Israel idea was called for in which a Jewish State would be the best means of fostering, in the language of the prophet, the Torah that would go out from Zion and the word of the Lord from Jerusalem. Precisely because Conservative Judaism stresses the idea of peoplehood, this movement has never had difficulties with Zionism and embraces it without reservation.

The depletion in the number of Jews world-wide during World War II and the establishment of the State of Israel made many of the debates about Zionism academic. Few contemporary Jews, whether Orthodox or Reform, see the emergence of the State of Israel in anything other than the most positive terms. Jewish thinkers are far from unanimous, however, on whether the establishment, after two thousand years, of a Jewish State demands a rethinking of the role of peoplehood in Judaism. Perhaps the dominant tendency is to see the State of Israel as a centre for Jews and Judaism without rejecting the role Diaspora Jews have to play both in supporting Israel and in their understanding and furtherance of Judaism in the world at large. From time to time the spectre of dual loyalties raises its head, but here, too, it has become generally accepted that Jews, as citizens of their own countries, can help and support the State of Israel without having their loyalties impugned, since even if there are dual loyalties they are not conflicting ones.

Jews are also divided into the two groups of Sephardim (whose ancestors came from Spain and the oriental lands) and Ashkenazim (Jews whose ancestors came from Germany and Poland). But the differences between the two groups are in no way doctrinal; they are based chiefly on different customs and authorities followed in the two centres in former times. There are very few instances of Ashkenazi Jews crossing the divide to become, as it were, honorary Sephardim. But many Sephardi Jews have studied in the Lithuanian-type Ashkenazi Yeshivot and, while not forsaking their own customs, have adopted many of the Ashkenazi ways, studying the Torah in Yiddish, for example. Sephardim are not known for becoming Hasidim but there is no doubt that some have been influenced by Hasidic teachings and treat the Hasidic books as sacred literature. A few practising Kabbalists are still to be found, especially among the Sephardim. The theoretical study of the Kabbalah, however, is engaged in by both Sephardi and Ashkenazi Jews. It is doubtful, though, whether one can speak of actual circles of Kabbalists on the contemporary scene on the lines of those that existed in the past. A fairly recent phenomenon is the emergence of the Baaley Teshuvah ('Returners'), young men and women of non-Orthodox background who have resolved to adopt the strictly Orthodox way of life. Special Yeshivot exist for these 'Returners' and a good deal of literature has been produced to cater to their special needs. Naturally, there are to be found on the contemporary Jewish scene secularist Jews who are indifferent to the question of religious belief. Yet there are only a few professed atheists among Jews and here and there are to be found advocates of a secular form of Judaism in which some of the observances are kept not for the religious beliefs they were intended to foster but as beautiful ceremonies which link the unbeliever to his people. Finally, it should be noted that a Jewish feminist movement has come to the fore, demanding a rethinking of some hitherto male-dominated attitudes.

The above is no more than a brief sketch of what is happening in the Jewish religious world, Each of the themes mentioned in it receives closer attention in the book itself. There may be some small degree of repetition here, but this introduction has been necessary so that the reader will be able to see both the wood and the trees.

## *The Question of Objectivity*

Works on religion are of two kinds: those which advocate that a particular religion or religious outlook be followed, and academic treatises, such as the encyclopaedias of religion, the authors of which need not be followers at all of the religion they describe. This book belongs in neither category or, possibly, in both. I have tried to be objective, referring to all the points of view among Jews on matters that are the subject of controversy. At the same time, I owe it to the reader to state from the outset that I am committed to a particular view of the Jewish religion and cannot pretend to be entirely dispassionate in surveying religious attitudes different from my own. For what it is worth and to declare my bias, I share the view described above as Conservative/Masorti, namely, that in which the human element discernible in the revelation of the Torah cannot be ignored, although this does not affect loyalty to Jewish practices and observances. Some German Jews, as in the Breslau School, used to refer to such an attitude as Orthopraxy, that is, Orthodox in practice but non-fundamentalist in theory. Nevertheless I have striven for objectivity while fully aware, (and the reader should be aware) that my bias may intrude on occasion. In this sense the writing of the book has involved a kind of balancing-act between what I hope is scholarly objectivity and personal commitment. In the saying attributed either to the Hasidic master, Nahman of Bratslav, or to one of teachers belonging to the Musar school: 'The world is a narrow bridge and the main thing is to cross it without any fear at all.' I have approached the compiling of the book with a strong degree of trepidation. The crossing of this particular narrow bridge has not been made without fear but I have tried to cross it notwithstanding; whether or not I have done so successfully is for the reader to decide.

# The Jewish Religion

A COMPANION

**Aaron** Brother of Moses; Aaron together with his sister *Miriam, features in the Bible among the three leaders of the Israelites from Egyptian bondage: 'For I brought thee up out of the land of Egypt, and redeemed thee out of the house of servants; and I sent before thee Moses, Aaron, and Miriam' (Micah 6: 4). Aaron and his sons were consecrated to be the *priests in the sanctuary (Leviticus 9). On the basis of this and other biblical passages, the descendants of Aaron are held to be the priestly cast, although there has been much discussion among modern scholars on the actual historical development of the Aaronic priesthood. In the Rabbinic tradition, Aaron's role in the making of the *golden calf is played down and he becomes the prototype of the peace-loving, not to say compromising, leader, unlike Moses, the stern, uncompromising lawgiver. In an ancient Rabbinic homily it is noted that when Aaron died, *'all the house of Israel'* mourned for him (Numbers 20: 29), whereas when Moses died it is said only that the children of Israel (not *all*) wept for him (Deuteronomy 34: 8). The advice given to the Jewish teacher in Ethics of the Fathers (1. 12) is: 'Be of the disciples of Aaron, loving peace and pursuing peace, loving all people and bringing them near to the Torah.'

**Abba** Aramaic equivalent of the Hebrew *Av* ('Father') with Imma (Hebrew *Em*) for 'Mother'. There is thus no support for the view that these are terms of endearment like 'Daddy' and 'Mummy' and that Jesus was using Abba in this sense (Mark 14: 36). In modern Hebrew these two are the usual forms of address to parents. In Jewish literature Abba is sometimes used as a title: 'Abba Benjamin', 'Father Benjamin', and it is also found as a personal name, Rabbi Abba. The term is also used frequently as referring to God. Since the letters of Abba are the first two letters of the alphabet, it was the custom in medieval Germany for the

beadle, who went round the houses in the early morning to summon people to the synagogue, to knock on the door of the house with his stick once, twice, and once again, as if to say: 'Rise up to the worship of Abba', (the Father in heaven). According to the Kabbalistic doctrine of the *Sefirot, both Abba and Imma represent processes in the divine unfolding; the former is equivalent to the divine Wisdom, the latter to the divine Understanding.

**Abbaye and Rava** Two fourth-century Babylonian teachers whose debates in matters of Jewish law appear frequently in the Babylonian Talmud; so much so that from the Middle Ages the term 'the debates of Abbaye and Rava' was used as a synonym for Talmudic dialectics as a whole. In the early thirteenth century, when David *Kimhi was criticized for neglecting his study of the Talmud in his preoccupation with philosophy, he retorted that he did not allow a day to pass without engaging in 'the debates of Abbaye and Rava'. For Maimonides (*Mishneh Torah*, 4. 13) 'the debates of Abbaye and Rava' represent the study of that which is forbidden and that which is permitted and of the other practical laws of Judaism, which constitute the 'bread and wine' of the meal that is offered the student; they are the prior but essential elements in a sound Jewish education before the higher (for Maimonides) study of Jewish philosophy can be undertaken.

**Abortion** There is no actual prohibition in the Bible against aborting a foetus. In the only biblical reference (Exodus 21: 22) it is implied that if a man strikes a pregnant woman and brings about the destruction of the child she is carrying, he has to compensate her husband financially. Nevertheless, in the unanimously accepted Jewish consensus, abortion is a very serious offence, though foeticide is not treated as homicide. Consequently, the Mishnah (*Oholot* 7: 6) rules that if a woman's life is endangered by the child she is carrying, it is permitted to abort the foetus in order to save her life. But once the greater part of the child has emerged from the womb, to destroy it would be an act of murder and it is not permitted to murder one human being in order to save another human being. Arguments against abortion, such as the ensoulment of the foetus or that the foetus has potential life or, in favour of abortion, that a woman has a right to do what she wishes with her own body, are not found in the classical Jewish sources in which the question is discussed, where the basic distinction is between the destruction of a 'life' (a person) and that which is not a 'life'. All the authorities agree that an abortion may be carried out only for the weightiest of reasons, though they differ on what would be considered to be a 'weighty' reason. Many would permit it where when the birth of the child might endanger the mother's sanity. Many would also permit it if, in the doctor's opinion, the child, if allowed to be born, would be seriously deformed or an imbecile. Some would permit it where the pregnancy is the result of rape, especially the rape of a married woman by a man other than her husband. None permit an abortion, as a means of *birth-control, for economic reasons, or where the child is simply unwanted. Thus traditional Jewish attitudes to abortion are stricter than those obtaining in many contemporary societies but less strict than in Catholicism.

David M. Feldman; *Marital Relations, Birth Control and Abortion in Jewish Law* (New York, 1974).

**Abraham**  First of the three *patriarchs of the Jewish people, father of *Isaac and grandfather of *Jacob. The story of Abraham is told in the book of Genesis (11: 27–25: 18) Critical scholarship sees in this account a welding-together of different traditions, and the migrations of Abraham as a later attempt at mirroring the journeys of the children of Israel towards the land of Israel in order to provide a theological scheme in which later events are anticipated through the divine promise to Abraham and his seed. The suggestion made by nineteenth-century scholars that Abraham is not an historical figure at all has been abandoned by the majority of contemporary scholars who detect behind the stories and myths a real historical figure living in approximately the eighteenth

century BCE. In the Jewish tradition, Abraham is the father *par excellence* of the Jews and Judaism. The numerous legends that have been woven around Abraham's life from the earliest times were partly intended to depict him as the ideal 'Jew'. As H. L. Ginzberg has put it, Abraham is in Judaism a figure akin to John Bull in England or Uncle Sam in the USA. On the basis of the verse: 'In olden times, your forefathers—Terah, father of Abraham and father of Nahor—lived beyond Euphrates and worshipped other gods' (Joshua 24: 2), the Rabbis depicted Abraham as the great iconoclast, destroying his father's idols once he had come unaided to a belief in the true God. God's covenant with Abraham was given its expression in the rite of *circumcision (Genesis 17) The circumcision rite of Jewish male children is called 'entry into the covenant of Abraham our father', and the name of the rite itself is the *berit*, the 'covenant'. But the idea of Abraham as the 'father' of the Jews is not understood only in terms of physical parenthood. Abraham is the spiritual father of all who are converted to Judaism. At the *conversion ceremony, the convert is given a Hebrew name and is called a 'child of Abraham our father'.

As with all prototypes, that of Abraham is made to serve different, even contradictory, ideals. On the one hand he is the probing seeker after truth, the philosopher who calmly discovered God by the application of his reasoning powers even before God addressed him directly when he became, according to Maimonides (*Guide of the Perplexed*, 2. 45), the highest of all the prophets with the exception of Moses. On the other hand, he represents the lovable man (Kierkegaard's 'knight of faith') who trusts his God unquestioningly and follows Him whenever He calls. In the old Jewish tale a man says that he does not want his son necessarily to become a famous scholar or saint but 'a simple Jew like our father Abraham'.

Another of Abraham's traits held up for admiration and emulation is his *hospitality. Abraham sits at the door of his tent ready to welcome weary travellers and provide them with food and drink (Genesis 18: 1–8). The Rabbinic *Midrash imagines Abraham's tent as having openings on all four sides so that anyone seeking help could enter immediately from whichever direction he came. In Eastern Europe, a home famed for its hospitality was called 'a house with Abraham's doors'. To follow

Abraham's magnanimity and humility is the ideal stated in Ethics of the Fathers (5. 19): 'He in whom are these three things is of the disciples of Abraham our father: a good eye and a humble spirit and a lowly soul.' In the same work (5. 3) Abraham is depicted as one who does not retreat from the worship of God no matter how severe the temptation, as when Abraham was tempted in the incident of the binding of Isaac, the *Akedah. 'With ten temptations was Abraham our father tempted, and he stood steadfast in them all, to show how great was the love of Abraham, our father.' For recitation during the daily morning service the *Prayer Book contains the verses (Nehemiah 9: 7–8): 'Thou art the Lord the God, who didst choose Abram, and broughtest him forth out of Ur of the Chaldees, and gavest him the name of Abraham: and foundest his heart faithful before thee.' Curiously enough, none of the Talmudic Rabbis has the name Abraham, perhaps because every Jew has to strive to become an 'Abraham', so that this name was not considered to be suitable for a particular individual. But from the Middle Ages onwards Abraham became a very popular name for Jewish boys.

**Abravanel, Isaac** Don Isaac Abravanel, prominent statesman in Portugal and later in Spain, Jewish philosopher, and biblical exegete, born Lisbon, 1437, died Venice, 1508. Abravanel objected to the attempt by thinkers such as Maimonides to draw up lists of *principles of the faith. These thinkers, he declares, thought of the Torah as a science operating with certain axioms or principles from which everything else can be derived, whereas the God-gven Torah is complete in itself with every detail of its precepts a principle and none more important or more axiomatic than the others. More than any other Jewish biblical exegete, Abravanel was influenced in his commentary to the Bible by his own background and personal experiences. For instance, disillusioned by the oppressive regime in Spain and the comparatively free atmosphere in Venice under the doges, he interprets the biblical statement about the king (Deuteronomy 17: 14–20) not as advocating the monarchy as an ideal system but as a concession to human weakness. The passage concerning the appointment of the king does not mean, he argues, following a Talmudic opinion, that the Israelites were duty-bound to have a king; only

that if they wished to have a king, his powers must be curtailed by the regulations stated in the passage. For the same anti-authoritarian reason Abravanel comments that the sons of Jacob, Moses, and David at first were simple shepherds, an occupation that gave them the opportunity to earn an honest living away from the distractions of urban life. Abravanel claims to have discovered why there is a prohibition against 'seething a kid in its mother's milk' (Exodus 23: 19; Exodus 34: 26; Deuteronomy 14: 21). He sees this prohibition as a protest against idolatrous practices and he remarks in passing that it is the custom in Spain and in England 'to this day' for the shepherds, when they meet together to take counsel with one another, to eat the meat of a goat cooked in the goat's milk, such food being a delicacy. As an extra precaution the Torah forbids, as the Rabbis declare, the cooking of any meat and milk together. In a rationalistic spirit, Abravanel points out that not every prophecy of the biblical *prophets came to pass and he concludes that prophecy should not be understood solely in terms of an accurate foretelling of future events, but rather in the nature of a divine message to contemporaries of the particular prophet. More startling is his contention that occasionally the literary style of Jeremiah and Ezekiel could be less than perfect without this affecting their claim to be true prophets of God; he is thus virtually rejecting the notion of verbal *inspiration.

B. Netanyahu, *Don Isaac Abravanel, Statesman and Philosopher* (Philadelphia, 1968).

**Abudarham, David** Pupil of *Jacob ben Asher, who compiled in Seville in 1340 an influential commentary to the *liturgy, every detail of which he expounds on the basis of traditional teachings but with original ideas of his own. In this work he suggests that the reason why *women are exempt from carrying out those precepts that can only be carried out at a particular time is that married women have a prior obligation to attend to the needs of their husbands and family and cannot be expected to be ready to perform time-conditioned precepts.

**Adam and Eve** The first parents of the human race, whose story is told in the opening chapters of the book of Genesis. There is no doubt that until the nineteenth century Adam and Eve were held to be historical figures, but with the discovery of the great age of the earth and of human civilization many modern Jews have tended either to read the story as a myth expressing important ideas about the human condition in non-historical form or to identify Adam with prehistoric man in general. In the traditional sources, too, the story of Adam and Eve serves as a paradigm for human conduct in general. The *Mishnah, for example (*Sanhedrin* 4: 5), suggests a number of lessons to be derived from the fact that the whole world is said to be descended from one man:

'Therefore but a single man was created in the world, to teach that if anyone brings about the death of even one person Scripture considers it as if he had brought about the destruction of the whole world and whoever saves the life of a single person Scripture considers it as if he had saved the whole world. Again for the sake of peace among human beings, that none should say to his fellow: "My father was greater than your father"; also that the heretics should not say: "There are many ruling powers in heaven". Again to proclaim the greatness of the Holy One, blessed be He, for man stamps many coins with the same seal and they are all like one another; but the King of kings, the Holy One, blessed be He, has stamped every man with the seal of the first man, yet not one of them is like another. Therefore every person must say. For my sake was the world created.'

At the *marriage ceremony, one of the benedictions reads: 'O make these loving companions greatly to rejoice, even as of old thou didst gladden thy creature in the garden of Eden. Blessed art Thou, O Lord, who makest bridegroom and bride to rejoice.'

The opinion is recorded in the Talmud (probably based on the recognition that there are some female characteristics in every male and male characteristics in every female) that Adam was created as an *androgenos*, a creature half male and half female and that it was a 'side', not a 'rib', that God took from Adam to create Eve. According to an old tradition Adam and Eve are buried in the Cave of *Machpelah.

**Adam, Fall of**   While it is incorrect to say that post-biblical Judaism attaches no special significance to Adam's fall or knows nothing of *original sin, it is certainly true that, with the exception of the Kabbalah, the fall does not occupy an important place in Jewish theology. There are many interpretations of Adam's sin

and of the tree of knowledge from which he ate after having been forbidden by God so to do. Opinions range from that which understands the knowledge of good and evil as having a sexual connotation to that according to which the tree was no different from any other tree and was simply set aside as a test of obedience. In the Talmud there is a view that it was not a tree but wheat from which Adam and Eve ate, since an infant only acquires the knowledge that enables it to speak when it has begun to eat bread. Another view in the Talmud is that it was the vine from which Adam and Eve ate, since so many of the troubles of the world result from drinking wine. No apple!

According to the Kabbalah the Tree of Life is the Tree of the *Sefirot on high and Adam's sin was to detach the lowest of the Sefirot from the others, thus creating a cosmic flaw, a disturbance of the harmony which ought to prevail in the upper worlds (see HOLY SPARKS). All human souls were contained as sparks in the great souls of Adam and were involved in his sin. Since one of these sparks now inheres in every one of Adam's descendants, their task is to help restore cosmic harmony by the elevation of soul that stems from good deeds. This constitutes the salvationary scheme leading to the restoration of souls and of cosmic harmony at the coming of the *Messiah.

**Adam Kadmon**   Primordial man, a term used in the Kabbalah to denote the stage of the divine unfolding which provides the link between *En Sof and the *Sefirot. This stage is conceived of in anthropomorphic terms as cosmic 'man'. As the Infinite emerges from Its utter concealment It produces the entity Adam Kadmon containing the Sefirot in potentia. Spiritual entities, known on the analogy with physical illumination as 'lights', stream forth from various organs of Adam Kadmon's 'body' to produce the vessels into which further lights then flow so as to form the Sefirot. Behind all this is the ancient idea that the human body is written large in the cosmos, man being created literally in the *image of God.

**'Adon Olam'**   'Lord of the universe', the title, after the opening words, of a popular hymn of uncertain authorship. In many liturgies this hymn forms the beginning of the daily morning services and the closing hymn on the Sabbath and festival services. Because the final stanza reads: 'My soul into His hand divine | Do I commend: I will not fear, | My body with it I resign, | I dread no evil: God is near', this hymn is often recited as part of the night prayers before retiring to sleep and, where possible, on the deathbed after the *confession. A number of melodies with which to chant the hymn have become universally popular among Jews. 'Adon Olam' is built around the idea that God rules before and after His creation of the world and will reign for ever. He is, was, and will be through all eternity. Another stanza reads: 'And at the end of days shall He | The dreaded one, still reign alone, | Who was, who is, and still will be | Unchanged upon his glorious throne.' Since the hymn is poetry, not a statement about *eschatology, this stanza is not usually interpreted to mean that at 'the end of days' no creatures will exist, only God alone.

**Adoption** Although legal adoption was recognized in the ancient Near East as far back as the Code of Hammurabi around 1700 BCE, there is no clear evidence that this institution existed in ancient Israelite law. Pharaoh's daughter adopted Moses as her son (Exodus 2: 10) but this is stated in the context of Egyptian norms. Similarly, the statement in the book of Esther (2: 7) that Mordecai took his orphaned cousin Esther to be his daughter may be intended to reflect conditions in the Persian Empire. The Talmudic Rabbis rely on the biblical stories of Pharaoh's daughter and Esther to teach that if anyone brings up an orphan in his household, Scripture considers it as if he had actually given birth to the child; but nowhere in Talmudic law is real legal adoption recognized, despite the fact that the Romans certainly knew of it. It may even be that the Rabbinic refusal to introduce adoption into the legal system was a conscious reaction to Roman law, almost as if the Rabbis were saying that precisely because the Romans recognized it, they must not. But this is mere conjecture. There is nothing in Jewish law to prevent the drawing-up of new legislation in such matters and the Adoption of Children law of 1960 in the State of Israel empowers a court to grant an adoption order for children under the age of 18. However, an adopted child is not treated as a natural child in every respect. If a couple adopt a boy and a girl unrelated to one another the laws of consanguinity do not apply and, when they grow up, they are free to marry, the fact that they are

brother and sister by adoption being irrelevant. Strictly speaking, the laws of *mourning to be observed after the death of a parent do not apply to a child in respect of his adopted parents, but if adopted children wish to observe the mourning rites for their adopted parents they may do so and this is in fact normal practice. Whether a child is a *Kohen or a *Levite depends on the status of his natural, not his adopted, father.

**Adret, Solomon Ibn** Spanish Rabbi, theologian, and Kabbalist (1235–1310), known, after the initial letters of his Hebrew name, as Rashba. Adret was one of the most outstanding scholars of medieval Jewry. During the fierce debates on the question of the study of *philosophy, Adret steered a middle course, discouraging this study ('What did the Greeks know of God?') and yet, in a ban he pronounced in Barcelona (1305), he declared it forbidden only to those under the age of 25. Similarly, with regard to the Kabbalah, although Adret was a Kabbalist and composer of a famous Kabbalistic prayer, he took pains to conceal his Kabbalistic leanings as much as possible. He is best known as a prolific writer of *Responsa on all aspects of Jewish law. Typical of Adret's understanding of Judaism—traditional but not uninfluenced by philosophical formulations—is his statement regarding inwardness:

'The first stage in the matter of intention, to which every Jew attains, is that all know and acknowledge that there is a God, blessed be He, whose existence is necessary [not contingent]. He created the world by His will and gave the Torah to His people Israel at Sinai, a Torah of truth with righteous judgements and statutes. To Him do we belong and Him we worship. He commanded us to offer ourselves up to Him when we call on His name Him we acknowledge and to Him we do pray since everything is from Him. His providence extends over us all and He looks down upon our deeds to requite us for them and grant us our recompense. Every Jew should have this in mind when he prays.'

Isidore Epstein, *The 'Responsa' of Rabbi Solomon ben Adreth of Barcelona (1235–1310)* (London, 1925).

**Afikoman** This word of uncertain etymology but of Greek origin means 'dessert' and is now used to denote the piece of unleavened bread, *matzah*, eaten at the end of the *Seder on the first night of *Passover. It is customary not to eat anything else after the *afikoman* in order for the taste of *matzah* to remain in the mouth all night. There is a folk-belief that if a piece of the *afikoman* is kept in the house after Passover the house will not be visited by burglars during the year.

**Age** Respect for the aged is an important principle in Judaism. 'Thou shalt rise up before the hoary head and honour the face of the old man, and thou shalt fear thy God: I am the Lord' (Leviticus 19: 32). This is understood in the Talmud to mean that whenever an old man or woman passes by one should rise to one's feet as a token of respect. It is recorded in the Talmud that the third-century Palestinian teacher, Rabbi Johanan, would rise to his feet in respect even before heathens who were old because, he declared, they had experienced so many trials and tribulations in their long life and this entitled them to respect. The prophet Isaiah, speaking of a corrupt generation, describes it (Isaiah 3: 5) as one in which: 'The child shall behave insolently against the aged, And the base against the honourable.' Remarkably for the age in which he lived, the Psalmist (Psalms 90: 10) defines by implication what constitutes old age: 'The days of our years are threescore years and ten, or even by reason of strength fourscore years; yet is their pride but travail and nothingness; for it is soon gone by and we fly away.' Based on this Psalm is the statement in Ethics of the Fathers (5. 21) that of the fourteen ages of man (not seven as in Shakespeare): '60 is for to be an elder, 70 for grey hairs, 80 for special strength.' Since Moses is said to have lived for 120 years (Deuteronomy 34: 7) it is the custom, when someone mentions his or her age, to express the wish: 'May you live until you are 120.'

In most Jewish communities there is a special old-age home (*moshav zekenim*) in which the old people are adequately cared for. The thirteenth-century biblical exegete *Bahya, Ibn Asher, commenting on the verse Exodus 20: 12): 'Honour thy father and thy mother, that thy days may be long upon the land which the Lord thy God giveth thee', remarks that it is undoubtedly true that care of aged parents can be a severe burden but in return the Torah promises longevity to those who shoulder the burden. A Talmudic saying has it that if the young tell you to build and the aged to destroy, listen to the aged; for the construction of the young is destruction, but the destruction of the aged is construction.

**Aggadah** The aspect of Jewish, especially Talmudic, literature that embraces all non-legal topics. Aggadah treats of Jewish history, ethics, philosophy, folklore, medicine, astronomy, popular proverbs, pious tales, and so forth. Aggadah is thus best defined as including any subject of relevance to Judaism that is not embraced by the term *Halakhah, the legal side of Judaism. Statements in the Talmud about *etiquette, for example, belong to Aggadah, whereas a ruling, say, that the victim of an assault has to be compensated in a particular way belongs to Halakhah. In a famous essay on the subject, H. N. Bialik described Aggadah as the poetry of Judaism, Halakhah as the prose. This is not to say, however, that Aggadah is treated less seriously than Halakhah, only that the former is less precise than the latter, as poetry is less precise than prose. Although, as a result of the distinction between the two, a reluctance can be observed to base legal decisions on Aggadic statements, some such rulings did find their way into the standard Jewish Code, the *Shulḥan Arukh. Broadly speaking, the Spanish authorities in the Middle Ages tended to stress the distinction between Aggadah and Halakhah, while the French and German authorities tended to play it down, giving almost as much weight to the Aggadah as to the Halakhah. In later Jewish parlance Aggadah often means a 'legend', as when *Herzl' is reported as saying of *Zionism: 'If you wish it, it is no Aggadah'; in other words, not a hazy dream or a legend but sober fact capable of realization.

H. N. Bialik and Y. H. Ravitzlcy, *The Book of Legends: Sefer Ha-Aggadah* trans. William G. Braude (New York, 1992).

**Agnosticism** A term coined by T. H. Huxley to denote that attitude which, unlike theism (conviction that God exists) and *atheism (conviction that God does not exist), maintains that it cannot be known whether or not God exists. Judaism, as a monotheistic religion, obviously rejects the agnostic attitude as it does that of atheism. This is not to say, however, that there are no unexplored areas in matters of *belief.

Some Jewish thinkers advocate the *via negativa* in which it is affirmed that while God exists His true nature can never be grasped by the human mind. In the Rabbinic literature there are references to people weak in faith, believing and yet not believing, but faith in this context means trust in God rather than belief that God exists. It is this capacity for trust in God that is said to vacillate.

**Agunah** A woman bound or 'chained' either to a missing husband or to one who refuses to *divorce her. In Jewish law the State cannot intervene to grant a couple a divorce. The only way a married woman can become free to remarry is by obtaining a release from her husband by his death or by him delivering to her, of his own free will, the *get, the bill of divorce. From early Rabbinic times efforts have been made to help the *agunah* obtain release from the tragic situation in which she is prevented from marrying another by a husband who is no husband. Where the husband is missing the laws of evidence are relaxed somewhat so that his death can be presumed. Husbands who disappeared in the Nazi *Holocaust were presumed dead, after a reasonable time had elapsed, and their wives were permitted to remarry on the grounds that the vast majority of Jews under Nazi rule who did not reappear probably perished, the probability principle being accepted in Jewish law.

Remedies are not so ready to hand for the woman whose husband refuses to divorce her, either out of spite or because she is unwilling or unable to raise the sum of money he exorbitantly demands before he will agree to the delivery of the *get*. *Reform Judaism, with some exceptions, relies on the civil divorce to terminate the marriage so that, for Reform, there is no *agunah* problem. *Orthodox Judaism often adopts other tactics to release the woman whose husband refuses to grant her a divorce. In the State of Israel, for example, if a husband has been ordered by the court to grant the divorce and refuses to do so, he may be held in prison for contempt of court until he does the right thing. In other countries, other means of coercion, social pressure, for example, may be brought to bear on the recalcitrant husband. In some cases a way out may be found by establishing that, for various reasons, the original marriage was invalid and, consequently, no divorce is necessary for the woman to remarry.

*Conservative Judaism, unwilling to depart from the tradition in such a serious matter as marriage and divorce but wishing Jewish law to be more flexible than it needed to be before civil divorce was known, relies on indications in the Talmud that in certain cases the drastic measure of nullification of marriage is a valid option and, after a stern warning has been given to the husband, will obtain release for the *agunah* by declaring her marriage retrospectively null and void. The status of the children of the marriage would not be affected by the nullification of the marriage since, in Jewish law, children born out of wedlock are not illegitimate and suffer no disabilities. The Orthodox Rabbis hold, on the other hand, that, despite Talmudic precedents, contemporary courts do not have the power to nullify a marriage. It should be noted that it is not only the *agunah* herself who suffers. If she did decide to ignore the law and remarry, the child she had from the second union would be a *mamzer.

**Ahad Ha-Am** 'One of the People', pen-name of Asher Ginsberg (1856–1927), Hebrew essayist and Zionist thinker. For Ginsberg, *Zionism was important not only because it sought to provide a physical homeland for the Jewish people but because this homeland had the potential of becoming a spiritual centre for world Jewry. Ginsberg saw what he called 'absolute spirituality' (*ruḥani ha-muḥlat*) as the very essence of Judaism, which had always set its face against material concepts of the divine. The Talmud tells of the prospective proselyte who came before *Hillel asking to be given first a statement about the essential meaning of the Torah 'while standing on one leg' (i.e. in capsule form). Ginsberg observes that if such a would-be proselyte had come to him his reply would have been to quote the verse: 'Thou shalt not make a graven image.' But it has to be appreciated that 'spiritual' in these contexts has an intellectual and ethical connotation rather than a religious one. Ginsberg, though brought up in a strictly traditional home, was a freethinker in religious matters, admiring Judaism for the stress it puts on intellectual and cultural pursuits and, especially, on a strictly ethical approach. In an essay directed against the views of C. G. *Montefiore, who argued for the incorporation into Judaism of some of the higher (for Montefiore) ethical aspects of *Christianity,

Ginsberg tried to show, not very successfully, that this was not possible since, apart from the doctrinal aspects, the Christian ethic based on love was incompatible with the Jewish ethic based on justice. Ginsberg's generalization overlooks the obvious facts that in both the Christian and the Jewish ethic the tension exists between justice and love and that it is, in any event, precarious to speak of specifically Jewish *ethics, ethics being a universal concept. Ginsberg's personal life was of a high moral character and, through his writings, he influenced strongly ethics-orientated Jewish thinkers such as Mordecai *Kaplan. With the establishment of the *State of Israel, Ginsberg's thought became somewhat academic. If his essays are still studied in Israel and elsewhere, it is now far more for their fine literary style than for the relevance of the ideas they express.

Ginsberg recognized that the ethical and intellectual aspects of Judaism can only be understood as part of the religious tradition. The modern Jew cannot disown his religious heritage. He must live with it and extrapolate from it the values that have shaped his life. In a famous essay on Moses, Ginsberg remarks that he remains unmoved by scholarly attempts at showing that Moses never existed. His Moses, the Moses of the Jewish tradition, still lives on as the powerful advocate of righteous living.
   Leon Simon, *Ahad Ha'am-Asher Ginzberg: A Biography* (London, 1960).

**Akedah** 'Binding of Isaac', the account in the book of Genesis (22: 1–19) of *Abraham, at the command of God, taking his son, *Isaac, to be offered as a sacrifice on Mount Moriah. Abraham *binds* his son (hence 'the Binding of Isaac') to the altar and is ready to perform the dreadful deed when an angel appears to tell him to stay his hand and to promise him that his seed will increase. There is no reference to this episode anywhere else in the Bible. Nor does it feature very prominently in post-biblical Jewish literature until the third century CE. Some biblical scholars, Jews included, have read the story as a protest against human sacrifice, the significant point being that the angel intervenes to prevent the murder as an obscene act that God, unlike the pagan deities, hates and could never really have intended. But in traditional Jewish thought, the *Akedah* is used as a paradigm for Jewish *martyrdom; the Jewish people are ready at all times to give up life itself for the sake of the

sanctification of the divine name (*Kiddush Ha-Shem) On the judgement day of *Rosh Ha-Shanah at the beginning of the year, God is entreated to show mercy to His people in the merit of Abraham's willingness to sacrifice his son. A prayer of the day reads:

'Remember unto us, O Lord our God, the covenant and the loving-kindness and the oath which Thou swore unto Abraham our father on Mount Moriah; and consider the binding with which Abraham our father bound his son Isaac on the altar, how he suppressed his compassion in order to perform Thy will with a perfect heart. So may Thy compassion overbear Thine anger against us; in Thy great goodness may Thy great wrath turn aside from Thy people, Thy city, and Thine inheritance.'

'Thy city' in the prayer is a reference to the ancient tradition that Mount Moriah, the site of the *Akedah*, is the place in Jerusalem where the Temple was built. Thus, contrary to the 'happy ending' theory mentioned above, the traditional view, whether historically accurate or not, is close to that of Kierkegaard, who reads the *Akedah* as an illustration of how far the 'knight of faith' is ready to go in his 'teleological suspension of the ethical'.

The commentators find some features of the *Akedah* puzzling. Why, for instance, is there no mention of Isaac returning with his father after the ram had been substituted for him? Abraham is said to have returned together with the lads who accompanied him but nothing is said of Isaac. Abraham *Ibn Ezra records an opinion that the angel's call came too late and that Isaac was, in fact, killed by Abraham. (On this opinion, Isaac, who reappears in the later narratives, was resurrected from the dead.) Ibn Ezra rejects this as contrary to the plain meaning of the biblical text. But Shalom Spiegel, in a famous essay, shows that such an opinion came to be widely held in the Middle Ages, possibly in order to deny that the sacrifice of Isaac was in any way less than that of Jesus; or as a reflection of actual conditions in the Middle Ages when the martyrdom of Jewish communities demanded a more tragic model than that of a mere intended sacrifice. Nevertheless it is constantly stressed in the literature that God never intended that Abraham should actually sacrifice Isaac. A Talmudic comment on Jeremiah 19: 5 states: ' "which I commanded not"; this refers to the sacrifice of the son of Mesha, the king of Moab (2 Kings 3: 27); "nor spake it"; this refers to the daughter of Jepthtah (Judges 11: 31); "neither came it to My mind"; this refers to the sacrifice of Isaac, the son of Abraham.' *Philo goes to the opposite extreme, defending the *Akedah* against the charge that it is by no means unique since, in the history of mankind, many people have been prepared to lay down their lives and the lives of their children for a cause in which they believed: Moloch-worshippers for instance, who are condemned by Moses, and Indian women who gladly practise suttee. Philo replies that Abraham's sacrifice was unprecedented in that he was not governed by motives of custom, honour, or fear, but solely by his love of God.

Another puzzling feature of the *Akedah* is the opening statement that God tested Abraham, as if the purpose were to provide God with information about Abraham's trust He did not previously possess. According to Maimonides (*Guide of the Perplexed*, 3. 24) the words 'God tested Abraham' do not mean that God put Abraham through a test but that He made the example of Abraham serve as a test case of the extreme limits of the love and fear of God. *Nahmanides, on the other hand, states that God did indeed know beforehand how Abraham would behave but, from Abraham's point of view, the test was real since he had to be rewarded not only for his potential willingness to obey the divine command but for actually complying with it. The implications of the *Akedah* are that, despite what appears to be a contradiction, divine foreknowledge is compatible with human *free will.

There are Midrashic statements that *Sarah died of a broken heart when she learned that Abraham had taken her son to be sacrificed. Since Sarah gave birth to Isaac at the age of 90 (Genesis 17: 17) and she died at the age of 127 (Genesis 23: 1) Isaac must have been, on this view, 37 years of age at the time of the *Akedah*. (Ibn Ezra rejects this opinion too as contrary to the plain meaning of the biblical text in which Isaac is depicted as a pliant and docile little boy.) This leads the Talmud to ask why Isaac submitted to what virtually amounted to an act of suicide. The legal conclusion the Talmud draws from the episode is that when a true prophet of God, like Abraham, speaks in God's name, he is to be obeyed even if the act he commands would otherwise be the most serious crime.

That Abraham went to the *Akedah* in 'fear and trembling' (the title of Kierkegaard's work on the subject) is expressed in the Talmudic legend that as Abraham went on his way he was met by *Satan, who tried to stop him by arguing that God had promised him that his future and the future of all his teachings about the One God would depend on Isaac and now he was about to frustrate that promise.

Louis Jacobs; 'The Problem of the *Akedah* in Jewish Thought', in Robert L. Perkins (ed.), *Kierkegaard's Fear and Trembling: Critical Appraisals.* (University, Ala. 1981), 1–9.

Shalom Sprefel; *The Last Trial* (New York 1969).

**Akiba, Rabbi** Foremost teacher of the Torah who lived in the second half of the first century and the first half of the second century CE. As is the case with so many of the *Tannaim and Amoraim, it is has proved difficult for historians to disentangle the facts of Akiba's life from the pious legends with which it is surrounded. The statement, for example, that Akiba was an ignoramus (*am ha-aretz*) until, at the age of 40, he was encouraged by his wife to study the Torah for forty years, after which he taught for forty years, is obviously far too neat to be anything but legendary, and was presumably intended to place Akiba among the great teachers who wore the mantle of Moses who lived to be 120. The same applies to the dialogues Akiba is supposed to have engaged in with Turnus Rufus, the Roman Governor of Palestine, though these might reflect early Rabbinic associations with the Gentile authorities and the kind of queries Roman nobles might have addressed to the Rabbis. Turnus Rufus is supposed to have asked Akiba why, if God loves the poor, He does not make them rich and why, if God wants man to be circumcised, He created him with a foreskin. Akiba replies that God allows the poor to remain in a state of poverty in order to provide the rich with the capacity to acquire merit by helping the poor, and He creates man with a foreskin in order for Jews to acquire merit by observing the rite of *circumcision. In similar vein, when Turnus Rufus asks Akiba which is greater, the work of God or the work of man, Akiba replies that the work of man is greater in that God provides the wheat but it is man who has to do the sowing, harvesting, and baking before bread can satisfy the human need for food. The line running through such stories is that of human co-operation with the divine; it is a rejection, fathered on Akiba, of the philosophy of *quietism. Akiba studied under Rabbi *Eliezer and Rabbi *Joshua and among his foremost disciples were Rabbi *Judah, Rabbi *Meir and Rabbi *Simeon. Akiba is also acknowledged as an early compiler of teachings later used by Rabbi *Judah the Prince in his compilation of the Mishnah. There is no doubt a kernel of truth in the accounts of Akiba acknowledging *Bar Kochba as the Messiah and of him continuing to teach the Torah when it had been proscribed by the Roman authorities, for which he suffered a martyr's death, his soul expiring while he joyfully recited the *Shema. In matters of *Halakhah, too, it is difficult to know for certain how much is Akiba's own and how much has simply been attributed to him as a pioneering teacher. There was an important difference, it is reported, on the question of *hermeneutics, between the school of Akiba and the school of Akiba's contemporary, Rabbi *Ishmael. The latter taught that even in the legal portions of the Pentateuch some words have no legal significance but are simply stylistic—'The Torah speaks in the language of men.' But the school of Akiba held that there are no superfluous words in the legal passages, every word being intended to convey some additional rule. Words like 'also' are intended to include some addition to the law not stated explicitly in the text and words like 'however' are intended to exclude laws that it might otherwise have been imagined are embraced by the implications of the text.

Akiba is quoted as saying that 'Love thy neighbour as thyself' is a great principle of the Torah. A saying attributed to him in a more universalistic vein is: 'Beloved is man because he has been created in the image of God.' Akiba is also depicted as belonging to the mystical tradition in ancient Israel. Of the four sages who entered the *Pardes ('Paradise') Akiba alone is said to have emerged unscathed by the tremendous experience. Akiba is held to be of the utmost significance in laying the foundations of Rabbinic Judaism after the destruction of the *Temple. He is the exemplar of complete devotion to the study, practice, and teaching of the Torah. He is described in the Talmud as 'one of the fathers of the world'.

Louis Finkelstein, *Akiva: Scholar, Saint and Martyr* (New York, 1962).

**Albo, Joseph** Spanish philosopher (fifteenth century), author of *Sefer Ha-Ikkarim* (*Book of the Principles*), an eclectic work based on the ideas of earlier teachers such as his own mentor, Hasdai *Crescas, but important as the last great system of medieval Jewish philosophy. In this work, part *theology, part *apologetics, Albo sets out the principles of the Jewish religion by which Judaism differs from other religions, especially Christianity.

In the course of his analysis Albo observes that, in a religion, only that without which the religion would lose its distinctiveness can be considered to be a principle. Contrary to Maimonides, who states that there are thirteen principles of faith in Judaism, Albo holds that Judaism has only three principles. These are: belief in the existence of God; belief that the Torah is from Heaven (i.e. belief in *revelation, that Judaism is a revealed religion); belief in *reward and punishment. There are other beliefs to which the Jew is obliged to give his assent, belief in the coming of the *Messiah for example, but, since Judaism can be conceived of without it, this belief cannot be said to be a principle of the faith. One who denies belief in the coming of the Messiah, though he is in grievous error, cannot be read out of Judaism as Maimonides declares. (The apologetic note is here clearly sounded: Judaism, unlike Christianity does not stand or fall on belief in the Messiah.) Moreover, according to Albo, a person can only be termed an unbeliever if he wilfully rejects a principle which he knows to be laid down by the Torah. It is the act of rebellion against the clear doctrine of the Torah that constitutes unbelief.

'But one who upholds the Torah of Moses and believes in its principles, yet when he undertakes to investigate these matters with his reason and when he scrutinizes the texts, is misled by his speculation and interprets a given principle otherwise than it is taken to mean at first glance; or denies the principle because he thinks that it does not represent a sound theory which the Torah obliges us to believe; or erroneously denies that a given belief is a fundamental principle, which, however, he believes as he believes the other *dogmas of the Torah which are not fundamental principles; or entertains a certain notion in relation to one of the miracles of the Torah because he thinks that he is not thereby denying any of the doctrines which it is obligatory upon us to believe by the authority of the Torah—a person of this sort is not an unbeliever. He is classed among the sages and pious men of Israel, though he holds erroneous theories. His sin is due to error and requires atonement.'

It is hardly possible for a Jewish thinker to go further than this in tolerance of freedom of thought. Although Albo's unbeliever of the class he describes is in error, he is like any other person who sins in error and can still be counted among the 'sages and pious men of Israel'.

Albo, in fact, extends his three basic principles to others derived from them, so that including the three he first mentions there are in all eleven basic principles. These are: the existence of God; the unity of God; His incorporeality; His independence of time; His perfection; prophecy; the authenticity of God's messenger, the prophet; revelation; God's knowledge; providence; and reward and punishment.

Although only these are principles, according to Albo's definition, there are six further dogmas the wilful rejection of which, with full knowledge that it is a dogma of Judaism, renders a person a heretic who has no share in the *World to Come. These are: belief in *creatio ex nihilo*; the superiority of Moses' prophecy; the immutability of the Torah; that human perfection can be attained by fulfilling even a single one of the commandments of the Torah; the resurrection of the dead; the coming of the Messiah. Although this might be seen as Albo taking back with one hand what he has given with the other, it has to be realized that Albo, as he remarks, is thinking only of a wilful rejection of a belief which a person knows to be taught by the Torah. For all that, Albo's distinction between a principle and that which is not a principle remains purely in the realm of semantics, without any practical consequences. In the uncensored version of his work, Albo refers to a discussion he had had with a Christian scholar who maintained that Christianity is superior to Judaism with regard to the duties a man owes to God, the duties a man owes to his fellows, and the duties a man owes to himself. Albo seeks to demonstrate that the opposite is true, that Judaism is superior in all three categories. In the process, Albo accepts that there is a third category, that of duties a man has to himself, a category not found in any of the earlier Jewish sources in which *precepts

are divided solely into the two categories of 'between man and God' and 'between man and his fellow'.

Joseph Albo, *Sefer Ha-ʿIkkarim Book of Principles*, trans. and ed. Isaac Husik (Philadelphia, 1946).

**Alfasi, Isaac**  Alfasi (1013–1103) lived for most of his life in Fez in Morocco (hence the name Alfasi, 'from Fez' or the Rif, '*R*abbi *Y*itzhak *F*esi') and was the author of one of the great *Codes of Law, the *Sefer Ha-Halakhot* (*The Book of the Laws*). By the time of Alfasi the Babylonian Talmud had become the supreme source of Jewish Law, but the Talmud is not a Code; rather, it is a corpus of the discussions by the Rabbis on numerous questions, most of them of law. Alfasi's method was to give the basic debates in matters of law in the original form in which they appear in the Talmud but omitting all the elaborate discussions, stating simply, in his own words, at the end of each passage: 'This is the law'. Alfasi's Code had an influence on all subsequent Codes such as that of Maimonides. Alfasi's work is often called: 'the Talmud in miniature'.

**Allegory**  The method of scriptural interpretation in which persons and events mentioned in the Bible are understood not in a literal sense but as referring to stages in the religious life of the Jews. *Philo, the greatest of the allegorists, understands, for example, the command to Abraham to obey Sarah and send away his handmaiden Hagar (Genesis 21: 10) to mean that in order to achieve perfection a man has to obey the voice of reason and banish the passions that control his life. In the fourteenth century, Solomon Ibn *Adret took strong issue with the allegorists of his day who were so enamoured of their interpretations that they were indifferent to the question of whether biblical figures such as *Abraham and *Sarah ever really existed. The best-known interpretation of Scripture in this vein by the ancient Rabbis is that of the *Song of Songs, understood not as a simple love poem about a youth and a maiden but as a dialogue between God, the Lover, and Israel, His beloved.

**Alphabet, Hebrew**  The Hebrew alphabet has twenty-two letters, five of which have a slightly different form when they occur at the end of a word to close the word. The letters are:

| | | | | | | |
|---|---|---|---|---|---|---|
| *alef* | א | = | 1 | *ayin* | ע | = 70 |
| *bet* | ב | = | 2 | *pey* | פ | = 80 |
| *gimel* | ג | = | 3 | *tzade* | צ | = 90 |
| *dalet* | ד | = | 4 | *kof* | ק | = 100 |
| *hey* | ה | = | 5 | *resh* | ר | = 200 |
| *vav* | ו | = | 6 | *shin* | ש | = 300 |
| *zayin* | ז | = | 7 | *tav* | ת | = 400 |
| *het* | ח | = | 8 | | | |
| *tet* | ט | = | 9 | The five final letters are: |
| *yod* | י | = | 10 | *kaf* | ך |
| *kaf* | כ | = | 20 | *mem* | ם |
| *lamed* | ל | = | 30 | *nun* | ן |
| *mem* | מ | = | 40 | *pey* | ף |
| *nun* | נ | = | 50 | *tzade* | ץ |
| *samekh* | ס | = | 60 | | |

These letters are all consonants, to which the vowels have to be added in order to form words. In the *Sefer Torah, for instance, only the consonants are written, the reader supplying the vowels. The vowels and the signs by which they are recorded are:

*patah* (–) = a as in hat.
*segol* (∵) = e as in let.
*hirek* (.) = i as in lit.
*kibbutz* (∴) = u as in bull.
*kametz*, short (ㄒ) = o as in top.
*kametz*, long (ㄒ) = a as in yard (sign the same for both short and long).
*tzere* (..) = e as in they.
*shurek* (וּ) = long u as in flute.
*holem* (וֹ) = long o as in role.

Each of the twenty-two letters also represents a number, hence the method of interpretation known as *gematria in which one word can be made to represent a different word because they have the same numerical value. The letters *alef* to *yod* represent the numbers 1 to 10. The numbers 11 to 99 are represented by *yod* and *alef* = 11; *yod* and *bet* = 12, and so on up to *tzade* and *tet* = 99. The letter *kof* = 100; *resh* = 200; *shin* = 300; *tav* = 400. The numbers from 401 to 999 are represented by adding the desired letters. Thousands are represented by the letters *alef* and so forth, with a stroke over them before the other numbers. Thus the year 5,755 is represented as: *hey* (stroke), *tav, shin, nun, hey*.

In the Midrashic literature comments on the letters of the alphabet abound. The Torah begins with the letter *bet* (Genesis 1: 1, 'In the beginning', Hebrew *bereshit*) because this letter is the first of the word *berakhah*, meaning 'blessing'. The letter *bet* (ב) is closed on three sides and only open to the left (Hebrew is read from right to left) to denote that speculation is futile on 'what is above and what is below, what is before and what is behind', that is, speculation on the mysteries which it is beyond the mind of man to grasp. The opening of the *bet* represents the future, indicating that man should move onwards. The letter *hey* (ה) is open at the bottom to denote that freedom of choice is given by God and none is coerced into accepting the way of the Torah. The opening of the *hey* at the bottom hints at the possibility of a man leaving the Jewish way, since there is an opening for him so to do. But if, later on, he repents, his repentance is accepted and he can re-enter, as is indicated by the small opening at the top of the *hey*. Similarly, there are many interpretations of those letters traditionally written larger than the others in the Sefer Torah and those written smaller than the others. The simplest way of understanding the large letters is that this is for emphasis (much as we underline words or letters) and as for the small letters, S. D. *Luzzatto has noted that these are usually found where the same letter is repeated. According to Luzzatto's plausible theory the scribe may have written only one letter where two were required and when he came to put it in the line, the space was such that he had to write it small. This has never prevented commentators reading ideas into the large and small letters.

In the *Kabbalah the letters of the alphabet are not mere conventions but represent on earth those spiritual entities on high by means of which God created the world. For the Kabbalists God really did 'say' 'Let there be light' (Genesis 1: 3) in the sense that He combined those entities represented by the letters *alef, vav, resh* to form the word *or* ('light'), the spiritual entity that is both the cause on high of physical light and the form this entity assumes as it descends into the material universe. In practical Kabbalah the adept is able to repeat the divine creative activity by combining the letters of the alphabet to bring new creatures into being, even to create a *golem, a human-like creature with great physical power of its own; but this practice is frowned upon for all but the greatest of saints and is said to be fraught with danger, both spiritual and physical.

A. E. Cowley (revised), *Gesenius' Hebrew Grammar as Edited and Enlarged by the Late E. Kautzch* (Oxford, 1949), i. 24–98.

**Amalek** The name of a tribe that attacked the Israelites in the wilderness (Exodus 17: 8–16; Deuteronomy 25: 17–19), whose memory was to be 'blotted out'. In the later Jewish tradition the actual identity of this tribe is unknown but Amalek becomes the symbol of wanton cruelty and murderous intent. The Jewish moralists speak of the need to eradicate the Amalek residing in the human heart—that is, aggressive tendencies in general.

**Amen** The liturgical response now used not only in Judaism but also in *Christianity and *Islam. The word has the same Hebrew root as *emunah* ('faith') and is also connected with the word *emet* meaning *'truth'. The idea expressed is of firm trust, acceptance, and reliability. Amen is found in a variety of contexts in the Bible (Numbers 5: 22; Deuteronomy 27: 15; 16, 17, 18, 19, 20, 21, 22, 23, 24, 25, 26; 1 Kings 1: 36; Isaiah 65: 16; Jeremiah 11: 5; 28: 6; 1 Chronicles 16: 36; Nehemiah 5: 13; 8: 6; Psalms 41: 14; 72: 19; 89: 52; 106: 48). Louis Ginzberg has translated Amen as 'So be it' or 'So shall it be' and has described it as 'perhaps the most widely known word in human speech'. A late second-century teacher in the Talmud takes the initial letters of Amen to represent *el melekh neeman*, 'God, Faithful King'. A later Jewish commentator to the *Prayer Book interprets homiletically the initial letters as: *ani moser nafshi*, 'I offer up myself as a sacrifice'. A Rabbinic saying has it that one who responds Amen to a benediction is greater than the one who recites the benediction. The reason given for this statement by the medieval 'sages of England' is that the one who responds with Amen also hears the benediction itself and, since 'to hear is akin to pronouncing', he has to his credit both the Amen and the benediction. It may also be that the statement is intended to express the thought that it is more praiseworthy, because more difficult, to give assent to a truth first seen by others than to be a pioneer in discovering the truth for oneself. On the other hand, it is said that Amen should not be recited in a louder voice than that of the one who recites the benediction, perhaps because this would imply a 'holier than thou' attitude.

A saying attributed to the second-century teacher Rabbi *Meir has it that a child merits the *World to Come from the day it first says Amen. Another Rabbinic saying is that all the gates of heaven open to one who recites Amen with all his strength, explained by the great French commentator *Rashi as meaning with all his powers of concentration. The rules in the Codes regarding the response Amen are that it must not be 'orphaned' from the *benediction to which it is the response by coming too soon or too late; it should not be slurred but perfectly distinct; and it should only be recited after a benediction pronounced by someone else, not after one's own benediction. When said in response to a prayer of petition the intention should be: 'May it be Thy will that this purpose be realized.' Among Jews Amen is never used at the beginning of a sentence as it is in the Gospels (Matthew 5: 18, 26; 6: 2; Luke 4: 24; John 1: 51).

David *Abudarham, in his commentary to the Prayer Book, compares the response of Amen to the validation of a bond by a court of law. Without such validation the bond may be a forgery or otherwise incapable of performing its proper function.

Some of the later Rabbis discuss whether Amen should be said to a benediction heard over the radio. The ruling is that there is no need for the one who recites Amen to be in the same room as the one who recites the benediction. Nor is it necessary for the one who recites Amen actually to hear the benediction. It is sufficient if he knows that the benediction has been recited. In a humorous Talmudic passage it is told that a synagogue in Alexandria was so huge that at the end of each benediction by the prayer leader a flag had to be waved so that those at a distance would know when to say Amen.

Joshua Alter Wildman, *And Let Us Say Amen*, trans. Charles Wengrov (Jerusalem and New York, 1979).

**Am Ha-Aretz** An ignoramus, in contradistinction to the *Talmid Ḥakham*, the scholar. The term, meaning literally 'the people of the land', is found in the Bible (e.g. in Genesis 23: 12–13), perhaps referring to the governing body of the people, the Parliament. In post-biblical times the 'people of the land' were the farmers and agricultural labourers and later still the terms was applied to the individual in the sense of the ignorant man, by much the same process as in the development of the English words 'peasant' and 'commoner'. In the first century CE, the *am ha-aretz* was suspected of laxity with regard to tithing and ritual purity so that produce purchased from him required to be tithed and his garments were held to be ritually impure. In the Rabbinic period, the *am ha-aretz* came to mean the man who had little or no learning. It has to be appreciated that the Talmud was compiled by scholars, so that the picture conveyed in it is biased against those hostile to learning. This explains, if it does not justify, such Talmudic hyperboles as these stating that it is permitted to kill an *am ha-aretz* even on *Yom Kippur that falls on the Sabbath, and that whoever marries off his daughter to an *am ha-aretz*, it is as if he had tied her up to be devoured by a lion.

The post-Talmudic teachers known as the *Geonim were embarrassed by these extreme statements. It is on record that in Geonic times a young scholar, on the basis of the Talmudic statements, argued that it is permitted to steal from an *am ha-aretz*; whereupon his teacher declared that in that case, on his own showing, it was permitted to steal from him, since by his perverse misunderstanding of the Talmudic ethic he had demonstrated that he was himself an *am ha-aretz*, Other attempts were made throughout the ages to treat all Jews, whether learned or ignorant, as equals. The German authority Rabbi Jair Hayyim Bacharach (1638–1702) remarks that the Talmudic references are not to be applied to contemporary ignoramuses, so that no one now takes any notice of the Talmudic disapproval of the marriage of the daughter of an *am ha-aretz* to a scholar. The Hasidic master and Halakhic authority Rabbi Jekutiel Judah Teitelbaum (1808–82) goes so far as to say that 'nowadays' everyone has at least sufficient learning to enable him to avoid being stigmatized as an *am ha-aretz*.

For all that, in everyday Jewish parlance the name *am ha-aretz* is used as an epithet of scorn by learned Jews, often by scholars against other scholars with whom they happen to disagree, rather like the term 'Philistine' in English.

**Amos** The first of the literary prophets who lived, according to the biblical book which bears his name, during the reigns of King Uzziah in Judah and Jeroboam in Israel, in the Northern Kingdom, in the eighth century BCE. Amos came from the village of Tekoa in the Southern Kingdom of Judah and he is de-scribed (Amos 7: 14) as 'a herdman and a dresser of sycamore trees', which probably means that he was a kind of gentleman farmer. Because of his occupation, Amos uses in his prophetic utterances similes taken from agricultural and farming life. Students of the prophetic books have seen this phenomenon of a prophet expressing himself in language drawn from his own personal status and type of life as showing that however *prophecy is to be understood, it does not mean that in his experience of the divine and the inspiration to which it gives rise, the personality of the prophet is taken over or obliterated. When Amos says (Amos 7: 14): 'I was no prophet, neither was I a prophet's son', he is not declaring that his father was not a prophet but that he had never belonged among the 'sons of the prophets', the guild of prophetic disciples. Like other prophets, Amos claims to have been called by God to prophesy without having either prepared himself for the experience or even desired it. Amos, though living in Judah, came to the Northern Kingdom to prophesy against the house of Jeroboam, whereupon Amaziah, priest of Bethel, said to him: 'O thou seer, go, flee thee away into the land of Judah, and there eat bread, and prophesy there' (Amos 7: 12), as if to say: 'If you must earn your living by foretelling calamities, do it in your own community and leave us alone'—an ancient version of 'Over here we keep religion out of politics'.

Amos is seen more than any other as the prophet who places the emphasis on justice and fearlessly attacks the powerful, when they are guilty of injustice, even at risk to his own safety. 'Thus saith the Lord: For three transgressions of Israel, Yea for four, I will not reverse it: Because they sell the righteous for silver, And the needy for a pair of shoes.' Because the book of Amos is full of prophecies of catastrophe, many modern scholars see the final verses (Amos 9: 13–15), in which great material prosperity is promised, as a later addition for the purpose of providing a happy ending. But the majority of Jewish commentators see no reason why the prophet should not end on an optimistic note, assuring the people that if they will repent God will look favourably on them. Amos's attitude towards his people is certainly not that they have been rejected by God. On the contrary they are God's *Chosen People and precisely because of this have a greater degree of responsibility for their conduct: 'You only have I known of all the families of the earth; Therefore I will visit upon you all your iniquities' (Amos 3: 2). This has been called the greatest 'therefore' in all human history.

A Rabbinic legend, based on a possible meaning of his name as 'the one with a burden', has it that Amos had a speech handicap. Although he stuttered and was taunted as a stutterer, he felt compelled to speak out against injustice. This legend may have originated in an attempt to compare Amos with Moses, who had a similar defect (Exodus 4: 10).

S. M. Lehrman, 'Amos', in A. Cohen (ed.), *The Twelve Prophets* (London, 1970), 81–124.

**Amulet** Heb. *kamea*, a magical charm to protect from harm the one who possesses it or wears it. Despite the strong biblical opposition to magic and *divination, white magic in the form of the amulet was tolerated by the Talmudic Rabbis, who allowed a tried amulet (one written by an expert in the art, which had worked successfully on three different occasions) to be carried even on the Sabbath when carrying objects in the public domain is normally forbidden. Even the rationalist thinker Maimonides records this rule in his Code; although he scorns any belief in the amulet's efficacy and holds that it is only permitted because of the psychological relief it offers to the disturbed mind. Even Rabbis were not entirely free from superstition (SEE MAGIC AND SUPERSTITION) and many not only tolerated the use of amulets but actually wrote them themselves. The belief in amulets persisted widely among Jews until, along with similar superstitious practices, it was attacked by the *Haskalah and *Reform movements in the eighteenth century. To this day the belief is still held in some circles, where amulets are worn as a protection against the *evil eye and are hung around the room of a woman in childbirth to protect her against the machinations of *Lilith.

The inscriptions on amulets in ancient times would appear to have been various scriptural passages that spoke of healing or protection. In the practical *Kabbalah, various combinations of divine names are used for the writing of amulets on parchment. Contrary to Maimonides and some of the *Geonim, who were strongly opposed to the writing of amulets, the notable Halakhic authority Solomon Ibn *Adret could

say that the amulet works according to special properties with which *nature is endowed by the Creator. For Ibn Adret the cures and protection from harm afforded by amulets are governed by natural, though incomprehensible, law. If the Greek-influenced philosophers had never actually observed a magnet, says Ibn Adret, they would have scorned any belief that an object can attract to it other objects without any direct contact with them. In other words, if the empirical test is applied, amulets work, or so it was believed in the Middle Ages, and that gives us the right to resort to them.

**Angels** Supernatural beings who perform various functions at God's behest. The Hebrew word *malakh* comes from a root meaning 'to send' and is used both in the ordinary sense of a messenger and in the sense of an angel 'sent' by God. (The English word 'angel' is derived from the Greek *angelos* with the same meaning of messenger.) In Genesis 32: 2 *Jacob meets the angels of God (*malakhey elohim*) but in verse 4 he sends messengers (*malakhim*) to is brother Esau, though in a Midrashic fancy it is the angels mentioned in verse 2 that Jacob sends to Esau.

References to angels are found throughout the Bible but with the exception of Gabriel (Daniel 8: 16; 9: 21) and Michael (Daniel 10: 13; 12: 1) in the late book of Daniel, the angels in the Bible have no name. When Manoah asks the angel to tell him his name, the angel replies that it is secret (Judges 13: 17–18). The interesting observation is found in the Talmud that, in fact the names of the angels came into the possession of the Jews from Babylon. The word *el* appended to an angel's name means God; thus Gabriel (from *gevurah*, 'power') means 'power from God'. In the later Jewish tradition the angel Michael is the angel of mercy; Gabriel the angel of justice; Raphael the angel of healing; and Uriel the angel of illumination. In the prayer before going to sleep the words occur: 'In the name of the Lord, the God of Israel, may Michael be at my right hand; Gabriel at my left; Uriel before me; Raphael behind me; and the *Shekhinah of God be above my head.' As in the Bible, there are numerous references to angels in the Rabbinic literature. But there is not a single reference to angels in the Mishnah, although it is hard to tell whether this silence is simply because the Mishnah had no cause to refer to angels or whether, as some scholars think, the editor of the Mishnah wishes to discourage belief in angels. Angels are never the objects of worship. This is severely condemned by the Rabbis as idolatry. The Palestinian Talmud remarks that there is no need for Jews to pray to God through the mediation of the angels, but in the Babylonian Talmud it is implied that one of the angelic functions is to bring the prayers of Israel to the throne of God. Some later Rabbis disapproved of the few passages in the liturgy in which angels are invoked, but others defended these prayers on the grounds that the angels are only entreated to be the messengers of Israel as they are the messengers of God. A device found in a number of Talmudic passages is to place apparent moral objections to God's conduct of the world into the mouths of the ministering angels, as if to say that these objections seem to be weighty and have spiritual force, although, eventually, God provides the answer. Good men are said to be higher in rank than the angels. The angels are not allowed to sing their praises of God on high until Israel has done so on earth.

The medieval thinkers, though believing in the existence of angels as found in the Bible and the Rabbinic literature, tend to interpret the whole subject of angelology in a highly spiritual and more or less rationalistic manner. According to Maimonides, angels are creatures possessing form without matter. They are pure spirits differentiated from one another not by any bodily distinctions but solely by spiritual form and purpose. For Maimonides, the angels are only seen in the Bible as creatures of fire and in human form with wings as a feature of the prophetic vision. Wherever it is said in the Bible that angels appear to men in human guise, the meaning is that they so appear in a dream, which leads Maimonides, to the consternation of *Nahmanides and others, to explain away some biblical passages as relating not actual events but dreams. Jacob did not really wrestle with the angel (Genesis 32: 25–30), but only dreamed that he did so. Other commentators take the biblical passages literally, accepting that the angels actually become men when they appear on earth. The Zohar adopts a compromise position. For the Zohar the angels are pure spirits and in their natural form they cannot appear in the natural world, for the world could not contain them if they did. They are obliged to assume the garments,

as the Zohar puts it, of this world. The Kabbalah as a whole is full of references to angels and in the practical Kabbalah names of angels are used in *amulets. Interestingly, Maimonides (*Guide of the Perplexed*, 1. 49) quotes a Midrashic comment on the words (Genesis 3: 24): 'the flaming sword that turns every way' which suggests that this refers to the angels who change constantly, sometimes appearing as men, at other times as *women*.

In one passage in the Talmud it is said that angels accompany a man wherever he goes except when he goes to relieve himself. Before a man enters the privy he should address a special apology to the angels for his having to take leave of them.

Among many modern Jews, belief in the existence of angels is very peripheral. Even when those parts of the liturgy referring to angels are still maintained, they are understood more as sublime poetry than as theological statements. However, there are comparatively few outright denials of the actual existence of angels and some Jews, even today, look upon belief in angels as an important part of religious life.

Louis Jacobs, *A Jewish Theology* (New York, 1973), 107–113.

**Anger** Most of the rules and regulations of Judaism have to do with actions rather than with character traits. Emotional states cannot be made subject to categorical injunctions. The standard Code of Jewish law, the *Shulḥan Arukh*, offers no guidance on when and why not it is permissible to fly into a rage. There are many expressions, however, in the non-legal sources—the moralistic literature, for example—where it stated again and again that anger is an ugly emotion and has to be avoided; but the appeal here is to character-cultivation and it is acknowledged that individual temperament is involved. Some persons have a calm, easy-going disposition and for them it is easy to avoid flying into a rage. Others are more readily prone to anger and for them the struggle against their natural disposition is more severe. Hence the statement in Ethics of the Fathers (5. 14): 'There are four kinds of tempers: he whom it is easy to provoke to anger but easy to pacify, his loss disappears in his gain; he whom it is hard to provoke to anger but hard to pacify, his gain disappears in his loss; he whom it is hard to provoke to anger and easy to pacify is a saintly man; he whom it is easy to provoke to anger and hard to pacify is wicked.'

Anger is disapproved of because it betokens loss of self-control and a failure to acknowledge God's providential care. A Talmudic saying has it that a man who breaks things when he loses his temper is like an idolater. Another saying is that a person's true character can be discerned through his anger (*kaaso*), his cup (*koso*), and his pocket (*kiso*). This punning formulation is intended to convey the thought that the inner man is revealed when external restraints are removed; when he loses his temper, when he is drunk, and when he fails to put his hand into his pocket to relieve the sufferings of the needy; by the same token, when a man exercises a measure of self-control even when in a rage and even when in his cups and gives generously to charity, his benevolent inner self is exposed. Nevertheless, the Talmud states that it is permitted for parents and teachers to pretend to be angry in order to express their displeasure at the misconduct of their children and pupils.

Those who are quick tempered, say the Rabbis, have nothing to show for it except the temper itself, and the life of such persons is not worth living because they rarely experience the calmness of spirit that alone can promote a serene and happy life.

**Animals, Attitudes to** There is no single theological view in Judaism on the purpose of the animal creation. *Saadiah Gaon, discussing why God created animals, gives three possible reasons. The first is that God simply willed it so and it is not for man to try to fathom the divine will. Secondly, it may be that God created the wondrous animal kingdom in all its variety so that His wisdom could be revealed to man. Thirdly, it may be that animals have been created for man's benefit. Maimonides (*Guide of the Perplexed*, 3. 13), on the other hand, does not consider the question of why God created animals a significant one, since we must eventually fall back on the idea that it is God's will, as it is with everything else in creation. Maimonides refuses to interpret the creation narrative in Genesis (Genesis 1: 26–8) as implying that animals, sun, moon, and stars were created solely for man. True, argues Maimonides, the Genesis account states that man can rule over the animals but this in no way implies that God created them for this specific purpose. Maimonides (*Guide of the*

*Perplexed*, 3. 17) also ridicules the notion that animals will be recompensed in the Hereafter for the sufferings they have to undergo on earth. This view is held by Saadiah but Maimonides believes it to be foreign to Judaism. The Rabbinic literature was not composed by systematic theologians like Saadiah and Maimonides. In this literature there are teachings about animals which do seem to imply that everything in creation, including animals, exists for the sake of human brings. In Midrashic comment on the creation narrative in Genesis, an analogy is made between God's creation of animals, birds, and fishes and a king who has a tower stocked with all good things. If the king receives no guests, what pleasure does he derive from so stocking it? Human beings are God's guests and the animals are 'stocked' for his benefit. In even more startling form, the Talmud observes that nothing in creation is useless: the snail can be used as a cure for a scab, the fly as a cure for the sting of a wasp, and so on. We are not told what use the snail itself has in being used as a cure for a scab but then, as has been said, the Rabbis were not systematic theologians exploring fully the reasons for *creation, and are best understood as religious poets trying to give human beings a sense of importance because the whole creation revolves around them.

The ancient compilation known as *Perek Shirah* (*Chapter of Song*), is based on the idea that each species of animal sings its own particular hymn to the Creator. Appropriate scriptural verses are listed for each of God's creatures who 'sing' His praises by their very being. For instance, the song of the birds is: 'Even the sparrow hath found a house, and the swallow a nest for herself, where she may lay her young' (Psalms 84: 4). *Dogs sing: 'O come, let us bow down and bend the knee; let us kneel before the Lord our Maker!' (Psalms 95: 6). Another theological problem in connection with animals, discussed particularly by Judah Halevi, is that of animal suffering: why Nature is 'red in tooth and claw'. Although this is part of the more general question of *suffering, of why God tolerates evil in His creation, the problem is especially acute with regard to animals who have no moral sense that might be refined and developed through suffering. Halevi admits that it is hard to explain why animals should have to find their food by preying on one another. But in the very act of the spider spinning its web to catch the fly there is to be seen the wondrous wisdom of the Creator and faith must then sustain us in the belief that, in a way beyond our grasp, this same wisdom is benevolent and in the divine plan all is well and truly put.

Louis Jacobs, *A Jewish Theology* (New York, 1973), 107–9.

**Animals, Cruelty to**   While Judaism does not advocate *vegetarianism and permits the killing of animals for human use, causing unnecessary pain to animals is strictly forbidden, whether by biblical *law, according to some teachers in the Talmud, or by Rabbinic law, according to others. The Talmud urges a man to feed the animals in his care before he himself sits down to eat. Some teachers explain the existence of the law of *shehitah, the killing of animals in a special way on the grounds that this method causes the least pain to the animal. The biblical injunctions against taking the young from the nest before sending away the mother bird (Deuteronomy 22: 6–7) and against slaughtering an animal and its young on the same day (Leviticus 22: 28) have been similarly explained. This would certainly seem to be the reason for the prohibition against muzzling an ox when it treads the corn (Deuteronomy 25: 4). While *hunting animals for food is permitted, many authorities frown on hunting for sport.

The book of *Jonah concludes with the words 'and also much cattle' (Jonah 4: 11). God wishes to spare not only the human inhabitants of Nineveh but the beasts as well. In a remarkable passage in the Talmud it is related that Rabbi *Judah the Prince ordered a calf being led to the slaughter: 'Go, for this thou wast created.' He was afflicted with sufferings and these only left him when he prevented his maidservant from destroying some weasels, saying: 'His tender mercies are over all his works' (Psalms 145: 9). The point of the story is that while it is permitted to kill animals for food, it is a callous attitude to be unaware of the suffering to the animals that this entails.

It cannot be denied that the fine line between the necessary use of animals and the avoidance of unnecessary cruelty is not always drawn successfully. Is it permitted, for instance, to wear fur coats? Is battery farming permitted? Is it permitted to train animals to perform in the circus or to keep them in a zoo? Is vivisection of animals permitted in order to obtain information of benefit to humanity? The tendency is to leave a good deal of freedom to individuals to make up their minds, always being aware that wanton cruelty to animals is forbidden. Very revealing is the ruling by Rabbi Moses *Isserles in his gloss to the *Shulhan Arukh* (*Even Ha-Ezer*, 5. 14): 'Wherever it is for the purpose of healing or for some other purpose there is no prohibition against cruelty to animals. It is consequently permitted to pluck feathers from living geese [for quills] and there is no objection to it on the grounds of cruelty to animals. Nevertheless, the [Jewish] world avoids this because it is cruel.' Isserles nevertheless implies that whatever the law says, Jewish communities have not tolerated practices they perceive intuitively to be contrary to the spirit of Judaism.

Louis Jacobs, 'Animals', in his *What Does Judaism Say About . . . ?* (Jerusalem, 1973), 24–9.

**Annihilation, of Selfhood**   The mystical state in which the ego, confronted by the divine, especially in prayer, loses its separate identity; Heb. *bittul ha-yesh*. The doctrine of self-annihilation is prominent in *Hasidism in general but is stressed particularly in the *Habad group. In cultivation of this attitude some Hasidim would try never to use the 'I' pronoun in conversation. *Bittul ha-yesh* has strong affinities with the *unio mystica* in general mystical theology and it is therefore incorrect to say, as some scholars do, that in Judaism the gulf between God and human beings is so vast that no version of the religion teaches the possibility of the soul of the mystic being absorbed in the divine.

**Antediluvians**   The men before the *Flood who lived to fabulous ages (Genesis 5). According to Maimonides, it was only particular individuals who lived to these great ages but *Nahmanides considers this view to be untenable; all men of those generations lived to a great age and it was only the deterioration of the atmosphere after the Flood that brought about a gradual shortening of human life. Some students of the Bible have suggested that the numbers of 'years' are really those of 'months' but the Hebrew word *shanah* used here always means a 'year' in the Bible and a different word is used for 'month'. The Jewish Bible scholar U. Cassuto has noted that in many ancient Near Eastern cultures there are tales of great men who lived for a very long time and eventually became gods. On this view the significant expression in the biblical use of the ancient myths is 'and he died'. None of them, not even *Methuselah who lived for 969 years, were in any way divine; none of them reached the thousand years that is said by the Psalmist (Psalms 90: 4) to be like a day in the eyes of God. Ethics of the Fathers (5. 2) notes that there are ten generations of the antediluvians from *Adam to *Noah and this is said to teach that God was patient with all these generations even though they provoked Him; He did not bring the waters of the Flood upon them until their sins had reached the point where they could no longer be overlooked.

U. Cassuto, *A Commentary on the Book of Genesis*, i. *From Adam to Noah*, trans. I. Abrahams (Jcrusclem, 1959), 249–72.

**Anti-Semitism**  Hatred of Jews or unreasonable prejudice against them; a term coined in 1875 but with the reality behind it going back virtually to the beginnings of Judaism itself and culminating in the Nazi persecution of the Jews and the *Holocaust in which six million Jews perished. Anti-Semitism has assumed various forms. Greek and Latin authors ridiculed the Jewish religion and the Jews who adhered to it either because the Jews were 'atheists' in refusing to acknowledge the Greek and Roman deities, or because they thought of themselves as superior. One example of an ancient diatribe of this nature is the accusation that the Israelites were driven out of Egypt because they were a nation of lepers. Another is that the Jews keep the Sabbath because they are too lazy to work. Christian anti-Semitism, often, it has to be said, denounced by Christian authorities, was based on the Church seeing itself as the new Israel, with the consequent role for the Jews as a people rejected by God. The charge of deicide was often levelled against the Jews for killing Jesus. Jews were accused of desecrating the host and, in the *blood libel, of using Christian blood in the baking of *matzah, or of poisoning the wells and thus wilfully causing the death of Christians. In the political versions of anti-Semitism, Jews were accused of organizing a conspiracy to take over the world. Some anti-Semites pointed to the alleged undue influence of Jews in the commercial life of Western nations; others saw them as communists bent on the destruction of capitalist society. The list is unending and the outrageous and contradictory accusations are seen by most unbiased observers as based on sheer prejudice.

The cause of anti-Semitism is a question much discussed in modern times. If the phenomenon is due to prejudice, how does the prejudice arise? Opinions have varied from simple dislike of the unfamiliar to the objection to Jews foisting their religious values on the non-Jewish world with a resulting conflict of conscience for the betrayal of these values. It would be too much to say that anti-Semitism has disappeared in civilized society today but, once its horrific consequences in the Holocaust have been perceived, very few decent men and women view it as anything but an aberration. Jews have naturally co-operated with non-Jews in fighting anti-Semitism but Jewish teachers have urged that the fear of anti-Semitism should not be allowed to dominate Jewish life. Jews, they advocate, should be far more concerned with furthering positive Jewish values than with seeking to present Judaism negatively in terms of anti-anti-Semitism. Nor should everyone who dislikes Jews be dubbed an anti-Semite. Simple prejudice, unfortunate though it is, hardly constitutes a philosophy of Jew-hatred and is, of course, directed against other minorities or people seen as foreigners. An ironic feature of this whole sorry affair is the existence of self-hating Jews who come perilously close to admitting that the anti-Semite is sometimes right. It is only a generalization, but it has been said that while the anti-Semite hates the Jewish people as a whole but likes individual Jews ('Some of my best friends are Jews'), there are Jews who love the Jewish people as a whole but cannot stand the sight of their Jewish neighbours.

Léon Polialcov, *The History of Anti-Semitism*, vols. i–iii (London, 1974–5); vol. iv (The Littman Library of Jewish Civilization; Oxford, 1985).

**Apocrypha**  The books produced by Jewish writers during the period of the Second *Temple but not included in the Bible as part of sacred Scripture, as they are in Catholicism but not in the Protestant Church. The statement in the Mishnah (*Sanhedrin* 10: 1) that one who reads 'external books' has no share in the *World to Come probably refers to the books of the Apocrypha and 'reading' means reading them in public as a liturgical act, which might make them appear to enjoy the sacred status of the biblical books. Jewish scholars today have relied on the Apocrypha to uncover details of Jewish life in the Second Temple period and for comparative purposes. The books of the Apocrypha are: the first book of Esdras; the second book of Esdras; Tobit; Judith; the rest of the chapters of the book of Esther; the Wisdom of Solomon; Ben Sira (Ecclesiasticus); Baruch; a letter of Jeremiah; the Song of the Three; Daniel and Susanna; Daniel, Bel, and the Snake; The Prayer of Manasseh; the first book of the Maccabees; the second book of the Maccabees. None of these books is quoted in the Talmud or the Midrash with the exception of *Ben Sira, from which there are occasional quotations with approval. Other works from more or less the same period are embraced by the term Pseudepigrapha, a name given to them because they are attributed to early saints. These, like the Apocrypha, were unknown in Jewish literature until the Renaissance period. Apart from the circles of historians and objective scholars, all these works are largely ignored entirely by Jews today. By the same consensus by which they were excluded from the Bible they have been made to seem, if not heretical, not quite right in Jewish eyes so that rarely, if ever, will one find quotations from them in, say, books of devotion.

**Apologetics, Jewish** The systematic defence of the Jewish religion against its detractors from within and without. Numerous examples of apologetics are found in the Rabbinic literature in which the Jewish sages frequently engage in controversy with heretics or with pagan philosophers and rulers. The dialogues between Rabbi *Akiba and Turnus Rufus, the Roman Governor of Palestine, are examples of keen apologetics advanced by the former, or, more correctly, put into his mouth by later editors. Turnus Rufus asks Rabbi Akiba, for instance, why if his God loves the poor, He does not make them rich, and Akiba gives the typically Jewish reply that if there were no poor, how could the rich gain the merit afforded by alms-giving? The Rabbis often use the ministering *angels as an apologetic device. The angels are made to ask God why He shows favour to Israel and why He allows Rabbi Akiba, who had devoted himself to the study and teaching of the Torah, to be tortured to death by the Romans. Usually God is made to give an explanation but in the instance of Rabbi Akiba, all that God says is: 'Be silent. This is how it has entered My thought.' In the history of Jewish apologetics, both these types of response are prominent: those matters capable of a reasonable explanation are elaborated on, while there is always an acknowledgement that some matters are beyond human comprehension and must be left to faith. Many of the apologetics in the Rabbinic literature have the aim of expounding biblical texts in such a way that, contrary to what appears to be the surface meaning, they do not conflict with standard Jewish teachings; note the use of the plural form, for example, in the creation narrative (Genesis 1: 26): 'Let *us* make man', which is explained as meaning that God took counsel with the angels in order to teach human beings not to be hesitant in seeking advice, even from inferiors.

In the Middle Ages many works of apologetics were directed against the claims of *Christianity and *Islam that Judaism had once been a true religion but had now been superseded. The Kuzari of Rabbi *Judah Halevi, the subtitle of which is 'A Defence of the Despised Faith', is of this nature. The *Guide of the Perplexed* by *Maimonides consists of a sustained apologetic to meet the objections of Greek *philosophy. In this work, Maimonides seeks to give a rational explanation of the *dietary laws and other precepts of the Torah which appear to be opaque to human reason. In modern times *Orthodox Judaism has produced a number of apologetic works to meet the attacks of *Reform.

Apologetics only flies in the teeth of scholarship when it twists or obscures the facts in order to present the Jewish tradition in the most favourable light. Many scholars today are, however, somewhat suspicious of apologetics and, even when they themselves are committed Jews, refuse to engage in it for fear of compromising their scholarly objectivity. Yet, when the inevitable bias of apologetics is taken into account the discipline is not without value in preventing a distorted picture of Judaism from being uncritically accepted.

**Aramaic** A sister language of Hebrew (from Aram, the ancient name of the country now Syria). The Bible contains some portions in Aramaic. The language of scholarship in *Palestine in the Mishnaic period was Hebrew and the Mishnah itself is in Hebrew, but the the language of the common people was Aramaic.

In the post-Mishnaic period (from the beginning of the third century CE) the scholars used both Hebrew and Aramaic in their debates and discussions so that both the Palestinian *Talmud and the Babylonian Talmud are in Aramaic (the former in the Western dialect of Aramaic, the latter in the Eastern dialect) with a strong mixture of Hebrew, especially for legal maxims and similar formulations. As an important legal document, the *ketubah is in Aramaic, the language the people knew and understood. To the present day, in *Orthodox Judaism, the original Aramaic form is retained in the ketubah.

The language of official *prayer has always been Hebrew. Only a very few items in the *liturgy are in Aramaic—the *Kaddish, the *Kol Nidre formula recited on *Yom Kippur, and a few, much later, liturgical hymns. The language of the *Zohar is an artificial Aramaic, evidently composed by *Moses de Leon by drawing on elements·in the Talmud and the *Targum, the Aramaic paraphrase of the Bible. In Talmudic times, during the reading of the *Torah, a verse-by-verse translation was given in Aramaic for the benefit of those unable to understand the original Hebrew. Under the influence of the Talmud, many Aramaic words and expressions found their way into spoken and written Hebrew.

**Architecture** From the earliest times Jews were influenced by the various architectural styles used by the surrounding peoples, so that no specifically Jewish architectural style ever developed. But Jewish teaching has always been in favour of sound building techniques for aesthetic reasons and for reasons of safety and security. An oft-quoted Midrashic comment (Genesis Rabbah 1: 1) on creation compares the Torah to the architect's blue-print. Before God created the world, He 'looked into the Torah' like an architect who consults his plans before he begins to build. The idea here is that the world was created to be in harmony with the teachings of the Torah, but such a simile could not have been used unless the skill of the architect was admired. Incidentally, it can be seen from this passage that in ancient times the roles of architect and builder were combined in the same person. The fact that, in the Talmud, scholars are compared to builders also implies that a high value was placed on construction techniques. The Talmudic tractate Eruvin,

which treats of the *eruv, has much to say about the construction of houses, courtyards, and other enclosures and, from the Middle Ages, editions of this tractate have many diagrams to illustrate the nature of these constructions. In the Talmudic tractate Bava Batra there are many laws about the care householders have to take, when building or making additions to their houses, in order not to obstruct neighbouring residences. They must not, for instance, block the view from neighbouring houses, a Talmudic version of the English law of 'ancient lights'.

Even with regard to the construction of a *synagogue there is nothing like official regulations. Often synagogues in Islamic lands were built in a similar style to mosques and in, Christian lands, synagogues were frequently built on the pattern of churches, though not, of course, with any cruciform pattern. Many synagogues in the nineteenth century were built in a mixture of Gothic and oriental styles; the latter apparently because this was felt appropriate for a religion which came originally from the East. In modern times there has been considerable experimentation in synagogue building, though some feel that the newly built synagogues have occasionally substituted the novel for the numinous.

It remains true that considerable licence is given to the architect when building a synagogue. There is a relevant Responsum on the question by Rabbi Ezekiel *Landau of Prague. The old synagogue in Trieste was destroyed by fire and a magnificent new synagogue was erected in 1787. Before the actual building, a scholar in Trieste noticed that the plans called for an octagonal building and he turned to Rabbi Landau to enquire whether it was permitted for a synagogue to have this unusual shape. Rabbi Landau's reply is found in his *Responsa collection entitled Noda Biyhudah (Second Series, Orah Ḥayyim, no. 18). Rabbi Landau says that there is no ruling in either the Talmud or the *Codes about the shape and form a synagogue ought to have. There is nothing sacred about the conventional oblong shape of a synagogue and it is permitted to have an octagonal-shaped synagogue or, for that matter, any shape a congregation wishes. Suspicious of innovations in the traditional pattern of Jewish life and disliking the kind of ostentation that might upset the non-Jewish authorities, Rabbi Landau adds, however, a cautionary note:

'All that I have said is in accordance with the strict letter of the law. But I wonder why they should want to do this. I thought to myself, it may be they had seen something like it in palaces of princes or some other houses they wished to copy. But the truth is that it is not proper for us in our exile to copy princes and to be envious of them. If this was the reason, I recite for them the verse [Hosea 8: 14]: "For Israel has forgotten his Maker, and built palaces". It is better, therefore, not to change any of the old customs, especially in this generation. But if their reason was that there would be more room if the synagogue were to be built according to these specifications, there is not the slightest fear of there being any wrong in it.'

Few communities took Rabbi Landau's advice on the question of ostentatious synagogue buildings, possibly because conditions had changed, but his general ruling that there is no official law as to how a synagogue should be built was followed to allow a rich variety of architectural styles.

**Aristotle**   Renowned fourth-century BCE Greek philosopher. Astonishingly, there is no reference in the Talmudic literature to Aristotle or to any other famed Greek thinker even though the Palestinian Rabbis, at least, appear to have had some familiarity with Greek thought (see HELLENISM). It is possible that Aristotle and the others were not mentioned by name intentionally in order to avoid too much contact and concern with Greek opinions. In the Middle Ages, when Greek thought in its Arabic garb had penetrated the circles of the Jewish philosophers, Aristotle is quoted and his opinions discussed. Maimonides goes so far as to write that with regard to mundane topics Aristotle's views are superior to the opinions on such topics of the prophet Ezekiel, in other words it is not the task of a prophet, but of a philosopher and scientist, to explore and explain the natural world; the prophet's task is to bring God to the world. Maimonides' *Guide of the Perplexed* is largely devoted to an attempt at reconciliation between Aristotelian thought and the teachings of the Torah. Maimonides does not follow Aristotle blindly, however, and adopts the traditional Jewish view on such matters as *creation rather than the Aristotelian view that matter is eternal with God. Other medieval Jewish philosophers such as *Crescas were far

more critical of Aristotelianism. Unwilling to grant Greek thought originality over Jewish thought, later Jewish legend makes Aristotle a member of the party that is supposed to have visited Jerusalem with Alexander the Great, where the philosopher met with Jewish sages whose pupil he became. Thus there is no conflict between Greek philosophy and Judaism because Greek philosophy is really nothing but Jewish philosophy. Jewish thinkers who opposed the whole philosophical enterprise scorned the notion that Aristotle had anything to teach the Jews, although even in these circles there is a kind of grudging admiration for the attainments of the Greek thinker.

**Ark, Biblical**   The chest containing the two *tablets of stone on which the *Decalogue was inscribed. The account is given in the book of Exodus (25: 10–22) of Moses being commanded by God to instruct the people to make an Ark (*aron*) into which the 'testimony' (understood as the two tablets on the basis of other passages in the Bible) was placed. The Ark was a chest of acacia wood overlaid inside and outside with pure gold, its length 2 1/2 cubits, its width 1 1/2 cubits, and its height a 1 1/2 cubits. On top of the Ark there was a cover of pure gold to which were affixed two golden figures with outstretched wings, the *cherubim. Four golden rings were attached to the Ark into which two staves of acacia wood were placed so that the Ark could be carried from place to place. Many modern biblical scholars, while not denying the essential historicity of this account, believe that many of the details belong to a later elaboration. For instance, it has been estimated that, according to the details given, the ark would have weighted about 10 tons—a load too heavy to carry.

The numinous power of the holy Ark was such, it is related in the second book of Samuel (ch. 6), that when Uzzah saw that it was slipping from the cart in which it was being brought, and he stretched out his hand to steady it, he was stricken dead.

In Solomon's *Temple the Ark was placed in a special shrine (the 'holy of holies') but the cherubim figures were no longer attached to it, being placed on the floor of the shrine (2 Kings 6 and 8: 6). Some time during the First Temple period, the Ark is said mysteriously to have disappeared and there was no Ark in the holy of holies in the Second Temple.

In the Talmudic/Midrashic literature symbolic meanings are read into the Ark, representing the students of the Torah. The measurements of the Ark are all in half-cubits because the work of the student of the Torah is never finished. There is always more for him to study. The Ark was gold within and without and so, too, must the scholar be sincere; his outward appearance of piety and learning should not contradict what he really thinks within and he should never be a hypocrite. The staves of the Ark represent the patrons of learning who, though not necessarily learned themselves, have an important role to play in the preservation of the Torah when they shoulder the burden of the Torah by supporting needy scholars. Those who carried the Ark were not required to exert themselves too much since as soon as they put their shoulders to the staves of the Ark, the Ark carried them aloft: 'the Torah carries those who carry it'.

Nahum M. Sarna, *Exploring Exodus* (New York, 1986), 209–13.

**Ark, Noah's** See FLOOD.

**Ark, Synagogue** Following the pattern of the biblical *Ark, every *synagogue has an Ark containing the Scrolls of the Torah (*Sefer Torah). In Talmudic times the Ark was a portable chest, like the biblical Ark, and was also used as a stand upon which the Scroll was placed for the reading of the *Torah. In post-Talmudic times down to the present day, the Ark is a built-in cupboard at the eastern wall of the synagogue, covered by a curtain. (*Sephardim usually have the curtain inside the Ark, *Ashkenazim outside.) Scriptural verses concerning the biblical Ark are chanted when the Scrolls are taken from the Ark for the reading and when they are returned to the Ark. At the opening of the Ark to take out the Scroll, the verses chanted are: 'And it came to pass, when the Ark set forward, that Moses said, Rise up, O Lord, and thine enemies shall be scattered, and they that hate Thee shall flee before Thee' (Numbers 10: 35–6). At the return of the Scroll the verse is chanted: 'And when it rested, he said, Return, O Lord, unto the tens of thousands of the families of Israel' (Numbers 10: 36).

**Arrogance** A sense of brazen superiority or sheer effrontery; Heb. *azut*. In Ethics of the Fathers (5. 20) it is said: 'The arrogant [*az panim*, lit. "brazen faced"] is destined for Gehinna but the shamefaced is destined for Gan Eden' (see HEAVEN AND HELL). Arrogance is a more pejorative term than *chutzpah for which there is occasionally a kind of grudging admiration; as in English, cheek is a less objectionable expression than arrogance. In the confession of sin recited on *Yom Kippur there occurs the phrase: 'For the sin we have committed by arrogance' (*azut metzah*, lit. 'brazen forehead'). In a curious Talmudic passage (*Betzah* 25b) it is said that the people of Israel are more arrogant than any other people and, it is implied, they would be insufferable if the Torah had not been given to them so that their arrogance is controlled and disciplined. In the same passage it is stated that three are excessively arrogant: the dog among animals, the cock among birds, and Israel among the nations. Behind such sayings is presumably the idea that Jews would not have survived were it not for their stern refusal to knuckle under, but that the emotion itself is unworthy and, if unbridled, can be destructive.

**Art** It has been said that while the Greeks taught the holiness of beauty, the Hebrews taught the beauty of holiness. This is an unfortunate generalization, although it is true to say that the ancient Hebrews did see holiness as beautiful. It would be way off the mark to say, however, that Jews have been indifferent to the creation of beautiful things. A typical Talmudic saying, albeit slightly male chauvinistic, is: 'Three things broaden a man's mind: a beautiful wife, a beautiful home, and beautiful furniture.' The ancient Hebrews had a keen appreciation of beauty as can be observed in the account in the book of Exodus (ch. 25 to the end of the book) describing the erection of the *Tabernacle containing so many things of great beauty. The sacred garments for the *priests were to be made 'for splendour and for beauty' (Exodus 28: 2). According to the ancient Rabbis, special attention has to be given not only to carrying out the *precepts but also to their adornment. A *Sefer Torah, Scroll of the Torah, for instance, has to be written by a skilful scribe so that the writing is clear and pleasant to the eye. It has to be covered with a finely embroidered mantle and have attached to it the silver ornaments of bells, breastplate, crown, and pointer. Artists provided illustrations for the *Passover *Haggadah and craftsmen fashioned exquisitely wrought cases for the *mezuzah, plates for use at the Passover *Seder, candelabra for the festival of *Hanukkah and other such ritual objects, many of which are now prized collector's items.

With regard to pictorial representation there is an erroneous but widespread notion that Judaism is opposed to portrait-painting and sculpture. This notion is supposedly based on passages in the Pentateuch. The two passages quoted in this connection are the second commandment (Exodus 20: 4): 'Thou shalt not make unto thee a graven image, nor any manner of likeness, of anything that is in heaven above, or that is in the earth beneath, or that is in the water under the earth'; and Deuteronomy 4: 16–19, which forbids the making of any graven image: 'Lest ye deal corruptly, and make you a graven image, even the form of any figure, the likeness of male and female, the likeness of any beast that is on the earth, the likeness of any winged fowl that flies in the heaven, the likeness of anything that creepeth on the ground, the likeness of any fish that is in the water under the earth.'

In fact, as the context shows in both passages, the prohibition is against fashioning these likenesses for the purpose of worshipping them. It is true that some Jews have understood the prohibition as directed against any plastic representation even when it is not for the purpose of worship, just as Islam is very strict in this matter. But Jewish *law is actually far more lenient, as we shall see.

The main Talmudic passage on which the law is based is in tractate *Rosh Ha-Shanah* (24b). Rabban *Gamaliel is said to have had a tablet on which were engraved the various phases of the moon for the purpose of instructing witnesses who had come to him to testify that they had seen the new moon. The Talmud discusses how such a thing can have been permitted since there seems to be a biblical prohibition, and makes the distinction between fashioning images for the purpose of worship and fashioning them for other harmless purposes as in the case of Rabban Gamaliel. However, while the full prohibition is not incurred where the purpose is other than worship, the Talmud states that there are lesser prohibitions in certain circumstances—where, for instance, there is a full three-dimensional representation of the complete human form.

Nevertheless, the passage continues, the Rabbis in the Babylonian town of Nehardea had no hesitation in praying in a synagogue which contained a statue, although it was not fashioned by a Jew. The statue might have been erected in honour of the Gentile ruler of the town. This precedent was never followed anywhere else and it is nowadays quite unthinkable for Jews to have statues in a synagogue. The reason given for prohibiting a three-dimensional representation of the human form is that, since man is created in God's image, to represent the full human figure comes close to an attempt at representing the divine. Whatever images of God human beings have in the mind, they are only imaginary and must not be given the kind of fixed permanence they would have if they were to be fashioned as statues.

On the basis of the above, the ruling in the standard Code of Jewish law, the *Shulḥan Arukh* (*Yoreh Deah*, 141. 4–7) is clear: 'It is permitted to paint, draw, or weave in a tapestry the figures of creatures and even the figures of human beings but not to make statues of the complete human form.' An incomplete human figure is allowed—the head on its own, for instance, or the torso on its own. Henry Moore's work would be allowed on this definition and practically all modern art and sculpture. This is not to say that the *Shulḥan Arukh* is always followed in this matter. Some Jewish authorities are more puritanical, forbidding any representation even in the form of a painted portrait and there are some, fewer still, who frown even on *photography where the subject is a human being. But the majority of Jews see no need to prohibit art forms except for the three-dimensional representation of the complete human figure.

**Artificial Insemination** The question of whether Judaism permits artificial insemination has been much discussed in the *Responsa of twentieth-century Rabbis. There are two kinds of artificial insemination: (*a*) where the semen is the husband's, AIH; (*b*) where the semen is from a donor other than the husband, AID. AIH is generally allowed. The objection that AIH involves the husband in an act of *masturbation in order for the semen to be produced is generally disregarded, since no 'waste of seed' is involved, the 'seed' being used to make the wife fertile. With the sole exception of the great Orthodox authority Rabbi Moshe *Feinstein,

Orthodox Rabbis frown on AID on two grounds. First, there is the legal objection that the donor may have donated his semen to more than one woman, which might result in 'a brother marrying his sister'; that is, the donor is the natural father of all the children born as a result, and the children are brothers and sisters in Jewish law. In addition to the possibility of incest, there is the moral objection that for a married woman to become impregnated by a man other than her husband, while it is not, in the absence of actual intercourse, technically an adulterous act, does none the less constitute what is termed 'mechanical adultery' and is hence forbidden on moral grounds. Many *Reform Rabbis adopt a more lenient stance and permit AID, especially where the woman is single, though here the question of allowing a child to be brought up without ever knowing the identity of his natural father is not easily dismissed.

**Asceticism** Self-denial for a religious purpose; Heb. *perishut*, 'separation' from worldly things. As in other religions there are ascetic trends in Judaism. At the end of tractate *Kiddushin* in the Palestinian Talmud, the saying is found that a man will be obliged to render account before his Maker in the Hereafter for every legitimate pleasure he denied himself. But it is absurd to quote this stray saying, as is often done, to show that Judaism is opposed to any kind of asceticism. As we might have expected, the Talmud contains statements both in favour of asceticism and against the tendency. There is, for instance, a debate among the Talmudic teachers on whether one who fasts is a sinner or a holy man. The debate depends on how the biblical institution of the *Nazirite is understood. One teacher holds that the Nazirite is a holy man, and this teacher argues that if the Nazirite, who only took a vow to abstain from drinking wine, is a holy man, then the one who fasts and denies himself all food and drink is *a fortiori* a holy man. The other teacher holds that the Nazirite should be seen as a sinner in that he rejects God's gift of wine, and this teacher holds that one who denies himself all food and drink is an even greater sinner. The truth is that a good deal depends on individual temperament and the social conditions of the time. Teachers living in a dissolute age will try to redress the balance by advocating the ascetic ideal. (It has been said that Rabbis always appear to live in dissolute

ages!) And religious people who feel themselves tempted to overindulgence will naturally be moved to compensate for it by a regimen of abstinence. Judaism is no stranger to these conflicting tendencies and it is ridiculous to draw any neat distinctions between the so-called sane attitude of Judaism and the unbalanced hatred of the body supposedly prevalent in other religions such as Christianity.

In the Middle Ages, Maimonides' advocacy of the golden mean—a man should avoid extremes; he should not be a glutton and wear ostentatious clothes nor should he starve himself and dress in rags—was offset by the teachings of the German saints (see SAINTS OF GERMANY) who went so far as to mortify the flesh by such practices as rolling naked in the snow in winter and allowing themselves to be stung by bees in summer after smearing their naked bodies with honey in order to invite the attention of the bees. The contention of the historian F. Baer that the German saints were influenced by Christian monasticism cannot be dismissed, but this only goes to show how precarious it is to speak of a normative Judaism expressing itself in monolithic terms throughout its history. If the Germans were influenced by Christian trends in their society, Maimonides was influenced by the Greek ideal of a harmonious life which had come to him from his Islamic background.

The student of the Torah in Rabbinic times was especially encouraged to lead a life of self-denial in the pursuit of his aim. The advice to the student given in Ethics of the Fathers (6. 4) is: 'This is the way of the Torah. You must eat bread with salt and drink water by measure, and you must sleep on the ground and live a life of pain while you toil in the Torah.' A similar saying in a late Midrash has it that the student, instead of praying that the words of the Torah should enter his innards, should pray that food and drink should not enter his innards.

If, in spite of what has been said above, one can speak of the 'normative' Jewish attitude in this matter, an approximation of this was best expressed by the eighteenth-century mystic and moralist Moses Hayyim *Luzzatto in his *The Path of the Upright*, a manual for progress in the spiritual life. In this work Luzzatto devotes a whole section to the theme of abstinence and writes (ch. 9):

'You may accept as a true principle that a man should abstain from worldly things which are not absolutely necessary. But if, for whatever reason, something is physically indispensable, he who abstains from it is a sinner. To this there is no exception but how each particular thing is to be regarded must be left to each person's discretion. "A man shall be praised according to his understanding" [Proverbs 12: 18]. It is impossible to set down a rule for all the possible instances, because these are innumerable, and the human mind, not being able to grasp all of them at the same time, must deal with each case as it presents itself.'

Because *Hasidism believes that to engage in worldly matters in a spirit of sanctity is an act of worship in which the *holy sparks inherent in the material universe are reclaimed for the sacred, the Hasidic masters are, on the whole, opposed to asceticism. A grandson of the *Baal Shem Tov, the founder of the Hasidic movement, is reported to have said that the Baal Shem Tov introduced a new mystical way, in which mortification of the flesh is negated and in which the three essentials are: the love of God, the love of the Jewish people, and the love of the Torah. Yet, ascetic practices are certainly not unknown even in Hasidism. R. 'Arele' *Roth used to wear sackcloth under his shirt and whip himself regularly with a small strap, though never to the extent of endangering his health. One of the Hasidic masters of *Belz defended his extremely ascetic life by declaring that one who serves God while eating only does so during the act of eating, but one who serves God by fasting does so all the time.

In modern versions of Judaism, whether *Orthodox, *Reform, or *Conservative, there has developed a tendency to view any but the mildest forms of asceticism as bordering on the morbid and masochistic and to see as 'healthier' the more balanced life of religion.

**Ashkenazim** Jews whose ancestors lived in the Middle Ages in Germany and the surrounding countries, as distinct from those with a Spanish or oriental ancestry, the *Sephardim. The name Ashkenaz in the Bible (Genesis 10: 3) was identified in the Middle Ages with Germany, hence Ashkenazim, 'Germans'. There are no doctrinal divisions between Ashkenazim and Sephardim but each community preserves its own traditions. There are differences between the two communities in matters of *customs and, in some instances, of law. These differences are due either to different traditions

or to the different legal authorities that are followed. To give one example among many, Ashkenazim do not eat rice on *Passover while Sephardim do, a divergence arising out of the fact that medieval Ashkenazi authorities placed a ban on rice for Passover use because it might resemble leaven, forbidden on Passover. *Alfasi and Maimonides are the main authorities followed by the Sephardim, while the Code of Jacob ben *Asher is the main authority for the Ashkenazim. The *Shulhan Arukh* of Joseph *Karo records the Sephardi practices, the glosses of Moses *Isserles the Ashkenazi practices.

In matters of *liturgy, there are Ashkenazi prayer books and Sephardi prayer books, essentially the same so far as the prayers themselves are concerned but differing in some of the wordings and the arrangement. There are also differences in the pronunciation of *Hebrew. Since the Sephardim were already in Palestine at the time of the rise of Zionism, their pronunciation was followed by the creators of modern Hebrew and is still followed in the State of Israel. There is still a close rivalry between the two communities, though nowadays it rarely goes so far as to object to intermarriage between one community and the other. Attempts have been made in recent years to bring about a closer relationship between the two communities even while each remains loyal to its own traditions.

**Ashmedai** King of the *demons, as this strange figure is described in the Talmud, where he is provided with a consort, Igrat, 'queen of the demons'. Ashmedai, in Jewish folklore, is not identified with the Devil or *Satan but is rather like Shakespeare's Puck, a mischievous prankster but not evil. In a famous legend, Ashmedai succeeds by his *magic in banishing King *Solomon from his palace and taking his place disguised as Solomon on the royal throne until the wise king, after much effort, is able to prove to the elders that he and not the demonic usurper is the real Solomon.

**As If** The philosophical theory of Hans Vaihinger (1852–1933) according to which ideas, the truth of which cannot be determined, can still be of value when treated *as if* they are true. The nearest approach to this theory in the Jewish tradition is the ancient Rabbinic attempt to heighten certain concepts by treating these as if they represented concepts of greater significance. Examples of this Rabbinic 'as if' are: one who unfairly takes away another's livelihood, it is as if he had taken his wife from him; one who puts his neighbour to shame in public, it is as if he had shed his blood; if three people eat at a table and speak words of Torah, it is as if they had eaten at God's table; whoever saves the life of a single human being, it is as if he had saved alive the whole world; whoever brings up an orphan in his household, it is as if he had given birth to the child. In the last instance, the Rabbis may have intended to compensate for the fact that there is no legal *adoption in the Jewish legal system. Later teachers, however, warned against taking the Rabbinic 'as if' too literally because to do so might have the opposite to the desired effect. Instead of treating the lower concept as having a higher significance, the result might be to treat the higher concept as less significant than it really is because of its comparison with the lower concept. The Jewish moralists, on the other hand, often invent 'as ifs' of their own for leading a good life.

**Astrology**  The belief that human destiny is determined or at least affected by, the stars and planets in the ascendancy when a person is born. The ancient Egyptian and Babylonian astronomers studied the movements of the heavenly bodies and as a result the astrologers claimed to be able to predict the fate of human beings born under this or that star. The prophet Jeremiah inveighs against the people of Israel resorting to the astrologers: 'Thus saith the Lord: Learn not the way of the nations, And be not dismayed at the signs of heaven; For the nations are dismayed of them' (Jeremiah 10: 2). In the book of Isaiah the prophet declares: 'Thou art wearied in the multitude of thy counsels; Let now the astrologers, the star-gazers, the monthly prognosticators, stand up and save thee from the things that shall come upon thee' (Isaiah 47: 13). Yet neither in these two passages nor in any other biblical passage is there an explicit prohibition against consulting astrologers and there is certainly no denial that astrology actually works. Before the rise of modern science, astrology was itself believed to be an exact science. It was accepted as true by the Talmudic Rabbis, for example, who debated only whether the Jewish people are immune, in miraculous fashion, to the influence of the stars: 'There is no *mazal* ["planet" and its influence] for Israel.' Even the medieval Jewish

philosophers were not inhibited by their rationalistic approach from believing in the power of the stars. Maimonides was an exception, but he rejected astrology on theological grounds, that such belief was contrary to the doctrines of divine *providence and human *free will. When Maimonides was asked in a letter how he could deny the truth of astrology since the Talmudic Rabbis held to this belief, he replied that man was created with eyes in the front of his head, not the back! Maimonides does refer to the *zodiac but only in the astronomical, not the astrological, sense. In addition, Maimonides holds that the biblical objections to *magic and *divination extend to astrology. He is followed in this by the *Shulḥan Arukh* (*Yoreh Deah*, 179. 1) where the ruling is given: 'One must not enquire of the astrologers and not consult lots.' But *Isserles, gloss to this (179. 2) quotes *Nahmanides to the effect that while one must not consult the astrologers but rely on God without being concerned about what the future will bring, nevertheless, if a man knows some undertaking to be contrary to his *mazal*, his fate as determined by the stars, he should take the necessary precautions and should not rely on a miracle to save him. It follows that there has been in the past a somewhat ambivalent attitude towards astrology, only Maimonides declaring it to be complete nonsense. The other authorities advise strongly against actually consulting the astrologers but believe, none the less, that the forecasting of horoscopes can be accurate if carried out by an expert. The majority of Jews today are not much affected by astrological beliefs one way or the other, although in Yiddish parlance the expression *mazal tov* for 'good luck' is still used, more as a convention than as a matter of belief. Similarly, the Yiddish term for an unfortunate, like the English 'one on whom the stars do not shine', is *shlimazal*, 'one without *mazal*'. That it is all not taken very seriously can be seen from the old Yiddish humorous definition of the *shlimiel* ('the clumsy') and the *shlimazal*. The former is the man who spills the cup of tea, the latter the man who gets it on his trousers.

**Atheism**  The attitude that affirms there is no God. Until the Middle Ages, when the philosophers, Jewish, Christian, and Muslim, who in response to atheistic attacks sought to prove by rational argument the existence of God, theoretical atheism was unknown. When the

Psalmist (Psalms 14: 1) castigates the fool for saying in his heart there is no God, he is thinking of practical atheism: that, so far as human conduct is concerned, God does not matter, that God is unconcerned about whether or not human beings practice justice and right-eousness. When St Anselm of Canterbury (1033–1109), presenting his famous ontological argument for the existence of God, quotes this Psalm against his 'fool' and understands the fool to be saying that God does not exist, his understanding of the Psalm is consequently anachronistic, as the verse goes on to say: 'They have dealt corruptly, they have done abomina-bly; there is none that doeth good.' The 'fool' in the Psalm is guilty of moral, not intellectual, turpitude. Similarly, such ancient Rabbinic ref-erences to one who 'denies the basic principle' or one who says that 'there is neither judge nor judgement', mean not that these do not believe in the existence of God but rather that they deny that God is at all concerned with how human beings behave. They deny divine *provi-dence and that God is a 'judge'. In the Middle Ages, however, it is clear that the atheistic philosophy in its more extreme form was held by some Jews and it was to counter their arguments that the philosophers sought to prove the existence of God. After Kant's demonstra-tion that the existence of God can only be determined by the practical reason, not by the theoretical, atheism as a philosophy became popular in some circles and has persisted in modern times. It goes without saying that Judaism, which stands or falls on the belief in the existence of God, is totally incompatible with atheism, though Jewish *secularism does try to preserve Jewish *values and even some Jewish rituals together with an atheistic atti-tude. In a Jewish tale, a man refuses to come to the synagogue for the afternoon prayer so as to make up the quorum required, on the grounds that he is an atheist. The president of the synagogue wryly remarks: 'And if he is an atheist does that mean that he must not recite the afternoon prayer?'

The word *epikoros, from the Greek, origi-nally had a number of meanings denoting a denial of one or other aspect of the Jewish religion, but nowadays the term is often used to denote the out-and-out atheist.

**Authority** That by which the beliefs and prac-tices of Judaism are sanctioned. To quote first the biblical text on which the question of authority in Judaism is based:

'If there arise a matter too hard for thee in judgement, between blood and blood, between plea and plea, and between stroke and stroke, even matters of controversy within thy gates; then shalt thou arise, and get thee up unto the place which the Lord thy God shall choose, And thou shalt come unto the place which the Lord thy God shall choose, And thou shalt come unto the priests the Levites, and unto the judge that shall be in those days; and thou shalt inquire; and they shall declare unto thee the sentence of judgement. And thou shalt do according to the tenor of the sentence, which they shall declare unto thee from that place which the Lord thy God shall choose; and thou shalt observe to do all that they shall teach thee. According to the law which they shall teach thee, and according to the judgement they shall tell thee, thou shalt do; thou shalt not turn aside from the sentence which they shall tell thee, to the right hand, nor to the left.' (Deu-teronomy 17: 8–11.)

In the context the passage refers to cases in law, disputes between two parties, with which, because of their difficulty and complexity, the local judges cannot cope and on which they require guidance from a higher authority. The case must be brought to a supreme court (later identified with the *Sanhedrin) composed of the *priests, the custodians of the Torah, which sat in the place chosen by God (identified with Jerusalem).

In traditional Jewish thought, the passage is extended so as to confer authority on the sages of Israel (especially the Talmudic *Rabbis) whose interpretation of the Torah is the only authentic interpretation of the text, from which no faithful Jew may depart 'to the right hand, nor to the left', understood in the Midrash as meaning: 'even if they seem to be telling you that your right hand is your left, or your left hand your right'. The ultimate authority is, then, the God-given Torah as interpreted by the Talmudic Rabbis, so that the Talmud, as the sole authentic interpreter of the biblical text, became, in one sense, more authoritative than the bare text itself.

Many medieval Jewish thinkers, especially after the rise of the *Karaites, lumped together everything in the Talmud as the opinion of the sages in Israel, treating the Talmudic Rabbis as infallible, spiritual supermen whose teachings must be obeyed as if they were the very word of God. Maimonides, on the other hand, locates the authority of the Talmudic Rabbis not in their supposed gift of inspiration but in the fact that the Jewish people had taken it upon themselves to accept the teachings of the Talmud. On this view, the ultimate authority is the tradition of the Jewish community as a whole, the consensus of Jews throughout the ages by which the Talmud itself enjoys authority.

With regard to *belief the matter is more complicated. There are *dogmas in Judaism but the position is very different from, say, that in Christianity, since there has never emerged in Judaism an authoritative body to define the beliefs a Jew is expected to hold. Furthermore, belief cannot be coerced and in matters of doubt the believer has no course but to work it out for himself. This is why *Bahya, Ibn Pakudah, in his work with the, in this connection, revealing title *Duties of the Heart*, noted that the Deuteronomic passage speaks only of problems in law, not of problems in theology. For Bahya as well the Talmudic is authoritative in all matters, including matters of belief, but each person must try to arrive at the truth by himself, guided, naturally, by the wisdom contained in the Talmud.

While the Talmud constitutes the final Court of Appeal in Jewish *law, later Rabbis were obliged to deal in their *Responsa with new questions where the Talmudic rulings are opaque and with matters on which the Talmudic Rabbis engage in debate. Various *Codes of law were compiled, the one enjoying the greatest authority in *Orthodoxy from the date of its compilation in the sixteenth century down to the present day being the *Shulḥan Arukh. *Reform Judaism in the early nineteenth century rejected the authority of the Talmud, but, especially after the *Holocaust in the twentieth century, came to pay greater heed to Talmudic teachings and to Rabbinic law, at least where these are not seen as contrary to the modern spirit.

For the Kabbalists a different type of authority emerged, that of the new revelations of religious truths conveyed by the great mystical teachers and believed by the Kabbalists to contain the inner meaning of the Torah. For the Kabbalists, the Zohar took its place beside the Bible and the Talmud as an infallible, sacred text of supreme importance. The followers of *Isaac Luria, the Ari, from the sixteenth

century onwards, saw the teachings of this master as secrets communicated to him from on high which were therefore to be followed as the word of God. There was even produced a *Shulḥan Arukh* of the Ari in which were set forth the special practices and rituals based on Kabbalistic teachings. The problem that arose was what the devout Kabbalist was to do when rules based on Kabbalistic ideas were in conflict with those in the Talmud and the Codes. The later codifiers generally laid down the rule that where the Talmud and Codes are in conflict with the Kabbalah, the Kabbalah should not be followed. But where a Kabbalistic rule is not found at all in the Talmud or the Codes, that rule should be followed. The Kabbalists themselves naturally followed the Kabbalah as their ultimate authority whether or not its rules were in conformity with the Talmud; although the great Talmudist and Kabbalist, *Elijah, Gaon of Vilna, is reported to have said that it was impossible for the Talmud and the Kabbalah to be in conflict and if they appeared to be, it was because one or the other had been misunderstood.

In *Hasidism yet another type of authority emerged, that of the *Rebbe, the particular master to which the Hasid owed his allegiance. The source of this new kind of authority lies not only in the charismatic quality of the leader but also in local Hasidic *custom.

**Autopsies** The dissection of corpses in order to discover the cause of death. Whether autopsies are allowed in Judaism has been much discussed in recent years. There are two possible objections to autopsies according to *Orthodoxy (*Reform Judaism is usually more permissive): 1. It is forbidden to mutilate a corpse. 2. It is forbidden to enjoy any benefit from a corpse. But against these objections is the principle that the saving of *life overrides most prohibitions of the Torah, so that logically autopsies should be allowed since they help to increase medical knowledge of benefit to mankind in the saving of many persons who would otherwise die. But the famous eighteenth-century Halakhic authority, Rabbi Ezekiel *Landau, in a Responsum on the subject at a time when the dissection of corpses was an innovation, ruled that an autopsy is only permitted where a sufferer from the same disease which caused the death of the person on whom the autopsy is performed is still alive and where there is, consequently, an immediate saving of life. Some more recent authorities have advanced the argument that, nowadays, with greater means of communicating the results of medical research, sick persons who will benefit directly are always present. Yet, so far, this argument has not been accepted in Orthodox circles who still frown very severely on autopsies.

**Av, Ninth of** The ninth day of the month of Av (tisha be-av), the fast day commemorating the destruction of the *Temple and other calamities in Jewish history. Tisha Be-Av is treated with greater severity than the minor *fast days in that it begins at sunset of the previous night and on it are forbidden not only eating and drinking but also marital relations, bathing, and the wearing of leather shoes. The book of *Lamentations is chanted in the *synagogue in a mournful tune. Since the study of the Torah is thought of as the greatest joy, it is forbidden to study the Torah except for the book of *Job and Talmudic and Midrashic passages which deal with the destruction of the Temple. Special dirges, kinnot, composed in former times in mourning for tragic events, are chanted. The *tefillin, a sign of Israel's glory, are not put on until the afternoon. The Torah *reading in the morning is from the book of Deuteronomy (4: 25–40) and the *Haftarah from the book of Jeremiah (8: 13–9: 21), both dealing with warnings of disaster. *Reform Judaism in the last century abolished this fast on the grounds that to mourn for the destruction of the Temple, thus implying that it will one day be rebuilt, runs counter to the Reform interpretation of the doctrine of the Messiah in terms of progress as was evident at the time in Western society. *Orthodoxy sees the day as one of hope of restoration and redemption from exile. The ancient legend has it that the *Messiah was born on Tisha Be-Av. Many contemporary Reform Jews do keep the fast in commemoration of the greatest tragedy that befell the Jewish people in all history, the *Holocaust.

Voices have been raised, even in the Orthodox camp, to the effect that following the establishment of the State of Israel there is no longer any need to fast on Tisha Be-Av and given the repopulation of its cities it is unfitting, and might even seem ungrateful, to pray for the rebuilding of Jerusalem. These voices are now mute but many Jews have altered the phrase in the special Tisha Be-Av prayer, 'the city that is desolate' to read 'the city that was desolate'. Tokens of mourning are out of place on the Sabbath, so if the Ninth of Av falls on Sabbath, the fast is postponed for a day, taking place from sunset on Saturday night to nightfall on Sunday night.

**'Avinu Malkenu'** 'Our Father our King', a prayer attributed in the Talmud to Rabbi *Akiba and recited during the penitential season from *Rosh Ha-Shanah to *Yom Kippur and on fast days. God is referred to as both the stern King and the loving Father and is entreated to show mercy to His people.

**Azazel** The place, according to the Jewish tradition, to which the scapegoat was taken on *Yom Kippur in Temple times. The relevant biblical passage reads: 'And Aaron shall cast lots upon the two goats; one for the Lord, and the other lot for Azazel. And Aaron shall present the goat upon which the lot fell for the Lord, and offer it as a sin-offering. But the goat, on which fell the lot for Azazel, shall be set alive before the Lord, to make atonement over it, to send it away for Azazel into the wilderness' (Leviticus 16: 8–10). All the commentators are puzzled by this rite and the actual meaning of Azazel is very uncertain but, according to the Mishnah (Yoma 6: 2–6), the goat was taken to a rock, Azazel, from which it was pushed to be killed and thus atone for the sins of the people. Abraham *Ibn Ezra and *Nahmanides in the Middle Ages connected Azazel with the worship of *demons, as a kind of protest against such worship. Among popular insults, 'Go to hell' is rendered as lekh le-azazel and, with more fancy than accuracy, the guides in modern Israel take unsuspecting tourists on a visit to hell, that is, to the supposed rock of Azazel. In some ancient legends Azazel is connected with one of the fallen angels in the book of Genesis (6: 1–4). These and similar fanciful ideas remain purely in the realm of speculation and have no relevance to Jewish theology of any variety.

**Azikri, Eleazar** Safed Kabbalist (1533–1600), author of Sefer Haredim (The Book of the God-fearers), in which the *precepts are given an original classification corresponding to the various organs and limbs of the body with which they are carried out. In his introduction to the book, Azikri draws up seventeen necessary conditions for a precept to be performed in the ideal manner; among them that it should be carried out with proper intention to do God's will; that it should not be half done or in a half-hearted manner but with joy in the service of God; that it should be carried out by the worshipper himself and not delegated to others; and that, wherever possible, it should be carried out in the company of other worshippers. Azikri's poem of mystical yearning, *Yedid Nefesh*, is very popular and has been incorporated into many prayer books.

**Azulai, Hayyim Yosef David** Jerusalem Kabbalist, bibliographer, Talmudist, and traveller (1724–1806), especially known for his *Shem Ha-Gedolim*, a bibliographical and biographical lexicon of Rabbinic authors and their works. His travel diary is also well known. Azulai (called, after the initial letters of his name, *Ḥida*) has good claim to the title of first modern Jewish bibliographer, even though he often has an uncritical approach to his sources.

# B

**Baal Shem Tov** 'Master of the Good Name', the title given to Israel ben Eliezer (1698–1760), founder of the Hasidic movement (*Hasidism). The title (often abbreviated to Besht, after its initial letters) refers to the use, as in the *Kabbalah, of various combinations of divine names ('*names of God') in order to effect miraculous cures. Like other miracle-workers of the time, the Besht was first known as a practitioner of white magic but this aspect of his life is usually played down by the Hasidim, who prefer his role as spiritual master and guide to predominate.

The life of the Besht is so surrounded by legends that some historians doubted his existence. The legendary biography *Shivhey Ha-Besht* ('Praises of the Besht') was not published until around fifty years after his death, by which time numerous legends had proliferated, and it was thought of as pure fiction. But recently it has been established beyond doubt that there is a strong core of fact in the hagiographical material. As M. J. Rossman has shown, the name Israel ben Eliezer appears in Polish archives with the addition of the words 'doctor and Kabbalist'. We now know that the Besht lived in the town of Miedzyboz in Podolia for many years, where he received a handsome stipend from the Jewish community (thus giving the lie to the notion that Hasidism was anti-establishment from its inception). In Miedzyboz there gathered around him a group of pneumatics out of which the new movement emerged. It has to be appreciated that at the time in Eastern Europe there were a number of charismatic leaders, of whom the Besht was only one. However, the Besht's teachings and way of life so influenced like-minded followers that the other groups eventually vanished from the scene. Hasidism became Beshtian Hasidism.

It is also difficult to distinguish the original ideas of the Besht from those taught in later varieties of Hasidism. The sayings attributed to him in *Toledot Yaakov Yosef,* by his disciple Jacob Joseph of *Polonoyye, and in *Degel Mahaney Efrayim,* by his grandson, Ephraim of Sudlikov, have an air of authenticity about them but come to us at second or third hand. The Besht stressed the divine immanence, contemplation of which is bound to fill the heart with religious joy and enthusiasm. In *Zangwill's essay 'The Master of the Name' (in his *Dreamers of the Ghetto*) the Besht appears as a jolly coachman full of the love of life who strikes the narrator as a mere simple man of faith until he stands in prayer, lost in profound contemplation. Zangwill's portrait is not without value but ignores the numinous quality of life as perceived by the master.

The figure of the Besht became the prototype of the Hasidic *Zaddik and is treated in every variety of Hasidism with the utmost veneration, although, at the same time, he is seen as caring passionately for the well-being of the Jewish people as the people of God. In later Hasidism to tell the story of the Besht is itself a means of bringing down the divine grace from on high. The curious early Hasidic legend that the heavenly mentor of the Besht was Ahijah the Shilonite (1 Kings 11: 29–39) is undoubtedly based on the need to link the novel ideas of the Besht to the Torah of Moses (according to Rabbinic legend, Ahijah was present at the time of the *Exodus as a contemporary of Moses and he lived on for hundreds of years).

Dan Ben Amos and Jerome R. Mintz (eds. and trans.), *In Praise of the Baal Shem Tov* (Bloomington, Ind., and London, 1970).

**Baal Teshuvah** Repentant sinner, literally 'one who returns' from his evil ways. That a sinner is to be encouraged to return to God and repent of his sins is stressed by the Talmudic Rabbis, following the biblical teachings about sin and *repentance. According to one opinion in the

Talmud, the repentant sinner is greater than one who has never committed any grievous sin. There are two kinds of penitents: the sinner who repents out of fear and the sinner who repents out of love for God. Once the former has repented his sins are considered as if he had committed them unintentionally, but when a sinner repents out of love his very sins are counted as if they had been virtues. The Rabbis teach that it is a serious offence to taunt a penitent with his former evil deeds.

For the *Saints of Germany *sin and repentance are seen as stages in the spiritual life. Even the saints, for these medieval teachers, can only advance in spirituality by repenting of minor sins which for lesser mortals would be mere peccadilloes, the *baal teshuvah* thus becoming one highly advanced in the spiritual way.

In times when conversions to other religions were not unknown among Jews, the name *baal teshuvah* was given especially to a convert to Christianity or Islam who had returned to the Jewish fold.

In the second half of the twentieth century, there has emerged a strong *baal teshuvah* movement in which the name is given to those, especially young persons, formerly estranged from or ignorant of full Jewish observance, who have now returned to the fully *Orthodox way of life. The name *baal teshuvah* has here lost its original meaning, which bordered on the pejorative, to denote something of a status symbol. There are, nowadays, special *Yeshivot for the training of such 'returners', in which they are introduced gradually to all the niceties of Jewish rituals and observances. It is not uncommon for people belonging to this movement, once they have seen the light, to become intolerant zealots with the result that they are sometimes viewed with suspicion and hostility by their parents and former teachers, who are appalled at their *fundamentalism. However, the teachers at these institutions do try hard to promote tolerant attitudes on the part of their pupils, urging them not to look down on those who do not have their advantages. In contemporary American slang, the *baal teshuvah* is called, after the initial letters, a BT, in contradistinction to the FFB, 'frum ["pious"] from birth'. BTs now wear their name with pride, feeling superior to the FFBs; the latter react, as might have been expected, with derision.

Louis Jacobs, *A Jewish Theology* (New York, 1973), 243–59.

**Babylon** The country between the rivers Tigris and Euphrates, now Iraq, to which the Jews were exiled by Nebuchadnezzar after the destruction of the First *Temple and by the rivers of which the exiles refused to sing 'the Lord's song in a strange land' (Psalms 137). In Talmudic times the Jews and their religion were not at first viewed with tolerance. Ardeshir, the first of the Sassanian rulers of the whole Persian Empire, of which Babylon was the centre, held sway over forty million people. The official religion of the empire was *Zoroastrianism and the Magi, the Zoroastrian priests, had great power, their hostility to Judaism expressing itself in severe denunciation and even persecution. Under King Shapur I (241–72), however, a far more tolerant attitude emerged. The Jews came to be relied on, together with the Armenians, by the Sassanian rulers for trade and commerce in the empire. In this period Babylon became, next to Palestine, the greatest centre of Jewish life in the world. Under the early third-century teachers *Rav and Samuel, Babylon became a centre of Jewish learning, a keen rivalry existing between the Babylonian and Palestinian scholars. The Babylonian Talmud became more authoritative than the Palestinian under the influence of the *Geonim, who looked upon themselves as the heirs of the Talmudic sages.

The Jewish community in Babylon in Talmudic and Geonic times was headed by the *exilarch who was virtually a Jewish prince, with his own law-enforcement agencies.

In Jewish literature, many a reaction to the official religion in Babylon can be observed: to Zoroastrianism in the Talmudic period and to *Islam in the Geonic period. The very names of the Jewish months have a Babylonian origin, as the saying in the Palestinian Talmud acknowledged, because the names of the months and the names of the *angels were brought by the Jews out of Babylon. It is generally held that. *Sephardim are influenced by the Babylonian rites, *Ashkenazim by the Palestinian.

**Baeck, Leo** German Reform Rabbi, preacher and thinker (1873–1956). Baeck was deported by the Nazis to the Theresienstadt concentration camp where his great courage in the face of adversity was an encouragement to the other inmates. Baeck was a renowned preacher but it was said of him that he never used the personal pronoun 'I' in his sermons. This fondness for objectivity and abstract thought is evidenced in all Baeck's works, making them difficult reading despite the importance and wide influence of his ideas. In Baeck's major work *The Essence of Judaism*, Judaism is described in strongly ethical, albeit God-inspired and God-directed, terms. Baeck became the acknowledged leader of *Reform Judaism in the first half of the twentieth century, claiming that only in Reform can the Torah be termed 'the Torah of truth' because it faces up squarely to the challenges presented by modern thought.

Albert A. H. Friedlander, *Leo Baeck: Teacher of Theresienstadt* (London, 1968).

**Bahir** 'Brightness', the earliest book of the Kabbalah, of unknown authorship, which first appeared in southern France at the end of the thirteenth century and in which the doctrine of the *Sefirot is adumbrated. Like its successor, the Zohar, the Bahir is a pseudepigraphic work, sayings being attributed in it to various *Tannaim and Amoraim who could not have been the actual authors.

**Bahya, Ibn Asher** Thirteenth-century Spanish biblical exegete and Kabbalist, author of a commentary to the Pentateuch written in the year 1291. Bahya was a disciple of Solomon Ibn *Adret, whose Kabbalistic ideas as well as those of Adret's teacher, *Nahmanides, are expressed more or less openly in his commentary. Bahya accepted the notion of *cycles according to which the history of the world proceeds in a series of 6,000 years followed by a thousand-year Sabbath and then another series and so on, until the great Jubilee at the end of 49,000 years. In the introduction to the commentary, Bahya remarks that the Torah is bound up with the Supernal Wisdom and it therefore embraces all the sciences. Bahya employs in his commentary the fourfold method of exegesis. Verses are explained according to their plain, their homiletical, and their allegorical meanings, and their 'mysteries', the Kabbalistic meaning. The popularity of his commentary can be gauged from the title given to it by later generations, *Rabbenu Bahya*, 'our master Bahya', that is, master *par excellence*.

**Bahya, Ibn Pakudah** Spanish philosopher of the eleventh century. Bahya's *Duties of the Heart* is a treatise of morals and religion, translated into *Yiddish, sure evidence of the

work's popularity among ordinary devout Jews, although the opening section on the unity of God is strictly philosophical and written for thinkers. In this section Bahya stresses that the nature of God cannot be apprehended by the human mind. The biblical anthropomorphic expressions do not mean that God can be described in human terms. Indeed, God cannot be described at all. The biblical descriptions are necessary, however, for the psychological reason that if humans are to worship God they must have some picture of God in the mind, always with the proviso that 'the Torah speaks in the language of men' (a Talmudic expression which Bahya has adapted for his purpose); that is, the language used in the Torah does not and cannot convey the Reality but provides humans with a vocabulary of worship. For Bahya, when Judaism teaches the unity of God this should not be understood only to mean that God is one not many, but to indicate particularly that God is unique, totally different from His creatures and completely beyond the imagination.

In his introduction, Bahya states his aim of calling attention to the inwardness that Judaism demands of its adherents. Religious Jews are fully aware of the external rites, ceremonies, and other external obligations and perform these, the duties of the limbs, diligently. It is with regard to the duties of the heart that they often fall short. These duties include the love and fear of God, prayer with proper intentions, love of the neighour, and pure, sincere and disinterested worship of God with all the heart. These, far from being incidental, belong to the very essence of Judaism. Bahya was influenced by Sufi teachings (see SUFISM) even in the title he gave to his work. He is not averse to quoting favourably non-Jewish pietists, as when he tells with approval the tale of the non-Jewish saint (*ḥasid*) who slept outdoors where he was in danger from wild beasts and robbers because his fear of God was too profound to allow him to entertain any fear of God's creatures.

The *Duties of the Heart* is ascetic in tone, although it rejects extreme forms of *asceticism in which a man shuns the society of others. Bahya's ideal is for man 'to mix freely with others but be alone with his Maker in his mind'. Man must engage in battle at all times with his great foe, the evil inclination within his heart that seeks to prevent him following the way of the Torah. The maxims in the book are often quoted in the literature of Jewish piety.

One of these is that prayer without inwardness is like a body without a soul.

Bahya Ben Joseph Ibn Pakudah, *The Book of Direction to the Duties of the Heart*, trans. and ed. Menahem Mansoor (London, 1973).

**Balaam** The heathen soothsayer and prophet whose story is told in the book of Numbers (22: 1–24: 25). This strange biblical passage, giving rise to a number of problems, has been widely discussed by Jewish commentators throughout the ages. How Balaam's curses could have been effective and why it was necessary for God to turn them into blessings, for example, troubled Jewish thinkers, who generally treat the topic as part of the wider problem regarding the efficacy of *blessings and curses. Another problem, that of of Balaam's talking ass, for long an object of ridicule by foes of the Bible, has been considered by Jewish exegetes; the more miraculously inclined among them see no reason why God should not have endowed an ass temporarily with the power of speech, while the rationalists interpret the whole episode as having taken place in a dream, or suggest that Balaam imagined the noises made by the ass to be human speech.

With regard to ancient Rabbinic attitudes, a distinction has to be made between the story and Balaam's oracles, as these appear in the Bible, and the character of Balaam himself. The former, as part of the Pentateuch, enjoys the full authority of the divinely revealed Torah. In tractate *Bava Batra* (14b) of the Talmud, there is even an opinion that Moses wrote the book of Balaam; an alternative opinion evidently holds that the actual words of the oracles are Balaam's own, and were incorporated by Moses into the Torah. Concerning the character of Balaam, there is considerable ambiguity in the ancient Rabbinic literature. In the ancient Rabbinic Midrash known as the Sifre (Deuteronomy 34: 10) it is said that while no prophet arose in Israel like Moses, among the nations of the world there did arise such a one, namely Balaam. On the other hand, in Ethics of the Fathers (5: 19) a distinction is drawn between the disciples of Father *Abraham, who have a good eye, a humble mind, and a lowly spirit, and the disciples of Balaam, who have an evil eye, a haughty mind, and a proud spirit. At the beginning of the morning service in the *synagogue, the verse from Balaam's oracles (Numbers 24: 5) is recited: 'How goodly are thy tents, O Jacob, Thy dwelling places, O Israel'; 'tents' and 'dwelling places' are taken to mean the synagogues.

The suggestion made by *Geiger and others that sometimes in the Rabbinic literature the name Balaam refers to *Jesus is very unlikely. In some versions of the Christian Kabbalah, however, Balaam is identified with Jesus and becomes a figure to be venerated instead of treated with opprobrium as in the Jewish sources, where he is usually called 'Balaam the wicked'.

**Bare Head** It would be difficult to find a more trivial matter that was the source of greater controversy in Jewish life than the question of whether or not it is permitted for males to pray with uncovered head. From the very few references in the Talmud it would appear that only men noted for their piety covered their heads, not only for prayer but at all times, out of respect for God 'on high', that is, above their head. As late as the eighteenth century *Elijah, Gaon of Vilna could write (note to the *Shulḥan Arukh, Oraḥ Ḥayyim*, 8) that according to the strict law there is no need to pray with covered head and that to cover the head is no more than an act of piety. For all that, especially in reaction to Christian worship, it became the universal practice among the *Orthodox to cover the head (either with a hat or with the *yarmulka) at all times. Certainly, it is now unheard of for worshippers in an Orthodox synagogue to have their head uncovered. In the early days of *Reform Judaism it was often the practice to pray with bared head even in the synagogue but this is rare nowadays, and some Reform Jews have adopted the Orthodox practice of wearing a head-covering at all times.

The ancient practice for married *women was to wear a head-covering at all times as a token of modesty. Many, but by no means all, Orthodox married women still follow this custom, usually by wearing a wig, the *sheitel*. Rabbi Moses *Sofer, in the nineteenth century, argued that since one of the reasons why males should have their heads covered in the synagogue is not to copy Christian forms, single women should, on the contrary, pray in the synagogue with uncovered head because in the Christian Church women normally have a head-covering during worship. From the many studies that have been made on this vexed topic, it is clear that what was originally a simple matter of extraordinary piety has become, for many, a badge of allegiance to Judaism. As the nineteenth-century Orthodox leader, Israel *Salanter, is reported to have remarked: 'There is no law that a Jew must have his head covered but, nevertheless, a Jew covers his head.' It is customary for a Jew who takes an oath on the Bible in a non-Jewish court to do so with his head covered.

**Bar Kochba** General in Judaea who led a great revolt against Roman dominion (d. 135 CE). Letters written by Bar Kochba (and the coins he struck during his early successes against Rome) have been discovered. From these we learn that the real name of this leader was Simeon bar Kasivah. The name Bar Kochba ('son of the star') was evidently given to him later on the basis of the verse in the oracles of *Balaam (Numbers 24: 17): 'There shall step forth a star out of Jacob', said to be a forecast of the brave warrior who will arise to save the Jewish people from its oppressors.

In two Talmudic passages it is stated that, at first, Rabbi *Akiba hailed Bar Kochba as the *Messiah. While there may well be a core of truth in this, it has to be appreciated that these passages are very late and belong more to legend than to history. Speculations by historians that Rabbi Akiba played an important role in the revolt led by Bar Kochba are pure fancy.

In Jewish thought the episode of Bar Kochba was often seen as a warning against forcing God's hand and against realized *eschatology, but with the rise of *Zionism and the established of the State of Israel the tendency emerged to see Bar Kochba as the hero who fights for his people against all odds. It is probably true, none the less, to say that for Jews Bar Kochba is more important for historical studies than he is for present-day Jewish theology or religious life.

**Bar Mitzvah** 'Son of commandment', a boy who has reached, at the age of 13, his religious majority, that is, the age at which he is responsible for his actions and hence obliged to keep the *precepts of the Torah. The word 'bar' ('son') means in this context 'belonging to', associated with the precepts. In the older tradition there was no special initiatory rite for the new status of *bar mitzvah*. When he reached the age of 13 a boy simply lost his status as a minor not responsible enough to carry out any

religious duties and became, in law, a responsible adult, although, according to some authorities, God did not hold him to be fully responsible until he reached the age of 20. In the Middle Ages, especially in German communities, the transition was marked by special ceremonies. The boy was called up to read the *Torah; he began to put on the *tefillin*; and a party was held in his honour at which he delivered a learned discourse, displaying his learning or, in some cases, his lack of it. In Western lands, much has been made (some Rabbis hold, too much) of the Bar Mitzvah ceremonies. It is a common mistake to imagine that, in the absence of these ceremonies, the boy is not fully Jewish. The plain fact is that every male Jew becomes automatically responsible and the ceremonies are irrelevant. Yet the ceremonies and the party are usually seen as a pleasant way of introducing the boy into a fuller Jewish life, harmless and even admirable provided there is no ostentation.

The usual procedure for a Bar Mitzvah nowadays is for the boy to attend the Sabbath service in the synagogue together with his parents. During the reading of the Torah from the *Sefer Torah, the boy will chant a portion and then chant the prophetic portion of the day, the *Haftarah, after which he is addressed by the Rabbi who will remind him of his new obligations as a Jew. When the boy is called up to read from the Torah, his father recites the *benediction: 'Blessed be He who hath freed me from the responsibility of this child', expressing the thought that until now the father has been held blameworthy for any sins of commission or omission of the boy; he is now free of this responsibility and the boy stands on his own, so to speak. The Torah is read on Mondays and Thursdays as well as on the Sabbath and in some communities the boy reads his Bar Mitzvah portion on one of these days. In recent years, a Bar Mitzvah has often been taken to *Jerusalem for the Monday or Thursday reading at the *Western Wall. Visitors to the Western Wall on these days can see Oriental Jews carrying the boy around after he has read his portion, accompanied by the beating of drums and full-throated song.

Strictly speaking, it is not the age of 13 that determines whether or not a boy is Bar Mitzvah, but the onset of puberty. However, the ruling of one of the Talmudic Rabbis is accepted that, in the absence of any evidence to the contrary, there is the presumption that a boy who has reached the age of 13 has the signs of puberty.

Moira Paterson (ed.), *The Bar Mitzvah Book* (London, 1975).

**Bat Kol** 'Daughter of a voice', an echo, the term given in the Talmudic literature and Jewish mystical thought to a communication from heaven, the lowest form of direct divine *inspiration. The Talmud (*Eruvin* 13b) states that for three years the rival schools of *Hillel and *Shammai debated whose authority was to be accepted in Jewish *law until a Bat Kol decided that, while the words of both schools were 'the words of the living God', the actual rulings in practice were to be in accordance with the school of Hillel. On the other hand, in the Talmudic tale (*Bava Metzia* 59b) where a Bat Kol decides that the ruling is in accordance with the view of Rabbi *Eliezer against that of the sages, Rabbi *Joshua protests that the Torah is not in heaven (Deuteronomy 13: 12), and so a heavenly voice must not be allowed to overturn the clear ruling of the Torah that the majority opinion of the sages is to be adopted. The medieval commentators discuss at length why in the one case the Bat Kol is heeded but ignored in the other. Some argue that a Bat Kol is only ignored, as in the case of Rabbi Eliezer and the sages, where it runs counter to a definite ruling of the Torah. In any event, the consensus in Jewish thought is that no appeal to a heavenly voice can be made to decide matters of *Halakhah where human reasoning on the meaning of the Torah rules is alone determinative. In non-legal matters, however, a Bat Kol is to be heeded.

Occasionally the term Bat Kol is used in a purely figurative manner, as when the early third-century Palestinian teacher, Rabbi Joshua ben Levi, said (Ethics of the Fathers 6: 2): 'Every day a Bat Kol goes forth from Mount Sinai to proclaim: "Woe to mankind for contempt of the Torah"' a way of declaring that the very fact of the revelation of the Torah at *Sinai is a permanent protest against those who hold the Torah in contempt. But the belief persisted in the Middle Ages that the *saints can actually attain to the mystical state known as the Bat Kol. *Judah Halevi (*Kuzari*, iii. 11) observes that the truly religious person sees himself always in God's presence and then he can, at times, see the *angels and hear the Bat Kol, as did the most prominent of the sages during the period of the Second Temple. But Judah Halevi qualifies this by saying that the place in which the saint stands has to be a *holy place, in this context the Holy Land, which is why there are few references to later saints hearing a Bat Kol. In modern Jewish thought, even among the *Orthodox, claims to have heard a Bat Kol would be treated with extreme suspicion and dismissed as chicanery or hallucination.

**Bat Mitzvah** 'Daughter of the commandment', the status of religious obligation to keep the *precepts which a girl attains at the age of 12 as a boy becomes *Bar Mitzvah at the age of 13. While a boy marks his religious majority by putting on the *tefillin and by being called up to the reading of the *Torah, until recent times there were no special ceremonies for the Bat Mitzvah. With the greater trends towards equality of the sexes, ceremonies such as special prayers and a party have been introduced in many communities. In *Reform and *Conservative Judaism the girl reads a portion in the synagogue just as a boy does on his Bar Mitzvah but the *Orthodox object, in any event, to *women reading the Torah. Some Orthodox Rabbis even object to any special celebration of Bat Mitzvah on the grounds that this is unknown in the tradition, but some Orthodox communities get round the problem by having a special service in the synagogue on a week day for a number of girls who have reached the age of Bat Mitzvah, at which the girls recite passages from Scripture and prayers for the occasion.

**Beard** The verse: 'Ye shall not round the corners of your heads, neither shalt thou mar the corners of thy beard' (Leviticus 19: 27) is understood by the Talmudic Rabbis not to mean that it is wrong for a man to be clean-shaven, but only that facial hair must not be removed with a razor. The standard Code of Jewish law, the *Shulḥan Arukh* (*Yoreh Deah*, 181. 10) rules that it is permitted to remove all facial hair with scissors even when this is done as closely as if with a razor. On the basis of this, many *Orthodox Jews shave with an electric razor on the grounds that technically this machine, with its two blades, is not to be treated as a razor. The reason for the prohibition of shaving is not stated in the Bible but Maimonides understands it as a protest against idolatry, conjecturing that the heathen priests shaved their beards. Others have seen it as a means of distinguishing between males and females. Neither of these reasons would explain why the distinction is made between shaving with a razor and by other means, but this distinction still holds as a matter of law, although some later authorities do invoke both reasons not as a matter of law but of piety. Consequently, it has been the practice among many Jews to wear a beard and sidelocks (*peot*). The Talmud describes the beard as an 'adornment of the face' and implies that a beardless man cannot be said to be handsome.

In the Kabbalah the beard is said to represent on earth the 'beard of the Holy Ancient One' on high, that is, the stage in the unfolding of the *Sefirot at which the divine grace, symbolized by the strands of the beard, begins to flow throughout all creation. In Kabbalistic circles the beard becomes a sacred object and some Kabbalists would not even remove a single hair from their beard. The statement that, according to the Kabbalah, there is no need to wear a beard outside the Holy Land, is unwarranted. *Hasidism follows the Kabbalah and all Hasidim wear long beards and sidelocks. Most westernized Jews do not wear beards, including many Orthodox Rabbis, who shave with an electric razor but sometimes sport a small goatee beard as a bow in the direction of the tradition. Yet it can be observed that the wearing of a full beard is coming increasingly into fashion among the Orthodox. *Reform Jews do not consider the prohibition on shaving with a razor still to be binding.

**Belief** Heb. *emunah*. In the Bible and the Rabbinic literature this term denotes 'belief *in*', that is, trust in God and in His Torah, but in the Middle Ages the term is more generally used to denote 'belief *that*' God exists and that the *dogmas of Judaism are true. Although the emphasis in Judaism is on action, there are principles of *faith in which the Jew is expected to believe. Lack of belief is considered sinful, though *Crescas and others have discussed how anyone can be blamed for something beyond his control. Some later teachers have suggested that all unbelief is only in the category of unwitting sin (see ATHEISM and EPIKOROS).

**Belz** Name of a small town in Galicia and of the Hasidic dynasty founded there by Rabbi Shalom Rokeah (1779–1855). Shalom was succeeded as both the Rebbe and the town Rabbi of Belz by his son, Joshua, who was in turn succeeded by his son, Issachar Dov, succeeded by his son, Aaron (1880–1957) who escaped the *Holocaust to set up his 'court' in Tel Aviv. When Aaron died, his nephew, Issachar Dov II, was a little boy, but the Belzer Hasidim adopted him as the rightful Belzer Rebbe, which post he still occupies.

The Belzer Rebbes published very little, so that it is hard to define the particular doctrines of this branch of *Hasidism. If there is a specific Belzer approach to Hasidic life, it can be detected in strict observance of Jewish law so that the term 'a Belzer Hasid' became synonymous with strict, uncompromising piety which tolerates no departure from the traditions of the past.

Belz is also known for its institution of the *yoshevim* ('sitters'), chosen Hasidim who live a celibate existence at the Rebbe's court, devoting themselves to prayer and study and distinguishing themselves by total loyalty to the Rebbe whose every word, for them, is law.

**Benedictions** Blessings in which thanks are offered to God for spiritual and physical benefits He has bestowed. The benediction (Heb. *berakhah*) begins with the words: 'Blessed art Thou, O Lord our God, King of the universe, who . . .' and then goes on to state the particular matter for which the benediction is recited; for example, over wine: 'Blessed art Thou, O Lord our God, King of the universe, who creates the fruit of the vine'; over *tefillin*: 'Blessed art Thou, O Lord our God, King of the universe, who hath sanctified us with His commandments and hath commanded us to put on *tefillin*.' The medieval thinkers were puzzled by the words 'Blessed art Thou' in the benediction, as if God can be blessed by humans. The usual solutions are that 'Blessed' means 'the Source of all blessing' or that it means simply: 'thank you'. But *Elijah, Gaon of Vilna sees no reason why the expression should not be taken literally, since God requires the co-operation of humans for the fulfilment of His purposes just as the *soul, pure spirit though it is, requires, while in the body, the food by which the body is kept alive.

Examples of benedictions (all beginning with 'Blessed art Thou, O Lord our God, King of the universe') over physical enjoyment are:

over wine; over bread ('who brings forth bread from the ground'); over fruit ('who creates the fruit of the tree'); over vegetables ('who creates the fruit of the ground'); over smelling fragrant plants ('who creates odorous plants'); over water, meat, fish, and other things for which there is no specific expression ('by whose word all things have come into being'). Just as there are benedictions before enjoying food and drink there are benedictions after them, *grace after meals, for example. The theological principle behind these benedictions, as stated in the Talmud, is that the whole world belongs to God and must not be enjoyed by humans without acknowledgement of His bountiful goodness in satisfying their needs. These benedictions are all recorded in the Talmud and the authorities are uneasy about introducing benedictions not found there, over smoking a pipe or a cigar, for example. Some of the Hasidic masters even go so far as to discuss why no benediction has been ordained for the enjoyment of sex (!) and suggest that, none the less, God should be thanked, albeit not in the usual form of the benediction, for giving humans this pleasure, and this despite the somewhat negative attitude to *sex in Hasidism.

The purpose of the benedictions before the performance of the precepts is for the act to be carried out in full awareness that one is obeying a divine command. However, this type of benediction is limited to purely religious obligations. There is no benediction before, say, giving charity or honouring parents, probably, it has been suggested, because ethical conduct is universal. Gentiles also lead ethical lives and 'who hath sanctified *us* with His commandments', implying that these are only for Jews, is grossly inappropriate.

A third category of benedictions is that in which God is praised in more general terms, for example in the *Kiddush recited on the Sabbath, where thanks are given for the great gift of the Sabbath, or in the benediction at a *marriage ceremony, in which God is praised for the institution of marriage. A fourth category of benedictions is that in which God is praised when one observes marvellous or unusual sights. Examples of these are: over lofty mountains ('who has made the creation'); on hearing thunder ('whose strength and might fill the world'); over the sea ('who has made the great sea'); on seeing giants or dwarfs ('who varies the forms of His creatures'); on seeing a

monarch ('who has given of His glory to flesh and blood'); on seeing a person learned in the Torah ('who has imparted of His wisdom to those who fear Him'); on seeing a person distinguished in other than sacred knowledge ('who has given of His wisdom to flesh and blood'); when one receives bad news ('who is the true Judge'); and when one receives good tidings ('who is good and dispenses good').

Israel Abrahams, Blessings on Various Occasions, in his *A Companion to the Authorized Daily Prayerbook* (New York, 1966), 211–12.

**Ben Sira** The name of the ancient author (second century BCE) and of his book, also called Ecclesiasticus, one of the books of the *Apocrypha. The book was written originally in Hebrew but translated into Greek by Ben Sira's grandson. Although the Talmudic Rabbis had a somewhat ambivalent attitude towards this work and the other books of the Apocrypha, a number of quotations from the book are found in the Talmud.

**Beruriah** Wife of Rabbi *Meir. She is reported to have been a woman very learned in the Torah, although the few details about her in the Talmud and the *Midrash are vague and belong largely to legend. Naturally, in modern Jewish *feminism the figure of Beruriah occupies a prominent place, especially in her role as scholar. In feminist circles it is argued that if the ancient Rabbis could praise Beruriah for her learning, this demands, nowadays, a thorough revision of the conventional picture of women's role in Judaism.

**Bet Din** 'House of Law', that is, court of law, composed of three judges learned in the law. According to the Talmud, a court had to be composed of three fully ordained *Rabbis but since Semikhah, *ordination, was reserved for the Jews in the Holy Land, the courts of the *Diaspora, in *Babylon and other lands, operated by the legal fiction that they functioned on behalf of the Palestinians. Most authorities hold that a Bet Din has to be composed of three males but some medieval French teachers ruled that a woman could serve as a judge (witness *Deborah), an opinion followed by *Reform and *Conservative Jews, who have women judges as they have women Rabbis.

The main functions of the Bet Din are to decide in matters of civil law; to supervise the *divorce proceedings; to see that *conversion to Judaism is carried out in accordance with the law; and, in many communities, to give a seal of approval that foodstuffs are *kosher, that is, that they have been prepared in such a manner that people who buy them will not offend against the *dietary laws.

**Bible** The collection of books constituting sacred literature, which Christians refer to as the Old Testament to distinguish it from the New Testament. The Hebrew Bible is divided into three: 1. *Torah (the five books of Moses, the *Pentateuch); 2. *Neviim* (*Prophets', embracing the books of the literary prophets and the historical books); 3. *Ketuvim* ('Writings', the books of the Hagiographa). After the initial letters of these words, the Bible is called the *Tanakh*. Jewish tradition sees these three divisions as composed under different degrees of *inspiration. The Torah, as the very word of God, is seen as possessing the highest degree of inspiration; the prophets as having the degree of prophecy, that is, the word of God mediated through the personality of the prophet; and the Hagiographa as composed under the lower degree of inspiration known as the *Holy Spirit. But for all practical purposes no distinction is made between one part of the Bible and another so far as its *authority is concerned.

The books of the Bible are:

*Torah*

Genesis, Exodus, Leviticus, Numbers, Deuteronomy.

*Prophets*

Joshua, Judges, Samuel, Kings (known as the 'early prophets').
Isaiah, Jeremiah, Ezekiel, the Twelve Prophets (the 'later prophets') (the Twelve are Hosea, Joel, Amos, Obadiah, Jonah, Micah, Nahum, Habakkuk, Zephaniah, Haggai, Zechariah, and Malachi).

*Hagiographa*

Psalms, Proverbs, Job, Song of Songs, Ruth, Ecclesiastes, Lamentations, Esther, Chronicles, Daniel, Ezra, and Nehemiah.

In the later Jewish tradition there are said to be twenty-four books of the Bible. This number is arrived at by counting the Twelve as a single book and Ezra and Nehemiah as a single book, thus:

1. Genesis; 2. Exodus; 3. Leviticus; 4. Numbers; 5. Deuteronomy; 6. Joshua; 7. Judges; 8. Samuel; 9. Kings; 10. Isaiah; 11. Jeremiah; 12. Ezekiel; 13. The Twelve; 14. Psalms; 15. Proverbs; 16. Job; 17. Song of Songs; 18. Ruth; 19. Ecclesiastes; 20. Lamentations; 21. Esther; 22. Chronicles; 23. Daniel; 24. Ezra and Nehemiah.

The division of Samuel, Kings, and Chronicles into two books, that is, 1 and 2 Samuel, 1 and 2 Kings, 1 and 2 Chronicles, is not known among Jews until the age of printing. The reason why the Twelve are counted as a single book is that they were too small in size to be written on separate scrolls and were hence written together so that they would not be lost, as the Talmud states. The colloquial expression 'a minor prophet' (not used, incidentally, by Jews), refers only to the size of, say, the book of Hosea, and does not indicate that Hosea was any less of a prophet than, say, Isaiah.

The term used in modern biblical scholarship for the process by which some writings were included in the Bible, others excluded, is canonization and the whole collection is called the canon. This term is not used in the Jewish tradition but this does not mean that there was no defining process among the Jewish teachers in post-biblical times. The term used for the process in the Mishnah is 'contamination of the hands'. If a book was considered to be sacred literature (part of the 'canon') it had the property of rendering the hands of those who touched it ritually unclean, that is the hands, before ritual washing, might contaminate sacred food such as the meat of sacrifices in Temple times. The Mishnah states that this rule of the *Pharisees was ridiculed by the *Sadducees who protested the oddness of treating sacred literature as having this property while secular literature did not contaminate the hands. The Pharisees replied, in so many words, that a taboo was placed on sacred writ so that it would not be handled in too familiar a fashion. (To this day, the *Scroll of the Torah has handles affixed so that these are touched but not the Scroll itself, although, of course, the actual rules about contamination of this sort applied only in Temple times.) Thus the discussion in the Talmudic literature on whether a book belongs to sacred Scripture is recorded in the form: 'Does it contaminate the hands?' As late as the second century CE, there were opinions that the *Song of Songs and *Ecclesiastes did not contaminate the hands and, it is said, the sages wished to hide away the book of Ezekiel because some of the laws recorded in the book seem to be in conflict with the laws recorded in the Pentateuch. There was also some doubt whether the book of *Esther was written under the inspiration of the holy spirit. Eventually, however, all these books were included in the 'canon'.

From the historical point of view, all this means that there was no actual official body to determine which books of the Bible belonged there and which did not. The Pentateuch was accepted as the sacred Torah from the earliest times, the Prophets somewhat later, and the books of the Hagiographa later still. In effect it was by a kind of mysterious consensus among the Jewish people that these twenty-four books and no others came to be held as *the* Bible. Ultimately the Bible is sacred Scripture because the consensus in the Jewish community, operating over a long period, declared it to be such. As Isaiah Leibowitz has put it: 'It is not the *Written Torah that determines the *Oral Torah. It is the Oral Torah that determines what is the Written Torah.' The practical consequence is that, for Jews, the *authority of the Bible depends on how the Bible has been interpreted by the sages of Israel. This is why a naked biblicism, in which the biblical text is examined for direct guidance, is foreign to the Jewish tradition.

The chapter divisions of the Bible, though now used by all Jews, are originally Christian, adopted by Jews in the Middle Ages for convenience when discussing the Bible with Christians. There is evidence that in the more ancient biblical texts there were no divisions at all into chapters or even into verses. The Pentateuch is usually divided by Jews in accordance with the reading of the *Torah into fifty-four portions, one to be read each week. There are also traces of an older division of the Pentateuch into smaller units in obedience, it has been conjectured, to the Palestinian practice of reading the Torah in a triennial rather than an annual cycle. It is astonishing that devout Jews still use the Christian divisions, since these often follow Christian doctrine. For instance, it is clear that Genesis 2: 1–3 is the end of chapter 1, the first creation narrative; it was obviously made into a separate chapter in order to detach these verses about God completing His work by the seventh day, so as to

detract from the sacredness of the Jewish *Sabbath. Similarly, a new chapter was made to begin with: 'Now the serpent was more subtle' (Genesis 3) because of the importance of the serpent's tempting of Eve and the *fall of Adam in the Christian theological scheme. In the nineteenth century, Meir Friedmann, lecturer at the Rabbinical College in Vienna, tried to organize Jewish opinion to have Bibles printed without the chapter divisions deriving from Christian usage on the grounds that it is surely highly undignified for believers in the truth of Judaism to apply the forms, and even the doctrines, of another religion to their sacred Scriptures. But Friedmann's was a lost cause. Traditionalists retorted that after the invention of printing and the publication of the Bible in printed Hebrew editions containing these divisions, the great Jewish teachers such as Joseph *Karo and the Kabbalist Isaac *Luria had accepted them, so what was good enough for them should be good enough for everyone.

Who wrote the various books of the Bible? A distinction has to be drawn between the claims of authorship made in the books themselves and the understanding of later generations. In the Pentateuch itself, for instance, there is no statement that all five books were written by Moses or in the book of Psalms that all the Psalms were written by David, yet the tradition developed that the five books are the books of Moses and the whole book of Psalms the Psalms of David. This question of authorship was only scientifically examined with the rise of *biblical criticism. The ancient Rabbis made many references to the authors of the various books, yet in doing so they were not stating any dogma but simply referring to the general views of their day.

There is a much-discussed statement in the Babylonian Talmud (*Bava Batra* 14b–15a) on the question of authorship. Here it is said that Moses wrote his book; that Moses is the author of the Pentateuch is taken for granted everywhere in the Rabbinic literature and in medieval Jewish thought. But it has to be appreciated that, in Rabbinic times, even the heretics believed that Moses was the author of the Pentateuch; they, however, held that Moses did not record the word of God but made up everything out of his own head. It was the divine nature of the communication that the Rabbis wished to preserve, not the Mosaic authorship of the Pentateuch. According to one Rabbi mentioned in the Talmudic passage, Moses even wrote the last eight verses of the Pentateuch dealing with his own death and burial; but another Rabbi holds that these eight verses were added, after Moses' death, by Joshua, Moses' successor.

In the Talmudic passage it is further said that the books named after a person were actually written by him, except for additions obviously made after his death. It is only in the Pentateuch that, according to one opinion, even the additions were by Moses himself. (For further details on the question of authorship, see GENESIS, EXODUS, LEVITICUS, NUMBERS AND DEUTERONOMY.)

**Biblical Criticism** The close examination by modern biblical scholars of the composition, authorship, and text of the biblical books. The 'lower criticism' or textual criticism seeks to discover the original text as this left the hands of the final editors. The 'higher criticism' seeks to discover how the books were compiled, their sources, whether oral or written, and the process by which they came to assume their present form. The text handed down from generation to generation is known as the Masoretic Text, after the *Masorah, the traditional form of the text. But, while the Masoretic Text is very reliable, great care having been taken in its transmission, the evidence of early versions such as the *Septuagint, which contain variant readings, shows that before the Masoretic Text had been established, readings which differ from it had been widely known, and modern scholars are certainly not averse to suggesting their own emendations of the text where these seem plausible. The higher criticism seeks to detect, by noting anachronisms, for example, the sources behind the particular books.

All this activity has presented a considerable challenge to traditional views. Reform and Conservative Jewish scholars usually accept the results of biblical criticism and acknowledge that it demands a revision of traditional views, without necessarily affecting the view of the Bible as inspired. Many Orthodox scholars still reject all biblical criticism in the belief that its untraditional opinions constitute *heresy but a few hold that its findings can be accepted for all the books of the Bible except the Pentateuch, which, they affirm, as the very word of God, cannot be subjected to critical examination as if it were a book produced by human authors.

Hardly any Orthodox scholar will say otherwise than that the doctrine of 'Torah from Heaven' implies that the whole of the Pentateuch is a unified, not a composite, text, communicated directly by God to His faithful servant Moses.

**Bimah** The elevated platform in the *synagogue at which the *reading of the Torah takes place. The bimah has steps on its two sides so that those called to the reading ascend at the side nearest to them and descend, after their portion has been read, by the steps at the other side; the principle is that one should ascend for the reading of God's words by the swiftest route and leave, as if reluctant to depart, by the longest route. In Sephardi synagogues the *Cantor leads the prayers from the bimah (also called the almemar) but in some Ashkenazi synagogues it is held to be inappropriate to pray to God on an elevated spot, and the Cantor stands at a desk on the floor below the *ark. In many of the older synagogues the preacher (see PREACHING) delivered his sermon from the bimah.

The bimah, according to Maimonides, has to be situated in the centre of the synagogue but *Karo defends, on aesthetic grounds, the Sephardi practice of his day of siting the bimah at the western end of the synagogue, provided that all the congregants can hear the reading.

With the rise of the *Reform movement at the beginning of the nineteenth century, some synagogues located the bimah at the eastern end of the synagogue adjacent to the ark. This innovation met with fierce opposition from *Orthodox authorities such as Moses *Sofer, who argued that it was a conscious attempt by the Reformers to copy the practice of the Christian church where the altar is at the east end of the building. Hungarian Orthodox Rabbis placed a ban on entering a synagogue where the bimah was located at the eastern end of the synagogue. Nowadays, however, even some Orthodox synagogues have the bimah adjacent to the ark, mainly because, in larger synagogues, this enables the congregation to have more space for seats in the body of the building. The whole controversy about the siting of the bimah, like the question of the use of the *organ, obviously had more to do with the general question of innovations in the forms of Jewish worship than with the strict application of Jewish law in the particular instances. It was all part of the suspicion by the Orthodox that the Reformers were prone to imitate Gentile forms of worship.

**Bioethics** The branch of ethics concerned with the preservation of human life; sometimes referred to as medical ethics, since many of the issues arise as a result of advances in modern medicine. Among the questions considered in Jewish bioethics are: preference for medical treatment; *abortion; *autopsies; *birth-control; withholding treatment from the terminally ill (see EUTHANASIA); *genetic engineering; cosmetic surgery; organ transplants, and *artificial insemination. These and similar questions are discussed at length in the *Responsa of contemporary Orthodox Rabbis on the basis of the *Halakhah, the Jewish legal system, in which new situations, unenvisaged in the classical sources of the *Talmud and the *Codes, are discussed by means of analogy. The questions are rarely discussed on the basis of general ethical principles since, for the Orthodox, these have no standing when they are in conflict with the Halakhic norms.

*Conservative and *Reform Rabbis are uneasy with this purely legal approach, among other reasons because the Halakhah is sometimes uncertain or ambiguous. For instance, on the question of access to a kidney machine, one reading of the Halakhah might suggest that preference be given always to a man over a woman because a man has more religious obligations to perform than a woman. On general ethical principles it can be held that a young mother with children to care for should be given precedence over an old man with a rich and full life behind him. In a different reading of the relevant Halakhah a first-come, first-served attitude ought to be adopted; but what if the need of a later patient is more urgent than one who has applied first, to say nothing of the administrative difficulties? All Jewish thinkers, Orthodox or Reform, operate in accordance with the general principle that human life is precious and the need to preserve it overrides religious prohibitions. Where life is at stake, forbidden food may be eaten and the Sabbath profaned. Further discussion is to be found under the particular headings mentioned above.

Fred Rosner and J. David Bleich (eds.), *Jewish Bioethics* (New York, 1979). Immanuel Jakobovits, *Jewish Medical Ethics*, (second edn.; New York, 1975).

**Birth-Control** The prevention of the birth of unwanted children either by total abstinence from sexual relations or by engaging in them in a way that frustrates conception. There are two objections to birth-control in the Jewish tradition. The first is based on the biblical injunction to be fruitful and multiply (Genesis 1: 28; 9: 1), interpreted by the Talmudic Rabbis as a command, a *mitzvah. The Mishnah (*Yevamot* 6: 6) records a debate between the rival schools of *Hillel and *Shammai. According to the School of Hillel the *mitzvah* is fulfilled when a couple (the accepted opinion, however, is that the full *mitzvah* is binding only on the husband) produces a son and a daughter, while the School of Shammai holds that to fulfil the *mitzvah* the couple must produce two sons. The law follows the opinion of the School of Hillel. Thus it would seem to follow that once a son and daughter have been born the couple can voluntarily agree not to have marital relations. For all that, the Talmudic sources quote two further verses, of lesser import, which seem to reject this form of family planning. These are the verses: 'Not for void did He create the world, but for habitation did He form it' (Isaiah 45: 18); and 'In the morning sow thy seed, and in the evening do not withhold thy hand, for you know not which will succeed, this or that, or whether they shall both alike be good' (Ecclesiastes 11: 6). But according to the Rabbinic extension based on these two verses a good deal of discretion is left to individuals on how far they are obliged to contribute further (following the birth of a son and daughter) to the peopling of the world and how much they are obliged to 'sow' in the 'evening' as well as in the 'morning'.

Abstinence from marital relations, however, is notoriously difficult to maintain. Nor does the tradition consider such a regimen to be at all desirable, both because sexual pleasure in marriage is considered to be a legitimate and worthy goal and because total abstinence may lead to sinful conduct outside marriage. Consequently, most of the discussions are about when artificial methods of contraception are allowed: whether a couple may have sex while adopting devices or stratagems to prevent this resulting in the birth of a child, and whether, in fact, resorting to artificial methods of contraception is intrinsically sinful.

The objection to artificial contraception after the *mitzvah* of *procreation has been fulfilled is on the grounds of what the Talmud terms 'wasting seed', that is the emission of semen which, if deposited in the womb, could have resulted in the birth of a child. This does not mean that sexual relations are forbidden unless they can lead to a birth. There is no objection whatsoever to sex where conception is impossible, for instance, where the wife is already pregnant or where she is beyond the childbearing age. In these instances, the semen is not actively destroyed, whereas the use of artificial methods of contraception positively destroys the seed. This is the Orthodox position, equating contraception by artificial means with *masturbation. The Orthodox view will now be described, although it must be added that Reform and Conservative Rabbis generally refuse to make the equation and are consequently more lenient in the matter of artificial birth-control.

In general the Orthodox authorities permit the use of artificial contraceptives only where the life of the wife might be endangered by a pregnancy. Social or economic reasons for avoiding childbirth in this way are not countenanced, since these reasons are held to be insufficient to warrant the sin of 'wasting seed'. Some authorities, however, interpret danger to the life of the wife in a liberal manner. Where there is risk to the wife some authorities permit the use of a condom, but others permit only the use of devices by the wife, such as the coil or cap, on the grounds that the sin of 'wasting seed' applies more to the man than the woman. For this reason *coitus interruptus* is not allowed. Many authorities advocate the contraceptive pill as the most favoured method and, since this does not involve 'waste of seed' as defined above, some would permit the use of the pill on grounds other than danger to life.

As in other intimate areas of life, the actual practice of Orthodox couples is uncertain. It is something of a puzzle, granted that total abstinence has always been viewed with disfavour, and granted the extent of infant mortality in the past, that many of the great authorities, so far as we can tell, seem to have had comparatively small families.

David M. Feldman, *Birth Control in Jewish Law* (New York and London, 1968).

**Birthdays**  There is only a single reference to a birthday in the Bible: 'And it came to pass on the third day, which was Pharaoh's birthday, that he made a feast unto all his servants'

(Genesis 40: 20). The Mishnah (*Avodah Zarah* 3: 1), too, refers only to the birthday celebrations of pagan rulers but is silent on birthday celebrations among Jews. It has even been suggested that, in ancient times, Jews saw a birthday as a gloomy reminder that life is drawing closer to its end; a day for solemn reflection and repentance rather than festivity. It is reported that, on these grounds, the famous Russian Rabbi Isaac Elhanan Spektor (1817–96) refused to allow his community to organize a celebration in honour of his jubilee in the Rabbinate. On the other hand, the Talmud (*Kiddushin* 72b) gives a list of Rabbis each of whom was born on the day when another famous Rabbi died and whom he replaced, implying that there is cause for rejoicing when a good man is born. In more recent times birthday celebrations have become the norm among many Jews. Even if this practice was copied from the non-Jewish world, it is held that there is no harm in it since questions of doctrine are in no way involved. In some synagogues, Orthodox as well as Reform, special prayers of thanksgiving are recited for someone reaching the age of 70 or 80 or at his 'second *Bar Miztvah*' when he reaches the age of 83! It is customary to greet an elderly man or woman on their birthday with the wish: 'May you live to be 120' (the age at which Moses died; Deuteronomy 34: 7).

Relevant in this connection is the Talmudic statement (*Moed Katan* 28a) that the fourth-century Babylonian teacher Rabbi Joseph made a party for the scholars on his sixtieth birthday to celebrate his having passed the age of *karet* ('excision'). In the same Talmudic passage the verse is quoted: 'The days of our years are three score years and ten, or even by reason of strength four score years' (Psalms 90: 10) to suggest that it is good for one who has reached the age of 70 or 80 years to give special thanks to God for having spared him. The German Rabbi Jair Hayyim Bacharach (1638–1702) has a Responsum in which he lists the occasions when a party has religious significance, one such occasion being when the age of 70 is reached (by coincidence the number of this Responsum in his collection is 70). Interestingly, some *Hasidim, especially those of *Lubavitch, celebrate annually the birthday of the *Rebbe. Aware that this is something of an innovation, they argue that not all innovations are taboo.

Also relevant is the Rabbinic statement, in Ethics of the Fathers (5. 21) on the ages of man (fourteen, not seven as in Shakespeare): 'The age of five for the study of the Bible; then ten for the study of the Mishnah; thirteen for the commandments; fifteen for the study of Talmud; eighteen for marriage; twenty for earning a living; thirty for power; forty for understanding; fifty for giving advice; sixty for old age; seventy for grey hairs; eighty for special strength; ninety for bowed back; a hundred—it is as if he had died and passed away.'

**Blasphemy** Reviling God; Heb. *birkat ha-shem*, literally 'blessing [euphemism for "cursing"] the Name [of God]'. The one guilty of this offence is called a *megaddef* ('blasphemer'). In the two main passages in the Bible (Leviticus 24: 10–23 and 1 Kings 21: 8–13) the penalty for this offence is stoning to death. It is, however, none too clear what exactly is involved in the offence. Does it mean to insult God, or does it mean to curse God? According to the Gospels of Matthew (26: 63–6) and Mark (14: 53–64) Jesus was tried by the *Sanhedrin on a charge of blasphemy, but New Testament scholars have puzzled over both the question of the historicity of the event and the precise nature of the offence. Even more puzzling is the definition given in the Mishnah (*Sanhedrin* 7: 5) that the penalty of stoning for the blasphemer applies only where he used the *Tetragrammaton with which to curse God by this name: 'Let the Tetragrammaton curse the Tetragrammaton.' This would make the whole offence impossible in practice, to say nothing of the extreme psychological difficulty involved in the whole idea of requesting God to curse Himself. To be sure, the Jewish tradition obviously holds that it is a severe offence to revile God and the medieval courts placed a ban on anyone guilty of this, but so far as the full offence of blasphemy is concerned it all remained purely theoretical. The same applies to Talmudic statements that the prohibition of *birkat ha-shem* is one of the seven *Noahide laws.

To insult the Torah or Moses, the other prophets, or the sages of Israel is also held to be a serious offence but this is, at the most, an extension of the original blasphemy law and is not covered by the death penalty, even in theory. In Christian Europe the Church, on the other hand, extended the law of blasphemy to cover any denial of God or denigration of the Christian religion, and Islam regarded it as covering any attack on the personality of Muhammad, as in the Salman Rushdie case. The whole subject is more than a little obscure so far as Jewish law is concerned and there is hardly any evidence that trials for blasphemy took place among Jews in post-biblical times.

Leonard W. Levy, *Treason Against God: A History of the Offense of Blasphemy* (New York, 1981).

**Blessings and Curses** The invocation to God to bestow goodness and happiness (the blessing) or to visit evil and suffering (the curse) upon others. There is no doubt that in both the Bible and the Rabbinic literature the belief was strongly held that the word of blessing and curse possessed power so that, unless there was direct divine intervention, it would automatically take effect. Particularly noteworthy is the story of *Balaam (Numbers 23, 24). The clear implication of the whole narrative is that Balaam's curses would have had their effect on the Israelites if God had not turned them into blessings. In the *priestly blessing it is the priests who bless the people with the threefold blessing, God giving his assent, so to speak (Numbers 6: 22–7). Moses instructs the people, when they crossed the Jordan, to station themselves on Mount Gerizim to bless the people and on Mount Ebal to curse the wrongdoers. Modern biblical scholars have detected in this echoes of the custom in the ancient Near East of vassal-kings entering into a pact with a mightier ruler and sealing it by calling down on themselves dire curses if they fail in their loyalty to him. In the story of Jacob and Esau (Genesis 27) the brothers contend in order to secure their father's blessing and Jacob protests to his mother that his attempt to obtain the blessing by trickery might bring upon him Isaac's curse. The patriarch Jacob blesses his sons on his deathbed (Genesis 49) and Moses blesses the people before his death (Deuteronomy 33). The Talmud is full of tales of Rabbis blessing others. Typical is the tale (*Taanit* 5b–6a) of Rabbi Isaac who was asked by Rabbi Nahman to bless him: 'Shall I bless you with knowledge of the Torah, this you already have. Shall I bless you with wealth or children, these you already have. I bless you that all your offspring shall be as you.' In one Talmudic passage (*Megillah* 15a) it is said that the blessings or curses even of an ordinary man, let alone those of a saint or sage, should not be treated lightly. The biblical injunctions against cursing princes (Exodus 22: 27) and a deaf person (Leviticus 19: 14) were extended by the Rabbis to include cursing any Jew (*Sanhedrin* 66a). The Mishnah (*Bava Metzia* 4: 2) states that while a contract of sale is not legally binding until the goods have been taken into the possession of the buyer, yet if either party wishes to go back on his word, the court has to inform the one who wishes to retract that the God who brought retribution to the generation of the Flood will bring retribution on the man who does not keep his word. According to one view in the Talmud this is a simple statement by the court, but according to another interpretation the court issues this as a curse.

To this day parents bless their children on the eve of the Sabbaths and festivals, and teachers their pupils. The usual form of blessing for boys (based on Genesis 48: 20) is: 'God make thee as Ephraim and Manasseh'; for girls: 'God make thee as Sarah, Rebecca, Rachel, and Leah.'

**Blood Libel**   The calumny that Jews murder Christian children in order to use their blood for ritual purposes such as the baking of *\*matzah* for *\*Passover. The accusation is an amalgam of pagan notions of human sacrifice and ignorance about the nature of the Jewish religion and its utter abhorrence of consuming blood, wedded, in Christian Europe, to the alleged desecration of the Host by Jews. As the legend developed Jews were said to use Christian blood for all kinds of bizarre rituals and magical practices, for anointing Rabbis, for curing eye ailments, in stopping menstrual blood, removing bodily odours, and warding off the evil eye. The earliest appearance of the blood libel in the middle ages was in the case of the boy William of Norwich in 1144. The boy, William, was said to have been tortured by the Jews and then murdered and hanged on the cross in imitation of the Passion of Jesus. The libel spread throughout Christian Europe despite the opposition of Church leaders who condemned it in the strongest terms. The libel persisted even in modern times, especially in Russia.

An echo of the fear aroused among Jews as a result of the blood libel is found in the commentary to the *Shulḥan Arukh* by the Polish Rabbi David Ha-Levi (1586–1667). In his

commentary *Turey Zahaz* (n. 9) to the ruling in the *Shulḥan Arukh* (*Oraḥ Ḥayyim*, 472. 11) that it is preferable to have red wine for the Passover *\*Seder, Rabbi David remarks: 'Nowadays, however, we do not use red wine because, for our many sins, of the false libels.'

The whole sorry history of this absurd libel with its tragic consequences has been told many times. A good survey is given in the article 'Blood Libel' in the *Encyclopedia Judaica*, iv. 1120–31, and there is no need to repeat it here. Perhaps the final word on the subject so far as Jews are concerned is the remark by *\*Ahad Ha-Am that Jews can obtain a melancholy satisfaction from blood libel. Every Jew knows that there is no basis whatsoever in the calumny and yet it was believed by so many. The conclusion to be drawn, he observes, is that if such a widespread belief about Jews and Judaism is really nonsensical, Jews, lacking in confidence, should not be too ready, when they meet with *\*anti-Semitism, to say to themselves that there is no smoke without fire. In the blood libel there was so much smoke without even the tiniest spark of real fire.

R. Po-Chia, *The Myth of Ritual Murder: Jews and Magic in Reformation Germany* (New Haven, 1988).

**Books**   Of the many aspects of books and book-production in the history of Judaism considerations of space preclude a comprehensive study. This entry is devoted to some of the main features.

Although Jewish *\*literature embraces many fields, Jewish books, until modern times and the rise of Jewish *\*secularism, were complied chiefly to further the aim of *\*study of the Torah and were looked upon as religious works to be treated with a special respect and regard. There are references to books in the Bible and the Bible itself is a collection of books produced over a long period. It has been said that there are three distinct periods: 1. that of the Sefer (the Book), the Bible as a whole; 2. that of the Soferim ('Scribes', the period when the sages of Israel commented on the Bible; see ORAL TORAH); 3. that of the *sefarim* ('books'). Originally books were compiled in the form of scrolls written on parchment. Under Roman influence, the codex form was introduced and this was the norm in works compiled in the Middle Ages. These handwritten books were costly because of the shortage of paper and the scarcity of skilful copyists. With the invention of *\*printing the

Jewish book came into its own, thousands of copies being produced of the ancient texts, together with numerous original works. Rabbi J. L. Maimon (1875–1962), a great book-collector, estimated that up to the year 1955 no less than 20,000 different Hebrew books had been printed. There were 2,500 *Responsa works in Maimon's own vast library and he estimated that at least another 150 had been printed. Many others have been published since then. It is not always appreciated that in the earlier, Talmudic period the study of the Torah was largely by word of mouth, hence the many references to the need for mastering the texts by heart and to studying with companions. It was not until the Middle Ages that it became essential for the scholar to have a good library of books to assist him in his studies. Judah Ibn Tibbon's advice to his son, written around the year 1190, has often been quoted: 'My son! Make thy books thy companions, let thy cases and shelves be thy pleasure-grounds and gardens. Bask in their gardens, gather their fruit, pluck their roses, take their spices and myrrh. If thy soul be satiate and weary, change from garden to garden, from furrow to furrow, from prospect to prospect. Then will thy desire renew itself, and thy soul be filled with delight.' It might be supposed that such advice is calculated to put anyone off books for ever yet the son, Samuel, became, like his father, one of the great scholars and translators of the Middle Ages. Centuries later a Rabbi who preferred to study on his own could argue that the Talmudic injunction against solitary study can be ignored, 'since our books are our study companions'.

### Subjects

Although such topics as biblical and Talmudic commentaries and *Halakhah in all its ramifications formed its core, the subject-matter of the Jewish religious book was very wide. There are books on *philosophy, *geography, *history, *science and mathematics, *ethics, *folklore; books of poetry and sermons (see PREACHING); and, of course, all the works on *Kabbalah and *Hasidism. All these were termed *sefarim*, meaning religious books, the tradition believing with William Temple that God is interested in many things other than religion in its narrower sense. Naturally, some of these topics were of peripheral interest, the books on these catering only to the specialist

reader, and some were viewed with suspicion by the traditionalists (see CENSORSHIP), A tendency can also be observed to limit the term *sefarim kedoshim*, 'holy books', to works on Kabbalah and Hasidism. But the broader term *sefarim* (without the adjective) was used for all the works mentioned. In addition to the Hebrew books, many more popular books were published in *Yiddish and *Ladino.

### Introductions

While a Jewish proverb has it that a book without an introduction is like a body without a soul, the formal introduction to a book in which the author states his aim was unknown in the ancient period. None of the books of the Bible has an introduction (although, according to some scholars, the first Psalm is really an introduction to the whole collection), nor do any of the Talmudic books. The reason for this may be because most of these works grew, so to speak, gradually and are really collections of earlier material. It is also possible that the ancient authors, for whom the idea of an author acquiring fame for work which God gave him the ability to produce seemed somewhat preposterous, kept themselves in the background. They may have considered their work as a divine gift not to be squandered through the self-indulgence of a personal introduction. How helpful it would have been for scholars puzzling over the dating of the ancient books if their authors or editors had supplied a 'Dear Reader' type of preface with precise dates, provenance, and all, but nothing of the sort is available because that kind of preface was never thought of. From the Middle Ages and onwards, however, books were generally provided with an introduction or preface. Even when the author wished to remain anonymous he usually stated his aim in writing the book and, perhaps, why he preferred anonymity. Rabbi A. Amiel (1993–46), in an introduction to one of his books, wittily remarked that, like the Passover *Haggadah, introductions usually 'begin with disparagement and end with praise'; the author first declares the inadequacy of the book and his own unworthiness to write it but then goes on to say that, for all that, the work is well-worth publishing because of its many virtues.

From introductions we obtain much information about the overt reasons why the authors have seen fit to publish their works. Like authors everywhere, the authors of *sefarim* no doubt often wrote to court fame or wealth, but such pandering to selfish motives is never admitted, particularly since the Rabbinic tradition frowns on the study and teaching of the Torah with ulterior motives. Some authors declare that they wrote their books as thanksgiving for having escaped danger. Childless authors wrote their works to gain immortality through these substitute offspring. The Talmudic saying (*Yevamot* 97a) is often quoted by authors in this connection that when the Torah words of a scholar are repeated after his death, his lips move in the grave.

*Titles*

The biblical and Talmudic books, with few exceptions such as the headings of the Psalms, did not have titles, probably for the same reasons that they did not have introductions. (The titles we now have, Genesis, Exodus, and so forth, were given to them long after they had been compiled.) Ancient books were often later given titles with no reference to their contents of the book but simply after their opening word. The book of Genesis is known in Hebrew as *Bereshit*, 'In the beginning', after the word with which the book opens. Similarly, a tractate of the Talmud was given the name *Betzah* ('Egg') not because, as a monk scornfully remarked in the Middle Ages, the Rabbis had nothing better to do than to devote a whole tractate to eggs, but because the tractate opens with this word. Even in later times some books are given their title by their opening word or words, which explains the oddity of a book on Jewish rituals being called: 'Meat on Coals.'

Many books do, of course, have titles describing their contents, such as *Saadiah's Beliefs and Opinions*; Maimonides' *Guide of the Perplexed*; *Albo's Book of the Principle of Faith*, *Meiri's Treatise on Repentance*, or the works produced from time to time with titles such as *Jewish Customs*, or the many works of commentary entitled simply: 'Commentary to . . .'. Titles are often given not because of the contents of a book but because the title refers to the author by a biblical verse containing his name. Examples are: *And Isaac Sowed*; *And Jacob Said*, *And Moses Began*, by authors with these names. A book on Hebrew grammar by Jacob Bassani is called *Jacob Shall Take Root* (Isaiah 27: 6) because it deals, among other grammatical topics, with the 'roots' of Hebrew words. Especially in the Kabbalah, flowery and grandiose titles are popular. Cordovero's *Orchard of Pomegranates* has two commentaries on it, one called *The Rind of the Pomegranate*, the other *The Sweet Juice of the Pomegranate*. Hayyim *Vital's work on Kabbalistic theory is called *The Tree of Life* and the work in which this author describes the application of the theory to practice is called *The Fruit of the Tree of Life*.

Clever and punning titles abound. A popular moralistic work by Zvi Hirsh Kaidonover (d. 1712) is called, in Hebrew, *Kav Ha-Yashar* ('The Upright Path') because the book contains 120 sections, the numerical value (see GEMATRIA) of *Kav*. Moreover, if the letters of *Ha-Yashar* are transposed they form the word Hirsh, the author's name. In his humility Israel Isserlein (1390–1460) called his Responsa collection after the expression used for the removal of the ashes from the altar, *Terumat Ha-Deshen* ('Removal, or Contribution, of the Ashes') but, by using the Hebrew word *Deshen* in the title, he hints that the numerical value of *Deshen*, 354, is the number of Responsa in the book. Rabbi Moshe *Feinstein called his Responsa collection *The Letters of Moshe*. A book attacking his opinions by a Rabbi Schwartz was published, in exactly the same format, entitled *In Reply to the Letters*.

*Regard for Books*

It is the practice among Jews that when a religious book is no longer fit for use it is not destroyed but reverentially buried in the cemetery, often in the grave of a scholar or pious man at his interment. There is a statement in the Talmud (*Sanhedrin* 21b) that every Jew is obliged to write (or buy) a *Sefer Torah ('Scroll of the Torah') yet, following earlier authorities, the *Shulḥan Arukh* (*Yoreh Deah*, 270) rules that, nowadays, when Scrolls are not lacking in the synagogue, the obligation can better be satisfied by acquiring books from which to study. It is held to be of high religious value to supply poor students with books. Israel Isserlein disbarred from his lectures a student who had refused to lend a book to a fellow-student. When a sacred book falls to the ground it is not left there. A pious Jews will pick it up and kiss it before restoring it to its proper place. According to a medieval superstition, when a reader of a sacred book has to leave the room for a time he should close the book. If he leaves it open during his absence the demon of forgetfulness will cause him to forget his learning.

This was later given the rationale that it is disrespectful to a book to leave it open when one is not studying from it; moreover, an open book gathers dust.

Leonard Singer Gold (ed.) *A Sign and a Wonder: 2,000 Years of Hebrew Books and Illuminated Manuscripts* (Oxford, 1988).

Raphael Posner and Israel Ta-Shema (eds.), *The Hebrew Book: An Historical Survey* (Jerusalem, 1975).

**Buber, Martin** Existentialist Jewish philosopher, educationist, and Zionist thinker, born Vienna, 1878, died Jerusalem, 1965. Buber's main contribution to philosophy is the distinction, made in his justly famous philosophical poem *I and Thou*, between the *I–It* relationship and the *I–Thou*. In the former man relates to others and to things in an objective, detached manner, as when the physical scientist examines his data and the social scientist the life of a community. In the latter relationship, man meets others as those to whom he says 'Thou'. That is to say, his approach to the other is as person to person, where the other is not a thing to be manipulated or even to be used for the satisfaction of his benevolent instincts, but a fellow creature with whom one can engage in dialogue, a favourite Buberian word. On the religious level, according to Buber, man cannot talk *about* God but can only encounter Him, not only in the dialogue of prayer but also by encountering the divine Thou behind all particular Thous.

Buber's further distinction, in his book *Moses*, between history and saga is important for biblical studies. Many of the biblical narratives, such as the Exodus, are best seen not as sober, factual histories but rather as a retelling, a *Heilsgeschichte* or a kind of sacred poetry, of past events in which the mighty acts of God were observed by men and women of faith.

In his early career Buber was profoundly interested in Jewish mysticism but as his thought developed he came to view mysticism with a degree of suspicion. The mystic's ideal of *annihilation of selfhood tends to negate the all important I–Thou relationship in which the human soul is not lost in God but encounters Him in dialogue. Buber's retelling of *The Tales of the Hasidim* (the title of the work in which Buber brought *Hasidism to the attention of the Western world) tends to make the leaders of the movement advocates of the I–Thou approach. A favourite quote of Buber was from the master of *Kotsk who commented on the verse: 'And ye shall be holy men unto Me' (Exodus 22: 30) that this means: 'Be holy *men*'; or, as Buber put it, the ideal is to be 'humanly holy', a Jewish humanism which does not urge its followers to flee the world but to become involved in the world. Gershom *Scholem has criticized Buber for relying only on the Hasidic tales while ignoring Hasidic doctrine as taught in the works of its foremost teachers who did advocate the mystical way. Buber also wrote a novel on Hasidism, *For the Sake of Heaven*, a narrative of the conflict between the early masters of the movement when, during Napoleon's invasion of Russia, some were on Napoleon's side and, others on the side of the Tsar.

A question often put is whether Buber can be considered a Jewish thinker. Buber certainly considered himself to be speaking from within the Jewish tradition. 'I can stand beside my father's house,' said Buber, 'and yet see the whole world go by.' But it was often remarked that while Buber enjoyed unbounded admiration in the Christian world his reception among Jews was less enthusiastic, partly because there is a strong element of antinomianism in Buber's thought that places him outside the Jewish traditional approach to religion in which the Torah and its precepts are imposed heteronomously upon the Jew and are not dependent on whether he personally can appropriate them by saying 'Thou' to them. An attempt at appointing Buber to a chair in religious studies at the Hebrew University in Jerusalem was abandoned because of opposition by the *Orthodox. Eventually he was appointed instead Professor of Social Philosophy where his influence was keenly felt in educational and other spheres and where he was idolized by generations of students.

Buber was a Zionist from his youth and was highly admired when he moved to Jerusalem in 1938, yet his political views which looked forward to an eventual bi-national commonwealth of Jews and Arabs were thought naïve, unrealistic, and dangerous. It is said that during his life in Israel he never entered a synagogue in his refusal to accept any kind of external, and hence for him, unauthentic, forms of religious activity.

Buber's literary style, except in his Hasidic tales and his novel, hardly makes for easy reading. At times it seems almost as if he believed that the only way to give expression to profound ideas is to be obscure. The story is told that, soon after he had settled in Jerusalem, a woman complimented him on his excellent Hebrew, saying that it was so good that she understood everything he said. Buber is reported to have replied (though he denied this):

'I shall not be satisfied with my Hebrew until you cannot understand a word I say.'

Martin Buber, *I and Thou*, trans. R. Gregor Smith (Edinburgh, 1937).

Paul Arthur Schilpp and Maurice Friedman (eds.), *The Philosophy of Martin Buber* (La Salle, Ill., 1967).

# C

**Cain and Abel**  The two sons of *Adam and Eve (Genesis 4). Cain is a tiller of the soil and Abel a keeper of sheep. (The suggestion that the narrative contains echoes of a conflict between the settled farmers and the nomadic shepherds has no evidence to support it, since there is no record of such a conflict in ancient Israelite society.) Cain brings an offering to the Lord from the fruit of the soil and Abel from the choicest of the firstlings of his flock. God rejects Cain's offering but accepts Abel's. When Cain and Abel are in the field Cain attacks Abel and kills him, whereupon God condemns Cain to a life of wandering and puts a mark on him, as a sign that he is protected and no one must kill him. (The expression 'the brand of Cain' for a murderer is based on a misunderstanding. Cain was not 'branded' in order to mark him as a murderer but rather to protect him from himself becoming a victim of murder.)

The name Cain, in Hebrew *kayin*, is said to have been given by Eve because she declared: 'I have gotten [*kaniti*, from *kanah*, "to acquire"] a man from the Lord.' Of Abel the text simply says that Eve gave birth to him, without stating that she named him. It is interesting that the Hebrew word, translated as Abel, means 'vapour' and this is a probably an instance, of which there are many in the Bible, of a name describing the subsequent fate of a person; in this case it means, perhaps, that his life was short and insubstantial because he was cut off in his prime.

The narrative is unclear about why God rejected Cain's offering and accepted Abel's. One interpretation is based on the word 'choicest' of Abel's offering. Abel brought his very best, whereas Cain was satisfied with the leftovers.

In a Midrash (Genesis Rabbah 22: 7) there are three opinions as to why the brothers quarrelled. According to one opinion the brothers divided the world between them, one taking all the land, the other all the movables. The one who took the land ordered the other to get off his land and fly in the air. The one who took the movables ordered the other to strip naked because the clothes belonged to him. Another opinion is that the quarrel was about in whose territory the *Temple was to be built. A third opinion is that Cain had a twin sister (Genesis 4: 17 says that Cain took a wife and otherwise whom did he marry?) but Abel had two sisters born at the same time as him (i.e. they were triplets). Abel claimed both his sisters for himself but Cain wanted the additional one by his right as a first-born to have a double portion. It is fairly obvious that the Midrash uses the original narrative as a paradigm for human conflict. Why do people engage in violence and what are the basic causes of war? One reason is disputes over land and property, another arguments over women, and a third disagreements over religion.

In the Jewish tradition Cain is a bad character and Abel a virtuous one, but occasionally there is to be found, if not a justification of Cain's act, at least an attempt to understand it on the grounds that Cain had had no experience of killing or death and must have been unaware of the seriousness of what he was doing. Cain also features as one of the biblical characters who admitted their fault and hence is a prototype of the penitent, although his repentance is sometimes described as less than totally sincere. In the Kabbalah Cain's soul belongs to the *Sitra Aḥara*, the demonic side (see DEMONS), while Abel's soul came down to earth again (see *Reincarnation) as the soul of Moses! There is a legend (Zohar, (i. 9b) that Cain's descendants live in the netherworld as two-headed monsters. This legend was known in the Middle Ages in the non-Jewish world as well.

**Calendar**  The Jewish religious year with its feasts and fasts. Whatever its origins (the question of which is extremely complicated) the Jewish calendar, from at least the beginning of the present era, was a lunar calendar. The very word for 'month', *hodesh*, means 'that which is renewed' and refers to the waning and waxing of the moon; hence the biblical name *Rosh Hodesh, the 'head of the month', for the beginning of the month, observed as a festival in biblical times (I Samuel 20: 24). In the Mishnah (*Rosh Ha-Shanah* 1. 1–3–1) the elaborate details are given for the calculation of the months. The beginning of the month was determined by the sighting of the new moon by witnesses. A month could have either twenty-nine or thirty days. If the new moon was sighted on the night of the thirtieth day (the night belonging to the next day in the Jewish calendar) and the Supreme Court, accepting the testimony of the witnesses as valid, declared that day to be Rosh Hodesh, the previous month would be one of twenty-nine days. If no witnesses were forthcoming the thirty-first day would automatically be Rosh Hodesh and the previous month would be one of thirty days. The calendar was, however, fixed in the fourth century and from that time onwards there is a fixed succession of 'full' months (having thirty days) and 'defective' months (having twenty-nine days). Rosh Hodesh, so important a feast in biblical times that it is compared to the Sabbath (e.g. in Isaiah 1: 13), is, nowadays, celebrated only as a minor festival. When the previous month has twenty-nine days, Rosh Hodesh is celebrated for two days (this is because of the uncertainty about the sighting of the moon in the earlier period). When the previous month has a full thirty days, Rosh Hodesh is celebrated for only one day.

The problem at the heart of the Jewish calendar is that while it is lunar, there is a need to bring it into relationship with the solar year. This is because the months are to be counted from the month in which the Exodus from Egypt took place (Exodus 12: 2) and yet the festival of *Passover, celebrating the Exodus, is said (Deuteronomy 16: 1) to fall in the month Aviv ('ripening' of the corn); Passover must fall in spring. Since the lunar year is shorter than the solar, something had to be done to prevent Passover moving through the solar year so as to fall in other than the spring month. The method adopted was to intercalate the lunar year, that is, to add an extra lunar month to seven years in a cycle of nineteen lunar years.

(The leap years, the years which have an additional month, are the third, sixth, eighth, eleventh, fourteenth, seventeenth, and nineteenth of the nineteen-year cycle, the beginning of the cycle being established by tradition.) Simeon ben Tzemah Duran (1351–1444), Rabbi in Algiers, proudly remarked in a Responsum (Responsa *Tashbetz*, Pt. 2, no. 250), that the Jewish calendar is superior to both the Christian and the Muslim calendars. The Christians, who have a solar calendar, are obliged to fix the months arbitrarily so that some have thirty days, others thirty-one. The beginning of each month is decided purely by convention and is not based on nature, as in a lunar calendar. The Muslims, who do have a lunar and hence a 'natural' calendar, pay the price for it of having Ramadan movable through the solar year. Jews have the best of both worlds. Their calendar is lunar and natural and yet their festivals always fall in more or less the same period of the year. Since, however, the Jewish calendar is based on a calculation of the solar year that is out by about six minutes, Passover moves in the direction of summer by almost a day every 200 years. When it moves, in about 8,000 years' time, to as late as 1 June, the Rabbis of that future age will have a problem on their hands. Many would say, let them worry about it!

The names of the months of Babylonian origin, as we now have them, are found only in late books of the Bible such as the book of *Esther. These names, used universally by Jews, are, counting from the first month, the month in which Passover falls: Nisan, Iyyar, Sivan, Tammuz, Av, Elul, Tishri, Marheshvan, Kislev, Tevet, Shevat, Adar. In a leap year the added month is always the one before Nisan and is called Adar Sheni, 'Second Adar'.

*Dates*

In Talmudic times, legal documents and the like were dated from the beginning of the Seleucid Empire in 312 BCE. But in the Middle Ages the custom arose of dating from the creation of the world. As can be seen from the French commentary to the Talmud known as the *Tosafot (Gittin* 80b), this method of dating from the creation was already well established in twelfth-century France. There is a debate in the Talmud on whether the world was created in Nisan or in Tishri and the view is followed that it was in Tishri. Consequently, the first of Tishri is *Rosh Ha-Shanah, the beginning of the year for purposes of dating. (The first day of Tishri is called the New Year for certain other purposes in the Mishnah, *Rosh Ha-Shanah* 1: 1, but the idea that the year is counted from the creation on this day is later.) There is a tradition that the year 1240 CE is the year 5000 from the creation. Thus the year 5753 corresponds to the year 1992 from Tishri to December and to 1993 from 1 January until the next Tishri. Few traditionalists feel themselves bound by this method of dating to reject the scientific picture of the vast age of the earth (feeling free to interpret the creation narrative in Genesis in a non-literal fashion—see EVOLUTION), since this dating is not a matter of dogma but purely one of convention. For the same reason they have no objection to using, in letters, for example, the general date, although some do object to its use on the grounds that the counting is from the birth of Jesus and might, therefore, be considered to be of a doctrinal nature. No one seems to object to the use of Wednesday (Woden's day) or Thursday (Thor's day), since the pagan associations have long been forgotten. For that matter, the month Tammuz originally bore the name of the god Tammuz, and yet is used by Jews because it no longer has any pagan associations.

## Night and Day

Most modern biblical scholars understand the refrain in the first chapter of Genesis: 'and it was evening and it was morning' to mean that when the day had turned into evening and then the night into morning a full day had past; that is, the day begins in the morning and continues until the next morning. Some commentators even in the Middle Ages acknowledged that this was the plain meaning of the verses. Nevertheless, the tradition understands the verses to mean that the day begins at nightfall and lasts until the next nightfall. Thus it is universally accepted by all Jews that for religious purposes the 'day' begins on the previous 'night'. The Sabbath begins on Friday at nightfall and terminates at nightfall on Saturday. The same applies to the festivals. Since the twilight is a doubtful period and there is, in any event, a Rabbinic injunction to add to the Sabbath, the calendar usually gives the times for the beginning of the Sabbath (and the festivals) as a little before sunset and the time of termination when it is fully night. Pious Jews, uncertain when the Sabbath ends in the absence of a calendar, will follow the Talmudic rule that it is not considered to be night until three average-sized stars can be seen in the night sky.

## Second Days of Festivals

Since, as noted above, Rosh Hodesh, the first of the month, from which the festivals of the month are counted, could be either on the thirtieth day of the previous month or on the thirty-first day, this meant that there was always a doubt as to which day had been declared *Rosh Hodesh* and hence from which day the festivals falling in that month were to be counted. For the Jews of Palestine there was no problem. There was time to inform them before the festival. But the Jews of the *Diaspora, who lived too far away for the communication to reach them, had to keep the two days as a festival in order to be sure that they were keeping the right day. Even the Jews in Palestine kept the festival of *Rosh Ha-Shanah for two days, since this day coincides with the beginning of the month. Unless they lived adjacent to the court they, too, would not know which day was the day of the festival and they, too, kept two days. Once the calendar was fixed in the fourth century there was no longer any doubt, but the Talmud states that the Diaspora Jews were urged by the Palestinian authorities to continue to keep the two days as did their ancestors. There was considerable debate whether this applied to the keeping of two days of Rosh Ha-Shanah in Palestine, but the standard *Orthodox practice is to keep the 'two days of the [other] festivals' in the Diaspora and the two days of Rosh Ha-Shanah in Israel. There is much discussion regarding the position of a Diaspora Jew on a visit to Israel for one of the festivals and that of an Israeli who pays a visit to a Diaspora community. Does he follow the practice of the place he comes from or that of the place where he is staying on the festival?

The three festivals affected by the second-day problem are: Passover (in the Bible to be observed with the first and seventh day as a full festival); *Pentecost (in the Bible to be observed as a one-day festival); and *Tabernacles (in the Bible a festival on the first day and on the eighth). Jews in Israel follow the times laid down in the Bible but Diaspora Jews celebrate Passover for eight days, the first and second and seventh and eighth, as full festivals; two days of Pentecost; and the first and second days of Tabernacles and the eighth and an additional ninth day. The intermediate days of Passover and Tabernacles have the status of a festival but of a lesser kind (see FESTIVALS). Reform Jews do not keep the second days of the festivals and some Conservative Rabbis have argued for their abolition in order to bring the Diaspora into line with Israel. Conversely, some Reform congregations have reintroduced, for the same reason, the observance of a two-day Rosh Ha-Shanah.

*The Religious Year*

The major festivals are: Passover, Pentecost, Tabernacles, Rosh Ha-Shanah, and *Yom Kippur; the minor festivals: *Hanukkah and *Purim from Talmudic times and *Lag Ba-Omer from the Middle Ages. There are also a number of *fast days. The following is a list, month by month, of the dates of festivals and fasts in the Jewish religious year:

*Nisan* 15–22 (15–23 in Diaspora): Passover.

*Iyyar* 18: Lag Ba-Omer.

*Sivan* 6 (6 and 7 in Diaspora): Pentecost.

*Tammuz* 17: Fast of *Tammuz.

*Av* 9: Fast of *Av, Ninth.

*Tishri* 1–2: Rosh Ha-Shanah.
3: Fast of *Gedaliah.
10: Yom Kippur.
15–23 (15–24 in Diaspora): Tabernacles.
22: *Hoshanah Rabbah,
23: *Shemini Atzeret,
24: *Simhat Torah.

*Kislev* Hanukkah begins on the 25th and lasts for eight days.

*Tevet* 10: Fast of *Tevet.

*Shevat* 15: New Year for *Trees.

*Adar* 13: Fast of Esther.
14: Purim.
15: *Sushan Purim.

In recent years 27 Nisan has been introduced as Yom Ha-Shoah, the Day of the *Holocaust, when this terrible event is commemorated and 5 Iyyar as *Yom Ha-Atzmaut, Israeli Independence Day.

From the Middle Ages there are: the *Omer period of mourning from the end of Passover to Pentecost; the fast of the *First-Born on the eve of Passover; the month of *Elul as a period of preparation for the repentance period in Tishri; the Ten Days of *Penitence, the first ten days of Tishri. The *Safed mystics introduced the eve of each Rosh Hodesh as a Minor Day of Atonement, *Yom Kippur Katan.

Abraham Bloch, *The Biblical and Historical Background of the Jewish Holy Days* (New York, 1978). Hayyim Schauss, *The Jewish Festivals*, trans. Samuel Jaffe (New York, 1962).

**Candles** Candles of wax or tallow took the place of lamps used in various Jewish *rituals such as the *Sabbath lights; in the *Havdalah ceremony; and the *Hanukkah lights. A *synagogue had to be well lit and pious folk used to denote candles for the purpose. Now most synagogues use electric lights, but in some two candles are placed before the Cantor at the reading-desk. The *Sephardi synagogue, Bevis Marks in London, still preserves its original candelabrum containing 613 candles corresponding to the 613 *precepts of the Torah, which is used for *Yom Kippur and on other ceremonial occasions. On the basis of the verse: 'The soul of man is a candle of the Lord' (Proverbs 20: 27) a special candle which burns for twenty-four hours is kindled on the anniversary of the death of a near relative (*Yahrzeit) and often two lighted candles are placed at the head of a corpse awaiting burial. In some communities the bride is escorted under the *ḥuppah with lighted candles. The practice of having votive candles for *saints is totally rejected.

**Cannibalism** The natural human revulsion against consuming the flesh of other human beings and the fact that examples of it in practice are only very rarely found, explains, perhaps, why the topic is virtually ignored in the Jewish sources. The sole reference to it in the Codes is that of *Isserles in his gloss to the *Shulḥan Arukh* (*Yoreh Deah*, 79: 1), Discussing the *dietary laws, Isserles simply states: 'It is forbidden to eat human flesh by the law of the Torah.' In the much-discussed cases of human beings saving their lives by eating the flesh of their dead companions, Judaism would permit the practice on the grounds that only three prohibitions (those of murder, incest or adultery, and idolatry) demand that life be sacrificed rather than offend against them.

**Cantillation** The mode of chanting for the *reading of the Torah and the other Scriptures in the synagogue and the system of musical notation for this. Scripture was not simply declaimed in the synagogue, but chanted. The Talmud (*Megillah* 32a) implies that a simple reading of Scripture without the accompanying melody is lifeless. This shows that in Talmudic times the Torah was chanted, but there is no indication anywhere in the Talmud of the type of melody used for the chant. In post-Talmudic times various systems of notation were developed, one of which became standard; that is to say, there eventually arose a universally accepted system of musical notation with special signs for the different notes. All communities follow this system, although the actual form of the melodies is not the same in all communities. The *Ashkenazi melodies, for instance, are in a different mode from the *Sephardic, the latter having distinct traces of Arabic musical styles.

The signs for the various notes are called *neginot* ('melodies') or *teemim* ('flavours', i.e. giving flavour to the words). These notes have a double purpose. In the first instance they serve as punctuation similar to the full stop, colon, semi-colon, and comma in English, these not being shown in the original Hebrew. The notes also serve as a commentary to the text. For instance, the note *shalshelet* ('chain') is a wavering note, placed, for example, over the Hebrew word for 'But he lingered' (Genesis 19: 16) to denote tarrying and uncertainty. A particularly interesting use of this note is the placing of it over the Hebrew word for 'But he refused' (Genesis 39: 8), describing Joseph's rejection of the blandishments of Potiphar's wife, perhaps to suggest that Joseph's eventual 'refusal' came only after a degree of struggle with himself during which he vacillated before he actually resisted temptation.

In the Scroll of the Torah (*Sefer Torah) itself there are no notes; the reader is obliged to learn these by heart beforehand and supply them as he reads. The notes for the prophetic readings (see HAFTARAH) and for the books of *Esther, Song of *Songs, *Ruth, *Lamentations, and *Ecclesiastes are the same in form as those of the Pentateuch but are chanted in different modes. The Haftarah mode is suited to admonition; the books of Song of Songs, Ruth, and Ecclesiastes are chanted in a more joyous mode; Esther and Lamentations in, respectively, a jolly and a sad tone, as befits the theme of these books. There is a different system of notation for the book of *Psalms but it is no longer known what this represents and the actual chant for the book of Psalms depends nowadays on the tradition of the various communities. While, from the Talmudic passage referred to above, it appears that the Mishnah, too, was chanted and some ancient manuscripts of the Mishnah have signs for the notes, this system is no longer known. Yet in traditional circles, the Talmud is chanted, not simply read, in the '*Gemara *nigun*', chiefly as an aid to memory.

In the Talmudic passage (*Berakhot* 62a) on proper conduct in the privy a number of reasons are given why one should wipe with the left not the right hand. One of these is that it is improper to use the right hand for the purpose since it is with this hand that 'one shows the notes of the Torah'. The great French commentator *Rashi remarks that he had personally observed readers who came from Palestine who, as they read from the Torah, would make the signs of the notes with their right hand. It has been suggested that this old custom, still observed in some Oriental communities, was not that the reader himself made these signs with his hand but that someone standing beside him made them in order to remind the reader which notes to use.

*Reform Jews tended to give up the whole method of cantillation, preferring to follow the practice in Protestant churches of declaiming Scripture, in the belief that this was more decorous in Western society. But, as part of a definite swing towards greater traditionalism, many Reform congregations have reintroduced the old system of cantillation.

In the Kabbalah the *teemim* represent higher worlds than those which are represented or can be reached by the words themselves. The Zohar has a detailed exposition on the musical notes, referring to them by the names they came to have. This was one of the arguments presented against the Kabbalistic contention that the author of the Zohar was Rabbi *Simeon ben Yohai in the second century CE, since it is virtually certain that this system of notation is much later.

**Cantor** The prayer leader in the synagogue. In Rabbinic times, many people were unfamiliar with the prayers, and so in public worship a man well versed in the *liturgy would recite the prayers aloud with the congregation responding to his benedictions with *Amen, this being considered as if they themselves had offered the prayers. Even after the wide dissemination of the *Prayer Book, the institution of the prayer leader was continued, so that the prayers were then recited by both the congregation and the reader. In the Mishnah, the leader is called 'one who descends before the chest'. (The *Ark in the ancient synagogue was not built into the wall of the synagogue but consisted of a portable chest containing the *Sefer Torah.) Other terms found in the sources are sheliah tzibbur ('messenger of the congregation'), abbreviated to shatz (hence the Jewish surname Schatz) and hazan (originally meaning 'overseer'), the name most frequently used. The hazan was not a special functionary. Any member of the congregation was qualified to lead the congregation in prayer. But in the course of time, specially qualified persons were favoured to act as hazanim. The term 'Cantor', adopted by Western Jews in modern times, is not found in the traditional sources and is used chiefly for a man with special musical qualifications who sings accompanied by a choir (see CHOIRS). The modern Cantor is a special salaried official. In this entry the term 'Cantor' is used to denote every variety of prayer leader.

A section in the Shulhan Arukh (Orah Hayyim, 53) is devoted to the qualities ideally required for a hazan. He should be without sin (comparatively speaking, of course, since no one is free from sin); he should be free of rumours that he had a bad reputation in his youth; he should be a modest man and acceptable to the people for whom he deputizes; and he should have a pleasant voice. If such a paragon is not to be found, this source adds, somewhat laconically, that the man chosen should be the most pious and learned in the congregation. (For this reason it is customary in *Hasidism for the *Rebbe, the Hasidic master, to act as prayer leader.) The hazan should be at least 13 years old (see BAR MITZVAH) and should be male. (*In Reform and many *Conservative congregations women Cantors are appointed; see WOMEN.) Ideally a hazan should have a full *beard but this was later interpreted to mean that he should be of an age when the beard is fully grown, that is, he should be a mature person, who is then acceptable even if he does not actually sport a beard.

The Rabbinic authorities tended to look askance at Hazanim monopolizing the service (and there was no doubt a degree of envy when the hazan, who pleased the congregation with his sweet singing, was more popular than the learned Rabbi) but most attempts at curbing the exuberance of the prayer leader were doomed to failure. On the whole the people loved cantorial versatility (hazanut). Very revealing is the statement in the Shulhan Arukh (53. 11):

'A shatz who prolongs the service so that people will hear how pleasant is his voice, if it is because he rejoices in his heart that he is able to praise God with his sweet voice, let a blessing come to him, provided that he offers his prayers in a serious frame of mind and stands in God's presence in awe and dread. But if his intention is for people to hear his voice and he rejoices in this, it is disgraceful. Nevertheless, it is not good for anyone to prolong the service unduly because this imposes a burden on the congregation.'

A number of modern Cantors have been very gifted musically, some being also expert composers whose liturgical compositions were collected and used by Cantors all over the world. With the invention of the gramophone, there was a proliferation of Cantorial records and, later, tapes, enjoyed by Jews in their own homes. Among the more famous of modern Cantors were Yossele Rosenblatt, Gershon Sirota, Mordecai Herschman, and Zavel Kwartin. It is not unknown for Cantors to use melodies from well-known operas adapted to the words of the prayers. The more discriminating regard this as vulgar but others see no harm in it. They point to the Responsum of the Polish Rabbi Joel Sirkes (1561–1640), who is so lenient (Responsa Bayit Hadash, no. 127) as to permit even the use of church melodies, except for those especially associated with Christian hymns. The offence of copying *Gentile ways, the Rabbi remarks, applies only to doctrinal matters belonging to the practices of other religions. *Music is not specifically Christian but is the common heritage of all mankind.

A. Z. Idelsohn, *Jewish Music in its Historical Development* (New York, 1944).

**Capital Punishment** The Bible prescribes the death penalty for a large number of offences including religious offences such as idol worship and the profaning of the Sabbath. But the question of capital punishment in actual practice in ancient Jewish society is extremely complicated.

According to the Mishnah (*Sanhedrin* 1: 4) the death penalty could only be inflicted, after a trial, by a *Sanhedrin composed of twenty-three judges and there were four different types of death penalty (*Sanhedrin* 7: 1): stoning, burning, slaying (by the sword), and strangling. A bare reading of these and the other accounts in the tractate would seem to suggest a vast proliferation of the death penalty. Yet, throughout the Talmudic literature, this whole subject is viewed with unease, so much so that according to the rules stated in that literature the death penalty could hardly ever have been imposed. For instance, it is ruled that two witnesses are required to testify not only that they witnessed the act for which the criminal has been charged but that they had warned him beforehand that if he carried out the act he would be executed, and he had to accept the warning, stating his willingness to commit the act despite his awareness of its consequences. The criminal's own confession is not accepted as evidence. Moreover, circumstantial evidence is not admitted. The extreme case is referred to of a man running after another man with a drawn sword, the victim being found slain by that sword and no one else being present who could have done the deed what greater evidence of his guilt could there be? It has to be appreciated, however, that practically all this material comes from a time when the right to impose the death penalty had been taken away from the Jewish courts by the Roman authorities. According to one report in the Talmud (*Sanhedrin* 41a) the power of the Jewish courts to impose the death penalty ceased around the year 30 BCE; according to another report (*Sanhedrin* 52b) it could only have been imposed while the Temple stood and must have come to an end not later than 70 CE when the Temple was destroyed.

This means that, although earlier traditions may be present in the Mishnaic formulations, the whole topic, including the restrictions, is treated in the Mishnah and the Talmud in a purely theoretical way. It is hard to believe that when the courts did impose the death penalty they could only do so when the conditions mentioned above obtained. Who would commit a murder in the presence of two witnesses when these had solemnly warned him that if he persisted they would testify against him to have him executed for his crime? That the Mishnaic material is purely on the theoretical level can be seen from the oft-quoted statement (Mishnah *Makkot* 1: 10): 'A Sanhedrin that puts a man to

death once in seven years is called destructive. Rabbi Eliezer ben Azariah says: even once in seventy years. Rabbi *Akiba and Rabbi Tarfon say: had we been in the Sanhedrin none would ever have been put to death. Rabban Simeon ben Gamaliel says: they would have multiplied shedders of blood in Israel.' This Mishnah is a kind of reflection on the whole law of capital punishment. Faced with the clear biblical injunctions, the Rabbis mentioned could not simply have said that capital punishment was wrong. After all, the Bible states that it is right and has to be imposed on the guilty. But the statement seems to imply that the Rabbis welcomed the development by which the Sanhedrin no longer functioned with the power to impose the death penalty and Rabbi Akiba and Rabbi Tarfon speculate that even when the Sanhedrin did possess this power, various legal means could have been adopted to negate the imposition of the penalty. It is not so much, as Jewish apologists maintain, that the Rabbis consciously attempted to reform the law, but rather that when the power to inflict the death penalty fell into abeyance in any event this development was interpreted as being fully in accord with the Torah's regard for all human life, including the life of the criminal; so in a sense it was felt to the good that the death penalty could no longer actually be imposed but was simply left in the books for theoretical discussion. Once the matter was discussed on a purely theoretical basis the gruesome details could be described in all their starkness while, at the same time, restrictions could be piled on in order to make the death penalty virtually impossible. In practice it became illegal for a Jewish court to impose the death penalty.

Against all this is the Talmudic statement (*Sanhedrin* 46a) that as an emergency measure, 'when the generation requires it', a court has the power to 'act against the Torah' and to order an execution or other 'illegal' physical penalties. In other words, although it is illegal to impose the death penalty, the court can, on rare occasions, act illegally if the aim is to protect the Torah. Naturally, it all depends on the circumstances that would warrant executions without the due processes of law. The statement was never interpreted as meaning that what the Law took away with one hand it gave back with the other. The German and French communities in the Middle Ages ignored the statement altogether and never imposed the death penalty, not even when circumstances seemed to call for it. Not so in Muslim Spain, where the Gentile authorities gave the Jewish courts a good deal of autonomy. In Spain, albeit on rare occasions, the courts did rely on the Talmudic statement and imposed otherwise illegal penalties such as mutilation (found nowhere in the classical sources) of certain offenders; they also executed offenders such as informers who endangered the community. When Asher ben Yehiel (d. 1327) came from Germany to Toledo in Spain he expressed his horror at the Spanish practice, totally unknown in Germany, although later on he himself conformed to the Spanish norm.

There the matter rested until the establishment of the *State of Israel. There are rumours of Jews very occasionally taking the law into their own hands and executing dangerous criminals among them on the basis of the Talmudic statement. The Israeli scholar Reuben Margaliot (d. 1971), in his massive commentary to tractate *Sanhedrin* entitled *Margaliot Ha-Yam* (Jerusalem, 1958, p. 182, comment on this Talmudic statement), writes that his father told him that in his home town near Lemberg in the nineteenth century members of the community one Yom Kippur took a notorious informer who threatened their survival, smothered him in his prayer shawl, and drowned him in the river. But these rumours are few and far between and largely unsubstantiated.

The remarks of Rabbi Isaac Herzog (1888–1959) in an article on the Sanhedrin published in 1932 (republished in Herzog's *The Main Institutions of Jewish Law* (London, 1936, pp. xxii–xxiv) are worth noting. Herzog begins: 'I have often heard it remarked that the restoration of the Jewish State in accordance with Jewish law would isolate the Jewish people from the modern civilized world; for the Hebrew penal code includes the death-penalty for purely religious offences such as the wilful desecration of the Sabbath, etc.' Herzog, quoting the material mentioned above and other Talmudic sources which make the re-establishment of the Sanhedrin dependent on the rebuilding of the *Temple in the Messianic age, demonstrates in his reply that until the advent of the *Messiah it is illegal to impose the death penalty for any offence, even for murder. There follows this statement:

'The difficulty in question is therefore a matter which could only arise in the *Messianic* age and need not enter into any practical calculations affecting the reconstitution of the Jewish State in Palestine. But, of course, in view of the actual position the idea of a Jewish State in Palestine (as distinct from a National Home), quite irrespective of the restoration of the Temple, is, in itself, rather a *Messianic* hope than a question of practical politics.'

Little did Rabbi Herzog think when he wrote this that the State of Israel would be established and that he would become its Chief Rabbi. When the State of Israel was established the Israeli Parliament, the Knesset, did debate whether or not to retain the death penalty as in the law established under the British mandate but the Knesset was not acting as a religious court or Sanhedrin, only as a secular body, albeit one influenced in its decisions by the Jewish religious tradition. The debate between Rabbi Akiba and Rabbi Tarfon and Rabban Simeon ben Gamaliel was referred to in the Knesset debate, and it was eventually decided to abolish capital punishment entirely except for treason committed in time of war.

David Menaham Shohet, *The Jewish Court in the Middle Ages* (New York, 1931), 135–38.

**Celibacy** It is a high religious obligation to marry and have children (see PROCREATION, MARRIAGE and BIRTH-CONTROL), so that the question of whether it is religiously proper to be celibate is really a question of whether there are circumstances when the religious injunction of procreation can be set aside. The classical text in this connection is in the Talmudic tractate *Yevamot* (63b). Here the story is told of the Palestinian teacher Simeon ben Azzai (early second century CE), who preached an eloquent sermon on the duty of procreation. When his colleagues reproached him for not practising what he preached since he himself was unmarried, he replied: 'What can I do? My soul is in love with the Torah. The world can be populated through others.' Ben Azzai's vocation as a diligent student of the Torah did not allow him to shoulder the responsibilities of married life. His love of the Torah prevented him from being a proper husband to a human wife. (The idea of the Torah as Israel's bride is found in many Talmudic and Midrashic passages.)

Does the Jewish tradition extend this exemption from the duty to marry to other students of the Torah, or is the case of Ben Azzai treated as unique because of his exceptional qualities?

A number of medieval authorities did not treat the case of Ben Azzai as exceptional. They are followed in the ruling of the *Shulḥan Arukh* (*Even Ha-Ezer*, 1. 4): 'Anyone whose soul is constantly in love with the Torah like Ben Azzai so that he cleaves to it all his days without ever taking a wife such a one commits no sin, provided that his [sexual] inclination does not get the better of him.' The later commentators, however, do tend to see Ben Azzai as exceptional and some point to the less than categorical formulation in the *Shulḥan Arukh*: 'commits no sin', implying, perhaps, that if such a student were to ask his Rabbi whether he might remain single he should be told that it is his duty to marry. Others again note the qualification that celibacy is only allowed where the student is fully able to control his sexual urge and they hold that 'nowadays' such total dedication to the ideal of chastity no longer exists. Even among his Rabbinic colleagues Ben Azzai's attitude was not accepted. Evidently, although they were also in love with the Torah, they did not feel that a celibate life was possible for them. In practice, throughout the ages, only a very few scholars remained unmarried and there are only a very few instances of a community seeing no objection to appointing a bachelor as its Rabbi (but this is not entirely unknown). The weight of the tradition is against the celibate life even for the most dedicated students of the Torah. With the possible exception of the *Essenes, there has never been anything like a religious order of celibates in Judaism.

**Censorship** The control of Jewish books to make sure that they do not contain material considered by those exercising the control to be injurious to religion and morals or harmful to the reputation of the Jewish people.

In considering the question of censorship in Judaism, it must first be noted that there has never been anything like a universally recognized body of Rabbis responsible for controlling the kind of literature that Jews produce. This is not to say that individual Rabbis never sought to ban certain books but their power to do so was limited by the willingness of authors, publishers, and readers to obey the dictates of these Rabbis.

The censorship that did exist was of two kinds—external and internal. External censorship was exercised by governmental bodies who ordered the excision from Jewish publications of passages held to be attacks on *Gentiles or on the Christian faith. The Jewish authorities, too, anticipated this type of intervention by themselves deleting or altering such 'dangerous' passages. For instance, the words *oved avodah zarah* ('a worshipper of strange gods') in the Talmud was altered to read *oved kokhavim u-mazalot* ('a worshipper of stars and planets'), usually abbreviated to *akum*, an obviously 'safe' reading since neither in the Roman Empire nor Babylon in Talmudic times nor in Christian Europe in the Middle Ages were Gentiles star-worshippers. It is ironic that some Christian would-be censors read the word *akum* itself as an abbreviation of *oved Christus u-Miriam* ('worshipper of Christ and Mary'). The Talmudic saying (*Yevamot* 62b): 'Any man without a wife lives without joy and without blessing' was changed to: 'Any Jew without a wife', presumably to avoid giving offence to Christian celibates (see CELIBACY).

Internal censorship was imposed by Rabbis who had the necessary power over books believed to contain heretical or immoral ideas. Whatever the meaning of the statement in the Mishnah (*Sanhedrin* 10: 1) that one who reads external books has no share in the World to Come (it probably referred to treating the books of the *Apocrypha as sacred Scripture by *reading* them in public in the synagogue), it was extended by some in the Middle Ages and beyond to include all manner of books they held to be unwholesome. The standard commentary to the Mishnah by the fifteenth-century Italian scholar Obadiah Bertinoro remarks on 'external books': 'By this is meant the works produced by heretics, for example, the works of the Greek *Aristotle and his associates. This prohibition extends to anyone who reads the histories of Gentile kings, love poems, and erotic writings, works which contain neither wisdom nor advantage but are simply a waste of time.'

When the Italian historian Azariah de Rossi (*c*.1511–*c*.1578) claimed, in his book *Meor Eynayyim*, that the Talmudic Rabbis were sometimes ill informed in matters of history, Rabbi Joseph *Karo, author of the *Shulḥan Arukh*, tried unsuccessfully to have the book burned. Karo writes in the *Shulḥan Arukh* (*Oraḥ Ḥayyim*, 307. 16):

'It is forbidden to read on the Sabbath the mocking poems and parables of secular works, and erotic works such as the book of Immanuel [of Rome]. The same applies to works of military exploits. Even on a weekday it is forbidden on the grounds of "sitting in the seat of scoffers" [Psalms 1: 1] . . . In the case of erotic works there is further the offence of inciting the evil inclination. The authors of such works, and those who make copies of them, and, it goes without saying, those who print them, are guilty of causing the public to sin.'

A more liberal view is stated in the gloss to this passage by *Isserles, who permits the reading of secular works even on the Sabbath provided they are written in Hebrew. But in his gloss elsewhere (*Yoreh Deah*, 246. 4) Isserles, too, comes down heavily against the reading of heretical works.

It was chiefly in this area of supposed *heresy that numerous attempts at banning books were made. Maimonides' *Guide of the Perplexed* was proscribed by many Rabbis opposed to the sage's rationalistic approach. The books of the followers of Shabbetai *Zevi were banned by the Rabbis for their mystical heresy. The tendency emerged to treat Kabbalistic works as taboo for immature readers even among the Kabbalists themselves. *Hasidism was condemned as heresy by its opponents, the *Mitnaggedim, and there are reports of the public burning of the first Hasidic work to be printed: the early master *Jacob Joseph of Polonnoye's *Toledot Yaakov Yosef*.

With the rise of the *Haskalah movement, many Rabbis banned the writings of Moses *Mendelssohn and the commentary to the Torah known as the *Biur*, produced by the members of his circle, because of their rationalistic and untraditional tendencies. The works of *Reform Rabbis had been banned by the *Orthodox. The Prayer Book edited by Mordecai *Kaplan, from which references to the *Resurrection and the *Chosen People had been deleted, was symbolically burned (set alight, it is said, on a silver tray) at a meeting of Rabbis at the Waldorf Astoria Hotel in New York in 1945. It is consequently quite incorrect for Jewish apologists to maintain that Judaism knows nothing of the censorship or burning of books. However, apologists are probably correct when they point to the fact that Jews, compared with the adherents of Christianity and Islam, have been rather less tempted to condemn works compiled by other Jews. Especially after the burning of books by the Nazis,

most Jews have acquired a horror at the notion of burning books; cold comfort perhaps, but a measure of comfort nevertheless. Certainly most modern Jews have been influenced by the idea of religious *tolerance that has emerged in Western society through the writings of Milton, *Spinoza, John Locke, John Stuart Mill, and other thinkers in the liberal mode. See also HEREM.

Moshe Carmilly-Weinberger, *Censorship and Freedom of Expression in Jewish History* (New York, 1977).

**Chariot** The vehicle seen by the prophet *Ezekiel (Ezekiel 1), representing, in Jewish *mysticism, the realms on high into which the soul of the mystic is transported. The Hebrew for 'chariot' is *Merkavah*, and the Rabbinic name for this type of mystic gnosis is *Maaseh Merkavah* ('the Work of the Chariot'), as distinct from speculation on the theme of the divine creation, which is called *Maaseh Bereshit* ('the Work of Creation'). The mystics who attempted this ascent of soul are known as the *yoredey Merkavah*, the literal meaning of which is: 'those who *descend* the Chariot', possibly because the 'ascent' is through the depths of the mystic's psyche, or, perhaps, simply because one goes down into a chariot in order to ride in it rather like one who goes into a car today. In any event, the usual term in English is 'Riders of the Chariot'.

The mystical activity of riding the Chariot extended for the whole first millennium CE. As late as the tenth century, this mystical ascent was attempted, but gave way eventually to the different form of Jewish mysticism known as the *Kabbalah. The foremost Babylonian teacher, Rav *Hai Gaon (939–1038), describes (*Otzar Ha-Geonim*, vol. 4, to tractate *Ḥagigah*, ed. B. M. Lewin (Jerusalem, 1932), pp. 13–15) the techniques employed by the Riders of the Chariot:

'You may perhaps know that many of the Sages hold that when a man is worthy and blessed with certain qualities and he wishes to gaze at the heavenly chariot and the halls of the angels on high, he must follow certain exercises. He must fast for a specified number of days, he must place his head between his knees, whispering softly to himself the while certain praises of God with his face towards the ground. The result will be that he will gaze in the innermost recesses of his heart and it will seem to him as if he saw the seven halls with his own eyes, moving from hall to hall to observe that which is found therein.' Hai is very circumspect here, throwing out hints of the techniques without explaining them in any detail. It is hard to tell whether Hai is speaking from personal experience but with reserve due to his unwillingness to impart the teaching to unworthy followers, or whether he has gained his information by hearsay.

Gershom G. Scholem, *Jewish Gnosticism, Merkavah Mysticism and Talmudic Tradition* (New York, 1965).

**Charity** Alms-giving and care for the poor; Heb. *tzedakah*. This word in the Bible denotes 'righteousness' in general but in post-biblical Judaism it is used to denote charity, as if to suggest, according to many exponents of the idea, that there should be no condescension in alms-giving. The poor are not to be patronized but given the assistance they need because they have a just claim on the wealthy. The Jerusalem Talmud records that in ancient Palestine a poor man when asking for help would say to his would-be benefactor: 'Acquire merit for yourself', as if to say: 'I am doing you a favour.' In a popular Jewish tale, when a rich man excuses the small size of his donation by protesting that he is unable to afford to give more generously because he has been obliged to pay his son's gambling debts, the poor man retorts: 'If your son wants to gamble let him do so with his own money, not with mine.' In a revealing Midrashic anecdote, the Roman Governor, Turnus Rufus, puts the question to Rabbi *Akiba: 'If, as you maintain, your God loves the poor, why does he not make them rich?' to which Akiba replies: 'It is in order to give the rich the means of acquiring merit', a quaint way of coping with the theological problem of why a beneficent God has created a world in which people suffer. A world without poverty would be an uncaring world; without those to whom compassion must be shown it would be a world without compassion. A Hasidic master, in the same vein, once asked: 'Since everything in God's world must have a purpose, what purpose is served by the phenomenon of atheism?' God allows the possibility of unbelief, he concluded, because otherwise the rich would have so much faith that God will help the poor that they would not themselves think of trying to alleviate their suffering. Faith is admirable when exercised on one's own behalf. Where the needs of others are concerned it is essential to act as if there is no God to intervene.

*Charity and Benevolence*

The theory that the rich acquire merit by charity might suggest that alms-giving is no more than a calculated attempt at storing up good deeds in a spiritual bank in order to draw on them in the future. There is little doubt that for many, perhaps for most, there is an element of self-seeking in charitable endeavours: giving to have one's name in the list of prominent donors or, on a slightly higher level, to help one go to heaven. It is interesting to find that the Talmudic Rabbis, while generally stressing the importance of disinterested action, are tolerant of impure motivation when it comes to helping the poor, since, after all, the needs of the poor are redressed whatever the motivation of the benefactors. A Talmudic saying has it that if one says: 'I give this coin to the poor so that my sick child may recover', or: 'I give so that I shall merit the World to Come', there is no fault in this, even if it falls short of the ideal. Yet in order to widen the scope of charity the Rabbis introduce the much broader concept of benevolence (Heb. *gemilut ḥasadim*, lit. 'bestowing kindnesses').

In a Talmudic saying the differences between charity and benevolence are said to lie in three areas. 1. Charity can only be carried out by giving money, whereas benevolence involves giving of one's person, for example by a kindly word or a pat on the shoulder or by generally offering words of comfort and consolation. 2. Charity is directed to the poor, whereas benevolence involves the expression of goodwill to all, rich or poor, healthy or sick, to the successful as well as to those who fall short of success. 3. Charity is given to the living. Benevolence can be extended to the dead by attending to the burial and going to the funeral. In reality the difference is one of disposition. The charitable person may give as an obligation imposed from without; his generosity may stem solely from his sense of duty. Benevolence, on the other hand, comes from within, from the compassionate heart. As the old Jewish saying has it: 'Charity awaits on the cry of distress. Benevolence anticipates the cry of distress.' Among acts of benevolence especially singled out in the Jewish tradition are: visiting the sick, attending funerals, comforting mourners, and, very pressing in ancient communities, redeeming captives held to ransom by kidnappers.

Associated with charity and benevolence is the cultivation of the charitable disposition. 'Judge everyone in the scale of merit' is the advice given in Ethics of the Fathers, meaning find excuses for the apparent ill behaviour of others and be charitable in your assessment of their conduct. A similar saying is: 'Judge not your neighbour until you have been in his situation.' Even with regard to charity itself, a Hasidic master read the verse (Leviticus 19: 17): 'Thou shalt not hate thy brother in thine heart' to mean 'Do not hate another because you have a good heart.' Generous persons should be charitably disposed even to the niggardly and ungenerous who have not been blessed with the good heart they are fortunate enough to possess. That is how God has made them. This shows an admirable religious advocacy of tolerance, an area in which religious people have often been among the worst offenders. Naturally, it can be overdone. Judaism certainly does not encourage an attitude of benevolent acceptance of evil and the question is obviously one of achieving the correct balance. Many Jewish teachers, for all that, have preferred to err on the side of goodwill. When another Hasidic master gave some money to a poor man and his followers expressed surprise, pointing out that the man was thoroughly disreputable, the master replied: 'How can I discriminate? God did not discriminate when He gave the money to a reprobate like me in the first place.' To achieve a balanced attitude is notoriously difficult. The Talmud reads the verse: 'There shall be no needy among you' (Deuteronomy 15: 4) to mean that your first duty is to see that there are no needy among your own, that is, first take care of your own and your own family's needs—an ancient version of 'Charity begins at home'. Yet the Talmud continues that anyone who goes through life with this as his maxim will eventually become poor, since few will place any confidence in one whose attitude is grasping and completely selfish.

## The Laws of Charity

Typically, Judaism, with its emphasis on action, has a system of laws governing the exercise of charity, including those intended to control the exuberance of the charitable and the importunities of the charity collectors. While, it is said, the collectors and distributors of charity, who risk the displeasure of both the donors and the poor themselves, have a more rewarding task than the actual donors, undue pressure which embarrasses the donors must be avoided. There are instances of Talmudic Rabbis compelling wealthy men to give generously but only when these are seen as attempting to avoid their social obligations. The collection of charity must be done by at least two persons. A single collector might be suspected of pocketing for himself some of the money raised. Since so much depends on the assessment of the different needs of the poor, the actual distribution of the funds requires three persons who form an *ad hoc* court of law (see BET DIN). Where a man and a woman require assistance, precedence is given to the man where money is to be distributed, the man usually being the breadwinner in Talmudic and medieval times. But where clothes are to be distributed the woman has precedence since a woman is more embarrassed than a man by lack of adequate clothing. There is a fully developed system of poor relief. Every Jewish community is required to have a charity organization to which all the inhabitants of the town are obliged to contribute according to their means. Each of the poor is to be provided with two square meals a day, three on the Sabbath. Each of the poor visiting a town is to be given a bed for the night and food each day.

According to Maimonides, if a man has a large sum of money for distribution to the poor, it is better for him to give in successive stages rather than all at once since giving by stages has a greater effect on the character than has a huge sum given in a moment when one is carried away by feelings of extreme generosity. Enthusiasm can wane but regular giving, even of small amounts each time, is habit-forming. Maimonides' eight degrees of charity are well known (*Mishneh Torah, Mattenat Aniyim*, 10. 7–14). The lowest degree of all is where the donor does give but is glum and appears to be reluctant to give. Next is when he gives cheerfully but not as much as he can afford. Next is where he gives cheerfully and as much as he can afford but only when his donation is solicited. Next in degree is where he gives without having to be asked. Higher still is where the donor does not know which of the poor he benefits, for example, where he leaves a sum of money in a place where the poor can take it. Higher still is where the poor do not know the identity of their benefactor, for example, where a donor sends a sum of money anonymously. Higher still is where the money is given to the charity collectors. Here the donor is not aware whom he benefits and the poor do not know to whom they are indebted. Highest of all is where a man is prevented from becoming poor by being given a job or a loan without interest so that he can adequately support himself and have no need to be the recipient of charity.

### The Limits of Charity

Although the biblical laws of tithing applied only to agricultural produce, it was extended by the ancient Rabbis to include money; a man was obliged (according to some there is no actual obligation but it is an act of piety) to give a tenth of his annual income to charity. The Talmud records an enactment drawn up by the High Court in the town of Usha in Galilee that even the most generous should not give away more than a fifth of his capital. This enactment probably had its origin at a time when the wars against the Roman occupation of Palestine had created havoc with the economy, so that self-impoverishment by people of comparative means would have a detrimental effect. Maimonides sees the enactment of Usha as applying only to ordinary folk. The saintly can give away even more than a fifth and there are numerous instances of Usha being ignored where the needs of the poor were great.

Since poverty is relative there is much discussion in the sources as to who is considered to be poor for the purposes of poor relief. The Mishnah (*Peah* 8) lays down the rule that one who has 200 *zuz* in ready cash or has invested 50 *zuz* in a business concern is no longer eligible to obtain poor relief. It is difficult to know the exact value of a *zuz* but some indication can be gained from the statement that it was possible to buy a small house for 50 *zuz* and the minimum requirement for the marriage settlement by a husband was 200 *zuz*. Naturally, these limits were frequently ignored both by those who were qualified to receive poor relief but refused to be recipients of charity, and by the unscrupulous who traded on the generosity of others even though they were not entitled to receive poor relief. Obviously in these matters much had to be left to the discretion of the poor and the courts. Of a man

who starved himself to death rather than accept charity a Rabbi remarked that this man did not die of hunger but of pride. The further statement of the Mishnah sums it up in general, somewhat mechanical, terms:

'One who does not need to accept charity yet takes it shall not depart from the world before he falls in need of charity; but he that needs to take charity yet does not take it shall not die in old age before he has come to support others. Of such a one it is written [Jeremiah 17: 7]: "Blessed is the man that trusteth in the Lord, and whose hope the Lord is." And if a man is not lame or dumb or blind or halting, yet makes himself like to one of them, he shall not die in old age before he becomes like to one of them.'

There are grades of charity obligation with regard to precedence. The general rule is that the prior obligation is to the poor of one's own family, then to the poor of one's own town, and then to the poor of other towns. The poor of the land of Israel take precedence over the poor of other places. In many Jewish communities there was a special fund for the relief of poverty in the Holy Land. Other charitable organizations in Jewish communities provided dowries for poor brides; hospices for the sick, the aged, and the infirm; and money for those who required interest-free loans.

The following quotations from the standard Code of Jewish Law, the *Shulḥan Arukh* (*Yoreh Deah*, 247–59) give some indication of further ideas about charity as recorded in a legal Code which was binding on all faithful Jews, and did not only represent pious sermonizing by the moralists.

'God has compassion on whomever has compassion on the poor. . . . A man should reflect that he asks of God all the time to sustain him and just as he entreats God to hear his cry so should he heed the cry of the poor. He should reflect that poverty is a fate that overtakes all sooner or later so that one day he or his son or his grandson will be in need and whoever has compassion on others compassion is shown to him. . . . Every person is obliged to give charity. Even a poor man who is himself supported by charity is obliged to give from that which he receives. If a man without adequate means gives more charity than he can afford or if he deprives himself in order to give to the charity collection because he fears embarrassment, it is forbidden to ask him for donations and the charity collector who puts such a one to shame by soliciting a donation will be punished by God. . . . A man should give charity cheerfully and out of the goodness of his heart. He should participate in the grief of the poor man and speak words of comfort to him. But if he gives in an angry and unwilling spirit he loses any merit there is in giving. . . . Once a man has given money to the charity collection neither he nor his heirs any longer have a say in the matter and the community can do with the money whatever they consider to be right in the eyes of God and man. . . . If a man asks to be fed no investigation should be undertaken to discover whether or not he is a fraud but he should be fed without further ado. But if a man ask to be clothed it is necessary first to investigate whether or not he is a fraud. If, however, his situation is known he must not be subjected to any investigation.'

Although the taking of *vows is generally discouraged, an exception is made where a man in trouble vows to donate a sum to charity. There is much discussion among the authorities on the conditions and binding nature of this kind of vow. For instance in the *Responsa of the outstanding Galician authority, Rabbi Shalom Mordecai Shvadron (1835–1911), questions of the following kind are discussed, addressed to him by questioners from many parts of the Jewish world. A woman took a vow to give a large sum to a poor Rabbi to pray for her sick son. The Rabbi did offer his prayers but these were of no avail and the son died. Is the woman obliged to fulfil her promise? A man vowed to give a sum of money to a charitable cause and he died before fulfilling his vow. Are his heirs obliged to carry out his wishes? A man whose wife was pregnant vowed to give 25 roubles if she gave birth to a boy and half this amount if she gave birth to a girl and she gave birth to twins, a boy and a girl. Is he obliged to give only the amount he had promised for a boy or must he give for both the boy and the girl? And what if she gave birth to twin boys? It is clear that this kind of question was taken seriously.

### Charity and Social Justice

All the powerful appeals to give generously to charity are directed chiefly to individuals. There was nothing like a welfare state in former times when the classical sources were formulated. A question much discussed in modern times is the extent to which such individual efforts are required in a country with a welfare state. Maimonides' eighth degree, the highest of all, would seem to support the view that the best form of charity, nowadays, is to help create and support institutions catering for the needs of the poor and the sick on a social basis. The State of Israel is a fully developed welfare state and yet here and in other advanced countries there is still room for private donations; moreover, the complementary ideal of benevolence is highly personal and cannot be relegated to governmental bodies. Although our whole social system is very different from that which obtained when the sources were compiled, Jews have followed the implication in those sources that charity and benevolence are among the highest values of the religion. One of the distinguishing features of the Jewish people, according to the ancient Rabbis, is that they are generous and compassionate.

Louis Jacobs, *What Does Judaism Say About . . .?* (Jerusalem, 1973), 79–84.

Solomon Schechter, 'Notes of Lectures on Jewish Philanthropy', in his *Studies in Judaism* (Philadelphia, 1945), iii. 238–76.

**Cherubim**  The winged creatures mentioned frequently in the Bible; Heb. *keruvim*, the etymology of which is uncertain. In a Midrashic source the folk etymology is given according to which the singular form *keruv* means *ke-ravya*, 'like a young child', hence the depiction in art and literature of the cherubim as baby angels.

In the Bible God sets the cherubim at the entrance of the *Garden of Eden, after the expulsion of *Adam and Eve, to guard the way to the Tree of Life (Genesis 3: 24). Two cherubim overlaid with gold with outstretched wings were placed facing one another on the cover of the *Ark in the Tabernacle (Exodus 25: 18–20) and figures of cherubim were embroidered on the veil and the curtains of the Tabernacle (Exodus 26: 1, 31). In Solomon's Temple the two gilded cherubim were not attached to the Ark, as in the Tabernacle, but were placed as figures each 10 cubits high in front of the Ark (1 Kings 6: 27–8). A curious Talmudic legend has it that the cherubim in Solomon's Temple were in the form of male and female. When the Israelites came to the Temple on pilgrimage, the curtain in front of the Ark was drawn aside and the cherubim were seen interlocked as if in sexual congress. This was said to be a miraculous indication that

God's love for Israel resembles the love of man and woman. Elsewhere in the Bible (2 Samuel 22: 11; Psalms 18: 11) God is described very anthropomorphically as riding on a cherub. The resemblance of the cherubim to the winged creatures depicted in the religious art of the ancient Near East has often been noted.

The whole matter of the cherubim was a source of puzzlement and embarrassment to the Jewish teachers. In another Talmudic legend, when the Ammonites and Moabites entered the Temple at its destruction they pulled out the cherubim and attempted to expose the hypocrisy of the Israelites who pretended to worship the invisible God and yet had figures of a man and a woman having sex in the very holy of holies. The Jewish philosophers, in particular, tried to rationalize the subject. In Philo's discourse on the cherubim these represent two aspects of God, His goodness and His authority. For Maimonides the cherubim represent a species of the angelic hosts. In Maimonides' scheme there are ten grades of *angels, and the cherubim belong to the ninth degree. Angels are seen by Maimonides as the various spiritual forces God uses for the control of the universe. The angles adjacent to the Ark represent the operation of these spiritual forces in the revelation of the Torah and are a symbolic representation of the dogma that the Torah is from heaven. There were two cherubim on the Ark because had there been only one it might have been confused with a representation of the One God (Maimonides, *Guide of the Perplexed*, 3. 45).

Except in the Kabbalah, there is not much interest in the cherubim in Jewish thought. It is perhaps significant in this connection that while the liturgy contains references to other forms of angels, the ophanim and seraphim, for example, there is no reference to the cherubim anywhere in the liturgy. See also ARK.

Nahum M. Sarna, *Exploring Exodus* (New York, 1986), 211–13.

**Chess**  Playing chess has long been a popular pursuit among Jews, although most scholars reject the notion that there are references to the game in the Talmud. Chess was favoured even by staid Rabbis who considered games to be a waste of time which would be better spent on the study of the Torah, since the game stimulated the mind and honed it for that very study. Thus most authorities permitted the playing of chess even on the Sabbath, provided, of course, that the game was not played for money. Some pious folk had a special silver chess set for use on the Sabbath. The association of chess with keenness of mind is no doubt behind the legend that the wise King Solomon played chess.

**Children and Parents**  From biblical times onwards children are considered to be God's greatest gift. The first precept of the Torah is to engage in *procreation. A common Jewish blessing is: 'May you enjoy *naches* [Yiddish: satisfaction and pleasure] from your children.' Jewish parents have always claimed preeminence in their care for children and while no doubt the boast is often a vain one, the claim is not entirely without justification. And for children, the fifth commandment: 'Honour thy father and thy mother' (Exodus 20: 12) is a key text. Yet the Freudian insight into the conflict between parents and children is echoed in many a Jewish source. It is noteworthy that, apart from the general injunction to *love the neighbour, there is no special command for children to love their parents, only to pay them the respect due to them, which is construed by the Jerusalem Talmud as the simple payment of a debt to those who brought the children into the world. The Zohar observes that the patriarch Jacob blessed his grandsons before he blessed his own sons because grandparents have greater love for their grandchildren than parents have for their children. In a wry Jewish comment, parents love their children more than children love their parents because Adam and Eve, having no parents, could not bequeath the love of parents to their offspring. In the popular Yiddish saying, a father can support ten of his children yet ten children cannot adequately look after a single parent.

*In Jewish Law*

An illustration of how Jewish law deals with the question of possible conflict between children and parents is provided in what came to be seen as the classical text on the subject, a Responsum by the Italian authority, Rabbi Joseph Colon (d. 1480). Colon was asked whether a young man, who wishes to marry someone of whom his father disapproves, must give up the young lady in obedience to the fifth commandment. In a closely reasoned argument, Colon comes down on the side of the son and this ruling is recorded by *Isserles in the *Shulḥan Arukh*, thus giving it wide authority. The Talmud, Colon points out, discusses whether the fifth commandment means that a son is obliged to provide his parents with food and clothing out of the son's pocket and comes to the conclusion that the son is not so obliged (unless the son is wealthy and the parents poor). Now if a son is not, strictly speaking, obliged to give up even his money for his parents, how can he be obliged to sacrifice his own happiness by giving up the woman he loves? Secondly, to have children is a religious obligation, one that the son can only carry out by marrying the particular woman he wants to marry. Consequently, the father's attempt is akin to a parent ordering his son to commit a sin and there the fifth commandment certainly has no binding force. Thirdly, Colon argues, the fifth commandment means that a son has to show respect to his parents. It does not mean that he has to obey them except when the order by a parent is one from which the parent will enjoy a direct benefit. When a father requests his son to pour him out a glass of wine or to help him on with his coat (examples stated in the Talmud) the son must certainly do so but that is because the father's needs are directly satisfied by the son. Where a parental order is simply that, an order based on personal whim, the fifth commandment does not apply. This ruling of Colon had far-reaching consequences. If the ruling is accepted (which, with few dissenting voices, it is) it refuses to allow dictatorial parents to invoke the fifth commandment in order to impose their will on their children. Children have a life of their own and are entitled to opinions of their own. There are, in fact, numerous instances of great Jewish scholars debating with their fathers and teachers in matters of Torah learning; taking issue with the opinions of their elders and betters, respectfully to be sure, but firmly and decisively none the less.

*In Hasidism*

*Hasidism, at its inception, was a movement of rebellion against the established order. The movement was seen as challenging the authority of the traditional Rabbis in favour of the new authority of the charismatic Hasidic master. As the movement developed, young men would leave their parental home and, often, their young wives and children, to stay for long periods at the master's 'court' and some of the new doctrines taught by the Hasidic masters

were seen as heretical by their opponents. Such a movement inevitably had to face the protest that it flies in the teeth of the implications of the fifth commandment. The Hasidim tended to be looked upon as upstarts with no reverence for the past. Avigdor ben Hayyim, a fiery opponent of Hasidism, went so far as to invoke the Russian authorities in his attempt to have Hasidism declared illegal. In a document Avigdor presented for the consideration of the Russian authorities, he drew up nineteen counts against the new movement, the twelfth of which reads: 'They [the Hasidim] have no respect whatever for their parents. For, they argue, a father only brings his child into the world in order to satisfy his own lusts and there is, consequently, no obligation for a son to honour his father. The same applies to the mother but [they say] some measure of respect is due to the mother from the heart of the child she suckled.' The Hasidim, for their part, tended to rely on the ruling of Colon that a parent has no right to prevent his son from pursuing his own religious way even if it meets with parental opposition.

Gerald Blidstein *Honor Thy Father and Mother: Filial Responsibility in Jewish Law and Ethics* (New York, 1975).

Louis Jacobs, ' "Honour Thy Father": A Study in Hasidic Psychology', *Cambridge Opinion* 39 (1965), 4–8.

**Choirs** When the *sacrifices were offered in the *Temple they were accompanied by the Levites playing musical instruments and singing psalms but the institution of a choir assisting the *Cantor in synagogal worship is not found before the early seventeenth century in Italy, where it was almost certainly introduced under Renaissance influence. There is a choir, nowadays, in most of the larger Western synagogues. *Hasidism tended to view the institution of the choir with distaste both because it seemed to be a copy of Christian forms of worship and because it was altogether too formal and lacking in spontaneous fervour.

A question much discussed was whether a mixed choir of male and female voices was in accordance with Jewish law. The opposition was not on the grounds that the sexes were 'mixed' but rather because of the Talmudic objection to a man listening to a woman's voice. Orthodox synagogues did not have mixed choirs, with the exception of the United Synagogue in

England, whose argument was that, according to some authorities, the Talmudic prohibition only applies when a man is reciting the *Shema and will be distracted by a woman singing at the time and that the Talmud, in any event, only refers to where the woman is singing a secular song. In more recent years, as part of a definite swing to the right in Anglo-Jewry, all Orthodox synagogues have rid themselves of their mixed choirs. Reform and Conservative synagogues have no objection to mixed choirs. (See SYNAGOGUE.)

**Chosen People** The idea that the people of Israel, later called the Jews, have been given a special role to play in the divine scheme is pervasive in the Bible and in all subsequent Jewish thought. There has been a rich variety of interpretation of this idea throughout the history of Judaism since, it has to be acknowledged, the whole doctrine appears, at first glance, to be in conflict with the belief in the One God whose care and providence extends equally, if it can be expressed in this way, to all human beings He has created in His image. In the now famous jingle:

> How odd
> Of God
> To choose
> The Jews

the oddness is not so much in the choice of the Jews but in the very idea of a divine choice. Western thought, especially, is accustomed to seeing questions of truth in universalistic terms. It seems incongruous that the greatest truth of all taught by Judaism, God's self-disclosure, should have become manifest among the members of a particular group. Basically, in considering this question of Israel's election, we are confronted with the vexed problem of particularism versus *universalism the problem of the tensions that are bound to exist in the very notion of a world religion centring on a small, comparatively insignificant, group of human beings making this astonishing claim to the scandal of all others. In one sense this problem has to be confronted by the adherents of every religion, each of which lays claim to insights regarding ultimate reality greater than those found in other religions. Yet the problem is especially acute for what have been called 'religions of revelation' (Judaism, Christianity, and Islam) in contradistinction to the 'religions

of wisdom' (the Far Eastern religions). It is in the doctrine of divine *revelation that the heart of the problem lies.

The witty stock replies to the question posed in the jingle hardly constitute a theology of election. The best known of these is:

> It isn't odd.
> The Jews
> Chose God

This does take us some way towards an appreciation that, in *Zangwill's words, the chosen people is a choosing people, but requires much elaboration to be theologically sound. The other counter-jingle is even more unsatisfactory:

> It isn't
> Odd.
> The *goyyim*
> Annoy Him

Why should the goyyim (the *Gentiles) annoy Him more than the Jews? The Bible is full of castigations by the prophets of Israel of the shortcomings of their own people. To quote *Zangwill again: 'the Bible is an anti-Semitic book'.

The two passages in the Bible most relevant to the question are (English translation of the Jewish Publication Society edition):

'Now then, if you will obey Me faithfully and keep My covenant, you shall be My treasured possession among all the peoples. Indeed, all the earth is Mine, but you shall be to Me a kingdom of priests and a holy nation.' (Exodus 19: 5–6.)

'Mark the heavens to their uttermost reaches belong to the Lord your God, the earth and all that is on it. Yet it was to your fathers that the Lord was drawn in His love for them, so that He chose you, their lineal descendants, from among all peoples—as is now the case.' (Deuteronomy 10: 14–15.)

On the critical view (see BIBLICAL CRITICISM), shared here, these passages are not a verbatim record of God's actual utterance, so to speak, but are the reflections of later generations of Israelites grappling with the problem of God's choice of their people and His covenant with them in the face of the clear reality that there are other peoples over whom His providential care extends. The Jewish philosopher Isaac Heinemann (1876–1957) has called attention to the fact that in these two passages, and elsewhere in the Bible where the election of Israel is mentioned, it is stressed that it is the God of all the earth, the universal God, who chooses. Only the God to whom all peoples belong can choose one of them for a special contribution towards the fulfilment of His purposes. However the doctrine of election is understood, the God of Israel is in no way a 'tribal god' whose residence is confined to the territory the tribe occupies. A tribal god does not choose his tribe. He is the tribe and suffers defeat when the tribe is defeated. A tribal god has no independent existence for tribes beyond his jurisdiction.

The historical note is sounded in the Deuteronomic passage. God so loved the *patriarchs, Abraham, Isaac, and Jacob, who were faithful to Him and obeyed His word, that He made a covenant with them and chose their offspring who themselves became bound to the ancient covenant. Historically speaking, the doctrine that God has chosen Israel emerged out of the growing realization among generations of the Hebrew people, the Israelites and later the Jews, that among all the peoples around them they were the only monotheists.

*The Meaning of the Choice*

The significance of Israel's election has been variously understood. Maimonides, in obedience to his general, strong, universalistic and individualistic thrust, hardly considers the topic at all and when he does raise the question, while discussing creation in time, of why God chose to reveal the Torah to Israel rather than implant the truth into all human nature, he falls back on the view that it belongs to the unfathomable will of God (*Guide of the Perplexed*, 2. 25). At the other end of the scale, the modernist, Mordecai *Kaplan, interprets the whole concept in functionalistic terms since, in Kaplan's naturalistic philosophy, God is not a person who can exercise choice. For Kaplan, the idea of Israel's election did serve the purpose of promoting the Jewish will to survive but, he maintains, this function is now neither necessary nor desirable and references to Israel's election no longer have any place in the liturgy.

Among other Jewish thinkers, interpretations of Israel's election tend to be of two different kinds; these can be termed the associative and the qualitative. The associative thinkers do not believe (or, at least, do not refer to the idea) that the Jewish soul is inherently different from the Gentile soul. The election of Israel does not mean that Jews form a special category of the human race but rather that the Jews are special in that the Torah was given to them in its fullness, although there is a Torah for Gentiles contained in the *Noahide laws. Saadiah *Gaon expressed this thought in a famous statement: 'Our people is only a people by virtue of its Torah.' Thinkers such as Judah *Halevi, on the other hand, understand the election of Israel to mean that the heirs of the faithful patriarchs have had bequeathed to them a special quality of soul, inherently superior to the souls of Gentiles. The Hasidic master, Rabbi *Shneur Zalman of Liady, basing his thought on the writings of Hayyim *Vital, goes so far as to say that there is a divine spark deep in the recesses of the Jewish, and only the Jewish, psyche. Even among the modernists, the Reform thinker, Abraham *Geiger, interprets the doctrine of election in qualitative terms when he understands it to mean that the Jewish people have a special genius for religion out of which, in ancient times, belief in God erupted spontaneously among them without any influence from other cultures.

*The Consequences of the Choice*

The average Jew takes pride in his conviction that he belongs to a people with a special role to play in God's world. Rarely has such pride gone beyond the harmless boasting most people engage in with regard to the particular group to which they belong, their nation, their religion, their country, even their club or football team. And virtually all Jewish teachers stress that the choice of the Jews is not for privilege but for service. (Kaplan once retorted that to be chosen to serve is itself the greatest privilege.) In the best Jewish thought, the election of Israel is by God and for God and for the fulfilment of His plan for all mankind (see AMOS). And the doctrine was never racist. There is nothing like a pure Jewish race and *conversion to Judaism is possible, based on the idea that anyone who joins voluntarily the Jewish people and embraces the Jewish religion is a 'child of Abraham' and hence a full member of the Chosen People.

Henri Atlan, 'Chosen People', in Arthur A. Cohen and Paul Merdes-Flohr (eds.), *Contemporary Religious Thought* (New York, 1987), 55–9.
Daniel H. Frank (ed.), *A People Apart: Chosenness and Ritual in Jewish Philosophical Thought* (Albany, NY, 1993).

Louis Jacobs, *A Jewish Theology* (London, 1973), 209–75.
——*God Torah Israel: Traditionalism without Fundamentalism* (Cincinnati, 1990), 57–80.

**Christianity** In its very earliest days, Christianity was seen by the Jewish teachers as a Jewish heresy; its adherents were Jews who believed in the divinity of Christ. But when Christianity spread and became a world religion, with numerous converts from the *Gentile world, it became a rival religion to Judaism. Christians were then seen as Gentiles not because they were Christians but because, in the main, they were, in fact, Gentiles (i.e. not Jewish). In the Talmud and Midrash, the comparatively few references to Christianity (these only appear in uncensored versions; see CENSORSHIP) are to this religion as an heretical sect believing in a form of dualism, God the Father and God the Son. Typical is the comment of the late third-century Palestinian teacher, Rabbi Abbahu, on the verse (Isaiah 44: 6): 'I am the first, and I am the last, and beside Me there is no God.' As Rabbi Abbahu spells it out: ' "I am the first", for I have no father; "and I am the last", for I have no son, "and beside Me there is no God", for I have no brother.' Since the doctrine of the Trinity did not emerge fully until a later period, there are no references to this doctrine in the Talmud or Midrash, despite far-fetched attempts to find hints of it in these sources. It was not until the Middle Ages that the status of Christianity (and of *Islam) as a rival religion was considered from the Jewish point of view.

*Attitudes to Christianity in the Middle Ages*

Attacks on Christian dogma are found in medieval Jewish writings from the biblical commentaries of *Rashi and *Kimhi, refuting the Christian claim that the *Old Testament contains prophesies anticipating the coming of Jesus, through works of apologetics such as the *Kuzari* of Judah *Halevi and the *Faith Strengthened* of Isaac of Troki (d. 1593) to the records drawn up by Jews of the various *disputations they had with Christians. In these and similar works the main thrust was to deny that the *Messiah had come in the person of Jesus (the world gave no evidence that this glorious age had arrived, it was frequently protested) and especially to take issue with the doctrine of the Incarnation and the Trinity. As *Leon da

Modena noted, it was not the doctrine of the Trinity in itself that was objectionable (after all, in the Kabbalistic doctrine of the *Sefirot there is much talk of three, and more, aspects of Deity) but its elaboration, in which the Trinity is composed of three divine Persons, one of which became incarnate in a human being. The medieval thinkers who held Christianity but not Islam to be an idolatrous faith did so particularly because of the worship of the Cross; to bow before an icon or a crucifix was held to be akin to bowing to idols. The basic question in practice was whether the older Talmudic regulations against social intercourse and business dealings with pagans on the days of their festivals (because they might offer praise to their gods at the successful outcome of the deal) applied to Christians. With Jews living among Christians to apply these regulations would have been catastrophic, if not impossible. The French scholars tended to adopt casuistic arguments in order to circumvent some of the more onerous rules; they argued, for instance, that any money given by Christians to the Church is largely for the benefit of the clergy and there are certainly no actual sacrifices of animals or birds to idols as there were in Talmudic times. Menaheem *Meiri went much further to argue that the references to pagans in the Talmudic literature could not apply to what he called 'people whose lives are governed by religion'. Eventually, a distinction was made, unknown in the Talmudic sources, according to which Christianity did constitute idolatry for Jews but not 'for them' (i.e. Christians). A Christian did not offend against the *Noahide laws since the Torah allows a Gentile, but not a Jew, to worship another being in addition to God. This concept was known as *shittuf* ('association', of another together with God) and the oft-quoted legal maxim, allowing for a more liberal attitude towards Christians, is: 'A Noahide is not enjoined to reject *shittuf.'*

Social needs obviously called forth this artificial distinction which was by no means universally accepted. As late as the end of the eighteenth century, *Elijah, Gaon of Vilna ruled that, since it is forbidden to mention the name of an idol, a Jew may refer to Jesus but never use the name Christ. In the twentieth century the Halakhic authorities debated whether it is permitted to use an abandoned church as a synagogue, or for a Jew to give a donation to a church or even enter a church, or wear a medal in the shape of a cross. In the last instance permission was given, on the grounds that the medal is a decoration, not an object of worship. Some authorities permitted a Jew to trade in the sale of crosses to Christians provided these were to be worn not for purposes of worship but simply as decorations.

*Modern Attitudes to Chistianity*

In modern times there has been far greater co-operation between Jews and Christians, many Jews welcoming Jewish–Christian dialogues in which the aim of each side is to understand the position of the other, and even learn from it, without in any way moving from its own. Some Jews believe that Judaism and Christianity have so much in common that it is permissible to speak of a Jewish Christian tradition. But there is the strongest opposition on the part of all Jews, Orthodox, Conservative, and Reform, to the attempts by Christian missionary groups to convert Jews to Christianity. The Jews for Jesus movement is very much a fringe phenomenon and has justly been condemned by all faithful Jews as trying to introduce Christianity to Jews through the back door, so to speak. A single, contemporary, Orthodox Jewish theologian, in the USA, has argued that Judaism does not oblige Jews to reject the doctrine of the Incarnation as impossible in itself. For him, Jews reject Christianity not because God could not have become incarnate in a human being, since that would compromise God's omnipotence, but because, in fact, He did not do so in the person of Jesus. This eccentric view is rejected by all other Jewish theologians on the grounds that God, being God, can as little become human as He can wish Himself out of existence. As Aquinas said, and he was anticipated by Jewish thinkers, it is no compromise of God's omnipotence that He cannot do the absolutely impossible.

C. G. *Montefiore, while insisting that a Jew cannot be at the same time a Christian, argues that some aspects of the Christian ethic are superior to the Jewish, for which he was attacked by *Ahad Ha-Am. On the scholarly level, there have been Jewish investigations into the Jewish background of Christianity but in a purely objective way with the theological questions seen as irrelevant to scholarship. It would certainly be incorrect to say that the suspicions of the two religions of one another are a thing of the past. What can be said is that, in an age of greater religious tolerance, there has been a growing realization that the two have enough in common to enable them to work in harmony for human betterment.

Eugene B. Borowitz, *Contemporary Christologies: A Jewish Response* (New York, 1980).
Walter Jacob, *Christianity Through Jewish Eyes* (Cincinnati, 1973).
Jacob Katz, *Exclusiveness and Tolerance* (Oxford, 1961).
James Parkes, *The Foundations of Judaism and Christianity* (London, 1960).
Lawrence H. Schiffman, *Who Was a Jew?: Rabbinic and Halakhic Perspectives on the Jewish–Christian Schism* (Hoboken, NJ, 1985).

**Chronicles, Book of** The biblical book dealing with the history of the people of Israel; Heb. *divrey ha-yamim*, lit. 'the accounts of the days', the usual biblical term for an historical account, although it is impossible to tell whether this title is the author's own or was given later. In current editions, Chronicles is divided into two, 1 and 2 Chronicles, but originally it was a single book, later included into the third section of the *Bible, the Hagiographa or Sacred Writings, and hence held to be of a lower order of inspiration than the other historical books, *Samuel and *Kings, which belong to the Prophets. According to the passage in the Talmud on the authorship of the various biblical books, Chronicles was compiled by *Ezra with additions by *Nehemiah. Modern biblical research tends to accept this connection and maintains that the three books of Chronicles, Ezra, and Nehemiah were originally a single book but that Chronicles in the form we now have is a separate and reworked account.

The strong connection between Chronicles and the books of Samuel and Kings is obvious. In fact the author of Chronicles often gives a reconstruction of the earlier histories to suit his particular theological aims. He pays far greater attention to the role of the *Levites, the musicians in the Temple, and it has even been conjectured that he himself was a Temple musician. A particularly instructive example of revision is the Chronicler's substitution (1 Chronicles 21: 1) of *Satan as the being who enticed David to count the people of Israel, instead of God as in the same narrative in the book of Samuel (2 Samuel 24: 1); this appears to be due to the Chronicler's reluctance to ascribe this enticement directly to God.

Among his sources, the Chronicler mentions two accounts which he calls a Midrash (2 Chronicles 13: 22; 24: 27). In later Jewish literature a *Midrash consists of a rather free homiletical exposition of Scripture and it is possible that the Midrashic method was used in earlier times. Many modern scholars, on the basis of these two passages and also because of the exaggerated numbers in the book, treat the whole of Chronicles as an early Midrash on the history of the people, that is to say, not so much as history as saga (see BUBER). The book of Chronicles affords some insight into how the ancient Hebrew writers compiled their works; they used earlier sources, often in their original words, but with elaborations, insertions, and alterations of their own.

The Book of Chronicles, with commentary by I. W. Slotki (Soncinco Books of the Bible; London, 1952).

**Chutzpah** Arrogance, impudence; a Talmudic word that made its way into *Yiddish from which it was adopted into American slang and has now entered the English language and is recorded in the Oxford English Dictionary as an English word. It comes from a root meaning 'to peel' and hence 'to be bare'; chutzpah means barefacedness, sheer cheek. The classical definition of chutzpah is given in the story of the boy who killed his parents and then threw himself on the mercy of the court on the grounds that he was an orphan.

Chutzpah is seen on the whole as as undesirable trait. The Talmud, interpreting events in its own day in Messianic terms, observes that just before the advent of the *Messiah chutzpah will be found in abundance—the young will show no respect to the old. In a later Talmudic source, when a boy was exceedingly disrespectful to venerable Rabbis, the Rabbis concluded that since he had so much chutzpah it was obvious that he was a bastard. In another Talmudic passage chutzpah is said to be royalty without a crown; it possesses regal power even though it has no regal backing and can prevail even against kings.

Yet, as in other cultures, there is often a grudging admiration for chutzpah in the Jewish tradition. The Rabbis ironically remark that chutzpah seems to be effective even when directed against God Himself in the case of *Balaam, who was at first told by God not to go on his mission to curse Israel, but when he persisted was told by God to carry on (Numbers 22: 12, 20). Chutzpah is particularly admired when it consists of standing up bravely against the powerful or when it is an expression of sheer determination to overcome seemingly insurmountable odds. The many tales of the saints arguing with God on behalf of their people, with their basis in the story of Abraham bargaining with God on behalf of the men of Sodom (Genesis 18: 22–32), have been seen as a kind of holy chutzpah.

**Circumcision** The removal of the foreskin in order to make manifest the 'sign in the flesh' of the *covenant made with *Abraham and hence called in Hebrew berit milah, 'covenant of circumcision' or, in everyday parlance, simply 'the Brit'. The covenant of circumcision is first recorded in the book of Genesis (17: 9–13), where Abraham is instructed to circumcise all his male descendants, just as he himself had been circumcised, as a sign of the covenant God had made with him and through him with them: 'Thus shall My covenant be marked in your flesh as an everlasting pact.' Here as well as in the book of Leviticus (12: 1–3) the age of circumcision is stated to be when a boy is eight days old. The Jewish tradition understands this to mean that while the ideal is for the child to be circumcised at this age, the rite is valid even if carried out later. If the child shows signs of jaundice, for example, it is the practice to postpone the circumcision until the doctor declares him to be fit enough for the operation. An adult whose parents did not have him circumcised is obliged to have the operation carried out as soon as possible and must not remain uncircumcised. A male convert (see CONVERSION) must be circumcised before he becomes a member of the covenant but for one born a Jew the rite is an initiation not into Judaism, but only into the covenant, since Jewish status is established by birth. A boy born of a Jewish mother is automatically Jewish, whether or not he has been circumcised.

*Reasons for Circumcision*

In a Midrashic anecdote, the Roman Governor of Palestine, Turnus Rufus, asks Rabbi *Akiba: 'If God dislikes a man having a foreskin why did He create him with one in the first place?' This is a serious question to the logical Roman mind and one echoed by early Christians. Akiba replies that God has created an incomplete world, leaving human beings to bring it to greater perfection (see CHARITY). Jewish teaching rejects the idea, put forward by those hostile to aeroplanes, that if God wanted men to fly He would have provided them with wings. The rite of circumcision is seen as the removal by man of an appendage to his body for which there is no purpose except its removal as a symbol of total obedience to God's will. Jewish teachers were not unaware that other peoples had circumcision rites but saw the Jewish rite, as the Bible states, as the special sign of the covenant with Abraham. Widespread though the rite may have been in some ancient cutures, it became the distinguishing mark of the Jew, especially, since many of the peoples surrounding the people of Israel did not practice circumcision. The Philistines and others are described in the Bible with abhorrence as the uncircumcised.

The medieval Jewish philosophers, with their strong rationalizing tendencies, were moved to ask why, granted that circumcision is a sign of the covenant, the sign had to be on this particular organ of the body. Maimonides (*Guide of the Perplexed*, 3. 49) advances two reasons. The first (which Maimonides considers to be the best) is that circumcision weakens, without actually harming, the organ of generation so that the sexual desires of the circumcised man are moderated. (Maimonides, more than any other medieval Jewish thinker, had an aversion to *sex.) The bodily injury caused to that organ, he says, does not interrupt any vital function, nor does it destroy the power of generation but it does counteract excessive lust. Maimionides' second reason is that the sign of the covenant had to be in that particular organ in order to prevent those who did not believe in the unity of God claiming to be members of the covenant for reasons of their own. The operation is so difficult and so disagreeable that no one would undergo it unless he sincerely wished to belong to the people of faith. *Philo of Alexandria was the first to advance the hygienic reason. The foreskin is literally unclean and can be a cause of disease. The more usual reason given by Jewish thinkers is the obvious one that the sign of the covenant through all the generations has to be in the very organ of generation. But, whatever the origin and the reasons for the practice, faithful Jews have circumcised their male children as the most distinctive sign of their loyalty to God.

Even *Spinoza can remark: 'Such great importance do I attach to the sign of the Covenant, that I am persuaded that it is sufficient by itself to maintain the separate existence of the nation for ever.'

*The Ceremony*

There are no special rules about the place in which the rite is to be carried out, although, if possible, pious Jews prefer it to be done in the synagogue during the morning service. The infant is taken into the room where the circumcision is to take place by a godmother who hands him to a godfather who, in turn, hands him to the *sandek* (a word of uncertain origin but meaning the man who holds the infant on his knees during the rite). In some communities the honour of acting as godfather and godmother is given to an engaged couple or to a childless married couple in the belief that their participation in the rite will provide a blessing for the couple themselves in the form of a child. The function of the *sandek* is usually performed by a grandfather of the infant or by a man learned in the Torah. The *sandek* is instructed by the man who performs the rite, the Mohel, to grasp the infant firmly so that the circumcision can more easily be performed. Only a man highly skilled in the performance of the rite is qualified to be a Mohel. Nowadays, there are special organizations for the training of Mohalim. A doctor, provided he is Jewish, can serve as a Mohel but many doctors admit that a trained Mohel is best qualified to perform the delicate operation.

Before carrying out the circumcision, the Mohel recites the benediction: 'Blessed art Thou, O Lord our God, King of the universe, who hast sanctified us with Thy commandments, and hast given us the command concerning circumcision.' As soon as the Mohel begins the circumcision the father recites: 'Blessed art Thou, O Lord our God, King of the universe, who hast sanctified us with Thy commandments, and hast commanded us to make our sons enter the covenant of Abraham our father.' All present then respond: 'Even as this child has entered into the covenant, so may he enter into the Torah, the nuptual canopy, and into good deeds.' The Mohel then takes a cup of wine and recites over it a prayer for the infant in which he gives the infant his Hebrew name. (A girl is named in a special prayer in the synagogue on the Sabbath after her birth.)

A drop or two of the wine is placed in the infant's mouth and the father drinks some of the wine, sending the rest to the mother who is not normally present in the room when the rite takes place. Afterwards there is a festive meal and special prayers are recited in the *grace after meals, blessing the parents, the infant, the Mohel, and the *sandek*. According to the Talmud a circumcision consists of three separate acts: 1. *milah*, the actual removal of the foreskin with a knife reserved for the purpose; 2. *periah*, the tearing-off and folding-back of the mucous membrane to expose the glans; 3. *metzitzah*, the suction of the blood from the wound. With regard to the third stage there has been considerable controversy in modern times. In the Talmud the suction was done by mouth, the Mohel actually sucking the blood from the wound. But the Talmud does not advocate this third stage as belonging to the rite itself but only as a hygienic measure. In the present stage of medical knowledge suction by mouth is the opposite of hygienic; germs can be transmitted from the Mohel to the infant and from the infant to the Mohel. Yet some Orthodox Jews still perform suction by mouth, arguing that the hygienic reason is not the only one and that suction is an integral part of the rite. Many Orthodox Jews, however, adopt the compromise of using an orally sucking tube where the mouth does not come into direct contact with the infant's penis.

*Opposition*

In the early days of the *Reform movement, some of the Reformers advocated the abolition of circumcision, protesting that the rite was too particularistic and too cruel to be retained since the Reformers did not believe that it had divine sanction. The Reform leader, Abraham Geiger, notoriously described circumcision in a private reference as 'a barbaric, bloody act, which fills the father with fear'. But today all faithful Jews, Reform, Conservative, and Orthodox, do have their sons circumcised, among other reasons because contemporary Reform Jews are less suspicious of particularism than were their nineteenth-century predecessors at a time when the call of the age was so strongly universalistic. Some Reform and Conservative congregations have devised ceremonies for a daughter to correspond to the circumcision ceremony of the son. One of the reasons for early Reform opposition was that there was no equivalent for

a Jewish girl. Although in more recent years a few voices have been raised in opposition to circumcision because of the alleged harmful psychological effect it may have on the infant, very few Jews take this objection sufficiently seriously even to think of abolishing a rite of such importance to Judaism.

J. H. Hertz, *Authorised Daily Prayer Book* (London, 1947), 1024–28.

Bernard Homa, *Metsitsah* (London, 1966).

Isaac Klein, *A Guide to Jewish Religious Practice* (New York, 1979), 419–32.

Michael A. Meyer, *Response to Modernity: A History of the Reform Movement in Judaism* (New York, 1988); see index: 'Circumcision'.

William Rosenau, *Jewish Ceremonial Institutions and Customs* (New York, 1929), 129–44.

**Cleanliness** The Talmudic Rabbis understand the verse: 'Ye shall not make yourselves abominable' (Leviticus 11: 43) as forbidding anything from which normal people recoil in disgust— eating from dirty plates, for example, or eating rotten food, or leaving the body unwashed. Passing water and movement of the bowels must be attended to as soon as the need becomes urgent and there are even instructions in the Talmud about wiping thoroughly afterwards. The story told in the ancient sources about the great sage *Hillel is typical. Hillel, on his way to the bath-house, met some of his disciples who asked him where he was going. 'To carry out a religious duty,' he replied. 'Is it a religious duty to go to the bath-house?' 'Yes,' replied Hillel. 'If the statues of the emperor are regularly washed and scoured to keep them clean, how much more should a human being, created in God's image, keep himself clean.' The Talmud forbids a scholar to live in a town which has no bath-house and states that everyone should wash his face, hands, and feet every day out of respect for his Maker. There are to be found in the Talmud and Codes detailed regulations about keeping clean towns in which Jews resided. People were not allowed to throw their refuse into the streets except in the rainy season when the unpaved streets were muddy in any event.

Abraham Cohen, *Everyman's Talmud* (London, 1949), 238–59.

**Codes, Alphabetical** A mode of expounding the Bible by means of various codes in which one Hebrew letter is substituted for another so that a word can have, in addition to its plain meaning, one or more hidden meanings depending on the code used. This kind of code is found especially in the Kabbalah (see GEMATRIA) and in the writing of *amulets where, to avoid writing the actual divine names, these were written in code. The codes are based on various arrangements of the letters of the Hebrew alphabet on the lines of the following illustration in the English alphabet:

ABCDEFGHIJKLMNOPQRSTUVWXYZ
ZYXWVUTSRQPONMLKJIHGFEDCBA

The word CAT can be written in code as XZG. To form the code other arrangements of the letters are possible, for example:

ABCDEFGHIJKLMNOPQRSTUVWXYZ
CDEFGHIJKLMNOPQRSTUVWXYZAB

but the most usual is where the letters in the second line are in reverse order, as in the first illustration. This is known as the AT BASH code, *alef* (the first letter of the Hebrew alphabet) being represented by *tav* (the final letter) ; *bet* (the second letter) by *shin* (the penultimate letter), and so on. These codes were used in private communications as well, though they were obviously fairly easy to crack. There is very little, if any, resort to code-writing and code-interpretation of Scripture in contemporary Jewry except, perhaps, among a few Kabbalists or simply for amusement.

**Codes of Law** The Talmud is the ultimate *authority in Jewish *law but the Talmud is not itself a Code of Law. Besides containing much non-legal material, the Talmud, even in its legal portions, which constitute by far its major part, is generally concerned with theoretical discussion and debate rather than with practical decisions. For practical Jewish religious life, rules and regulations are required to be culled from the Talmud, a very difficult task considering the purely theoretical thrust of the work, and then presented in systematic fashion in a Code. When Codes were drawn up in post-Talmudic times, their authority was not based on the opinions of their compilers. Whatever authority they enjoyed was due to their correct assessment of the relevant Talmudic passages. This means that it was possible for the Codes to disagree with one another, since there can be various understandings of what the Talmud is saying and the decisions to be drawn from this gigantic work. In a famous passage,

*Nahmanides observes that the study of the Talmud is not comparable to an exact scientific enquiry in which hypotheses can be empirically tested. Moreover, new conditions often obtained after a Code had been compiled. The whole of the *Responsa literature consists of questions and answers on topics for which there is direct guidance neither in the Talmud nor in earlier Codes. Later codifiers were obliged to take these into consideration when drawing up a fresh and more comprehensive Code of their own, and so the process has continued down to the present day, at least, in *Orthodox Judaism, of codification, Responsa, and further codification. This entry will deal only with the major and most influential Codes.

Not all the great Talmudists engaged in codification. Some were more interested in producing commentaries and works of exposition, although, naturally, legal decisions are often present in their works as well. The conventional division of traditional Talmudists is between the *mefareshim*, 'commentators', such as *Rashi and the *Tosafot, and the *posekim*, 'deciders', such as the authors of the Responsa and the codifiers. The division must not be drawn too neatly. Just as there are legal decisions in the works of the *mefareshim*, there is a good deal of theoretical discussion in the works of the *posekim*. The latter have to grapple with the theories before they can arrive at decisive practical rulings.

The *Sefer Ha-Halakhot* ('Book of the Laws') compiled in the eleventh century by Isaac *Alfasi, known as the Rif, is really a reworking of the Talmud in such a way as to give, wherever possible, the practical rulings while omitting the elaborate discussions where these do not serve the practical aim. The Rif often provides a digest of the Talmud in the form: 'Rabbi *A* says . . . but Rabbi *B* says . . . And the law follows Rabbi *A*', whereas, in the Talmud itself, elaborate reasons may be given and discussed on why Rabbi *A* said what he did and why Rabbi *B* dissents from his opinion.

A century after the Rif, Maimonides compiled, in an exquisite Hebrew style, his great compendium, the *Mishneh Torah*, a Code which embraces every aspect of the law, including topics, like that of how animal sacrifices are to be offered in the Temple, that were of no practical consequence whatsoever in his day.

In the fourteenth century, Jacob ben *Asher constructed his Code on that of his father

Asher ben Yehiel, known as the Rosh (abbreviation of Rabbi Asher). Jacob ben Asher divided his Code into four sections which he called Arbaah Turim ('Four Rows'). This was abbreviated to 'Tur' and Jacob ben Asher's Code is known as the Tur. Although Asher and his son Jacob later settled in Spain, the laws they recorded were mainly in the German tradition to which they had belonged before coming to Spain—that of the *Ashkenazim, in contradistinction to the Rif and Maimonides who were *Sephardim.

There were thus three great Codes in the Middle Ages, those of the Rif and Maimonides, and the Tur. Each of these was commented on by later scholars who defended and, where they thought it necessary, attacked their decisions as unwarranted.

In sixteenth-century Safed, Rabbi Joseph *Karo wrote a detailed commentary to the Tur which he called Bet Yosef ('House of Joseph'). After the fashion of referring to authors by the names of the books they wrote, Karo is still often referred to as the Bet Yosef. As Karo states in his introduction, his work had a severely practical aim. He has noticed, he remarks, that because Jewish law developed in different ways in various centres of Jewish life, it is unfortunately possible to find Jewish communities governed so differently by the laws that the Torah seems to have become not one but many Torahs. On the practical level, it was almost as if there were as many systems of the Jewish religion as there were Jewish communities. Karo's methodology in the Bet Yosef, in the brave attempt to promote the emergence of a unified system, was to treat the Rif, Maimonides, and the Rosh as his authorities but, where these were in conflict, he would decide in favour of the majority and where such a majority was not to be found, other authorities would be relied on in order to render clear, unambiguous decisions in all practical matters. Since, however, both the Rif and Maimonides belonged essentially to the same Spanish tradition and the Rosh (and the Tur) to the German tradition, Karo's whole methodology was strongly biased in favour of the Sephardic tradition to which he belonged.

In the Bet Yosef, Karo elaborates on all the topics he discusses but, for the benefit of his disciples, as he remarks, he later produced a compendium in which the bare decisions arrived at in the Bet Yosef were stated without the full reasoning behind them. Karo called this latter work the *Shulhan Arukh ('Arranged Table'), as if to say: here is all the spiritual food the Jew requires for his practical life. Karo's Code was widely disseminated, being produced after the invention of printing, but, as has been noted, it is weighted in favour of the Sephardic practices.

To redress the balance, the Polish Rabbi Moses *Isserles, known, after the abbreviation of his name, as the Rama, produced glosses to the Shulhan Arukh: 'the Tablecloth', as it was called, to cover Karo's table so that Ashkenazim as well as Sephardim could enjoy the spiritual repast. The Shulhan Arukh, now comprising Karo's original text together with Isserles' glosses, became the standard Code for the majority of Orthodox Jews, the Sephardim relying on the original text of Karo and the Ashkenazim on the glosses of Isserles, since the two were now set side by side in the same work.

The matter did not rest there, however. The Shulhan Arukh soon found a number of outstanding commentators, all of them Ashkenazim, who, with the acumen, love of debate, and, it might be added, the occasional dose of sheer cussedness, all features of the Rabbinic mind, took issue not infrequently with the decisions of Isserles, a fellow Ashkenazi, as well as with those of Karo, the Sephardi. And, again, new problems, unenvisaged in the earlier sources, arose and were dealt with in the Responsa, with the result that new Codes were called for to incorporate all this new material. Among the more influential of the later Codes are the Shulhan Arukh compiled by the Hasidic master Rabbi *Shneur Zalman of Liady in the eighteenth century and the Arukh ha-Shulhan by the Russian Rabbi Y. M. Epstein (1829–1908). On the Sephardi side, Rabbi H. H. Medini (1832–1904) produced his very comprehensive digest of Jewish law entitled Sedey Hemed. Of a more popular nature are the Code Hayye Adam by Abraham Danziger (1748–1820) and the Kitzur Shulhan Arukh ('Abridged Shulhan Arukh') of Rabbi Solomon Ganzfried (1804–86). The last-named has gone into innumerable editions and is still used as a handy guide by Orthodox Jews all over the world, interestingly enough receiving its own commentators who often take issue with its decisions. The Mishnah Berurah of Israel Meir Kagan, the *Hafetz Hayyim, still enjoys great authority. Since World War II, the great digest Otzar Ha-Posekim on the laws of marriage and divorce has gone into many large folio volumes in which all the opinions of the *posekim* are recorded with all their arguments and disagreements. Conservative Rabbis have begun to produce their own Codes and even contemporary Reform is no longer as hostile as Reform used to be to the codification of Jewish law.

**Cohen, Hermann** German Jewish philosopher (1842–1918). Cohen, the son of a Cantor, received a traditional Jewish education and studied for a time at the Breslau Jewish Theological Seminary with the intention of becoming a Rabbi, but he gave up this plan to study philosophy at the universities of Breslau and Berlin, receiving a doctorate from the University of Halle. Cohen's place in the history of general philosophy is as the founder of the Marburg school of neo-Kantianisne, in which the general Kantian position is subjected to critique and a reworking.

The question of Cohen's understanding of Judaism is complicated, his philosophical universalism tending to be in conflict with his fulsome acceptance of the great value of the Jewish ethical stance and the importance of the traditional Jewish practices. In Cohen's earlier work, God is seen as an idea produced by the human mind to give coherence to man's ethical strivings. The story has often been told of how, when Cohen delivered a lecture in which he described God in very abstract terms, a pious Polish Jew declared: 'Fine. But where is the Ribbono Shel Olam ['Sovereign of the universe', the name used in the prayer life of the devout] in all this?' In his later life, however, Cohen moved closer to the traditional Jewish conception of God. Cohen took issue with Kant's view that Judaism is an obsolete religion. On the contrary, Cohen affirmed, Judaism's teachings regarding ethical monotheism are as relevant and as needed as ever they were.

Cohen's thought is universalistic in scope, for all his insistence that God has a special relationship with the Jewish people. The sufferings of the Jews, far from being evidence that God has rejected them, is evidence of His love for them since God loves those who suffer. Yet Cohen's understanding of the doctrine of the *Messiah is in universalistic terms. The attempts by various communities to achieve better human conditions will lead eventually to the emergence of a world in which the ideal will

triumph of social justice for all human beings. Cohen's opposition to *Zionism was based on his universalistic, Messianic thought, which he saw as frustrated by a particularistic movement like Zionism.

Cohen's influence on contemporary Jewish thought is more indirect than direct. Only one of his works has been translated into English and none into Hebrew and, after the establishment of the State of *Israel, his anti-Zionism has become totally unrealistic. Yet his reaffirmation in philosophical terms of the significance of the Jews as the bearers of ethical monotheism has taught many Jews how to live with dignity as Jews and, at the same time, as citizens of the world.

Hermann Cohen, *Religion of Reason out of the Sources of Judaism*, trans. Simon Kaplan, with an introduction by Leo Strauss (New York, 1972).

**Communism** When considering communism from the Jewish point of view, a distinction must be drawn between the political theory, developed by Karl *Marx, of a classless society based on common ownership of the means of production, and the practice of Communism in societies such as that of Soviet Russia after the Russian revolution. In the latter, where all religion is seen as opium for the masses, God is dethroned, and Judaism is subject to considerable restraint, there is obviously no room for any kind of Jewish acceptance. But the idea in itself of common ownership is not necessarily at variance with the ideals and practices of Judaism. According to Jewish teaching, a *community is entitled to make its own arrangements with regard to the management of its economy, provided that these are established by proper democratic means. The Israeli *kibbutz is basically a communist form of social organization. While there has been opposition to the institution of the kibbutz on the part of religious Jews this was because the members of the kibbutz were themselves irreligious, not because of the organization in itself. There have been, in fact, some few religious kibbutzim and to these there has been no opposition on dogmatic grounds. In a remarkable letter, Rabbi A. I. *Kook advised a religious Jew not to disinherit his Communist and hence atheistic son, among other reasons because the atheism of many of the young Communists of his day was not based so much on sheer unbelief but rather on the mistaken view that the Jewish religion is a hindrance to the pursuit of social justice. They were in gross error in this, but not in their dream of a more just society.

A prominent Rabbi once remarked that Communism would be a good thing if controlled by Rabbis; a very dubious proposition, but one can see his meaning. What is wrong with Communism is the dictatorship to which it seems inevitably to lead, which overrides the needs and opinions of individual human beings created in the image of God and results, indeed, in rejection of God Himself.

Louis, Jacobs, *What Does Judaism Say About . . .?* (Jerusalem, 1973), 214–18.

**Community** The Hebrew word *tzibbur* (from a root meaning 'to gather') is used both for the Jewish people as a whole and for a particular group of Jews organized as a community. The expression 'the Synagogue', sometimes used in English as a collective, on the analogy of 'the Church', is incorrect. The term *synagogue refers only to the building in which prayers are offered. The nearest equivalent to 'the Church' is 'the Jewish Community', the *tzibbur*. Another term used both for the Jewish Community as a whole and for a particular community of Jews is *kehilah* ('assembly'). This entry deals with the particular Jewish community, the social institution through which a number of Jews organize their Jewish life, say, in a Jewish town or around a particular synagogue. Significantly, the fuller term for this is *kehilah kedoshah*, 'holy congregation', the idea being that while individual Jews may be far from the ideal of holiness there is an element of the sacred when Jews work together for the furtherance of Judaism.

Most of the information regarding the *kehilah* in ancient times is found in the Talmud. Later Jewish communities in the larger towns organized themselves on the basis of the Talmudic regulations. The Talmud, for instance, speaks of important transactions such as the sale of the town synagogue being conducted by 'the seven good men of the city in the presence of the men of the city', which probably means that the affairs of the community were attended to by a council of seven elected members who were obliged to consult all the other members before undertaking anything of great importance. It is bothersome to historians of the Jewish community that details are lacking in the Talmudic sources as to how the 'seven good men' were

elected. The general impression gained is that this town council was democratically elected by majority vote, but there is little indication of whether every citizen had a vote or only those who paid for the upkeep of the communal institutions. From the sixteenth century onwards in the great Polish towns, no one was appointed to leadership of the community unless he was both wealthy and learned in the Torah (see DEMOCRACY). The honorary officers of synagogues and other communal organizations are, nowadays democratically elected, with all that involves: standing for office, canvassing votes before the election, baby-kissing and so on.

*The Communal Enactment*

In Jewish law the community, through its representatives, the local Rabbi and the communal officers, is empowered to introduce legislation to the benefit of the community. The *takkanah* ('enactment') of the community is binding on all its members as a condition of their membership by contractual arrangement. To give just one example, if the communal leaders saw that fishmongers were charging exorbitant prices for their wares because Jews consider it good to eat *fish on the Sabbath, they would issue a *takkanah* that for a given period all the members must abstain from eating fish on the Sabbath and this would speedily bring down the prices. Offenders against the enactments were treated very severely, in dire cases being threatened with the *herem*, the ban preventing offenders from participation in communal life. Nowadays, failure to comply with the particular rules of the community often results in loss of membership, as with most social organizations.

Members of a community are expected to pay their dues but it is left to the representatives to fix these, perhaps in a graded scale according to the economic circumstances of the members. It all depends on the regulations of the particular group. In many Jewish communities today the synagogues have their own administration but there are, in addition, charitable and educational institutions for which appeals are made to the whole community, each having its own administrative body.

*Communal Prayer*

The Rabbis, stressing the importance of communal prayer, say, no doubt with a degree of hyperbole, that when prayers are offered in a congregation God will never reject them. Some of the more sacred prayers can be recited only where a quorum of ten, the *minyan, is present. The prayers in the standard *liturgy are in the plural form: 'Help *us*'; 'Pardon *us*'; 'Bless *us*'; '*We* give thanks to Thee'.

Various reasons are given by the Jewish teachers for the advantage of communal over private *prayer. Menahem *Meiri stresses the psychological advantage: 'Whenever a man is able to offer his prayers in the synagogue he should do so since there proper concentration of the heart can be achieved. The Rabbis laid down a great rule: Communal prayer has especial value and whenever ten pray in the synagogue the *Shekhinah is present.' Judah *Halevi's *Kuzari* is in the form of an imaginary dialogue between the king of the *Khazars and a Jewish sage. The king asks, why all this emphasis on communal prayer? Would it not be better if everyone recited his prayers for himself where, on the contrary, there is greater concentration and purity of thought without distraction? The sage replies that an individual, praying on his own, may pray for others to be harmed, but a community will never pray for harm to come to one of its members. Furthermore, an individual may make mistakes when mouthing the words of the prayers whereas when people pray together they make up for one another's shortcomings. The Zohar gives a mystical reason. When an individual prays, his prayers do not ascend to God until there has first been a heavenly investigation to determine whether he is worthy for his prayers to be accepted. Communal prayers, on the other hand, ascend immediately to the heavenly throne without any prior investigation.

In an astonishing Rabbinic saying, when communal prayers are offered on a fast day in a situation of dire necessity such as failure of the rains to come, there must be sinners among the supplicants, otherwise the prayers will not be answered. As the Rabbis put it, among the ingredients of the incense prepared in Temple times, one was the evil smelling galbanum, which had none the less to be mingled with the other sweet-smelling spices before the incense could be used. The Jewish community is not a community of saints but is composed of all types of persons who, including the notorious sinners, find strength in coming together for a common purpose. A Jewish folk etymology understands the initial letters of the word *tzibbur*, 'community', as representing the words *tzaddikim* ('righteous'); *benonim* ('average'); *reshaim* ('wicked'). It takes all sorts to make a Jewish community as it takes all sorts to make a world.

### Communal Fellowship

Strife and contention were no strangers to the Jewish community (see CONTROVERSIES). Wherever there are two Jews, the wry saying has it, there are three different opinions. All the more reason why the Jewish teachers, often not averse to a good dose of controversy themselves, repeatedly stressed the importance of communal harmony and cohesion, especially when the community was attacked from without. In Rabbinic and medieval times, the Jew who was disloyal to his community or who deserted it when it was in trouble or, worst of all, who sought to curry favour with the governmental authorities by pointing to the faults of its members so as to endanger their lives, was treated as an outcast. Within the community the danger was ever present of powerful leaders taking unfair advantage of the other members or seeking to lord it over them. In a Talmudic saying, no man should be appointed a community leader unless he has behind him a box of vermin, presumably meaning that ideally he should not have an aristocratic background so that when he seems to be getting beyond himself his followers will be able to remind him of his base ancestry.

Going back at least as early as the second century CE, Ethics of the Fathers has a number of acute maxims on the subject of Jews working together in a community. Attributed to Rabban Gamaliel son of Rabbi *Judah the Prince, a communal leader himself who knew where the shoe pinches, is the saying: 'Let all who labour with the community labour with them for the sake of Heaven [not for personal advantage]. For the merit of their ancestors is their support, and their righteousness endures for ever.' *Hillel is quoted as saying: 'Do not separate yourself from the community', which may have been directed against the sectarians of Hillel's day, although Travers Herford, in his commentary to Ethics of the Fathers, is too conjectural when he understands Hillel as referring to the *Essenes. An anonymous saying in Ethics of the Fathers is: 'Anyone who makes many virtuous, no sin will result from his actions. But anyone who makes many sin, no opportunity will be given him to repent.' The Talmud contains a virulent denunciation of those who have abandoned the ways of the community; those who 'spread terror in the land of the living' (based on Ezekiel 32: 2 and referring to leaders who are tyrants); and those who sin and make others sin. These will go to hell to be punished there for all generations.

When the community is in trouble the individual should participate in its distress even if he himself is not affected. In another Talmudic saying: 'If an individual separates himself from the community when it is in distress, the two ministering angels that accompany every man, place their hands upon his head and say, such and such a man has separated himself from the community, let him not live to witness the comfort of the community.'

A good example can be given of the way in which Jewish teaching seeks to achieve a proper balance between the needs of the individual and those of the community to which he belongs. Taking the verse: 'And unto Joseph were born two sons before the year of famine came' (Genesis 41: 59) as the key, the Talmud states that conjugal relations must not be engaged in time of famine, which is understandable not only because there will then be less mouths to feed but also because personal pleasure of the more intense kind should be avoided when the community suffers. However, the passage goes on to say that people who have no children may perform their marital duty even in a time of famine. It can be generally said that the tensions between the individual and his community have been resolved neither in Jewish thought nor in Jewish practice, yet Jews have always felt the need to belong to a community and, on the wider scale, to the whole Jewish community, even when to do so was costly.

Salo W. Baron, *The Jewish Community* (Philadelphia, 1945).

Louis Jacobs, *Religion and the Individual* (Cambridge, 1992), 31–41.


**Compassion** Fellow feeling, the emotion of caring concern; in post-biblical Hebrew *raḥamanut*, interestingly from the word *reḥem*, 'womb', originating in the idea of either motherly love or sibling love (coming from from the same womb); in biblical Hebrew *raḥamim*. The Talmudic Rabbis (*Yevamot* 79a) considered compassion to be one of the three

distinguishing marks of Jews. A Talmudic term frequently used of God, particularly in legal discussions, is the Aramaic *Raḥamana*, 'the Compassionate', denoting that the Torah, the Law, is God's compassionate gift to Israel.

In Jewish teaching compassion is among the highest of virtues, as its opposite, cruelty, is among the worst of vices. The prophet Jeremiah speaks of the people from the north country who 'lay hold on bow and spear, they are cruel, and have no compassion' (Jeremiah 6: 23). The people of *Amalek, in particular, are singled out in the Jewish tradition as perpetrators of wanton cruelty and an uncompassionate Jew is called an Amalekite.

Compassion is to be extended to *animals as well as to humans. It is strictly forbidden to cause unnecessary pain to animals. There is a Talmudic rule (*Gittin* 62a), still followed by pious Jews, that before sitting down to a meal one must first see that the domestic animals are fed. The Midrash remarks that Moses proved his fitness to be the shepherd of Israel by the tender care with which he treated the sheep when he tended the flock of his father-in-law. Commenting on the law against killing an animal and its young on the same day (Leviticus 22: 26), the Zohar (iii. 92b) says:

'Thus if a man does kindness on earth, he awakens loving-kindness above, and it rests upon that day which is crowned therewith through him. Similarly, if he performs a deed of mercy, he crowns that day with mercy and it becomes his protector in the hour of need. So, too, if he performs a cruel action, he has a corresponding effect on that day and impairs it, so that subsequently it becomes cruel to him and tries to destroy him, giving him measure for measure. The people of Israel are withheld from cruelty more than all other peoples, and must not manifest any deed of the kind, since many watchful eyes are upon them.'

There is, in this connection, a revealing tale in the Talmud (*Bava Metzia* 85a). A calf, being led to the slaughter, ran for protection to Rabbi *Judah the Prince, but the Rabbi said to the calf: 'Go! For this you were created', whereupon the Rabbi was visited with great suffering. Some time later, Rabbi Judah noticed his servant sweeping out a nest of weasels from the corner of his palace. 'Let them be,' he ordered, 'it is written [Psalms 145: 9] "His tender mercies are over all His works"', whereupon the suffering departed from him. The point of the story seems to be that cold calculation, even when justified, is no substitute for compassion. The story is not told in support of *vegetarianism. There is no suggestion that the calf should not be killed to provide humans with food. But the compassionate man, even when he can do nothing to prevent suffering, will still have pity for those that suffer, even if they are dumb animals. The Rabbi's response was unfeeling, as he came to realize when his suffering departed after he showed compassion to the weasels, even though here, too, he had no actual obligation to spare them.

Louis Jacobs, *Jewish Values* (London, 1960), 135–44.

**Competition** Jewish law accepts the principle that commercial activities are, in the nature of the case, competitive but draws the line between fair and unfair competition. The key biblical text is: 'Thou shalt not remove thy neighbour's landmarks' (Deuteronomy 19: 14).' In the context this refers to a man moving the marker between his and his neighbour's field so that he takes to himself some of his neighbour's land. In Rabbinic law this is applied to every attempt to encroach, unfairly, on a neighbour's property or his means of earning a living. The operative word here is 'unfair' and the sources discuss at length how this is to be defined.

The Mishnah (*Bava Metzia* 4: 11) records a debate between the second-century Palestinian Rabbi Judah and the sages on whether a shopkeeper is allowed to distribute burnt ears of corn and nuts to children who are sent by their parents to buy provisions. Rabbi Judah considers this to be unfair to the other shopkeepers in that it encourages the children to buy from him and not from them, The sages disagree. There is nothing wrong in this practice since the other shopkeepers can themselves compete by providing the children with even better goodies. Rabbi Judah also holds that it is forbidden for a shopkeeper to sell his goods below the standard market price but the sages say: 'Good for him' (literally, 'May he be blessed'). Clearly, the debate revolves around the question of whose interests the law should seek to preserve, those of the other traders or those of the general public. The law, as recorded in the Codes, follows the opinion of the sages. Economic conditions in second-century Palestine were very different from those which obtain today but it is not difficult to see how the debate can

have some relevance even in our different form of society to the question of price controls and, say, issuing gift vouchers to customers.

What of other forms of competition? The key passage is in the Talmud tractate *Bava Batra*, 21b. The third-century Babylonian teacher Rabbi Huna ruled that if a resident of an alley sets up a hand-mill and another resident of the alley wishes to set up one next to him, the first has a right to stop him, because he can say: 'You are interfering with my livelihood'. Rabbi Huna ben Joshua (not the same Rabbi Huna), however, disagrees and permits a resident of the same alley to compete, but not a resident of another town. He is uncertain what the law is with regard to the resident of another alley. The Codes decide in favour of the second Rabbi Huna and are less tolerant of protectionist policies. Later authorities make a distinction between ruinous and non-ruinous competition. Where the competition only reduces the profits of the one who protests against the intrusion, the view of the second Rabbi Huna is followed. But where the competition will result in his financial ruin the view of the first Rabbi Huna is adopted. Indeed, it is suggested, where the competition is ruinous the second Rabbi Huna would agree that it is not allowed.

Contemporary Jewish scholars have tried to discover in these earlier sources principles that can be applied in the modern urban market, but to transfer and apply rules originally formulated against a far more primitive economic background to the social order of today with its monopolies, organized labour, and large co-operations is bound to result in vagueness.

Jewish communities often issued special enactments (see COMMUNITY) to protect interests considered to be vital to the Jewish life of that community or, in certain instances, to Jewish life as a whole. For instance, kosher meat imported from butchers who lived elsewhere was declared forbidden by communal edict in order to protect the supply of kosher meat by the local butcher, which would cease if he went out of business. Printers who risked their money to print Jewish works would often print in the frontispiece a stern prohibition by a famous Rabbi, or Rabbis, against another publisher publishing the same work within a stated period. The dispute between the printers of the Vilna and Slavita editions of the Talmud in the nineteenth century made case history in the discussion of monopolies in Jewish law.

Aaron Levine, *Free Enterprise and Jewish Law* (New York, 1980).

Stephen M. Passamaneck, *The Traditional Jewish Law of Sale* (Cincinnati, 1983).

**Confession** In Judaism (see SIN AND REPENT-ANCE) a penitent sinner must give verbal expression to his remorse: he must confess his sin before God pardons him. Strictly speaking, the confession is acceptable even in the bare formulation: 'I have sinned', but more elaborate forms have been compiled and used. Maimonides (*Teshuvah*, ch. 1–2) holds that the more the sinner confesses at length the better, but gives as the basic form: 'O God! I have sinned, I have committed iniquity, I have transgressed before Thee by doing such-and-such. Behold now I am sorry for what I have done and am ashamed and I shall never do it again.'

Although Jewish apologists have affirmed that in Judaism confession is to God alone not to a priest, as in Catholicism, and although it is true that, on the whole, the Jewish teachers frown on public confession as brazen (on this there is a discussion in the Talmud, *Berakhot* 34b), it is incorrect to say that confession of sin addressed to another human being is entirely unknown in any version of the religion. In the circle of the thirteenth-century German pietists who produced the *Sefer Ḥasidim*, the idea is found of confessing sins to a spiritual mentor, a 'father confessor', who would give the sinner a penance to perform. The *Sefer Ḥasidim* is fully aware that the Talmud does frown on confession to others, but holds that this does not apply where the confession is made to a discreet sage who can be relied upon not to publish the sin abroad and who can instruct the sinner how to do penance for his particular sins so that he may inherit eternal life. There may well be a Christian influence in all this, although it is cast in a Jewish form. In some versions of *Hasidism, too, confession to a mentor, in this case the Hasidic master, the *Zaddik, is advocated.

The Hasidic master Elimelech of Lizansk (1717–87) writes, in his list of spiritual counsels:

'A man should tell his mentor who teaches him God's way, or even a trustworthy friend, all the evil thoughts he has which are in opposition to our holy Torah, which the evil inclination brings into his head and heart, whether while he is studying the Torah or offering his prayers or when he lies on his bed or at any time during the day. He should conceal nothing out of shame. The result of speaking of these matters, thus actualizing the potential, will be to break the hold over him of the evil inclination so that it will possess less power to entice him on future occasions, quite apart from the sound spiritual guidance, which is the way of the Lord, he will receive from his friend. This is a marvellous antidote to the evil inclination.'

Another Hasidic master, *Nahman of Bratslav (1772–1811), in his anthology of spiritual maxims, *Sefer Ha-Middot*, writes: 'Good thoughts are the result of confession of sin to scholars.'

Confession of sin is an integral part of the *Yom Kippur liturgy. At various stages during the service of this great Day of Atonement, a standard confession is repeated by the Cantor and the congregation, in some congregations accompanied by a joyous melody. As the *Baal Shem Tov is reported to have put it: 'The charlady who cleanses from their dirt the floors of the king's palace, sings sweetly as she works.' Originally the form of the Yom Kippur confession was not stereotyped, it being left to the individual to give expression in his own way to his inner hurt. But eventually a formal confession was introduced in which a variety of sins are mentioned in alphabetical order. This alphabetical acrostic form has been a source of puzzlement to many authors. Does it not frustrate the whole purpose of confession when it is turned into a purely mechanical act devoid of inwardness? One answer is that, before the days of printed prayer books, the alphabetical form was an aid to memory. Another reason given for the stereotype formula is that, when the whole congregation adopts the same form of confession, the individual is spared the embarrassment he might have suffered if his particular listing of his sins were to be overheard. In this connection the Talmudic saying is quoted that, in Temple times, the sin-offering was slaughtered in the same place as the burnt-offering in order not to expose the sinner to public shame. The individual is encouraged, however, to think of his particular sins while reciting the standard confession with the congregation.

*Deathbed Confessions*

As in other religions, the notion is scorned in Judaism that a man can sin with impunity throughout his life and all too easily make up for it by expressing remorse on his deathbed when he is incapable of sinning in any event. Nevertheless, and since no man is without sin, the Talmud (*Shabbat* 32a) observes: 'When a man is sick and near to death, they say to him: Make Confession.' The Talmud here, too, leaves it to the individual, but *Nahmanides records in his writings a special form, which he says is of long standing, and this, in more or less the same words, is found in the Prayer Book. It reads:

'I acknowledge unto Thee, O Lord my God and God of my fathers, that both my cure and my death are in Thy hands. May it be Thy will to send me a perfect healing. Yet if my death be fully determined by Thee, I will in love accept it at Thy hand. O may my death be an atonement for all the sins, iniquities and transgressions of which I have been guilty against Thee. Bestow upon me the abounding happiness that is treasured up for the righteous, Make known to me the path of life: in Thy presence is fulness of joy; at Thy right hand, bliss for evermore.'

Israel Abrahams, *A Companion to the Authorized Daily Prayerbook* (London, 1966), 225–226.
Louis Jacobs, *A Jewish Theology* (London, 1973), 243–59.

**Conservative Judaism** The form of the Jewish religion that occupies the middle ground between *Orthodoxy and *Reform, with its centre in the United States, where it is the largest of the three movements, and with adherents in other parts of the world. The main institution for the training of Conservative Rabbis is the Jewish Theological Seminary in New York, with branches in Los Angeles and Jerusalem. *Conservative Judaism*, published as a quarterly in New York, is the house organ of the movement. Conservative Rabbis are organized in the Rabbinical Assembly of Conservative Rabbis, the RAC, which meets annually in conference, publishing the proceedings in *Proceedings of the Rabbinical Assembly*.

*Ideology*

The two key thinkers of Conservative Judaism are Zachariah *Frankel and Solomon *Schechter; the former describes his religious position as that of 'positive historic Judaism', the latter stresses the idea of 'Catholic Israel', that the ultimate seat of *authority in Judaism resides in the consensus of the Jewish people as a whole on the meaning of Judaism.

The attitudes of Frankel and Schechter were by no means novel in Europe in the nineteenth and twentieth centuries, where it became obvious to many thinking, observing Jews that, in the light of modern historical investigation into the Bible and the classical sources of Judaism, a reappraisal was required of the whole idea of *revelation. For these Jews, the too-neat picture of the doctrine 'the Torah is from Heaven', as presented in Orthodoxy, was unacceptable, since historical research has demonstrated the developing nature of the Jewish religion as it came into contact, throughout its history, with various and differing systems of thought. On the other hand, these Jews saw Reform as too ready to accommodate Judaism to the *Zeitgeist* and to abandon practices and doctrines hallowed by tradition, especially in Reform's indifference, if not hostility, to the system of Jewish law, the *Halakhah. The attitude of such Jews was articulated in Frankel's maxim: positive historic Judaism—'positive' in its acceptance of the tradition and the Halakhah, 'historic' in that it conceived of these in dynamic rather than in static terms. Schechter spelled it out further in his writings. Since, ultimately, as historical research has demonstrated, the dual process of acceptance and adaptation of ideas in conformity with the spirit of the religion was determined by the way Jews actually lived their religion, the Judaism of tradition *is* Judaism, although expressed in different ways in different times. On this view, the Jew can have an open mind on the question of origins. He may come to the conclusion, as Bible critics argue, that some of the institutions of Judaism such as the Sabbath and the *dietary laws originated in primitive taboos. It is not origins that matter but what the institutions actually became in the Jews' long quest to discover the will of God.

In the USA, a number of prominent Rabbis and laymen became increasingly disturbed by the excesses of American Reform. When, in 1883, non-kosher food was served at the banquet in honour of the first graduates of Hebrew Union College, the Reform institution for the training of Rabbis, these more 'conservative' leaders founded the Jewish Theological Seminary for the training of a modern but strictly traditional Rabbinate. At a later date the United Synagogue of America was founded, embracing synagogues of this traditional cast. A third movement was thus established and since its chief motivation in reaction to Reform's untraditionalism, it gave itself the name 'Conservative Judaism', namely, a movement adopting a more conservative and more traditional approach than Reform.

Not everyone who joined the new movement was attracted by its ideology. Many Jews, sentimentally attached to the traditions of their forebears, most of whom came from Eastern Europe where Reform hardly existed as a movement, felt comfortable in a movement which preserved traditional norms without rejecting modernism and the American way of life. For all that, a galaxy of outstanding Jewish scholars, members of the faculty at the JTS, demonstrated, on the intellectual level, that it was possible to wed critical scholarship to full observance of the Torah laws, and constant attempts have been and are being made to produce a satisfactory theology of Conservative Judaism.

Schechter's 'Catholic Israel' means, as has been frequently noted, that, historically considered, God does not so much reveal His will *to* the Jewish people as *through* them. The Jews are not simply passive recipients of the Torah. In a sense they are the creators and authors of the Torah under divine guidance, the latter being the operative phrase. But the emphasis on the concept 'Catholic Israel' can result in an interpretation of Judaism in naturalistic terms, as in *Reconstructionism, an offshoot of Conservative Judaism in which the *precepts of the Torah are seen not as the revealed will of a personal God but as folk-ways and pleasant ceremonies created entirely by the Jewish people which are still capable of enriching the Jewish spirit. This was certainly not the view of Schechter, although in his admiration for Mordecai *Kaplan, the founder of Reconstructionism, Schechter appointed him to a Professorship at the Jewish Theological Seminary where Kaplan influenced generations of Rabbinic students. It can perhaps be said that the thinker who more than any other restored the traditional thrust of Conservative Judaism was Abraham Joshua *Heschel, whose thought, influenced by his Hasidic background, gave Conservative Judaism not only a more traditional but also a powerful mystical direction. Heschel also taught at the Seminary, where he influenced especially the younger generation of students.

The definition of Conservative Judaism as 'middle of the road' is unfortunate in its unspoken implication that the movement lacks the vigour and loyalty of Orthodoxy and the courage and progressiveness of Reform. Conservative Jews are fond of telling the story of the woman who approached a Conservative Rabbi to officiate at the marriage of her daughter. The woman said: 'I do not want either a Reform or an Orthodox service but a Conservative one that is mediocre.' Rightly understood, however, Conservative Judaism, while rejecting both what it sees as the fundamentalism of Orthodoxy and the untraditionalism of Reform, adopts a positive religious position of it own in which Jewish piety can be fully at home in minds open to the best of modern thought. If it is middle of the road, this is not because it lacks both courage and conviction but because it believes that truth is rarely to be found in two towering but virtually inaccessible mountains rather than in the broad valley that lies between them.

### Conservative Judaism and Jewish Law

The major problem that a movement which accepts the Halakhah while seeing it in dynamic terms has to face is how to apply Jewish law in the conditions of modern life. Reform does not have to face this problem. Even though there has emerged in contemporary Reform a greater appreciation of the values enshrined in the Halakhah, Reform, basically, does not operate with traditional Halakhic categories. Orthodoxy does not have to face the problem because Orthodoxy sees the Halakhah in all its details as the very word of God, so that where the Halakhah is in conflict with modern life it is the latter that has to yield. Conservative Halakhists seek to operate within the system so far as they can but where the need is pressing will create new Halakhic categories, based on the traditional Halakhah to be sure, but without being bound, as much as Orthodoxy is, to precedent.

Some illustrations can be given of how the Conservative approach to the Halakhah works and the way in which this differs from Orthodoxy. An extremely vexing problem today for Jews who accept the Halakhah as binding is that of the *agunah, the wife who has obtained a civil divorce but whose husband refuses to give her the *get*, the religious bill of *divorce, without which she is not free to remarry. The husband may withhold the *get* out of sheer spite or he may blackmail the wife to give him a large sum of money before he gives his assent. Clearly, the perpetration of an injustice in which the poor woman is neither married nor remarried should not be tolerated in a religion like Judaism, which is based on justice. While the Halakhah gives this power to the husband, according to the Talmud, in cases where the wife is entitled to a divorce, say, because the husband refuses to live with her as man and wife, he can be compelled to divorce her, his assent under duress being considered assent for the purpose. But to compel the husband nowadays is not really possible, although Orthodox Rabbis will, it must in fairness be said, strain every nerve to persuade the husband to act decently and grant the divorce. Another remedy is to nullify the marriage. There are instances where the Talmudic Rabbis exercised this right to nullify a marriage for social reasons. The Orthodox refuse to adopt this remedy for the *agunah* problem, since there is an extreme reluctance among post-Talmudic Rabbis to accept the idea that later generations also have the same right as the Talmudic giants. Conservative Rabbis, at first, tried various other remedies, all within the Halakhic framework, but eventually came to realize that in dire cases the only remedy is that of annulment. Since the precedent is found in the Talmud and the Talmud is the final Court of Appeal for Halakhah, Conservative Rabbis do not see this as a rejection in any way of the Halakhic process but rather as an extension of it to prevent the Halakhah itself becoming an instrument of injustice.

In many large cities, some Jews do not live within walking distance of the synagogue. What are they to do on the Sabbath, since the Halakhah forbids riding in a motor car? Orthodoxy either turns a blind eye to how the members of Orthodox synagogues arrive there on the Sabbath or else says: too bad, they should live nearer to the synagogue. At first most Conservative Rabbis agreed with the Orthodox, stressing the sanctity not only of the Sabbath itself but also of all the Halakhic rules which give it life. More recently, many Conservative Rabbis, appreciating the importance of regular attendance at the synagogue for Jewish life today, as much, or even as more so, than in the past, try to follow Halakhic precedents to permit travelling to the synagogue on the Sabbath; they say, for instance, that to ride in a motor car is a comparatively minor

offence, one that can be set aside for the sake of the Sabbath itself.

An illuminating example of the way in which Conservative Rabbis apply Halakhic categories concerns calling up women to the *reading of the Torah. The Talmudic source is ambiguous, stating at first that a woman can be called to read the Torah but then expressing disapproval. A woman should not be called up to read the Torah 'out of respect for the congregation'. This expression has been understood to mean that the men in the congregation will be shown up if a woman can read while the men are too ignorant to read. The *Shulḥan Arukh* rules that a woman cannot be called up to the reading of the Torah and there the matter rests so far as Orthodoxy is concerned. Conservative Rabbis, after much debate and discussion, decided that, nowadays, when women are emancipated and have a right to an equal share in Jewish worship (see FEMINISM and WOMEN), the original approval of women being called to the Torah should be reintroduced and the Talmudic qualification ignored.

Thus Conservative Judaism does not advocate a new Halakhah and no attempt has been made to compile a Conservative *Shulḥan Arukh*. The major difference between Conservative Judaism and Orthodoxy is on the question of Halakhic flexibility. It should also be noted that Conservative Halakhists differ among themselves on many issues, as do the Orthodox. Orthodoxy sees this more flexible approach on the part of the Conservatives as a tampering with the Halakhic system, the result of which is to undermine the system itself. Many an Orthodox Rabbi has expressed the opinion that the Conservative approach poses a greater threat to traditional Halakhah than Reform, which is avowedly outside the Halakhic process.

## Masorti

Conservative Judaism, originally an American tendency, as noted above, now has adherents in the State of Israel, where the movement is called the Masorti movement. Masorti means 'traditional' and has the same connotation as 'Conservative' in the USA, but with an Israeli slant. In order to avoid too close an association with the specific needs and approaches of American Jews, a few Anglo-Jewish congregations, sympathetic to the philosophy of Conservative Judaism, have adopted the Israeli term Masorti.

This whole question of traditionalism has recently exercised Conservative Rabbis in the USA. When the Jewish Theological Seminary decided to train women for the Rabbinate and when the Rabbinical Assembly accepted women Rabbis as members (women now officiate as Rabbis in a number of Conservative synagogues), some Rabbis and some teachers at the Seminary formed themselves into the Union for Traditional Conservative Judaism. At the present time there is thus a definite swing towards greater traditionalism in the whole Conservative movement. In point of fact, Conservative Rabbis have long been divided into three groupings, adopting, respectively, the right, left, and centrist positions.

Despite these wide divergencies and pluralistic tendencies, all Conservative congregations agree in affirming the basic institutions of traditional Judaism—observance of the Sabbath and the festivals, the dietary laws, circumcision, daily prayer, marriage and divorce, *conversion in accordance with Jewish law, the centrality of Hebrew in the synagogue service, and, above all, the study of the Torah as a high religious obligation.

Aware of the inevitable vagueness in certain important areas of belief and practice, the leaders of Conservative Judaism met in commission in 1985 and eventually produced a booklet, with the participation of representatives of all three groupings, containing a statement of principles of Conservative Judaism. Rabbi Kassel Abelson, the then President of the Rabbinical Assembly, conveys in his introduction the tensions which still exist, and are bound to exist, in a movement that seeks to combine diversity with cohesion, tradition with change:

'Bitter debates had taken place at Rabbinical Assembly conventions, and we appeared to be a movement in danger of division. Seated on the Commission were intellectual advocates of the most extreme positions, while in between were the rest of us, reflecting the broad spectrum of opinion within the Conservative movement . . . As we began to talk to each other informally, we found that "the other side" was neither as "wrong" nor as extreme as it may have appeared at Rabbinical Assembly debates. We soon discovered that not only were we all sincerely interested in producing a Statement of Principles of Conservative Judaism, but that we had much more in common than

we realized. All of us, whether on the right or the left, were Conservative Jews. We all accepted the results of modern scholarship. We agreed that historical development of the tradition had taken place, and that the tradition continues to develop. We all agreed on the indispensability of Halakhah for Conservative Jews, but a Halakhah which responds to changing times and changing needs.'

Elliot Dorf, *Conservative Judaism: Our Ancestors to Our Descendants* (New York, 1979).

Neil Gillman, *Conservative Judaism* (West Orange, NJ, 1993).

Seymour Siegel (ed.), *Conservative Judaism and Jewish Law* (New York, 1977).

Marshall Sklare, *Conservative Judaism* (New York, 1955).

*Emet Ve-Emunah: Statement of Principles of Conservative Judaism* (New York, 1988).

**Contemplation** The great emphasis placed in Judaism on the *study of the Torah, involving reflection, discussion, and debate, especially on the niceties of Talmudic and post-Talmudic legal topics, towards which practically all intellectual efforts were directed, was bound to result in a degree of indifference to religious contemplation of the more mystical kind. The medieval philosophers, represented particularly in this context by Maimonides, did however, see contemplation on the wondrous world in which God is manifest as a high religious value. For Maimonides (*Mishneh Torah, Yesodey ha-Torah*, 2. 1–2), the *love and fear of God is attained through profound reflection on the created universe:

'How does man come to love and fear God? No sooner does man reflect on His deeds and on His great and marvellous creatures, seeing in them His incomparable and limitless wisdom, than he is moved to love and to praise and to glorify and he has an intense desire to know the great Name, as David said [Psalms 42: 3]: "My soul thirsteth for God, for the living God". When man reflects on these very things he immediately recoils in fear and dread, aware that he is only a puny creature, dark and lowly, standing, with his minute fraction of unstable thought, in the Presence of the Perfect in Knowledge.'

This is reminiscent of Pascal's 'The eternal silence of these infinite spaces terrifies me'.

Maimonides is true to his general view that God Himself is beyond human intellectual grasp. Contemplation can only be on God as

He is manifest in the universe. In Jewish *mysticism, on the other hand, there are to be found various forms of contemplation on God Himself; from the vision of the divine throne seen by the Riders of the *Chariot through to the contemplation of the divine names by the later Kabbalists. The latter is best described as meditation rather than contemplation since in it the mind is directed to particular words and expressions. The Kabbalists believed that by concentrating the mind on the various combinations of divine names the mystic releases the divine energy latent in them to strengthen the spiritual powers of both his own soul and the whole of the created universe. In *Hasidism, to some extent, the Kabbalistic meditations on the divine names yielded to the more direct ideal of *devekut, communion with God, in which the devotee has God Himself constantly in mind.

In the branch of Hasidism known as *Habad, the attempt is made to combine mystical contemplation with the Kabbalistic meditations. In the type of contemplative prayer favoured by the Habad practitioners, the mind reflects on the whole of the Kabbalistic scheme of the divine unfolding, from the mystery of *En Sof through to the detailed emanations of the *Sefirot and then to the emergence of all the lower worlds. The second master of Habad, *Dov Baer of Lubavitch, compiled for his followers a guide, known as *Tract on Contemplation*, in which the whole scheme is set out in rich detail; it is one of the very few guides to contemplation found in Jewish sources. Certainly in Hasidism in general but also in Habad, the ultimate aim in contemplation is to reach to the divine Nothingness, that aspect of the divine that is beyond all comprehension, so as to attain to the state known as *annihilation of selfhood, paradoxically, contemplation bringing about its own extinction.

Moshe Idel, *The Mystical Experience in Abraham Abulafia* (Albany, NY, 1988).
Aryeh Kaplan, *Meditation and Kabbalah* (York Beach, Me., 1982).
Daniel C. Matt, 'Ayin: The Concept of Nothingness in Jewish Mysticism', in Robert K. C. Forman (ed.), *The Problem of Pure Consciousness: Mysticism and Philosophy* (Oxford, 1990).

**Controversies** There have been numerous controversies in the history of Judaism. This entry considers the main controversies regarding Jewish belief and practice, some of which

threatened to split Jews into two separate religious denominations or even, in the more extreme instances, into two different religions.

The earliest controversy, in the Second Temple period, was that between the Jews and the *Samaritans, the latter claiming that they were the true descendants of the biblical Israelites. According to the Samaritans, the Pentateuch had been falsified so as to omit all the supposedly original references which supported their claim.

The dispute between the *Sadducees and the *Pharisees was chiefly, according to the Talmudic records, on the doctrine of the *Oral Torah, a doctrine which the Sadducees rejected, claiming that the *Written Torah, the Bible, alone contained the word of God. Also, according to both the Talmud and Josephus, the Sadducees rejected belief in the *World to Come. The Sadducean beliefs re-emerged in the later dispute between the *Karaites and the followers of the Talmud, the Rabbanites. While the Sadducees were vanquished, their ideas lived on in the Karaite '*heresy', which rejected the authority of the Talmud, the depository of the Oral Torah, and a small group of Karaites is still to be found in the State of Israel.

Within the Pharisaic tradition, at the beginning of the current era, the rival schools of *Hillel and *Shammai were so divided in matters of law and, to some extent, in doctrine, the Talmudic legend has it, that there was a danger of the Torah becoming 'two Torahs', that is, of being split up into the religion of the Hillelites and that of the Shammaites, until a heavenly voice, a *Bat Kol, declared: 'Both these and these are the words of the living God but the law [*Halakhah] follows the School of Hillel.' In this instance, however, the opinions of the Shammaites were not completely ignored. These opinions are recorded and discussed in the Talmud side by side with those of the Hillelites. It was only for practical purposes that the Hillelites were followed since, in practice, there can only be a single authority. A statement of the famous Kabbalist Isaac *Luria has it that in the Messianic age the law will follow the stricter Shammaites rather than, as now, the more lenient Hillelites.

Although *Christianity was, at first, a Jewish heresy, once it had become the religion of a large part of the Gentile world, the dispute between Judaism and Christianity, like that between Judaism and Islam, was no longer a controversy within Judaism but became one surrounding the truth-claims of rival religions.

In the Middle Ages the Jewish world, after the death of Maimonides in the early thirteenth century, was divided over the vexed question of whether the philosophical approach to Judaism was legitimate. 'What did the Greeks know about God?' the anti-Maimonists roundly declared; to which the Maimonists retorted that even if *Joshua himself were to come down from heaven to forbid the study of philosophy he would not be heeded, so much had philosophy become part of their very being.

The controversy surrounding the Kabbalah, from its rise in the twelfth century, was far less vehement since the Kabbalists pursued their mystical way in small, discrete circles, apart from the major groupings. Moreover, great figures belonging to the Talmudic establishment such as *Nahmanides and Solomon Ibn *Adret, were themselves Kabbalists as well as renowned Talmudists, making the study and practice of the Kabbalah perfectly respectable and legitimate, even though rumblings did not cease over the Kabbalistic claim that their secret lore was vastly superior because it continued the 'soul of the Torah', as they called it. The main bone of contention in this dispute was whether the Kabbalistic doctrine of the *Sefirot, of ten powers or potencies in the Godhead, constituted a radical departure from the pure monotheism taught by Judaism.

The controversy in sixteenth-century Palestine between the Rabbis Jacob Berab and Levi ben Habib over the question of restoring Rabbinic *ordination was ostensibly a purely legal debate but it certainly had doctrinal aspects in that there was a Messianic motivation for restoring the form of ordination that was the norm in Temple and later times in the Holy Land. Berab, who favoured the reintroduction of the old form, held that this would bring nearer the coming of the *Messiah.

The great controversy which erupted in the seventeenth century over the claims of *Shabbetai Zevi to be the Messiah became considerably, but not entirely, muted when the false Messiah converted to Islam. After Shabbetai's apostasy, and even after his death, there were secret Shabbeteans who believed in him and his mission because, they maintained, the Messiah was obliged to descend into the depths of impurity in order to reclaim the *holy sparks

captured by the demonic forces. Crypto-Shabbeteans were still to be found here and there as late as the nineteenth century. The controversy between Jacob *Emden and Jonathan *Eybeschitz, which divided the Rabbinic world in the eighteenth century, was conducted to the sound of echoes from the Shabbetean controversy, Emden accusing Eybeschitz of being a crypto-Shabbetean. The other controversy of the eighteenth century and later, between *Hasidism and its opponents, the *Mitnaggedim, also had Shabbetean overtones. Together with other doctrinal matters, such as the Hasidic doctrine of *panentheism and the alleged scorn by the Hasidim of the Talmudic scholars, Hasidism was viewed with suspicion as a movement strongly infected with the poison of Shabbeteanism. This dispute largely came to an end when Hasidim and Mitnaggedim were compelled to unite in combating their common foe, the *Haskalah.

It seems almost as if a major controversy has to erupt in each century. The great divide in the nineteenth century was between *Reform and *Orthodoxy. The central issue, at first, was the comparative minor matter of changes in the liturgy but eventually at stake was the doctrine of the immutability of the Torah. If the Torah is God's will, can it ever be 'reformed'? However, apart from Samson Raphael *Hirsch, who described the differences between Orthodoxy and Reform as akin to those between Protestantism and Roman Catholicism, no one thought of Reform and Orthodoxy as two separate religious denominations.

**Conversion** Something of a convention has emerged in which a convert to Judaism is described in English as a proselyte, while a Jew converted to another religion is referred to as a convert. In Hebrew, too, different terms are used: *ger* for the proselyte and *meshumad* (from a root meaning of 'to destroy') for the convert to another religion.

*History*

The word *ger*, with a root meaning of 'to dwell', means, in biblical usage, 'sojourner', and refers to one coming to the Holy Land not as a casual visitor but as a permanent settler who identifies with the people of Israel. When the Moabite Ruth resolves never to be parted from Naomi and Naomi's people she gives expression to her new loyalties by declaring: 'Do not urge me to leave you, to turn back and not follow you, For wherever you go, I will go; wherever you lodge, I will lodge; your people shall be my people, and your God my God' (Ruth 1: 16). First, the people of Israel become Ruth's people and then Israel's God becomes her God. In the biblical period it was inconceivable for, say, an Egyptian or a Babylonian, to remain in their native land and yet embrace the Israelite religion. But as Judaism took root in the post-biblical period, numbers of *Gentiles became attracted to Judaism as a religion. The principle was gradually established of accepting converts to Judaism as a religion and then the term *ger* came to denote the proselyte (the feminine form *giyoret* for a female proselyte). There has been much discussion on the question of whether Jews ever engaged in missionary activity. A good deal of the evidence indicates not only that Jews did accept proselytes who came forward of their own free will but that they also consciously sought to convert others to their religion. However, when Jews lived under Gentile rule, it often became extremely hazardous for them to seek converts and thereby challenge the dominant religion. For this reason, in the Middle Ages, the extremist opinion the Talmud attributes to Rabbi Helbo (a Palestinian teacher of the third–fourth centuries): 'Proselytes are as harmful to Israel as a scab', was increasingly quoted not as a minority opinion but as the authoritative Jewish ideal, thus making a virtue of necessity.

Two other factors have contributed towards the Jewish aversion to engaging in conversionist activities among Gentiles. First, Jews in Western lands suffered from the conversionist tactics of sometimes unscrupulous Christian missionaries who sought to win Jews away from their ancestral religion either by bribes or by physical coercion. Jews acquired a horror of such activity which they refused to adopt on the principle: 'Since we do not like it when it is directed against us, we should not do it when directed against them.' The second reason was that the doctrine: 'The righteous of all peoples have a share in the *World to Come' became official teaching so that there was no need for a Gentile to embrace Judaism in order to be 'saved'. Judaism itself did not demand that Gentiles become Jews, only that they keep the *Noahide laws. For all that, some few Reform Rabbis have recently argued that, nowadays, in an age more open to religious cross-

fertilization, not to say indifference, Jews ought to encourage missionary activity directed, at least, to Gentile atheists or followers of idolatrous faiths. This suggestion has not caught on. The general position among the majority of Jews is that Judaism should not consciously seek converts but should still welcome into its ranks the sincere proselyte.

*Procedures*

There are two requirements for admission into the Jewish fold: circumcision (for a male) and immersion in the ritual bath, the *mikveh, for both males and females. The applicant is interviewed by a court, *Bet Din, of three (nowadays usually composed of three Rabbis) who first test his or her sincerity. In fact, the practice is for the court first to discourage the applicant and only to permit entrance into Judaism when the applicant is determined to be admitted. The main Talmudic source (*Yevamot* 47a–b) states the standard procedure:

'If at the present time one wishes to become a proselyte, they [the members of the Court] say to him: "Why should you wish to become a proselyte; do you not know that the people of Israel at the present time are persecuted and oppressed, despised, harassed and overcome by afflictions?" If he replies: "I do know it and yet am unworthy [of the privilege]", he is accepted forthwith, and is given instruction in some of the minor and some of the major precepts . . . If he accepts [to keep the precepts] he is circumcised forthwith . . . As soon as he recovers [from the circumcision] he is immediately immersed; two scholars standing beside him to acquaint him with some of the minor and some of the major precepts. When he comes up after his immersion he is considered to be an Israelite in every respect. In the case of a woman proselyte, women instruct her to sit in the water up to her neck, while two scholars stand outside to acquaint her with some of the minor and some of the major precepts.'

Maimonides adds that the proselyte has also to be informed of the major principles of the Jewish religion such as belief in the unity of God. Although from this Talmudic passage it would seem that the proselyte is accepted as soon as he or she demonstrates willingness and sincerity, the usual procedure, nowadays, is to require a period of study before admittance so that the basic doctrines and practices of Judaism will not be overlooked out of ignorance.

The acceptance of the precepts is understood by Orthodoxy to mean that the proselyte must give an undertaking to keep all the rules and regulations of Orthodox Judaism, which often means that the probationary period can last for a year or even longer. *Reform is less strict, insisting only on compliance with those rules that Reform itself does not reject. Conservative Judaism follows the same procedures as Orthodoxy but usually with a lesser demand of total acceptance. Many Reform Rabbis did not always insist on circumcision for male proselytes or on immersion for male and female proselytes but in contemporary Reform some, though by no means all, Rabbis tend to adopt the traditional requirements.

After acceptance, the proselyte is given a Hebrew name and is called son or daughter of our father *Abraham: 'Moshe ben Avraham Avinu' or 'Ruth bat Avraham Avinu'. The tradition is very insistent that the proselyte be made welcome, treated with great love, and never taunted with his or her pre-Jewish conduct.

Maimonides' famous letter to Obadiah the proselyte, who was called a fool by his teacher for defending Islam against the charge of idolatry, is no doubt too intolerant towards other religions for contemporary taste, yet his attitude is typical of the regard Jews have for proselytes:

'As for your teacher calling you a fool, I am utterly astonished. A man capable of leaving his father and his birthplace and the protection afforded by the government of his people; a man capable of so much understanding as to attach himself to a people, which today is despised by others and a slave to rulers, because he appreciates that theirs is the true religion; a man capable of so understanding the ways of Israel as to recognize that all the other religions have stolen from this one, one adding, the other subtracting, one changing, the other lying and attributing to God things that are not so . . . a man capable of casting this world from his heart, not turning to lies and falsehood; shall such a man be called a fool? God forbid! No fool has God called you but wise, understanding, upright, a disciple of Abraham our father who left his father and his birthplace to go after God.'

## Conversion to Another Religion

The question of the status of a Jew converted to a religion other than Judaism did not arise and could not have arisen before the emergence of Judaism's two daughter and rival religions, Christianity and Islam. In the Roman period in Palestine, for instance, a Jew might worship the Roman gods but there was no Roman religion to which he could be converted. Such a Jew would be treated very severely as as idolater but he remained a Jew; a Jewish sinner of the worst kind, to be sure, but a Jew none the less. But the Jew who converted to Christianity or Islam had actually embraced a religion other than Judaism and it might have been held that by so doing he had severed all his connections with Jews and Judaism and had lost his Jewish status according to Jewish law. The homiletical Talmudic saying: 'Even when he has sinned an Israelite is an Israelite', did not refer to apostasy but simply to a Jewish sinner who, the homily observes, still retains the high title 'Israel' despite his sinfulness. In the Middle Ages, however, perhaps in order to stem the tide of apostasy, the saying was given a completely new turn. Sin being understood as the sin of apostasy, the saying was taken to mean: 'Once a Jew always a Jew', namely, Jewish law does not acknowledge that a Jew's conversion to another religion can be in any way effective in changing his Jewish status.

The implications were very far-reaching. For instance, the wife of a convert who retains her loyalty to Judaism is held to be still married to a 'Jew' and cannot remarry until she obtains a religious divorce from him. Some of the *Geonim, however, ruled otherwise, arguing that when the husband converts to another religion he is considered in law to be as one dead, since he has died Jewishly, so to speak, and his wife can remarry without requiring a divorce just as if he had physically died. But the generally accepted view is that conversion to another religion cannot sever a Jew's connection with his Judaism. All this is, of course, seen from the purely legal aspect. Jews have looked upon the *meshumad* as a traitor to his people, far more so than the Jewish atheist who has taken no positive steps to sever his connection with Judaism. Some Jewish converts to Christianity would defend their apostasy by ridiculing the Jews and Judaism and some became virulent anti-Semites. Others, like the Russian orientalist Professor Daniel Chwolson (1819–1911), retained a high regard for the faith they had abandoned and were staunch defenders of the Jews. When Chwolson celebrated his seventieth birthday, a number of Russian Rabbis, in gratitude for his efforts on behalf of the Jewish community, sent him a telegram to wish him many happy returns. Rabbi Hayyim *Soloveitchik was more typical of the standard Jewish abhorrence of apostasy when he refused to participate, saying: 'I do not send congratulatory telegrams to a *meshumad*.' The wry remark attributed to Chwolson himself in the following story is probably apocryphal. Chwolson is reported to have said that he became a Christian out of conviction. 'Who are you kidding?' said a Jewish friend. 'How can you of all people, a learned Jew, be convinced that Christianity is true and Judaism false?' To which Chwolson is supposed to have replied: 'I was convinced that it is better to be a professor at the university than to be a Hebrew teacher in a small town.'

B. Bamberger, *Proselytism in the Talmudic Period* (New York, 1968).
William G. Braude, *Proselytising in the First Five Centuries of the Common Era* (New York, 1940).
Max Eichhorn (ed.), *Conversion to Judaism: A History and Analysis* (New York, 1965).
Sidney B. Hoenig, *Jewish Identity* (New York, 1965).

**Cordovero, Moses**   Safed Kabbalist (1522–70) whose family probably came from Cordoba in Spain. Cordovero was a disciple of Joseph *Karo in Talmudic and Halakhic studies and of his brother-in-law, Solomon Alkabetz, in the Kabbalah, in which subject he soon became the acknowledged master of all the Safed Kabbalists. Cordovero's literary output was amazing. The Kabbalists were fond of saying that he wrote by 'conjuration of the pen', that is, by means of magic power in which the pen seemed to write effortlessly and automatically. Cordovero wrote his *magnum opus*, the *Pardes Rimmonim* ('Orchard of Pomegranates') at the age of 27! (The conventional picture of Kabbalists as aged mystics, rich is life's experiences, owes much to the ban, after the débâcle of Shabbetai *Zevi, on the study of the Kabbalah before the student has reached the age of 40— a ban that did not exist in sixteenth-century Safed). Among Cordovero's other works on the Kabbalah is his *Or Yakar* ('Precious Light'), a voluminous commentary to the Zohar which remained in manuscript, appearing only very recently in print. His *Tomer Devorah* ('Palm Tree of Deborah'), a moralistic work on the idea of *Imitatio Dei* according to the Kabbalah, still enjoys great popularity among Jewish pietists, non-Kabbalists as well as Kabbalists.

Cordovero's renown is due to his genius for systemization. He, more than any other Kabbalist, presents all the complex ideas of the Zohar and the Kabbalah in clear, well-arranged form. The *Pardes* is, in reality, a Kabbalistic encyclopaedia, treating, for instance, all the various terms and symbols for the *Sefirot in alphabetical order. Cordovero was familiar with the philosophical tendency in Jewish thought and was influenced by it in his negation of attributes from the divine, as when he writes:

'When your intellect conceives of God, do not allow yourself to imagine that there is a God as depicted by you. For if you do this you will have a finite and corporeal conception, God forfend. Instead, your mind must dwell only on God's existence and then recoil. To do more than this is to allow the imagination to reflect on God as He is in Himself and such reflection is bound to result in imaginative limitation and corporeality. Put reins, therefore, on your intellect and do not allow it too great a freedom, but assert God's existence and deny your intellect the possibility of comprehending Him. The mind should run to and fro—running to affirm God's existence and recoiling from any limitations produced by the imagination, since the human intellect is pursued by imagination.'

Of the relationship between God and the universe Cordovero writes: 'He is in everything and everything has come into being from Him and nothing is empty of His divinity, God forfend. Everything is in Him and He is in everything and beyond everything and there is nothing beside Him.' It would be small wonder if, as has been plausibly suggested, Cordovero's thought had a strong influence on *Spinoza. In *Hasidism the doctrine of *panentheism seems also to be heavily indebted to Cordovero.

Cordovero's scheme eventually yielded to that of his contemporary (and, it would seem, originally his disciple) Isaac *Luria. But the later Kabbalists tended to see both systems, the Lurianic and the Cordoveran, as complementary. The two systems, say the Kabbalists, are both true but they refer to two different aspects of the divine, to two different 'worlds', as they put it.

Moses Cordovero, *The Palm Tree of Deborah*, trans. Louis Jacobs (London, 1960).

**Corporal Punishment** Flogging as a judicial punishment is mentioned in the book of Deuteronomy (25: 2–3) where it is stated that 'if the guilty person is to be flogged' he must be given forty stripes and no more. Since the verse does not define which type of guilty person is to be flogged, the Rabbinic tradition understands the reference to be to one who has transgressed a negative *precept in which a physical act is involved; eating forbidden food, for example. The forty stripes was understood as the number approaching forty, that is, thirty-nine; a third on the chest and two-thirds on the back. This whole procedure is known as *malkut* ('flogging'). But such flogging could only be administered by an ordained court, and *ordination was limited to courts in the Holy Land. However, as with *capital punishment, what the law took away with one hand it gave with the other. On the basis of the Talmudic statement (*Sanhedrin* 46a) that, where it is required by circumstances, a court can avail itself of extra-legal remedies and can flog offenders, a 'Rabbinic' flogging was introduced, known as *makkat mardut* ('flogging for rebellion'), to be exercised at the discretion of the court, even a non-ordained court.

Consequently, in the Talmudic and post-Talmudic periods, flogging as a punishment was inflicted for various types of offences, among them insulting scholars; wife-beating; adultery; disregarding communal enactments; and, often, as a penance accepted voluntarily by a sinner. It has to be appreciated that corporal punishment and the ban ('*herem') were the only means available to the *community of exercising its authority and preserving its autonomy. Nowadays, judicial flogging and other forms of corporal punishment are totally unknown.

Corporal punishment was also practised in schools, following the biblical injunction: 'Do not withhold discipline from a child; If you beat him with a rod he will not die. Beat him with a rod and you will save him from the grave' (Proverbs 23: 13–14). Fathers would beat their sons and teachers their pupils, often with great severity, in spite of the fact that the Talmud advises that discipline in the school should only be carried out by means of a light strap; a shoelace is the illustration given. The cruelty of schoolteachers, especially the incompetents, became a byword in many communities.

Here, too, times have changed. With few exceptions, the modern educational theory, 'children should be seen and not hurt', is followed and corporal punishment is discouraged, although it would be too much to claim that it is completely unknown.

Nathan Morris, *The Jewish School* (London, 1937), 166–77.

David Menahem Shohet, *The Jewish Court in the Middle Ages* (New York, 1931), 138–142.

**Corpse** A dead body is considered in the Bible to be a source of ritual contamination. Anyone who came into contact with a corpse or a grave in which a corpse lay buried became contaminated and was forbidden to enter the Sanctuary until he had undergone the rites of purification by the ashes of the *red heifer (Numbers 19). A priest, *Kohen, was forbidden to come into contact with a corpse other than of one of his near relatives (Leviticus 21: 1–4). Various conjectures have been made as to why a corpse contaminates. It has been suggested, for example, that the priestly prohibition was a reaction to the preoccupation with death in Egyptian religion, where the priests had an important role to play in escorting the dead to the realm of the gods.

Respect for a corpse is another matter. The Talmud compares a corpse to a Scroll of the Torah, a *Sefer Torah, that has been destroyed; meaning, presumably, that, while the person was alive he carried out the precepts of the Torah with the body, now lifeless, and hence the body, like the scroll, must be buried with reverence. Thus a corpse must not be left unattended before the funeral (see DEATH AND BURIAL) and must be ritually cleansed and dressed in special white shrouds. It is forbidden to enjoy any benefit from a corpse or to make use of a grave or shrouds. The Talmudic saying that worms in the grave are as painful to the dead as a needle piercing living flesh has been interpreted figuratively. It is not the unfeeling corpse that suffers pain but the soul of the dead when it witnesses what is happening to the body it once occupied. Similarly, the saying that when the words of Torah uttered by a scholar while alive are repeated in his name, his lips move in the grave, has also been understood as a poetic way of saying that the scholar's teachings live on after the death of the physical body. Behind all this there appear to be the mixed emotions felt when confronted with a dead body: horror that the soul has fled, reverence for what was the house of the soul. The Talmud speaks of the thoroughly wicked as corpses, bodies without souls.

**Cosmology** Strictly speaking, there has never been in the history of Jewish thought a Jewish cosmology in the sense of a specifically Jewish way of understanding how the universe is constructed. Judging by the classical sources of Judaism, the preoccupation of the Jews was with the God of the cosmos, not with the cosmos itself. Jews simply adopted or accepted the cosmologies of the various civilizations in which they lived. They were interested in natural phenomena but chiefly as pointers to God whose glory fills the universe, as when the Psalmist pronounces: 'The heavens declare the glory of God, and the firmament showeth forth His handiwork' (Psalms 19: 2). The vivid description of the universe and its creatures in Psalm 104 begins: 'O Lord my God, Thou art very great; Thou art clothed with glory and majesty.' It is more correct, therefore, to speak not so much of Jewish cosmology as of cosmologies that have been entertained by Jews.

The cosmological picture in the Bible, for instance, clearly owes much to the ancient Mesopotamian cosmologies, especially the Babylonian. The universe is conceived of in geocentric terms. The earth has the shape of a flat disc, so that if one were able to travel far enough one would eventually arrive at 'the ends of the earth' (Deuteronomy 13: 8; 28: 64; Isaiah 5: 26; Psalms 135: 7). The 'corners' or 'wings' of the earth (Isaiah 11: 12; Ezekiel 7: 2; Job 37: 3) may be a synonym for the 'ends of the earth'. But if the earth is not conceived of as a disc but as a square strip, the 'corners' may be understood literally. The earth rests on pillars (Job 9: 6). Stretched above the earth is the sky, the 'heaven' or the 'firmament', a solid substance (Genesis 1: 6–8) also resting on pillars (Job 26: 11). The sun, moon, and stars are positioned in, or just beneath, the firmament (Genesis 1: 14–17) and they move across it (Psalms 19: 1–7). Beneath the earth is Sheol, the abode of the dead (Numbers 16: 28–34; 1 Samuel 28: 13–15; Isaiah 14: 9–11; Ecclesiastes 9: 10). There are waters above the firmament (Genesis 1: 6–7) as well as beneath it. Some of the waters beneath the firmament were gathered together at the beginning of creation to form the seas (Genesis 1: 9–10) but, in addition, these waters flow

beneath the earth (Exodus 20: 4; Deuteronomy 4: 18; Psalms 24: 2) where they are connected to the waters of Tehom, the great deep (Genesis 1: 2). The Deluge was caused by a tremendous outpouring of the fountains of Tehom as well as by the opening of the windows of heaven (Genesis 7: 11). Above the waters that are above the firmament is the area called 'the heaven of heavens' (Deuteronomy 10: 4; 1 Kings 8: 27). These details are mentioned here to demonstrate the remarkable uniformity in the biblical material produced over a long period, which is only natural as the picture is the usual Mesopotamian one. It is difficult to know to what degree the biblical authors took all this literally, or whether they simply used the standard vocabulary derived from the ancient cosmic myths.

In the Talmudic literature there is a strong attempt to discourage speculation on cosmic origins and on cosmic matters that are beyond human experience, in all probability because of the heretical, especially dualistic, views which could follow from these. The Rabbis quote, with approval, the saying of *Ben Sira: 'Do not pry into things too hard for you or examine what is beyond your reach. Meditate on the commandments you have been given; what the Lord keeps secret is no concern of yours' (Ecclesiastes 3: 21–22). The Mishnah (*Ḥagigah* 2: 1) states: 'Whosoever reflects on four things, it were better for him if he had not come into the world—what is above; what is beneath; what is before; and what is after.' The Jerusalem Talmud, however, comments on this Mishnah that the opinion expressed there is not unanimous and that others hold that it is permitted to 'expound the work of creation'. In any event, there are to be found in the Rabbinic literature discussions on the manner of God's creation and on the nature not only of the terrestrial but also of the celestial realms. The Rabbis are fond of describing the immense size of the universe with the aim of praising God and pointing out Israel's worth in the cosmic scheme. Here, too, it is difficult to know how far these descriptions were taken literally and how far they were purely metaphorical. One Rabbi, for instance, disagrees with his colleagues who hold that the world rests on twelve or on seven pillars, and says that the earth rests on a single pillar the name of which is 'Righteous', for it is said: 'But *Righteous* is the foundation of the world' (Psalms 10: 25). When

Israel is apprehensive that God has forgotten her, He is made to reply (significantly in terms taken from the Roman army):

'My daughter, twelve constellations have I created in the firmament, and for each constellation I have created thirty hosts, and for each host I have created thirty legions, and for each legion I have created thirty cohorts, and for each cohort I have created thirty maniples, and for each maniple I have created thirty camps, and to each camp I have attached three hundred and sixty-five thousands of myriads of stars, corresponding to the days of the solar year, and all of them I have created only for thy sake, and thou sayest, Thou hast forgotten me and forsaken me.'

This is obviously Rabbinic hyperbole and the aim is certainly not to describe the cosmos 'scientifically' but to encourage the Jewish people not to feel cowed into insignificance when reflecting on the vastnesses of the heavens and their own inferior position among the nations (See CHOSEN PEOPLE).

Medieval Jewish cosmology, generally speaking, is the standard Greek cosmology in its Arabic garb. The first four chapters of Maimonides' *Mishneh Torah*, for instance, are devoted to a description of the universe, based on his conviction that *contemplation of the vastness and marvels of God's creation would evoke man's sense of awe and lead him eventually to the love and fear of God. Maimonides' notion of the spheres is the common medieval one. There are in all nine spheres. The nearest to earth is the sphere to which the moon is attached. In ascending order there are then the spheres of Mercury, Venus, the Sun, Mars, Jupiter, and Saturn. Above these is the eighth sphere to which all the other stars are attached and above all is the great ninth sphere which revolves each day from east to west; through its revolutions the other spheres revolve. The spheres are translucent so that when seen from the earth all the stars appear to be attached to a single sphere. Some of the stars seen in the sky are smaller than the earth, some of them larger. The earth is forty times larger than the moon but the sun is 170 times larger than the earth. The smallest of the stars is Mercury and none of the stars is larger than the sun. The stars and spheres are intelligent beings who offer praises to their Creator—Shakespeare's 'music of the spheres'. All sublunar beings are composed of the four elements: fire, air, water, and earth.

It can be seen to what extent Jewish teachers were dependent for their cosmological views on the particular cosmologies dominant in their age, whether Babylonian, Greek, or Arabic. There has never been an official Jewish cosmology dictated by Jewish Orthodox belief. Cosmology was the domain of science, although its study had the profoundest religious implications. When the ancient Ptolemaic system was compelled to yield to the Copernican, only a few Jewish die-hards persisted in their defence of the older view on the grounds, also behind the Church's opposition to Galileo, that revealed religion depended on a geocentric universe. When the plain meaning of the Bible seemed to contradict the findings of the astronomers, the biblical accounts were usually interpreted in non-literal fashion so as to be in conformity with the scientific picture (but see EVOLUTION). The same applies to modern cosmological views such as the Big Bang theory. Jews have considered themselves free to accept or reject cosmological theories without seeing any of these matters as belonging to the area of religious faith. Cosmology has on the whole been viewed by Jews as a religiously neutral subject.

Louis Jacobs, 'Jewish Cosmology', in Carmen Blacker and Michael Lowe (eds.), *Ancient Cosmologies* (London, 1975), 66–86.

**Covenant** A pact or contract of mutual obligation, especially between God and Israel; Heb. *berit*. In the Bible (Genesis 9: 8–17) God, after the Deluge, establishes His covenant with Noah and his offspring and with every living thing upon the earth, promising never again to bring a flood to destroy the earth. The *rainbow in the sky is made to be the sign of this covenant. To this universal covenant is added the special covenant made with *Abraham (Genesis 15: 7–21). Since this was established, as the passage states, by Abraham passing through the pieces of animals that had been cut up, the term for it, in the Jewish tradition, is 'the covenant between the pieces'. *Circumcision, known particularly as the *berit*, is made the sign of the further covenant with Abraham (Genesis 17). A further covenant is made with Israel at *Sinai (Exodus 19: 5; 24: 1–8), in which God promises that Israel will be His special people if they will keep His commandments. At the entrance to the Promised Land, Moses repeats that God has made a covenant with the people and all their offspring (Deuteronomy 29: 9–14). Modern scholarship has succeeded in drawing parallels between God's covenant with Israel and the Hittite procedures in which a vassal king promises to be faithful to his overlord in return for the latter's protection. The parallel is too close to be accidental but the biblical covenant is unique in that it is between the God of all the earth and a particular people.

A number of Christian biblical scholars have developed a 'covenant theology' in which the previous covenants lead up to the 'New Covenant', the 'New Testament'. Obviously, Jews accept neither this reading nor the New Testament itself. But, apart from this, while the covenants of 'the pieces' and of circumcision and that made at Sinai are highly significant in Jewish religious thought, the idea of a particular covenant theology does not loom at all large in traditional Jewish sources, being discussed only incidentally in the context of the obligation of the *Chosen People to keep the Torah.

M. Weinfeld, 'Covenant', in C. Roth and G. Wigoder (eds.), *Encyclopedia Judaica*, v. 1012–22.

**Creation** That God is the Creator of the universe is accepted as a basic belief in the Jewish religion but the precise meaning of this doctrine has been disputed. The discussion revolves around the meaning of the Hebrew word *bara* in the very first verse of the Bible (Genesis 1: 1): 'In the beginning God created [*bara*] the heaven and the earth.' While this word is used throughout the Bible for God's creative activity alone (the word is never used of human creativity), it does not necessarily imply that He created the world out of nothing (*creatio ex nihilo*). Abraham *Ibn Ezra, in his commentary to the Pentateuch, points to the use of this word, in the same narrative, of the creation of man (verse 27), even though man is said, in Genesis 2: 7, to have been formed from the dust of the earth. The earliest reference to *creatio ex nihilo* is found in a book of the late second–early first century CE, 2 Maccabees (7: 28). But, contrary to this view, the Wisdom of Solomon (11: 17) speaks of God creating the universe 'out of formless matter'. *Gersonides (*Wars of the Lord*, 6) similarly accepts the notion, going back to Plato, that God created the universe out of a 'hylic substance'. *Maimonides (*Guide of the Perplexed*, 2. 13–21) even discusses whether the Aristotelian view that matter is eternal can be accommodated

within the biblical account. For Aristotle, the relationship of God to the creation can be compared to a tree and its shadow, where, although the shadow is of the tree and could not exist were it not for the tree, the shadow is always present together with the tree. Maimonides, in a remarkable passage, states that if the Aristotelian argument had proved to be conclusive, he would have accepted the argument and interpreted the Bible accordingly. But since, on grounds of reason, Aristotle is not convincing, Maimonides prefers to accept the doctrine of creation out of nothing, which he considers to be the Jewish traditional view. For all the variety of opinions on this subject, the standard view did eventually become that of creation out of nothing. In reply to the stock objection that it is impossible for something to come out of nothing, the tradition generally replies that God cannot be bound by what seems possible or impossible to the human mind.

The Kabbalah has its own understanding of the doctrine of *creatio ex nihilo*, of 'that which is' from 'that which is not'. This refers, according to the Kabbalah, to the emergence of the divine creative powers, the *Sefirot, 'that which is', by a process of emanation, from 'that which is not', namely, the *En Sof, the Limitless Ground of being, called 'that which is not' because it is beyond all human comprehension and has no existence in the human mind.

Thus, while the doctrine of God as the Creator is an essential belief in Judaism, there is no official doctrine regarding the manner of creation. From this point of view, modern scientific theories about the origin of the universe, such as the Big Bang theory, are irrelevant to Jewish belief (see COSMOLOGY).

*The Significance of the Doctrine of Creation*

The question of why God created the universe receives various answers. The conventional view is that God created the universe in His goodness since it is in the nature of the All-good to have recipients for His bounty, even though there would obviously be no deprivation if the creatures who now enjoy the good did not exist that they should suffer deprivation. On this view, God is compelled, as it were, by His own essential being to produce creatures on whom He can bestow His goodness. Another view is that God created the universe for His glory to become manifest in it, a view that fails to explain why the glory requires to become manifest. Maimonides (*Guide of the Perplexed*, 3. 13) believes that every explanation, other than that it is simply God's will, is question-begging. Whatever answer is given, the question 'why' can be posed, and ultimately it is necessary to fall back on the idea that it is God's inscrutable will. In obedience to this view that everything is the result of God's will, Maimonides cannot accept the opinion (put forward by *Saadia-Gaon, *Beliefs and Opinions*, i., 4) that man is the ultimate purpose of creation. To be sure, man has a highly significant role to play in God's world, but it is clearly God's will that there be other creatures in the universe and these do not enjoy existence merely in order to benefit human beings. It is certainly hard to believe that the animal creation, in all its rich and marvellous variety, is intended solely for the purpose of affording man delight, or other benefits, or even for invoking his sense of wonder.

Yet there is a special significance for man in the doctrine that God is the Creator of the universe. In many a Jewish teaching the idea is prominent that, since God is the Creator, the whole universe, deriving from Him, is subordinate to Him. The gifts He has bestowed upon man, the skills by means of which man is allowed to adapt the universe to his own purposes, are given to him in a stewardship in which he is obliged to render a full account of what he does with God's world. Some see this idea behind the institution of the *Sabbath, the day when God is hailed as the Creator. By refraining on the Sabbath from all creative activity, the Jew demonstrates that he uses his skills not as of right but by permission of the Creator, with the corollary that he uses them for the benefit of mankind, not to its detriment. The whole notion of a planning God, as described in the creation narrative at the beginning of the book of Genesis, is said to be for the purpose that man should see the world as a purposive and highly organized system to which he is expected to contribute as a co-worker with God. God does not need to plan a universe emerging by stages, but man requires it in order to impress on him the importance of his role. As Ethics of the Fathers (5. 1) puts it: 'The world was created by ten sayings. But could it not have been created by a single saying? It was to punish the wicked who destroy a world that was created by ten sayings, and to

grant reward to the righteous who sustain a world that was created by ten sayings.'

Louis Jacobs, *A Jewish Theology* (London, 1973), 93–113.

**Cremation** The disposal of a corpse by reducing it to ashes. While cremation was known in the ancient world, the universal Jewish practice, until the late nineteenth century when cremation became popular, was to bury the dead in the ground or in mausoleums (see DEATH AND BURIAL). In modern times, Reform Judaism has little objection to cremation, although it normally favours burial. Orthodox and, to a very large extent, Conservative Judaism frown severely on cremation. Orthodox Rabbis have been especially virulent in their opposition to the practice.

The following are the objections to cremation, some more convincing than others:

1. Cremation was a pagan practice in ancient times and is consequently associated with the idolatrous beliefs against which Judaism set its face. Even an otherwise innocent practice can become tainted by association.

2. The Talmud (*Sanhedrin* 46b), after a lengthy discussion, comes to the conclusion that it is a religious obligation to bury the dead and when cremation takes place this obligation has not been fulfilled.

3. The Talmud (*Ḥullin* 11b) states that it is forbidden to mutilate a corpse. When a dead body is buried, decomposition takes place as a natural process, whereas in cremation the human remains are intentionally destroyed. A comparison is made with a Scroll of the Torah, a *Sefer Torah. Even when this is no longer usable, because the letters have faded, it is reverentially buried in the soil rather than destroyed directly. The analogy is far from exact since the Scroll is a sacred object. Nevertheless, the point of the analogy is that there should be reverential disposal of what was once a human being, created in God's image, who carried out the precepts of the Torah while he was alive.

4. A Talmudic legend (*Gittin* 56b) has it that the emperor Titus ordered that his corpse be cremated and his ashes scattered in order to escape God's judgement. It is therefore argued that anyone who wishes his body to be cremated thereby demonstrates a lack of belief in the *resurrection of the dead and in God's

judgement. This is the weakest of the arguments against cremation. For one thing, many believing Jews do not understand the doctrine of the resurrection in a crude literal sense, and even those who do can hardly believe that it is beyond God's power to reconstitute a body that has been cremated, just as it is in His power to reconstitute a body that has become decomposed in the grave. The notion that there is a tiny bone in the human body which does not suffer decay in the grave and from which the resurrected body is reconstituted (making cremation forbidden because this bone is destroyed by fire) belongs more to folklore than to Jewish doctrine. The corpses of Jews who perished in the gas chambers were burnt in crematoria. Surely these Jews are not denied their place in the Hereafter because they were not buried.

5. The strongest argument against cremation is on grounds of tradition, that it is wrong to depart from the custom of burial practised by Jews for thousands of years.

The argument of the cremationists that burial takes up too much space which is better used for the living does not have much to commend it. The amount of land involved is very small, and graveyards are usually situated in the countryside. In any event, crematoria usually have spacious gardens attached to them which also take up space. Another argument is that the quick disposal by cremation, which the bereaved family do not witness, spares their feelings. Even if this were true, a dubious proposition, Judaism does not encourage any refusal to acknowledge either the facts of life or the facts of death. In more recent years, cremation has become far from popular among ecologists concerned that the atmosphere should not be polluted.

Some Orthodox Rabbis, in their opposition to cremation, do not permit burial in the Jewish cemetery of the ashes of one who has been cremated, but others do allow it. It has long been the practice in the Orthodox community of Great Britain to permit this practice provided the ashes are placed in a normal coffin.

Louis Jacobs, *What Does Judaism Say About . . . ?* (Jerusalem, 1973), 103–4.

**Crescas, Hasdai** Spanish Jewish philosopher (d. 1412). Crescas, communal leader of the Aragonian Jewish communities, was one of the most influential personalities of Spanish Jewry,

in particular in his efforts to prevent Jews from being lured away from Judaism in the wake of Christian persecution. His own son was killed during a persecution in 1391. Not surprisingly, therefore, Crescas devoted a good deal of his literary endeavours both to defending Judaism against theological attacks by Christians and to offering a critique of the popular philosophical trends. His work in Spanish (later translated into Hebrew), *Refutation of the Principal Dogmas of the Christian Religion*, came to occupy a prominent place in the literature of Jewish–Christian polemics.

Crescas's major work, on which his fame as a philosopher rests, is his *Or Adonai* ('Light of the Lord') in which he takes issue with the dominant Aristotelian philosophy and Maimonides' reliance on this for the interpretation of Judaism. Among other topics discussed in the book is the question of *dogma in Judaism, where Crescas has a different arrangement from that of Maimonides. In this Crescas was followed by his disciple Joseph *Albo.

Crescas's views on the question of human freedom are startling for a Jewish thinker. The medieval philosophers grappled with the problem of reconciling divine foreknowledge with human *free will. Crescas, anxious not to qualify in any way the doctrine of divine foreknowledge, puts forward a deterministic view. Man is not fated to act in the way he does. He does have freedom of choice. But the exercise of this freedom of choice is determined by God's foreknowledge. God knows how man will choose. Man's choice is guided by the promise of reward for doing good and the threat of punishment for doing evil. Thus, what is determined by God's foreknowledge is the whole process by means of which man arrives at his particular choices. There would be no justice in God granting reward to the righteous and punishing the wicked if rewards were in the nature of gifts for virtuous living and punishments were deprivations for evil living. Rewards and punishments are only the means by which a man is spurred on to choose to lead a virtuous life and to reject a vicious life, and they operate as cause and effect. Crescas is not unaware of the difficulties in his position, a very unusual one in Jewish thought, which attaches the greatest significance to human free will. If all is determined by God's foreknowledge, why does Jewish law make a distinction between sins committed voluntarily and sins committed under compulsion, since the 'voluntary' acts are also done under the compulsion of the divine foreknowledge? Crescas replies that there would be no point in rewarding or punishing acts done under compulsion since, as he has argued, the whole purpose of rewards and punishments is to influence man's choice. In that case, why is a man punished for entertaining false beliefs, since he is compelled to hold these beliefs by the arguments which have led up to them? Crescas replies that punishment in this area is not for entertaining the false beliefs but for lack of care in accepting the faulty arguments on which the beliefs are based.

Crescas differs from Maimonides on the question of the divine attributes. According to Maimonides' doctrine of negative attributes, to say that God is good or wise does not mean that His nature can be described in any positive way. The attributes of God found in Scripture are to be understood only as negating their opposite. When it is said that God is good, this refers solely to His actions, which, if performed by a human being, would be said to be good. When it is said that God is wise, the meaning is that He is not ignorant. Crescas disagrees. For Crescas, the divine attributes are to be understood in a positive sense. God really is good and wise. Such an idea does not compromise the doctrine of the divine unity, since multiple qualities do not imply a compound subject if these qualities are interconnected.

Julius Guttmann, *Philosophies of Judaism* (Philadelphia, 1964), 224–41.

Isaac Husik, *A History of Mediaeval Jewish Philosophy* (New York, 1940), 388–405.

**Cripples** Priests afflicted with physical deformities were disbarred from officiating in the Temple: 'Whoever hath a blemish, he shall not approach: a blind man, or a lame, or he that hath any thing maimed, or any thing too long, or a man that is broken-footed, or broken handed, or crook-backed, or a dwarf, or that hath his eye overspread, or is scabbed, or scurvey, or hath his stones crushed' (Leviticus 21: 18–20). The usual explanation of this disbarment is that the dignity of the sacred spot is impaired if those who officiate there are deformed. Whether the disqualification applies to a *Cantor, who leads the prayers in the *synagogue, was discussed in the Middle Ages. The famed German authority, Rabbi Meir of Rothenburg (d. 1293), was asked whether a cripple can act as the

Reader in the synagogue. The Rabbi replies that no conclusions can be drawn from the disqualification of a cripple from service in the Temple. Apart from in the Temple, he observes, God wishes particularly to be served by the physically deformed. A human king uses only whole vessels whereas the King of kings prefers to use broken vessels. The Rabbi quotes in this connection the verse: 'A broken and contrite heart, O God, Thou wilt not despise' (Psalms 51: 19). The man broken in body has the broken heart that God wants. Against Rabbi Meir's ruling, later authorities quote a passage in the Zohar (iii. 90b–91a) in which it is stated that the spirit of holiness cannot rest on a deformed person, a statement coming close to the Latin tag: *mens sana in corpore sano*. In this passage the Zohar explicitly draws a distinction between the broken heart, admired by the Psalmist, and a broken body.

Rabbi Hayyim Eleazar Shapira of Munkacs (d. 1937) is astonished at the Zoharic statement; some of the greatest saints were physically deformed, and he believes that the Zohar cannot possibly be taken literally. In practice some communities did insist that the Reader be whole in body, while others preferred to follow the ruling of Rabbi Meir of Rothenburg.

Interesting in this connection is the Talmudic passage (tractate *Berakhot* 58b) that if one sees a negro or a redskin or a dwarf one recites the benediction: 'Blessed . . . who varies the form of His creatures.' But on beholding a person with an amputated limb, or blind, or lame, one recites: 'Blessed be the true Judge.' Implied in the subsequent Talmudic discussion on these two different types of benediction is that for a person to be born different from others in the colour of his skin and so forth is not a calamity; that is how God, who varies the form of His creatures, has made him. On the other hand, the disability suffered by some is a calamity but not one which should lead to a denial of God's justice, hence the benediction: 'Blessed be the true Judge.' In a number of Midrashic passages it is stated that in the Hereafter all cripples will be made whole again.

**Cruelty** *Compassion is high among Jewish virtues while its opposite, cruelty, is especially prominent among the vices. *Amalek was later understood to be the symbol of wanton cruelty. To utter cruel and wounding words is a serious offence; it is wrong to taunt, for instance, a reformed criminal with his past misdeeds or to suggest to one who suffers that it is because he has sinned, or to call a man a bastard or other insulting names. The Italian scholar Samuel David *Luzzatto understands the Hebrew word for the cruel, *akhzar*, as a compound standing for *akh*, 'only' and *zar*, 'stranger'. Only a stranger to others, only one who lacks the imagination and fellow feeling to put himself into another's place, will behave cruelly to others.

**Customs** Jewish rituals, ceremonies, and practices adopted by particular Jewish communities or by the Jewish people as a whole. Originally, the term *minhag*, 'custom' (from a root meaning 'to follow', i.e. that which people follow) referred to a practice about which the law was unclear, perhaps where certain details were the subject of debate by the legal authorities. When it was observed that the people followed a particular interpretation or ruling, the practice of the people was decisive and this practice acquired full legal status. As the Talmud (*Berakhot* 45a) puts it: 'Go out and see what people actually do.' But in the Middle Ages, especially in Germany, the people followed certain practices for which there was no support in the law; sometimes, such practices were adopted from the customs of the peoples among whom Jews resided. At times, the Rabbinic authorities were suspicious of this kind of folk-custom, but when it became too deeply rooted to be eradicated, even this type of custom was also incorporated into Jewish law, on the principle, evidently, of 'if you can't beat them join them', and a new Jewish interpretation was given to the custom so as to render it innocuous. A good example is the practice of breaking a glass at a marriage ceremony. It seems that this practice took root among German Jews, the *Ashkenazim, because they were enamoured of a similar practice they observed among German folk which was intended to trick the *demons into believing that a catastrophe rather than a celebration was taking place; the demons would then leave the couple alone and do them no harm. The practice was eventually accepted by the Rabbis; the Jewish interpretation given to it was that it reminded the couple, on their happy day, that they should reflect on the destruction of the Temple, in other words, they should be aware, even on this day, of the sufferings of their people and not selfishly ignore them.

There was constant tension over the adoption of new customs. On the one hand, there was the need to cater to the masses and keep them faithful, but on the other hand, the pagan origin of some customs was too blatant to be ignored. This tension resulted in two contradictory sayings. One saying has it that the custom of Israel is Torah, that is, custom has the binding force of Jewish law. Against this is the saying that when the letters of *minhag* are transposed they form the word *gehinom*, Gehinna ('hell'). But, generally speaking, more of the folk-customs were accepted than were rejected. Many of these eventually found their way into the *Shulḥan Arukh*, the standard Code of Jewish law, through the glosses of *Isserles, the great recorder of Ashkenazi customs. In addition to the differences in matters of law proper between the Ashkenazim and the *Sephardim, different folk-customs developed in the two communities so that there are Sephardi *minhagim* (plural of *minhag*) and Ashkenazi *minhagim*, in matters of prayer and its melodies, for example, and here the ruling is that the members of a particular community must follow that community's custom and not adopt the different customs of another community. In *Hasidism customs took root in accordance with the specific ideas of the movement. Even in Hasidism, each master, the *Zaddik, tended to have his own custom with regard to the practice of certain rituals and this became the norm for his faithful followers. The Kabbalists developed their own customs through which specific Kabbalistic ideas were given expression.

Considerations of space do not allow anything like a complete survey of the manifold Jewish customs. Some of these are, in any event, referred to in this book under specific entries such as those on the *Sabbath and *death and burial. The following is no more than a sampling of customs for the purpose of elucidating the concept.

On the eve of *Yom Kippur, Ashkenazi Jews perform the custom of *Kapparot, 'atonements'. The procedure is to take a cockerel, and wave it round the head while saying: 'May this cockerel, which is to be killed, be an atonement for my sins.' The cockerel is then killed and cooked and some, at least, of its meat is given to the poor. Rabbi Joseph *Karo records in the *Shulḥan Arukh* (*Oraḥ Ḥayyim*, 605) that this is a superstitious practice and should be abolished, but in Isserles' gloss the practice is not only accepted but all its details are recorded as if it were a matter of law rather than custom.

When the book of *Esther is read on the festival of *Purim it is the custom, Karo states in the *Shulḥan Arukh* (*Oraḥ Ḥayyim*, 690. 17) to fold the megillah, the Scroll of the book, as if it were a letter, since the book refers to the 'letter' Esther wrote to describe the events which led to the delivery of the Jews from the plot of Haman to destroy them. Isserles, in his gloss, refers to other customs in connection with the reading of the megillah, including the practice of the children to 'boo', bang stones together, or wave rattles whenever Haman's name is mentioned. Some evidently objected to the practice as indecorous but Isserles typically observes: 'No custom should be abolished or laughed at for it was not established without purpose.' Interestingly enough, this observation that the custom should not be scoffed at is made by Karo in his work on the Tur, though Karo does not record the practice in the *Shulḥan Arukh*.

These last two customs were the subject of debate, as were many others. Some folk-customs, however, became the norm in the majority of the Jewish communities such as the custom of bride and bridegroom fasting on their wedding day. When a Jewish couple marry and begin a new life together their sins are forgiven so that the day is, for them, a kind of *Yom Kippur. Another universally adopted custom is to wash the hands ritually when rising from sleep, by pouring water over them from a glass. Two reasons are given. One is that just as the priests in Temple times washed their hands from the hand-basin before beginning their service, so, too, a Jew should wash his hands as he rises to serve his Maker. The other reason is that a 'spirit of impurity' rests on the finger-nails during sleep and this has to be removed by the pouring of pure water over the fingers. The ritual is, in fact, called in Yiddish *neggel wasser*, 'water of the nails'. This too is evidently an attempt at providing a more respectable reason for a custom that probably had its origin in superstition, although here the 'rational' and the 'superstitious' reasons appear side by side.

It is obvious that in many of the instances cited the 'reasons' are given *post factum*. It is not a case of the customs being based on the reasons but rather of reasons being given for customs that were, in any event, deeply rooted in the practices of the people. Reform Judaism tends to ignore customs which clearly have their origin in superstition. But Orthodox Judaism, even when it acknowledges the base origin of some of the customs, holds that these have become part of the Jewish lifestyle and act as a bulwark against assimilation.

Abraham Chill, *The Minhagim: The Customs and Ceremonies of Judaism, their Origins and Rationale* (New York, 1979).

William Rosenau, *Jewish Ceremonial Institutions and Customs* (New York, 1929).

**Cycles** The notion, found in early Kabbalistic works, that the history of the world proceeds in series of thousands of years. The doctrine runs that our present world will last for 6,000 years after which it will cease to exist during a 'Sabbath' of 1,000 years. After this, the cycle will begin afresh and this process will continue until 49,000 years have elapsed, after which there will be a great Jubilee of 1,000 years. In some versions, after the great Jubilee, the whole process will be set in motion once again. The startling feature of the doctrine is the further affirmation that there is a different Torah for each cycle of 6,000 years. For instance, our present cycle is one in which the Torah of judgement prevails, so that in this Torah there are more negative precepts than positive. But in the next cycle the Torah of love will prevail and there will then be more positive than negative precepts. *Luria and the later Kabbalists rejected the whole notion as challenging the doctrine of the immutability of the Torah.

The notion of cycles virtually disappeared from Jewish thought in later years, apart from the attempt by Israel Lipschutz (1782–1860), in his famous commentary to the Mishnah, *Tiferet Yisrael* (end of vol. v), to invoke the theory to explain away the evidence that man existed on earth long before the 5,600 years of the Jewish tradition based on the biblical record. The skeletons uncovered, argued Lipschutz, were those of men from an earlier cycle. This essay caused Lipschutz's commentary, for all its brilliance, to be treated with reserve by some of the Orthodox.

# D

**Damages** Compensation imposed by the court for injury to a person or to property. Included in the command to *love the neighbour is the obligation not to harm a neighbour or a neighbour's property. This is taken for granted in all the sources of Jewish law, which discuss mainly the nature of the compensation to be imposed by the court in particular cases. (The main Talmudic source in this connection is the first six chapters of tractate *Bava Kama*.)

For injury to property the compensation is assessed in accordance with the actual damage done and this applies not only to where a man is himself responsible for the damage done, for example where *A* himself destroys or impairs *B*'s property, but also to where *A* fails to look after his property, say, his animal, so that it causes harm to *B* or to *B*'s property. Where *A* himself injures *B* by a direct assault, there is a more complex type of compensation. Here, in addition to *A* having to compensate *B* for the damage itself, he is obliged to pay the doctor's fees for *B*'s healing; compensation for the pain *B* has suffered; compensation for the amount *B* would have earned while he is incapacitated; and compensation for the embarrassment *B* has suffered. The elaborate means of assessing these various forms of compensation is described in the sources.

Suppose, for example, that *A* assaulted *B* and broke his arm. *B*, prior to the assault, earned his living in a manner that required him to use both his arms. *B* can now no longer be employed in his former job but he is still capable of obtaining a less remunerative job, that of night-watchman, for example. During *B*'s recovery from the attack, even this form of employment is not available to him and *A* will have to pay the doctor to heal him; in addition, *B* will have suffered the indignity of being the victim of an attack. Thus *A* is obliged to pay *B* for the initial loss of his working arm; for the time he loses in being unable to work at any job

during his incapacity; for the healer's fees; for the pain he suffered through the breaking of his arm; and for the embarrassment he suffered from the attack itself. But if *A*'s dog caused *B* to lose the use of his arm, *A* is only obliged to compensate *B* for his incapacity to work in the job he had before the attack. In this instance of damage by *A*'s property (his dog), *A* is not obliged to pay for the loss of *B*'s secondary earnings (as a night-watchman). Nor is he obliged to compensate *B* for the pain and embarrassment *B* has suffered and *B* cannot claim compensation from *A* for his doctor's fees.

The full assessment of damages where *A* himself attacks *B* was, at first, confined to the authorities in Palestine (see ORDINATION). But courts outside the Holy Land did use their discretion in going beyond the legal norms where necessary. For instance, in cases of serious embarrassment, the courts in medieval Spain did impose a fine on the perpetrator.

All this refers to legal actions. The Talmud expresses admiration for saintly folk who take the utmost care not to injure others or damage the property of others. The '*saints of old', it was said, would bury any pieces of broken glass they had in their possession so deep in the ground that it would be impossible for the plough to bring them up again to cause damage.

**Dance** Dancing as a form of religious celebration is referred to in a number of biblical passages. After the deliverance at the Red Sea, Miriam leads the women in a dance of glory (Exodus 15: 20). The fact that, in the narrative of the golden calf, the people are said to have danced (Exodus 32: 19) demonstrates that dancing was a customary form of celebration in an idolatrous context, as does the dancing of the priests of Baal when challenged by *Elijah (1 Kings 18: 26). When the *Ark was returned to the city of David, the king 'whirled with all his might before the Lord' (2 Samuel 6: 14). In the light of this it is surprising that, so far as we can tell from the sources, biblical and Talmudic, religious dancing, unlike the playing of musical instruments by the *Levites, had no part in the services in the *Temple, probably because of the idolatrous associations. A vestige of the ancient practice was, however, preserved in the *Water-Drawing Ceremony on the festival of *Tabernacles, when, the Mishnah (*Sukkah* 5: 4) states, 'Men of piety and good works used to dance before them with burning torches in their hands, singing songs and praises.'

Another vestige of ancient practices is contained in the statement of the Mishnah (*Taanit* 4: 8) that in Temple times, on two occasions of the year (one of these being *Yom Kippur!), the daughters of Jerusalem used to dance in the vineyards and themselves propose marriage instead of waiting for a proposal to be made to them. The association of the dance with marriages is also found in the Talmudic accounts of 'dancing before the bride', when the bride's praises were sung. The Talmud (*Ketubot* 17a) tells of saintly Rabbis who used to dance before the bride, one of them going so far as to take the bride on his shoulder while he danced. When his disciples asked this Rabbi if they were allowed to do likewise, he replied that they might only do so if the bride affected the male dancer no more than would a beam of wood on his shoulder, that is, if there were not the slightest risk of sexual arousal. Dancing at weddings became an important part of the celebrations. The busybody who is always poking his nose into other people's affairs is described in Yiddish as one who dances at every wedding (i.e. whether he is invited or not).

Dancing plays no part in the service in the *synagogue, except for the late custom of dancing with the Scrolls of the Torah on the festival of Rejoicing in the Law (*Simhat Torah). This practice is now well-nigh universal, although in some westernized congregations the dance with the Torah is considered to be indecorous and 'foreign' to the Western society to which they belong and which, no doubt, has an influence on their conduct even during worship.

*Mixed Dancing*

Mixed dancing was severely frowned upon by the Rabbis. The Rabbinic interpretation of the verse: 'Hand to hand shall not go unpunished' (Psalms 11: 21) was to prohibit a man and woman not married to one another to hug or kiss, and 'hugging' was held to apply to any touching of hands or other parts of the body; this was quite apart from the conviction that mixed dancing leads inevitably to lewd conduct. At weddings the men danced while the women looked on. The sole exception was the practice of some saintly men (following the Talmudic precedent) to dance with the bride but, even here, there was no actual touching. The bride would hold a handkerchief at one end while the man held the other end without ever actually touching the bride herself. In many communities, especially among the Hasidim, this practice continues to the present day. In the Kabbalistic teaching, to dance with the bride was to dance with the *Shekhinah, of whom the bride is the representative on earth. Many medieval Jewish communities had a special 'dancing-hall' (*Tanzhaus*), chiefly for use when marriages were celebrated, but voices were sometimes raised against the dancing-house because of the mixed dancing which often took place there. Rabbi Jonathan *Eybeschitz writes that he was once asked by a bishop of the Church why Jews object to mixed dancing, since the verse says: 'Then shall the virgin rejoice in the dance, and the young men and the old together' (Jeremiah 31: 13). The Rabbi replied that, on the contrary, the verse implies that there will no mixed dancing, since the virgin is said to dance apart from the youth and old men who dance together. The prohibition of mixed dancing is still applied rigorously by most Orthodox Jews, although a few see no harm in the practice nowadays, evidently because such a widely accepted form of social behaviour in the West hardly involves the kind of embrace forbidden because it is the prelude to sexual intercourse.

*Hasidic Dancing*

In *Hasidism the ancient religious dance comes to its own again. The dance as a form of worship occupies a prominent role in the movement whose favourite text in this connection is: 'All my bones shall say, Lord, who is like unto Thee?' (Psalms 35: 10). The Hasidim say that in the dance one foot at least is nearer to heaven than to earth. The usual form of the Hasidic dance is in a circle, with the hands of each Hasid on the shoulders of his neighbour. In the circle there is no beginning and end, no higher and lower, so that the dance expresses that all are equal members of the fraternity. The staid opponents of Hasidism, the *Mitnaggedim, scorned Hasidic dancing as a wild excess unknown in Jewish tradition. The followers of the Hasidic masters Abraham of Kalisk and Hayyim Haikel of Amdur, two disciples of the the great Hasidic leader, *Dov Baer of Mezhirech, used to turn somersaults during their prayers, though their master strongly disapproved of this corybantic behaviour. It is remarkable that, at approximately the same time, the Shakers sect emerged in Manchester. The Shakers practised a rolling exercise which consisted of doubling the head and feet together, and rolling over like a hoop. Despite the resemblance, there was, naturally, no contact whatsoever between the Hasidim and the Christian sect. When the Hasidim of Hayyim Haikel turned their somersaults, they would say: 'For the sake of God and for the sake of the master', that is, in obedience to the Hasidic doctrine of the *annihilation of selfhood. The self was overturned, so to speak, seeking nothing for itself and desiring only the glory of God. As part of the process, the Hasid would deliver himself up completely to the master through whose prayers he would be led to God. In a defence of the practice of somersaults the Hasidim who believed in them would declare: 'When a man is afflicted with pride he must overturn himself.'

Israel Abrahams, *Jewish Life in the Middle Ages* (London, 1932); see index: 'Dance'. Louis Jacobs, *Hasidic Prayer* (London, 1972), 56–9.

**Daniel**   The biblical hero, living in the sixth century BCE in Babylon, where his people had been exiled, and whose story is told in the book of Daniel. The first six chapters of the book of Daniel tell of how Daniel and his companions, Hananiah, Mishael, and Azariah, were faithful to their religion despite the allurements and threats they were offered to forsake it. The second part of the book contains the visions of the future seen by Daniel, and their interpretation. Part of the book is in Hebrew but most of it is in *Aramaic. Modern scholarship, on philological and other grounds, does not accept the traditional view that Daniel himself was the author of the book but holds that, while early material was undoubtedly incorporated into the book, the second part of it was compiled by an author who lived during the time when the *Maccabees fought the anti-Jewish decrees of the Syrian ruler Antiochus Epiphanes in the second century BCE. On this now generally

accepted view, the last vision of Daniel hints at the reign of Antiochus as it does at a *resurrection of the dead limited to the saints, the earliest reference to the resurrection in Jewish writings; and all for the purpose of encouraging the Jews of that time to remain steadfast in their loyalty to their religion.

The stories in the book of Daniel are among the best known in the Bible: the three young men cast into the fiery furnace for refusing to bow to the image of the king but emerging unscathed (ch. 3); King Belshazzar and the writing on the wall which only Daniel can interpret (ch. 5); and Daniel in the lion's den (ch. 6).

The visions of Daniel were believed to contain hints of the time when the *Messiah will come but generally the Rabbis discouraged attempts to discover from the book the time of the advent of the Messiah, since it might lead to loss of faith if the date said to be predicted came and went without the anticipated event happening.

In the Rabbinic tradition Daniel did not possess the higher degree of *inspiration known as *prophecy, but only the lower degree known as the *Holy Spirit, which is why the book of Daniel belongs in the third section of the Hebrew *Bible, the *Hagiographa, rather than in the second section, the Prophets.

Judah J. Slotki, *Daniel Ezra and Nehemiah* (Soncino Bible Series, London, 1953).

**David**   The second king of Israel (tenth century BCE) whose story is told in the biblical book of *Samuel and whose descendants reigned successively for the four centuries until the Babylonian exile. At the end of the book of *Ruth, David's ancestry is traced back to this Moabite heroine. The narrative in the book of Samuel tells how the prophet Samuel was ordered by God to anoint David as king after the first king, Saul, had been rejected by God. David, in his youth, defeated the giant Goliath in a battle against the Philistines and eventually he was given the hand of Saul's daughter. In a different version in the book of Samuel, David came to Saul's attention because of his prowess as a musician in dispelling Saul's melancholy. David became the friend of Jonathan, Saul's son and heir, but this caused Saul to be jealous of David, who had to flee for his life and remained a fugitive until the death of Saul and Jonathan in battle. David first became king over

Judah and then king over all Israel and he reigned for forty years. David resolved to build a *Temple in Jerusalem, the 'City of David', but, as a man of war, he was told by the prophet Nathan that he could not be the builder of the Temple (1 Chronicles 22: 8). The Temple was built by David's son and successor, King *Solomon. David was attracted to Bathsheba, wife of Uriah, and he ordered Uriah to be sent to the battle-front where he was killed. For this Nathan, in the famous parable of the poor man and his ewe lamb, caused David to pronounce sentence of death upon himself (2 Samuel 12).

These are the bare bones of the biblical narratives about the life of David. The question posed in modern scholarship is: what proportion of all these sometimes contradictory stories are historical since, outside the Bible, there are no references anywhere to David? It has proved impossible to disentangle fact from legend in sources produced over a long period of time, although hardly any scholars go so far as to suggest that David is a purely legendary figure. With regard to the book of *Psalms, for instance, attributed to David, the 'sweet singer in Israel', there has long been a tendency to reject the previously held view that David did not compose any of the Psalms, all of which were attributed to him only at a much later date. It is now acknowledged that while many of the Psalms are undoubtedly much later than David, there is no reason for denying that the core of the book originated from David himself. In any event, it is not the historical David that is important for the Jewish religion, but the David of tradition, David as the prototype of the saintly psalmist who pours out his heart in supplication to God on his own behalf but, especially, on behalf of his people. In this respect, David is contrasted with Moses, the one the graceful singer of God's praises, the other the stern lawgiver. One Rabbi in the Midrash observes that the world was created only for the sake of Moses, while another Rabbi states that it was created, for the sake of David, thus giving expression to the perennial conflict in Judaism between the rival claims of law and piety to be the supreme value.

### David in the Jewish Tradition

In the Jewish tradition, God's promise to David that his kingdom will endure for ever means that the future *Messiah will be a scion of David. Even in the New Testament, *Jesus, as

the Messiah, is called 'son of David'. One of the benedictions recited after the reading of the *Haftarah reads:

'Gladden us, O Lord our God, with Elijah the prophet, thy servant, and with the kingdom of the house of David, thine anointed. Soon may he come and rejoice our hearts. Suffer not a stranger to sit upon his throne, nor let others any longer inherit his glory; for by Thy holy Name Thou didst swear unto him, that his light should not be quenched for ever. Blessed art Thou, O Lord, the Shield of David.'

Reform Jews, believing in a Messianic age rather than in the coming of a personal Messiah, do not recite this benediction and generally treat the traditions about the Messiah as the son of David as belonging not to Jewish *dogma but to poetic fancy.

Various tendencies are to be found in the Rabbinic literature with regard to the character of David. Thus David's saintliness is often stressed but he is also turned into a learned Rabbi who renders decisions in Jewish law. Some Rabbis follow the plain biblical record in holding that David sinned grievously in the Bathsheba episode, although Bathsheba was destined for David from the six days of creation and even in his sin he showed the way to repentance for other sinners. Other Rabbis say that David did not really sin, since Uriah had given a bill of divorce to Bathsheba before he departed to the battle in which he was slain, so that David's sin was not one of adultery. As for David causing Uriah's death, Uriah was guilty in law because he refused to obey David's orders, the penalty for defying the orders of a king being death. The Rabbis were puzzled by David's rise to become king, since the law does not permit the descendant of a Moabite even to enter the congregation of the Lord (Deuteronomy 23: 4), and they imagine David's enemies taunting him that he was unfit to marry into the congregation, let alone be king over it. The solution which, Boaz, Ruth's husband, is said to have found so that he could marry her was that the verse speaks only of a Moabite, not a Moabitess. Female Moabites do not taint their descendants.

In the Kabbalah David represents on earth the quality of Sovereignty, the *Shekhinah, the tenth of the *Sefirot, which has both a male and female aspect—male in its relationship to the lower worlds and female in retaining and absorbing the light of the other Sefirot. The

Kabbalists introduced a special meal in honour of King David, which was celebrated after the departure of the *Sabbath, symbolizing the Shekhinah. According to the Kabbalah, the union of David and Bathsheba represents the male and female aspects of the tenth Sefirah, sovereignty. Of the seven celestial guests invited to the *sukkah on the festival of *Tabernacles, the guest for the seventh day is David, on the same principle that the seven days of the festival represent the seven lower Sefirot.

The figure of David exercised a powerful fascination over artists, musicians, and literary men, non-Jewish as well as Jewish. Joseph Heller's *God Knows* is a clever, semi-obscene, some would say blasphemous novel in which the aged king David reminisces on his life, crossing the time-barrier as he does so (referring to Freud, for example). Heller is not too distant from the refusal in the Jewish tradition to pin down a heroic, and for that matter lovable, figure like David to the particular age in which he lived. David spans the ages.

S. Goldman, *Samuel* (Soncino Bible Series; London, 1951).

Louis Ginzberg, *The Legends of the Jews* (Philadelphia, 1942), iv. 79–122.

**Dead Sea Scrolls** Documents found in 1947 around *Qumran, near the Dead Sea in the Judaean Desert. The Jewish sect to which these documents belonged has been identified by some scholars with the *Essenes. The sect had its own solar calendar instead of the normal lunar *calendar, it had a monastic social order; great emphasis was placed on the life of purity; and, most startling of all, it was completely opposed to the Jerusalem *Temple which it termed an abomination. The scrolls of the biblical books found in Qumran, some complete, others only as fragments, resemble very closely the Masoretic Text but differ from it occasionally.

The Qumran material has rightly been investigated with the utmost care by scholars fascinated by discoveries which throw fresh light on Judaism in the centuries before the destruction of the Temple, on the text of the biblical books, and on the methods of scriptural exegesis in the period when the method later known as the Midrashic began to emerge. Since their discovery the Dead Sea Scrolls have been the subject of much debate among scholars, some of whom even declared that, despite the date of the jars in which they were found, clearly second century

BCE, the Scrolls themselves were medieval and of *Karaite origin. This view is no longer held by the experts, who none the less have quarrelled vehemently over the details. It is all very exciting stuff but, it has to be said, of hardly any relevance to contemporary Jewish religion since it was known, long before the discoveries, that there are variant readings in the Bible and that in the period before the destruction of the Temple in 70 CE there was a proliferation of Jewish sects.

R. K. Harrison, *The Dead Sea Scrolls* (London, 1961).

**Death and Burial** The Jewish religion encourages neither a morbid preoccupation with death nor any refusal to acknowledge the fact of human mortality. Judaism teaches that life on earth is a divine gift to be cherished in itself not only as a prelude to the *World to Come. Death is seen as a tragic, though inevitable, event. There are many tales of Jewish pietists weeping on their deathbed because it is only in the here and now that the precepts of the Torah can be carried out. As the Talmudic Rabbis put it: 'This World is the place in which the *mitzvot are performed. The World to Come is the place of reward for keeping them'; implying that the devout Jew should think more of the joy of living as a servant of God than dwell on the rewards for righteous living which are best left to God Himself. Yet, while positive *euthanasia is condemned in Jewish law, some Jewish thinkers hold that it is permitted to pray for the death of a person suffering from an incurable and extremely painful disease. Moreover, the eighteenth-century Kabbalist Hayyim *Ibn Atar writes that a good Jew should not be afraid to die or be angry when his time comes but should surrender his soul willingly in confidence that it is about to enter into eternal life. When death does come, the *corpse has to be treated with respect as the vehicle of the soul while the deceased was still alive on earth. A whole series of regulations have developed around the arrangements necessary for the dead to be given a decent burial. Some of these regulations belong in the area of folklore and superstition but since they are recorded in the *Shulḥan Arukh*, the standard Code of Jewish law, they have acquired the dignity of law to be observed by faithful Jews and they are followed today very scrupulously, at least by Orthodox Jews.

*Regulations to be Observed*

There are no special 'last rites' in Judaism but a dying person is required, if his state permits it, to recite the *Shema and make *confession of his sins. After it has been ascertained that death has taken place, the eyes of the corpse are closed, by his sons if possible, on the basis of the verse which speaks of the death of the patriarch, *Jacob: 'And Joseph shall put his hand upon thine eyes' (Genesis 46: 4). The corpse is then taken from the bed and placed on the floor, care being taken that it remains decently covered. The corpse is not left alone but 'watchers' remain with it until the burial. It appears from the earlier sources that the reason why 'watchers' are required is to protect the corpse from attack by rats, but a later reason given is to ward off the demonic powers who are attracted by death.

In preparation for burial the corpse is washed from head to foot, the hair and beard combed and the toe- and finger-nails cleaned. There are elaborate details of this 'purification' of the corpse, most of which have their origin in the Kabbalah and are recorded in the special manuals drawn up for the purpose. The most popular of these manuals is the *Maavar Yabbok* ('The Crossing of the Jabbok', see Genesis 32: 22) by the Italian Kabbalist Aaron Berachiah of Modena (d. 1639). For instance, there is a reference to the washing of the head of the corpse with an egg beaten up with wine or water to symbolize the revolving wheel of fortune in this world. However, the custom in some places of sprinkling a small amount of the beaten egg on the head of the deceased is frowned upon because it resembles the Christian practice of anointing the dead.

In early times, the Talmud relates, families would compete with one another to dress the corpse in splendid, costly garments, and people were in danger of becoming impoverished through the heavy funeral expenses. Rabban *Gamaliel, prince of his people, therefore left instructions in his will that he be buried in simple linen shrouds and this custom was followed. It became the custom for the mourners after the funeral to drink a toast to the memory of Rabban Gamaliel. The shrouds are, nowadays, made of muslin, cotton, or linen. The usual items of the shrouds are: a headdress; trousers; a chemise; an upper garment known as a kittel (this is worn by pious Jews

during the *Yom Kippur services as a symbol of purity and as a reminder of death); a belt or girdle; and a wrapping sheet. Men are clothed in addition with the *tallit, the prayer shawl they wore while alive, although it is the custom to remove one of the fringes to render the tallit unfit for use; otherwise the deceased is mocked since he is no longer capable of carrying out the precepts. In many communities all these rituals are carried out by members of a special society, the Chevra Kaddisha, 'Holy Brotherhood', to belong to which is considered to be a high honour. On the seventh day of the month of Adar, the anniversary of the death of Moses, the Chevra Kaddisha partakes of a festive meal in gratitude for having been given the privilege of attending to the dead.

*The Burial*

The coffin should be a plain wooden casket. The Jewish tradition frowns on elaborate caskets for the dead for the same reason that it objects to the use of costly shrouds. In death all are equal and ostentation is out of place. In the State of Israel the old custom is still preserved of not using a coffin at all, the dead being buried directly in the ground.

The laws of *mourning do not come into operation until the body has been buried, except for the rending of the garments carried out before the funeral. The practice of rending garments as an expression of grief is mentioned in the Bible. The rending is done by the nearest relatives, usually by cutting and then tearing the part of one of the garments worn at the lapel. Nowadays, the rending (Hebr. *keriah*) is often done more as a mere token of grief on, say, a cardigan or even a tie. Reform Jews have given up the practice of *keriah*. For parents the rending is done at the left side of the garment, for other relatives (brother, sister, son, daughter, husband, wife) at the right side. The rationale for this difference is that the heart is situated at the left side and the emotions of grief at the loss of a parent are to be expressed in a more intense form in obedience to the fifth commandment: 'Honour thy father and thy mother.'

It is considered to be a special act of benevolence to pay the last respects to the dead by attending he funeral. This is called 'true kindness' in that it is completely disinterested because the dead cannot repay the living for the kindness shown to them.

The funeral itself is simple in form. The

body is escorted to the cemetery where the prayer acknowledging God's justice is recited. A eulogy, in former times, was only recited over persons distinguished for their learning or piety but, nowadays, the Rabbi eulogizes practically every person lying dead before him. Incidentally, funerals do not require a Rabbi to be present at all (the Rabbi is not a priest and, in any event, a Jewish funeral bears nothing of the sacramental) but it has become the function of the Rabbi to officiate at funerals, probably in an unconscious accommodation to Christian mores. In some communities the body of a very distinguished person is taken before the funeral into the synagogue, where the eulogy is recited.

After the funeral service in the cemetery, pallbearers bring the body to the grave, stopping seven times on the way to represent the seven 'vanities' mentioned in the book of *Ecclesiastes. The coffin is lowered into the grave and first the immediate relatives and then all those present shovel the earth into the grave. All then return to the hall of the cemetery where the mourners recite the *Kaddish. It is customary to wash the hands before leaving the cemetery. Two reasons are given for this washing of the hands. One is that it amounts to a symbolic declaration that the hands are clean of having done anything so to distress the deceased as to hasten his death. The other reason is to encourage the living symbolically to wash their hands clean of preoccupation with death, since life must go on. In this and in all the other rituals expression is given to both grief at the loss of a dear one and faith that death is not the end. Death, in a Talmudic saying, is the occasion when two worlds 'kiss' one another. The deceased departs on the journey to eternity while the living, accepting God's will, carry on with their lives.

The mourners return to their home after the funeral to observe the *shivah* ('seven'), the seven days of mourning, where they sit on low stools and where they are visited by their friends and offered words of comfort and consolation. The psychological effect has often been noted. Where the grief is shared and where it is not kept bottled up but given expression in concrete forms, the burden becomes a little lighter and utter despair is overcome.

H. Rabinowicz, *A Guide to Life: Jewish Laws and Customs of Mourning* (London, 1964, and New York, 1967). Maurice Lamm, *The Jewish Way in Death and Mourning* (New York, 1969).

**Death, Angel of** The angel sent by God to bring about death; Heb. *malakh ha-mavet*. There are no references in the Bible to a specific angel of death but the concept is found frequently in Rabbinic literature and in Jewish folklore. In the latter, for instance, the practice of pouring out all the water in pots and so forth when a death occurs is said to be based on the belief that the Angel of Death dips his sword in the water and poisons it. Maimonides (*Guide of the Perplexed*, 3. 22) demythologizes the concept, understanding it as the life-denying, evil force that lurks in the human psyche. Maimonides quotes with much approval the Talmudic saying (tractate *Bava Batra* 16a) that *Satan, the evil inclination (see YETZER HA-TOV AND YETER HA-RA) and the Angel of Death are one and the same. In Yiddish slang a man with destructive tendencies or one who is always running down others is called an Angel of Death.

**Deborah** The female prophet and leader whose story is told in the book of *Judges 4 and 5. Deborah's famous song of triumph is recited as the *Haftarah on the Sabbath when the Song of Moses (Exodus 15) forms part of the Torah reading for the day The name *devorah* means 'bee' in Hebrew and it is difficult to know why she should have been called by such a curious name. According to one opinion in the Talmud, this was not her real name but was given to her because, like a busy bee, she took pride in calling attention to her worth, calling herself, in her song, 'a mother in Israel'. In the Middle Ages there was considerable discussion on whether a woman can serve as a judge. Some of the French authorities argue that a woman can obviously serve as a judge, witness Deborah: 'She used to sit under the Palm of Deborah. . . . and the Israelites would come to her for judgement' (Judges 4: 5). Others argue that the case of Deborah is exceptional either, because she acted only in an emergency capacity by special dispensation or because both parties in the dispute agreed to abide by her decisions. According to a Talmudic statement Deborah judged under a palm tree in the open air in order to avoid being secluded with the men who came to her to be judged.

**Decalogue** The ten words, better known as the Ten Commandments, given by God to the people of Israel at *Sinai, as recorded in the book of Exodus (20: 1–14) and in the book of

Deuteronomy (5: 6–18). The two versions are very similar but there a few differences such as '*Remember* the Sabbath' in Exodus and '*Keep* the Sabbath' in Deuteronomy. The discrepancies between the two versions are explained by the critics on the grounds that Exodus and Deuteronomy are two separate sources and by *Ibn Ezra on the ground that the Deuteronomic version is reported speech which is not necessarily exact. The accepted Jewish numbering of the items in the Decalogue is:

1. I am the Lord thy God;
2. Thou shalt have no other gods;
3. Do not take the Name of the Lord in vain;
4. Remember and keep the Sabbath;
5. Honour thy father and mother;
6. Thou shalt not murder;
7. Thou shalt not commit adultery;
8. Thou shalt not steal;
9. Thou shalt not bear false witness;
10. Thou shalt not covet.

Each of these receives very detailed treatment in the tradition. Maimonides understands the first item as a command to believe in God. Maimonides cannot have been unaware of the logical flaw, to which his critics call attention, in the notion of a command to believe in God. If one believes in God there is no need for the command so to do. If one does not believe in God there is none to issue the command. Maimonides may mean that once belief in God has been attained a 'command' of the Torah, a *mitzvah*, has been carried out. Be that as it may, *Nahmanides sees the first item not as a command at all but as a preamble to the others. As has been noted above, the traditional form is not the Ten Commandments but rather the ten words, although the other nine are certainly understood as divine commandments.

The second commandment is directed against every form of idolatry. The Israelite is to have no other gods and must never worship idols; he must be prepared, if necessary, to suffer *martyrdom rather than be false to the One God. Contrary to the conventional view, however, the second commandment was not understood in the tradition as forbidding any representation of human and other figures in *art. Some forms of representation are forbidden but these are not discussed under the heading of the second commandment.

The third commandment is understood as directed against false oaths, 'taking the name of the Lord in vain', that is, by swearing falsely, but the tradition also understands 'in vain' to mean that no meaningless oaths must be made. An example given is to take an oath that wood is wood or gold is gold. It is forbidden to invoke the majesty of the divine name for the purpose of establishing as true that which is known by everyone to be true in any event.

The fourth commandment enjoins strict observance of the *Sabbath by refraining from work on the sacred day. This is the meaning of 'Keep the Sabbath'. Remembering the Sabbath is understood to mean that the Sabbath day must be celebrated at its beginning with the hymn of praise known as the Kiddush, 'sanctification'.

The fifth commandment is self-explanatory. Parents are to be respected and Talmudic tradition defines at length what respect means in this context. Later traditions extended the fifth commandment to embrace respect for step-parents, parents-in-law, grandparents, and older siblings, though not to the same extent as parents themselves.

The sixth commandment is directed against murder but does not rule out killing in self-defence, or *capital punishment as a penalty imposed by the court. *Abortion, too, while a serious offence, is not covered by the sixth commandment. Foeticide is not treated as homicide in Jewish law.

The seventh commandment is directed against a man having sexual relations with a married women. Until polygamy was banned by Rabbenu *Gershom of Mayyence, for Ashkenazi Jews at least, a man was allowed to have more than one wife, so that for a married man to have sex with an unmarried woman would be an act of fornication, forbidden, naturally, but not coming under the heading of the seventh commandment.

The tradition understands the eighth commandment as directed against kidnapping, 'stealing' another human being. There are, of course, other scriptural injunctions against stealing another's property but this offence, while very severe, is not said to be included among the basic commandments of the Decalogue.

The ninth commandment refers initially to giving false testimony against another in a court of law, although the moralists extend it, on the ethical if not the legal level, to issuing any false report about a neighbour's conduct.

The tenth commandment, not to covet, is

generally understood in the legal context to mean that one should not take steps to acquire the wife or the property of another, even if these steps do not in themselves involve any illegal action. Examples would be where a man seeks to encourage a neighbour to divorce his wife so that he can marry her legally, or where a man persists in entreating his neighbour to sell him his house or his land, even though he wishes the actual purchase to be done legally. But here, too, the moralists step in to extend the tenth commandment to the mere desire to have something that belongs to someone else. Some of the later moralists make a distinction between coveting the object owned by the neighbour and wishing to have one like that which the neighbour has. I must not say: 'I would like to have *A*'s Rolls Royce', but I am allowed to say: 'I, too, would like to have a Rolls Royce.' In this connection, *Ibn Ezra discusses how emotions can be commanded. How can a man prevent himself from coveting a neighbour's goods, since it is all in the mind? Ibn Ezra replies that the command implies that the man of faith should realize that all is apportioned by God in such a way that it is impossible to imagine that something which divine *providence has allotted to *A* can ever be transferred to *B*. With this kind of realization no man would ever experience a psychological need to wish to obtain that which does not and cannot possibly belong to him, just as (the illustration is Ibn Ezra's) a peasant, convinced that he can never gain the hand of a princess, will experience no psychological need to wish to have her. That which is absolutely unobtainable is never the object of desire. The command refers to the cultivation of this kind of awareness of the all-pervasive divine providence, which is bound to inhibit feelings of covetousness.

The Decalogue was inscribed on two tablets of stone (Exodus 31: 18; 32: 15-16). In art these are usually depicted as two oblongs joined together with a copula on each. The copula, the invention of Christian artists, has been adopted in Jewish representations, although it is certainly unknown in any of the Jewish sources. As a matter of fact, the two tablets themselves do not appear at all as a specific Jewish symbol until around the year 1300 and were copied from the representation in Christian illuminated manuscripts. The older Jewish symbol for the Torah was not the Decalogue but the seven-branched candelabrum, the *Menorah, the symbol of spiritual light. In the Midrashim various suggestions are put forward regarding the arrangement of the words on the tablets. Some say that the two were separate tablets on each of which all ten of the commandments were written, but others see them as having the first five commandments on one stone, the second five on the other.

In a Midrashic comment, the first five commandments are, in the Rabbinic phrase, 'between man and God' while the second five are 'between man and his neighbour', to suggest that the religious and ethical commands are both essential and that a religion without *ethics or an ethical system without religion is a distortion. On this reading, the fifth commandment is seen as 'religious' rather than 'ethical' because, as the Rabbis say, there are three partners in the creation of a child, God and the father and mother. The command to honour parents is, therefore, seen as having to do with reverence for God, the Creator of all life.

According to the Rabbinic sources, the Decalogue was recited daily by the priests in the Temple. There is some evidence that, in the early period, the Decalogue formed part of the *tefillin. Later, the Talmud (*Berakhot* 12a) observes, a strong degree of opposition developed against giving too much prominence to the Decalogue 'because of the sectarians', defined, by the commentators, as those who believed that only the Ten Commandments are the word of God not the whole Torah. There is, in fact, considerable tension in the history of Jewish thought between special reverence for the Decalogue and too strong an attachment to it, this tending to demote the Torah as a whole from its supreme position. Maimonides and other authorities are opposed, for this reason, to people standing when the Decalogue is read in the synagogue on the festival of *Shavuot, the anniversary of the giving of the Torah, and when the passages from Exodus and Deuteronomy are read from the Torah. The custom, nowadays, is nevertheless for the congregation to stand when the Decalogue is recited on these occasions, it being argued that, since they are recited as part of the Torah reading, there is no fear that the special reverence afforded the Ten Commandments will result in a lesser regard for the rest of the Torah. In most synagogues today the Ten Commandments are displayed above the *Ark, although some few Rabbis object to this as well. In many prayer books the Decalogue is printed for recital by individuals as an adjunct to the morning service. Since this is not for public recitation, the old objection does not apply.

Brevard S. Childs, *Exodus* (New York, 1974), 385–439.

Solomon Goldman, 'The Ten Commandments', in his *From Slavery to Freedom* (New York, 1958), 585–689.

Nahum M. Sarna, *Exploring Exodus* (New York, 1986), 130–57.

**Democracy**  A democratic form of society was unknown before the modern period but the Jewish *community in the Middle Ages came close to this form in that the communal leaders were elected by a majority vote of those who paid taxes for the upkeep of the community. The poorer people, who made no contribution, did not evidently have a vote and had no representatives in the governing body. It is, consequently, futile to try to read modern democratic ideals into Jewish sources produced under different social structures. Yet majority rule was the norm even in these sources with regard to the decisions of judges and also in connection with communal enactments. The State of Israel is a democracy and the majority of communal bodies and synagogues are today organized on democratic lines. The general principle here is that any form of society favoured by the members is allowed according to Jewish teaching. A majority can, if it so wishes, vote to give its minorities the right to be represented, all of which means that modern democratic principles, albeit new in human society, can be and are adopted in Jewish life without this involving any real departure from the tradition.

**Demons**  Supernatural, malevolent beings with the power to cause hurt to humans. (See MAGIC AND SUPERSTITION.) Belief in demons, though not very pronounced in Jewish life and thought, is still prevalent, in a semi-comical way, at the level of folklore. Even some of the learned feel compelled to accept, perhaps not too seriously, belief in demons because this belief is implied in the Talmud in many places. The Babylonian Talmud, in particular, produced against a Zoroastrian background in which the belief was strongly rooted, contains stories of visitations by demons and spells to ward them off. There is even a report of a Rabbi conversing with a demon prince. It is completely unhistorical to maintain, as did *Krochmal, that all these references were inserted into the Talmud by ignorant copyists or by those influenced by folk-beliefs said to have been repudiated by the Rabbis themselves.

Some of the medieval thinkers accepted the belief in demons. Others rejected the belief as contrary to the doctrine of divine *providence. Why should God have surrendered His control of the universe, on some occasions, into the power of such creatures? Abraham *Ibn Ezra rejects entirely the notion that demons really exist. Maimonides either ignores the Talmudic references to demons or gives these a rationalistic explanation; as, for example, when he understands the Mishnaic reference to an 'evil spirit' against which a light can be put out even on the Sabbath, to mean a spirit of melancholy. Menahem *Meiri generally follows a similar demythologizing tendency when he understands the Talmudic reference to warding off the demons by reciting the *Shema before retiring as meaning that evil thoughts invade the mind at bedtime and these can successfully be dispelled through the recitation of the Shema. Meiri also understands the Talmudic reference to Joseph the demon, who was able to traverse great distances through the air, to mean that there was a skilled acrobat who could vault over great distances and who was known as 'Joseph the devil' in the sense that he was a devil-may-care character.

The Kabbalah has a vast demonology of its own. The demonic powers constitute an unholy parody of the sacred realms against which they are in constant battle. In a very revealing illustration, the Zohar compares the 'Other Side', the domain of the evil powers, to a vicious dog held by its owner on a long lead. The dog, though it appears to enjoy independent power, is pulled back whenever it is in danger of getting out of control. Under the influence of the Kabbalah, especially, belief in the existence of demons became widespread. Although there is no official Jewish rite of *exorcism, there are numerous tales of saintly men exorcizing demons from houses and persons.

Belief in demons is thus generally present but very peripheral in the Jewish scheme. No representative thinker, for instance, ever thought of dubbing Ibn Ezra a heretic because he refused to believe in demons. Needless to say, sophisticated Jewish thinkers who did believe in the existence of demons did not think of these as little devils with forked tails breathing fire but as spiritual forces which God has unleashed in the world for purposes of His own, or as harmful psychological processes which take place in the human mind.

Joshua Trachtenberg, *Jewish Magic and Superstition: A Study in Folk Religion* (New York, 1970), 25–60.

**Dessler, E. E.** Religious thinker and prominent figure in the *Musar movement (1881–1954). Dessler was born in Homel in Russia where he received a traditional Jewish education leading to his Rabbinic ordination, *Semikhah. After trying his hand, unsuccessfully, in business, Dessler obtained a Rabbinic position in the East End of London. He was later instrumental in establishing in the town of Gateshead a Kolel, an institution in which married men with families are supported by patrons of learning while they devote themselves entirely to advanced Talmudic studies on the Lithuanian pattern; an institution now popular everywhere in the ultra-Orthodox world, but, at that time, unheard of in England. Dessler used to say that even the Orthodox Jews in England looked upon members of the Kolel as if they were Martians newly arrived on the planet. Dessler, though the principal of the Kolel, received no salary from the institution, earning his living by privately teaching the sons of Jews who were concerned that the young men should be trained in the old-style Talmudic learning. Dessler later was appointed to the prestigious position of spiritual guide to the great *Yeshivah of Ponivezh in Israel. Both in Gateshead and in Ponivezh, Dessler influenced generations of students, two of whom, L. Carmel and A. Halpern, published his discourses under the title *Mikhtav me-Eliyahu* (*Writing of Elijah*; Bene Berak, 1976 and Jerusalem 1983), in four volumes. This work has become a standard text for devotees of the Musar tradition.

Dessler belongs firmly in the Musar tradition (he was a great-grandson of Israel *Salanter, the founder of the Musar movement), most of his thought being based on the ideas of this movement. But he also acquired an extensive knowledge of Kabbalah and *Hasidism and, to a lesser extent, of modern psychological theories, often referring in his lectures to Freudian theories, for example. In this respect he was a highly original Jewish theologian whose views were respected even by thinkers with no allegiance to his form of traditional Judaism.

Dessler's religious thought is of the otherworldly kind, although, through his early business experience, he came to know the world, its temptations and allurements, and was far removed from the ideal of the world-losing saint. The purpose of Judaism, for Dessler, is to equip the Jew to enjoy the nearness of God in life everlasting, which, he taught, can be achieved only through the rigorous, unselfish study and practice of the Torah. Great attention is paid, in his thinking, to the subconscious mind, which Dessler comes close to identifying with the 'evil inclination' of Rabbinic thought (see YETZER HA-TOV AND YETZER HA-RA). God has endowed man with the instincts of self-preservation and self-regard, without which human life would lack its driving force, but it is through the discipline afforded by the Torah alone that these instincts are prevented from becoming entirely self-serving and ultimately destructive. Dessler understands *Heaven and Hell in purely spiritual terms. For him, Heaven and Hell are not 'places' but spiritual states: the one of the nearness to God acquired in this life by disinterested, and hence God-like, service and worship; the other of remoteness from God, the pain of which is described in terms of physical torment because, in this life, it is it is beyond the human mind otherwise to picture intense spiritual loss.

Dessler postulates that life, rightly understood, consists of that towards which an individual directs his strivings. When a man directs all his strivings towards what Dessler calls 'worldly vanities', that man's self is empty and insignificant. But if the self directs its strivings to spiritual, other-worldly concerns, that self enjoys the life of the *World to Come even here on earth. It is only by the individual's free choice of the good, in his struggle with temptation in this life, that the good becomes part of his very being and his choosing of it the root of his eternal bliss in the World to Come. A good given as a gift, even if the gift is from God Himself, cannot become part of the soul's very being since a gift, by definition, is an external endowment and is not self-acquired. This is why the Rabbis speak frequently of this life as a preparation for eternal bliss in the Hereafter.

In Dessler's subtle thought, the austerity of his Musaristic belief is only partly offset by his frequent appeal to the writings of the Hasidic masters. Dessler seems to be attempting the impossible when he seeks to blend the rigours of Musar with the joyousness of Hasidism and the very different Freudian-type analysis of the psyche.

> L. Carmel, 'Rabbi E. E. Dessler', in Leo Jung (ed.), *Guardians of Our Heritage* (New York, 1958), 675–99.

**Deuteronomy, Book of** The fifth book of the *Pentateuch in which Moses delivers his final addresses to his people, reminding them of the events of their wanderings in the wilderness for forty years after the Exodus from Egypt and repeating and elaborating on the laws given to them. The older Hebrew name for the book is *Mishneh Torah* ('Repetition of the Law'), rendered in Greek as *Deuteronomion* and in the Latin Bible as *Deuteronomium*, hence the present English title, Deuteronomy. All this is based on the *Septuagint rendering of the word 'Torah' as *nomos*, 'law' rather than 'doctrine'. The other Hebrew name for the book is *Devarim*, 'Words', after the opening verse: 'These are the words which Moses spoke unto all Israel.'

*The Traditional View*

According to the tradition all five books of the Pentateuch were written by Moses at the 'dictation' of God and are really a single book. The Talmudic Rabbis (see BIBLICAL CRITICISM) found difficulties in the last eight verses of the book dealing with Moses' death. How could Moses have written the account of his own death after this had taken place? One Rabbi holds that Moses did write these eight verses, none the less, but with tears in his eyes, while another Rabbi holds that these verses were added, after Moses' death, by Moses' disciple, *Joshua. Abraham *Ibn Ezra hints that all the last twelve verses, from the verse which describes Moses' ascent to the mount on which he died, must have been added later since, as Ibn Ezra says, 'once Moses ascended he did not return [to write the account]'. In the Middle Ages other voices were heard occasionally to suggest that there are some few post-Mosaic additions in the book but, until the rise of modern biblical criticism, the traditional view was that Moses is the divinely inspired author of, at least, by far the major part of Deuteronomy.

*The Critical View*

*Spinoza relies on Ibn Ezra's comments to suggest that the whole of the Pentateuch was compiled much later than Moses, although it is obvious that Ibn Ezra himself refers only to a small number of post-Mosaic additions and certainly would have repudiated Spinoza's radical departure from the traditional view.

This is what Ibn Ezra actually says or rather hints at indirectly. The opening verse of Deuteronomy states that Moses spoke these words 'beyond the Jordan', which seems to mean on the eastern side of the river Jordan. This makes sense if the author of Deuteronomy lived on the western side of the river at a time when the people had lived there after the death of Moses. But if Moses is the author, he was actually on the eastern side when he wrote the book of Deuteronomy. Why, then, does he refer to it as 'the other side of the Jordan'? Defenders of the tradition reply that the other side of the Jordan is not a geographical location but can apply to either side. Ibn Ezra is evidently unhappy with this solution. His cryptic comment on the verse is: 'If you know the secret of the twelve; and of "And Moses wrote"; "And the Canaanite was then in the land"; "Behold his bedstead was a bedstead of iron"; you will discover the truth.' Spinoza is undoubtedly correct in deciphering Ibn Ezra's hints. Ibn Ezra means that if one examines the Pentateuchal passages at which he hints it becomes clear that these are post-Mosaic additions to the Pentateuch. The 'secret of the twelve' refers to the last twelve verses of Deuteronomy, as above. Since they refer to Moses' ascent to the mount on which he died, they could not have been written by Moses. In Deuteronomy 31: 9 the verse states: 'Moses wrote down this Torah and gave it to the priests', implying that a later author wrote these words; otherwise one would have to postulate that Moses wrote down *that he wrote down* which seems absurd and does not fit in at all with the plain meaning of the text. 'And the Canaanite was then in the land' (Genesis 12: 6) is hard to explain if Moses wrote the verse, since in Moses' day the Canaanites were still in the land. (Traditionalists have replied that the meaning is either that the Canaanites were still in the land or that the Canaanites had just then entered the land.) 'Behold his bedstead was a bedstead of iron' (Deuteronomy 3: 11) speaks of the bedstead of Og, king of Bashan, who was slain by Moses towards the end of Moses' life, while the verse seems to suggest that the bedstead of Og was pointed to as a curiosity many years after Og had been slain. (S. D. *Luzzatto suggested, in reply, that the word used means not a 'bedstead' but a 'cradle'. Og was such a giant babe that his cradle was kept as a curiosity even while Og was still alive.)

Driver, in his commentary to Deuteronomy, gives a very comprehensive account of how later scholarship develops the theory of a post-Mosaic authorship of the whole of Deuteronomy and, for that matter, of the rest of the Pentateuch. Modern biblical scholarship is virtually unanimous in accepting a date for Deuteronomy much later than the time of Moses and has added numerous refinements of its own, attempting to fix the date when the book was composed and discussing whether the book itself is a composite work. Chief Rabbi J. H. *Hertz, on the other hand, persists in defending the traditional view that Moses is the author of the whole of the Pentateuch including Deuteronomy.

### Does it Matter?

If the critical view is correct, what significance does this have for the Jewish religion? Reform and Conservative Jews hold that the question of the Mosaic authorship of Deuteronomy (and of the other four books of the Pentateuch) is purely a matter of scholarly investigation and has no significance for the Jewish religion. What matters, they hold, is the teachings of Deuteronomy—its affirmation that there is only one God; that a great aim is the love of God; that man should have a passion for justice; that the Jewish people has no future unless it obeys God's word. As for the laws, produced, on the critical view, in response to particular conditions which no longer obtain, Reform Judaism does not consider all the Pentateuchal laws to be permanently binding in any event, while Conservative Judaism locates the authority of the laws in the way these have been interpreted and developed in the Jewish tradition, not in the bare biblical text (see CONSERVATIVE JUDAISM).

Orthodoxy, on the other hand, is faced with a severe problem since, on the Orthodox view, that God gave to Moses the whole Torah, Deuteronomy included, is a basic dogma of the Jewish religion, as recorded in Maimonides' *principles of faith. While some few Orthodox scholars are prepared to admit that the attribution of authorship of biblical books in the traditional sources—say, *David as the author of the book of Psalms—has now to be abandoned, or taken in a non-literal way, in the light

of modern scholarship, fewer still are prepared to accept the verdict of the critics, plausible though it may seem, with regard to the Pentateuch, the holy of holies, the ultimate source of the Jewish religion. Orthodox scholars either take on the critics on their own ground by trying to demonstrate that modern biblical scholarship is flawed as scholarship or tend to dismiss the critical views as pure guesswork, mere hypotheses which it is folly to prefer to the certain truth of a tradition established and accepted throughout Jewish history. There the matters rests for the time being.

S. R. Driver, *A Critical and Exegetical Commentary to Deuteronomy* (Edinburgh, 1902).

J. H. Hertz, 'Deuteronomy: Its Antiquity and Mosaic Authorship', in his *Pentateuch and Haftorahs* (London, 1960), 937–41.

**Devekut** Attachment to God, having God always in the mind, an ideal especially advocated in *Hasidism but found, too, in earlier Jewish writings. The term *devekut*, from the root *davak*, 'to cleave', denotes chiefly this constant being with God but sometimes also denotes the ecstatic state produced by such communion. The relevant verse is found in the book of *Deuteronomy, a book replete with the summons to love God, in the verse: 'To love the Lord thy God, to walk in all His ways and to cleave unto Him' (Deuteronomy 11: 22). The Talmudic Rabbis understand the 'cleaving' to God mentioned in the verse as referring to the Torah and its students. Being attached to the Torah and its study constitutes the only possible cleaving to God at all applicable to finite human beings who can never actually 'cleave' to God Himself. But in a notable passage, Maimonides (*Guide of the Perplexed*, 3. 51) develops the idea that it is possible for the greatest saints to have God always in the mind. Such saints, says Maimonides, are immune from the common mishaps of human life. As their minds are on the highest, nothing on earth can affect them; they can even walk through fire and water without suffering any harm. Hasidism relies on this passage but, following a comment by *Nahmanides to the verse, extends the ideal as attainable by lesser mortals, although, in its fullest sense, it can only be attained by the Hasidic master, the *Zaddik.

Nahmanides writes in his Commentary:

'The verse warns man not to worship God and a being beside Him; he is to worship God alone in his heart and in his actions. And it is plausible that the meaning of "cleaving" is to remember God and His love constantly, not to divert your thought from Him in all your earthly doings. Such a man may be talking to other people, but his heart is not with them since he is in the presence of God. And it is further plausible that those who have attained this rank, do, even in their earthly life, partake of the eternal life, because they have made themselves a dwelling place of the *Shekhinah.'

The Hasidic ideal of 'serving God in corporeality', that is, serving God by having the mind on Him even when engaging in business or other worldly pursuits, is based on Nahmanides' understanding of the ideal of *devekut*. It was also in obedience to this ideal that Hasidism understood the Rabbinic doctrine of 'Torah for its own sake' to mean that when studying the Torah the mind should be on God. This attempt to convert the study of the Torah from an intellectual into a devotional exercise angered the *Mitnaggedim, the opponents of Hasidism, because, for them, to study with anything in mind other than the subject studies, is not to study at all.

Hasidic fondness for song and melody is based on this ideal. A particular melody of plaintive yearning, 'soul music', is called a *devekut niggun*, 'an attachment melody', which Hasidim repeat over and over again in order to cultivate this state to the highest degree possible for ordinary worshippers.

Gershom Scholem, 'Devekut, Or Communion with God', in his *The Messianic Idea in Judaism* (New York, 1971), 203–26.

**Dialogue** Discussions and conversations between two parties holding different views on some matters of high significance but who believe that it is fruitful for them to talk to one another and thus come fairly to understand why the other sincerely holds to his opinion, as well as to assist one another in the furtherance of the aims they have in common. Dialogue on the contemporary scene usually refers to discussions between Jews and Christians, hence the term Christian–Jewish dialogue. In the Middle Ages, Jews were at times compelled to engage in *disputations with Christians with the ultimate, hoped-for result being to convince the Jews that Christianity was true and Judaism false. In these disputations, it has to be said, the Jews were rarely defeated despite the one-sidedness

of a debate in which the Jews were all too well aware that a Jewish victory could place the Jewish community at risk. In an age of greater religious tolerance, many Jews and Christians have come to the realization that representatives of the two faiths can try to understand one another's beliefs while respecting the other's integrity and without any motivation, conscious or unconscious, of trying to convert Jews to Christianity or Christians to Judaism. A clear distinction is thus drawn between disputations, where there is hostility between the two sides, and dialogue, where respect and the need to understand prevails. Nevertheless, some Jewish thinkers do not believe that the sorry history of the disputations can so easily be sloughed off and hold that it is unhelpful to both Jews and Christians to engage even in the much milder form of dialogue; although, naturally, Jews and Christians can work together to further social justice and other worthy causes such as the promotion of peace and harmony in human society.

So far, few attempts have been made to create a serious dialogue between Jews and Muslims or between Jews and adherents of the Far Eastern religions, although such bodies as the World Council of Faiths have enjoyed a limited success in bringing together followers of the major religions of the world.

Jews who do accept the validity of interfaith dialogue steadfastly refuse to see this as any kind of attempt to blur the distinction between the religions. As Chief Rabbi J. H. *Hertz once remarked: 'There is little difference between the religions of the world but it is the little differences which really count.'

Another form of dialogue is that between God and man, especially prominent in the thought of Martin *Buber. Buber holds that man cannot talk much about God but he can address God directly; in Buber's terminology, man's 'I' can say 'Thou' to God.

**Diaspora** The communities of Jews dispersed in countries outside *Palestine; Heb. Golah or Galut ('Exile'). Originally, the term denoted the community formed by the Jews exiled to *Babylon after the destruction of the First *Temple in 586 BCE. The book of *Ezekiel begins with the words: 'In the thirtieth year, on the fifth day of the fourth month, when I was in the community of exiles [*ha-golah*] by the Chebar Canal.' The book of *Esther (2: 5) speaks of 'the group that was carried into exile [*ha-golah*] along with King Jeconiah of Judah which had been driven into exile by King Nebuchadnezzar of Babylon'. After the destruction of the Second Temple in 70 CE, the Diaspora consisted mainly of the communities of Babylon, Egypt, Rome, and other parts of Europe. At the present day the Diaspora consists of all the Jewish communities outside the State of Israel, the most prominent of which is the American community, which has a Jewish population larger than that of Israel.

Each of the Diaspora communities in the Talmudic period developed its own cultural patterns and, to a degree, its own interpretation of Judaism. The Greek-speaking community of Alexandria in Egypt was strongly influenceed by Greek philosophy and its Bible was in Greek translation. The Babylonian community had its own approach to Torah study, the results of which are found in the most notable and influential work of Diaspora Jewry, the Babylonian Talmud.

As the name 'Exile' implies, Diaspora Jews, while often quite content to remain such, never completely gave up the hope that one day they would return 'home'. It was this hope, kept alive in many of the prayers and ceremonies, that paved the way for *Zionism and the establishment of the State of Israel. Ben Gurion, the first Prime Minister of Israel, went so far as to say that eventually the Diaspora will fade away entirely; the Diaspora Jews will either become so assimilated as to lose their Jewish identity or they will bid farewell to the Diaspora by emigrating to Israel. Very few Jews accepted this negative view, arguing that, as in the past, the Diaspora has its own specific contributions to make.

**Dietary Laws** The rules and regulations governing which items of food are forbidden and which permitted. The word kosher (*kasher* in the Sephardi and modern Hebrew pronunciation) means simply 'right' or 'fit', as in the verse: 'The thing seems right [*kasher*] in the eyes of the king' (Esther 8: 5) and originally had no special association with the dietary laws. (In American slang, derived from the Yiddish, a kosher business deal means one that is perfectly above-board.) But the term kosher is now used particularly for food that is permitted and the abstract noun kashrut is used as a synonym for the observance of these laws. Another biblical

verse states: 'Ye shall be holy men unto Me; therefore ye shall not eat any flesh that is torn [*terefah*] of beasts in the field' (Exodus 22: 30). This term, terefah, often abbreviated to tref, was extended to include any food forbidden by the dietary laws. Thus, in current parlance, the observance of kashrut involves eating only kosher food and rejecting terefah food.

*Animals, Birds, and Fishes*

From two biblical passages (Leviticus 11 and Deuteronomy 14: 3–21) the following rules are extracted regarding which animals, birds, and fishes are kosher and which terefah.

Only animals which have cloven hooves and which chew the cud are permitted. The pig does have cloven hoofs but does not chew the cud and is, consequently, forbidden. In the course of time, Jews came to have an aversion to the pig in particular, especially after Jews, in the period of the *Maccabees, were ready to give their lives rather than eat pig-meat when ordered by tyrants to do so as an expression of disloyalty to the Jewish religion as a whole. Many a Jew today, otherwise not too observant of the dietary laws, will still refuse steadfastly to eat swine-flesh. It might be remarked, however, it is only eating of the pig that is forbidden. Surprising though this may seem at first glance, there is no objection, in Jewish law, to a Jew having a pigskin wallet. The passage in Deuteronomy (14: 4–5) gives a list of the animals which chew the cud and have cloven hooves and are thus kosher: oxen, sheep, goats, deer, gazelles, roebuck, wild goats, ibex, antelopes, and mountain sheep. It is interesting to note that whale-meat and whale-oil are forbidden not because the whale is a forbidden fish but because the whale is a mammal which, obviously, does not have cloven hooves and does not chew the cud.

With regard to birds, the Bible gives a list of the forbidden birds, implying that all others are kosher. But since the exact identity of the birds mentioned is uncertain, it is the practice only to eat birds which are known by tradition to be kosher, such as chickens, turkeys, ducks, geese, and pigeons. The eggs of forbidden birds are terefah, but quails' eggs are permitted since the quail is a kosher bird (see Numbers 12: 31–2).

Nowhere in the whole of the Bible is there any reference to a particular fish, only to fish in general. In the two passages dealing with the dietary laws it is stated that only fish which have fins and scales are kosher. The Talmud lays down the rule that a fish that has scales also has fins, so that what actually determines which fishes are kosher is the existence of scales, A problem arises as to how 'scales' are defined. *Nahmanides understands that only scales that are detachable from the skin of the fish qualify as scales. Where they cannot be detached they are not considered to be scales at all but part of the fish itself. This is the reasoning behind a fierce debate which took place between Rabbinic authorities in the eighteenth century regarding the permissibility of caviar, derived from the sturgeon, since the scales of the sturgeon cannot easily be detached from the skin of the fish, although they can be removed by the application of a lye solution. Some Orthodox Jews today do consider caviar to be kosher, others do not. There are similar problems regarding turbot and swordfish. Conservative Rabbis have ruled that swordfish is kosher, since the Talmud states explicitly that it is kosher. Most Orthodox Rabbis, however, are doubtful whether the fish mentioned in the Talmud as kosher is the swordfish. English Rabbis in the nineteenth century ruled that the turbot is a kosher fish but their opinion is now generally rejected by Orthodox English Jews.

Worms, frogs, eels, and all shellfish such as crabs and prawns are not kosher. With regard to locusts, the Bible (Leviticus 11: 21–2) does state that four species of locust are kosher but it is difficult to know how these can actually be identified so that, nowadays, very few observant Jews eat locusts, although in some oriental countries the kosher type of locusts are eaten, as they were in the biblical period.

*Other Dietary Laws*

As noted above, the Bible forbids the eating of the meat of an animal torn (*terefah*) by wild beasts and it also forbids (Deuteronomy 14: 21) the meat of an animal that has died of its own accord, called *nevelah*, a carcass. The Rabbinic understanding of these two terms is that any animal that has not been killed in the manner known as *shehitah* is treated as *nevelah* and any animal that has serious defects in its vital organs is treated as a terefah, so that its meat is forbidden even if it has been killed in the proper manner. This applies to birds as well as to animals. There is a vast literature on how to determine which type of organic disease renders an animal or bird terefah. Observant Jews, for

instance, will bring to a Rabbi a chicken which seems to have some defect when it is opened up. After an examination, the Rabbi will declare it to be either kosher or terefah. Similarly, after an animal has been killed, the *shohet*, the one who performs the act of *shehitah*, is required carefully to examine the lungs of the animal to see whether there are adhesions, some of which render the animal terefah. Not all adhesions on the lungs render the animal terefah and a Rabbi is called upon to decide in doubtful cases. But the practice has developed among the more observant of permitting only animals the lungs of which have no adhesions at all. Such an animal is called glatt kosher, from the Yiddish 'glatt' meaning smooth (i.e. the lungs are smooth without adhesions). A curious development from this in more recent years is to extend the term glatt kosher to all products, so that when a product is stated to be 'smooth' the meaning is free of any possible taint that can render it terefah; glatt kosher has thus come to mean something like very kosher or strictly kosher.

Pots and pans in which non-kosher food has been cooked render any kosher food cooked subsequently in them terefah, on the principle that 'the flavour of a forbidden substance is as the substance itself', that is, not only is the actual terefah food forbidden but also kosher food to which the terefah flavour has been imparted. However, the flavour of the terefah food can be ejected from a utensil by a process known as 'kashering' (making kosher). This is done by immersing the tainted utensil in a cauldron of boiling water or by heating up water in the utensil until the water boils over. The kashering of utensils that come into direct contact with the fire, ovens, spits, and so forth, is achieved by subjecting them to a degree of heat equivalent to the degree through which the flavour of the forbidden food was absorbed in the first instance. Since they are very absorbent, the kashering process cannot operate with regard to utensils of china or porcelain. There is also a rule that if a small amount of terefah food becomes mixed with kosher food and can no longer be identified to remove it, it becomes neutralized in a proportion of 1: 60.

The strict prohibition of blood in the Bible (Leviticus 7: 26–27; 17: 10–14) is the basis for the laws governing the preparation of the meat of animals and birds for food. The usual practice is first to soak the meat in cold water for half an hour and then to salt it thoroughly and leave it covered in salt on a draining-board so that as much as possible of the blood is drained off. An alternative method is to roast the meat over a naked flame. In many communities, nowadays, the butcher attends to this process, relieving his customers from having to do it themselves. The blood of fishes is permitted so there is no process of 'salting' for fish.

The biblical text repeats three times the prohibition of 'seething a kid in its mother's milk' (Exodus 23: 19; 34: 26; Deuteronomy 14: 21). This might originally have been intended to prohibit an act of such callousness or to ban any attempt at influencing nature by some kind of sympathetic magic, but in the Rabbinic tradition the prohibition means that no meat of any animal may be cooked in any milk (the 'kid' and the milk of the 'mother' referring only to the type of the forbidden mixture, i.e. the milk and meat of animals like a 'kid' and its 'mother'). As for the threefold repetition, this is said to forbid the initial cooking-together of meat and milk; to forbid the eating of meat and milk cooked together; and to forbid any benefit from the mixture: by selling it, for example, to a non-Jew to whom these laws do not apply. According to one opinion in the Talmud it is permitted to cook the meat of birds in milk but the accepted opinion is that this, too, is forbidden by Rabbinic law on the grounds that if such is permitted, people may conclude that it is also permitted to cook in milk the meat of animals. This is an example of the Rabbinic principle of 'making a fence around the Torah'. A further Rabbinic extension is to forbid the eating of meat and milk together even when they have not been cooked or boiled together; for example, to have a glass of milk together with meat, or to eat meat together with buttered bread. Derived from this is the current practice of waiting, after a meat meal, before having a dairy meal. Some devout Jews wait for one hour between a meat and a dairy meal; in Anglo-Jewry, people often wait for three hours; and, in the usual custom among Orthodox Jews, the waiting period is as long as six hours. The basic reason for this waiting period is to make sure that no meat is lodged in the teeth, and so it is permitted to have a meat meal almost immediately after a dairy meal (generally after only half an hour). Because of these rules it is the usual practice among Orthodox Jews to have two separate sets of cooking utensils, crockery, and cutlery for meat and dairy meals.

Because of the verse prohibiting the sciatic nerve (Genesis 32: 33), this nerve must be removed from the animal by the process known as 'porging'. In communities like that of Anglo-Jewry, where there is a lack of skilled porgers, the hindquarter meat is not eaten at all. In Israel and most other countries, porging is done and the meat of the hindquarters eaten, though the fat of the stomach and that on the kidneys is forbidden, since these were offered as a sacrifice in Temple times (see Leviticus 7: 22–24).

## Reasons for the Dietary Laws

Unlike the ethical and moral precepts of Judaism the dietary laws seem to defy human reasoning. Why should it matter to religion what a man eats and, if it does matter, why are these particular items of food singled out as forbidden? The reason given for the prohibition of the sciatic nerve is that this was the site of Jacob's wound when he wrestled with the angel; fat and blood are forbidden because these were offered on the altar; but no reasons are given for the other dietary laws. Generally in the Talmudic tradition no special reasons are advanced. The Torah repeats that these laws are essential in promoting a life of holiness (Exodus 22: 30; Leviticus 11: 44–5; Deuteronomy 14: 21) and that it is God's will that they be obeyed. Why should man wish to fathom the divine will? God has His reasons and the devout Jew will obey these laws for this entirely sufficient reason. In fact, there is a definite tendency in Rabbinic thought to consider the quest for reasons for the precepts as bordering on the impious or as a questioning of God's wisdom. In a famous Rabbinic statement: 'A man should not say: I dislike intensely the meat of the pig. But he should rather say: I would like to eat it but my Father in heaven has declared it to be forbidden.'

Nevertheless, the medieval Jewish philosophers did try to provide a rationale for the mysterious details of the dietary laws. These thinkers had a threefold motivation in trying to demonstrate rationally why the otherwise obscure precepts of the Torah must be seen to be reasonable. They argued that if a Jew knows the reasons for the dietary laws he will be more enthusiastic in following them than if he simply followed them as an act of blind obedience. Secondly, to stress unreasoning obedience tends to lead men to think of God as tyrannically imposing unreasonable laws on His creatures.

Thirdly, there is the apologetic motivation: Jewish thinkers felt themselves obliged to react to attacks from without on Judaism on the grounds that some of its laws seem to be unreasonable and even bizarre.

Maimonides (*Guide of the Perplexed*, 3. 48) understands the dietary laws chiefly as a means of keeping the body healthy. The meat of the forbidden animals, birds, and fishes is unwholesome and indigestible. Surprisingly, Maimonides says that, at first glance, this does not apply to pork, to eat which does not seem to be harmful. Yet, Maimonides observes, the pig is a filthy animal and if swine were used for food, market-places and even houses would be dirtier than latrines, as may be seen, continues Maimonides, among the Franks in Western Europe; he is obviously contrasting the Muslims who do not eat pork with the Christians who do. Maimonides refuses to see the signs for the permitted animals and fishes as anything more than simple indications of the types of animal and fish that are permitted. An animal is not kosher because it chews the cud and has cloven hooves nor is a fish kosher because it has fins and scales. These are only the means of identifying which species are wholesome and which unwholesome. The prohibition of eating meat cooked in milk is similarly seen ·by Maimonides to be because such a mixture constitutes gross and very filling food. But he surmises that a reaction to idolatry may have something to do with the prohibition in that the idolatrous priests may have mingled meat and milk to encourage the earth to give its yield.

Nahmanides, in his Commentary to the Pentateuch, tends to see the dietary laws as beneficial to the soul rather than the body. Nahmanides observes that the forbidden animals and birds are predators so that for man to eat of their flesh will have an adverse effect on his character, whereas the permitted animals and birds are calmer and far less violent. As for fishes, those which have fins and scales are able to swim nearer to the surface of the water where they can inhale the fresher air, whereas the other fish lurk in the murky waters of the deep and their flesh is less clear and refined. In the Kabbalah this idea of human refinement is developed in a mystical way. The forbidden animals, birds, and fishes are in the realms of the demonic powers. To eat their flesh is to imbibe a spirit of impurity, making the mind dull and the soul impure. Modern thinkers, on the other hand, tend to dwell not so much on the reasons why these laws were first introduced but rather on the effect they have had and on the part they have played in Jewish self-discipline and in the preservation of the Jewish people as a people apart, as a holy people, in the language of the Bible (Exodus 19: 6).

## Extent of Observance

Where the view obtains, as it still does among Orthodox Jews, that the dietary laws are directly ordained by God, these laws will be unreservedly obeyed. But, affected by *biblical criticism and general uncertainty regarding the Bible as the direct word of God, modern Jews have adopted a variety of attitudes towards the observance of the dietary laws. *Conservative Judaism, with its emphasis on revelation *through* the people, not only *to* the people, tends to accept the findings of the critics that many of the dietary laws may have had their origin in primitive taboos, but still maintains that these laws must be obeyed as the most powerful means of preserving the Jewish people. This is not necessarily to leave God out of the picture or to say that these laws have no divine origin, although, no doubt, some Conservative Jews would say this. Other Conservative Jews still see the dietary laws as coming from God, albeit in an indirect way, through the experiences of the Jewish people in its quest for holiness. Because of its emphasis on *Halakhah as the distinguishing feature of the Jewish religion, Conservative Judaism advocates obedience to the rules and regulations of kashrut as laid down in the *Shulḥan Arukh*, though interpreted in a more liberal fashion than Orthodox Judaism normally allows. A Conservative Rabbi may eat kosher food in a non-kosher restaurant without being too fussy about the utensils in which the food has been cooked. On the other hand, in some Conservative circles, nowadays, especially in towns where there are kosher restaurants and where a large variety of kosher food-products is readily available, Conservative Jews will be as strict as the Orthodox in observing the dietary laws.

The attitude of *Reform Judaism, in the earlier period, was more or less one of indifference to the dietary laws. In 1888 a number of leading American Reform Rabbis adopted the 'Pittsburgh Platform' in which is contained the declaration:

'We hold that all such Mosaic and rabbinical

laws as regulate diet, priestly purity, and dress originated in ages and under the influence of ideas entirely foreign to our present mental and spiritual state. They fail to impress the modern Jew with a spirit of priestly holiness; their observance in our days is apt rather to obstruct than to further modern spiritual elevation.'

Nevertheless, some Reform Jews do keep the dietary laws, especially those found directly in the Bible such as that on the forbidden animals. To the taunts of those who scathingly dubbed observance of the dietary laws as 'kitchen religion', Morris Joseph, himself a Reform Rabbi but one who kept the dietary laws, retorted: 'It is better to have kitchen religion than drawing-room irreligion.' Rabbi Gunther Plaut summarizes the modern Reform attitude: 'The spokesmen of Reform Judaism rarely find it necessary either to attack or defend these observances. They do not regard such provisions as the literal word of God; they hold that they are no longer religiously meaningful and therefore need not be followed. But they have no quarrel with those who choose to observe the dietary laws'—to which final sentence one can only say: 'Jolly decent of them!'

It cannot be maintained that all Jews who call themselves Orthodox are strict observers of the dietary laws. Some, for example, will keep a 'kosher home' in which the separation of meat and milk and the other laws are strictly observed, but will not be too particular about eating non-kosher food outside the home in restaurants or in the homes of non-Jewish friends. Against this is the marked tendency in Orthodoxy, nowadays, to be excessively strict. Various organizations exist to provide Rabbinic supervision of prepacked foods to ensure that these contain not the slightest trace of terefah ingredients. In right-wing Orthodox circles, there is a tendency to go rather over the top in matters of kashrut, ignoring even the leniencies found in the standard Codes of Jewish law.

J. H. Hertz, 'Dietary Laws', in his *The Pentateuch and Haftorahs* (London, 1960), 448–54.

I. Grunfeld, *The Jewish Dietary Laws* (London, Jerusalem, and New York, 1972).

W. Gunther Plaut, 'The Dietary Laws', in his *The Torah: A Modern Commentary* (New York, 1981), 898–913.

**Discipleship**   The acceptance by a person of another as master, tutor, and spiritual guide. The two chief examples of discipleship in the Bible are those of *Joshua and Moses (Exodus 33: 11; Numbers 12: 28; 27: 12–22; Deuteronomy 34: 9) and *Elisha and Elijah (1 Kings 19: 19–21; 2 Kings 2). The 'sons of the prophets' mentioned in the biblical narrative of Elisha (2 Kings 2: 3–11; 4: 1; 38) appear to have been a guild of aspirants to prophecy who gathered around prophets to be instructed in the art. The word 'son' (*ben*) should be understood in the sense of a close pupil and the Hebrew is best translated as 'disciples of the prophets'. Elisha's special disciple and retainer, Gehazi, is not viewed with complete favour in the narrative because of his interference in the master's affairs (2 Kings 4).

The Talmudic Rabbis, with the study of the Torah as their highest value, attached the greatest significance to discipleship. In the opening section of Ethics of the Fathers, the chain of tradition from Moses to Joshua and down to the Men of the *Great Synagogue is first recorded and these are then quoted as advising: 'Raise many disciples.' The Talmud contains numerous admonitions to teachers to impart their knowledge of the Torah to their disciples and to disciples to pay great respect to their masters. The disciple was urged to 'serve scholars', this 'service' being interpreted both literally, as acting as a valet to the master, and figuratively, as observing closely the conduct of the master as a guide for the disciple's own way of life. There are stories of disciples secreting themselves in the master's bedroom to see how he behaved when he had relations with his wife, or in the privy to see how the master attended to his natural functions. In these stories, when the master protests at this invasion of his privacy, the disciple replies: 'What can I do? It is Torah and it is my duty to learn.' A disciple was forbidden to render decisions in Jewish law in the presence of his master. When a master passed in front of his disciple, the latter was obliged to rise to his feet and remain standing until the master had passed out of sight. It was extremely rare for a scholar to be entirely self-taught. To study at the feet of a master was seen as of the essence. In Jewish biography, the most distinguished Rabbis are always described as the disciples of this or that teacher.

In the Kabbalah it is frequently stressed that the devotee must not gain his knowledge of the 'secret science' simply from books but by word of mouth from a trusted teacher who himself had received the teaching from a master.

In *Hasidism, in particular, discipleship is

given the utmost priority. By definition, the Hasid is a follower of a particular Rebbe, the *Zaddik, whose approach to Judaism he tries to follow in every detail. In the earlier period of the Hasidic movement, it was the disciple of the master, not, as later, the son, who became the master's successor in the leadership of a particular group. The story has often been told of the disciple of *Dov Baer, the Maggid of Mezhirech, who declared that he did not journey to the master in order to learn Torah from him but to witness how the master tied his shoelaces.

*Scholem is not quite correct when he sees this as an entirely new form of charismatic leadership and discipleship. As mentioned above, there are parallels in the Talmudic period. Yet it is correct that in Hasidism the emphasis is on the charisma of the Rebbe, which has the greatest influence on his followers. It is no coincidence that the model of discipleship in Hasidism is often Elisha in his relationship to his master, Elijah, the holy man of God, a state Elisha himself eventually attained. Most of the Hasidic Rebbes had a Gabbai, an assistant whose function it was, to some extent, to act as a go-between and to protect the Rebbe from the clamour of the Hasidim to be given frequent audiences with the holy man. In Hasidic lore, the Gabbai often sees himself as the real power behind the Rebbe's throne and he is often revealingly dubbed a 'Gehazi'.

In the *Musar movement, too, discipleship is of supreme importance. All the Musarists described themselves as the disciples of Israel *Salanter, the founder of the movement, but each was also a follower of a later teacher whose philosophy he had chosen to follow. Salanter himself is reported to have said that both the Hasidim and the *Mitnaggedim, their opponents, are in error—the Mitnaggedim because they believe they have no need for a Rebbe, the Hasidim because they believe they have a Rebbe.

> Louis Ginzberg, 'The Disciple of the Wise', in his *Students, Scholars and Saints* (New York, 1958), 35–8.

**Disinterestedness** The mystical ideal of detachment from personal striving and ambition, also called equanimity. The Hasidic doctrine of *annihilation of selfhood comes very close to the ideal of disinterestedness. Disinterestedness has its origin in Western thought in the Stoic doctrine of ataraxy, the absence of passion. This originally non-religious ideal had an effect on the ascetic tendencies in early Christianity and, later, influenced the Sufi movement in Islam. Under the influence of Sufism, the doctrine appears in *Bahya, Ibn Pakudah's *Duties of the Heart* (v. 2, 5). Bahya describes ten principles by means of which believers can draw near to God's service free from the taint of self-interest. As the sixth of these principles, Bahya notes: 'It should be all the same to him whether others praise him or denigrate him.' Without reference to Bahya, the Kabbalist Isaac of Acre (thirteenth–fourteenth centuries) tells of a certain sage who came to one of the hermits requesting to be admitted into their fraternity. The hermit said to him: 'My son: "It is clear to God that your motives are worthy, but tell me this, have you attained to the state of equanimity?" ' When the would-be initiate asked the hermit what he meant, the hermit replied: 'Supposing there are two men, one of whom pays you honours, while the other insults you, are both the same in your eyes?' The aspirant replied: 'No master. When honours are paid me I am pleased and experience a sense of bliss, but when I am insulted I feel aggrieved, although I have no wish to take revenge or to hate the one who has insulted me.' 'Go in peace, my son,' said the hermit. 'For as long as you have not attained to equanimity, to the extent that insults to your person leave you totally unaffected, you are not yet ready for your thoughts to be bound to the One on high that you may be admitted into membership of our fraternity. However, go away and humble yourself still more in true humility until you do attain to equanimity and then you will be able to become a hermit.'

It is obvious from the context that the hermit in the passage was not a Jew. There were no fraternities of Jewish hermits in Isaac or Acre's day, nor is the existence of groups of Jewish hermits attested anywhere else in the history of Judaism. Yet, as often happened in the history of Jewish thought, an idea from without became accepted as an ideal worthy of emulation by Jewish mystics at least. The ideal is mentioned with approval by the famous Safed Kabbalist, Hayyim *Vital. Vital, in his work *Gates of Holiness*, writes: 'Humility should become so much part of his nature [lit. "the heart"] that he experiences no joy from honours paid to him and no distress from insults, and the two should be the same in his eyes.'

*Dov Baer of Mezhirech, disciple of the *Baal Shem Tov and the real organizer of the Hasidic movement, extends the ideal of equanimity to embrace an attitude of indifference to all worldly pleasures, though his philosophy is not one of *asceticism:

'Whatsoever befalls a man, it should be all the same to him, whether people praise him or despise him. And so, too, with regard to all other matters. And so too, with regard to eating, whether he eats delicacies or other food, it should be all the same to him since his evil inclination has gone entirely from him. Whatever befalls him he should say: "Behold this is from God and if it is good in His eyes, so be it", but his intention should be for the sake of Heaven so that in essence there is no difference. This is a most elevated stage.'

In his final remarks, Dov Baer seems aware that it is possible to cultivate the attitude of disinterestedness as a form of escapism from life's problems and without any religious motivation, hence his qualification that it should all be 'for the sake of Heaven'. It is also possible that the ideal of disinterestedness had a powerful psychological effect in *Hasidism, a movement constantly under attack by its opponents, the *Mitnaggedim. To be indifferent to praise and blame was essential if the Hasidim were to follow their new way of worship undeterred by how others saw them. Be that as it may, the ideal reoccurs in Hasidic works and many followers of the movement were as 'stoically' impervious to what others thought of them as they were to success and failure and to the world and its pleasures.

A disciple of Dov Baer, the 'Seer' of Lublin (d. 1815) analysed still further the ideal of equanimity in an anecdote told by his disciple, Moses of Sambur. A man was heard to say in the presence of the 'Seer', that he violently disliked it when people praised him. Upon hearing this, the 'Seer' shock his head, as if in protest. 'From this I understood,' remarks Moses of Sambur, 'that the ideal of equanimity, referred to in *The Duties of the Heart*, in the name of the saint, does not mean that it should be as unpleasant to a man when he is praised as it is when he is denigrated. Rather, the ideal means that he should be in his own eyes as if he were nothing at all, so that whether he is praised or denigrated he remains totally unaffected by it all, as if it were all said of a piece of wood or a stone. That is the ideal of true equanimity.'

It cannot therefore be said that Judaism knows nothing of the drastic negation of selfhood implied in the ideal of disinterestedness. But the ideal is confined to the circles of the more world-losing mystics. Those with a more traditional approach not only fail to realize the ideal but view it with a degree of suspicion as leading to its opposite, the pride which calmly dismisses as beneath contempt the opinions of others.

Louis Jacobs, 'The Saintly Ideal of Equanimity', in his *Holy Living: Saints and Saintliness in Judaism* (Northvale, NJ, and London, 1990), 59–64.

**Disputations** Debates between representatives of the Jewish and Christian religions in the Middle Ages in which Jews were compelled to engage with the aim of persuading them that Christianity not Judaism is the true religion. Three of these disputations, unlike the others, have been placed on record, though it is not too easy to determine what actually happened since, naturally, each side presents itself in its account in the most favourable light. In all three the main spokesman for *Christianity was a converted Jew, anxious to defend his conversion to the dominant faith. The Jewish representatives were forced into a defence of their religion that was bound to result in a denigration of Christianity and in this they risked their own lives and the lives of their co-religionists.

The first of these three disputations was staged in Paris under King Louis IV in 1240. Actually, this was not so much a real disputation as a defence of the Talmud by Rabbi Jehiel of Paris and other Rabbis against the accusation by Nicholas Donin that the Talmud contains ludicrous and perverse statements and denigrates the character of Jesus. Rabbi Jehiel has little difficulty in disposing of the first objection but, with regard to the second, he is obliged to postulate, unconvincingly, that the Talmudic references to 'Jesus' were to an earlier Jesus. not to *Jesus of Nazareth. The disputation had a sorry ending. Twenty-four cart-loads of the Talmud were consigned to the flames—one of the reasons why there is great scarcity of early Talmudic manuscripts.

The second disputation was between Pablo Christiani and the great Talmudic scholar *Nahmanides and took place in Barcelona in 1263, presided over by King James I of Aragon, who saw to it that the Jews received fair treatment, allowing Nahmanides to be completely open about his beliefs. Much of this disputation centred on the Christian claim that Jesus was the hoped-for *Messiah and was divine. Nahmanides, in the course of his argument, calls attention to the fact that the whole doctrine of the Messiah has a less prominent place in Judaism than in Christianity. Nahmanides himself wrote an account of the disputation and writes that the king rewarded him with a purse of 300 gold coins. Nevertheless, severe pressure was brought on Nahmanides to leave Spain and he did depart to settle in Palestine.

The third disputation was held in Tortossa over the years 1413–15, between Geronimo de Santa Fe and a number of learned Rabbis, among them Rabbi Astruk Halevi and Rabbi Joseph *Albo. Albo's views on Christianity were later incorporated into his *Sefer Ha-Ikkarim*, although this section is missing from the censored editions of the work.

In addition to the direct confrontations in the disputations, many polemical Jewish works were compiled to defend Judaism and to demonstrate its superiority over Christianity. But Jews had to engage in all this activity with great caution and restraint. It was not until the twentieth century that any kind of real *dialogue emerged between Jews and Christians.

A number of stock themes appear with regularity in both the disputations and the written works: Was Jesus the Son of God? Did the prophets foretell the coming of Jesus? Is not the New Testament the fulfilment of the Old Testament? If Judaism is the true religion, why is the Church so successful and why do the Jews suffer so greatly? It was all done on both sides with a hurling of biblical texts, an approach that has virtually ceased except in a few fundamentalist circles since *biblical criticism has been applied rigorously to the New as well as to the Old Testament. If there is still debate between the adherents of Judaism and Christianity, it is on the theological level.

Hyam Maccoby, *Judaism on Trial: Jewish–Christian Disputations in the Middle Ages* (London and Toronto, 1982).

**Divination** The practice of forecasting the future, especially by magical means (see MAGIC AND SUPERSTITION). A biblical text seems to condemn every form of divination: 'Let no one be found among you who consigns his son or daughter to the fire, or who is an augur, a soothsayer, a diviner, a sorcerer, one who casts spells, or one who consults ghosts or familiar spirits, or one who inquires of the dead. . . . But you must be wholehearted with the Lord your God' (Deuteronomy 18: 10–13). The famous French commentator, *Rashi, understands the last verse to mean that the man of faith should so rely on God's providence that he should have no urge to know what the future will bring, safely leaving his destiny in God's hand. Yet there are references in the Bible to apparently approved methods of divination. Joseph used a silver goblet for the purpose of divination (Genesis 44: 5), though this was said of Joseph in his capacity as ruler in Egypt, the land of magical practices. Eliezer, Abraham's servant, when he was sent to find a wife for Isaac, practised divination in order to know which maiden would be the one God had chosen.

The Talmudic Rabbis try to distinguish between actual divination and the use of a sign. The distinction seems to be based on the idea that while certain events may provide some indication of what is to happen, it is wrong to treat these as actually having power to influence the future. For instance, if a ferry-boat did not come along at the time when it was expected, it was permitted to rely on this as a sign that the intended journey would not be worth while. This very far from clear distinction paved the way for a whole range of practices, especially in medieval Germany. Another illustration of the permitted 'sign' is the practice of eating apples dipped in honey and other sweet things on the New Year festival as an augury of a sweet year to come. It is not that the eating of the sweet things guarantees a good future, but it is psychologically helpful to begin the year with tokens of the sweet, at least that is the rationale for the practice. No doubt some do believe that the practice does have some kind of magical effect.

A particularly interesting type of permitted divination consists in using the Bible to indicate what the future has in store. There are references in the Talmud to Rabbis, wishing to know which line of conduct they should successfully pursue, asking a little child which biblical verse he has just read in the Hebrew school, the verse providing the course to be taken. There are also references to a biblical verse that falls into the mind as being a kind of minor prophecy. Even such a stern opponent of all magical practices as Maimonides permits

(Responsa, no. 173) bibliomancy, since this has Talmudic support and, in any event, relies on the holy book. A teacher was in the habit of opening the Bible at random to discover a verse that foretold the future. The teacher used this method when requested to do so by Christians and Muslims. Is this permitted, Maimonides was asked, and should the man be removed from his office? Maimonides replies that the man must be deterred from using this method in the future on behalf of non-Jews, but he does not have to be deposed for having done so in the past.

Lithuanian Rabbis were in the habit of using a type of bibliomancy known as 'the Lot of *Elijah, Gaon of Vilna', although there no evidence whatsoever that the attribution is correct. So far as one can tell, the usual method was to flip through the pages of the Hebrew Bible at random and then count seven pages from the place where a particular page opened. Seven lines from the top of this page provided the verse for the divination. Rabbis are very cagey about their use of this method, but some use it even today.

Joshua Trachtenberg, 'Divination', in his *Jewish Magic and Superstition* (New York, 1939), 208–99. Yaakov Hillel, *Faith and Folly: The Occult in Torah Perspective* (Jerusalem, 1990).

**Divorce** Jewish divorce procedures are based on the Rabbinic understanding of Deuteronomy (24: 1–2): 'When a man hath taken a wife, and married her, and it come to pass that she find no favour in his eyes, because he hath found some uncleanness in her, then let him write her a bill of divorcement, and give it into her hand, and send her out of his house: And when she is departed out of his house, she may go and be another man's wife.' In the Rabbinic scheme, the 'bill of divorcement' is a document, known as the *get, in which it is stated that *A* hereby divorces his wife *B* and she is now permitted to marry whomsoever she pleases. The *get* is not a mere formal document of intent, but is the instrument through which the divorce is effected.

The most significant difference between the Jewish religious law of *marriage and divorce, and the law in this area in Western societies, is that the State or the court in Jewish law have the power neither to create a marriage bond nor to sever it. Both these actions can only be achieved by the two persons concerned. Even when the Jewish court, the *Bet Din, does

supervise the writing and delivery of the *get*, this is only for the purpose of seeing that the procedures are carried out correctly.

It has to be appreciated that, while a man obviously cannot marry a woman without her consent, it is she who is married to him not him to her, since, in the polygamous system which obtained until the ban on polygamy by Rabbenu *Gershom of Mayyence in the eleventh century, a man could have more than one wife. The husband is bound to his wife with regard to loving her, caring for her, and supporting her, but not in the sense that he cannot henceforth take another wife. The wife, on the other hand, from the time of her marriage, has bound herself entirely to this particular man and if, while still married to him, she has sexual relations with another man, it constitutes adultery (see *Decalogue). Thus, in traditional Jewish law, it is the husband who divorces his wife, not the wife her husband.

*Protection of the Wife*

Throughout the history of the Jewish divorce-laws various measures were introduced by Rabbinic authorities to prevent abuse by the husband of the rights the law gives him. The most important of these measures was the institution of the *ketubah*, the marriage settlement; this is a sum, determined by husband and wife when they marry, to be claimed by the wife from her husband's estate when he dies or from the husband himself when he divorces her. Thus, even though the wife's consent is not required for the divorce to be valid, there is the greatest check against hasty divorce by the husband since, when he divorces his wife, he is obliged to pay her the amount stated in the *ketubah* and this settlement is, naturally, enforceable by the courts.

Once the ban on polygamy was introduced, a husband was further banned from divorcing his wife without her consent since, otherwise, he could have avoided the ban against having more than one wife by divorcing his first wife. Furthermore, in Talmudic law, which became the norm, a wife can, in certain circumstances, petition for divorce. An illustration is where the husband earns his living by engaging in an unpleasant, malodorous occupation such as a tanner, which is more than the wife can reasonably be expected to bear. In these instances, the legal fiction was introduced that, although the consent of the husband is required, consent

given under duress is sufficient for the purpose
and the court can exercise coercion to force the
husband to give his assent to the divorce. There
can still be no divorce without the husband's
consent, but how such consent is obtained is
treated in a liberal fashion. For all that, the wife
is still at a disadvantage in countries where
there is civil divorce. Here it is possible for a
husband who has obtained a civil divorce still to
refuse to release his wife by delivering the *get*
and, in modern societies, the courts have no
power to coerce the husband to do the right
thing by his wife. This results in the vexed
*agunah* problem, where an unfortunate wife is
still bound to a husband who is no husband to
her but who refuses to deliver the *get* in order
to release her. Various attempts have been
made to solve the problem of the *agunah* but so
far with little success in Orthodox circles.

*Attitudes to Divorce*

The statement above of the purely legal position must not be taken to mean that there is no
stigma attached to divorce in Judaism. On the
moral and religious level a divorce should be
resorted to only as a last option where the
marriage has irretrievably broken down. The
union of man and wife is used by the prophets
in illustration of the unbreakable bond between
God and Israel. In a Hasidic homily it is noted
that the Hebrew term for divorce, *gerushin*,
means 'driven forth', the same word used for
Adam and Eve when they were driven from
Paradise. A divorce frustrates the divine purpose that husband and wife live harmoniously
in the 'Paradise' in which God has planted
them without having to leave it to pursue their
individual destinies. The prophet states that
God Himself testifies against the man who
breaks faith with the wife of his youth (Malachi
2: 14–15), upon which the Talmud (*Gittin* 90b)
comments that the very altar of God sheds tears
over the man who divorces his first wife.
Nevertheless, if both husband and wife believe
that they cannot continue to live together as
man and wife, there is no objection to divorce
by mutual consent, although the Rabbinic courts
will usually try to bring about a reconciliation
where this is possible. Orthodox and Conservative Jews follow all the rules regarding divorce
but Reform Jews generally dispense with the
whole *get* procedure, relying solely on the civil
divorce to dissolve the marriage. This radical
departure from the tradition in a matter of such

importance as divorce is seen as totally unacceptable in traditional circles.

*The Delivery of the* Get

Where there is no possibility of reconciliation
—say, where a civil divorce has already been
given—husband and wife attend a meeting of
the court for the *get* to be written and delivered.
Since the sole function of the court is to see
that the correct procedures are followed, in
some communities a single Rabbinic expert
serves in this capacity; but usually three Rabbis
serve as the court.

The *get* is written in Aramaic but with some
sections, the names for instance, in Hebrew.
Since writing a *get* requires skill, it is done by a
special scribe, the *sofer*, delegated by the husband to write the *get* on his behalf. The *get* has
to be delivered in the presence of two witnesses
and these have to sign the document. In Talmudic times the *get* was written on parchment
but any material may be used and nowadays it
is often written on heavy white paper. The *get*
is normally written by the scribe with a goose
quill. It is customary for a *get* to have twelve
lines of written text with margins at both sides
and at the top and the bottom.

The presiding Rabbi first asks the husband
whether he is prepared to give the *get* to his
wife of his own free will. The husband then
instructs the scribe to write the *get*, which the
scribe does. The witnesses read the text and
append their signatures. The *get* is then folded
and the husband takes it and declares that he is
about to deliver it in order to release his wife to
marry another, and he drops it into the wife's
palms which she holds together but open to
receive it. The *get* is then cut at its four corners
and kept in the Rabbi's archives. Husband and
wife are given a document which states that
they have been divorced according to Jewish
law.

David Werner Amram, *The Jewish Law of Di-
vorce* (London, 1897).
Isaac Klein, *A Guide to Jewish Religious Practice*
(New York, 1979), 449–508.

**Doctors** The statement in the Mishnah
(*Kiddushin* 4: 14), in the context of the kind of
trade and occupation a father should train his
son to pursue, that 'the best of doctors will go
to hell', was not taken seriously in practice by
subsequent Jewish teachers, many of whom
were themselves skilled physicians, and who

argued that the Mishnah denigrates only unscrupulous and unskilled healers. Yet the fact that the Talmud can comment on the biblical rule that an assailant must pay for his victim's cure (Exodus 21: 18), 'we can derive from this verse that a physician has been granted permission to heal', shows that there was an awareness of the theological problem in the pursuit of healing by natural means. The Talmudic observation seems to have been directed against a prevalent view that if God brings illness upon a person, it is an act of impiety for the doctor to attempt to frustrate the divine will. Such arguments were not accepted, however, and the Talmud even went so far as to advise a scholar not to reside in a town which had no doctors. To an extent, the problem resurfaced in some branches of *Hasidism where belief in the efficacy of the *Zaddik's prayers for the sick came into conflict with the claim of the physicians to effect cures in a natural way. Even so, very few Hasidic masters refused to allow their followers, when sick, to have recourse to skilled physicians.

In Jewish law, the opinion of a skilled physician is relied upon even in matters affecting the Jewish religion: when, for instance, a doctor advises strongly that a sick person should eat and not fast on *Yom Kippur, or where he urges that the Sabbath be profaned in order to care adequately for a dangerously sick person.

**Dogmas** In the eighteenth century, Moses *Mendelssohn and his followers tended to imply that Judaism does not, in the manner of the Christian Church, lay down that there are certain beliefs which a Jew must hold in order to be counted among the faithful. Judaism, on this view, is not a revealed religion at all but a revealed law. (The logical fallacy that to speak of a 'revealed law' is itself the formulation of a dogma is ignored.) Beliefs such as that in the immortality of the soul and belief in God are true, on this view, because reason tells us so, not because these and similar beliefs are expressed in any form of a Jewish catechism. This view, 'the dogma of dogmalessness', as it is called by Solomon *Schechter in a celebrated essay, is far too sweeping. That areas of dogma are the subject of considerable discussion; that, for instance, there have been many debates around Maimonides' *principles of the faith; that, in Judaism, a bare belief in a dogma or doctrine without any attempt to abide by its

consequences is valueless; cannot be taken to mean that Judaism has no fixed beliefs of any kind. If that were so, it is hard to see how Judaism itself can be defined at all. Schechter concludes: 'It is true that every great religion is "a concentration of many ideas and ideals", which make this religion able to adapt itself to various modes of thinking and living. But there must always be a point round which all these ideas concentrate themselves. This centre is Dogma.'

Solomon Schechter, *The Dogmas of Judaism*, in his Studies in Judaism (first series, Philadelphia, 1945), 147–81.

**Dogs** Rabbinic attitudes to dogs are somewhat ambiguous. On the one hand, it is permitted and even advisable to have guard dogs where there is danger of attack (a Midrash states that God gave Cain a dog to protect him in his wanderings) but, on the other hand, there are stern warnings against a Jew keeping a vicious dog in his house. The earliest reference to keeping dogs as pets is found in a German work of the fifteenth century, although, in the apocryphal book of Tobit, it is said that the hero had a dog.

In the Kabbalah the dog is the symbol of the demonic powers. In a remarkable statement in the Zohar, evil in the universe can be compared to a vicious dog on a long lead. The dog seems to enjoy full, independent power to bark and harm, but when there is a risk of it getting out of control the owner pulls it back in time. Influenced by the Kabbalah, Hasidic Jews never keep dogs as pets but many Orthodox Jews in Western lands see no objection whatsoever to this.

**Dov Baer of Lubavitch** Hasidic master (1773–1827), successor to his father, R. *Shneur Zalman of Liady, in the leadership of the intellectual tendency in *Hasidism known as *Habad. He is also known as *Dov Baer of Lubavitch (the Russian town where he settled) and as the Middle Rebbe, that is, the master who came in the middle between his predecessor and his successor as Habad leaders. By all accounts, Dov Baer was a genuine mystic (his valet reported that he would not infrequently go into a trance-like state in which he was totally unaware of his surroundings) but was also a capable organizer who drew up plans for a farming enterprise through which his followers would be able to earn an honest living while having sufficient time to devote to *contemplation.

Dov Baer developed in a host of works the contemplative ideas of his father. Especially noteworthy in this connection are the two lengthy missives he wrote for the guidance of his followers: *Tract on Contemplation* and *Tract on Ecstasy*. The latter is one of the most remarkable documents on Jewish spirituality in the whole history of Jewish thought, a unique analysis of the mystical mind. In this tract, Dov Baer, while believing in the high value of ecstatic states that result from profound contemplation on the divine, sternly warns his followers against the forms of sham *ecstasy in which there is too much of selfhood (see ANNIHILATION OF SELFHOOD) or which are sought by the worshipper with the express intention of obtaining cheap thrills from the ecstatic state, as he would from imbibing alcohol. Like his father, Dov Baer believed that deep in the recesses of the Jewish psyche there is a 'divine spark' of God Himself so that, at the highest stage of contemplation, this spark is rekindled and God meets Himself, so to speak.

In Dov Baer's scheme, contemplation on the whole Kabbalistic scheme in which all worlds evolve from the *En Sof through the *Sefirot down to our lowly world, is not only an extremely elevated form of divine worship but has the effect of refining the character of the worshipper. Contrary to the opinions of some moralists that character-defects can be rectified by a direct onslaught, Dov Baer taught that it is only through contemplation on the divine glory and majesty that the character can really be improved and strengthened.

Opponents of Habad were especially critical of Dov Baer's attempt to explain the Kabbalistic mysteries in a rational way. Such an attempt, they protested, turned the Kabbalah into a philosophical system entirely accessible to the human mind instead of a body of revealed truth which the human mind can only hope to apprehend, but never actually comprehend.

Louis Jacobs, *Tract on Ecstasy* (London, 1963).
Naftali Loewenthal, *Communicating the Infinite: The Emergence of the Habad School* (Chicago, 1990).

**Dov Baer of Mezhirech** Hasidic master (d. 1772), leader, theoretician, and organizer of *Hasidism after the death of Israel *Baal Shem Tov. Although Dov Baer was a competent Talmudist he was never a town Rabbi, occupying only the secondary Rabbinic position of 'Maggid' (the word means 'preacher') in the towns of Rovno and Mezhirech in Volhynia, and is hence known by the Hasidim either as 'the Mezhirecher Maggid' or as 'the Rebbe, Reb Baer'. Dov Baer only got to know the Baal Shem Tov during the last two years of the latter's life and while he quotes, very occasionally, sayings of the Baal Shem Tov, he never refers to him as 'my teacher'. Dov Baer is therefore more correctly to be seen as an original thinker with his own emphasis on what it is that Hasidism teaches.

The Maggid published nothing of his own but his teachings are found in works published by his disciples, especially Solomon of Lutzk, whose *Maggid Devarav le-Yaakov*, is an anthology of the Maggid's sayings with an introduction which provides a succinct account of the Maggid's thought.

According to the Maggid, man's central aim is to be constantly aware that God, as stated in the Zohar, 'surrounds all worlds and fills all worlds and no space is unoccupied by Him'. The Hasid must learn to perceive the divine energy with which all things are infused and in whatever he does he should intend to elevate all things to their divine Source.

Solomon Maimon (1753–1800), in his autobiography, describes in detail a visit he paid to the Maggid's 'court' and the goings-on he witnessed there, including the pranks the Hasidim played on one another in order to awaken joy for divine worship. Maimon tells of a homily of the Maggid which, in fact, is also found in early Hasidic writings in the Maggid's name and is typical of his thought. A scriptural verse (2 Kings 3: 15), with a degree of homiletical licence, is made to read: 'And when the minstrel became like the instrument he played then the hand of the Lord rested upon him.' When man considers himself to be nothing more than a passive instrument upon which God can play as He wishes, then the spirit of the Lord will rest upon him. In this and in other homilies of the Maggid, expression is given to the ideal of '*annihilation of selfhood'.

Joseph Weiss, 'The Great Maggid's Theory of Contemplative Magic', in *Studies in Eastern European Jewish Mysticism* (The Littman Library of Jewish Civilization; Oxford, 1985), 126–30.

**Dreams** In the Bible there is evident throughout a belief that dreams can contain revelations
from on high, as in the dreams of *Jacob,
*Joseph, and Pharaoh in the book of Genesis.
The prophetic vision, the Bible states (Numbers
12: 6), comes in a dream. A Rabbinic saying has
it that a dream is a sixtieth of prophecy.
Maimonides (*Guide of the Perplexed*, 3. 36–8)
develops his theory that in the dream the
imaginative faculty is awakened, without which
prophecy is impossible.

There is a good deal of material on dreams in
the Talmud but a degree of ambiguity about
the efficacy of dreams. In one Talmudic passage it is implied that dreams are a manifestation of the unconscious, as *Freud suggests, or,
at least, this is the meaning that can be given to
the Talmudic statement: 'A man is only shown
in a dream that of which he thinks during the
day.' In matters of law, information obtained in
a dream is disregarded. The illustration is given
of a man whose father appeared to him in a
dream and informed him that a sum of money,
hidden in such-and-such a place had been
designated by him for charity and it belonged
to the poor. The ruling given was that the
dream could be disregarded and the son could
keep the money for himself. While a Rabbinic
scholar might occasionally claim that a suggested interpretation of a biblical or Talmudic
text came to him in a dream, the habit of Jacob
of Marvege (thirteenth century) of using information conveyed to him in dreams as authoritative in law was extremely unusual. After fasting
and employing other techniques, Jacob would
present Halakhic queries to heaven, to which
he received replies in dreams. These replies are
recorded in Jacob's work entitled: *Responsa
from Heaven*. We should not be surprised that,
according to the work, 'Heaven' always had
the same Halakhic opinions as the French
Talmudists. The Talmudic statement that a
dream depends on how it is interpreted, puzzling to the more philosophically minded, is
discussed in the *Responsa of Solomon Ibn
*Adret. Based on a Talmudic passage, a special
ceremony developed of 'interpreting for good'
a bad dream. The procedure was for the man
who had the dream to say to three other
persons: 'I have had a dream and do not know
what to make of it'; and they would reply: 'The
dream is a good one and is for your good.'
Many people, disturbed by a bad dream, would
fast in order to ward off the possible evil

effects. The Rabbis allowed such a fast to be
undertaken even on the Sabbath in order to
release the man from his anxiety but they
required him to undertake another fast for
having fasted on the Sabbath.

Joshua Tractenberg, 'Dreams', in his *Jewish Magic
and Superstition* (New York, 1939), 230–48.

**Dress** There are three biblical laws regarding
dress: that fringes (*tzitzit) are to be attached to
the corners of garments (Numbers 15: 37–41);
that a garment containing a mixture of wool
and flax (*shaatnez*) is not to be worn (Deuteronomy 22: 11); and that a man must not wear a
woman's apparel or a woman a man's (Deuteronomy 22: 5). The reason given for the last
prohibition is either that this might lead to men
and women gaining entrance in disguise into
companies of the opposite sex for immoral
purposes, or else because of the need to distinguish clearly between male and female in God's
creation. In sixteenth-century Italy, because of
the influence of the Italian carnival, men used
to dress up as women on *Purim and women as
men, and the Rabbis permitted this on the
grounds that, since this is done, for men and
women to wear the other's clothes on Purim is
not to wear the garments of the opposite sex
(see CUSTOM).

Otherwise, there are hardly any rules about
the kind of dress Jewish men and women
should wear. The principle of avoiding *Gentile
ways only applies to practices associated with
pagan rites or with the doctrines of a religion
other than Judaism. In a famous ruling, Rabbi
Joseph Colon (d. 1480) permitted a Jewish
doctor to wear the special doctor's robe used by
non-Jewish physicians since it was only a mark
of his craft and has no doctrinal significance.
Jews were not normally distinguished from
their Gentile neighbours in matters of dress;
otherwise there would have been no need for
the introduction of the infamous Jew badge to
identify Jews as such when they walked abroad.
The special Hasidic garb is in a class on its own
and, interestingly enough, appears to have been
adopted from the clothes worn by the Polish
noblemen in the eighteenth century (see
HASIDISM and STREIMEL).

The Rabbis generally discouraged the wearing of ostentatious or loud garments. It is
nowadays a distinguishing feature of the ultra-
Orthodox that the menfolk wear dark jackets
and coats and black hats, except on the Sabbath

when some wear white or golden robes. Women were urged to be especially modest in their clothing, wearing ankle-length dresses with sleeves reaching to the wrist and with the head entirely covered by a *sheitel or a kerchief. The majority of modern Jews, even the Orthodox, see no harm in adopting the less outrageous fashions in dress, but stop short of mini-shirts and see-through blouses.

**Dubnow, Simon** Russian Jewish historian (1860–1941). Dubnow wrote his great *World History of the Jewish People* in Russian but it was published in German translation in ten volumes in Berlin (1925–9) and subsequently in Hebrew. Inevitably, Dubnow's thought with regard to Jewish history has been compared with that of the other famous modern Jewish historian, *Graetz. It has been said, perhaps too simplistically, that while Graetz sees the thrust of Jewish history chiefly in terms of great men and their ideas, Dubnow sees Jewish history as the expression of the rich and varied life lived by the Jewish people as a whole, not only its great heroes. Religion is an important element in Jewish history for Dubnow but, in his view, it is more a case of the history shaping the religion than the religion shaping the people. Dubnow's *History of Hasidism* was written in Hebrew (published 1930–2) and is the first comprehensive attempt to treat the movement with scholarly objectivity. In this area, too, Dubnow differs from Graetz for whom the Kabbalah, Hasidism, and, indeed, Jewish mysticism as a whole were delusions beneath the contempt of a rational Jewish thinker. Dubnow sketches with great accuracy the earliest stages of the movement and provides full annotated bibliographies of Hasidic sources and anti-Hasidic polemics.

**Dybbuk** Sometimes spelled *dibbuk*, the soul of a person pursued by *demons that has found temporary security in the body of a living person. References to evil spirits entering human bodies are frequent in early Jewish literature but the notion of the *dybbuk* is not found until the sixteenth–seventeenth centuries where it appears in the writings of the Kabbalist Hayyim *Vital. Tales of *dybbuk* possession are numerous among Oriental and Eastern European Jews. In the usual version of these stories, a sinner dies and the demons or destructive angels hurry to bring him before the judgement

throne. In order to escape for a time he can enter the body of a living person if that person has committed some sin, albeit of a minor nature, at the time. The *dybbuk* (from the root *davak*, 'to cleave', see DEVEKUT) generally overtakes, to some extent, the personality of the one whose body it has entered, speaking in a strangled, muffled tone as if from a vast distance. In the ceremony of *exorcism a holy man orders the *dybbuk* to leave the body in which it has found lodging.

The whole subject was made popular through the play *The Dybbuk* by S. An-ski, of which many productions and a classic film have been made. Not only Hasidic Rebbes, as in An-ski's play, were called upon to drive out a *dybbuk*. In the sober circles of Lithuanian Jewry, the tale is often told of the *Hafetz Hayyim exorcizing a *dybbuk* through his disciples. On the other hand, when the Sotmarer Rebbe was approached by a father to drive out a *dybbuk* from his daughter, the Rebbe laconically said: 'Take her to a psychiatrist. There are no *dybbuks* in America.'

Gershon Winkler, *Dybbuk* (New York, 1981).

**Dynastic Succession** The transfer of power and authority from father to son throughout the generations. Jewish history knows of royal dynasties, especially the dynasty of King *David from whom all the kings of Judah were descended in direct succession. The *Messiah is thought of as a descendant of David who will reign as the legitimate scion of this royal house. The dynasties of the Maccabees and of Herod were viewed somewhat ambiguously by the later Rabbis. The Princes in Palestine during the first two centuries CE claimed descent from *Hillel: Rabban *Gamaliel I; his son, Simeon ben Gamaliel; Rabban Gamaliel II; his son, Simeon ben Gamaliel II; and his son, Rabbi *Judah the Prince. There are echoes in the Talmud of conflicts between the Princes and scholars such as Rabbi *Joshua and Rabbi *Meir who were not of aristocratic birth. Although the High Priesthood was not necessarily a hereditary office, if the son of the High Priest was capable of assuming the office he was to be given preference over all others. Here, too, there appear to have been conflicts between holders of the highest positions in the Jewish community who were of noble birth and the scholars of far lower rank. Extremely revealing is the ruling of the Mishnah (*Horayot* 3: 8), theoretical though it undoubtedly is, that a scholar, even if he is a bastard (*mamzer) takes precedence over a High Priest who is an ignoramus.

Although *Hai Gaon is said to have sat on the 'throne' of his father, *Sherira Gaon, and Hai's 'coronation' with great pomp and ceremony is described, the Gaonite does not appear to have been a hereditary office. In the later period, as the office of *Rabbi developed, mainly from the sixteenth century on, there was considerable discussion as to whether, when a Rabbi died, his son was entitled automatically to succeed him, even though other candidates might be more learned and more suitable for the post. Some authorities argued that, since Maimonides states that hereditary succession is to be the rule for all communal positions, the office of Rabbi is hereditary. Others refused to accept the argument, since the Torah cannot be the special preserve of a Rabbi to the extent that he can bequeath it to his sons. At present it is not the practice to accept that the office of Rabbi is hereditary. Nevertheless, many communities do tend to offer the position to the son or son-in-law of the previous Rabbi. There are even instances where, at the graveside of the previous Rabbi, his son is declared his successor and congratulated, on the lines of: 'The king is dead, long live the king!'

In later *Hasidism, dynasties of Rebbes proliferated. During the nineteenth century, the comparison between the Rebbe and a king was taken almost literally, in the use of the term 'the Rebbe's court', for instance. There were often dynastic rivalries as to which son would inherit his father's 'throne' and much 'palace' intrigue. It was certainly not unknown for the sons of a Rebbe, when he died, to set themselves up as Rebbes in their own right, each claiming to be the true heir of the departed saint. And there were a number of instances of the Hasidim appointing a regent where the heir apparent was too young to assume office when his father died.

# E

**Ecclesiastes** Biblical book, one of the Five Scrolls (Megillot) in the third section of the *Bible, the *Hagiographa; Heb. name, Kohelet (usually translated as 'Preacher'). The opening verse of the book: 'The words of Kohelet, the son of David, king in Jerusalem' were understood in the Jewish tradition to mean that the author was none other than King Solomon but modern biblical scholarship is unanimous in holding that the book was compiled at a much later date, although opinions differ as to when and by whom the book was actually composed. The Talmud (*Shabbat* 30b) states that, at first, the sages wished to hide the work (i.e. they refused to endow it with the sanctity of sacred Scripture) because some of its statements contradict the Torah and are even self-contradictory. Eventually, however, the book was accepted as a biblical book on the grounds that it begins and ends with 'the fear of heaven'. In other words, for all the book's scepticism and pessimism about the human condition, the teaching which shines through is: 'Fear God and keep His commandments' (12: 13). The usual Midrashic interpretation of the book is that the description of all human life 'under the sun' as 'vanity of vanities' applies only to earthly pursuits ('under the sun'), not to the way of the Torah, which is 'above the sun', eternal and beyond time.

Ecclesiastes is read in the synagogue on the festival of *Tabernacles, the festival of joy; an odd choice, on the face of it, for a book that seems to question life's values. But, here again, the interpretation holds good that the philosophical probings of the book do not lead ultimately to unbelief but, on the contrary, to an appreciation of the higher values which promote true happiness. The book has served as a reminder that Judaism does not necessarily frown on a sincere quest for life's meaning and significance. For this reason, the book is, in a sense, the earliest encounter between faith and reason, a debate which has been continued by the philosophically inclined throughout the history of Jewish thought. The very admission of such a book into the Bible demonstrates how precarious it is to try to draw a picture of Judaism in simple terms.

Victor E. Reichert and A. Cohen, 'Ecclesiastes', in their *The Five Megilloth* (London, 1952), 104–91.

**Ecology** Concern with the preservation of the planet, especially acute in the twentieth century. The proliferation of vast industries; the successful fight against disease, creating the danger of overpopulation; the use of nuclear energy; building activities on a scale unimagined in the past; the risk of global warming or the greenhouse effect, as it is called: all these factors contribute to anxiety about the ecological state of the world. The classical Jewish sources, coming from a time when the problem was hardly a serious one, cannot offer any kind of direct guidance. The argument, on the basis of the verse: 'And replenish the earth, and subdue it; and have dominion over the fish of the sea, and over the fowl of the air, and over every living thing that creepeth upon the earth' (Genesis 1: 28), that, from the beginning, Judaism was opposed to ecological concerns, is extremely faulty. When this verse was written, there was no problem of ecology. On the contrary, at that time, man's problem was how to master the environment. This is quite apart from the fact that Jewish interpretations of the verse have never understood it to mean that man's right and duty to conquer nature is unlimited.

Concern with the cultivation of a wholesome environment is evident in the older Jewish sources, although these do not deal with the problem on a global scale, requiring the co-operative efforts of many nations, but with the more limited problem of how city-dwellers are to come to terms with their environment and how the individual is to avoid wasting nature's resources.

Waste-disposal, for instance, was a major concern in Rabbinic times. Care was to be taken, the Rabbis urged, that bits of broken glass should not be scattered on public land where they could cause injury. Saintly men, the Talmud (*Bava Kama* 30a) remarks, would bury their broken glassware deep down in their own fields. Other rubbish could be deposited on public land, but only during the winter months when, in any event, the roads were a morass of mud because of the rains. In the Mishnah (*Bava Batra* 2), Rabbinic concern for a peaceful and clean environment was given expression in definite laws. A dovecote must not be kept within 50 cubits of a town and no one may keep a dovecote on his own property, unless his land extends at least 50 cubits in every direction around it. The reason is to prevent the doves from consuming the seeds sown in the neighbouring fields. Since a city is more attractive with a wide open space around it, no trees may be planted within a distance of 25 cubits from the city. If the trees were there before the city was built they can be cut down, but the owner is entitled to compensation for the loss of his trees. (All this obviously does not refer to the planting of trees as an adornment of the city, a concept unknown in Mishnaic times.) Carcasses, graves, and tanneries must be kept at a distance of at least 50 cubits from the city. A tannery must not be set up in such a way that the prevailing winds waft the unpleasant odour to the town.

A prohibition known as *bal tashḥit*, 'do not destroy' is based by the Rabbis on the biblical injunction not to destroy fruit-bearing trees (Deuteronomy 20: 19), but it is extended by them to include wasting anything that can be used for the benefit of mankind. For instance, while it was the custom to rend the garments on hearing of the death of a near relative (see DEATH AND BURIAL), to tear too much or too many garments violates this rule (*Bava Kama* 91b). Maimonides formulates this as: 'It is not only forbidden to destroy fruit-bearing trees but whoever breaks vessels, tears clothes, demolishes a building, stops up a fountain or wastes food, in a destructive way, offends against the law of "thou shalt not destroy".' Maimonides' qualification, 'in a destructive way', is intended to convey the thought that if, say, a fruit-bearing tree is causing damage to other trees, it

may be cut down since then the act is constructive. A Midrashic homily has it that the reason why the wood used for the Tabernacle in the wilderness was not from fruit-bearing trees, was to teach human beings that when they build their own homes they should use wood from other than fruit-bearing trees.

Norman Lamm, 'Ecology in Jewish Law and Theology', in his *Faith and Doubt* (New York, 1971), 162–85.

**Economics** In economic matters Jews have generally adapted themselves to whichever economic system was in vogue in the particular country in which they resided. There has never emerged anything like a specifically Jewish form of economics. This is not to suggest that Judaism has nothing to say on the subject. The principles of social justice and compassion are repeatedly stressed in the Bible, the Talmud, and the moralistic literature. But the problem today is how these principles can best be applied in the conditions that obtain in the age of capitalism—organized labour, the machine, and advertising on the widest scale, even if one does not go so far as to dub our society a ratrace. While all Jews accept the principles, how they are to be realized is a matter on which men and women of goodwill differ profoundly. It is consequently futile to invoke Judaism in any direct fashion in trying to cope with economic problems. A useful analogy is provided by attitudes to health and combating disease. Judaism is on the side of health, but it is the experts in this area, the physicians and, to a large extent, the politicians, who can best help to provide the needed health-care for the greatest possible number of people. That is why, in the State of Israel, there has so far not emerged a religious party with an economic programme of its own based on Jewish teachings. It is hard to see on what such a party, if it did emerge, would base its claims.

In the area of business ethics, for example a number of attempts have been made in recent years to extrapolate from the Jewish sources modes of conduct to be followed by the believing Jew. But these, inevitably, have to contend with the sober fact that the sources were produced mainly in a feudal system of society, which was so different from modern forms of society that whatever guidance is available is bound to be of an indirect and purely theoretical nature (see COMMUNISM).

Aaron Levine, *Free Enterprise and Jewish Law: Aspects of Jewish Business Ethics* (New York, 1980).

**Ecstasy** Intense exaltation of spirit at the nearness of God, in which the worshipper transcends his self in wonder. Ecstasy is closely associated with *devekut, the ideal stressed in particular in *Hasidism. Since there is a marked reluctance on the part of Jewish mystics to record their most intimate religious experiences, very few accounts of ecstasy are found in the literature of Jewish worship. In fact, the only comprehensive analysis of the phenomenon is the *Tract on Ecstasy* by *Dov Baer of Lubavitch, in which an attempt is made to distinguish between true ecstasy and various spurious forms. At a lower level, Hasidism speaks frequently of the state of *hitlahavut* (from *lahav*, 'flame'), the state of burning enthusiasm during prayer in which the soul of the worshipper reaches out to God in yearning. In some versions of Hasidism, it is believed that when the *Zaddik delivers his discourse (his 'Torah') during the third meal on the Sabbath, the *Shekhinah takes over, as it were, and speaks through him, the Zaddik himself being unaware of what he is saying.

**Ecumenism** The attempt by religious groupings with divergent views to discuss the things they have in common and work together for the furtherance of these things. On the Jewish–Christian scene the old antagonism of the *disputations has largely yielded to greater co-operation in *dialogue.

The question of a purely Jewish ecumenism between Orthodoxy, Conservative, and Reform Judaism has exercised the minds of thinkers belonging to the three groupings. As long ago as 1913, Solomon *Schechter, in an address he delivered as spokesman for the Jewish Theological Seminary of America (the Conservative College) at the Hebrew Union College (the Reform College), put forward his programme of Jewish ecumenism, although the actual term was not used by Jews at that time. Schechter drew on the analogy of the British Parliament, in which the governing party is known as His (Her) Majesty's Government and the opposition as His (Her) Majesty's Opposition, and yet both His Majesty's Government and His Majesty's Opposition form one large community, working for the welfare of the country and the prosperity of the nation. Schechter observed:

'Of course, it will always be a question as to which is which; we Conservatives maintaining that we are His Majesty's Government and you His Majesty's Opposition. But this is one of the differences. For reduce your differences as much as you want, and, indeed, I hope and pray that the difference of aims is not as deep as we sometimes think, the fact remains that we are unfortunately divided both in questions of doctrines—at least certain doctrines—and even more in practice. But, thank God, there are still a great many things and aims for which both parties can work in perfect harmony and peace, and unite us.'

After the *Holocaust and an astonishing revival of Orthodoxy in the USA, the view of Schechter became increasingly unpopular among the Orthodox. But there, and in other countries such as Great Britain, the country that provided Schechter with his illustration, while Orthodox, Conservative, and Reform Jews continue to co-operate in many areas, working together for the State of Israel and Jewish and general welfare, there is now an extreme reluctance on the part of the Orthodox to engage in ecumenism on a religious level. Indeed, a number of influential heads of Yeshivot in the USA pronounced a ban against Orthodox Rabbis belonging to Rabbinic bodies in which Reform or Conservative Rabbis participated as Rabbis, since these Rabbis are said to reject the doctrine 'the Torah is from Heaven'.

Solomon Schechter, 'His Majesty's Opposition', *Seminary Addresses* (New York, 1959), 239–44.

**Education** In Rabbinic Judaism, *study of the Torah is the highest of Jewish values, for men at least (see WOMEN). The need to study made education at every level a divine imperative. During the past two thousand years, Jewish communities saw it as a prime aim to establish elementary schools and, in the larger cities, Yeshivot (see YESHIVAH), at which young men engaged in advanced Jewish learning. In many communities, people would gather in study-groups, the members of which would meet regularly to study, at a less advanced level, the more basic texts of Bible, Talmud, and Codes. In addition, many Jews devoted a good deal of their leisure time to studying on their own, helped by the standard commentators. The past should not be idealized. Not every Jew was educated. Indeed, the constant refrain of the Jewish moralists, that everyone must devote time to study, suggests that the injunction was often needed. It remains true that parents would scrimp and save in order for their children to be given a sound education. No one could be elected to high office in the Jewish *community unless he possessed a considerable degree of learning.

Side by side with education in the Torah, the elementary schools usually provided the children with the rudiments of a general education— simple arithmetic, a smattering of history, and, in some instances, knowledge of languages other than Hebrew. But at every level, there was a conflict between the total demands of Torah learning and the thirst for general knowledge. The *Haskalah movement, often with the disapproval of the traditional Rabbis, had, as a main aim, the cultivation of a broader, more hospitable attitude towards general education. Samson Raphael *Hirsch, in Germany, developed his doctrine of 'Torah and Derekh Eretz' ('the Way of the Land', denoting, in Hirsch's thought, Western culture and its values where these were not incompatible with Torah). Today, with the exception of a comparatively few ultra-Orthodox, it is accepted that it is both possible and desirable for a Jew to have a good general education without this compromising his loyalty to the traditional ideal of Torah education.

Norman Lamm, *Torah Umadda: The Encounter of Religious Learning and Worldly Knowledge in the Jewish Tradition* (Northvale, NJ, and, London, 1990).

**Eighteen Benedictions** The series of benedictions recited thrice daily; Heb. Shemoneh Esreh ('Eighteen'), later also known as the Amidah ('Standing Prayer') because, while reciting it, the worshipper has to stand in respect. There is considerable confusion regarding the history of the Eighteen Benedictions. In some Talmudic sources they are attributed to the Men of the *Great Synagogue, in others to Rabban *Gamaliel II. To the original eighteen, the benediction directed against the sectarians (*minim*) was added, so that there are now nineteen benedictions. Similarly, the term Eighteen Benedictions is used for the Sabbath and festival Amidah, even though this only has seven benedictions.

The Amidah is in three parts. There are three benedictions of praise at the beginning,

three of thanks at the end, and thirteen in the middle. The idea behind this form is that a petitioner to a king first praises the king, then states his request, and finally thanks the king for granting him an audience. The nineteen benedictions, each ending with: 'Blessed art Thou, O Lord Who . . .', are:

1. 'Fathers', praising God for choosing the patriarchs, Abraham, Isaac, and Jacob.
2. A benediction referring to the *resurrection.
3. Praise of God's holiness.
4. Prayer for wisdom and knowledge.
5. Prayer for repentance.
6. Prayer for pardon of sin.
7. Prayer for redemption from personal troubles.
8. Prayer for healing.
9. Prayer for sustenance.
10. Prayer for redemption of the Jewish people.
11. Prayer for the restoration of true judges.
12. Prayer for the downfall of the sectarians.
13. Prayer for the righteous.
14. Prayer for God to dwell in the rebuilt Jerusalem.
15. Prayer for the coming of the *Messiah, son of David.
16. A prayer for all prayers to be heard and answered.
17. Prayer for the restoration of the Divine Glory to the rebuilt Temple.
18. Thanksgiving.
19. Prayer for Peace.

All the benedictions are in the plural form: 'Grant us'; 'We praise Thee'. The prayer for the downfall of the sectarians was introduced for the purpose of separating heretics from the community. Crypto-heretics would obviously avoid reciting a benediction which calls for their own downfall and they would stop coming to the synagogue for prayer. Some scholars think that the 'sectarians' referred to were the early Jewish Christians. Out of fear of the censor, the wording of this benediction has been changed over the years so as to render it less offensive or so as to make it refer only to the excessively wicked. Reform prayer books preserve the basic pattern of the Eighteen Benedictions but with the omission of references to a personal Messiah.

The Eighteen Benedictions are recited with upright posture, except for the first and eighteenth benediction. At the beginning and end of these two the body is bent gently downwards from the waist and then raised slowly again in token of submission to God's will. The Eighteen Benedictions are first recited by the worshippers very quietly (hence the name the 'Silent Prayer') and then repeated, in the morning and afternoon service (but not in the night service) in a loud chant by the *Cantor, the members of the congregation responding with 'Amen' after each Benediction. The 'Silent Prayer' does not require a congregation and can be recited in public, but the repetition by the Cantor requires a quorum of ten, the *minyan.

Israel Abrahams, *A Companion to the Authorized Daily Prayer Book* (New York, 1966), 55–71.

**Electricity** The Hebrew word *ḥashmal*, used in Ezekiel's vision of the *Chariot (Ezekiel 1: 4, 27), is usually translated as 'amber' or 'electrum' and may be based on the recognition by the ancients that rubbing amber produces sparks. This word is, in fact, used for 'electricity' in modern Hebrew. Israeli children are astonished to find, as they think, that the prophet knew of electricity! Once this mysterious power was discovered and harnassed to cater to human needs, a host of problems became acute in connection with Jewish religious law. With regard to the Sabbath, for instance, on which the law forbids kindling fire (Exodus 35: 3), the question arose of whether this meant that it was wrong to switch on an electric light on the Sabbath. In the early days, some Rabbis tried to argue that electric lights may be switched on on the Sabbath, since there is no combustion in the filament and, in any event, the electric power is already present, the switching-on of the light being only an indirect cause. Conservative Jews accept this argument and permit the switching-on of electric lights but do not allow cooking by electricity on the Sabbath, since to cook food is a separate prohibition. In the Reform system there is generally a relaxation of the strict Sabbath laws. Orthodox Judaism, today, does not permit any use of electricity on the Sabbath. Orthodoxy sees it as wrong not only to switch on electric lights but even to open the door of a refrigerator so that the light will come on. Most Orthodox authorities today also ban the use of a microphone or a telephone on the Sabbath on the grounds that sparks are produced and that the flow of the current is changed through the speaking voice.

But Orthodoxy has no objection to having a time-switch fixed so that the lights will go on and off automatically on the Sabbath.

Another question with regard to electricity is whether electric lights can be used for religious ceremonies in which hitherto oil lamps or tallow candles were used; the lights of *Hanukkah, for instance, or the memorial, *Yahrzeit, light, or the *perpetual light in the synagogue. The tendency is to be lenient in these matters and to permit the use of electric lights for these purposes.

Another question in connection with electricity is whether the prohibition of shaving with a razor (see BEARD) applies to an electric shaver. It used to be the practice in most Orthodox circles to permit this, but there is now a definite tendency to frown upon the removal of facial hair by an electric shaver.

In practically every collection of contemporary *Responsa questions of electricity according to Jewish law, the *Halakhah, are discussed. A two-volume compendium has been published on the subject in Hebrew, entitled *Ha-Ḥashmal Ba-Halakhah* (Jerusalem, 1978–81).

**Eliezer, Rabbi** Rabbi Eliezer ben Hyrcanus (*c*.40–120 CE), one of the five most distinguished disciples of Rabban Johanan ben *Zakkai, later to become one of the leading Rabbinic figures of his day and teacher of Rabbi *Akiba. The Mishnah records around 300 laws in the name of Rabbi Eliezer. The difficulty to be faced in attempting to reconstruct the life of Rabbi Eliezer is that he is, like all the other early Rabbinic figures, a hero of Jewish legend, from which it is far from easy to disentangle the facts. It is surprising that practically all the historians accept at face-value the Talmudic story (*Bava Metzia* 59b) that, in a certain case, Rabbi Eliezer held fast to his opinion even against the majority ruling and even against a voice that came from heaven, as a result of which he was placed under the ban (see HEREM). Very curious is the story told of Rabbi Eliezer that he was falsely accused of heresy because he had once heard a saying, of which he approved, recorded by a disciple of Jesus. The truth is that these stories are very late and were told possibly centuries after Rabbi Eliezer so that, at the most, the only conclusion that can be drawn from them is that Rabbi Eliezer, for all his great learning, may have been viewed at times with a degree of suspicion. Yet Rabbi Eliezer is one of the most revered of the *Tannaim, the teachers who flourished in Palestine in the first two centuries CE, and he is often called 'Rabbi Eliezer the Great'.

**Elijah** The ninth-century BCE prophet active during the reign of King Ahab and Ahaziah as told in the book of *Kings (1 Kings 17–19; 21; 2 Kings 1–2. In Elijah's confrontation with the prophets of Baal (1 Kings 18) the prophet presents to the people his famous either/or: 'How long will you waver between two opinions? If the Lord is God, follow Him; and if Baal, follow him!' Elijah, even in the Bible, is a mysterious figure, whose sudden appearance is announced without preamble and without the name of his father or any other details of his early life: 'Elijah the Tishbite, an inhabitant of Gilead, said to Ahab, "As the Lord lives, the God of Israel whom I serve, there will be no dew or rain except at my bidding"' (1 Kings 17: 1). In the book of Malachi (3: 24), Elijah is the figure who will reappear on the great judgement day of the future; on the basis of this, Elijah, who did not die but was taken up to heaven in a chariot of fire (2 Kings 2), becomes, in later Jewish thought, the herald of the *Messiah.

In the Talmudic period, it was believed that Elijah frequently returns to earth to teach and converse with certain Rabbis of special merit. Two later Midrashim, *The Great Teaching of Elijah* and *The Lesser Teaching of Elijah*, purport to be the record of these discourses of Elijah and the Talmudic Rabbis. At a *circumcision a special chair is set aside for Elijah who is present at every such happy event. At the Passover *Seder, a special 'cup of Elijah' is placed on the table and, at a stage in the proceedings, the door is opened to welcome the prophet. (In later Jewish apologetics, when Christians derided the notion that Elijah appears at the same time in different places, the retort was: 'You Christians believe that Jesus is present in the host in different places!')

In Jewish mysticism, Elijah appears to the saints and imparts to them new mystical ideas. This appearance of Elijah is often understood literally, that is, that the mystic sees a vision of the prophet, but, on a more sophisticated level, it is understood as a mystical state in which the soul of the mystic is in close association with the soul of the prophet. Elijah is thus the device used by the Kabbalists for the purpose of

proclaiming that while some of their teachings are undoubtedly new, they are still true because they are guaranteed by the appearance of Elijah, the true disciple of Moses.

When a problem is left unsolved in the Talmud, the word used is TEYKU, 'Let it stand', that is, there is no solution. This term is often said to be an abbreviation of: 'The Tishbite will solve all problems and difficulties' and the belief developed that, in the Messianic age, Elijah will provide the solution to every Halakhic problem. But this is, in reality, a folk-etymology, not found before the seventeenth century. In the older Talmudic and Rabbinic tradition, Elijah, when he teaches the Rabbis, does so only as a human teacher, not as a prophet with supernatural powers. Indeed, the idea that an appeal can be made to the supernatural when matters of Halakhah are in doubt is very dubious. Maimonides even goes so far as to declare that a prophet who claims to have been told in a prophetic vision that the ruling is so is a false prophet.

Aharon Wiener, *The Prophet Elijah in the Development of Judaism: A Depth-Psychological Study* (London, 1978).

**Elijah, Gaon of Vilna** Famed Rabbinic scholar (1720–97). Elijah lived for most of his life in the Lithuanian town of Vilna, his renown being such that he was given, even in his lifetime, the title Gaon (see GEONIM). Judaism knows nothing of hermits but Elijah came closest to the hermit ideal, although he did marry at the age of 18 and had a family. Secluded in his study for most of the day and night, he engaged unceasingly in profound investigation into all the classical Jewish texts. He occupied no official Rabbinic position but was supported very generously by the Vilna community.

The Gaon believed that it was essential for a Jewish scholar to have sufficient knowledge of secular subjects such as mathematics, astronomy, botany, and zoology, to be able to understand the many Talmudic passages which take such knowledge for granted. Secular learning, however, was for the Gaon only a means to the supreme task of 'toiling in the Torah', as the Rabbis call this intense activity.

Elijah was gifted with a keen critical sense. He perceived that many of the difficulties Jewish scholars have to face in their studies are the result of faulty texts which he did not hesitate to emend, many of his emendations later finding support in manuscripts in libraries to which he had no access. The Gaon was a Kabbalist and, in his youth, decided to embark on the creation of a semi-human figure, a *golem, by white magic, but when he saw a strange shadow hanging over him he understood it as a warning for him to desist.

The Gaon's many works are largely in the form of notes to the standard Jewish sources. His notes on the Talmud and the *Shulḥan Arukh* are now printed together with the text in most editions.

The Gaon allowed a small number of Talmudists, distinguished in their own right, to become his disciples. The most prominent of these, Hayyim of *Volozhyn, established the great Yeshivah of Volozhyn at which hundreds of highly gifted young men followed in the Gaon's footsteps to study the Torah for its own sake.

The Gaon is one of the three key figures belonging to the transitional period from medievalism to modernity in Jewish life and thought (the other two are the *Baal Shem Tov and Moses *Mendelssohn). The *Haskalah movement, founded by Mendelssohn, sought, mistakenly, to claim the Gaon for themselves. To be sure, the Gaon was a critical scholar, in the limited sense referred to above, but he was far removed from any attitude of broad tolerance towards views which diverged from the traditional path. It is on record that the Gaon was instrumental in having one of the early Maskilim placed in the pillory for daring to express criticism of a passage in the Midrash and of *Rashi. Nor had the Gaon any use for Jewish *philosophy. In a note to the *Shulḥan Arukh*, he is very critical of Maimonides for rejecting belief in *demons, incantations, and *amulets. Maimonides was misled, remarks the Gaon, by his study of the 'accursed philosophy'.

Although the Gaon took little part in communal affairs, he led the opposition to the Hasidic movement, convinced that the Hasidic doctrine of *panentheism, that everything is in God, is a heretical doctrine. It is not going too far to say that the Gaon persecuted the Hasidim, placing their leaders under the ban (see HEREM). Some of the Hasidic masters, nevertheless, revered the Gaon and even acknowledged that were it not for his opposition the movement might have gone astray. Respect for the Gaon in Lithuanian circles was unbounded. Some Lithuanian Rabbis declared that the Gaon really belonged to the generation of the *Tannaim whose word was law.

Louis Ginzberg, 'The Gaon, Rabbi Elijah Wilna', in his *Students, Scholars and Saints* (New York, 1958), 125–44.

**Elisha** Successor to the prophet *Elijah (1 Kings 19: 19–21). The story of Elisha and the *miracles he performed is told is the book of *Kings (2 Kings 2–6). Elisha, more than any other prophet, is the prototype of the holy man of God endowed with the power to alter the ordinary course of nature. In *Hasidism, Elisha is the biblical forerunner of the miracle-working Hasidic saint, the *Zaddik. On the other hand, there is a tendency in medieval Jewish *philosophy, to rationalize Elisha's miracles; for example, it is said that the child Elisha revived from the dead (2 Kings 4: 32–7) was not really dead but in a coma in which he appeared to have died.

**Elul** The twelfth and final month of the Jewish year (see CALENDAR), the month of spiritual preparation for the coming New Year. At the end of the daily service during Elul the ram's horn, the *shofar*, is sounded as a call to repentance, and Psalm 27 is read. Devout Jews are especially punctilious in their religious observances during this month.

**Emancipation** The recognition in Western societies that Jews are entitled to equal rights together with other citizens of the State, beginning with the State Constitution in Virginia in the USA in 1776 and the aftermath of the French Revolution and continuing during the nineteenth century. The Emancipation is often and rightly seen as the emergence of Jewry from the *Ghetto in order to play its full part in Western society. The Emancipation led to the formation of the *Haskalah movement, the main aim of which was to demonstrate that Jews could and should remain true to their own religion and culture while accepting Western mores and values. The problem was rarely quite as simple as that. Some Jews found the strain of living in two worlds too great to bear and they became totally assimilated in the surrounding culture. The Reform movement sought to deal with the problem by 'reforming' the system, adapting it so as to remove those features the Reformers saw to be at variance with what the Emancipation demanded. The Orthodox German thinker, Samson Raphael *Hirsch, sought to deal with the problem by developing his idea of 'Torah and the Way of the Land', that is, the combination of the traditional learning and way of life with the new values. Yet Hirsch saw fit to remark that if the Emancipation were to result in wholesale defection from Judaism and its values, it would have been better for it not to have taken place at all.

**Emden, Jacob** Renowned Talmudist and polemicist (1697–1776). Emden lived for most of his life in Altona, Hamburg, where he occupied no official Rabbinic position, earning his living by printing books, especially his own, including his Prayer Book (known as the 'Jacob Emden Siddur'), his collection of Responsa, his autobiography (very unusual for a Rabbi), and his valuable notes to the Talmud.

Well known in the history of Jewish *controversies is that between Emden and the Rabbi of Altona, Jonathan *Eybeschitz, whom Emden suspected of being a follower of the false Messiah, *Shabbetai Zevi. Like his father, Zevi Ashkenazi, known as the Hakham Zevi, Emden fought the crypto-Shabbeteans and their works, finding traces of this heresy in books hitherto considered to be completely religiously respectable. Though a Kabbalist and believer in the Zohar as sacred literature, Emden, aware that Shabbeteanism based itself on the teachings of the Zohar, sought to prove that Rabbi *Simeon ben Yohai is not, as he is reputed to be, the author of the Zohar. His arguments against the antiquity of the book show that he had a keen critical sense and are still widely used in modern Zoharic scholarship.

Emden's opinions were often extremely unconventional. He could not believe that the pious and orthodox Maimonides could have written the *Guide of the Perplexed* and maintained, contrary to all the evidence, that the real author of this work was an unknown heretic. Emden believed that Christianity has an important role to play in God's plan for mankind and was on friendly relations with a number of Christian scholars, as he was with Moses *Mendelssohn the founder of the *Haskalah movement.

Emden has been criticized for his undue interest in sexual matters but while it is true that, for instance, he provides, in his Prayer Book, details of how the marital act is to be carried out, this is in the context of the Friday-night section of the Prayer Book which, for the Kabbalists, is the occasion for sexual congress between husband and wife in order to repeat and assist the union on high between the male and female principles in the Godhead. In his autobiography, Emden is very frank in describing how he was tempted in his youth to have sex with his cousin, a temptation he resisted. He believed that the ban on polygamy by Rabbenu *Gershom of Mayyence was a serious mistake in that it followed Christian mores; although, he states, he does not have the power to urge the ban to be repealed. He even advocates a scholar taking a mistress since, he says, the Rabbis hold that 'the greater the man, the greater his sexual urge'. Nevertheless, it is extremely precarious to conclude from this, as does Mortimer Cohen, that Emden was sexually maladjusted. He never carried out his theories in practice and was looked upon by later Jewish teachers as a holy man. The Hasidim often refer to Emden as 'the Holy Old Man', even though there is what seems to be an attack on early *Hasidism in a work by Emden.

Mortimer Cohen, *Jacob Emden, Man of Controversy* (New York, 1937).

**Enoch** In the list of the generations from Adam (Genesis 5), Enoch belongs to the seventh generation. Unlike the other antediluvians mentioned in the passage, who reached the age of over 900, Enoch lived 'only' 365 years (the connection of this number with that of the days in the solar year has often been noted). The narrative does not say that Enoch died but, mysteriously, that 'he walked with God, and then he was no more, for God took him' (Genesis 5: 23), on the basis of which later Jewish legend considers Enoch to have been taken up to heaven, while still alive, to become an angel. In a medieval Midrash, Enoch was a cobbler who, when he stitched the lower part of the shoes he made to the upper part, 'performed unifications'. This is usually taken to mean that Enoch's mind, during his earthly activities, was engrossed with the heavenly task of uniting the lower with the upper worlds. Typical of R. Israel *Salanter's ethical stance is this moralist's remark that if Enoch's mind had been engaged with heavenly matters instead of on his work as a cobbler, he would have produced poor pairs of shoes and would have defrauded his customers. Salanter, therefore, understands the Midrash to mean that by doing honest work as a cobbler he 'performed unifications' by that very activity.

**En Sof** 'Without Limit', the Kabbalistic name for God as He is in Himself, utterly beyond all human comprehension. In the Kabbalah, God as He is in Himself produces, by a process of emanation, the ten *Sefirot, the powers or potencies in the Godhead through which En Sof becomes manifest in creation. Since En Sof is beyond all comprehension, It (the impersonal pronoun is usually preferred by implication, though Hebrew does not have any impersonal pronouns) cannot be spoken of at all. Elijah, Gaon of *Vilna remarks that, strictly speaking, one cannot even refer to En Sof as En Sof. Indeed, if one is to speak strictly in Kabbalistic vein, one cannot even say what the Vilna Gaon says! True to this idea, the Zohar rarely speaks of En Sof and some early Kabbalists boldly remark that En Sof is only referred to in the Bible itself by hint. The God of whom the Bible speaks is God in manifestation. All this presents a severe problem for the Kabbalists. Does this not mean that a dualistic concept has been introduced into the monotheistic faith that is Judaism? In reply the Kabbalists seek to preserve the unity of En Sof and the Sefirot by drawing on various analogies, for example that En Sof can be compared to colourless water poured into vessels of different hues, thus partaking, as it were, of the colour of the particular vessel into which it is poured. Another illustration is taken from the human psyche which is one but which expresses itself in different intellectual and emotional forms. Yet another illustration is provided by the varied hues in a single glowing coal.

**Envy** The state of being jealous or of being distressed at the success of others. Envy sours the life of its possessor. In Ethics of the Fathers (4. 21) the maxim occurs: 'Envy, lust and ambition drive a man out of the world.' Basing themselves on the Talmudic saying: 'The envy of scribes increases wisdom', many of the Jewish moralists, however, do not decry every kind of envy. To be envious of those who are intellectually superior or those more advanced in spiritual matters is held by the moralists to be no vice but, on the contrary, to act as a powerful spur to the living of the good life. Yet, in *Hasidism, the serene mind accepts its intellectual and spiritual limits, refusing to succumb to any pangs of envy, not even of those who have reached higher rungs on the ladder of perfection. When envy is more than a state of mind and results in the attempt to obtain, even by legitimate means, that which belongs to another, this is seen in the Rabbinic tradition as a breach of the tenth commandment: 'Thou shalt not covet' (see DECALOGUE).

**Epikoros** An atheist or unbeliever in the Torah. The name *epikoros* is obviously derived from that of Epicurus, yet the term is used in the Rabbinic literature without reference to Epicurus. (It is an interesting fact that while the Talmudic Rabbis do refer to Greek thought, the names of none of the Greek thinkers appear in the Rabbinic literature, possibly in order to avoid too close an association with Greek ideas.) *Josephus, on the other hand, does apply the term to the followers of Epicurus, writing that: 'the Epicureans exclude Providence from human life and refuse to believe that God governs its affairs or that the universe is directed by a blessed and immortal Being to the end that the whole of it may endure, but say that the world runs by its own movement without knowing a guide or another's care' (*Antiquities* 10. 11. 7). Maimonides, in his commentary to the Mishnah (*Sanhedrin* 10: 1), where the term is employed, follows the Talmudic Rabbis in deriving the name from the Hebrew root *pakar*, 'to be abandoned' and defines the *epikoros* as the person 'who abandons and despises the Torah and its students'; although in his *Guide of the Perplexed* (3. 17) Maimonides does refer to the Greek philosopher Epicurus by name. The term has thus had a chequered history but in the Middle Ages and onwards it was used in various senses and eventually became a general term of opprobrium to denote anyone guilty of entertaining heretical opinions. For some of the Kabbalists, a person who rejects the Kabbalah is an *epikoros*. Despite the astonishing statement in the Talmud that the life of the *epikoros* is forfeit and he may be murdered, this statement is seen as pure hyperbole by the authorities and there is no instance of the theory ever having been put into practice. Twentieth-century Rabbis such as Rabbi I. *Kook have argued that, in any event, nowadays, unbelievers are not governed by a spirit of revolt against Judaism. Their unbelief is often based on sheer ignorance of what Judaism teaches, so that the pejorative term *epikoros* is inapplicable to them.

Louis Jacobs, *Principles of the Jewish Faith* (Northvale, NJ, and London, 1988), 11–13.

**Equity** The practice of righteousness in a civil dispute even where there is no strict legal obligation to be righteous. In Rabbinic teaching the requirement to go 'beyond the line of the law' is based on the biblical injunction to 'do what is good and right in the sight of the Lord' (Deuteronomy 12: 28). *Nahmanides understands this requirement as being in itself part of the law. That is to say, every person has an obligation to go beyond the line of the law, different from the law only in that the law is categorical and binding upon all, whereas when and when not to go beyond the letter of the law depends on the particular person and situation. For instance, the Talmud relates that a Rabbi once hired porters to transport some casks of wine, and they broke the casks through negligence. The Rabbi's teacher ordered him not only to refrain from exacting payment but also to pay the porters their wages. When the Rabbi protested that the law entitles him to compensation and certainly does not demand that he pays them their wages, the teacher quoted the verse concerning doing that wĥich is good and right in the eyes of the Lord, stating that *it was the law*. The meaning is, of course, that the law itself makes no demands of equity and for ordinary folk the law undoubtedly stands. But for a scholar of renown the practice of equity is a *legal* demand so that what is not a law for others is a law for him. In a remarkable Talmudic passage (*Berakhot* 7a) God Himself is said to pray to Himself that His mercy prevails over His justice so that He behaves towards His children beyond the line of the law. Portia's 'the quality of mercy is not strained' is sound Jewish teaching.

Aaron Kirschenbaum, *Equity in Jewish Law* (New York, 1991).

**Eruv** 'Mixing' or 'mingling', a legal device by means of which two areas or periods are mixed or combined in order to provide a relaxation of the Sabbath and festival laws; plural *eruvin*. There are three different types of *eruv*.

*1. The* Eruv *of Limits or Boundaries*

According to the *Halakhah, a person is allowed to walk any distance he wishes on the Sabbath and festivals provided he keeps within the town boundaries. In addition he is allowed to walk 2,000 cubits (rather more than half a mile) on all sides outside the town boundaries. This extra area is known as the 'Sabbath

boundary'. Now, supposing a person wishes to walk beyond the 2,000 cubits in one direction, say, to the east of the town. The device permitting him to do this is the '*eruv* of boundaries'. Before the Sabbath (or the festival) he places a small amount of food at the eastern boundary, that is, at the end of the 2,000 cubits, and this becomes his domicile from which he now has a 2,000-cubit boundary at that spot. He is now able to walk on the Sabbath through the town itself and a further 4,000 cubits, 2,000 to his *eruv* and a further 2,000 to the east. But, since his domicile is now to the east, he has forfeited his right to walk to the west beyond the actual limits of the town. The *eruv* thus 'mingles' the two areas so that they are treated as a single area. All this is relevant to a compact town with open country all around. In a built-up city like London, with houses and other buildings extending for a great distance, it is permitted to walk many miles in the city without needing to resort to the *eruv*.

*2. The* Eruv *of Courtyards*

This applies only on the Sabbath when it is not permitted to carry objects from a private domain into a public domain. (On the festivals carrying is permitted.) Where houses surround a courtyard it is not permitted to carry objects from the houses into the courtyard unless, before the Sabbath, the *eruv* 'mingles' them so that the whole courtyard and its houses are treated as a single private domain in which it is permitted to carry. The ideal *eruv* for this purpose would be a surrounding wall but, by a legal fiction, if the area is enclosed by a series of posts and wire this counts as a wall, as do natural boundaries such as rivers or streams. The walls of the houses also contribute to the necessary partition. Most authorities hold that it is possible to convert a large area or even a whole town into a private domain by means of the *eruv*. The principle here is that anything that has the appearance of an entrance or door counts as contributing to the required surrounding 'wall'. Consequently, a wire stretched over the top of two posts, no matter how distant the two are one from the other, counts as a 'door'. Thus it is possible to create an *eruv* around a district in a city by erecting this system of poles and wires where there are open spaces between the houses or the natural boundaries. In Jerusalem, and other Israeli cities, there is such an *eruv*. If a visitor goes outside the city to the surrounding hills he will see this system of poles and wires. If, in a storm for instance, the wires snap or the poles fall down, the *eruv* is rendered null and void. The stricter authorities frown on the *eruv*, originally intended for the use of people residing in a courtyard, being applied so as to permit carrying in a large city. But the consensus even among Orthodox is to permit this.

### 3. The Eruv for Cooking

Although cooking and baking are forbidden on the Sabbath, they are permitted on a festival, provided the food is intended to be eaten on the festival. It is forbidden to cook on the festival for the following weekday. The question rises whether, when a festival falls on Friday, the eve of the Sabbath, it is permitted to cook on the festival for the Sabbath. By the device of the *eruv* it is permitted. The procedure is to set aside, on the day before the festival, two simple cooked dishes, say a boiled egg and a small piece of fish or a piece of bread. This is the *eruv*, in that it 'mingles' the festival with the weekday which precedes it and the principle then obtains that just as the two dishes are the beginning of the preparations for the coming Sabbath, all cooking on the festival is merely a continuation of the process begun on the weekday. The dishes prepared are eaten on the Sabbath.

Reform Jews are generally critical of the whole institution of the *eruv* and none of the three types of *eruv* is known at all in Reform Judaism. Many Conservative Jews are in agreement with the Orthodox in the matter of the *eruv*.

**Esau** The son of Isaac and twin brother of Jacob (Genesis 35, 36). Esau is identified with Edom (Genesis 36: 1) and, on the critical view (see BIBLICAL CRITICISM), the Esau–Jacob narratives reflect the conflict between the Israelites and the neighbouring people of Edom. In the later Rabbinic period, Edom is identified with *Rome and the narratives are read as a foretelling of the love–hate relationship between Rome and the Jewish people. Later still Edom (Rome) is identified in Jewish literature with the Christian Church, the narratives now being read as reflecting the rivalry between the two religions of Christianity and Judaism.

Gerson D. Cohen, 'Esau as Symbol in Early Medieval Thought', in A. Altmann (ed.), *Jewish Medieval and Renaissance Studies* (Cambridge, Mass., 1967), 19–48.

**Eschatology** The doctrine of the 'last things'. The actual term eschatology is found only in Christian theology but the themes embraced by the term—the doctrine of the *Messiah, the *resurrection of the dead, the immortality of the *soul, the *World to *Come, *heaven and hell—are discussed in detail in the classical Jewish sources, albeit in a non-systematic way. Throughout the ages Jewish thinkers have reflected on what is to happen in the world of the future but much of this reflection is more in the nature of speculation than dogmatic formulation (see DOGMAS). It is, therefore, hazardous to speak of an official Jewish eschatological scheme. What one can do is describe what came to be the conventional view in the Middle Ages, after various tendencies, often contradicting one another, had come together in the believing mind.

According to the commonly held view, at a time in the not too distant future there will be a series of wars and catastrophes, 'the birth pangs of the Messiah', after which *Elijah will come to herald the advent of the Messiah. The Messiah will succeed in rebuilding Jerusalem and the Temple, where the sacrificial system will be re-established. Warfare, hatred, and enmity will cease and a new era will be ushered in during which all mankind will acknowledge that God is the sole Ruler and the Jewish people will study the Torah and observe its precepts in a spirit of total dedication. Human beings in the Messianic age will live for a very long time but, eventually, all will return to the dust to await the resurrection of the dead. The resurrected dead will be judged in a great Day of Judgement after which those declared righteous will live on in a new earth and will enjoy the unimaginable bliss of the nearness of God. In the language of the Rabbis they will 'bask in the radiance of the *Shekhinah'. The souls of those who have died before the advent of the Messiah as well as the souls of those who died afterwards will enjoy the nearness of God in heaven but the less righteous will first be punished in hell. All souls will await the resurrection when they will be reunited with the bodies they formerly occupied.

This amalgam of various eschatological notions is, naturally, far too simplistic to provide anything more than a vague picture. Even in the medieval period, Jewish thinkers such as

Maimonides felt themselves obliged to introduce various qualifications and there were considerable debates around some of the details. Will the Messiah and his associates rebuild the Temple themselves or will the Third Temple drop down ready-made from heaven? Will the resurrected dead live for ever on the new earth or will they, too, eventually die, their souls alone enjoying immortality? Will the Messiah establish his claim to be such by performing miracles or will his success in bringing about the new age be itself the guarantee that he is the true Messiah? What precisely is the role of Elijah in the process, and what of the idea that before the advent of the Messiah son of David, a forerunner, the Messiah son of Joseph, will appear but will be murdered? If one can speak of a general tendency in these matters, it is that the details must be left in God's hands.

In the modern period, the whole picture tended to become even more opaque. Reform Jews abandoned the whole doctrine of a personal Messiah and thought instead of the emergence of a Messianic age, often identified with the creation of a just society in which all men will be able to realize their full potential. On this view the only eschatological doctrine that endures is that of the immortality of the individual soul. Even the Orthodox accept, in the main, the idea that the establishment of the State of Israel has introduced a new dimension into the Messianic vision; only they usually qualify this by suggesting that the Jewish State is the 'beginning of the redemption', that is, it is paving the way for the advent of the Messiah. Moreover, historical research has succeeded in demonstrating that all the eschatological doctrines have developed gradually over long periods in response to particular challenges and concerns at different periods in Jewish history. The result has been that even among some believing Jews an attitude of religious *agnosticism has become dominant. This attitude is one of patient resignation to the will of God, to whom the future and its mysteries belong.

Abraham Cohen, *Everyman's Talmud* (London, 1949), 346–89.
C. G. Montefiore and H. Loewe, *A Rabbinic Anthology* (London, 1938), 580–608.

**Essenes** A Jewish sect which flourished at the end of the Second Temple period, from the second century BCE. *Philo, *Josephus, and the Roman author Pliny all make mention of this sect but while references to the other two sects of this period, the *Pharisees and the *Sadducees, are frequent in the Talmudic literature, there is no mention of the Essenes anywhere in this literature, unless the references to the 'pious men of old', *hasidim harishonim*, are to the Essenes. (A number of modern scholars, in fact, understand the name Essenes to be a Greek form of the word Hasidim.) The community that produced the *Dead Sea Scrolls seems to have been a community of Essenes or one with some association with the Essenes. Probably because there is no clear reference to them in the Rabbinic literature, the Essenes are not mentioned at all in later Jewish religious literature and they have had no direct influence on the development of the Jewish religion.

**Esther** Heroine and, according to tradition, author of the book of Esther, the *Megillah read on the festival of *Purim. The book tells how Esther is chosen by King Ahasuerus to be his queen and how she and her cousin, *Mordecai, succeed in foiling Haman's plot to destroy the Jews. Esther in Jewish life and thought is the valiant woman who risks her life to save her people. She is not described in the book of Esther as beautiful, as are other biblical heroines, and one Rabbi, rather ungallantly, remarked that she had a sallow complexion and was only attractive because 'a thread of grace' was extended to her from on high. According to an opinion in the Talmud, Esther was Mordecai's wife and this gave rise to the question of how could she be unfaithful to her husband by living openly with the king, the answer given is that Esther was threatened with death if she did not yield, but she was not obliged to suffer martyrdom in the circumstances since the woman's role in the sex act is passive and martyrdom is only demanded where there is a positive action. In the Kabbalah, Esther represents, among the *Sefirot on high, *Malkhut* ('Sovereignty'), the *Shekhinah.

**Esther, Fast of** Minor fastday held on 13 Adar, the day before *Purim, so called because it is stated in the book of Esther that Esther and her people fasted in order to avert Haman's decree. The fast is not mentioned anywhere in the Talmud. The earliest reference to it is in the eighth century CE. Because of its comparatively late origin, the Codes treat this fast less stringently than the other minor fasts (see CALENDAR).

**Ethics** The philosophy and systematic treatment of the theory of moral conduct The actual term ethics is not found in the Jewish sources, since classical Jewish thinking is organic rather than systematic. The practice of justice, for example, is advocated uncompromisingly in every variety of Judaism but there is hardly to be found in Jewish thought anything like a Socratic analysis of the nature of justice. The implication always is that a person, whether Jew or Gentile, man or woman, does not have to be a skilful philosopher to recognize that justice and righteousness are categorical imperatives. On the question of how these ideals are to be put into practice, the reply of traditional Judaism is that this is provided in the *Halakhah, the legal system worked out over the ages by its acknowledged representatives. Even if the whole Halakhic system is seen, as it should be, as a process of development through human agency, as a quest rather than as a given, the human quest involves a search for the will of God in the complex situations, many of them new, in which human beings find themselves. It would seem to follow that one can as little speak of a specific Jewish ethic as one can speak of kosher mathematics. Two problems have to be addressed in this connection: 1. The relationship between ethics and religion; 2. The relationship between ethics and Jewish law.

*1. The Relationship between Ethics and Religion*
At the most basic level the question here is whether it is possible for a person to lead the good life in the ethical sense if that person has no religious commitment. The answer must surely be that it is possible, as everyday experience demonstrates. There are numerous instances of men and women without any profound religious belief leading good ethical lives, just as there are religious persons lacking in sound ethical sense. Allied to this is the question of whether a religious person ought to lead an ethical life because it is the will of God. Some theologians have taken the extreme view that the reason why a man must, say, honour his parents and refrain from stealing is because God has so commanded and had God commanded: 'Do not honour your parents' or 'Do steal', it would have been right and proper to

dishonour parents and to steal. While such a view is not entirely unknown in Judaism, the more usual view is that God, being God, could not possibly have commanded that parents be dishonoured or that it is good to steal. The better way of looking at the question from the religious point of view is to say not that it is wrong to steal because it is the will of God but that it is the will of God that we do not steal. Ethical autonomy is best seen not as in conflict with religion but as a part of the total religious imperative. A prominent teacher of the *Musar School put it in this way. When I behave with care and compassion for my neighbour I should not do so in order to carry out a precept of the Torah, a *mitzvah*, for that would imply that I need the spur of a divine command to make me the caring person God wishes me to be. The *mitzvah* involves the refinement of the character that results in an automatic attitude of care and compassion for others.

Relevant here is Maimonides' well-known analysis. Maimonides (introduction to Ethics of the Fathers in his commentary to the Mishnah) discusses, in this context, what appear to be the differing attitudes of the Greek philosophers and the Talmudic Rabbis on the good life. Who is a better person, the one who has no desire to do wrong or the one who wishes to do wrong but exercises self-control? The Greek thinkers argue that the man with murder in his heart, even if he does not actually kill anyone, is inferior to the man who has no murder in his heart. The Talmudic Rabbis, on the other hand, say that a man should not declare: 'I dislike swine-flesh' but should rather declare: 'I like it but what can I do if my Father in heaven has forbidden it to me?' Maimonides draws a neat, perhaps too neat, distinction. The Rabbis are speaking about the *dietary laws. Here the motivation must be obedience to God's will, otherwise what religious significance is there if a man abstains from forbidden food because he simply finds it distasteful? The Greek thinkers speak of ethical conduct and here they are right in affirming that unethical desires are unworthy even if they are not put to work.

That religion can be seen as the ground of ethics is quite a different matter. Even though religious belief does not necessarily result in sound ethical conduct or lack of such belief in ethical malfunction, yet, it can be argued, the 'ought' that is the basis for all ethical conduct cannot be grounded in the person who acts, but is outside him. This is where the divine imperative comes in. The moral argument for the existence of God is that the very sense of duty must have been implanted in man by a source beyond him and that source is God. This is a position adopted by many a Jewish thinker.

## 2. The Relationship between Ethics and Jewish Law

While it is true that ethics are universal, there are specific Jewish laws governing human conduct. What, then, is the relationship between obedience to these laws and the ethical character? The Talmudic Rabbis know, of course, of the principle of *equity, of the need to go 'beyond the line of the law', but this in itself is seen traditionally as a demand of the law, albeit a demand in which, unlike with regard to the law itself, scope is left for individual decision and choice. Furthermore, there are many instances, in the Talmud and the Codes, where certain types of conduct are declared to be legally permitted but morally reprehensible.

A few of these instances can be quoted. A appoints B as his agent to buy for him a certain property. B, on seeing the property, takes a liking to it and buys it for himself. Since A has suffered no direct loss the law declares B's purchase of the property to be valid. Yet, the Talmud states, B has behaved 'in a fraudulent fashion'. The Codes extend this principle to one who steps in to obtain a job that is being offered to someone else. If a notorious robber desires to give up his way of life, the Talmudic sages disapprove of his victims accepting compensation because, if all the victims did this, it would effectively prevent the robber from expressing remorse and being obliged to return his ill-gotten gains to their rightful owners. A victim who, nevertheless, does accept compensation commits no legal offence but, the Talmud states, 'the spirit of the sages is displeased with him', in other words, his conduct is unsocial and un-Jewish. In a more remarkable instance, the Talmud states that the 'spirit of the saints' (ḥasidim) is displeased with anyone who kills snakes and scorpions on the Sabbath but goes on to state: 'And the spirit of the sages is displeased with these saints.'

A significant anecdote is told in the Jerusalem Talmud. The Mishnah rules that if a company of Jews is attacked by heathen, they may save their lives by handing over one of their company if the heathen have specified that man by name, in other words, if they have declared that they have no wish simply to kill any member of the company, only that particular man. Rabbi Joshua ben Levi, following the Mishnaic rule, saved the lives of the citizens of the town in which he resided by handing over a man specified by name, whereupon *Elijah, a regular visitor to Rabbi Joshua ben Levi, visited him no more. After the Rabbi had fasted for many days, Elijah did appear to him and reproached him for his conduct. The Rabbi defended his act by appealing to the unambiguous ruling of the Mishnah. 'Yes,' retorted Elijah, 'but is that a teaching suitable for saints?' In this anecdote it is implied that a saint should have his own ethical code which he is expected to obey even where both logic and the law sees his actions as extreme. They are extreme, it is implied, but a saint is bound to be extreme by his very vocation.

For all that, the interdependence of law and ethics was not allowed to blur the distinction between the two. The verse 'neither shalt thou favour a poor man in his cause' (Exodus 23: 3), and the verse: 'Ye shall do no unrighteousness in judgement; thou shalt not respect the person of the poor, nor favour the person of the mighty; but in righteousness shalt thou judge thy neighbour' (Leviticus 19: 15) form the basis of the principle that justice must be administered impartially. A Rabbinic Midrash puts it in this way, addressing a judge: 'You must not say, since this man is poor and both I and the rich man are obliged to support him, I shall decide the case in his favour so that he will find his sustenance in a clean manner. That is why Scripture declares "thou shalt not respect the person of the poor".' If the judge wishes to help a poor man, as he should, he must not do it by tampering with the law so as to decide unjustly in the poor man's favour. Where justice demands it, the judge must decide against the poor man and then, if he so wishes, compensate the poor man out of his own pocket. King David is said to have acted in this way when judging his people.

Reference should be made to the relationship of law to good character. It is all too easy for a man never actually to offend against the law and yet to be a thoroughly disreputable character; in a famous comment of *Nahmanides, he can be a 'scoundrel with the permission of the Torah'. The Talmudic Rabbis even go so far as to say that if a man is unworthy, that is, if he has a bad character, the Torah itself becomes for him a deadly poison, meaning, presumably, that he will use the law to further his own nefarious ends. For the person who has merits, that is, a good character, the Torah becomes an elixir of life, refining his character still further. The dietary laws have been seen by many Jewish teachers as a means of refining the character.

> Louis Jacobs, 'The Relationship between Religion and Ethics in Jewish Thought', in Gene Outka and John P. Reeder Jr. (eds.), *Religion and Morality* (New York, 1973), 155–72.
> Menachem Marc Kellner (ed.), *Contemporary Jewish Ethics* (New York, 1978).

**Ethics of the Fathers** A treatise, compiled not later than the end of the second century CE, containing Rabbinic maxims of various kinds. In reality this treatise is not a separate work at all but a tractate of the Mishnah. Its original name is *Avot*, 'Fathers', so-called because its sayings are those of successive generations of Jewish teachers, the 'fathers' of Rabbinic Judaism. In current editions of the Mishnah, *Avot* belongs in the order of the Mishnah known as Nezikin, but the association with this order, which deals with jurisprudence, is far from clear. It has been suggested that originally *Avot* was an appendix at the end of the whole Mishnah corpus, since it is in the nature of a summary of the teachings of the Mishnaic 'fathers'. The treatise was often published as a work on its own and was given the full name, *Pirkey Avot*, 'Chapters of the Fathers'. The name Ethics of the Fathers is not of Jewish origin but was given by Christian writers who found the book attractive and read it as a series of ethical maxims. The truth is, however, that while the book does contain such maxims, it is not an ethical treatise in the strict sense, its main thrust being to provide a series of statements of the basic ideas of each particular teacher mentioned.

*Avot* originally consisted of five chapters. But since the custom arose in the Middle Ages of reading the book on the six Sabbaths between *Passover and *Pentecost, a further chapter, taken from earlier Rabbinic teaching, was added so as to provide a chapter for each of the six Sabbaths. This additional chapter was given the name, after its basic theme, 'The Acquisition of the Torah', that is, the means by which proficiency is attained in Torah learning.

In a number of passages in this little book a set of three sayings is attributed to particular teachers with the formula: 'He used to say.' Obviously each of the teachers said much more in his lifetime but careful study of these sayings demonstrates that the final editors have endeavoured to summarize each teacher's life's work by representing it in a series of three, as if to say, he stood for these ideas, these were the basis of his particular teaching, these are what he 'said' by being what he was. For instance, the saying attributed to the very early teacher Simeon the Just at the beginning of the book is: 'The world stands on three things: on the Torah, on the Temple service, and on acts of benevolence.' The meaning here is that if one is to give a summary of what Simeon the Just stood for, it would be that he saw the significance of Judaism as consisting of study of the Torah, the sacrificial system of the Temple, and the practice of benevolence since, for Simeon the Just, the whole world only endures because of these three things.

The book begins with the chain of tradition: 'Moses received the Torah at Sinai and handed it down to Joshua and Joshua to the elders, the elders to the prophets, and the prophets handed it down to the Men of the *Great Synagogue.' The meaning of 'Torah' in this context is almost certainly the *Oral Torah of which the later Rabbis were the bearers. It is clear that the whole aim of the book is to see Judaism as a living tradition, the core of which is divinely revealed but with each generation adding something of its own. That some of the sayings recorded are of an ethical nature does not justify the name 'Ethics of the Fathers'. It is not the main aim of the treatise to advocate ethical conduct alone and, in any event, the Jewish tradition does not know of any system of ethics separate from the religion as a whole (see ETHICS).

Ethics of the Fathers has been extremely popular throughout the history of Jewish learning and piety, receiving a number of commentaries from prominent Jewish teachers, each of whom used the book as a vehicle for his own ideas and so, in a sense, continued the theme of the book itself. Ethics of the Fathers is in Hebrew, like the rest of the Mishnah, with one or two Aramaic sayings but it has been translated into many other languages.

> Judah Goldin, *The Living Talmud: The Wisdom of the Fathers* (New Haven, 1955).
> Charles Taylor, *Sayings of the Jewish Fathers* (Cambridge, 1877).

**Etiquette** Correct behaviour, good manners; Heb., *derekh eretz*, 'the Way of the Earth', that is, how people on earth ought to conduct themselves. The term 'the Way of the Earth' suggests that the rules of decent, courteous conduct are not specifically Jewish but belong to humanity as a whole and are appreciated by all human beings without the need for them to be revealed as the precepts of the Torah are revealed to Israel. Nevertheless, each culture and society has its own particular norms of what is fitting, and Judaism is no exception. Two of the minor tractates of the Talmud ('minor' in the sense that, in their present form, they are post-Talmudic, though they contain a good deal of material from Talmudic times) are devoted to matters of etiquette: *Derekh Eretz Rabba* (*The Larger Treatise of Derekh Eretz*) and *Derekh Eretz Zuta* (*The Smaller Treatise of Derekh Eretz*). Maimonides devotes a section of his Code to good manners, especially for the scholar, whose standards have to be of the highest. Maimonides in this gives etiquette a semi-Halakhic status. It would appear that in Talmudic times there existed a collection of rules of conduct in matters of etiquette but these did not enjoy full legal status and are expressly stated to be of lesser importance than the law itself. Later on, however, many of the Talmudic statements about etiquette, precisely because they are in the Talmud, came to be incorporated into Codes of law such as the *Shulḥan Arukh*.

Table etiquette features prominently in the Jewish sources. To engage in conversation while eating is frowned upon because this may cause the food to enter the windpipe and cause choking. This rule, it is said, is generally disregarded, although many Jewish mothers, like mothers everywhere, do urge their children not to talk with food in the mouth because it is unseemly. If two men are seated at the same table and one interrupts his meal to sip the wine, the other should wait until his friend resumes eating before he continues with his own eating. Two men need not wait, however, for a third and it is not improper for them to eat while he sups. Interestingly, this rule is also generally disregarded since, the commentators say, we do not normally eat from the same dish, as they did when the rules were formulated. A host should not display any bad temper during the meal for this will cause embarrassment to his guests. To quaff a cup of wine in a single gulp is to be a guzzler; two gulps is the norm; to take three gulps is to be overly fastidious. The commentators wisely observe that all depends on the size of the cup and the strength of the wine. If two men are seated at the same table, the one of higher rank should reach first for the food. If one of lesser rank reaches first for the food, he is said to be a guzzler. A later commentator remarks, on the basis of a Talmudic passage, that it is good form for the host to pour out the wine for his guests.

When putting on the shoes the right shoe should be put on first, right being a universal symbol for righteousness. But, since the *tefillin* are wound around the left hand, the lacing of the shoes should be in the opposite order: the left shoe should first be laced and then the right. Many of the authorities see all this as pernickety, but many pious Jews still follow the rule. Some Hasidic Jews, in order to avoid complications, do not wear shoes with laces and simply slip on the right shoe first.

It is hardly necessary to give further examples of good manners as seen by the Jewish teachers. The sources themselves imply that everything depends on the mores of a particular community and its cultural background. But the principle behind it all is the typical Jewish idea that nothing is too trivial to be invested with religious significance, in which due care is taken not to be offensive to others.

**Etrog** See TABERNACLES.

**Eulogies** Funeral orations in which the praises of the departed are sung (in the older Jewish tradition literally 'sung', in a special mourning chant); Heb. *hesped*. There are references to eulogies in the Bible; the two best known are Abraham's lament over Sarah (Genesis 23: 2) and David's lament over Saul and Jonathan (2 Samuel 1: 12). The Talmud (*Moed Katan* 21b) gives a list of eulogies over famous Rabbis from which it appears that eulogies were in poetic form. The Talmud has a lengthy discussion (*Sanhedrin* 46b–47a) on whether the eulogy is in honour of the dead or of the living. The practical difference here is seen where the deceased left in his will that he was not to be eulogized. If the eulogy is out of respect for the living, the man's instructions can be disregarded since the honour being paid is not to him but to his family. The conclusion is that the eulogy is to pay respect to the dead, so that if such an instruction in made it must be heeded. One hears, occasionally, of prominent scholars who, out of humility, left instruction that no eulogies were to be recited over them.

The Talmud contains advice for those who deliver the eulogy. Its aim should be to call attention to the achievements of the deceased. A little exaggeration was felt to be in order. In a eulogy it is permitted to imply that the deceased was rather more generous and pious than he really was, but the kind of insincere praise which everyone present knows to be false must be avoided. One Talmudic Rabbi said to a man well known as a gifted eulogizer: 'Give warm expression to your feelings when you eulogize me for I shall be present there.' Nowadays the eulogy is delivered in the hall of the cemetery or, sometimes, at the grave-side. In ultra-Orthodox circles it is not unusual for many eulogies to be given over a famous scholar.

**Euthanasia** Taking the life, at his request, of a person suffering from an extremely painful and terminal illness who will die very soon even if nature is allowed to take its course. Jewish law strongly condemns any act that shortens life and treats the killing of a person whom the doctors say will die in any event to be an act of murder. Positive euthanasia is thus ruled out. Switching off the life-support machine is rather more debatable. For one thing, a person who has suffered brain-death and has only a vegetable form of existence through the machine is held, by many authorities, to be actually dead so that the question of killing him does not arise. Furthermore, it has been argued, when the machine is switched off, the person dies because nature takes its course and there is no positive act of shortening life. The standard Code of Jewish law, the *Shulḥan Arukh*, rules (*Yoreh Deah*, 339. 1), for example, that it is forbidden to move the limbs of a person on his deathbed if this will have the effect of hastening his death, but it is permitted to remove any external cause, such a the noise of a hammer in an adjacent room, which prevents the departure of his soul. There are also references to persons committing *suicide, to avoid severe torture, whose act is not condemned. As a result of all this, a case can certainly be made out to permit the switching off of a life-support machine. The majority of Orthodox Rabbis are, however, very uneasy about this and, in any event, Jews are obliged to follow the law of the countries in which they reside; if the law forbids even passive euthanasia Jews must obey the law of the land.

A different case is that of praying for the death of an incurable patient who suffers greatly. Some authorities frown on this as an attempt to frustrate the divine will. Others hold that such prayer, as an appeal to the divine will, is permitted and may even be laudable, though they would limit such prayers to those who are not actual members of the sufferer's family. The members of the family could be motivated not so much by their desire to spare the sufferer as to be rid of the burden of looking after him.

Orthodox Rabbinic authorities, today, are opposed to doctors shortening life by such direct intervention as the injection into the patient of a drug that will directly bring his life to an end. But it is also generally held that pain-killing drugs may be administered even though these will have the indirect effect of shortening his life. It is again generally agreed that doctors are not obliged to resort to artificial means of keeping alive an incurable patient suffering severe agony.

**Evil Eye** The ability to bring about evil results by a malicious gaze. In most cultures the belief is prevalent that some human beings have the power of sending destructive rays, so to speak, in order to cause harm to those of whom they are envious or otherwise dislike. The concept of the evil eye seems to have come about in stages in Jewish thought. Originally, in the Mishnah, for example, the 'evil eye' simply denoted that its possessor could not bear with equanimity the good fortune of others. In this sense the term is used in contrast to the 'good eye', the possessor of which enjoys seeing others happy and successful. But, especially in the Babylonian Talmud, the notion developed that some persons do have this kind of baneful power and there are a number of superstitious practices to ward off the harmful effects of the evil eye, for example spitting out three times when a person seems to be at risk. Even today some people, when praising others, will add: 'let it be without the evil eye' (in the Yiddish form, *kenenhora*), meaning I do not intend my praise to suggest that I am enviously casting a malevolent glance.

There was a widespread belief that the descendants of the biblical hero *Joseph, were immune from the effects of the evil eye; hence the curious incantation found in the Talmud (*Berakhot* 55b) to ward off the effects: 'Take the thumb of the right hand in the left hand and the thumb of the left hand in the right hand, and say: "I, so-and-so, am of the seed of Joseph over whom the evil eye has no power."'

In view of this, it cannot be said that Judaism knows nothing of the belief in the malevolent power of the evil eye. But it has also to be said that Jewish thinkers such as *Maimonides fought against all kinds of superstition, both because they seem totally unreasonable and because of the theological difficulty that since God is in control of His universe it can hardly be possible for human beings to frustrate His will by supernatural means.

**Evolution** The theory, associated especially with Charles Darwin, that all living creatures have evolved, from the lowest forms, over an immense period of time, by a process of natural selection. In the science versus religion debates in the nineteenth century, Darwinism was rejected by some Christian theologians on two grounds. First, it was in conflict with the *creation narrative in the first chapter of Genesis, in which God is said to have created the world in six days. Secondly, and more significantly, the idea that species have evolved by natural processes appears to be in conflict with the whole doctrine of God as the Creator. Jewish theologians remained, at first, very much on the periphery of the discussion but later on thinking Jews were bound to react to the new challenges which affected the Jewish religion as they did the Christian religion. No official Jewish response has emerged. Indeed, it is doubtful whether one can speak of an official Jewish view in such matters (see DOGMAS).

Many Orthodox Jewish thinkers still feel obliged by their faith to reject not only Darwinism but the whole scientific picture of the vast ages of the earth. The Jewish *calendar is still dated from the creation, which is said to have taken place some 5,700 years ago. Other Orthodox thinkers have attempted to deal with the problem of the age of the earth as uncovered by science by postulating, as did many Christians at the time of the debate, that the 'days' of Genesis represent vast periods of time; though, if that is the case, what is the meaning of 'evening and morning' in Genesis? On the question of natural selection, many Orthodox Jews totally reject the theory in favour of the idea that God created the separate species directly. Some few, however, have even accepted the theory of natural selection, arguing, again as do many Christian thinkers, that it is God who set the whole process in motion; that even if species have been produced through the survival of the fittest, it is God who is responsible for the arrival of the fittest.

Reform and Conservative Jews find no difficulty in the theory of evolution since they reject, in any event, the idea that the Bible is the inerrant word of God and hold that the human authors of the Bible, though divinely inspired, had only the science of their day.

Unusually for an Orthodox Rabbi, Rabbi A. I. *Kook warmly accepted the theory of evolution. As a Kabbalist, Kook believed, corresponding remarkably with the thought of Teilhard de Chardin, that the theory was fully in accord with the Kabbalistic view that the whole of creation is constantly evolving from lower to higher forms. As for the Genesis narrative, Kook points out that it is generally held that this narrative belongs to 'the secrets of the Torah', namely, that it contains ideas about the mystery of creation which go far beyond any superficial literal reading. The surface reading of Genesis is no doubt in conflict with the theory of evolution but, in connection with this narrative in particular, the surface meaning is not the true meaning.

Aryeh Carmel and Cyril Domb, 'Creation and Evolution', in Carmel and Domb (eds.), *Challenge: Torah Views on Science and Its Problems* (Jerusalem and New York, 1978), 124–287.

**Exilarch** Head of the Jewish community in *Babylon. The origins of the office are obscure but there is clear evidence that the exilarchs, traditionally descended from King David, functioned virtually as Jewish kings under the Persian rulers in Babylon in Talmudic times and under the Islamic rulers in the period of the *Geonim. The exilarch had his own police force and prisons. He regulated the economic life of the Jewish community by imposing strict market controls. Throughout the period of the exilarchs there was often rivalry between the holders of the office and the Rabbinic scholars, though it was not unknown for an exilarch to be himself a distinguished scholar.

**Exile** The banishment of the Jewish people from their homeland and the state of mind produced by this; Heb. Galut. Especially after the destruction of the Second Temple in 70 CE, Jews began to see the Galut as a catastrophic punishment for their sins. In the additional prayer recited on festivals the phrase occurs: 'because of our sins we have been exiled from our land and removed far from our country'. Tensions inevitably developed between the idea that Jews in the *Diaspora are in exile and the desire for Jews to accommodate themselves to the life of the countries in which they reside. After the expulsion of the Jews from Spain at the end of the fifteenth century, the concept of exile became increasingly powerful. In the great Kabbalistic system of Isaac *Luria in sixteenth-century Safed, exile received a cosmic dimension. According to the Lurianic Kabbalah, the whole creative process began by *En Sof withdrawing from Himself into Himself so that the finite world could emerge and the subsequent stages in the process of emanation consist of transmitting the divine energy and then recoiling. The exile of the Jewish people mirrors forth the exile of the *Shekhinah, conceived of as an exile of part of God from God, so to speak. The whole human drama is seen in this system as a process of restoration from exile of the *holy sparks. When the process is complete the *Messiah will come and exile will be no more.

Reform Judaism in the nineteenth century tended to reject the whole idea of exile, believing that life in Western Europe is no catastrophe but in itself the realization of the ideal of Israel becoming a 'light to the nations'. *Zionism, on the other hand, placed great emphasis on the idea that Jews were strangers in lands outside Palestine, and Zionists often spoke of the acceptance of the situation as exhibiting a servile, contemptible Galut mentality. With the establishment of the State of Israel, there emerged an even stronger implicit rebuke of Jews living outside the Jewish State who saw no reason to leave the countries in which they were comfortably at home. David Ben Gurion, the first Prime Minister of Israel, even looked forward to the time when the vast majority of Jews will reside in Israel and spoke of this as 'the negation of the Galut'. Such an attitude was later seen to be impossible and, it was further argued by many Jews, Israel needs the support of the Diaspora for its continued

existence. On the theological level, exile is interpreted as remoteness from God so that, in some religious sources, redemption from exile means not alone the salvation of the Jews from oppression and persecution, but the restoration, in the individual soul, of the harmony and bliss that are the fruit of nearness to God. This emphasis is particularly strong in *Hasidism.

In Kabbalistic circles, there was a practice of engaging in exile as a penance. Basing their belief on the Rabbinic saying that exile from home atones for sin, these Kabbalists undertook journeys to distant places where they lived incognito for a time. This is known as 'suffering Galut' (*laiden golus* in Yiddish). The practice was also said to re-enact the exile of the Shekhinah, the *Weltschmerz* felt, as it were, by God Himself at the sorry condition of an unredeemed humanity. Based on the Lurianic Kabbalah is the practice of rising at midnight to sit on the ground and shed tears over the exile of the Shekhinah and to pray for the restoration of the divine glory that has been dimmed.

**Existentialism** The intensely personal philosophy in which the individual responds not to a philosophical system, which he surveys from the outside, but to what is true for him. In religious existentialism, the believer adopts monotheism not because his reason has demonstrated that there is a God but, as Kierkegaard puts it, by a 'leap of faith'. *Heschel's suggestion that Judaism substitutes a 'leap of action' for the 'leap of faith' sounds good but is unhelpful from the philosophical point of view in that it ignores the question of belief upon which, presumably, the action is founded. The two best-known Jewish religious existentialists are Martin *Buber and Franz *Rosenzweig. These two have been followed, rather too blindly, by a number of contemporary Jewish religious thinkers whose attitude has not unfairly been dubbed 'Kierkegaard with a *yarmulka'.

An atheistic existentialist like Sartre affirms that existence precedes essence. This means that there is no essence outside man to which he must conform. Man creates his own values, which is to say that he determines his own essence through his existence and not the other way round. The man who allows others to determine his way of life is being false to himself if he simply acquiesces in it. He must make his own individual choice if he is to be true to himself. Thus, for the atheistic existentialist there is no God who has created man and provided the pattern of human existence. Obviously, such an attitude is totally opposed to Jewish belief. But even the religious existentialists place great emphasis on man's free choice. For them, the choice comes first. The essence or pattern provided by theistic belief is there because the individual has freely chosen to embrace the theistic way. Indeed, for thinkers like Kierkegaard religious faith is not something that can be achieved once and for all. The tensions between belief and unbelief are ever present in the human situation. Again and again the believer must opt for faith, grasping it as a freely choosing human being just when it seems most elusive.

Whether religious existentialism is compatible with Judaism is a complicated question. From the point of view of traditional Judaism, at least, God is a 'given'. He is ever present and the pattern He has created for humans is there in the Torah whether or not humans choose to accept it. The essence of faith does precede human existence. That is why some Jewish thinkers have seen even religious existentialism as a form of atheism.

Caution should certainly be exercised. Jews should not swallow existentialism whole. But, undoubtedly, some of the insights provided by the existentialists are in full accord with the traditional Jewish approach. Judaism does believe in freedom of choice, as it believes in the value of the individual soul in the eyes of God. And it has often been remarked that speculative system-building is foreign both to the Bible and Rabbinic Judaism, in both of which God is to be met and experienced rather than merely thought about or discussed.

Eugene B. Borowitz, *A Layman's Introduction to Religious Existentialism* (New York, 1965).

**Exodus, Book of** The second book of the Pentateuch, called Exodus, after the Greek, meaning 'the Departure' (from Egypt) and in Hebrew *Shemot*, 'the names of' (the Children of Israel), after the book's opening words. The book of Exodus tells of the sojourn of the Children of Israel in Egypt where they were enslaved by Pharaoh and afflicted by his taskmasters; the birth of Moses and his election by God to entreat Pharaoh to let the people go; the ten plagues visited on Pharaoh; the actual exodus of the people from Egypt; the crossing

of the Red Sea and Moses' song of deliverance; the theophany at Sinai and the *Decalogue; the Code of law given to the people; the episode of the *golden calf; and the detailed instructions for erecting the *Tabernacle. The traditional Jewish view is that the book, like the rest of the Pentateuch, was written down by Moses at the dictation of God, forming the Torah of Moses. *Biblical criticism sees the book, again like the Pentateuch as a whole, to be a composite work produced at different times in Israel's history.

Brevard S. Childs, *Exodus* (London, 1974).

Nahum M. Sarna, *Exploring Exodus* (New York, 1986).

**Exorcism** The driving out of a *dybbuk, demons, or evil spirits. The belief that a holy man can order the expulsion of evil spirits that have invaded a place or the body of a person is ancient. It is referred to in Josephus, the New Testament, and the Talmud. Some commentators see a form of exorcism in David playing the harp to drive out Saul's evil spirit (1 Samuel 18: 10). In Jewish folklore there are numerous tales of exorcism by saintly persons. There is, however, no actual rite of exorcism in Judaism. The whole notion of exorcism, bound up as it is with *magic and superstition, is found only very rarely in contemporary Jewish life, but instances do occur.

Gershom Winkler, *Dybbuk* (New York, 1981).

**Eybeschitz, Jonathan** Talmudist, Kabbalist, preacher, and Rabbi (d. 1764). Eybeschitz's fame as a Talmudist rests chiefly on his *Urim ve-Thummim*, a work of keen analysis of legal concepts in the form of a commentary to the *Shulhan Arukh, Hoshen Mishpat*. In his early career Eybeschitz was the head of a *Yeshivah and a preacher in Prague, where he was on friendly terms with Christian prelates with whom he discussed and debated theological question. Many of his sermons were collected in his *Yaarat Devash*, a work that provided generations of Jewish preachers with sermonic material.

While in Prague, Eybeschitz was accused of being a follower of the false Messiah, Shabbetai Zevi, an accusation he strongly denied; together with other Prague Rabbis, *he signed a *herem* issued against the Shabbeteans. After Eybeschitz had been appointed Rabbi of the three communities of Altona, Wandsbeck, and Hamburg, he issued *amulets for the protection of women in childbirth. His opponent, Jacob *Emden, claimed to have discovered in these amulets a coded reference to Shabbetai Zevi. One of the fiercest *controversies in Jewish history erupted as a result, the Rabbinic world being split between defenders of Eybeschitz and his detractors. A number of modern scholars have argued that there was some truth in the accusation, hard to believe though it is that a prominent Rabbi would see anything in the strange heresy. Eyebeschitz's son did become a Shabbetean prophet. But it has to be appreciated that to call someone a Shabbetean, in those days, was rather like calling someone today a Marxist, meaning not necessarily an actual disciple of Marx but one with Marxist leanings. Both Emden and Eyebeschitz are revered in *Hasidism, the Hasidim referring to Eybeschitz as 'the Rebbe, Rabbi Jonathan', almost as if he were a Hasidic Rebbe before his time.

> Israel Bettan, 'Jonathan Eybeschitz: Passionate Pleader', in his *Studies in Jewish Preaching* (Cincinnati, 1939), 317–368.

**Ezekiel** The priest who was exiled in 597 BCE to Babylon, where he began to prophesy. Dwelling beside the Chebar canal, he saw the vision of the *Chariot as told in the opening chapter of the book of Ezekiel and thus his prophetic vision contradicts the idea that *prophecy is limited to those who reside in the Holy Land. The Talmudic Rabbis compare the vision of the Throne of God seen by *Isaiah with Ezekiel's vision of the same throne carried on the chariot. Ezekiel, say the Rabbis, can be compared to a villager who, unfamiliar with the sight, waxes eloquent after he has seen the king. Isaiah's account is less elaborate and more subdued since he can be compared to the townsman for whom the sight of the king is not so rare that he is moved to share his experience with others at great length.

The book of Ezekiel was the subject of much discussion, according to the Talmudic sources, before it was admitted into the *Bible as sacred Scripture. The reason for the doubts about the book is that some of its statements appear to contradict those of the Torah. For instance, Moses states in the Torah (Exodus 34: 7) that God visits the sins of the fathers upon the children whereas Ezekiel (18: 4) states: 'The person who sins, he only shall die.' But eventually the book of Ezekiel did become part of the Bible, the apparent contradictions with the Torah being resolved in various ways.

On the critical view (see BIBLICAL CRITICISM) the contradictions are real but present no problem, since the critics do not see the whole of the Bible as a unit. The older critical view was that the book itself is a unit and that it was actually compiled by the prophet himself. This view no longer holds good but there is still considerable discussion on whether the book is a composite work and who were its final editors. Interestingly, the Talmud (*Bava Batra* 15a) states that the book of Ezekiel was written down by the Men of the *Great Synagogue, although the oracles are the prophet's own.

> G. A. Cooke, *The Book of Ezekiel* (Edinburgh, 1936).

**Ezra** The biblical leader of the exiles who had returned to Jerusalem in 458 BCE. Ezra's associate was *Nehemiah and the story of these two leaders is told in the books of Ezra and Nehemiah. He is described in the book of Ezra (7: 6, 11) as a scribe and is known in the Jewish tradition (which gives each of the biblical heroes his own particular appellation) as Ezra the Scribe. As told in the book of Ezra (chs. 9 and 10) Ezra fought against the marriage of Jews with foreign women, evicting these men and their children from the community.

In the Rabbinic sources, Ezra is placed alongside Moses as the great teacher of the Torah. *Spinoza, a pioneer of *biblical criticism, suggested that Ezra was the actual compiler of the Torah of Moses, the Pentateuch—a view that is obviously at variance with the tradition, although the Rabbis do speak of Ezra placing dots over certain letters in the Pentateuch because he was uncertain whether the words over which the dots were placed belonged to the original Torah. A number of ancient enactments such as the reading of the Torah on Sabbath afternoon, Mondays, and Thursdays are attributed, to Ezra. In the tradition Ezra is held to be responsible for changing the old cursive script, in which the Torah was originally written, into the square script now used universally. Another Rabbinic saying has it that if the Torah had not been given to Moses it would have been given to Ezra. Ezra is also said to belong among the Men of the *Great Synagogue. In one source Ezra is identified with the prophet *Malachi.

> Judah J. Slokki, *Daniel, Ezra and Nehemiah* (London and Bournemouth, 1951), 107–77.

# F

**Faith** The Hebrew word for 'faith', *emunah*, is used in the Bible and Talmud to denote trust in God (see BELIEF) The Talmud (*Makkot* 24a), for instance, observes that the prophet Habakkuk based the whole of the Torah on one principle, when he said: 'But the righteous shall live by faith' (Habakkuk 2: 4). This observation suggests that the whole Torah is based on trust in God, from which everything else in the Torah follows. It was not until the medieval period, when the Jewish thinkers were obliged to confront atheistic opinions (see ATHEISM), that these thinkers used the term 'faith' to denote belief in the existence of God, though the meaning of trust in God was not abandoned. The Jewish sources in the earlier biblical and Talmudic period addressed themselves to the central problem in their day, trust in God, whereas medieval and modern Jewish thinkers grappled with the problem of the very existence of God, so that before discussing the need for trust in God they sought to demonstrate that there is a God in whom to trust. Faith now acquires a cognitive connotation, involving assent to certain propositions such as that God exists, and lack of faith implies a rejection of these propositions.

The medieval thinkers, Jewish, Christian, Muslim, held that it is possible to demonstrate the existence of God by rational argument, hence the traditional proofs for the existence of God—the ontological, the cosmological, and the teleological. The first is not found in any of the Jewish sources but the other two are used for what seemed to these thinkers to be knock-down arguments which were bound to be accepted by every rational person. As a result of Kant's critique of the ability of the human reason to arrive at conclusions beyond its scope and experience, many religious Jews have followed the arguments more as pointers than as proofs. Others have been attracted to religious *existentialism, to Kierkegaard's 'leap of faith', in which the human will has a role to play. The

mystics, on the other hand, tend to speak of faith as 'higher than reason', treating it almost as a divine gift given to those who seek God with all their heart, mind, and will. In a sense this mood is closer to the biblical insight into the nature of faith than is the rationalistic approach of the medieval thinkers. The Bible deals with faith in terms of passionate concern and commitment. It recognizes the needs of the individual face to face with God. It stresses that the whole of man and not only his reason must be involved in the life of faith. It is non-systematic and God is both nearer and yet more mysterious than in the too-tidy schemes of the medieval thinkers.

Generally speaking, the Jewish way to faith is through the tradition. To find God through tradition, however, is not at all the same thing as to argue that there must be a God because people in the past have believed in Him. People in the past, even millions of them, may have been as wrong in this as in believing that the earth is flat, or in the possibility of a flying ship (this latter was a frequently adduced illustration in medieval literature of the clearly impossible). The appeal of faith to tradition is that human beings in the past (particularly as evidenced in the biblical record) have claimed to have met a Being who endowed their lives with moral worth and significance. They have handed down what the encounter meant for them so powerfully that their heirs relive the tremendous meeting and hear God speaking to *them* when, for instance, they read of how He had spoken to Isaiah, Jeremiah, and Micah.

This is, in fact, how the vast majority of Jews obtained their concept of God in the first instance. Hardly any Jews are moved to reflect on God's existence as if this were a question they had come to consider entirely for themselves. Born as they were into a particular theistic tradition, one which has been severely challenged in modern times, Jews find themselves obliged, as soon as they reflect on life's meaning, to decide whether the tradition speaks truth or not, whether there is a God or not. If Jews (naturally a similar process can be observed among Christians and Muslims) finally decide that the tradition is true for them, this is because it provides the most adequate key to unlock life's secrets, because it answers their own profoundest stirrings of soul. Jews who opt for God on the basis of tradition do so because the knowledge found there coheres with the rest of their knowledge. Believing Jews do not argue that their faith is true because it is in the tradition, but have come to appreciate that faith is in the tradition because it is true.

Faith in the sense in which it has been discussed above denotes faith in God. In some Orthodox circles in recent years, however, notably in the Aggudat Israel movement, faith has also come to mean belief that certain charismatic personalities, acknowledged as outstanding teachers of the Torah, have a kind of built-in guarantee that their opinions are infallible and are to be heeded even when these opinions are on political matters. The term for this is 'faith in the sages', an expression found in Ethics of the Fathers (ch. 6) where it is mentioned as one of the ways by which knowledge of the Torah can be gained. But in that passage the expression simply denotes reliance by the student on the ability of his teachers. Unless a student has confidence that his teachers really know the Torah he will not make make the effort to understand what they are saying. There is nothing in the passage to justify the notion that the devout Jew is obliged to follow blindly and uncritically the opinions of certain sages no matter how eminent, to say nothing of the sobering fact that there is no agreement among Jews on which personalities qualify as the 'sages of Israel'.

Louis Jacobs, *Faith* (London, 1968).

**Faith-Healing** The cure of disease by methods that invoke religious belief either as a complement to natural methods or as a substitute for them. Judaism is obviously opposed to this kind of healing where it belongs to the practices and beliefs of another religion: in the name of Jesus, for example, or as part of a Christian service. The question of the legitimacy of recourse to faith-healing from the Jewish point of view arises where this is undertaken in the name of God. Traditionally, Judaism has viewed

with suspicion supposedly supernatural intervention to cure human ills because this might be associated with *magic and superstition. Nor does Judaism usually countenance the belief, as in the Christian Science movement, that all disease is in the mind and is really an illusion that can be addressed by exposing its illusory nature. The rival Jewish movement of Jewish Science, founded by Morris Lieberman in 1922, has found very few adherents among Jews. There is nevertheless a recognition in some of the classical Jewish sources that the mind has an influence on bodily heath.

It is tempting, for instance, to understand the Talmudic accounts of certain sages taking the hand of a sick person and raising him from his sick-bed (*Berakhot* 5b) as examples of faith-healing, although the motif in these tales appears rather to be the power of the saint to work miracles. Many of the Hasidic masters were claimed by their followers to possess supernatural powers of healing—one of the reasons why the *doctors were opposed to *Hasidism. Nowadays, when many diseases are seen by doctors themselves in psychosomatic terms, a distinction is often drawn between Rabbis and others co-operating with doctors to apply the healing powers of faith as an aid to recovery, and faith-healing as a cult. This kind of distinction is behind the tale told of the Hasidic master, Simhah Bunem of Pzhysha (d. 1827). This master, who suffered severely from bad eyesight, was once advised, after the doctors had declared they could do nothing to help him, to consult a faith-healer. The master is said to have retorted that the Torah advises the Jew to consult doctors who heal by natural means. But where the healer invokes faith it is wrong to go to a healer who does not accept Judaism. Instead, the sick person should have resort to a Jewish saint or master of prayer to pray that he be healed. Similarly, the Central Conference of American [Reform] Rabbis, after discussing, in 1927, the question of 'spiritual healing', issued a report reaffirming belief in the healing powers of the synagogue but disapproving of cults that deny reality to all human ailments.

**Falashas** A tribe of black Jews in Ethiopia, many of whom have now emigrated to Israel. The name 'Falashas', meaning 'strangers', is pejorative and is never used by the Beta Israel ('House of Israel') as these Ethiopian Jews call themselves. The origins of this ancient community are shrouded in obscurity. Some scholars believe that they are the remnant of a Christian sect, others that they are the descendants of Yemenite Jews. They themselves claim descent from some notables from Jerusalem who accompanied the son of King Solomon and the Queen of Sheba when he returned to the land of his ancestors. The religion of these Jews is a form of Judaism without the *Oral Torah that is, the traditions contained in the Rabbinic literature. They have their own liturgy, offer animal sacrifices, segregate menstruating women in special huts, and, in addition to the standard Jewish feasts and fasts, they have some of their own.

When the Ethiopian Jews began to settle in Israel, the question, discussed already in the sixteenth century by Rabbinic authorities, arose of whether they are Jews: are Jews permitted to intermarry with them or must they first undergo *conversion, involving circumcision for males (actually only a token circumcision since these Jews practise circumcision) and immersion for both males and females. The Chief Rabbinate in Israel, following the sixteenth century precedent, declared that the Ethiopian Jews were the descendants of the ancient tribe of Dan and were, consequently, true members of the House of Israel. Nevertheless, a token conversion was required of them before they could marry Jews, a Rabbinic decision which has caused much conflict; the Ethiopian Jews refuse to undergo immersion, as they consider this to be a denial of their Jewish status.

**Fame** Judaism does not normally encourage an attitude of contempt and disdain for fame and renown achieved by legitimate means. Fame is the spur to achievement. Yet a well-known statement in the Talmud (*Eruvin* 13b) warns: 'Whoever runs after fame, fame runs way from him. But whoever runs away from fame, fame runs after him.' In a delightful Hasidic tale, a man protested to a Hasidic master that while he had always followed the Talmudic advice to run away from fame, fame somehow did not run after him. Why was this? The master replied: 'Your trouble is that you are always looking behind you to see if fame is running after you!'

In connection with religious matters any conscious attempt to achieve a reputation for piety, learning, or benevolence tends to come into conflict with the Rabbinic ideal of *lishmah* ('for its own sake'), serving God without thought of reward (see DISINTERESTEDNESS). The proper attitude is expressed in another Rabbinic saying: 'Act out of love and fame will come to you in the end', implying that there is nothing to be ashamed of in a well-deserved reputation, even in religious matters, but his should come of its own accord and never be consciously cultivated. Nevertheless, the Rabbis were sufficiently aware of the allure of impure motivation when they urged a person not to desist from carrying out his obligations merely because his motivation is one of self-seeking. 'Let a man busy himself with studying the Torah and carrying out the precepts even if his motive is impure. For as a result of acting out of ulterior motives he will eventually come to act out of pure motivation' (*Pesaḥim* 50b).

In *Hasidism, however, not only is the conscious pursuit of fame denigrated but fame itself is seen as having a corrupting effect on the character (see ANNIHILATION OF SELFHOOD). Many of the Hasidic masters were extremely unwilling to assume office and only yielded reluctantly to the importunities of their followers. Some of the masters longed to live in obscurity and looked upon their elevation to high office as a punishment for their sins. This attitude is reflected in the tales of the *Lamed vovniks, the thirty-six hidden saints upon whose shoulders the world is carried while they themselves remain completely unknown.

**Family** Judaism attaches great importance to the family. In the Bible (Genesis 10) the whole human race is presented as a family of nations and even the most obscure and trivial family relationships of the patriarchs are recorded in detail (see e.g. Genesis 22: 20–4; 26). The family both circumscribes and broadens the horizons of its members, each individual having a dual role: as a person in his or her own right and as father or mother, son or daughter, brother or sister, husband or wife, with the extended relationships of grandparents, grandchildren, uncles, aunts, nephews, nieces, cousins, parents-in-law, children-in-law, step-parents and stepchildren.

These family relationships are carefully graded in the Jewish tradition. The *mourning rites, for example, to be observed when a near relative dies, are limited to the seven nearest relatives—father, mother, son, daughter, brother, sister, husband, wife. Of these seven, the mourning period for a parent extends for a whole year, while for the other five for one month. Similarly with regard to *charity, the nearer a relative the greater the obligation to assist him or her when in need. Poor parents take precedence over other relatives, closer members of the family over more distant relatives, and members of the family over strangers.

Yet individual needs and rights are safeguarded by the tradition. While, for instance, the fifth commandment: 'Honour thy father and thy mother' is binding upon children, *Isserles rules that if a father objects to his son marrying the woman of his choice, the father's wishes can be disregarded (see CHILDREN AND PARENTS).

In the *marriage relationship, too, as everybody knows, husband and wife have to surrender some of their individuality if the marriage is to work: 'Therefore shall a man leave his father and his mother, and shall cleave unto his wife, and they shall be one flesh' (Genesis 2: 24). On the verse: 'It is not good that the man should be alone: I will make him a help meet for him' (Genesis 2: 18), the nineteenth-century commentator Rabbi Naftali Zevi Judah Berlin observes that the Hebrew for 'meet for him' can have the meaning of 'opposed to him', yielding the thought that husband and wife are of 'help' to one another because of their differences, not in spite of them. The same would apply to other members of the family. Shaw's 'family stewing in love' is not the traditional Jewish family.

In Jewish law near relatives are disqualified from testifying in a court of law not only in each other's favour but also against one another. Some of the commentators see this rule as a means of avoiding the kind of terrible conflicts engendered by the Nazis who encouraged children to betray their parents. Others see in it an expression of abhorrence that a member of a family should be a cause of another member's disgrace, even when the one against whom the testimony is given is guilty.

The notion of family pride has been prominent in Jewish life from the earliest periods; at times, it is not unfair to say, it has amounted to an obsession. The families of the *priests and the *Levites were held to be especially aristocratic. The ruling is given in the Mishnah that if a man betroths a woman, assuring her that he is a priest when, in fact, he is only a Levite, the betrothal is invalid because this amounts to misrepresentation. The same rule applies if the man says that he is a Levite but is really a priest, since the woman may not wish 'to wear a sandal too large for her foot'. When a new aristocracy of learning emerged, pride in belonging to a scholarly family was encouraged. A scholar whose family are ignorant, remarks the Talmud, tends to parade his learning just as a single stone in a large otherwise empty jar makes a loud rattling noise. Matchmakers in most pre-modern Jewish communities would set great store on good family background. Yet, the Talmud advises, before a community elects someone to serve as its leader they should make sure that he has 'a box full of vermin hanging behind him', that is, disgraceful episodes in his family history with which he can be taunted whenever he abuses his power.

Against undue emphasis on family pride, the story is often told of a famous Rabbi whose father was a humble tailor. At a meeting of Rabbis each quoted something of Torah learning, prefacing his remarks with: 'My saintly father said.' When his turn came the Rabbi wryly declared: 'My saintly father said, it is better for a boy to have a suit tailored specially for him than to give him his father's reach-me-downs.'

Louis Jacobs, 'Family Relationships', in his *Religion and the Individual* (Cambridge, 1992), 20–4.

**Fanaticism** Excess of zeal in religious matters, especially when directed against others. Judaism, like most other religions, has had to face the problem of how to achieve a balance between complete, uncompromising loyalty, pursued with enthusiasm and utter conviction, and unbridled zeal, the possessor of which ignores some of the values of the religion itself. The problem is to distinguish between religious zeal and fanaticism. The scriptural prototype of the zealot is Phinehas who slays Zimri, the prince of Israel, and the Moabite woman with whom Zimri had intercourse in the presence of all the people (Numbers 25: 1–15). Building on this scriptural passage, the Talmudic Rabbis remark that 'Zealots slay one who has intercourse with a Syrian woman' but this is 'a law that must not be taught'. That is to say, Phinehas was not guilty of murder but had he asked Moses beforehand for a statement of the law, Moses would have been obliged to reply that it is an act of murder. Indeed, the Rabbis go on to say, if Zimri had defended himself by slaying Phinehas, he would have acted in self-defence and would not have been guilty of murder, since Phinehas had designs on Zimri's life (*Sanhedrin* 81a–82b). Scholars are surely correct in hearing in all this echoes of the discussions around the activities of the *Zealots during the war with Rome in 66–72 CE, towards whom the later Rabbis had an ambivalent attitude.

In the later tradition, the Talmudic passage was used to convey the principle that if a man has to ask whether his fanaticism is lawful; if, that is, he has to weigh up his actions beforehand and is sufficiently calm to do this; then his act is not carried out by an ungovernable religious impulse and he is to be blamed for his fanaticism. The idea appears to be that fanaticism, especially when it flies in the teeth of Jewish values, is to be rejected and can only be tolerated, but not necessarily admired, when completely spontaneous. There have been Jews throughout the ages who took pride in their fanaticism. But against such fanatics the verse was generally applied: 'Be not righteous overmuch' (Ecclesiastes 7: 16). It is said that a man complained to the Hasidic master, Menahem Mendel of *Kotsk, that people called him a fanatic, saying. 'Why am I called a fanatic and not a Jew zealous for his religion?' The Kotsker replied: 'A fanatic is one who turns a minor issue into a major one.'

**Fast Days**   The days in the Jewish *calendar set aside for fasting by the whole community. In addition to the major fasts of *Yom Kippur and the Ninth of *Av, there are three minor fasts commemorating events connected with the downfall of Jerusalem and the destruction of the *Temple in ancient times. These are the fasts of 10 *Tevet, the 17 *Tammuz, and the Fast of Gedaliah on 3 Tishri. The Talmud (*Rosh Ha-Shanah* 18b) comes to the conclusion, based on the passage in the book of *Zechariah (18: 19), where the prophet states that in the future these fasts will be turned into days of joy and gladness, that there are three distinct periods. In periods of persecution the fasts have to be observed with full rigour. In the Messianic age they will become days of joy and gladness. In a period where there is neither 'joy' nor persecution these fast days are optional. Eventually, the suggestion was put forward that the Jewish community should take the option

of fasting on these days, thus creating a new obligation based on the consensus of the community. Nevertheless, these days were not treated as definite public fasts but like the private fast that an individual undertakes as a penance. Such a private fast does not begin on the previous night but at dawn on the day of the fast. The three fast days are thus public–private fasts; public in that they are now obligatory, private in that they only begin at dawn. With the establishment of the State of Israel some Jews, even among the Orthodox, have tended towards greater leniency with regard to these three fasts although they are still observed strictly by the majority of the Orthodox.

In addition to these three there is another public fast day on the day before *Purim known as the Fast of *Esther. Curiously enough, this fast day is observed by the Ethiopian Jews (see FALASHAS) but while the *Shulhan Arukh* does refer to the Fast of Esther as obligatory, it allows certain relaxations. The Fast of the *First-Born on the eve of Passover is much later and is treated in even more lenient fashion.

Hyman E. Goldin, 'Public Fast Days', in his *Code of Jewish Law* (New York, 1961), iii. 54–6.

**Fatherhood of God**   It is often said that Judaism speaks of God as the Father of all human beings who consequently are all brothers and sisters. This idea is often described as the doctrine of the Fatherhood of God and the Brotherhood of Man. The fact is, however, that this formulation is modern and highly apologetical. There is much discussion on the whole question of *universalism and particularism in Judaism (and see CHOSEN PEOPLE) but this particular formulation finds no support in the Jewish sources. The Bible does not speak directly anywhere of God as Father but the idea is found by implication in the verse: 'Ye are the children of the Lord your God' (Deuteronomy 14: 1). Since 'ye' are His children it follows that He is 'your' Father. But the 'ye' in the verse refers to the people of Israel. The intimate relationship described in father–children terms is reserved for God's relationship to Israel, not for mankind as a whole.

Modern exponents of the Fatherhood of God and the Brotherhood of Man are fond of quoting the verse: 'Have we not all one father? Hath not one God created us?' (Malachi 2: 10) but even a cursory glance at the verse in its context shows that the prophet refers to his own people's relationship with God, as the verse concludes: 'Why do we deal treacherously every man against his brother, profaning the covenant of our fathers?' It is even doubtful whether 'father' in this verse refers to God. Many scholars understand 'father' to mean the patriarch Jacob from whom all the people are descended.

Rabbi *Akiba (Ethics of the Fathers, 3. 14) long ago gave expression to the authentic Jewish attitude in this matter:

'Beloved is man for he was created in the *image [of God]; still greater was the love in that it was made known to him that he was created in the image of God, as it is written: "For in the image of God made He man" [Genesis 9: 6]. Beloved are Israel for they were called children of God; still greater was the love in that it was made known to them that they were called children of God, as it is written: "Ye are the children of the Lord your God" [Deuteronomy 14: 1].'

Rabbi Akiba, to be sure, affirms that every human being is created in God's image but he understands the special, intimate father–children relationship to be reserved for God in relation to Israel. Like many a Rabbinic saying, Rabbi Akiba's calls attention to both the universalistic and the particularistic elements in Judaism.

**Feinstein, Moshe** Rabbi, teacher, and foremost authority in Jewish law (1895–1986). Feinstein was born in Russia and received his Talmudic education in the Yeshivot of Lithuania. He was Rabbi of the town of Luban in Russia from 1921 until 1937, at which date he emigrated to the USA where he served as the head of the Yeshivah Tiferet Yerushalayim in New York. Feinstein followed the methods of keen analysis of legal concepts as taught in the Yeshivot of Lithuania, with the emphasis on legal theory rather than on its application in practice. He published commentaries in this vein on a number of Talmudic tractates. But Feinstein's fame rests chiefly on his collections of *Responsa under the name Iggerot Moshe, 'Letters of Moses'. His decisions in these Responsa are widely held to be authoritative for the whole world of Orthodoxy.

Feinstein's general stance is one of strictness in connection with non-Orthodox tendencies in Judaism, even declaring that it is not permitted to answer 'Amen' to a benediction uttered by a Reform Rabbi. But within Orthodoxy he is very lenient, coming close, for instance, to permitting *artificial insemination by a donor, to the consternation of his Orthodox colleagues. Although the law only permits milk from Gentile farms if a Jew has been present at the milking (lest non-kosher milk be substituted), Feinstein argued that since there are strict rules against the adulteration of milk in the USA and most countries today, it is always a case of a Jew being 'present'. He ruled that an aged, pious man could stay with his irreligious daughter and need have no fear that she will give him non-kosher food to eat. He saw no reason why a blind man should not be allowed to bring his guide-dog into the synagogue during prayers.

Feinstein also discusses theological questions in his Responsa; for instance, whether to take out life *insurance betokens lack of trust in God. Feinstein declares that, like any other business transaction, insurance is not only allowed but advocated on the principle that human endeavour is required before God's help is forthcoming. Trust in God here means reliance on God to help a man who has taken out insurance to do well enough to be able to pay the premiums. In another Responsum he discusses whether a Gentile is obliged to pray to God, according to the Torah, since this is not one of the *Noahide laws. The reply is that a Gentile has no obligation to offer prayer to God but it is counted to him as meritorious if he does.

Feinstein was often referred to as 'the Great One of the generation', in other words, the world authority in Jewish law. In 1974, a Rabbi Schwartz published the work Reply to the Letters, in which he sought to demonstrate that Feinstein made many errors of judgement in his works and does not deserve the high title. Schwartz's critique was generally seen as unfounded and had no effect on Feinstein's reputation.

Shimon Finkelman, Reb Moshe: The Life and Ideals of HaGaon Rabbi Moshe Feinstein (New York, 1986).

**Feminism** The movement to obtain equal rights and opportunities for women in Jewish religious life. Following on from the general feminist movement in the 1960s, voices of Jewish men as well as women began to be raised, especially in the USA, that Judaism is too male-oriented. The Jewish woman is at a disadvantage, for instance, in matters of *divorce and a woman cannot be counted in the quorum required for communal prayer, the *minyan. The claims of Jewish feminism in these and similar areas of practice have been acceded to in Reform Judaism and, with some exceptions, in Conservative Judaism. Orthodoxy rejects any departure from the tradition in this area, although some Orthodox Rabbis see no objection to women coming together for services conducted by them in a separate women's minyan.

Jewish feminism, however, goes much further in its advocacy of a Jewish feminist theology. Jewish feminist theologians maintain that sexist language used in Jewish prayers and in statements about the Deity tend to be implicitly weighted in favour of the understanding of Judaism as a religion for men. True, the argument runs, *women are given an important role in the religion, but it is a role given to them by the hitherto male interpreters of the tradition. For instance, according to the traditional *Halakhah, women are exempt from performing positive precepts dependent on a particular time, so that they have no obligation to wear a *tallit or don *tefillin, and women are not obliged to study the Torah. But these limitations are based on the teachings of the Talmudic Rabbis who were men with a masculine way of looking at things. An innovation of Jewish feminism is to add to the expression in the standard liturgy 'God of Abraham, God of Isaac and God of Jacob' the names of the *matriarchs: 'God of Sarah, God of Rebecca, God of Rachel and God of Leah.'

Some Jewish feminist theologians have tried to adopt insights they claim to be found in the Kabbalah. In the Kabbalistic doctrine of the *Sefirot, the divine Wisdom is referred to as Abba, 'Father', and the divine Understanding as Imma, 'Mother'. Here, as well as in the Kabbalistic doctrine of the *Shekhinah, there is a female element in the Godhead, demonstrating that, in some varieties of Judaism at least, there is room for God to be referred to as a 'She' as well as a 'He'. It has to be said, however, that, in the Kabbalah, it is the male principle that represents mercy while the female principle is the source of severity and judgement and that the Kabbalah, too, was produced by men; scholars have often noted the absence of female mystics in Judaism.

With the rise of Jewish feminism, the question began to be debated whether women could be ordained as *Rabbis. There is little Halakhic objection to having women serve as Rabbis since, traditionally, the Rabbi's function is to render decisions in Jewish law and, if a woman is competent to do so, there appears to be no reason why she should not exercise this function. There are a few Halakhic problems with regard to a woman serving as a modern Rabbi; for instance, whether she can act as a prayer leader in the synagogue. But basically it is a matter of traditional norms, as many of the Orthodox admitted when they declared that to have women serving as Rabbis is 'contrary to the Jewish spirit', an opinion hardly Halakhic in nature. Reform Judaism ordained women as Rabbis and accepted women as *Cantors in the 1970s and the majority of Conservatives soon followed suit. Orthodoxy and some Conservative congregations accept women neither as Rabbis nor as Cantors.

In this connection it should be noted that the question of whether women can serve as Rabbis is quite different from the Christian debate on whether women can be priests. As noted above, the Jewish debate does not revolve round doctrinal issues as does the Christian discussion of whether women can belong in the Apostolic succession or whether the priest is in the stead of Jesus. A good deal of confusion has been caused by trying to equate the Jewish with the Christian debate and both with the cause of feminism.

Simon Greenberg (ed.), *The Ordination of Women as Rabbis* (New York, 1988).
Susannah Heschel (ed.), *On being a Jewish Feminist* (New York, 1983).

**Festivals** The festivals of the Jewish year are treated under the separate headings: *Passover, *Pentecost, *Tabernacles, *Rosh Ha-Shanah, *Yom Kippur, *Hanukkah, *Purim, and the New Year for *Trees (see CALENDAR). The last three are minor festivals compared with the first five, Hanukkah and Purim dating from ancient times, New Year for Trees being introduced as a festival at a much later date. Essentially, there are five major festivals and two minor in the sense that the major festivals are biblically ordained, the minor festivals only by Rabbinic law.

In connection with forbidden work, a distinction is drawn between the *Sabbath on the one hand and the major festivals on the other, with a further distinction between the major and the minor festivals. On the Sabbath all work is forbidden but on the major festivals (with the exception of Yom Kippur which is treated on a par with the Sabbath) work required for the preparation of food is permitted. It is permitted, for instance, to light a fire on the festivals and to cook and bake, but building operations, weaving and sowing, writing, and business activities are forbidden. On Hanukkah and Purim there is no prohibition at all of work or business dealings. The days between the first and last days of Passover and Tabernacles are known as semi-festivals and have rules of their own. Even work not required in the preparation of food is permitted on these days but only where loss will be incurred if it is not carried out. In biblical times the day of the new moon, *Rosh Hodesh, seems to have been treated as a major festival with regard to the prohibition of work but is now treated as a minor festival like Hanukkah and Purim, although pious women do not work on this day, possibly as a response to the day's original status.

S. J. Zevin, *The Festivals in Halakhah*, trans. Meir Fox-Ashri (New York, 1981).

**Fire** The Bible explicitly forbids kindling a fire on the Sabbath (Exodus 35: 3). At the *Havdalah ceremony at the termination of the Sabbath, when fire can again be kindled, a special benediction is recited over a lighted candle, praising God for the gift of fire. In contrast to the Prometheus legend in which the hero was punished by the gods for introducing fire to mankind, a Jewish legend tells how Adam, when he first saw the sun going down and night beginning to set in, thought the world was coming to an end until God taught him to rub two sticks together to make fire.

Fire is used frequently as a symbol of the divine, based on the verse: 'For the Lord your God is a consuming fire' (Deuteronomy 4: 24), which a Rabbinic comment understands to mean that man must strive to come near to God but not too near. In the narrative of the theophany at Sinai, the verse states that God descended upon the mount in fire (Exodus 19: 16), expressing the numinous quality of fire. Another Rabbinic comment has it that the Torah, given at Sinai, is compared to fire because, like fire, the Torah is freely available to all.

Evelyn Underhill has noted that the connection of fire with the divine presence runs right through the Hebrew Bible, for instance, in the burning bush seen by Moses, the pillar of fire which led the Israelites by night through the wilderness, the flame and smoke of Sinai, as in the verse mentioned above, in the sacrifice of *Elijah on Mount Carmel, the visions of *Ezekiel and *Daniel. Underhill remarks that for Semitic thought fire and *light were essential attributes of the divine self-disclosure. Examples of the use of fire and light in Jewish rituals, in addition to the Havdalah ceremony, are: the *Hanukkah lights, the light kindled in a house of *mourning and on the anniversary of a death, the candles before the reading-desk in the *synagogue, and the burning of leaven on the eve of *Passover. In the Kabbalah, fire is the symbol of divine judgement as water is the symbol of the divine mercy.

**First-Born, Fast of** The fast on 14 Nisan, the day before *Passover. The earliest reference to the first-born fasting on the eve of Passover is in the post-Talmudic tractate *Soferim* (ch. 21). This fast is said to commemorate the deliverance of the first-born Isaelites when the Egyptian first-born were slain and is therefore unique as a fast not of mourning or penance but of thanksgiving. Traditionally, the completion of a Talmudic tractate in study is an occasion for a 'religious meal' in which it is a religious obligation to participate. This obligation overrides the need to fast on this day, which is an unusual fast in any event. It is consequently the well-nigh universal custom that a Talmudic scholar arranges to complete the study of a Talmudic tractate on this day after which the celebratory meal (usually just drinks and cakes) is partaken of by the first-born and this releases him from the obligation to fast. A Hasidic master is reported to have said that the original reading in tractate *Soferim* was 'the first-born enjoy themselves'—*mitangin*—and this was changed to 'the first-born fast'—*mitanim*—by a spoilsport omitting the letter *gimmel*; an unlikely tale, but one that expresses the mood of solemnity yielding to joyousness.

**First-Born, Redemption of** The ceremony at which the first-born male child is symbolically purchased from a priest; Heb. *Pidyon Ha-Ben*, 'Redemption of the Son'. This ceremony is carried out in the following manner.

The first-born child, if a male, is brought into the room (often on a silver platter) and presented by his father to the priest, a *Kohen, a descendant of *Aaron the priest (see PRIESTS). The ceremony has to be performed on the thirty-first day after the child's birth unless this day is a Sabbath. The father makes the following declaration:

'This my first-born son, is the first-born of his mother, and the Holy One, blessed be He, has given command to redeem him, as it is said: "And those that are to be redeemed of them from a month old shalt thou redeem, according to thine estimation, for the money of five shekels, after the shekel of the sanctuary, the shekel being twenty gerahs" [Numbers 18: 16]; and it is said: "Sanctify unto Me all the first-born, whatsoever openeth the womb among the children of Israel, both of man and of beast it is mine" [Exodus 13: 2].'

The father then places before the Kohen silver to the amount of 5 *shekalim*. The Kohen asks the father: 'Which would you rather, give me your first-born son, the first-born of his mother, or redeem him for 5 shekels, which you are bound to give according to the Torah?' The father replies: 'I desire rather to redeem my son, and here you have the value of his redemption, which I am bound to give according to the Torah.'

The Kohen receives the redemption money, and returns the child to his father, and the father recites two *benedictions: 'Blessed art Thou, O Lord our God, King of the universe, who hast sanctified us by Thy commandments, and commanded us concerning the redemption of the son', and 'Blessed art Thou, O Lord our God, King of the universe, who hast kept us in life, and hast preserved us, and enabled us to reach this season.'

The Kohen then takes the redemption money, and, holding it over the head of the child, says: 'This is instead of that, this in commutation for that, this is in remission for that. May this child enter into life, into the Torah and the fear of Heaven. May it be God's will that even as he has been admitted to redemption, so may he enter into the Torah, the nuptial canopy, and into good deeds. Amen.' The Kohen then places his hand on the head of the child and recites the priestly benediction. It is the usual practice for a festive meal to be arranged in celebration of the redemption.

There is some uncertainty about the value of

5 shekels. The usual assessment is that the amount is equivalent to the value of a silver object, such as a candlestick, containing at least 96 grams of silver. An enterprising firm has produced sets of 5 shekels for the Pidyon Ha-Ben. But the amount need not be particularly in silver coins. Any silver object will suffice. In fact, if no silver is available the redemption can be carried out with anything worth an equivalent amount. One of the Talmudic Rabbis who was a Kohen accepted a turban for the redemption. The redemption money belongs to the Kohen and he is entitled to keep it for himself. But if he wishes he can return it to the father as a gift or he can donate it to charity.

The redemption itself is biblical, as stated in the verses quoted in the father's declaration, but the benedictions recited by the father are Talmudic and the ceremony in its present form dates from the period of the *Geonim.

The reason given in Exodus 13 for the redemption of the first-born is that when Pharaoh refused to let the people go God slew every first-born in Egypt, taking the first-born Israelites to Himself, and they have therefore to be redeemed. Many scholars have noted that in ancient societies the first-born son served as a priest and this may be the origin of the redemption law. There has also been read into the rite the idea that by dedicating the first-born to God's service the whole family is set on the right course.

'First-born' in this context means the first-born of the mother, since the Bible speaks of 'the opening of the womb'. Thus, even if the father already has children from another wife the rite of redemption has to be carried out when his present wife gives birth to her first-born. Conversely, if the child is not the first-born of the mother no redemption is to be carried out even if he is the first-born of his father. If the wife has had a previous pregnancy that resulted in a miscarriage, there is no redemption of the first-born since the child, though a first-born, did not 'open the womb', unless the miscarriage happened during the forty days from the conception. If the father is a Kohen or a *Levite or the mother the daughter of a Kohen or a Levite, no redemption takes place, since these have themselves a priestly role of a kind.

Reform Judaism has generally abandoned rites associated with the ancient priesthood and many Reform Jews do not observe the ceremony of Pidyon Ha-Ben, but others do. Some feminists (see FEMINISM) have sought to introduce a parallel ceremony for a first-born girl.

Isaac Klein, 'Redemption of the Firstborn', in his *A Guide to Jewish Religious Practice* (New York, 1979), 430–2.

**Fish** It is somewhat surprising that while there are many references to fish and fishing in the Bible there are no names for particular fish. According to the *dietary laws only fish that have fins and scales may be eaten: 'These you may eat, of all that are in the waters. Everything in the waters that has fins and scales.' (Leviticus 11: 9–11). The use of the general term 'of all that are in the waters', instead of 'all the fish that are in the waters', might be meant to imply that the species without fins and scales are not considered to be fish at all. The Israelites in the wilderness complained to Moses that while they were slaves in Egypt they ate fish 'for nothing' (Numbers 11: 5), perhaps because fish were plentiful. The Hebrew word for fish is *dag* (plural *dagim*) on the basis of which it used to be conjectured that Dagon, worshipped by the Philistines (Judges 16: 23), was a fish-god but it is now seen as more tenable that Dagon was an agricultural deity (from *dagan*, 'corn'). There are many references to fish and fishing in the Talmudic literature.

The Talmud (*Pesaḥim* 76b) states that it is forbidden to eat meat and fish together on the grounds that this can be injurious to health. Maimonides, however, does not record this prohibition in his Code, probably because, from his experience as a doctor, he concluded that in his day there was no risk to health.

From Talmudic times it became the custom to eat fish on the Sabbath. One reason given for this preference is that in the creation narrative in the first chapter of Genesis three are blessed after they had been created: the Sabbath, fish, and human beings. A curious reason was advanced by some of the Kabbalists. Some righteous persons, after death, are sentenced to be reincarnated (see REINCARNATION) in fish and when these are eaten by a holy man on the sacred day the soul finds its rectification. It would sometimes happen that fishmongers, knowing of the practice of eating fish on the Sabbath, would charge exorbitant prices, whereupon the Rabbinic authorities would ban the eating of fish until the prices came down. There was a widespread Jewish belief that

eating fish is good for the mind. Jews are said to be clever because they eat plenty of fish!

**Flattery** In the Jewish tradition flattery as a real vice applies only to any attempt to win the favour of a wrongdoer by justifying his evil deeds or by lauding him and paying him respect. The medieval authors refer especially in this connection to the verse: 'But what I see in the prophets of Jerusalem is something horrifying: adultery and false dealing. They encourage evildoers, so that no one turns back from his wickedness' (Jeremiah 23: 14). It is the encouragement of wrongdoing that is chiefly condemned. Insincere praise of a neighbour or praising a neighbour for virtues he does not possess or simply 'buttering him up' is not forbidden by the strict letter of the law. Nevertheless the moralists frown on such activities as well, but much depends in this grey area on the aim and purpose of the flattery and on its social effects. Thus even the moralists advise a husband to promote peace and harmony in the home by flattering his wife, rather ungallantly implying that it is the wife not the husband from whom disharmony generally stems. Similarly, they suggest that a teacher should flatter his pupils in order to encourage them to progress in their studies and pupils should flatter their teacher in order for him to pay greater attention to them. Flattery does no harm, it is intimated, when it serves a good cause.

Rabbi H. H. Medini (1832–1904), in his great compendium of Jewish law and morals entitled *Sedey Ḥemed* (under *ḥanufah*) discusses at length whether the practice of Rabbis, when corresponding with one another, to use exaggerated *titles, falls under the heading of forbidden flattery. His conclusion is that there is no harm in it since it has become the norm and no one takes it too seriously, and to omit such flowery praise amounts, nowadays, to an insult. Obviously in such matters much depends on sensitivity and good taste and there can be no hard-and-fast rules.

**Flood** The deluge in which God destroyed all mankind (with the exception of *Noah and his family) because of their evil deeds, as told in the book of Genesis (6: 9–9: 28). The mythical nature of the Flood narrative has often been noted, especially in the account of the animals coming in two by two into Noah's Ark, which is not a huge ship but a comparatively small, box-like structure. Moreover, parallels to the Flood story are found in ancient Babylonian myths, especially in the *Gilgamish Epic* in which the gods decide to destroy mankind because people are disturbing them by making too much noise! Orthodox Judaism, stressing that the whole of the *Pentateuch is the very word of God, accepts the narrative as factually true in all its details; although Chief Rabbi J. H. *Hertz is prepared to admit that the Pentateuchal narrative is paralleled in the Babylonian myth. Hertz's view is that the narrative is factual. There really was a Flood of universal proportions and Noah is a historical figure, both the Babylonian myth and the Genesis narrative being no more than different versions of the same facts. Even on the critical view (see BIBLICAL CRITICISM) that the Genesis narrative is mythical and that there is more than one account combined in the present form of the narrative, the critics readily note the vast difference between the monotheistic account of the Torah and the polytheistic Babylonian account. In the Babylonian myth, for instance, Ut-Napishtim, the Babylonian Noah, is saved by the god of whom he was a special favourite and he himself eventually became a god, unlike in the biblical account in which Noah is a righteous *man*, saved because of his righteousness. On this view, the biblical authors used the ancient myth to create a myth of their own, but one infused with moral concern in the monotheistic vein.

Many modern Jewish scholars and thinkers, while acknowledging the mythical elements in the Genesis narrative and its indebtedness to the Babylonian epic, maintain that the narrative is in part at least factual, although, naturally, it is impossible to determine how much is history and how much legend.

Beyond the particular problem of the Flood, the whole discussion centres on the question of the degree to which the Bible conveys infallible information on all matters, and this questions turns on how the traditional doctrine 'the Torah is from heaven' is to be understood (see FUNDAMENTALISM).

J. H. Hertz, 'The Flood', in his *The Pentateuch and Haftorahs* (London, 1960), 196–7.

Nahum M. Sarna; 'The Flood', in his *Understanding Genesis* (New York, 1966), 37–66.

**Folklore** The notions, tales, fancies, legends, proverbs, *magic and superstition, which stem from the people rather than the learned circles, although the Jewish teachers often have recourse to these. There is a good deal of folklore in the Bible and the Talmud and some of the folk-customs eventually found their way into the *Codes. The folklore of the Jews is obviously indebted to folk-beliefs current in the various civilizations in which Jews lived. These were taken over, often in their original vocabulary, but generally given a Jewish slant. Belief in the power of the *evil eye, for instance, is widespread among many cultures and is found in many a Jewish source, but Jewish theological thinking prevented this belief from being expressed in a form contrary to the Jewish religion that God wishes His creatures to be harmed because He is jealous of the success of His creatures.

It cannot be denied that the line between religious belief and folklore is often very finely drawn in Judaism, naturally so since Judaism is a religion that centres on the Jewish people. Both Jewish theology and Jewish law are coloured by ideas that stem from the beliefs of the people and there is considerable tension among the Jewish teachers between the struggle to eradicate folk-beliefs and the wish to adopt them into Judaism by reinterpretation. A good example is the practice of the bridegroom breaking a glass at the marriage ceremony. Like many a folk-custom, this practice originated in Germany where it was copied from the practice of the German peasants which aimed to fool the *demons that a tragic, rather than a happy, event was taking place. The Jewish interpretation given to the practice is that it is a symbol of mourning for the destruction of the *Temple. Similarly, the custom of eating sweet things on the eve of the *Rosh Ha-Shanah festival, a popular practice in many cultures as a sign of a good New Year, was accepted by the Rabbis but only as a means of setting out in good spirits, not as an attempt to guarantee a good year by magical means.

Angelo S. Rappoport, *The Folklore of the Jews* (London, 1937).

**Forgiveness** Under this heading is discussed the question of forgiveness when someone has been wronged by another. (For God's forgiveness of sin, see SIN AND REPENTANCE and YOM KIPPUR.)

The Mishnah (*Bava Kama* 8: 7), after describing the amount to be paid in compensation by an attacker to his victim, draws on the story of Abimelech's taking Sarah, Abraham's wife, and then returning her to him (Genesis 20) to declare that monetary compensation is not enough. The attacker must beg forgiveness. But when he does so the victim should grant it readily: 'Even when he pays, he is not forgiven until he seeks forgiveness from him, for it is written: "Now, therefore, restore the man's wife . . . [and he shall pray for thee]". And whence do we learn that if he does not forgive him he is cruel? Because it is written: "And Abraham prayed unto God and God healed Abimelech."' Implied in this is that someone who has been wronged by another has no obligation to forgo his legitimate claim to compensation. To make this an obligation would encourage attacks on the victims through the knowledge that they would not seek redress in a court of law and it would undermine the pursuit of justice. Moreover, even after compensation has been made, as assessed by the court, this does not release the attacker from his religious and moral obligation to ask the victim to forgive him. This obligation to ask for forgiveness applies to a wrong committed against another even where the question of compensation does not arise; where, for instance, the victim suffered no financial loss. Yet, the Mishnah concludes, the victim should be ready to forgive, otherwise his attitude is cruel and unfeeling.

This is the general Jewish attitude in which justice and mercy are combined; justice in that the victim is entitled to compensation, mercy in that once the wrong has been redressed the victim should forgive and forget. Maimonides elaborates on this theme in his Code.

'Repentance and Yom Kippur can only win pardon for offences against God such as eating forbidden food or illegal cohabitation and so forth. But there is no forgiveness for offences against one's neighbour such as assault or injury or theft and so forth until the wrong done is put right. Even after a man has paid the restitution due to the victim he must beg his forgiveness. Even if all he did was to taunt his neighbour he must still appease him and beg his forgiveness. If the victim does not wish to forgive him he should go to him in the company of three friends and they should beg him to grant his pardon. If their efforts were of no avail he should repeat the procedure with a second and a third group but if the victim still persists in his attitude he should be left alone and the victim is then sinful in refusing his pardon . . . It is forbidden for a man to be so cruel as to refuse to forgive those who have wronged him but he should forgive them wholeheartedly and willingly. Even if they have wronged him grievously he should not take revenge or foster hatred. This is the way of the seed of Israel and their trustworthy heart. But the heathen of uncircumcised heart are different, their wrath being preserved for ever . . . If the victim had died in the meantime he should bring ten men to his grave and declare: "I have sinned against the Lord God of Israel and against this person whom I have wronged in such-and-such a way." If he owed him money because of the wrong done he should give it to the victim's heirs. If these are unknown he should hand over the money to the court.'

It is the custom in many communities for people, on the eve of Yom Kippur, to ask forgiveness from one another if they have offended against them during the past year. Sigmund Freud retells the wry Jewish story of two enemies who declared to one another on the eve of Yom Kippur: 'Let bygones be bygones.' After Yom Kippur one said to the other: 'I wish you everything you wish me.' 'Starting again already?' was the reply. There is also the custom in many places that, at a funeral, the acquaintances of the deceased beg him to forgive them.

A delicate question in this connection is discussed by the famous moralist, Israel *Salanter. Supposing *A* has wronged *B*, say, by speaking ill of him behind his back, and *B* does not know of it. Should *A*, in his desire to win forgiveness, inform *B* that he has wronged him and now wishes to be forgiven? Salanter argues that *A* should not confess to *B* that he has wronged him because *B* will then suffer distress from the knowledge that *A* disliked him so much. *A* has no right to win pardon for himself at the expense of *B*'s humiliation. Not every Jewish moralist agrees with Salanter.

The question much discussed after the *Holocaust, whether the Jewish people should forgive the Germans, is extremely complex and raises further difficult questions. Is it right for a whole people to be condemned for the atrocities perpetrated by a comparatively few, even though many were guilty by ignoring the dreadful events that were taking place before their eyes? Many present-day Germans were not even alive during the Nazi period; it has also been argued that if any forgiving is to be done it can only be by the victims themselves and they are no longer alive. For those who did not perish to offer forgiveness is to usurp the divine prerogative. Judaism certainly believes that the perpetrators of these and similar horrors will be punished by God. It is hard to believe that God will not punish Hitler in *hell, to use the language of tradition. But that must be left to God. Furthermore, it is often argued, forgiveness is a state of mind so that it makes no sense to speak of forgiveness by one group for the actions of another. Consequently, doubts have been raised over whether the language of forgiveness is appropriate in this case.

What is really involved in the question of attitudes to Germany after the Holocaust is not forgiveness but forgetting. Should Jews forget the Holocaust? Here undoubtedly the majority of Jews would say that it is wrong to forget the terrible event, not least because there are still Nazis and their emulators with the destructive ambition to repeat the event or to deny that it ever took place. If humanity forgets, similar horrors can happen again with the victims being not only or even primarily Jews. (See AMALEK.)

The moralists, for all their emphasis on the high value of forgiveness, do, however, make one exception. If *A* has been slandered by *B*, who has spread untrue rumours about his conduct that might destroy his reputation, *A* is not only not obliged to forgive *B* but is forbidden to forgive where the result of his readiness to forgive will be construed as an admission that there is something in the rumours, that there is no smoke without fire. Yet even here much depends, naturally, on the circumstances in each individual case.

It is also important to note that the idea of 'turning the other cheek' is found in Jewish sources and the distinction often made by Jews as well as Christians that in this lies the difference between Christianity and Judaism is unfounded. An oft-quoted Talmudic passage (*Shabbat* 88b) reads: 'Our Rabbis taught: Those who are insulted but do not insult, hear themselves reviled without answering, act through love and rejoice in suffering, of them Scripture says: "But they who love Him are as the sun when he goeth forth in his might" [Judges 5: 31].' And the Safed mystic, Moses *Cordovero, in his work on the Kabbalistic understanding

of *Imitatio Dei* (*Palm Tree of Deborah*, 1.1) remarks that God does not withhold His goodness even from those who use the power He gives to them to provoke Him. Implied, therefore, says Cordovero, in the ideal of imitating God is that 'this is a virtue man should make his own, namely, to be patient and allow himself to be insulted even to this extent and yet not refuse to bestow of his goodness to the recipients'. Mystics like Cordovero are undeterred by the protest that such attitudes will turn them into doormats, since they see no harm and only good in becoming a doormat. As in other areas, self-evaluation and honest scrutiny of motive are necessary before embarking on saintly living. *Saints can take it; for others to seek to emulate them can have an adverse effect on the character. For all that, the Rabbinic ideal remains: 'Whoever overrides the dictates of his character [in forgiving those who have wronged him] God will override all his transgressions.'

**Frankel, Zechariah** Rabbi, theologian, and historian of the Talmudic period (1801–73). Frankel studied Talmud in his native Prague under Rabbi Bezalel Ronsberg and philosophy, natural science, and philology in Budapest. His combination of traditional and general learning equipped Frankel to become one of the leading lights of the *Jüdische Wissenschaft movement in which the tools of modern historical criticism were used to explore the development of the classical sources of Judaism. Frankel became principal of the Jewish Theological Seminary in Breslau in 1854. In 1871 he founded the learned journal *Monatsschrift für Geschichte und Wissenschaft des Judenthum*, the foremost organ of modern Jewish scholarship. Frankel's major works, in which he employed successfully the new methodology, are: *Darkhey Ha-Mishnah* (*The Way of the Mishnah*) and *Mevo Ha-Yerushalmi* (*Introduction to the Jerusalem Talmud*). He also published important essays on the *Septuagint and on the relationship between Alexandrian and Talmudic exegesis of the Bible. In all these works, Frankel demonstrated that Judaism had developed in response to the different conditions of Jewish life in various civilizations.

The Breslau school, as Frankel and his associates came to be called, played an important role in its insistence that while freedom to investigate the origins of Jewish beliefs and institutions is granted and must be granted, this does not affect the need for strict observance of the *precepts, since such observance belongs to the living religion, as accepted in a kind of mystical consensus by the Jewish people, and this is independent of origins. Frankel coined the expression 'positive-historical' for his approach to Judaism; 'historical' because it acknowledges that Judaism did not simply drop down from heaven ready-made, so to speak, but has had a history; 'positive', because, whatever the origins, this is what the religion has come to be under the guidance of God. The Breslau school did not rule out the possibility of further development and change in Judaism but held that the development must be in accordance with Judaism's own organic nature. Artificial changes, as introduced by Reform, were not in the true spirit of Judaism, especially when these involved the jettisoning of hallowed traditions. Prayers in languages other than Hebrew, for instance, while permitted according to the law, if introduced on a regular basis in the synagoue, as in Reform, involve a far too radical departure from the Judaism of the past.

Frankel was opposed to Reform radicalism, as he saw it, but was also opposed to the neo-Orthodoxy of Samson Raphael *Hirsch because of its rejection of the historical-critical method. Revealing is the great debate between Frankel and Hirsch on the meaning of the Rabbinic expression 'A law from Moses at Sinai', for example when it is said that it is a law from Moses at Sinai that the *tefillin have to be black. Hirsch took this literally, that Moses was given at Sinai all the instructions about the tefillin. Frankel held that the term denotes a very ancient rule, the origins of which are lost in time. But true to his philosophy, Frankel wore tefillin and his tefillin were black because, for him, that is how Jews should follow the tradition of how God is to be worshipped. Frankel is thus rightly seen as the real founder of what later came to be called *Conservative Judaism.

Louis Ginzberg, 'Zechariah Frankel', in his *Students, Scholars and Saints* (New York, 1958), 195–216.

**Frankists** The followers of Jacob Frank (1726–91) in Podolia, south-east Poland, who formed themselves into a Shabbetean sect (see *Shabbetai Zevi). Frank, a charismatic figure but also, by all accounts, something of a charlatan and bold adventurer, boasted of his ignorance of the Talmud, claiming that the true, higher Torah is found only in the Zohar; hence the name Zoharists by which the sect was known in the eighteenth century. The name Frankists was not given them until the early nineteenth century, after Frank's death. The Frankists conformed outwardly to the *Halakhah, the legal side of Judaism, but in secret believed it essential to disobey the law. They even went so far as to indulge in orgies at which the sexual prohibitions of adultery and incest were cast aside.

The Rabbis, appalled by their excesses, placed a ban (see HEREM) on the Frankists and this led them to attempt to curry favour with the Catholic clergy in order to win their protection. The Frankists claimed that the Rabbinic opposition to their views was due to the fact that elements in their creed were close to Christian beliefs. This was at first only a pretence but eventually the sect actually embraced Catholicism, developing a new theology of accommodation.

Frankist theology, as it later developed, is a curious amalgam of Kabbalistic, Shabbatean, and Christian beliefs, an antinomian mystery religion which seeks to transcend all the religions. Frank maintained that the true and good God has no links with the finite and insignificant world but conceals Himself behind the 'King of Kings' whom Frank calls the 'Big Brother'. The *Shekhinah of the Kabbalists, the female element in the Godhead, becomes, in Frankist theology, the 'Virgin', an obvious adaptation of the Catholic doctrine. The Frankists believed that their function was to lead the way to the life of freedom from the restraints of the law. This process had begun with Shabbetai's conversion to Islam and was now to be followed still further by conversion to Christianity and, through Christianity, to the future religion of freedom of which Frank was the true *Messiah. This whole bizarre doctrine was naturally rejected by both Jews and Christians and Frankism vanished entirely from the scene of Jewish life.

Gershom Scholem, 'Jacob Frank and the Frankists', in his *Kabbalah* (Jerusalem, 1974), 287–309.

**Fraud** The key text against fraudulent dealing is: 'Do not wrong one another' (Leviticus 25: 14), upon which text is based the Rabbinic term *onaah*, 'wronging', a term embracing any action by which unfair advantage is taken of another.

The Talmud thus observes that there are two kinds of wronging: 1. wronging in monetary matters; 2. wronging with words. The first denotes chiefly an unfair overcharge on the part of the seller or undercharge on the part of the buyer in commercial transactions. How an unjust charge is to be defined is a subject of much discussion in the Talmud but the general principle is that an overcharge or undercharge of a sixth or more of the market price of the goods sold constitutes 'wronging'. Examples given in the Talmud of other kinds of fraudulent dealing besides overcharging or undercharging are: polishing old utensils to make them look new and selling them as new; tipping the scales when weighing out food; and raising prices for essential commodities by cornering the market.

Wronging with words applies to misleading statements and insults. Examples given in the Talmud are: taunting a sinner with his past misdeeds; taunting a convert to Judaism from idolatry with his pagan background; and suggesting to a person who suffers that he has only himself to blame for his sufferings which are the result of his sinfulness. In their conviction that words can hurt severely, the Rabbis declare that the sin of wronging with words is greater than the sin of wronging in monetary matters.

**Free Will**    That human beings have free will is axiomatic in Judaism. As many Jewish teachers have said, unless a man is able freely to choose, how can he be commanded in the Torah to do good and not evil? Even those thinkers, like Maimonides, who drew up *principles of Jewish *faith have no need to include among the principles belief that the human will is free, since this is implied in the very appeal to follow the principles, which are meaningless if those to whom the principles are addressed and the authors of the creeds themselves are under compulsion to think and act as they do. Robot-like creatures with no will of their own cannot be issued with commands, not the kind of commands of the Torah at any rate.

For this reason, Jewish law is not binding on those such as minors or imbeciles who are not fully aware of what they are doing. According to Jewish law, acts done under compulsion, such as when heathen forces a Jew to transgress the precepts of the Torah, are in no way culpable. Accidental homicide, for instance, is held to be culpable but only where there is a degree of negligence, failure to take proper care being

considered itself to be the result of an unsound will. An imbecile whose powers of distinguishing between right and wrong are weak and inadequate is not guilty even if he commits 'intentional' murder. Naturally, many fine distinctions are made between the degree of free will present and hence the degree of culpability in certain circumstances, for instance, between a man who does work on the Sabbath, knowing that it is the Sabbath and that the work he does in forbidden, and the man who does work on the Sabbath but has forgotten that the day is the Sabbath or that the particular type of work is forbidden. And the Jewish moralists acknowledge that two men may have different degrees of responsibility for carrying out the same act, so that each has his own area in which his free will can come into operation. While the law is bound to be categorical, brooking no exceptions, the moralists cannot believe that, say, a child brought up among thieves has the same freedom to choose not to steal when he grows up as a man whose childhood was spent among honest people. So far as the law is concerned both are deemed culpable but God will not judge the two as if they both had the same will.

### The Problem of Divine Foreknowledge

A problem that exercised the minds of the medieval Jewish philosophers was that of reconciling God's foreknowledge with human free will. This problem, called the problem of 'knowledge versus free will', can be baldly stated. If God knows, as presumably He does, long before a man is born how he will behave throughout his life, how can that man be blamed and punished for his sinful acts and how praised and rewarded for his virtuous acts?

*Gersonides, unwilling to compromise in any way human free will, posits as a solution (*The Wars of the Lord*, iii. 6) that God does not know beforehand how a man will behave in particular circumstances. God knows beforehand all the choices open to a man but which of these he will follow depends entirely on his own free will. Gersonides' 'solution' does provide for free will but from the theological point of view it is surely odd to deny God's knowledge of the future in all its details.

*Crescas attempts to deal with the problem (*The Light of the Lord*, iv. 5) by distinguishing between fatalism, the notion that man must act in the way he does, and determinism, the notion that man is free to choose which acts he performs but the choice itself is determined. God's foreknowledge is of the choices man actually makes of his own free will. Crescas admits that, since his choices are determined by God's foreknowledge, man is not really free, and is obliged to face the problem of why, if this is so, there are rewards for virtuous living and punishments for vicious living. Crescas tries to deal with this further problem by suggesting that the promise of reward and the threat of punishment are only to spur a man on to choose virtue and reject sin. The good man thus does not really deserve his reward nor the wicked man his punishment. Crescas is as unconventional in his qualification of human free will as is Gersonides in his qualification of divine foreknowledge.

Maimonides (*Mishneh Torah, Teshuvah*, 5. 5) holds that man has free will and God has foreknowledge so that there is, indeed, a problem but it is one incapable of solution by the finite mind of man. Maimonides is not simply saying that there is an insoluble problem. If he were saying that, his critics would have been right in protesting that a wise man does not formulate problems of faith for which he has no solution and Maimonides should have kept silent on the whole question. But, in reality, Maimonides is putting forward a solution of his own, as is clear from his actual formulation. According to Maimonides, the problem is due to the fact that God's knowledge is incorrectly understood as akin to human knowledge, albeit of an infinitely greater degree. If a human being were to know beforehand how a man will behave, and know it beyond all doubt, that man would not be free to do otherwise. But God, says Maimonides, does not 'know', as humans do, that which is outside of Him. God is a Knower but never a Learner. God's knowledge is not something added to His essence but is God Himself. God's foreknowledge is as incomprehensible as God Himself since God's knowledge is God Himself. Consequently, the whole formulation of the problem, employing human ideas and human language, is logically meaningless. When we ask how God's foreknowledge can be reconciled with human freedom, we are operating within the human universe of discourse in referring to human freedom and attempting to go beyond the human universe of discourse in speaking of God's foreknowledge. The question is as meaningless as if we were to ask: 'How can $X$ be reconciled with human freedom' without any possibility of stating what the $X$ factor is. Maimonides is

insistent that the Jew must hold fast to both propositions. God does have foreknowledge and man has free will, though it is utterly beyond our scope to comprehend what the first proposition means. All this is in line with Maimonides' view that of God only negative attributes can be postulated. We can say what God is not but can never know what God is.

Isaac ben Sheshet Perfet (1326–1408), in his Responsa collection (no. 118), is severely critical of Gersonides' attempted solution. According to Gersonides, God does not know beforehand which choice a man will make in the future but, presumably, Gersonides must hold that the act the man chooses does become known to God once it has been performed. This means that God acquires knowledge of that of which He had been previously ignorant, which is surely theologically impossible. Perfet's own solution is that God knows beforehand not only the act but the choice upon which the act is based. God knows beforehand how man will choose in his freedom. It is not the foreknowledge that determines that choice but the choice which, as it were, determines that foreknowledge. God knows how man will choose in his complete freedom. Perfet believes that his is the best solution to the problem but the difficulty remains of how God's foreknowledge can fail to be determinative.

Some of the Jewish mystics deal with the problem by invoking the mystical idea of the Eternal Now (see TIME AND ETERNITY). It is incorrect to speak of God knowing now what a man will do in the future since past, present, and future are all seen by God, as it were, at once. God does not have foreknowledge of how man will behave in the future but he sees him when he acts in His Eternal Now.

Among contemporary Jews the problem does not loom very large, since the majority of Jews prefer not to dwell on the mysteries known only to God but on the present duties imposed upon them by the Torah. For naturalist Jewish thinkers such as Mordecai *Kaplan the problem is in any event a pseudo-problem since God as 'the power that makes for righteousness' cannot be said to have any 'knowledge' at all, let alone foreknowledge. Only in Crescas is there to be found in Jewish thought ideas that approximate to those of Kismet in Islam and Calvinism in Christianity.

Louis Jacobs, 'God and Personal Freedom', in his *Religion and the Individual* (Cambridge, 1992), 79–93.

**Friendship** The two extreme examples of friendship in the Bible are to be found in the story of *David and Jonathan (1 Samuel 20) and the story of *Ruth and Naomi (Ruth 1). In both these stories one of the friends (Jonathan and Ruth) is ready to sacrifice everything out of loyalty to the bond of friendship. In both instances the friendship is between persons of the same sex. No doubt this is because close friendships between men and women were exceedingly rare, on the grounds of sexual morality, so that 'friendship' between a man and a woman was expressed in *marriage. In the benediction recited under the marriage canopy, God is praised for having created 'friendship' as well as other qualities the couple require for their marriage to be blessed. Some have concluded in the case of David and Jonathan that a homosexual element was present, on the strength of David's lament over the death of Jonathan (2 Samuel 126): 'I grieve for you, my brother Jonathan, you were most dear to me. Your love was wonderful to me more than the love of women.' But 'more than the love of women' means different from and more wonderful than the erotic love men have for women, quite apart from the fact that these words are not David's own but were put into his mouth by the author of the book of *Samuel, also, Jonathan says to David when they part (1 Samuel 20: 42): 'May the Lord be between you and me, and *between your offspring and mine, for ever.*' In Ethics of the Fathers (5. 16) the friendship of David and Jonathan is held up as the supreme illustration of how love that does not depend on any ulterior motive is everlasting; 'love' being used here, as it is often used in both the Bible and the Rabbinic literature, to denote strong affection and deep friendship. Nowhere in the classical sources of Judaism is there any reference to a man establishing a kind of permanent marriage relationship with another man, or a woman with another woman (see HOMOSEXUALITY).

The value of friendship is mentioned frequently in the Rabbinic literature. When Rabbi Joshua was asked by his teacher to discover the best and worst thing in the striving towards self-improvement, he replied that the best thing is to have a good friend and the worst to have a bad friend (Ethics of the Fathers, 2. 9). A very early teacher is reported in Ethics of the Fathers (1. 6) as advising: 'Make someone your teacher and acquire for yourself a friend.' A

famous tale is told in the Talmud (*Taanit* 23a) of the miracle-working saint, Honi the Circle-Drawer who slept for seventy years. When he awoke he was given the cold shoulder by the scholars who had nothing in common with him because of the 'generation gap'. When Honi observed this he prayed to be released from his agony by death (see EUTHANASIA). The Talmud adds the comment of a later teacher: 'Either friendship or death', meaning a life without friends is no life.

That friendship should not, however, be too possessive and overpowering is taught in the book of *Proverbs: 'Visit your neighbour sparingly, lest he have his surfeit of you and loathe you' (Proverbs 25: 17).

In *Hasidism friendship is especially valued, all the followers of a particular master banding themselves into a close fraternity in which they assist one another materially and spiritually.

**Fundamentalism** The attitude towards the sacred texts of a religion in which these are taken literally and treated as infallible. The term fundamentalism has its origin in the United States at the beginning of the twentieth century, when a group of Protestant Christians formed an alliance to oppose liberalism in the Church. Liberals held that *biblical criticism and modern science have made untenable the idea that Scripture, taken at its face value, conveys accurate information regarding such matters as the age of the earth and the way animals and human beings have evolved (see EVOLUTION). The fundamentalists adopted this name in the belief that to accept liberalism was to deny *fundamental* Christian doctrine. For fundamentalists the *Bible is the very word of God and as such is inerrant in all its details.

It has often been argued that the term fundamentalists is inapplicable to Jews both because it is taken from Christian debates and because no traditional Jew can be a literalist since it is not the literal meaning of the Bible that is authoritative for Jews but the Bible as expounded and applied in the Talmudic literature. This argument is untenable. To be sure, the term is taken from Christian discussions but the phenomenon it represents is to be found among Jews. As for the question of literal meaning, the main thrust of fundamentalism is not so much in the direction of literalism as towards inerrancy. Jewish fundamentalists believe that the Bible, as interpreted in the Rabbinic tradition, is infallible. Jewish fundamentalism can be defined as that attitude in which all notions of historical development are rejected. For Jewish fundamentalists there can be no acknowledgement of any human element in the Bible as understood by the Rabbinic tradition. In any event, there is no point in a semantic quibble. The term Jewish fundamentalism is no more than convenient shorthand for the attitude described above.

It is important to appreciate that in Jewish religious life, unlike in Christianity and Islam, there is no identifiable, organized group consciously adopting the fundamentalist position to distinguish itself thereby from the rest of the believing community. Moreover, unlike in some contemporary versions of Islam, Jewish funda-mentalists rarely if ever use violent means to achieve their aims and there is among them a *de facto* acknowledgement, at least, of religious tolerance. From this point of view, Jewish fundamentalists rightly object to being called fanatics (see FANATICISM). Basically, what is involved in the question of fundamentalism on the Jewish scene is whether or not modern historical scholarship has anything to say on the way Judaism has developed (see ZECHARIAH FRANKEL and JÜDISCHE WISSENSCHAFT). With these qualifications in mind it is not unfair to describe Orthodox Judaism as leaning far more in the direction of fundamentalism than *Conservative Judaism and *Reform.

Louis Jacobs, 'World Jewish Fundamentalism', in William Frankel (ed.), *Survey of Jewish Affairs 1987* (London and Toronto, 1988), 221–34.

# G

**Gamaliel, Rabban** The name and title of six holders of the office of Nasi, Prince, in Palestine during the first five centuries CE. The title Rabban, 'Our Master', was used to distinguish the Nasi from other *Rabbis. The office of Nasi was primarily one of religious authority but the Nasi also played an occasional political role in representing the Jewish community to the Roman authorities. Since practically all the references to the office are in sources compiled later and are far from being contemporary records, it is difficult to know for certain how the office came about and the precise way in which the affairs of the Nasi were conducted. From the later sources (Talmudic and Midrashic) it appears that the first Nasi was Rabban Johanan ben *Zakkai, a disciple of *Hillel, after whom Rabban Gamaliel, a grandson of Hillel, served as Nasi; the office then became a hereditary one held by Gamaliel's descendants.

A list of princes until the end of the Mishnaic period, that is, until the beginning of the third century CE, can now be given:

1. Rabban Gamaliel the Elder (Gamaliel I), first half of the first century.
2. Rabban Simeon ben Gamaliel (Simeon ben Gamaliel I), son of (1).
3. Rabban Gamaliel of Yabneh (Gamaliel II), son of (2).
4. Rabban Simeon ben Gamaliel (Simeon ben Gamaliel II), son of (3).
5. Rabbi *Judah the Prince, editor of the Mishnah, son of (4).
6. Rabban Gamaliel (Gamaliel III) son of (5).

The other three Gamaliels are referred to only very infrequently. Gamaliel VI died in 426 CE, after which the office of Nasi was abolished.

Granted that, as above, the majority of the sources are late, there are echoes in these sources of a degree of conflict between the Nasi, the representative of the establishment, and certain other scholars. According to the Mishnah (*Rosh Ha-Shanah* 2: 8–9), in a dispute between Rabban Gamaliel II and Rabbi *Joshua regarding the exact date of *Yom Kippur, Gamaliel ordered Joshua to appear before him on 'his' Yom Kippur carrying his stick and his money-bag so as to establish the Nasi's authority. According to a Talmudic account (*Berakhot* 27b–28a), after further humiliations of Rabbi Joshua by Rabban Gamaliel, the latter was deposed, for a time, from the office of Nasi. In another Talmudic account (*Horayot* 13b) Rabban Simeon ben Gamaliel II had a dispute with Rabbi *Meir and Rabbi Nathan, resulting in the exclusion of these two teachers from participation in the debates in the House of Learning.

In the first chapter of Ethics of the Fathers and in the beginning of chapter 2, a list of sayings of the various Princes is given from Gamaliel I to Gamaliel III but no saying at all of Gamaliel II is quoted. This may be because of Gamaliel II's deposition but it is more likely that sayings of this teacher were originally in the list and were simply slipped out by accident. Although Rabban Gamaliel I is sometimes referred to as 'the Elder', he is often referred to simply as Rabban Gamaliel, making it difficult to know whether a source refers to him or to his grandson, Gamaliel II. With regard to extra-Talmudic sources, there is only a single reference to Gamaliel I in the New Testament (Acts 22: 3) where he is said to have been Paul's teacher. All this only goes to show how difficult it is for the historian of Talmudic times who attempts to use sources compiled later for a reconstruction of events in an earlier period.

Echoes are also to be found of the close relationship between the princes and the Romans. It is said, for instance, that many young men of the house of Rabban Gamaliel studied 'Greek wisdom' (*Sotah* 49b), a statement that was much discussed in the medieval debates on the study of *philosophy. Gamaliel is also said to have bathed in a bath-house in which there was a statue of Aphrodite (Mishnah *Avodah Zarah* 3: 4), which practice he defended on the grounds that the statue was purely decorative and in no way dedicated to the goddess. There is also an account of Rabban Gamaliel, Rabbi Joshua, and other Rabbis visiting Rome. Especially interesting in this connection are the Talmudic tales, largely legendary, of the close friendship between Rabbi Judah the Prince and 'Antoninus', though it is none too clear which Roman emperor is referred to by this name in these tales.

**Gambling** That there are no references to gambling in the Bible can hardly lead to the conclusion that this activity, found in all cultures both ancient and modern, was unknown in the biblical period; although it can be concluded that gambling was not widespread enough to constitute a social evil, otherwise its condemnation would have been recorded somewhere in the biblical records. The casting of lots is mentioned not infrequently in the Bible but this has more to do with *divination rather than with gambling proper. Lots were cast to determine which of the two goats were to be offered to God and which to *Azazel (Leviticus 16: 8–10); in the affair of Jonathan (1 Samuel 14: 42–3); and to divide up the land (Numbers 26: 55 and Joshua 15). Among non-Israelites, the sailors cast lots in order to determine who was responsible for the storm ( Jonah 1: 7) and Haman cast lots to determine the most suitable month in which to realize his plan to destroy the Jews (Esther 3: 7). The famous German Halakhist Jair Hayyim Bacharach (1639–1702) did, however, apply the biblical references to casting lots to gambling, even going so far as to conclude that a raffle is a legitimate means of allowing divine *providence to operate in favour of the winner (Responsa, *Havvot Yair*, no. 61). Bacharach quotes in support the verse: 'The lot is cast into the lap; but the whole disposing thereof is of the Lord' (Proverbs 16: 33).

From the legal point of view, the Mishnah (*Rosh Ha-Shanah* 1: 8 and *Sanhedrin* 3: 3) states that two types of gamblers are untrustworthy and therefore disqualified from acting as witnesses in a Jewish court of law. These are the dice-player and, according to one opinion, the man who bets on pigeon-racing. The reason why the gambler is disqualified is discussed in the Talmud (*Sanhedrin* 24b). One Rabbi holds

that it is only the gambler who has no other occupation, that is, the professional gambler who earns his living by gambling, who is disqualified and the reason is because he makes no useful contribution to society. Another Rabbi holds that the disqualification applies even to the occasional gambler, even if he does have a useful occupation. According to this Rabbi the gambler is disqualified because in betting, the one who bets believes that he is going to win so that there is no firm determination, as there is in other contractual obligations, by the loser to pay out. The winner is disqualified because, by pocketing his winnings, he is a thief, taking that to which he has no legal entitlement. The codifiers follow the first opinion and permit a 'mild flutter' and even a not so mild one. Thus, according to the strict letter of the law, it is permitted to play cards for money, to bet on horses, and to organize and participate in a raffle. It is certainly the practice of many Jewish charitable organizations to raise money by raffles and the like but for bingo to take place on synagogue premises is frowned upon by many Rabbis even if the proceeds will go to charity, on the grounds that such games of chance are unsuitable for premises attached to a house of worship. The Galician Rabbi Meir Arik (1855–1926) allows a Jew to breed race-horses and does not consider such an occupation to be akin to that of the professional gambler whom the Mishnah disqualifies as a disreputable person (Responsa, ii, no. 65).

Whenever gambling got out of hand, the Jewish moralists condemned it as a frivolous pursuit (almost everything was a frivolous pursuit for some of the moralists) and, especially, because it could easily lead to impoverishment and destroy family life.

**Games and Sport** Jews, like all other people, played many kinds of games and engaged in sporting activities. Especially popular were card games, ball games, dominoes, *chess, archery, athletics, and swimming. From time to time, however, the Jewish moralists voiced a number of objections to overindulgence in games and sport on the grounds that these are a waste of time that could be better spent on the study of the Torah. When bets were taken on the outcome, the question of *gambling arose. There were strong reservations over games and sports involving any mingling of the sexes on the grounds that this might lead to immoral conduct.

*Hunting and other sports involving cruelty to *animals were decried. Macaulay's saying that the Puritans hated bear-baiting not because it gave pain to the bear but because it gave pleasure to the spectators, is no doubt unfair to the Puritans. A Jewish objection would be on both grounds: because it gave pain to the bear and because to take pleasure in animal pain is an ugly emotion. Another religious objection had to do with Sabbath-observance but here, provided no actual forbidden work and no exchange of money were involved, the Codes permit games and sport even on the Sabbath. Nowadays, for instance, most authorities permit the playing of Scrabble on the Sabbath, since the forming of the letters into words in this game cannot be considered 'writing'. But it is forbidden to write down the score. There is evidence that some Jews had special silver chessmen used only on the Sabbath to distinguish the sacred day from weekdays.

In modern times, even the most Orthodox see no objection to games and sports such as athletics, tennis and table tennis, cricket, football, baseball, billiards and snooker. Boxing and wrestling are in a slightly different category. Contemporary Rabbis have discussed whether it is permitted for a Jew to be a professional pugilist. Those who permit it do so on the grounds that, while the sport involves risk to mind and body, many other occupations involve a degree of risk and are permitted if they are undertaken in order to earn a living. Others disagree, arguing that consciously to set out to earn a living by maiming other human beings is not at all in the spirit of Judaism. The general opinion among many of the Orthodox is that to take lessons in boxing, wrestling, judo, and karate might be permitted if the aim is training in self-defence, but on the whole these are not suitable activities for a good Jew. Naturally in all such matters a good deal must be left to individual taste and discrimination and there can be no hard-and-fast rules.

Israel Abrahams, *Jewish Life in the Middle Ages* (London, 1932), 397–422.

**Garden of Eden** Heb. *Gan Eden* (Eden is a place-name but the word means 'fruitful'), the abode of *Adam and Eve before they were driven out as a result of their sin (Genesis 2, 3). The prophet *Ezekiel refers to Eden as the Garden of God (Ezekiel 28: 13). From the description in Genesis it is obvious that the

Garden of Eden is situated on earth. But during the Rabbinic period, Gan Eden and its opposite *Gehinnom were names given to the places, respectively, of reward and punishment of the soul after the death of the body (see HEAVEN AND HELL). In Ethics of the Fathers (5. 20), for instance, it is said that the shameless are destined for Gehinnom but the modest are destined for Gan Eden. In the prayers for the dead an entreaty is made that the soul of the departed should rest in Gan Eden. Maimonides thinks of Gan Eden not as a place but as a state, equating the term with the soul's immortality. In various Midrashim, on the other hand, there are vivid descriptions of the delights of Gan Eden being enjoyed in what is presumably a place on earth. There is, consequently, considerable ambiguity on whether the souls of the righteous are in what later came to be called 'the higher Gan Eden' or in the 'lower Gan Eden' on earth, conceived of as a 'Shangri-La', though not for the bodies of the righteous but their souls. In Kabbalistic sources these two Gardens of Eden are also set on high. The term Paradise is very rare in the Jewish sources for the Hereafter as is heaven, for which these sources either use Gan Eden or the *World to Come. Yet the famous Rabbi and Kabbalist, Yosef Hayyim of Baghdad (1835–1909) can still discuss in a Responsum (vol. iii, no. 1) whether legends such as that of Alexander the Great knocking at the door of Gan Eden are to be taken literally. Hayyim goes so far as to say that Gan Eden is a place on earth even though the explorers have not discovered it. There the lower part of the soul resides clothed in refined spiritual garments but the higher parts are in the Gan Eden on high. Hayyim thus has the best of both worlds.

**Gedaliah, Fast of** A minor fast on 3 Tishri to commemorate the murder of Gedaliah ben Ahikam, the Governor of Judah appointed by Nebuchadnezzar after the exile of the majority of the population to Babylon, as told in the Bible (Jeremiah 40: 5–41; 2 Kings 25: 22–6). Had Gedaliah not been killed the people remaining in the Holy Land might have rebuilt it but when Gedaliah was killed, they fled to Egypt. In the old Jewish joke a man says that he has two reasons for not fasting on this day: first, because if Gedaliah had not been murdered he would have died eventually; secondly, 'If I had been killed would Gedaliah have fasted?' It is obvious, of course, that the fast really commemorates the exile of the people, not the death of Gedaliah.

**Gehinnom** Abbreviated form of *Gey Ben Hinnom*, 'Valley of Ben Hinnom', a place where children were burned in fire in the worship of *Moloch (2 Kings 23: 10). Because of the association with burning in fire the name Gehinnom (or, from the Greek, Gehenna) became the name in post-biblical Judaism (and in the New Testament) for the place of torment of the wicked after death. Thus Gehinnom and its opposite *Gan Eden are synonymous with *heaven and hell. Lurid descriptions are found of the punishments of fire and ice in Gehinnom (there even exists a treatise called *Tractate Gehinnom*, in which these physical torments are described), though the whole concept is often treated in a metaphorical manner, to represent the remoteness of the souls of the wicked from God. Maimonides seems to hold that 'punishment' in Gehinnom means the total annihilation of the most wicked sinners, so that Gehinnom is not a place of positive torture but denotes the painless extinction of the soul. Sometimes Gehinnom is used simply to denote adverse characteristics, as when the Rabbis say that when a man flies into a rage every kind of Gehinnom rules over him or, in our parlance, 'he has a hellish temper'.

**Geiger, Abraham** Reform Rabbi and scholar (1810–74). Geiger, born in Frankfurt, received the traditional Talmudic education of his day and later studied at various German universities and was thus well equipped to become one of the pioneers of the *Jüdische Wissenschaft movement, in which the historical-critical method was employed to uncover the sources of Judaism and the way in which the religion developed. After occupying various Rabbinic positions (serving in Breslau as an Orthodox Rabbi where he met with determined opposition on the part of the Orthodox), Geiger became the Director of the Hochschüle in Berlin, a position he occupied until his death. Geiger's two major works are: *Was hat Mohammed aus dem Judenthum aufgenommen?* (showing the influence of Judaism on Islam and the Koran) and *Urschrift und Übersetzungen der Bibel* (in which the text and contents of the Bible were examined in the spirit of modern *biblical criticism, then in its infancy).

For all his scholarly eminence, Geiger was not content to live and work in an academic ivory-tower but believed his researches and those of his colleagues demonstrated that the Reform movement followed in the tradition of Judaism as a developing religion and this impelled him to struggle for the recognition of Reform as the tendency demanded once Jews had become members of Western society. As Geiger saw it, the nationalistic and particularistic aspects of Judaism reflected no more than stages in Judaism's progress towards, *universalism. He advocated, therefore, the substitution of German for the Hebrew of many prayers and the rejection of the idea of a return to Zion and the rebuilding of the *Temple, in favour of the idea that Jews have a mission to all mankind; although he did believe in a version of the *Chosen People idea according to which Jews had been especially gifted with the powerful religious sense that resulted in the emergence of ethical monotheism. Geiger was strongly opposed to the neo-Orthodoxy of S. R. *Hirsch, a friend of his youth, and to the conservative philosophy of Zechariah *Frankel, but he was less radical in his Reform stance than S. *Holdheim, whose ideas seemed to Geiger to destroy continuity with the Jewish past. Unlike Holdheim, Geiger steadfastly refused to countenance the transfer of the Sabbath to Sunday. Such a step would imply that Judaism was moving closer to Christianity. Any move in this direction was vehemently opposed by Geiger. For the same reason Geiger refused to countenance any attempt to abolish *circumcision, despite the fact that, in a private letter, he once described it as a 'barbaric act'. Orthodox Jews to this day consider Geiger to be an archheretic, though there is often to be observed, even among the Orthodox, a grudging admiration for his great learning.

W. Gunther Plaut, *The Rise of Reform Judaism* (New York, 1963); see index: 'Geiger, Abraham'. Michael A. Meyer, *Response to Modernity: A History of the Reform Movement in Judaism* (Oxford, 1988); see index: 'Geiger, Abraham'.

**Gemara** 'Teaching', synonymous with Talmud. The term *gemara* originally meant a unit of teaching, a text upon which commentary was made. The term is often used in this sense in the Talmud. When, however, Christian polemicists claimed that the Talmud contains anti-Christian statements (see DISPUTATIONS), the printers, anxious to avoid any banning of the Talmud, substituted for this allegedly 'guilty' word the 'innocent' term Gemara (see CENSORSHIP). Thus, nowadays, the study of the Talmud is called the study of the Gemara.

**Gematria** The exegetical method by which a word is equated with a different word because the two words have the same numerical value. Gematria is derived from the Greek and its resemblance to the word geometry had often been noted, but scholars are now uncertain about this etymology.

An illustration of how gematria operates can be given from comments on Jacob's dream of a ladder set on the ground with its top reaching to heaven (Genesis 28: 12). The Hebrew word for 'ladder', *sulam*, is formed from the letters *samekh, lammed, mem*. Since the Hebrew letters also serve as numerals, the total of *sulam* is 130, i.e. *samekh* (60) + *lammed* (30) + *mem* (40) = 130. Now the Hebrew word for *\*'Sinai'*, also has the numerical value of 130, i.e. *aamekh* (60) + *yod* (10) + *nun* (50) + *yod* (10) = 130. Hence, one interpretation of Jacob's ladder is that it represents the giving of the Torah on Mount Sinai and the 'angels' who ascend and descend are Moses and Aaron. In another interpretation, it is noted that the word for 'money', *mamon*, has the numerical value of 136, i.e. *mem* (40) + *mem* (40) + *vav* (6) + *nun* (50) = 136 and if *sulam* is spelled in full, as it can be, with a *vav*, it also has the numerical value of 136, yielding the thought that wealth can drag a man down if acquired dishonestly but can reach to the very heavens if used for charitable purposes. The artificial nature of the exercise is readily admitted even by those who follow it, the adding of the *vav* in one interpretation and its omission in the other; and *mamon* is a postbiblical word for 'wealth'. The possibilities of gematria are endless. To give just one further example, the Hebrew word for 'wine', *yayyin*, has the same numerical value as the word *sod*, 'secret', yielding the thought that when a man is in his cups there is a risk that his secret thoughts will be revealed.

Even in matters of *\*Halakhah the Talmudic Rabbis resort at times to gematria. For instance, in the biblical account of the *\*Nazirite vow the word *yiheyeh*, 'he shall be' is used (Numbers 6: 5). This word has the numerical value of 30, i.e. *yod* (10) + *hey* (5) + *yod* (10) + *hey* (5) = 30. Thus the Rabbis say that if a man undertakes to be a Nazirite without specifying for how long period, he is to be a Nazirite for thirty days. Here, however, it is highly likely that the gematria is not used as an actual derivation but as a peg on which to hang a law established on other grounds, that thirty days, for instance, is a reasonable minimum period where there has been no actual specification.

In the Kabbalah the gematria principle is applied to produce an extremely complicated series of divine names, believed to represent various aspects of divine creativity.

There are numerous ways in which gematria can be worked out in addition to the simple form mentioned above. If we imagine that gematria could operate with regard to English, e.g. a = 1, b = 2, and so forth, two among many of these complicated forms can be mentioned: 1. The process known as 'filling', in which each letter is first spelled out in full. The word 'cat' in the simple form has a total of 24 (c (3) + a (1) + t (20) = 24) but in the 'filling' method this is: ce = 3 + 5 = 8; ay = 1 + 25 = 26; te = 20 + 5 = 25; = 8 + 26 + 25 = 59. The process is known as 'adding', e.g. c = 3, ca = 3 + 1 = 4; cat = 3 + 1 + 20 = 24; 3 + 4 + 24 = 31. It is possible to combine the two methods, e.g. 59 + 31 = 88, and so on *ad infinitum*. Advocates of gematria rarely take it all too seriously, although, especially among the Kabbalists, the process of gematria is said to be part of the divine revelation in which the words of the Torah, as the very word of God, are capable of being understood in these complex ways. Yet even the Kabbalists are occasionally obliged to resort to artificial constructions, When, for instance, one of the two words has a numerical value of one less than that of the other, the word itself is counted as one to make up the total. Gematria thus often becomes a kind of religious, mathematical game, with an element of sheer playfulness. In his critique of the Kabbalah, *\*Leon de Modena observed that the use of gematria makes everything possible. It can yield the thought, for instance, that a woman can be addressed as 'honey', since the numerical value of *devash* ('honey') and *ishah* ('woman') is the same.

**Genealogy** From biblical times pride was taken in tracing ancestry back to prominent families (see DYNASTIC SUCCESSION, FAMILY). The Mishnah (*Kiddushin* 4: 1) states *\*Ezra, when he went up to the Holy Land, took with him all ten of the different genealogical classes, the highest of which was that of the \*priests, the lowest, those of the \*_mamzer_ and the slave. But, apart form the last two, there was no objection to people marrying out of their class, so that a caste system was largely avoided. In modern times many Jews are fond of working out their family trees. In some circles advice on this exercise virtually amounts to an industry of its own.

**Generosity**   Jews have always placed the generous disposition high among the virtues. In Ethics of the Fathers (5. 10) human dispositions are divided into four types: the one who says: 'Mine is mine and thine is thine'; the one who says: 'Mine is thine and thine is mine' (this is said to be an ignorant stance); the one who says: 'Mine is mine and thine is mine' (this is said to be a wicked stance); and that of the saintly person who says: 'Mine is thine and thine is thine'. \*Job is praised by the Rabbis for being 'generous with his money', sometimes explained as that he always told the shopkeeper to keep the change. The ancient Rabbis observe that \*compassion and generosity are among the distinguishing marks of the Jewish people (see CHARITY). It would be absurd to pretend that there have never been ungenerous Jews but it is true to say that generosity has always been upheld as an ideal among all sections of Jewry.

**Genesis, Book of**   The first of the five books of Moses, the \*Pentateuch. The name Genesis is from the Greek, meaning 'origin' (i.e. of the universe). The usual Hebrew name for the book is _Bereshit_ 'In the beginning', after the opening word. The book tells of the history of the world and mankind from the earliest beginnings down to the patriarchs, Abraham, Isaac, and Jacob, and Jacob's son, \*Joseph, who became ruler in the land of Egypt where he received Jacob and his family. The story is taken further in the book of \*Exodus, which tells of the sojourn of the children of Israel in Egypt and their eventual redemption from Egyptian bondage.

On the traditional view, the book of Genesis, like the Pentateuch as a whole, was conveyed by God to Moses and thus constitutes the infallible word of God. \*Biblical criticism, on the other hand, sees the Pentateuch as a composite work, the parts of which were produced at various stages in the history of ancient Israel. The \*creation narrative in Genesis is, if taken

literally, at variance with modern scientific theories regarding the vast age of the earth and the origin of species through \*evolution. Orthodox Judaism still maintains the correctness of the traditional view, but Reform and Conservative Judaism generally accept the critical view, or, at least, some version of it, and believe that the acceptance of this view need not affect the sacredness of the Pentateuch as a divinely inspired work, while acknowledging that the older doctrine of direct, verbal inspiration has to be abandoned in the light of the new knowledge.

Nahum M. Sarna, _Understanding Genesis_ (New York, 1966).

**Genetic Engineering**   The possibility of experimenting on human embryos in order to remove genetic defects and increase human fertility is still a new science, and no consensus has so far emerged as to its advisability. It can be said, however, that hardly any Jewish authorities have dismissed the whole project as an illegal tampering with nature. Judaism generally believes that God has created an unfinished world which it is the task of human beings to bring to greater perfection.

**Genizah**   'Hiding away', the storing of sacred Hebrew texts that are no longer capable of being used; also, 'hiding place'. The usual custom is to bury sacred books in the cemetery, not to destroy them directly, even when they can no longer be used because the writing has faded. In some communities, however, they were placed in a special room either to be buried later or simply left there untouched. The most famous genizah was situated in an attic in the Ben Ezra synagogue in Cairo. Much of the material of the Cairo genizah was brought to Cambridge by Solomon \*Schechter at the end of the nineteenth century and is now studied by scholars in the Taylor Schechter Institute under the directorship of Dr Stefan Reif. This genizah contains a wealth of material from medieval times and has succeeded in enriching knowledge of the Jewish medieval world.

**Gentiles**   Persons who are not Jews. Precisely because Judaism centres on a particular people (see CHOSEN PEOPLE) the tendency has been to define all non-Jews as belonging to the 'nations' of the world. The Hebrew for 'nation' is _goy_ (a term used, incidentally, in the Bible for the Israelites as well), hence an individual Gentile is referred to as a goy and a number of Gentiles or Gentiles in general as goyyim. Originally the term goy was used simply as a designation and had none of the pejorative meanings it later often assumed. In the Rabbinic literature, Gentiles are often lumped together as 'the nations of the world' but in this literature, too, the term goy is used. In censored editions of the Talmud (see CENSORSHIP) various substitutes for this term have been inserted in order to avoid any suggestion that the references are to Christians. Thus we find very odd references to an 'Egyptian' doing or saying this or that in a context that has no reference at all to Egyptians.

The key text for Jewish–Gentile relationships is Leviticus 20: 23: 'You shall not follow the practices of the nations [ḥukkot ha-goy] that I am driving out before you. For it is because they did all these things that I abhorred them.' A second verse with the same import is: 'You shall not copy the practices of the land of Egypt where you dwelt, or of the land of Canaan to which I am leading you, nor shall you follow their laws' (Leviticus 18: 3). In the context, 'the practices of the nations' (ḥukkot ha-goy) refer to the sexual offences listed in Leviticus 18 and 20 but this was extended in the Rabbinic literature to practices prevalent in Roman Palestine in the first two centuries of the Common Era which were held to be 'un-Jewish'; the Rabbinic Midrash known as the *Sifra gives the revealing illustrations of attendance at 'theatres, circuses, and arenas', or of stabbing an animal to death.

The whole concept of ḥukkot ha-goy was variously interpreted by teachers who wished to keep the Jews apart from their Gentile neighbours where religious issues were at stake and who, at the same time, accept that complete separation was neither possible nor desirable. Where the surrounding culture presented little danger to Judaism or where certain practices adopted from the non-Jewish environment had become too deeply rooted among the people to be easily eradicated, a lenient interpretation of the concept becomes evident (see CUSTOMS). Where the danger was real or where certain practices could easily be eradicated the stricter interpretation tends to prevail. Thus Rabbi Eliezer of Metz (d.1198) lays down the firm rule that the concept applies only to *religious* practices of Gentiles, and Rabbi Isaac ben

Sheshet Perfet (1326–1408) of Algiers holds that the concept applies only to practices for which there is no reason (i.e. taboos and the like). If, Perfet argues, we are to ban certain practices simply because they are carried out by Gentiles, we ought to ban such things as funeral orations. *Isserles in his gloss to the *Shulḥan Arukh* (*Yoreh Deah*, 178. 1) records the generally accepted view in this matter:

'All these things are only forbidden when idolaters do them for the sake of loose conduct, for example, when it is their intention to wear red garments, the garments of noblemen, and the same applies to immodest dress. The same applies to any practice which has become their custom without any reason so that one must fear that it belongs to the ways of the Amorites [a Talmudic term] and that there inheres in it a trace of idolatry inherited from their ancestors. But it does not apply to a practice the advantage of which is evident. For example, if it is their habit for every skilled physician to wear a special cloak to denote that he is proficient in his craft, a Jewish physician is permitted to wear such a cloak.'

In the nineteenth century, a century that witnessed the *Emancipation of the Jews in Europe and the rise of Reform Judaism, great tension surrounded the concept of ḥukkot ha-goy. No Jews thought of adopting forms of worship associated with Christian dogma but Reform generally tended to play down the differences between Jewish and Christian worship where doctrinal issues were not involved, such as the use of the *organ in the synagogue service. In Orthodox circles, the new challenges to Jewish separatism were faced by allowing the concept of ḥukkot ha-goy to embrace not only the use of the organ in the synagogue but even such innocent practices as adopting Gentile names, using the general instead of the Jewish date, not growing a *beard, and among the more extreme, not wearing a tie. It has been wittily remarked that for some Jewish extremists to be punctual in attendance at a meeting is to be guilty of ḥukkot ha-goy.

On the wider question of Jewish attitudes to Gentiles, it is important to have a proper historical perspective. There is no doubt that the Talmudic Rabbis, living among pagans, had a poor opinion of the Gentile world around them even while admiring some of its features. At times some of the Rabbis gave vent to the harshest feelings, as in the notorious statement:

'Kill the best of the goyyim'. Johann Andreas Eisenmenger (1654–1704) in his *Endecktes Judenthum (Judaism Unmasked)* collected such adverse passages in order to prove to his satisfaction that the Jews hate all Gentiles. It became an important aspect of Jewish *apologetics to demonstrate that Eisenmenger had either misunderstood many of the passages he quotes or had taken them out of context. One often finds in published Jewish texts a note in which it is declared that all references to goyyim in the work refer only to the ancient pagan idolaters. The truth of the matter is that attitudes towards Gentiles have been favourable in countries in which Jews were treated well, albeit as second-class citizens, and unfavourable in conditions of persecution, and the personal temperament of individual teachers was also determinative. It is certainly easy to 'do an Eisenmenger' in reverse. The Talmudic Rabbis, for example, develop the concept of 'ways of peace', stressing that Jews should strive to live in harmony with their Gentile neighbours. Pursuing the 'ways of peace', Jews are expected to give charity and perform acts of *benevolence to their Gentile neighbours as they do for other Jews. According to the Rabbinic doctrine of the *Noahide laws, the seven rules of decent conduct, the Torah for Gentiles so to speak, a Gentile who observes these is to be classed among 'the righteous of the nations of the world' who have a 'share in the *World to Come'. Gentile wisdom is admired to the extent that when meeting a learned Gentile a special benediction is recited in which God is praised for 'bestowing of His wisdom to flesh and blood'. A Rabbinic saying, in which Edom is identified with Rome, has it that if someone tells you there is wisdom is Edom, believe it but if he tells you that there is Torah in Edom, do not believe it. The eighteenth-century Kabbalist Hayyim *Ibn Atar goes so far as to say that Gentiles are generally superior in wisdom to Jews! The Torah, Ibn Atar remarks, was given to Israel not because of Israel's superiority to Gentiles in wisdom but solely because of the merits of Israel's righteous ancestors, the *patriarchs. Most authorities hold that a convert of Judaism should respect his Gentile parents (see *Decalogue) and many a Hasidic *Zaddik would offer his prayers on behalf of his Gentile neighbours. In this area both the denigrations of the anti-Semites and the fulsome praise of the apologists are out of place. The history of

Jewish thought, in this and in many other areas, is too rich, too varied, too complex, and often too contradictory, to permit cosy generalizations.

Joseph S. Bloch, *Israel and the Nations* (Berlin and Vienna, 1927).
Louis Jacobs, 'Responses to the Gentile World', in his *A Tree of Life* (Oxford, 1984), 91–103.

**Geography** Geographical details are imparted only indirectly in the Bible, for instance in the verse: 'I will set a sign among them, and send from them survivors to the nations: to Tarshish, Pul, and Lud—that draw the bow—to Tubal, Javan, and the distant coasts, that have never heard My fame nor beheld My glory. They shall declare My glory among the nations' (Isaiah 66: 19). In the table of the nations (Genesis 10) the geographical area in which the seventy nations live covers the whole of Arabia, Syria, and Asia Minor and extends as far as Greece, but, of course, there is no mention of the Far East. Similarly, the numerous geographical references in the Talmud are incidental to the information conveyed. In the Middle Ages, a number of Jewish travellers brought back accounts of life in distant lands and these, supplemented by legends such as that of the Lost Ten *Tribes residing on the other side of the River Sambation, contributed to the medieval Jewish picture of the world, which from the tenth century was known by Jewish thinkers to be a globe (and see COSMOLOGY).

As late as the eighteenth century in some parts of Russia and Poland there were to be found Rabbinic scholars who could not believe that America existed since, they argued, if it did, why is there no mention of it in the Bible? But a summary of the new discoveries was provided for Jewish readers by Abraham Farissol (d. 1525) in his *Iggeret Orḥot Olam (Letter on the Ways of the World)* in which there is a chapter on America. An edition of Farissol's work with a Latin translation and learned notes by Thomas Hyde was published in Cambridge in 1691 with the title *Itinera Mundi*. It seems that until modern times, while Jewish intellectuals had a good deal of interest in astronomy, few of them had an interest in geography, possibly because astronomy encouraged man to look upwards whereas geography by definition is earthbound.

**Geonim** Plural of Gaon, the heads of the two great colleges of Sura and Pumbedita in

Babylonia from the seventh to the eleventh centuries, though a minor Gaonite flourished also in the land of Israel and, after the tenth century, in Baghdad. The word Gaon means 'excellency' or 'pride', based on the verse: 'For the Lord has restored the pride of Jacob' (Nehemiah 2: 3.). Each Gaon enjoyed authority within his own area, with the head of Sura occupying something of a superior position resembling, if the analogy is permissible, the administrative functions of the Archbishop of Canterbury and the Archbishop of York in the Anglican Church. With the Arabic conquest of Babylonia, the old office of *exilarch was reinstated under the Caliphate who, in principle, had the right to appoint the Geonim. There were often keen rivalries between the exilarch and the Geonim and between the Geonim of Sura and Pumbedita. In the tenth century the seat of the two colleges was located in Baghdad, though the original names were retained. The two last and most famous of the Babylonian Geonim (with the exception of those belonging to the minor Gaonates mentioned earlier) were *Sherira, Gaon of Pumbedita (968–98) who was succeeded by his son *Hai Gaon (998–1038). Hai's father-in-law, Samuel ben Hofni, Gaon of Sura (1003–13), was the author of a commentary to the Bible in Arabic in which he expressed a number of rationalistic views, for instance, that the *Witch of Endor did not really bring up the prophet Samuel from the dead but only made King Saul to hallucinate that she did so. This rationalization, contrary to the opinion of the Talmudic Rabbis, angered Hai who attacks it in a Responsum.

The Geonim looked upon themselves as the legitimate successors to the Babylonian teachers of the Talmudic period and it was largely owing to them that, for purposes of Jewish *law, the Babylonian Talmud—'our Talmud' as the Geonim called it—came to enjoy greater *authority than the Palestinian Talmud. It was said of the Geonim that all their words were 'words of tradition'. Jewish communities in other parts of the world acknowledged the authority of the Geonim, questions being addressed to them from scholars everywhere. In point of fact, the Geonim came the closest to a central authority in the history of the Jewish religion, without there being any kind of formal contractual arrangement to this effect. The *Responsa of the Geonim have been published in a number of collections. The majority of these Responsa are from Sherira and Hai. These Responsa are not only important for the legal decisions they contain but also for the theological views given expression in them and for light they throw on conditions in the Talmudic period. Yet modern scholarship has noted that a degree of caution must be exercised in using the Geonic material for the reconstruction of life in the Talmudic period since, at times, the Geonim tend to read back into the Talmudic period the more highly developed conditions and institutions of their own day.

It was largely because of the battle of the Geonim with the *Karaites over the doctrine of the *Oral Torah and the Talmud based on the doctrine that the Talmud became established as the final court of appeal in Jewish law, ethics, and religion. Yet, for all their reverence for the Talmud and its teachers, the Geonim were prepared to depart from some of its ideas and institutions in obedience to the different social conditions of their own day. With regard to the medical cures found in the Talmud, for example, the Geonim warned that the Talmudic Rabbis did not have any real tradition that these cures were efficacious. The Rabbis, out of the goodness of their hearts, simply shared with their followers the medical knowledge of their day so that in these matters one should go to expert contemporary physicians whose skill is far more advanced. The Talmudic rule that a wife's *ketubah*, her marriage settlement, can only be claimed from real estate was set aside by the Geonim. In the different economic conditions of their day, they argued, the need to secure the interests of the wife could only be satisfied if movables were also placed in lien. The Talmud is very strict on forbidding any use of Gentile wine but the Geonim appreciated that the prohibition, though later extended to all Gentile wine, had its origin in the fact that Gentiles in Talmudic times were suspected of offering their wine as a libation to the gods. Muslims, the Gentile neighbours of the Geonim, were not idolaters, so that while the prohibition against actually drinking Gentile wine was preserved, the Geonim held that the prohibition against deriving any benefit from the wine, by selling it, for example, could be set aside. The Geonim were also responsible for some liturgical innovations. Amram Gaon of Sura (853–6) compiled the first Prayer Book (*Siddur) and a similar order of service was drawn up by *Saadiah.

After the tenth century the title Gaon was given to many scholars by their admirers, although it was purely honorific and conveyed no authority on the scholars. The famous *Elijah, Gaon of Vilna, in the eighteenth century, came to be known as the 'Gaon'. In more recent years the title Gaon became virtually an adjunct to the title Rabbi, so much so that it came to be held to be an insult to refer to a Rabbi simply as 'Ha-Rav', the Rabbi. He had to be addressed as 'Ha-Rav Ha-Gaon'. Some have protested at this debasement of the currency of learning, but to no avail. There is now often found the title 'the true Gaon', implying that the Rabbis to whom this superior title is not given are false Geonim. The whole thing has become something of a joke (see TITLES).

**Gershom of Mayyence** Prominent German Jewish leader and legal authority (960–1028), also known as Rabbenu ('Our Master') Gershom and as 'Light of the Exile'. The great French commentator, *Rashi, remarked that all French and German scholars are the disciples of Gershom's disciples. Gershom considers in his writings some of the problems that arose for Jews in Christian society. He was asked whether a *Kohen, a *priest, who had been converted to Christianity but later returned to the Jewish fold can enjoy the priestly privileges of being called up first to the reading of the Torah and reciting the priestly blessing in the synagogue. Gershom's reply is in the affirmative. Apostates must be encouraged to return and welcomed, not disbarred from exercising the rights they previously enjoyed. There is an ancient report to the effect that a son of Gershom was forcibly converted to Christianity and yet Gershom mourned for him. The meaning is that Gershom mourned for the son when the son died, since he was still his son. But, at a later date, the report was misunderstood to mean that Gershom mourned for his son when he heard of the son's apostasy as if the son had died. This led in some circles to the bizarre practice of a family observing the rites of *mourning when a member of the family became a convert to Christianity, even while the apostate was still alive.

There are a number of communal enactments attributed to Gershom, although some scholars believe that these were only fathered on him later. In any event each of these is known as the 'the *herem (ban) of Rabbenu Gershom'. One forbids a postman opening a letter to read its contents. But the two most famous of the bans are that on a man having more than one wife at the same time and that on divorcing a wife against her will. The latter was introduced to prevent a man who wished to take a second wife divorcing his first wife whether or not she agreed to the *divorce. The ban of Rabbenu Gershom was only binding on Ashkenazi Jews since Gershom, as an Ashkenazi leader, had no power to impose his rulings upon Sephardi Jews.

**Gersonides** Levi ben Gershom (1288–1344) of Provence, Talmudist, philosopher, and astronomer. Gersonides wrote a lengthy commentary on the Bible in which his general methodology is to give a list of 'advantages' to be gained from the biblical narratives, that is, the moral lessons to be derived from them. His philosophical approach in this work and particularly in his *Wars of the Lord* follows the rationalistic mode of Aristotelian philosophy in its Arabic garb. He understands, for instance, the fall of the walls of Jericho (Joshua 6) to have been caused by the weakening of the walls by the tramping feet of the priests and the blowing of the trumpets. According to Gersonides, the sun did not stop for Joshua (Joshua 10: 12–14) but only appeared to do so because the battle was over so soon. Similarly, the shadow on the sundial did move 10 degrees backwards (2 Kings 20: 11), though not because the sun really moved but as a result of the arrangement of the clouds at the time. In all this Gersonides' principle is that the Torah does not oblige us to accept things that are contrary to reason. In his *Wars of the Lord*, Gersonides understands the doctrine of *creation as meaning not that God created the world 'out of nothing' but rather that he created it out of a formless substance. On the problem of *free will and divine foreknowledge, Gersonides advances the startling theory that God knows beforehand only the possibilities open to a man but, since man is free to choose, not the actual choice he will make. These views seemed so startling to later theologians that they dubbed his work heretical, calling it 'The Wars against the Lord'. It is noteworthy, however, that Gersonides' works became acceptable even to Orthodox Jews as representing the rationalistic tendency in Jewish thought, which has a legitimacy of its own.

Isaac Husik, 'Levi Ben Gerson', in his *A History of Mediaeval Jewish Philosophy* (New York, 1958) 328–61.

**Gestures** Gestures and special posture in prayer are known in Judaism as in other religions from the earliest period. The biblical record refers to bending the knees (1 Kings 8: 54; Isaiah 45: 23); prostration on the face (Exodus 34: 8; Psalms 29: 2); the spreading of the hands heavenwards (1 Kings 8: 23; Isaiah 1: 15); and, possibly, the placing of the face between the knees (1 Kings 18: 42). In the Talmud bowing the head and body is advocated at the beginning and end of the *Eighteen Benedictions and this is now the standard practice. Of Rabbi *Akiba it is said that he would cut short his prayers in public but when he prayed alone he would bow and prostrate himself so much that he would begin his prayers in one corner and finish them in another corner. The practice of *swaying during prayer and the study of the Torah is frequently mentioned. In *Hasidism in particular there was a tendency to move the body vigorously during prayer, to the scandal of the staid Rabbinic opponents of the movement. Some of the early Hasidim used to turn somersaults in their prayers rather like their contemporaries, the Shakers in America. Part of the aim of this exercise was for it to symbolize the doctrine of *annihilation of selfhood. The self was overturned, as it were, seeking nothing for itself and desiring only the glory of God. In present-day Orthodoxy, except among the Hasidim, there is considerable restraint in the matter of gesture. Reform Judaism looks askance on bodily movement in prayer as indecorous by Western standards, although many young Reform Jews are attracted to the wilder types of enthusiasm favoured by the Hasidim.

**Get** The bill of *divorce given by the husband to the wife in order to dissolve the marriage. Just as a Jewish marriage is established by the delivery of the ring together with the declaration of marriage in the presence of two witnesses, an instrument, the *get*, is required to be given before the marriage can be dissolved. Thus the *get* is not merely a record of dissolution of the marriage but the means of dissolution. There are many rules about the *get*, especially that it be written specifically for this particular husband and wife whose names have to be recorded with complete accuracy. The word *get* means a document and is used in the Talmud for other types of document, but the term generally denotes the bill of divorce.

The universal procedure is for the *get* to be wrtten in Aramaic, the language with which ordinary people were familiar in Rabbinic times, and there is now a standard form for the document, of which the following is an English translation:

'On the——day of the week and——day of the month——in the year——from the creation of the world, according to the mode of reckoning in this place——by the River——, do I——son of——of the town of——and by whatever other name or surname I or my father may be known, and my town and his town, thus determine, being of sound mind and under no constraint; and I do release and send away and put aside thee——,daughter of—— and by whatever other name or surname thou and thy father are known, and thy town and his town, who have been my wife from time past hitherto; and hereby I do release thee and send away and put thee aside that thou mayest have permission and control over thyself to go to be married to any man whom thou desirest, and no man shall hinder thee in my name from this day and forever. And thou art permitted to be married to any man. This shall be from me to thee a bill of dismissal, a document of release, and a letter of freedom, according to the law of Moses and Israel.

——son of——a witness
——son of——a witness'

**Ghetto** The part of a town in which Jews were segregated from the rest of its citizens. The name is derived from the foundry, known as the ghetto, in Venice, where, by papal decree, the Jews were forced to live. The name ghetto was used for all such places of segregation; the ghetto in Germany was called the *Judengasse*. With the Emancipation of the Jews the ghettos were abolished, although Jews still tended to live in certain Jewish districts for purposes of convenience—proximity to the synagogue, stores providing kosher food, and Hebrew schools for the children. Life in the old ghetto was usually grim, squalid, and restricted but in it the Jew found a measure of protection from a hostile world and the ability to assimilate his own spiritual heritage. As has been remarked: 'The Jews in the ghetto had nowhere else to go, so they went upwards.'

The ghettos created by the Nazis were for the purpose of concentrating the Jews in particular places so as to make the 'final solution' easier. There were a number of ghetto uprisings, doomed to failure but conducted with heroism and the determination to show the Nazis that Jews could live and die with dignity. The story of the Warsaw ghetto uprising has been told in song and writing as one of the greatest examples in human history of the power of the freedom-loving to resist tyranny.

**God** The Supreme Being, Creator of the world and all its creatures. Judaism stands or falls on belief in God. In the philosophical formulation of Maimonides (*Yesodey Ha-Torah*, 1. 1–3) with which the master's great Code opens:

'It is the basis of all foundations and the pillar on which all wisdom rests to know that there is a Prime Being who brought into being everything that exists and that all creatures in heaven and earth and between them only enjoy existence by virtue of His existence. If it could be imagined that He did not exist, then nothing else could have existed. But if it could be imagined that all beings other than He did not exist, He alone would still exist and He would not suffer cessation in their cessation. For all beings need Him but He, blessed be He, needs not a single one of them. It follows that His true nature is unlike the nature of any of them [i.e. His is necessary being, whereas theirs is contingent].'

In the \*'Adon Olam' hymn this is expressed poetically (in the translation by Israel \*Zangwill) as:

Lord of the world, He reigned alone
While yet the universe was naught,
When by His will all things were wrought;
Then first his sov'ran name was known.
And when the all shall cease to be,
In dread lone splendour He shall reign,
He was, He is, He shall remain
In glorious eternity.

Centuries later the Hasidic master Zevi Elimelech of Dinov (1785–1841), in his compendium of the precepts of the Torah entitled *Derekh Pikkudekha* ('The Way of Thy Precepts', no. 25), formulates belief in God to mean:

'to believe in the heart in very truth that God exists. He, blessed be He, it is who, out of nothing, has brought all creatures into being, By His power and will, blessed be He, there has come into existence everything that was, is and will be and nothing exists except by His will

and desire. His providence extends over all, in general and in particular, so that even the natural order is the result of His desire to use nature as the garment of His providence.'

All three formulations, even that of the Hasidic master, are the result of philosophical reflection. The very terms they use, 'Prime Being', 'existence', 'providence', belong to the medieval coinage in Hebrew of Greek philosophical terms. The very attempt at abstract formulation is in stark contrast to the simple, direct, and concrete statement with which the Hebrew Bible opens: 'In the beginning God created the heavens and the earth', and the even more direct opening verse of the \*Decalogue: 'I am the Lord thy God who brought thee out of the land of Egypt and out of the house of bondage.' Formulations of belief in God have varied in the history of Judaism; the belief itself has remained constant.

*The Existence of God*

The average theist, Jewish, Christian, or Muslim, believes in the existence of God, in the first instance, because he accepts this belief as part of the package delivered to him by the particular tradition in which he has been nurtured. When, however, he discovers that there are atheists or agnostics around (see ATHEISM and AGNOSTICISM) who challenge his childhood certainties, he may, if he is philosophically minded, seek to demonstrate that his belief can be defended on rational grounds; that, indeed, belief in God is the only conclusion to be drawn from rational reflection on the nature of the world in which he lives. Hence, from the time of the medieval philosophers (or, better, theologians) attempts have been made to prove the existence of God. This whole way of thinking is foreign to the biblical authors. In their day everyone believed in the existence of divine beings. The contribution of biblical monotheism (whether this arose spontaneously among the people of Israel or whether, as many biblical scholars maintain, it developed gradually from a belief in a supreme being over and above the other gods) is that there is only one God. It has to be appreciated that theoretical atheism, in biblical times, was not what William James calls 'a live option'. Abstract thought in systematic form comes to us in any event from the Greeks, but even if the biblical authors had engaged in this kind of thinking, they would have as little thought to prove the existence of God as they would have thought to prove that their human neighbours or they themselves existed. When, in the Middle Ages, atheism did become a live option, one chosen by some speculative thinkers, it became essential, at least so the theologians imagined, to try to adduce conclusive proofs that God really exists and is not a figment of the imagination or an illusion thought up by the tradition to dupe the credulous. The basic issue was whether biblical monotheism was no more than a powerful negation of the gods, from which there should follow the ultimate negation of the whole God concept, or whether it was rather a tremendous affirmation that the one God is, in the language of the Bible, the 'living God' by whose word everything came into existence.

The three main proofs or arguments in Christian thought for the existence of God are: 1. Anselm's ontological argument; 2. the cosmological argument; 3. the teleological argument or the argument from design. Briefly stated, the ontological argument is that anyone who uses the word 'God' has, in his mind, the most perfect being but a being who actually exists is more perfect than one who does not exist so that the very notion in the mind is of the God who actually exists. What this really amounts to is that the innate idea which men have of the perfect being they call God presupposes that such a being actually exists, otherwise whence came the idea itself into the human mind? The Jewish medieval thinkers never refer to this argument, either because they were ignorant of it or, as H. A. Wolfson has suggested, because they did not recognize in their theory of knowledge any such thing as an innate idea in the sense of an idea that comes from within rather than from without.

The cosmological argument holds that since everything must have a cause, the only way to explain the existence of the universe as a whole is to postulate an ultimate, uncaused being, a being beyond causation who is the Cause of causes and this, as Aquinas says, is God.

The teleological argument holds that evidence of design in the universe, in plant and animal life and in the workings of the human mind itself, points to the existence of Mind written large in the universe.

The Jewish thinkers generally prefer the cosmological argument—all motion in the universe, for instance, pointing to the Unmoved Mover—but they also use the teleological argument to supplement the cosmological. In a tale told of *Saadiah Gaon, some sages came to him to ask that he prove to their satisfaction that God exists. Saadiah left them alone in his room, where they saw a marvellous document full of ripe wisdom. 'Who wrote this?' they asked when Saadiah returned. Saadiah replied that the inkwell simply spilled over and the words formed themselves. 'How can such a thing be possible?' the sages asked. 'Exactly,' replied Saadiah. This is a variation of the old conundrum that if a host of monkeys were busy tapping at typewriters over millions of years they could never produce the plays of Shakespeare.

Another popular argument among Christians and Muslims is that of universal assent. All peoples seem to have believed in some form of deity. The Jewish thinkers do not use this argument, again according to Wolfson, because they do not believe in the gods but in the One God and for this there is certainly no universal assent. Ibn *Gabirol, however, does observe in his poem 'The Royal Crown' that even the idolaters, in their very act of worship, are worshipping the true God without knowing it:

Thou art the Lord,
And all beings are Thy servants, Thy domain;
And through those who serve idols vain
Thine honour is not distracted from,
For they all aim to Thee to come.

Since Kant's critique, the power of the traditional arguments have lost a good deal of their power. Kant rejects the notion that any experience of the universe can lead to anything beyond the universe. Many modern Jewish theologians accept the Kantian critique and tend to rely instead on the Kierkegaardian 'leap of faith' (see EXISTENTIALISM). But in more recent years, other Jews have followed thinkers such as A. C. Ewing and Richard Swinburne and many Roman Catholics who hold that the traditional arguments still have power, not so much as knock-down proofs but as indications. If all the arguments are presented together as pointers, then the very idea of God in the human mind, the facts of causation and design in the universe, and the consensus of human beings that there is in the universe That to be worshipped, all combine to render theism the most cogent way of approaching ultimate Reality. It is not, in any event, as if the believing

Jew starts from scratch. Even when he argues for the existence of God, what he is really doing is making sense of his long tradition that there is a 'living God'. The God He seeks is not an abstract Final Cause but the God who gave the Torah to His people Israel and through them to all mankind; in Pascal's famous cry from the heart, not the God of the philosophers but the God of Abraham, Isaac, and Jacob.

## The Nature of God

Jewish thinkers are divided on the matter of trying to understand what God is like. Some believe that it is possible for humans to have some apprehension of God but no real comprehension. Others have favoured the way of complete negation. *Bahya, Ibn Pakudah in his 'Duties of the Heart' (Gate One) remarks that in every subject of enquiry two questions have to be asked: 1. whether the subject exists; 2. what its nature is. But of God one can only ask if He is and one cannot then seek to know what He is. Or, as a sage quoted by *Albo remarks: 'If I knew Him I would be He', that is, only God can have knowledge of Himself so that His being can only be apprehended through His manifestation in the universe.

Both Bahya and Maimonides develop the idea of negative attributes applied to God. Attributes of God, as found in the Bible, are of two kinds, those referring to His essence and those referring to His activity. According to Maimonides, only the attributes referring to God's actions can be used in a positive sense. God can be described as good, not because it is possible to say anything about His true nature, but because such acts as that of bringing the embryo to birth as a human child, if they could have been performed by humans, would be attributed to human goodness. Attributes referring to God's essence, on the other hand, that He exists, that He is One, that He is wise, must be understood not as saying anything positive about His nature but only a negating their opposites; that is, God is not non-existent, not ignorant, and there is no multiplicity in His being. *Crescas, on the other hand, refuses to accept this negative way. For Crescas, all the attributes must be applied to God in a positive way. God is really wise and good in the sense in which these terms are used of humans, although unlike those of humans, His wisdom and goodness are infinite. Crescas points to the logical difficulty in Maimonides' stance. There

is no logical difference between saying that God is not not-knowing and saying that He is knowing.

The Kabbalists deal with the whole problem by drawing a distinction between God as He is in Himself and God in manifestation. God as he is in Himself is the *En Sof, the Limitless, and of this aspect of Deity nothing at all can be said, even negative attributes being totally impermissible. But God as manifest in the powers or potencies known as the *Sefirot is sufficiently accessible to the human mind to allow even positive attributes to be used.

## God as a Person

The term 'a personal God' is not found in the classical Jewish sources, although the biblical anthropomorphisms in which God is described certainly suggest that, for the biblical authors, God meets human beings, as *Buber puts it, in the life of dialogue in which person addresses person. 'The Lord would speak to Moses face to face, as one man speaks to another' (Exodus 33: 11). But Jewish naturalists such as Mordecai *Kaplan, under the influence of scientism, believe that God can no longer be described in personal terms at all. God, on this view, is not a being or a person but the name people have given to the 'force that makes for righteousness', the principle in the universe which gurarantees that righteousness will ultimately win out. This naturalistic understanding is not only a complete reversal of the traditional view but is less coherent in that it fails to explain how this affirmation that there is such a force in the universe can be 'cashed', as the linguistic analysts would say. As William Temple puts it, when God is described as a 'He' the meaning is that He is not an It. He is more than a 'He', not less. God can only be described, if spoken of at all, in human terms but that is because we are obliged to describe God in terms of the highest that we know and this is in terms of the human personality, always with the qualification that He is infinitely more than anything we can say of Him. Since Hebrew has no neuter gender, the biblical writers use the masculine 'He' when speaking of God and this term has persisted. Feminists believe that God should be spoken of, too, as a 'She' (see FEMINISM) but both 'He' and 'She', when used of God, are only a poor attempt to describe that which is beyond description and to define that which is utterly beyond all definition. Some religious folk may think of God as the old man in the sky, but surely even the most immature do not really think that God is located only somewhere 'up there'—they, too, know that the whole earth is full of His glory. Even Moses of Taku, Maimonides' near contemporary, who takes issue with Maimonides' rejection of the corporeal concept of the Deity, only maintains that, as the plain meaning of Scripture seems to have it, God can and does assume the form of a king seated on His throne surrounded by His angels, not that He is limited to this particular form of manifestation.

In all this the problem for the believer is how to speak of God without saying either too much or too little. To say too much is to come close to idolatry, to describing as God that which is less than God. To say too little is to come close to atheistic negation. Francis Bacon, in his essay on superstition, remarks: 'It were better to have no opinion of God at all than such an opinion as is unworthy of him; for the one is unbelief, the other is contumely: and certainly superstition is the reproach of the Deity.' It is interesting that almost at the same time when Bacon wrote this, the Safed Kabbalist Moses *Cordovero could write to the exact opposite effect: 'His [the atheist's] character is inferior to that of the idolater who admits that there is a God but is in error as to who is God, making a god for himself according to his belief and opinion. This heretic, on the other hand, does not even worship idols since according to his premiss there is no God.' But Cordovero, while acknowledging that false beliefs about the divine are better than no belief at all, also states that as soon as the worshipper of the One God has a picture in his mind (as he must have, as a psychological necessity, if he is to engage in worship) he must recoil in the realization that whatever he depicts is utterly remote from the reality. The average Jewish believer follows naturally Cordovero's advice about 'running to and fro' in worship. He affirms the existence of God and is bound to have some picture flashing in his mind but recoils from any suggestion that he can really have any grasp whatsoever of the divine nature. One of the main reasons why Judaism takes issue with *Christianity is that Judaism refuses to believe that God, as in the doctrine of the Incarnation, can have assumed human flesh. And this is why Judaism forbids the making of an image of God. To have an image of God in the mind is inevitable, but when the image is given a concrete and hence more permanent form there can be none of the immediate recoil of which Cordovero speaks.

*Transcendence and Immanence*

Traditional Jewish thought about God takes issue both with a thoroughgoing pantheism in which God is the universe and the universe He, God being the name given to the totality of things, and with deism, the theory that God did create the universe but then left it to its own devices, so to speak, like a clock-maker who, once the clock has been put together, no longer exercises any control over it. Deism leaves no room for any interaction between the divine and the universe and hence no possibility of divine intervention in the affairs of the universe, ruling out divine *providence and *revelation. On the Jewish view, God is both transcendent and immanent, beyond the universe and apart from it but working within it. Terms like 'beyond' or 'outside' in this connection are very misleading in that they suggest a spatial location. On any sophisticated view, the doctrine of divine transcendence does not mean that God resides in outer space, as a Russian astronaut imagined theists to believe; he returned to declare that his voyage had demonstrated that there is no God, otherwise he would have seen some evidence of His presence out there. Such terms really denote that God is wholly other than the universe, that if there were no universe God would still be. In C. S. Lewis's analogy, which should not be pressed too far, God's presence in the universe can be compared to Shakespeare's presence in his plays. Shakespeare is not a character in his plays but he is present in all the characters and in the plays themselves.

Jewish thought has long interpreted a Talmudic passage (*Berakhot* 10a) as expressing, though in less abstract terms, the transcendence and immanence of God. In this passage there are said to be five points of resemblance between the human soul and God: God 'fills the world' and the soul 'fills the body'; God 'sees, but is not seen' and the soul 'sees, but is not seen'; God 'sustains the world' and the soul 'sustains the body'; God is 'pure' and the soul is 'pure'; God 'resides in the innermost recesses' and the soul 'resides in the innermost recesses'. The poetic conclusion is: let the soul which has these five characteristics praise the God who has the same five. The doctrine of divine immanence and transcendence is expressed in many a biblical passage but nowhere so powerfully as in the verses: 'Thus saith the Lord, The heaven is my throne, and the earth my footstool: where is the house that ye build unto me? And where is the place of my rest? For all these things hath mine hand made, and all these have been, saith the Lord; but to this man will I look, to him that is poor and of a contrite spirit, and trembleth at my word' (Isaiah 66: 1–2). The non-Jewish biblical scholar S. R. Driver comes close to the deeper significance of Jacob's dream of the ladder with its feet on the ground and its head reaching to the heavens (Genesis 28: 10–22) when he comments that the truths that find expression in the narrative are: 'that heaven and earth are not spiritually parted from one another, that God's protecting presence accompanies His worshippers, and that He is ever at their side, even when they are away from their accustomed place of worship, and are tempted by circumstances not to realise the fact.'

The paradox of divine transcendence and immanence is given its expression in a famous poem by *Judah Halevi:

> Lord where shall I find thee?
> High and hidden is thy place;
> And where shall I not find thee
> The world is full of thy glory.

## Omnipotence and Omniscience

That God is all-powerful and knows everything is implied in all the sources of Judaism, though both medieval and modern Jewish thinkers have explored the meaning of 'all' and 'everything' in this context. Two biblical passages, in particular, touch on the question of divine omnipotence. When Abraham is told that his wife, Sarah, then 90 years of age, will give birth to a child (Genesis 18: 1–15), Sarah laughs at the very thought of such an impossibility but she is rebuked for her laughter: 'Is anything too hard for the Lord?' (v. 14). God says to the prophet Jeremiah, who has faith even though the situation in which he finds himself seems an impossible one: 'Behold, I am the Lord, the God of all flesh; is there anything too hard for Me?' (Jeremiah 32: 27). The root meaning of the Hebrew word translated as 'too hard' is that of 'separation', that is, something extraordinary, totally different from normal human experience and expectation. Implicit in these two

passages, typical of the general biblical view, is that God can do anything He chooses. Nothing is too marvellous for Him. His power is exalted far above that of humans. That which seems impossible for humans is not impossible for Him.

The biblical writers were not bothered by the kind of problems regarding divine omnipotence discussed with much subtlety by the medieval thinkers, Jewish, Christian, and Muslim. The biblical authors were content to affirm that God can do everything and leave it at that. But, under the impact of Greek philosophy, the medieval thinkers asked, is it really true to say that God can do anything He chooses? If He can, does this mean that He can, for example, create a stone which even He cannot lift up? Can He create another God? Can He will Himself out of existence? The answer to this kind of question is surely in the negative, but is not then this answer a denial or qualification of divine omnipotence?

*Saadiah Gaon is the first Jewish thinker to face this problem in a systematic way (*Beliefs and Opinions*, ii. 13). Saadiah says that some people ask whether God can put the world through the hollow of a signet ring without making the one narrower and the other wider. Saadiah replies that while God can do the impossible (for humans) He cannot do the absurd, not because of any lack of power but because there is no such thing. To put the world through the ring means either that the world has become smaller or the ring larger, so that the question is a nonsense question, as if it were: can God make the world smaller without making it smaller? Centuries later, *Albo (*Ikkarim*, i. 22) discusses the same question. Some things are impossible for us even to imagine, since they involve us in contradiction. It is impossible even to imagine that God could create another being like Him in every respect for that would involve one being the cause and the other the effect, so they would not be similar in every respect. We cannot declare, on the other hand, says Albo, that the *resurrection of the dead, though it seems impossible for us, is impossible for God, since the idea can be grasped in the mind and does not involve any inherent contradiction. As Aquinas puts it on the Christian side (*Summa Theologica*, I, q. 25. 4): 'Nothing that implies a contradiction falls under the scope of God's omnipotence.' Nonsense words do not make sense simply because the word 'God' is tagged on to them. When it is asked whether God can make another being like Him in every respect who is not like Him in every respect this is no different from asking: 'Can God . . .?' without completing the question.

Whatever the doctrine of omnipotence means, therefore, it does not mean that nonsense propositions can be predicated of God. But Judaism does insist that God is omnipotent and that a being lacking the power to do anything He chooses would not be God. However, there have been religious thinkers, including some Jews in modern times, who would deny that God is omnipotent, though He is exceedingly powerful. John Stuart Mill argued that the very idea of God as Designer of the universe implies that He is only able to work on the stuff out of which the universe is formed, otherwise why should God have to design or plan the universe? Albo (*Ikkarim*, ii. 4) gave the Jewish answer to this when he noted that, in Jewish teaching, God 'designed' the universe, not because He needed to create a universe that He had planned beforehand, but in order to impress upon humans the importance of God's creation as if it were the result of a well thought-out process. Other thinkers have seen God as limited by His own nature which is infinite in some respects but finite in others. Alone among Jewish thinkers, *Gersonides anticipated, to some extent, the idea of God as finite in some respects. Gersonides, for example, holds that there is a formless material coexistent with God from all eternity upon which He has to work and that God does not know beforehand the particular choices man will make. But few religious minds are satisfied with the doctrine of a limited God, a doctrine that borders on dualism and is open to the same objections as that now discredited religious philosophy.

Judaism also insists that God is omniscient, knowing all things; as the Psalmist says: 'From the place of His habitation He looketh intently upon all the inhabitants of the earth; He that fashioneth the hearts of them all, that considereth all their doings' (Psalms 33: 14–15). Yet there is no clear statement in the Bible that the doctrine of omniscience means that God knows all that is to be in the future and the Talmudic Rabbis acknowledge that this is so when they ask: 'How do we know from Scripture that God knows that which will come to pass in the future?' (*Sanhedrin* 90b). Yet it became axiomatic among Jews in the post-Talmudic age that God knows not only the past and the present but all the details of the future. This gave rise in the Middle Ages to the vexed problem of how divine foreknowledge can be reconciled with human *free will.

## God and Evil

While Maimonides can hold that God is described as 'good' in the Bible only on the analogy of human conduct, not that His essential nature, of which nothing can be known, can be described as 'good', it is postulated in all the Jewish sources that God desires the good for His creatures and urges them to struggle against evil. The biblical and Rabbinic authors are concerned, however, with the human struggle against evil and when the problem of evil is discussed it is generally, as in the books of *Ecclesiastes and *Job and in many a passage in the Rabbinic literature, in the context of why the righteous suffer and the wicked prosper. The abstract problem of why the benevolent Creator should have created evil and suffering in the first place is not touched upon until the age of the medieval thinkers. As the problem has often been expressed: theistic faith, in its traditional version, asserts three propositions: 1. God is wholly good; 2. evil is real; 3. God is omnipotent. The problem is how these three propositions can all be maintained at the same time. For if God can prevent evil and does not choose to do so, He cannot be good and if, on the other hand, He wishes to prevent evil but cannot do so, He cannot be omnipotent. One of these three propositions would seem to demand some qualification. The problem is severe and has been presented in modern times in a particularly acute form as a result of the *Holocaust in which six million Jews perished at the hands of the Nazis.

No representative Jewish thinker has sought to grapple with the problem by denying the second proposition, that evil is real. Even if it be postulated that the existence of evil is an illusion, the illusion is itself evil. Nor does it help to argue, as some Jewish thinkers have argued, that evil is only a negation, the absence of the good, since this is in itself an evil. Nor have Jewish thinkers believed that the first proposition can be qualified, even if some, like Maimonides, refrain from ascribing goodness to God's essential nature. From the human angle, at least, God is good and hates evil. The only way out for the traditional theist would seem to be to qualify in some way the doctrine of divine omnipotence. This is the famous free-will defence. God, as noted above, cannot do the absurd. If He is to grant free will to His creatures, the world must be the arena in which free will can be exercised and this involves the creation of a world that provides for the conflict between good and evil and hence the existence of evil. Some thinkers see no logical contradiction between God making man free and yet always seeing to it that he chooses the good. But if God always saw to it that man freely chooses the good, there would be no value in the choice.

This is how the majority of Jewish thinkers have tried to cope with the problem, although they usually add to the equation that by choosing the good, man makes it his own and so can enjoy it as his own creative achievement for all eternity (see IMMORTALITY, HEAVEN AND HELL, WORLD TO COME). The world is seen, in Keats's famous phrase, as 'a vale of soul-making'. Jews can have no quarrel with F. R. Tennant's analysis of why there must inevitably be evil in a world in which moral values can be realized. For the world to be a theatre of the moral life there must be a regular operation of natural forces, there must be a law-abidingness in the universe. A topsy-turvy world in which anything can happen or a fairy-tale world in which the ugly brute always turns into a prince would not be the requisite background for the emergence of moral qualities.

Tennant's discussion, and that of John Hicks who pursues a similar line, is helpful; but the average theist protests, granted that a degree of evil is necessary, why so much? Is the Holocaust a price worth paying for the world to be a moral theatre? The majority of believing Jews hold that there is no solution to the problem of evil capable of being grasped by the human mind in this life. This would agree with Browning's illustration (in 'Bishop Bloughram's Apology') that the world is a checkerboard containing black and white squares. The sceptic holds that the board is black but contains white squares. The believer holds that the board is essentially white but contains black squares.

Nowhere in the history of Jewish thought is the reality of evil more pronounced than in the Kabbalistic notion of the *Sitra Aḥara*, the Other Side, the side of the demonic forces, constantly at war with the holy from which it is nourished. But, even in the Kabbalah, there is

no final dualism, no permanent battle between a god of light and a god of darkness. In a remarkable Kabbalistic simile, the *Sitra Aḥara* is compared to a vicious dog on a very long lead. The dog appears to be out of control and have total power to cause harm but when it is in danger of getting completely out of hand the owner pulls it back by the lead in his hands. The struggle against dualism was especially prominent in Babylonia in Talmudic times, where the Zoroastrian religion of Ormuzd and Ahriman, the god of light and the god of darkness, reigned supreme among the Gentile population. There are numerous Rabbinic rules that were introduced for the purpose of combating this religious view; for instance, that in prayer one must not repeat the words: 'We give thanks to thee' because this might imply that thanks were being given to two gods. It is possible that Deutero-Isaiah's strong affirmation of the divine unity is directed against early Persian dualism: 'I form light, and create darkness; I make peace, and create evil; I am the Lord that doeth all these things' (Isaiah 45: 7). This verse was inorporated into the liturgy, with 'all things' substituted for 'evil' in order to avoid the direct ascription, in daily prayer, of evil to God. The Talmud (*Sanhedrin* 39a) has a little tale to illustrate the theological difficulty with any dualistic view. A Magus said to Amemar: 'From the middle of your body upwards you belong to Ormuzd; from the middle downwards, to Ahriman.' Amemar replied: 'In that case why does Ahriman permit Ormuzd to send water through his territory?'; in other words, how are the digestive and excretory processes possible, how can the human body or the world as a whole function as a unity, if it belongs to two contending powers?

Samuel S. Cohon, *Jewish Theology: A Historical and Systematic Interpretation of Judaism and its Foundations* (Assen, 1971).
Louis Jacobs, *A Jewish Theology* (New York, 1973).
Kaufmann Kohler, *Jewish Theology Systematically Arranged*, with new material by Joseph L. Blau (New York, 1968).
Arthur Marmostein, *The Old Rabbinic Doctrine of God* (reprint; New York, 1968).
Milton Steinberg, *Anatomy of Faith*, ed. Arthur A. Cohen (New York, 1960).

**Gog and Magog**  The peoples who will wage war against the Jews before the advent of the *Messiah. These two names appear in the vision of the prophet *Ezekiel (Ezekiel 38, 39) where Gog is the ruler of the country of Magog. Gog will lead his people in war against the land of Israel but will be defeated and God alone will reign supreme. Since Ezekiel prophesied in *exile about the return of the Jewish people to its land, it is possible that he was thinking of contemporary events. Attempts have been made to identify Gog and Magog with nations whom the prophet may have thought to pose a threat in the immediate future to the Jews who were to return to the land. On the other hand, as a number of biblical scholars understand it, the prophet himself may have had in mind events in the remote future as part of his apocalyptic vision. In subsequent Jewish *eschatology, both Gog and Magog are understood to be persons and the 'wars of Gog and Magog' become part of the whole eschatological scheme. As with regard to Jewish eschatology as a whole, there is a considerable degree of uncertainty about what is said to happen at the 'end of days'; the picture is really an amalgam of various folk-beliefs, some of them contradictory. In the eschatological account given by *Saadiah Gaon (*Beliefs and Opinions*, viii. 6) an attempt is made to accommodate the wars of Gog and Magog into the scheme. Interestingly enough, however, in Maimonides' scheme at the end of his great Code, the *Mishneh Torah*, in which Messianism is interpreted in largely rationalistic terms, there is no reference to the wars of Gog and Magog only to the Messiah fighting 'the battles of the Lord' in order to reconquer the land of Israel, rebuild the Temple, and establish God's reign on earth. Even in Orthodox Judaism, the details of these terrible events are vague and the whole notion of the wars of Gog and Magog does not feature at all prominently in Orthodox theology. Yet, at the time, World Wars I and II did tend to be seen as the 'wars of Gog and Magog', as the essential prelude to the coming of the Messiah. Some of the Hasidic masters saw the struggle between Napoleon and Russia as the 'wars of Gog and Magog'. Martin Buber's novel *For the Sake of Heaven*, based on historical fact, is constructed around the conflict between the Hasidic masters on whether Napoleon was to be identified with Gog. Reform Judaism, in any event, has substituted belief in a Messianic age for belief in the coming of a personal Messiah and has given up entirely all such notions as the wars of Gog and Magog, viewing these as fevered responses in the past to severe calamities, rather than as any kind of revelation about what is to happen in the future.

**Golden Calf** The calf fashioned out of gold worshipped by the Israelites in the wilderness. The narrative of the golden calf is found in the book of *Exodus (32: 1–33: 23) where it is told how the people, seeing that Moses had tarried in his descent from Mount *Sinai, stripped off the golden ornaments from their womenfolk, and persuaded *Aaron, Moses' brother, to make for them a calf who would lead them in Moses' stead. When Moses came down from the mount and saw the people dancing before the calf, he shattered the two *tablets of stone containing the *Decalogue which he had brought down with him, destroyed the calf, and forced the people to drink the water into which its fragments had been scattered. The Levites, who had not taken part in the worship of the calf, then killed 3,000 of the worshippers and God punished the people with a plague. The traditional explanation of the narrative is that the calf was actually worshipped as a god, but recent biblical scholarship sees behind the narrative an ancient Semitic practice in which the figure of a bull was fashioned not as a god but as the seat of the god. For this reason, it is suggested, the narrative of the golden calf is placed in the Pentateuch in between two accounts of the *Tabernacle, the place in which God is said to reside with the holy *Ark as His seat.

In the book of Kings (1 Kings 12) there is another golden-calf narrative. Here it is stated that *Jeroboam, after he had successfully led the rebellion against the house of *David, resolved to set up a golden calf in Dan and another in Beth-el so that the people would forsake David's *Jerusalem and come to worship instead at these shrines. Jeroboam declares: 'Ye have gone up long enough to Jerusalem; behold thy gods, O Israel, which brought thee out of the land of Egypt.' These words are identical with the words of the Israelites who made the calf in the time of Moses (Exodus 32: 4). The plural form 'these' is appropriate in the Jeroboam narrative, since there were two calves, but why is 'these' used in the wilderness narrative where there was only one? The Jeroboam narrative contains no reference to the earlier episode of the golden calf. There are further associations between the two narratives.

Jeroboam appoints priests from among the people 'that were not of the sons of Levi' (1 Kings 32: 4) and in the earlier episode the Levites do not worship the calf. In both narratives there is a reference to a feast and sacrifices. Aaron, who made the golden calf, had two sons, who 'died at the instance of the Lord' (Leviticus 10: 1–2), named Nadab and Abihu and Jeroboam's sons were also called Nadab and Abihu (1 Kings 14: 1 and 15: 25). These strong resemblances have led some critics to view the Exodus narrative as pure fiction, intended to reflect and discredit the rebellion of Jeroboam. This is unlikely, since, on the critical theory, the Exodus passage belongs to a very early strand in the *Pentateuch (see also BIBLICAL CRITICISM), one that must have been composed long before the book of Kings. Moreover, the details are too circumstantial for them to be fiction. Others scholars, therefore, suggest that the Exodus narrative is the original one. Much later, these scholars suggest, when Jeroboam's rebellion had been discredited, the account of what he did was reinterpreted, in the book of Kings, so as to make Jeroboam guilty of a repetition of the ancient sin of the golden calf. Whatever the critical solution to the problem may be, the tradition understands both narratives to be accurate accounts of what transpired so that Jeroboam simply repeated the ancient act of apostasy.

In subsequent Jewish literature the 'sin of the calf' becomes the prototype of national apostasy and idolatrous worship. In the Kabbalistic scheme, when Adam sinned death was decreed for him and his descendants but when Israel accepted the Torah the people rectified Adam's original sin and were destined to live for ever. When they worshipped the golden calf, they repeated Adam's act of apostasy, and were thus delivered unto death. The taint of sin and death will not be removed until the final 'rectification' provided in the Messianic age and the *resurrection.

Jewish and Christian preachers often use the golden-calf narrative to call attention to the sin of greed and the unbridled pursuit of wealth. But this idea that an unworthy pursuit of wealth is to worship the golden calf is, of course, homiletical. Later Midrashim, noting that the women were extremely reluctant to give their ornaments for the making of the calf, state that women are more steadfast in faith than men. As a reward for their loyalty the women were given Rosh Hodesh, the New Moon day, as a special festival for women. Some pious Jewish women are still known to abstain from work on Rosh Hodesh.

It is traditional, when the golden-calf narrative is read from the *Scroll in the synagogue, to chant it in softer voice than is usual in the *reading of the Torah in order to express the embarrassment of the congregation at the sin of their ancestors.

Nahum M. Sarna, 'The Golden Calf', in his *Exploring Exodus* (New York, 1986), 215–20.

**Golem** A creature made out of clay into which life has been injected by magical means. The Hebrew word *golem* means something incomplete or unfinished, as in the verse (Psalms 139: 16) referring to the human embryo: 'Thine eyes did see mine unfinished substance [ *golmi* ].' While the notion that it is possible to bring to life an artificial semi-human figure is found in the Talmud, the term golem for such a creature was not used until centuries later. In Ethics of the Fathers (5. 7) the golem is contrasted with the wise man and thus denotes a stupid person, like 'dummy' in English slang.

In a Talmudic passage (*Sanhedrin* 65b) it is stated that the Babylonian teacher Rava (fourth century CE) created a man and sent him to Rabbi Zera who tried to converse with him but when he saw that the man could not speak he said: 'You belong to that crew [of the magicians] go back to dust.' The passage continues that the two third-century Palestinian teachers Rabbi Haninah and Rabbi Oshea, with the aid of the *Sefer Yetzirah* (*Book of Creation*) created a calf every eve of the Sabbath which they ate on the Sabbath. This passage implies that the Rabbis brought these creatures into being by white magic (see MAGIC AND SUPERSTITION) in which, as it was later spelled out, divine names, the creative powers in the universe, were utilized. This formed the basis of the post-Talmudic legends of the golem. In a manuscript of Rabbi Eleazar of Worms, discovered by Gershom Scholem, the technique for creating a golem (this is the earliest reference to the term for the creature) is described: 'He who consults the Sefer Yetzirah must first perform a ritual immersion and put on white garments. He then takes virgin soil from a mountain which has not been dug by men, soaks it in water from a well and makes the golem, forming each limb by reciting alphabetical permutations.' In the year

1808, Jakob Grimm, of fairy-tale fame, wrote: 'After saying certain prayers and observing certain fast days, the Polish Jews make the figure of a man from clay or mud, and when they pronounce the divine name over him, he must come to life. He cannot speak, but he understands fairly well what is said or commanded. They call him Golem and use him as a servant to do all sorts of housework.' This kind of legend evidently enjoyed a wide circulation. Mary Shelley is supposed to have based her story of Frankenstein on the golem legend.

The legend reached the city of Prague not earlier than the year 1730 where the famous *Maharal of Prague was said to have created a golem in order to protect the Jews of Prague from pogroms. When the golem began to get out of hand, the Maharal took the divine name from his forehead and restored the golem to his dust which is now supposed to reside in an attic in the Altneuschul. For the benefit of tourists, shops in Prague now sell models of the golem which closely resemble the figure of the Frankenstein monster.

When Gershom Scholem heard that the Weitzmann Institute at Rehovot had completed the building of a new computer, he suggested that in his opinion the computer should be called Golem I.

Behind all the golem legends lies the belief, especially prominent in the Kabbalah, that the mystics, by using the creative energy inherent in the divine names, repeat the divine creative processes. The whole fascinating legend owes its importance to this belief in which the doctrine of the imitation of God is applied to the creative as well as the ethical sphere.

Moshe Idel, *Golem: Jewish Magical and Mystical Traditions on the Artificial Anthropoid* (Albany, NY, 1990).
Gershom G. Scholem, 'The Idea of the Golem', in his *On The Kabbalah and its Symbolism* (London, 1965), 158–204.
Byron L. Sherwin, *The Golem Legend: Origins and Implications* (Lanham, 1985).

**Grace Before and After Meals** The special benedictions with a wording of their own recited before and after partaking of a meal. *Benedictions are recited before and after enjoying any food or drink, but the Rabbis introduced special forms for a full meal. A meal in this context is one at which some bread, the staple diet in biblical and Rabbinic times,

is eaten. Even nowadays, when meals do not necessarily include bread, this special grace is not recited if bread is not eaten, no matter how many courses in the meal.

The following is the traditional procedure, still observed by all religious Jews, although Reform Judaism has modified some of the regulations, having, for instance, a shorter form of grace after meals worded more in accordance with Reform theory. There is also a different, traditional, shorter form of grace, consisting of the main features of the longer form. This is only to be recited in an emergency when there is no time for the full grace to be recited.

The first step is the ritual washing of the *hands. Then the grace before meals is recited, ideally over a whole loaf: 'Blessed art Thou, O Lord our God, King of the universe, who has brought forth bread from the earth.' The bread is broken, dipped in salt, and distributed to the participants. The original reason for dipping the bread in salt was that salt was considered essential as a hygienic measure, since bread was usually baked in ancient times without salt being added. Another reason given is that the table is said to resemble the altar in the Temple (in this sense every meal is a sacred meal), where salt was offered together with the sacrificial meat. Since the altar is said to promote peace, for the same reason the custom developed of removing all the knives, the symbol of war, from the table before the grace after meals is recited. The grace before meals over bread suffices for everything partaken of at the meal, except for wine and fruit. If, say, the meal consists of fish, meat, and vegetables, these are covered by the benediction over bread. But when wine or fruit is partaken of during the meal, the benediction over these should be recited and these are not covered by the benediction over the bread. The Hebrew word for bread, *lehem*, also denotes 'food' in the Bible, as in the verse (Psalms 104: 14) upon which the wording of the grace before meals is based: 'He causeth the grass to grow for the cattle, and herb for the service of man; that he may bring forth bread [*lehem*] out of the earth.'

The form of grace after meals goes back to early Talmudic times and consists of four parts: 1. a benediction in which God is thanked for providing all His creatures with their food (for 'food' here the word *mazon*, 'sustenance', is used, hence grace after meals in Hebrew is *birkat ha-mazon*) 'benediction over food';

2. thanksgiving for the land of Israel; 3. a prayer for the city of Jerusalem and its rebuilding; 4. a hymn of general praise and various petitions, some of which were added in post-Talmudic times. In one of these, guests at the table recite a special prayer for their host and hostess. Another prayer of this kind is recited by guests at a wedding banquet or at the meal following a circumcision in which prayers are offered for the celebrants. The wording of the grace after meals is essentially the same in all the rites with only minor variations. There are suitable additions, referring to the special day, on Sabbaths and festivals.

Where three or more adult males eat together at the same table, the practice is for one of them to preface the grace after meals with an invitation to the others to join with him in the recitation, saying: 'We will bless Him of whose bounty we have partaken', to which they respond: 'Blessed be He of whose bounty we have partaken, and through whose goodness we live.' Reform and Conservative Jews count women in the quorum required for this invitation to say grace.

There are a number of melodies, traditional and modern, by which grace after meals is chanted, especially on Sabbaths, festivals, Bar Mitzvah, and wedding celebrations. From the seventeenth century it became the practice to recite, on Sabbath and festivals, as a prelude to grace after meals, Psalm 126: 'When the Lord brought back those that returned to Zion we were like unto them that dream', with a joyous melody.

It can be seen that grace before and after meals follows a traditional pattern. The practice of the host composing his own form of thanksgiving, as in many Christian Protestant circles, is not normally countenanced by Jews for that very reason.

Israel Abrahams, *A Companion to the Authorized Daily Prayerbook* (New York, 1966), 206–11.

**Graetz, Heinrich** German Jewish historian (1817–91). Graetz received a traditional Jewish education in his youth but read widely in private works of general learning and early on was obliged to grapple with the problem of religious belief arising out of the conflict in his mind between traditional beliefs and the new ideas. Graetz was assisted in his struggle by the famous neo-Orthodox Rabbi Samson Raphael *Hirsch. Hirsch became Graetz's mentor for a time but eventually the two became estranged, partly because Hirsch was dissatisfied with Graetz's standards of Jewish observance (when Graetz married, Hirsch observed with displeasure that the young wife did not cover her hair in the manner of Orthodox Jewish matrons) but mainly because Graetz's historical approach to Judaism was not to the Orthodox master's dogmatic taste.

Graetz, at one time, had an ambition to become an Orthodox Rabbi but neither the congregation where he delivered his trial sermon nor Graetz himself believed that he possessed the necessary ability to assume such a role, in that he was a fine writer but a poor speaker. Instead, Graetz decided to pursue an academic career. He studied for his Ph.D. at Breslau University, presenting his thesis on the relationship between Gnosticism and Judaism at the University of Jena. Graetz found a kindred spirit in Zechariah *Frankel, the founder of the Breslau school in which the historical approach to Judaism predominated but was wedded to a deep respect for the Jewish tradition. After occupying a number of teaching positions, Graetz was appointed lecturer in Jewish History and Bible at Frankel's Jewish Theological Seminary in Breslau.

Graetz was a biblical scholar in the critical mode. He had no hesitation in putting forward untraditional views regarding the dating of some of the biblical books but, as in the Breslau school generally, adopted the completely traditional view on the authorship of the *Pentateuch. In Graetz and in other members of the school, including Frankel himself, *biblical criticism, then in its infancy, was allowed its head with regard to the rest of the Bible and the critical approach was certainly pursued with regard to Rabbinic literature, but a halt was called when it came to the holy of holies, the Pentateuch. This dichotomy was to haunt traditionalist historians well into the twentieth century. Graetz's historical and critical studies did not affect his Orthopraxy, as this stance came to be called. To the end of his life Graetz was opposed to the Reform movement and remained a strictly observant Jew. It is reported that when Graetz visited London, he was invited to read the *Haftarah at the Great Synagogue and read it with his own critical emendations of the text. Yet, it was observed, when he left the synagogue he tied his handkerchief around his wrist in order to avoid carrying it in the public domain on the Sabbath.

Graetz's fame rests on his monumental *History of the Jews*. Drawing on sources in many languages and building on the researches of the Jüdische Wissenschaft school, Graetz surveys in the work Jewish history from the earliest times down to his own day, presenting it all in systematic fashion together, in the original German edition, with learned footnotes in which he gives his sources. Graetz emerges as an objective historian but one with a profound belief in God and in the contribution of the Jewish people in realizing the divine will. Graetz's emphasis, and here he differs from the later Jewish historian, *Dubnow, is on Jewish spirituality as expressed in literary sources and on the spiritual strivings of the Jewish people as the essential feature of their political and social life. There is very little social history in the work and hardly any use of archival material.

Graetz's overall view of Judaism and the role of the Jewish people is best conveyed in an essay entitled 'The Significance of Judaism for the Present and the Future', published, towards the end of his life, in the year 1889 as the opening essay of the first issue of the *Jewish Quarterly Review*, edited by Israel Abrahams and C. G. *Montefiore. Here Graetz's rationalism is well to the fore. He is unhappy, for instance, about the term 'faith' as applied to Judaism since such a term, for him, denotes acceptance of an inconceivable miraculous fact. He quotes with approval Renan's aphorism that Judaism is 'a minimum of religion', which Graetz finds illustrated in Micah's 'What doth the Lord require of thee? Only to do justly, and to love mercy, and to walk humbly with thy God' (Micah 6: 8) and in the Talmudic ruling that martyrdom is demanded of the Jew only when an attempt is made to force him to worship idols or commit adultery, incest, or murder. In all this Graetz sees the essence of Judaism as containing two elements, the ethical and the religious, each possessing a positive and a negative side. The ethical includes in its positive side, love of mankind, benevolence, humility, justice, and in its negative aspects, respect for human life, care against unchastity, subdual of selfishness and the beast in man, holiness in deed and thought. The religious element in its negative aspects includes the prohibition of worshipping a transient being as God and to consider all idolatry as vain and to reject it entirely. The positive side is to regard the highest Being as one and unique, to worship it as the Godhead and the essence of all ethical perfection. Graetz claims that in this union of the ethical and the religious consists the unique character of Judaism, and this doctrine of ethical monotheism has lost none of its significance. The elaborate rituals of Judaism are, of course, required but these were intended to surround ideals themselves of an ethereal nature. Unfortunately, he remarks, owing to the tragic course of history, the ritual has developed into a fungoid growth which overlays the ideals. Graetz's rationalistic views are pervasive in his *History of the Jews* which, for all his profound belief in God, is very weak on the question of Jewish *dogmas.

Graetz's rationalistic approach is particularly evident in his treatment of the Kabbalah and Jewish mysticism for which he seems to have had a blind spot. Typical of his approach is his treatment of the Zohar, the supreme work of the Kabbalah. By means of careful scholarship, Graetz demonstrates that the Zohar could not have been written, as the Kabbalists claim, by the second-century Palestinian teacher, Rabbi *Simeon ben Yohai. The true author of the book is the man who claimed to have 'discovered' the work, *Moses de Leon, in the thirteenth century. Modern scholarship, thanks to the researches of Gershom *Scholem, has accepted Graetz's argument. That Moses de Leon is the author would not have led Graetz to call the Zohar 'the book of lies' were he not convinced, on other grounds, that the Kabbalah is nonsense. He does not appear to have had any appreciation that a pseudepigraphic work is not 'false' on that account and he fails to see what many have seen, that one does not have to swallow the Kabbalah whole in order to recognize the many religious insights it contains. Similarly, with regard to *Hasidism, Graetz sees this mystical, revivalist movement, solely as a superstition.

Despite the legitimate criticisms by later scholars of Graetz's *History*, the book retains its importance as a pioneering work of modern Jewish historiography and for the proud advocacy of the importance of Judaism to the world at large. In the memoir of Graetz contributed by Dr Phillip Bloch to the English translation of the *History of the Jews*, the anecdote is told of a meeting between Graetz and the great Leopold *Zunz. Graetz was introduced as a scholar who was about to publish a Jewish history. 'Another history of the Jews?' Zunz pointedly asked. 'Another history,' was Graetz's retort, 'but this time a *Jewish* history.'

Heinrich Graetz, *A History of the Jews*, trans. Bella Lowy *et al.* (Philadelphia, 1946).

**Gratitude** In the ethical literature of Judaism, gratitude is a great virtue, ingratitude a great vice. It is not that there is any actual precept to express gratitude for favours done. To be grateful is rather seen as what is involved in being a decent human being for which no precept is required. In a Rabbinic comment on the story of the ten plagues, it is noted that Moses is told to tell Aaron to hold his staff over the waters of the Nile (Exodus 7: 19). Moses himself was not allowed to strike the waters, even symbolically by holding the staff over them, because they had protected him after his mother had hidden him in the bulrushes when he was an infant (Exodus 2: 2–3). This principle of gratitude is expressed in the folk-saying the Rabbis quote in this connection: 'Do not cast clods of earth into the well from which you drink water.' A key text for the principle of gratitude is: 'You shall not abhor an Egyptian, for you were a stranger in his land' (Deuteronomy 23: 8), as if to say, despite the bondage to which the Egyptians subjected the children of Israel, the latter must never forget that, after all, at first, they were offered hospitality in the land of Egypt and for this they should be eternally grateful. A text quoted by the Jewish moralists against ingratitude is: 'Whoso rewardeth evil for good, evil shall not depart from his house' (Proverbs 17: 13).

In this connection, a case is quoted in the *Responsa* (no. 202) of Joseph Ibn Migash (1077–141). When Ibn Migash's teacher, Isaac *Alfasi, fell ill, a man looked after him and saw to it that he was given medicinal baths in the man's house until he recovered his strength. Later on, the man fell heavily into debt and was obliged to have his bath-house evaluated in order to pay his creditors. Alfasi refused to be a judge in the case. He argued that it would obviously be wrong to make an unfair evaluation in favour of the man who had benefited him, since that would be to exercise bias. But if honesty compelled him to decide against the man, while this would be a sound legal decision, it would still constitute ingratitude to a benefactor. Ibn Migash ends on a religious note. If gratitude is to be expressed to this extent to human benefactors, how much more should it be expressed to God, the Source of all human life?

**Great Synagogue, Men of** The body of sages said to have flourished during the early days of the Second *Temple. The Men of the Great Synagogue or Great Assembly are mentioned as belonging to the chain of tradition at the beginning of Ethics of the Fathers: 'Moses received Torah from Sinai and delivered it to Joshua, and Joshua to the Elders, and the Elders to the Prophets, and the Prophets delivered it to the Men of the Great Synagogue. They said three things: Be deliberate in judgement, and raise many disciples, and make a fence for the Torah.' This sets the date of the institution in the time of *Ezra and, indeed, in some Rabbinic sources, Ezra is said to have been a member of the body. But in the following section of Ethics of the Fathers it says that Simeon the Just was one of the survivors (or remnants) of the Men of the Great Synagogue. Now Ezra's date is around the year 444 BCE, while Simeon the Just died around the year 270 BCE. How, then, could Simeon have been a survivor of the Men of the Great Synagogue? As a result of this kind of chronological problem and the evident legendary elements in many Rabbinic accounts of the Men of the Great Synagogue, some Christian scholars used to assert that the whole institution is fictitious, an idealized source for later Rabbinic Judaism. Many modern scholars, however, Jewish and non-Jewish, tend to see the references to the Men of the Great Synagogue as allusions not to a body that existed only at a particular time but to an ongoing activity extending over the first two centuries of the Second Temple. On this view, that they 'said' three things has to be understood as meaning that their activity can be summed up as establishing a successful administration of justice, teaching the Torah to as many students as possible, and protecting the laws of the Torah by building a fence around them, that is, by introducing safeguards against encroachment on the forbidden realm; they forbade, for instance, the handling of an axe on the Sabbath lest it be used to chop wood. In any event, references in the Rabbinic literature to the Men of the Great Synagogue can be taken to mean that ideas, rules, and prayers, seen to be pre-Rabbinic but post-biblical, were often fathered on them.

**Greetings** The best-known Jewish greeting is: 'Shalom alekhem' ('Peace to you') to which the reply is: 'Alekhem Shalom', 'To you be peace'. In modern Hebrew the form is usually simply Shalom. Greetings are known as *sheilat shalom* ('asking peace' or 'requesting welfare'), after the biblical verse (Exodus 18: 7): 'Moses went out to meet his father-in-law; he bowed low and kissed him; each asked after the other's welfare.' Since Shalom is said to be a divine name, this form of greeting is not used in the communal bath-house where people are naked. On the Sabbath people greet one another with: 'Good Sabbath' and on a festival with: 'Good Yom Tov'. In modern Israel the usual greeting for the Sabbath is 'Shabbat Shalom' and on a festival, 'Hag Sameah', 'A joyous festival'. '*Mazal tov' (literally 'A good star') is the standard form of congratulation. The greeting to one embarking on a journey by ship or plane is: 'Nesiah tovah', 'A good journey'. Every community has its own form of greetings for special occasions in addition to the above. For instance, English Jews greet a person who has lost a near relative with: 'I wish you long life', a form found nowhere else in the Jewish world.

# H

**Habad** The movement and tendency within *Hasidism which places particular emphasis on the role of the intellect in the life of religion. Habad (often spelled Chabad in English) is an acronym formed from the initial letters of the three Hebrew words: *Ḥokhmah, Binah, Daat*, standing, respectively, for Wisdom, Understanding, and Knowledge; in this context these refer to the three unfoldings of the divine mind taught in the Kabbalistic doctrine of the *Sefirot. Because of its special thrust, Habad is sometimes described by modern writers as the intellectual movement in Hasidism. There is some truth in this designation but it is a little misleading. Habad does attach great significance to contemplative thought and its writings do contain many profound religious ideas but it can by no stretch of the imagination be seen as rationalistic. The Habad thinkers build all their theories on ideas given in the Jewish sources and never try to reason out for themselves the basics of Judaism. They never feel the need, for example, to argue for the existence of God or that the Torah is revealed truth.

## History of Habad

The founder of the Habad tendency, *Shneur Zalman of Liady (1745–1813), became a foremost disciple of *Dov Baer, the Maggid of Mezhirech (d. 1772), disciple of the *Baal Shem Tov and organizer of the developing Hasidic movement. Shneur Zalman evidently owes many of his specific ideas to the Maggid and his son, known as Abraham the Angel; ideas to which Shneur Zalman gave systematic form. Although an offshoot of Hasidism, Habad is essentially a movement of its own, looked at with a degree of indifference and, on occasion, hostility, by the other Hasidic masters who, while admiring Shneur Zalman himself, believed that the Habad understanding of Hasidism is too intellectually orientated and too close to philosophy for comfort. Shneur Zalman's

successor in the leadership of the Habad group was his son, *Dov Baer of *Lubavitch (1773–1827). Shneur Zalman's chief disciple, Aaron of Starosselje (1766–1829) differed from Dov Baer in his interpretation of his master's teachings and set up as a Habad master in his own right, producing some of the most subtle writings in the Habad corpus. Dov Baer was succeeded by his son-in-law and nephew, Menahem Mendel of Lubavitch (1787–1866). Menahem Mendel's descendants served in the main as successive masters of the Lubavitch dynasty but a few established Habad schools of their own in opposition to Lubavitch, although their followers were eventually absorbed in Lubavitch. Thus, although the terms Lubavitch and Habad are now interchangeable, originally Habad was the more embracing term. Naturally, each of the Habad masters added nuances of his own, as did some of the Habad thinkers who were followers of the masters without being themselves masters. The essential Habad ideas are common to all the expositions.

## Habad Theology

Habad theology involves a radical interpretation of the Kabbalistic ideas of the famed sixteenth-century Safed mystic, Isaac *Luria, known as the Ari. In the Lurianic Kabbalah, the first step in the divine creative process is a withdrawal or contraction of the *En Sof, the Infinite ground of being, God as He is in Himself, 'from Himself into Himself'. This act of divine limitation is known as Tzimtzum. As a result of the Tzimtzum an 'empty space' is left into which the light of En Sof then streams forth eventually to produce, through a further series of contractions, the Sefirot and through these all the worlds on high and the material world experienced by the senses.

The basic problem is how the Tzimtzum and especially the 'empty space' are to be understood. The Kabbalists generally understand the 'empty space' in other than spatial terms, as a metaphor for that which is other than God, very few entertaining the bizarre notion that there really is a kind of immense circular hole in En Sof into which the universe has emerged. But even if the Tztimtzum is understood in more sophisticated terms to denote spiritual processes in the divine realm taking place outside space and time, humans do have the experience of space and time and the physical world certainly seems real enough. Since this is so, the problem the doctrine of Tzimtzum was intended to solve, how there can be a universe apart and separate from the limitless and infinite En Sof, still remains as obdurate as ever. In Habad thought the extremely radical solution is that, from the point of view of ultimate reality, there is no universe. The universe and the creatures who inhabit the universe only appear to enjoy existence. From our point of view, the world is indeed real, but not from God's point of view, as the Habad thinkers put it. The meaning of Tzimtzum is not that it results in a real world, only that God allows the apparent existence of that which is other than He. The all-pervasive divine light is screened from view and this screening is what Tzimtzum denotes. The Habad thinkers stop short of saying that the world is an illusion, as in some varieties of Far Eastern thought, since such a view would tend to deny the reality of the practical laws and observances of the Torah which only have meaning in a real world. Instead, the distinction is drawn between the universe from God's point of view and the universe from our point of view, a concept difficult to grasp, and one which renders opaque the meaning of 'real'. The Habad view is basically one of acosmism ('there is no universe') or *panentheism ('all is in God').

Shneur Zalman gives the illustration of the sun and its rays. We see the sun's rays because we are so far distant from the sun but there are no rays in the sun itself. Similarly, creatures are sufficiently remote, in a non-spatial sense, from God to enable them to perceive the material world as real and as apart from Him but through which His glory is manifested. It follows that the nearer humans are to God in spirit, the closer they approximate to the mystical ideal of *annihilation of selfhood. The more humans perceive the ultimate reality that is God, the less they become aware of themselves and the world of the senses. Habad

teachers like to tell of Shneur Zalman being asked what he saw when he lay on his deathbed. 'I see only the divine light that pervades all that there is,' was his reply.

Habad contemplation involves a survey in the mind of the whole complicated process described in the Kabbalistic scheme, the gradual unfolding and screening of the divine reaching from En Sof to the Sefirot, from the Sefirot to the lower worlds on high, and from these to our material world. All the complex details of the process as described in the Lurianic Kabbalah are to be followed in the mind with a view to grasping the divine unity, that in all the multiplicity of being there is only the One. When the Sefirotic map is perceived in the mind in descending order, from En Sof through all the worlds, this is termed 'the higher unification'. When the map is drawn in the mind in the opposite direction, in ascending order, from the material universe through to the En Sof, it is termed 'the lower unification'. The Habad contemplatives try to achieve both unifications especially when they recite the *Shema, their minds undertaking the long and hazardous journey up on high and back again. The more zealous of the Habad devotees have been known to spend a whole hour and more lost in contemplation while reciting the first verse of the Shema.

*Habad Psychology*

According to the Kabbalistic doctrine of the Sefirot, Hokhmah and Binah (and Daat as a harmonizing principle between the two) represent the process of the divine mind as it unfolds to create the universe. These are the higher Sefirot. The seven lower Sefirot belong to the divine emotions, so to speak, the divine love and power and the various manifestations of these. Since the process begins in the divine mind, in the will to create and to 'plan' the details of creation, the divine emotions can be said to result from the divine thought. The Sefirotic processes are found, too, in the human soul, man being created in God's image. Among humans, too, the ideal is for the emotions to be stirred by thought, not thought by the emotions. Habad does not believe that moral and spiritual improvement of the character can be realized by any direct assault on the emotions. Where the love and fear of God seem to erupt without prior contemplation on the divine glory and majesty, the emotions are spurious. It is only through profound reflection on how the divine light pervades all that the religious emotions can be authentically awakened and the heart leap for joy and in numinous fear. Critics of the Habad approach among the Hasidim refuse to believe that the emotions cannot be tackled head-on and maintain that the Habad claim can easily result in a failure adequately to control lustful or vicious feelings. When a young Habad Hasid described with great learning and profundity to the fiery *Rebbe of *Kotsk the details regarding the relationships among the powers of the upper worlds, the Kotsker brought the young man down to earth by coarsely protesting: 'And what is with the navel?'

The most startling aspect of Habad psychology is its doctrine of the two souls, a doctrine derived, like other Habad ideas, from the Lurianic Kabbalah but given a more radical thrust. Every Jew, the doctrine runs, possesses two souls. The first of these is the 'animal soul', the vital force by which man lives and through which he gives expression to his will, thoughts, emotions, and actions; hence it is also called the 'intellectual soul'. In the Kabbalah, the impure forces in the spiritual world are known as the *kelipot*, 'shells' or 'husks', which surround the domain of the holy and are nourished by it. The 'animal soul' of the Jew derives from one of the *kelipot* that is not totally impure but contains an admixture of good and evil. There is a taint of evil, produced by the 'animal soul' stemming from the realm of the *kelipot*, in all willing, thinking, feeling, and doing. This is the Habad version of 'original sin'. Attempts have been made, not very successfully, to equate the notion with Freudian theories about the id, the ego, and the super-ego (see PSYCHOLOGY).

In addition to the 'animal soul', there is a 'divine soul', a portion of En Sof, deeply hidden in the recesses of the Jewish psyche. When the 'divine soul' is bestirred, through contemplation on the divine by the 'animal soul', God meets Himself, so to speak. Thus in Habad contemplative exercises the tremendous effort is made not only to cause the all to be embraced by the divine unity but also for the divine in man to meet itself, as it were. All this was seen as scandalous and heretical by opponents of Habad. The scandal is aggravated by Habad's further elaboration that only Jews possess a 'divine soul'. Moreover, the 'animal soul' of *Gentiles, according to Habad, derives from

the wholly impure *kelipot*, unlike the 'animal soul' of Jews which at least contains an admixture of the good. The conclusion drawn in Habad is that a Gentile is incapable of complete *disinterestedness, every thought, emotion, and deed, no matter how worthy in itself, being tainted with love of self. More recent Habad thinkers have tried to remove or weaken the offensiveness of this version of Jewish superiority by demythologizing the whole concept in order to render it more palatable; pointing out, for example, that a convert to Judaism acquires the 'divine soul' on his conversion and that very few Jews are capable of a completely disinterested thought or deed (see CHOSEN PEOPLE).

For all the criticism that has been levelled against it, Habad thought has won the admiration of many religious thinkers for its profound probings of the mystery of the divine in its relationship to human beings and to the world as a whole.

> Roman A. Foxbrunner, *HABAD: The Hasidism of R. Shneur Zalman of Lyady* (Tuscaloosa, Ala. and London, 1992).
> Louis Jacobs, *Seeker of Unity: The Life and Works of Aaron of Starosselje* (London, 1966).
> Naftali Loewenthal, *Communicating 'the' Infinite: The Emergence of the Habad School* (Chicago, 1990).

**Habakkuk** A prophet whose date is uncertain, although a number of scholars draw the conclusion from the book that bears his name that he prophesied towards the end of the seventh or at the beginning of the sixth century BCE. The unusual name of the prophet has been connected with an Assyrian word meaning 'fragrant herb'. In the Zohar the name Habakkuk is said to be derived from the Hebrew root *havak*, 'to embrace' and the prophet is identified with the son *Elisha promised to the Shunnamite woman, saying: 'At this season next year, you will be *embracing* a son' (2 Kings 4: 16). The son of the Shunnamite woman was revived by Elisha from the dead, so, according to the legend, when Habakkuk speaks of apprehending the fear of God he is recalling his own death and revival.

The book of Habakkuk is the eighth in the book of the Twelve Prophets (see BIBLE) and consists of two chapters of prophetic narration and a third chapter in the form of a psalm. Habakkuk boldly challenges God on why the wicked seem to prosper while the righteous are victimized, but he affirms that God's justice will eventually triumph. Habakkuk's declaration, 'the righteous shall live by his faith' (2: 4) is described in the Talmud (*Makkot* 24a) as a statement upon which all the precepts of the Torah are based.

S. M. Lehrman, 'Habakkuk: Introduction and Commentary' in A Cohen (ed.), *The Twelve Prophets* (London, 1970), 211–29.

**'Had Gadya'** 'One kid'; the song, printed in the final pages of the Passover *Haggadah, with which the *Seder ends. 'Had Gadya' is in *Aramaic, in a form that lends itself easily to the jingling melodies in which it is sung. Some use the tune of 'Three Blind Mice'. The doggerel resembles in form such nursery rhymes as 'This is the House that Jack Built'. 'Had Gadya' begins with: 'One kid, one kid, that father bought for two *zuzim*' and then goes on to tell of the cat that ate the kid, the dog that bit the cat, the stick that beat the dog, and so on until the final stanza: 'Then came the Holy One, blessed be He, and smote the angel of death, who slew the slaughterer, who slaughtered the ox, that drank the water, that quenched the fire, that burned the stick, that beat the dog, that bit the cat, that ate the kid, that father bought for two *zuzim*. One kid, one kid.'

The song first appeared in the Middle Ages and was adopted by Ashkenazi Jews as what they evidently considered to be a suitable ending to the Seder, probably in order to keep the children happy and awake during the long service. The motif of holding the interest of the children is prominent in Rabbinic discussions of the Passover celebrations. Sephardi Jews did not have the 'Had Gadya' as part of the Seder and some Sephardim, we learn, ridiculed this intrusion on the solemnities of the occasion. The Sephardi Rabbi J. D. H. *Azulai, however, relates that a ban had been placed on such spoilsports. It is wrong, he remarks, to call any well-established Jewish custom 'stupid'. In this connection, 'Had Gadya' is often quoted in the discussions regarding Jewish *customs of doubtful origin. Once they have been widely accepted, they should not be negated.

Nevertheless, Rabbinic commentators to the Passover Haggadah sought to read various religious ideas into the Had Gadya, treating it, for example, as an allegory of the survival of the Jews, the 'one kid' who still lives at the end when their oppressors have vanished from the scene. Others have interpreted the 'kid' to be

the Torah which the Father, God, bought for the children of Israel for two *zuzim*, representing the love and fear of God by which the Torah is 'acquired'.

**Hafetz Hayyim** Israel Meir Kagan (1838–1933), Talmudic and Rabbinic scholar, ethical and religious teacher, venerated by Jews all over the world, especially those in the Lithuanian tradition, for his saintliness and learning. Israel Meir (his original surname was not Kagan but Poupko) is universally known by the title of his first book directed against the evils of slander and malicious gossip. He published this work anonymously, its title taken from the verses: 'What is he that delighteth in life [*he-ḥafetz ḥayyim*], and loveth many days that he may see good? Keep thy tongue from evil, and thy lips from speaking guile' (Psalms 34: 13–14). Although the Hafetz Hayyim occupied no official Rabbinic position, his later reputation as an authority in practical Jewish law rested secure on his work on the subject. His life of extreme piety caused him also to be acknowledged among Lithuanian Jews as a charismatic personality akin to the *Zaddik in *Hasidism around which numerous legends accumulate. He has good right to be considered as the most influential figure in twentieth century Orthodox Judaism, appealing also in his homely approach to ordinary Jews with no pretensions to learning. With his gifted pen he produced both scholarly and popular works, all of which are still assiduously studied and some of which, a sure sign of popularity, have been translated into *Yiddish.

The Hafetz Hayyim, though the supreme patron of the Lithuanian *Yeshivot, did not himself study in a Yeshivah. Indeed, in his youth he was not an outstanding Talmudist and showed little promise of his future greatness in this field. A reliable report has it that the Maskilim, followers of the *Haskalah movement of enlightenment, tried to win the young boy over to their camp but he resisted their blandishments, and remained indifferent to general studies and modern scholarship all his life. His approach to Judaism was other-worldly. When an American visitor to his home saw how bare was the sage's room, he asked him: 'Where is your furniture?' 'Where is *your* furniture?' the Hafetz Hayyim asked the man. 'I am only a visitor here,' was the reply. 'I, too, am a visitor to this world,' was the typical reply. After his marriage, he and his wife owned a shop in the Lithuania town of Radin, she serving the customers and he keeping the books. Numerous stories are told of his scrupulous honesty. He once discovered that a non-Jewish customer had paid for a herring but had not taken it away with him. The Hafetz Hayyim had forgotten the man's identity, so for a time he gave every non-Jewish customer a free herring. He remained in Radin for the rest of his life, students at first coming to his home to imbibe his wisdom. At a later date, a large Yeshivah was established at Radin, which became a metropolis of Jewish learning in the old style. He was also a leader of the Orthodox movement, Aggudat Israel, and became very active in the support of Yeshivot everywhere. When his fame as an author spread, he earned his living by the sale of his books, seeing to it at all times, in order not to defraud the buyers, that the books were in the best condition and offered at a very fair price.

*Works*

As noted, the Hafetz Hayyim's first work on the laws of slander and malicious gossip has the title by which he became subsequently known. He was, it seems, led to compile the work because he had witnessed fierce quarrels in Lithuanian Jewry that caused communities to be torn apart. The novelty in the work consists in an attempt to provide detailed rules on when and where not to speak, a subject that had hitherto been confined to the moralistic literature. Critics of the work argued that it was a mistake to apply the rigidities of the *Halakhah to a subject that should really be treated under the heading of *Aggadah with its more flexible approach. There is substance in the criticism yet the work proved to be a very useful guide in this sphere. A critic from the ranks of the Haskalah, on the other hand, protested that the work seemed to be saying that the only thing for a Jew to do was never to speak at all. Such a criticism is grossly unfair, though it must be admitted that the Hafetz Hayyim comes down strongly even against the pleasure of harmless gossip. All gossip is harmful, the sage maintains. For all that, the work demonstrates from the Rabbinic sources that it is permitted to speak ill of persons when to remain silent will result in harm to others. For instance, if it is noticed that a naïve person is about to enter into partnership with a man one knows to be a

rogue, it is one's duty to tell the truth to avoid advantage being taken of the innocent. Presumably, the Hafetz Hayyim would not have disapproved of investigative journalism of the right kind.

The Hafetz Hayyim's most famous work is his Halakhic compendium, entitled *Mishnah Berurah (Clear Teaching)*, on the practical religious life. This work, in six volumes, is in the form of a commentary to the first section of the *Shulḥan Arukh, the standard Code of Jewish law, and, as the name implies, purports to guide the student through the labyrinth of differing views and opinions to enable him to discover the actual rule to be followed in practice. Although Rabbis have occasionally contested some of the rulings in the work, it has come to be the standard guide in this branch of Jewish law. The author rarely gives his own unsupported opinions but generally prefers to state the law as this appears by conflating the opinions of the great authorities and by noticing how pious Jews actually conduct themselves in matters of doubtful procedures.

The Hafetz Hayyim was a *priest, a *Kohen (hence the name Kagan, the Russian form of Cohen) and he believed without reservation that soon the *Messiah would come, the *Temple would be rebuilt, and the sacrifices would be offered, for which events the priests, in particular, had to be ready and to know all the correct procedures. Although Maimonides had recorded the laws of the Temple sacrifices in his great Code, and although the Talmudic tractates dealing with these topics had always been studied, the whole subject was naturally purely academic in the pre-Messianic age. The Hafetz Hayyim's *Likkutey Halakhot (Collection of Laws)* had the aim of providing clear Halakhic rulings for life in the Messianic age!

Two other guides by this prolific author are *Maḥaney Yisrael (Israel's Camp)*, a manual for Jewish soldiers in the Russian army, and *Nidḥey Yisrael (the Dispersed of Israel)* in which advice is given to immigrants to America on how to remain faithful to Orthodox Judaism in the new hostile environment in which the task was extremely difficult. In both these works, the author is prepared to find leniencies whenever possible, appreciating that conditions in the army and in America are such that too strict an application of the law is bound to result in failure because of excessive demands.

The Hasidic masters of his day also had a

high regard for the Hafetz Hayyim even though his legalistic approach was not to their taste. Reform and Conservative Jews, while recognizing that the Hafetz Hayyim's simplistic approach and fundamentalism were not for them (this applied, to a large extent, to the neo-Orthodox as well), never attacked him and still saw him as a saintly figure, whose integrity, practical wisdom, and deep piety made him a model of traditional Jewish living at its best. In point of fact, the Hafetz Hayyim's simple style was misleading. It was said of him that his piety served to cloak his immense learning. He was not only a saint, it was said, but a Gaon (see GEONIM), a genius in Talmudic studies.

M. M. Yosher, *Saint and Sage* (New York, 1937).

**Haftarah** The 'termination', the prophetic reading which follows the *reading of the Torah. When the practice arose of adding a reading from the prophets after the reading of the Torah in the synagogue is uncertain. A popular view, which goes back to David *Abudarham, is that in a time of persecution, perhaps that of Antiochus in the days of the *Maccabees, when a decree was issued against the reading of the Torah in public, readings from the prophets, not covered by the decree, were substituted. The practice is, in any event, ancient, seemingly referred to in the *New Testament's reference (Acts 13: 15) to the reading of the law and the prophets in the synagogue. The Haftarot for the festivals are given in the Talmud but the current arrangement for the Sabbath by Sabbath readings is medieval and there is, in fact, no universal scheme; on occasion the Haftarah for a particular weekly reading is different in the Ashkenazi and Sephardi rites. Since the Talmud advises against certain prophetic readings being adopted for the Haftarah, it would appear that, in Talmudic times, each community picked its own readings from the prophetic books.

There is always some association, however slight, between the particular Torah portion and the Haftarah. On occasion, a particular Haftarah was chosen simply because of a similarity of expression, but usually it was selected because of a similarity of theme. For instance, the Haftarah chosen for the Sabbath when the account of the theophany at *Sinai is read from the Torah, is Isaiah 6, describing the prophet's vision in the Temple; in the Torah portion, God appears to the people, in the Haftarah to the prophet. The Haftarah is chanted with a different melody from that used for the Torah reading (see CANTILLATION).

The Haftarah for each of the Sabbaths and festivals is provided in editions of the *Pentateuch intended for liturgical use, for instance, in *The Pentateuch and Haftorahs* edited by J. H. Hertz (London, 1960; Hertz uses the incorrect 'Haftorahs' because of the similarity in sound to 'Torah').

**Haggadah** 'The telling', the book containing the passages dealing with the theme of the Exodus, recited at the Passover *Seder. The reading of the Haggadah is based on the verse: 'You shall tell your son on that day: it is because of what the Lord did for me when I came forth out of Egypt' (Exodus 13: 8). Although the Talmud mentions some features of the 'telling' by the father at the Seder, no formal Haggadah was produced until the Middle Ages, when the current form was established in essence and became universally accepted. The Haggadah now contains passages from early and late sources dealing with the Exodus, instructions for the conduct of the Seder, psalms and other songs of praise, *grace before and after meals, concluding in the Ashkenazi version with a number of table songs (see *'Had Gadya'). It has been estimated that no fewer than 2,000 different editions of the Haggadah have been published. No other Jewish sacred book has enjoyed such popularity. The Haggadah is, of course, a sacred book. Its theme, the delivery of the people of Israel from Egyptian bondage, is more than a celebration of freedom as such; it is a celebration of the freedom the people of Israel attained in order to become God's people and receive His Torah. Yet even secular Jews enjoy the Passover Seder and read the Haggadah as the ancient manifesto of liberty for all. Very few secular Jews, however, have gone so far as to produce an edition of the Haggadah, like the notorious 'Godless Haggadah', from which all the references to God and His deliverance have been removed.

Many Haggadot have been published with commentaries by outstanding scholars and many are richly illustrated (see ART). Illuminated manuscripts and early editions of the Haggadah are now highly prized collectors' items.

Joseph Elias, *The Haggadah* (New York, 1980). Chaim Raphael, *A Feast of History* (London, 1972).

**Haggai** Prophet after the return of the people from the Babylonian exile at the time of the process of rebuilding the Temple. Although details of Haggai's life are not given in the book that bears his name, the date of his prophecies is clearly implied. The prophecies in this little book of only two chapters were delivered in the year 520 BCE. This does not mean, however, that the book itself, which is the tenth in the book of the Twelve Prophets (see BIBLE), was composed at that date or that it was necessarily composed by the prophet himself. In the Rabbinic tradition, Haggai, together with *Zechariah and *Malachi, are the last of the prophets. After them, the Holy Spirit ceased in Israel. Thus these three are often described as the last of the great prophets. The name Haggai seems to be associated with the Hebrew word *ḥag*, 'festival'; perhaps the name means 'one born on a festival'. The prophet urges the people, who had delayed for too long, to continue to build the Temple, whose glory in the future will exceed the glory of Solomon's Temple.

To illustrate his message, Haggai (2: 11) puts a question to the *priests regarding the laws of ritual contamination. This question and whether or not the priests gave the correct ruling is discussed at length in the Talmud and it is probably on the basis of this that the Talmud attributes to Haggai a number of other rulings and so turns him into a legal authority as well as a prophet (see *Halakhah).

Eli Cashdan, 'Haggai', in A. Cohen (ed.), *The Twelve Prophets* (London, 1970); 253–64.

**Hai Gaon** Head of the college of Pumbedita at the end of the Geonic period (see GEONIM) (939–1038). Hai served in the Gaonite of Pumbedita together with his father, *Sherira Gaon. When Sherira died, Hai was inducted formally into the office with the pomp and ceremony typical of the institution. It is reported that there was read in the Babylonian synagogues the narrative of *Solomon's succession to the throne of *David (1 Kings 2: 10–12), adapted to the occasion: 'And Sherira slept with his fathers . . . And Hai sat upon the throne of Sherira his father; and his kingdom was established firmly.' Hai was the son-in-law of the Gaon of Sura, Samuel Ibn Hofni, whose rationalism in Bible interpretation was not to Hai's taste.

A large proportion of the extant Geonic *Responsa consists of the replies of Hai to his questioners not only in Babylon but in North Africa and Europe. These Responsa throw much light on Hai's activity as the foremost legal authority of his day. Hai had a strong mystical bent, describing in a Responsum the techniques to be employed for the ascent of the soul.

As a theologian of note, Hai was among the earliest Jewish thinkers to discuss, in a Responsum, the vexed question of how to reconcile God's foreknowledge with human freedom, a problem of concern to the Arabic thinkers in Hai's day. In another Responsum, Hai reacts to Islamic fatalism when he considers the idea that every man has a life-span fixed beforehand. When a man is murdered, Hai was asked, does this mean that even had he not been slain, he would have died, in any event, at that particular moment? Hai replies that we simply do not know. We can either suppose that if he had not been murdered he would have died at that moment in any event, or we can suppose that if he had not been murdered he would have lived on until a later date. But, it might be objected, supposing a murderer killed a large number of persons on the same day, is it plausible to suggest that they would all have died in any event on the same day? 'Why not?' replies Hai. Experience shows us that a large number of people do sometimes die at the same time, when, for example, a building collapses or when a ship goes down and all the passengers are drowned. But if the victim of a murder would have died in any event, Hai asks, why is the murderer punished for his crime? Hai replies that it is the act of murder that constitutes the crime. The murderer deserves to be punished for the evil act that was his and his alone.

This Responsum has been quoted at length to demonstrate Hai's theological approach, one in which he is thoroughly familiar with the Islamic thought of his day (he knew Arabic and some of his writings are in this language) but proudly defends Judaism against its critics. The Talmudic Judaism, of which Hai was the great representative, was attacked also from within the Jewish camp by the *Karaites.

The Karaites poured scorn on the Talmud for its grossly anthropomorphic descriptions of the Deity. The Talmud even says that God prays, wears *tefillin, and wraps Himself around with a prayer shawl. Hai's reply is that the meaning is that God taught Moses how to pray and how to use the *tefillin* in prayer. When the

Talmud gives God's prayer as: 'May it be My will that My mercy may suppress My anger, and that My mercy may prevail over My attributes so that I may deal with My children in the attribute of mercy', the meaning is not that God prays to Himself but that He taught Moses how to recite the kind of prayer that will result in the flow of the divine mercy. Hai is not original here. This interpretation goes back, in fact, to Hai's predecessor, *Saadiah. On the general question of apparently strange Talmudic statements, Hai observes that these belong to the *Aggadah and it is a sound principle that one does not learn from the Aggadah. It has to be appreciated, moreover, that, in their Aggadah the Talmudic Rabbis were often like poets who describe natural phenomena in anthropomorphic terms. Hai draws attention to Greek mythology in which natural phenomena are endowed with personality. This statement of Hai amounts to an acknowledgement that there is a mythological element in Rabbinic thought.

> Louis Jacobs, *Theology in the Responsa* (London, 1975), 1–13.

**Halakhah** The legal side of Judaism, in contradistinction to *Aggadah; the latter embracing all the non-legal ideas. In the earliest Rabbinic period, the term Halakhah (from the root *halakh*, 'to go' or 'to walk') was confined to a particular ruling or decision. But, subsequently, while the original meaning was retained, the term Halakhah was also and chiefly used for the whole system. The Halakhah came to denote that aspect of Judaism which is concerned with Jewish *law as a whole; the rules and regulations by which the Jew 'walks' through life. Traditional Jews, brushing aside the charge of legalism often directed against Judaism by hostile critics, have always seen the Halakhah as the most distinctive feature of the Jewish religion. Judaism is not content only with providing broad religious, social, and ethical principles, but expects its adherents to give body to the principles through the concreteness and precision of the Halakhah. In this sense, Judaism has correctly been described, by a non-Jewish thinker, as 'the religion of doing the will of God', a religion with its emphasis on the deed. This is not to say, however, that Judaism is only a religion of law and is indifferent to questions of belief and truth (see DOGMAS). A. J. *Heschel has coined the term 'pan-Halakhism'

for the view, often held by some contemporary Orthodox Jews that nothing matters apart from Halakhah. In point of fact, the supremacy of the Halakhah can itself only be defended on extra-Halakhic grounds, by a philosophy of the Halakhah. Just as a Judaism of Aggadah without Halakhah is traditionally unsound, it is an equal distortion of the religion to postulate a Halakhic Judaism without Aggadah.

*Sources of the Halakhah*

The main source of the Halakhah is, of course, the *Pentateuch, which contains three Codes of law (Exodus 21–3; Leviticus 19; Deuteronomy 21–5) and particular laws in other parts of the work. The prophets also refer here and there to laws not found in the Pentateuch but, in the Rabbinic scheme, no prophet was ever authorized to introduce new laws and, on this view, the prophets are simply recording the 'law of Moses'; that is, although these laws are not actually found in the Pentateuch, they, too, were given, together with the laws found there, by God to Moses, either on Mount *Sinai or subsequently during the forty-year journey through the wilderness. This is the Rabbinic doctrine of the two Torahs, the *Written Torah of the Bible, supplemented and interpreted by the *Oral Torah. The Oral Torah denotes both those interpretations of the Pentateuchal laws handed down by tradition from Moses and the exegesis of the laws by the Jewish sages. In addition, the sages of Israel are seen as possessing the *authority to introduce new legislation. Laws which stem from the Written and Oral Torah are referred to as biblical laws; laws introduced by the sages are termed Rabbinic laws. There are technical differences between the two types of law—for instance, cases of doubt with regard to biblical law are treated strictly, those with regard to Rabbinic law, leniently. All this material, the oral law and the Rabbinic legislation, are found in the Talmuds, Babylonian and Palestinian, and in the other Rabbinic sources known as the Halakhic Midrashim. Although, in the early period, the *Sadducees rejected the whole doctrine of the Oral Torah, and much later, the *Karaites rejected the Talmud, it is the Talmud that became the ultimate source of the Halakah as traditionally conceived.

The problem is that in the Talmud and the Rabbinic literature in general, there are numerous debates among the Rabbis on questions of interpretation so that, as the Talmud states, it is difficult to find a clear Halakhah anywhere. The Talmud is not a code of law but a gigantic work containing all the debates and elaborations, largely in a purely academic form. Yet, occasionally, the Talmud does gives a final ruling, the *halakhah* in particular instances. For example, according to the Talmudic accounts, the great debates between the House of *Hillel and the House of *Shammai are, with just a few exceptions, always to be decided in practice in favour of the House of Hillel. Where such clear rulings are not given in the Talmud, attempts had to be made to discover the mind of the Talmud, so to speak, as this could be gauged from the Talmudic academic dialectics. This exercise leaves room for considerable differences of opinion. On the academic level, it is possible to say that Rabbi *A* says this and Rabbi *B* says that and to discuss the reasons why, without any guidance being given as to which view is to be followed in practice. It became necessary for codes of law to be drawn up in which the practical laws would be stated with precision (see CODES OF LAW). The three main Codes, the *Mishneh Torah* of Maimonides, the Tur of Jacob ben Asher, and the *Shulḥan Arukh* of Joseph *Karo, all had their antagonists who gave, in many instances, rulings different from theirs. This is true even of the *Shulḥan Arukh*, although this, at the most widely accepted of the three Codes can be seen, in a loose sense, as the standard Code of the Halakhah.

The above is, in broad outline, the traditional understanding of Halakhic transmission—from God to Moses, through the prophets, through the Men of the *Great Synagogue, the Talmudic Rabbis and the Talmudic literature, down to the Codes. In addition to the Codes, the various *Responsa collections enjoy authority as sources of the Halakhah, as do the commentators to the Talmud, and, to some extent, the *customs of the Jewish people. 'Transmission' is the key word in the traditional scheme. From Moses onwards, through the whole chain of tradition, the Halakhah is seen as the word of God handed down intact from generation to generation. The debates themselves were seen as part of this static process. Although, obviously, only one opinion could be decisive for practice, the whole system, debates and all, was seen in terms of static transmission. A Talmudic saying about the

debates between the houses of Hillel and Shammai has often been quoted in this connection. This statement, attributed in the Talmud (*Eruvin* 13b) to a heavenly voice, has it that 'Both these and these are the words of the living God but the Halakhah [the ruling] follows the opinions of the House of Hillel.' A number of distinguished Talmudists in the Middle Ages and many in contemporary Orthodoxy have understood this in literal fashion to mean that when God gave the Torah to Moses He gave both opinions, even though only one can be followed in practice.

## Development of the Halakhah

The static picture described above has been challenged by modern historical-critical scholarship (see JÜDISCHE WISSENSCHAFT). Scholarly research has succeeded in demonstrating that the Halakhah, like other religious institutions, Jewish and non-Jewish, has had a history. Judaism, in different periods, has reacted to the conditions of the time, so as to produce the particular Halakhah required by the time. The three law Codes in the Pentateuch are seen by the critics (see BIBLICAL CRITICISM) as stemming from three different periods, the laws of each being governed by conditions obtaining when the Code was compiled. So, too, the Halakhah itself and the doctrine of the Oral Torah upon which it is based are now seen not as dropping down from heaven ready-made but as evolving as the result of a lengthy process. And there is the problem of the manner in which the Halakhah is derived from Scripture. There are numerous instances where the scriptural support given in the Talmudic literature for a particular law is so weak that the law was obviously established on other grounds and then support for it was discovered in Scripture. This can only mean that the real basis for many of the laws is in the life of the people. Throughout the history of the Halakhah, scholarship has shown, the Halakhists were not only concerned with discovering what the law is but with what it must be if the other values of Judaism are to be realized. Research has now shown, too, that in extra-Talmudic sources such as the *Apocrypha, *Josephus, the *Dead Sea Scrolls, and *Philo, details of the early Halakhah are different from Talmudic Halakhah. Moreover, the most formative era of the Halakhah is from the return from the Babylonian exile down to the age of the Maccabees, and this period is shrouded in obscurity. For all the difficulties inherent in the attempt to discover how the Halakhah developed, and the difficulties are formidable, without any consensus having emerged among scholars, it has become fairly clear that there is a history of the Halakhah and the static picture of the tradition is not a true picture of the tradition itself. Yet, as in every legal system, the Halakhah proceeds by its own principles in which the law is established by precedent and consensus. The traditional Halakhists cannot allow historical considerations to obtrude when rendering their Halakhic discussions, the law having an internal life of its own. The problem of reconciling the static notion of the tradition with the dynamic notion revealed by modern scholarship has become particularly acute for contemporary Jews. This conflict is partly responsible for the differing attitudes to the Halakhic among religious Jews, especially when there are increasing numbers of religious Jews who enjoy expertise in both the profundities of traditional Jewish learning and the subtleties of modern scholarship.

### Attitudes towards the Halakhah

In every version of Orthodox Judaism, the Halakhah in its traditional form is sacrosanct as the sole guide for the application of the law to Jewish life. Some Orthodox scholars, fully aware of the findings of modern scholarship, tend to draw a distinction between theory and practice. The scholar can and should have an open mind on the question of how the Halakhah has come to be, while following scrupulously the demands of the Halakhah in practice. The one is a matter of pure scholarship, the other of religion in action. To take an illustration from the Hebrew language, a scholar may investigate the origin and development of Hebrew as a Semitic language but his researches will in no way affect his use of Hebrew in prayer and worship since this language and no other, whatever its origins and development, became the 'sacred tongue'. Reform Judaism, from the beginning, had a far lesser appreciation of the role of the Halakhah in Judaism, preferring to see the religion more in terms of the prophetic thrust in the direction of ethical monotheism. In more recent years, however, as evidenced in the work of Rabbi Solomon B. Freehof, Reform has acquired a new respect for the Halakhah, at least in those areas, such as in synagogal life, where many Reform Jews wish to follow the traditional norms where these are not in conflict with Reform ideology. Conservative Judaism adopts a middle-of-the-road stance, accepting the traditional Halakhah in broad terms but feeling free to allow historical considerations to have a voice in Halakhic application.

Boaz Cohen, *Law and Tradition in Judaism* (New York, 1959).
Solomon B. Freehof, *Reform Responsa and Current Reform Responsa* (New York, 1973). Louis Jacobs, *A Tree of Life: Diversity, Flexibility and Creativity in Jewish Law* (Oxford, 1984).

**Halitzah** 'Taking off' the shoe, the rite by means of which a widow whose husband has died without issue is released from the bond of levirate *marriage. In the book of Deuteronomy (25: 5–10) the law is promulgated that the widow of a childless man is obliged to marry his brother but if the levir ('brother-in-law') refuses to marry her he has to undergo the rite of Halitzah:

'But if the man does not want to marry his brother's widow, his brother's widow shall appear before the elders in the gate and declare, "My husband's brother refuses to establish a name in Israel for his brother; he will not perform the duty of a levir." The elders of his town shall then summon him and talk to him. If he insists, saying, "I do not want to marry her", his brother's widow shall go up to him in the presence of the elders, pull [from the root *halatz*, hence the name Halitzah] the shoe off his foot, spit in his face, and make this declaration: "Thus shall be done to the man who will not build up his brother's house!"' (Verses 7–9.)

From this it appears that the purpose of Halitzah was to put the levir publicly to shame for refusing to do his duty of marrying his brother's widow. The widow is considered bound to the levir in that she cannot marry anyone else until she has been released by Halitzah.

In the Rabbinic sources the opinion is expressed that while it is clear from the biblical passage that the ideal is for the levir to marry the widow, 'nowadays', he should not be allowed do so but must release her through Halitzah. The reason for the change is that since levirate marriage involves a man marrying his brother's widow, an act otherwise forbidden, the levir must be motivated solely by his wish to carry out his religious obligation and it can no longer be assumed that the levir's intention is 'for the sake of heaven'. Another opinion is recorded, however, that levirate marriage has priority over Halitzah. The difference of opinion continued for centuries, some Sephardi and Oriental communities following the opinion which prefers levirate marriage to Halitzah. The Chief Rabbinate of the State of Israel introduced the law that Halitzah is always to be preferred for all Jews in the State, whatever their original practice was. Obviously, once the ban on polygamy had been established, Halitzah was the only option in any event where the levir already had a wife. There is evidence that sectarians in early Rabbinic times understood literally the reference to the widow spitting in the levir's face but, according to the Rabbis, the word be-fanav has to be translated not as 'in his face' but 'to his face' and the widow simply spits on the floor in front of the levir.

The Halitzah rite, as now practised with great solemnity, is based on the elaborations found in the Talmud and the Codes. A court of three Rabbis, to which two others who need not be Rabbis are added, meet on the previous day to establish the place where the rite is to be carried out, usually but not necessarily in the court-house. On the next day, the widow is expected to fast until after the Halitzah has been performed. She and the levir appear before the court and she recites in Hebrew the words in the Deuteronomic passage and he recites the declaration that he does not wish to marry her. A special shoe made of leather with straps, the property of the court, is given formally as a gift to the levir, who puts the shoe on his right foot and walks in it a few paces. The widow then bends down, holds the levir's foot in her left hand, unties the shoe with her right hand, removes the shoe, and casts it aside. She then spits in front of the levir and recites the Deuteronomic declaration: 'Thus shall be done to the man who will not build up his brother's house.' The court then offers the prayer: 'May it be God's will that the daughters of Israel will never have to resort to levirate marriage or Halitzah.'

Orthodox and Conservative Jews still observe this time-honoured rite, requiring the widow to obtain the Halitzah release before she can remarry. Some, perhaps many, Jews have given expression to a marked aversion to Halitzah on the grounds that the levir is humiliated for failing to do his duty when he is no longer allowed to carry it out. The spitting has also been seen as repugnant and some people have morbid superstitions about the rite, aggravated by the custom in Eastern European communities for the levir to rest his back against the board upon which the dead was washed before burial. Against this, widows left without a child by a deceased husband have been known to value the rite as affording them psychological relief by denoting a complete severance with the past in order for a new life to begin. The problem of the *agunah can arise where the brother-in-law refuses to participate in the Halitzah rite unless he is given a substantial sum of money. Rabbis usually seek to persuade the brother-in-law not to engage in this form of blackmail but their efforts are not always successful. The Chief Rabbinate in the State of Israel has coped with this problem by introducing a law according to which the brother-in-law is obliged to undertake the maintenance of the widow until he agrees to participate in the Halitzah rite. Another instance of agunah in connection with Halitzah is where the only brother of the deceased is a minor. Since a minor cannot perform Halitzah, the widow has to wait until the boy reaches the age of 13 before she is free to remarry. So far no legal remedy has been found for this problem.

Reform Judaism in the nineteenth century rejected the requirements of either levirate marriage or Halitzah, although Reform Rabbis have been known to participate in the rite if the widow feels herself bound by conscience not to remarry without Halitzah.

William Rosenau, 'Divorce and Chalitzah', in his *Jewish Ceremonial Institutions and Customs* (New York, 1929), 163–78.

**Hallel** 'Praise', the joyous recital of Psalms 113–18 during the morning service on festivals. The benediction which precedes the Hallel is: 'Blessed art Thou, O Lord our God, who has sanctified us with Thy commandments and has commanded us to recite the Hallel.' Even though the institution is Rabbinic, the words 'who has commanded' are deemed appropriate because Rabbinic ordinances are believed to enjoy biblical sanction since the Torah itself is said to give the sages of Israel the right to introduce new religious obligations (see HALAKHAH). Others say that, in any event, the obligation to praise God is implied in the Torah. On *Rosh

Hodesh, the New Moon minor festival, only part of the Hallel is recited (the first eleven verses of Psalm 115 and Psalm 116 are omitted). Half-Hallel is also recited on Passover, except on the first day (the first two days in the *Diaspora), when the full Hallel is recited. An interesting reason given for this is that the Passover celebrations should be somewhat muted in that the deliverance of the Israelites was brought about by the drowning of the Egyptians in the sea. Hallel is not recited on the solemn judgement days of *Rosh Ha-Shanah and *Yom Kippur. Nor is it recited on *Purim, either because the miracle of Purim took place outside the Holy Land or because the reading of the *Megillah on Purim takes the place of Hallel. The full Hallel is recited on *Hanukkah. After the establishment of the State of Israel, the Chief Rabbinate ruled that the full Hallel with the benediction should be received on Israeli Independence Day (5 Iyyar) This has been adopted in practice by the majority of Jewish communities, though in some the benediction is omitted. Some few communities refuse to recite hallel on this day either out of anti-Zionist sentiment or because they believe that no contemporary sages have the right to introduce a new religious practice. Full Hallel is included in the Passover *Haggadah, part of it being recited before the meal and the remainder after the meal at the *Seder but without the special benediction.

Another form of Hallel, known as 'the Great Hallel', consists of Psalm 136. This hallel is also recited at the Seder on Passover and is included in the Passover Haggadah. It is also recited, together with other additional Psalms, during the early morning service on Sabbaths and festivals.

The Talmudic sages frowned on any recital of Hallel on days when it has not been ordained, probably on the principle that it is unfitting to sing God's praises when the mood of the day is not one of particular joy.

Israel Abrahams, 'Hallel', in his *A Companion to the Authorized Daily Prayerbook* (New York, 1966), 184–8.

**Hallelujah** 'Praise ye Yah' (one of the *names of God). The current English form is from the transliteration of the letter 'yod' as 'J'. A more correct transliteration is Halleluyah and this is, in fact, how the word is universally pronounced. The word occurs twenty-three times in the book of Psalms but is not found in the Bible outside this book. Hallelujah has become, like 'Amen', a liturgical expression in Christian as well as in Jewish hymnody. Numerous musical compositions have been created around this word, the best known, of course, being the Hallelujah Chorus in Handel's *Messiah*. The Talmud records a debate on whether Hallelujah is composed of two words—Hallelu Yah, 'Praise ye Yah'—or whether it is a single word the meaning of which is 'Praise ye with numerous praises', in which case the word does not contain a divine name. But the former meaning has been generally accepted as correct.

**Haman** See PURIM

**Ḥametz** 'Leaven', in contradistinction to *matzah*, 'unleavened bread'. As recorded in the book of Exodus, chapter 12, no leaven must be eaten during the 'feast of unleavened bread', *ḥag ha-matzot*. Although, on the critical view (see BIBLICAL CRITICISM) this feast was originally distinct from the feast of *Pesaḥ* ('Passover'), on the traditional view, Passover and the 'feast of unleavened bread' are the same festival during which no leaven may be eaten or even kept in the house. 'Seven days you shall eat unleavened bread; on the very first day you shall remove leaven from your houses, for whoever eats leavened bread from the first day to the seventh day, that person shall be cut off from Israel' (v. 15; on 'cut off', see *karet*). And again (vv. 19–20); 'No leaven shall be found in your houses for seven days. For whoever eats what is leavened, that person shall be cut off from the assembly of Israel, whether he is a stranger or a citizen of the country. You shall eat nothing leavened; in all your settlements you shall eat unleavened bread.' Tractate *Pesahim* in the Talmud is devoted to the laws of Passover, including the prohibition of *ḥametz*. The Codes state the rules regarding *ḥametz* in great detail and these are followed by all traditional Jews. (Here the rules regarding *ḥametz* are given in outline; for further details see MATZAH and PASSOVER.)

On the night preceding the festival (the night belonging to the following day of 14 Nisan) the house is searched for *ḥametz* and any found is removed from the house. In addition, a declaration is made that any *ḥametz* that may have been overlooked is rendered null and void. This declaration and the whole procedure of searching for the *ḥametz* is found in all editions of the Passover *Haggadah.

The prohibition of *ḥametz* extends, according to the Rabbis, to any benefit obtained from it. Thus it is not only forbidden to eat *ḥametz* but also to sell it to a non-Jew or even to give it to him on Passover. It can, however, be given or sold to a non-Jew before Passover and can then be kept in the house over Passover. The principle here is that the prohibition only applies to *ḥametz* owned by a Jew to whom the laws of Passover apply. This is why the declaration that the *ḥametz* be null and void is effective. As a result of the declaration the *ḥametz* becomes ownerless and hence is not Jewishly owned *ḥametz*. In the earlier period it was, in fact, the usual practice to give away or to sell to a non-Jew before Passover all *ḥametz* in one's possession. When, however, Jews, in Eastern Europe particularly, often earned their living as innkeepers, it was obviously impossible for them to give away or even to sell all the alcoholic drinks containing *ḥametz* (whisky and beer, for example, contain fermented grain that is treated as *ḥametz*) and the Rabbis, sympathizing with their plight, introduced a bill of sale in which all *ḥametz* was sold and a legal document drawn up for the purpose, but with the implicit understanding that, after Passover, the non-Jew would sell it back again. Eventually, this 'sale of *ḥametz*' became the established practice for most householders. The local Rabbi draws up a formal bill of sale and sells all the *ḥametz* in the houses of his flock on their behalf. The friendly non-Jew does not, of course, pay the full amount, only a very small deposit, but the transfer is effected by legal means so that in the unlikely event of him wishing to retain his ownership of the *ḥametz* he can do so provided he pays for it in full. Naturally, this never happens so that, in essence, the sale is a legal fiction. The criticism of the whole procedure by Reform Jews that it is a dishonest evasion of the law, an attempt to fool God, is based on a misunderstanding. No ethical question is involved. In ethical matters it is surely wrong to skirt around the law. But with regard to *ḥametz* the Torah, at least in the Rabbinic understanding, does allow *ḥametz* of a non-Jew to be kept in the house. There can be no objection to introducing machinery through which the *ḥametz* is kept without the law being abrogated. The *ḥametz* sold is kept away from all other food in a locked room. Nevertheless,

not all Orthodox Jews avail themselves of this remedy.

A further strictness with regard to *ḥametz* on Passover is that if even a minute quantity of leaven is mixed in a dish, the whole dish is forbidden. The usual rule that a quantity of forbidden food becomes neutralized in a ratio of 1 : 60 (see DIETARY LAWS) does not apply to *ḥametz*. Many authorities hold, however, that if the *ḥametz* had been mixed in the dish before Passover the usual rule of neutralization applies. Nevertheless, it has become the practice for manufactured products that may, even remotely, contain a very small portion of *ḥametz*, to be supervised by a Rabbinic authority; hence the many products sold in the shops before Passover with a label stating that they are 'Kosher for Passover', although what leaven can possibly be in packets of tea, for example, is hard to grasp.

In the Torah the prohibition of leaven is connected with eating unleavened bread; unleavened bread is to be eaten on Passover, leavened bread is not to be eaten. This is implied throughout Exodus 12. Why unleavened bread should be eaten is also stated in the same chapter (v. 39): 'And they baked unleavened cakes of the dough that they had taken out of Egypt, for it was not leavened, since they had been driven out of Egypt and could not delay; nor had they prepared any provisions for themselves.' In the moralistic literature a more individualistic interpretation is also given for the prohibition of *ḥametz*. *Ḥametz* is said to represent the *yetzer ha-ra*, 'evil inclination' (see YETZER HA-TOV AND YETZER HA-RA), lust, pride, and ambition, which are necessary for human survival as the ferment of human life, but which have to be controlled. Hence *ḥametz*, fermented dough, is not forbidden during the rest of the year, only on the festival of Passover, the festival of freedom, which ought to include freedom from domination by the *yetzer ha-ra*. This idea of leaven representing the evil impulse in man is very old among Jews, since it is referred to as early as the New Testament period (Corinthians 5: 6–7). In this context the moralists refer to the private prayer of the third-century Palestinian teacher Rabbi Alexander, recorded in the Talmud (*Berakhot* 17a): 'Lord of the universe! It is revealed and known before Thee that it is our will to perform Thy will; but what stands in the way? The leaven that is in the dough and the servitude of the kingdom [religious oppression by the Roman government]. May it be Thy will to deliver us from their hand, so that we may again perform the statutes of Thy will with a perfect heart.'

**Hands, Washing of** The ritual washing of the hands on various occasions. In Temple times there were elaborate rules in connection with ritual impurity. If a person had been rendered impure through having come into contact, say, with a dead rodent, he contaminated sacred food such as the tithe given to the *priests, which must then not be eaten. The way in which contamination of this kind could be removed was through immersion in a ritual bath (see MIKVEH). But the sages imposed in certain circumstances the minor form of contamination known as 'hand contamination', in which only the hands, not the whole body, was contaminated and for this to be removed total immersion was not required, only the ritual washing of the hands. Since there was a good deal of priest's tithe in ancient Palestine which could easily come into contact with the hands, the sages eventually ordained that the hands of every Jew, not only the hands of a priest, must be washed ritually before meals. It has to be appreciated that this ritual washing of the hands has nothing to do with physical cleanliness. On hygienic grounds, the hands are obviously to be clean of dirt before food is eaten. Even when the hands are physically clean they are still required to be ritually washed.

Although the original reason for washing the hands no longer applies, since there is no sacred food to be eaten, the ritual was continued on the grounds that the ideal of *holiness demands a special, ritualistic washing of the hands. The act of washing the hands in this sense is seen as the introduction of the holiness ideal into the mundane life of the Jew. This ritual washing is only required before a meal at which bread is eaten (see GRACE).

The procedure is to pour water out from a cup or glass first twice over the right hand and then twice over the left hand, care being taken that the unwashed hands do not touch the water used for the washing. The hands are then dried with a towel before partaking of the meal. A benediction is recited over the washing of the hands: 'Blessed art Thou, O Lord our God, King of the universe, who has sanctified us with Thy commandments and has commanded us concerning the washing of the hands.' The

reference to the command has to be understood in the context that Rabbinic ordinances are also 'commanded' by God (see HALLEL). Observant Jews are very strict in this matter of washing the hands before meals.

The Talmud also refers to washing the hands after meals but here the reason given is that people used to eat with their hands and a certain salt added to food in those days might cause injury to the eyes if it came into contact with them. The French authorities in the Middle Ages argued that this hygienic reason no longer obtains, since this kind of salt is no longer used. Many observant Jews follow this line of thinking and do not wash the hands after the meal, not as a ritual in any event. But many authorities introduce the holiness motif here as well, although no benediction is recited over *mayyim aḥanonim*, 'afterwards water'. For those who observe it, the procedure is simply to pour a little water out of a cup or glass over the fingers of the two hands.

There is a further ritual washing of the hands on rising from sleep. This is a later innovation for which two reasons are given. One is that during sleep an unclean spirit rests on the body. This departs on waking, except for a residue left on the fingernails (see MAGIC AND SUPERSTITION) and to remove this the hands have to be washed. The second reason (perhaps introduced as a rationalization) is that a Jew, a member of the 'kingdom of priests' (Exodus 19: 5), must, when he rises from his bed to serve his Maker, follow the practice of the priests in the Temple who would wash their hands from the hand-basin (Exodus 30: 17-21). The procedure for this washing of the hands is to pour the water first on the right hand and then the left and to repeat this three times. Some of the more scrupulous have a cup of water and a basin at the bedside so as to wash the hands immediately on waking. Following the first reason, they will pour out the 'nail water' (*neggel wasser* in Yiddish) and not allow it to come into contact with food or drink.

Many pious Jews also carry out the ritual of washing the hands before performing any religious act, especially before prayer. It is also the custom to perform the ritual of washing the hands on returning from the graveside after a burial (see DEATH AND BURIAL).

**Hannah** Biblical heroine, mother of the prophet *Samuel. Hannah's story is related in the first two chapters of the book of 1 Samuel. Here it is told how Hannah, who was barren, prayed to God to give her a son whom she promised to give to the Lord. Her prayer was answered and when the boy Samuel was 2 years old she brought him to the High Priest, Eli, to serve in the Sanctuary. Many biblical scholars hold that Hannah's hymn of praise at the beginning of chapter 2 was originally an independent composition that was added later to the Hannah narrative.

The Talmud (*Berakhot* 31a–b) considers the story of Hannah and her prayer to be the supreme biblical model for how individual prayers are to be offered. The story of Hannah was chosen as the *Haftarah for the first day of *Rosh Ha-Shanah.

**Hanukkah** 'Dedication', the minor winter festival that begins on the twenty-fifth day of Kislev and lasts for eight days, to celebrate the victory of the *Maccabees over the forces of Antiochus after a three-year battle in the second century BCE, as related in the two apocryphal books, 1 and 2 Maccabees. In the well-known Talmudic legend (*Shabbat* 21b) the Maccabees, when they rededicated the *Temple, found only a small jar of oil, sealed with the High Priest's seal, for the kindling of the *menorah, the candelabrum. This jar contained sufficient oil for only one night but, by a miracle, it lasted for eight nights until fresh, uncontaminated oil could be produced. There are thus two separate ideas behind the celebration of Hanukkah: 1. the victory of the Maccabees; 2. the miracle of the oil.

The problem of the origin of Hanukkah is complicated. According to some historians, the origins are to be found in pagan celebrations of light in the mid-winter season. This motif is naturally ignored in the Jewish tradition. But even according to the tradition, the celebration of Hanukkah as a festival of light may not have depended solely on the Talmudic legend of the oil, to which, incidentally, there is no reference in the Hanukkah liturgy which speaks only of the victory of the Maccabees. Moreover, in the second book of the Maccabees (10: 6–8) it is stated that the eight-day festival was introduced because during the war it was impossible to celebrate the eight-day festival of *Tabernacles. Yet it is undoubtedly the miracle of the oil that has captured the Jewish imagination through the ages. Some scholars see the

emphasis on the miracle as due to the disillusionment of later generations with the Maccabees, so that the victory came to be interpreted in terms of the spiritual power of the Torah symbolized by the oil that burns miraculously even when, according to the natural order, the light should have gone out. Many Orthodox Jews refuse to speak of the Talmudic story as a 'legend', believing it to be historical fact.

*The Kindling of Hanukkah Lights*

According to Jewish practice, based on Talmudic sources, lights are to be kindled in each Jewish house during the eight nights of Hanukkah. These lights are kindled in a special eight-branched candelabrum which used to be called a menorah (although the menorah in the Temple had only seven branches) but is more usually called, nowadays, a Hanukkiyah. In many households, each member of the family has his or her own Hanukkiyah. The more pious Jews use olive oil for the Hanukkah lights, since this was used in the Temple for the kindling of the menorah. Most Jews use candles and the consensus of Rabbinic authorities is that electric lights can also be used. One light is kindled on the first night of Hanukkah, two on the second, three on the third, and so on until eight lights are kindled on the last night. An additional light is used to do the kindling. This is known as the Shamash ('servant'). Before the kindling of the lights two benedictions are recited: 'Blessed art Thou, O Lord our God, King of the universe, who has sanctified with Thy commandments, and has commanded us to kindle the light of Hanukkah', and 'Blessed art Thou, O Lord our God, King of the universe, who wrought miracles for our fathers in days of old, at this season.' On the first night the benediction is added: 'Blessed art Thou, O Lord our God, King of the universe, who has kept us in life, and has preserved us, and enabled us to reach this season.' After the lights have been kindled the declaration is recited: 'We kindle these lights on account of the miracles, the deliverances and the wonders which Thou didst work for our fathers, by means of Thy holy priests. During all the eight days of Hanukkah these lights are sacred, neither is it permitted us to make any profane use of them; but we are only to look at them, in order that we may give thanks unto Thy name for Thy miracles, Thy deliverances and Thy wonders.'

The hymn *'Maoz Tzur' is then sung to a popular melody.

The Hanukkah lights are kindled during the service in the synagogue as well as in private homes. In the State of Israel (nowadays, in other countries as well on occasion) huge, electrically operated menorahs are placed in public squares and on prominent buildings.

### Celebration of Hanukkah

Hanukkah, as a minor festival on which it is permitted to work, is chiefly celebrated by the kindling of the lights and through additions to the liturgy. Because the motif of spiritual light is prominent—the saving of the Jewish soul, so to speak, rather than, as on *Purim, the saving of the body—there is no special Hanukkah feast. The addition to the prayers and to Grace after Meals on Hanukkah thanks God for delivering 'the strong into the hands of the weak, the many into the hands of the few, the impure into the hands of the pure, and the wicked into the hands of the righteous'. The *reading of the Torah in the synagogue on each of the days of Hanukkah is from the portion dealing with the gifts of the princes at the dedication of the Tabernacle (Numbers 8: 1–7) and, on the last day, the command to kindle the lights of the menorah. The *Haftarah on the Sabbath of Hanukkah is from the vision of the menorah in the book of Zechariah (ch. 2).

It is the custom of children to play a game with a spinning top (dreidel) on each side of which the various moves of the game are represented by a letter. These letters are said also to represent the Hebrew words for: 'A great miracle took place there.' In the State of Israel, by a slight change, the letters represent: 'a great miracle took place *here*'. Adults sometimes participate in the game but, among many adults, for some unknown reason and to the consternation of the more staid Rabbis, cardplaying is especially indulged in on Hanukkah. Because of the association with oil, there is a widespread custom to eat oily potato pancakes (*latkes*) on Hannukkah.

*Light is the symbol of Torah and of *charity, so that the Jewish teachers stress the special requirement to study the Torah and give alms on Hanukkah. But the custom now prevalent of giving Hanukkah presents to children finds no support in the classical sources and, fairly obviously, has been introduced so that the children would not feel upset if they are left out

of the giving of presents to their Christian friends at this season. Rabbis frown, however, on presents being distributed by a 'Father Hanukkah' and on Jews having in their home a 'Hanukkah bush'.

> Oliver Shaw, *The Origins of the Festival of Hanukkah* (Edinburgh, 1930).
> Simon Maurice Lehrman, *A Guide to Hanukkah and Purim* (London, 1958).

**Hasidism** The revivalist movement founded by Israel *Baal Shem Tov (in abbreviated form, the Besht) in eighteenth-century Podolia (southeastern Poland), later extending to the whole of Eastern Europe and beyond. There are adherents of Hasidism (Hasidim) today in the State of Israel, the USA, England, France, and many other countries.

### History of Hasidism

The Hebrew for Hasidism, *hasidut*, denotes piety or saintliness, an extraordinary devotion to the spiritual aspects of Jewish life. The term itself did not originate with the eighteenth-century movement. Groups of Hasidim were found in Talmudic times and even earlier. The *Saints of Germany in the Middle Ages were called the Hasidim of Ashkenaz. In the early eighteenth century, the group surrounding the Baal Shem Tov was, at first, only one of a number of such groups of pneumatics. But eventually the Beshtian group became the dominant one; the others either vanished from the scene or became absorbed in the Beshtian group. From the beginning, Hasidism centred on a charismatic personality, the *tzaddik* (*Zaddik in the usual English transliteration). This term has an interesting history of its own. In the Bible and the Talmudic literature, the *tzaddik* ('righteous man') is the ordinary good man to whom the *hasid* is superior. But since the members of the group were themselves termed Hasidim, a different term had to be found for the spiritual leader and for this the old term *tzaddik* was adopted. In this way the older roles were reversed. The Hasid is the follower of the Zaddik, with the latter being the superior pietist.

Hasidism was, at first, an élitist movement, consisting of a small company of pietists seeking the proximity of the Baal Shem Tov in order to be guided by him in the spiritual path. But since the idea of loving every Jew was stressed by the Baal Shem Tov and his disciples as a highly significant religious ideal, it is not surprising that, as the movement spread, it attracted to itself Jews with no pretension to excessive piety who believed in the power of the Zaddik's prayers to help them in their distress. The Zaddik then came to function both as a spiritual guide to the few thirsting for a closer relationship with God and as a man of prayer and a miracle-worker for the masses. Not to be overlooked, however, is that the masses, too, had mystical yearnings which they believed the Zaddik could satisfy. The description of Hasidism as 'mysticism for the masses' ignores the élitist aspects of the movement but is, none the less, a fair representation of the appeal of Hasidism as it came to be.

*Dov Baer of Mezirech, the foremost disciple of the Baal Shem Tov, sent out his own chosen disciples to spread his understanding of the Baal Shem Tov's teachings abroad and these men became Zaddikim in their own right in different Eastern European centres. Personalities such as *Levi Yitzhak of Berditchev, *Shneur Zalman of Liady, the 'Seer' of Lublin and other disciples of Dov Baer are the spiritual heroes of Hasidism. The spread of the movement was assisted by another disciple of the Baal Shem Tov, *Jacob Joseph of Polonnoye, author of the first Hasidic book to be published. Jacob Joseph's *Toledot Yaakov Yosef* was published in the town of Koretz in 1780 and this was followed by a spate of works by the masters in which the new doctrines were expounded. Through these works and through the missionary activities of Dov Baer's disciples, Hasidism spread rapidly to Volhynia, Poland, Russia, and Lithuania, despite, or perhaps because of, the opposition of the *Mitnaggedim, the Rabbinic and communal leaders who tended to see the new ideas as rank heresy. It has been estimated that by the beginning of the nineteenth century Hasidism had won over to its ranks almost half the communities of Eastern Europe.

The movement developed as a variety of groups each owing allegiance to a particular Zaddik. In the early days, when a Zaddik died he was succeeded by his most outstanding disciple, acknowledged as such by his companions. But, towards the end of the eighteenth century, the idea of *dynastic succession took root. The Zaddik was called a 'king' with his own 'court' and when he died he was succeeded by his son, the 'crown prince', or, where he had left no son suitable to succeed him, by his son-in-law, brother, or other close relative. Each

Zaddik (or Rebbe, as he was called to distinguish him from the traditional Rav, the town Rabbi) had his own court to which his devoted followers journeyed periodically, especially to be with the Zaddik on the great festive occasions of the year. There were often fierce rivalries between the different dynasties and, occasionally, struggles for the succession in a dynasty itself. When Mordecai of Chernobil died in 1837, each of his eight sons founded a new dynasty, as did his sons-in-law. It was far from unusual for a Hasid to ask another Hasid: 'To whom do you journey?' meaning, to which Zaddik do you owe allegiance?

While some Hasidim settled in the land of Israel in 1777 and a very few settled in Western Europe and America, the vast majority remained in Eastern Europe, where, before World War II, hundreds of Hasidic dynasties flourished. The pattern was for the Rebbe to reside in a small town with his followers meeting for prayer, study, and companionship in a small conventicle, the *stiebel*. These small meeting-houses were found everywhere in the villages and in the larger towns. The dynasties were known by the name of the town in which the Rebbe resided. After the *Holocaust and the resulting destruction of the great European communities, the Rebbes who survived created a new home for themselves in the State of Israel and the USA, taking care to preserve the name of the European centres at which they and their ancestors had held court. The Hasidic master who held court in Boston was the exception in that he became known as the Bostoner Rebbe. The best-known and influential Hasidic dynasties on the contemporary scene are those of *Belz, Ger (see KOTSK), Sotmar, and *Lubavitch (and see HABAD).

*Hasidic Ideas*

Hasidism is less a movement with ideas of its own than one in which ideas found in the classical Jewish sources, especially the Kabbalah, are given new life and fresh emphasis. The task of discovering in what this emphasis consists is rendered difficult because each of the early masters has his own interpretation of Hasidic doctrine. In some respects, for instance, the teachings of Dov Baer of Mezhirech are at variance with those of Jacob Joseph of Polonoyye, those of Habad different from those of *Nahman of Bratslav. Moreover, the Hasidic works do not normally present their ideas in any systematic form but are in the form of stray comments on biblical verses and Talmudic sayings. Students of the movement are consequently obliged to try to note which teachings are common to all the versions and which belong to the particular bent of individual teachers. The Baal Shem Tov himself conveyed his ideas in the form of brief aphorisms in Yiddish so that even sayings in Hasidic works that are attributed to the first master come to us at second or third hand and it is often desirable to question their authenticity. The most one can do when describing Hasidic doctrine is seek the ideas that are not found in the Hasidic form in earlier Jewish sources and upon which there is a fair degree of consensus among the Hasidic masters no matter to which group they belong. Only with these reservations in mind is it possible to speak of *the* doctrine of Hasidism.

An idea common to every variety of Hasidism is that of pervasiveness of the the divine presence. Behind and in all created things is the divine energy that keeps them in being. The Kabbalistic doctrine of the '*holy sparks' inherent in all things is laid under tribute in Hasidism to reject *asceticism (though a few Hasidic masters did pursue the ascetic way). The ascetic, by abstaining from food and drink and other worldly pleasures, fails to set free the holy sparks clamouring to be released from the demonic forces. The task of the true Hasid is to rescue the holy sparks by engaging in worldly pursuits in a spirit of sanctity. This is the meaning of the older ideal of *devekut, 'attachment to God' as applied in Hasidism. The Hasid is to have God constantly in his mind even when going about his daily affairs. In a work attributed to Baruch of Meziboz (1757–1830), grandson of the Baal Shem Tov, it is said that the Baal Shem Tov introduced a new way, without mortification of the flesh, in which the three essentials are love of God, love of the Jewish people, and love of the Torah. In the earliest period, the masters relied on the doctrine of the 'holy sparks' to introduce the teaching regarding 'strange thoughts'. When sinful thoughts invade the mind of the Hasid at prayers, the doctrine runs, he should not reject these entirely since even these contain holy sparks to be elevated by thinking of their source on high. For instance, if the Hasid thinks during his prayers of a pretty woman he has met, he should contemplate that her beauty is

but a pale reflection of the divine beauty on high and instead of allowing his mind to dwell on the woman herself he should see the thought that has entered his mind as calling him to contemplate the spiritual Source of all beauty. The staid Mitnaggedim were horrified at the very idea which was, in fact, eventually abandoned by the Hasidim themselves on the grounds that only the great masters of the past were sufficiently strong in soul to succeed in elevating the strange thoughts without allowing simple lust to obtain lodging in the mind.

*Humility and *joy are virtues prominent in Hasidism but these are understood in a particular Hasidic way. Humility does not mean that a person should think little of himself but that he should not think of himself at all (see ANNI-HILATION OF SELFHOOD). Humility means for Hasidism that perception of God's glory and majesty leads inevitably to self-transcendence. A Hasidic master observed that there is no precept urging humility and there cannot be such a precept since a conscious striving for humility is self-defeating. In true humility there is no self to be commanded. Joy in Hasidism denotes the attitude of intense spiritual delight in being a servant of God. Since the divine is everywhere present, how can the heart help leaping in joy? Another Hasidic master said that to be joyful is not an actual *mitzvah, a religious obligation, nor is it an actual sin to be miserable. Yet joy leads to the performance of all the Jew's obligations and misery leads to despair and every kind of sin. *Jacob Joseph of Polonnoye writes in this vein that one should not be overscrupulous in the the performance of the precepts because this can easily lead to a morbid striving for perfectionism that frustrates the ideal of joy. The Hasidim were, of course, observant Jews but, for them, the precepts of the Torah were to be carried out in love and fear of God and were, at the same time, the means to love and fear. Fear, in Hasidism, usually refers to the sense of awe (Rudolf Otto's 'the numinous') in God's presence. In the classical works of Hasidism there is little reference to the fear of punishment in hell or in this world as the motivation for leading a good life. Love and fear, as the Baal Shem Tov is reported to have put it, are the two wings by which the soul soars upwards.

Hasidism generally considered prayer as superior in the scale of Jewish values to the *study of the Torah, a reversal of the traditional picture in which no religious activity is more sublime than the study of God's word. Kalonymus Kalman Epstein of Cracow (d. 1827) writes in his book *Maor Va-Shemesh*, a book that came to assume classical status among Hasidic works and which can be said to express authoritative Hasidic doctrine, if there is such a thing:

'From the time of his coming, the holy Baal Shem Tov, may the memory of the holy and saintly be for a blessing, caused the tremendous sanctity of prayer to illumine the world for whoever wishes to draw near to God's service. However, in order for a man to attain to pure prayer it is necessary for him to engage in much service of the sages, to labour long, night and day, in the study of the Torah and in the performance of good deeds so that, as a result, he may learn how truly to pray with fear and great love, as those who have discernment know full well.'

In this passage prayer is not said actually to supersede Torah study, yet the latter is considered important as a means to an end, unlike in the Rabbinic tradition where the study of the Torah is an end in itself with prayer, for all its importance, only secondary. The reversal in Hasidic thought is due to the Hasidic doctrine of *devekut*, an ideal more readily realized in prayer than during study. In most early versions of Hasidism the further step was taken of treating the study of the Torah itself as a devotional exercise. In this version, the Rabbinic ideal of Torah study for its own sake does not mean, as it does for the Mitnaggedim, study with the Torah in mind but with God in the mind. The Mitnaggedim retorted that the student of the Torah will never be able to master whatever subject he studies if his mind is on God instead of being immersed in the complexities of the subject.

### Opposition to Hasidism

Hasidism was attacked by the Mitnaggedim, the Rabbis, and communal leaders on the right, and by the Maskilim, the followers of the *Haskalah movement of enlightenment, on the left. The Mitnaggedic opposition was on various grounds. Whether or not the suspicion had any substance, the Mitnaggedim believed that the new movement was simply Shabbeteanism in disguise and the Hasidim crypto-followers of the false Messiah *Shabbetai Zevi. On the social level, the Hasidim, with their separate conventicles and comparative independence of the Kahal, the governing body of the community, were often seen as dangerous rebels against the authority that held the community together. On the theological level, the Mitnaggedim saw Hasidic *panentheism, the doctrine that all is in God, to be a heretical understanding of 'The whole earth is full of His glory'; one which blurs the distinction between good and evil, the holy and the profane, the pure and the impure. The Mitnaggedim were strongly opposed to the doctrine of the Zaddik as an intermediary between God and man. In its more extreme form, the Mitnaggedim protested, Hasidic veneration of the Zaddik borders on idolatrous Zaddik worship. And the interpretation of Torah study by the Hasidim in terms of devotion was seen by the Mitnaggedim as a denigration of the Torah and those who spent their lives studying the Torah. There is, in fact, in early Hasidic literature, much criticism of the scholars who, the Hasidim maintained, studied out of ulterior motives, to gain fame or wealth. The Mitnaggedim thus saw the new movement with its emotional excesses as threatening the old order in which the community was governed by sober, learned Rabbis and lay leaders.

The Maskilim attacked Hasidism for its obscurantism, as they saw it. Instead of the masses trying to improve their financial position by their own efforts and taking care of their health by consulting and being advised by the physicians, they were encouraged to leave everything to the prayers of the Zaddik on their behalf. The Hasidic masters were generally opposed to Jews learning foreign languages and adopting any of the mores of Western society, all in direct opposition to the Haskalah, whose main aim was to encourage accommodation to the Gentile world where this did not affect loyalty to the Jewish religion. Furthermore, the Maskilim maintained, Hasidic life was governed by a superstitious belief in the supernatural powers of the Zaddik to change the natural order. Eventually, the Mitnaggedim made common cause with the Hasidim in opposition to the Haskalah, which was not slow to hurl similar accusations against the traditionalist Mitnaggedim.

### Hasidic Life

There is a lifestyle common to all Hasidim but with variations according to the patterns and traditions of particular dynasties. All Hasidim wear a girdle for prayer to divide the upper part of the body from the lower. The majority of Hasidim wear on the Sabbath the squat fur-trimmed hat known as the *streimel* but the Hasidim of Ger substitute for the *streimel* the tall fur hat known as the *spodik*, while the Hasidim of Lubavitch wear neither. Some Hasidim wear white socks on the Sabbath as a symbol of purity; others allow only the most distinguished Hasidim to wear white socks; and others do not know of the custom at all (see DRESS). All Hasidim usually sport beards and cultivate long ear-locks, *peot*, but some Hasidim have straight, others 'corkscrew', *peot*.

When a Hasid pays his regular visit to the Rebbe's court, he presents a written petition, the *kvittel*, to the Rebbe, in which he requests the Rebbe to pray for his needs and those of his family to be satisfied. In return the Hasid donates a sum of money known as a *pidyon* ('redemption'). The Rebbe uses the moneys he receives from the *pidyon* and from collections made in the various towns not only for his own use and the upkeep of his court but also, perhaps primarily, for charitable purposes, the wealthier Hasidim contributing in this way to the maintenance of their poor associates. The Rebbe is usually consulted before the Hasid arranges marriages for his children and whenever he is about to undertake an important business transaction. The Rebbe acts as a spiritual guide to his followers and if possible will advise them in private audience on the more intimate aspects of their religious life. Although some writers have overplayed the role of *women in Hasidism it remains true that Hasidic women are allowed access to the Rebbe for him to guide them in the conduct of their affairs, whether spiritual or material.

The Hasid's access to the Rebbe is usually through the Gabbaim ('Overseers'), the facto-tums whose role it is to see that protocol is observed and to protect the Rebbe from too many intrusions on his privacy. Some Hasidic courts are run on comparatively frugal lines but others are conducted with great opulence. Nowadays, for instance, the Rebbes often travel in great style in chauffeur-driven automobiles and with first-class seats on trains and planes.

At the sacred meal on the Sabbath the Hasidim sit in awesome silence around the Rebbe's 'Tish' (table) until he gives them the sign to sing the traditional Sabbath songs. Some Rebbes are themselves gifted composers, others have Hasidim who compose melodies which then form the repertoire for all the Hasidim of the particular group and, often, for other Hasidim as well. After the Rebbe has tasted a little from the dish placed before him, the 'leftovers' (*shirayim*) are distributed among the Hasidim in the belief that to eat of the food that has been blessed by the Rebbe brings material and spiritual blessings. At the Tish the Rebbe delivers a discourse on the Torah portion of the week read in the synagogue. The majority of Hasidic works consist in the main of the Rebbe's discourses which were recorded, after the Sabbath, by Hasidim who retained the Rebbe's ideas in their memory. In the early days of Hasidism, and to a lesser degree later as well, it was believed that when the Rebbe 'says Torah', it is the *Shekhinah that takes over and 'speaks through his throat', so that it was often said that the Rebbe himself was later unaware of his words. Some Rebbes dressed all in white on the Sabbath but this is nowadays looked upon as religious ostentation and is very unusual. There is also a custom, still practised by only a few, for there to be twelve loaves at the Rebbe's table, corresponding to the twelve tribes of Israel. The Hasidic *dance is a regular feature of Hasidic life; the Hasidim place their arms around their neighbours' shoulders and whirl around in a circle in obedience to the Psalmist's call to 'serve the Lord with gladness' (Psalms 100: 2). For the same reason, on the Sabbath and other festive occasions no Hasidic gathering is complete without a generous supply of alcoholic drinks.

## The Literature of and on Hasidism

It has been estimated that some 3,000 Hasidic works have been published since the appearance of Jacob Joseph of Polonoyye's *Toledot Yaakov Yosef* (Koretz, 1780) and Dov Baer of Mezhirech's *Maggid Devarav Le-Yaakov* (Koretz, 1781). This corpus consists in the main of works by the masters, early and late. The language of these works is Rabbinic Hebrew but with numerous terms adopted from the Kabbalah. Generally speaking, while the Kabbalistic vocabulary is maintained in these classical works, they cannot really be considered to be in the older Kabbalistic tradition since the masters interpret the Kabbalah, as they do the Bible and the Talmud, in the spirit of Hasidism. *Scholem speaks of Hasidism as the 'interiorisation of the Kabbalah'. That is to say, the Hasidic teachers are far less interested in the relationships among the *Sefirot on high than in the human psychological processes on earth. In fact, many of the masters, but not all, tend to see too much concentration on the older, extremely complex Kabbalistic system as frustrating the Hasidic ideal of *devekut*. The mind of the worshipper cannot realistically be on the details of the Sefirotic map and at the same time on God.

The major works of the masters have gone into numerous editions and are studied assiduously by the Hasidim, whatever particular dynasty they happen to belong to. These works are called 'holy books', taking their place, for the Hasidim, beside the Bible, the Talmud, and the Zohar, as sacred literature the study of which counts as the study of the Torah. Some of the masters were accomplished Talmudists and Halakhists, producing works in this genre. But in this activity they function as traditional Talmudists and Halakhists, making hardly any reference to specifically Hasidic themes.

Hasidism from the beginning saw great value in the stories told by the Hasidim of the mighty deeds of the Rebbes. The older Hasidim would tell these tales to the younger men, who would sit around the teller with bated breath. While the tales are full of ethical and religious sayings of the Zaddikim, they are chiefly intended to demonstrate the power of the saints to work miracles. Both the Mitnaggedim and the Maskilim poured scorn on the exaggerations in Hasidic hagiography, considering the telling of the tales as nothing but a frivolous waste of time. At first, these tales circulated by word of mouth but, in the nineteenth century, numerous collections of Hasidic tales were published, some more sophisticated and religiously significant than others.

In addition to the expository and hagiographical works, letters of the Rebbes and accounts of their lives have been published. These have been used extensively, but with caution, by the historians of Hasidism in their attempts to reconstruct Hasidic life in the past.

The literature on the Hasidic movement is similarly vast. The Maskilim Isaac Erter and Joseph Perl published satires, often biased and unfair, on Hasidic life. S. M. *Dubnow's *History of Hasidism* is the only complete history of the movement. Dubnow's study has to be supplemented by the scholarly researches of Scholem and his school. There are numerous studies, in Hebrew and English, of individual masters and their teachings. Two helpful anthologies of Hasidic sayings are: *The Hasidic Anthology* by Louis I. Newman (New York, 1944) and the two volumes by Martin *Buber: *Tales of the Hasidim: The Early Masters* (New York, 1947) and *Tales of the Hasidim: The Later Masters* (New York, 1948). Buber is the founder of neo-Hasidism, the attempt to apply Hasidic teachings to the religious life of Western man. It has to be noted, however, that Buber largely ignores the Hasidic works of doctrine and relies mainly on the Hasidic tales, which he retells to suit his own I and Thou philosophy.

> Gershon David Hundert (ed.), *Essential Papers on Hasidism*, (New York, 1991).
> Louis Jacobs, *Hasidic Thought* (New York, 1976).
> —— *Hasidic Prayer* 2nd edn, The Liltman Library of Jewish Civilization; London and Washington 1993).
> Gershom G. Scholem, 'Hasidism: The Latest Phase' in his *Major Trends in Jewish Mysticism* (London, 1955), 325–50.

**Haskalah** 'Enlightenment', the movement which originated in eighteenth-century Germany with the aim of broadening the intellectual and social horizons of the Jews to enable them to take their place in Western society. The term Haskalah, in medieval Jewish literature, is from the Hebrew word *sekhel*, 'the intellect', but, as here applied, refers to the attitude of attraction to general knowledge, secular learning, and Western culture. The followers of the Haskalah movement were called Maskilim. This latter term is found in the verse: 'And the intelligent [*ha-maskilim*] shall shine as the brightness of the firmament' (Daniel 12: 3), although, in this verse, the meaning is simply 'the wise', the men of wisdom. These terms did not become prominent until the middle of the nineteenth century, though the trend they represent is a century earlier.

*History*

The historian Leopold *Zunz remarked that the Jewish Middle Ages did not come to an end until the French Revolution, when the new ideas of liberty were reflected in the German *Aufklarung*. During the eighteenth century, a number of middle-class German Jews had begun to shake off the intellectual fetters, as they saw it, of the *ghetto and had begun to take their place in German society, often meeting with hostility and having to fight against prejudice. There was, of course, considerable intellectual activity in the life of the ghetto but this was in the traditional mode of study, chiefly the study of the Talmud and the Codes, with no desire for instruction in the new learning that followed on the Renaissance, to which the Jews, with few exceptions, had no access. Nevertheless, there were a number of German Jews in the middle of the eighteenth century who had managed to acquire a degree of general education and 'enlightenment'. Out of their ranks the Haskalah emerged. The central figure here is Moses *Mendelssohn, the great thinker who was an observant Jew fully trained in the traditional Jewish learning, and yet thoroughly at home in German philosophy and culture. A group of enthusiastic seekers gathered around Mendelssohn in Berlin to be guided by him in their pursuit of the new knowledge. It is not, therefore, correct to speak of Mendelssohn as the founder of the Haskalah movement. He has been more accurately described as the 'Father of the Haskalah', the central figure who helped to organize the movement and who, together with his associates, encouraged its spread.

One of the aims of the Maskilim was to help Jews to acquire equal rights in German society. This, they maintained, was impossible and would not be granted by the German government, unless the blinkers of the ghetto mentality had been removed from Jewish eyes. As part of their educational programme, the Maskilim sought to encourage Jews to substitute for the Yiddish they commonly spoke the German language of culture, a language that would give them access to German and other European literature and open their minds to new ideas. But, aware that this aim could easily lead to a rejection of the rich Jewish literary heritage, the Maskilim also stressed the need to cultivate the Hebrew language of the Bible so that Judaism could be expressed on its own terms as a philosophy of life in no sense inferior to that of their neighbour. The programme required Jewish schools to be established in which the children would be taught both Hebrew and general science and literature. An associate of Mendelssohn, Naftali Herz Wesseley (1725–1805), published his *Divrey Shalom Ve-Emet* (*Words of Peace and Truth*), often described as the manifesto of the Haskalah, in which he made a typical Haskalah distinction between 'the law of man' and the 'law of God'; the former denoted Western patterns of life and secular learning, the latter, the traditional Jewish way of religious life and study. The Maskilim had to struggle for the realization of these two, often conflicting, aims. As late as the mid-nineteenth century the Russian Maskil, Judah Laib Gordon, could still proclaim as the Haskalah ideal: 'Be a Jew in your home and a man outside it', as if a Jew could only make his way as a 'man' by concealing his Jewish identity when associating with his non-Jewish neighbours. The tensions arising out of the virtually overnight emergence of the Jew from the confines of the ghetto were bound to be acute. Jews had to try to achieve an accommodation with modernity in a single generation, a task in which their Christian neighbours had been involved for several centuries. The German Jews found themselves suddenly precipitated from medievalism into the modern world with hardly any time to reflect on the totally unfamiliar, new situation in which they found themselves. No wonder the efforts of the Maskilim were often fraught with peril. No wonder the more traditional saw the Haskalah as subversive and preferred to remain within the confines of the old ways in all their cosiness and with all their certainties.

The first major contribution of the Haskalah to modernization was the translation of the Bible into German by Mendelssohn, provided with a Hebrew commentary by a number of his associates called the *Biur* (*Commentary*). Through the translation, Jews, familiar with the Hebrew of the Bible, acquired a fair knowledge of the German language. Through the *Commentary*, they were introduced to a new approach to the Bible since the *Commentary* departed radically from the fanciful homiletical style, popular for centuries, in favour of what they felt was the plain meaning of the biblical text. This is not to say that the *Commentary* is truly inconoclastic. Writing before the rise of BIBLICAL CRITICISM, the Biurists adopted a stance that was completely traditional with regard to such things as the authorship of the biblical books and was in fact fully in line with the exegesis of the medieval commentators such as Abraham *Ibn Ezra and *Rashbam, who tried to understand the Bible on its own terms unencumbered by Midrashic elaborations. In further pursuit of their aim, the Maskilim arranged for the first modern Jewish school to be opened in Berlin in 1778 and, in 1784, the periodical, *Hameasef* (*The Gatherer*), began to be published.

The German Haskalah may have been welcomed by some of the traditional Rabbis but when they observed that the new tendency led many to a rejection of Judaism and even to apostasy they opposed it vehemently, forbidding any devout Jew to read the *Biur*, for example. The Rabbis saw clearly that the Haskalah was engaged in a transformation of Judaism, a shifting of its centre from the religious ideal of Torah study 'for its own sake', with secular learning at the most an adjunct, to secular learning 'for its own sake' with the study of the Torah as an adjunct. The Rabbis perceived the Haskalah as a modern version of the old struggle between Judaism and *Hellenism, as in one sense it was. The Maskilim were repeating in new form the medieval attempt to reconcile Judaism with Greek philosophy, with all the dangers to faith in the enterprise. The Maskilim admitted the charge. It was no accident that Maimonides was the great hero of the Maskilim, who were seeking to do for their age what the sage did for his.

From Germany the Haskalah spread to Galicia and later to Russia. In these countries the Jews were far more deeply immersed in the traditional Jewish learning and far more observant of Jewish practices than their German co-religionists and had little reason to feel culturally inferior to their Polish or Russian neighbours. Nevertheless, the Haskalah ideal proved extremely attractive to a number of thoughtful Jews in the Galician towns of Lemberg and Brody. Nahman *Krochmal, the foremost exponent of Haskalah ideas, was born in Brody in 1785, a year after the death of Mendelssohn, but lived for most of his life in Zolkiew, where, like Mendelssohn in Berlin but less overtly, he gathered around him a small group of young 'seekers of light'. Krochmal was also a pioneer of the *Jüdische Wissenschaft movement, the movement in which Jewish history was studied not as mere chronology but as a discipline pursued by the critical method developed in modern studies. Krochmal's *Guide for the Perplexed of Our Time* is an interpretation of Judaism in philosophical and rationalistic terms. Another historian in the critical vein in Galicia was Solomon Judah *Rapoport, whose biographical studies of the luminaries of the past display the keenest scholarly acumen. Both Krochmal and Rapoport were strictly observant

Jews; Rapoport served, in fact, as a traditional Rabbi in Tarnopol and Krochmal as the head of the Jewish community in Zolkiew. The special foe of the Galician Haskalah was *Hasidism, against which the Maskilim Isaac Erter and Joseph Perl published works of satire. The Hasidim retaliated by dubbing the Maskilim heretics and free-thinkers whose sole aim was to cast off the yoke of the Torah and the precepts.

As in Galicia, the Haskalah in Russia took root in a very learned and traditional Jewish society. Especially in sober, rationalistic Lithuania, with its great tradition of Talmudic learning, the Haskalah was attractive to many in that it opened up exciting new intellectual vistas, but the Lithuanian Jews saw nothing anti-intellectual in the traditional scheme of studies. On the contrary, the profound study of the Talmud provided ample stimulus of the mind and had the advantage of being a sublime religious activity, which could be supplemented but not superseded by the Haskalah. Thus the Lithuanian Haskalah was much more a movement within Judaism than the Berlin version of the movement. Although the early Russian Maskilim saw signs that the Czarist government might eventually grant Jews equal rights and their strivings were directed to the achievement of this aim, disillusionment soon set in and the Maskilim themselves became increasingly suspected of being no more than lackeys of the Russian government whose real intention was to persuade Jews to adopt Christianity. The result was a greater emphasis on Hebrew; and to some extent Yiddish, too, far from being scorned as in the Berlin Haskalah as an uncouth jargon, was welcomed as a truly 'Jewish' language. Final disillusionment with the Haskalah's confidence in the Russian government set in with the Russian pogroms in 1881–2. The thrust of the Haskalah became even more Jewishly pronounced with an emphasis on *Zionism as the solution to the problem of the Jew in a hostile environment.

Max Lilienthal (1815–82), believing the Czarist government to be serious in wishing to grant equal rights to the Jews if only they would abandon their outlandish ways, devoted much effort to spreading the ideas of Haskalah in public meetings and discussions but he eventually felt that he was being used by the Russians and left for the United States. Another leading figure in the Russian Haskalah was Isaac Baer Levinsohn (1788–1860), the 'Russian Mendelssohn' as he was called. Levinsohn's *Teudah Be-Yisrael* (*Testimony in Israel*) is an appeal for the Haskalah ideal based on passages in the writings of past sages who favoured the pursuit of general knowledge and the learning of foreign languages in addition to the traditional scheme of studies. The Russian Maskilim published a number of journals with revealing titles such as *Hamelitz* (*The Defender*) and *Hashahar* (*The Daybreak*) to which gifted Hebraists contributed essays and news items of what was going on in the world outside as well as in the Jewish world. Seminaries were established by the Maskilim with governmental approval in Vilna and Zhitomir for the training of modern Rabbis, in which aim they met with scanty success. The novels of Abraham Mapu and the poems of Judah Laib Gordon exercised a powerful influence on Hebrew readers. In this way the Haskalah idea gathered momentum throughout Russia. Even in the great *Yeshivah of *Volhozhyn, the fortress of traditional Talmudism, it was far from unknown for the students to read surreptitiously the 'little books' of the Haskalah. It has been noted that in the great Vilna publishing house of Romm, authors could be seen reading the proofs of their works in the traditional mode side by side with the authors of Haskalah works.

*Influence of Haskalah*

It is all too easy to decry the superficiality of the Haskalah and its unconscious encouragement of assimilation, yet the movement undoubtedly had a positive influence on Jews facing the challenge of modernity. The Reform movement had its origin in the German Haskalah as did the neo-Orthodoxy of Samson Raphael *Hirsch. After the Haskalah, there was no longer any need to argue that a Jew could be loyal to his religion without ignoring the values of Western society. Zionism can be said to be a more Jewish version of the Haskalah and, of course, the State of Israel is a modern state in which the liberal values of the West are accepted without reservation. After the *Holocaust, however, many traditionalists did reject the argument in favour of Western culture which, for them, reached its *reductio ad absurdum* in the terrible catastrophe unparalleled in all Jewish, and indeed human, history. If this is the fruit of Western civilization, they argued, it is a civilization the Jew can well do without. In

contemporary ultra-Orthodox circles, there is a reversal to pre-Haskalah days. Most of the traditional Yeshivot (see YESHIVAH) discourage the students from engaging in secular studies, except for the purpose of earning a living. Only the Torah is to be studied 'for its own sake'. Yet, for all that, the modern Orthodox still hold that it is both possible and desirable for the intelligent Jew to be educated in Torah and also in general science and literature. It is a moot point whether the Lithuanian method of Talmud study, now followed in the majority of the Yeshivot, does not itself owe much to the Haskalah. This new method, involving keen logical analysis of legal concepts, is certainly new in Talmudic studies and appears to have been influenced, at least indirectly, by the Haskalah's advocacy of the role of reason in understanding the classical Jewish sources.

It is not widely known that the Haskalah literature in Hebrew had an influence on the far-flung Jewish community of the Yemen. From the circle of Yihya Kafah (1850–1932), Halakhist and traditional scholar, a Yemenite Haskalah developed, known as the Darda (short for Dor Dea, 'Generation of Knowledge'). The Dardaim rejected the predominance of the Kabbalah and encouraged secular studies, even establishing a modern Jewish school in San'a in 1910.

The final verdict on the Haskalah has not yet been given. For all their attacks on some aspects of the traditional way of life, the Maskilim were, in the main, religious men who wished to further the cause of Judaism in the new environment. They saw their struggle as directed against what they considered to be the superstitious and reactionary elements in the tradition, not against the tradition itself and certainly not against the Jewish religion. Despite their espousal of secular learning, the Maskilim were remote from secularism. It is going too far to see the Haskalah as a religious movement, but the religious motivation was rarely absent from their thinking and activities.

Jacob Salman Raisin, *The Haskalah Movement in Russia* (Philadelphia, 1923).

Alexander Altmann, *Moses Mendelssohn* (London, 1973), 346–420.

**Havdalah** 'Division', the ceremony performed at the termination of Sabbaths and festivals to mark the division between the sacred day and the ordinary days of the week. The ceremony is performed in the synagogue at the end of the evening service and especially in the home. A cup of wine is taken in the right hand and the benediction is recited: 'Blessed art Thou, O Lord our God, King of the universe, who createst the fruit of the vine.' (If wine is not available, the benediction can be recited over other liquids but not over water.) Then the Havdalah benediction is recited: 'Blessed art Thou, O Lord our God, King of the universe, who makest a distinction [*hamavdil*] between holy and profane, between light and darkness, between Israel and other peoples, between the seventh day and the six working days. Blessed art Thou, O Lord, who makest a distinction between holy and profane.' These two benedictions alone form the Havdalah ceremony at the termination of a festival. At the termination of the Sabbath two further benedictions are recited, one over sweet-smelling spices, the other over a candle. Over the spices the benediction is: 'Blessed art Thou, O Lord our God, King of the universe, who createst various kinds of spices.' Over the candle, the benediction is: 'Blessed art Thou, O Lord our God, King of the universe, who createst the lights of the fire.'

The reason for reciting the benediction over light is obvious. Fire may not be kindled on the Sabbath, so that when the sacred day is over fire is kindled and God praised for the gift of light and fire. A number of reasons are given for the benediction over spices, the most popular being that on the Sabbath the Jew is endowed with an extra soul. Sweet spices refresh the soul, sad at the departure of the 'over soul', since the sense of smell is the most ethereal of the five senses and hence closest to the spiritual. It is customary to have the Havdalah spices in a special spice-box, usually made of silver. Since the benediction over light is also over the gift of fire, more than one candle is used. The custom is to use a special plaited Havdalah candle containing more than one wick. It is also customary to spread the fingers of the two hands towards the light. The main reason for this is to have some use of the light over which the benediction is recited, just as one drinks the wine and smells the spices over which these benedictions are recited. Another idea behind the spreading of the hands is that now the Sabbath is over, the hands may be employed in work forbidden on the Sabbath.

A shorter form of Havdalah is added to the benediction in the evening service in which

God is thanked for the gift of knowledge, since, as the Talmud says, without knowledge there is no capacity for making distinctions between the holy and the profane. This addition reads:

'Thou hast favoured us with a knowledge of Thy Torah, and hast taught us to perform the statutes of Thy will. Thou hast made a distinction, O Lord our God, between holy and profane, between light and darkness, between Israel and other peoples, between the seventh day and the six working days. O our Father, our King, grant that the days which are approaching us may begin for us in peace, and that we may be withheld from all sin and cleansed from all iniquity, and cleave to the fear of Thee.'

There are various liturgical compositions for recital in the home after the Havdalah ceremony including references to the prophet *Elijah, the herald of the *Messiah, and a hymn, the first stanza of which reads: 'May He who maketh a distinction between holy and profane pardon our sins; our offspring and our possessions may He multiply as the sand, and as the stars in the night.' Because of the reference to pardon of sins, some scholars believe that this hymn was originally intended to be recited not after the Sabbath but only after *Yom Kippur.

Israel Abrahams, 'The Habdalah', in his *A Companion to the Authorized Daily Prayerbook* (New York, 1966), 182–184.

**Health** Jewish teaching advocates strongly that proper care be taken for the health of mind and body, since life is God's precious gift. The Talmud forbids a scholar to reside in a town in which there is no physician to care for the health of its citizens (see DOCTORS) and the Talmud contains much advice on how a person is to keep in good health. Maimonides, himself a physician, devotes a section of his great Code to the subject in which he adds to the Talmudic prescriptions hygienic measures deriving from his own experience and the medical knowledge of his day. Maimonides prefaces this section of his Code with the observation: 'Since it is God's will that a man's body be kept healthy and strong, and because it is impossible for a man to have any knowledge of his Creator when ill, it is, therefore, his duty to shun anything which may waste his body, and to strive to acquire habits that will help him to preserve his health.' Jews have usually been careful (at times, it must be said, this borders on hypochondria) to preserve mental and physical health. The following are typical regulations found in the Talmud and Codes which, whatever the original reason, have had beneficial hygienic effects.

The body must be bathed regularly and the bodily functions attended to as soon as they become necessary. To withhold evacuation of the bowels and passing water is considered sinful. Washing the *hands before meals is a ritualistic prescription but the hands are also to be washed after visiting the privy and after touching parts of the body that are usually covered. Over and above the *dietary laws, some of which themselves have occasionally been understood on hygienic grounds, there are rules which prohibit the eating of food that may cause ill health. Nowadays, as a result of researches into the harm that is caused by smoking cigarettes, many Rabbis frown upon smoking (see TOBACCO). Alcohol is nowhere proscribed as such but caution must be exercised not only to avoid drunkenness but also to ensure that imbibing alcoholic beverages should not cause mental or physical ill health. Taking drugs, unless prescribed by the doctor, is certainly frowned upon for this and for other sound reasons. Regular exercise is advocated for the purpose of keeping the body strong and healthy.

Naturally, it is generally acknowledged, some of the regulations found in this context in the ancient sources are not necessarily sound and may be positively harmful in the light of medical advances. But the principle of health-preservation still holds good, although it is the voice of the contemporary physician that should be heeded rather than any appeal to ancient sources.

Hyman E. Goldin, 'Rules Concerning Physical Wellbeing', in his *Code of Jewish Law* (New York, 1961), 101–8.

**Heaven and Hell** The places in which, respectively, the righteous are rewarded after death and the wicked punished. The usual terms in Jewish literature are the *Garden of Eden for heaven and *Gehinnom for hell. The Hebrew word *shamayyim* means either the sky, the firmament, as in the first verse of Genesis, or God, as in the Rabbinic expression: 'the fear of heaven'. In the earlier literature, the term never refers to the location of souls after the death of the body. In this literature, too, the

term Paradise is not used to denote heaven. However, possibly under the influence of Christian usage, both these terms are found in medieval literature. For instance, on the famous Talmudic account (tractate *Ḥagigah* 14b) of the 'four who entered the Pardes' (the 'Orchard' of the King) the standard French commentator, *Rashi, comments: 'They ascended to Heaven by means of a divine name.' In this article the conventional English names heaven and hell are used.

*The Talmudic Literature*

There are so many references in the Talmudic literature to 'the *World to Come' and so much is inevitably vague in any discussion of the subject that it is not really possible to present a coherent picture of Rabbinic *eschatology. A major problem is whether 'the World to Come' is to be identified with the world of the future after the *resurrection of the dead or with the fate of the soul in the Hereafter. The idea of this life as a preparation for life in the Hereafter is prominent in Rabbinic thought, as the following quotations show. 'This world is like a vestibule before the World to Come. Prepare yourself in the vestibule that you may enter the hall' (Ethics of the Fathers, 4. 16). 'This world is compared to the eve of the Sabbath, the World to Come to the Sabbath. Only one who has toiled on the eve of the Sabbath has food to eat on the Sabbath' (*Avodah Zarah* 3a). The saying of the third-century Babylonian teacher, Rav, has often been quoted in discussions of the question: 'Not like this world is the World to Come. In the World to Come there is neither eating nor drinking; nor procreation or business transactions; no envy or hatred or rivalry; but the righteous sit enthroned, their crowns on their heads, and bask in the radiance of the *Shekhinah' (*Berakhot* 17a). It is uncertain whether this refers to the world after the resurrection of the dead or, as Maimonides understands it, to the fate of the soul in heaven. But an anecdote told in the Talmud (*Pesaḥim* 50a) undoubtedly refers to the souls in heaven. The son of Rabbi Joshua ben Levi, it is said, expired. When he came back to life, his father asked him what kind of a world he saw. The son replied that he saw an upside-down world: those who were highly esteemed here on earth were held in little esteem there but those of little esteem here were held in high esteem there. And what of us, the scholars, the father asked. The son replied that their status there is the same as their status here, presumably meaning that students of the Torah do not delude themselves as to their real status.

The notion of harp-playing in heaven is not found anywhere in the Jewish sources. But, especially for scholars, heavenly bliss consists of the study of the Torah in 'the Yeshivah on High', where they will be taught by God Himself and even debate matters of Torah with Him. These descriptions are in a form suggesting that the events are taking place 'now' in heaven, not in the remote future. On the other hand, there are references to the great banquet God will prepare for the righteous 'in the future to come'. In one version (*Bava Batra* 75a) at this wonderful banquet the righteous will eat the meat of the *Leviathan and drink 'wine stored in the grape from the six days of creation' (*Berakhot* 34b). In another version (*Pesaḥim* 119b) after the righteous have eaten at the banquet the cup of blessing will be offered to the great heroes of the Bible for them to say Grace over it. They will all refuse except David, who will accept the honour saying: 'I will lift up the cup of salvation, and call upon the name of the Lord' (Psalms 116: 13).

The usual expression, in the Rabbinic literature, for going to hell is to 'descend' to hell, suggesting that hell is located beneath the earth, but there are statements that hell is located in the mysterious realm known as 'beyond the mountains of darkness'. The chief element for the torment of the wicked in hell is fire, which is said to be sixty times hotter than our fire (*Berakhot* 57b). But there are also references to snow and brimstone in hell, which is said to be a place of utter blackness. There are implications that the excessively wicked will be punished in hell for all eternity, a view adopted by *Saadiah. But the accepted view, if one can speak of such a thing in this context, is that, as the Mishnah (*Eduyot* 2: 10) states, the punishment of the wicked lasts for twelve months. On the basis of this statement, the custom arose that a son recites the Kaddish to benefit his father's soul, for only eleven months after the death of his father. If he were to recite the Kaddish for a whole year it would imply that his father belongs in the ranks of the wicked. Remarkable, and also much discussed, is the saying of the third-century Palestinian teacher Resh Lakish that there is no hell in the future but the Holy One, blessed be He, will

remove the sun from its sheath and scorch the earth with its rays. The wicked will be punished and the righteous healed thereby (*Avodah Zarah* 3b).

It is difficult to know to what degree all these speculations were taken literally by the Talmudic Rabbis. The medieval thinkers generally demythologize the statements in the Talmudic literature about heaven and hell, interpreting them in terms of purely spiritual bliss and spiritual torment.

*Medieval Jewish Thought*

While it is true that the Talmudic statement about heaven and hell influenced considerably the folk-view, ordinary people undoubtedly believed in heaven and hell as actual places and in physical pleasures and torments; the thinkers generally understood heaven in terms of the unbounded bliss afforded to the souls of the righteous by the nearness of God and hell as the terrible torment of being remote from Him—as states of soul rather than as spatial locations. The tendency is also to be observed among the medieval thinkers to understand many of the Talmudic references to be to the world after the resurrection, with only a few referring to heaven in the sense of the soul's bliss and the sinner's sufferings immediately after the death of the body. Maimonides (*Teshuvah*, ch. 8) is unique in totally identifying the Rabbinic 'World to Come' with the fate of the soul immediately after death.

Maimonides appears to identify hell with the annihilation of the wicked soul, not at all with a place or even a state of torment. 'The good which is treasured up for the righteous is the life of the world to come; it is a life which is deathless and a happiness free from all adversity. The punishment of the wicked is that they do not merit this higher form of life, but are cut off and die. Whoever does not merit that life suffers death without ever recovering life again; he is cut off in his wickedness and perishes like the beast.' This may be a harsh statement, but it is gentle when compared with statements about the actual lurid tortures inflicted on the wicked in a real hell. On heaven, with which he identifies the Rabbinic 'World to Come', Maimonides remarks: 'In the World to Come there is no bodily form, but the souls only of the righteous without a body, like the ministering angels. Since there are no bodies in it, there can likewise be neither eating nor drinking nor any of the other things which the bodies of men need in this world. Nor can any of the accidents to which bodies are subject in this world, such as sitting, standing, sleep, death, pain, laughter, and so on, occur there.' Maimonides must have been aware that the sophisticated Muslims of his day hardly took literally the statements in the Koran (Sura 55) about the houris in Paradise and is no doubt only attacking popular notions when he goes on to say:

'Perhaps that bliss will be lightly esteemed by you, and you will think that the reward for fulfilling the commandment and for being perfect in the ways of truth consists in nothing else than indulging in fine food and drink, enjoying beautiful women, wearing raiment of fine linen and embroidery, dwelling in apartments of ivory, and using vessels of silver and gold or similar luxuries, as those foolish and ignorant Arabs imagine who are steeped in sensuality. But wise and intelligent men know that all these things are nonsense and vanity and quite futile; since with us, in this world, they are only considered desirable because we possess bodily form, and because all these things are needs of the body, so that its desires may be gratified and it be preserved . . . But the bliss of the World to Come is exceedingly great and cannot bear comparison with the happiness of this world except in a figurative manner. Actually, however, to compare the bliss of the soul in the World to Come with the happiness of the body in this world by means of eating and drinking is quite incorrect. That heavenly bliss is great beyond limit, and there is nothing to be compared or likened to it.'

Elsewhere, Maimonides observes that for persons in this life to try to grasp the nature of heavenly bliss is like a man born blind trying to grasp the nature of colour.

The heaven of the Jewish mystics is similarly all spiritual. According to the Zohar (i. 90b–91a) when the righteous depart from the world their souls ascend and God prepares for them a garment woven from the good deeds they performed while on earth and the great banquet of the future is the feasting of the righteous on divine mysteries never before revealed (Zohar, i. 135b). In this vein the eighteenth-century mystic Moses Hayyim *Luzzatto begins his work of moral perfection, *The Path of the Upright*: 'Our Sages have taught us that man was created only to find delight in the Lord, and to bask in the radiance of His Shekhinah

for this is the true delight and a pleasure far greater than every imaginable pleasure. But the real place for such delight is the World to Come, which has been created for that very purpose. The present world is only a path to that goal.' Other Kabbalistic sources speak of a lower and a higher heaven (Garden of Eden). In the lower heaven the saints can recognise one another as they do on earth. After a period in this lower heaven they ascend to the higher heavens by means of a special pillar, but only the greatest saints can ascend directly to the higher heaven. There is much speculation in Hasidic thought on the nature of heavenly bliss. According to some Hasidic texts, the saints in heaven are provided with a limiting element, called the spiritual 'body', in order for them to retain their individual identity; otherwise they would become absorbed in the divine splendour they witness there. The first Hasidic author to have his work published, *Jacob Joseph of Polonoyye, endeavours to explain in that work why the delights of Heaven do not pall:

'The difference between physical pleasure and the delight enjoyed by the soul is well known. Since the body is confined and restricted, any experience a person enjoys eventually becomes part of his natural capacity so that he enjoys the experience no longer. It is quite otherwise with regard to the delights enjoyed by the soul which, as a spiritual entity, has neither limits nor constraints. Such delight is infinite and unending and exists permanently.'

### Contemporary Religious Thought

Contemporary religious Jews usually prefer not to dwell on the geography of heaven and hell. Even believers in the immortality of the soul tend to speak of the 'hope' of immortality and to leave the details to God. Religious Jews, even the Orthodox, have been influenced by the general shift in religious thought from an otherworldly to a this-worldly stance. Yet this is not the whole story and the statement in the article 'Death' in Arthur A. Cohen and Paul Mendelssoh (eds.), *Contemporary Jewish Religious Thought* (New York, 1987; p. 132) is far too sweeping: 'Orthodox Judaism still clings staunchly to such notions, but other strands of modern Jewish thought are uncomfortable with the notion of an afterlife.' If this is correct, why is it that at funerals and in the house of *mourning (see DEATH AND BURIAL) prayers are recited by all religious Jews, whether Orthodox or not, for the repose of the soul of the departed, even by those who constantly stress that Judaism is primarily concerned with the conduct of life here on earth and who consider the speculations on heaven and hell in the traditional sources to be precisely that, vague speculations, incomprehensible and largely irrelevant to Jewish life in the here and now? Are they all simply playing an elaborate game? It cannot be overlooked that the thinker who has good cause to be considered the first modern Jew, Moses *Mendelssohn, the 'Father of the *Haskalah', wrote his *Phaedon* with the express intention of defending belief in immortality. And the modernist thinker, Franz *Rosenzweig, concludes his *Star of Redemption* with the words: 'To walk humbly with thy God—the words are written over the gate, the gate which leads out of the mysterious miraculous light of the divine sanctuary in which no man can remain alive. Whither, then, do the wings of the gate open? Thou knowest it not? INTO LIFE.' Vague though this conclusion is, it gives expression to the thinking of many a modernist Jew.

Abraham Cohen, 'The Hereafter', in his *Everyman's Talmud* (London, 1949), 346–89.

Louis Jacobs, 'The Hereafter', in his *A Jewish Theology* (New York, 1973), 301–22.

Aryeh Kaplan, 'On Immortality and the Soul', in his *The Aryeh Kaplan Reader* (New York, 1983), 175–83.

**Hebrew**   The language spoken and written by the ancient Israelites and, in various forms, throughout the history of the Jewish religion. The *Bible (the 'Old Testament') is in Hebrew with the exception of parts of the books of *Ezra and *Daniel, a single verse in *Jeremiah, and two words in the *Pentateuch. These are in the sister language of Hebrew, Aramaic. Both Hebrew and Aramaic belong to the Semitic branch of languages. Scholars have detected various forms of Hebrew in the Bible itself; the poetic portions, for example, preserve traces of archaic Hebrew case-endings and have other disinguishing features.

Attempts have been made from time to time to read religious ideas into the very forms of biblical Hebrew. A good deal of Samson Raphael *Hirsch's work is based on the supposed uniqueness of biblical Hebrew in conveying religious ideas by its structure and vocabulary. Such attempts are bound to fail once it is appreciated that Hebrew is only one among the Semitic languages, all of which have basically the same forms and structures. Yet even a non-Jewish scholar, A. B. Davidson (called by his colleagues 'Rabbi' Davidson) can write, in his *An Introductory Hebrew Grammar* (Edinburgh, 1923; p. 3) that there is a unique regularity in biblical Hebrew so that the student 'will find its very phonetic and grammatical principles to be instinct with something of that sweet reasonableness, that sense of fair play, we might almost say that passion for justice, for which the Old Testament in the sphere of human life so persistently and eloquently pleads'.

Post-biblical Hebrew has developed forms of its own. This is the scholarly language used by the *Tannaim, the teachers of the first two centuries CE, while the language of the people was Aramaic. Since the *Mishnah is in this form, it is known as Mishnaic Hebrew, although its use is attested before the actual Mishnaic period.

The two Talmuds, Babylonian and Palestinian, are largely in Aramaic but with portions and numerous quotations in Hebrew as well as loan words from the Greek and Persian, and the same is true of the Midrashim, but with a greater preponderance of Hebrew in the latter works. Post-Talmudic Jewish literature, influenced by the Talmudic and Midrashic forms, is in Rabbinic Hebrew, an amalgam of Hebrew and Aramaic, that is, a Hebrew with many words and expressions taken from the Talmud. The *Responsa literature is in Rabbinic Hebrew, except for some of the earlier Responsa written in Arabic. For medieval Jewish philosophical writings, a new vocabulary had to be invented, since classical Hebrew is lacking in terms for the expression of abstract ideas such as 'essence', 'existence', and 'categories'. A more or less successful attempt was made by the *Haskalah to produce poetry, novels, and other 'secular' writings in Hebrew. This paved the way for the development of Hebrew as a modern language spoken now in the State of Israel and all over the Jewish world, and called Ivrit ('Hebrew'). This name, Ivrit, is not new. It is found in the Mishnah (*Gittin* 9: 8) and has been described as 'Hebrew reborn' but is, in many ways, a new language. In Ivrit, numerous new words and forms have been introduced into the language, many of them adaptations from earlier Hebrew forms and many based on

European languages. In the context of religious discussion Hebrew is not usually referred to as Ivrit but by the term found in the Talmud (*Berakhot* 13a; *Sotah* 49b; *et passim*): *lashon ha-kodesh*, 'the sacred tongue'.

### Religious Aspects

The standard Jewish *liturgy and the majority of the later additions to it are in Hebrew. The early Reformers introduced a new liturgy, a good deal of it in the vernacular. The Orthodox Rabbis, while admitting that according to Jewish law prayers can be recited in any language, argued that this only applies to an individual worshipper who does not know Hebrew. To substitute German or other European languages for Hebrew in public worship involves a radical departure from tradition and cannot be tolerated. When a conference of Reform Rabbis decided, on a majority vote, that the substitution was acceptable, Zechariah *Frankel left the hall in protest. Contemporary Reform congregations, however, have tended to reintroduce a good deal of Hebrew into the liturgy. Conversely, it has long been the practice among the Orthodox in Western countries to read some of the prayers in the vernacular as well as in Hebrew. The Yiddish-speaking Jews preferred this language for ordinary purposes, reserving Hebrew for religious matters. Similarly, Sephardi Jews used *Ladino for ordinary purposes and Hebrew for sacred purposes. For this reason, many ultra-Orthodox Jews were opposed to the use of Ivrit, treating it as Hebrew and hence not to be used for secular discourse. But the opposition to Ivrit was, at times, advanced on the grounds that, on the contrary, Ivrit was a totally different language from 'the sacred tongue' of Hebrew and was the invention of the Maskilim and the Zionists whose philosophy was taboo. Only a very few of the ultra-Orthodox, nowadays, refuse to converse in Ivrit.

In mystical texts, Hebrew is the original language of mankind and is God's language, the language in which He 'spoke' to Moses and the prophets. A Christian lady is said to have observed that she was studying Hebrew in her old age so that when she went to heaven she would be able to speak to God in His own language! For the mystics, Hebrew letters are not mere conventions, as are the letters of other languages, but represent on earth spiritual, cosmic forces. Maimonides (*Guide of the*

*Perplexed*, 3. 8) writes that Hebrew is called 'the sacred tongue' because it contains no words with which to designate the male and female genitals, the sex act itself, sperm, urine, or excrement, for all of which euphemisms are used. *Nahmanides (commentary to Exodus 30. 13), as a Kabbalist, finds Maimonides' reason unconvincing. The reason why Hebrew is called 'the sacred tongue', says Nahmanides, is because God spoke in this language to His prophets and created the world by means of the letters of this language. One imagines that for the majority of Jews today, Hebrew is the 'sacred tongue' because, whatever its origin, it is in this language and in no other that the classical works of the Jewish religion have been written. For Jews, the Hebrew language is not intrinsically sacred, as Nahmanides and the mystics would have it, nor is it sacred in the sense of 'pure', as Maimonides would have it. It is sacred because of its association with all that Judaism holds sacred.

E. Kautzsch and A. E. Cowley, (eds.), 'Sketch of the History of the Hebrew Language', in *Gesenius' Hebrew Grammar* (Oxford, 1949), 8–17.

**Height** Height as a symbol for the spiritual is found very frequently in Judaism as it is in all cultures. It seems that early on in the history of the human race, the sublime was thought of as spiritually rather than spatially transcendent. In the Bible, God is often said to reside in heaven, the firmament above the earth (Genesis 1: 8), but it is hard to believe that this was taken literally even though the older spatial connotation is reserved in the language used (see COSMOLOGIES), as when, for instance, the prophet *Isaiah says that he saw the Lord 'sitting on a throne, high and lifted up, and his train filled the temple' (Isaiah 6: 1). Similarly, when Deutero-Isaiah (Isaiah 66: 1) declares: 'Thus saith the Lord, the heaven is my throne, and the earth is my footstool', the 'throne' on high is as little to be taken literally as the 'footstool' on earth. Particularly significant in this connection is the Psalmist's declaration (Psalms 113: 4–6): 'The Lord is high above all nations, and His glory above the heavens. Who is like unto the Lord our God, that dwelleth on high; that looketh down so low upon the heavens and the earth?' As Edwyn Bevan has noted, the first chapter of Genesis demolishes in a single phrase in the first verse, any idea of God as coinciding with the sky: 'In the beginning God created the heavens'. If God created the heavens, He must have existed in almighty power before there was any heaven there at all. No doubt many Jews did, and still do, like many non-Jewish believers, think of God as somehow located 'up there', but ordinary folk as well as the thinkers generally qualify this by, consciously or unconsciously, treating height in this connection as a metaphor. As late as the twelfth century CE, Maimonides is obliged to devote a section of his *Guide of the Perplexed* (i. 20) to a demonstration that 'high', when used of God in the Bible, is a homonym and denotes rank, quality, and power.

Height as a metaphor for spiritual excellence is found in other contexts throughout the history of Jewish thought. The soul *ascends* to heaven and *descends* to *hell; the land of Israel is said to be 'higher than all other lands' (this may originally have been meant literally but was certainly later understood in terms of value); the saints are said to be 'inhabitants of the heights'; the angels are higher than human beings (and in some respects lower); a book of the prophets may be sold in order to buy a Scroll of the Torah but not vice versa because 'one ascends in sacred matters and one does not descend'.

> Edwyn Bevan, 'Height', in his *Symbolism and Belief* (London, 1962), 25–72.

**Hellenism** Greek culture, which spread from the end of the fourth century BCE to influence Jews in the land of Israel and in the *Diaspora, to some features of which many Jews became increasingly attracted and to some of which they reacted with hostility in the name of their religion. The *Maccabees fought against the armies of Antiochus in his attempt to introduce Greek culture to the detriment of Judaism but it was Jewish Hellenizers who encouraged the tyrant in the first place. Hellenism in the Greek and later the Roman period in Palestine made heavy inroads into the life of the Jews. Buildings, public highways, bath-houses, and markets all followed the Hellenistic pattern. It is highly revealing that the highest court in the land became known by the Greek name, Sanhedrin. An early teacher mentioned in the first chapter of *Ethics of the Fathers had a Greek name, Antigones. Rabban *Gamaliel, the Mishnah (*Avodah Zarah* 3: 4) states, bathed in a public path-house in which there was a statue of Aphrodite, excusing his conduct on the grounds that the statue was erected there purely

as an adornment, not as an object of worship. According to a Talmudic account (*Sotah* 49b), Rabban Simeon ben Gamaliel said: 'There were a thousand young men in my father's house, five hundred of whom studied the Torah, while the other five hundred studied Greek wisdom.' Even if this report is legendary, as might be concluded from the artificial round numbers, it must have had some basis in fact. Of the same Rabban Simeon ben Gamaliel the Mishnah (*Megillah* 1: 8) states that, while he took issue with the sages who ruled that the Torah can be written in other languages than Hebrew, he still ruled that it could be written in Greek. The Babylonian Talmud (*Megillah* 9b) suggests, in support, the verse: 'God enlarge Japheth, and he shall dwell in the tents of Shem' (Genesis 9: 27), taken to mean: 'Let the words of Japheth [identified with the ancestor of the Greeks] dwell in the tents of Shem.' By a pun on Japheth and the Hebrew word for 'enlarge', *yaft*, the further elaboration is given: 'Let the beauty [from *yafeh*] be in the tents of Shem.' Originally applied to the question of whether a *Sefer Torah may be written in Greek, this saying became a slogan for Jews in the *Haskalah period who saw the need for Judaism to effect some accommodation with Western civilization, the eighteenth and nineteenth-century version of Hellenism. Saul Lieberman has shown that some of the Talmudic Rabbis were not averse to quoting, in their discussions, Greek proverbs and sayings in the original Greek.

Yet the influence of Hellenism on the Rabbis must not be exaggerated. There are statements in the Talmudic literature warning of the dangers of Greek wisdom and the temptations afforded by circuses, arenas, and theatres. And while some of the Rabbis evidently had an acquaintance with Greek thought, this cannot have been very profound since the great Greek thinkers, Socrates, Plato, and Aristotle, are never referred to in the whole of the Rabbinic literature.

The Greek-speaking Jews of Alexandria, whose greatest representative is *Philo, produced the *Septuagint, the translation of the Bible into Greek. In Philo the two cultures, Judaism and Hellenism, met and, for the first time, an attempt was made to interpret, or at least to defend, the religion, in the light of Greek thought. The conflict between the Maimonists and anti-Maimonists in the Middle

Ages over the desirability of studying Greek *philosophy contained many echoes of the earlier struggle between Judaism and Hellenism. Those who favoured the study of philosophy justified their stance by referring to the legend, known already to Philo, that Alexander the Great was a disciple of Socrates, who travelled with him when he came to the land of Israel. There Socrates sat at the feet of Jewish sages who taught him all he came to know, so that Greek philosophy is, in fact, Jewish philosophy.

Saul Lieberman, *Hellenism in Jewish Palestine* (New York, 1962).

——*Greek in Jewish Palestine*, New York, 1965.

——'How Much Greek in Jewish Palestine?', in Alexander Altmann (ed.), *Biblical and Other Studies* (Cambridge, Mass., 1963), 123–41.

**Herem** A ban imposed on an individual to separate him from the other members of the community. The Hebrew word *herem* denotes a setting-apart for a particular purpose, when, for instance, property is devoted for Temple use. In Arabic the harem is the place set aside for the women. When *Joshua destroyed the city of Jericho, he pronounced a *herem* on anything appertaining to the city and when Achan took of that which was proscribed he was severely punished for his disobedience of the ban (Joshua 6–7). In the book of *Ezra the *herem* takes the form of confiscation of property and exclusion from the community: 'Then a proclamation was issued in Judah and Jerusalem that all who had returned from the exile should assemble in Jerusalem, and that anyone who did not come in three days would, by decision of the officers and elders, have his property confiscated and himself excluded from the congregation of the returning exiles' (Ezra 10: 7–8). In the Talmud, these verses are used in support of the right of a court to confiscate property where this is seen as necessary for the preservation of communal life but the *herem* proper applied only to excommunication of the person, with no confiscation of his property.

In the Middle Ages, among the offences for which the *herem* was invoked were: disobedience to court orders; refusal to pay damages; insulting an official of the court; reviling scholars; and preventing the community from discharging its duties. The *herem* was thus an effective method of maintaining communal cohesion and authority. There are rare instances of a *herem* imposed on an individual for his heretical views, of which the best-known instance is the ban on *Spinoza by the court in Amsterdam. The ban on polygamy attributed to Rabbenu *Gershom of Mayyerce became known as the *herem* of Rabbenu Gershom, although there is no evidence that this enactment took the form of a *herem*.

According to the Talmud (*Moed Katan* 16a) the first stage was for the offender to be placed under a minor form of the ban for thirty days. If he persisted in his error he was banned for another thirty days. If he still persisted the full *herem* was imposed on him. A man under *herem* had to observe the laws of *mourning as if a near relative of his had died. He was not allowed, for instance, to wear shoes and bathe his whole body. Apart from the immediate members of his family, no one was allowed to come within 4 cubits of him and those who did became themselves liable to the *herem*. He was not to be taught the Torah but was allowed to study on his own. He could no longer qualify to make up a *minyan, the quorum of ten required for prayer. If he died while under the ban his coffin was to be stoned but this was understood to mean that a stone was placed symbolically on the coffin. In extreme cases, the *herem* was pronounced in the synagogue, where black candles were kindled, the Ark opened, the *shofar* sounded, and the offender solemnly cursed.

In modern times the whole institution of the *herem* has largely fallen into desuetude. On the threshold of the modern period, Moses *Mendelssohn, on grounds of religious tolerance, expressed his opposition to the right of the Rabbis to impose the *herem*. In many European communities, the governments declared the imposition of the *herem* to be illegal and Jews obeyed the laws of the countries in which they resided. Excessive resort to the *herem* was, in any event, self-defeating. When *herem* met with counter-*herem*, it often happened that so many people we were under the ban that it became totally unenforceable, nothing more than an expression of strong disapproval. The sporadic attempts, nowadays, to impose a *herem* are treated as something of a joke.

David Menahem Shohet, 'Excommunication', in his *The Jewish Court in the Middle Ages* (New York, 1974), 142–50.

**Heresy** The holding of beliefs contrary to the Jewish religion. Any attempt to study the phenomenon of heresy in Judaism has to take note of the differences in this matter between Judaism and the Christian Church. The various councils of the Church met in order to define Christian doctrine, any departure from which was seen as heresy. In Judaism, on the other hand, while there are Jewish *dogmas, there has never been any officially accepted formulation of these, no meeting, say, of authoritative Rabbis, to decide what it is that Judaism teaches in matters of faith. It is no accident that Maimonides, who drew up his thirteen *principles of the Jewish religion, was the first noted Jewish thinker to attempt a systematic treatment of the various types of heresy. Ironically, Maimonides himself was accused of heresy because of his declaration that anyone who believes that God is corporeal is a heretic! What actually happened in the history of Judaism was that a kind of consensus emerged among the faithful that there are limits in matters of faith, broad to be sure, to step beyond which is heretical.

There are a number of terms corresponding to heretic in the Rabbinic sources. There are references to Jews who 'deny the root principle', denoting *atheism in its practical sense, that is, the attitude which, while not necessarily denying that God exists, denies that God is concerned with human life and its conduct. Another widely used term is *epikoros, not connected, strangely enough, in the Rabbinic literature with the Greek philosopher Epicurus, but understood as referring to people who entertain false beliefs about the Torah and who revile its teachers. But the most frequent term for heretic is min. This word (plural minim) means a 'species' and is used to denote a sectarian. For 'heresy' the word, coined from min, is minut. To give one example among many, the Talmud (Berakhot 12b) observes that when Scripture states 'do not follow your own hearts' (Numbers 15: 39) it refers to heresy (minut) since in another verse it is said: 'the fool hath said in his heart there is no God' (Psalms 14: 1). The minim mentioned in the Rabbinic literature may be the early Christians or the Gnostics but the term minim embraces all sectarians who hold dualistic views contrary to pure Jewish monotheism.

In the post-Talmudic period, among the groups to be declared heretical by the Rabbinic upholders of the tradition were the *Karaites; some of the rationalistic philosophers; the *Shabbeteans, and the *Frankists. Some of the Kabbalists dubbed opponents of the Kabbalah heretics for denying the 'true science', while these opponents considered the Kabbalah to be heretical because of its belief in the *Sefirot. The *Mitnaggedim regarded the Hasidim as heretics for their belief that all is in God (see *Hasidism and *Panentheism) and in the powers of the *Zaddik, and the Hasidim the Mitnaggedim for denying, among other things, these selfsame powers. Both Hasidim and Mitnaggedim often called followers of the *Haskalah heretics. Some Rabbis denigrated the Zionists as heretics who took matters into their own hands instead of waiting patiently for the *Messiah. The early Reformers were seen as heretics by the Orthodox Rabbis; the term 'Orthodox' itself is adapted from Christian discussions of orthodoxy versus heresy. On the contemporary scene, many of the Orthodox consider Reform, Conservative, and *Reconstructionist Jews to be heretics, albeit unintentional ones.

Heretics were treated with opprobrium but were only rarely excommunicated; the *herem was reserved largely for practical breaches of communal discipline. On the other hand, *Spinoza was excommunicated by the Amsterdam Rabbis for his pantheistic beliefs. The statement in the Talmud (Avodah Zarah 26b) that if heretics fall into a pit they need not be rescued and may even be pushed in the pit to die, is obviously hyperbole. There is no instance of it ever having been followed in practice. Even Maimonides, not particularly noted for his religious tolerance, states that this was the law.

Louis Jacobs, *A Tree of Life: Diversity, Flexibility, and Creativity in Jewish Law* (Oxford, 1984), 104–21, 137.

**Hermeneutics** The science of biblical exegesis by the early Talmudic Rabbis in accordance with certain rules. The idea behind the system is that the full implications of the biblical laws can only be ascertained by a close scrutiny of the text for which the hermeneutic principles provide the key. A question much discussed in modern scholarship is whether the application of these rules was believed by the Rabbis to convey the true meaning of the law, so that the laws were seen as actually derived from the texts examined, or whether the laws were arrived at by other means, either by tradition or by independent reasoning, and the hermeneutical rules were intended to show that the laws have a basis in the Torah. It is impossible to provide a simple solution to this extremely complicated question. It often seems that when the Rabbis engaged in detailed exegesis in order to arrive at the law to be followed, they saw their conclusion as actually one demanded by the exegesis. On the other hand, where the exegesis was too unlikely for it to be believed to be the actual source of the law, it seems probable that the Rabbis knew this and were really saying, this is what the law must be and we can attempt to show that our understanding has a basis in Scripture. The *Karaites, in their opposition to the Talmud, alleged that the hermeneutical principles were a foreign importation into Judaism and were no more than Jewish adaptations of Greek reasoning methods.

The employment of seven hermeneutical principles is attributed in the sources to *Hillel. But the formulation of thirteen principles by the first- to second-century teacher, Rabbi *Ishmael, is the usually accepted formulation, appearing in the standard Prayer Book as part of the morning service. This inclusion in the Prayer Book is based on the idea that every Jew, in addition to his prayers, should study each day something of the Torah, which the rules provide in capsule form, although it cannot be imagined that the average worshipper has an inkling of what he is saying when he recites these difficult rules.

Considerations of space permit only a brief outline of Rabbi Ishmael's thirteen principles. The earliest source in which they are found is the Midrash known as Sifra (see MIDRASH), the introduction to which begins with: 'Rabbi Ishmael says, by means of thirteen principles the Torah is expounded' and then gives the following list.

1. The inference from the minor to the major: If $A$ is so then $A2$ is certainly so.

2. An inference by a similar expression used in two different texts. A law found in one text applies also to the other text.

3. A conclusion derived from a construction stated in a single verse or from one stated in two verses.

4. A general statement followed by a statement of a particular instance. Only this particular instance is intended by the general statement.

5. A particular statement followed by a general statement. The general statement is intended to include instances other than that in the particular statement.

6. A general statement followed by a particular statement followed by another general statement. Other instances than those in the particular statement are to be included but only if these are similar to that in the particular statement.

7. A general statement requires a particular statement for its meaning or a particular statement requires a general statement for its meaning. Here the general and the particular complement one another.

8. A general statement is followed by a particular statement but something new is mentioned in the particular. This new addition is to be applied to the general statement.

9. Particular instances of a general rule are treated specifically in details similar to those in the general rule; then only the relaxations, not the severities, of the general rule are to be applied in these instances.

10. When particular instances of a general rule are treated specifically in details dissimilar to those included in the general rule, then both relaxations and severities are to be applied in those instances.

11. When a particular instance of a general rule is singled out for completely fresh treatment, the details contained in the general rule must not be applied to this instance unless Scripture does so specifically.

12. The meaning of a passage can be derived either from its context or from a statement later on in the same passage.

13. When two verses appear to contradict one another, a third verse can be discovered which reconciles them.

In addition to Rabbi Ishmael's thirteen, other hermeneutical principles are found in the Talmudic literature. For instance, it is generally accepted that the portions of the Torah are not arranged necessarily in chronological order, so that events related in a later passage may have taken place before those related in an earlier passage. Another principle is that while there can be additional interpretations of a scriptural verse, the verse does not lose entirely its plain meaning.

Once the Talmud had become authoritative, the later teachers developed hermeneutic principles for the interpretation of the Talmud itself but did not apply new principles to Scripture.

H. L. Strack and G. Stemberger, 'Rabbinical Hermeneutics', in their *Introduction to the Talmud and Midrash* (Edinburgh, 1991), 17–34.

**Hertz, Joseph Herman** Orthodox Rabbi, communal leader, and author (1872–1946). Hertz was born in Romania but emigrated when young to America where he studied, obtaining his Ph.D. degree from Columbia University. He was the first Rabbinic graduate of the Jewish Theological Seminary. Later he was greatly influenced by Solomon *Schechter's ideas on the desirability of allowing the Jewish tradition to be open to the findings of modern scholarship. Hertz served first as a Rabbi in Syracuse, New York State, and later as Rabbi in South Africa, where he was a powerful advocate of human rights. In 1913 Hertz was appointed Chief Rabbi of the United Hebrew congregations of the British Empire, a post he occupied for the rest of his life. Among his many political activities, Hertz, a deeply committed Zionist, was instrumental in frustrating the efforts of some leaders of the Anglo-Jewish community to prevent the Balfour Declaration being issued.

In his written works, Hertz defended Orthodox Judaism (of the moderate Anglo-Jewish type) against its detractors from outside and from within the Jewish camp. Hertz was never one to pull his punches, whether in his role of Chief Rabbi or in his writings. It was said of him that he preferred the peaceful way if no other was available. His *Affirmations of Judaism* (Oxford, 1927) contains three sermons, entitled 'The New Paths: Whither Do They Lead?', in which he attacked the thinking of the Liberal movement, an English version of radical Reform. His *Book of Jewish Thoughts*, of which many editions have been published, is an excellent anthology of writings on Jews and Judaism culled from both Jewish and non-Jewish works. His commentary to the Prayer Book is a superb devotional work in the modern spirit.

Hertz's best-known and most influential work is his *Pentateuch and Haftorahs*, written in collaboration with other Anglo-Jewish scholars. In his introduction to this work, Hertz defends his particular stance:

'Jewish and non-Jewish commentators—ancient, medieval and modern—have been freely drawn upon. "Accept the truth from whatever source it come", is sound Rabbinic doctrine—even if it be from the pages of a devout Christian expositor or of an iconoclastic Bible scholar, Jewish or non-Jewish. This does not affect the Jewish Traditional character of the work. My conviction that the criticism of the Pentateuch associated with the name of Wellhausen is a perversion of history and a desecration of religion, is unshaken; likewise, my refusal to eliminate the Divine either from history or from human life.'

In the book, Hertz is prepared to accept the theory of *evolution; sees no dogma involved in the suggestion that the second part of Isaiah was composed by an unknown prophet during the exile; and quotes an opinion that the plague of darkness in Egypt was caused by a partial eclipse of the sun. Yet his attitude towards *biblical criticism proper is very one-sided. With great zest he sets up supposedly critical views in order to demolish them, so that his work has to be seen more as a exercise in apologetics than as one of objective scholarship. Reform Rabbis saw the work as too Orthodox, Orthodox Rabbis as too Reform. But Hertz was disturbed neither by critics of the Pentateuch nor by his own critics and went on his way undaunted.

Isidore Epstein (ed.), *Joseph Herman Hertz 1872–1946: In Memoriam* (London, 1947).

**Herzl, Theodor** Foremost leader of political *Zionism (1860–1904). Herzl belonged to a fairly assimilated Jewish family in Vienna. He took a law degree at the university but earned his living as a playwright and particularly as a successful journalist on the *Neue Freie Presse*. The story has often been told of how Herzl, reporting for his paper in Paris on the Dreyfus Affair, in which the thoroughly assimilated Captain Dreyfus, in an anti-Semitic plot, was falsely accused of treason, came to realise that the *Emancipation of the Jews, far from solving the Jewish problem, only aggravated it by creating severe tensions between the Jews and their neighbours in European society. In Herzl's view, the Jews had to consider themselves to be not only a religious body but also a nation capable of developing its own political institutions in a land of its own.

Herzl gave expression to his views in 1896 with the publication of *Judenstaat* ('Jewish State'). He eventually came to appreciate that the creation of such a Jewish State could be

feasible only in Palestine, the traditional homeland of the Jewish people. Herzl has been
described as a 'practical dreamer' and it is true
that, with considerable organizing ability, he
worked for the practical realization of his aim,
succeeding in winning many Jews to co-operate
with him in, at the time, a seemingly impossible
task. The first Zionist Congress was held in
Basle in 1897 at which the World Zionist
Organization was founded and Herzl elected
as its President. In 1902 Herzl published his
utopian vision of the Jewish State, the *Altneuland*
('Old New Land'). Herzl died, at the early age
of 44, in Vienna, where he was buried. In 1949
Herzl's remains were taken to Jerusalem where
they were buried on a hill, now called Mount
Herzl. More than any other thinker and politician, Herzl was indirectly responsible for the
emergence of the State of Israel and is acknowledged to be the State's true founder.

It is undeniable that Herzl's ideas, while
contributing immensely to the survival of the
Jewish people, created problems for the Jewish
religion. For Herzl and for political Zionism as
a movement, the Jews were a nation like other
nations, and this raised questions about the
nature of Judaism. The majority of the Rabbis
in Herzl's day, whether Orthodox or Reform,
were opposed to his views on precisely these
grounds. The Reformers believed that the new
emphasis on nationhood frustrated the universalistic thrust of Judaism as a world religion
independent of nationality. The Orthodox, at
the opposite end of the spectrum, believed that
the particularistic elements in Judaism were
contained in the Torah and the practice of its
laws, not in any form of secular nationalism;
though the *Mizrachi movement sought to
combine the ideas of nationalism and religion
for Jews in a modern State. Once the State of
Israel had been established, the whole debate
became purely academic, which is not to deny
that many of the problems still await their
solution.

Alexander Bein, *Herzl* (New York, 1975).

**Herzog, Isaac** Outstanding Rabbinic leader
(1888–1959). Herzog was born in Lomza, Poland, but was brought up in Paris and lived
later in Leeds, the cities in which his father
served as a Rabbi. Unusually for his time in
Orthodox circles, Herzog was largely self-
educated. It is said that at the age of 16 he
succeeded in completing the study of the whole

of the Talmud. Herzog also studied general
subjects, obtaining the D.Litt. degree from
London University for a thesis on 'The Dyeing
of Purple in Ancient Israel'. After serving as
Chief Rabbi in Ireland, Herzog was elected, in
1936, Ashkenazi Chief Rabbi of Palestine, succeeding Rabbi Abraham Isaac *Kook. When
Herzog was asked whether he had the ability to
follow such an illustrious, charismatic figure, he
replied that while he was undoubtedly inferior
to Kook as a religious thinker, he was Kook's
superior in knowledge of the Talmud and the
Codes. When the State of Israel was established, Herzog became the first Ashkenazi Chief
Rabbi of the new State. His Rabbinic decisions
in this role have had a good deal of influence on
religious life in Israel. Many of these rulings
were published in Herzog's *Responsa collections. Herzog's son, Chaim (b. 1918), was
elected President of Israel in 1983.

Herzog wrote *The Main Institutions of Jewish
Law* (1st edn., 1936; 2nd edn., London, 1967),
a work remarkable for the author's extraordinary familiarity with English law and the whole
range of traditional Jewish law. It is outstanding in its analytical approach and for pointing
out uncanny resemblances between the Halakhic
authorities and the English jurists, but has
been criticized by modern Jewish scholars for
its failure to employ a historical methodology.
Jewish law is treated in static fashion with
hardly any reference to the idea of development
in response to external conditions and outside
influences.

For all his immense secular learning, Herzog
was deeply religious and completely Orthodox
in his outlook. In the introduction to his *Main
Institutions*, Herzog discusses (pp. xxii–xxiv)
the problems that might arise if a Jewish State
were restored. Herzog quotes an article he
wrote on the subject in 1932. It is clear from
the discussion, and was known to all who knew
him, that Herzog believed implicitly in the
coming of the *Messiah and in the divine
origin of Jewish law as revealed in the Torah.
Some ask, he remarks, would not the restoration of a Jewish State isolate the Jewish people
from the modern civilized world, since the
death penalty would be imposed for purely
religious offences such as desecration of the
Sabbath? In reply, Herzog demonstrates that
for the death penalty to be imposed, a
*Sanhedrin is required. This institution cannot
legally be restored before the Temple is rebuilt

and the Temple cannot be rebuilt until the Messiah comes. In an astonishing conclusion (written in 1932 and repeated in 1937) Herzog writes: 'The difficulty in question is therefore a matter which could only arise in the *Messianic* age and need not enter into any practical calculations affecting the reconstitution of the Jewish State in Palestine. But, of course, in view of the actual position the idea of a Jewish State in Palestine (as distinct from a Jewish National Home), quite irrespective of the restoration of the Temple, is, itself, rather a *Messianic* hope than a question of practical politics.' Little did Herzog realize, when he wrote this, that not only would a Jewish State be established but that he would become its first Chief Rabbi.

> Chaim Herzog (ed.), *Judaism Law and Ethics by the late Chief Rabbi Dr Isaac Herzog* (London, 1974).

**Heschel, Abraham Joshua** Religious philosopher (1907–72). Heschel was descended on both his father's and mother's side from a long line of Hasidic *Zaddikim. Heschel himself seemed destined to occupy the role of a Hasidic Rebbe but, while intensely loyal to Hasidism, he preferred, at an early age, to follow in the path of modern philosophy and scholarship, leaving his native Poland to study in Berlin at the university and at the Jewish Hochschule für die Wissenschaft des Judenthums. He was deported by the Nazis in 1938 but eventually escaped to London and was later invited to occupy a Chair at the Hebrew Union College in Cincinnati, the main institution for the training of Reform Rabbis. Heschel was not really at home in a Reform seminary and in 1946 he was appointed to the Chair of Jewish Ethics and Mysticism at the Conservative Jewish Theological Seminary in New York, a position he occupied for the rest of his life.

Heschel was never one to believe that a religious thinker can afford to live in an ivory tower. He played a significant role in connection with the Second Vatican Council where his views on Judaism and Christian–Jewish dialogue were treated with great respect. He marched together with Martin Luther King for civil rights and became a leading Jewish spokesman in the USA on issues of social justice.

Heschel was a prolific author. All his works have a strong mystical tinge, owing much to his Hasidic background. In his book on the Hebrew *prophets (Die Prophetie)*, published in English as *The Prophets* (New York, 1962), Heschel broke new ground in biblical studies in seeing the prophets as participants in the divine pathos; an idea criticized by some thinkers as too anthropomorphic. This idea was developed further in Heschel's *Man is Not Alone: A Philosophy of Religion* (New York, 1951) and *God in Search of Man: A Philosophy of Judaism* (New York, 1955). In these works Heschel sees the sense of wonder, which modern man is in danger of losing, as essential to any religious outlook on life. Heschel once began a lecture by saying: 'An hour or two ago the greatest event in human history took place. The sun set!' Heschel's study of Polish Jewry, *The Earth is the Lord's* (New York, 1950), is a prose poem on the spirituality of the religious community of Poland; a community in which, as Heschel observes, carriers could be seen to pitch their waggons outside the synagogue each night while they themselves repaired to study the Torah. In his book *The Sabbath: Its Meaning for Modern Man* (New York, 1951), Heschel puts forward the somewhat one-sided view that, unlike the pagan religions, in which the 'gods of space' are worshipped, in Judaism it is sacred time that is significant; time representing religious dynamism with touches of eternity. In his study of the Hasidic master Menahem Mendel of *Kotsk, *A Passion for Truth* (New York, 1973), Heschel compares this unconventional master with his near contemporary, Kierkegaard.

Heschel, in his Hebrew work on the doctrine 'the Torah is from heaven' and in his other works, develops the idea that the Torah, while it should not be understood in any fundamentalistic way—that God literally delivered all the precepts to Moses at Sinai—is, none the less, the record of the divine will. Taking issue with Mordecai *Kaplan and other religious naturalists, Heschel refuses to think of God in terms of function, as the power that makes for righteousness. God, for Heschel, is a Person, or, rather, more and not less than a Person. Heschel, while accepting that Jewish institutions, including the *Halakhah, did not simply drop down from heaven but have had a history, yet thinks of the Halakhah as the most significant element in Judaism, and Heschel was himself a strictly observant Jew. In this Heschel represents the thinking of *Conservative Judaism but with mystical nuances of his own. Yet, Heschel argues, pan-Halakhism, a term he coined for the attitude in which only the Halakhah is seen to be important, is a distortion of Judaism. In Judaism, the non-legal element, the *Aggadah, is at least as important. Heschel, in treading the middle road between fundamentalism and religious liberalism, between the mystical and rational, between the prosaic Halakhah and the poetic Aggadah, does not really succeed in doing justice to the extremes and his work, for all its high value, has justly been criticized for its vagueness in places, a vagueness not helped by the numerous purple passages in his writings. Yet to Heschel's credit, he has demonstrated that the mystical approach to Judaism and the observance of the precepts is possible for the modern Jew without any sacrifice of intellectual integrity.

Heschel's daughter, Susannah, is a leading Jewish feminist (see FEMINISM).

Fritz A. Rothschild (ed.), *Between God and Man: An Interpretation of Judaism from the Writings of Abraham J. Heschel* (New York, 1976).

**High Priest** Chief among the *priests who officiated in the *Temple; Heb. *kohen gadol*, lit. 'great priest'. The High Priest was distinguished from ordinary priests in a number of respects. Based on Exodus 28, the Talmudic sources state that every priest, while performing the Temple service, had to wear four garments: a tunic, a girdle, a turban, and breeches reaching from the hips to the thighs. These four were worn by the High Priest as well but in addition he wore four further garments. These were: the *ephod*, a kind of apron, worn from behind with a sash in front around his middle; the *meil*, a coat reaching from his neck to his feet with bells and pomegranate-shaped adornments at its hem; the *ḥoshen*, a breastplate to which were affixed twelve precious stones containing the engraved names of the twelve tribes; and the *tzitz*, a gold forehead piece on which was engraved the words: 'Holy to the Lord.' The breastplate is said in the Exodus account to contain the *Urim Ve-Thummim, an oracle. Whatever the original meaning of the Urim Ve-Thummim, in the Talmudic tradition it was not a separate object but represented the miraculous illumination of certain letters of the stones on the breastplate so as to yield information about the fate of the people.

Unlike ordinary priests, the High Priest (Leviticus 21: 10–14) was only allowed to marry a virgin who had not before been married.

Unlike ordinary priests, who, while not permitted to come into contact with a corpse, were allowed to come into contact with the corpse of a near relative, the High Priest was not allowed to come into contact even with the corpse of his father and mother. The Kabbalist Hayyim *Ibn Atar, explains this latter rule in an interesting, though unhistorical, comment. The High Priest, by virtue of his elevated role as the totally committed servant of God, had already severed his emotional ties with his parents from the moment he assumed office.

On the basis of Leviticus 16, it is stated in the Talmudic sources that all the services in the Temple on *Yom Kippur could be carried out only by the High Priest. No one was allowed to enter the Holy of Holies at any time except the High Priest on this awesome day, when he entered to atone for his people.

It is difficult to know how far all these details developed out of the rules as stated in the Pentateuch or how the Pentateuchal rules themselves were originally formulated, since there is hardly any information about the role of the High Priest in the period of the First Temple. It seems that towards the end of the Second Temple period, under Roman rule, the office of the High Priest was often a political appointment and there are Talmudic references to the unworthiness of the High Priests in this period. There are echoes of this in the statement of the Mishnah (*Horayot* 3: 8) that a *mamzer ('bastard') who is a scholar takes precedence over an ignorant High Priest and in the Talmudic statement attributed to Rabbi *Meir (*Bava Kama* 38a) that even a *Gentile who occupies himself with the Torah is equal to the High Priest. In other words, a new aristocracy, that of learning, was established. With the destruction of the Temple, the office of High Priest vanished entirely from Jewish life.

**Hillel** Foremost teacher in Palestine in the first century BCE. Together with *Shammai, Hillel is mentioned in the first chapter of Ethics of the Fathers as the last of the 'Pairs' (see ZUGOT), the five sets of two spiritual heads in succession until the leadership of the people was in the hands of Hillel's descendants, of the house of Rabban *Gamaliel. A number of Hillel's descendants were also named Hillel, of whom the best-known is the fourth-century Hillel to whom is attributed the fixing of the *calendar.

The problem scholars have had to face in attempting to put together a biography of Hillel is that the major sources for Hillel and his activity are the Talmud and the Midrash and a good deal of the material in these sources dates from no earlier than the time of their compilation, often centuries after Hillel. Great caution is therefore necessary when using these sources for a reconstruction of Hillel's life and work. For instance, much has been made of the Talmudic story (*Shabbat* 31a) in which Hillel, when asked by a prospective convert to Judaism to teach him the whole Torah while he stood on one leg, replied: 'That which is hateful unto you do not do to your neighbour. This is the whole of the Torah. The rest is commentary. Go forth and study.' Theologians, Jewish and non-Jewish, have compared this version of the Golden Rule, stated in negative form, with that of *Jesus, in the positive form. There is a total failure to appreciate that this story is told, in Babylonian Aramaic, at least two hundred years after Hillel and probably much later. Moreover, in the same set of stories related in a Midrash, the hero is not Hillel at all but Rabbi *Joshua. Similarly, when it is said of Hillel and other key figures that they lived for 120 years, it is as obvious as can be that this is not factual but a way of saying that these teachers followed in the footsteps of Moses who was 120 years old at his death (Deuteronomy 34: 7). Yet while there is little authentic information about Hillel and Shammai themselves, the Mishnah and Talmud are full of the great debates between the House of Hillel and the House of Shammai, Bet Hillel and Bet Shammai.

### The Two Houses

That there were two houses, in the sense of schools, formed of the disciples of the two sages, is undeniable but even with regard to these houses the sources have to be approached with caution. Although, in the Talmudic sources, the House of Hillel generally gives lenient rulings in matters of law and the House of Shammai stricter rulings, it can hardly be suggested that the three hundred and more cases debated by the two great schools depended solely, or even mainly, on whether the law should be decided strictly or leniently. We are told nowhere, in fact, why two separate schools should have emerged at all and we are largely left in ignorance both of their composition and of the principles by which they operated. In an oft-quoted Talmudic passage (*Eruvin*, 13b), dating not earlier than the third century CE and obviously containing strong elements of pure legend, it is said that for three years the two houses debated whether the law should be decided in accordance with the House of Hillel or the House of Shammai and there was a danger that the Torah would become two Torahs; in other words, there was a danger of schism in which the religious practices and the laws of one group of Jews were quite different from those of another group of Jews. The issue was finally decided by a *Bat Kol, a voice from heaven, which declared: 'Both these and these are the words of the living God but the law [the *Halakhah] is in accordance with the rulings of the House of Hillel.' All this has left modern scholarship with the extremely difficult and purely conjectural task of discovering the guiding principles behind the decisions and debates between the two houses.

Some modern scholars suggest that the two houses operated by different exegetical methods, interpreting Scripture in ways which led to different practical conclusions. In one version of this theory, the House of Shammai favoured a more literal meaning of Scripture, while the House of Hillel tended to interpret Scripture in a less than literal manner. Louis Ginzberg (1873–1953) advanced the ingenious thesis that the two houses really represented two social classes: the House of Shammai legislating for the wealthy landowners, the 'patricians', the House of Hillel for the working classes, the 'plebeians', as these are called by Ginzberg's disciple, Louis Finkelstein. To give one example among many, the Mishnah (*Gittin* 9: 10) states: 'The House of Shammai say: A man may not divorce his wife unless he has found her to be unfaithful, for it is written (Deuteronomy 24: 1) "because he has found some indecency in her". But the House of Hillel say: Even if she spoiled a dish for him, for it is written: "because he has found *some* [i.e. 'any'] indecency in her".' On the theory of difference in exegetical principles, the different rulings of the two houses are based solely on how literally the verse is to be interpreted. But on the Ginzberg-Finkelstein hypothesis, the scriptural exegesis is secondary and derives (see *Hermeneutics) from the different needs and attitudes of two different social classes. The two houses, each legislating for a different social class, are bound to interpret Scripture in the way they do, since the position of women among the aristocracy is far better than among the lower social classes. The trouble with all the theories, is that they can only be made to work by selective quotations and are far too neat. And what is one to make of the purely theological debates between the two houses upon which neither the exegetical nor the sociological theory has any bearing? Why, for example, did the House of Shammai say (*Eruvin* 13b) that it were better for a man not to have been created than to have been created and the House of Hillel say it were better for man to have been created than not to have been created, and why did the House of Hillel eventually agree with the House of Shammai on this matter? To date, no satisfactory theory has been advanced which convincingly explains the reason or reasons for the emergence of two separate schools.

It remains true that, because of the Bat Kol, Jewish law is usually decided in favour of the House of Hillel. In the sixteenth-century Lurianic Kabbalah, it is stated that in this world, the law generally follows the more lenient views of the House of Hillel, but in the Messianic age, when people will have greater spiritual stamina, the law will follow the tougher rulings of the House of Shammai.

> Louis Ginzberg, 'The Significance of the Halachah for Jewish History', in his *On Jewish Law and Lore* (New York, 1877, 77–124).

**Hirsch, Samson Raphael** German Rabbi and religious thinker (1808–88). Hirsch was born in Hamburg where he received a general as well as a traditional Jewish education. His teacher in Hamburg was Isaac Bernays and in Mannheim Rabbi Jakob Ettlinger, the most distinguished Talmudist in German Jewry. Both these teachers were men of a comparatively broad outlook. Influenced by them, Hirsch saw his life's task as being to demonstrate that traditional Judaism is fully compatible with Western culture. Hirsch studied classical languages, history, and philosophy for a short time at the University of Bonn but he did not take a university degree. Abraham *Geiger was a fellow-student of Hirsch at Bonn but later their paths diverged, Geiger becoming leader of the Reform movement to which Hirsch was relentlessly opposed. In 1830 Hirsch was appointed Rabbi of Oldenburg and in 1846 he was appointed District Rabbi of Moravia, living in the town of Nikolsburg. A small number of Orthodox families in Frankfurt-on-Main, disturbed by the assimilated tendencies of the general Jewish community, invited Hirsch to become their Rabbi in 1851. This new Orthodox community flourished under Hirsch's guidance.

Hirsch believed that the only way to preserve the Orthodoxy of his community was to obtain permission from the German authorities to establish a separatist organization. To further this aim, Hirsch argued that the differences between Orthodoxy and Reform were akin to those between Catholicism and Protestantism in Christianity: two religious attitudes that could not exist side by side. Hirsch's community soon became the model for communities ready to be both open to general culture and strict in adherence to Orthodox practices, hence the term *neo-Orthodoxy by which this tendency is known. In a real sense, Hirsch was a child of the *Haskalah but his 'enlightenment' had a far greater thrust in the direction of Orthodox Jewish beliefs and observances. In his early work *The Nineteen Letters of Ben Uziel*, Hirsch typically remarked that it would have been better for the Jews not to have been emancipated if the price they had to pay was assimilation.

Hirsch's *Nineteen Letters* was written while he was Rabbi in Oldenburg. The work made a great impression in wide circles of German Jewry and beyond. The historian *Graetz, then a young man, was so impressed that he came to Oldenburg to study under Hirsch for three years, but later Hirsch and Graetz came to differ widely in their views, chiefly on the historical approach to Judaism, an approach for which Hirsch had no sympathy because it tended to produce a relativistic attitude towards the Torah. At Oldenburg, Hirsch also wrote his *Horeb: Essays on Israel's Duties in the Diaspora*, in which he set out all the precepts of the Torah in a way that would commend itself to the cultured Jews of his time. Among Hirsch's other writings is his commentary to the Pentateuch published in Frankfurt-on-Main in 1867–78. The *Nineteen Letters* was published in an English translation by Bernard Drachman (New York, 1942); his *Horeb* by I. Grunfeld (London, 1962); and an abridged version of his commentary to the Pentateuch by Isaac Levy (London, 1958–62). Grunfeld also published *Judaism Eternal: Selected Essays from the Writings of S. R. Hirsch* (London, 1956). More recently the Samson Raphael Hirsch Publications Society published the *Collected Writings of Rabbi Samson Raphael Hirsch* (New York, 1985–8).

## Hirsch's Philosophy of Judaism

The statement in Ethics of the Fathers (2. 2) of Rabban *Gamaliel III: 'Torah is good together with *derekh eretz*', formed the basis of Hirsch's understanding of Judaism for modern Jews. In the context, *derekh eretz* (literally, 'the way of the earth') refers to a worldly occupation. But Hirsch develops the concept to embrace Western culture. This is the 'way of the world' which has to be combined with the study and the practice of the Torah. Hirsch states that *derekh eretz* refers not only to ways of earning a living but also to the social order that prevails on earth, the mores and considerations of courtesy and propriety arising from social living and things pertinent to good breeding and general education. Hence Hirsch speaks of the ideal Jew as the 'Israel-Man', that is, the Jew who is proudly Jewish, a believer in the eternal values and precepts of the Torah as divinely ordained, and is, at the same time, a cultured 'man', a human being belonging to the modern world. Hirsch certainly does not avoid the problem facing the modern Jew when he makes his imaginary protagonist remark in the first of the *Nineteen Letters*: 'How can anyone who is able to enjoy the beauties of a Virgil, a Tasso, a Shakespeare, who can follow the logical conclusions of a Leibnitz and Kant—how can such a one find pleasure in the Old Testament, so deficient in form and taste, and in the senseless writings of the Talmud?' Before Hirsch, no Orthodox Jew had ever expressed such sentiments, even as a prelude to their rebuttal.

Hirsch seeks to demonstrate in all his writings that the combination of Torah and *derekh eretz* is not only possible but essential if Judaism is to come to grips with the challenge of modern life. Basically, his approach is to see the divinely revealed Torah as the means for the ennoblement of the human spirit by bringing it closer to the divine will for the Jews and, through them, to the whole of mankind. The Jewish people have a divinely ordained role to play in the world, one that can only be realized when the Jew belongs to the world and is, in the best sense, a man of the world. This is not to say that Hirsch tolerates any watering-down of the full Jewish tradition. He fought Reform in his belief that this movement pandered to

the *Zeitgeist*, 'the spirit of the age'. Hirsch wrote in the *Nineteen Letters*:

'Was Judaism ever "in accordance with the times"? Did Judaism ever correspond with the views of dominant contemporaries? Was it ever convenient to be a Jew or a Jewess? . . . Was that Judaism in accordance with the times, for which, during the centuries following the Dispersion, our fathers suffered in all lands, through all the various periods, the most degrading oppression, the most biting contempt, and a thousand-fold death and persecution? And yet *we* would make it the aim and scope of Judaism to be always "in accordance with the times!"'

There is no doubt that Hirsch was highly successful in winning over more than one generation of German Jews to a deeper appreciation of the meaning of Judaism for modern man. In Hirsch's congregation in Frankfurt and elsewhere there were to be found cultured men and women, bankers, university professors, physicians, artists, scientists, and men of letters, thoroughly at home in Western society and yet strictly observant in their daily lives. These men demonstrated that Hirsch's philosophy was viable. To the present day, neo-Orthodoxy is an acceptable Jewish way of life and for this most of the credit goes to Hirsch and his vision.

## Critique of Hirsch's philosophy

For all the power and undoubted success of Hirsch's philosophy in the nineteenth century, it can be questioned whether Hirsch really managed to show how the Torah can be reconciled with his understanding of *derekh eretz*. Often, in Hirsch's writings, apparent contradictions between the two are resolved by reading the ideas of German romanticism into the Torah. Hirsch's approach to traditional Judaism has been criticized for its lack of scholarly method. If, for example his somewhat fanciful interpretation of biblical Hebrew words can be sustained, it would have to apply to other Semitic languages such as Arabic, whereas Hirsch sees in it the uniqueness of Hebrew. Hirsch took issue with the historians *Frankel and Graetz, because his picture of Judaism presupposes that the Jewish religion has been preserved intact from generation to generation and this runs counter to the findings of all modern historical research. Hirsch's attempt to distinguish between the basics of Judaism, which are unchanging, and the externals which can and should be changed, fails in that no criteria are provided to distinguish one from the other. Many of the Orthodox thought that Hirsch's preference for teaching the Bible rather than the Talmud, his wearing of a robe at the services, and his attempt to abolish the recital of *Kol Nidre, to be themselves Reformist and a tampering with the essentials.

On the right, Hirsch's accommodation came to be seen as no more than an emergency measure introduced in order to stem the tide of assimilation in his day, which had now to be abandoned. On any reading of Hirsch such a view cannot be defended. Hirsch was obviously enamoured of Western culture and thought of it as a good in itself, not as a necessary evil. But he fails to demonstrate adequately how such an approach is possible, granted that Judaism as he constantly affirms is unchanging.

The attitude of the Hirschean school to Zionism has been much discussed. While it is true that Hirsch saw the Jews as a people and stressed the idea of Jewish peoplehood, he refused to understand this in nationalistic terms, believing, as did the Reformers, that the Jews would find their place in Western lands once they had achieved the necessary degree of assimilation. Hirsch differed from the Reformers, however, in believing in the coming of a personal *Messiah; yet, for him, the Messianic age was a matter of the future and the culmination of human history, which is why the Hirschean school was later opposed to political Zionism.

> Zoah H. Rosenbloom, *Tradition in an Age of Reform: The Religious Philosophy of Samson Raphael Hirsch* (Philadelphia, 1976).

**History** With the exception of *Josephus, it was not until the sixteenth century, that scholars emerged to study the Jewish religion historically. Even then, David Ganz had to justify his historical approach by quoting the verse: 'Remember the days of old' (Deuteronomy 32: 7) and when Azariah de Rossi dared to examine Jewish history with reference to the Greek and Roman authors, Joseph *Karo sought, unsuccessfully, to have his book banned for its rejection of some Talmudic statements about the past as pure legend. For the medieval thinkers, truth was in no way time-conditioned. Maimonides' observation in his commentary to the Mishnah (*Sanhedrin* 10: 1) is typical. It is simply a waste of time, remarks Maimonides, to read the chronicles of the past. The historical

study of Judaism by historical-critical methods did not, in fact, begin until the rise of the *Jüdische Wissenschaft movement in the early nineteenth century when *Zunz, *Krochmal, *Rapoport, and *Frankel pioneered the critical approach to the classical Jewish sources, followed by *Graetz, *Dubnow, and many others.

From the religious point of view, the new historical approach to the Jewish religion has created problems. To study Judaism historically, rather than simply to chronicle the Jewish past, results inevitably in a degree of relativism. If it can be shown that Judaism has had a history, has responded to external conditions in various ways, this seems to strike a blow at the traditional view in which Judaism is seen as a static body of divine truth conveyed without change from age to age. Instead of reading the religion of the Bible with Talmudic eyes and the Talmud with medieval eyes, the historians tried to see each period with its own particular stresses, hopes, and fears. Reform and Conservative Judaism have largely accepted without qualification the historical approach and have sought to understand Judaism in the light of the new knowledge. Orthodox Jews, with some exceptions at the extreme right, have also been prepared to accept this approach with regard to the Talmud and even, to some extent, to the rest of the Bible with the exception of the *Pentateuch, the Torah. Here, for Orthodoxy, all *biblical criticism is still taboo.

**Holdheim, Samuel** German Reform leader (1806–60). Holdheim received a thorough traditional Jewish education in his native Poland where he was looked upon as an infant as a Talmudic prodigy; he later supplemented his early knowledge by his reading of general literature and his studies in the University of Prague. Together with Abraham *Geiger, Holdheim provided much of the intellectual vigour for the Reform movement, although Geiger, for all his radicalism, did not see eye to eye with some of Holdheim's excesses. For Holdheim, the Jewish religion contained in the past two elements: the universalistic—ethical monotheism and the doctrine of the immortality of the soul, and the nationalistic—the rituals such as the sacrificial system in Temple times and institutions such as the *dietary laws. Holdheim was fond of quoting the verse: 'One generation goes, another comes, but the earth remains the same for ever' (Ecclesiastes 1: 4), which he interpreted to mean that the universalistic element in Judaism is the 'earth', permanent and unchanging, while each 'generation' has to supply its own understanding of how this element is to be realized. Far from denigrating the *Zeitgeist*, Holdheim saw this as essential for the interpretatión of Judaism in a new light. Holdheim claimed, with scant historical justification, that his theories were supported by the Talmudic dictum: *dina de-malkhuta dina*, 'the law of the [Gentile] government is law'. In the context, this applies only to civil law; the Jew is under an obligation to obey the laws of the country in which he resides. But Holdheim extended the principle to cover religious laws, to suggest that the 'nationalistic' elements of Judaism, that is, many of the rules of the *Halakhah, are no longer binding according to Judaism itself. If this were so, the historian *Graetz protested, it would mean that Judaism provides itself with a silken halter with which to commit suicide. Undeterred, Holdheim roundly proclaimed: 'The Talmud was right in its day and I am right in mine.'

From 1847 Holdheim was the Rabbi of the Berlin Reform Temple, in which the most extreme reforms were introduced. Hebrew was largely eliminated from the prayers, Sunday services were eventually substituted for the Sabbath services, on the grounds that in Western society many Jews had to earn their living by working on the Sabbath, and intermarriage between Jews and Gentiles was not discouraged. Holdheim's extremism was not viewed with favour in Germany, apart from in his own congregation, but found an echo in the USA version of radical Reform towards the end of the nineteenth century.

> Michael M. Meyer, *Response to Modernity: A History of the Reform Movement in Judaism* (Oxford, 1988); see index: 'Holdheim, Samuel'.

**Holiness** The Hebrew word for 'holiness', *kedushah*, conveys the twin ideas of separation *from* and dedication *to* something and hence holiness as a religious ideal refers to the attitude and state of mind in which certain activities and thoughts are rejected in order to come closer to God. The concept is found in a general sense in two biblical verses. At the theophany at *Sinai, the ideal of holiness is expressed in the words: 'And ye shall be unto Me a kingdom of priests, and a holy nation' (Exodus 19: 6). The

introductory verse to the Holiness Code (as it is called by modern scholars) states: 'Speak unto all the congregation of the children of Israel, And say unto them: Ye shall be holy; for I the Lord your God am holy' (Leviticus 19: 2). In the first verse, Israel is to be separate from other nations as a holy nation dedicated to God. In the second verse, the plain meaning would seem to be: separate yourselves from the illicit practices mentioned later in the Holiness Code in order to be holy because God is holy. The Rabbinic Midrash known as the Sifra (see MIDRASH) comments on 'Ye shall be holy': 'Ye shall be separatists'. *Rashi, the great French commentator, understands the Sifra as meaning that to be holy involves separation from the illicit, particularly from sexual unchastity. On this reading, holiness is virtually synonymous with obeying the laws of the Torah and has no special connotation of extraordinary cultivation of sanctity. The latter is an ideal for the saints, the holy men, not for 'all the congregation of the children of Israel'.

However, in a famous analysis of the holiness ideal, *Nahmanides (commentary on Leviticus 19: 2) takes issue with Rashi and understands the separation mentioned in the Sifra to mean not only from the illicit but also, to some degree, from the licit. Holiness, according to Nahmanides, involves a measure of abstinence even from things permitted by the Torah. This author follows the Talmudic saying: 'Sanctify yourself with regard to that which is permitted to you' (*Yevamot* 20a). Even the average Jew, let alone the holy man, is not to be content with simple obedience to the law but must go beyond the law in his cultivation of holiness:

'The principle is that the Torah forbids illicit sexual relations and forbids certain foods but permits the sexual act in marriage and permits the eating of meat and the drinking of wine. Consequently, the libertine would have found many opportunities for unlimited sexual indulgence with his wife or with his many wives, for unrestrained gluttony and drunkenness, for speaking obscene things to his heart's desire, for these things are not explicitly forbidden in the Torah. Such a man would be a scoundrel with the full permission of the Torah. Therefore, after the Torah had detailed those things which are categorically forbidden, it enjoins a man to separate himself from that which is unnecessary.'

Holiness, then, according to Nahmanides,

and he is followed by other Jewish teachers, is the attitude of the Jew who has no wish, in Nahmanides' pungent expression, to be 'a scoundrel with the full permission of the Torah'. Nahmanides' point is that the rules and regulations of the Torah constitute the bare minimum of decent behaviour expected of every Jew, a standard below which none should fall. But an essential part of the Torah discipline is that the Jew is obliged to go beyond these minimum rules. For this there can be no hard-and-fast rules, since all depends on individual character and temperament. What may be morbid indulgence, leading to a softening of the moral fibre, for one, may be a necessity for another. For all its insistence on rules, Judaism, according to Nahmanides, acknowledges that there is a whole area of life, the area of the licit, where man's freedom of choice must operate in determining those things which will help him to live more worthily and those which can pollute his soul. In life today, for example, how many drinks a man should have in one evening, how much time he should spend watching television, which kind of films he should see, which type of books he should read, and what stand he should take on the moral issues of the day—all such matters cannot belong to Torah legislation. But that a man's religion compels him to put such questions to himself is basic to a sound religious outlook on life and it is the asking of the questions and the sincere attempt to answer them in the spirit of Judaism that is meant by the command to be holy. Clearly a balance has to be achieved between self-indulgence and priggishness, a balance that can only be achieved through individual choice.

Judaism does know, of course, of the higher reaches of holiness and it does speak, albeit very occasionally, of men distinguished for their sanctity. But the title *ha-kadosh*, 'holy man', is reserved for a handful of men of the most saintly type. The editor of the Mishnah, Rabbi *Judah the Prince, is known as Rabbenu Ha-Kadosh, 'Our Holy Master'; Isaac *Luria, as the Ari Ha-Kadosh, and the founder of Hasidism, the *Baal Shem Tov, as the Baal Shem Tov Ha-Kadosh. Martyrs, who gave up life itself for their faith, are called *kedoshim*.

Of these higher reaches, Moses Hayyim *Luzzatto writes (*The Path of the Upright*, ch. 26):

'See, then, that in order to attain holiness it is essential for a man to practice abstinence, to meditate intently upon the mysteries of Providence and the secrets of nature, and to acquire a knowledge of the majesty and attributes of God, blessed be He, so that he comes to cleave devotedly to Him and to carry out His purpose even when engaged in worldly pursuits . . . It is impossible to attain the trait of holiness in any other way, and anyone who attempts to do so remains, in all respects, as gross and earthly as the rest of mankind. And the things that will greatly help a man in his quest after holiness are solitude and abstinence, for where there are no distractions, the soul is able to gather strength, and to commune with the Creator.'

Luzzatto, a Kabbalist and mystic, is insistent on the need for solitude as a prerequisite for the higher reaches of holiness. When two people meet, Luzzatto argues, the physical element in one is awakened and reinforced by the physical element in the other. But the man who courts solitude will find that with God's help his soul will become strong and he will be able to conquer all corporeal desires to become a holy man. Luzzatto's statement here comes as close to the hermit ideal as anything found in Jewish writings.

Luzzatto reserves the most elevated role for the holy man, putting it beyond the grasp of most mortals. The holy man's power of comprehension, Luzzatto observes, will exceed mortal limitations until in his communion with God he will be entrusted with the power of reviving the dead, as were *Elijah and *Elisha. The *Zaddik in *Hasidism is an example of the holy man as conceived of by Luzzatto and it is possible that this section of Luzzatto's work is one of the sources of the Hasidic doctrine. Hasidim refer in Yiddish to the Zaddik as *der heilige Rebbe*, 'the holy Rabbi'.

In the literature of Jewish piety, then, holiness is conceived of in three ways: as obedience to all the stern demands of the Torah (Rashi); as the striving to go beyond the strict letter of the law (Nahmanides); and as extraordinary sanctity possible only for the very few (Luzzatto). But no neat division is possible and in many Jewish texts the three overlap.

Louis Jacobs, 'Holiness', in his *Jewish Values* (London, 1960), 99–107.

**Holocaust** The destruction of six million Jews by the Nazis during World War II. It is not known who coined the English name 'Holocaust' for this, the most terrible event in all

Jewish history. In all probability the term, meaning a 'burnt-offering', was used because of the crematoria in which the bodies of the victims were burned. The Hebrew terms are *Shoah* ('Catastrophe') and *Ḥurban* ('Destruction', obviously based on the term used in the tradition for the destruction of the *Temple). It is unnecessary to spend any time discussing the pernicious view of revisionist 'historians' that the Holocaust never took place. This final insult to those who perished is too absurd to require refutation. Sober historians have documented all the details of the Holocaust. This entry considers chiefly the various Jewish theological responses to the Holocaust and other horrors of the twentieth century.

*Theological Responses*

It is generally acknowledged in contemporary theological discussion that, while the daunting problem of how *God, the all-good and all-powerful, can tolerate evil in His creation has always been the most stubborn the theist has to face, the problem as it confronts twentieth-century man is so acute as to render banal most of the earlier attempts at a solution. This is so for a number of reasons. First, there is the sheer nakedness of evil in the twentieth century. Babies have suffered cruel deaths throughout human history, but it was left to the Nazis to hurl them alive into gas-chambers and burn their bodies in the crematoria. The horrors of Hiroshima and the napalm bomb seem too monstrous to cope with, so that the more subtle the defence, the greater appears the affront. Secondly, the colossal scale of evils embracing large areas of the earth's surface tends to weight the dice against the possibility of ever finding a satisfactory solution. It is much harder now to believe with Maimonides (*Guide of the Perplexed*, 3. 12) that there is more good than evil in the universe, even while granting that human beings are incapable of knowing whether or not this is the case. Thirdly, the emergence of such evils in the century when human beings had been thought to have reached a high stage of mature and moral development, has shattered the hopes of those thinkers who were groping for a solution in evolutionary terms.

For many sensitive Jews there is the strongest distaste for even considering the problem. Haunted by feelings of guilt at having been spared when the six million were foully destroyed, these Jews discover within themselves a psychological block which prevents them from contemplating any explanation of such insanity on a cosmic scale, and this reinforces the natural Jewish reticence which has ever frowned on justifying God's judgement of others. Against any understanding of the mind, the heart cries out at a desecration of the memory of those who perished. Yet, though reluctant to suggest that solutions can be found, Jewish thinkers have grappled with the special problem posed for the Jewish religion by the fact of the Holocaust.

There is considerable agreement among Jewish thinkers that any neat solution amounts to a callous unawareness of the magnitude of the disaster and that, for example, it would be an insufferable insult to the memory of the six million to dare even to try to see their sufferings within a tidy scheme of reward and punishment. The tit-for-tat solution had to contend with serious difficulties even in former ages. How did it explain the suffering of those immune from fault and the escape of those prone to it? How did it understand the torture of innocent children? Very few indeed are prepared to suggest, as did some of the Kabbalists, that children were being punished for sins they had committed in a previous existence as adults (see REINCARNATION). There has emerged among the majority of Jewish thinkers a consensus that God is not to be defended by laying any blame at the doors of European Jewry. With a kind of spontaneous religious insight, the Jewish people has given the murdered innocents the name *kedoshim*, standing for 'martyrs'.

The most extreme response to the Holocaust on the part of Jewish thinkers is that of Richard Rubenstein who holds that no theodicy is now possible and all that the Jew can do is to hold on courageously, in the face of what Rubenstein calls the divine Nothing, to faith in the survival of the Jewish people and in the goodness still inherent in mankind. A theological idea that has frequently been revoked in discussions of the Holocaust is that of *hester panim*, 'the hiding of [God's] face'. It is argued that at certain periods in human history God removes His providential care to leave human beings to their own devices, as it were. It is as if God says: if you imagine you can get along without Me just try and see how badly it works out. But this idea merely aggravates the problem of divine *providence in general—the problem of why God refuses to intervene and allows naked evil to triumph.

Some feel that Holocaust theology has been overworked and can be positively harmful because it might encourage an attitude of total despair; for this reason many agree with Emil Fackenheim that the most significant affirmation with regard to the Holocaust is not to allow Hitler to have the last word, although, of course, such a response does not really belong to theology.

Dan Cohn-Sherbok, after surveying the views of various Jewish thinkers, expresses surprise that there is so little reference in Jewish thinking on the subject to the traditional doctrine of the Hereafter. The problem is by no means solved but is reduced in scale if it is believed that only the bodies of the victims were destroyed, their immortal souls remaining unaffected by anything that Hitler and the Nazis could do (see ESCHATOLOGY and HEAVEN AND HELL).

Eliezer Berkovits, *With God in Hell* (New York, 1979). Dan Cohn-Sherbok, *Holocaust Theology* (London, 1989).
Emil L. Fackenheim, *To Mend the World* (New York, 1982).
Richard Rubenstein, *After Auschwitz: Radical Theology and Contemporary Judaism* (Indianapolis, 1966).

**Holy Places** The Jewish religion, like any other, has its holy places, locations possessing a special degree of sanctity, some to a greater extent than others. In polytheistic religions, where the earth is seen as inhabited by a multiplicity of gods, it seems natural to assume that each god has his own particular abode, the plot where he actually resides, zealously maintaining his right of possession. For Judaism and the other monotheistic religions, on the other hand, it is hard to understand how the God whose glory fills the whole earth can be said to reside in one place more than another. Why is the building in which He is worshipped more His 'house' than any other spot on earth? And what meaning can be given to the idea that there are degrees of sanctity in which one place is more holy than another? Does this mean that there is a greater degree of in-dwelling in the holier place, and if it does, how can it be said that God is located more definitely in one spot, less in another? Any attempt to deal with this kind of question from the Jewish sources is rendered difficult by the absence of anything

like a systematic treatment of the topic. What exists are voluminous rules and regulations regarding the practical consequences which result from the sanctity of certain places; casual theological deliberations on the idea that God dwells in those places; observations on the psychological effects of man's confrontation with the numinous; and mystical speculations on the spiritual realm invading the secular.

There are basically two different ways within monotheism of understanding the concept of a holy place. The first is to see the divine as actually located in a quasi-physical manner in the sacred spot, or, better, as especially manifested there. The second way is to see the holy place as hallowed by experience and association. On the second view there is numinous power in the holy place, due not to any special in-dwelling of the divine but to the evocation of intense religious emotion resulting from the fact that the place has been the scene of divine revelation or of sustained and fervent worship. It is history that hallows the shrine. These two ways of looking at the question can be termed, respectively, the objective and the subjective (see CHOSEN PEOPLE for a similar distinction). Both attitudes are found among Jewish theologians.

There are many references in the Bible to sacred spots, the most famous being: Mount Moriah, the place of the binding of Isaac (Genesis 22: 14), which the later tradition identified with the *Temple site in Jerusalem; Beth-el where Jacob dreamed of the ladder linking heaven and earth (Genesis 28: 10–22); the burning bush where Moses was instructed to remove his shoes because the place on which he stood was holy ground (Exodus 3: 1–5); and Mount *Sinai upon which the Lord descended upon in fire (Exodus 19: 1–25). Interestingly enough, however, Sinai was only held to be sacred during the actual theophany. In subsequent Jewish tradition Sinai possesses no sanctity whatsoever; probably because, as the Rabbis say and it was believed, the command for the people to keep away from the Mount was rescinded once the *Decalogue had been given. The land of Israel is the Holy Land (Leviticus 18: 24–30; Zechariah 2: 16) and the Temple Mount the most sacred part of the land (Psalms 15: 1; 24: 3). Only the *High Priest on the Day of Atonement was allowed to enter the Holy of Holies in the Sanctuary (Leviticus 16: 1–34). Anyone who entered the Sanctuary in a state of unfitness committed a grave offence (Leviticus 21: 21–23). The Mishnah (*Kelim* 1: 6–9) gives a list of ten places in the Holy Land in ascending order of sanctity from the Land itself and culminating in the Holy of Holies in the Temple. All this might suggest that the objective understanding is the one adopted in ancient times. Yet any attempt at really confining God to a particular spot on earth is repudiated in Solomon's prayer when he dedicated the Temple: 'But will God in very truth dwell on the earth? Behold, heaven and the heaven of heavens cannot contain Thee, how much less this house that I have built' (1 Kings 8: 27). And the unknown prophet of exile declares: 'Thus saith the Lord: The heaven is My throne and the earth is My footstool. Where is the house that you may build unto Me? Where is the place that may be My resting place? For all these things has My hand made. And so all these things came to be, says the Lord. But on this man will I look, even on him that is poor and of a contrite spirit, and trembles at My word' (Isaiah 66: 1–3).

With regard to the lesser sanctity of the *synagogue, the emphasis does seem to be on the subjective understanding. The place is sacred because people worship there. They do not worship there because it is sacred. Very revealing in this connection is the Talmudic ruling (*Megillah* 26b–27a) that the House of Study (*bet ha-midrash*) has a higher degree of sanctity than a synagogue, since the study of the Torah occupies a higher rung than prayer on the ladder of Jewish piety. Jewish law has it that the sanctity of the synagogue is conditional upon its use, so that when it is no longer in use it may be sold even for secular purposes. It is true that some of the Jewish mystics did see the synagogue as sacred in the objective sense but they, too, accepted the provisions of Jewish law with its clear implication that the sanctity of the synagogue derives from association and use.

It thus appears from the sources that there is considerable tension between the objective and subjective understanding of the phenomenon of holy places. Indeed, a close reading of the sources suggests that, while a more objective understanding is appropriate for a place of higher sanctity, it is less appropriate for one of a lower degree of sanctity. Although an objective understanding is unpopular with modern thinkers, such an interpretation cannot be ruled out. A religion like Judaism, with its strong emphasis on the material as the vehicle for the spiritual and on the physical world as the arena for the struggle with evil and the pursuit of the good, cannot necessarily reject the objective understanding as too materialistic, literally too earth-bound. For it is on earth that in this life man meets his God.

Yet even if it be granted that there are no cogent reasons for rejecting the objective interpretation, the question still remains of how one can possibly know whether or not holiness or the divine influence dwells in a particular place. The traditional answer, so far as Judaism is concerned, is that this is known by revelation; it has been told in the divine Torah. The modernist Jew, however, has learned to see the Torah more as a divine–human encounter than as a direct communication by God to passive recipients (see BIBLICAL CRITICISM and CONSERVATIVE JUDAISM). For the modernist the Torah, though still God's Torah, has a human element, The sources, including the biblical sources, in which it does seem to be implied that the divine glory actually resides in the holy place, are themselves seen by the modernist as profound *human* reflection on events. Historically speaking, these sources are themselves subjective and do not convey anything like a divine guarantee that this or that place is sacred. The Jewish modernist will have an open mind on the question of whether or not a presence is really there in the holy place, while treating the spot as sacred, none the less, because, as a historical reality, that place has been associated with the most significant religious experiences of his tradition. In fact, there is not much practical difference between the objective and the subjective views, except that the subjective view might encourage a more tolerant and more respectful attitude towards the holy places of theistic religions other than one's own. This is not to adopt a relativistic position. The adherents of all the monotheistic faiths continue to have their own holy places of supreme significance to them. There is no need for triumphalism in this matter, not, at least, in the pre-Messianic age (see ⁷/₈ESSIAH).

Louis Jacobs, 'Holy Places', *Conservative Judaism*, 37/3 (1984), 4–16.

**Holy Sparks** The spiritual illuminations inherent in all things. The doctrine, as found in the Kabbalistic system of Isaac *Luria, the Ari, runs that when the light of *En Sof, the

Limitless Ground of Being, poured into the vessels which were to receive this light in order to produce the *Sefirot, the powers or potencies in the Godhead, the light was too strong to become limited in the vessels of the seven lower Sefirot, those at a greater distance, so to speak, from the infinite light of En Sof. As a result, there took place the 'breaking of the vessels'. When the vessels were broken, the lights returned to their source; but not all the lights returned. 'Sparks' of the lights remained, adhering to the broken shards in order to keep them in being.

The Sefirot were reconstituted after the breaking of the vessels, reinforced so that they could contain the light, using in the process the further light that streamed forth but also the holy sparks in the broken shards. This restoration resulted in an overspill of the light in the highest of the four worlds, the World of Emanation. From this overspill the World of Creation was constituted but here, too, there was an overspill and this constituted the World of Formation and here again there was an overspill to constitute the lowest world of the four, the World of Action. The idea behind all this is that fewer sparks are required for the formation of the worlds as they descend; less energy is required to keep lower worlds in existence, so that as the sparks flash out those which are redundant so far as that world is concerned spill over to create the next, lower world. There is a further overspill from the World of Action and it is this which nourishes the *kelipot*, the 'shells' or 'husks', the demonic forces which feed on the sacred realms while attacking them. In this way the effect of the breaking of the vessels results in holy sparks being imprisoned among the *kelipot*. It is the human task to reclaim these sparks for the holy and by so doing to assist the fallen worlds to be restored to their former harmony. The reclaiming of the holy sparks from the *kelipot* is achieved by rejecting evil, that is, by obeying the negative *precepts of the Torah. The highest of the *kelipot* is not totally evil, as are the others, but is ambiguously holy and unholy and the sparks therein are reclaimed by directing aright the natural drives of the body and so bringing this *kelipah* into the realm of the holy. Every evil deed keeps the holy sparks imprisoned among the *kelipot*. Conversely, every good deed assists in the reclaiming of the holy sparks and ultimately the restoration of cosmic harmony. When

the task of restoration is complete, when all the sparks have been reclaimed for the holy, the *Messiah will come and the disharmony resulting from the breaking of the vessels will be no more and cosmic redemption will have been achieved.

At first it was intended for the reclaiming of the holy sparks to be performed by *Adam, whose great soul embraced all the souls of humanity. If Adam had obeyed God, harmony would have been restored throughout all creation. But, as a result of Adam's disobedience, there took place a second cosmic fall, repeating, as it were, the original breaking of the vessels. Adam's soul became fragmented, each of his descendants having a mere spark of Adam's mighty soul. Thus the Lurianic School thinks of two kinds of sparks. The first are those which fell when the vessels were shattered. The second are the sparks of Adam's soul. It is not only the sparks in creation that require reclamation, but, in addition, every soul has its own task, the perfection of that particular spark of Adam's soul. A vast cosmic drama is being played out with the human being in the central role. Each human being has his or her own holy spark, an inheritance from the first father of the human race, and each has to reclaim the holy sparks in creation, both of which tasks are achieved by keeping the precepts of the Torah. When Israel was given the Torah and accepted it, humanity was given a second chance to produce harmony in the Sefirotic realm. But when the people worshipped the *golden calf the catastrophic breach was repeated and all was in disarray again. The process of reclaiming the sparks now had to be a gradual one, to be completed only in the far-off Messianic age. The risk of a third catastrophic failure could only be averted by a step-by-step restoration rather than an immediate storming of the heavens.

The followers of the false Messiah, Shabbetai *Zevi, in the seventeenth century, when the supposed Messiah embraced Islam, developed a radical theology based on the doctrine of the holy sparks. In this system the final reclamation of the holy sparks could only be achieved by the Messiah himself descending into the realm of the *kelipot*, consciously embracing Islam in order to rescue the sparks still awaiting their redemption there. Long after Shabbetai's death, his still-faithful followers were captivated by this intoxicating notion of the holy sin, adopting it as a task to be undertaken not only by the Messiah but by all believers. These later Shabbateans outwardly kept all the observances of the Torah but secretly endeavoured to rescue, by the performance of illegal acts, the holy sparks imprisoned among the *kelipot*. This involved a complete reversal of the Lurianic Kabbalah. In the Lurianic scheme it is never permitted to rescue the holy sparks through sinful acts. On the contrary, refraining from sin was one of the ways in which the sparks were to be rescued and the restoration completed.

The doctrine of the holy sparks occupies a prominent place in *Hasidism. But in this movement the whole doctrine was further developed in two ways. First, unlike in the Lurianic Kabbalah, which makes little of the holy sparks residing in food and other worldly things, except when the discussion has to do with the performance of the precepts, Hasidism taught that it is incumbent on the Hasid to be fully engaged in worldly affairs in order to reclaim the holy sparks inherent in the food, drink, and other worldly things. Secondly, in Hasidism each individual has his own holy sparks, as in the Lurianic system, but, in addition, his own sparks in creation which only he and no other can reclaim. Because of this one finds many Hasidic tales of a master being propelled by a force beyond his control to journey to distant places for no other purpose than to carry out there some task, otherwise neutral or insignificant, that would have the effect of rescuing the holy sparks held there captive by the *kelipot*—those sparks awaiting the one rescuer whose soul-root is close to them in the divine scheme, like the princess in the ogre's castle who will only consent to be rescued by the particular knight in shining armour to whom she has plighted her troth.

Louis Jacobs, 'The Uplifting of Sparks in Later Jewish Mysticism', in Arthur Green (ed.), *Jewish Spirituality: From the Sixteenth Century Revival to the Present* (New York, 1987), 34–63.

**Holy Spirit** Inspiration or the attainment of a degree of prophecy; Heb. *ruah ha-kodesh*. The Hebrew word *ruah* means both wind and spirit. The translation of Genesis 1: 2 as: 'and the spirit of God [*ruah elohim*] moved upon the face of the waters' is a Christian translation influenced by the doctrine of the Trinity. The correct meaning is probably either a 'wind from God' or a 'mighty wind' or, at the most, 'a

spirit which came from God'. Nowhere in the Hebrew Bible is there any reference to a spirit divine in itself or 'Holy Ghost', as distinct from a spirit that comes from God to inspire human beings. For instance, when it is said of Bezalel, the architect of the Tabernacle, that he was filled with *ruah elohim* (Exodus 35: 31) the meaning is that he was filled with a spirit which came from God to guide him in his task. This is the meaning of *ruah ha-kodesh* in the Rabbinic literature, where the term denotes a level of divine inspiration. The books of the Hagiographa such as Psalms and Proverbs (see BIBLE) are said to have been compiled under the Holy Spirit, that is, by a degree of inspiration somewhat less than the degree of prophecy, although, on occasion, the prophetic vision itself is also said to be by means of the Holy Spirit.

The Holy Spirit is often seen as a divine gift to certain persons distinguished for their learning and saintliness. In the addition to the Mishnah at the end of tractate *Sotah*, however, it seems that techniques were known by which a man might attain to the Holy Spirit. This addition reads: 'Rabbi Phinehas ben Jair said: Energetic care leads to [spiritual] cleanliness, and cleanliness leads to purity, and purity leads to abstinence, and abstinence leads to holiness, and holiness leads to humility, and humility leads to the shunning of sin, and the shunning of sin leads to saintliness, and saintliness leads to [the gift of] the Holy Spirit, and the Holy Spirit leads to the resurrection of the dead.' Moses Hayyim *Luzzatto devoted his *Path of the Upright* to a detailed description of these stages on the sacred path and it is possible that Luzzatto believed that even in his day (the eighteenth century) is was possible for people to attain to the Holy Spirit if they followed this strict regimen. In pious legends throughout the Middle Ages and even later, some rare individuals were said to have been given the gift of the Holy Spirit, despite the general Talmudic statement (*Yoma* 9b) that when the last of the prophets, Haggai, Zechariah, and Malachi, died, the Holy Spirit ceased from Israel. This statement was evidently understood as referring to the prophetic degree of the Holy Spirit not to occasional flashes of inspiration. The difference between the Holy Spirit and the heavenly voice, the *Bat Kol, appears to be that the latter comes by more external means.

Maimonides (*Guide of the Perplexed*, 2. 45) lists the Holy Spirit as a degree of prophecy but understands it in a more or less rationalistic manner as a certain thing that descends upon an individual, 'so that he talks in wise sayings, in words of praise, in useful admonitory dicta, or concerning governmental or divine matters —and all this while he is awake and his senses function as usual'. The Kabbalists believed that the Kabbalistic system of Isaac *Luria, the Ari, was compiled under the influence of the Holy Spirit.

**Homosexuality** Homosexual conduct between males (putting it bluntly, anal intercourse) is mentioned much more frequently and is more heavily condemned in the traditional Jewish sources than homosexual practices between females. There is no reference to a homosexual tendency or mental condition. It is the act itself that is forbidden, as in Leviticus 19: 22: 'Thou shalt not lie with mankind, as with womankind; it is an abomination'; and in Leviticus 20: 13: 'And if a man lie with mankind, as with womankind, both of them have committed abomination; they shall surely be put to death; their blood shall be upon them.' Some scholars have suggested (though whether they are right is another matter) that the 'price of a dog' in Deuteronomy 23: 19 ('Thou shalt not bring the hire of a harlot, or the price of a dog, into the house of the Lord thy God for any vow: for even both of these are an abomination unto the Lord thy God') refers to the hire of a man by a man for sexual purposes. While the men of Sodom (Genesis 19: 5) wished to abuse the two men who stayed with Lot, the main sin of Sodom, according to the Jewish tradition (see Ezekiel 16: 49) was its injustice and cruelty, so that a term like 'sodomy' for homosexual acts between males is not found in the Jewish sources. The term *kadesh* in Deuteronomy 23: 18 is rendered in some English versions as a 'sodomite' but the New English Bible renders the verse more correctly as: 'No Israelite woman shall become a temple-prostitute, and no Israelite man shall prostitute himself in this way.'

A debate, dating from the second half of the second century CE, is recorded in the Mishnah (*Kiddushin* 4: 14) in which Rabbi Judah forbids two unmarried males to sleep together in the same bed, while the sages permit it. The Talmud to this Mishnah states that the reason why the sages disagree with Rabbi Judah is that Jews are not suspected of engaging in homosexual practices. Although the standard Code of Jewish law, the *Shulḥan Arukh*, records the opinion of the sages as the law (*Even Ha-Ezer*, 24), it continues: 'But in these times, when there are many loose-livers about, a man should avoid being alone with another male.' The two standard Polish commentaries to the *Shulḥan Arukh* argue that the author of the work was thinking of his own milieu but 'in our lands', they say, it is only a special act of piety to refuse to be secluded alone with another male, although they do advise against two males sleeping together in the same bed.

According to Rabbinic teaching, *Gentiles, too, are commanded by the Torah to abstain from male homosexual acts. This belongs to the *Noahide laws binding on Gentiles as well as Jews. A Talmudic passage (*Ḥullin* 92a–b) states that even those Gentiles who indulge in these practices at least have the decency not to draw up a formal marriage-contract between two males. In a Rabbinic legend (*Shabbat* 149b) Nebuchadnezzar used to submit the kings he had conquered to sexual abuse.

The sources are far less clear on the question of lesbianism. The Rabbinic Midrash known as the Sifra (see MIDRASH) comments on the verse: 'After the doings of the land of Egypt wherein ye dwelt shall ye not do; and after the doings of the land of Canaan, whither I bring you, shall ye not do; neither walk in their statutes' (Leviticus 18: 3) that the reference is to the sexual practices of the Egyptians and the Canaanites: 'What did they do? They married off a man to a man and a woman to a woman.' The Talmud (*Yevamot* 76a) rules that women who perform sex acts with one another are not treated as harlots but only as indulging in lewd practices. Maimonides rules (*Issurey Biah* 21: 8) that while lesbian practices are forbidden, a married woman guilty of them is not treated as an adulteress forbidden to her husband. Nevertheless, Maimonides continues, a husband should object to his wife indulging in such practices and should further prevent his wife from associating with women who are known to be addicted to such pursuits.

It is clear from the above sources that homosexual practices are severely frowned upon but that female homosexuality is treated far less severely than male homosexuality. Why this should be so is not stated in the sources but would appear to be because it is in the nature of the case that full sexual contact is not possible for two females. The sources, moreover, do not seem to recognize either male homosexuals or lesbians as distinct groups, or in any event there is reference only to practices, not to some men and some women having homosexual tendencies.

Orthodox Judaism continues to maintain that homosexual acts are sinful although many Orthodox Jews might accept the view that since, nowadays, homosexuality is seen to be a condition, it should be left to God to determine whether a homosexual can or cannot help himself. Orthodox Jews certainly do not countenance 'gay synagogues'. The Reform movement in the USA has allowed gay synagogues to be affiliated to the movement but would not ordain a gay man or a lesbian as a Rabbi. Only a very few Reform Rabbis would agree to officiate at a 'marriage' of two males or two females. Among prominent Reform Rabbis who have condemned homosexual practices is Solomon B. Freehoff. Freehoff argued that while Reform Jews do not see the Bible as the very word of God, they still pay the greatest heed to the Bible and the Jewish tradition, where such practices are described as an abomination.

Louis Jacobs, 'Homosexuality', in his *What Does Judaism Say About . . . ?* (Jerusalem, 1973), 171–3.

**Horowitz, Isaiah** Polish Rabbi, Kabbalist, and author (1570–1630). Horowitz was born in Prague but studied in Poland under distinguished Talmudists. After serving as Rabbi in Frankfurt-on-Main, Horowitz returned to Prague in 1614 to become Rabbi there. In 1621 he journeyed to Palestine where he became Rabbi of Jerusalem. Horowitz died in Tiberias where he was buried near to the tomb of Maimonides.

Horowitz's major work is his *Sheney Luḥot Ha-Berit*, 'The Two Tablets of Stone', published in Amsterdam in 1649. The title of this book was abbreviated, after its initial letters, to *Shelah* and Horowitz himself is usually referred to as 'the Holy Shelah' (see HOLINESS). The work, encyclopaedic in range, consists of biblical commentaries, Kabbalistic discourses, explanations of the precepts and rituals of Judaism, ethical teachings, liturgical notes, and a treatment of Talmudic methodology. The work had a great influence on Jewish pietists, especially in *Hasidism.

As an example of Horowitz's stance can be quoted his analysis of the Talmudic concept *derekh eretz* ('good conduct'). Horowitz writes,

in the section of his work arranged in alphabetical order:

'The meaning of Derekh Eretz is correct behaviour, extraordinary humility, improvement of the character and all delightful things, to love all creatures and to be loved by them, to be a man of peace and a perfect man, contributing to the world in general and in particular in both spiritual and worldly matters. Derekh Eretz is conducted in three ways: 1) the way of perfect conduct by a man for himself; 2) the way of perfect conduct for a man in his home; 3) the way of perfect conduct by a man in relation to his fellows.'

Eugene Newman, *Life and Teachings of Isaiah Horowitz* (London, 1972).

**Hosea** The prophet whose book is the first and largest of the books of the Twelve Prophets. From the the superscription of the book and later passages, we learn that Hosea prophesied during the reigns of Uzziah (769–733 BCE), Jotham, Ahaz, and Hezekiah, kings of Judah (727–698 BCE) and Jeroboam and Menahem, kings of Israel (784–737 BCE). The only details of his life recorded in the book are that he received a command to marry a harlot in order to symbolize Israel's faithlessness to God and God's love nevertheless. He did marry a harlot named Gomer and had three children by her. The medieval Jewish commentators are divided on whether this incident actually took place or whether the story is part of Hosea's prophetic vision. Many modern biblical scholars believe that the consolatory portions of the book of Hosea come from a different prophet.

While the prophet *Amos places the stress on justice, Hosea speaks of loving-kindness (*hesed*). God loves His people but they have repaid that love by going a-whoring after Baal, the Phoenician god. The concluding portion of the book of Hosea, beginning with: 'Return O Israel, unto the Lord thy God' (Hosea 14: 4) is read as the *Haftarah for the Sabbath which falls during the *Ten Days of Penitence between *Rosh Ha-Shanah and *Yom Kippur. This Sabbath is consequently known as *Shabbat Shuvah* ('Sabbath of Return').

The Talmud (*Pesaḥim* 87a–b) has a lengthy account of the dialogue that is supposed to have taken place between God and Hosea. When God said to Hosea: 'Thy children have sinned,' Hosea replied: 'Change them for another people,' whereas he should have replied: 'Are they my children and not Thine?' That is why God told him to marry a harlot. Even though she was so unworthy Hosea came to love her and could not send her away permanently. God, too, could never exchange His people for another. This passage is one of a number of such criticisms made by the Rabbis even of the great biblical prophets.

S. M. Lehrman, 'Hosea: Introduction and Commentary' in A. Cohen (ed.), *The Twelve Prophets* (London, 1970), 1–55.

## Hoshanah Rabbah

'Great Hoshanah', the seventh day of the festival of *Tabernacles. According to the Mishnah (*Sukkah* 4: 5), in Temple times, on the festival of Tabernacles, huge willow branches were placed around the altar and a circuit was made around the altar while the worshippers recited: 'Hoshanah' ('O Lord, deliver us') (Psalms 118: 25). On the basis of this Temple practice, it became the custom on Tabernacles for the worshippers to hold the four species (the palm-branch, the etrog, the willows, and the myrtles), and make a circuit around the *Bimah, while reciting Hoshanah hymns in which God is entreated to deliver His people, especially from famine and drought, since Tabernacles is the festival on which the divine judgement for rain is made. On the seventh day of the festival, there are seven circuits, at each of which a special Hoshanah hymn is recited; hence the name, Hoshanah Rabbah. After the seven circuits, the four species are put aside and bunches of willows are taken in the hand and these are beaten on the ground three times so that the leaves fall off. The usual explanation of this rite is that it is a symbolic representation either of the rain, required at this season, which beats on the leaves, or of the leaves which fall from the trees until these are revived by the rain.

Further elaborations were introduced under the influence of the Kabbalah in which this day is seen as the culmination of the penitential season beginning on *Rosh Ha-Shanah and continuing through to *Yom Kippur. Part of the service is chanted in the solemn mode of Rosh Ha-Shanah and Yom Kippur, the Reader wears white robes, and references are made to the 'sealing' of human destiny for the year ahead. There was a widespread *superstition that if a man failed to see his shadow by the light of the moon on Hoshanah Rabbah night

he would not live out the year. The mood of Hoshanah Rabbah, falling as it does on Tabernacles, the special season of rejoicing, is thus a blend of joy and solemnity. Hoshanah Rabbah belongs to the intermediate days of the *festivals on which there are fewer restrictions on work being done.

Isaac Klein, 'Hosha'na Rabbah', in his *A Guide to Jewish Religious Practice* (New York, 1979), 167–8.

## Hospitality

Offering hospitality to guests, *hakhnasat oreḥim* ('bringing in guests') in Hebrew, is considered to be a *mitzvah*, a high religious obligation. The prototype is the patriarch *Abraham who sits at the door of his tent ready to welcome hungry and thirsty travellers (Genesis 18: 18). Since the narrative states that the Lord appeared to Abraham and yet Abraham ran to welcome his guests, a Rabbinic comment has it that to welcome guests is greater than to welcome the Divine Presence, the *Shekhinah. Another Rabbinic comment is that Abraham's tent had an opening on all four sides so that he could run to welcome guests from whichever direction they came. In Eastern Europe a house in which generous hospitality is provided was known as 'a house with Abraham our father's doors'. Although, naturally, friends visit one another and entertain one another in their homes, this is a private matter and is not considered to fall under the heading of hospitality, which applies to guests who are poor and needy. Many Jewish communities in the past had special societies for providing the poor with food and lodgings in hostels or in a room adjacent to the synagogue (see CHARITY). In the *Grace after Meals there is a special insertion for a guest in a private home to bless his host and hostess.

The Jewish moralists often refer to the *etiquette to be observed by both host and guest. The host should have considerations for the feelings of his poor guests and not embarrass them. The guests should not conduct themselves in a manner likely to cause embarrassment to their host. Naïve but typical of conditions in medieval German Jewry, is the advice given to hosts and guests in the *Sefer Ḥasidim*.

'A guest eating in a house in which he has been offered hospitality should leave something on his plate in order to show that he was given enough. If he eats everything, people might say it is because he was not given sufficient. If, however, the host said to him: "Please do not leave anything; what is the good of throwing food away to the dogs," he should listen to the host and leave nothing on his plate. It once happened that a certain guest regularly took no notice of his host who urged him to eat well. When the host observed this he naturally gave him smaller portions and then the guest complained. A sage said to the guest: your host was quite right for you should have listened to him in the first place. Your intention was to pay him honour but the best way of honouring a man is to do what he wants. A guest should not bring into the home which offers hospitality another, uninvited, guest.'

The moralists advise a host that he should not take issue with any opinions expressed by his guest at the table because this might result in further humiliation for a poor man humiliated in any event by having to accept hospitality. A poor man who can easily obtain his needs in the special communal guest-house should not insist on being given hospitality in a private home even if he senses that a private householder is willing to provide this. To trade without good cause on another's generosity smacks of theft. A husband should not bring the poor into his house without his wife's approval, since the burden is far heavier on the mistress of the house than on the master.

There is no doubt, granted the considerate treatment of poor Jewish travellers, that there often arose what Israel Abrahams calls 'that troublesome feature of modern Jewish life, the professional mendicant traveller, who is less a tramp than a licensed blackmailer'. Yet, for all the abuses to which it has been subject, hospitality remains a prominent feature of Jewish life.

Israel Abrahams, *Jewish Life in the Middle Ages* (London, 1932), 156–7.

**Humility** In the Jewish tradition, humility is among the greatest of the virtues, as its opposite, pride, is among the worst of the vices. Moses, the greatest of men, is described as the most humble: 'Now the man Moses was very meek, above all the men that were on the face of the earth' (Numbers 12: 3). The patriarch *Abraham protests to God: 'Behold now, I have taken upon me to speak unto the Lord, who am but dust and ashes' (Genesis 18: 27). When Saul was chosen as Israel's first king, he

was discovered 'hid among the baggage' (1 Samuel 10: 22), a phrase which became current among Jews for the man who shuns the limelight. The Hebrew king was to write a copy of the law and read therein all the days of his life, 'that his heart be not lifted above his brethren' (Deuteronomy 17: 20). Greatness and humility, in the Jewish tradition, are not incompatible. They complement one another. For a man to be humble he does not have to be someone who 'has plenty to be humble about', as Churchill is reported to have said of a political opponent who was praised for his humility. The greater the man the more humble he is expected to be and is likely to be. The Torah, say the Rabbis (*Taanit* 7a), is compared to water for just as water only runs downhill, never uphill, the word of God can only be heard in a humble heart.

The Jewish moralists are fully aware that any conscious attempt to attain to humility is always self-defeating and that pride can masquerade as humility. Crude vanity and self-glorification are easily recognized for what they are. Mock modesty is less easy to detect. It is not unusual for a man to take pride in his humility; nor is it unknown for a man to indulge in the more subtle form of self-deception in which he prides himself that he is not a victim of false modesty. In his *Path of the Upright*, Moses Hayyim *Luzzatto has an amusing analysis of various forms of false modesty:

'Another imagines that he is so great and so deserving of honour that no one can deprive him of the usual signs of respect. And to prove this, he behaves as though he were humble and goes to great extremes in displaying boundless modesty and infinite humility. But in his heart he is proud, saying to himself: "I am so exalted, and so deserving of honour, that I need not have anyone do me honour. I can well afford to forgo marks of respect." Another is the coxcomb, who wants to be noted for his superior qualities and to be singled out for his behaviour. He is not satisfied with having everyone praise him for the superior traits he thinks he possesses, but he wants them also to include in their praises that he is the most humble of men. He thus takes pride in his humility, and wishes to be honoured because he pretends to flee from honour. Such a prig usually goes so far as to put himself below those who are much inferior to him, even below the meanest, thinking that in this way he displays the utmost humility. He refuses all titles of greatness and declines promotion in rank, but in his heart he thinks, "There is no one in all the world as wise and as humble as I." Conceited people of this type, though they pretend mightily to be humble, cannot escape some mishap which causes their pride to burst forth, like flame out of a heap of litter.'

A Hasidic tale tells of a man who came to the *Zaddik with a complaint. 'All my life,' he said, 'I have tried to follow the advice of the Rabbis that one who runs away from fame will find that fame pursues him, and yet while I run away from fame, fame never seems to pursue me.' The Zaddik replied: 'The trouble is that while you do run away from fame you are always looking over your shoulder to see if fame is chasing after you.'

It is a paradox in the whole matter of humility that when a man knows his own worth he comes close to being a victim of pride and yet humility cannot mean that a man has to imagine that he is less worthy than he really is. Self-delusion is no virtue and is presumably to be as much avoided as any other delusion by the seeker after truth. 'The last infirmity of great minds' is not easily conquered.

This is how *Nahmanides deals with the problem of humility in a famous letter he wrote to his son:

'I shall explain how you should become accustomed to the practice of humility in your daily life. Let your voice be gentle, and your head bowed. Let your eyes be turned earthwards and your heart heavenwards. When you speak to someone do not look him in the face. Let every man seem superior to you in your own eyes. If he is wise or rich you have reason to respect him. If he is poor and you are richer or wiser than he, think to yourself that you are therefore all the more unworthy and he all the less, for if you sin you do so intentionally whereas he only sins unintentionally.'

Modern readers will no doubt find Nahmanides' treatment extreme. Is it possible or even desirable never to look another in the face? Such an attitude will often be insulting. Basically, what Nahmanides seems to mean is that God alone knows the true worth of a man and the extent to which he faces life's challenge with the gifts, or lack of them, that are his fate. The *religious* basis for humility is that only God knows the true worth of each human being.

On the deeper level, the notion is found, especially in Hasidism, that humility is not the mere absence of pride. Rather it consists not so much in thinking little of oneself as in not thinking of oneself at all. When the Hasidim and other Jewish mystics speak of *annihilation of selfhood, they are not thinking of a conscious effort of the will. To try to nullify the self by calling attention to it is bound to end in failure. Instead, the mystics tend to suggest, the mind should be encouraged to overlook entirely all considerations of both inferiority and superiority.

Louis Jacobs, 'Humility', in his *Jewish Values* (London, 1960), 108–117.

Moses Hayyim Luzzatto, *Mesillat Yesharim: The Path of the Upright*, trans. Mordecai M. Kaplan (Philadelphia, 1936), 102–6, 192–210.

**Humour** It is often said that the biblical authors took their activities too seriously to indulge in jest. There is some truth in this contention yet there is humour in the Bible, as when the prophet *Elijah mocks the prophets of Baal: 'And it came to pass at noon, that Elijah mocked them, and said: "Cry aloud, for he is a god, either he is musing or he has gone aside, or he is on a journey, or peradventure he sleepeth, and must be awakened"' (1 Kings 18: 27). There is similar irony in the prophet's mocking of the idolater who carves a god for himself, out of part of a block of wood, while using the other half for fuel (Isaiah 44: 13–17). The Talmudic Rabbis (*Megillah* 25b) sensed an apparent contradiction between such biblical passages and the Psalmist's injunction against scoffing (Psalms 1: 1) and suggest that while scoffing is usually unworthy it is permitted to make fun of idols and idolaters. However, the Talmudic reference is to coarse jests in which obscene language is used. That the Rabbis had a keen sense of humour, sufficiently close to ours for us to appreciate it, is evident from numerous witty sayings in the Talmudic and Midrashic literature. A fourth-century Babylonian teacher, we are told (*Shabbat* 30b), would always preface his lectures with a joke or a witticism in the belief that by making his pupils smile he would help prepare them for the difficult theme he was about to expound to them.

A Talmudic legend (*Taanit* 22a) tells of Elijah pointing out to a Rabbi two men in the market-place who were assured of a place in *heaven. When the Rabbi asked the men the nature of their occupation, they said that they were comedians who brought cheer into the lives of sufferers by amusing them with their jests. Even in the difficult legal passages in the Talmud humour is often introduced into the argument to strengthen the case. People secure in their religious convictions do not believe that in order to treat religion seriously it is necessary to treat it solemnly.

During the Middle Ages parodies of various kinds were written, especially for use on *Purim. In the famous tractate *Purim* the Talmudic rules governing the search for leaven before *Passover are parodied. The search is not for leaven but for water which must be entirely removed from the house before Purim; wine alone is to be kept there to gladden the heart. Many later Rabbis were renowned for their humour. A number of collections have been made of humorous Rabbinic tales and sayings. The folk-humour of Eastern European Jews is well known—some of it sick humour in which Jews poke fun at their misfortunes and stupidity. The psychological value is fairly obvious. If Jews had lacked the courage to laugh at themselves, the crushing burden of poverty and alienation would have become intolerable. To the question: 'Why does the Jew always answer a question with a question?' the traditional answer is either: 'Does he?' or 'Why not?'

Henry D. Spalding, *Joys of Jewish Humor* (New York, 1985).

**Hunting** The Bible refers to hunting for food (in Leviticus 17: 13 for example) and sees no objection to this. The principle, as established by the Rabbis, is that while wanton cruelty to *animals is strictly forbidden, it is permitted to kill animals for food or for their skins and the same would apply to hunting animals for this purpose. Nevertheless, the only two persons mentioned in the Bible as hunters are Nimrod (Genesis 10: 9) and Esau (Genesis 25: 27), neither of whom is held up for admiration in the Jewish tradition. There is no reference at all in the whole of the biblical and Rabbinic literature to hunting for sport.

There are, however, two frequently quoted *Responsa on the question of hunting for sport. The Italian physician and Rabbinic scholar, Isaac Lampronti (1679–1756) discusses, in his encyclopaedia of Jewish law entitled *Paḥad Yitzhak*, whether it is permitted to hunt animals and kill them when they are caught.

Lampronti forbids this on the grounds that it is forbidden to waste anything in God's creation (see ECOLOGY). Rabbi Ezekiel *Landau of Prague, in a Responsa (second series, *Yoreh Deah*, no. 19), argues that, in addition to the reason given by Lampronti, hunting for sport is forbidden because it involves unnecessary cruelty to animals and the hunter risks life and limb in the pursuit. Landau points out that the Talmudic discussion on the duty to kill wild animals even on the Sabbath (*Shabbat* 121b) only applies to wild animals that come among men and endanger human life and not to pursuing the animals in their own haunts. Walter Rathenau's remark has often been quoted in this connection: "When a Jew says he's going hunting to amuse himself, he lies.' There are Jews, of course, perhaps even some religious Jews, who do enjoy taking part in the hunt, advancing the usual arguments for why this is thought to be desirable. Yet there is no record of Rabbis in any age hunting animals for sport.

There is no logical reason for distinguishing between hunting animals and catching fish, apart from the question of risk to human life, yet some Jews who would not hunt animals see no harm in angling as a hobby. Perhaps they hold that the fish caught will be eaten and fishing therefore is not purely for sport, or perhaps they believe that fish feel less pain than animals.

Louis Jacobs, 'Hunting', in his *What Does Judaism Say About . . .?* (Jerusalem, 1973), 182.

**Ḥuppah** The wedding-canopy under which bride and groom stand during the *marriage. The *ḥuppah* represents symbolically the groom's dwelling into which the bride is escorted but from ancient times it was the custom for the marriage ceremony to be conducted under an actual canopy and this is the universal practice to the present day. There are no rules about the materials from which the *ḥuppah* is made. The usual form is of a canopy stretched over four posts. In many communities it is the custom to have four post-holders, one at each corner of the *ḥuppah*. Eventually the name '*ḥuppah*' became synonymous with the marriage ceremony itself. At a *circumcision, for instance, the parents of the infant are given the blessing that they should have the joy of escorting the child under the *ḥuppah* when he grows up.

**Hypnotism** Rabbi Zevi Hirsch Spira (d. 1913), in his compendium, *Darkhey Teshuvah* (179. 6) discusses whether resort by a physician to hypnotism constitutes a natural and hence legitimate form of healing or whether it is supernatural and hence might fall under the heading of *magic and superstition. Spira quotes a Responsum, dated 1852, by Rabbi Jakob Ettlinger (1798–1871). A pious Jew had fallen ill and was advised by his physician to resort to a hypnotic cure (more specifically, to 'magnetism'). Ettlinger replies that he consulted the experts and received contradictory answers from them. Some of the experts dismissed the whole method as charlatanism but others were less sceptical. Ettlinger permits it on the grounds that those who practise it do believe that it is a perfectly natural form of healing. Since Ettlinger, hypnotism has been widely used by reputable physicians, especially in treating various kinds of mental illness, and it is agreed that there is no reason nowadays to forbid a pious patient from submitting to hypnotism. More recent authorities have discussed whether an act performed by a person who has been hypnotized can be held to be an intentional act in Jewish law.

Louis Jacobs, 'Hypnotism', in his *What Does Judaism Say About . . .?* (Jerusalem, 1973), 183.

**Ibn Atar, Hayyim** Rabbi and Kabbalist, born Morocco, 1696, died Jerusalem, 1743. Ibn Atar studied with his grandfather, also called Hayyim Ibn Atar (Oriental Jews often gave their children the names of living relatives), and acquired even in his youth a reputation for advanced Talmudic learning and, through his ascetic life, for saintliness (see SAINTS). A strong believer that Messianic redemption was at hand and seeing his destiny in helping to hasten the redemption by living in the Holy Land, Ibn Atar resolved to establish there a *Yeshivah and he left Morocco in order to fulfil his dream. On his way Ibn Atar stopped in Leghorn, Italy, in 1739, where he resided for two years, teaching a small group of keen disciples and preaching to large audiences. In 1741 Ibn Atar set out for the land of Israel and eventually founded a Yeshivah for ascetic Talmudists in Jerusalem. His house, with an adjacent ritual bath (*mikveh) can still be seen in the Old City. He was buried on the Mount of Olives where his two wives were also buried. He seems to have had these two wives at the same time since the ban on polygamy (see RABBENU *GERSHOM) was only accepted by Ashkenazi Jews and did not apply to Oriental Jews. Israel ben Eliezer, the *Baal Shem Tov, founder of the Hasidic movement, is reported to have had a high regard for Ibn Atar in whom he saw a kindred spirit. Certainly, Ibn Atar's writings had a marked influence on *Hasidism in which he is revered as a great saint, a forerunner of the Hasidic *Zaddik.

Ibn Atar's Halakhic work, *Peri Toar* (*Fruit of Good Appearance*), published in Amsterdam in 1742, displays his vast knowledge of the Talmud and Codes. But he is renowned chiefly for his mystical commentary to the Torah, entitled *The Light of Life* (*Or Ha-Ḥayyim*, a pun on his name, Hayyim). This work was published in Venice in 1742 together with the text of the *Pentateuch, a sure sign of the high regard in which he was held even while he was still alive. After the fashion of calling Rabbinic authors after the title of their major work, Ibn Atar is, in fact, known as 'The *Or Ha-Ḥayyim*' or, among Hasidim, 'The Holy *Or Ha-Ḥayyim*'. The work has gone into many editions either together with the biblical text or as a work on its own, and a number of scholars have written commentaries on it.

*Ideas*

Ibn Atar draws on the Kabbalah which he interprets in a personal, individualistic manner similar to the later Hasidic approach. He interprets biblical texts allegorically in order to convey what he considers to be their deeper meaning. For example, he is obviously aware that the verse: 'neither shalt thou favour a poor man in his quarrel' (Exodus 23: 3) has the plain meaning that a judge should not show favour to a poor man in his lawsuit with a rich man if the poor man is in the wrong, yet he comments that the verse has a meaning applicable to all, not only to a judge. Every poor man, he remarks, has a quarrel with God for having made him poor. When the poor man is assisted (see CHARITY) and his poverty diminished, his otherwise legitimate cause for his quarrel with God is removed. Of a similar allegorical nature is Ibn Atar's comment on the injunction to restore to its rightful owner a brother's ox or sheep that has gone astray (Deuteronomy 22: 1–3). The 'brother' is daringly understood to be God and the lost oxen and sheep are the sinners. The good, for whom God is a Brother, should not be indifferent to sinners but should seek to restore them to the good path and hence bring them back to 'Brother God'.

Ibn Atar develops the Kabbalistic idea that the conduct of human beings on earth has cosmic effects, influencing the upper worlds. Relying on the Aristotelian and medieval theory of the four elements, he observes that, of the four, earth is the most gross and the lowest. Every creature has in its composition its special element, the other three being subsidiaries. The element of the birds is air, of fish water, of fire the Salamander (a mythical creature coming out of fire), and of earth man. This is why man can only live on earth and cannot survive in the air or in water or in fire. Man was created as the lowest of creatures for his task is to refine the whole cosmos from the lowest to the highest. Ibn Atar's understanding of the image of *God in which man is created is that God has endowed man with His two attributes of mercy and justice so that man can be godlike in having compassion on others and also in his capacity to pass judgement on others.

In his Halakhic work Ibn Atar exhibits a keen critical sense but in his *Or Ha-Ḥayyim* he accepts uncritically statements found in earlier works, such as the odd postulate that in the Messianic age the pig will be permitted to Jews. It is almost certain that this notion has a Christian origin yet Ibn Atar accepts it and, since the Torah is eternal, he remarks, a miracle will happen and the pig's nature will be changed so that it will chew the cud and thus become a kosher animal (see DIETARY LAWS).

The attainment of mystical and ecstatic states features often in Ibn Atar's work. It was widely believed among the Hasidim that the *Or Ha-Ḥayyim* was an inspired work, compiled under the influence of the *Holy Spirit. The famed nineteenth-century Hasidic master, Hayyim Halberstam of Zans, goes so far as to discuss whether a teacher of children, who scoffed at the idea that the work was inspired in this way, should be given the sack for entertaining heretical ideas. Ibn Atar himself remarks (commentary to Genesis 6: 3) that nowadays no one has even the fragrance of holiness (*reaḥ ha-kodesh*, let alone the Holy Spirit (*ruaḥ ha-kodesh*) but this was dismissed as extreme humility on the holy man's part. In a remarkable comment on the verse: 'after the death of the two sons of *Aaron, when they drew near before the Lord, and died' (Leviticus 16: 1), Ibn Atar remarks that these two, like all the saints, died by a divine kiss; the only difference was that for the other saints, the 'kiss' drew near to them, whereas the two sons of Aaron drew near to the kiss. These two saints did not cease from drawing nearer to the sweet, delightful longing of their attachment (*devekut) to God, even though they knew that they would expire in longing as a result. When such an experience presents itself to the saint, he is torn between his longing and his natural instinct to resist its death-inviting allure, and he struggles against this compelling force. That is why the prophets are sometimes described as insane.

There then follows this comment:

'I shall explain to whoever reflects on the innermost comprehension of that which is comprehended that the comprehension of that which is comprehended does involve comprehension but when it is comprehended the one who comprehends comprehends that the object of his comprehension cannot be comprehended. When he comprehends of his own accord, and yet it is not of himself, he then comprehends that that which is comprehended is so comprehended from a source that cannot be comprehended by the intellect, and it is conveyed to those who comprehend by their becoming united with the comprehension, in accord with the mystery of a soul added to a soul. At this stage, all human comprehension becomes superfluous, like the king's crown and his throne in relation to the king himself. One who has reached this stage will sense that there is a life above life, concerning which Moses said: "choose life" [Deuteronomy 30: 19], the ultimate destiny, not that which is generally understood as such, and he will bless the living God who has given this treasure to His people.'

However this is to be understood, and for all the difficulties the commentators find in this passage, it obviously involves an analysis of the raptures experienced by the saints, and it would certainly seem that Ibn Atar here, and in much of his work, is writing from personal experience. This kind of analysis is extremely rare in the literature of Jewish mysticism in that it seeks to examine mystical experience in a more or less detached manner. In the whole of his *Or Ha-Ḥayyim*, Ibn Atar similarly appears as a commentator who reads the Torah in the light of personal experience. He is undoubtedly a believer in the Kabbalah as divine truth and frequently refers to Kabbalistic terms, but he is more than a mere exponent of Kabbalistic ideas. The Hasidim rightly saw in the work a guide to spirituality and the mystical love of God.

Louis Jacobs, *Holy Living: Saints and Saintliness in Judaism* (Northvale, NJ, and London, 1990), 73–5.

**Ibn Ezra, Abraham** Poet, philosopher, grammarian, and biblical exegete (1089–1164). Ibn Ezra was born in Tudela, Spain, where he lived until he left in 1140 to wander to other lands. His life is consequently divided by historians into two periods, that of his residence in Spain, where he wrote many of his poems, and that of his sojourn in various Jewish communities outside Spain in which his other works were compiled. Few details of his personal life in Spain are known, or why he left that country. It has been conjectured that the reason for his 'troubled spirit', as he puts it, in Spain was that his son, Isaac, was converted to Islam, though the son later returned to Judaism. His wife seems to have died after he had left Spain. Details of Ibn Ezra's wanderings are, however, known from the names of the places he recorded in his works. Through these it is known that he lived for a time in Italy, France, and England. He appears to have earned his living in these places by teaching the sons of wealthy Jews and, though of a fiercely independent temperament, he allowed himself also to be supported by a number of patrons of learning. He writes that, from time to time, he tried to engage in various business enterprises but met with no success in these. In a satiric poem, he writes that if he manufactured candles it would never get dark and if he sold shrouds no one would die! The picture which emerges is of a hugely gifted wandering scholar (he was, in addition to his other attainments, a mathematician and astronomer of note and he dabbled in astrology) who, undeterred by the odds, somehow managed to survive to compile works of permanent value. He is the hero of Browning's poem 'Rabbi Ben Ezra'.

Ibn Ezra's poems, both secular and religious, are among the choicest examples of Hebrew poetry. One of his liturgical compositions is printed at the beginning of many prayer books. His theological works include *Sefer Ha-Shem* (*Book of the Name*), on the names of God, and *Yesod Mora* (*Foundation of Fear*) on the meaning of the precepts of the Torah. His *Iggeret Ha-Shabbat* (*Letter on the Sabbath*) was written while he was staying in England. The Sabbath, he says, came to him in a dream to urge him to compile the work as a refutation of the heretical opinion that the Sabbath begins in the morning and ends on the next morning in contradiction to the traditional view that it begins at sundown and ends at sundown of the next day. But Ibn Ezra is chiefly important and influential in the history of the Jewish religion for his commentaries to the Bible, chief of which is his commentary to the *Pentateuch. This work was first published in Naples in 1488, has since been printed many times in editions of the Pentateuch together with the text, and has taken its place beside the works of *Rashi, *Rashbam, and *Nahmanides among the standard Jewish commentaries to the Pentateuch, the Torah, upon which work everything in Judaism is based.

*Commentary to the Pentateuch*

Ibn Ezra, a man of boundless curiosity, often draws on his own experiences in his travels to elucidate biblical texts. In his comment on the command to eat unleavened bread (*matzah) on *Passover, he notes that when he visited a prison in England, he saw that the prisoners were provided with unleavened bread, so he sees the command as symbolic both of the Israelites' redemption from Egyptian bondage and of the bondage itself, surmising that they, too, were obliged to eat this kind of 'prison' bread while in Egypt. Also while in London, he saw the thick mist rising from the Thames and this led him to explain the plague of darkness in terms of a mist rising from the Nile. As a skilful grammarian, Ibn Ezra is profoundly concerned in his commentary with Hebrew philology and syntax. In his comment to the first verse of Genesis, for example, he denies that the word *bara* ('created') must mean, as others have argued, *creatio ex nihilo* (see CREATION), since the same root is used for the creation of man and man was created out of the dust. Ibn Ezra usually writes in a cryptic style, leaving much room for conjecture as to his meaning, probably because he was aware of the daring nature of some of his ideas which might lead the ignorant to unbelief. He is not averse to suggesting original interpretations of biblical events, as when he suggests that divine *providence had so ordered it that Moses was raised in Pharaoh's palace. Had Moses been brought up among his fellow Israelites, they would have been too familiar with him from his youth to have respect for him as their leader. Moreover, the future leader had to have a regal upbringing and an aristocratic background to endow him with the nobility of character suitable for a leader.

In his rhymed introduction to his commentary to the Pentateuch, Ibn Ezra rejects the four different exegetical methods current in his day: the diffuse method; the untraditional and too individualistic methods of the *Karaites; the allegorical method; and the homiletic method pursued by the Rabbis of the *Midrash. Ibn Ezra himself favours a fifth method in which, wherever possible, the plain meaning of the text is uncovered and accepted as the true meaning, except, with regard to the laws of the Torah, when this runs counter to the Jewish tradition. His guiding principle is that the human intellect is 'an angel sent from God'. Legend and homily should be accepted for what they are, pure poetry and fancy, often valuable in themselves but impossible to accept as factual where they are contradicted by reason and common sense. For instance, the Midrashic comment that the Torah was created 2,000 years before the creation of the world is all very well as a pleasant way of pointing to the superiority of the Torah above all things; but such a notion cannot be taken literally, since there cannot have been any 'years' *before* the creation of the world, years themselves being part of the creation.

In a sense Ibn Ezra was the forerunner of *biblical criticism. He held that the second part of the book of *Isaiah could not have been written by the prophet Isaiah, since it speaks of events that occurred well over a hundred years after Isaiah's death and there is no indication that these were prophesies about future events. *Spinoza maintained with justice that Ibn Ezra hints that there are post-Mosaic additions to the Pentateuch. In a comment to: 'These are the words which Moses spoke unto all Israel beyond the Jordan' (Deuteronomy 1: 1) he hints that this verse could not have been written by Moses since the words 'beyond the Jordan' imply that the writer was in the land of Israel, whereas Moses would not have referred to his location as 'beyond the Jordan'. He then proceeds to hint at other verses, such as the last twelve verses of the Pentateuch which tell how Moses went up on Mount Sinai to die there, which could not have been written by Moses. More Orthodox interpreters of Ibn Ezra declare that he believed that these verses were written by Moses but as a prophesy of future events. Spinoza (he was anticipated by the fourteenth-century Joseph Bonfils in his commentary to Ibn Ezra) understands Ibn Ezra to be saying that these verses are post-Mosaic additions. The sixteenth-century Italian historian Azariah

de *Rossi also understood Ibn Ezra in this way and attacked him for daring to depart from the established Jewish tradition that the whole of the Pentateuch was written by Moses.

Moses Friedlander, *Essays on the Writings of Abraham Ibn Ezra* (London, 1877).
Louis Jacobs, 'Ibn Ezra', in his *Jewish Biblical Exegesis* (New York, 1973), 8–21.

**Ibn Gabirol, Solomon** Poet and philosopher (1020–57). Few details of Ibn Gabirol's life are known. He was born in Malaga, Spain, where a modern statue of him is to be found near the sea-shore. But the statue depicts him as a tall, venerable old sage, whereas, in fact, he died before reaching the age of 40. It is known that while Malaga was his native city (he signs some of his poems as Malki, meaning 'from Malaga'), he was taken as a child to Saragossa where he received a sound education and acquired a reputation as a scholar. Ibn Gabirol's poems, together with those of Judah *Halevi, are considered to be the choicest of medieval Hebrew poetry. Some of his poems were composed when he was no more than 16 years of age.

Ibn Gabirol's philosophical poem, *Keter Malkhut* (*The Kingly Crown*) is still recited by Sephardi Jews at the Neilah service on *Yom Kippur. This poem is in three parts: 1. a hymn celebrating the divine attributes; 2. a description of the wonders of creation, rising from contemplation of the sun, moon, stars, and planets to the ultimate mystery of the Godhead; 3. confession, penitence, and supplication.

Ibn Gabirol's philosophical work, *Mekor Hayyim* (*Source of Life*), composed under the influence of Neoplatonic thought, was written in Arabic and translated into Latin as *Fons Vitae*. This work, treating of the relationship between form and matter, makes no reference to the Bible or to the Rabbinic literature and is so universalistic in character that it was attributed by Christian writers to an unknown Christian or Muslim philosopher operating solely in philosophical categories. It was not until the nineteenth century that S. Munk identified Ibn Gabirol as the author. Ibn Gabirol also wrote an ethical work, *Tikkun Middot Ha-Nefesh* (*Improvement of the Soul's Qualities*). This work, also written in Arabic, was translated into Hebrew and was widely read by Jews seeking edification.

The influence of Ibn Gabirol's thought on subsequent Jewish religious thought is largely indirect, except for the ideas found in his religious poems. Many of the ideas found in the Kabbalah, especially that of emanation and God as wholly other, are found in Ibn Gabirol. Some of the sentiments expressed in *The Kingly Crown*, for instance, are found in almost the same form in the *Zohar; although in Ibn Gabirol's scheme God's will stems from His wisdom, whereas in the Zohar Will belongs to the highest of the *Sefirot, and from it Wisdom emanates.

An oft-quoted stanza in *The Kingly Crown* sees all men as worshipping God without knowing the object of their worship; the act of worship itself is sufficient evidence that this is so:

Thou art God, and all creatures are Thy slaves and worshippers,
and Thy glory is not diminished by those who worship others
than Thee, for the goal of all of them is to attain to Thee.

*Selected Poems of Solomon Ibn Gabirol*, trans. Israel Zangwill, ed. Israel Davidson (Philadelphia, 1933).
Solomon Ibn Gabirol, *The Kingly Crown*, trans. Bernard Lewis (London, 1961).

**Idolatry**   The worship of any being other than God; Heb. *avodah zarah* ('strange worship'). The Hebrew prophets fought against the worship of Baal and the other foreign gods but nowhere in the Bible are the other nations condemned for worshipping their gods, only for the 'abominations' attendant on that worship. However, in the Rabbinic doctrine of the *Noahide laws, the Torah for all mankind so to speak, idolatry is as serious offence for *Gentiles as it is for Jews, although, in the nature of the case, this was purely academic. It was unlikely in the extreme in Rabbinic times that a Gentile would ask a Rabbi whether or not he was allowed by the Torah to worship his gods. A whole tractate of the Talmud, tractate *Avodah Zarah*, is devoted to the laws against idolatry and idolatrous practices. Hardly any attempt is made in the classical Jewish sources to distinguish between different kinds of pagan or primitive worship such as animism, fetishism, and polytheism. All forms of worship that are not purely monotheistic are treated together as idolatry and severely condemned.

Maimonides' fifth *principle of faith, that God alone is to be worshipped, is directed

against idolatry. In his *Guide of the Perplexed*, Maimonides was the first Jewish teacher to attempt a systematic presentation of biblical prohibitions in the light of contemporary idolatrous practices. With sure insight, Maimonides was the first to see fully that many of the biblical regulations, of the sacrificial system, for example, can only be understood against the pagan background to which they were a reaction. In this he influenced John Spencer, who acknowledges his debt to the great medieval thinker. Spencer, in turn, influenced both Robertson Smith and James Fraser, so that Maimonides has been heralded, with some justice, as the real founder of comparative religion. In his *Mishneh Torah* (*Laws of Avodah Zarah* 2: 1) Maimonides defines idolatry: 'The chief command with regard to idolatry is that one should not worship any creature, neither angel nor sphere nor star, neither one of the four elements nor anything formed from them.'

Opposition to anything which savoured of idolatry was very fierce during the Roman period. According to *Josephus (*Antiquities* 18: 3. 1), when Hadrian introduced the Roman ensigns into Jerusalem the vehement protest was such that he was compelled to remove them. Some of the ways in which the Rabbis viewed idolatry can be gleaned from the Mishnah, tractate *Avodah Zarah*. For three days before pagan festivals it was forbidden to have any business dealings with pagans (1: 1). It was forbidden to sell articles to pagans before their festivals which they might use in idolatrous worship, for example, fir-cones, white figs, frankincense, or a white cock (1: 5). It was strictly forbidden to cast a stone at a *Merkolis* (4: 1), which appears to have been a pillar to Mercury, the Roman equivalent of Greek Hermes, who was the patron deity of travellers and at whose shrine the grateful passers-by cast a stone. It is stated (4: 7) that the Jewish elders were asked in Rome why God does not destroy idols, if he hates them so. To this the elders replied that men worship the sun, moon, and stars and God refuses to destroy the world He has created 'because of fools'. If, on the other hand, He were to destroy only those idols for which the world has no use, this would confirm the worshippers of the idols that were not destroyed that these alone had power.

Among further numerous details of Rabbinic abhorrence of idolatry, the following can be given as illustrations. The early third-century teacher Menahem ben Simai was given the appellation 'the son of the holy' because he refused to gaze even at the image of a pagan god or a deified emperor on a coin (*Pesaḥim* 104a). Not only idolatry itself was treated with the greatest severity by the Rabbis, but anything appertaining to it was strictly prohibited. It was forbidden to use the leaves of an idolatrous grove, even for their medicinal properties because leaves from another place could serve the same purpose (*Pesaḥim* 25a). No use might be had of an idol, but if it had been desecrated by its worshipper, by being defaced, for example, it was permitted to have use of it. This only applied to an idol belonging to a non-Jewish idolater. An idol worshipped by a Jew was permanently forbidden even after its defacement by the owner (*Avodah Zarah* 52a). If a person saw a place in the land of Israel from which idolatry has been uprooted he should say: 'Blessed is He who uprooted idolatry from our land, and as it has been uprooted from this place, so might it be uprooted from all places belonging to Israel; and do Thou turn the heart of those that serve them [the pagan gods] to serve Thee' (*Berakhot* 57b). Although the mere intention to commit a sin is not counted as a sin this does not apply to idolatry, where even the mere intention to worship idols is sinful (*Kiddushin* 40a). The Rabbis were not unaware, however, that the older pagan cults had lost much of their force, hence the saying of the third-century Rabbi Johanan that Gentiles outside the land of Israel are not true idolaters but simply continue in the ways of their ancestors (*Ḥullin* 13b)

In the post-Talmudic period, there was no longer any threat to Judaism from the pagan religions and a certain relaxation was granted of some of the stricter rules against relations with idolaters. The discussion among the Jewish teachers then centred on whether *Islam and *Christianity, the two daughter religions of Judaism, as they were called, and the new rivals to the Jewish religion, were to be treated as idolatrous religions. Islam was seen as a purely monotheistic religion but opinions differed with regard to Christianity. Eventually, the consensus emerged that while Christianity did not constitute idolatry 'for them', that is, a Gentile Christian did not offend against the Noahide laws, it did constitute idolatry 'for us'. Many Jews suffered martyrdom rather than embrace the Christian faith. To worship the gods of the Far Eastern religions is, of course, held to be idolatrous by all Jewish authorities.

In modern times, when very few Jews are tempted to worship idols in the older sense, Jewish thinkers have called attention to different forms of idolatry—the worship of the State, for instance, as in totalitarian regimes, or the worship of causes, persons, and 'isms' of various kinds. For Jews to substitute Jewish nationhood for the Jewish religion would be a species of idolatry in this wider sense. In the Jewish tradition even the Torah is to be seen as a means to God, never as an object of worship. Some authorities go so far as to forbid Jews to bow to the Torah since this might seem to treat the Torah as an object of worship. The custom is to bow to the Torah but only as one bows, as a token of respect, to a human being. The Torah in Judaism is more akin to *Muhammad in Islam than to *Jesus in Christianity. A constant complaint of the *Mitnaggedim against *Hasidism was that the Hasidic veneration of the *Zaddik bordered on idolatry, although, in fact, while the Hasidim revere the Zaddik they never worship him.

The Hasidic master, Shneur Zalman of *Liady sees idolatry not as a denial of God but as an attempt at insubordination. Man desires to have a little corner of life apart from God's all-embracing power and the idols he sets up are his means of effecting the separation between God and that part of life man wishes to call completely his own. Hence, for the Rabbis, pride is equivalent to idolatry because both commit the same offence of insubordination. 'Pride is truly equivalent to idolatry. For the main root principle of idolatry consists in man's acknowledgement of something existing in its own right apart and separate from God's holiness, and does not involve a complete denial of God' (*Tanya*, ch. 22). Rabbi A. I. *Kook, in his work *Orot Ha-Kodesh* (ii. 411–12) considers the idolatry involved in self-worship or the worship of humanity. According to Kook, there is to be found deep in the human psyche a bizarre form of envy—envy of God. Man, in the wretchedness of his finite situation and human plight, envies God His infinite nature and bliss. This leads, among other things, to a denial of God and a deification of man. There are two antidotes, remarks Kook, to this poison, the first intellectual, the second moral. The intellectual antidote consists in the recognition that the difference between God and the world depends on degrees of comprehension. The greater a man's comprehension of truth, the fuller will be his comprehension that God is in all, that the happiness and well-being of each individual belongs to the happiness which pervades all things, since all have their source in God. The moral antidote is to be found by the man who freely develops his own nature so that of his own accord he longs for the triumph of justice and righteousness in the world. Man's free longing is then in accord with the nature of true reality and there is no longer any reason for envy of the divine.

Louis Jacobs, *Principles of the Jewish Faith* (Northvale, NJ, and London, 1988), 175–83.

**Image of God** The idea that all human beings, whether male or females, are created in a form that in some way resembles the Creator: 'So God created man in His own image; in the image of God created He him; male and female created He them' (Genesis 1: 25). In a saying attributed to Rabbi *Akiba in Ethics of the Fathers (3. 15) the doctrine is elaborated on: 'Beloved is man for he was created in the image [of God]; still greater was the love in that it was made known to him that he was created in the image of God.' It should be noted that here and elsewhere, and in the clear implications of the verse, all human beings are said to have been created in God's image (see CHOSEN PEOPLE). In the biblical narrative, man is distinguished from all other creatures in being created in God's image.

The Jewish commentators differ as to the meaning of the image of God in which man has been created. The concept is not normally taken literally, since God has no 'image', though there are exceptions to this in the Middle Ages, when Talmudists like Moses of Tachau did understand the anthropomorphic expressions in the Bible and Talmud as suggesting a correspondence in some way to a corporeal conception of the divine nature. The medieval philosophers sought to combat such notions, Maimonides going so far as to state that a Jew who believes that God is corporeal in any way is a heretic and has no share in the *World to Come. There is no evidence that Jews ever actually made an image of God for the purpose of worship (but see GOLDEN CALF). Some take the reference to the 'image' to mean the form God envisaged for man, not that there is any resemblance between God and man. For them

the image of God means no more than an image made by God. But the more usual interpretation is that in some way there is a point of resemblance between God and man, in the human intellect, for example, or in the kind of relationships that can only exist between 'persons'.

In the Kabbalistic doctrines of *Adam Kadmon and the *Sefirot there really is an 'image of God' but this refers to the divine, spiritual entities which are the source of all creation and which are mirrored in the human mind and body. Thus the human right arm, for example, is the form in which the spiritual entity known by this name appears when it descends into the world of matter.

Nehama Leibowitz, 'Man in the Image of God', in her *Studies in the Book of Genesis*, trans. from the Hebrew by Aryeh Newman (Jerusalem, 1972), 1–8.

**Imitatio Dei** Latin for the imitation of God, the doctrine that man can and should be godlike in his conduct. Although there are anticipations of the doctrine in such biblical passages as: 'Speak unto all the congregation of the children of Israel, and say unto them: Ye shall be holy for I the Lord your God am holy' (Leviticus 19: 2), it is in the Rabbinic literature that this teaching receives its most definite form. The Rabbinic Midrash known as the Sifre (see MIDRASH) to the verse in Deuteronomy (11: 22) which speaks of 'walking in God's ways' (in the context, walking in the ways laid down by God) takes 'walking in God's ways' to mean: 'Just as He is called "Merciful" be thou merciful; just as He is called "Compassionate" be thou compassionate.' Following in the same tradition, the third-century teacher Hama bar Hanina taught:

'What is the meaning of the verse: "Ye shall walk after the Lord your God" [Deuteronomy 12: 5]? Is it possible for a human being to walk after the *Shekhinah? For has it not been said: "For the Lord thy God is a devouring fire" [Deuteronomy 4: 24]? But the verse means to walk after the qualities of the Holy One, blessed be He, as He clothes the naked, for it is written: "And the Lord God made for Adam and his wife coats of skin and clothed them" [Genesis 3: 21], so do thou clothe the naked. The Holy One, blessed be He, visited the sick, for it is written: "And the Lord appeared to him by the oaks of Mamre" [Genesis 18: 1], so do thou also visit the sick. The Holy One, blessed be He, comforted mourners, for it is written: "And it came to pass after the death of Abraham that God blessed Isaac his son" [Genesis 25: 11], so do thou comfort mourners. The Holy One, blessed be He, buried the dead, for it is written: "And He buried him in the valley" [Deuteronomy 34: 6], so do thou also bury the dead' (*Sotah* 14a).

In his Code (*Deot*, 1. 16) Maimonides observes that this is the reason God is called by the prophets 'long-suffering ', 'abundant in mercy', 'righteous', 'upright', 'perfect', 'mighty', and so forth, that man might imitate Him in possessing these qualities.

Maimonides follows here his general stance that it is not permissible to apply positive attributes to *God. God is only 'called' compassionate but nothing can be known of his true nature. From the Rabbinic quotations, however, it would appear that the Rabbis mentioned did believe that God can really be described as compassionate so that man is actually godlike in some sense when he follows in God's ways. It is also significant that Maimonides (*Guide of the Perplexed*, i. 54) extends the notion of imitating God to the anger and vengeance required at times in dealing with criminals and sinners, whereas for the Rabbis the doctrine is applied only to the gentler virtues.

The doctrine is often said to be the foundation of Jewish ethics. Dr A. Cohen, for instance, writes: 'The doctrine of the Imitation of God is, accordingly, not only the actual foundation of Talmudic ethics but its motive and inspiration. It created the feeling in man that when his life was morally right, he gained the approval of his Maker, but more important than that, established his kinship with God. It therefore provided the all-sufficient incitement to righteous conduct.' Much of this statement can be accepted but it is questionable whether the expression 'foundation of Talmudic ethics' is correct. The doctrine does not apply to Talmudic ethics as a whole but only to the virtues of compassion and so forth. For the Talmudic Rabbis, there is, in fact, no independent *ethics as such, only ethical conduct as ordained in the Torah. Acts of *benevolence, on the other hand, are not explicitly enjoined in the Torah and it is for these that the doctrine of the imitation of God is invoked.

According to the Kabbalah, the imitation of God acquires a mystical meaning. To imitate God means, for the Kabbalists, to imitate and

thus bring into play the *Sefirot. Moses *Cordovero's *Palm Tree of Deborah* is a manual of guidance on how to imitate the Sefirot.

A. Cohen, 'Imitation of God', in his *Everyman's Talmud* (London, 1949), 210–12.

**Incense** A mixture of aromatic herbs burnt twice daily on the golden altar in the Temple; Heb. *ketoret*, from a root meaning 'to smoke'. The burning of the incense also formed an important part of the ritual performed by the *High Priest when he entered the Holy of Holies on *Yom Kippur (Leviticus 16: 12–13). The biblical instructions for the preparation of the incense are found in Exodus 30: 34, where four ingredients are mentioned—stacte, onycha, galbanum, and pure frankincense. But the Talmud (*Keritot* 6a) records an ancient tradition according to which there were eleven ingredients in the incense. This passage is known, after its opening words, as *pittum ha-ketoret* ('compound of incense'):

'The compound of incense consisted of balm, onycha, galbanum and frankincense, each in the quantity of seventy manehs; of myrrh, cassia, spikenard and saffron, each sixteen manehs by weight; of costus twelve, of aromatic rind three, and of cinnamon nine manehs; of lye obtained from leek nine kabs; of Cyprus wine three seahs and three kabs; though, if Cyprus wine is not available, old white wine may be used instead; of salt of Sodom the fourth of a kab, and of the smoke raiser [a herb that makes the smoke of the incense rise] a minute quantity. Rabbi Nathan says: Also of Jordan resin a minute quantity. If, however, honey is added, the incense is rendered unfit; while if one omits one of the ingredients he is liable to the death penalty [not by the human court but by the "Court of Heaven"]. Rabban Simeon ben *Gamaliel said: Balm is nothing but a resin which exudes from the wood of the balsam-tree; the lye obtained from leek was rubbed over the onycha in order to render it beautiful, and in the Cyprus wine the onycha was steeped that its odour might be intensified. In fact urine might well serve this purpose, but urine may not be brought within the precincts of the Temple.'

A Rabbinic comment on this is that galbanum has an unpleasant smell and yet is included in the ingredients of the incense, to teach that when the community assembles for prayer on public fast days the sinners, too, must be included. According to the Mishnah (*Yoma* 3: 11) the incense in the Second Temple period was manufactured by the House of Abtinas who zealously kept their method secret. The Mishnah states that the sages objected to the House of Abtinas having a monopoly on the preparation of the incense but the Talmud comments that the reason for keeping it a secret was that it should not be manufactured by unscrupulous persons for profane purposes. The womenfolk of the House of Abtinas never used any perfume in case people would imagine that they were using the incense compound.

Incense is found in the worship of most ancient societies, no doubt because of the pleasant aroma ascending upwards towards heaven and as a symbol of purification. Maimonides' explanation of the incense (*Guide of the Perplexed*, 3. 43) scandalized the pious who considered it far too banal an explanation for so numinous a rite:

'Inasmuch as many beasts were slaughtered daily in that holy place, the flesh cut into pieces, and the intestines burnt and washed, there is no doubt that if it had been left in that state its smell would have been like that of a slaughterhouse. Therefore it was commanded in regard to it that incense would be burnt there twice daily in the morning and in the afternoon in order to improve its smell and the smell of the clothes of all who served there . . . This also preserved the fear of the Sanctuary. For if it has not a pleasant smell, and all the more if the contrary were the case, the result would have been the opposite of glorification. For the soul is greatly solaced and attracted by pleasant smells and shrinks from stench and avoids it.'

For the *Zohar the incense has a profound mystical meaning. The smoke of the incense represents the ascent of all creation to the *Sefirot and of the Sefirot to their Source in *En Sof. The Zohar observes (ii. 218b): 'It is a firmly established ordinance of the Holy One, blessed be He, that whoever reflects on and recites daily the section of the incense will be saved from all evil things and sorceries in the world, from all mishaps and evil imaginings, from evil decrees and from death; and no harm will befall him that day, as the "Other Side" has no power over him. But it must be read with devotion.' Following this, the Talmudic passage of *pittum ha-ketoret*, referred to above, is recited in many rites at the beginning of the morning and afternoon services.

Incense itself, however, is never used in the synagogue, probably in order to distinguish the synagogue from the Temple, although synagogues have been known to spray the building with aromatic herbs, not as any kind of ritual but solely for aesthetic reasons. Some of the Hasidic masters used to smoke a pipe of fragrant *tobacco when they meditated before their prayers.

Isaiah Tishby, 'Incense', in his *The Wisdom of the Zohar*, trans. David Goldstein (Oxford, 1989), 933–7.

**Individual** Although it is often said that the emphasis on Judaism is on the group rather than the individual, on the *Chosen People rather than on particular Jews, this glib generalization is not supported by the evidence. Where the emphasis lies in a religious tradition is notoriously difficult to determine. The possibility always exists that some ideas are rarely mentioned not because they are considered unimportant but, on the contrary, because their importance is taken for granted. Yet even if the yardstick of frequency of mention is applied, it becomes clear from the classical Jewish sources that, while there are numerous passages centred on the role of the people, passages are certainly not lacking in which the role of the individual is stressed. In any balanced picture of the Jewish religion, what the individual does with his life has eternal significance for him or her, not only for the Jewish people, which is itself made up of individuals.

It is no doubt true that the Talmudic Rabbis, anxious for the survival of their people against what seemed to them the heaviest odds, constantly appeal to group loyalties. Yet the Mishnah (*Sanhedrin* 4: 5) can give expression to the supreme significance of the individual. This Mishnah comments as follows on the creation narrative in the book of Genesis, according to which *Adam, the first man, is the ancestor of all human beings: 'Therefore but a single man was created in the world, to teach that if anyone has caused a single person to perish Scripture imputes it to him as though he had caused a whole world to perish; and if anyone saves the life of a single person Scripture imputes it to him as though he had saved a whole world.' This is the reading in the original text. The insertion of a 'Jewish life' (*yisrael*) in current texts has support neither in the original manuscripts nor in the Adam narrative on which the

Mishnah comments. The reference is to the significance of every human being, Jew or *Gentile.

With regard to the biblical period, the contention of some Old Testament scholars that all the stress was on the nation until the later *prophets taught individual responsibility, must be rejected even on a superficial reading of the earlier sources. In the patriarchal narratives, for example, while it is now axiomatic that these often reflect tribal motifs, yet each of the *patriarchs and *matriarchs appears as a person with the strongest individual characteristics. The pioneering *Abraham is different from *Isaac who follows in his father's footsteps and both are different from *Jacob who relies on his grandfather's and father's teachings to build 'the house of Israel'. Of the three leaders of the people through the forty years of wandering in the wilderness, *Moses is the stern lawgiver, *Aaron the priestly figure bent on compromise for the sake of peace; while *Miriam adopts the feminine role, watching over her infant brother and eventually leading all the women in singing her own song of deliverance at the shores of the sea.

Both the first paragraph of the *Shema (Deuteronomy 6: 4–9) and the *Decalogue are in the singular and are addressed to each individual; the same is true of the majority of the laws in the three Pentateuchal Codes (Exodus 21: 1–23: 19; Leviticus 18: 1–37; Deuteronomy 21: 1–25: 19) and was so understood in subsequent Jewish teaching. Though in some instances the singular form is used for the people as a whole, these are instances in which a social context is apparent in the texts themselves.

As for the prophets, each of these speaks as an individual, his communication from God expressed in terms of his own temperament and particular circumstances. And while the prophetic message is generally to the people as a whole, the call of the prophets is for the individuals of that people to be governed by justice, righteousness, holiness, and compassion. *Ezekiel 18 is a powerful plea for individual responsibility. *Micah's famous declaration of what it is that God demands is in the singular and is addressed to each member of the group: 'It hath been told thee, O man, what is good, and what the Lord doth require of thee; only to do justly, and to love mercy, and to walk humbly with thy God' (Micah 6: 8). In the Psalms the 'I' does often refer to the people but in many of the Psalms the 'I' is the Psalmist's own.

In the Talmudic and Midrashic literature, the emphasis is generally on peoplehood but statements regarding individual duties, responsibilities, and needs are found throughout this literature. Each of the Rabbis is an individual with his own particular virtues and failings, so much so that it has been possible, with a fair degree of success, to reconstruct Rabbinic biographies from the hints scattered in this vast literature.

In the philosophical tradition in the Middle Ages, especially in Maimonides, Judaism is so interpreted that the aim of the religion is ultimately for the individual, the social thrust of Judaism being regarded as a means to an end; a sound social-order helps the individual to rise towards perfection. Maimonides' *principles of faith are directed towards the individual Jew. It is no accident that Maimonides does not list belief in Israel as the *Chosen People among his thirteen principles. It is not that Maimonides does not believe that Israel has been chosen by God, but that such a belief is not so prominent a feature of the Jewish religion that it can be designated a principle of the faith.

In the Kabbalah, every human soul is a spark of Adam's soul, bound to engage in the task of restoration of the '*holy sparks' that fell into the demonic realm when Adam sinned. In the Kabbalistic doctrine of 'rectification', each individual has his own special part to play in accordance with his particular soul-root. In *Hasidism the soul-root idea is developed still further. Not only does the Hasid have to find the Zaddik whose personality is in accord with his particular soul (because they both belong to the same 'root') but there are fallen sparks in creation which only a particular individual can raise because these, too, belong to his soul-root. In their different ways both the *Haskalah and the *Musar movement have the strongest individualistic thrust.

Moreover, in every version of Jewish *eschatology, it is the individual who lives for ever, whether in the doctrine of the *resurrection or of the immortality of the soul. In the otherworldly Judaism that was the norm until modern times, the whole of life upon earth was seen as a preparation by the individual for his life in the Hereafter and all the precepts of the Torah have this as their ultimate purpose.

All the above, of course, presents only one side of the picture. Throughout all periods there has been considerable tension between peoplehood and individualism in Judaism as there has been between Jewish particularism and *universalism. And individual needs are often made subordinate to the obligations to family, other individuals, community, the Jewish people, and the world at large. To the question: 'does Judaism centre on the people or on the individual?' the only answer possible is that it centres on both.

Louis Jacobs, *Religion and the Individual: A Jewish Perspective* (Cambridge, 1992).

**Insanity** Mental instability, of which state a number of instances are recorded in the Bible. Among the curses threatened for faithlessness to the covenant is 'so that thou shalt be mad [*meshugga*] for the sake of thine eyes which thou shalt see' (Deuteronomy 28: 34). King Saul was terrified by an evil spirit and David was invited to play the harp so that Saul could find relief (1 Samuel 16: 14–23). David feigned madness when he fled to the court of Achish the king of Gath (1 Samuel 21: 13–16: Psalms 31: 1). A Midrashic comment on this is that David questioned why God should have created such a purposeless state as insanity. But when he saved his life by pretending to be mad, David came to see that madness also has a purpose. In one passage (Hosea 9: 7), the prophet is described as 'mad', though it is clear from the context that this term is used ironically. Some moderns have understood the biblical record here and elsewhere to imply that a man who has received a vision from on high is bound to have had a profound disturbance of his mental equilibrium. In the Rabbinic literature madness or melancholia is often attributed to an evil spirit, *ruahyaah*.

It is axiomatic in Jewish law that an imbecile, *shoteh* in Hebrew, is held responsible for his actions neither by a human court nor by the divine judgement. But there is considerable uncertainty about the degree of mental instability required for a person to be considered a *shoteh*. The classical definition stated in the Talmud (*Hagigah* 3b) is one who goes out alone at night, stays overnight in the cemetery, and rends his garments. The Talmud discusses this further but the definition remains more than a little opaque. Maimonides, in his Code (*Edut*, 9. 9–10), after stating that a *shoteh* is disqualified

from acting as a witness in a court of law, observes that in this context a *shoteh* is not only one who walks about naked or breaks vessels or throws stones but whoever is mentally disturbed. Evidently, Maimonides understands the Talmudic definition to be in the nature of a broad, general assessment so that for practical purposes the term denotes anyone whose mind is disturbed with regard to any one matter and Maimonides proceeds to extend the scope of the law as follows: 'Those especially stupid in that they cannot note contradictions and cannot understand any matter in the way normal people do, and so, too, those who are confused and hasty in their minds and behave in an excessively crazy fashion, these are embraced by the term *shoteh*. This matter must depend on the assessment of the judge since it is impossible to record in writing an adequate definition of insanity.' Thus Maimonides, perhaps because of his knowledge of medicine, finds the notion of insanity too complicated and too vague to be recorded in a precise legal definition, so that the decision must be left to the discretion of the judge in each particular case.

The problem of defining insanity is particularly acute in connection with *divorce. An insane wife cannot be divorced. Freehof is wrong in stating that the reason for this is because it amounts to divorce by force since the ban on a husband divorcing his wife without her consent (see GERSHOM OF MAYYENCE) did not obtain in Talmudic times. The reason given in the Talmud is that a divorce involves sending the wife away, in the language of Deuteronomy (24: 1–4), and an insane wife cannot be 'sent away' since she will continue to consider herself to be married and will constantly return to her husband. Yet the problem of the insane wife is usually resolved by granting a dispensation of the ban against polygamy; in other words, the husband is required to make adequate provision for the support of his insane wife and he is then permitted to take another wife. In practice this dispensation is not given unless 100 Rabbis residing in three different lands examine the case and sign the dispensation.

An insane husband cannot divorce his wife because he lacks the requisite degree of mental stability to know what he is doing. An insane person cannot effect a valid marriage but it is possible for a man whose mental capacity is weak to contract a valid marriage in his lucid periods. It follows that it is possible, because of the difficulties inherent in the problem of defining insanity, that a man of weak mind may have possessed a sufficient degree of mental stability for his marriage to be valid and yet lack that degree when he attempts to divorce his wife. Such a marriage would result in the wife becoming an *agunah*, a woman technically married to a husband from whom she cannot obtain a legal divorce. All this became the subject of the *cause célèbre* in the eighteenth century known as the Get of Cleaves. Here the various Rabbis who took part in the debate were often divided on the question of the state of mind required for a man to be held to be insane. The tendency among Rabbis today is to be lenient with regard to some forms of mental illness such as split personality or manic depression, so as to allow the divorce provided the husband's mind is sufficiently lucid to enable him to know what he is doing when he authorizes the delivery of the *get*, the bill of divorce.

In everyday parlance, when it is said of someone that he is *meshugga* or a *shoteh*, these terms are used very loosely and resemble the English use of 'barmy' or 'daft'.

Solomon B. Freehof, 'The Divorce in Cleaves', in his *The Responsa Literature* (New York, 1973), 158–61.

**Inspiration** Enlargement of the human psyche so as to produce an increase in vision and knowledge of the will of God. Though the actual word 'inspiration' is never used in the traditional sources, the idea that God endows spiritually gifted persons with insights that are not available to ordinary mortals is found frequently throughout the Bible, the Rabbinic literature, and among the standard Jewish thinkers. According to the tradition there are various degrees of inspiration: *prophecy; the *Holy Spirit; the heavenly voice (*Bat Kol); the appearance of *Elijah; and *dreams. Some modernists, influenced by the scientific picture of the universe, have abandoned the concept of *God as a transcendental being and have understood inspiration in purely naturalistic terms—that, for instance, the Bible is inspired in the way that Shakespeare or Mozart are said to be 'inspired'. But, while critical investigation (see BIBLICAL CRITICISM) has succeeded in raising powerful objections to traditional views, and while there is a greater acknowledgement

of the human element, there is no valid reason for rejecting the idea of inspiration itself. It can be put in this way: modern Jews are far less certain that works considered to be the result of divine inspiration are really so, yet a belief in God surely cannot rule out that human beings have encountered God in the special manner implied by the idea of inspiration.

**Insurance** In the medieval and Renaissance world, the question was widely discussed of whether taking out insurance on ships' cargoes and the like involved any infringement of the laws against *usury. Legal arguments were advanced by the authorities to allow merchants to secure their goods against risk while avoiding the prohibitions, treating insurance like any other commercial transaction but not like a loan on interest where the borrower gives back the lender more than the amount he borrowed purely in return for the loan itself. On the theological level, no one seems to have imagined that to take out insurance was to lack faith in God's power to provide. It was not until the late twentieth century that Rabbi Moshe *Feinstein raised the question, coming to the obvious conclusion that according to sound Jewish teaching God only provides when human beings play their part.

S. M. Passamaneck, *Insurance in Rabbinic Law* (Edinburgh, 1974).

**Intermarriage** Marriage between a Jew and a non-Jew. In Jewish law there is no validity whatsoever to a marriage between a Jew and a non-Jew so that no *get (bill of divorce) is required to dissolve the union. The Jewish status of the children depends on the status of the mother, not the father. If a non-Jewish man marries a Jewish woman, the children are Jews; but if a Jewish man marries a non-Jewish woman, the children are not Jewish. However it evolved, this became the traditional position from early Rabbinic times. This principle of matrilineal descent, as it is termed in contemporary discussions, is still adhered to strictly by Orthodox and Conservative Jews, as well as by many Reform Jews. But, in recent years, some Reform Rabbis in the USA (and this is the position of the Liberal movement in the UK) have adopted the rule that, provided the intention of the parents is to bring the child up as Jewish, the child of a Jewish father and a non-Jewish mother also has Jewish status.

All Jewish groups frown on intermarriage, not only because of the law which forbids such unions, but primarily because intermarriage poses a severe threat to Jewish survival. There is hardly any intermarriage between Jews and non-Jews in the State of Israel, for obvious reasons, but in the *Diaspora intermarriage is the most acute problem facing Jews. A large proportion of Jews do fall in love with non-Jews and do 'marry out'. Attitudes to Jews who have married out differ widely. Every effort is made by Rabbis to discourage intermarriage and, when it happens, to encourage the non-Jewish spouse to convert to Judaism. Nevertheless, where these efforts fail, the Jewish spouse is treated as a full member of the Jewish people and is accepted as a member of the synagogue, even in many Orthodox communities.

J. David Bleich, 'The Prohibition against Intermarriage', in his *Contemporary Halakhic Problems* (New York, 1983), ii. 268–82.

**Isaac** The second of the three *patriarchs, son of Abraham and father of Jacob, whose story is told in the book of Genesis. The Hebrew name Yitzhak, from *tzaḥak*, 'to laugh', was apparently given to him because his mother Sarah laughed when it was foretold that she would give birth at her advanced age (Genesis 18: 12). Abraham was 100 years old at Isaac's birth and Sarah 90 years (Genesis 21: 5). The traditional commentators take this literally but the suggestion has been made that by 'years' in the narrative only half-years are meant, so that Abraham was 50 and Sarah 45. It is extremely unlikely, however, that years should mean half-years since that meaning is found nowhere else in the Bible. The story of the *Akedah*, the binding of Isaac, is told in Genesis 19. Isaac married Rebecca when he was 40 years of age and she bore him twin boys, Jacob and Esau, when he was 60 years of age (Genesis 25: 19–26). Isaac died at the age of 180 and was buried by his sons in the Cave of *Machpelah (Genesis 35: 27–9). The chronological details of Isaac's life are confusing and difficult to put together as a coherent whole. On the critical view, the narratives stem from different sources, though hardly any biblical scholars fail to treat Isaac as a historical figure.

Commentators have noted that Isaac appears in the narratives chiefly in a passive role. He becomes in the Jewish tradition the 'one in the middle' whose activities are more constricted than those of his father and son. Isaac is the man whose function it is to preserve the tradition intact. In the Kabbalah, Isaac represents the Sefirah of Power, *Gevurah*, because of his willingness to be sacrificed at the *Akedah*. In this he represents the counterpart to the Sefirah of Love, *Hesed*, represented by Abraham.

Nahum M. Sarna, *Understanding Genesis* (New York, 1966), 154–90.

**Isaiah** Prophet of the eighth century BCE during the reigns of four kings of Judah, Uzziah, Jotham, Ahaz, and Hezekiah. Although the book of Isaiah begins with the prophet's vision of the future, in which he foretells the catastrophes that will befall his people if they practice injustice and fail to put their trust in God, Isaiah's first prophetic vision is recounted in chapter 6 of the book: 'In the year that King Uzziah died, I beheld the Lord seated on a high and lofty throne and the skirts of His robe filled the Temple' (6: 1). In this vision the prophet sees the Seraphim proclaiming one to the other: 'Holy, holy, holy! The Lord of Hosts! His presence fills all the earth' (6: 3). This verse constitutes the main section of the *Kedushah recited in the synagogue. In the same chapter (6: 13) the prophet declares that a remnant of the faithful will remain come what may, an idea that was to prove influential in Jewish thought. No matter how far the Jewish people have strayed from the true path, a faithful remnant will always be found to preserve the covenant with God.

Isaiah's vision of a 'shoot' growing out of the stump of Jesse, father of King *David, who will usher in a new era of peace when 'the wolf shall dwell with the lamb' (11: 1–15), became a key passage for the doctrine of the *Messiah.

The political background to Isaiah's activity is the alliance of Syria with the Northern Kingdom of Israel against Judah in 735 BCE and the threat presented by the advance of Assyria. Isaiah's two sons were given names to represent these dire events. The first son was called Shear-yashuv (7: 3), meaning: 'a remnant shall return'. The second son was called Maher-shalal-hash-baz (8: 1–4), meaning: 'the spoil speeds, the prey hastens', usually understood as referring to the downfall of Syria and the conquest of the Northern Kingdom by Assyria.

All this provides an illustration of the nature of the prophesies by the great literary prophet. While, in subsequent Jewish interpretation, their visions were interpreted in Messianic terms—that they foretold events that would come about 'at the end of days'—it is abundantly clear that prophesies like those of Isaiah were directed chiefly to events of their own day. The statement that the prophets were forthtellers rather than foretellers is far too glib. While the prophets did bring the message that God wants righteousness and justice from His people in the here and now, they also spoke of the future. But it was the immediate future to which they addressed themselves and it was only much later that their visions came to be understood as prophesies of what was to happen at the culmination of human history.

Abraham *Ibn Ezra in the Middle Ages and the majority of biblical scholars today believe that the second part of the book of Isaiah (from ch. 40 onwards) could not have been composed by the prophet Isaiah since this section of the book speaks, as if it were actually taking place, of the return from the Babylonian exile. Cyrus, the king of Persia who defeated the Babylonians in 539 BCE and issued his edict to permit the Jews to return to Jerusalem, is mentioned twice by name (44: 28; 45: 1). Diehards such as S. D. *Luzzatto remained unconvinced and even went so far as to say that anyone who denies that the second part of Isaiah was composed by the prophet Isaiah, denies altogether the power of a prophet to gaze into the future. The consensus of scholarly opinion is that the second part of Isaiah, 'Deutero-Isaiah', makes no claim to foretell events of the remote future and was compiled by an unknown prophet or prophets. As for the strong resemblance in style between the two halves of the book, scholars have suggested that a kind of Isaianic school persisted long after the death of Isaiah himself.

J. H. Hertz, 'The Authorship of the Second Part of Isaiah', in his *The Pentateuch and Haftorahs* (London, 1960), 941–2.

**Ishmael** Son of Abraham and his concubine Hagar (Genesis 16) and half-brother of Isaac. To some extent in the Pentateuchal narrative itself, and especially in the Rabbinic literature, Ishmael is seen in a very unfavourable light, but eventually, according to the Midrash, he repented of his evil deeds. In Islam, Ishmael is the ancestor of Muhammad and is venerated as a prophet and the true son of Abraham. In the Koran (*Sura*, 37) it is Ishmael, not Isaac, who was bound on the altar at the *Akedah. Later

Muslims accused the Jews of falsifying the Torah by substituting Isaac for Ishmael. Many of the Rabbinic Midrashim which speak of the life and conduct of Ishmael have, in fact, the Muslims in mind. This fact has helped scholars in dating some literary works. When, for instance, the Zohar states that the time will come when Edom (the name for Rome and later for Christians) and Ishmael will fight over the Holy Land, the reference is fairly obviously to the Crusades. In the *Targum attributed to Jonathan ben Uziel, the names of Ishmael's two wives are given as Ayesha and Fatima, the names of Muhammad's wife and daughter, thus demonstrating that the work could not possibly have been compiled by Jonathan ben Uziel who lived in the first century BCE and could not have known these names.

Louis Ginzberg, *The Legends of the Jews* (Philadelphia, 1940), i. 263–9.

**Ishmael, Rabbi** Tanna (see TANNAIM AND AMORAIM) who lived in the first half of the second century CE and contemporary of Rabbi *Akiba, with whom he often engaged in debate. He is sometimes referred to as Rabbi Ishmael ben Elisha but usually simply as Rabbi Ishmael. That a Rabbi should have the name of a biblical villain is probably to be explained on the grounds that since it was believed that eventually Ishmael* repented and was, after all, the son of Abraham, Jewish parents saw no objection to giving this name to their sons. There are references to the 'school' or 'house' of Rabbi Ishmael, meaning no doubt a group of disciples who followed his teachings. Unlike Rabbi Akiba, who held that every word of the legal passages in the Torah must be interpreted to convey its own nuances, Rabbi Ishmael held that some words have a purely stylistic significance because 'The Torah speaks in the language of men'. Rabbi Ishmael is the author of the thirteen principles of *hermeneutics.

**Islam** The religion whose prophet is Muhammad. Islam and Christianity are sometimes referred to as the 'daughter religions' of Judaism because both affirm that God did reveal His will to the Jews and many of their ideas are adopted from Judaism, although the term 'daughter religions' is never found in any of the standard Jewish sources. The accepted view among the medieval thinkers is that Islam, though false from the standpoint of Judaism, is a pure monotheistic faith so that a non-Jew who is a Muslim does not offend against the *Noahide laws, one of which is the prohibition of idolatry. Maimonides goes so far as to rule that if a Jew is ordered to embrace Islam or be killed, he is not obliged to suffer martyrdom. Others disagree. It is true, they argue, that a convert to Islam is not an idolater but, by becoming a Muslim, he rejects the *Torah and to avoid this act of apostasy, too, martyrdom is demanded.

In a famous Responsum (no. 448) Maimonides admits that the pre-Islamic Arabs were idolaters, but states that the pilgrimage to Mecca by contemporary Muslims can in no way be construed as idolatrous worship:

'If someone were to argue that the house in which they worship is a house of idolatry and an idol is hidden therein which their ancestors used to worship, what of it! Those who worship there today have only God in mind. Our Rabbis have already explained in tractate Sanhedrin [61b] that if a man bows down in a house of idolatry thinking it is a synagogue his heart is directed towards God. The same applies to these Arabs today. Idolatry has been cut off from the mouths of all of them including the women and children. Their folly is only with regard to other matters which I cannot state explicitly out of fear of wicked and iniquitous Jews, but with regard to the unity of God they are in no way in error . . .'

In his *Epistle on Martyrdom* Maimonides is less circumspect. The Muslim rulers had refused to allow the Jews of Morocco to continue to reside there unless they embraced Islam and many Jews did succumb, living outwardly as Muslims but secretly observing as many of the practices of Judaism as they could. Maimonides, seeking to encourage the Jews who were not strong enough to give their lives, asserts that Islam is not an idolatrous faith. These Jews who have allowed themselves to become Muslims do commit a serious sin and if they can escape from the country must make every sacrifice in order to do so. Yet they have not gone over to idolatry and should persist in their Jewish observances, contrary to the opinion of a Rabbi that since they have become Muslims all their Jewish practices are worthless. But Maimonides here is careful not to allow the faintest suggestion that Islam is in any way a true religion. He pours scorn on the Islamic claim that the Jews have falsified the Torah which originally

had prophesied the birth and teachings of Muhammad, whom he calls 'the madman'.

Maimonides has been quoted at some length because his attitude became the prevailing one among the Jewish teachers. As late as the twentieth century, Rabbi A. I. *Kook repeats Maimonides' ruling. A Responsum (*Daat Kohen*, no. 16) dated Jerusalem 1925 concerns the Muslim authorities who only allow *sheḥitah* (see DIETARY LAWS) to be carried out if the *shoḥet* faces east and acknowledges Allah. Kook rules that if possible this must be avoided but otherwise it is permitted, since Muslims worship God alone and are not idolaters.

While there is a good deal of Jewish–Christian *dialogue on the contemporary scene there is hardly any Jewish–Islamic dialogue, no doubt because of the strained relations between Jews and Muslims after the establishment of the State of Israel.

Abraham Halkin and David Hartman, *Crisis and Leadership: Epistles of Maimonides* (Philadelphia, 1985).

**Israel, State of** The literature on the State of Israel is vast. The *Encyclopedia Judaica* alone has over a thousand pages and an extensive bibliography on Israel, to say nothing of books and newspaper articles published all over the world on what, on any showing, is one of the most momentous creations in all human history. In this entry all that can be attempted is a brief glance at Jewish religious attitudes to the State of Israel and the implications of its establishment for the Jewish religion. From the days of *Herzl and the rise of political *Zionism, this new movement was hailed by many as the only solution to the Jewish problem and attacked by others as an attempted substitution of nationalism for religion. With the establishment of the State of Israel, these debates became academic and, with the exception of a few religious anti-Zionists, there has been a wholehearted acceptance of the State not only as a refuge for Jews but as being in some way of the highest significance for the future of Judaism.

The Declaration of Independence of the State of Israel, signed by David Ben Gurion and members of the provisional council of state and members of the provisional government, reads in part:

'Eretz-Israel was the birthplace of the Jewish people. Here their spiritual, religious and political identity was shaped. Here they first attained to statehood, created cultural values of national and universal significance and gave to the world the eternal Book of Books ... The catastrophe which recently befell the Jewish people—the massacre of millions of Jews in Europe—was another clear demonstration of the urgency of solving the problem of its homelessness by re-establishing in Eretz-Israel the Jewish State, which would open the gates of the homeland wide to every Jew and confer upon the Jewish people the status of a fully-privileged member of the community of nations ... On 29 November 1947, the United Nations General Assembly passed a resolution calling for the establishment of a Jewish State in Eretz-Israel; the General Assembly required the inhabitants of Eretz-Israel to take such steps as were necessary on their part for the implementation of that resolution. This recognition by the United Nations of the right of the Jewish people to establish their State is irrevocable ... Accordingly we, members of the people's council, representatives of the Jewish community of Eretz-Israel and of the Zionist movement, are here assembled on the day of the termination of the British mandate over Eretz-Israel and by virtue of our natural and historic right and on the strength of the resolution of the United Nations General Assembly, hereby declare the establishment of a Jewish State in Eretz-Israel to be known as the State of Israel ... We appeal—in the very midst of the onslaught against us now for months—to the Arab inhabitants of the State of Israel to preserve peace and participate in the upbuilding of the State on the basis of full and equal citizenship and due representation in all its provisional and permanent institutions. We extend our hand to all neighbouring States and their peoples in an offer of peace and good neighbourliness, and appeal to them to establish bonds of co-operation and mutual help with the sovereign Jewish people settled in its own land. The State of Israel is prepared to do its share in common effort for the advancement of the entire Middle East ... Placing our trust in the Almighty, we affix our signatures to this proclamation at the session of the provisional Council of State on the soil of the homeland, in the city of Tel Aviv, on this Sabbath eve, the 5th day of Iyar, 5708 [14 May 1948].'

In this historic document, visionary and noble in its aims and comparable to the American Declaration of Independence, there can already be heard echoes of the older conflict between Jewish secular nationalism and Judaism as a religion. It is not necessary to see the words 'placing our trust in the Almighty' as a sop to the religious and it was almost certainly intended as a sincere declaration of religious faith, whether or not a faith subscribed to by all the signatories. Yet it is significant that, perhaps to appease the secularists, very little is said about religion and it is the Jewish people, not God, who shaped 'their spiritual, religious and political identity' and it is they 'who gave to the world the eternal Book of Books'. This ambivalence was inevitable granted that some Jews saw Israel as a modern, democratic, secular State while others saw it in semi-numinous terms as, in the language of the religious Zionists, 'the beginning of the Redemption', that is, as paving the way for the coming of the *Messiah.

In the debates and discussions ever since, Israelis have been divided, or have divided themselves, into secularists (*ḥilonim*) and religionists (*datiim*). This distinction is unfortunate in that religion is identified with Orthodoxy, and all those Israelis who are not fully observant are placed in the camp of the 'secularists'. Many are not secularists at all, but deeply religious people whose conscience does not allow them to adopt completely the traditional ways. A large proportion of the so-called secularists fast and attend services on Yom Kippur; observe the Sabbath and festivals, though not necessarily in the traditional manner; and keep the *dietary laws with varying degrees of strictness. With regard to Jewish law, the compromise was reached that in matters of personal status and marriage and divorce the sole authority is the Orthodox Rabbinate. There is no civil marriage or divorce in the State of Israel. This means that marriages cannot take place where the religious law is opposed to them, for instance, the marriage of a *Kohen (*priest) to a divorcee; this is one example among many of the difficulties facing a democratic State that guarantees human rights and yet wishes to preserve traditional religious values. Disputes erupt from time to time on such matters as well as on comparatively less significant issues such as the performance of *autopsies in Israeli hospitals; the closing of religious districts to cars on the Sabbath; archaeological digs which might disturb the resting-place of the dead of ancient times; and even the appearance on bus-shelters of posters advertising beach-wear which display scantily clad models.

There are a number of political parties representing religious Jews, with a variety of religious affiliations. The Aggudat Israel party, anti-Zionist in pre-State days, now accepts, somewhat uneasily, that the State of Israel is at the centre of Jewish life everywhere and is represented in the Israeli Parliament, the Knesset, and sometimes even in the government. Aggudat Israel has established its own independent religious school system. To the left of Aggudat Israel is the Mafdal, the National Religious Party, formerly the Mizrachi movement of religious Zionism. This party is totally committed to the Zionist ideal. An offshoot of Mafdal is the Gush Emunim movement. This is not a political party but a tendency among religious Zionists to try to make sure that the land promised to Abraham, as the members often say, will never be surrendered; so that trading land for peace with the Arabs, even if this is feasible, is ruled out by divine fiat. The religious parties are generally opposed to the extremist and hawkish attitudes of the Gush Emunim. Sephardi religious Jews, believing Aggudat Israel to be too dominated by the Ashkenazim, have formed themselves into the Sephardi Torah Guardians' Party (Shas). The Degel Ha-Torah party represents Ashkenazi Jews sympathetic to the Aggudat Israel philosophy but who believe that Aggudat Israel is too dominated by Hasidic Jews. Reform and Conservative Jews are not organized on party-political lines but have their own organizations and synagogues in Israel. Conservative Judaism in Israel is known as Masorti ('Traditional').

Of non-Jewish religions in Israel there are the Druzes, with a secret religion, Muslims, and Christians of many denominations, all of whom are given complete freedom to worship in accordance with their own beliefs and to further their own institutions.

The Chief Rabbinate of Israel, with two heads, a Sephardi Chief Rabbi and an Ashkenazi Chief Rabbi, goes back to the days of the British Mandate for Palestine and is modelled, in fact, on the British Chief Rabbinate, itself owing much to the office of Archbishop in the Anglican Church. The ultra-Orthodox, known as the Haredim ('God-fearing') do not recognize the Chief Rabbinate and have their own Rabbinic authorities. Since there is no doctrinal significance to the office of Chief Rabbi, voices

are raised from time to time to abolish the whole institution of two Chief Rabbis, irreverently called by Israelis 'the Heavenly Twins'.

Beyond all the practical considerations are the challenges to traditional Jewish thought presented by Jewish Statehood in its modern form. While the vast majority of Jewish thinkers have welcomed the centrality of the State of Israel for Jewish religious life everywhere (Isaiah *Leibowitz is a notable exception), severe problems still await their solution: how Jewish nationalistic aspirations are to be reconciled with *universalism, the secular with the sacred, belief in divine *providence with human endeavour, justice for the Jews with the rights of the Arabs, love for the Holy Land with the loyalty owed by Jews outside Israel to the lands in which they reside. There are no easy solutions. Rabbi A. I. *Kook's: 'Let the old be renewed and let the new be sanctified' is all very well as a slogan, but slogans are no substitute for solid thought, any more than is the old maxim of the Mizrachi: 'The land of Israel for the people of Israel according to the Torah of Israel.' It is obviously far too soon after the establishment of the State of Israel for anyone to offer precise solutions. Much is in a state of flux and will remain so for some time. These problems must be faced by religious Jews in the spirit of their faith, which attaches the greatest significance to what has happened in Israel and entertains the highest hopes for Israel in the future, but which has God alone as its, in Paul Tillich's phrase, 'ultimate concern'.

'Israel', in Ian Harris, Stuart Mews, Paul Morris, and John Shepherd (eds), *Contemporary Religions: A World Guide* (Harlow, 1992), 427–8.

Zvi Sobel and Benjamin Beit-Hallahmi (eds), *Tradition Innovation Conflict: Jewishness and Judaism in Contemporary Israel* (Albany, NY, 1991).

**Isserles, Moses** Polish authority, Rabbi in Cracow (d.1572). Isserles had a good knowledge of philosophy, Kabbalah, and history. He was the author of *Responsa and other Halakhic works but his chief claim to fame rests on his glosses to the *Shulḥan Arukh* of Joseph *Karo. Karo's work, meaning 'Arranged Table', was intended to provide, a clear ruling on all matters of *Halakhah. But since Karo generally followed the Sephardi rulings, Isserles resolved to compile glosses in which Ashkenazi opinions and customs would be recorded. Isserles gave his work, which appeared together with the *Shulḥan Arukh* in 1569–71, the name *Mappah*, 'Tablecloth' (i.e. to Karo's 'Table'). Since that time every edition of the *Shulḥan Arukh* contains the glosses of Isserles, and the two, Karo and Isserles, are referred to as the authors of the *Shulḥan Arukh*. Isserles is generally known, after the initial letters of his name, as Rema—*Rabbi Moshe Isserles*. It is thanks to Isserles that numerous Jewish *customs have been preserved; he believed that, as the old maxim has it, 'The *minhag* ["custom"] of Israel is Torah.'

# J

**Jacob** The third patriarch of the Jewish people, son of Isaac and Rebecca, grandson of Abraham, whose story is told in the book of Genesis (25: 19 to the end of the book). On the critical view (see BIBLICAL CRITICISM), the Jacob saga in Genesis is an amalgam of various sources and traditions. For all that, most critics believe that there is a core of historical fact to all the traditions; only a very few accept the notion that Jacob and the other two *patriarchs are fictitious persons. From the point of view of the Jewish tradition, it is not, in any event, the historical Jacob who matters most but Jacob as he appears in Genesis as the progenitor of the twelve tribes constituting the 'children of Israel'. In the Genesis narrative, Jacob, Yaakov in Hebrew, is so called because at his birth he seized hold of the heel (*akev*) of his twin brother, *Esau (Genesis 25: 25), while the name Israel was given to him by the angel with whom he wrestled (Genesis 32: 25–33).

Among the salient features in Jacob's life, as told in Genesis, are that Esau sold him his birthright for a 'mess of pottage' (24: 27–34); that, at the instigation of his mother, Rebecca, he tricked his father, Isaac, into giving him, instead of Esau, the blessing (ch. 27); that he fled from Esau's wrath to his uncle Laban whose two daughters, Rachel and Leah, he married and by whom, and by the two concubines Bilhah and Zilpah, he had twelve sons in all (chs. 29 and 30); that he came to sojourn in the land of Egypt (chs. 45 and 46); and that he was taken after his death to be buried in the land of his fathers ('the land of Israel') in the Cave of *Machpelah (ch. 50).

It is a moot point whether the Genesis narrator approves or disapproves of Jacob's subterfuges in wresting the birthright and the blessing from his brother. The prophet Hosea certainly indicts Jacobs for 'supplanting' (*akav*, a pun on the name Yaakov) his brother and in subsequent Jewish commentary on the narrative there are echoes of disapproval of Jacob's stratagems, if not of his right to both the birthright and the blessing. On the other hand, there are many attempts to defend Jacob as acting honourably given the circumstances in which he found himself. It has to be appreciated that Jacob is seen in the Jewish tradition as representing the Jewish people so that attacks on the character of the patriarch are often seen as, and, indeed, sometimes are, motivated by anti-Jewish sentiment.

In the Rabbinic literature in particular, the figure of Jacob is made to represent the people as a whole, the conflict between Jacob and Esau being seen as a reflection of the love–hate relationship between Rome and the Jews—fierce enemies and yet, after all, brothers. Later, this conflict is interpreted as the struggle for supremacy between Christianity—Esau and Judaism = Jacob. The description of Jacob as a man who dwells in tents, in contradistinction to Esau, the skilful hunter, the man of outdoors (Genesis 25: 27), is made to signify that while the Roman ideal is to get things done in the world at large the Jewish ideal is to remain apart from the world to study God's words in the 'tents of Torah'. Much of the same is behind the Rabbinic identification of the angel who wrestled with Jacob as the guardian angel of Esau, that is, the narrative represents the struggle between the different spiritual ideals of Rome and Judaea. This episode, in which the angel dislocates the thigh of Jacob, concludes with the verse (32: 33): 'That is why the children of Israel to this day do not eat the thigh muscle that is on the socket of the hip, since Jacob's hip socket was wrenched at the thigh muscle.' Among the *dietary laws is the rule that the muscle or sinew of the thigh (*gid ha-nasheh*) must not be eaten and the sinew is skilfully extracted from the meat of the animal (a process known as 'porging') before it is sold as kosher meat. In some communities, because of the difficulty of porging correctly, the hind-quarters of an animal are not eaten at all.

The statement in the Talmud (*Taanit* 5b) that Jacob did not die, since Scripture, while speaking of Jacob's embalming and burial, does not actually say, as it does of the other patri-archs, that he died, was undoubtedly meant to be figurative. Yet in the Middle Ages it was taken literally and the legend developed that Jacob did not, in fact, die and that he awaits patiently, in the Cave of Machpelah, the final redemption of his children; there is a resem-blance here to the legends about King Arthur and similar folk-heroes in other cultures.

In the Kabbalistic doctrine of the *Sefirot, the powers in the Godhead, Jacob represents the power known as *Tiferet* ('Beauty'), the male principle, so to speak. The Zohar, for instance, sees each of the patriarchs as representing one of the Sefirot: Abraham, *Ḥesed*, the divine loving-kindness; Isaac, *Gevurah*, the divine judgement; and Jacob, *Tiferet*, the power through which harmony is brought about between loving-kindness and judgement. Hence Abraham is 'the pillar of loving-kindness'; Isaac, 'the pillar of judgement'; and Jacob, 'the pillar of truth', since truth is arrived at when apparently contra-dictory principles are reconciled. In the Lurianic Kabbalah, the two wives of Jacob represent two different aspects of the female element in the Godhead, the Sefirah *Malkhut*, Sovereignty, also known as the *Shekhinah. Already in the Rabbinic literature there is found an attempt to elevate Jacob to what comes close to a divine rank, as when it is said that the image of Jacob is engraved on the divine throne. Yet here it is only the 'image' of Jacob that is on the throne. The Kabbalah is somewhat less reserved. While in the Kabbalah generally the patriarchs are no more than symbols for the Sefirot, yet with regard to Moses (also representing *Tiferet*) and Jacob it is said in the Zohar that they became 'the consort of the Shekhinah', Moses even during his lifetime, Jacob at his death. On this Tishby remarks: 'Here we can see the process of transition from a normal symbolic state to an identification of symbol with the thing sym-bolized, and this leads almost to the deification of the most outstanding men.' Tishby rightly qualifies this extraordinary idea by using the word 'almost' since nowhere in Jewish litera-ture and thought do we find anything even remotely like the Christian doctrine of the Incarnation.

Nahum M. Sarna, *Understanding Genesis* (New York, 1966), 181–231.

Isaiah Tishby, *The Wisdom of the Zohar*, trans. David Goldstein (Oxford, 1989), 288–9.

**Jacob ben Asher** German Halakhist (d. 1340), son of Asher ben Jehiel, the outstanding au-thority in German and later Spanish Jewry, known as the Rosh (after the initial letters of his name, Rabbi Asher). Under threat of persecu-tion, Jacob with his father left Germany for Spain in 1303. The Rosh became Rabbi of Toledo but Jacob refused to take up a Rabbinic appointment and lived a life of poverty, only partly relieved by money he received from time to time from patrons of learning.

Jacob is chiefly renowned for his great Code of Jewish law (first published in Piove di Sacco in 1475 and thus one of the very earliest Jewish works to be printed), known as *Arbaah Turim* ('Four Rows'). The name is based on the four rows of precious stones in the breastplate of the High Priest (Exodus 28: 17), usually abbrevi-ated to *Tur*, so that in Halakhic literature both Jacob himself and his Code are called 'the Tur'. The work consists of four sections, hence the 'four rows'. These are: 1. *Oraḥ Ḥayyim*, 'Path of Life' (after Psalms 16: 11), dealing with prayer, the Sabbath, and festivals, and with general religious duties; 2. *Yoreh Deah*, 'Teaching Knowledge' (after Isaiah 28: 9), dealing with the *dietary laws and other topics required chiefly for Rabbinic decisions on more complex matters; 3. *Even Ha-Ezer*, 'Stone of Help' (after 1 Samuel 5: 1 and Genesis 2: 20, where woman is the 'help' meet for man), dealing with the laws of marriage and divorce; 4. *Ḥoshen Mishpat*, 'Breastplate of Judgement' (after Exo-dus 28: 15), dealing with civil law and jurispru-dence in general, The Tur quickly took its place beside the Codes of Isaac *Alfasi and that of Maimonides as a major textbook of Jewish law.

Jacob uses as his sources the two Codes which preceded him, other Halakhic works produced by both Sephardim and Ashkenazim, and, especially, the rulings of his father, the Rosh, all of whom he treats with great deference while often pursuing a line of his own, dis-agreeing, on occasion, even with his father. In the introduction to the 'Laws of the Sabbath', Jacob remarks, in a revealing aside, that he had discussed many times with his father, the Rosh, whether someone in a similar situation to his, who has to rely for his support on charitable donations, is obliged to spend money on extra food and drink for the Sabbath meals. The father's replies were far from clear, he observes, and he had to make up his own mind. Later authorities relied on the Tur's disagreement with the Rosh to demonstrate that the fifth commandment (see DECALOGUE) does not mean that a son is duty-bound to agree with his father's opinions in matters of Torah learning.

Rabbi Joseph *Karo compiled his *Bet Yosef* (*House of Joseph*), as a commentary on the Tur and the *Bet Yosef* formed in turn the basis of Karo's own Code, the *Shulḥan Arukh*.

Jacob also compiled a commentary to the Torah in which , as in his Code, he draws on earlier teachers to give what he calls 'the plain meaning' of the text. In the introductions to each section of the Torah, Jacob playfully adds, partly for the reader's amusement, ingenious asides in which *gematria and other plays on words are utilized in an admittedly fanciful manner. It is ironical that while the commentary itself was largely ignored (it was not published until the nineteenth century) these playful comments were printed together with the text in many editions of the Torah, under the title *Baal Ha-Turim* (*Author of the Turim*). These became exceedingly popular among students who resorted to them for intellectual relaxation from their more arduous studies. The following are two typical examples of Jacob's method. On the very first verse of Genesis, Jacob notes that the final letters of *bara elohim et* ('God created') are *alef, mem, tet*, forming the word *emet*, 'truth'. The world was created by truth. He observes that many words in the Torah have these three as their final letters to hint at the pervasiveness and importance of truth. On the patriarch Jacob's dream of a ladder with its feet on the ground and its head reaching to the heavens (Genesis 28: 10–22), Jacob notes that word for ladder, *sulam*, has the numerical value of 136 and the word for wealth, *mamon* and the word for voice, *kol*, also have the numerical value of 136. This is to teach that a man's wealth can lead him heavenwards, if he uses it properly, as can the use of his voice in prayer and supplication.

Meyer Waxman, *A History of Jewish Literature* (South Brunswick, NJ, 1960), ii. 32–4, 140–2.

**Jacob Joseph of Polonnoye**   Disciple of the *Baal Shem Tov and foremost Hasidic author.

Jacob Joseph (d. *c.*1784), when serving as the Rabbi of Shargorod, came under the influence of the Baal Shem Tov whose doctrines he began to disseminate to the consternation of his congregation; he was obliged to relinquish his post, eventually becoming a Maggid, 'Preacher', in the town of Polonnoye. Jacob Joseph's work *Toledot Yaakov Yosef* (*The Generations of Jacob Joseph*), based on Genesis 37: 2, was the first Hasidic work to be published (in Koretz, 1780) and as such set the tone and style for subsequent Hasidic publications as well as bearing the brunt of the attacks on Hasidism by opponents of the new movement, the *Mitnaggedim. The scorn Jacob Joseph poured out on Rabbinic scholars who studied with impure motives and his statement that one should not be overscrupulous in observing the precepts because this diverted the mind from true devotion to God, were seen as a special cause of offence.

Jacob Joseph is known among the Hasidim as 'the Toledot', after his first work. Three other works of this author, each having a title with an allusion to the biblical hero Joseph whose name he bore, are: *Ben Porat Yosef* (*Joseph is a Fruitful Vine*), after Genesis 49: 22; *Tzafenat Paneaḥ* (the name given to Joseph by Pharaoh, Genesis 41: 45); and *Ketonat Passim* (*Coat of Many Colours*), after the coat Jacob made for Joseph, Genesis 37: 3. The first two of these works were published in Koretz, respectively, in 1781 and 1782. The third did not see the light of day until it was published in Lvov as late as 1866. The *Toledot* is in the form of a running commentary to the whole of the Pentateuch. *Ben Porat Yosef* is a commentary to Genesis, *Tzafenat Paneaḥ* to Exodus, and *Ketonat Passim* to Leviticus and Numbers. There is evidence that Jacob Joseph also wrote a commentary to Deuteronomy but this has not survived.

Purity of heart and joy in the service of God are essential ingredients in the Hasidic life as understood by Jacob Joseph. A man should learn how to worship God even from clowns or the stony-hearted. The clown, for the few pennies he receives from the onlookers, is prepared to make a fool of himself in order to make people laugh. How, then, can a man stand on his dignity rather than abandon himself with joy to God's service? The hard-hearted will do all in their power to avoid having to give to charity and to do evil. The wise man will learn from them to use every stratagem in order to do good. Jacob Joseph realistically advises the Hasid to approach gradually the ideal of complete purity of motive in his service of God. To try to attain to purity of motive from the beginning is bound to be self-defeating. At first, the Hasid must persevere in his devotion, even if his motivation is in part selfish. Only after hard and long training and constant struggle against selfishness can complete purity be attained.

Jacob Joseph stresses that God is omnipresent. The Hasid should not lead an ascetic life. He should eat and drink and participate in social life but always with his mind on God. The masses, too, can be brought nearer to God through their attachment to the *Zaddik, the holy master, who is, in turn, attached to God; as the Talmud states, 'the fear of God was but a small thing' to the people in the wilderness who were closely attached to Moses. The Zaddik is, moreover, the channel through which the divine grace and blessing flows.

It appears that Jacob Joseph had hoped to be the Baal Shem Tov's successor but it was the other chief disciple of the master, *Dov Baer of Mezhirech, who became the acknowledged leader. Jacob Joseph retreated into himself to some extent and established no Hasidic following of his own. Yet his *Toledot Yaakov Yosef* is seen by all later Hasidim as the main record of the authentic teachings of the Baal Shem Tov, whose sayings Jacob Joseph quotes repeatedly with the formula: 'I have heard from my master.'

Samuel H. Dresner, *The Zaddik: The Doctrine of the Zaddik According to the Writings of Rabbi Yaakov Yosef of Polnoy* (New York, 1966).

**Jacob's Ladder** The dream Jacob had when he left Beer-sheba to set out for Haran (Genesis 28: 10–27) has exercised a powerful fascination over all readers of the Bible. In his dream, Jacob sees a ladder or stairway (Heb. *sulam*) set on the ground with its top reaching to heaven, and angels of God going up and down on it. In the context, the dream is of Jacob's own future: a divine promise that God will be with him, and send His angels to protect him. A Rabbinic comment notes that the angels first ascend and then descend, although the angels come from on high and the descent should have preceded the ascent. But the angels who attended Jacob in the Holy Land, the land of his fathers, ascend to be replaced by different angels who

come down to guide him outside the Holy Land. Yet, in Jewish exegesis and homiletics, the dream is chiefly interpreted as a vision in which Jacob gazes into the future of his seed, the children of Israel.

In one Midrashic interpretation, for instance, the ladder symbolizes Mount *Sinai, on which the Torah was given, the angels representing Moses and Aaron who go up on the mountain (see Exodus 19). In another Midrashic interpretation, the vision is of the guardian angels of the empires of Babylon, Media, Greece, and Rome, which are destined to have successive dominion over the people of Israel. These will be in the ascendancy for a time but will later suffer decline, the permanent survival of Israel alone being assured.

The medieval thinkers have their own interpretations. For Maimonides (*Guide of the Perplexed*, 1. 15) the angels are the prophets. This is why the verse states that the angels ascend before they descend. The prophet has first to ascend to God on the ladder of perfection and then he can come down from on high to bring God's message to the people. *Nahmanides, on the other hand, does understand the reference as being to real angels. These first ascend to report on events on earth and then return to carry out God's instructions. The statement that God is on the ladder denotes that all is determined by divine providence. *Bahya, Ibn *Asher comments that all being is divided into the three categories of earth, the realm of the spheres, and the realm of the angelic hosts; thus the ladder has its feet on earth, its head reaches to the spheres and the planets, and the angels are on the ladder, all under the direct control of God. Bahya also quotes a Midrash according to which the top of the ladder reached to what was later to be the site of the *Temple, the 'house of God' referred to in the narrative. This idea that all prayer ascends on high through the 'gate of heaven' that is the Temple became prominent in later Jewish thought. Finally, Bahya quotes a Kabbalistic interpretation, according to which the Hebrew word *bo*, usually translated as 'on it', can mean 'through him' (i.e. through Jacob), yielding the typical Kabbalistic notion that the upper worlds depend on the deeds of humans on earth. When man sins he brings down the spiritual powers but when he is virtuous he upholds the very heavens.

The moralists have an individualistic interpretation. Angels are created by good deeds.

But a man must first send these angels upwards and only then do the angels, representing God's help, descend from on high. God assists man in his spiritual efforts but the divine help depends on man's own prior attempt to lead a good life.

In Hasidic thought, the angels are the Zaddikim, the spiritual masters who engage in the struggle to come closer to God. But even these 'angels', spiritual supermen though they are, have their ups and downs, suffering the mystical 'dark night of the soul' or the state of 'smallness' as it is called in the Kabbalah, when all is dry and man seems remote from God. Yet this descent of the *Zaddik is not really a descent but an ascent. As a result of his struggles during his periods of spiritual dullness, fresh illuminations of spirit are given to him to raise him to even greater heights. Another Hasidic interpretation sees the ladder in terms of the life of prayer. The 'descent' in prayer refers to reflection on human frailty and earthiness. Only after man has considered his lowliness can he rise in his prayers to contemplate God's majesty and glory.

Nehama Leibowitz, 'Jacob's Dream', in her *Studies in the Book of Genesis*, trans. Aryeh Newman (Jerusalem, 1973), 298–304.

**Jeremiah** The prophet born in Anathoth, about 3 miles north of Jerusalem, whose ministry began in the thirteenth year of Josiah king of Judah (i.e. 627 BCE), and extended for a period of over forty years. The book of Jeremiah contains much biographical and autobiographical material, so that more is known about Jeremiah's life than about any other of the great literary prophets. Little is told of Jeremiah's activity during the reign of Josiah, whose grandfather Manasseh, during a reign of forty years, had led the people astray from monotheism to idolatrous worship on the 'high places'. Josiah's reformation consisted of the restoration of monotheism and the centralization of worship in the Temple. Many of the people, however, continued to follow the ways to which they had been accustomed during the reign of Manasseh and against them were directed Jeremiah's castigations. From the beginning Jeremiah witnessed the downfall of the Assyrian Empire in 606 BCE; the death of Josiah in 605 BCE; the destruction of the Jewish State by the Babylonians in 586 BCE; and the carrying-away of most of the people in captivity to Babylon.

Jeremiah himself was taken to Egypt by fugitive Judaeans where he died, according to the legend, a martyr's death.

Biblical scholars have seen the book of Jeremiah as comprising four major collections: 1. chapters 1–25, consisting of smaller units centred on the judgement announced against the nation; 2. chapters 26–36, comprising oracles and sayings within a narrative framework; 3. chapters 37–45, dealing with Jeremiah's life from the siege of Jerusalem to his final ministry in Egypt; 4. chapters 46–51, a separate section containing oracles against the nations. The book ends with a chapter (52) consisting of a historical appendix. This last section has a close parallel in the historical account in the second book of Kings (24: 18–25: 30). Jeremiah is held by tradition to be the author of the book of *Lamentations.

Jeremiah is fearless in denouncing the faithlessness of both the people and the noblemen. It is righteousness and knowledge of Him that God wants and it is in these alone that man can take pride: 'Thus saith the Lord: Let not the wise man glory in his wisdom, neither let the mighty man glory in his might, let not the rich man glory in his riches; But let him that glorieth glory in this, That he understandeth, and knoweth Me, that I am the Lord who exercises mercy, justice and righteousness in the earth; For in these things I delight, saith the Lord' (Jeremiah 9: 22–3). How can Israel, the prophet declares, forsake their true God when the pagan nations, though they worship worthless gods, remain true to the religion of their ancestors? 'Hath a nation changed its gods, Which are no gods? But My people hath changed its glory for that which does not profit' (2: 11). 'For My people have committed two evils; They have forsaken Me, the fountain of living waters, and hewed them out cisterns, broken cisterns, that can hold no water' (2: 13).

In English a 'Jeremiah' is a person given to woeful complaining but, in fact, for all the denunciations of his people, Jeremiah sounds a note of encouragement and of hope. God, he says, remembers the loyalty of their ancestors and He will restore the exiled people to their land in the future. 'And the word of the Lord came to me saying: Go, and cry in the ears of Jerusalem, saying: Thus saith the Lord: I remember for thee the affection of thy youth, the love of thine espousals; how thou wentest after Me in the wilderness; in a land that was not sown' (2: 1–2). 'But fear not thou, O Jacob My servant, neither be dismayed, O Israel; For, lo I will save thee from afar, and thy seed from the land of their captivity; and Jacob shall again be quiet and at ease, and none shall make him afraid' (46: 27).

Jeremiah preaches not only to the nation but to the individual who is acceptable to God when he repents of his evil deeds. Even while addressing the nation as a whole, he breaks off to address himself to the individual whose temptations he recognizes: 'The heart is deceitful above all things, And it is exceeding weak— who can know it? I the Lord search the heart, I try the reins, Even to give every man according to his ways, According to the fruit of his doings' (17: 9–10).

Jeremiah 32 tells how, in the year 587, during the siege of Jerusalem, when Jeremiah had been put in prison because he had foretold that the city would fall, he redeemed a piece of land so as to keep it in his family, as evidence of brighter days to come when the people would once again have possessions in the land of their fathers. This chapter, containing details of how lands were bought and sold in ancient times, is used in the Talmudic literature as a source for the laws of buying and selling property. The final verse of this chapter became a key text for Jewish philosophical reflection on the doctrine of divine omnipotence: 'Behold, I am the Lord, the God of all flesh; is there any thing too hard for Me?'

H. Freedman, *Jeremiah* (London, 1949).

Ernest W. Nicholson, *The Book of the Prophet Jeremiah* (Cambridge, 1973).

**Jeroboam** Son of Nebat, first king of the Northern Kingdom after the death of Solomon, reigning for twenty-two years until around 907 BCE. When Rehoboam, Solomon's successor, refused to release the people from excessive taxation, the tribes, apart from Judah and Benjamin, broke away from the House of David to establish their own kingdom with Jeroboam as king. In order to encourage the people to worship outside Jerusalem, in the territory of the House of David, Jeroboam set up two golden calves, one at Dan and another at Bethel. The resemblance between this episode and that of the *golden calf in the wilderness has often been discussed. In the Rabbinic tradition, Jeroboam is the most grievous of sinners because he caused many others to sin by setting up the calves (Ethics of the Fathers, 5. 18): 'Jeroboam the son of Nebat sinned and caused others to sin; the sin of the many is ascribed to him, as it is said "The sin of Jeroboam who sinned and made Israel to sin" [1 Kings 14: 16].' In the Mishnah (*Sanhedrin* 10: 2) Jeroboam is listed as one of the three kings who have no share in the *World to Come. The Rabbis use the figure of Jeroboam to depict the highly gifted man who in his pride can never take second place to anyone, even when it is to his advantage so to do. When God said to Jeroboam: 'Repent and I, you and David will walk together in the Garden of Eden,' Jeroboam asked: 'Who will go in front?' and when God said: 'David will go in front,' Jeroboam retorted: 'In that case I do not want it.'

**Jerusalem** The holy city, Heb. *ir ha-kodesh*; sacred in itself and in that it contained the site of the *Temple (see HOLY PLACES). There is no explicit reference to Jerusalem in the *Pentateuch but the city Salem of which Melchizedek, priest of God Most High, was king (Genesis 14: 18), is identified by the tradition with Jerusalem, of which Salem is said to be an abbreviated or earlier form. The 'land of Moriah' (Genesis 22: 2), at which the *Akedah took place, is also traditionally identified with Jerusalem. After King David had reigned in Hebron for seven years he moved his capital to Jerusalem (2 Samuel 5: 1–13), so that another name for Jerusalem is 'the city of David' (2 Samuel 6: 12). David planned to build the Temple in Jerusalem but it was David's son, Solomon, who actually built and dedicated the Temple there (1 Kings 7 and 8). Jerusalem remained the holiest of cities during the period of the First and Second Temples. Even after the destruction of both the Temple and Jerusalem the city remained the focus of Jewish prayers, a special benediction being added to the *grace after meals in which God is entreated to rebuild Jerusalem.

Later passages in the Bible are full of the praises of Jerusalem as God's city. The Songs of Ascents in the Psalms are generally considered to have been originally the songs of the pilgrims who went up to Jerusalem. 'Our feet stood inside your gates, O Jerusalem, Jerusalem built up, a city knit together, to which tribes would make pilgrimage . . . Pray for the peace of Jerusalem, may those who love you be at peace' (Psalm 122). 'Jerusalem, hills unfold it, and the Lord enfolds His people now and for ever' (Psalms 125: 2). Zion is largely synonymous with Jerusalem but refers specifically to the Temple Mount—Mount Zion. 'Blessed is the Lord from Zion, He that dwells in Jerusalem, Hallelujah' (Psalms 137: 21). The Psalmist's oath was often repeated throughout Jewish history: 'If I forget thee, O Jerusalem, let my right hand forget its cunning; let my tongue cleave to my palate if I cease to think of thee, if I do not keep Jerusalem in memory even at my happiest hour' (Psalms 137: 5–6). The prophet, witnessing the exiles returning from the Babylonian captivity, declares: 'Rejoice with Jerusalem and be glad for her, all you who love her. Join in her jubilation all who mourned over her' (Isaiah 66: 10). In the prophetic vision of the time to come (later thought of in Messianic terms) the verse occurs, used in the liturgy when the Scroll of the Torah is taken from the Ark: 'For Torah will go out from Zion and the word of the Lord from Jerusalem' (Isaiah 2: 3).

The significance of Jerusalem is repeatedly stressed in the Rabbinic literature. A typical Rabbinic saying is that ten measures of beauty came into the world, of which Jerusalem took nine (*Kiddushin* 49b). In the Rabbinic Midrash to the book of Lamentations a number of stories are told to illustrate the superior wisdom of the Jerusalemites; even their little children score over sophisticated Athenians. The 'noblemen' of Jerusalem are said to have conducted themselves always with fastidiousness, delicacy, and tact. There was a widespread belief, shared by Philo of Alexandria, that Jerusalem was at the exact centre of the earth—the 'navel of the earth'. It was also said that the land of Israel is higher than all other lands and Jerusalem the highest spot in the land of Israel. This obviously hyperbolic statement puzzled Moshe Hayyim *Luzzatto in the eighteenth century who advanced the anachronistic interpretation that since the world is a globe, any spot designated for a particular purpose can be said to be the 'highest' spot and God has designated Jerusalem for His purpose. Aggadic passages refer to a 'heavenly Jerusalem' (*yerushalayim shel maalah*) which God declares He will not enter until He enters first the earthly Jerusalem (*Taanit* 5a).

During the Middle Ages, Jerusalem, now also a holy city for Christianity and Islam, was fought over by the adherents of these two religions but from the fall of the Crusaders until 1917 Muslim rule over the city was uninterrupted. In 1917 the British conquered Palestine and established a mandatory government there with Jerusalem as its capital. By this time there had been created a new city of Jerusalem outside the area of the Old City. During Israel's War of Independence in 1948 the Old City fell to the Jordanian Arab Legion and Jerusalem was divided into the New City and the Old City with access denied to Jews to the Old City. In the Six Day War, on 28 Iyar 5727 (7 June 1967) the city was reunited and the day declared Jerusalem Day, now celebrated as a festival by many religious communities in all parts of the Jewish world. A large space was cleared in front of the *Western Wall, the surviving wall of the Temple, and services are held there, thronged with worshippers and curious onlookers.

Jerusalem is now acknowledged as occupying a special place in the heart and mind of every Jew. In the nineteenth century, the marked tendency among Reform Jews was to see Jerusalem as a spiritual ideal rather than in spatial terms. With Reform advocacy of Jewish accommodation to Western society and with its universalistic thrust, Jerusalem tended to be thought of much along the lines of Blake's: 'Till we have built Jerusalem in England's green and pleasant land.' With the establishment of the State of Israel and the rebuilding of Jerusalem, such attitudes are exceedingly rare. Reform, like Orthodoxy, though to varying degrees, sees Jerusalem as a, if not the, spiritual centre of Judaism.

There are inevitable tensions between Jerusalem as both the holy city and the capital city of a modern secular state. There is no public transport on the Sabbath in Jerusalem but private cars are naturally allowed to go on their way, except through the districts occupied by the more strictly observant. There have been protests against this infringement of human rights but Jerusalemites, including the secularists, accept begrudgingly these restrictions on their freedom. The 'peace of Jerusalem' on the Sabbath has a mystical quality which is often remarked on. There are hundreds of synagogues in which a variety of liturgies are used, the spirit of prayer pervading the quiet streets.

Freedom of worship is given, obviously in a democratic state, to all religious bodies, non-Jewish as well as Jewish. Severe tensions often erupt here too but, given the extremely difficult situation, the accommodation has worked more or less successfully, especially under Mayor Teddy Kollek, who wrote in 1990: 'It may take several generations to eradicate fear, resentment and religious fanaticism. But only a united city can ensure that Jerusalem, too often the background of holy wars, will be a city of peace, a city with sufficient spiritual space to embrace its multiplicity of faiths and ideologies.'

*Jerusalem* (Israel Pocket Library; Jerusalem, 1973). F. E. Peters, *Jerusalem* (Princeton, 1984).

**Jesus** There is comparatively little in the Talmudic literature on Jesus of Nazareth. Uncensored editions of the Babylonian Talmud do contain a few allusions to Jesus and his disciples but these are of a clearly legendary nature; the Babylonian Jews had only a very hazy picture of Jesus or, for that matter, of Christianity as whole. Their religious challenge was presented chiefly by Persian dualism, which they attacked whenever they had the opportunity to do so. Palestinian sources are less vague but still not really informative. From the few Talmudic references we have, it would seem as if the figure of Jesus was of very little interest to the Rabbis and could largely be ignored. The suggestion by some scholars that *Balaam in the Talmudic literature is a veiled name for Jesus has largely been discounted, as has the suggestion that the word Peloni, meaning So-and-so, is sometimes a reference to Jesus, the circumlocution being used because there was a reluctance to use the real name. Followers of Jesus, on the few occasions when these are mentioned in the Talmud, are called Minim, 'sectarians', a general term applying to all sectarians, not only to believers in the Christian heresy. A direct attack on the Christian dogma such as the homily of the third-century teacher Rabbi Abbahu is rare and it must be remembered that this Rabbi lived in Caesarea where he came into regular contact with Christians. Rabbi Abbahu comments on the verse: 'I am the first, and I am the last, and beside Me there is no God' (Isaiah 44: 6); ' "I am the first" since I have no father; "And I am the last" since I have no son; "And beside Me there is no God" since I have no brother', the last phrase referring to the doctrine of dualism.

It was not until the Middle Ages, when the Church had become triumphant, that the figure of Jesus was widely discussed in the medieval Jewish–Christian *disputations and in polemical works produced by Jews in defence against

Christian attacks, such as the *Toledot Jeshu* (*The History of Jesus*). In this work it is accepted that Jesus did perform miracles, but drew on the black arts for the purpose.

It is obvious that the Christian belief in Jesus as the Son of God (see CHRISTIANITY) is incompatible with Judaism, as is the belief that Jesus was the Messiah. The claims of the American 'Jews for Jesus' movement, that one can believe in Jesus and still remain a Jew, are rightly rejected by all religious Jews, who see the new movement as no more than a thinly disguised Christian mission seeking to mislead the unwary. Beyond that, attitudes towards the personality of Jesus, and on how Jews should view Jesus from the point of view of Judaism, vary from the belief that Jesus is not a historical figure at all to the acceptance of Jesus as an ancient Jewish 'Rabbi' or profound ethical teacher, a view rejected by all Orthodox Jews and by many Reform Jews. The whole question is befogged by the impossibility of disentangling the historical Jesus from the Jesus of Paul and the Synoptic Gospels, and by the central role that Jesus occupies in the Christian religion. Among the majority of Jews, the fear exists that to acknowledge in any way, however this is qualified, that Jesus has something of value to say to Jews, is to open the door to apostasy to a religion which Jews have given up their lives rather than embrace.

Thomas [T] Walker, *Jewish Views of Jesus*, with a new introduction by Seymour Siegel (New York, 1973).

**Jew** The English word 'Jew' is derived from the Latin which, in turn, is based on the Hebrew word Yehudi, meaning 'from the tribe of Judah' (Judah = Yehudah). From the time of *Jeroboam's revolt, the division came about between the Northern Kingdom, called 'Israel', and the Southern Kingdom of the House of David. The latter was located in Judaea, the territory of the tribe of Judah. After the conquest of the Northern Kingdom by the Assyrians, the *ten tribes were carried away and all the members of the people, wherever they were found and whatever their origin, adopted the name 'Judah', hence the name 'the Jews'. In the book of *Esther (2: 5) *Mordecai is described as a 'Jew' (Yehudi) even though he belonged to the tribe of Benjamin. A Talmudic comment on this (*Megillah* 13a) has it that Mordecai was called a Yehudi because anyone who rejects idolatry is called a Yehudi. This homily became in later times a means of Jewish self-identification, as if to say, no matter how far a Jew has gone along the road to assimilation, provided he does not worship idols and retains his belief in the One God, he is still a Jew; although, from the point of view of the *Halakhah, a Jew retains his Jewish status even if he has been converted to another religion (see CONVERSION), and the principle obtains: 'Once a Jew always a Jew'.

The Law of Return of the State of Israel gave the right to every Jew to become a citizen of the State. The problem arose of defining the term 'Jew' in this context. According to the traditional Halakhah, Jewish status depends either on the status of the mother or on conversion to Judaism. Thus the child of a Jewish mother and a non-Jewish father is Jewish, but not the child of a non-Jewish mother and a Jewish father. A non-Jew who has been converted by the due processes of Halakhah is a Jew. Furthermore, as above, a Jew never loses his Jewish status even if he has been converted to another religion. This gave rise to certain problems with regard to the Law of Return. Father Daniel, a Christian priest, born a Jew, who has been converted to Christianity, claimed Israeli citizenship as a Jew (non-Jews can, of course, be granted Israeli citizenship, but Father Daniel claimed the right by the Law of Return). By a majority decision, the Israeli court denied Father Daniel this right, arguing that it is not a question of what the Halakhah says but what was in the minds of those who framed the Law of Return. These, it can be presumed, never intended the Law of Return to apply to Jews converted to another faith. And what is the position of a Jew converted by Reform Rabbis where the Halakhic procedures have not been carried out in the proper manner? In this case, it could be argued that, while the Halakhah does not consider that person to be a Jew, those who framed the Law of Return presumably did consider such a person to qualify as a Jew. All this gave rise to the 'Who is a Jew?' controversy, as it has been called, although the persons affected were very few in number. On the whole this problem had been dealt with adequately, although voices are still raised protesting that the Law of Return must be interpreted in accordance with Halakhic categories.

Another problem arose for Jews everywhere, not only in the State of Israel, when a number of Reform Rabbis in the USA introduced the new category of patrilineal descent, ruling that as long as one of the parents of a child is Jewish, whether the mother or the father, the child has Jewish status. Here again, Halakhically the child is not Jewish if only the father is Jewish and the mother is not Jewish. Orthodox Rabbis obviously refuse to depart from the Halakhah in this matter and would require the child of a Jewish father and non-Jewish mother to be converted to Judaism by the due Halakhic processes.

With regard to the semantic question, the term 'Jew' in English has been used as a term of contempt and obloquy and has been so rendered in standard English dictionaries. While some Jews have protested and while some dictionaries have added terms like 'pejorative' to this kind of definition, it is now widely accepted that it is not the job of dictionaries to express moral opinions but simply to record popular usage even where this is based on false opinions or perverse attitudes. The same applies to the Yiddish word 'Yid' for a Jew. This, too, sometimes has a pejorative connotation, although Yiddish speakers use the term as one of praise. In *Hasidism, one of the names for the Hasidic *Zaddik, is *gutter yid*, 'a good Jew', that is, one who has reached the acme of Jewish perfection, one who lives as the ideal Jew is expected to live, with the additional connotation that he is a miracle-worker As a result of the *Holocaust, when were seen the terrible results of *anti-Semitism, there has been a marked reluctance on the part of non-Jews to use the term 'Jew' in its pejorative sense and most Jews, today, are happy with the term Jew in every sense of the word 'happy'.

'A Symposium on Patrilineal Descent', *Judaism* 34/1 (1985), 3–135.

**Job** Heb. Iyov, the central figure in the book of Job, the third book of the Hagiographa in the Hebrew Bible. Job is a good man, blessed with a wife and children and with great wealth. *Satan seeks permission of God to test Job by bringing sufferings on him to see whether he will relinquish his good way, since it may be that he is only righteous because it pays him so to be. Job loses his children and his wealth and is afflicted with a loathsome illness. Job's friends come to visit him and they imply that God has visited the torments on him because, despite outward appearances, he is not really a good man but a sinner who deserves to suffer. Job protests that his sufferings are undeserved. Eventually God appears to Job 'out of the whirlwind' to demonstrate the impossibility of humans grasping the mysterious ways of God. Job bows to the divine will and accepts his fate. The book concludes with Job's prosperity being restored to him and he is blessed with beautiful daughters. All this is presented in exquisite poetic style, except for the prologue and the ending which are in prose, to make the story of Job one of the greatest masterpieces of world literature. Many scholars have felt that the 'happy ending' is too much like the: 'and they all lived happily ever after' of the fairy story, spoiling the effect of the great drama, and must have been added at a later date by an unsophisticated pietist.

The book of Job is completely universalistic in thrust. Job is not described as a Jew and some of the Rabbis hold that he was, in fact, an Edomite, while another opinion has it that Job is a fictitious person and the whole story is pure fiction of the most elevated kind and was intended as such. These and other opinions on the book are presented in the Talmud (*Bava Batra* 15a–b), where the authorship of the book is also discussed; according to one view, the author was none other than Moses! Modern biblical scholarship is similarly divided on the question of authorship, some scholars dating it from the very early period, others believing it to be post-exilic.

Commentaries on Job have been written by Jews and non-Jews, most of whom see in the book a classical statement of the problem of why the righteous suffer. Rudolf Otto's interpretation of God's reply to Job has been widely accepted as close to the original meaning. According to Otto, when God brings to Job's notice that He has created beasts like the crocodile and the hippopotamus, this is far removed from any teleological argument for design in creation but refers to the 'numinous' quality of existence. These strange beasts are evidence of a wisdom of God as Wholly Other, utterly beyond the power of the human mind to fathom. This is the sentiment expressed in Blake's: 'Tyger! Tyger! burning bright | In the forests of the night, | What immortal hand or eye | Could frame thy fearful symmetry?'

In the Talmudic passage referred to, Job is compared to Abraham who was similarly tested

at the *Akedah*. In this line of interpretation the book has, as part of its aim, the demonstration both that there are to be found pious individuals among non-Jews and that, for all their worth and trustworthiness, these are inferior to the 'Jewish' saints represented by Abraham. The verse in which Job accepts, at first, God's judgement: 'The Lord hath given and the Lord hath taken away; blessed be the name of the Lord' (Job 1: 21), became, in the tradition, the supreme declaration of resignation to the will of God. The verse is recited at funerals by those who have lost a near relative. The Rabbis frown on a man behaving like 'Job's comforters' in hinting to those who suffer that they have only themselves to blame.

Victor E. Reichert, *Job* (London, 1946).

**Joel** The prophet whose book is the second of the book of the Twelve Prophets in the Hebrew Bible, placed between the books of Hosea and Amos who lived in the eighth century BCE. Beyond the prophet's name, Joel son of Pethuel, the book gives no indication of who the prophet was and when he prophesied. Scholars differ widely on the matter. The suggestion that he lived at the time of Hosea and Amos is based on the placing of his book between the books of these two prophets but this is no indication at all, since the placing of the books in this order is very late and has no significance for dating purposes. Many scholars prefer the much later date of the fifth century BCE. All this is, in any event, pure conjecture.

The book of Joel contains four chapters; the first two describe a plague of locusts which the prophet declares God will remove in His compassion for his people; the third and fourth chapters speak of events that will take place 'at the end of days'. Scholars are also divided on whether the plague of locusts is to be understood literally or whether it is an allegory for a foreign invasion of the land. In many rites, the second half of Joel 2, with its message of repentance, is read as the *Haftarah on the Sabbath of Repentance, the Sabbath between *Rosh Hashanah and *Yom Kippur, concluding with the message of hope: 'And ye shall know that I am in the midst of Israel, and that I am the Lord your God and there is none else; and My people shall never be ashamed.'

S. M. Lehrman, 'Joel', in A. Cohen (ed.), *The Twelve Prophets* (London, 1978), 57–79.

**Johanan Ben Zakkai** First-century CE disciple of *Hillel. Johanan took a prominent part in the controversies between the *Pharisees, of which group he was leader, and the *Sadducees. He is said to have been responsible for a number of new enactments and to have abolished the ordeal of the wife suspected of adultery (Numbers 5: 11–31) and the rite of the beheaded heifer (Deuteronomy 21: 1–9). Although not of the Princely House, Johanan was given the title usually reserved for the Nasi (the Prince), Rabban, '*Our* Master', in contradistinction to the simple title 'Rabbi'. 'Master' Johanan's two outstanding disciples, Rabbi *Eliezer and Rabbi *Joshua, succeeded him in the leadership of the Pharisaic party and, together with him, belong to the early teachers known as the *Tannaim, who developed what later came to be known as Rabbinic Judaism.

As with other early Rabbinic figures it is difficult to disentangle fact from pious legend when trying to reconstruct Johanan's history. For instance, when it is said of him, Hillel, and *Akiba that each lived for 120 years, it is as clear as can be that this is simply a device for calling attention to the significance of the teacher for later Judaism. Each lived for the lifespan of Moses, the first great leader and lawgiver. The same applies to the legend for which Johanan is especially known. According to this very late legend, during the siege of Jerusalem in 70 CE, Johanan was smuggled out of Jerusalem to meet Vespasian, then a general but greeted by Johanan as the emperor he was destined to become. Johanan requested Vespasian to spare the city of Yavneh as a home for scholars and to preserve the House of the Nasi by affording protection to the young *Gamaliel, later to become the Nasi, Rabban Gamaliel II. Apart from the fact that this story is told in the language of the Babylonian Talmud compiled centuries after Johanan, its legendary nature is obvious. But the legend is extremely significant in suggesting Johanan's importance in contributing to the continuing study of the Torah and protecting the legislative body, the *Sanhedrin, and thus assuring the survival of Judaism.

**Jonah** Son of Amittai; a prophet whose story is told in the book of Jonah, the fifth book of the book of the Twelve Prophets. Elsewhere in the Bible (2 Kings 14: 25) there is a reference to a prophet of the eighth century BCE named Jonah son of Amittai but even if this prophet is the same person as the Jonah of the book of Jonah this leads in no way to the conclusion that he is the author of the book. The book, quite different in form from any other prophetic book, seems to be a short story, composed much later, of which the historical Jonah is the hero, not the author. Traditionally, however, the events recorded in the book are not seen as fictitious. The religious value of the book and its message are not affected either way, any more than by (a question still discussed by fundamentalists) whether a 'big fish' (not a whale) can swallow a man. Most moderns prefer to read the book as a profound tale with the most significant religious message, from which message the attention is only diverted when the book is taken literally. As someone has remarked: 'The fish that swallowed Jonah was a red herring.'

The story of the book of Jonah has passed into world literature. The prophet receives a summons from God to go to Nineveh, the capital city of Assyria, to preach that unless its king and citizens repent of their evil deeds the city will be .overthrown. Jonah is reluctant to obey the summons because he fears that the people of Nineveh may repent and this will be to the detriment of the prophet's own people of whom Assyria was the sworn enemy. Jonah seeks to flee from before the Lord. He embarks at the port of Jaffa on a ship bound for Tarshish, located in an exactly opposite direction from that of Nineveh. A terrible storm rages at sea and the God-fearing sailors cast lots to determine which of the passengers is responsible for God's wrath. The lot falls on Jonah who urges the sailors to cast him into the sea, which they do reluctantly. Jonah is swallowed by a big fish and he cries out to God in the belly of the fish. The fish spews out Jonah and he makes his way to Nineveh where he preaches his message of repentance. The king and his people fast and pray to God and God spares the city. Jonah departs from the city to take refuge under a gourd but this is smitten by a sultry east wind and Jonah, fainting in the heat, asks God to let him die. God asks Jonah whether he is deeply grieved about the plant and Jonah replies that he is so grieved that he wishes to die. The book concludes with God's reply: 'You cared about the plant, which you did not work for and which you did not grow, which appeared overnight and perished overnight. And should not I care about Nineveh, that great city, in which there are more than a hundred and twenty thousand persons who do not yet know their right hand from their left, and many beasts as well!'

Throughout the ages the book has been read as containing a twofold message: first, that it is impossible for a man to escape from doing God's will; and secondly, perhaps more significantly, that God is concerned with all His creatures, even if they are heathen, whose sincere repentance He accepts. By a stroke of religious genius, the tradition has set aside the book of Jonah, with its universalistic message, for reading as the *Haftarah on the afternoon of *Yom Kippur, the special Day of Atonement when the Jewish people becomes reconciled with its God. It is considered a high honour to be given the privilege of reading 'Maftir Yonah' on Yom Kippur; in some communities the privilege is 'bought' by a large donation to charity or for the upkeep of the synagogue.

Midrashic comments on the book of Jonah abound. According to one line of Midrashic interpretation, Jonah represents the people of Israel since Israel is compared to a dove, the gentle bird that is often the prey of more ferocious birds. (The Hebrew *yonah* means 'dove'.) The Jewish people can never escape its destiny as the people that proclaims God's unity. Another Midrash discusses how Jonah, a prophet of God, could have imagined that he could flee from God's presence. The answer given is that Jonah imagined that outside the Holy Land the prophetic vision would depart from him and he would no longer be under its burden. The illustration is of the slave of a priest who seeks refuge from his owner in a graveyard because he knows that a priest must not come into contact with the dead. Another Midrashic fancy has it that the fish that swallowed Jonah was made for the purpose from the very beginning of the creation and that Jonah was as comfortable in it as if he were in a spacious synagogue. The Rabbis note, too, that the verse does not say that God saw the fasting or the sackcloth of the men of Nineveh but that He saw their deeds. The external trappings of repentance are of no value unless they are tokens of sincere repentance. In one Midrashic comment, however, the people of Nineveh, after their forty days of repentance, reverted to their wicked ways and became, indeed, even more wicked than before and God did eventually destroy the city. This line, so much at variance with the story itself, seems to have been pursued in defence of the Jewish people. Some of the Rabbis of the Midrash could not bear the thought that Gentiles were more ready to repent of their evil deeds than the Jews. Contrary to the view that Jonah was extremely comfortable in the belly of the fish is the opinion that he suffered so greatly there that he was exempted from death and was allowed to enter Paradise while he was still alive. All these are, of course, pure fancy— speculations that easily arise from this marvellous book.

The Hasidic master Mordecai Joseph Leiner (d. 1854) utilized the story of Jonah to convey the lesson that it is forbidden for a good man to feel frustrated when his intention to honour God is set at naught, since his obligation is to submit to the divine will wherever it leads. Jonah should not have prayed for death when he realized that his will to pay homage to God was at variance with God's true will.

Louis Ginzberg, *The Legends of the Jews* (Philadelphia, 1942), iv. 237–53.

Solomon Goldman, 'Jonah', in A. Cohen (ed.), *The Twelve Prophets* (London, 1978), 137–50.

**Joseph**  Son of Jacob and Rachel; his story is told in the book of Genesis (chs. 37–50). Joseph, Jacob's favourite son, is hated by his brothers because of his dreams that one day they will all bow and pay homage to him. The brothers plot to kill Joseph but he is saved by passing merchants who sell him in Egypt where he becomes the slave of Potiphar, a high-ranking Egyptian. Potiphar's wife tries to seduce Joseph but he resists her blandishments. As a result Joseph is put in prison where he interprets successfully the dreams of two Egyptian officials who are imprisoned with him. Pharaoh has a disturbing dream which no one can interpret until Joseph is brought from prison for the purpose. According to Joseph's interpretation, there will be seven years of plenty in Egypt followed by seven lean years. Pharaoh, impressed by Joseph's interpretation, appoints him vice-regent to prepare the country for the ordeal of the seven lean years and Joseph rises to a position of great power. Joseph's brothers come to buy corn in Egypt where they are brought into Joseph's presence without recognizing that he is their long-lost brother. On a second visit, the youngest son of Jacob, Benjamin, is accused of stealing Joseph's magic cup. *Judah, Joseph's older brother, protests vehemently and Joseph is eventually moved to disclose his identity and urges his brothers to bring Jacob and all his family down to Egypt. Jacob settles in Egypt, dies there, but is buried in the Cave of *Machpelah in Canaan, the land of his fathers. Before his death, Joseph requests that when God redeems His people from Egypt, his bones should also be taken to be buried in Canaan.

The story of Joseph is thus the prologue to the story of the children of Israel's sojourn in Egypt and the subsequent Egyptian bondage from which they were redeemed by Moses, as told in the book of Exodus. Biblical scholars have discussed at length how far the events in the Joseph saga are historical and how far they are a reading-back of the events of later times. But from the point of view of the tradition, the Joseph episode is seen as part of the divine plan for the children of Israel to be refined by their sufferings in Egypt in order to merit the land of Canaan promised to the *patriarchs. Joseph is seen as the man of destiny, the instrument of divine providence. Joseph's resistance to temptation in the affair of Potiphar's wife is seen as the supreme example of chastity, no matter how strong the allure of sex. Joseph is consequently called the 'righteous' in the Rabbinic tradition. For the same reason, in the *Kabbalah, Joseph represents the Sefirah (see *Sefirot) of Yesod, 'Foundation', the source of all cosmic energy, represented by the organ of generation in the human body, the place of *circumcision, the *covenant, and hence Joseph and every male who is sexually pure is known as a 'guardian of the covenant'.

Nahum M. Sarna, 'Joseph', in his *Understanding Genesis* (New York, 1966), 211–31.

**Josephus, Flavius** Historian, soldier, and political figure (first century CE). Josephus, born to a priestly Palestinian family, was learned in the Torah but was also at home in the Roman culture of his day. While still quite young he visited Rome to intercede with the authorities on behalf of some Judaean priests who had been taken prisoner. In Rome Josephus was captivated by the rich cultural life he witnessed but while acquiring a typical Roman outlook on life he remained true to his own people and completely faithful to Judaism. During the Jewish War against Rome, which culminated in the destruction of the Temple in 70 CE, Josephus was at first commander of the Jewish forces in Galilee but, saving his own life by trickery when his colleagues killed themselves rather than give in to Rome, accompanied Titus and Vespasian on the Roman side and advocated that the Jews abandon as futile their resistance to Rome. Josephus ended his days in Rome close to the circle of the emperor. In addition to his autobiography, Josephus wrote *The Jewish War*, *Antiquities of the Jews*, and *Against Apion*.

Attitudes to Josephus vary. Some consider him a traitor to the Jewish cause in his support of Rome. Others defend Josephus as taking what he saw as the only possible course if the Jewish people were to survive and he personally live proudly to tell the tale. Josephus naturally presents himself in a favourable light and he is not always too careful always to get his facts right. For this reason, historians treat his works with caution. Nevertheless, together with the New Testament writers, Josephus is important for the true picture he presents of life as it was lived in first-century Palestine.

Josephus, *The Jewish War*, ed. G. R. Williamson (Harmondsworth, 1959).

**Joshua** Disciple and successor of Moses whose story is told in the Pentateuch and in the book of Joshua. Joshua is described as the assistant of Moses (Exodus 24: 13) and as the lad 'who would not stir out of the Tent' (Exodus 33: 11). When Moses, before his death, entreats God to appoint a leader in his stead, God replies: 'Single out Joshua, son of Nun, an inspired man, and place your hand upon him' (Numbers 27: 18) and when Moses dies it is recorded: 'Now Joshua son of Nun was filled with the spirit of wisdom because Moses had laid his hands upon him; and the Israelites heeded him, doing as the Lord had commanded Moses' (Deuteronomy 34: 9). The book of Joshua takes up the story, God saying to Joshua: 'My servant Moses is dead. Prepare to cross the Jordan, together with all this people, into the land which I am giving to the Israelites' (Joshua 1: 2). The rest of the book contains the account of how Joshua conquered the land. The traditional view is that Joshua is the author of the book that bears his name, except for the account of the events which took place after Joshua's death. Modern biblical scholarship generally sees the book as a later compilation. In any event Joshua belongs, according to the tradition, in the line of the transmission of the

Torah. Ethics of the Fathers (I. 1) begins: 'Moses received the Torah at Sinai and handed it over to Joshua who handed it over to the elders.'

Joshua is thus the prototype of the faithful disciple. In a famous Rabbinic comment, the face of Moses is like the face of the sun, the face of Joshua like the face of the moon; in other words, Moses' illumination was original to him while Joshua possessed only a reflected glory. (Because of this comment, there was a curious folk-belief in Eastern Europe that Joshua is the man in the moon!) Moses' laying-on of hands became the basis for Rabbinic ordination, *semikhah*, 'resting' (of hands), from generation to generation.

> H. Freedman, 'Joshua', in A. Cohen (ed.), *Joshua and Judges* (London and Bournemouth), 1950, pp. xi–151.

**Joshua, Rabbi** First to second centuries CE, one of the most distinguished of the early Rabbinic teachers known as the *Tannaim. Rabbi Joshua was a disciple of Rabban *Johanan ben Zakkai and a colleague of Rabbi *Eliezer; the debates between these two teachers are found throughout the Talmud. Rabbi Joshua appears to have had a somewhat conciliatory attitude towards the Romans after the destruction of the Temple in 70 CE. In a famous parable attributed to him, a fox put its head into a lion's mouth in order to remove a bone that had lodged in the lion's teeth and was troubling the lion. When the fox demanded a reward for his pains, the lion replied that for a creature to have its head in a lion's mouth and yet remain unscathed was in itself sufficient reward. When some zealots wished to give expression to their mourning over the destruction of the Temple by abstaining from wine and from marriage, Rabbi Joshua is said to have advocated less severe tokens of mourning, since one does not impose on the community regulations impossible for the majority to follow (*Bava Batra* 60b). On a number of occasions Rabban *Gamaliel is said to have behaved in an autocratic manner towards Rabbi Joshua, as a result of which Rabban Gamaliel was deposed for a time from his position as Nasi and head of the Sanhedrin. As with Rabbinic biography generally, these and similar statements about Rabbi Joshua's life and career have to be treated with a degree of caution since they are not eyewitness accounts but stories told much later.

Nevertheless, the stories do reflect the high regard in which Rabbi Joshua was held by later generations as a foremost teacher of the Torah.

**Joy** Joy, Heb. *simhah*, is a term used in Jewish literature to denote both the sense of physical well-being and various states of religious feeling from simple happiness in carrying out the will of God to *ecstasy and intense rapture. The Psalmist urges: 'Serve the Lord in gladness; come into His presence with shouts of joy' (Psalms 100: 2) and speaks of the precepts of the Lord as 'rejoicing the heart' (Psalms 19: 9). A notable passage in the Talmud (*Shabbat* 30b) contrasts two verses in the book of Ecclesiastes. One verse states: 'I said of laughter, it is mad: and of mirth, what doeth it?' (2: 2) while another verse states: 'Then I commended mirth' (8: 15). This is, in fact, one of the many inconsistencies in Ecclesiastes but the Talmud uses the apparent contradiction to postulate that there are two kinds of joy, religious and secular, the one advocated by the Preacher, the other denigrated. This leads to the typical Rabbinic idea of *simhah shel mitzvah*, 'joy in the precepts', that is, taking delight in obeying God's will by carrying out His laws. It is important to appreciate that 'joy in the precepts' is a more steady emotion than that described by the Christian writer, C. S. Lewis, in his autobiography *Surprised by Joy*. The Jewish mystics are certainly familiar with the sudden sense of spiritual awakening described by Lewis but the more normative Jewish approach is to take delight in the opportunities the precepts afford to worship God in the daily routine.

The great Safed Kabbalist, Isaac *Luria, was fond of quoting the verse: 'because thou didst not serve the Lord thy God with joyfulness, and with gladness of heart' (Deuteronomy 28: 47). In the context the verse means: 'because you did not serve the Lord when you were prosperous and in a state of well-being', but Luria gives the verse a new turn by understanding it to mean 'because you did not serve the Lord and rejoiced in so doing'. *Hasidism in particular stresses the importance of religious joy. The early Hasidic master Menahem Mendel of Vitebsk used to say that a Jew should rejoice at all times in that he has so many opportunities of serving God and in the very fact that he is a Jew who can sing constantly God's praises.

There is no essential contradiction between joy and *asceticism. Luria advocated the ascetic life while emphasizing the supreme need for joy. But to a large degree in Hasidism the ascetic way is seen as a positive hindrance to joy in God's service. Judah *Halevi's analysis of the relationship between fear and joy is germane to this issue:

'Our law, as a whole, is divided between fear, love, and joy, by each of which one can approach God. Thy contrition on a fast day does nothing the nearer to God than thy joy on the Sabbath and holy days, if it is the outcome of a devout heart. Just as prayers demand devotion, so also is a pious mind necessary to find pleasure in God's command and law; that thou shouldst be pleased with the law itself from love of the Lawgiver. Thou seest how much He has distinguished thee, as if thou hadst been His guest invited to His festive board. Thou thankest Him in mind and word, and if thy joy lead thee so far as to sing and dance, it becomes worship and a bond of union between thee and the Divine Influence.' (*Kuzari*, ii. 50)

**Jubilee** The institution described in the book of Leviticus (25: 8–24) where it is stated that series forty-nine years were to be counted (there is considerable uncertainty as to the date from when the counting is to begin, but traditionally it is from the creation of the world) and every fiftieth year declared a special year during which there was to be no agricultural work; all landed property was to revert to its original owner; and slaves were to be set free. The name Jubilee is from the Hebrew word *yovel*, 'ram's horn', the year being so called because a ram's horn was sounded when it was proclaimed (Leviticus 25: 9). Since this verse says: 'throughout the land for all its inhabitants', the Talmudic view is that the Jubilee was not observed during the Second Temple period because the majority of Jews no longer lived in the land of Israel.

The celebration as a Jubilee of such events as a special wedding anniversary or the anniversary of the founding of a synagogue is modern and has no basis in the Jewish tradition. On the other hand, there is nothing in the tradition to reject an innovation in which people give thanks for a special landmark in their lives. Numerous Jubilee volumes have been published in honour of notable Jewish scholars. When the noted Talmudic scholar Rabbi Simeon Shkop (1860–1940) had served fifty years as a *Yeshivah head in various Lithuanian towns, a Jubilee volume, *Sefer Ha-Yovel*, was published in his honour (Vilna, 1936). Following this example in more recent years the publishing of Jubilee (and Memorial) volumes has become something of an industry among the Orthodox.

**Judah** Fourth son of the patriarch Jacob from his wife Leah and the progenitor of the tribe of Judah which gave its name to the territory known as the 'land of Judah' or Judaea, hence the name *Jew. The story of Judah and Tamar is told in chapter 38 of the book of Genesis, where the name of Judah's son is given as Perez (v. 29). In the book of Ruth (4: 18–21), King David's ancestry is traced back to Perez. Since the *Messiah is a descendant of David, the story of Judah was often read as conveying hints of Messianic expectations.

**Judah Halevi** Spanish poet and religious philosopher (d. 1141). Judah Halevi's poems, secular and religious, are recognized as belonging to the foremost examples of Hebrew poetry. His Songs of Zion, giving expression to the poet's yearning for the land of Israel, are still used in synagogues during the Ninth of *Av service to introduce a note of consolation after the recital of the dirges on this day of mourning for the destruction of the Temple and for other calamities of the Jewish past. Obedient to the call of the Holy Land, Halevi, at the age of 60, resolved to leave Spain in order to settle in the country of his dreams. Legend has it that he did arrive in the Holy Land only to be murdered there but recent research has established that, in fact, on his way he stayed in Egypt, where he died.

In addition to his poems, Halevi is renowned for his very influential philosophical treatise, the *Kuzari*, originally written in Arabic but later translated into Hebrew. Halevi structured this work around the accounts of a heathen tribe, the *Khazars, whose king and people became converted to Judaism; the *Kuzari* consisting of a dialogue between a Jewish sage and the king of the Khazars. The book opens with a dream in which the king is told that while his intentions are admirable his deeds fall short of what God demands of him. Perturbed by the dream, the king first consults a philosopher but the latter tells him that God is so far above all human thought that He can be concerned neither with the king's intentions nor with his deeds. The king receives a similar dusty answer when he consults a Christian and then a Muslim sage. In despair, the king consults the Jew who then embarks on a reasoned defence of Judaism. The *Kuzari* is thus a work of Jewish *apologetics, a defence of the Jewish religion against the challenges of Greek philosophy, Christianity, and Islam from without, and against those presented by the *Karaites from within.

Halevi's thrust throughout the book, as well as in his poems, is particularistic. It is no accident that, at the beginning of the *Kuzari*, the king dismisses the philosopher in dissatisfaction with the notion that God has no concern with the particular. Halevi had a good knowledge of Greek philosophy in its Arabic garb and knew how alluring this universalistic trend could be for thinking Jews. But he refuses to yield to what he considers to be a superficiality that never penetrates to the depths of human existence. In one of his poems, Halevi urges that a Jew should not be enticed by Greek wisdom 'which has only flowers and produces no fruit'. Further in the particularistic mode is Halevi's contention that both the land of Israel and the people of Israel are intrinsically holy and set apart by God to fulfil His special purpose. On the Holy Land, Halevi's 'Ode to Zion' declares: 'Thine air is life for the souls, like myrrh are the grains of thy dust, and thy streams are like the honeycomb. It would be pleasant for me to walk naked and barefoot among thy desolate ruins, where once thy temples stood, where the ark was hidden, and where thy Cherubim dwelled in thy innermost shrines.' As for the Jewish people, they are endowed, through their righteous ancestors, with a special spiritual nature that marks them off from the rest of mankind as different not only in mere degree but in kind. Following this line, Halevi denies that a non-Jew, no matter how morally and intellectually gifted, can ever be a prophet.

On revelation, Halevi remarks that Judaism, unlike Christianity and Islam, affirms that God revealed Himself not to a single person but to the 600,000 Israelites who came out of Egypt. He implies that an event witnessed by so many people must be true, whereas a claim by an individual to have received a divine revelation can easily be the result of sheer delusion. That Halevi did not see that he was begging the question, since we are informed that the 600,000 were present only in the Torah itself, is to be explained on the grounds that Christianity and Islam, Judaism's rivals, admitted that the original revelation to Israel took place, but, they claimed, it had been superseded by the revelation to Jesus or Muhammad. Halevi's basic point here is that the onus of proof, that the original revelation has been superseded, rests on those who make the claim not on those who cling fast to the faith of their fathers, since God does not change His mind. By the Torah Halevi understands both the *Written and the *Oral Torah, the latter found now in the Rabbinic literature. A considerable portion of the *Kuzari* is devoted to a defence of the Talmud against the Karaites who rejected the Talmud and with it the whole doctrine of the Oral Torah. Obviously influenced by Muslim claims for the Koran, Halevi goes so far as to say that the Mishnah must have been inspired by God since no unaided human mind could have produced a work compiled in such exquisite style.

Some moderns have seen Halevi's particularism as racist in that it sees the doctrine of the *Chosen People in qualitative terms. It has to be appreciated, however, that Halevi never suggests that God is unconcerned with the rest of mankind. On the contrary, in Halevi's view, Israel is the 'heart of mankind'. When the heart is healthy the whole body is sound. When the heart is sick the whole body is affected adversely. And while Halevi does see the Jews as endowed with a superior spiritual nature, he adds that just as a dead plant is more repulsive than stagnant water, a dead animal more than a dead plant, and a human corpse more than a dead animal, so a Jewish sinner can be far worse and far more repulsive than a non-Jew who falls from grace. It can be put in this way. For Halevi, no adherent of another religion can ever be as good as a good Jew but, by the same token, none can ever be as bad as a bad Jew.

The influence of Halevi, always very strong, became felt especially, for obvious reasons, with the rise of *Zionism.

Hartwig Hirschfeld, *Judah Hallevi's Kitab Al Khazari*, trans. from the Arabic (new revised edn., London, 1931).

Isaac Husik, 'Judah Halevi', in his *A History of Mediaeval Jewish Philosophy* (New York, 1958), 150–83.

**Judah the Prince**  Nasi ('Prince') of the Palestinian community (d. *c.*217 CE), known simply as Rabbi, that is, Rabbi *par excellence*. Rabbi

Judah the Prince was the son of Rabban Simeon ben *Gamaliel II. Many tales are told in the Talmudic literature of his close friendship with the Roman emperor Antoninus, but the legendary nature of these tales is so blatant that attempts by some scholars to identify him with this emperor seem utterly pointless. The tales are obviously intended to illustrate the comparatively less strained relationships between the Jewish community and the Roman government in Rabbi Judah's time. Rabbi Judah the Prince was evidently a man of great wealth and position. As the Talmud puts it, he possessed both Torah and 'greatness' in other words, he enjoyed both religious and political authority. This dual function enabled him to embark on compiling the authoritative digest of Jewish law and practice, the *Mishnah, containing the teachings of the earlier Tannaim, which became the standard source for the Oral Torah, upon which the Amoraim commented in bóth Palestine and Babylonia (see TANNAIM AND AMORAIM).

The details of how Rabbi Judah compiled the Mishnah are somewhat obscure. He is best described as the editor of the Mishnah, not its author, since it is obvious that the Mishnah contains not only much earlier material but actual compilations of this material. The Talmud recognizes, in fact, traces of an earlier Mishnah in Rabbi Judah's Mishnah which were left by him intact even when this resulted in contradiction. There are also passages in the Mishnah that must have been added by others such as the statement that when Rabbi Judah died, humility came to an end (*Sotah* 9: 15). The numerous teachings of Rabbi Judah himself recorded in the Mishnah in the third person seem to indicate that these were added later; though this is by no means conclusive since it is not impossible that he himself recorded his teachings in this way for the sake of uniformity.

**Judah the Saint** Mystical teacher and moralist of Regensburg (d. 1217), prominent leader of the *Saints of Germany, and main author of the *Sefer Ḥasidim*. Judah's system is a blend of the homely and the austere and in it the ideal of suffering martyrdom for the faith occupies a prominent place.

**Judges** See BET DIN.

**Judges, Book of** The biblical book in which is recorded the history of the 'Judges', the leaders of the people, after Joshua down to the prophet *Samuel, who, according to the Talmud (*Bava Batra* 14b) is the actual author of the book. Modern biblical scholarship is divided on the question of date and is uncertain about the authorship of the book. Some scholars follow more or less the Talmudic view that the book is early, though not that it was compiled by Samuel. Others believe that the final editing of the book dates from the period after the Babylonian exile in 586 BCE. Although one of the Judges, *Deborah, functioned as a judge in the usual sense of the term, she and the others mentioned in the book were chiefly Judges in the sense of political and military leaders. The superscription to the book of *Ruth has it that the events recorded there took place in the days of the Judges.

Judah J. Slotki, 'Judges', in A. Cohen (ed.), *Joshua and Judges* (London and Bournemouth, 1970), 152–333.

**Jüdische Wissenschaft** 'Jewish Science', the German name for the historical-critical school which arose in the first half of the nineteenth century and whose main practitioners were Leopold *Zunz, Abraham *Geiger, and Zechariah *Frankel in Germany; Samuel David *Luzzatto in Italy; Nahman *Krochmal and Solomon Judah *Rapoport in Galicia (see HASKALAH and HISTORY). Jüdische Wissenschaft was not a consciously organized movement. Rather, a number of traditionally educated Jews who became familiar with the languages of Western European culture resolved independently, though in close communication with one another, to investigate by these new methods the classical sources of Judaism. The aim of Jüdische Wissenschaft was to demonstrate how the Jewish religion, literature, and philosophy had developed in response to the different civilizations with which Jews had come into contact through the ages. A prior aim of the movement was to establish correct texts by comparing current texts with those found in libraries open to Jews for the first time. Instead of the piecemeal treatment typical of the older approach, texts were studied as a whole and set in their proper period. The Greek and Latin classics were studied for comparative purposes in order to shed light on the Talmudic sources; Arabic and Islamic thought for the better understanding of the medieval Jewish works; the ancient Semitic tongues for a keener appreciation of the Bible and its background; and, above all, world history for the purpose of showing how Jewish history formed part of general historical trends. Indeed, the whole movement can be said to have called attention to the fact that Judaism, like all human institutions, has had a history and did not simply drop down from heaven to be transmitted without change from generation to generation. New questions were asked. What does the text really mean? Why does it say what it says and why just at that particular time? Does the text represent normative Jewish thinking or is it peripheral or contradicted by other texts and if so, what has caused the difference?

The movement undoubtedly had in part an apologetic aim, at first, in which the Wissenschaft scholars sought to show that Judaism, too, is normal and 'respectable' in having a history, a literature, and a philosophy like other cultures and that the great men of the Jewish past were not mere cyphers or irrational isolationists but creatures of flesh and blood responsive to the world around them. Yet the followers of the movement did try to study their sources as objectively as possible, paving the way for the use of the new methodology in higher institutions of Jewish learning and in learned journals in which articles of impeccable scholarship appeared.

Nathan Stern, *The Jewish Historico-Critical School of the Nineteenth Century* (repr.; New York, 1973).

**Justice** The biblical injunction: 'Justice, justice shall you pursue' (Deuteronomy 16: 20), addressed originally to judges and those who appoint them, became a key text in Judaism for the pursuit of justice by all in daily living. The repetition of the word 'justice' denotes, as has been frequently noted, what amounts to a passion for justice, as if the cry is: 'Justice, only justice, shall you pursue.' The pursuit of justice is urged throughout the Bible. Of the prophets, *Amos in particular calls on his own people and on the surrounding nations to practise justice. Amos declares: 'Let justice well up like water, righteousness like an unfailing stream' (Amos 5: 24). The patriarch Abraham, when pleading on behalf of Sodom, challenges God Himself to practise justice: 'Shall not the judge of all the earth deal justly?' (Genesis 18: 25).

In the Rabbinic scheme, the divine name Elohim (translated as 'God') denotes the divine justice while the *Tetragrammaton denotes the divine mercy. Noting that the creation narrative uses the name Elohim at first, and the Tetragrammaton only at a later stage, the Rabbis remark that it was God's intention, so to speak, to create the world only with His attribute of justice but when He perceived that His creatures could not live solely under the divine judgement, He associated mercy with justice so that the world might endure. (See AHAD HA-AM, BET DIN, LAW.)

# K

**Kabbalah** The mystical, theosophical system developed in the eleventh and twelfth centuries, culminating in the *Zohar, and later reinterpreted and recast by Isaac *Luria, the Ari, in sixteenth-century Safed. Essentially, there are two distinct Kabbalistic systems, the Zoharic and the Lurianic, though the latter sees itself as no more than an elaboration of the former. The word Kabbalah means 'tradition'. This term was used in the earlier Jewish sources for the Jewish tradition as a whole but was appropriated by the Kabbalists to denote their own secret doctrine, believed to be preserved by the initiates as the true, inner meaning of the Torah reaching back to Moses and even, in some versions, to Adam. Another name for the Kabbalah is, in fact, *Hokhmah Nistarah*, 'Secret Science'. Abraham Abulafia (1220–c.1290) developed his own system of prophetic Kabbalism in which the mystic uses certain techniques such as profound concentration on divine names in order to be the recipient of illuminations from on high. But while Abulafia's system is also known as Kabbalah, Abulafia remained a somewhat peripheral figure in the history of the Kabbalah; generally, and in this entry, the term Kabbalah covers the systems of the Zohar and Luria. Abulafia's writings, studied at length recently by Professor Moshe Idel, have had an influence on many of the later mystics and Kabbalists, though not as conveying a separate Kabbalistic system.

The Kabbalah as found in the Zohar had its origin in twelfth-century Provence in the circle of Isaac the Blind, though various, much earlier, philosophical and mystical trends, Gnostic and Neo-platonic in particular, found their way into the system. From Provence, the doctrine spread to Spain where in Gerona, around the person of the great Halakhist *Nahmanides, who gave it a respectability it might not otherwise have won for itself, the Kabbalah became known to wider circles. At the end of the thirteenth century, the Zohar was compiled, eventually taking its place as the supreme depository of the secret lore and, for many, as the sacred book of Judaism together with the Bible and the Talmud.

## The Doctrine

The medieval Jewish philosophers discuss at length the question of the divine attributes. What meaning can be given to statements such as 'God is wise' or 'God is good' since such anthropomorphic descriptions are totally inapplicable to that which is beyond all human experience? How is the God of the philosophers to be reconciled with, as Pascal puts it, the God of Abraham, Isaac, and Jacob, the Living God of the Bible, immediately accessible to His creatures in His loving care and concern for them? Maimonides and other thinkers develop the doctrine of negative attributes. One can only say what God is not, never what He is. On this view, to say that God is wise is to say no more than whatever God is, and this cannot be known, He is not ignorant. To say that God is good refers only to God's acts in the universe, which, were they to be performed by humans, would be the outcome of their good nature.

The Kabbalah, evidently impressed by the arguments of the philosophers and at the same time longing for the Living God of the Jewish religion, adopts a different and far more radical solution to the problem. According to the Kabbalah, there are two aspects of Deity: God as He is in Himself and God in manifestation. God as He is in Himself is known as *En Sof, the Limitless, the Infinite, the ineffable Ground of Being, so far removed from all human apprehension that of It (the impersonal term is sometimes used) nothing can be said at all. En Sof becomes manifest through a process of emanation in the ten *Sefirot, the powers and potencies in the Godhead, from which all creation stems. All worship of En Sof is directed through the Sefirot. These descend through all creation to become manifest in the human psyche so that man is the final link in the great chain of being which he can influence by his deeds. When man is virtuous, he sends beneficent impulses on high to promote harmony among the Sefirot and then the divine grace can flow freely to all creation. When man is vicious he sends baneful impulses on high to disturb the harmony of the Sefirot and then the flow of divine grace is impeded. It has convincingly been argued that, despite its strangeness and seeming incompatibility with pure monotheism, the Kabbalah won acceptance among Jews because of this idea, typical of Judaism, though not in the Kabbalistic form, that man is at the centre of God's world with a role to play given to no other creatures. For the Kabbalists, man literally holds up the heavens.

The Kabbalists deny that their doctrine is dualistic. The One God comprises both En Sof and the Sefirot or, as the Kabbalists are fond of saying, En Sof is always present in the Sefirot and apart from En Sof the Sefirot have no existence. For all that, the Kabbalists were bothered by the apparent dualism and multiplicity in their concept. If the Sefirot are totally identical with En Sof, there is what appears to be a decatheistic belief, ten divine powers in the one. (Abulafia and other opponents of the Zoharic Kabbalah accused the Kabbalists of entertaining a belief 'worse' than the Christian doctrine of the Trinity.) If, on the other hand, as some Kabbalists hold, the Sefirot are only the instruments used by En Sof, why are they treated, as they often are in the Kabbalah, as if they are divine in themselves? *Cordovero adopts a kind of compromise position. According to Cordovero, while the 'bodies' of the Sefirot are only the instruments of En Sof, these 'bodies' have 'souls' and these are part of En Sof, so to speak.

A startling element in the Kabbalistic doctrine is the division of the Sefirot into male and female. The Sefirot on the right are male and represent the divine love; those on the left are female, and represent the divine judgement. There are also Sefirot in the middle which represent the harmonization of love and judgement. Two Sefirot belonging to the divine mind, Ḥokhmah ('Wisdom') and Binah ('Understanding'), give birth to the lower Sefirot belonging to the divine emotions, and hence

called, respectively, *Abba ('Father') and Imma ('Mother'). Moreover, six of the lower Sefirot are grouped around *Tiferet* ('Beauty'), known as the 'Holy One, blessed be He', a male principle. The harmony among the Sefirot is brought about when *Tiferet* is united with *Malkhut* ('Sovereignty'), the female principle, also known as the *Shekhinah. In the liturgies composed by the Lurianic Kabbalists, the formula to be recited before carrying out the precepts of the Torah is: 'For the sake of the unification of the Holy One, blessed be He, and His Shekhinah.'

Just as there are holy Sefirot there are Sefirot belonging to the *Sitra Aḥara*, the 'Other Side', the demonic side of existence. The inhabitants of the demonic realm are known as the *kelipot* ('shells' or 'husks'), so called because they surround the holy and feed on it and, at the same time, protect it in a way, as does the shell of a nut its kernel and the bark of the tree the tree itself. Man is at the very centre of the struggle between the holy and the unholy, his role being to enable the holy Sefirot to gain the victory over the demonic forces. In the Lurianic Kabbalah, man's task is to rescue the *holy sparks imprisoned among the *kelipot*. For the Kabbalah every detail of the precepts of the Torah corresponds to some detail in the Sefirotic realm. The process of promoting cosmic harmony and vanquishing the *kelipot* through the performance of the precepts, is known as a Tikkun ('Rectification') while its opposite, through sin, is known as a Pegam ('Flaw'). The whole of human history is seen by the Kabbalah as the playing-out of a tremendous cosmic drama in which every act and every detail of the precepts, no matter how trivial in itself, has its effect in enabling human history to attain its final goal in the advent of the *Messiah.

### Theoretical and Practical Kabbalah

The Kabbalah is a theosophical system which can be studied objectively and with no practical consequences being aimed for, like many other subjects of enquiry. Students of the Kabbalah have included non-Jews as well as Jews who have pursued the study of Kabbalah in the belief that it contains ideas hospitable to their own philosophy. It was left to Professor Gershom Scholem and his school at the Hebrew University in Jerusalem to create what amounts to a new scholarly discipline, the objective study of the Kabbalah and Jewish mysticism in general by the application of rigorous standards of philological and historical investigation.

From the eighteenth century onwards, there existed a Christian Kabbalah in which Christian dogmas were read into the system. The Jewish Kabbalists themselves obviously had not the faintest intention of advocating Christian ideas and were, in fact, strongly opposed to Christianity as a religion, though this is not to say that they were totally uninfluenced by ideas which came to them from a Christian background. Knorr von Rosenroth's Latin version of Kabbalistic texts, *Kabbala Denudata*, was published in 1677–84 and influenced Madame Blavatsky (1831–91) the founder of the Theosophical movement, whose writings on the occult can hardly qualify as anything like any known version of the original Kabbalah. A. E. Waite's *The Holy Kabbalah*, on the other hand, despite the author's connections with the occult world of Blavatsky, has a far truer insight into the original meaning of the Zoharic texts, which Waite nevertheless sometimes misunderstands; he also cavalierly dismisses the Lurianic Kabbalah, about which he appears to be totally ignorant. There has been a recent spate of works of pop-Kabbalah, sold in shops dealing with the occult, but these are largely worthless for anyone wishing to know what the Kabbalah is really like.

Since, according to the Kabbalah, every aspect of cosmic energy stems ultimately from the power of the Sefirot and from various combinations of divine names, the Kabbalists believed that adepts who were thoroughly familiar with these mysteries could bring the higher powers into play to change the course of nature. To perform miracles in this way and change the laws of nature for good was seen by the practitioners of practical Kabbalah as a legitimate form of white *magic, unlike the black art in which attempts were made to contact the *kelipot* and which was sternly forbidden. However, recourse to practical Kabbalah was only tolerated for the most saintly. For lesser mortals the whole enterprise was seen as fraught with danger to body and soul. For this reason there are very few practical Kabbalists nowadays but many charlatans to prey on the gullible.

### Attitudes towards the Kabbalah

Attitudes towards the Kabbalah differ among religious Jews. In the nineteenth century, many shared the view of the historian Heinrich *Graetz that the Kabbalah was a foreign importation into Judaism, a resurrection of the old pagan gods, and that the idea of God as both male and female amounted to sheer blasphemy. *Hasidism adapted the Kabbalah to its own philosophy, though believing in the Kabbalah as divinely revealed truth. After the débâcle of Shabbetai *Zevi, the false Messiah whose ideas were based on the Kabbalah, the study of the Kabbalah was discouraged in most Orthodox circles except for those who had amassed a good deal of Talmudic and Halakhic learning and who had reached at least the age of 40, considered to be the age of complete maturity. Many a Jewish teacher, accepting the Kabbalah as true, still recoiled from actual study of the Kabbalah texts. Although, to some extent, *Halakhah and Kabbalah were rivals for the attention of students of the Torah, a number of customs and practices based on the Kabbalah found their way into the standard Codes and are followed by Orthodox Jews even if they are non-Kabbalists or anti-Kabbalists. In more recent years there has been something of a revival in Orthodox circles of Kabbalistic studies. A number of Kabbalistic textbooks have been published and a few Yeshivot established in which Kabbalah has its place in the curriculum. Yet it would be a mistake to make belief in the truth of the Kabbalah a test of Orthodoxy. It is possible for an Orthodox Jew to reject the Kabbalah without being accused of heresy. It was in no way startling for Professor Saul Lieberman, an outstanding Talmudist and a strictly Orthodox Jew, to say, when introducing a lecture on the Kabbalah by Scholem, that the Kabbalah is nonsense but the scientific study of Jewish nonsense constitutes Jewish scholarship. Reform Judaism in the nineteenth century tended to see the Kabbalah as nothing more than superstition and irrationalism but, nowadays, many Reformers acknowledge that the Kabbalah contains a wealth of insights still of value for the cultivation of Jewish spirituality.

Moshe Idel, *Kabbalah: New Perspectives* (New Haven, 1988).

Gershom Scholem, *Kabbalah* (Jerusalem, 1974).

—— *Origins of the Kabbalah* (Princeton, 1991).

**Kaddish** 'Sanctification', the doxology in Aramaic in which the hope is expressed that God's great name will be sanctified in the whole world He has created and the *Kingdom of Heaven be established on earth. Originally the Kaddish was recited after an Aggadic homily was delivered by a teacher, since the *Aggadah generally sounds a note of consolation and hope for the future. From the period of the *Geonim the Kaddish was introduced into the *liturgy of the synagogue to mark the end of a section or subsection of the prayers. The subsections conclude with what is known as half-Kaddish, that is, a shorter form containing only the first half of the doxology, and the larger sections with the full Kaddish which contains a prayer for the supplications of Israel to be acceptable to God. After the section in the liturgy that is in the form of a brief Rabbinic discourse, the older, school version of the Kaddish is recited. This contains a prayer for the well-being of students of the Torah and hence is known as Kaddish De-Rabbanan ('Kaddish of the Rabbis'). At a funeral the sons of the deceased recite an even longer version of the Kaddish in which reference is made to the *resurrection.

In the Middle Ages in Germany Kaddish Yatom ('Mourner's Kaddish') was introduced and this has been adopted by Jews everywhere. A son (in some communities a daughter as well) recites this special Kaddish for eleven months after the death of a parent and on the anniversary (*Yahrzeit) of the death. The principle behind the Mourner's Kaddish is that when the child sanctifies God's name in public by reciting the doxology, merit is accrued to the parent's soul. Very many Jews, otherwise not particularly observant of the rituals, observe meticulously 'saying Kaddish', as it is called, attending services for the purpose each morning and evening since, according to Orthodox practice, Kaddish can only be recited in a *minyan, the quorum of ten males (in Conservative synagogues females count as well).

Israel Abrahams, 'The Kaddish' and 'The Mourner's Kaddish', in his *A Companion to the Authorized Daily Prayerbook* (New York, 1966), 39–41, 88–9.

**Kaplan, Mordecai M.** Rabbi and influential religious thinker and teacher (1881–1983). Kaplan was born in Svencianys, Lithuania, but emigrated at the age of 9 with his parents to the USA. Kaplan's father, a Rabbi and renowned Talmudist, saw to it that his son received a sound, traditional Jewish education. Young Kaplan also attended general schools in New York and studied at Columbia University and

at the Conservative Jewish Theological Seminary in New York, where he received Rabbinic ordination.

Kaplan served as Rabbi of the Orthodox Kehillat Jeshurun synagogue in New York, but, increasingly influenced by the findings of modern science and the critical study of the Bible, began to have serious doubts about Orthodox theology. Kaplan, an intensely honest thinker, found himself unable to continue to serve as a Rabbi in an Orthodox synagogue, where, when the Scroll of the Torah (*Sefer Torah) is elevated, the congregation sings: 'This is the Torah which Moses set before the children of Israel', implying the Mosaic authorship of the whole of the Pentateuch (see BIBLICAL CRITICISM). Kaplan resigned from his position at the synagogue despite the urging of his congregation who were quite prepared to tolerate his un-Orthodox views provided he kept these to himself. Solomon *Schechter, Principal of the Jewish Theological Seminary, was so impressed with Kaplan's originality and pedagogical ability that he invited him to become Head of the Seminary's Teachers' Institute. Kaplan was later appointed Professor of Homiletics and the Philosophies of Religion at the Seminary. Kaplan influenced more than one generation of Conservative Rabbis, and this influence was extended to wider circles through his writings and through *Reconstructionism, the movement he founded to cut across across the divisions of Orthodoxy, Conservative, and Reform Judaism.

As a religious thinker, Kaplan adopted a naturalistic philosophy. His somewhat mechanistic view of science did not allow him to think of God as a Person or Being outside and beyond the universe. God, Kaplan maintained, is best understood by modern Jews as the power that makes for righteousness, that which is present in the universe and in the human psyche which guarantees that righteousness will eventually win out. Prayer, thought of as an appeal to a divine being whom one can influence, belongs, according to Kaplan, to a prescientific age. Prayer is rather, for him, reaching towards the highest in the universe and in oneself. The precepts of Judaism are commanded, according to Kaplan, not by the God of tradition but by the God within the Jewish soul, that is, by the ability Jews have to enrich their lives by drawing on all the sources of their glorious past. In Kaplan's famous work,

*Judaism as a Civilization*, published in New York in 1934, Judaism is depicted as more than a religion in the narrow sense. Judaism is a whole civilization, at the heart of which, to be sure, is the Jewish religion, but which embraces art, literature, music, folk-ways, in all of which the Jewish spirit finds its fulfilment.

Kaplan's naturalistic views of God have been attacked, with some justice, as being atheistic or, at least, very different from what Jews have hitherto believed about God. From the philosophical point of view, it is hard to see how Kaplan knows that there is a power that makes for righteousness in the universe and why it is more in accord with the scientific picture to believe in the existence of such a power than to believe in the God of traditional theism.

'Mordecai Kaplan on his Hundredth Year', *Judaism*, 30 (1981), 5–103.

Moshe Davis (ed.), *Mordecai M. Kaplan Jubilee Volume* (New York, 1953).

**Kapparot** 'Atonements', 'expiations'; the rite in which a live cock is waved around the head on the eve of *Yom Kippur and the words recited: 'This is my substitute, this is my vicarious offering, this is my atonement. This cock will go to its death, but I shall have a long and pleasant life of peace.' The superstitious and even pagan elements in the rite were recognized as early as the thirteenth century, when it was opposed by such outstanding Halakhic authorities as *Nahmanides and Solomon Ibn *Adret. *Karo, in the *Shulḥan Arukh* (*Oraḥ Ḥayyim*, 605), follows Ibn Adret in declaring that the rite should be abolished but *Isserles, in his gloss, records the rite as a worthy custom and provides the details of its observance. As a result, the rite is still performed by the more strictly Orthodox Jews, although some now substitute a sum of money, later given to charity, for the cock and alter the wording accordingly. Where a cock is used, it is slaughtered and given to the poor or its value given to the poor. The rite of Kapparot features strongly in discussions of which Jewish *customs should be retained and which abolished.

Jacob Z. Lauterbach, *Rabbinic Essays* (Cincinnati, 1951), 354–76.

**Karaites** The sect which arose in the eighth century CE; Heb. *Keraim*, from the root *kara*, 'to read', and so called because they relied on the 'reading' of Scripture in itself, rejecting the Rabbinic interpretations of Scripture found in the Talmud. The story that the sect was founded by Anan ben David when he was passed over for the position of *exilarch in Babylonia, is viewed with a degree of scepticism by modern scholars while they acknowledge that Anan was a prominent Karaite leader. The Karaites themselves trace their origin back to much earlier times. Maimonides identifies the Karaite *heresy with that of the *Sadducees. This view is not accepted by scholars in the field although certain Sadducean ideas appeared to have enjoyed a subterranean existence until they emerged among the Karaites.

The Karaites have their own liturgy, different from the standard Rabbinic form; they are very strict with regard to the degrees of forbidden marriages, extending these, contrary to the Rabbinic view, to relatives such as cousins; they do not wear *tefillin*; and do not permit food to be kept hot on the stove on the Sabbath in obedience to their understanding of: 'You shall kindle no fire throughout your settlements on the Sabbath day' (Exodus 35: 3). As a result of this Karaite interpretation, the medieval Rabbis ruled that anyone who refuses to eat hot meals on the Sabbath is to be suspected of heresy. It has been conjectured that the institution of kindling special Sabbath candles in the home before the Sabbath arose in reaction to the Karaites who, originally, forbade the lighting of candles to burn on the Sabbath, although later they, too, adopted the custom.

The Karaites naturally stressed the importance of the study of the Bible, upon which their religious outlook was based. This led to followers of traditional Rabbinism devoting some of their energies to the study of the Bible as well as the Talmud. In such biblical commentaries as that of Abraham *Ibn Ezra, the Rabbinic interpretation is defended against that of the Karaites but in the process the Rabbinites were led back to a deeper understanding of the plain meaning of the biblical texts.

The Karaites were treated as full, though heretical, Jews in the Middle Ages; many Rabbinic authorities permitted marriages between Rabbinites and Karaites. But eventually the breach between the two communities so widened that neither saw the other as belonging to the same religion. It has been estimated that there are around 20,000 Karaites in the State of

Israel, organized as a separate religious community with its own religious authorities.

Jacob Mann, *Texts and Studies*, ii. *Karaitica* (New York, 1972).

Leon Nemoy, *Karaite Anthology* (New Haven, 1952).

**Karet** 'Excision', 'cutting off', the biblical penalty, for certain offences, of being 'cut off from the people'; for example, for failing to be circumcised (Genesis 17: 14); for eating leaven on Passover (Exodus 12: 19); and for committing incest (Leviticus 20: 17). The Mishnah (*Keritot* 1: 1) lists thirty-six offences for which the penalty is *karet*. The chief problem here is the meaning of *karet*. Josephus (*Antiquities of the Jews* 3. 12: 1) remarks: 'To those who were guilty of such insolent behaviour, he [Moses] ordered death for his punishment', implying that *karet* is identical with other death penalties in the Pentateuch. This view is accepted by many biblical scholars but fails to explain why this term is used instead of 'he shall be put to death', that is, by the hands of the court. Other modern scholars hold that *karet* denotes some kind of exclusion from the community, the offender being 'cut off', that is, excluded from the community. But, as Milgrom has rightly pointed out, the penalty of *karet* is limited to purely religious offences and is never enjoined for offences such as murder, the penalty for which is judicial execution. Consequently, the unanimous Rabbinic view, as stated in the Talmud, has much to commend it, that *karet* is a form not of human but of divine punishment, though it is unclear how *karet* differs from the other divine penalty mentioned in the sources, 'death by the hand of Heaven'. In one view, *karet* means a divine punishment of death before the age of 60, which is why a Talmudic Rabbi had a party on his sixtieth *birthday. In another version *karet* means that the offender will die childless. In the confession of sin on *Yom Kippur one sentence reads: 'For the sins for which we are liable to the penalty of *karet* and childlessness.' The medieval philosophers endeavour to explain how the penalty of *karet* fits into the scheme of divine *providence. Maimonides (*Teshuvah*, 8: 5) identifies *karet* for the worst sinners as total annihilation of the soul in the Hereafter. This whole area is very obscure and is largely ignored in present-day Jewish theology.

Jacob Milgrom, 'The Penalty of "Karet"', in Nahum M. Sarna (ed.), *The JPS Torah Commentary: Numbers* (Philadelphia and New York, 1990), 405-8.

**Karo, Joseph** Outstanding lawyer and mystic (1488-1575). Karo was probably born in Toledo but, after the expulsion of the Jews from Spain in 1492, his family settled in Turkey where Karo lived for around forty years, acquiring a great reputation as an authority on Jewish law. In 1536 he left Turkey for Safed, serving there until his death as a Rabbi and Head of a Yeshivah*. In Safed he became closely associated with the mystical circle that flourished there.

Karo wrote a commentary, entitled *Kesef Mishneh*, to Maimonides' Code and another commentary, his greatest work, on the Tur of *Jacob ben Asher, to which he gave the title *Bet Yosef* (*House of Joseph*), because in it he provided a home for all the legal opinions held by the jurists of the past. In his introduction to the *Bet Yosef*, Karo remarks that he was moved to compile it because there was so much uncertainty about the actual law in practice, each Jewish community seeming to have its own 'Torah'. The Tur, he thought, is the best starting-point for the task he had set himself, since in this work, too, many different opinions are recorded. But Karo seeks to go further than the Tur in an analysis of the law as it developed from Talmudic times down to his own day. The *Bet Yosef* is probably the keenest work of legal analysis in the history of Jewish law.

Karo recorded the decisions in every branch of practical law at which he had arrived in his digest, the *Shulḥan Arukh*, which, together with the glosses of *Isserles, became the standard Code for all Orthodox Jews.

It is highly interesting that Karo, evidently in compensation for his powerful concentration throughout his life on acute legal subtleties, had strong mystical tendencies, believing himself to be the recipient of a heavenly mentor. This phenomenon was not unknown among the Kabbalists, who called the spirit which brought the revelation a Maggid ('Preacher' or 'Teller'). Karo identified his Maggid with the soul of the Mishnah and with the *Shekhinah. The revelations of the Maggid were sometimes in the form of automatic speech coming out of Karo's mouth. Solomon Alkabetz (d. 1576), author of the hymn *'Lekhah Dodi', sent an eyewitness account of Karo's visitation, in a letter from Safed to the mystic brotherhood in Salonika. Here Alkabetz states that during a mystic vigil on the eve of the festival of Shavuot the companions heard a voice speaking out of Karo's mouth. 'It was a loud voice with letters clearly enunciated. All the companions heard the voice but were unable to understand what was said. It was an exceedingly pleasant voice, becoming increasingly strong. We all fell upon our faces and none of us had any spirit left in him because of our great dread and awe.' Alkabetz then records what the voice said, evidently able to decipher the message.

Karo kept a mystical diary for around forty years in which he recorded the Maggid's revelations. This work, entitled *Maggid Mesharim* (*Teller of Upright Words*) was first published in Amsterdam in 1704. (The letter of Alkabetz is printed as the introduction to the work.) Followers of the *Haskalah, embarrassed that one of their heroes, with his keen logical mind, should have kept a mystical diary, denied that Karo was the author of the *Maggid Mesharim*. But, as Werblowsky has shown, its authenticity has been demonstrated beyond doubt. Students of religious psychology have found rich material for their investigation in the *Maggid Mesharim*, among other things that in its non-mystical sections the work falls far short of Karo's own acute reasoning. As Zevi Ashkenazi (1660–1718) is reported to have said: 'Karo was a far greater scholar than his Maggid.' Another fascinating feature of the *Maggid Mesharim* is the manner in which the Maggid addresses Karo, rebuking him for his shortcomings and holding out to him promise of his future greatness and assuring him that one day he would be worthy of suffering martyrdom for his religion. Whatever one is to make of Karo's mystical activities, the lie is given to the notion that legalism in religion is incompatible with the mystical approach.

Louis Jacobs, 'The Communications of the Heavenly Mentor to Rabbi Joseph Karo', in his *Jewish Mystical Testimonies* (New York, 1977), 98–122.
R. J. Z. Werblowsky, *Joseph Karo: Lawyer and Mystic* (Oxford, 1962).

**Kavvanah** 'Intention', 'concentration', directing the mind to the meaning of words uttered or acts performed. The question of Kavvanah is discussed with regard to prayer and with regard to the performance of the *precepts. In connection with the precepts, the Talmud, in a number of places, records a debate among the teachers about whether Kavvanah is essential. All agree that the ideal is to have the intention of carrying out a precept, *mitzvah, when one is

about to carry it out to demonstrate that the act is not a mechanical one but is carried out in order to do God's will. The debate is with regard to the *de facto* situation where the *mitzvah* has been carried out unwittingly. An example, referred to in the Mishnah (*Rosh Ha-Shanah*, 3. 7) is where a man passing by outside the synagogue on *Rosh Ha-Shanah at a time when the *shofar* was being sounded, heard the *shofar* sounds but did not listen to them with the intention of carrying out the *mitzvah*. Is he obliged to hear the *shofar* sounds again with full intention to carry out the *mitzvah* or does it suffice that he has heard the *shofar* sounds after all, albeit without intention? In other words, is a *mitzvah* carried out without the intention to carry it out, no *mitzvah* at all or, *de facto* at least, is the act counted as a *mitzvah* since it is the act in itself which ultimately counts? The Codes are divided on the question and the usual advice given is that the *mitzvah* should be carried out again but without the prior benediction: 'Who has commanded us to . . .'. It would seem, indeed, that the main purpose of the *benedictions recited before the performance of the *mitzvot* is to direct the mind to the act by stating beforehand that it is done in obedience to the divine command.

Kavvanah in prayer involves chiefly proper concentration on the meaning of the words uttered. A saying of *Bahya, Ibn Pakudah has often been quoted: 'Prayer without Kavvanah is like a body without a soul.' But here, too, the ideal is one thing, its realization in practice quite another. The medieval thinkers were fully aware of how difficult it is, especially since the prayers are in Hebrew, to concentrate adequately all or even most of the time. Although, strictly speaking, where Kavvanah was absent the prayers have to be recited again with Kavvanah, this stringency was relaxed so as to apply only to the first verse of the *Shema and the first paragraph of the Amidah (see EIGHTEEN BENEDICTION ). A passage in the Zohar (i. 243b–244a) states that when a man is in trouble and unable to concentrate on his prayer he should not refrain from prayer on that account. Even Maimonides, who is very insistent on the need for Kavvanah in prayer, can still acknowledge the need for long and arduous training. Maimonides writes (*Guide of the Perplexed*, 3. 51):

'The first thing you must do is this: Turn your thoughts away from everything while you read the Shema or during the Prayer [the Amidah], and do not content yourself with being devout when you read the first verse of the Shema or the first paragraph of the Prayer. When you have successfully practised this for many years, try in reading the Torah or listening to it, to have all your heart and all your thought occupied with understanding what you read or hear. After some time when you have mastered this, accustom yourself to have your mind free from all other thoughts when you read any portion of the other books of the prophets, or when you say any blessing; and to have your attention directed exclusively to the perception and the understanding of what you utter.'

Later religious teachers continued to grapple with the problem of Kavvanah in prayer. *Hasidism in particular is much concerned with the techniques of Kavvanah in prayer and with how to cope with distracting thoughts. A main reason why early Reform Judaism preferred that many of the prayers should be recited in the vernacular, rather than in the traditional Hebrew, was because of the conviction that proper concentration is only possible when prayers are recited in a language with which one is familiar from birth.

Among the Kabbalists, especially in the Lurianic system (see KABBALAH and LURIA, ISAAC) the whole ideal of Kavvanah in prayer is given a new turn. The Lurianic Kabbalists use the plural Kavvanot, by which they mean not concentration on the plain meaning of the words but on the map of the *Sefirot and the numerous combinations of these. Every word of the prayers hints at one or other of the details in the unfolding of the worlds on high and the mystic adept is expected to have these Kavvanot in mind as each stage of the prayers leads him from higher to ever higher world. A somewhat different type of mystical 'intentions' is found in the very popular manual of devotion called *Yesod Ve-Shoresh Ha-Avodah* (*The Foundation and Root of Divine Worship*) by Alexander Süsskind of Grodno (d. 1793). Alexander's 'intentions' are directed to the deeper meaning of the prayers in which the liturgy is used, in Alexander's words, 'to enflame the heart in the service of God'. For instance, in his comment on the quotation in the Prayer Book of Psalm 30: 3, Alexander gives this intention:

'For example, when a man has suffered some pain or has been sick, God save us, or when, God forbid, such has happened to a member of his family and, with God's help he has been healed, then when he recites the verse: "I cried unto Thee, and Thou didst heal me", he should give thanks and offer praise, with full concentration, to the Creator, blessed be He, who has sent him or his family healing from that pain or illness, God save us.'

This type of 'intention' is found at the foot of each page in some of the older prayer books.

H. G. Enelow, 'Kawwanah: The Struggle for Inwardness in Judaism', *Studies in Jewish Literature in Honor of Kaufmann Kohler* (Berlin, 1913), 82–107.

**Kedushah** Sanctification of God's name during the Reader's repetition of the Amidah (see EIGHTEEN BENEDICTIONS). During the Reader's repetition, when he reaches the third paragraph, the theme of which is God's holiness, he declares: 'We will sanctify Thy name in the world even as they sanctify it in the highest heavens, as it is written by the hand of Thy prophet: "And they called one unto the other and said, Holy, holy, holy is the Lord of hosts; the whole earth is full of His glory" [Isaiah 63].' From 'Holy, holy, holy' onwards is chanted by the congregation. The Reader continues: 'Those over against them say, Blessed', to which the congregation responds: 'Blessed be the glory of the Lord from His place' [Ezekiel 3: 12]. The Reader continues: 'And in Thy holy words it is written, saying', to which the congregation responds: 'The Lord shall reign for ever, thy God, O Zion, unto all generations. Hallelujah' [Psalms 146: 10].

The Kedushah is thus a re-enactment by the congregation on earth of the angelic praising of God on high. In one Talmudic passage it is stated that the *angels do not begin their song until Israel has recited the *Shema on earth and that, moreover, the divine name occurs in the Shema after only two words ('Hear' and 'Israel') whereas the angelic hosts are only permitted to give utterance to the divine name after three words ('Holy, holy, holy'). From the sixth century CE the Shema is added to the Kedushah in the Musaf (Additional) Prayer on the Sabbaths and festivals. This is reportedly because, the Byzantine authorities, whether Christians or Persian dualists, would not permit Jews to declare publicly the unity of God in the Shema. Consequently, the Shema was not recited in the usual place in the early morning service but only in the later Additional Prayer in order to avoid the watchful eyes of the governmental authorities. There is probably some historical truth behind this report.

Israel Abrahams, 'Kedushah' and 'The Kedushah for Musaf', in his *A Companion to the Authorized Daily Prayerbook* (New York, 1966), 60–1, 165–6.

**Ketubah** The marriage contract by which a bridegroom obligates himself to provide a settlement for his wife if he divorces her, or his heir if he predeceases her. *Ketubah*, from the root *katav*, 'to write', is the name for both the written contract itself and for the amount the husband is obliged to settle on his wife. The main purpose of the *ketubah* is to prevent a husband divorcing his wife against her will, which, in Talmudic times, he had the right to do (see DIVORCE). The knowledge that he had to pay his wife her *ketubah* would serve as a check against hasty divorce. The minimum amount for the *ketubah* is 200 *zuz* for a virgin and 100 *zuz* for a widow or divorcee. These amounts were by no means negligible since an average house in Talmudic times could be bought for 50 *zuz* and if a man had 200 *zuz* in ready cash he was no longer eligible for poor-relief. A groom could, of course, add to the *ketubah* any amount he wished. A whole tractate of the Mishnah and Talmud, tractate *Ketubot*, is devoted mainly to the laws of the *ketubah*. In addition to the basic settlement, the husband undertakes in the *ketubah* to protect his wife, work for her, provide her with her marital rights and with all that is necessary for her due sustenance. Since it was a legal document and had to be understood by both parties the *ketubah* was written in Aramaic, the vernacular in Talmudic times. This form is still preserved in the traditional *ketubah*, though in Anglo-Jewry and elsewhere there is an English translation on the back of the document.

In the State of Israel, the *ketubah* is still an enforceable legal document. In the USA, the UK, and most European countries, marriage arrangements are a matter for the secular civil law, so that the *ketubah* becomes a formality, every *ketubah* stating only the amounts of either 200 or 100 *zuz*. Nevertheless, since, in Rabbinic law, it is forbidden for a man to live with his wife unless she has a *ketubah*, the drawing-up and reading of the *ketubah* is part of every Jewish *marriage ceremony.

The *ketubah* is essentially a statement of the husband's obligations. The obligations of the wife to her husband are not recorded in the *ketubah*. Most Reform Jews today, therefore, prefer a different version of the *ketubah* which is more egalitarian. It has long been the practice in many communities to have illuminated *ketubot*, with paintings of birds, flowers, and other ornamental features. Illuminated *ketubot* from the nineteenth century and earlier are now collector's items.

Louis M. Epstein, *The Jewish Marriage Contract* (New York, 1927 repr. 1973).

**Khazars** A Turkish people whose kingdom endured from the seventh to the eleventh centuries. There is a solid basis in fact behind the stories circulating in the Middle Ages that a king of the Khazars and his people with him converted to Judaism. The mere fact that such a kingdom of Jews had existed provided medieval Jewry with hope for the future. Judah *Halevi's *Kuzari* consists of an imaginary dialogue between the king of the Khazars and a Jewish sage after which the king is moved to accept the Jewish religion in its Rabbinic formulation. Arthur Koestler's attempt (*The Thirteenth Tribe*, London, 1976) to show that all *Ashkenazi Jews are descended from the Khazars is purely speculative, has nothing to commend it, and is repudiated by all Khazar scholars.

**Kibbutz** 'Gathering', the collective, socialistic settlement in the State of Israel which had its origins in the early years of the twentieth century. The kibbutz movement believed that the establishment of kibbutzim was the best method of reclaiming the land of Israel. The influence of the highly idealistic kibbutzniks was enormous and their important contribution was acknowledged from the days of early Zionism. It has to be appreciated that the kibbutz was a secular movement, though obviously based on Jewish ideals, especially the ethical norms of Judaism. Most of the kibbutzim were and are largely unobservant of the Jewish rituals or, rather, they sought to develop a secular, nationalistic form of some observances and ritual, in the celebration of the festivals, for example, in a new form, and in the creation of new festivals based on the land. However, the Kibbutz Ha-Dati is an organization of religious kibbutzim, the slogan of which is 'Torah Va-Avodah' ('Torah and Work on the Land'), implying the socialist ideal wedded to full observance of Jewish law.

Henry Near, *The Kibbutz Movement: Origins and Growth, 1909–1939* (The Littman Library of Jewish Civilization; Oxford, 1992).

**Kiddush** Sanctification of the Sabbath. On Friday night, when the Sabbath begins, the Kiddush ceremony is carried out before sitting down to the Sabbath meal. A cup of wine is filled and held in the hand by the person presiding, usually but not necessarily the father of the house, and the benediction over wine recited (see BENEDICTIONS). Then the Kiddush proper is recited:

'Blessed art Thou, O Lord our God, King of the universe, who hath hallowed us by Thy commandments and hast taken pleasure in us, and in love and favour hast given us Thy holy Sabbath as an inheritance, a memorial of the creation—that day being also the first day of the holy convocations, in remembrance of the departure from Egypt. For Thou hast chosen us and hallowed us above all nations, and in love and favour hast given us Thy holy Sabbath as an inheritance. Blessed art Thou, O Lord, who hallowest the Sabbath.'

As a prelude to the Kiddush the verses of the creation narrative which speak of the Sabbath (Genesis 2: 1–3) are recited. After the drinking of the wine, the benediction over bread is recited and the family partakes of the Sabbath meal.

Strictly speaking, Kiddush is a home ceremony but in the Middle Ages Kiddush was also recited in the synagogue during the Friday-night service on behalf of visitors who often had their meals in a room adjacent to the synagogue. Even though, nowadays, guests are usually made welcome in the home, the older practice of reciting Kiddush in the synagogue as well as in the home is still retained. A shorter form of Kiddush is recited before the meal on the Sabbath day in the morning but this consists of verses in praise of the Sabbath (Exodus 31: 16–17, 29: 8–11) with no benediction other than that over the wine. This Kiddush is not recited during the synagogue service but in many synagogues a small celebration consisting of cakes and drinks is held over which the day-Kiddush is recited. This small repast came itself to be known as a Kiddush, to which the congregants are invited. For instance, people celebrating a happy event will often take the opportunity to invite their friends and fellow-congregants to 'a Kiddush' after the service.

Kiddush is also recited on the festivals with the wording altered so as to refer to the festivals instead of the Sabbath.

Israel Abrahams, 'Kiddush' and 'Sabbath Morning Kiddush', in his *The Authorized Daily Prayerbook* (New York, 1966), 139–41, 169–70.

**Kiddush Ha-Shem** Sanctification of the name (of God), the opposite of Hillul Ha-Shem, the profanation of the name (of God). These two concepts, prominent in Jewish thought from Talmudic times, are based by the Rabbis on the verse: 'You shall not profane My holy name, that I may be sanctified in the midst of the children of Israel—I am the Lord who sanctify you' (Leviticus 22: 32). In the Rabbinic interpretation, the verse implies that a Jew must so conduct himself that his actions increase reverence for God's name and that none of them should bring the divine name into disrepute. Israel must be a holy people because Israel has been sanctified by God (see CHOSEN PEOPLE) and bears His holy name. The stress is placed on the words 'in the midst of the children of Israel', that is, on public conduct. Not every sin constitutes Hillul Ha-Shem and not every virtuous act Kiddush Ha-Shem but only deeds, whether good or bad, that are carried out in public and thus either decrease or increase respect for Judaism. To suffer *martyrdom rather than be faithless to the Jewish religion is the supreme example of Kiddush Ha-Shem. If a man is ready to die in public for his faith, there can be no more powerful attestation to its truth. But to suffer martyrdom is obviously quite extraordinary and is only demanded by Jewish law in extremely rare instances. Numerous examples are given in the sources of Kiddush Ha-Shem and Hillul Ha-Shem in ordinary living by the light of Judaism.

Kiddush Ha-Shem in the daily round involves actions, not necessarily enjoined by strict law, which bring credit to Jews and through them to the Jewish religion given by God. The idea behind this is that a religion that can inspire men to act so justly and so sympathetically is a noble religion. An illustration given in the Jerusalem Talmud is of the early teacher Simeon ben Shatah, a poor man who earned his living by selling flax. His pupils, desiring to spare him from too much hard work, bought him a donkey from a Saracen and found that a pearl was attached to it. They told him that he would no longer have to work so hard because his sorry financial situation would be eased by his acquisition of a pearl of such great value. But Simeon insisted that the pearl be returned to its rightful owner, even though a case could have been made in strict law for Simeon to keep the pearl. Simeon declared that he would rather hear the heathen say: 'Blessed be the God of the Jews' than have any reward this world has to offer. Another story in similar vein is told in the same passage of some old Rabbis who bought a quantity of wheat from robbers and found there a bundle of coins. When they returned the money they had found the robbers exclaimed: 'Blessed is the God of the Jews!'

An example of Hillul Ha-Shem given in the Talmud (*Yoma* 86a) is of the great Babylonian teacher, Rav, who says that if he buys meat from the butcher without paying of it on the spot it constitutes a Hillul Ha-Shem since people may suspect him of not paying his bills. Another example given is of the Palestinian teacher Rabbi Johanan, who says that whenever he walks 4 cubits without studying the Torah and wearing his *\*tefillin* it constitutes a Hillul Ha-Shem. It is all a question of preserving standards of ethical conduct and religious practice. The more renowned a scholar, the greater the demands made on him. If the scholar appears to be lowering his standards of conduct, this calls into question all standards of conduct. Along those lines the nineteenth-century moralist Israel *Salanter says that he knows only too well that he is neither a really great scholar nor anything remotely approaching a great saint but since people mistakenly believe that he is both, then for him to behave in a way less than is expected of such a paragon constitutes a Hillul Ha-Shem.

The deeper theological meaning of Kiddush Ha-Shem is that God as He is in Himself is unknown and unknowable. God only becomes manifest in human life when human beings acknowledge Him by acting in such a way that His being is relevant to and influences their daily life. Professor Hugo Bergmann's famous essay entitled *Kiddush Ha-Shem* (translated into English in *Commentary* (March, 1952), 271 ff.) is rightly given the subtitle: *God Depends on Man, as Man on God.*

> Louis Jacobs, 'The Sanctification of the Name', in his *Jewish Values* (London, 1960), 74–85.

**Kimhi, David** Biblical exegete of Narbonne in Provence (*c.*1160–*c.*1235), known, after the initial letters of his name (*R*abbi *D*avid *K*imhi) as Radak. Kimhi was renowned as a philosopher and grammarian but his permanent claim to fame rests on his biblical commentaries, printed together with the text in many editions of the Hebrew Bible. These commentaries were so highly regarded by later generations that the saying in Ethics of the Fathers: 'Where there is no flour [*kemah*, i.e. no means of earning one's bread] there is no Torah' was adapted as: 'Where there is no Kimhi there is no Torah', that is, without Kimhi's commentaries the Bible is a closed book. The English translators of the King James Version relied heavily on Kimhi's insights.

Kimhi's aim, similar to that of Abraham *Ibn Ezra, is to elucidate the plain meaning of the text, that is, to see each text as a whole and discover the exact meaning of the words and the context in which they appear. Like other medieval exegetes who follow the plain meaning, Kimhi frequently notes that a biblical device in the poetic sections is to repeat the same idea in different words. This phenomenon is called 'parallelism' in modern biblical scholarship. Thus on the verse: 'And righteousness shall be the girdle of his loins, and faithfulness the girdle of his reins' (Isaiah 11: 5) Kimhi rejects the notion that the two causes refer to different matters, stating simply that: 'The verse describes the same thought twice, each time in different words.'

Kimhi belonged in the philosophical, rationalistic tradition. In his old age he travelled to Spain to defend Maimonides' *Guide of the Perplexed* and he often draws on Maimonides' views.

> Frank Talmage, *David Kimhi: The Man and the Commentaries* (Cambridge, Mass. 1975).

**Kingdom of Heaven** Heb. *Malkhut Shamayyim*, the Rabbinic expression for the sovereignty of God as acknowledged by human beings; hence the frequent expression: 'acceptance of the yoke of the Kingdom of Heaven'. The Mishnah (*Berakhot* 2: 2) understands the reading of the *Shema to be the 'acceptance' of the yoke of the Kingdom of Heaven'. The kingly metaphor is found in the Bible in the verse: 'The Lord shall reign for ever and ever' (Exodus 15: 18) and in the verse: 'And the Lord shall be king over all the earth: in that day shall the Lord be One and His name one' (Zechariah 14: 9). Both these verses are recited at the end of the Alenu prayer which looks forward to the day 'when the world will be perfected under the kingdom of the Almighty, and all the children of flesh will call upon Thy name'. The Alenu prayer, now recited at the end of every service, originally belonged to the introduction to the Malkhuyot ('Kingship verses') section in the Musaf Amidah (see EIGHTEEN BENEDICTION) on *Rosh Ha-Shanah, the festival when God is hailed particularly as king. One of the many interpretations of the sounding of the *shofar on Rosh Ha-Shanah is that trumpets are sounded at the coronation of a king. In the majority of the *benedictions God is referred to as 'King of the universe'. In Rabbinic times the kingly metaphor, with its overtones, in those days, of tyrannical power, proved somewhat embarrassing so that often the Rabbis, while preserving this metaphor, feel obliged to draw a distinction between a king of flesh and blood and the Divine King, as when it is said that an earthly king is not obliged to obey the laws he lays down for his subjects whereas God Himself obeys the laws He has promulgated; God refuses, for example, to accept as a sacrifice an animal that has been stolen. A more elaborate expression for God, in the Alenu prayer and elsewhere, is 'King of the kings of kings, the Holy One, blessed be He', obviously in reaction to the title given to the Persian rulers: 'the King of kings'; God is 'King of the kings of kings'.

Solomon *Schechter rightly detects three aspects of the Kingdom of God: 1. the personalistic and individualistic, the acceptance of the yoke, as when reading the Shema; 2. the universalistic, in which the establishment of the Kingdom over all is the hoped-for Messianic event; and 3. the nationalistic, in which the people of Israel is redeemed from subservience to earthly rulers to worship God in freedom. In the Kabbalistic doctrine of the *Sefirot, the lowest of the Sefirot is *Malkhut*, 'Sovereignty', the divine principle by which the world is governed.

Solomon Schechter, *Aspects of Rabbinic Theology* (new edn., New York, 1966), 65–115.

**Kings, Book of** The book in the Bible in which is related the histories of the kings of Judah and Israel from David and Solomon down to the last of the kings of Judah. In present editions of the Bible Kings is divided into two books, and this division has become the accepted one, although in the Jewish tradition the two form a single book. According to the Talmud (*Bava Batra* 15a) the author of the book is the prophet *Jeremiah. Modern biblical scholarship prefers a later date, since events recorded in the book took place after Jeremiah's death. The book itself states explicitly that some of its contents are derived from early histories such as 'the book of the acts of Solomon', 'the book of the chronicles of the kings of Judah', and 'the book of the chronicles of the kings of Israel'.

I. W. Slotki, *Kings* (London and Bournemouth), 1950.

**Kittel** From the German word meaning a 'smock'; a long white shirt worn over the outer garments. The kittel is one of the shrouds in which the corpse is dressed (see DEATH AND BURIAL). The kittel is also worn by the Reader, and by many congregants, during the service on *Rosh Ha-Shanah and *Yom Kippur, as a reminder of death on these penitential occasions; as a symbol of purity; and in order to resemble the *angels who are 'clothed in white'. For similar reasons, it is the custom in some communities for the bridegroom to wear the kittel during the marriage service. Some Jews also wear the kittel at the *Seder on *Passover. The wearing of the kittel on these occasions arose among German Jews and is still largely restricted to the *Ashkenazim.

**Kohen** 'Priest', a descendant of *Aaron the priest, plural Kohamin. The priestly case officiated in the Temple and have certain functions to perform even after the destruction of the Temple. The Jewish family name, Cohen, usually denotes that its members were *priests. In Temple times no one was admitted to the priesthood unless he could prove his priestly descent. In later times rigorous proof was no longer possible, so that Kohanim today act as such on the basis of presumptive status—the mere fact that a family tradition believes that it is formed of Kohanim is sufficient to establish its status as such. A Kohen may not come into contact with a corpse unless it is of a near relative (Leviticus 21: 1–4); and he may not marry a divorcee (Leviticus 21: 7). It is the Kohen's privilege to be the first of the persons called to the *reading of the Torah. Where a

Kohen is present at the table he has the right to recite the *grace after Meals, though he can waive this right if he chooses. Kohanim also recite the priestly *blessing in the synagogue. These rules are followed by all Orthodox Jews. Reform Jews reject the laws concerning Kohanim in the rather fanciful belief that they tend to perpetuate a caste system in Judaism. Conservative Jews are less categorical in the matter but many Conservative Rabbis also hold that the laws about the Kohanim are in abeyance today, especially since, nowadays, those who claim to be Kohanim only enjoy their privilege by presumptive status.

**Kol Nidre** 'All vows', the opening words of the declaration, largely in Aramaic, at the beginning of the evening service on *Yom Kippur in which all *vows that will be uttered in the coming year are declared null and void. The declaration applies only to religious vows and has no effect on *oaths taken in a court of law. If a person makes a vow, say, to deny himself wine for a certain period, perhaps as a penance, he must keep his promise, which is thought of as a promise to God. But this applies only if the vow is uttered with full intent. A person's declaration beforehand that all vows he will take in the year ahead are null and void means that any vow he will make is held to be without sufficient intention and hence without binding power. Because it was falsely assumed that Kol Nidre does apply to oaths taken in the court, Jews were suspected of unreliability in this matter and in a number of countries the infamous More Judaica, a special humiliating form of oath, was introduced when a Jew had to swear in court. Zechariah *Frankel and others in nineteenth-century Germany exposed the falsehood and explained the true meaning of Kol Nidre. In the Middle Ages a number of Rabbinic authorities were opposed to the Kol Nidre on the grounds that its effectiveness to nullify vows was very questionable. Yet the Kol Nidre is still recited in the majority of congregations, the night of Yom Kippur being referred to as 'Kol Nidre Night'. There is no doubt that it is the famous traditional melody, with its note of remorse, contrition, hope, and triumph, that has saved the Kol Nidre. Reform congregations often substitute a Psalm for the Kol Nidre formulation but retain the melody. The usual practice is for the Reader to chant the formula three times, raising

his voice each time. An interpretation given to the Kol Nidre is that the congregation declares, by implication, at the beginning of Yom Kippur: 'See, O Lord, what miserable sinners we are. We make promises to live better lives each year and yet always fall far short of keeping them. Therefore, help us, O Lord, and pardon us for our shortcomings.'

J. H. Hertz, 'Kol Nidre', in his *The Pentateuch and Haftorahs* (London, 1960), 730–1.

**Kook, Abraham Isaac** Rabbi, Kabbalist, and religious thinker, first Chief Rabbi of the Land of Israel (1865–1935). Kook was born in the small town of Greiva in Latvia. He studied at the famous Yeshivah of *Volozhyn. In 1904 Kook was appointed Rabbi of Jaffa. A strong religious Zionist, Kook travelled to Europe in the hope of persuading the recently formed ultra-Orthodox Aggudat Israel organization to adopt a more positive Zionist stance. Caught in Europe by the outbreak of World War I in 1914 he stayed in Switzerland until 1916 when he was appointed Rabbi of the Machzikei Ha-Dat synagogue in London. Despite brushes with the Jewish establishment in England, Kook was widely respected by all circles in Anglo-Jewry for his great learning and piety. It is reported that he mastered the English language by reading Rodkinson's (very poor) English translation of the Babylonian Talmud. In 1917 Kook published in London the little work *Rosh Milin* (*First Words*) on the letters, vowels, and notes for *cantillation of the Hebrew alphabet. Years later, Kook remarked in an aside that he believed he was gifted with the *Holy Spirit when he compiled the work. In this and in his other works Kook's style is obscure, inevitably so since he was searching for new forms of expression to give to old ideas. Fascinated by the paintings of Rembrandt, in which he saw traces of the Kabbalistic idea of the 'hidden light', Kook would go frequently to the National Gallery to study the works of the great master. In 1919 Kook was appointed Ashkenazi Chief Rabbi of Jerusalem and in 1921 Ashkenazi Chief Rabbi of Palestine as a whole.

Kook, a prolific author, wrote *Responsa, essays, religious poems, and Kabbalistic works, the most important in the last category being his *Orot Ha-Kodesh* (*The Lights of the Holy*). In some ways Kook was a controversial figure. The Rabbis of the old school, to which, in a sense, he himself belonged, were opposed to his encouragement of the secular Zionists and to his attempt at bridging the gap between the Jewish tradition and the world of science and technology. It cannot be supposed that Kook, a non-systematic thinker, was really successful in his bridging efforts, yet his influence is still felt in the world of Jewish thought, not only among the Orthodox. Kook's letters on all aspects of Jewish life were published posthumously and created a great stir among thinking Jews.

Virtually alone among Orthodox Rabbis, Kook warmly espoused the theory of *evolution, believing this to be in accord with the Kabbalistic doctrine that all worlds are moving gradually from the lower to the higher. Kook's thoughts in this area resemble those of Teilhard de Chardin's 'advance towards the Omega point'. In a remarkable passage (*Orot Ha-Kodesh*, v. 19–22) Kook writes:

'The theory of evolution, now so well known as a result of recent scientific researches, has revolutionized our thought patterns. This does not apply to the élite, who approach matters logically and reasonably, for they always tended to see things in terms of development, even the spiritual side of existence which is less tangible. For them it is not at all strange to understand by analogy that the material substance of the physical universe proceeds by the same method of development as the spiritual. It is natural for the physical universe to follow the course of development of the spiritual universe, in which no stage is bypassed or left unfulfilled.'

Kook's spiritual struggles are expressed in his poems:

My soul aspires
For the mysteries,
For the hidden secrets of the universe,
It cannot be content
With much knowledge
That Probes
The trivialities of life.

Profoundly influenced by Hasidic thought, especially by *Habad, Kook came closer than any other to being a Hasidic-type Rebbe in the non-Hasidic world.

Ben Zion Bokser, *Abraham Isaac Kook* (New York, and Toronto, 1978).

**Kosher** Ashkenazi pronunciation of the Hebrew world *kasher* meaning 'fit' or 'suitable', as in the verse: 'The thing seems right [*kasher*] in the eyes of the king' (Esther 8: 5). The most frequent use of the term kosher is in connection with the *dietary laws. A food that it is permitted for a Jew to eat is called kosher, hence the abstract name kashrut for the dietary laws. The term *glatt* ('smooth') kosher originally denoted that when the lungs of an animal had been examined they were found to be 'smooth', that is, without adhesions that might render the animal forbidden. But in recent years the term glatt kosher has come to refer to extreme punctiliousness in the preparation of food for Jews to eat, as when an establishment prides itself that it provides only glatt kosher food. The term kosher is applied to other matters as well, as when a Scroll of the Torah, *Sefer Torah, is declared to be kosher, that is, properly written. In modern slang the term is applied to anything that is right and aboveboard, as, for example, when a business deal is said to be kosher. An upright Jew is often described as a kosher Jew.

**Kotsk, Menahem Mendel of** Hasidic master (1787–1859), also known as 'the Seraph' because of his holy life and fiery temperament. In his youth Menahem Mendel was a follower of Simhah Bunem of Przysucha. The Przysucha branch of Hasidism placed the emphasis on intellectual ability, inwardness, and sincerity. When Simhah Bunem died, Menahem Mendel was elected by his colleagues to the leadership of the group. Menahem Mendel was a stern master, having little truck with the ordinary Hasidim who came to ask him to pray on their behalf for children, health, and prosperity. His appeal was chiefly to the select few, the sincere God-seekers willing to sacrifice everything to the quest. He once declared that his ambition was to raise 200 chosen disciples who would go onto the roofs loudly to proclaim: 'The Lord, He is God.' The Kotsker Hasidim were notorious for their disdain of outward religiosity and moral pretence. It was said of the Kotsker group that, unlike others who sinned in private and were virtuous in public, they were sinful in public and virtuous in private. Some Kotsker Hasidim would often sit up all night playing cards and then meet together in stealth to recite the morning prayers. Such a parade of apparent impiety was anathema to the staid, even in the Hasidic camp.

For the twenty years or so before his death, Menahem Mendel went into complete seclusion, allowing only an occasional visit to his mice-infested room to his more intense follow-ers. On the rare occasions when he did sud-denly burst into the synagogue, the Hasidim were so terrified by his awesome visage that they would try to jump out of the windows in order to avoid his wrath. Many tales have been told about this seclusion of the Rebbe and the reason for it, but they all lack any foundation. The rigours of Menaham Mendel's tormented life and his total disregard for the opinion of others (he is similar in this respect to the Danish thinker Kierkegaard) seem to have pro-duced in him severe traumas. The Kotsker regime, with all its severities, seemed doomed to failure but was saved through the activities of the Kotsker's brother-in-law, Isaac Meir Alter (1789–1866), who functioned as Hasidic master in the little town of Gora Kalwaria, known to the Hasidim as Ger. The Gerer dynasty, still very powerful, considers itself to be in the traditions of Kotsk but with a more humane face.

Menaham Mendel, hard on himself, brooked no relaxation of inner struggle to arrive at the truth on the part of his followers. Mere con-formity was taboo for him. His critique of the 'beautiful Jews', the middle-class pietists com-fortable in their social and religious life, resem-bles Kierkegaard's denunciations of the leaders of his church. The Kotsker once asked Jacob of Radzyman: 'What is the purpose of man's creation?' Jacob replied: 'Man was created in order to perfect his soul.' The Kotsker shouted: 'Jacob! Is this what we were taught in Przysucha? Man was created in order to increase God's glory.' The Gerer Rebbes and Hasidim had a more tolerant attitude towards the eatablishment dignitaries, but they, too, cultivated the wild piety typical of Kotsk.

Abraham Joshua Heschel, *A Passion For Truth* (London, 1973).

**Krochmal, Nachman** Philosopher, scholar, and leading figure (1785–1840) in the *Haskalah and *Jüdische Wissenschaft movements. Krochmal's father, a wealthy merchant in the Galician town of Brody, saw to it that his son received a traditional Jewish education in Bible, Talmud, and the Codes. At the early age of 14 Krochmal was married and, supported by his father-in-law after the fashion of those days, he continued his studies, acquiring a knowledge of German and German literature and philoso-phy, especially the works of Kant, Herder, and Hegel. Krochmal was entirely self-educated in general learning but his erudition was both extensive and profound. He would often be-moan the fact, however, that he never had an opportunity of studying at a university. In Brody, Lvov, and Zolkiew, Krochmal gathered around him a small group of earnest seekers after the new knowledge; some of these young men later followed in his footsteps as thinkers and historians of Judaism. Krochmal's *Moreh Nevukhey Ha-Zeman* (*Guide for the Perplexed of the Time*) was based on Maimonides' *Guide of the Perplexed*, although the title was given by *Zunz, who published the work in 1851 after Krochmal's death. What Zunz rightly saw as the difference between the two *Guides* lay in the very different challenges to which the authors responded. Maimonides' 'perplexed' were con-cerned with trying to reconcile Judaism with the Aristotelian philosophy dominant in the Middle Ages. No one was at all perplexed in this way in Krochmal's day when the source of confusion was the problem of 'Time', caused by the increasing awareness that Judaism, like all other religions and cultures, has had a history. Krochmal's intention was to show how Judaism had developed historically, contrary to the traditional view held in his day by his co-religionists in Galicia, that the Jewish religion was simply transmitted more or less intact from generation to generation.

In Krochmal's analysis in terms of the Hegelian thesis, antithesis and synthesis, the culture of every people undergoes a period of birth, growth, and decline and these are re-flected in the history of that people. The par-ticular idea on which the culture is based—the pursuit of beauty, for instance, by the ancient Greeks—first captivates that people and be-comes its guiding principle, its god, as Krochmal calls it. There follows a period of growth and the idea then spreads to become the common property of mankind. Once this happens the particular people loses its specific goal and suffers a decline. The Jewish people also un-dergoes periods of birth, growth, and decline but since the God Jews worship is the Absolute which embraces all particular ideas, the Jews never lose the reason and spur for their exist-ence and, even after a period of decline, re-emerge as the eternal people. Krochmal quotes in this connection the verse: 'For I the Lord change not; and ye, O sons of Jacob, are not consumed' (Malachi 36). Some students of

Krochmal's work believe that in his opinion the period of the *Emancipation and the emergence of the Jews into Western society heralded, though Krochmal does not state this explicitly, a new period of growth after decline for Judaism.

Although Krochmal was a strictly observant Jew, his ideas were viewed with disfavour by the Orthodox Rabbis of his day, who were suspicious of any attempt to see Judaism in terms of historical development because this suggested a degree of relativism. Krochmal believed that the modern Jew was bound by his sense of integrity to acknowledge the developing nature of his religion without surrendering his loyalty to traditional forms, especially those of the *Halakhah; although, in Krochmal's view, Halakhah, too, has had a history. Krochmal, at the beginning of his *Guide* quotes a passage from the Jerusalem Talmud in which it is stated that the Jew is confronted with two paths in life, one of fire, the other of ice. If he proceeds along the path of fire he will be burnt. If he proceeds along the path of ice he will be frozen. What should the wise man do? He should walk in the middle. This became Krochmal's slogan. The path of fire, of uncritical and unreasoning enthusiasm typical of Hasidism, a movement of which Krochmal was less than enamored, encourages ignorance and leads to all kinds of vagaries and superstitions. The path of ice, on the other hand, the path of cold reason uninspired by true religious feeling, leads to a rejection of Judaism and total assimilation. The wise man, for Krochmal the informed Maskil, follower of the Haskalah, knows how to walk in the middle. Such a Jew allows both his reason and his emotions to control his life.

It cannot be maintained that Krochmal's understanding of Judaism in the modern age is in any way the final word. Yet he was a pioneer and his ideas were seminal, influencing in their different ways Reform and Conservative Judaism and Zionism, and showing how the historical-critical approach can be adopted without detriment to the essential truth of the Jewish religion.

Solomon Schechter, 'Nachman Krochmal and the "Perplexities of the Time"', in his *Studies in Judaism* (first series; Philadelphia, 1945), 46–72.

# L

**Ladino** From Latino (Latin), the Judaeo-Spanish language spoken by Sephardi Jews, comparable to *Yiddish, spoken by Ashkenazi Jews.

**Lag Ba-Omer** The thirty-third day of (the counting of) the *Omer, the minor festival that falls on 18 Iyyar. Lag is formed from the combination of the Hebrew letters *lamed*, with the numerical value of thirty, and *gimmel*, with the numerical value of three. This minor festival goes back to the Geonic (see GEONIM) period but its origin is rather obscure. The traditional explanation is that the disciples of Rabbi *Akiba died in a plague during the Omer period and this ceased on the thirty-third day of the Omer. Some scholars understand the 'plague' to be a veiled reference to the war against Rome but there is no firm evidence for such a contention. Yet it is interesting that the folk-custom developed of teachers going out into the fields with their pupils on this day to play shooting-matches with bows and arrows.

According to the Kabbalah, Rabbi *Simeon ben Yohai, the reputed author of the Zohar, died on this day, his death being referred to as the 'marriage' of Rabbi Simeon, because his soul was reunited with its Source. From the seventeenth century pilgrimages were made to the grave of Rabbi Simeon in Meron near Safed on Lag Ba-Omer and these are still observed today. Various ceremonies take place at Meron, some of them bizarre, such as burning costly garments in honour of the saint. Bonfires are lit in other places in Israel on this day and the devotees dance around the fire while chanting hymns in Rabbi Simeon's honour. Prominent Rabbis in the last century looked askance at these practices but they were defended by the Rabbi of Safed. Little boys in Meron have their first haircut on Lag Ba-Omer. Although marriages do not take place during the Omer period, they are permitted on this day.

Hayyim Schauss, *The Jewish Festivals* (New York, 1938); see index, 'Lag Ba-Omer'.

**Lamedvovniks** Literally, 'thirty-sixers', from the Hebrew letters *lamed*, thirty, and *vav* (in Yiddish pronunciation, *vov*), six, together with the Russian ending 'nik', 'belonging to', popular in Yiddish. The notion of the Lamedvovniks goes back to the Talmud (*Sukkah* 45b) where it is said that there are never less than thirty-six *saints in each generation who are given a sight of the *Shekhinah daily. It is possible that thirty-six is significant here because this number represents a majority of the seventy judges in the *Sanhedrin, the Supreme Court in ancient times, possibly suggesting that these saints by their merits have a decisive role to play in sustaining the world. In the Talmud and other early sources there is no attempt to identify these saints. They are simply individual good men without any necessary relation to one another. But in later Jewish legend, from the eighteenth century, the idea took root that the Lamedvovniks are hidden saints, seemingly ordinary people, usually artisans living in little villages, who do not know the identity of the other thirty-five and may not even know that they themselves belong to the charmed circle and, if they do know, will deny it when questioned. Stories of saints who practise their piety in secret are certainly known in ancient Jewish sources but it is not suggested that they belonged to a special group of hidden saints. There arose many tales of these secret saints who intercede for the Jews when Jewish life is threatened. On occasion in Eastern Europe a strange tramp or other seemingly mysterious character would be suspected by the credulous of being a Lamedvovnik. In Hasidic legend the *Zaddik, the Hasidic master, is never himself a Lamedvovnik since everyone acknowledges his saintliness and he is not a saint by stealth. But Hasidic legend tells of some of the masters that they would know the identity of the thirty-six and even see to it that they were adequately supported without disclosing their true identity. Andre Schwartz-Bart's novel, *The Last of the Just*, is based on the Lamedvovnik legend.

Gershom Scholem, 'The Tradition of the Thirty-Six Hidden Just Men', in his *The Messianic Idea in Judaism* (New York, 1971), 251–6.

**Lamentations, Book of**   The biblical book consisting of elegies over the fall of Jerusalem and the destruction of the First Temple in 586 BCE; Heb., after the opening word, *Ekhah*, 'How'. In chapters 1, 2, and 4, each verse begins with a letter of the alphabet from *alef* to *tav* and in chapter 3 there are three verses for each letter of the alphabet. Chapter 5, the final chapter of the book, is not in the form of an alphabetic acrostic but contains twenty-two verses, the number of the letters of the alphabet. It can readily be seen, therefore, that the book is in contrived form, despite its sombre theme. Poetry is 'emotion recollected in tranquillity'. The traditional author of Lamentations is none other than the prophet *Jeremiah, who witnessed the destruction of the Temple. Modern scholars have found no support for the traditional view but largely agree that internal evidence does show that the book was composed by a contemporary or contemporaries of the events of which it tells. The book of Lamentations is chanted in the synagogue to a melancholy tune on the night of the fast of Tisha Be-Av, the Ninth of *Av.

Solomon Goldman, 'Lamentations', in A. Cohen (ed.), *The Five Megilloth* (London, 1952), 70–102.

**Landau, Ezekiel**   Prominent Rabbinic leader and authority (1713–93). Landau was born in Poland but in 1755 was invited to become Rabbi of Prague, a position he occupied until his death. Landau, although he had studied Kabbalah in his youth, was opposed to its study except by the most erudite because of the danger of Shabbateanism (see Shabbetai *Zevi), a movement which relied on the Kabbalah for its heretical approach to Judaism. He disliked the use of Kabbalistic terminology in *Hasidism and had little regard for the unlearned Hasidim whom he accused of spiritual arrogance in adopting the mystic way reserved for the initiates.

Landau's fame rests chiefly on his *Noda Biyhudah* ('Known in Judah'), a voluminous

collection of *Responsa in which he replied to Rabbis and other scholars from many parts of the Jewish world. Landau's legal decisions still enjoy great authority for Orthodox Jews (see AUTOPSIES and HUNTING). In addition, Landau's collection includes Responsa on theological topics. Typical of his sober approach is the Responsum in which he discusses the case of a young scholar who had had sexual relations with a married woman and later married her daughter. The young man wished Landau to give him a series of severe penances but Landau insists that too much mortification of the flesh must not be practised by a learned man because this will interfere with his studies. He should rather study the Torah twice as much as he was accustomed to do and donate large amounts to charity, this being the most effective means of repentance. Another Responsum discusses the case of a *Kohen who had married an Indian woman, the ceremony taking place in a Hindu temple. The man later divorced his wife and did penance for his sin and wishes to know whether he can deliver the priestly blessing in the synagogue or whether he is disbarred from this privilege on the grounds that he had once worshipped idols. Landau permits the man to deliver the priestly blessing since he has now repented and, in any event, he only went through the ceremony in order to please his bride and did not really believe in the Hindu gods.

Louis Jacobs, *Theology in the Responsa* (London, 1973), 173–81.

**Law**   The Greek translation of Torah as *nomos* is followed in the English versions of the Bible in which Torah is rendered as 'the Law' with the result that Judaism is often described as a religion of law and, contrasted by some authors with Christianity, said to be a religion of love (see AHAD HA-AM). While there is a degree of truth in this characterization, it is far too sweeping both with regard to Judaism and to Christianity. A passion for *justice, and respect and even love for the laws of the Torah, are remote from the legalism in which only actions count (see *Kavvanah). The charge of legalism is hotly denied by the majority of Jews. *Halakhah does occupy a prominent place in Judaism in the belief that there is a right and wrong way of doing things exemplified in the Halakhah. But Halakhah, the legal side of Judaism, is complemented by the *Aggadah, comprising the non-legal aspects of the Jewish religion. Judaism has its detailed laws but it also has its history, philosophy, ethics, and mysticism to redeem the religion from narrowness and rigidity. Moreover, discussions of the Halakhah itself are often conducted in a poetic spirit known to every student of the Talmud, the great depository of Jewish law. As Rabbi A. I. *Kook has remarked: 'Just as there are laws of poetry there is poetry in laws.' Even the committed Christian writer C. S. Lewis (*Reflections on the Psalms*, London, 1958) can give the title to his reflection of the Psalmist's love of the law: 'Sweeter than Honey', an expression taken from the Psalmist's praise of the Torah (Psalms 19: 10). Lewis writes of the Psalmist: 'The Law is "undefiled", the Law gives light, it is clean and everlasting, it is "sweet". No one can improve on this and nothing can more fully admit us to the old Jewish feeling about the Law; luminous, severe, disinfectant, exultant'; sentiments that could hardly be bettered by the most devout Jew.

Some of the greatest legal minds in Jewry had powerful interests beyond the Halakhah. Maimonides, author of the great Code, the *Mishneh Torah*, is also the author of the probing philosophical work, *Guide of the Perplexed*. The notable exponent of the Halakhah, *Nahmanides, was a Kabbalist and author of a comprehensive biblical commentary. Joseph *Karo, author of the standard Code of Jewish Law, the *Shulḥan Arukh*, kept a mystical diary for forty years in which he recorded his soul-searchings and his visions. This does not mean that Judaism has never known scholars and pietists who emphasized the legal aspect to the virtual exclusion of any other. But the Aggadah, too, has had its one-sided enthusiasts with little taste for law. Both Halakhah and Aggadah have their place in normal expressions of Judaism.

**Law, Rabbinic** Religious laws introduced by the Talmudic Rabbis and other early sages in order to create, as it is put in Ethics of the Fathers (1. 1), a 'fence around the Torah', that is, to add restrictions, over and above those found in the Bible, so as to keep people away from any risk of infringing biblical law. For instance, according to biblical law, it is forbidden to saw wood on the Sabbath but there is no prohibition against handling a saw or other such tools. This is forbidden by Rabbinic law on the principle that if one is not allowed even

to handle tools on the Sabbath, there is less risk that the tools will be used.

There is considerable discussion in the sources on the right of the Rabbis to introduce laws not found in the Bible. Authorities like Maimonides believe that the Bible itself provides the sanction for the sages of Israel to promulgate such laws. *Nahmanides, on the other hand, defends the right of the Rabbis on the grounds that their intention is to preserve the Torah. Nevertheless, Rabbinic law is treated less severely than biblical law. Doubt in cases of Rabbinic law is treated leniently while doubt in cases of biblical law is treated strictly. In any event, the principle of consensus of the Jewish community comes into operation and Rabbinic law is binding ultimately because Jews have accepted it as part of their religion (see AUTHORITY).

**Leah** The biblical matriarch, wife of Jacob, whose story is told in the book of Genesis (29–31). Leah is one of the four *matriarchs of the Jewish people.

**Leibowitz, Yeshayahu** Israeli scientist and controversial religious thinker (1903–94). Leibowitz's contribution to chemistry, biochemistry, and neurophysiology is immense. But his main claim to fame, others would say to notoriety, are his severe criticisms of Israeli policy. He believed that the sole advantage, a very considerable one to be sure, of the emergence of the State of Israel is that it has provided Jews with a homeland in which, as he was fond of saying, they no longer have to be bossed around by goyyim. For him, to see a deeper religious significance in the emergence of Israel verges on State-worship. There were fierce protests in Israel when, for example, at the time of the war in Lebanon, he called on the Israeli Army to refuse to serve there, and when he dubbed the *Western Wall a golden calf.

Leibowitz was a strictly observant Jew, believing the *Halakhah to be the sole guiding principle for Jews. Yet he accepted the findings of *biblical criticism in his conviction that the origin of the commandments is irrelevant to their binding force. Attempts at refuting Darwin and the Bible critics, he remarks, are to see God as a superior Professor of Biology or Semitics. For Leibowitz, a *mitzvah*, a precept of the Torah, constitutes an opportunity to serve God and any attempt to see it in terms of human betterment, even of a spiritual nature, is to prefer self-worship to worship of the Creator. He takes strong issue with the attempts of Maimonides and other medieval thinkers to give 'reasons' for the commandments. Religion is not *for* anything else but is an aim in itself. Leibowitz is critical of the Kabbalah the grounds that its pantheistic approach tends to obfuscate the distinction between the holy and the profane, as all mysticism tends to do. Mysticism is another name for idolatry, Leibowitz roundly declares. Even prayer should not be seen as asking God for favours. Leibowitz once remarked that in his synagogue people from every walk of life offer their prayers daily but if the worshippers were asked why they pray, they would all reply that they pray because a Jew is duty-bound to pray. Critics of this stance have not been slow in protesting that, if this is so, why use the words of the traditional prayers? Why not simply say: 'Blah, Blah, Blah' to the glory of God?

Typical of Leibowitz's approach, in which pure obedience is all, is his refusal to grasp why women should desire to carry out the precepts, such as wearing *tefillin, from which Jewish law exempts them. A Jewish male should not *want* to wear *tefillin* but should wear them because that is his duty. Since a woman has no such obligation it is as meaningless for her to wear *tefillin* as it is for a person who is not a *Kohen to refuse to marry a divorcee. The commandments, remarks Leibowitz, form the matrix of Judaism as one lives it and is capable of living it in the here and now, in the everyday life of the believing Jew who has bound his life to the rule of God's Torah. It is hard to see, given Leibowitz's acceptance of freedom from *dogmas and his refusal to treat seriously the question of *revelation, how he is able to know that the commandments form the matrix of Judaism. For all that, Leibowitz's stress on worship as the true end of Judaism is a salutary check on religious reductionism.

Yeshayahu Leibowitz, 'Commandments' and 'Idolatry', in Arthur A. Cohen and Paul Mendes-Flohr (eds.) *Contemporary Jewish Religious Thought* (New York, 1987), 67–80, 445–9.

**'Lekhah Dodi'** Heb. for 'Come my friend'; the hymn, of which these are the opening words, sung during the synagogue service on Friday night to welcome the Sabbath. The opening stanza reads: 'Come my friend, to meet the bride; let us welcome the presence of the

Sabbath'; and the other stanzas are in praise of the Sabbath and expressions of hope for the restoration of Zion and the Messianic redemption. The practice of welcoming the Sabbath as Israel's bride is mentioned in the Talmud, and on the basis of this the sixteenth-century Kabbalists in *Safed developed an elaborate ritual in which they would go out into the fields dressed in white garments to welcome the Sabbath, identified by them with the *Shekhinah. Solomon Alkabetz, the author of the 'Lekhah Dodi', was a member of this mystic brotherhood and composed the hymn especially for the ritual. The consecutive stanzas begin with the letters of his name to form the nominal acrostic, Shelomo Ha-Levi, 'Solomon the Levite'. 'Lekhah Dodi' is now recited in all Jewish congregations and various melodies have been composed with which to accompany it. The final stanza reads: 'Come in peace, thou crown of thy husband, with rejoicing and with cheerfulness, in the midst of the faithful of the chosen people; come, O bride, come, O bride.' Very few modern writers appreciate that, for the Kabbalists, the 'husband', for whom the Sabbath = Shekhinah is the crown, is, following the doctrine of the *Sefirot, the Sefirah *Tiferet*, the spouse of the Shekhinah. The hymn is now sung, however, with no awareness of the original Kabbalistic nuances. It is the universal custom to turn towards the door when this stanza is sung and bow to welcome the Sabbath.

Israel Abrahams, 'Lechah Dodi', in his *A Companion to the Authorized Daily Prayerbook* (New York, 1966), 124–27.

**Leon Da Modena** Italian Rabbi, prolific author, poet, and preacher (1571–1648). Da Modena, a typical Renaissance figure, was a man of many parts and contradictions. He was a staunch traditionalist and equally fervent modernist; having written, in his early youth, a treatise against gambling, he was addicted to the vice, which reduced him to penury, during his adult life. He acquired renown as a preacher in Venice, attracting Christians to his sermons as well as Jews. Da Modena had a thorough knowledge of the Talmud and wrote *Responsa, although these were not published from manuscript until as late as the twentieth century. His anti-Christian polemic, *Magen Va-Ḥerev* (*Shield and Sword*) also remained unpublished until the twentieth century. In this work he makes the observation that it is chiefly the doctrine of the Incarnation, which implies that there are three persons in the Godhead, that makes the Christian dogma highly offensive to Jews. The idea that there are three powers in the Godhead is found, in a sense, in the Kabbalah.

A curious work of Da Modena is in two parts: 1. *Kol Sakhal* ('Voice of a Fool') and 2. *Shaagat Aryeh* ('Roar of the Lion'). Da Modena attributes the former piece to an unknown opponent of Rabbinic law, and replies to it himself in the latter. But the attack covers many more pages than the refutation and some scholars suspect Da Modena himself of being the author of both. His little book *Ari Nohem* (*Growling Lion*) is a systematic attack on the Kabbalah, although in some of his other writings Da Modena is sympathetic to the Kabbalah. In all, Da Modena presents a severe problem to historians who are still unable to decide whether he was a confused genius or a deceitful scholar who hid his heretical views under the cloak of a defiant Orthodoxy. Some of Da Modena's untraditional views resurfaced in the Reform movement in the nineteenth century.

Salomone di Rossi had composed melodies for use in the synagogue service to which there had been objection by some Rabbis on the grounds that the tradition does not know of complicated musical arrangements, which, they argued, were copied from the Church. In a Responsum Da Modena supports di Rossi. If we prohibit, he says, the vocal efforts of gifted choirs, the Christians will ridicule the Jews for lacking all aesthetic appreciation. In another Responsum, Da Modena defends the right of preachers in their sermons to interpret the Bible freely. In Halakhic matters it is wrong, he observes, to depart from Rabbinic teaching and one must not depart from the Rabbinic understanding of scriptural verses when practice is based on these. But where it is simply a question of theoretical expositions, as in preaching, there is no harm in a preacher interpreting Scripture in accordance with what his mind tells him is the plain meaning.

Louis Jacobs, *Theology in the Responsa* (London, 1975), 154–60.

**Lesbianism**   See HOMOSEXUALITY.

**Leviathan**   Mythological sea-monster which will struggle with another monster, the Wild Ox, in the Hereafter. Both will be killed in the conflict and God will make a canopy of the skin of Leviathan under which the saints will sit to enjoy the meat of the Wild Ox. The general tendency is to interpret all this metaphorically.

**Levirate Marriage**   The marriage of a widow to a brother of her husband from the same father. According to Leviticus 18: 16 it is forbidden for a man to marry his brother's widow (the verse must be referring to a widow; if the brother is still alive he is forbidden to marry her in any event since she is a married woman). The exception as stated in Deuteronomy (25: 5–10) is where the brother dies without issue. Then one of his brothers is obliged either to take his place by marrying the widow or to release her to marry another by the rite of *Halitzah. There are two opinions in the Talmud as to whether levirate marriage is to be preferred over the release of the widow by the rite of Halitzah. But with the ban on a man having more than one wife (see Rabbenu *Gershom), Halitzah is the only option where the brother is already married and, nowadays, levirate marriage is no longer the rule in all circumstances, even when the brother has no wife. This is the law in the State of Israel. A whole tractate in the Talmud, tractate *Yevamot* ('sisters-in-law'), is devoted to the complicated laws of levirate marriage.

**Levites**   Members of the tribe of Levi, the third son of the patriarch Jacob. Members of the tribe are either *priests, Kohanim (see KOHEN), or Levites, their status being established by family tradition. The family name Levi or Levine generally denotes that the members of the family are Levites. In Temple times the offering of the *sacrifices was the function of the priests. The function of the Levites was to provide the musical accompaniment to the sacrifices, vocally and with musical instruments, and to act as gate-keepers and general guards. Nowadays, a Levite is given the privilege of being called, second to the Kohen, to the reading of the Torah in the synagogue and a Levite washes the hands of the Kohanim before the latter deliver the priestly *blessing. The redemption of the *first-born is not held where the father of the child is a Levite or the mother the daughter of a Levite.

Jacob Milgrom, in Nahum M. Sarna (ed.), *The JPS Torah Commentary* (Philadelphia and New York, 1990), Excursus 4, pp. 341–2.

**Leviticus, Book of** The third book of the *Pentateuch, called in Hebrew *va-yikra* ('And He called'), after the word with which the book begins. Another name is *Torat Kohanim* ('Priestly Torah') since the majority of the laws in the book have to do with the *sacrifices and other laws appertaining to the *priests. The current title, Leviticus, is derived from the *Septuagint and means 'of the *Levites'. There is very little in the book about the Levites but the name is not inappropriate since the priests also belonged to the tribe of Levi and were 'Levites' as well as Kohanim (see KOHEN). The book also contains laws and exhortations addressed to the people as a whole, including chapter 19, which contains the verse (18): 'Love thy neighbour as thyself' and other directions for holy living, which led the Talmudic Rabbis to declare that this chapter contains the main principles of the Torah. It was customary for school children to begin their studies with the book of Leviticus; as the Rabbis put it, 'Let the pure [the innocent children] busy themselves with purities' (the Levitical laws governing the sacrifices and other purities). This custom of starting off little children with Leviticus has now largely been abandoned except in ultra-Orthodox circles.

The book of Leviticus, in particular, was at the centre of the fierce debates between traditionalists and the critics (see BIBLICAL CRITICISM). The traditional view is that Leviticus, like the rest of the Pentateuch, was written by Moses at the 'dictation' of God. Defenders of the traditional belief point to the fact that throughout the book the words occur: 'And the Lord spoke to Moses.' Many of the laws are addressed to the situation in the wilderness: the sacrifices, for example, are offered in the Tabernacle, not in the Temple (chapters 1–17). And where the laws are addressed to the people when they will be settled in its land, this is stated explicitly (Leviticus 14: 34; 18: 3; 23: 10; 25: 2). The priests themselves are referred to as 'Aaron and his sons', the priests in the wilderness, not in the Temple. Moreover the book of *Ezekiel quotes or alludes to Leviticus which shows, at least, that the book, if not Mosaic, is pre-exilic.

On the older critical view, the laws in Leviticus are too complex to have been compiled in the days of Moses; but this argument has been considerably weakened by archaeological evidence that extremely complex rituals were the norm among ancient peoples in the days of Moses. There is thus nothing in the book of Leviticus which automatically rules out Moses as the author. Nevertheless, the standard critical view is that Leviticus and parts of Genesis, Exodus, and Numbers belong to a post-exilic work which the critics refer to as 'P' (standing for the Priestly Document). On the critical view the laws of Leviticus reflect the priestly system, with its hierarchy of Levites, priests, and a *High Priest, read back into the wilderness period. When the book of *Chronicles, the critics argue, is compared with the book of *Kings, the latter probably composed around the year 550 BCE, the former possibly two hundred years later, it can be seen that while Kings says little about worship in *Jerusalem, Chronicles describes a very elaborate cult with features akin to 'P'. The Israeli scholar Ezekiel Kaufmann has argued very plausibly for the view that 'P' is not post-exilic and is earlier than the book of *Deuteronomy, although Kaufmann and his school admit that 'P' is discernible as a unit in the Pentateuch different from other units.

The Orthodox scholar Dr J. H. Hertz holds that unless the Mosaic authorship of Leviticus is accepted, a great question mark is set against the whole doctrine: 'The Torah is from Heaven.' This is the general Orthodox view. Reform Judaism usually follows, with regard to Leviticus and the rest of the Pentateuch, the critical view and draws the conclusion that many of the ritual laws are a priestly and purely human creation no longer possessing any binding power. *Conservative Judaism holds that the origins of the laws of the Torah are irrelevant for the living religion that Judaism has become (see FRANKEL).

J. H. Hertz, 'The Book of Leviticus', in his *The Pentateuch and Haftorahs* (London, 1960), 554–9. Gordon J. Wenham, *The Book of Leviticus* (London, 1979).

**Levi Yitzhak of Berditchev** Rabbi and Hasidic master (d. 1810); Levi Yitzhak became a disciple of *Dov Baer the Maggid of Mezhirech in 1766, later becoming a foremost exponent of Hasidism in his writings and through his life. Levi Yitzhak, the most lovable figure among the Hasidic masters, belongs to the folklore of all Jews, not only the Hasidim, in his eloquent pleadings to the Almighty to look with favour on His people. A typical story told in this connection is that when Levi Yitzhak witnessed a Jewish coach-driver greasing the wheels of his carriage while wearing his *tefillin*, instead of upbraiding the man, the saint lifted his eyes heavenwards to proclaim: 'See how wonderful Jews are. Even while greasing the wheels of their carriages they wear *tefillin*.'

Levi Yitzhak, remained a staunch upholder of the Hasidic way all his life. He was appointed Rabbi of Zelichov, where he met with strong opposition on the part of the *Mitnaggedim for his Hasidic views. Eventually he was forced to relinquish his post, but met with the same fate when serving as Rabbi in Pinsk. He finally settled in Berditchev in 1785, after which town he is known as 'the Berditchever' or 'the Berditchever Rov', since he was one of the few Hasidic masters to serve also as a town Rabbi. There are tales, which seem to have a basis in fact, that, as a result of the opposition he met with, he suffered for a time from 'smallness of soul', in other words, he had a nervous breakdown; but he recovered and continued to teach the Hasidic ideas and ideals. There is also a basis in fact to the reports that he would travel with his company of followers from town to town in order to win souls for God.

Levi Yitzhak's work, *Kedushat Levi* (*Holiness of Levi*) is a commentary in the Hasidic vein to the *Pentateuch and other sacred books. The first part of the work was published in Slavita in 1798, the second part in Berditchev in 1816, since when it has gone into a number of editions and is acknowledged as a supreme Hasidic classic. A typical comment in the book is on the priestly *blessing. While delivering the blessing the priests hold their hands outstretched with the palm facing downwards. When a man prays for himself he is in the category of a recipient. When a man wishes to receive something he holds out his hand with the palm upward and the back of the hand downward. But when a man prays only for the sake of the delight that the Creator will have from his prayers, that man is a giver, giving something to God, so to speak. A giver holds his hand with the palm downward and the back of his hand upward. The priests thus bless the people that they themselves should be givers, that all their worship should be directed to the tremendous aim of giving delight to the Creator.

In Hasidic panentheistic vein (see PANENTHEISM) is Levi Yitzhak's remark on the first verse of Genesis:

'The general principle is that the Creator, blessed be He, created the all and He is the all and His influence never ceases. For He extends His influence at every moment to His creatures, and to all worlds, to all palaces, to all angels, and to all the Holy Hayyot. And this is why we say [in our prayers] that He forms light and creates darkness and not that He formed light and created darkness; "forms" in the present tense. For at every moment He creates, at every moment He bestows vitality to all living creatures and all is from Him, blessed be He, and He is perfect and He includes all.'

Levi Yitzhak stresses particularly the need for *humility. But for him true humility is attained not through a man thinking how unworthy he is, since in this process he is thinking of himself. True humility consists in profound contemplation on the majesty of God before whom all creatures are as naught. The book of Proverbs says: 'An abomination of the Lord is every lofty heart' (Proverbs 16: 5) from which it follows that pride is an idol, an abomination of which the Torah says: 'Thou shalt not bring an abomination into thy house' (Deuteronomy 7: 26).

Samuel H. Dresner, *Levi Yitzhak of Berditchev* (New York, 1974).

**Liberal Judaism** The English branch of Reform Judaism founded by C. G. *Montefiore. Liberal Judaism in England corresponds to American Reform Judaism and is to the left of both Reform Judaism in England and what used to be called Liberal Judaism in Germany, the last two being closer to left-wing Conservative Judaism in the USA. Such are the complexities of religious labels in contemporary Jewish life.

**Life, Book of** There is a reference to the Book of Life in Psalms (69: 29) where the Psalmist pleads that wicked men 'be erased from the Book of Life, and not be inscribed with the righteous'. During the *Ten Days of Penitence from *Rosh Ha-Shanah to *Yom Kippur prayers to be inscribed in the Book of Life are added to the *Amidah and on the eve of Rosh Ha-Shanah people bless one another that they be inscribed in the Book of Life. Very few Jews think of the Book of Life as a kind of huge ledger in which God inscribes the names of the righteous and from which He erases the names of the wicked. It is widely acknowledged that inscribing in the Book of Life is a powerful metaphor for God's judgement at the beginning of the New Year.

**Life, Saving of** Judaism places the highest value on the preservation of life. In order to save life the precepts of the Torah must be set aside (except for the offences of murder, idolatry, incest, and adultery). If, for example, the doctors order a man to eat on *Yom Kippur, otherwise his life may be endangered, he is obliged to eat on this sacred fast day. Every effort must be made to save life. The Talmudic Rabbis interpret the verse: 'Neither shalt thou stand idly by the blood of thy neighbour' (Leviticus 19: 16) to mean that if a man is in danger of drowning it is the duty of all who can swim to dive in to save him and the same applies to a man held to ransom by bandits or attacked by wild beasts. Included in the obligation to save life is to take adequate care of one's *health.

**Light** Light (and *fire) as a symbol for the divine is ubiquitous in the religious literature of Judaism. To refer only to the Psalms: 'light is sown for the righteous' (97: 11); 'the Lord is my light and my salvation' (27: 1); 'at the brightness before Him' (18: 23); 'the commandment of the Lord is pure, enlightening the eyes' (19: 9); 'thy word is a lamp unto my feet, and a light unto my path' (119: 105). In the vision of the divine *Chariot seen by the prophet Ezekiel (ch. 1) the divine is described in terms of flashing lights and the colours of the rainbow. The command to kindle the lights of the *menorah (Exodus 27: 20–1; Numbers 8: 1–4) was interpreted early on in the history of Judaism as symbolic of the need to bring the illumination of the Torah into human life. In the *Havdalah prayer, recited at the termination of the Sabbath, the benediction over light reads: 'Blessed art Thou, O Lord our God, King of the universe, who makest a distinction between between holy and profane, between light and darkness, between Israel and other nations, between the seventh day and the six working days.' In an oft-quoted passage in the Talmud (*Berakhot* 17a) the saints in the *World to Come are said to bask in the radiance of the *Shekhinah.

The symbol of light is drawn on repeatedly in the Kabbalah. The name Zohar for the classical work of the Kabbalah means 'Illumination'. The *Sefirot are described in terms of lights flashing, being reflected, producing *holy sparks, and the like. It is important to appreciate, however, that the Kabbalists are thinking of the spiritual sources of light. The Italian Kabbalist Joseph Ergas (1685–1710) is more rationalistic than many others, yet seems to be expressing the generally accepted Kabbalistic view when he writes (*Shomer Emunim* 2: 11): 'There are many who think of God as a great, pure, refined light, and the like, because they think that this is not to describe Him in corporeal terms. But this is the most extreme error and confusion. For although light is the most ethereal of all tangible things, it is still material. And there is nothing which can be imagined which is not an image of a material thing.'

Edwin Bevan, *Symbolism and Belief* (London, 1962), 111–33.

**Lilith** Queen of the demons, consort of Samael, the demon king. The word *lilith* occurs in the verse: 'Wildcats shall meet hyenas, goat-demons shall greet each other, there too the lilith shall repose and find herself a resting place' (Isaiah 34: 14). In the context Lilith seems to be the Assyrian Lilitu, a wind-spirit with long hair and wings. But in the Talmud the name is connected with the Hebrew word *lailah* ('night') and Lilith is a demon who is abroad at night. Later still, especially in the Kabbalah, Lilith becomes the demonic queen. In legends found in the later Midrashim Lilith is associated with Adam, either as Adam's demonic wife or as his original wife, created, like him but unlike Eve, from the dust of the ground. Lilith has designs on Eve's children and *amulets were written for women in childbirth to protect them from her evil designs. Some Jewish *feminists have adopted Lilith, the more aggressive and less docile wife of Adam, ad their heroine and have published a magazine called *Lilith*.

Joshua Trachtenberg, *Jewish Magic and Superstition* (New York, 1970), see index, 'Lilit'.

**Literature, Religious** The *Pentateuch and the other books of the *Bible are the sacred books *par excellence* for the Jewish religion although, traditionally, the Pentateuch was not treated as a human composition at all and the other biblical books were also acknowledged as being the product, in varying degrees, of divine *inspiration. Yet while the Bible was studied chiefly for its religious message and was not held to be like any other literature, the medieval biblical commentators, Abraham *Ibn Ezra, *Kimhi, and *Abravanel point to the stylistic elements in the Bible, treating it, to some extent at least, as if it were a literary work and adapting for this purpose the Rabbinic saying: 'The Torah speaks in the language of men.' The books of the *Apocrypha, on the other hand, whatever their literary value, were excluded from the canon of sacred Scripture because they were not held to be inspired works. The consensus at work in the Jewish community of believers decided that these books and works such as those of *Philo of Alexandria were undoubtedly religious works, in the sense that they were composed by religious men with a religious aim, but they were not held to belong to sacred, inspired literature. These works were never used as part of the synagogue *liturgy and Philo was not even mentioned at all in Jewish writings until the sixteenth century. The clear distinction between form and content in a book was continued throughout Jewish history. A book was judged by what its author had to say, rarely by the way he said it.

The *Septuagint, the Greek translation of the Bible, was largely unknown to Jews until modern times. The *Targum, the Aramaic translation (Targumim, 'translations', would be better, since there is more than one), took its place early on as a companion to Scripture and is printed together with the text in most editions of the Hebrew Bible. Among the standard commentators to the Bible, in addition to those mentioned above, are: *Rashi, *Rashbam, *Nahmanides, *Bahya *Ibn Asher, *Gersonides, and *Sforno in the pre-modern period, *Mendelssohn and his Biur, S. D. *Luzzatto, Samson Raphael *Hirsch, and J. H. *Hertz in the modern period. All these, in greater or lesser degree, belong in the traditional camp. From the nineteenth century onwards, the Bible had been studied objectively and a host of scholarly works on it have been produced by Jews. It is a moot point whether these many works can be said to be religious literature, since their authors claim, rightly or wrongly, that they engage in their task without any religious bias, simply studying the Bible as they would any other great literary work. These works of modern scholarship do, however, have important implications for the Jewish religion (see BIBLICAL CRITICISM).

Second only to the Bible (first, so far as *authority is concerned) is the Rabbinic literature: Mishnah, Talmud, and Midrash. The Mishnah was edited by Rabbi *Judah the Prince around the year 200 CE; the Jerusalem Talmud around the year 400 CE; the Babylonian Talmud around the year 500 CE; and the numerous Midrashim from this period down to the tenth–twelfth centuries CE. Commentaries to the Jerusalem Talmud and the Midrashim were not compiled in the early period, when the attention of scholars was given almost entirely to the Babylonian Talmud. The standard medieval commentators to the Babylonian Talmud are Rashi and the *Tosafot but to the present day commentaries and super-commentaries to this gigantic work have been and are being published. *Alfasi's great digest of the Babylonian Talmud belongs both to Talmud commentary and to the *codification literature. The other standard *Codes, are: the *Mishneh Torah* of Maimonides; the Tur of *Jacob ben Asher, and the *Shulḥan Arukh* of Joseph *Karo. The *Responsa literature is immense, the majority being the work of outstanding Halakhists replying to questions addressed to them; these replies were later collected to be published in separate volumes. Numerous commentaries were compiled over the ages on the Codes. It is customary to divide Halakhic authors, according to their particular aim, into commentators and codifiers, although the two often overlap. Rashi, for example, is chiefly a commentator but sometimes appears as a codifier. Solomon Ibn *Adret wrote many hundreds of Responsa but he also compiled standard commentaries to the Talmud.

Among the most influential works of the medieval philosophical literature are: *Saadiah Gaon's *Beliefs and Opinions*; *Judah Halevi's *Kuzari*; Maimonides' *Guide of the Perlexed*; *Gersonides *Wars of the Lord*; and *Crescas's *Light of the Lord*. Although such works are generally treated in the histories as works of philosophy, they are, in reality, theological works, employing reason in support and interpretation of a faith their authors already possessed. A modern thinker like the neo-Kantian Hermann *Cohen, on the other hand, works as a pure philosopher, although he by no means hides his sympathy for Judaism as the faith of his fathers.

Halakhic and philosophical literature was

produced by and for the few prepared to grapple with these difficult subjects. The moralistic literature, on the other hand, appealed to the masses as well as the élite. The best-known of the moralistic works and the most popular are: *Bahya, Ibn Pakudah's *Duties of the Heart*; The *Sefer Hasidim* produced in the circle of the *Saints of Germany; *Luzzatto's *Path of the Upright*; and the works produced by followers of the *Musar movement in the nineteenth and twentieth centuries. Collections of sermons (see PREACHING) were also widely read for instruction and edification and fall under the heading of moralistic literature.

Kabbalistic literature is also an élitist affair, produced by and for devotees of this 'secret science'. The *Bahir, an early Kabbalistic work, is less well known than the classical work of the Kabbalah, the *Zohar. For the Kabbalists, the Zohar takes its place beside the Bible and the Talmud as one of the three most sacred books of the Jewish religion. Among other significant Kabbalistic works are those of *Cordovero and the school of Isaac *Luria. The Hasidic movement (see *Hasidism) produced a vast literature in which Kabbalistic terminology is employed but used to further Hasidic doctrine. It is possible to mention only a few of the Hasidic works considered as classical statements of their theological position by all Hasidim. These are: *Jacob Joseph of Pulonnoye's *Toledot*; *Dov Baer of Mezhirech's *Maggid Devarav Le-Yaakov*; *Shneur Zalman of Liady's *Tanya*; *Levi Yitzhak of Berditchev's *Kedushat Levi*; and *Nahman of Bratslav's *Likkutey Moharan*. In addition to the Hasidic works of doctrine there are numerous collections of Hasidic tales about the masters.

Religious *poetry was composed by Judah Halevi, Ibn *Gabirol, and many others, some of their poems later being incorporated into the *liturgy. The standard Prayer Book, the *Siddur*, and the Festival Prayer Book, the *Mahzor*, contain hymns and prayers compiled over many centuries. In some editions of the Prayer Book there are notes containing brief instructions regarding the laws of *prayer and detailed expositions of the words of the prayers. (see also BOOKS; CENSORSHIP; HISTORY.)

Meyer Waxman, *A History of Jewish Literature*, 5 vols (South Brunswick, NJ, 1960).
Israel Zinberg, *A History of Jewish Literature*, trans. Bernard Martin, 12 vols (Cleveland and London, 1972–8).

**Liturgy** The order of the daily, Sabbath, and festival services. Scholarly investigation into the historical development of the liturgy began with the *Jüdische Wissenschaft school, especially by Leopold *Zunz and the early Reformers, the latter with an axe to grind. The Reformers wished to build their new orders of service around the traditional liturgy, rejecting whatever they considered to be outmoded, such as prayers for the restoration of the sacrifices and Israel's return to the Holy Land, and retaining some of the older forms while adapting them to what they saw as the new requirements. Among the outstanding historians of the liturgy in a more objective manner in the twentieth century were: Ismar Elbogen, Joseph Heinemann, Naftali Wieder, and Jakob Petruchowski. These scholars have skilfully traced the growth of the liturgy in general and the particular liturgies of various communities from the earliest period down to the present day.

At the core of the synagogue liturgy, dating from Talmudic times, are the *Amidah, the *Shema and its special benedictions, and the *reading of the Torah and the *Haftarah. Other prayers and *benedictions, some found in the Talmud but often only as individual songs and petitions, were added until the first *prayer books were compiled in the Geonic period. Other prayers and hymns and even passages from the Halakhah of the Talmud were added from time to time. The *Lekhah Dodi' poem, for instance, was composed by Solomon Alkabetz in the sixteenth century. The growth of the liturgy was never determined by anything as official as a synod of Rabbis but grew organically out of the customs of the various praying communities, so that a number of liturgies developed around the essential core as found in the Talmud. The Ashkenazi and Sephardi rites are the best known, but there are also Italian, Yemenite, and other rites. As noted above, Reform Judaism created its own forms of worship as did Conservative Judaism, the latter with only a very few departures from the traditional Prayer Book.

Stefan C. Reif, *Judaism and Hebrew Prayer: New Perspectives on Jewish Liturgical History* (Cambridge, 1993).

**Longevity** Long life is the blessing promised in a number of biblical passages (e.g. Exodus

20: 12; Deuteronomy 11: 21; 22: 7). Moses is said to have been 120 years of age when he died (Deuteronomy 34: 7) and the common, jocular Jewish blessing is: 'May you live for 120 years.' Another common blessing is to live long enough to see children and grandchildren engaging in the study and practice of the Torah. Statistics are not available of how long people lived in ancient times but, according to the Psalmist (Psalms 90: 10) the normal span of life was 70 years and, by reason of special strength, 80 years. Abraham *Ibn Ezra has an interesting comment on the verse which states that a priest may not come into contact with a corpse unless it is of his mother or his father (Leviticus 21: 1–2). Ibn Ezra remarks that the mother is mentioned before the father because females usually do not live as long as males. Whatever the situation in twelfth-century Spain, statistics now show that women generally have a longer life span than men.

**Love and Fear of God** In Jewish thought the love and fear of God are often understood as complementing one another. Fear without love can easily result in a too rigorous and ultimately stultifying approach to the religious life. Love without fear can just as easily degenerate into sheer sentimentalism. C. S. Lewis once remarked that some people do not want a Father in Heaven but a Grandfather in Heaven—a kindly, senile Deity who lets everyone off the hook. As it has been expressed homiletically, neither the excessively sour nor the excessively sweet, neither leaven nor honey, are acceptable as an offering on the Lord's altar (Leviticus 2: 11). And as the *Baal Shem Tov is reported to have said: 'Love and fear are the two wings with which the soul flies aloft.'

*The Love of God*

The great biblical text for the love of God is: 'You shall love the Lord your God with all your heart and with all your soul and with all your might' (Deuteronomy 6: 5). 'All your heart' in this context refers less to the emotions than to the mind: in the biblical idiom the intellect is located in the heart, the inner aspect of the human personality. 'With all your soul' means 'with all your being'; the Hebrew *nefesh*, translated as 'soul', really refers in the Bible to what we would call the person rather than the soul. The meaning of the verse is attachment to God without reservation. It speaks of what Paul

Tillich calls 'ultimate concern'. Tillich, in fact, quotes this verse, at the beginning of his *Dynamics of Faith* (London, 1957), as the most powerful expression in the Bible of 'ultimate concern'. But in early Rabbinic thought the love of God is understood less as an attitude of mind or as an emotional response than as advocating a course of action. The Rabbinic Midrash known as Sifre (see MIDRASH), for example, has the following comment on the verse: 'Take to heart these instructions with which I charge you this day' (Deuteronomy 6: 6). 'Why is this said? Because it is said: "You shall love the Lord your God with all your heart" and I do not know in what way God is to be loved, therefore it says: "Take to heart these instructions with which I charge you this day." Take these to heart and in this way you will come to recognise God and cleave to His ways.' In this passage, typical of the Rabbinic emphasis on doing the will of God, on the deed, love is understood to mean the practice of the precepts and the study of the Torah. This leads to, and, in a sense is identified with, the 'recognition' of God and attachment to His laws. There are passages in the Rabbinic literature which do speak of the love of God as an intense longing for God's nearness. But the main emphasis in the Rabbinic literature is on love as expressed in the deed.

The medieval thinkers, on the other hand, *Saadiah, *Bahya Ibn Pakudah, *Maimonides, and the Kabbalists, do place the emphasis on the mystical love of God. Maimonides devotes the opening chapters of his *Mishneh Torah* to an account of the marvels of the created universe, in the course of which he remarks (*Yesodey Ha-Torah*, 2. 2): 'How does man come to love and fear God? No sooner does man reflect on His deeds and on His great and marvellous creatures, seeing in them His incomparable and limitless wisdom, than he is moved to love and to praise and to glorify and he has an intense desire to know the great Name. As David said: "My soul thirsts for God, for the living God" [Psalms 42: 3].' The Kabbalists not infrequently use erotic symbolism for the love of man for God, this being compared to human love between a man and a woman, but the pure love of God is often described without any erotic overtones. The Zohar (iii. 267a) understands the love of God to mean that the one who loves is ready to sacrifice everything he has and even life itself in his love for the Creator: 'One who loves God is crowned with loving-kindness on all sides and does loving-kindness throughout, sparing neither his person nor his money.' In Hasidism the love of God generally means completely disinterested service of God with joy in the heart. Tales are told of a number of Hasidic masters who believed that they had forfeited their right to heavenly bliss. Becoming aware of this they declared that now they would have the opportunity of serving and loving God without any thought of self, not even that of the self enjoying the nearness of God for ever.

There is thus no single Jewish understanding of the concept of the love of God. On the whole, two distinct tendencies emerge. On the one hand, there are Jewish teachers, represented particularly in the Rabbinic tradition, who prefer to speak of the love of God in terms of the practical details of the religious life. For them, to study the Torah and keep its precepts *is* the love of God. On the other hand, there are those who understand the love of God in its mystical sense of intense longing for the nearness of God and for communion with Him. But even this latter group of teachers emphasize the great difficulties in the way of attainment of their ideal and teach that in its highest reaches it is only for a few very rare souls.

### The Fear of God

From the many references in the Bible to both the love and the fear of God, without any clear distinction being made between the two, it would seem, as many biblical scholars suggest, that the two are essentially identical with an intense relationship with God, especially as realized in high ethical conduct. The very expression 'the fear of God' often refers to an extraordinary degree of piety and moral worth. Of the Hebrew midwives who defied Pharaoh's order for them to kill the infants the verse says: 'The midwives, fearing God, did not do as the king of Egypt had told them; they let the boys live' (Exodus 1: 17). Job is described as 'wholehearted and upright, and one that feared God, and shunned evil' (Job 1: 1). In the Rabbinic literature, the usual expression for the fear of God is *yirat shamayyim*, 'the fear of Heaven', by which is meant the determination to carry out God's will and not to commit any of the sins. *Nahmanides understands the positive precepts of the Torah—commands to do this or that—as based on the love of God and the

negative precepts—not to do this or that—as based on the fear of God. Love is the motivation for action where this is demanded. Fear is the motivation for inaction where this is demanded.

In medieval Jewish thought a distinction is drawn between two kinds of fear: fear of punishment and fear in the presence of the exalted majesty of God. The latter comes very close to the feelings of awe and dread described in Rudolf Otto's phrase as the 'numinous'. *Bahya, Ibn Pakudah (*Duties of the Heart*, Gate 10, ch. 10) believes that only the second type of fear can lead to the pure love of God and is a necessary condition to it. One who attains to this degree will neither fear nor love other than the Creator. (A harsh saying this, reminiscent of George Orwell's 'You cannot love both God and man'.) Bahya relates that a God-fearing man slept in the desert. When he was asked by a 'saint': 'Are you not afraid of lions that you sleep in this place?' the man replied: 'I am ashamed that God should see that I am afraid of anything apart from Him.' The medieval thinkers, as Orthodox Jews, believed in *reward and punishment. It is not that they rejected the fear of punishment but that they believed this to be inferior to the higher fear of which they spoke. The Zohar (i. 11b) remarks: 'There are three types of fear; two of these have no proper foundation but the third is the main foundation of fear. A man may fear God in order that his sons may live and not die or because he is afraid of some punishment to be visited on his person or his wealth and because of it he is in constant fear. But it follows that such a man's fear has no proper foundation. There is another man who fears God because he is terrified of punishment in the next world, in dread of Hell. Both these types of fear do not belong to the main foundation of fear and to its root meaning. But the fear which does have a proper foundation is when a man fears his Master because He is the great and mighty Ruler, the Foundation and Root of all worlds and all before Him are accounted as nothing, as it is said: "And all the inhabitants of the earth are reputed as nothing" [Daniel 4: 32].'

Hasidic thought is generally free of references to the fear of hell-fire. In Hasidism the idea is often repeated that the fear of God has to be attained by human effort but the love of God is given to man by divine grace once he has attained fear. *Levi Yitzhak of Berditchev introduces into the whole concept of fear the Hasidic doctrine of *annihilation of selfhood. In the lower fear a man is necessarily aware of himself since he dwells on his sinfulness. But in the higher fear a man is so overawed by God's majesty that he has no self-awareness at all, not even a sense of his own unworthiness. In the *Musar movement the emphasis is placed on the lower fear. Taking a sombre view of human nature, the Musarists say that only simple reflection on the severe punishments in store for the transgressor can penetrate man's stony heart. It is somewhat surprising that in modern Jewish theological thinking there is very little on the fear of God. This is no doubt partly because of the move from a God-centred to a man-centred universe and partly because of the unwholesome emotions the concept of fear is said to generate. But it is an odd religious outlook that can blithely ignore, for all its difficulties, such a deeply rooted concept as the fear of God.

Louis Jacobs, 'The Love of God' and 'The Fear of God', in his *A Jewish Theology* (London, 1973), 152–73, 174–82.

**Love of Neighbour** The biblical injunction to love the neighbour occurs in the Holiness Code in the book of Leviticus. Readers of the Bible in English are familiar with the rendering of the King James Version: 'Thou shalt not avenge, nor bear any grudge against the children of thy people, but thou shalt love thy neighbour as thyself' (Leviticus 19: 18). The latter part of the verse has often been detached from the beginning as well as the 'but', so that among both Jews and Christians the injunction is read simply as 'love thy neighbour as thyself', meaning, so it has been understood, that man is obliged to love a neighbour as much as he loves himself, with the result that countless worthy people have been possessed with powerful guilt-feelings for failing to live up to this unrealistic expectation. Is it really possible to love a neighbour as one loves oneself? Is not the whole concept of 'love', by definition, directed to another, and do people, except those with split personalities, love themselves? Moreover, can love, an emotional condition, be coerced by divine command? A close examination of the passage yields a different understanding according to which the verse, in its context, is far more realistic and its goal more attainable than in the conventional understanding.

To appreciate what the verse actually says, the end should not be detached from the beginning and the 'but' should not be ignored. When the verse is read as a whole the meaning is clear: it states that instead of taking vengeance against the neighbour and bearing him a grudge, one should act lovingly to him. In spite of the fact, the verse is saying, that he has behaved badly towards you, you should not be tempted to retaliate but should behave decently towards him. Futhermore, the Hebrew *le-reakha* means not simply 'thy neighbour' but '*to* thy neighbour', And the Hebrew *kamokha* means '*who* is like thyself', the meaning being: behave lovingly towards him because he is like yourself, that is, with the same rights and feeling that you have. Thus in the original context the verse means: even when someone has behaved badly towards you, try to overcome your desires for revenge but rather behave lovingly towards him because, after all, he, too, is a human being and a member of the covenant people as you are and therefore entitled to be treated as you yourself wish to be treated.

As in other areas, however, the plain, original meaning of the text is not necessarily the meaning it bears in the long tradition of Jewish life and thought. In that tradition, the second clause is taken on its own as a command to love the neighbour as the self, even though it is the outcome of the love in deeds that is stressed rather than the loving feelings and emotions. Maimonides (*Mishneh Torah, Deot*, 6. 3) formulates it as follows: 'It is a religious duty incumbent upon every man to love every person in Israel as his own self, as it is said: "thou shalt love thy neighbour as thyself." It is necessary, therefore, to sing his praises and to have care for his money just as a man has care for his own money and wishes to be respected himself. But whoever gains respect through the degradation of his neighbour has no share in the World to Come.' Maimonides clearly understands 'as thyself' as qualifying 'love'; a man must love his neighbour as much as himself. Yet the meaning of this love, according to Maimonides, is expressed not in emotions but in deeds that demonstrate solicitude for the neighbour by singing his praises and having regard for his wealth and physical well-being.

Maimonides considers the neighbour who is to be 'loved' to be a fellow Jew. The verse itself speaks, in fact, of 'the children of thy people'. It has to be said that, on the whole, in the Jewish tradition, while there are many injunctions against treating *Gentiles in an unfair or unworthy manner and while there are demands that poor Gentiles be supported by the Jewish community, the golden rule to love the neighbour applies only to the neighbour who is a Jew. A number of Jewish teachers, however, have held that, whatever the restrictions in the context, the verse has to be applied to Gentiles as well as to Jews. In the Kabbalah the idea is found of the people of Israel as a mystical corporate body and hence the verse does refer only to members of this corpus. As *Cordovero puts it, 'love thy neighbour as thyself: because thy neighbour *is* thyself'; no Jew is an island, so to speak.

Generally speaking, the tradition demands only that a man should care for his neighbour as he cares for himself, not that he should be mindful of his neighbour's interests to the same degree as of his own. When there is a conflict of interests, the normal Jewish view is to give preference to the individual's own needs. The Talmud (*Bava Metzia* 33a) quotes two sayings of the early third-century teacher, Rabbi Judah, in the name of his teacher, Rav, on the question of whose needs are to be treated as paramount, those of the neighbour or those of the self. One saying has it that a man's own needs take precedence over the needs of others. This is derived from the verse: 'save that there should be no poor among you' (Deuteronomy 15: 4), understood to mean: you yourself have the prior right to prevent poverty coming to you. But the second saying adds that anyone who always insists on his rights in order to avoid poverty will find that his attitude is self-defeating and he will eventually become poor, naturally so since no one will wish to have too many business dealings with a man who always pursues only his own interests before those of others. And the tradition knows of the extraordinary magnanimity of the *saints who generally prefer to give to others than to keep things for themselves. As it is expressed in Ethics of the Fathers (5. 10): 'There are four types among men. One who says: "What is mine is mine and what is thine is thine", is a usual type of person, but some say this is the type of Sodom [the men of Sodom were said to have nothing to do with others and kept greedily to themselves]. "What is mine is thine and what is thine is mine", is an ignorant type of person. "What is thine is thine and and what is mine

is thine", is a saintly type of person. "What is thine is mine and what is mine is mine" is a wicked type of person.'

J. H. Hertz, 'Thou Shalt Love thy Neighbour as Thyself', in his *The Pentateuch and Haftorahs* (London, 1960), 563–4.
Louis Jacobs, 'Loving the Neighbour', in his *Religion and the Individual: A Jewish Perspective* (Cambridge, 1992), 25–30.

**Lubavitch** The branch of the *Habad tendency in Hasidism with many thousands of followers all over the Jewish world. The second Rebbe of Habad, *Dov Baer, settled in the Russian town of Lubavitch, after which this group of Hasidim is called. The sixth master, Rabbi Joseph Isaac Schneerson (1880–1950), settled in Brooklyn, USA, in 1940, where he was succeeded by his son-in-law, Rabbi Menahem Mendel Schneerson (1902–1994), the seventh Lubavitcher Rebbe, who established a worldwide network of educational institutions and a major publishing house. The original emphasis of Habad was on the intellectual approach to Hasidism but the Lubavitcher Hasidim in the USA and in countries under their influence employ highly emotional methods in order to win souls, with followers urging passers-by for instance, to put on *tefillin* and with vans from which the message is proclaimed through loudspeakers. The Rebbe's discourses at his headquarters in Brooklyn were broadcast on radio and television to followers and sympathizers in other parts of the Jewish world. Lubavitch also cultivated a high profile by erecting *Hanukkah menorahs in prominent public places. The result of these activities has been that many Jews, Orthodox and non-Orthodox, have either embraced the Lubavitch way entirely or have become, at least, fellow-travellers, admirers of the group's educational activities while drawing the line at going all the way to become Hasidim. Many of Rabbi Menahem Mendel's followers hailed him as the *Messiah, and went about singing in public places: 'We want the Messiah now', in the hope that God would reveal to the Rebbe his true identity as the hoped-for redeemer, to the consternation of most of the other Hasidim and traditional Orthodox Rabbis. The latter were not slow to point out the dangers of unbridled Messianic fervour, especially when the Messiah is identified with a particular, known leader. The Rebbe had a general education in his youth, studying at the University of Berlin and at the Sorbonne, but Lubavitch had a negative attitude towards secular studies unless they are pursued in order to earn a living.

Lubavitch rejected totally the theory of *evolution on the grounds that this seems to run counter to the creation narrative in Genesis and if a 'day' in Genesis is taken to mean a vast period of time, this would tend to reduce the significance of the Sabbath, the seventh 'day' on which God rested (see FUNDAMENTALISM). As for the fossil evidence, the Rebbe remarked that there is no reason not to suppose that God created fossil remains as He created everything else, in a single creative act.

A much-discussed question is the attitude of Lubavitch to the State of Israel. The Rebbe never actually set foot in Israel (the Hasidim who are gripped with Messianic fervour declared that he awaited his triumphant entry into Jerusalem as the Messiah) but the Lubavitcher are active in Israeli politics and the Rebbe was opposed to any surrender of the territories occupied and settled after the Yom Kippur War, since these lie within the traditional boundaries of the land of Israel and have now been returned to the Jewish people by divine providence.

*Challenge: An Encounter With Lubavitch-Chabad* (London, 1970).

**Lulav** see TABERNACLES.

**Luria, Isaac** The foremost Kabbalist after the Zoharic authors (see ZOHAR), founder of the Lurianic *Kabbalah (1534–72), known as the Ari ('the Lion') and his disciples as Gurey Ha-Ari ('the Lion's Cubs'). Legendary biographies of Luria convey little reliable information about his life. It seems that he was born in Jerusalem but, orphaned from his father at an early age, he was brought up in Cairo by his mother's brother, Mordecai Francis, a wealthy tax farmer. Luria received a good Talmudic education and also studied the Zohar which had recently been printed (Mantua, 1558–60; Cremona, 1560). At the age of 15 he married his cousin, Mordecai Francis's daughter. It is said that for seven years he lived in a little cottage on the banks of the Nile, where he meditated on Kabbalistic themes, returning to his home only for the Sabbath. The Kabbalists, aware of the unconventional and in some respects radical nature of Luria's ideas, believed

that he was visited by the prophet *Elijah who imparted to him new Kabbalistic mysteries, linking in this way the Lurianic system to the Zoharic. In the year 1569, Luria went to Safed where he became a member of the mystic circle around *Cordovero and soon after became the leading light among the Safed Kabbalists, attracting a small number of chosen disciples, of whom the chief was Hayyim *Vital. Luria wrote very little himself (a few of his poems were incorporated into Kabbalistic prayer books) but his teachings were recorded by his disciples, especially Vital, and the Lurianic scheme is described in elaborate detail in the various works known as 'the Writings of the Ari'.

*The Lurianic Kabbalah*

For Luria, living not long after the expulsion of the Jews from Spain, the idea of exile and Messianic redemption was highly significant, forming the main thrust of his thought. According to the Zohar, the whole creative process begins with the emanation of the *Sefirot from *En Sof. In Luria, the process begins at an earlier stage with the act known as Tzimtzum ('Withdrawal'). In order to allow for the emergence of the Sefirot and through them the emergence of all created things, En Sof 'withdraws from Himself into Himself' to leave a primordial 'empty space' into which the Sefirot, Space and Time as we know these, and all worlds, came into being. The idea of divine emanation, found in the Zoharic doctrine of the Sefirot, and that of divine withdrawal, basically contradictory though they are, become harmonized in the Lurianic system. This is achieved by postulating two stages in the process of God's self-revelation: first withdrawal and then emanation. The first step in the process was God's withdrawal, as a result of which the 'empty space' was created. When a line of the divine light later re-entered the 'empty space', as it had to do for the purpose of creation, it did so in the form of *Adam Kadmon, 'Primordial Man', from which the Sefirot emanated. The process as a whole is now seen as one of both withdrawal and emanation, of God withdrawing into Himself in order to allow finite creatures to exist and then sending forth the divine light in weaker form to sustain them. The drama of Israel's exile and redemption is thus provided with a cosmic mirror.

The doctrine runs further that lights stream from Adam Kadmon to produce containers or vessels for the Sefirot which have to emerge from potentiality to actuality. These vessels are formed by the divine light beaming forth and then bouncing back again. Once the vessels have been formed, further lights stream forth from the 'eyes' of Adam Kadmon to produce the lights of the Sefirot in the vessels. But this further light is too powerful for the vessels of the lower Sefirot to hold and there takes place the cosmic catastrophe known as 'the breaking of the vessels'. These vessels now have to be reconstituted in the form of Partzufim ('Configurations'). Since, after the breaking of the vessels, the Sefirot on their own are too weak to contain the divine light, they have to be reformed in a manner in which they can assist and strengthen one another. A Partzuf consists of an arrangement of all ten Sefirot around one of their number. There are five Partzufim in all, each containing all the Sefirot but with its own special emphasis, so to speak. What was formerly in disarray is now brought into harmony, but not complete harmony. It is the task of man to assist the Partzufim so as to bring about the Tikkun ('Rectification'). Moreover, as a result of the breaking of the vessels, *holy sparks have been scattered throughout creation and are held in thrall to the demonic forces, the *Kélipot*. All human deeds have cosmic significance in that they can either help or hinder the process of the Tikkun and the rescue of the holy sparks.

Exile and redemption, withdrawal and re-entry, are thus repeated in the whole process from the original act of Tzimtzum, through the beaming back and forth of the lights of Adam Kadmon, to the breaking and reconstitution of the vessels and the Tikkun provided by the Partzufim. It is not hard to see why the Lurianic scheme exercised a powerful hold on the Jewish imagination. In the Lurianic writings the extremely complex relationships between the Partzufim and the methods by which man helps in the Tikkun are all spelled out. The system was responsible for new Kabbalistic rituals and 'intentions' (see *Kavvanah), some of which found their way into the standard Codes.

The Lurianic Kabbalists, and Luria himself, did not see the system as new and original but as the authentic interpretation of the Zohar. After Luria, the Zohar itself was interpreted in Lurianic terms. Cordovero's massive works, on the other hand, seek to explain the Zohar on its own terms. Seeking to harmonize the two systems, the later Kabbalists claim that the two

are really one but are viewed as two different aspects. Luria describes the world of the Tikkun, Cordovero the pre-Tikkun world.

Later Lurianic Kabbalists were divided on how the doctrine of Tzimtzum is to be understood. The Italian Kabbalist Joseph Ergas (1685–1730) insists that since En Sof has neither image nor form, such as the form of a surrounding circle with an empty space in the middle, into which a line of light is injected, Tzimtzum is only a parable, otherwise En Sof would have an image. Ergas's contemporary, Immanuel Hai Ricchi (1688–1743) attacks Ergas. Since the whole purpose of the Tzimtzum idea, argues Ricchi, is to explain the emergence of the finite from the Infinite, the purpose is defeated unless the doctrine means what it says. If, as Ergas suggests, Tzimtzum is only a parable, it must follow that there is no real withdrawal and God is, therefore, present in material things, even in the unworthy and the evil. Rather than accept such a conclusion, Ricchi is prepared to interpret the doctrine to mean that God really did withdraw Himself and it is only His providence, not his true being, which extends to the 'empty space'. As Ricchi puts it somewhat crudely: 'It is one thing to say that the king observes from his window the filth outside but quite another to say that the king is himself immersed in filth.' Generally, in Hasidism, especially in the *Habad version, Tzimtzum is not understood literally. This was a main source of contention between the Hasidim and the *Mitnaggedim, the Hasidim adopting the doctrine of *panentheism.

Gershom G. Scholem, 'Isaac Luria and his School', in his *Major Trends in Jewish Mysticism* (London, 1955), 244–86.

**Luzzatto, Moses Hayyim** Italian Kabbalist, poet, and religious thinker (1707–47). Luzzatto was born in Padua. His father, a wealthy merchant, saw to it that his son received a good traditional Jewish education and a sound grounding in Latin, Italian, and the general culture of his day. In all his writings there is a remarkable blending of the two cultures. He composed, for example, allegorical dramas in the Italian style but in elegant Hebrew and has often been hailed as the father of modern Hebrew literature. A mystic, who claimed to have received, like Joseph *Karo, a heavenly mentor, he attracted around him a group of young enthusiasts with whom he studied the Kabbalah. These followers, and, possibly, Luzzatto himself, believed that he would be the longed-for Messiah. His activities were viewed with suspicion by the Rabbinic authorities and he was compelled to hide his Kabbalistic writings and to move to Amsterdam, where he earned his living as a diamond-polisher. He journeyed to the land of Israel in 1743 and died there at the early age of 40. His grave can still be seen in Tiberias.

Luzzatto was a prolific author, compiling works on theology, the Kabbalah, and Talmudic methodology. His Kabbalistic works are in the rationalistic vein in which the the Kabbalistic concepts are demythologized, to some extent at least. Luzzatto's major work is the *Mesillat Yesharim (Path of the Upright)*. In this work Luzzatto provides a step-by-step account of how the ladder of saintliness is to be scaled until the devotee attains to the *holy spirit. Luzzatto was held in the highest esteem by both the Hasidim and the *Mitnaggedim. The *Path of the Upright* became one of the most popular works of Jewish devotional literature, especially among the adherents of the *Musar movement. Luzzatto states in the introduction to the *Path of the Upright* that his aim is to demonstrate that saintliness is a science that can only be appreciated by the learned.

Moses Hayyim Luzzatto, *Mesillat Yesharim: The Path of the Upright*, trans. and ed. Mordecai M. Kaplan (Philadelphia, 1936).

**Luzzatto, Samuel David**  Italian historian, theologian, and biblical exegete (1800–65), known, after the initial letters of his Hebrew name, as Shadal. Shadal was one of the pioneers of the *Jüdische Wissenschaft movement, contributing many studies in Jewish history to learned periodicals and producing a critical edition of the Italian Prayer Book. An opponent of the *Kabbalah, he wrote a critique of this mystical lore in which he argued against the traditional ascription of the Zohar to the second-century teacher, Rabbi Simeon ben *Yohai. Shadal was also critical of Maimonides' attempt to interpret Judaism in the light of Aristotelian philosophy, which he dubbed Atticism. He was particularly severe on Maimonides' espousal of the Greek golden mean. The disciples of Abraham are required to go to extremes in generosity. In 1829 Shadal was appointed Principal of the Rabbinic College in Padua where he influenced more than one generation of Italian Rabbis.

Although Shadal's work on the Bible is not uncritical, he was not averse to *textual* criticism, for example, he believed that Moses was the author of the Pentateuch (see BIBLICAL CRITICISM) and that the whole of the book of *Isaiah was the work of the prophet whose name it bears. He believed that to deny that a prophet can foretell events that would take place long after his time was to deny prophecy altogether. He was not bothered by the command to exterminate the Canaanites, including the little children, since it was God's will, and God does sometimes allow the death of little children. In Shadal's understanding of divine *providence, each human being is given an equal degree of happiness and frustration, which should all be accepted in faith and trust. In his personal life, Shadal was an observant Jew but with reservations regarding some of the details of observance as laid down in the Rabbinic tradition. Shadal's religious philosophy has had virtually no influence on Jewish life and thought but his scholarly works are still acknowledged to be of much value.

Morris B. Margolies, *Samuel David Luzzatto: Traditionalist Scholar* (New York, 1979).

# M

**Maccabees** The military heroes, the leader of whom was Judah the Maccabee, in the struggle against the Syrian king Antiochus Epiphanes in 168 BCE; their victory is celebrated on the festival of *Hanukkah. The story of these heroes is told in the first and second books of the Maccabees in the *Apocrypha. The meaning of the name Maccabees, first given to Judah and then applied to the whole group, is uncertain. The popular explanation is that the name is derived from a Hebrew word meaning a hammer, hence: 'the Hammerers'. The Maccabees were also called the Hasmoneans, a name of similar uncertain meaning but possibly from a word meaning 'chieftain'. From a number of indications in the Rabbinic literature, it would seem that the ancient Rabbis had an ambivalent, not to say hostile, attitude to the Hasmonean dynasty because of the Hellenizing tendencies (see HELLENISM) of its members. With the rise of *Zionism and the establishment of the State of Israel the Maccabees regained their popularity as the prototype of those who battle against the loss of Jewish identity.

**Machpelah, Cave of** The burial place acquired by the patriarch Abraham from Ephron the Hittite (Genesis 23). According to the biblical record, Abraham buried his wife Sarah in the Cave of Machpelah and eventually Abraham himself, Isaac and Rebecca, Jacob and Leah were buried there. According to legend, Adam and Eve are also buried in the Cave of Machpelah. The Cave of Machpelah in Hebron is still a place of pilgrimage for both Jews and Muslims: for the latter because of the central place Abraham occupies in *Islam (see ISHMAEL).

**Magen David** 'Shield of David', the familiar six-pointed star, consisting of two interlocking triangles, said to be the shape of King David's shield and now serving as the most popular Jewish symbol. From the historical point of view, while the device itself is very ancient, as one among other magical symbols, and while it features occasionally in some earlier Jewish records and on some very few communal buildings, it did not begin to assume universal significance as a typical Jewish symbol until as late as the nineteenth century when it began to be used on synagogue buildings in Western lands on the analogy of a cross on a church building; nor was it called the Shield of David before this time. Jewish *objets d'art* claimed by dealers to be older than the nineteenth century should, consequently, be viewed with a strong degree of suspicion if they have a Magen David. There is no doubt at all that the popularity of the Magen David in the twentieth century is due to its adoption by *Zionism as a symbol of Jewish nationality. The device is depicted on the blue and white Israeli flag. In late Kabbalistic sources, the supposed Shield of David is the *menorah, the true, ancient, specifically Jewish symbol. Nevertheless, the Magen David has been interpreted to suggest various philosophical ideas; for example, the two interlocking triangles, the one pointing upwards, the other downwards, are supposed to represent the divine reaching downwards and the human response upwards. This kind of interpretation is the basis of Franz *Rosenzweig's famous work *The Star of Redemption*. The Nazis forced Jews to wear a badge in the form of the Magen David, since when it has become, as a reaction among Jews everywhere, a special symbol of pride in belonging to the Jewish people.

Gershom Scholem, 'The Star of David: History of a Symbol', in his *The Messianic Idea in Judaism* (New York, 1971), 257–81.

**Magic and Superstition** There are numerous references to magical practices in the Torah. At the beginning of Moses' confrontation with Pharaoh, he engages in a conflict with Pharaoh's sorcerers in which he performs greater acts of magic than they are able to do (Exodus 7: 8–13). It is commanded that a witch be put to death (Exodus 22: 17). Israel is enjoined that when the people enter their land they are to reject all magical practices: 'Let no one be found among you who consigns his son or daughter to the fire, or who is an augur, a soothsayer, a diviner, a sorcerer, one who casts spells, or one who consults ghosts or familiar spirits, or one who inquires of the dead. For anyone who does such things is abhorrent to the Lord and it is because of these abhorrent things that the Lord your God is dispossessing them before you' (Deuteronomy 18: 9–12). There are discussions in the Talmud on the precise meaning of these examples of magic and divination and various additional superstitious practices are added to the list by the Talmudic Rabbis under the heading: 'The Ways of the Amorites', the Amorites being one of the seven nations referred to in the verse.

The medieval Jewish thinkers discussed the question of whether magic really works, the majority of them holding that from the biblical references it appears that witchcraft and similar practices do have a real effect. Magic works and is a real danger and that is why the Torah is so strict in banning it. Moreover, it is clear that the Talmudic Rabbis believed in the existence of *demons, the power of witches to do harm by spells, incantations to ward off evil, and the *evil eye. Maimonides and some few other rationalists, on the other hand, believe that magic has no power to do harm and has no effect other than a psychological one. Maimonides remarks that the Torah does not forbid magic because it is true but because it is false, and, while he records in his Code the Talmudic advice that it is permitted to utter an incantation even on the Sabbath on behalf of one who has been bitten by a snake, finds it necessary to add that the incantation does no more than provide psychological relief to the one who has been bitten. Similarly, Menahem *Meiri comments on the Talmudic reference to the harm done by things in even numbers— eating an even number of cakes or drinking an even number of cups of wine, for example— that the harm only results for one who believes in such matters and is purely psychological so that, as the Talmud itself implies, anyone who does not believe in 'pairs' need have no qualms. Yet a host of superstitious practices were the norm in medieval Jewry, especially among the German Jews. Moreover, practical Kabbalah consists in the employment of divine names and combinations of these for the purpose of manipulating nature. Evidently the Kabbalists draw a distinction between white and black magic. Many Jewish *customs, some of which found their way into the Codes, are based on pagan superstitions. There is thus considerable confusion on the whole matter and the line between forbidden magical and superstitious practices and those that are permitted is very finely and often indistinctly drawn (see AMU- LETS, ASTROLOGY, DREAMS, and GOLEM).

The theological question of how magic can possibly operate to frustrate the divine will bothered those thinkers who believed in its efficacy. Maimonides was not bothered at all since magic does not work at all. The question is implied in the Talmudic tale (*Hullin* 7b) of a witch who tried to cast a spell over the late second-century teacher, Rabbi Hanina; the latter said to her: 'Try as you will, you will not succeed in your attempts, for it is written: "There is none else beside Him" [Deuter- onomy 4: 35].' Yet the same passage in the Talmud concludes that this applies only to a saint like Rabbi Hanina. For lesser mortals magic can have a baneful effect even when this is contrary to the divine will. Even Maimonides, for all his stern opposition to magical practices, still permits (*Avodah Zarah* 11: 5) bibliomancy, opening the Bible at random so that a verse or verses on the page opened offers guidance for a course of action, on the grounds that it is only an 'indication' and does not really involve the kind of divination forbidden by the Torah.

Even after the rise of modern science, and greater knowledge of cause and effect, super- stitions were not entirely abandoned. The *Mitnaggedim accused the Hasidim of resort- ing to superstition in their reliance on the power of the Hasidic masters to avert evil and bring blessing by supernatural means.

Joshua Trachtenberg, *Jewish Magic and Superstition: A Study in Folk Religion* (New York, 1970).

**Maharal of Prague** Acronym for *M*orenu *Ha*rav *R*abbi *Laib*, 'Our Teacher Rabbi Leow', Talmudist, theologian, Rabbi of Prague (d. 1609). It is unfortunate that the Maharal is known chiefly as the creator of the *golem and that his grave is one of the tourist attractions in the city, since he was an original and influential thinker who deserves better than a reputation as a vulgar miracle-worker. In his thought Maharal was influenced by the Renaissance and the emerging new scientific picture of the universe. A prominent theme in his writings is, consequently, the role of man in the creation. Following Rabbinic teachings on this theme, the Maharal develops the idea that God created an incomplete universe which it is the task of humans to bring to completion. This applies even to the Torah, which is incomplete and requires to be applied by the sages of Israel through their deliberations. The benediction recited before studying the Torah is: 'Blessed art Thou who hath commanded us to busy ourselves with words of Torah.' Why not simply, asks Maharal, 'to study the Torah'? His reply is that to study the Torah implies that the complete truth of the Torah is readily available, so that all the student has to do is to study the given texts. This is not the case, since the student of the Torah is aware of the many problems, debates, and discussions on the meaning of the various texts. The student's obligation is to be involved in the process. He has to busy himself with the words of the Torah, to engage in the constant quest for the truth. For this reason Maharal was opposed to the dialectic method (*pilpul), since this method involves basically no more than an ingenious manipulation of the texts when what is required is a sincere effort to arrive at what the texts are really saying and, above all, implying. The Torah and, for that matter, the Talmudic literature, have an inner meaning which is in no way contrary to the new scientific picture of the universe. When, for instance, the Talmudic Rabbis say that an eclipse is caused by a failure to respect sages, they do not mean that this is the immediate cause of an eclipse. An eclipse is a natural phenomenon which can be calculated beforehand. The Rabbis are thinking rather of the cause of the cause, of why God created a world in which there are eclipses. He created such a world, the Rabbis are saying, because the light of the Torah is eclipsed when sages are treated with disrespect.

Maharal was a staunch defender of the Jewish people, the custodians of the Torah. Against Christian charges that Jews are all too ready to engage in controversy and are often cantankerous, Maharal suggests that this is an indication of Jewish superiority. Men of small intellectual and spiritual calibre all too readily give in when their opinions are challenged. Great men fight for their strongly held opinions which they do not readily surrender. Only abject slaves obey their masters unquestioningly. Jews are princes, aristocrats of the spirit.

There is a strong mystical tinge to Maharal's thought. He was obviously influenced by the Kabbalah but formulates his thought in such a way that his theories are presented in his own style without any direct reference to Kabbalistic terminology. His presentation in his voluminous works is far from systematic and it is often difficult to see the wood for the trees. This probably accounts for the comparative neglect of this original thinker. In the Przysucha school of Hasidism (see KOTSK) the writings of Maharal were highly regarded because they provided an unusual blend of both the mystical and the philosophical approaches to Judaism.

Byron L. Sherwin, *Mystical Theology and Social Dissent: The Life and Works of Judah Leow of Prague* (London, 1982).

**Mahzor** See PRAYER BOOK.

**Maimonides** Known, after the initial letters of his name (*R*abbi *M*oshe *B*en *M*aimon, 'Rabbi Moses son of Maimon') as Rambam, generally acknowledged to be the greatest Jewish thinker, Talmudist, and codifier in the Middle Ages (1135–1204). Maimonides was born in Cordoba where his father was a Dayyan, a judge. Maimonides was later proud to trace his descent from judge to judge back through many generations. When Maimonides was 13 years of age he left Spain together with his parents under threat of religious persecution to wander in various places, but eventually he settled in Fostat near Cairo in Egypt. There he became the leader of the Jewish community and in 1183, by which time he had acquired skills in medicine and had practised as a physician, he was appointed physician to Saladin's vizier (not to Saladin himself as is often thought). He lived all his life in an Islamic society and had little knowledge of Christian life and thought. Maimonides died in Egypt but his body was taken to be buried in the land of Israel, where his grave in Tiberias is still a place of pilgrimage. For a lengthy period Maimonides was supported by his brother David, a dealer in precious stones, but when David perished at sea Maimonides earned his living as a physician. He thus was able to spend years in close study of the traditional sources of Judaism, of which he had an amazing knowledge, as well as Greek philosophy in its Arabic garb. He had no languages other than Arabic and, of course, Hebrew and Aramaic.

Maimonides in his lifetime met with a degree of opposition on account of some of his views but the great divide between the Maimonists, who favoured the study of philosophy, and the anti-Maimonists, opposed to this study, did not come about until after his death. Followers of the sage hailed him as the great thinker who demonstrated that Greek philosophy is compatible with Jewish teaching. His opponents thought his ideas dangerous to Jewish faith. Maimonides became the inspiration for Jews throughout the ages who wished to have a faith based on reason. Among non-Jewish authors he influenced Aquinas and Islamic theologians.

Maimonides was a prolific author. Among his published works are: letters, *Responsa, medical treatises, and works on *Halakhah. But his three major works are: his commentary to the Mishnah, compiled in his youth; his gigantic Code of law, the *Mishneh Torah*, compiled in his middle age; and, his best-known work among non-Halakhists, the *Guide of the Perplexed*, compiled in his old age. There is an astonishing consistency about Maimonides: the works of his old age depart hardly at all from his youthful works. Medieval authors rarely changed their minds—a pity, perhaps.

*Commentary to the Mishnah*

Maimonides' Arabic commentary to the Mishnah is part commentary proper, elucidating the meaning of each Mishnah in the collection, part philosophical reflection. Occasionally Maimonides' comments are at variance with the explanations of the Mishnah given in the Talmud (the *Gemara), in the belief, evidently, that the Mishnah, like the Bible, can be interpreted on its own terms; although Maimonides never bases his later Halakhic decisions on anything other than the Talmud. His philosophical asides are significant as an early attempt at reconciling Greek philosophy with the Jewish tradition. For instance, he prefaces his comments to Ethics of the Fathers with eight short chapters in which he compares Greek ethical standards with those of the Talmudic Rabbis. His formulation of the thirteen *principles of the faith occurs in his commentary to tractate *Sanhedrin*, chapter 10, where he discusses the question of *dogmas in Judaism, referred to indirectly in this section of the Mishnah. In his introduction to the work he provides a history of the *Oral Torah and a discussion on the relationship between learning and practice in Judaism.

*The* Mishneh Torah

The *Mishneh Torah* ('Second to the Torah') is Maimonides' great Code of Jewish law, written, unlike the other two works considered here, in Hebrew, of which he was a superb master. The implications of the title are that the work contains all that it is necessary for the Jew to know of the Oral Torah as found in the Talmudic literature and is thus a supplement to the *Written Torah, the Bible. The whole legal system of Judaism is presented without reference to the numerous debates and discussions found in the Talmud. Maimonides never records the names of the debaters, only the final ruling as this appears in the Talmud. His older contemporary, Abraham ben David, known as the Rabad, is very critical of this methodology, arguing that Maimionides has reduced the openness and flexibility of the Talmudic Halakhah to a bare, uniform series of categorical decisions with no room for legal manœuvre. The Rabad is similarly critical of many other statements in the *Mishneh Torah* and his strictures accompany the text in most editions of the work. Later scholars called the *Mishneh Torah* the *Yad Ha-Ḥazakah* ('Strong Hand') adapting the verse: 'And for all the strong hand and awesome power that Moses [i.e. Moses Maimonides] displayed before all Israel' (Deuteronomy 34: 12). There is a pun here on the word *Yad*, which has the numerical value of 14, since the work is divided into fourteen books. Unlike other Codes, the *Mishneh Torah* does not only include practical law for the guidance of Jews after the destruction of the Temple but also laws that were in operation in Temple times, such as the whole sacrificial system, in the Messianic hope that these laws, too, will one day come into operation. The *Mishneh Torah* has received standard commentaries of its own in which Maimonides' sources are uncovered and in which the sage is defended against the Rabad's strictures. It became a challenge to keen students of the Halakhah to defend Maimonides against the charge that he has either misunderstood or ignored Talmudic formulations, thus creating a new branch of

Halakhic studies. Joseph *Karo's *Shulḥan Arukh* is based on the *Mishneh Torah*, and Karo often quotes Maimonides verbatim.

Maimonides introduces his philosophical and theological ideas into the *Mishneh Torah* as well. Typically, for instance, he prefaces the work with four chapters on the marvels of the created world, reflection on which leads to the *love and fear of God. The apparent contradictions between the *Mishneh Torah* and the *Guide of the Perplexed* have often been discussed. While, for instance, in the former work Maimonides records all the laws of the sacrifices and the hope that the system will be reintroduced in the Messianic age, in the later work understands the whole system as a temporary measure introduced in order to wean the people away from idolatrous practices. A common, but essentially unconvincing, way of resolving the contradictions is to maintain that the *Guide* was compiled for the few, the philosophical enquirers, while the *Mishneh Torah* is for the guidance of non-philosophically minded Jews.

### The Guide of the Perplexed

The 'Perplexed' in the title of this three-part work are the students of Aristotelian philosophy puzzled and confused by the many apparent contradictions between philosophy (= human reasoning) and certain statements, especially about the nature of God, in the Bible and Talmud. The basic thrust of the *Guide* is to demonstrate that all truth is one so that the Bible, containing the revealed will of God, has to be interpreted not to be in conflict but to be in harmony with reason. In an oft-quoted passage in the *Guide*, Maimonides declares that he rejects the Aristotelian view that matter is eternal on the grounds of reason, not of faith. Had he have been convinced that the Aristotelian view is correct he would have had no difficulty in interpreting the biblical narrative of *creation to accord with this view. As it is, there is no 'reason' for rejecting the traditional Jewish view of *creatio ex nihilo*. The first part of the *Guide* deals similarly with the question of the biblical anthropomorphisms. It is true that the Bible describes God in human terms but these are not to be taken literally. In the third part of the *Guide*, Maimonides proceeds to give 'reasons' for those commands in the Torah which seem unreasonable at first glance such as the *dietary laws (see MITZVAH).

For all his reliance on reason Maimonides is not, however, a rationalist in the conventional sense. He believes beyond question in the Torah as divine revelation. Moreover, there is a strong mystical element in Maimonides' thought. In the remarkable account in the *Guide* (3. 51) of the man whose thoughts are always on God (see DEVEKUT), such a rare individual is said to be beyond the normal mishaps of nature. He can walk through fire without being burned and pass through water without being drowned.

The *Guide* is a very difficult work not only because of its subject-matter but also because Maimonides presents his thoughts, contrary to the precision he employs in his other works, unsystematically, evidently in his desire to prevent those incapable of following abstruse arguments from venturing into the dangerous field that might easily lead to loss of faith. He has even been accused of planting false clues for this purpose, so that it is often impossible to grasp what he is really saying. The commentators to the *Guide* often leave the student in a greater state of perplexity than he was when he began the study.

Abraham Cohen, *The Teachings of Maimonides* (London, 1927).
Maimonides, *The Guide of the Perplexed*, trans. Shlomo Pimes (Chicago, 1974).
Isadore Twersky, *Introduction to the Code of Maimonides (Mishneh Torah)* (New Haven, 1980).
David Yellin and Israel Abrahams, *Maimonides* (London, 1903).

**Malachi** The post-exilic prophet whose book of three chapters is the final book of the Twelve Prophets. It is uncertain whether Malachi is the actual name of the prophet, since the Hebrew word *Malakhi* can mean 'my messenger' and chapter 3 of the book begins with the words: 'Behold, I send My messenger [*malakhi*], and he shall clear the way before me.' In a Rabbinic legend Malachi is identified with none other than *Ezra. According to the Talmud (*Megillah* 15a) Malachi and his contemporaries *Haggai and *Zechariah were the last of the prophets, *prophecy coming to an end when they died. The book concludes with two verses which speak of God sending his prophet *Elijah to turn the heart of the fathers to the children— the earliest reference to the view that Elijah is the herald of the *Messiah. Malachi 1: 11 reads: 'For from the rising of the sun even unto the going down of the same My name is great among the nations; and in every place offerings are presented unto My name, even pure oblations; for My name is great among the nations, saith the Lord of hosts.' One Rabbinic interpretation has it that this verse refers to the *Jewish* scholars among the nations who offer the 'pure oblations' of Torah study. But the other interpretation which takes the verse literally and is thus universalistic is obviously the more probable. The meaning is then said to be that for all their worship of other gods the nations acknowledge a Supreme God, the one God worshipped by the people of Israel.

Eli Cashdan: 'Malachi', in A. Cohen (ed.), *The Twelve Prophets* (London, 1970), 335–68.

**Malbim** Acronym of *M*eir *L*aib *B*en *Y*ehiel *M*ichal, Russian Rabbi and biblical exegete (1809–79). The Malbim occupied a number of Rabbinic positions including the Rabbinate of Bucharest, which post he was compelled to relinquish because he fell out with the lay leaders of the community owing to his strict views concerning the *dietary laws and other observances, which were not to the taste of people with standards that fell far short of his own. Malbim's commentary to the whole of the Bible became one of the most popular commentaries for Orthodox Jews because its aim is to show, chiefly by philological investigation, that the teachings of the *Oral Torah, as found in the Talmud, are contained in the *Written Torah, the Pentateuch. Very few modern biblical scholars are at all enamoured of Malbim's methodology but acknowledge the many insights into the meaning of the biblical texts found in his commentary.

Malbim was well acquainted with the scientific and philosophical theories of his day which, he claims, are in no way in opposition to the Bible if the latter is correctly understood and interpreted. For instance, in his comment on the command to *love the neighbour, he points out that this cannot mean that a man is obliged literally to love others as he loves himself, but that the command means that others should be treated in the way one wishes to be treated oneself. Moreover, he maintains, the command does not only apply to other Jews but to all human beings. In his comment on the first Psalm, Malbim discusses, in a more or less modern fashion, the nature of happiness and how happiness in life is to be attained. Malbim studied the Kabbalah with an expert teacher and often makes use of Kabbalistic ideas in his interpretation of the Bible, especially in his comments to the creation narrative at the beginning of Genesis. Malbim's commentary is completely in the traditional mode. He has no use for the theories of *biblical criticism, though he does seem to accept the modern view that Psalm 137 was not composed by King David but by someone who lived through the events with which it deals, during the Babylonian exile.

Zvi Faier, *Malbim Commentary on the Torah* (Jerusalem, 1978).

**Mamzer** A child that is the issue of an adulterous or incestuous union. The law of the mamzer is stated in the verse: 'A mamzer shall not enter into the congregation of the Lord; even to his tenth generation shall he not enter into the congregation of the Lord' (Deuteronomy 23: 3). Whatever the original meaning of the word *mamzer*, in the Rabbinic tradition, as finally recorded after much discussion, the mamzer is the offspring of an adulterous or incestuous relationship, for example, of a man and a married woman or of a brother and sister, and 'entering the congregation of the Lord' is understood to mean that the mamzer (or mamzeret, for a female) is forbidden to marry a Jew. Since the verse states 'even to his tenth generation', this is taken to mean that the taint is transmitted over all the mamzer's generations so that the child of a mamzer, his grandchildren, and great-grandchildren may not marry into the Jewish community. Apart from the disqualification with regard to marriage, the mamzer suffers no disabilities in Jewish law. He inherits, for instance, the estate of his natural father. The translation of mamzer as 'bastard' or 'illegitimate child' is consequently incorrect so far as Jewish law is concerned.

The fact that an innocent child is penalized in this way through no fault of its own has always presented a severe theological and ethical problem. On the practical level, any proliferation of mamzerim could result in the Jewish community being split into two groups, the members of one being disallowed from marrying the members of the other. Because of these problems there is a distinct tendency throughout the history of Jewish *marriage law to discover legal remedies to prevent the mamzer being exposed or declared as such. *Isserles in his gloss to the *Shulḥan Arukh* (*Even Ha-Ezer*, 2. 15) states, on the basis of Talmudic rulings:

'If one who is unfit has become mixed in a particular family, then once it has become mixed it has become mixed and whoever knows of the disqualification is not permitted to disclose it and must leave well alone since all families in which there has been an admixture will become pure in the future.' The last remark refers to a Talmudic statement that in the Messianic age the taint of mamzerut (the abstract term for the mamzer situation) will be removed.

In lands where there is civil marriage it is not uncommon for a married woman who has been divorced in civil law to remarry in civil law without obtaining a *get, the Jewish bill of *divorce, from her first husband. Any children born to her from the second marriage are technically mamzerim, rendering the problem in modern times far more acute than in the time when civil marriage and divorce were unknown. Reform Judaism rejects the whole concept of mamzerut. Many Conservative and all Orthodox Rabbis do accept the traditional law in this matter but generally follow the Talmudic precedence of adopting various legal remedies in order to avoid the taint of mamzerut, and the ruling of Isserles is also followed that no investigation is to be made in order to expose mamzerut. It is certainly contrary to the tradition to compile, as unfortunately some few Orthodox Rabbis do, a register of mamzerim.

Louis Jacobs, 'The Problem of the Mamzer', in his *A Tree of Life: Diversity, Flexibility, and Creativity in Jewish Law* (Oxford, 1984), 257–75.

**Manna** The 'bread from heaven' with which the children of Israel were miraculously fed during their forty years in the wilderness (Exodus 16: 4–36; Numbers 11: 7–9). Some modern scholars, noting that the Arabs give the name *man* to a sweet, sticky, honey-like juice, exuding in heavy drops from a shrub found in the Sinai peninsula, understand the manna to have been a similar, natural substance. But it is obvious that the biblical account sees the manna as a miraculous substance dropping down from heaven. In a Rabbinic legend the manna had whatever taste those who ate it desired to experience but in the mystical lore the manna is the ethereal bread by which the angels in heaven are sustained. In the later tradition the manna became the symbol of man's need to trust in God for his sustenance. Devout Jews read the account of the manna in Exodus before going out to engage in their business activities and for this reason the account is printed after the morning service in a number of prayer books. The manna did not fall on the Sabbath but a double portion fell on the eve of the Sabbath (Exodus 16: 22). On the basis of this it is the universal custom to break bread for the Sabbath meals over two loaves. These are covered with a cloth while the Kiddush is recited over the wine, just as the manna in the wilderness was covered with dew (v. 13–14).

**'Maoz Tzur'** 'Fortress, Rock of my salvation', the hymn, of which these are the opening words, sung on *Hanukkah to a well-known melody in celebration of the deliverance by the *Maccabees, commemorated on this festival, and other deliverances from tyranny. The hymn itself dates from the thirteenth century, the melody from the fifteenth century, both in Germany, and were consequently used only by *Ashkenazi Jews until recently adopted by the *Sephardim as well.

**Marranos** The Jews of Spain and Portugal from the fifteenth century who submitted to baptism under threat of death or persecution, and many of whom kept Jewish observances in the secrecy of their homes. The Hebrew term for Jews forced to convert to another religion is *anusim* ('those who were forced'). Marranos means 'swine' in Spanish and is a term of opprobrium obviously resented by Jews even though this name is used in the history books. Many of the *anusim* later took up residence in Amsterdam where they formed a large proportion of the Jewish community (see CONVERSION).

**Marriage** In every interpretation of Judaism, marriage is the ideal state. The purpose of marriage is, in the first instance, for *procreation but the institution is also held in the highest regard in that it provides husband and wife with, in the language of one of the marriage benedictions, 'joy and gladness, mirth and exultation, pleasure and delight, love, peace and friendship'. Although *celibacy is not entirely unknown in Judaism, the vast majority of Jews favour marriage as the higher state. It used to be extremely rare, for instance, for the Rabbi of a community to be a bachelor. From the biblical story of *Adam and Eve and from the prophetic comparisons of the love of God and Israel to the love of husband and wife, it seems that monogamous marriage was the ideal, even though in early times a man could legally have more than one wife. From around the eleventh century CE polygamy was outlawed by the 'ban of Rabbenu *Gershom' for Áshkenazi Jews and this ban is now the norm for Sephardi Jews as well. In the State of Israel polygamy is proscribed by law for all citizens whether Ashkenazi or Sephardi. In the Kabbalah the union of husband and wife in marriage mirrors forth the union of the *Sefirot so that marriage comes to have a cosmic dimension. It is the dream of Jewish parents to stand beside their sons and daughters under the *huppah, the marriage canopy, and to arrange the wedding banquet, though generally speaking, the Rabbinic authorities frowned on too much ostentation in these practices.

In Talmudic times and beyond into the Middle Ages, the first stage in marriage was the betrothal, known as *kiddushin* or *erusin*. This involved the delivery, in the presence of two witnesses, of an object of value (now, universally, a wedding ring) by the bridegroom to the bride with the declaration: 'Be thou betrothed unto me by this ring.' This stage took place in the bride's home. Although the bride remained in her father's house while preparations for the wedding were being arranged, the couple became from that moment man and wife and the marriage could only be dissolved by the delivery of a bill of *divorce, the *get. The second stage was the marriage proper, known as *nisuin*. At this stage bride and bridegroom entered the *huppah*, the marriage lines (*ketubah*) were drawn up and the marriage benedictions recited in the presence of at least ten males, constituting a *minyan. During the Middle Ages, from at least as early as the time of *Rashi in France, and probably in order to exercise communal control over marriages, the two stages were combined to take place at the same time and this is the procedure in all communities nowadays.

### The Marriage Ceremony

The following is the traditional Jewish marriage ceremony, still observed in all its details by Orthodox Jews. Reform and some Conservative Jews have changed some of the details but essentially the traditional ceremony is identical with the Orthodox form. After the signing of the *ketubah*, bride and bridegroom are escorted under the *huppah* by their parents who stand beside them during the ceremony. In Western lands it is often the custom for the bride to be led 'down the aisle' in the synagogue by her father. Exceptionally traditionally-minded Jews do not follow this practice. Indeed, many ultra-Orthodox frown on marriages taking place in the synagogue on the grounds that this is to copy Christian practice (see GENTILES). The marriage ceremony proper begins, in many communities, with the recital of Psalm 100 and other verses from the Psalms and the blessing: 'He who is mighty, blessed and great above all, may He bless the bridegroom and the bride.' In most Western communities, the Rabbi delivers a brief address before the ceremony. This, too, is rejected by the ultra-Orthodox as a quasi-Christian practice.

The officiant is usually a Rabbi or another learned man but there is no such thing in Judaism as a priest 'marrying' people as in the sacraments of the Christian Church. The officiant takes a cup of wine and recites the benediction over wine. He then recites the benediction over the betrothal:

'Blessed art Thou, O Lord our God, King of the universe, who hast hallowed us by Thy commandments, and hast given us command concerning forbidden marriages; who hast disallowed unto us those that are betrothed, but hast sanctioned unto us such as are wedded to us by the rite of the nuptial canopy and the sacred covenant of wedlock. Blessed art Thou, O Lord, who hallowest Thy people Israel by the rite of the nuptial canopy and the sacred covenant of wedlock.'

Bride and bridegroom sip the wine and the groom then places the ring on the forefinger of the bride's right hand and declares: 'Behold thou art consecrated unto me by this ring, according to the law of Moses and Israel.' The *ketubah* is then read aloud.

The second stage consists of a further benediction over wine and the recital of the 'seven benefictions' (really six, but the benediction over the wine is also counted). In these God's blessing is called down on bride and bridegroom and a prayer for Zion is included. Bride and groom again sip the wine and the bridegroom stamps on a glass and breaks it. Whatever the origin of this custom, the official interpretation is that it is to remind bride and groom on their happy day of the destruction of the Temple (see CUSTOMS).

Unlike in the Christian marriage service, there is no reference in the Jewish service to procreation as a purpose of marriage. This is taken for granted and it was considered indelicate to refer to it in public Nor does Judaism know of marriage vows. It is understood that the provisions of the *ketubah* will be carried out and that husband and wife will remain faithful to one another until death parts them, but the Jewish tradition frowns on vows to fulfil one's obligations. In some communities the bride walks round the groom three or seven times under the *ḥuppah* before the ceremony. The custom is also observed in some communities of the groom covering the bride's face with the veil before the ceremony in an adjacent room. This is based on the story of the betrothal of Rebecca who covered her face with the veil when she saw Isaac for the first time (Genesis 24: 65). Where this custom is observed those present recite the blessing uttered by her father and brother to Rebecca: 'O sister! May you grow into thousands of myriads; may your offspring seize the gates of their foes' (Genesis 24: 60). Although in Western lands the bride usually has her maids of honour or bridesmaids and the groom his best man, these have no religious significance, so that there is no need for those who have these roles to be Jewish.

Israel Abrahams, 'Marriage Service', in his *A Companion to the Authorized Daily Prayerbook* (New York, 1966), 215–18.

Isaac Klein, 'The Laws of Marriage,' in his *A Guide to Jewish Religious Practice* (New York, 1979), 407–18.

**Marriages, Forbidden** The list of marriages forbidden by Jewish law is found in the book of Leviticus (18: 16–30; 20: 9–22). The union of a sister and brother or mother and son and the other instances mentioned have no validity whatsoever, so that if such a 'marriage' has taken place no *\*divorce* is required to dissolve it. While a nephew may not marry his aunt, a niece may marry her uncle and the marriage of first cousins to one another is allowed. A man's stepson may marry his wife's stepdaughter and his stepdaughter his wife's stepson since there is no blood relationship. The marriage of a *\*mamzer* to a Jew is not allowed but a mamzer may marry a mamzeret. The children of such a marriage, however, would be mamzerim. A *\*Kohen* may not marry a divorcee. A man may not marry his wife's sister while both are alive but may do so after the death of his wife.

**Martyrdom** Giving up life rather than being false to the Jewish religion; Heb. *\*Kiddush Ha-Shem*, 'Sanctification of the Divine Name'. There is considerable discussion in the Talmudic literature on when martyrdom is demanded of the Jew and when it is not, much of it purely academic but some of it severely practical. The Mishnah (*Berakhot* 9: 5) interprets the command to love God 'with all thy soul' (Deuteronomy 6: 5) to mean 'with all thy life', that is, love Him even at the cost of your very life. But against this is the verse (Leviticus 18: 5): 'by the pursuit of which man shall live', understood in the tradition to mean live and not die, implying that martyrdom is not demanded in pursuit of the precepts of the Torah. The resolution of this apparent contradiction is that a Jew is required to give his life for some of precepts but not for others. The question is then where to draw the line. Generally from the Talmudic discussions (e.g. *Sanhedrin* 74a) the rule emerges that all the other precepts of the Torah can be set aside rather than martyrdom be suffered, but a Jew is required to give up life rather than offend against three basic commandments. These are: idolatry, the forbidden sexual relations recorded in the book of Leviticus (see MARRIAGES, FORBIDDEN), and murder. Following the further details in the Talmudic discussion, Maimonides (*Yesodey Ha-Torah*, 5. 1–9) rules that a Jew may transgress the precepts of the Torah in order to save his life but that this does not apply to the three offences nor does it apply where the intention of heathens is to compel a Jew to commit an offence in order to demonstrate his disloyalty to the Jewish religion. Similarly, where there is a government decree against Jewish observance the Jew is obliged to suffer martyrdom rather than transgress a 'light precept' even in private. Where martyrdom is not demanded it is forbidden for a Jew to suffer martyrdom, according to Maimonides, and if he does he is guilty of the offence of suicide.

Obviously the above discussions are from the purely legal point of view. It is hard to imagine that in the actual situations in which Jews were called upon to give their lives for their religion they looked up the rules in the Talmud and the Codes. History records many examples of Jewish martyrdom in which the martyrs offered up their lives regardless of whether the law required them to do so. The converse is also true, that Jews whom the law required to be martyrs failed to be strong enough in their loyalty to their faith. Moreover, in the Middle

Ages, the period of the Crusades, for example, Jews were killed for professing the Jewish religion regardless of whether they were ready to submit to the sorry fate or escape it by surrendering. The awesome drama was always worked out against the particular situation. By a consensus among Jews, the six million victims of the *Holocaust are given the accolade of martyrdom and are known as *kedoshim* ('holy ones'), the name otherwise reserved for martyrs; they were, after all, murdered because they were Jews. Maimonides, when faced with the threatened destruction of Jewish communities by Muslim rulers, gave the ruling that since *Islam is not an idolatrous religion, martyrdom is not required if Jews are faced with the option of conversion to Islam or death. Other authorities took issue with Maimonides here, arguing that conversion to Islam involves a denial of the Torah of Moses and martyrdom is demanded for this very reason. The decision was naturally left to the individuals themselves. With regard to Christianity, the advice of the Rabbis was that martyrdom should be avoided by fleeing the places in which it was a threat and the tolerant attitude emerged according to which those who had been forcibly converted should be treated with respect as unwitting offenders and welcomed back into the fold, as happened with the *Marranos.

In the Talmudic tale (*Berakhot* 61b) Rabbi *Akiba, as he was being tortured to death for teaching the Torah, declared: 'All my life I said: when will I have the opportunity of suffering martyrdom and now that it has come should I not rejoice?' In the mystical diary kept by Joseph *Karo, this saint longed to be a martyr for the glory of God. But this longing for martyrdom is very unusual in the literature of Jewish piety. The more realistic attitude was to accept in love martyrdom if the need arose but not positively to long for it to come about. The prayer of Isaiah *Horowitz is germane:

'O Holy God! If it will be Thy will to bring me to this test, sanctify me and purify me and put into my thoughts and my mouth to sanctify Thy name in public, as did the ten holy martyrs [the Rabbis who are said to have been executed during Hadrian's persecution of the Jews] and myriads and thousands of Israel's saints . . . Our sages have taught us that whoever offers himself as a martyr for the sake of the sanctification of Thy name feels nothing of the great pain inflicted upon him. However, it is impossible to rely on these words of the sages. But come what may, be Thou with me that the torment should not prevent me having my thoughts on Thee and let me rejoice in my heart at the very moment of torture.'

Dirges for the martyrs were introduced into the liturgy of the synagogue for recital on certain Sabbaths of the year and on *Yom Kippur and the Ninth of *Av.

Israel Abrahams, 'The Dirge of the Martyrs', in his *A Companion to the Authorized Daily Prayerbook* (Now York, 1966), 162–3.
Abraham Halkin and David Hartman, 'The Epistle on Martyrdom', in their *Crisis and Leadership: Epistles of Maimonides* (Philadelphia, 1985), 13–90.

**Marxism** The economic and social doctrine propounded by Karl Marx (1818–83). Attempts have been made to see Marx's passionate concern with social justice as the heritage of the Hebrew prophets. Others have seen Marx's dialectic as derived not only from the philosopher Hegel but from the Talmudic reasoning of Marx's forebears—he was descended from Rabbinical families on both the paternal and the maternal side. These theories are purely speculative, however, and do not affect the question of the attitude taken towards Marxism by religious Jews. Marx was born a Jew but when the boy was only 6 years of age his father embraced Christianity. As soon as he grew to manhood, Marx declared himself to be an atheist. Marx's thought on religion is utterly at variance with theism. Marxism, as developed by Marx himself, his collaborator Engels, by Lenin, and in the Communist philosophy, treats belief in God as positively harmful. Marxism declares that men adhere to theistic religion not because it is true but because it serves as a tool for the preservation of the economic and social *status quo*. This is particularly so since in the theistic faiths man's final bliss is not in this world at all but is reserved for him in the Hereafter. The priests of theism, it is argued, help those in power to exploit the poor by directing their hearts to an other-worldly existence in which they will find compensation for their misery here on earth. By turning men's eyes heavenwards theism encourages indifference to the economic struggle in the here and now. Religion is thus the 'opium of the people'. The strong appeal of religion, which cannot be denied, is the appeal of any drug, providing contentment through vain dreams and producing a stupor from which man cannot awake to better himself.

It is the atheistic theory behind Marxism, not the Marxist economic doctrine, that is opposed to Jewish religious teaching (see COMMUNISM). A religious reply to the challenge of Marxism can point to the power religious belief has and its persistence against all odds, as evidenced by the upsurge of religious emotions among so many when the Soviet Union broke up. So far as Judaism is concerned, there is no doubt that some Jews as well as some non-Jews do use their religion to further their own grasping ends, to still their social conscience, to act as a palliative of guilt-feelings if they are exploiters, or as a tranquillizer if they are exploited. But the error of the Marxist is to imagine that all theists use their religion in this way and to overlook the fact that theists have been at least as condemnatory as Marxism of the abuses to which religion can be subjected. The sweeping denunciation that a man's philosophy of life is inexorably determined by his economic needs can all too easily be turned against Marxism itself. It is incredible that some Marxists speak as if the Communist philosophy is never used to further injustice, selfishness, and greed.

The Jewish doctrine of the Hereafter (see HEAVEN AND HELL and WORLD TO COME) rarely encourages Jews to be indifferent to the claims of social justice. The whole doctrine of the Hereafter occupies a very insignificant role in biblical thought. When the Hebrew prophets spoke in God's name, their chief interest was with justice and righteousness in the here and now. Rabbinic Judaism, which does have a strong other-worldly thrust, is, nevertheless, an heir to the biblical message; it could hardly have been anything else. For the Rabbis and their followers there is no contradiction between the claims of social justice and the longing of the individual for personal survival and spiritual bliss in the Hereafter.

Louis Jacobs, 'The Marxist Attack', in his *Faith* (London, 1968), 126–34.

**Masorah** 'Transmission', the establishment of the traditionally correct text of the Hebrew Bible by the group of scholars, the Masoretes, whose activity extended from the sixth to the tenth centuries CE. The Masoretes examined the many biblical manuscripts, noting divergences and seeking to determine which text is the more accurate. They noted where a traditional reading (*keri*) differs from the traditional written text (*ktiv*), for example, where the written text contains a coarse or vulgar expression. Such expressions were left in the text but the euphemisms required by the tradition are noted for the benefit of the reader in the synagogue. The Masoretes also noted where the tradition requires certain letters to be larger than the others and certain letters smaller than the others. They provided notes in which they conjecture that some words should have been written differently, for example, where the text has the singular form while the context seems to require the plural, but such conjectures were left in the margins and the text itself remained unchanged. A further activity of the Masoretes was to count the number of verses in each section of the Pentateuch. A list of these is now given at the end of each section. The current text of the Bible was established by the Masorete ben Asher in Tiberias in 930 CE and this is known as the the Masoretic Text (abbreviated in scholarly works as MT).

A major problem in biblical studies revolves around the accuracy and reliability of the Masoretic Text. It is known that from early Rabbinic times the greatest care was taken by copyists, especially when copying the Pentateuch text, the *Sefer Torah. There are detailed rules as to how the Sefer Torah is to be copied, with the result that there are no divergences in the text between one Sefer Torah and another in any part of the Jewish world. But, as the ancient versions—the *Septuagint, the *Targum, the Samaritan Pentateuch, the Latin version, the Vulgate, and the texts found among the *Dead Sea Scrolls—show, errors may have crept into the text before the Masoretic Text had been established or, rather, the ancient versions may be based on traditions different from that finally recorded in the Masoretic Text. Here and there even in the Talmud some biblical texts quoted differ in their wording from the current version. Modern biblical scholarship, consequently, while treating the Masoretic Text with the respect it deserves, is not averse to suggesting emendations to the text based either on the ancient versions or on plausible conjectures.

The problem for Orthodoxy presented by *biblical criticism applies only to what is known as the Higher Criticism, that is, the critical examination of how the Pentateuch came to be. The Lower Criticism, the critical examination of the text in the light of emendations and the ancient versions, is much less of a problem since there is no actual dogma which states that the Masoretic Text is entirely inerrant as the very word of God. Nevertheless, no Jewish community, Orthodox or Reform, has ever thought of emending the actual text of the Sefer Torah used in the synagogue, an attempt that would be considered to be sacrilegious by all Jews.

> Sid Z. Leiman (ed.), *The Canon and Masorah of the Hebrew Bible: An Introductory Reader* (New York, 1974).
>
> J. Weingreen, *Introduction to the Critical Study of the Text of the Hebrew Bible* (Oxford, 1982).

**Masturbation** Sexual self-abuse, often connected with the story of Onan who 'spilled his seed on the ground' (Genesis 38: 9); hence the term onanism, though the usual Rabbinic term for masturbation is 'waste of seed', meaning, presumably, the unlawful emission of semen which should be produced only in the procreative act, although normal marital relations are permitted even where no procreation can follow—where, for instance, the wife is too old to conceive (see BIRTH-CONTROL, SEX, and PRO-CREATION). The Kabbalah is particularly severe on 'waste of seed', treating this hyperbolically as the most severe of sins. To think lustful thoughts during the day is also forbidden in that it can lead to involuntary 'waste of seed' in dreams at night. Since the main objection to masturbation is because of 'waste of seed' there are hardly any references in the sources to female masturbation and, indeed, there is no explicit condemnation of this in the Rabbinic sources. Human nature being what it is, it is hard to believe that all observant Jews avoided the practice. From the references to 'the sins of youth', for which repentance is required in adult life, it would seem that masturbation was certainly not unknown even among pious young men.

> Louis M. Epstein, 'Wasting Nature', in his *Sex Laws and Customs in Judaism* (New York, 1948), 144-7.

**Matriarchs** *Sarah, *Rebecca, *Rachel, and *Leah. These four are the matriarchs of the Jewish people, since the majority of the sons of *Jacob were the offspring of Rachel or Leah and Jacob was the son of Rebecca and the grandson of Sarah. A Talmudic saying has it that only these four are called 'matriarchs' and only *Abraham, *Isaac, and Jacob are called *patriarchs'.

**Matzah** The unleavened bread that the Israelites ate when they went out of Egypt (Exodus 12: 39), after which the festival of *Passover, during which leaven (*hametz) is forbidden, is called *hag ha-matzot*, 'Festival of Unleavened Bread' (Exodus 23: 15; Deuteronomy 16: 16). As the law is expounded in the Talmudic literature and the Codes, the obligation to eat *matzah* applies only to the first night of Passover, when *matzah* is eaten at the *Seder. During the remaining days of the festival, leaven must not be eaten but there is no obligation to eat *matzah*; although some later authorities hold that it is meritorious to eat it. There are strict rules regarding the preparation of *matzah*; care must be taken that during the kneading and baking of the dough it is not allowed to become fermented. This care is known as *shemirah* ('watching over'). Most authorities hold that *shemirah* is only required from the time of kneading but some hold that it is required from as early as the time of reaping the grain. Many pious Jews only use on the first night of the festival *matzah* that has been watched over from the time of reaping, called *shemurah matzah* ('*matzah* that has been watched over'). The especially strict only eat *shemurah matzah* and no other during the whole of the festival. The watching over the *matzah* has to be done intentionally for the purpose of using it for the fulfilment of the precept (to eat it on the first night). This was one of the reasons why a fierce controversy arose in the nineteenth century over machine-manufactured *matzah*. It was argued that a machine cannot have intention. Those who favoured machine-made *matzah* argued that the intention of the man operating the machine is sufficient for the purpose and this is now generally accepted. Nevertheless, very strict Jews only use *matzah* that has been manufactured by hand.

**Mazal Tov** 'Good luck', the usual greeting or congratulations for a happy event or some particular achievement. The word *mazal* means a planet and the word *tov* means good so that the expression: 'Good Mazal' obviously has its origin in a belief in *astrology. Nowadays, the phrase has lost its astrological connotation and is no more than an expression of goodwill. In congratulatory telegrams the expression is usually in the form of a single word, Mazaltov. In Yiddish parlance an unfortunate person prone to mishaps is called a *shlimazal* ('one without luck') as in the English 'he is unlucky'.

**Meat and Milk**   See DIETARY LAWS for the rules against eating meat and dairy dishes together and for those against using the same cooking utensils for both meat and milk.

**Medicine**   See DOCTORS and HEALTH for physical cures. Frequently in the Rabbinic literature and in the moralistic literature there are references to the study of the Torah and the practice of its precepts as medicine for the soul.

**Megillah**   See PURIM.

**Meir, Rabbi**   Prominent teacher of the second century CE, the period of the later *Tannaim. Meir was one of the last disciples of Rabbi *Akiba. Like his master, he was responsible for collections of teaching that eventually found their way into the *Mishnah, a work in which Rabbi Meir often features. In one Talmudic account Rabbi Meir was engaged in a dispute with the Prince, Rabban Simeon son of Rabban *Gamaliel II, as a result of which he was expelled from the House of Learning. It was said that Rabbi Meir was so brilliant that his colleagues were incapable of fathoming the full profundity of his thoughts and for this reason where Rabbi Meir is in dispute with his colleagues, his rulings are not followed. There is something of a mystery about Rabbi Meir's background. Unlike the other Tannaim, his father's name is never given. A Talmudic legend has it that Rabbi Meir was descended from none other than the Emperor Nero; this is probably a folk-tale based on the resemblance between the name Meir, which means 'illumination', and a folk etymology of Nero from *ner*, a lamp. There are legends about Rabbi Meir's wife, *Beruriah, said to be a woman of great learning.

**Meiri, Menahem**   Talmudist and religious thinker of Perpignan in southern France (1249–1316). Meiri is chiefly renowned for commentaries to the tractates of the Talmud, the majority of which were in manuscript until the twentieth century. Meiri has an attractive style

and methodology which are all his own. For each individual tractate he first presents the framework and then comments on the tractate section by section, providing a résumé of the views of all earlier teachers of note, together with his own original observations. For contemporary students of the Talmud, Meiri is second only to *Rashi as a Talmudic commentator and is even superior to Rashi in comprehensiveness. Meiri is a religious rationalist, explaining away and occasionally ignoring completely apparently superstitious Talmudic passages such as those referring to *demons. Meiri also compiled a large work on repentance, moved, he remarks, by the accusation by a Christian friend that Judaism is weak in its treatment of *sin. Particularly important is his treatment of Christianity. As a devout Jew he was convinced that Christianity is false in its basic beliefs but he refused to treat Christians as pagans, calling Christians and Muslims, 'people whose lives are governed by religion'. Typical of both Meiri's rationalism and his tolerance is his explanation of the Talmudic saying that astrological forces have no effect on 'Israel'. A human being has been given free will and thus endowed can escape planetary influences. Since Christians and Muslims are encouraged by their religion to exercise their free will in order to live worthy lives, they, too, are immune to the fatalistic influences of the stars (see ASTROLOGY) and for this purpose are embraced by the term 'Israel'! In effect Meiri goes beyond the Talmudic division of human beings into Israelites and idolaters, creating a third category of his own in which 'peoples whose lives are governed by religion' occupy a position midway between Jews and pagans.

**Memorial Prayers**   The main prayer for the dead is known as Yizkor ('May He remember the soul of . . .)'. Memorial prayers originated in Germany in the form of martyrologies (see MARTYRDOM) for victims of the Crusades and from these Yizkor developed as a prayer for departed parents on *Yom Kippur. Later still it became the practice to recite Yizkor on the last days of the festivals. This practice, otherwise incongruous for a festive occasion, derives from the fact that on these days the portion read from the Torah concludes with the words: 'each with his own gift, according to the blessing that the Lord your God has bestowed upon you' (Deuteronomy 16: 17), on the basis of which donations to charity were promised, offered for the repose of the souls of the departed. A custom, regarded by some as superstitious, is for those whose parents are still alive to leave the synagogue during the recital of Yizkor on the grounds that others who have no parents may put on the more fortunate the *evil eye, or that those with parents may recite Yizkor together with the congregation and so harm their living parents by treating them as dead.

Another individual memorial prayer of seventeenth-century origin is the 'El Male Raḥamin' ('O God full of compassion') recited at a funeral or when visiting a grave and by the *Cantor in the synagogue on behalf of those who are observing the anniversary of the death of a near relative, the *Yahrzeit. These memorial prayers of German origin were recited until fairly recently only by Ashkenazi Jews but are now recited also by the majority of Sephardi Jews as well, though often in a slightly different form. Despite the remarks of some of the *Geonim that it is futile to offer prayers on behalf of the dead since a man can only gain merit by his deeds while he is alive, these memorial prayers are now exceedingly popular among all sections of Jewry (and see KADDISH).

H. Rabinowicz, *A Guide to Life: Jewish Laws and Customs of Mourning* (New York, 1974), 110–13.

**Mendelssohn, Moses** German Jewish philosopher (1729–86), often called the father of the *Haskalah. Mendelssohn was born in Dessau, where he received a thorough grounding in Bible, Talmud, and the Codes. He accompanied his teacher to Berlin in 1743 and, acquiring a comprehensive acquaintance with German culture, became a leading figure among the German intelligentsia. The hero of Lessing's *Nathan the Wise* is a thinly disguised Mendelssohn. In collaboration with other Maskilim, Mendelssohn produced his commentary to the Pentateuch, the *Biur*, in a modern idiom, interpreting Scripture in its plain meaning and providing a German translation. Typical of Mendelssohn's thinking is his *Phaedon*, published in 1767, a philosophical exposition, in universalistic terms, of the doctrine of the immortality of the *soul, a doctrine which Mendelssohn, like his contemporary Kant, believed to be based not on dogma but on the demands of reason. Mendelssohn's general treatment of Jewish *dogmas has been much discussed. For

Mendelssohn, it would seem, or at least so it has been understood by many of his exponents, Judaism is revealed law. It is the practices enjoined by *revelation that are significant for Judaism, questions of belief being left open to a large extent; though, as Mendelssohn's critics have not been slow to point out, belief in a revealed law is itself a dogma.

Mendelssohn's thought has rightly been seen as a pioneering attempt to find the correct balance between strong Jewish commitment and the necessary accommodation the modern Jew has to make in order to be at home in Western culture and civilization. Yet he has had a large number of detractors, who have viewed his approach as dangerous to Jewish faith, especially since a number of his children became converted to Christianity. In the circle of strict Orthodoxy in Hungary in the nineteenth century a ban was placed on the study of the *Biur*. It has been said with justice, none the less, that every Jew has been influenced, directly or indirectly, by the three great figures of eighteenth century Jewry—*Elijah, Gaon of Vilna, the *Baal Shem Tov, founder of *Hasidism, and Mendelssohn.

Alexander Altmann, *Moses Mendelssohn: A Biographical Study* (University, Ala., 1973).

**Menorah** The seven-branched candelabrum in the Tabernacle in the wilderness (Exodus 25: 31–8; 37: 17–24) and in the First and Second Temples. The *Maccabees, after their victory over the forces of Antiochus, celebrated on *Hanukkah, refashioned the menorah. The Hanukkah menorah used on the festival in Jewish homes, has, however, eight branches, one for each of the eight days of the festival. Nowadays, the Hanukkah menorah is often called a Hanukkiyah rather than a menorah. The menorah depicted on the Arch of Titus in Rome is not an accurate representation of the original. The menorah, as the symbol of spiritual light, is the most ancient and most powerful of Jewish symbols (SEE MAGEN DAVID). According to Jewish law it is forbidden to have a replica of the menorah outside the Temple, which is why many authorities frown on the representation of the seven-branched menorah found often in synagogues. Others see no harm in having a menorah of this kind in the synagogue, since it is never an exact replica of the Temple menorah. In a medieval interpretation, the central stem of the menorah represents the light of the Torah while the six branches represent the sciences—good to study provided the student treats them as secondary to the wisdom of the Torah.

**Menstruant** Hebr. *niddah* ('one set aside'). According to Jewish law, it is forbidden for husband and wife to have marital relations during the time of the wife's periods and for seven days after these have ceased. The practice is for the wife to examine herself for seven days after her flow has ended. If the examination during these seven 'clean days' shows that there is no longer any flow of blood, the wife immerses herself in the ritual bath, the *mikveh, after which marital relations may be resumed until just before the time when the next period is expected. This means that usually husband and wife can only be together for sixteen days in each month, making the laws of 'family purity' among the most difficult to observe, especially since strict observance of these laws involves no physical contact at all between husband and wife during this time. The majority of Orthodox Jews follow these laws and there is evidence that they are observed nowadays even in some Reform circles. As with the *dietary laws, the keynote in the sources for the observance of 'family purity' is holiness. It is surely wrong to threaten people into keeping these laws by the supposed but unwarranted claim that scientific findings show that women who observe the laws have a lesser chance of contracting cancer of the womb. The *Karaites were extremely strict in keeping a mentruant away from contact with sacred things. Against this, the Talmud states explicitly that 'the Torah cannot contaminate, so that the widespread notion that a woman in her periods should not handle a *Sefer Torah finds hardly any support in the Codes.

Isaac Klein, 'Family Purity', in his *A Guide to Jewish Religious Practice* (New York, 1979), 509-16.

**Messiah** 'The anointed one', the person believed to be sent by God to usher in a new era in which all mankind will worship the true God, warfare will be banished from the earth, and peace will reign supreme. With the strongest antecedents in the Bible, the doctrine of the Messiah was developed, elaborated upon, and given a variety of interpretations throughout Jewish history, but its basic affirmation is that human history will find its fulfilment here on earth. The doctrine of the Messiah denotes the this-worldly aspect of Jewish *eschatology, with the *World to Come as the other-worldly aspect (see also HEAVEN AND HELL).

The actual term *Mashiaḥ* was not used for the redeemer sent by God to release Israel from bondage until long after the biblical period. In the Bible the term refers not to a person who will come in the future to redeem Israel but to any person actually anointed with sacred oil for the purpose of high office, such as the king or the *high priest. The term is also applied to any person for whom God has a special purpose: Cyrus, king of Persia, for instance (Isaiah 45: 1). It would be totally erroneous, however, to conclude that the whole idea of a personal Messiah is post-biblical. While not referring to him as the Messiah, some of the Hebrew prophets (Isaiah, Micah, Jeremiah, and Zechariah) do speak of the future redemption as being ushered in by an ideal human leader possessed of lofty spiritual and ethical qualities. He is not, however, a redeemer. God alone is the redeemer and the Messiah-King, a scion of the House of *David, is only the leader of the redeemed people. In any event, redemption in this context is not redemption from sin for individuals, as in the redemptive role of Jesus in Christian theology. Redemption in Judaism, at least until quite late, refers to physical salvation of the Jewish people. Other prophets (Nahum, Zephaniah, Habbakuk, Malachi, Joel, and Daniel) do not speak of a human leader at all, the Lord alone being the redeemer. In other prophetic books (Amos, Ezekiel, Obadiah) there is only a collective 'Messiah', the kingdom of the House of David. In other words, the later distinction between the doctrine of a personal Messiah and the doctrine of a Messianic age has its origins in the Bible itself. Eventually, the various ideas regarding the Messiah were embellished in the *Apocrypha and other writings and a complex Messianic pattern emerged. A definite order of events was established and this order is found in the Rabbinic literature, although, as Maimonides recognized, much in this area belongs more to pure speculation than to doctrine or dogma.

The general view in the Rabbinic literature is undoubtedly of a personal Messiah. The sole exception is the opinion of the fourth-century Rabbi Hillel (not to be confused with the earlier teacher *Hillel) who declared (*Sanhedrin* 99a): 'There shall be no Messiah for Israel, because they have already enjoyed him in the days of Hezekiah'; that is to say, the prophetic vision referred to the tranquillity and stability in the days of King Hezekiah. *Rashi understands this to mean not that Rabbi Hillel denied the coming of a Messianic age, but only the doctrine of a personal Messiah. All the medieval thinkers believed in a personal Messiah, though they differ over whether the whole Messianic concept is to be understood in naturalistic or supernaturalistic terms. Maimonides (*Melakhim* 12: 1) for instance, states that it should not be imagined that a different order will prevail in the days of the Messiah or that nature will change. The apparent references in the prophetic writings to the marvels to take place in that time are to be understood figuratively not literally; for example, the lamb dwelling with the wolf (Isaiah 11: 6) refers to the 'lamb' of Israel living at peace undisturbed by Gentile 'wolves', who themselves will embrace the true religion and rob and plunder no more.

In the Kabbalistic doctrine of the *holy sparks, the Messiah will come when all the sparks have been rescued from the domain of the demonic powers. This doctrine paved the way for the false Messiah, Shabbetai *Zevi, whose followers believed in him even after he had been converted to Islam, since they saw his conversion as a valiant attempt to rescue the holy sparks inherent in that religion. Over the ages, Messianic speculation was rife; many tried to calculate from scriptural verses when the 'end' would be and, in addition to Shabbetai Zevi, other Messianic pretenders arose. The resulting frustrations caused the Rabbis to view with disfavour any attempt to calculate the date of the Messiah's coming. Ironically, some of those opposed to the practice were not averse to making such attempts themselves, especially when Jews were in great distress.

Modern Jewish thinkers were the heirs to all the previous notions. The fluctuating nature of the doctrine in former times; the accretion of legends and fanciful details; the debates among the sages on this or that detail; the possibility of a naturalistic as well as a supernaturalistic interpretation of the doctrine; the emphasis here on the personal Messiah and there on the Messianic age; all contributed to make this principle of the Jewish religion the one most fluid of all in its capacity for reinterpretation. Hardly any Jewish thinkers have been prepared to give up the doctrine entirely. Orthodox Jews

continue to believe in the coming of a personal Messiah who will lead all mankind back to God, even while acknowledging, as did Maimonides, that the details must be left to God. Classical Reform Judaism believed that the doctrine of a personal Messiah had to be abandoned. Moreover, the early Reformers in the nineteenth century believed that the Messianic promise would be realized not in a return of the Jews to the Holy Land but in the new world they saw beginning to emerge in Europe of sound education for all, greater liberalism in theory and practice, and greater opportunities for human betterment. The two world wars, the *Holocaust, and other horrors in the twentieth century dashed the hopes of the Reformers. Nevertheless, Reform Judaism still believes that the better world of peace and the acknowledgement by all of God the Creator will one day dawn and some Reform theologians refuse to reject the idea that God Himself will intervene directly to bring this happy state of affairs to fruition.

*Zionism is a modern secular version of Messianism. The early Zionists, too, rejected the doctrine of a personal Messiah but adopted those elements in the Messianic tradition that were hospitable to their efforts to restore the Jews to their ancient land. Religious Zionists have tried to adopt a compromise position, seeing, for example, the establishment of the State of Israel as the 'beginning of the redemption', that is, the new State cannot be identified with the Messianic hope, since, for all its achievements, it lacks the numinous quality associated with the Messianic hope, but it is, none the less, a sign that this hope is beginning to be realized. The Gush Emunim movement in Israel goes further and believes that the State itself has this numinous quality, so that the 'beginning' is the beginning of the final end of redemption. When this Messianic fervour is wedded to politics it can, of course, prove to be exceedingly dangerous.

In the light of all this, a not insignificant number of religious Jews have rightly adopted the view that an element of religious agnosticism is called for here: affirming that God will not allow His world to be surrendered to chaos and that the human drama will one day find its culmination on earth, but believing that more than this is opaque to humans and must be left to God.

Julius H. Greenstone, *The Messiah Idea in Jewish History* (Philadelphia, 1943).

(Abba Hillel Silver, *A History of Messianic Speculation in Israel* (Gloucester, Mass., 1978).
Louis Jacobs, 'The Messianic Hope', in his *A Jewish Theology* (New York, 1973), 292–300.

**Metatron** A supreme angel referred to in ancient Jewish writings. Many conjectures have been made on the meaning of this name—for instance, that it is a combination of the Greek *meta* and *thronos*, 'one who serves before the Throne [of God]' —but the name remains obscure. In some sources Metatron was created at the beginning of the creation of the world, in some even before the creation of the world. In later sources Metatron is the antediluvian, Enoch, who 'was no more, for God took him' (Genesis 5: 24). The figure of Metatron in the early literature and the Talmud aroused suspicions of *dualism, especially in the references to him being 'the lesser Lord'. The *Karaites attacked the Talmud on these very grounds. Although Metatron continues to appear in Jewish angeology (SEE ANGELS) he occupies a very peripheral role in later Jewish thought and has no real theological significance, testifying only to the persistence of semi-dualistic tendencies even in Jewish monotheistic thought.

Gershom Scholem, 'Metatron', in his *Kabbalah* (Jerusalem, 1974), 377–81.

**Methuselah** Grandfather of *Noah (Genesis 5: 21–5), who lived for 969 years, the longest lifespan of all the antediluvians. U. Cassuto has advanced the ingenious theory that in the biblical account of the fabulous ages reached by the antediluvians there is an implicit protest against the pagan notion that certain humans were admitted into the ranks of the gods. The Psalmist refers to a thousand years being as a day in God's eyes (Psalms 90: 4). Hence not even a Methuselah lives 1,000 years, thus stressing the gulf that exists between God and human beings. In Yiddish, as in English, the 'years of Methuselah' is an expression for extreme longevity.

**Mezuzah** Lit. 'door-post', the parchment scrip containing the two sections of Deuteronomy 6: 4–9 and 11: 13–21 and fixed to the door-posts of the house. The injunction in these two passages to write 'these words' on the door-posts (*mezuzot*) of the house was understood from early times to mean that these two should be inscribed on parchment and attached to the door-posts. The mezuzah is placed in a case (nowadays highly decorated cases that are works of art are often used) and fixed, either by nails or by glue, to the door-post of every room in the house, except the bathroom, toilet, and garage. The mezuzah is fixed to the right-hand door-post as one enters the room. It is placed about a third of the way down from the top of the door-post, slanting upwards. The reason given for the slanting positioning is that the medieval authorities are divided on whether the mezuzah is to be in a vertical or horizontal position and to place it diagonally satisfies both—an interesting illustration of the striving for compromise. Only houses in which people actually reside require a mezuzah. Synagogues, therefore, do not have a mezuzah. But the Bet Ha-Midrash, 'House of Study', does have a mezuzah since scholars sometimes eat and sleep there. A somewhat amusing debate centres on the question of whether prison cells require a mezuzah since residence there, it is hoped, is not permanent. In the State of Israel, the prison cells do have a mezuzah.

Modern biblical scholars have pointed to ancient and not so ancient practices of having some sign on the door-post of the house as a prophylactic to ward off the demonic powers. But, whatever its origin, the mezuzah in Judaism is a sign that those whose reside in the house are servants of the true God. There is no doubt that some Jews still see the role of the mezuzah to be to protect the house against harm. In Maimonides' day it was not uncommon for people to inscribe the names of angels on the mezuzah for the purpose of protecting the residents of the house from harm. Maimonides (*Mezuzah*, chs. 5–6) comes down heavily against the practice of writing the mezuzah so that its words taper to a point. 'For these fools not only nullify the commandment, but turn the great command of attesting the unity of God, of loving and serving Him, into an *amulet for their personal use in accordance with their foolish desires.' Maimonides would certainly have disapproved of fixing a mezuzah to the doors of an automobile to prevent accidents happening or of wearing a mezuzah around the neck as a charm. The purpose of the mezuzah is to remind the Jew of his obligations. (Women, consequently, are obliged to have a mezuzah on the door-posts of the house in which they reside, just as much as men.) As the Talmud (*Menahot*, 43b) puts it: 'Whoever has *tefillin* on his head and arm, *tzitzit on his garment, and a mezuzah on his door will surely not sin.' Maimonides remarks that a Jew should keep diligently the law of mezuzah since, then, every time he enters or leaves his house, he will encounter the name of God, be reminded of His love, and turn from the vanities of this world to choose the righteous path. The majority of Jews, Reform as well as Orthodox, take pride in the mezuzah, understand its symbolism, and have a mezuzah, if not on all the doors of the house, on the outer door facing the street at least.

Hyman E. Goldin, 'The Mezuzah', in his *Code of Jewish Law* (New York, 1961), i. 34–9.

**Micah** The prophet who prophesied during the reigns of Jotham, Ahaz, and Hezekiah (739–693 BCE) and whose book is the sixth in the book of the Twelve Prophets. The vision of the 'end of days' (see *Messiah) in Micah 4: 1–4 has an almost exact parallel in Isaiah 2: 2–5, suggesting either that Micah is quoting from Isaiah or Isaiah from Micah or, most probably, both are quoting from a common source, which shows that some passages in prophetic writings are not necessarily the prophet's own words but can be understood as direct quotations, throwing, in turn, some light on the nature of prophetic *inspiration. Micah's famous declaration of what God requires of man, 'only to do justly, and to love mercy, and to walk humbly with thy God' (Micah 6: 8) has been described as 'the noblest definition of true religion'.

Solomon Goldman, 'Micah', in A. Cohen (ed.), *The Twelve Prophets* (London, 1970), 153–89.

**Midnight Vigil** The practice, introduced by the followers of the famous Kabbalist Isaac *Luria, of rising at midnight to mourn for the destruction of the Temple and offer prayers for the exile of the *Shekhinah to come to an end; Heb. *Tikkun ḥatzot*, 'Arrangement [or Rectification] for Midnight'. The practice is still followed in some devout circles, especially among Kabbalists and Hasidim.

**Midrash** The method by which the ancient Rabbis investigated Scripture in order to make it yield laws and teachings not apparent in a surface reading. The word Midrash is from the root *darash*, 'to enquire', 'to investigate'. This searching of Scripture has been traced back to the book of *Ezra: 'For Ezra had set his heart to

seek [*lidrosh*] the Torah of the Lord, and to do it, and to teach in Israel statutes and ordinances' (Ezra 7: 10). In any event, the Midrash method was ubiquitous throughout the period of the *Tannaim and Amoraim. The doctrine of the *Oral Torah covers this discovery of new teachings as well as those believed to have been imparted to Moses at *Sinai. The *hermeneutics of *Hillel and Rabbi *Ishmael are part of the Midrashic process. It is highly significant that the House of Study is known, in Rabbinic times and later, as the Bet Ha-Midrash.

Collections of Midrash were made from time to time. These Midrashim are conventionally divided into two classes: 1. the Halakhic or Tannaitic Midrashim; 2. the Aggadic Midrashim. In the Halakhic Midrashim the Tannaim use the Midrashic method to derive laws (Halakhot) from Pentateuchal passages. Many of the debates in these works depend on the different methods used by the teachers for the elucidation of the texts. The Aggadic Midrashim (see AGGADAH) do not purport to convey the actual meaning of Scripture but usually employ the very different method of reading ideas into Scripture. To make clear the distinction between the two types of Midrashim an example must be given of each. A Halakhic Midrash, seeking to discover the law that the Sabbath can be profaned in order to save life (e.g. where the doctors say that hot food must be served to a dangerously sick person and no hot food is available) derives this from the verse: 'You shall keep My laws and My rules, by the pursuit of which a man shall live' (Leviticus 18: 5). Since the verse states 'shall live', it is implied that where death may result from the observance of the laws, the laws may be set aside. An example of the different Aggadic Midrash is the comment on the verse: 'God did not lead them by way of the land of the Philistines' (Exodus 13: 17). An Aggadic Midrash reads this as: 'God did not lead them by way of the land', that is, His providence over the Israelites in the wilderness was not through natural processes ('the way of the land'). In the natural order bread comes from the ground and water from the sky, whereas in the wilderness the *Manna came from heaven and water from the flinty rock. In the former instance, the verse is actually said to mean that the precepts can be set aside where life is at stake. In the latter instance, by no stretch of the imagination can the verse really be understood in the way the Midrash understands it, since the verse speaks of 'the way of the land of the Philistines'. The 'way of the land' in the Midrashic comment can be arrived at only by detaching 'the way of the land' from 'of the Philistines' and the author of this Midrash must have been aware of this fact. Clearly, then, the latter Midrash is in no way a matter of biblical exegesis but is rather a way of pegging on, so to speak, a pleasant idea to a familiar scriptural verse. Even with regard to the Halakhic Midrashim, however, there is the much-discussed question of whether the Midrash is the actual source of the law or whether the law had been arrived at independently by human reasoning (i.e. it seems reasonable that the laws can be set aside in order to save life) and then scriptural warrant was found through the Midrashic method.

The three main Halakhic Midrashim are: Mekhilta ('The Measure') to the book of Exodus; Sifra ('The Book'), also called Torat Kohanim ('The Law of the Priests') to the book of Leviticus; and Sifre ('The Books') to the books of Numbers and Deuteronomy. There is no Halakhic Midrash to Genesis since there is hardly any legal material in that book. The Halakhic Midrashim also contain some Aggadic material but this has a much closer connection with the biblical texts than in the Aggadic Midrashim. It might also be noted that Halakhic material is sometimes introduced in passing in the Aggadic Midrashim.

The activity of the Darshanim ('Expounders', those who engaged in Midrash) extended from the second century to the thirteenth century so far as the Aggadic Midrash is concerned. Eventually Midrashic-type commentary yielded to philosophy and Kabbalah, two very different ways of expounding the Torah. It is true that the *Zohar is a kind of Midrash, in the sense that, like other Midrashim, it is in the form of a running commentary to the Pentateuch, but its aim is to convey the secret meaning of the Torah, that is, the Torah as understood in the mystical sense of the Kabbalists. A good deal of the Midrashic material in the Aggadic Midrashim was no doubt based on sermons delivered by Rabbinic preachers but in the form we now have them these Midrashim bear all the marks of literary composition and breath the air of the school rather than the synagogue. The original sermonic material has been reworked to provide complete literary units. In addition to scriptural commentary, the

Aggadic Midrashim contain pious maxims, folklore, anecdotes about the Rabbis, theological observations, and many other topics, like the Aggadah in general.

There are numerous Aggadic Midrashim but the best known, most popular, and most intensively studied by the later scholars are: the Midrash Rabbah ('The Great Midrash'), on the Pentateuch and the books of Lamentations, Ruth, Ecclesiastes, Esther, and Song of Songs; the Midrash to Psalms; and the Midrash of Rabbi Tanhuma, known as the Tanhuma. Although it is customary to refer to a statement in one of the Midrashim as 'the Midrash says', this is far from accurate, since the various Midrashim come from different hands and from different periods. A major activity among modern scholars has been to date the various Midrashim and to study the different background against which each was produced. A passage in one Midrash may have its parallel in another Midrash or in the Talmud and scholars then consider where the two versions are in agreement and where they differ and why. The older view was that laws cannot be derived from statements in the Midrashim since these do not have the precision of legal formulations and are homiletical rather than prescriptive. Nevertheless, many later codifiers have incorporated into their systems rules found only in the Midrashim.

To sum up: the term Midrash denotes both the Midrashic method and the Midrashic collections. In the former sense the term is found in the Mishnah and the Talmud. In the early Rabbinic period the Midrash, in this sense, is distinguished from the Mishnah or the Halakhah. When a law is stated in abstract form, that is, where the bare law is stated without reference to its derivation from Scripture, this is known as a Mishnah ('Teaching') or Halakhah ('a Law'). When, on the other hand, both the law and its derivation from Scripture are given, this is known as a Midrash. Generally speaking, the Halakhic Midrashim give the various laws together with their derivation. In the Mishnah (the name given to the whole collection edited by Rabbi *Judah the Prince), on the other hand, the laws are stated in the abstract form without the scriptural derivation. But this distinction must not be carried too far. Occasionally a Midrash, in the sense mentioned, is found in the Mishnah and the Talmud. Once the Talmud had been accepted as the final arbiter in matters of law, it was considered unlawful by the post-Talmudic authorities to use the Midrashic method to discover new rules and regulations. Midrashic methodology yielded entirely to the method of pure Halakhic debate and discussion.

> H. L. Strack and G. Stemberger, 'Midrash', in their *Introduction to the Talmud and Midrash*, trans. Markus Bockmuehl (Edinburgh, 1991), 254–93.

**Mikveh** 'Gathering' of water, the ritual bath. The basic scriptural text for the mikveh is: 'Only a spring, cistern, or collection [*mikveh*] of water shall be clean' (Leviticus 11). 'Shall be clean' is understood by the Rabbis to mean 'shall be cleansing', that is, one who has suffered contamination remains unclean until he has immersed himself in the mikveh. In the context the reference is to one who has suffered contamination by coming into contact with a dead rodent or other sources of contamination mentioned in Leviticus. The law only applied in its fullness in the period of the Temple. One who had become contaminated was not allowed to enter the Temple or eat sacred food (e.g. sacrificial meat) until he had immersed himself in the mikveh. After the destruction of the Temple, the law of mikveh has had relevance chiefly to a *menstruant. After her period and after counting the seven 'clean days', a wife has to have immersion in the mikveh before she can resume marital relations with her husband.

The mikveh is constructed so that there is a tank of rain-water (ordinary water from the tap may not be used, since the water must not be poured from a container) which is connected to the waters of a small pool rather like a swimming-pool; the waters of the latter then acquire, so to speak, the purifying quality of the waters of the tank. The laws of mikveh-construction are very complex and, nowadays, the architect will consult with a Rabbi when a mikveh is being built. Orthodox Jews observe the laws of mikveh very strictly and every sizeable Jewish community has one or more mikvaot. Some Jews who observe the laws regarding menstruation use the bath in the house for the purpose of the ritual cleansing but, as stated, this is not allowed by Orthodox law. The laws of mikveh and menstruation are called the laws of 'family purity'. Although the law certainly allows marriage to a child conceived before the wife had visited the mikveh, a certain stigma is attached to such a child by the very Orthodox.

According to the strict law, crockery and cutlery bought from non-Jews have to be immersed in a mikveh before they can be used. This law is not widely observed nowadays even among the Orthodox. According to the Talmud, men must immerse themselves in the mikveh after they have had marital relations or other emission of semen before being allowed to study the Torah. This rule is attributed to *Ezra and is known, in fact, as 'the Immersion of Ezra'. However, the Talmud concludes that the original rule was relaxed on the grounds that it is too difficult for the majority of people to keep. Some pious Jews, nevertheless, still do observe 'the Immersion of Ezra'. Maimonides remarks in a letter that he always observed it. It is the custom for some pious Jews to have immersion in the mikveh on the eve of *Yom Kippur in readiness for the prayers of the sacred day. In Hasidism, the *mikveh is a very important means of cultivating purity of body and soul. All Hasidim immerse themselves in the mikveh on the eve of the Sabbath. Some Hasidim perform the ritual immersion daily before they offer their prayers. Since immersion has to be total, Hasidism sees the mikveh as representing the doctrine of *annihilation of selfhood, the person's self being abnegated by the complete immersion, in which he becomes one with the cleansing waters.

> Isaac Klein, 'Family Purity (II): The Miqweh', in his *A Guide to Jewish Religious Practice* (New York, 1979), 517–22.

**Minyan** 'Number', the quorum of ten males over the age of 13 for communal prayer and the reading of the Torah with the benedictions. Where no minyan is present in the synagogue some of the prayers can still be recited but not the *Kaddish, the *Kedushah and the *Cantor's repetition of the Amidah (see EIGHTEEN BENEDICTIONS). The Torah may be read even where no minyan is present but the benedictions over the reading must not then be recited. From Talmudic times it was considered especially meritorious to be among the first ten in the synagogue for the daily prayers. Some synagogues hire poor men to come there in order to make up the minyan. These are known as 'minyan men'. Many Reform Jews ignore altogether the need for a minyan and recite the prayers no matter how few are present. Conservative Rabbis now rule that women can be counted in the minyan as well as men.

**Miracles** In the Bible, the Talmud, and all other ancient and medieval Jewish writings it is taken for granted that miracles can and do occur, although a miracle was not thought of as a suspension of natural law since, before the rise of modern science, there was no such concept as a natural law that required to be suspended. A miracle was an extraordinary event which, precisely because it was so different from the normal course of events, provided evidence of God's direct intervention; hence the biblical term *nes*, 'sign', for a miracle. The miracle is an indication of divine intervention in particular circumstances. The whole question of miracles involves the doctrine of divine *providence, how the transcendent God can be said to become manifest in the particular events of the world, although this way of looking at the problem did not emerge in Jewish thought until the age of the medieval philosophers.

The Mishnah (*Berakhot* 9: 3) defines as a 'vain prayer' a cry to God to undo the past. Two illustrations are given. One is where a man's wife is pregnant and he prays that the child she is carrying should be a boy. The other is where a man hears from afar the sound of lamentation and prays that the sound should not be one that proceeds from his own house. In both these instances the prayer is futile since the event has already taken place. In the first instance, however, God can perform a miracle and *change* the sex of the foetus from female to male but that, as the Gemara states in its comment to the Mishnah, is to pray for a miracle to be performed and no man has the right to assume that he is worthy for God to perform a miracle on his behalf. Throughout the Rabbinic literature, the possibility of miracles occurring is accepted unreservedly while, at the same time, what is now called the natural order is seen as the usual manifestation of divine providence and the identification of a particular event as a miracle is viewed with caution. The medieval philosophers, too, acknowledge that miracles do occur but there is a tendency to explain even the biblical miracles in natural terms.

Despite the tensions in this matter, the power of holy men to work miracles is recognized in the Bible, the Talmud, and Midrash, and in subsequent Jewish hagiography down

to the Hasidic tales of the miracles performed by the Hasidic *Zaddik. Some modern Jewish theologians have incorrectly read a Talmudic debate (*Shabbat* 53b) as implying that there is a degree of spiritual vulgarity in hankering after miracles. The passage tells of a poor man whose wife had died, leaving him with a little babe. A miracle happened in that his breasts became as a woman's that he might suckle the infant. One Rabbi remarked: 'How great this man must have been that such a miracle was performed for him', but his colleague retorted: 'On the contrary! How unworthy this man must have been that the order of creation was changed on his behalf.' However, the second Rabbi is not denigrating holy men on whose behalf miracles happen, only this particular man and this particular kind of miracle involving a reversal of the roles and nature of male and female.

The real question for moderns is not *can* miracles happen, but did they and do they happen. As Hume recognized, the question is one of evidence. Many events that were seen in the past as miracles can now be understood as due to the operation of natural laws, even though Hume himself is less than categorical about the absolute necessity of cause *A* always to produce the effect *B* it usually seems to produce. Undoubtedly, a modern Jewish believer will be far less prone to attribute extraordinary events to a supernatural intervention, but his belief in God's power will not allow him to deny the very possibility of miracles occurring. A Hasidic saying has it that a Hasid who believes that all the miracles said to have been performed by the Hasidic masters actually happened is a fool. But anyone who believes that they could not have happened is an unbeliever. The same can be be said of miracles in general.

Louis Jacobs, 'Miracles', in his *We Have Reason to Believe*, 3rd edn. (London, 1965), 106–12.

Kaufmann Kohler, 'Miracles and the Cosmic Order', in his *Jewish Theology Systematically and Historically Considered*, new edn. with an introduction by Joseph L. Blau (New York, 1968), 160–6.

**Miriam** Sister of *Moses and Aaron, who, together with them, led the people of Israel through the wilderness (Micah 6: 4). Traditionally, the sister who watched over the infant Moses when he was placed in the Nile (Exodus 2: 2–8), although her name is not given, is Miriam. Miriam is described as a prophetess who led the women in a song of victory after the crossing of the sea (Exodus 13: 20–1). Miriam spoke ill of Moses, for which offence she became leprous until Moses prayed for her to be cured (Numbers 12). After stating that Miriam died at Kadesh and was buried there, Scripture goes on to say that the community was without water (Numbers 20: 1–2). On the basis of this juxtaposition of the verses, there is a popular legend, mentioned in Midrashic sources, that through the merit of Miriam a miraculous well accompanied the Israelites in their journeys but ceased when Miriam died. In a Talmudic passage (*Bava Batra* 17a) it is said that Miriam, like her two brothers and the *patriarchs, died by a 'divine kiss'.

**Mishnah** 'Teaching', the digest of the *Oral Torah compiled by Rabbi *Judah the Prince around the end of the second and the beginning of the third century CE. Rabbi Judah is best described not as the author of the Mishnah but as its editor, since he used earlier collections and other early material, often leaving these in their original form in his compilation. The Mishnah is in Hebrew, the scholarly language of the *Tannaim.

The Mishnah is divided into six orders:

1. *Zeraim*, 'Seeds' (agricultural laws).
2. *Moed*, 'Appointed Time' (Sabbath, festival and fast-day laws).
3. *Nashim*, 'Women' (laws of marriage and divorce).
4. *Nezikin*, 'Damages' (torts, buying and selling, jurisprudence in general).
5. *Kodashim*, 'Sanctities' (laws of the sacrificial system in the Temple).
6. *Tohorot* (the laws of ritual contamination and the means of purification, though the title may be a euphemism for 'impurities').

The titles of the six orders are not given in the Mishnah itself but by later teachers, and the titles do not all necessarily refer to the contents. The title of the fourth order, for example, seems to have been given after one of the opening words and is not descriptive of the order as a whole, just as the title of the first book of the Pentateuch is called *Bereshit* ('In the Beginning'), after its opening word. Similarly, the title *Nashim* may have been given after one of the order's opening words, since this order is primarily about marriage and divorce and not about all the laws appertaining to women found in other orders.

The six orders of the Mishnah are divided into tractates (*masekhtot*) and these are divided into chapters. Each chapter (*perek*) is made up of smaller units called *mishnayot* (plural of *mishnah*; see also MIDRASH). Thus the term Mishnah is used of the work as a whole and of its smallest unit; each of the units is a 'teaching', and the work as a whole is the teaching of Rabbi Judah the Prince. While many attempts have been made to discover why the tractates of the various orders are arranged in the 'order' in which these are found, *Geiger has noted that the arrangement is largely an artificial one, determined by the respective lengths of the tractates in that order, the lengthier ones coming first and the others in descending rank.

The *Hebrew of the Mishnah is known as Mishnaic Hebrew, to distinguish it from biblical and Modern Hebrew. A good deal of the material in the Mishnah (the last two orders, for example) was of no practical significance for Jewish religious life at the time when the Mishnah was compiled, since this material deals with conditions in the Temple, destroyed in the year 70 CE. Evidently, the aim of Rabbi Judah the Prince and his associates was to provide a complete digest of the whole of the Oral Torah, irrespective of its practical relevance. To study the Torah was a supreme religious aim in itself, quite apart from its practical consequences. Modern scholarship has been much concerned with the question of whether the Mishnaic formulations regarding conditions in the Temple times belong to actual traditions going back to Temple times, or whether they are are simply a reading-back of later ideas into the Temple period; some sections of the Mishnah, like those describing the measurements of the Temple precincts, do seem to be accurate reports dating from Temple times. There has also been much discussion, in both medieval and modern scholarship, of whether, as Maimonides holds, the Mishnah was committed to writing by Rabbi Judah the Prince or whether, as *Rashi holds, the Mishnah was originally an oral work and was not written down until much later.

Once the Mishnah had been compiled, it assumed the character of a canonical text upon which the Amoraim, the post-Mishnaic teachers in Palestine and Babylon, based their own teachings. Both the Palestinian (or Jerusalem) Talmud and the Babylonian Talmud are in the form of a running commentary to the Mishnah.

The Mishnah contains Aggadic (see AGGADAH) as well as Halakhic (see HALAKHAH) material. Tractate *'Ethics of the Fathers', for example, is a purely Aggadic tractate of the Mishnah and there are Aggadic asides in many other sections. The description of the Mishnah as a Code of law is consequently imprecise.

> Herbert Danby, *The Mishnah*, trans. from the Hebrew (Oxford, 1933). H. L. Strack and G. Stemberger, 'The Mishnah', in their *Introduction to the Talmud and Midrash*, trans. Markus Bockmuehl (Edinburgh, 1991), 119–66.

**Mitnaggedim** 'Opponents' or 'Protestants', the traditionalist Rabbis and communal leaders who opposed the ideas and practices of *Hasidism in the eighteenth century and beyond. It speaks volumes for the success of the Hasidic movement that, despite the fact that the movement was new, it was their foes, not the Hasidim, who were called, and called themselves, Mitnaggedim. The most prominent of the Mitnaggedim was *Elijah, Gaon of Vilna. The controversy between the Hasidim and the Mitnaggedim was at first conducted with vehemence and even violence but eventually the two groups made common cause against the inroads into traditional Jewish life made by the *Haskalah.

**Mitzvah** 'Command', the Hebrew for a precept of the Torah (pl. *mitzvot*). On the basis of a homily dating from the third century CE there are said to be 613 *precepts, 365 negative ('do not do this') and 248 positive ('do this') but this numbering of the precepts did not really come into prominence until the medieval period. The distinction, however, between positive and negative precepts is found throughout the Rabbinic literature. In that literature the term *mitzvah* is used for a negative precept as well as a positive but the *mitzvah* is more usually reserved for a positive precept, while the more usual term to denote a negative precept is *averah* ('transgression'); as when, for instance, it is said that a stolen palm-branch must not be used on the festival of *Tabernacles because it is a *mitzvah* that is the result of an *averah*.

A further classification of the precepts is that of 'between man and God' and 'between man and his neighbour', that is, religious and social obligations, although both are seen ultimately as having their sanction in a divine command. Another classification distinguishes positive precepts that depend for their performance on time (i.e. the precept of *tefillin* which is only obligatory during daytime) and precepts that are binding whatever the time in which they are carried out (love of the neighbour, for instance). Women are exempt from carrying out the former. Still another classification is between light and heavy precepts, that is, those that can easily be carried out and those that require much effort and are costly to carry out. In Ethics of the Fathers (2. 1) the advice is given to treat light precepts as seriously as one treats heavy precepts, 'since you do not know the reward for the precepts' and the performance of a light precept may win a greater reward from heaven than the performance of a heavy precept. Not that it is ideal to carry out the precepts in anticipation of reward for so doing. Against such a calculating attitude stands the Rabbinic doctrine of *lishmah* ('for its own sake'), of doing God's will without any ulterior motivation. For all that, it is advised to carry out the precepts even if the motivation is not entirely pure (*shelo lishmah*), since persistence in carrying out the precepts will eventually lead to performance out of pure motivation. The obligation to keep the precepts begins when a boy reaches the age of 13 and a girl the age of 12, hence the terms *Bar Mitzvah and *Bat Mitzvah.

The Rabbinic ideal is to carry out the precepts joyfully. It is generally assumed that Jews have *simhah shel mitzvah*, 'joy in the *mitzvah*' and that even sinners in Israel are as full of *mitzvot* as a pomegranate is full of seeds. (*Hagigah* 27a). The Jerusalem Talmud uses the term *mitzvah* to denote especially a deed of *charity, the *mitzvah par excellence*. In Yiddish a *mitzvah* often means any good deed just as an *averah* is anything bad or wasteful.

### Reasons for the mitzvot

For the Talmudic Rabbis the fact that God commanded the positive and negative precepts is sufficient reason for the Jew to keep them. But the medieval philosophers seek to provide reasons for those precepts such as the *dietary laws for which no reason is stated in the Torah. Maimonides devotes a large section of the third part of his *Guide of the Perplexed* to reasons for those precepts which seem on the surface to be irrational. Some thinkers were opposed to the whole attempt to discover reasons for the precepts, arguing that, apart from the Rabbinic stress on pure obedience, if reasons are suggested this could easily lead to neglect where it is assumed the reasons do not apply. If, for example, the dietary laws are explained on hygienic grounds, this could lead to Jews saying that the laws need not be kept where improved methods of food-production and the advance of medicine have made the risk to health more remote than it was in ancient times. On the other hand, those thinkers who did seek for reasons believed that unless it can be shown that the observance of the *mitzvot* is reasonable, Gentiles will taunt Jews as owing allegiance to an irrational faith in which God tends to be seen as a tyrannical ruler imposing arbitrary laws on His subjects. In the Kabbalah observance of the precepts has a cosmic effect, every detail of the precepts having its correspondence in the upper worlds, assisting the harmony of the *Sefirot so that the divine grace can flow unimpeded throughout creation. Many modern Jews are far less bothered about the reasons for the precepts or, for that matter, about the question of the origin of the precepts as suggested in biblical scholarship. What matters for such Jews is the opportunity the precepts afford for worshipping God (see CONSERVATIVE JUDAISM and FRANKEL).

Gersion Appel, *A Philosophy of Mizvot* (New York, 1975).

Daniel C. Matt, 'The Mystic and the Mizwot', in Arthur Green (ed.), *Jewish Spirituality from the Bible through the Middle Ages* (New York, 1986), 367–404.

Charles Vengrov, *Sefer haḤinnuch as Ascribed to Aaron haLevi of Barcelona* (New York, 1978).

**Mizrachi** Religious Zionist movement founded in 1902. The name Mizrachi is a shortened form of the Hebrew words *merkaz ruḥani,* 'spiritual centre,' and signifies that the aim of *Zionism to establish a Jewish State is highly laudable but this State should serve not only as a political focus but also as a spiritual centre for world Jewry. The Mizrachi maxim gives expression to the movement's special emphasis: 'The Land of Israel for the people of Israel in accordance with the Torah of Israel.' The essential problem for the Mizrachi is posed by the obscurity of the final statement of its programme. How was a modern democratic State, comprising both religious and non-religious Jews, to be conducted in accordance with 'the Torah of Israel'? With the establishment of the State of Israel, the Mizrachi became the National

Religious party (Mafdal) and still grapples, not very successfully, with this severe problem.

**Mizraḥ** 'East', the direction Jews living to the west of Jerusalem face in their prayers, the prayers speeding to heaven, so to speak, through the former site of the *Temple. Wherever possible synagogues in Western lands are built with the Ark containing the Torah Scrolls in the east, the *mizraḥ* of the building. Seats in the *mizraḥ* section of the synagogue are the most prized seats. Private homes sometimes have a plaque with the word *mizraḥ* in Hebrew on an eastern wall so that worshippers in the privacy of their homes can recognize the direction they should face.

**Molech** A god to whom there are a number of references in the Bible (Leviticus 18: 21; 20: 2–4; Deuteronomy 18: 10; 2 Kings 16: 3; 17: 17; 21: 6; 23: 10). In some of these references the worship of Molech consists of passing children through the fire. Whatever the original meaning of 'giving his seed to Molech', the Mishnah (*Sanhedrin* 7: 7) defines the offence of Molech-worship on the basis of the biblical verses in which passing through fire is mentioned. This definition is obviously purely theoretical, since the Mishnah deals with capital punishment for the offence and this form of punishment had long been abolished in the time of the Mishnah. The Mishnah reads: '"He that offers his seed to Molech" is not culpable unless he gives up [the child] to Molech and passes him through the fire; if he gave him up to Molech but did not pass him through the fire, or if he passed him through the fire but did not give him up to Molech he is not culpable; he must both give him up to Molech and pass him through the fire.' 'Passing through the fire' may have been originally a kind of formal dedication of the child to the worship of Molech, a fire-god. The Leviticus verses do not mention fire at all. The verse in Deuteronomy does speak of consigning children to the fire but makes no mention of Molech in this connection nor is there an unambiguous statement in the verse that the meaning is child sacrifice. But from the archaeological evidence it appears that child sacrifices were certainly known in Canaanite worship, so that it is plausible to understand Molech-worship as a practice in which children were actually burned to death in the fire. Giving children to Molech was understood homiletically by Jewish preachers and moralists to denote giving Jewish children the kind of bad education that would cause them to be estranged from Judaism when they grew up.

Baruch A. Levine, 'The Cult of Molech in Biblical Israel' in Nahum M. Sarna (ed.), *The JPS Torah Commentary: Leviticus* (Philadelphia, New York, and Jerusalem, 1989), 258–60.

**Moon, Blessing over** Heb. *Birkat Levanah*, 'Blessing over the Moon' or *Kiddush Levanah*, 'Sanctification of the Moon'; the ceremony, still observed by many Jews, in which God is praised, at the beginning of the month, for having created the moon, especially significant since the Jewish calendar is a lunar calendar. In Rabbinic times, before the calendar had been fixed, the date of *Rosh Hodesh, the New Moon minor festival, depended on the sighting of the new moon. The Supreme Court, after receiving witnesses of the sighting, declared that the day was sacred in the sense that the coming month and the festivals in it are counted from this day.

The procedure for the rite of blessing over the moon is for people to go outside on a night before the moon is full and recite the benediction found in its essentials in the Talmud:

'Blessed art Thou, O Lord our God, King of the universe, by whose word the heavens were created, and by the breath of whose mouth all their host. Thou didst assign them a statute and a season, that they should not change their appointed charge. They are glad and rejoice to do the will of their Master, the truthful Worker whose work is truth, who bade the moon renew itself, a crown of glory unto those who have been upborne by Him from the womb, who in time to come will themselves be renewed like it, to honour their Creator for his glorious kingdom's sake. Blessed art Thou, O Lord, who renewest the months.'

Various additions were made over the years. In the full rite the benediction over the moon is preceded by the recital of Psalm 148: 1–6, and followed by the recital of Psalms 121 and 150. The custom of dancing towards the moon may have had its origin in the festive dances that took place when the court proclaimed the day of the new moon. But, from the period of the *Geonim, the dance consists of a threefold spring towards the moon which is addressed directly with the words: 'Just as I dance towards thee but am unable to reach thee, so may mine enemies be prevented from reaching me to do harm.' After the landings on the moon, Rabbi S. Goren, the then Chief Rabbi of Israel, changed the formula to read: 'but I am not reaching thee', instead of: 'but am unable to reach thee'. The dancing towards the moon and the further practice of reciting, first forwards and then backwards, the verse: 'Terror and dread descend upon them, through the might of thine arm they stay still as stone' (Exodus 15: 16), obviously have a magical connotation.

Nosson Scherman (ed.), *The Complete ArtScroll Siddur* (New York, 1984), 612–17.

**Montefiore, Claude** Modernist Jewish theologian and author (1858–1938). Montefiore, a great-nephew of the famous philanthropist, Sir Moses Montefiore, studied at Balliol College, Oxford, where he came under the influence of the liberal Christian thinker, Benjamin Jowett, the Master of the College. From Oxford, Montefiore, resolving to increase his Jewish knowledge, went to study Judaism at the Hochschule in Berlin. There he met Solomon *Schechter, whom he brought to England to act as his private tutor. In 1902, Montefiore founded the radical Reform organization the Jewish Religious Union, which led to the establishment, in 1911, of the Liberal Jewish Synagogue, of which he became the President. A man of means, Montefiore was active in philanthropic endeavours, Jewish and non-Jewish. He refused, however, to give his support to *Zionism, a movement he thought too 'narrow' in its aims, and he even tried to prevent the signing of the Balfour Declaration.

Among Montefiore's many writings are works in which he compared Jewish and Christian thought. Together with Herbert Loewe, an Orthodox Jewish scholar, Montefiore published *A Rabbinic Anthology*, a collection of Rabbinic teachings to which he and Loewe added notes in which the teachings were assessed, respectively, from the Liberal/Reform and the Orthodox point of view.

Montefiore accepted the findings of *biblical criticism, which, he believed, had demonstrated that the Pentateuch was a composite work, produced at different periods in Israel's history. A convinced theist, Montefiore believed that Judaism's main contribution consisted in keeping pure monotheism alive. In this Judaism was superior to Christianity but, he maintained, Judaism, as a religion based on justice, was in some ways inferior to Christianity, a religion based on love, at least in the ethical sphere. In *Ahad Ha-Am's attack on Montefiore's attempt to see the religion of the future as a blend of the Jewish and Christian ethic, the view is put forward that there can be no marriage between a religion of justice and a religion of love. In point of fact, in their characterization of the two religions both thinkers are too facile, since Judaism knows of love as Christianity knows of justice. Montefiore looked upon Jesus as a great teacher but naturally refused to recognize him as in any way divine. For all his admiration for the Christian ethic and what he saw as an appealing, mystical note in the Gospels, Montefiore was opposed to any attempt at placing the New Testament on a par with the Hebrew Scriptures or at having readings from the New Testament in any act of Jewish worship.

Edward Kessler, *An English Jew: The Life and Writings of Claude Montefiore* (London, 1989).

**Mordecai** The hero of the book of *Esther who refused to bow to Haman, as a result of which Haman sought to persuade the king to destroy the Jews. The deliverance of the Jews is celebrated on the festival of *Purim. A degree of ambiguity is present among the Talmudic Rabbis about Mordecai's refusal to bow before Haman as the king had requested, thus endangering the life of his people. One excuse advanced for Mordecai's refusal is that Haman had set himself up as a god. In any event, in subsequent Jewish lore Mordecai is the prototype of the proud Jew who refuses to bow to tyranny.

**Moses** The most important figure in Judaism, the leader of the children of Israel from Egyptian bondage and, particularly, the great teacher of the Torah he received from God; hence the Torah is often called 'the Torah of Moses'. As told in the *Pentateuch from the beginning of Exodus to the end of Deuteronomy, the story of Moses begins with his birth to Amram and Jochebed in Egypt. When his mother had hidden him in the reeds of the Nile in order to save his life, because he was threatened by Pharaoh's decree that every Hebrew male be put to death, Pharaoh's daughter took pity on the infant and adopted him as her son. When Moses grew to manhood he went out of the royal palace, where he had been brought up as

an Egyptian prince, to see the afflictions of his Hebrew brethren toiling under the lash of the Egyptian taskmasters. Witnessing an Egyptian seeking to kill an Israelite, Moses slew the Egyptian, as a result of which he was obliged to flee for his life. Escaping to Midian, Moses served as a shepherd to Jethro, the priest of Midian, whose daughter, Zipporah, he married. During his stay in Midian, God appeared to Moses in the burning bush and ordered him to go to Pharaoh to demand that the people be released from their bondage; eventually, God said, Moses would lead them to the land of Canaan, the land of their fathers. When, after the ten plagues, Pharaoh finally let the people go, the Egyptians pursued the escaping Israelites but were drowned in the waters of the sea, whereupon Moses led the people in a song of victory. Arriving at Mount *Sinai, the people received the *Decalogue and, during his forty days' stay on the mountain, where he neither ate nor drank, Moses received further laws and instructions which he taught to the people. Moses led the Israelites through the wilderness for forty years until they came to the borders of the Promised Land. There Moses died at the age of 120 and there he was buried.

This is the bare outline of the Moses saga as told in much greater detail in the Pentateuch, and the whole is elaborated on in numerous Midrashic legends. According to the traditional view the Moses story, and, indeed, the whole of the Pentateuch, was compiled by Moses himself at the direct 'dictation' of God, a view that is still accepted in Orthodox Judaism despite the fact that it has been heavily assailed by *biblical criticism, in which discipline the Pentateuch is seen as a composite work produced in different periods of Israel's history. The question of the historical Moses has exercised the minds of biblical scholars, very few of whom, however, go so far as to deny completely that Moses is a historical figure. What requires to be discussed is not so much the question of the historical Moses but rather the role this towering figure occupies in the life and thought of the Jewish religion.

*Jewish Attitudes to Moses*

A marked ambivalence is to be observed in the Jewish tradition with regard to the personality of Moses. On the one hand, Moses is hailed as the intermediary between God and man, as the instrument of God's revelation of the Torah and the teacher of the Torah to Israel, as the father of all the prophets, with whom God spoke 'face to face' (Exodus 33: 11). On the other hand, strenuous efforts were made to reject any notion that Moses is divine or semi-divine. Even in the Pentateuch, Moses is described as a human being with human failings. He is reluctant to be God's messenger (Exodus 3: 11); he loses his temper (Numbers 20: 9–11; 31: 14); he marries and has children (Exodus 18: 2–4); and eventually, like all human beings, he dies and is buried (Deuteronomy 34). For all his role as the intermediary, it is not Moses but God who gives the Torah to Israel. There is even a Rabbinic saying that if God had not given the Torah to Moses, He could have given it, with the same effect, to *Ezra. Judaism is in no way 'Mosaism'. It is the religion of the Jewish people. In a Rabbinic comment (*Berakhot* 32a) on the words 'go down' (Exodus 32: 7), uttered by God when the people had been guilty of worshipping the *golden calf, these words are interpreted as: 'Go down from your lofty status since I have given you this greatness only because of Israel.' Yet in other statements in the Rabbinic literature Moses is declared to be equal in merit to all the people of Israel together. In the Middle Ages, there were a number of Jewish thinkers who, evidently in response to the claims made for *Jesus by Christians and for *Muhammad by Muslims, so elevated the role of Moses that the Jewish religion was made to centre on him. But the opposite tendency is also clearly to be observed. Precisely because Christianity and, to a lesser degree, Islam centre on an individual, these thinkers declared that Judaism, on the contrary, singles out no individual not even a Moses, as belonging to the heart of the faith. The stresses in the matter vary in proportion to the particular challenge in the period in which the role of Moses is considered. Throughout, the tension exists between an affirmation that Moses is supremely significant and the need to play down the role of Moses. Maimonides is extraordinary in laying down, as a *principle of the faith, that the Jew is obliged to believe that Moses is the greatest man who ever lived and, even, that his status is that of the *angels. But, as with his other principles, Maimonides is reacting, in a particularly strong emphasis, to the challenges to Judaism in his day and a careful reading of Maimonides' formulation shows that he hedges round his statement with a number of reservations.

In his formulation of the seventh principle in the commentary to the Mishnah (*Sanhedrin* 10: 1) Maimonides writes:

'The seventh principle of faith. The prophecy of Moses our Teacher. This implies that we must believe he was the father of all the prophets before him and that those who came after him were all beneath him in rank. He was chosen by God from the whole human kind. He comprehended more of God than any man in the past or future ever comprehended or will comprehend. And we must believe that he reached a state of exaltedness beyond the sphere of humanity, so that he attained to the angelic rank and became included in the order of the angels. There was no veil which he did not pierce. No material hindrance stood in his way, and no defect whether small or great mingled itself with him. The imaginative and sensual powers of his perceptive faculty were stripped from him. His desiderative power was still and he remained pure intellect only. It is in this significance that it is remarked of him that he discoursed with God without any angelic intermediary.'

It has to be appreciated that, in addition to the reservations Maimonides goes on to express, he is thinking only of Moses' perception of God through which he received the divine communication. It is only in this that Moses is greater than any other human being, and it is not to be thought that Moses in himself was faultless.

From Talmudic times the usual appellation of Moses is Moshe Rabbenu, 'Moses our Teacher'. A passage in the Talmud (*Yevamot* 49b) states that the difference between Moses and all the other *prophets is that they saw through a dim glass while Moses saw through a clear glass. Moses was chosen to be Israel's leader because he was so considerate to his flock when shepherding for Jethro (Midrash Exodus Rabbah 2: 2). In another passage (*Nedarim* 38a) Moses is said to have been wealthy, strong, and meek since the Holy One, blessed be He, only causes His spirit to rest on a person who has these endowments. Moses and his brother *Aaron are frequently mentioned together as the leaders of the people, Moses being the stern man of law, brooking no compromise, while Aaron is the leader who loves peace and pursues it. Moses died through a kiss of God (*Bava Batra* 17a) and God Himself buried him (*Sotah* 14a) in a grave that had been prepared for him since the eve of the Sabbath of creation (*Pesaḥim* 54a).

A curious legend about Moses circulated in the Late Middle Ages, which is quoted by some Rabbinic authors but attacked by others as a denigration of Moses. A certain king, hearing of Moses' fame, sent a renowned painter to portray Moses' features. On the painter's return with the portrait the king showed it to his sages who unanimously declared that the features portrayed were those of a degenerate. The astonished king journeyed himself to the camp of Moses and saw for himself that the portrait did not lie. Moses admitted that the sages were right and that he had been given from birth many evil traits of character but that he had held them under control and succeeded in conquering them. This, the legend concludes, was Moses' greatness; in spite of the tremendous handicap he managed to become the man of God. It is difficult to know when, where, and how this strange legend was invented.

There is thus no official Jewish attitude to Moses. What matters for Judaism is the role Moses plays in bringing the Torah to Israel and in interpreting the Torah for them. In this sense every teacher of the Torah follows in Moses' footsteps and adds something to the Torah of Moses. This appears to be the idea behind the oft-quoted Talmudic legend (*Menaḥot* 29b) that when Moses was miraculously transported into the school of Rabbi *Akiba he was at first dismayed that he was unable to understand what Rabbi Akiba was teaching. But when a disciple asked Akiba how he knew something and Akiba replied: 'It is tradition from Moses our Teacher', Moses' mind was set at rest.

Martin Buber, *Moses: The Revelation and the Covenant* (Oxford, 1946).
Louis Ginzberg, *Legends of the Jews*, iii (Philadelphia, 1942).
Louis Jacobs, *Principles of the Jewish Faith* (Northvale, NJ, and London, 1988), 206–15.
Nahum M. Sarna, *Exploring Exodus* (New York, 1986).

**Moses de Leon** Spanish Kabbalist (d. 1305). De Leon was the author of a number of Kabbalistic works but these pale into insignificance when compared to his major work, the *Zohar, or, at least, to the major portions of this work. There is hardly any doubt that Moses de Leon introduced the Zohar to the world of the Kabbalists but he is reported as saying that he copied the work from an ancient manuscript and that the true author was the second-century teacher Rabbi *Simeon ben Yohai. It is, however, the virtually unanimous view of modern scholarship, especially thanks to Gershom Scholem, that de Leon was the author of the bulk of the Zohar. De Leon obviously used earlier material but he compiled the Zohar in an Aramaic of his own and in this sense the work is highly original. The later additions were made by other hands and efforts have been made by scholars to point to the differences between these and the body of the Zohar.

Gershom Scholem, 'Moses ben Shem Tov de Leon', in his *Kabbalah* (Jerusalem, 1974), 432–4.

**Mountains** Mountains feature very frequently in the biblical narratives, the best known in the Jewish tradition being *Sinai, upon which the Torah was given; Moriah, upon which the *Akedah* took place (later identified with Mount Zion, upon which the *Temple was built); and Carmel, upon which *Elijah struggled with the prophets of Baal. Clearly to be observed in the biblical record is the attempt to wean the people away from the ancient practice of worshipping the gods on the mountains. 'You must destroy all the sites at which the nations you are to dispossess worshipped their gods, whether on lofty mountains and on hills or under any luxuriant tree' (Deuteronomy 12: 2). *Height, of which mountains are especially indicative, is used frequently as a symbol of the spiritual. 'Who may ascend the mountain of the Lord? And who may stand in His holy place? He that hath clean hands and a pure heart; who hath not set his desire upon vanity, and hath not sworn deceitfully' (Psalms 24: 3–4). 'I lift up mine eyes unto the hills; whence will my help come? My help is from the Lord, the maker of heaven and earth' (Psalms 121: 1–2). The mountains are invoked to describe God's love for His people. 'The mountains are round about Jerusalem, and the Lord is round about His people, from this time forth and for evermore' (Psalms 125: 2). 'For the mountains may depart, and the hills be removed; but My kindness shall not depart from thee' (Isaiah 54: 10). Implied in these verses and in other parts of the Bible is that God is the Lord of creation, in which the mountains are the most awe-inspiring evidence of His mighty acts. A special *benediction on seeing lofty mountains was introduced by the Rabbis: 'Blessed art thou, O Lord our God, King of the universe, who hast made the creation.' The Talmud (*Horayot* 14a) describes a scholar familiar with all the teachings of the Torah as a Sinai, while a scholar not so well versed but keener is called 'one who uproots mountains'.

J. H. Hertz, *The Pentateuch and Haftorahs* (London, 1960), 757.

**Mourning, Laws of** Jewish tradition enjoins that when a near relative dies mourning rites are to be observed (see DEATH AND BURIAL). A near relative is defined in this connection as: father, mother, son, daughter, brother, sister, husband, wife. The periods of mourning are closely defined. Maimonides (*Evel*, 13. 11–12) comes close to the original intention of the Rabbinic setting of a fixed period for mourning. To mourn, says Maimonides, beyond the allotted period is foolish since that would mean a failure to accept the inevitable fact of death, from which there is no escape. But not to mourn at all is cruel and unfeeling, evidence that the relative was insufficiently loved during his or her lifetime and is not really missed.

There are three periods of mourning: 1. the Shivah (seven days); 2. the Sheloshim (thirty days); and 3. the first year. The first two are observed by all relatives; the third only by sons and daughters on the death of their parents. The Shivah period is counted from the burial but a part of the day is counted as a day for the purpose. If, for example, the relative was buried on Tuesday afternoon, the rest of Tuesday is counted as the first day and the Shivah ends after one hour on the next Monday morning. During the Shivah the mourners sit on low stools (hence the expression 'sitting Shivah'); they do not bathe, shave, or have a haircut, they do not have marital relations; they do not study the Torah (because the latter is a great delight for the Jew); and they do not work or attend to their business affairs. If, however, the mourners are poor a dispensation is generally given them to go to work after the first three days of the Shivah. Mourners do not leave their homes during the Shivah but they may do so to go to the synagogue in order to recite the *Kaddish. It is the universal custom, however, wherever possible, to arrange for a *minyan to be present in the home of the mourners to obviate the need to leave the home. It is considered a high religious duty to visit mourners during the Shivah to offer them words of comfort and consolation. The manner of greeting mourners

during the Shivah is: 'May the Omnipresent comfort you in the midst of all other mourners over Zion and Jerusalem' (referring to Jewish mourning in general over the destruction of the *Temple). Since public expressions of grief are proscribed on the Sabbath the mourners attend the synagogue on the Sabbath but they are not called to the reading of the Torah and do not have marital relations. If a festival falls during the Shivah, the festival rejoicing overrides the Shivah. For example, if the burial took place two days before Passover, the Shivah period would last for only two, not seven, days. On the principle that, in these matters, any part of the day counts as a day, even if the burial took place on the eve of the festival, the hours until the festival count as the Shivah, which ends as soon as the festival comes in. It is customary to have a candle burning during the Shivah on the basis of the verse: 'The soul of a man is lamp of the Lord' (Proverbs 20: 27).

The Sheloshim period extends for thirty days but here, too, a part of the first day and a part of the thirtieth are counted in the total. During the Sheloshim mourners do not shave or have a haircut and do not listen to music, nor do they attend weddings or go to parties. At the end of the Sheloshim the period of mourning is over and there are no further restrictions, except for those who mourn the passing of parents, for whom the restrictions of the Sheloshim apply for a whole year. It seemed extremely onerous even in Talmudic times for people to go without a haircut for a whole year and the Talmud permits this if the appearance of the mourner is so unkempt that his friends rebuke him for his untidiness. Many people, nowadays, shave after the Shivah since it is the present custom to shave daily so that the 'rebuke' occurs as soon as the beard has a few days' growth.

Orthodox Jews observe the laws of mourning very strictly, as do the majority of Conservative Jews. Reform Jews, too, observe some of the laws but generally do not see all the mourning rituals as binding, believing that they should be adopted by free choice where they are psychologically helpful.

Isaac Klein, 'The Laws of Mourning', in his *A Guide to Jewish Religious Practice* (New York, 1979), 269–300.
Maurice Lamm, *The Jewish Way in Death and Mourning* (New York, 1966).

**Muhammad** The prophet and founder of the religion of *Islam (d. 612). After the rise of

Islam, many Jewish thinkers reacted to the claims made for Muhammad by elevating the role and personality of Moses. Maimonides, for example, lays down as one of the *principles of the Jewish faith that no prophet has ever arisen, even in Israel, greater than Moses, and thinkers like *Bahya, Ibn Pakudah tend to speak of Moses as 'the Prophet', adapting this form from the Islamic designation of Muhammad.

**Muktzah** 'Set aside'; an object that must not be handled on the Sabbath and festivals. The basic principle behind the laws of *muktzah* is that a fence is made around the Sabbath and festivals to prevent any infringement of the law. If, for instance, it would have been permitted to handle on the Sabbath working implements such as a saw or a chisel or to handle money or a pen, it would have been far easier to forget that the day is sacred and actually use the saw to saw wood or the money to buy and sell or the pen to write with it, all acts forbidden on the Sabbath. It is, however, permitted to touch *muktzah* objects, the prohibition extending only to handling them.

**Musar Movement** The movement was founded by Israel *Salanter in nineteenth-century Lithuania with the aim of promoting greater inwardness, religious piety, and ethical conduct among traditionally minded Jews. There can be little doubt that the impetus for the movement was given by the inroads the *Haskalah had made among Russian Jews as well as the success of the Hasidic movement (see HASIDISM) which taught that the traditional study of the Talmud and Codes, while highly significant, did not in itself suffice to promote a sound religious outlook on life. At first the movement sought to influence small circles of businessmen but it soon became a much more élitist movement, attracting, especially, the students in the Lithuanian *Yeshivot.

The word *musar* means 'reproof' or 'instruction', as in the verse: 'Hear, my son, the instruction [*musar*] of thy father' (Proverbs 1: 8). There developed in the Middle Ages and later, side by side with works on Talmud, Halakhah, Kabbalah, and philosophy, a Musar literature with the specific aim of encouraging religious awareness and character-formation. Classics of this genre are: Bahya, *Ibn Pakudah's *Duties of the Heart*, *Cordovero's *Palm Tree of Deborah*, and Moses Hayyim *Luzzatto's *Path of the Upright*. What was novel in Israel Salanter's approach, and that of his disciples, was the contention that the mere study of the Musar works was inadequate. In order for the ideas found in these works to penetrate the heart it was essential to reflect deeply on their implication. The new Musar movement encouraged the reading of a few texts over and over again, attended by a melancholy tune. Anticipating Freud, to some extent, Salanter and his followers believed that the subconscious mind has to be moved by severe introspection, as a result of which ethical and religious conduct become second nature. Salanter pointed out that observant Jews who would never dream of offending against the *dietary laws could still be unscrupulous in their dealings with others. This can only be, he maintained, because generations of Jews had become so accustomed to observance of the dietary laws that it was literally unthinkable for them to conduct themselves otherwise, whereas there had been no such habit-forming training in the ethical sphere.

At first the new movement met with determined opposition. The Maskilim, the followers of Haskalah, believed, rightly or wrongly, that while character-improvement was undoubtedly important and wholesome, the stress placed by the Musarists on severe introspection, as well as their insistence on total commitment to the traditional way, tended to produce narrow and bigoted personalities. The traditionalist Rabbis opposed the movement on the grounds that the Torah is in itself balm for the troubled soul and there was no need for any supplementary methods of self-improvement. The Rabbis were also afraid that the emotional thrust of the movement might lead to a loss of the intellectualism that was the hallmark of Lithuanian Jewry. This kind of critique was not without justification and the great Yeshivot only adopted the Musar regime after a fierce struggle. But eventually Musar did win out. Every one of the famous Lithuanian Yeshivot introduced Musar into its curriculum. Together with the Yeshivah principal, each Yeshivah appointed a *Mashgiaḥ* ('Overseer'), a spiritual guide and mentor who delivered regular Musar discourses as well as offering individual guidance to the students. For at least half an hour each day, the students closed their copies of the Talmud to sit in a darkened room while they rehearsed the Musar texts. To this day, the Lithuanian-type Yeshivah, in the USA, Israel, and other countries, has the dual function of training its students to become Talmudic and Halakhic scholars and teaching them to become personalities whose life is governed by *yirat shamayim*, 'fear of Heaven'.

As in Hasidism, there are various approaches in the Musar movement, in accordance with the particular emphasis of the individual teachers, all disciples of Salanter or disciples of his disciples. But the two main Musar schools are those of Slabodka, the Yeshivah headed by Nathan Zevi Finkel (the Old Man of Slabodka, as he is called) and Navaradok, headed by Joseph Horowitz (the Old Man of Navaradok). The majority of the contemporary Lithuanian-style Yeshivot follow largely the Slabodka way but a few follow the way of Navaradok. The Slabodka school places the emphasis on the dignity and sublime value of human beings created in the image of *God. The dedicated Torah scholar can attain to a rank higher than the angels. Navaradok, on the other hand, stresses the need for the scholar to overcome his worldly desires and to have no ambition other than to be a true servant of God and a student of His Torah. As an exercise in spiritual independence, the Navaradoks used to carry out bizarre practices, demonstrating, for instance, their contempt for worldly opinion by exposing themselves to ridicule. The difference between the two schools has been put in this way. In Slabodka they taught: man is so great, how can he sin? In Navaradok they taught: man is so small, how dare he sin?

The Musar movement has often been contrasted to its detriment with Hasidism, a much less austere and more joyous religious movement. While Hasidism frowns on too much introspection and encourages its adherents to think less of themselves and more of heavenly matters (see ANNIHILATION OF SELFHOOD), Musar is very severe on its followers in urging them constantly to look inwards, always to be dissatisfied with the stage they have reached in learning and piety. The Musarists claim that the Hasidic way is a form of escapism, a perpetual direction of the gaze outwards in fear of what is to be found within. Perhaps the most cogent description of the difference between the two movements is that while both Hasidism and Musar teach that this world is nothing and the next world everything, Musar dwells on the first part of the affirmation, Hasidism on the second.

Eventually, Hasidism had an influence on Musar, and the Musar teachers often used Hasidic material in their discourses. Even the main difference between the two movements, the doctrine of the *Zaddik, became blurred when the more famous Musar personalities were given the kind of veneration hitherto reserved for the Hasidic masters.

There is only one full-scale history of the Musar movement, that of Dov Katz, in Hebrew, in five volumes with an additional volume on the polemics surrounding the movement. The Musarists themselves wrote very little but in recent years a number of collections of Musar teachings have been published. The novels of the Yiddish writer Hayyim Grade contain heroes and anti-heroes taken from the Musar movement.

Louis Ginzberg, 'Rabbi Israel Salanter', in his *Students, Scholars and Saints* (New York, 1958), 145–94.

Kopul Rosen, *Rabbi Israel Salanter and the Musar Movement* (London, 1945).

**Music** Music has been associated with religion in Judaism from the beginning. The word *shirah* ('song') is often used in the Bible simply to denote a poem but there is enough evidence that it frequently refers to a chant or song, sometimes accompanied by musical instrument, as when *Miriam leads the women in the great song of victory at the sea with a tambourine (Exodus 15: 20). Especially noteworthy in this connection is the singing and playing of the *Levites in the *Temple. It is generally understood that the *Psalms were chanted by the Levites accompanied by the playing of instruments and this may be the meaning of Psalm 150 in which various instruments are mentioned. Biblical scholars see the superscriptions to the Psalms as indications of the various melodies to which they were sung. The Mishnah (*Arakhin* 2: 3–4) gives a detailed description of the Levites playing in the Second Temple and this is probably based on a reliable tradition. The medieval commentators were puzzled by the whole question of the introduction of a role for the Levites not referred to in the Torah, since this appears to contradict the doctrine of the immutability of the Torah. The usual defence is that the Torah itself made provisions for the innovation, which was said to have been conveyed orally to Moses at *Sinai.

Instrumental music was not used in the

traditional synagogue but the prayers and hymns were usually chanted (see CANTOR; CHOIR) and the reading of the Torah was done in a special chant (see CANTILLATION). The Lurianic Kabbalists sang sweet melodies while concentrating on the mystical meaning of the prayers (see *KAVVANAH). In Hasidism, in particular, music plays a prominent role as a high form of worship in itself. The Hasidic *niggun* ('melody'), often without words, is a regular feature of Hasidic life, together with the sacred dance. Some of the Hasidic masters composed their own melodies for their Hasidim to sing on the Sabbath, the festivals, and other happy occasions in the year. The *Habad master, *Dov Baer of Lubavitch had an expert choir and orchestra in his court, although, naturally, the latter did not play on the Sabbath. Some of the Hasidic masters used to play the violin to produce a 'prayer without words'.

Rabbi Dov Baer observes in his *Tract on Ecstasy*:

'First, it is necessary to understand the nature of ecstasy produced by melody. This is in the category of spontaneous ecstasy alone, without any choice or intellectual will whatsoever. This is an ecstasy that is felt, and yet the one who experiences it is not himself aware of it, because it does not result from the intention of the self to produce ecstasy, but is produced automatically and comes of its own accord without it being known to him. Since it is as if it is not felt or known to him at that very moment, it can be said that there is a total lack of self-awareness. But, for all that, it is an experienced ecstasy.'

This master refers here to the problem for the self-effacing Hasid who wishes to engage in ecstatic prayer and yet lose himself in the transcendent. In music the self can enjoy a profoundly ecstatic experience and yet be totally lost and immersed in the music.

There are numerous Hasidic sayings about the significance of melody in, as the Zohar puts it, opening those heavenly gates that firmly shut except to song and tears. The Habad master, Rabbi Solomon Zalman of Kopust (1830–1900), wrote a great deal on the philosophy of melody in prayer. He suggests, for instance, that the three colours of white, red, and green can be expressed in prayer. When the worshipper arrives in his prayer to the section in which God's mercies are related, he should sing a 'white' song, the colour of the divine mercy. When he arrives at more solemn passages, he should sing a 'red' melody, the colour of the divine judgement. A 'green' melody is suitable for the harmonizing principle between judgement and mercy, which, in the Kabbalistic scheme of the *Sefirot, is represented by this colour.

A. Z. Idelsohn, *Jewish Music in its Historical Development* (New York, 1944).

## Mysticism

**Mysticism** The difficulties encountered in attempting to define mysticism are well known. Dean Inge, in his *Mysticism in Religion*, quotes no fewer than twenty-six different definitions of mysticism to which he adds others. All of these refer to religious experience, more specifically, to communion with God, of an intense and direct nature. Jewish mysticism can be defined, therefore, as that aspect of Jewish religious experience in which the mind encounters God directly. The *Kabbalah is often identified with Jewish mysticism but, while undoubtedly the Kabbalistic doctrines were formulated by men who reflected profoundly on the divine and who were in this sense mystics, there were Jewish mystics before the rise of the Kabbalah and the Kabbalah itself is not limited to purely mystical speculations. Gershom Scholem, the great master of Jewish mystical historiography, attributes the reticence of Jewish mystics about their personal experiences, and the lack of mystical testimonies in Jewish literature, to the fact that Jews have always retained a sense of the incongruity between mystical experience and the idea of God as Creator, King, and Lawgiver. But personal mystical testimonies, though extremely rare in Judaism, do exist. Scholem also tends to deny that Jewish mystics know of the *unio mystica*, in which the soul of the mystic is absorbed in God. Here again, as Moshe Idel and others have recently pointed out, Scholem's generalization is too sweeping. The *unio mystica* is not entirely unknown even in a religion like Judaism which stresses the vast gulf between God and the individual soul.

Scholem has traced a number of major trends in Jewish mysticism, the earliest of which is that of the Merkavah ('*Chariot') mystics, extending over a thousand-year period from the beginning of the present era to around the year 1000. These mystics employed techniques by means of which they achieved an ascent of soul into the heavenly realms to behold God on the

Throne of Glory. The *Saints of Germany had different aims, leading an ascetic life and practising mortification of the flesh. Abraham Abulafia (1240–c.1291) believed in prophetic revelations which could be attained, he believed, through meditation on various combinations of divine names and by resort to music and breathing exercises. Then there are the two versions of the Kabbalah, that of the Zohar and that of Isaac *Luria in Safed. Scholem describes the Shabbetean form of mysticism (see *SHABBETAI ZEVI) as 'mystical heresy', in which the Lurianic Kabbalah received such a radical transformation that the whole Shabbetean movement read itself out of Judaism entirely. The final phase of Jewish mysticism found its expression in Hasidism. Among modern authors, Rabbi A. I. *Kook tried to develop a mystical approach to Judaism wedded to the traditional *Halakhah. But the majority of modern works on Jewish mysticism belong more to the realm of the occult than to the Jewish mystical tradition.

Louis Jacobs, *Jewish Mystical Testimonies* (New York, 1972).

Gershom G. Scholem, *Major Trends in Jewish Mysticism* (London, 1955).

# N

**Nahmanides** Spanish Talmudist, Kabbalist, and biblical exegete (1194–1270), known, after the initial letters of his name, as Ramban (*Rabbi Moshe ben Nahman*). Nahmanides was born in Gerona, Spain, where he lived for most of his life. An outstanding Talmudist, his work in this field still enjoys the highest esteem among students of the Talmud. As a Halakhic authority, he exercised a great influence on the *Codes of Jewish law, especially through the *Responsa of his most distinguished disciple, Solomon Ibn *Adret. Nahmanides was also the leading figure in the Gerona circle of Kabbalists. Indeed, it was through his renown as a Talmudist that respectability was won for the Spanish Kabbalah; though he was very circumspect in sharing his Kabbalistic insights, referring to them, for instance, in his Commentary to the Pentateuch, only by hint. Nahmanides was on very good terms with Christian notables, including King James I of Aragon. In the famous *disputation in Barcelona with the convert to Christianity, Pablo Christiani, in the presence of the king, Nahmanides emerged the victor and was rewarded by the king. But this victory aroused the ire of the Dominicans with the result that Nahmanides, at the age of 70, was forced to leave Spain for the land of Israel, where he settled in Acre, compiling there his great Commentary. During a stay in Jerusalem, Nahmanides worshipped in a synagogue that has recently been excavated and partially rebuilt and is now a tourist attraction in the Old City.

## Commentary to the Pentateuch

In his Commentary, one of the standard biblical commentaries which took its place side by side with that of *Rashi, Nahmanides tries, wherever possible, to arrive at the plain meaning of the text. At the same time, he believes that the Torah has a deeper, inner meaning as a mystical text. For instance, he accepts the Kabbalistic view that on one level the Torah is a series of combinations of divine names and goes far beyond the actual narratives, which is why, for him, the Torah, in this mystical sense, preceded the events of Moses' life, even though the book of Genesis, dealing with events before Moses was born, was also given by God to Moses. The mystical Torah actually preceded the creation of the world. Even on the level of the plain meaning, Nahmanides rejects the rationalizations of Maimonides. According to Maimonides all biblical references to angels appearing to men refer to their appearances in dreams. Nahmanides finds such a notion contrary to the meaning of the texts which clearly speak of actual appearances, as in Genesis 18: 1–15 and the continuation of the narrative.

The old puzzle of why the Torah, in the creation narrative, uses the plural: 'Let us make man' (Genesis 1: 26), Nahmanides solves by postulating that God is inviting the whole of creation to take part in the formation of man. Man has a body created out of the dust of the earth but he also has a soul from the heavenly realms. The soul spurs on man to acquire wisdom and perfection.

In his comment on the command to be holy (Leviticus 19: 2), Nahmanides understands this to mean that, in his pursuit of *holiness, a man has not only to avoid the illicit but, as the Talmudic Rabbis say, he must also sanctify himself by a degree of separation even from things permitted; otherwise he could become, in Nahmanides' powerful phrase, 'a scoundrel with the full permission of the Torah'.

Hyam Maccoby, 'The Barcelona Disputation', in his *Judaism on Trial: Jewish Christian Disputations in the Middle Ages* (London and Toronto, 1982), 97–150.
Solomon Schechter, 'Nachmanides', in his *Studies in Judaism* (first series; Philadelphia, 1945), 99–141.

**Nahman of Bratslav**   Hasidic master and religious thinker (1772–1811). Nahman, a great-grandson of the founder of *Hasidism, the *Baal Shem Tov, sought to reinvigorate the movement which he saw as having lost its original impetus. He gathered around him a small number of chosen disciples, among them Nahman of Tcherin and Nathan Sternhartz, the latter acting as his faithful Boswell, recording his life and teachings. Nahman undertook a hazardous journey to the land of Israel (1798–9). A year or two after his return he settled in Bratslav where he remained unto 1810. The last year of his life was spent in the town of Uman in the Ukraine where he died of tuberculosis at the early age of 39. In Uman, Nahman became friendly with followers of the *Haskalah movement of enlightenment. Although he is extremely critical of all secular learning, some of the ideas he seems to have obtained from these Maskilim do occasionally surface in his own works. Nahman's grave in Uman is a place of pilgrimage for his Hasidim to this day. The veneration in which the Bratslaver Hasidim hold Nahman is unparalleled even in Hasidic hero-worship. In the Bratslav synagogue, in the Meah Sharim district of Jerusalem, Nahman's original throne-like chair stands next to the Ark! Nahman promised his followers that he would be with them even after his death, so that no successor to him has ever been appointed and the Bratslaver are called the 'dead Hasidim' in that, unlike all others, they have no living master.

*Nahman's Thought*

Nahman's ideas on the Jewish religion were conveyed verbally, in Yiddish, to his disciples but were later written down by them, under the heading *Likkutey Moharan*, 'Collection of Sayings by Our Teacher Rabbi Nahman'. Basing his theory on the doctrine of Isaac *Luria that the *En Sof withdrew into Himself leaving an 'empty space' into which all worlds could emerge, Nahman draws the conclusion that, in a sense, the world is void of the full presence of God. That is why, he affirms, man is bound to have religious doubts and all his attempts at proving the existence of God are doomed to failure from the outset. The only way to find God is through faith which alone can raise the human soul beyond the void. Nahman seems to have had the kind of mind in which faith and reason cannot exist side by side. One of the two

must yield totally to the other so that Nahman, similarly to his contemporary, Kierkegaard, is a religious antirationalist, critical of the attempts of the medieval philosophers to work out a faith based on reason. Nahman speaks often of the 'true *Zaddik of the generation', which is understood by both his disciples and modern scholars as referring to himself. Obviously alluding to his own struggles against more conventional Hasidic leaders, Nahman remarks that God gives a man the desire to journey to the 'true Zaddik', but then he meets with obstacles. These obstacles are presented to him in order to awaken his desire, since whenever a man meets with obstacles in his desire to achieve something, the obstacles he has to overcome strengthen him in his resolve and his desire becomes even more powerful.

Nahman encouraged his followers to practice 'solitude'. Solitude is defined by Nahman to mean that a man sets aside at least an hour or more during which he is alone in a room or in the field so that he can converse with his Maker in secret, entreating God to bring him nearer to His service. This pouring-out of the heart in solitude should be in Yiddish, the ordinary language of conversation. Nahman also stressed the value of worshipping God in man's present circumstances. Too much planning for the morrow is inadvisable even in spiritual matters. 'For all man has in the world is the day and the hour where he is, for the morrow is an entirely different world.'

*The* Tales

Nahman's famous *Tales* (published by Sternhartz in 1815) are unique in Hasidic literature. The historian of Hasidism, Simon *Dubnow, dismisses these as 'fairy-tales' and certainly on the surface that is what they are: 'The Loss of the Princess'; 'The King Who Fought Major Wars'; 'The King's Son and the Maidservant's Son Who Were Switched', and so forth. Naturally, Nahman's followers read all kinds of mystical ideas into the *Tales*. Whatever their meaning, the *Tales* are admired for their literary merit.

Arnold J. Band, *Nahman of Bratslav: The Tales* (New York and Toronto, 1978).

Arthur Green, *Tormented Master: A Life of Rabbi Nahman of Bratslav* (University, Ala. 1979).

**Nahum**   Prophet whose book of three chapters is seventh in the book of the Twelve Prophets.

The superscription to the book reads: 'The burden of Nineveh. The book of Nahum the Elkoshite' (of Elkosh, a town mentioned nowhere else in the Bible). Nineveh fell to the Babylonians in 612 BCE and Nahum's prophecy is devoted entirely to this theme.

S. M. Lehrman, 'Nahum', in A. Cohen (ed.), *The Twelve Prophets* (London, 1970), 191–208.

**Names** From biblical times, much significance has been attached to the names given by parents to their children. The form of the name given to a boy is: 'X son of [ben] Y'; to a daughter: 'X daughter of [bat] Y'. The name is given to a boy at his *circumcision; to a girl in the synagogue when her father is called up to the *reading of the Torah soon after her birth. According to *Nahmanides, the father has the right to choose the name for the first-born child, the mother for the second child, but the custom is the opposite, the mother having the right to choose a name for the first-born, the father for the second child. Names are often given after relatives; among the *Ashkenazim only after deceased relatives, among the *Sephardim, even after living relatives. Thus a name like David ben David denotes for the Ashkenazim that the father died before the child was born. A child may have two or more names after different relatives. Names of biblical heroes and heroines are often chosen but it is interesting that, before the Middle Ages, Jews were not called Abraham or Moses, possibly because these names represent Jews as a whole who are all disciples of Abraham and Moses. The Talmudic Rabbis frown on giving children names of unworthy biblical characters such as Nimrod or Esau. A number of Rabbis have advised against giving a child an unusual name that will invite ridicule and cause the child embarrassment. Although disapproval is also expressed against giving children Gentile names, some of the Rabbis had such names; Antigonus or Symmachus, for example. In Western lands, Jews often have a Gentile name in addition to the Hebrew name, and this is often a form of the Hebrew: Arnold for Abraham or Maurice for Moshe (Moses). Hasidic children are often named after the particular *Zaddik to whom the family owes its allegiance. Except for a few families, family names were unknown until comparatively modern times. The custom of changing the name of a sick person, considered to be a supersition by many Jews, is still widely practised. The procedure is to add a name, usually a name like Hayyim, denoting life, for example: Hayyim David ben Moshe. The prayer is recited that if death has been decreed on David ben Moshe it has not been decreed on the now different person Hayyim David ben Moshe (see MAGIC AND SUPERSTITION).

**Names of God** The two divine names occurring most frequently in the Bible are the *Tetragrammaton—the four-letter name YHVH, and Elohim; the former is used of God in His special relationship to Israel, the latter in His relationship to the world and to human beings in general, as in the opening verse of Genesis: 'In the beginning God [Elohim] created the heavens and the earth.' In the Rabbinic literature, the Tetragrammaton denotes God in His attribute of mercy, Elohim in His attribute of justice. Other biblical names for God are: Adonai ('Lord'); El ('the Strong'); Shaddai ('the Almighty'); Elyon ('the Most High'); Yah (a shorter form of the Tetragrammaton); and Ehyeh ('I Am'). The Tetragrammaton occurs 6,823 times in the present text of the Bible. The book of *Esther is the only biblical book without any mention of a divine name.

In his study of the divine names in the Rabbinic literature, Marmorstein lists over ninety names for God in the literature. The most frequent names used by the ancient Rabbis are: Ha-Makom ('the Place' of the world, i.e. the Omnipresent); Shamayyim ('Heaven', as in the expression: 'The fear of Heaven'); Ha-Kadosh Baruch Hu ('The Holy One, blessed be He', used in indirect speech); Ribbono Shel Olam ('Master of the universe', used in direct speech); *Shekhinah (*Divine Presence, used of God's particular manifestations and His immanence); Avinu ('Our Father'); Malkenu ('Our King'); and Gevurah ('Power').

The medieval philosophers have a coinage of their own in accordance with their general fondness for abstraction when speaking of God. The more frequent terms used in the philosophical literature are: First Cause; Prime Being; Cause of causes; Beginning of beginnings; Creator; and Ha-Shem yitbarakh' ('The Name, blessed be he'), a name often used by contemporary Orthodox Jews, sometimes shortened simply to Ha-Shem.

The subject of divine names in the Kabbalah is too complicated to be discussed in any detail in a short entry. According to *Nahmanides, the whole Torah is a series of combinations of divine names. The term *En Sof denotes God as He is in Himself; the names of the *Sefirot are names for various aspects of God in manifestations. 'The Holy One, blessed be He' (Kudsha Berikh Hu, in its Aramaic form) denotes the male principle in the Deity, the Shekhinah, the female principle. There are also many references to the manifold different ways of spelling the divine names, each denoting a special aspect of the divine. Three especially significant names mentioned in the sources are: the 22-letter name; the 42-letter name; and the 72-letter name; the meaning of each is shrouded in mystery, although various explanations have been attempted.

Throughout the history of Jewish thought the tension is evident between the need to describe this or that aspect of Deity and the awareness that God is unknowable and cannot hence have any name.

The practice of some Orthodox Jews, writing today in English, to spell the word God as G–d is based on Rabbinic teachings about the need for reverence for the divine name. But many Orthodox Jews considered this pernickety, since there is no particular significance to the letter 'o' in English and G–d stands as much for God as the actual word God.

Louis Jacobs, 'Excursus: The Names of God', in his *A Jewish Theology* (New York, 1973), 136–151.

Arthur Marmorstein, *The Old Rabbinic Doctrine of God* (New York, 1968).

**Nature**　The idea of a natural order and natural laws is unknown in the Bible. The nearest reference to nature in the Rabbinic literature is the expression: 'The world follows its own habit', that is, events occur normally in an established pattern, though there is nothing of necessity in this and *miracles are possible as abnormal events under divine *providence. In the Middle Ages, however, the word *teva* ('implant' or 'impression') was coined for the idea of nature. Nature is the order imposed by God on His creation. At a later date the word *ha-teva* (literally 'the nature') was noted as having a numerical value (see GEMATRIA) equivalent to that of the word Elohim, God, thus identifying nature with God. On 20 November 1708, the Rabbi of the Sephardi congregation in London, David Nieto, preached an antideist

sermon which aroused the ire of some members of the congregation. In opposition to the deists, who taught that God, after having created the universe, left it to its own devices, so to speak, much as a watchmaker, after having manufactured his watches, does not intervene in their subsequent operations, Nieto declared that Judaism, on the contrary, teaches that God is involved directly in the workings of nature. It is God who causes the rain to fall and the crops to grow. As a result, Nieto was accused of being a follower of *Spinoza in identifying nature with God. The congregation applied for guidance to Rabbi Zevi Ashkenazi (1660–1718), the famed Rabbinic leader in Amsterdam. Ashkenazi, in a Responsum, springs to the defence of Nieto. Far from it being heresy to affirm, as Nieto did, that God works directly in the world, using nature as His instrument, the heretical view is that of the deists who see nature as existing independently of God.

Jakob J. Petuchowski, 'Nieto's Concept of God', in his *The Theology of Haham David Nieto* (New York, 1970), 106–27.

**Nazirite**　A man or woman who had vowed to be in a state of separation (from the root *nazar*, 'to separate'). The Nazirite vow was binding for as long as the one making it decided, but it could not be less than thirty days. The laws of the Nazirite are stated in the book of Numbers (6: 1–21) from which it emerges that the Nazirite was not allowed to drink wine or even eat grapes; he had to let his hair grow long; and he was not to come into contact with a corpse. Elaborate rituals are recorded for the termination of the Nazirite state. Once his term had been completed the Nazirite was obliged to bring to the Sanctuary a male lamb for a burnt-offering, a ewe lamb for a sin-offering, a ram for a peace-offering, and a basket of unleavened cakes and wafers spread with oil. It follows that the whole institution could only be in operation in the Temple period. Nevertheless, some few Jews, even after the destruction of the Temple, still undertook Nazirite vows, although this was then of the order of any other vow and did not fall under the heading of the Nazirite. David Cohen, a disciple of Rabbi A. I. *Kook, was a modern Nazirite in this sense, taking upon himself, in addition, an obligation never to leave Jerusalem.

No reasons are stated explicitly for why people undertook to be Nazirites but it seems fairly obvious that the Nazirite vow was often undertaken as a discipline against temptation. When a man felt that he was in danger of becoming addicted to wine, for example, he might resolve to become a Nazirite as an exercise in self-control. A whole tractate of the Talmud, tractate *Nazir*, is devoted to the Nazirite laws. The Talmudic Rabbis used the institution of the Nazirite, no longer in vogue in their day, as a paradigm for *fasting and for *asceticism in general. A debate is recorded (tractate *Taanit* 11a) on whether the Nazirite is a sinner or a holy man. One Rabbi argues that if the Nazirite, who only denied himself wine, is, on this Rabbi's interpretation, a sinner, a man who fasts and thus denies himself all food and drink, is an even greater sinner (in that he rejects God's gifts). But another Rabbi argues that if the Nazirite, on this interpretation, is said to be a holy man, then one who denies himself all food and drink is all the more a holy man. Obviously, it all depends on individual circumstances.

Jacob Milgrom, 'The Nazirite', in Nahum M. Sarna (ed.), *The JPS Torah Commentary: Numbers* (Philadelphia and New York, 1990) 355–8.

**Nehemiah** The Jewish governor of Judah in the fifth century BCE as told in the book of Nehemiah. Nehemiah is usually spoken of in the Jewish tradition together with the other great leader, *Ezra. In this tradition, Ezra's main role was to teach the Torah while Nehemiah was the political leader. Indeed, the Talmud (*Bava Batra* 15a) suggests that Ezra was the author of the book of Nehemiah as well as his own book, the book of Ezra. Modern scholarship tends to see the book as a much later compilation, from around 300 BCE. After the return from the Babylonian exile, Nehemiah is said to have built the walls of Jerusalem despite opposition on the part of the *Samaritans.

Judah J. Slotki, 'Nehemiah', in his *Daniel, Ezra and Nehemiah* (London, 1951), 179–269.

**New Testament** The second part of the Christian Bible, of which the first part is the *Old Testament. The expression is based on Jeremiah 31: 30 where the prophet speaks of a *berit ḥadashah*, 'new covenant', that God will make with Israel. In early Christian interpretation, the verse was read as a prophetic foretelling of the rise of *Christianity. Many modern Christians no longer understand prophecy quite in the sense that a prophet could see into the remote future and tell in detail what would happen then. In any event, the books of the New Testament are sacred for Christians. Jews, of course, accept neither the term Old Testament nor New Testament. As for attitudes towards the New Testament, no Jew accepts these books as in any way sacred and many see in some of them a strong anti-Jewish sentiment. Yet they were produced by Jews and constitute an important source for historians of first-century Jewry and Jewish life. Jewish as well as Christian scholars have studied the New Testament not as sacred literature but in the spirit of general scholarly investigation.

C. G. Montefiore, *Synoptic Gospels* (London, 1909).

**Nishmat** 'The breath of', the opening word of an ancient hymn, after which the hymn itself is called. The hymn begins: 'The breath of every living being shall bless Thy Name, O Lord our God, and the spirit of all flesh shall ever extol and exalt Thy fame, O our King', and continues with the praises of God. Thanksgiving for God's mercies is expressed with typical oriental hyperbole:

'Were our mouths full of song as the sea, and our tongues of exultation as the multitude of its waves, and our lips of praise as the wide-extended skies; were our eyes shining with light like the sun and the moon, and our hands were spread forth like the eagles of the air, and our feet were swift as the wild deer; we should still be unable to thank Thee and to bless Thy Name, O Lord our God and God of our fathers, for one-thousandth or one ten-thousandth part of the bounties which Thou hast bestowed upon our fathers and upon us.'

The hymn continues further with thanks for God's past deliverances from the time of the Exodus from Egypt, which is why the hymn is recited at the *Seder on Passover. Nishmat is recited in all rites during the morning service on Sabbaths and festivals. Parts of the hymn may go back to Temple times; other parts are later additions. By the Middle Ages, the whole hymn was known in its present form. A curious legend circulated in medieval France and Germany to the effect that Nishmat was composed by none other than the Apostle Peter, who is said to have built the Christian Church in order to remove Christians from the Jewish community, while believing himself that only Judaism is the true faith. The legend has no basis in fact but was often repeated.

J. H. Hertz, *The Authorised Daily Prayer Book* (London, 1947), 416–20.

**Noah** The biblical hero saved from the *Flood as told in the book of Genesis (5: 28–9: 28). Noah is described as 'a righteous man in his generation' (Genesis 6: 9). Some of the Rabbis understand this to mean that Noah was a good man even in his generation of evil-doers. But others understand it to mean that Noah's goodness was only relative. Compared with his evil generation Noah was a good man but had he have lived in the time of Abraham he would not have amounted to much when compared with the great patriarch. In the table of nations (Genesis 10) all the seventy nations are descended from Noah's sons, Shem, Ham, and Japheth. Thus, after the Flood, Noah takes the place of Adám as the father of all mankind. This is referred to in the Remembrance section of the liturgy of Rosh Ha-Shanah: 'Of Noah also Thou wast mindful in love, and didst remember him with a promise of salvation and mercy, when Thou broughtest the waters of the flood to destroy all flesh on account of their evil deeds. So his remembrance came before Thee, O Lord our God, to increase his seed like the dust of the earth, and his offspring like the sand of the sea.' The Rabbinic tradition has it that seven laws were given by God to Adam and then to Noah. These are the seven *Noahide laws which constitute, as it were, the Torah for a 'son of Noah' (Gentile) in contradistinction to the full Torah given to Israel.

U. Cassuto, *From Noah to Abraham*, trans. Israel Abrahams (Jerusalem, 1964).

**Noahide Laws** The seven laws given to *Noah, the father of all mankind after the *Flood. The doctrine of the Noahide laws is Rabbinic but is based on the constant appeals in the Bible to *Gentiles to behave justly and practise righteousness, implying that all human beings know either instinctively or by tradition what constitutes justice and righteousness. These seven laws seem to be basic rules by which all humans are expected to live. They constitute the Torah for the Gentile world. Opinions are divided in the Rabbinic literature on the precise formulation of these seven principles but the accepted view of the seven is that they consist of the

prohibition of *idolatry, *blasphemy, murder (see DECALOGUE), adultery and incest (counted as one, see MARRIAGES, FORBIDDEN), robbery (see DECALOGUE); the need to establish a proper system of *justice; and the prohibition against eating flesh torn from a living animal (see ANIMALS). A 'son of Noah' (*ben noaḥ*) is the name given to a Gentile. He is obliged to keep the Noahide laws and if he does he belongs among 'the righteous of the nations of the world' who have a share in the *World to Come. Maimonides (*Melakhim* 8: 11) is unusual in qualifying this that the 'son of Noah' is obliged to keep the laws because he believes that they have been revealed by God, otherwise he belongs among 'the wise of the nations of the world' and not among the 'saints' of the nations of the world.

David Novak, *The Image of the Non-Jew in Judaism: An Historical and Constructive Study of the Noahide Laws* (New York, 1983).

**Nudism** The modern movement which believes that the wearing of clothes is unnatural and that it is healthier for men and women to move about unrestricted by garments, allowing the beneficial rays of the sun to get to the body. Nudists or naturists have special camps in which their ideal can be followed without upsetting other people and there are special sections of beaches in some seaside resorts for nude bathing. Nudism conflicts with the Jewish ideal of *tzeniut*, 'modesty', in dress and comportment. No representative Jewish religious teacher, whether Orthodox or Reform, has ever advocated nudism. In the Genesis narrative (Genesis 2: 25) it is only in the pristine innocence of the Garden of Eden that *Adam and Eve are naked without feeling shame. After they had sinned 'the eyes of both of them were opened and they knew that they were naked' (Genesis 3: 7). Judaism does not frown on nudism because Judaism holds the body in contempt and therefore teaches that it should be concealed. On the contrary, the reason why Judaism would be opposed to nudism is that Judaism insists on human dignity. It befits a human being to be clothed and the wearing of clothes is one of the ways in which humans differ from animals.

Louis Jacobs, 'Nudism', in his *What Does Judaism Say About . . .?* (Jerusalem, 1973), 231–2.

**Numbers, Book of** The fourth book of the Pentateuch, usually called in Hebrew *bemidbar* ('in the wilderness') after one of its opening words. The English 'Numbers' is based on the Latin *numeri*, since the book records the musterings of the children of Israel. According to the traditional view the book of Numbers, like the rest of the *Pentateuch, was 'dictated' by God to Moses. On the critical view (see BIBLICAL CRITICISM) the book is a composite work with its sections deriving from different periods in the history of Israel. More recent scholarship, while acknowledging the composite nature of the book, tends to treat it as the unit it has become, that is the book is seen as a work of art, albeit one that has been reworked, so to speak, by an editorial process. The book describes the journey of the Israelites from *Mount Sinai to the the borders of the land of Canaan, a journey that took forty years,

Jacob Milgrom, *The JPS Torah Commentary: Numbers* (Philadelphia and New York, 1990).

# O

**Oaths** Jewish law recognizes two different types of oath: 1. the oath taken in a court of law; 2. the purely religious oath in which a solemn promise is made to do or not to do something. The judicial oath is imposed in civil cases on one of the parties to a dispute, usually on the defendant. The word of two witnesses is accepted on its own and they do not have to take an oath. The testimonial oath is unknown is Jewish law. Examples of the judicial oath are: where the defendant admits the truth of a part of the plaintiff's claim but denies part of the claim; where a bailee declares that the object deposited with him has been stolen; where the plaintiff has only one witness. The judicial oath involves holding a *Sefer Torah and swearing by God that the statement is true. To take a false oath is a serious offence. The third commandment (see DECALOGUE) is directed against taking God's name in vain by swearing falsely. Some pious Jews never take an oath and are prepared to lose the case rather than invoke God's name for their own purposes. Others, however, see no value in this self-imposed prohibition since the Torah explicitly permits the taking of an oath in support of a true statement.

The second type of oath, the religious oath, is really a form of a *vow. The technical difference between an oath (*shevuah*) and a vow (*neder*) is that the former is imposed on the person, the latter on the object. For instance, an oath is where a person swears that he will not drink wine. A vow is where he places a ban on wine. The key text in this connection is: 'If a man makes a vow to the Lord or takes an oath imposing a prohibition on himself, he shall not break his pledge; he must carry out all that has crossed his lips' (Numbers 30: 3). Oaths and vows of this kind are a form of religious offering.

Tractate *Shevuot* in the Talmud is devoted to both the judicial and the religious oath, tractate *Nedarim* to religious vows. The *Kol Nidre formulation embraces both religious vows and oaths.

**Obadiah** The book of Obadiah, fourth in the book of the Twelve Prophets, contains only one chapter of twenty-one verses and is thus the shortest book in the Bible. The first sixteen verses consist of an oracle against the kingdom of Edom, a fierce and violent people constantly at war with Israel. Verses 17–24 foretell the victory of Israel over Edom. Some scholars see these two sections as coming from different hands but there is no real reason for departing from the traditional view that the book forms a unit. While the book opens with the words: 'The vision of Obadiah', no indication is given of the identity of this prophet. According to a Rabbinic Midrash, Obadiah was an Edomite convert to Judaism. This Midrash obviously comes from a time when Edom was identified with *Rome. A prophecy, also against Edom, in the book of *Jeremiah (49: 9, 14–16) is expressed in virtually the same words as Obadiah, verses 1–5. This can either mean that Jeremiah was quoting from Obadiah or Obadiah from Jeremiah or, possibly, both prophets are quoting from the same source, demonstrating, in any event, that some prophetic utterances are in the form of quotations.

Solomon Goldman, 'Obadiah', A. Cohen (ed.), *The Twelve Prophets* (London, 1970), 127–35.

**Old Testament** The term used by Christians to denote the Hebrew Bible in contradistinction to the *New Testament. Jews do not normally use either of these terms because of their Christian significance and their implication that the Old Testament has been superseded by the New. Nevertheless, Jewish biblical scholars do use these conventional expressions purely as a matter of scholarship while rejecting anything in them of doctrinal significance.

**Omer, Counting of** The Omer ('sheaf') was a harvest-offering brought to the Temple on the second day of *Passover (Leviticus 23: 9–14). There is a further command that, from the day when the Omer was brought, seven weeks were to be counted and on the fiftieth day a festival was to be celebrated (Leviticus 23: 15–21). This festival was later called *Shavuot, 'the Feast of Weeks' (because it falls on the day after the seven weeks have been counted). In the Rabbinic tradition, all this was understood to mean that, even after the destruction of the Temple, each individual should actually count these days, by saying each day: 'This is the X day of the Omer.' Among the many interpretations given to counting the Omer is that Shavuot celebrates the giving of the Torah while Passover celebrates the Exodus from Egypt. The free man, as he reminds himself of the bondage in Egypt, counts each day towards the even greater freedom enjoyed by those who live by the Torah.

In the Middle Ages the Omer period became one of sadness and mourning. Various conjectures have been made about why what was presumably a joyous period in Temple times (see LAG BA-OMER) was transformed in this way. Orthodox Jews do not have a haircut during this period and weddings do not take place. There are, however, different customs regarding the duration of the mourning period. Some observe it from the end of Passover to Lag Ba-Omer (the thirty-third day), others from the end of Passover until Shavuot or until three days before Shavuot, and there are other variations.

In the Kabbalah each of the forty-nine days of the Omer represents one of the combinations of the seven lower *Sefirot (i.e. in each one there are all seven) and in a Kabbalistic prayer the worshipper entreats God to help him lead a pure life and pardon him for the flaw he has produced in the Sefirah of the day.

> Isaac Klein, 'Sefirah', in his *A Guide to Jewish Religious Practice* (New York, 1979), 142–5.

**Oral Torah** In the scheme developed in Rabbinic Judaism there is a *Written Torah, the *Pentateuch, and an Oral Torah. The doctrine runs that *Moses received at *Sinai a detailed elaboration of the laws and doctrines contained in the Written Torah and this is the Oral Torah. But the term denotes much more than the original revelation. All the later teachings of the sages and teachers of Israel are embraced by the Oral Torah, seen as a continuous process. The *Mishnah and the Talmud are thus the great depositories of the Oral Torah (see AUTHORITY, HALAKHAH, and TANNAIM AND AMORAIM).

**Ordination** The appointment of a disciple as a teacher of the Torah; Heb, *semikhah*, based on the verse: 'And he laid his hands [*va-yismokh*] upon him, and gave him a charge, as the Lord spoke by the hand of Moses' (Numbers 27: 23). In the verse, Moses, at the command of God, lays his hands on his disciple Joshua so that the latter can function in Moses' stead as the spiritual leader. In the early Rabbinic period only scholars who had received ordination, in the chain reaching back to Joshua, could act as judges and this was reserved for scholars in the land of Israel, the Babylonian scholars being given a minor form of authority as agents of the Palestinian scholars. After the close of the Talmud full ordination came to an end. Although the term *semikhah* is still used for the ordination of *Rabbis, this is not the full ordination but is only convention by which a scholar does not render decisions in Jewish law unless he has been authorized so to do by a competent Halakhic authority who has himself been ordained. There is no special ceremony for this type of Rabbinic ordination. The usual practice in Orthodox Judaism is for a student, after having mastered the texts, to present himself to a Rabbi for examination. If the Rabbi believes that the student is competent he gives him a document stating that he is qualified to render decisions and that he is now given permission so to do. Nowadays, even among many of the Orthodox, ordination takes place after a course of Rabbinic studies in a seminary and the certificate of ordination is given by the principal and other teachers of the seminary. This Rabbinic diploma is the usual form of ordination in Reform and Conservative seminaries. The major technical difference between the older *semikhah* and the later, simple ordination is that in the latter the ordinand cannot become a member of a court to inflict *capital and *corporal punishments. Since these were abolished, in any event, in early Rabbinic times, the distinction, nowadays, has no significance. Modern seminaries train their students in many disciplines other than that of pure Jewish law, so that ordination in these seminaries is a matter of attesting to the proficiency of the graduates to carry out all the other functions of a modern Rabbi such as preaching, counselling, and pastoral work, and there is often a service of ordination and a celebration with pomp and ceremony, rather like a university graduation ceremony, from which, in fact, it seems to have been copied.

In the year 1538, Rabbi Jacob Berav, on the basis of a passage in Maimonides' Code, sought to reintroduce the full ordination, but his efforts were frustrated by the Rabbi of Jerusalem, Levi Ibn Habib. This is the famous *semikhah* controversy (see CONTROVERSIES) about which much has been written. Voices have occasionally been raised to reintroduce the full *semikhah* and re-establish the *Sanhedrin but these have not been heeded by practically all Orthodox Rabbis, who believe that such an attempt can only meet with success with the coming of the *Messiah.

J. Newman, *Semikhah (Ordination)* (Manchester, 1950).

**Organ** The use of the organ to accompany the prayers in the synagogue was the subject of a fierce conflict between the traditional Rabbis and the early Reformers in the nineteenth century. Orthodox Rabbis to this day object to the organ in the synagogue service on the grounds that it constitutes a breach of the Sabbath laws when played on the sacred day and, even when played at a weekday service it is an example of aping Christian worship. Reform congregations use the organ and, nowadays, many Conservative synagogues see no objection to it. Some Conservative synagogues which do use the organ on the Sabbath have it played by a non-Jew. Some Orthodox Jews, who do not tolerate an organ in an ordinary service, do accept the use of this instrument in an occasional service—a wedding service, for example.

Michael A. Meyer, *Response to Modernity: A History of the Reform Movement in Judaism* (Oxford, 1988); see index: 'Organs, in synagogues'.

**Original Sin** The doctrine that, as a result of Adam's fall, all human beings are tainted with sinfulness. It is often said that Judaism does not know of the doctrine, believing that man does not sin because he is a sinner but is a sinner because he sins, as it has been neatly but inaccurately put. The truth is that, while the notion of original sin does not feature at all prominently in conventional Jewish theology, a

similar doctrine is found in the Kabbalah and even in the thought of some moderns. Of course, even in those versions of Judaism in which the idea of original sin is accepted, it differs from Christian dogma in that God alone, not a saviour like Jesus, helps man to overcome his sinful nature (see YETZER HA-TOV AND YETZER HA-RA).

**Orthodox Judaism** The trend in Jewish life and thought which accepts without reservation and in its literal sense the doctrine: 'The Torah is from Heaven.' The actual term Orthodox is derived from Christian theology and was, at first, a term of reproach hurled against the traditionalists by the early Reformers at the beginning of the nineteenth century to imply that those who failed to respond to the modernist challenge were hidebound. Eventually, however, the term was used by the traditionalists themselves as a convenient shorthand for the attitude of complete loyalty to the Jewish past, although some traditionalists prefer the term 'Torah-true' to describe their religious position. In any event, Orthodoxy came to mean for Jews faithfulness to the practices of Judaism, to the *Halakhah in its traditional formulation. Orthodoxy is none the less much more than Orthopraxy. It is far removed from the attitude: believe what you like as long you keep the laws. For all that, though the dogmatic assumptions are never ignored, the emphasis is on practice. A popular definition of the Orthodox Jew is a Jew who obeys the rules laid down in the standard Code of Jewish law, the *Shulḥan Arukh*. The Orthodox Jew is a *Shulḥan Arukh* Jew, which is not to say that all innovations introduced after the *Shulḥan Arukh* are never countenanced. These are allowed, and even encouraged, provided that the Halakhic process by which the *Shulḥan Arukh* itself was produced is faithfully observed.

Orthodox Judaism rejects the notion introduced by Reform that, in the light of modern thought and life in Western society, Judaism requires to be 'reformed'. Granted that the Torah is of divine origin, as the Orthodox affirm, to attempt to reform it is to imply that God can change His mind, to put it somewhat crudely. Orthodoxy also takes issue with Conservative Judaism which, unlike Reform, does accept the Halakhah but perceives it in a more dynamic fashion, according to which changes are legitimate if they are in the spirit of the

Halakhah. Naturally, the Orthodox disagree with the notion that there is a Halakhic spirit in obedience to which the letter of the law can be set aside where it is considered necessary. Ultimately, the difference between the Orthodox and the Conservative approach depends on whether or not there is a human element in the Torah.

There are, in fact, a variety of Orthodox approaches from the ultra-Orthodox to neo-Orthodoxy and it by no means follows that every Jew who belongs to an Orthodox synagogue is fully Orthodox in theory and practice. Yet all who subscribe, at least nominally, to Orthodoxy, have it in common that they believe the Torah is unchanging, so that while, here and there, minor changes do take place in the wake of new social and economic conditions, for the Orthodox these are not really 'changes' at all, but simply the application of the traditional law in new situations. To give a simple illustration of how the Orthodox attitude differs from those of Reform and Conservative Judaism, Reform maintains that the conditions of modern life demand a relaxation of the traditional Sabbath laws, Orthodoxy that no relaxation is at all possible, while Conservative Judaism allows those relaxations which can be defended on Halakhic grounds if the Halakhah itself is treated in a more flexible way than it was in the past. A Reform Jew will not usually be bothered at all by such prohibitions as that of producing light and fire on the Sabbath. A Conservative Jew will accept that the biblical prohibition of lighting a fire on the Sabbath is still binding but will not normally accept the view that to switch on an electric light involves lighting a fire. An Orthodox Jew will hold not only that the biblical prohibition still applies but that it embraces switching-on of electric lights. On the dogmatic side, Orthodoxy rejects totally the view of *biblical criticism that the *Pentateuch is a composite work and was not 'dictated by' God to Moses, although some Orthodox Jews are prepared to use the scholarly methodology in determining the dates of the other books of the Bible. For Orthodoxy, too, the Talmud, as the depository of the *Oral Torah, is the infallible source for Jewish practice and, to a large extent, for what Jews are expected to believe.

## The Ultra-Orthodox

This rather ridiculous term is often used, nowadays, to denote the attitude of strict adherence to all the details of the traditional law. A term favoured by the 'ultra-Orthodox' themselves is Haredim ('those who fear God') based on the verse: 'Hear the word of the Lord, ye that tremble [ha-haredim] at His word' (Isaiah 66: 5). In the ranks of the Haredim belong all the Hasidic groups; the *Yeshivah world; Ashkenazi Jews who try to preserve intact the way of life followed in Eastern Europe; and Oriental and other Sephardi Jews who follow faithfully the pattern of life in the pre-modern communities of the East. The actual pattern of life differs of course, among the Haredim. The Hasidic ideal is different from that of the Yeshivah world, an Oriental Jew hardly resembles a typical Jew of Eastern European background. But all the Haredim have in common a total dedication to the Torah in its traditional form and believe that the secular world is best kept at arm's length. Haredim are found in large numbers in Israel (especially in the Haredi districts of Mea Sharim in Jerusalem and Bene Berak near Tel Aviv) and in the USA and have strongholds in various European cities. A striking feature of Haredi life is the astonishing proliferation of colleges for higher Jewish learning in its traditional form. In these Yeshivot, most of them based on the old Lithuanian style, thousands of young men devote many years to the study of the Talmud and the Codes and they are followers, in the main, of the *Musar movement. Haredi men usually wear long black coats (though Yeshivah students usually wear short jackets in the modern fashion) and sport *beards. Haredi women dress very modestly (see DRESS) and have their heads covered (see BARE HEAD and SHEITEL). A number of young men and women from non-Orthodox backgrounds have adopted the way of life of the Haredim and special Yeshivot have been created to cater to their special requirements (see BAAL TESHUVAH). The more extreme Haredim are anti-Zionist and do not accept the State of Israel as other than a secular State. But the majority of the Haredim are organized in the Aggudat Israel party and, for Sephardim, the Shas party, and have come to terms with the State of Israel, even participating, with some reservations, in the political life of the State. The *Mizrachi, now the Mafdal, accepts the State of Israel without any reservations and is more open to the modern world and modern culture, but is, essentially, Haredi in outlook.

## Neo-Orthodoxy

The basic difference between neo-Orthodoxy and the Haredim is in the attitude taken toward modern culture. The founder of neo-Orthodoxy, Samson Raphael *Hirsch, though strictly observant, held that Western culture and other ideals of Western society should not be embraced solely in order to earn a living and the like, but welcomed as good in themselves. Neo-Orthodoxy, or Modern Orthodoxy as it is called in the USA, is represented in the majority of Orthodox synagogues in the USA and England, with its major institutions for the training of modern Orthodox Rabbis, being Yeshivah University in New York and Jews' College in London. Modern Orthodox Rabbis dress in Western fashion and usually have university degrees. They participate together with Christian clergymen in welfare movements, some even in Jewish–Christian dialogue. Many scientists of renown are Orthodox in this sense and often try to demonstrate how scientific views, the theory of *evolution for instance, can be squared with the *dogmas of traditional Judaism.

## Orthodox Self-Definition

Orthodoxy is less an organized movement than a reaction to other groups. There is much internecine feuding, for example, among the Orthodox and there is nothing like any official world organization for Orthodox Judaism. While *Hasidism is now accepted by the *Mitnaggedim as a legitimate expression of traditional Judaism and while, in the Council of Sages, the spiritual leaders of Aggudat Israel, there are Hasidic Rebbes as well as non-Hasidic Rabbis of the old school, the old conflict is not entirely a thing of the past. Ashkenazi Rabbis still tend to view their Sephardi opposite numbers as somewhat inferior in learning and Sephardi Rabbis often tend to see their Yiddish-speaking colleagues as uncouth and insufficiently flexible. Modern Orthodox Rabbis often have difficulties in matters of Halakhic interpretation with Rabbis of the pre-modern type. For instance, a number of Yeshivah heads placed a ban, which largely went unheeded, on participation by modern Orthodox Rabbis in organizations of which Reform and Conservative Rabbis are members. It is probably true to say that, for most of its adherents, Orthodoxy means simply that one's own religious traditions are followed, whether Hasidic or Mitnaggedic, Ashkenazi or Sephardi. The real issue on the level of practice between the Orthodox and the non-Orthodox is whether the tradition needs to be revised in some respects. The Orthodox rightly claim that theirs is the Judaism of tradition as followed in the pre-modern era. But this is precisely the question. Is the pre-modern tradition true to the tradition as it is now requires to be interpreted? To what extent, in other words, is 'traditional Judaism' traditional?

Reuven P. Bulka (ed.), *Dimensions of Orthodox Judaism* (New York, 1983).

Samuel Heilman, *Defenders of the Faith inside Ultra-Orthodox Jewry* (New York, 1992).

Norman Lamm, *Torah Umadda* (Northvale, NJ, and London, 1900).

# P

**Palestine** The non-Jewish name for the land of Israel, so called after the ancient Philistines who lived on the sea coast. Jews normally refer to the land as Eretz Yisrael, 'Land of Israel', When the State of Israel was established it shortened the name to 'Israel'.

**Panentheism** 'All is in God', the doctrine that all creation is embraced by God. Panentheism is quite distinct from pantheism (see *SPINOZA) or monism. According to pantheistic or monistic theory, God is the name given to the universe as a whole. The 'all' is identified with God, so that it is meaningless to speak of God as distinct from the universe. Pantheism means that all *is* God and monism (the theory of 'oneness') that God is a synonym for the 'stuff' or 'substance' of the universe. In panentheism, on the other hand, the 'all' is *in* God. The Being of God is both transcendent and immanent in relation to the universe, so that while it is inconceivable for there to be a universe without God it is not inconceivable for God to exist without the universe. The panentheistic doctrine is Jewishly unconventional but traces of it are found in some Jewish sources. The Zohar speaks of God both 'filling all worlds' and 'surrounding all worlds'. The Kabbalist Hayyim *Ibn Atar writes, in his Commentary, Or Ha-Ḥayyim (to Genesis 2: 1): 'The world is in its Creator and the light of the Creator is in the whole world.' The German Talmudist Moses of Taku (early thirteenth century) attacked the medieval hymn *Shir Ha-Yiḥud* ('Song of Unity') for its panentheistic leanings. In the section of this hymn for recital on the third day of the week the words are found: 'All of them are in Thee and Thou art in all of them' and: 'Thou surroundest all and fillest all and when all exists Thou art in all.'

The panentheisic doctrine surfaced again in *Hasidism, especially in the *Habad version. While the *Mitnaggedim understood the verse:

'The whole earth is full of His glory' (Isaiah 6: 3) to mean no more than that God is manifest in the universe and His providence extends over all, in the Hasidic understanding the verse means that God is literally in all things. This doctrine was one of the main theological counts against Hasidism, the Mitnaggedim believing that the panentheistic doctrine, according to which God is literally in all things, to be sheer heresy. Any tendency to blur the distinction between the sacred and the profane, the clean and the unclean, good and evil, poses the greatest threat to a monotheistic religion like Judaism. If God is in all and all is in God, what is to be made of the laws of the Torah based on these distinctions? Habad makes an attempt to deal with the problem by postulating that, from God's point of view, so to speak, there is no universe at all. It is only from the point of view of God's creatures that the universe appears to enjoy an existence apart from God.

Louis Jacobs, *A Jewish Theology* (New York, 1973), 34–7.

**Parapet** The small wall that has to be erected around a flat roof as a protection against people falling off. The law of the parapet is stated in the verse: 'When you build a new house, you shall make a parapet for your roof, so that you do not bring bloodguilt on your house if anyone should fall from it' (Deuteronomy 22: 8). The parapet had to have a minimum size of 10 hand-breadths. The law of the parapet applies only to flat roofs on which people can walk. The Talmud (*Bava Kama* 15b) records that the second-century teacher, Rabbi Nathan, extended the law of the parapet to prohibit keeping a vicious dog or a precarious ladder in the home. Obviously, it would apply today to the need to keep away from children medicines that could cause them harm or to failure to repair faulty electrical appliances. Another instance would be failing to check the brakes of an automobile. The Talmudic Rabbis discuss the theological question of why this kind of care against accidents should be so important, since if the victim of the accident is destined to suffer harm it is bound to happen, and if it is not so destined it will not happen, even if no care is taken. The stock reply to this kind of problem is that although it must have been destined, otherwise the accident would not have happened, it is wrong to be the instrument of divine *providence in such a situation.

Hyman E. Goldin, 'Protection of Life and Property', in his *Code of Jewish Law* (New York, 1961), iv. 83-4.

**Parveh** A word of uncertain etymology to denote food that is neither meat nor milk. According to the *dietary laws, meat and milk foods must not be eaten when mixed and the two must not even be eaten together. *Parveh* food such as eggs, fish, vegetables, and fruit, can be eaten together with either meat or milk. In Yiddish parlance the term *parveh* is often applied to an in-between person, as in the English expression 'neither fish nor fowl'.

**Passover** The spring festival, celebrating the Exodus from Egypt, beginning on 15 Nisan and lasting for seven days (eight for Jews outside the land of Israel). The Hebrew word, *Pesah*, means the Paschal lamb offered on the eve of the festival in Temple times (Exodus 12: 1-28; 12: 43-9; Deuteronomy 16: 1-8) and is so called because God passed over (*pasah*) the houses of the children of Israel when He slew the Egyptian first-born (Exodus 12: 23). Later on the festival itself came to be called Passover, although the usual biblical name is *Hag Ha-Matzot*, 'the Festival of Unleavened Bread', because of the command to eat only *matzah* ('unleavened bread') and to refrain from eating *hametz* ('leavened bread') during these seven days (Exodus 23: 15; Leviticus 23: 6; Deuteronomy 16: 16). Many biblical critics (see BIBLICAL CRITICISM) believe that originally there were two separate festivals, *Hag Ha-Pesah*, a pastoral festival (taking the word *Pesah* as referring to the gambolling of the lambs) and *(Hag-Matzot,* an agricultural festival. It goes without saying that this is opposed to the traditional view according to which the two names refer to the same festival. After the destruction of the Temple the Paschal lamb could not be offered and the Passover rituals centred entirely on the avoidance of leaven and the celebration of the *Seder on the first night (and the second outside Israel) during which the *Haggadah is recited.

In the synagogue liturgy for Passover the festival is referred to as: 'the season of our freedom', freedom from bondage being the keynote of the celebrations..The readings from the Torah and the prophetic readings are from passages dealing with the Exodus. On the seventh day, traditionally the anniversary of the parting of the sea, the passage dealing with this event (Exodus 14: 17-15: 26) is read. Some pious Jews, on the eve of the seventh day, used to pour water on the floor in the home and walk through it as a symbolic re-enactment of the ancient crossing of the sea, but this ritual is carried out nowadays by only a very few super-traditionalists. On the Sabbath in the middle of the festival, Ezekiel's vision of the dry bones (Ezekiel 37: 1-14) forms the prophetic reading (the *Haftarah), appropriate because of the theme of renewal and the final redemption in the Messianic age (see MESSIAH). It is customary in many synagogues to read the *Song of Songs on this Sabbath since there is a reference in the book to the spring (2: 11-13) and to the Exodus (1: 9). On the first day a prayer for dew is recited. The rainy season being over, supplication is made for the more gentle dew to assist the growth of produce in the fields.

Philip Goodman, *The Passover Anthology* (Philadelphia, 1961).

Isaac Levy, *A Guide to Passover* (London, 1958).

**Patriarchs** The three fathers of the Jewish people, *Abraham, *Isaac, and *Jacob, who, together with the *matriarchs, are acknowledged as the ancestors of all Jews born to a Jewish mother. Proselytes, however, are called son or daughter of Abraham (see CONVERSION) because Abraham and his wife *Sarah, who taught the monotheistic faith, are the spiritual ancestors of all who embrace the Jewish religion even though converts are not the physical descendants of the patriarchs. The first benediction of the *Amidah is called *Avot* ('Fathers') because in it God is described as the God of Abraham, Isaac, and Jacob. Jewish feminists (see FEMINISM) add the names of the matriarchs, *Sarah, *Rebecca, *Rachel, and *Leah. In the Kabbalah, each of the patriarchs represents on earth one of the divine qualities (see SEFIROT). Abraham is the 'pillar of loving-kindness'; Isaac 'the pillar of judgement'; Jacob the 'pillar of truth'.

**Peace** Heb. *shalom*. From the earliest times, Jews have considered peace to be among the highest values. The Talmudic Rabbis refer to peace as the vessel in which all blessings are contained. The traditional Jewish greeting is: 'Shalom alekhem' ('Peace to you'), to which the response is: 'Alekhem Shalom' ('To you Peace'). Nowadays, this is often shortened simply to Shalom. Typical of the high regard Jews have for peace is the ruling that Jews must not use the Shalom greeting in the public bath-house because Shalom is one of the *names of God. Although Judaism does not advocate total pacifism, the Messianic vision (see MESSIAH) looks forward to the time when *warfare will be banished from earth: 'And he shall judge among the nations, and shall rebuke many peoples; and they shall beat their swords into plowshares, and their spears into pruninghooks; nation shall not lift up sword against nation, neither shall they learn war any more' (Isaiah 2: 4).

Among the acts of *benevolence listed by the Talmudic Rabbis is making peace between husband and wife, parents and children, man and his neighbour. For all the value set on *truth, a white lie can be told for the sake of peace. Peace, for the Rabbis, is not a mere absence of strife but a positive, harmonizing principle in which opposites are reconciled. The verse: 'he maketh peace in His high places' (Job 25: 2), repeated at the end of the *Amidah and the *Kaddish prayers, is interpreted in the Midrash as referring to the high *angels Michael and Gabriel. Michael is the angel of mercy, Gabriel, the angel of justice, yet God 'makes peace in His high places' by combining the aspects of both Michael and Gabriel, mercy and justice. A late homily reads the verse as: 'He maketh peace to be among His highest things', that is, God, so to speak, places peace among the highest of values.

The pursuit of peace does not mean that a man must never fight for what he believes to be the truth. There is a dark side to the numerous *controversies in Jewish history but those who engaged in them often but not always believed that they were occupied with a 'controversy for the sake of heaven', as the Rabbis (Ethics of the Fathers, 5. 17) call it, giving the example of the controversies between the schools of *Hillel and *Shammai. The passage continues: 'Any controversy that is for the sake of heaven shall in the end be of lasting worth.' 'Battles of the Torah' occupy an important role in the history of Jewish learning. A Talmudic saying (*Kiddushin* 30b) expresses the ideal with a degree of hyperbole: 'Even father and son, teacher and disciple, who study Torah in the same gate become enemies of one another, yet they do not stir from there until they come to love one another.'

Peace also means that the individual character is not pulled too much in opposite directions. A Hasidic master observed: 'You cannot find peace anywhere save in your own self.' Cantankerousness is often a manifestation of inner feelings of instability and inferiority for which compensation is sought in combat with others. Another Hasidic saying notes that the verse says: 'The Lord will give strength to His people; the Lord will bless His people with peace' (Psalms 29: 11). Peace is the fruit of inner strength.

Louis Jacobs, 'Peace', in his *Jewish Values* (London, 1960), 155–60.

**Pentateuch** The five books of Moses—*Genesis, *Exodus, *Leviticus, *Numbers, and *Deuteronomy—called, in the Jewish tradition, the Torah, as distinct from the other two divisions of the *Bible, the Prophets and the Writings. On the traditional view, the Pentateuch is a single book, 'dictated' by God to Moses, with the exception, according to one opinion in the Talmud, of the last eight verses of Deuteronomy which describe the death of Moses. The still prevailing theory in *biblical criticism is the documentary hypothesis, according to which the Pentateuch stems from different periods in the history of Israel. On this hypothesis there are four 'documents' (many modern critics prefer to speak of oral 'strands' rather than actual 'documents')—J, E, D, and P—later combined by a redactor, hence the symbol 'R'. J represents the source in which the divine name used is JHVH (the Tetragrammaton*), hence, after the first letter, the symbol 'J'. E is the source which uses the divine name Elohim (see NAMES OF GOD). D represents the book of Deuteronomy; and P, the priestly strand. The documentary hypothesis purports to discover these strands throughout the Pentateuch and many critics, extending the analysis to the book of *Joshua, prefer to speak of a Hexateuch rather than a Pentateuch.

Some of the critical theories tend to be unbalanced. One critic, for example, has suggested that 'J' was composed by a woman. It hardly needs saying that this discovery of 'Ms J' is based on the flimsiest of evidence. Nevertheless, the whole theory cannot so easily be dismissed, as traditionalists often try to do (see FUNDAMENTALISM). Even if the documentary hypothesis is completely overthrown, as it may be one day, the verdict of all modern biblical scholarship is that the Pentateuch is a composite work. That this poses problems for the tradition is undeniable. The major difference on the question of divine *revelation between Orthodox Judaism, on the one hand, and Reform and Conservative Judaism on the other, depends on whether the traditional view of the Pentateuch must yield to critical theories.

J. H. Hertz, *Pentateuch and Haftorahs* (London, 1960)

M. H. Segal, *The Pentateuch: Its Composition and its Authorship* (Jerusalem, 1967).

**Pentecost** See SHAVUOT.

**Peot** 'Corners', the sidelocks worn in obedience to the injunction: 'Ye shall not round the corners of your heads' (Leviticus 19: 27). The Talmudic Rabbis interpret this to mean that the hair of the head must not be removed in such a way that there is no hair between the back of the ears and the forehead. Maimonides gives as the reason for growing *peot* that the idolatrous priests used to 'round the corers of their heads' and thus the practice symbolizes rejection of idolatry. In the Kabbalah great importance is attached to *peot*, which are said to represent on earth the stream of divine mercy from the 'Head of the Holy Ancient One'. Hasidim tend to cultivate long, corkscrew *peot*, although this is not required by law. A typical description of a Hasid is 'a Jew with *beard and peot*'.

**Perpetual Light** The light kept burning over the *Ark in the synagogue; Heb. *ner tamid*. The actual expression *ner tamid* is used of the *menorah in the Tabernacle (Exodus 27: 20) but the light of the menorah was not left burning all the time—it burned only during the night and was allowed to go out in the morning (v. 21)—whereas the perpetual light in the synagogue is kept burning all the time. In point of fact there is no reference at all in the sources

to the perpetual light in the synagogue before the late sixteenth century. Nevertheless, it is the established practice to have this light in the synagogue. Some synagogues still use an oil lamp for the purpose but in the majority of synagogues an electric light is used.

Solomon B. Freehof, 'The Eternal Light', in his *Current Reform Responsa* (Cincinnati, 1969), 8–14.

**Pharisees** One of the three sects mentioned by Josephus as having flourished from the second century BCE to the early second century CE, the other two being the *Sadducees and the *Essenes. There is considerable uncertainty about the meaning of the term Pharisees, in Hebrew, *Perushim*. The Hebrew word seems to mean 'separatists', which might have meant originally 'separation' from the Sadducees or, possibly, people who led a life separate from worldly concerns. But, as Ellis Rivkin has noted, this term is often used for 'separatists' in general, so that it is precarious to assume that all the Talmudic passages about the *Perushim*, except those in which the Pharisees are mentioned together with the Sadducees, refer to the Pharisaic party. This explains why, on the one hand, the Pharisees are hailed in the Talmudic literature as the forerunners of what became Rabbinic Judaism, while there are other references to the *Perushim* as hypocrites, as in the *New Testament, although it is obvious that the New Testament does refer to the Pharisaic party. Under the influence of the New Testament accounts, the term Pharisee came to denote among Christians a person excessively scrupulous with regard to the rituals and the niceties of the law but without any real inner depths. Needless to say, the Jewish tradition, in which the Pharisees are the forerunners of Rabbinic Judaism, rejects as totally biased this picture of the Pharisees. Indeed, Christianity itself owes much to the Pharisaic background of Jesus—the Christian doctrine of the Hereafter and the *resurrection of the dead, for instance.

According to both Josephus and the Talmud the two main theological differences between the Pharisees and the Sadducees were: the Pharisaic belief that Israel was given by God an *Oral Torah, and the Pharisaic belief in the reality of the *World to Come. A number of differences in practical law between the Pharisees and the Sadducees are recorded in the Mishnah and the Talmud. From all the accounts it emerges that the Sadducees were the wealthy landowners and aristocratic priests while the Pharisees belonged more to the lower classes. Nevertheless, scholars view with extreme caution the attempt by Louis Finkelstein to see the two groups as influenced in their attitudes by class distinctions.

Louis Finkelstein, *The Pharisees* (Philadelphia, 1940).

Jacob Neusner, *The Rabbinic Traditions about the Pharisees before 70* (Leiden, 1871).

Ellis Rivkin, *A Hidden Revolution: The Pharisees' Search for the Kingdom Within* (Nashville, 1978).

**Philo** Of Alexandria, Jewish philosopher (d. 50 CE). Philo wrote in Greek and used, for his biblical comments, the Greek translation of the Bible, the *Septuagint. Philo's main endeavour is to reconcile the Platonic philosophy, popular in his day and place, with Judaism. His usual method is allegorical. For instance, the biblical narrative that Abraham sent away his handmaiden Hagar at the request of his wife Sarah (Genesis 21: 9–21) is interpreted as referring to the good man, Abraham, sending away (i.e. avoiding), the lure of his bodily passions, represented by Hagar, in obedience to his intellect, represented by Sarah. Generally, Philo adopts the Greek view that the body is the tomb of the soul. Only that soul is immortal which refuses to become trapped in bodily desires. Such a soul returns to its source at the death of the body. Philo quotes the Greek philosopher, Heraclitus, who says: 'We live their death, and are dead to their life', meaning that during earthly life the soul is entombed in the body as in a sepulchre but at the death of the body the soul lives its proper life released from the corpse to which it was bound. This notion is found in Rabbinic literature as well, the Rabbis saying that the righteous are alive even when their body has died but the wicked are dead even while they are alive in the body.

According to Philo, God created the world out of a primordial substance but it is not clear whether he believes that this, too, was created 'out of nothing'. In any event, Philo holds that God created the world and all its creatures in a spontaneous act and the *creation narrative in Genesis speaks of the logical order of things, not of creation by stages.

It is a moot point whether Philo knew Hebrew. If he did his knowledge was not at all extensive. His works were known to Christians in the Middle Ages but there was no reference to him at all in Jewish literature until the sixteenth century, when he is mentioned by Azariah de *Rossi. In his book *Maor Eynayyim* de Rossi refers to Philo by a Hebrew translation of his name, Yedidiah.

Philo, *Works*, with an English translation by F. H. Colson and G. H. Whitaker (The Loeb Classical Library; Cambridge, Mass), 1929–62.

David Winston, *Philo of Alexandria* (London, 1981).

**Philosophy** Although philosophical ideas are found, of course, in the Bible—monotheism itself is such an idea—philosophy proper, in the sense of a systematic examination of the teachings of the Jewish religion in the light of what was considered to be pure human reasoning (see RATIONALISM) did not emerge fully until the Middle Ages, although it was anticipated by *Philo of Alexandria. The philosophy of the medieval thinkers such as *Saadiah Gaon, *Bahya Ibn Pakudah, *Judah Halevi, *Maimonides, *Gersonides, and *Crescas, was either Aristotelian or Neoplatonic or a mixture of both. None of these thinkers were acquainted with Greek thought at first hand but only knew it from Arabic translations, which enjoyed a wide circulation. Although the medieval thinkers employed philosophical method, their main aim was to demonstrate that the Jewish religion can be reconciled with the truth, as they saw it, of Greek philosophy. Their endeavours were not directed to the question: is Judaism true? Rather the thrust of their thinking was to show that the true religion, in which they believed and to which they subscribed without reservation, can be interpreted so as to conform with philosophical truth. In this sense, these thinkers are best described as theologians rather than philosophers. In their various ways, they tried to show that the truth conveyed through *revelation is the same truth taught by the Greek thinkers, except where the two clearly diverge. When the divergence became apparent, philosophy had to yield to revelation, since there is only one truth.

Many Jews in the Middle Ages believed the philosophical approach to be dangerous to faith. Once human reasoning is given its head, they argued, it can easily lead to a surrender of religious faith in those areas where faith seems to be unsupported by reason. Faith might even come to be seen as irrational. After the death of Maimonides, the Jewish intellectual world was split between the Maimonists and the anti-Maimonists; the former held fast to the philosophical approach, the latter denied its value and denigrated its pursuit. In Spanish Jewry, however, it was impossible to forbid entirely the study of philosophy. In Barcelona in the year 1305, Solomon Ibn *Adret was only able to issue his famous ban against the study of philosophy by limiting the ban to young men under the age of 25.

With the rise of science, the challenge presented to Judaism by Greek philosophy became a thing of the past. Western thinkers turned to science for the solution of many of the problems considered important by the ancient and medieval philosophers. The new philosophers—*Spinoza, Descartes, Hume, Kant, Hegel, and Nietzsche, later the existentialists, and later still the linguistic philosophers, all developed their own original approach, presenting new challenges to traditional Judaism. But in the modern period philosophy was largely pursued by Jews as a discipline independent of religion. It is far less accurate to speak of Jewish philosophers than philosophers who happened to be Jews. Only in the ranks of the comparatively few Jewish theologians were attempts made to work out a Jewish philosophy. The foremost Jewish philosophers of modern times, that is, philosophical theologians who worked more or less within the confines of the Jewish religion, are Moses *Mendelssohn, Nahman *Krochmal, Samson Raphael *Hirsch, Abraham *Geiger, Martin *Buber, and Franz *Rosenzweig. The majority of the traditionalists preferred to devote their intellectual efforts solely to the study of the traditional sources, Bible, Talmud, and the Kabbalah. But the approach of the Maskilim (see HASKALAH) had as its aim the development of an 'enlightened' approach to Judaism and can be considered to be in the Jewish philosophical tradition. The same applies to the thinkers of Reform and Conservative Judaism. Orthodox Jews also felt themselves obliged to interpret Judaism in a philosophical manner, if only in reaction to Reform. It is better, therefore, from the religious point of view, to speak of various philosophies (in the plural) of Judaism: the philosophy of Reform Judaism, of Conservative Judaism, of Orthodox Judaism, of *Zionism, and so forth.

Side by side with these Jewish philosophical trends, scholars have investigated the philosophical ideas contained in the classical sources, so that one can speak of the philosophy of the Bible, of the Talmud, of the *Halakhah, of the Zohar. But here it has to be appreciated that the attempt involves imposing on these sources a system basically foreign to their organic nature.

Julius Guttmann, *Philosophies of Judaism*, trans. David W. Silverman (Philadelphia, 1964).
Isaac Husik, *A History of Mediaeval Jewish Philosophy* (New York, 1958).

**Photography** The invention of photography has given rise to a number of Halakhic problems (see HALAKHAH). Can a photograph be relied on for the purpose of identifying a corpse so that the wife can be permitted to remarry? (The photograph can be relied on together with other criteria, according to many authorities). Is a photographed *mezuzah valid? Rabbi Ben-Zion Ouziel (1880–1953) takes issue, in a Responsum, with a Rabbi who held that a photograph of a handwritten mezuzah can be used, since this counts as a written mezuzah. Ouziel holds that it obviously does not qualify as a written mezuzah and this is the accepted ruling. In view of the opposition to representation of the human figure in *art, is it permitted to take photographs of people? While a few authorities were, at first, strict in this matter, nowadays hardly anyone takes exception to the practice. Photographs of famous Rabbis abound and presumably they allowed themselves to be photographed. The verse: 'Thine eyes shall see thy teacher' (Isaiah 30: 20) has been taken out of context by many contemporary Jews to encourage the taking of photographs of prominent Rabbis and Hasidic masters. The extreme veneration of saintly figures in which their photographs are affixed to baby-carriages seems thoroughly un-Jewish to many Jews. Ultra-Orthodox Jews, on the other hand, can sometimes be seen to protest when tourists try to take their photograph. This is based on the Kabbalistic notion that when a man dies he should leave behind nothing to represent his person on earth.

**Pig** The prohibition of swine-flesh is stated explicitly in the Pentateuch (Leviticus 11: 7; Deuteronomy 14: 8). According to the Rabbinic tradition the prohibition covers only the eating of pig's meat, but not other benefits from the animal. It is permitted, for instance, for a Jew to have a pigskin wallet. There is, however, a Rabbinic ban on pig-breeding. Maimonides suggests that the prohibition is on hygienic grounds; the pig is an excessively dirty animal. The prophet connects eating swine-flesh with idolatrous practices (Isaiah 66: 17). Since the time of the *Maccabees, when Jews were forced to eat pig as a sign of their disloyalty to the Torah, Jews have had a special abhorrence for the pig. Even Jews who do not observe strictly other *dietary laws usually draw the line at eating bacon or ham.

**Pilgrimages** The book of Deuteronomy (16: 16–17) states: 'Three times a year—on the Feast of Unleavened Bread [*Passover], on the Feast of Weeks [*Shavuot], and on the Feast of *Tabernacles—all your males shall appear before the Lord your God in the place that He will choose. They shall not appear before the Lord empty-handed, but each with his own gift, according to the blessing that the Lord your God has bestowed upon you.' In the book of Exodus (23: 14–17) the same command is given. The Mishnah (Ḥagigah 1: 1) understands the words 'not appear . . . empty-handed' to mean that every male Jew is obliged, when he appears in the Temple on the pilgrim festivals, to bring two offerings, a festival offering and an 'appearance' offering. The Israeli scholar Samuel Safrai has argued convincingly that Talmudic statements which suggest that three times a year every Jew was actually obliged to make the pilgrimage and bring these offerings are purely academic, and were made long after the Temple had been destroyed. It is hard to imagine that in Temple times all Jewish males left their farms and homes to travel to Jerusalem on all three festivals. It would seem that in the Temple period, while it was certainly considered meritorious to visit the Temple on these three occasions, especially on Passover when the Paschal lamb had to be offered, there was no actual obligation so to do. It seems probable that the pilgrimage was undertaken only by those who lived near to the Temple.

Even after the destruction of the Temple, pilgrims, over the centuries, visited Jerusalem, chiefly to mourn the loss of the past glories. Nowadays tourists who visit Jerusalem to pray at the *Western Wall and at other holy sites often describe their visit as a pilgrimage.

Another form of pilgrimage is to the graves of famous saints of the past; to the tomb of Rabbi *Simeon ben Yohai, for example, at Meron on *Lag Ba-Omer. Many Hasidim travel to the grave of their departed Rebbe on the anniversary of the master's death. The followers of *Nahman of Bratslav travel as far as Uman in the Ukraine. Rabbis insist that on such pilgrimages the prayers must not be directed to the saint, but should ask only that his merits protect the worshipper. Nevertheless, it cannot be denied that there is a superstitious element in this kind of pilgrimage, especially when coach trips are organized to visit a particular saint who is 'good' for sustenance, or healing, or finding a suitable match.

**Pilpul** Keen argumentation, sharp-witted discussion, especially of Talmudic and Halakhic themes, probably from the word pilpel, 'pepper', hence a peppery argument. In Ethics of the Fathers (6. 6) the pilpul of disciples is mentioned as one of the ways in which learning is advanced. Generally speaking, the method of keen dialectics represented by pilpul is highly prized. A distinction must, however, be drawn between pilpul with the aim of arriving at the truth (by a close examination of the various moves in an argument) and pilpul for its own sake as a kind of game in which far-fetched analogies are produced by a scholar with the aim of demonstrating his skill in debate. The latter form, prevalent in the Middle Ages, met with strong opposition on the part of some teachers, although others encouraged it as a means of sharpening the mind. The term pilpul is often used, nowadays, to denote hairsplitting.

Louis Jacobs, 'The Talmudic Argument', in his *The Talmudic Argument* (Cambridge, 1984), 1–17.

**Plagiarism** While there is little about plagiarism in the sources compiled before printed books were known, the practice of passing off another's thoughts as one's own was frowned upon as a form of theft. In Ethics of the Fathers (6. 6) one of the ways of learning with which the student of the Torah is expected to be familiar is the repetition of a thing in the name of the one who said it originally. 'For whoever tells a thing in the name of him that said it brings deliverance into the world. As Scripture says: "And Esther told the king thereof in Mordecai's name" [Esther 2: 22].' Throughout the Talmud the greatest care is taken to attribute teachings to those originally responsible for them. While there is no legal redress for stealing an author's ideas, this is certainly held to be a severe moral offence. The Hasidic author, Zevi Elimelech of Dynov, went so far as to consider plagiarism a form of kidnapping, since an author puts his very self into his ideas and to use them without acknowledgement is to offend against the principle if not the actual law that prohibits kidnapping. It is, in fact, rare, though not entirely unknown, for Rabbinic authors to claim as their own ideas they have appropriated from the works of other scholars.

**Pornography** In the Jewish sources disapproval of pornographic literature and obscene talk is expressed largely in the moralistic rather than the legalistic literature. So far as the ancient Rabbis and later Jewish moralists are concerned, there is no doubt that they frown on lewd or foul talk and on sexual thoughts other than those relating to husband and wife. The Rabbis, for instance, comment on the verse: 'Thou shalt keep thee from every evil thing' (Deuteronomy 23: 10) that this implies that one should not gaze intently at a beautiful woman, even if she is unmarried, or at a married woman even if she is ugly, nor at a woman's gaudy garments, nor at animals when they are mating (*Avodah Zarah* 20b). In another Talmudic passage (*Ketubot* 8b) there is a comment on the verse: 'And every mouth speaking wantonness' (Isaiah 9: 16), which runs: 'Everyone knows why the bride enters the bridal chamber, but whoever disgraces his mouth and utters a word of folly—even if a decree of seventy years' happiness were sealed for him, it is turned for him into evil.'

Naturally, in this area, it is all a matter of drawing the line. Blue jokes have been told by Jewish scholars and pietists through the ages; what one man considers to be obscene another might consider to be simply erotic and opinions are divided on the question of eroticism itself. The extent to which pornography should be made illegal in a modern State is the subject of debate and on this there is no specific Jewish view.

Louis Jacobs, 'Pornography', in his *What Does Judaism Say About . . .?* (Jerusalem, 1973), 244–7.

**Poverty** Jewish attitudes to poverty vary. Throughout Jewish history the poor are treated with respect, and alleviation of their sufferings is strongly advocated (see CHARITY). But this does not necessarily mean that poverty is seen as something of value. There is nothing in Judaism to correspond to the Christian monastic ideal of taking poverty vows. In the Bible possessions are usually seen as a blessing. Generally speaking, much depended on the economic conditions in which Jews found themselves. In Eastern Europe, for example, where the economic conditions were on the whole very low, poverty was accepted with resignation to the will of God but with a degree of irony. There are numerous Jewish jokes about the *shlimazal* (see MAZAL), the unfortunate poor man, for whom nothing seems to go right, who has a quarrel with the Almighty. Tevye in *Fiddler on the Roof* protests: 'Would it spoil some vast eternal plan, if I were a wealthy man?' This is based on the Talmudic tale of the Rabbi who asked God to make him rich, only to be told that God could not create the world anew in order to change his status. In Yiddish there are no fewer than thirty different terms for a poor man.

This explains the contradictory statements about poverty found in the Talmud. On the one hand, there is the saying: 'Poverty befits Israel like a red trapping on a white horse' (*Ḥagigah* 9b). On the other hand, the early third-century Babylonian teacher, Rav, used to pray that he be given 'a life of riches and honour' (*Berakhot* 16b), a prayer which, incidentally, has been incorporated in the liturgy for recital by all Jews on the Sabbath before the New Moon. It has been noted that, in the prayer, 'riches' are associated with 'honour'. Dishonourable means of acquiring wealth were severely condemned from the time of the great Hebrew prophets onwards.

The theological question of why some are rich and others poor has to do with the general question of divine *providence. The normal, though obviously less than satisfactory, attitude among Jewish theologians is to invoke the idea of the Hereafter in which the poor will be compensated for their sufferings on earth (see WORLD TO COME). When Rabbi Eleazar wept in distress at his poverty, his colleague replied: 'Not everyone has the merit of having two tables' (*Berakhot* 5b).

**Prayer** The most striking difference between prayer as it is found in the Bible and prayer as developed in post-biblical Judaism is that in the Bible the prayers are of private persons in their individual needs, whereas, from the earliest

Rabbinic times onwards, while there is an acknowledgement that private prayers are also essential, the emphasis is on public prayer. All the standard prayers are in the plural: 'Grant *us*'; '*We* praise Thee'; '*We* give thanks unto Thee', and so forth. Some prayers can only be recited where a quorum of ten—the *minyan—is present. The Jewish tradition would certainly view with sympathy the remarks of Friedrich Heiler (*Prayer*, p. 306): 'The prayer of the congregation is meant to lift the individual to a higher stage of devotion. Narrow self-seeking wishes should be silenced in the presence of the congregation.' For this reason the Talmudic Rabbis quote the verse: 'In the multitude of the people is the King's glory' (Proverbs 14: 28) in support of their contention that, whenever possible, people should come together in one large synagogue rather than worship in a number of small synagogues. The Rabbis praise congregational worship in the highest terms; one Rabbi goes so far as say, with obvious hyperbole, that prayer is only heard when it is offered in the synagogue (*Berakhot* 6a). Yet the fact that congregational prayer is not even mentioned in the Bible does not permit an either/or attitude. The standard prayers can be recited at home and Jewish masters of prayer, from Talmudic times, added to them private prayers of their own at an appropriate stage.

*Prayer as Obligation*

A typical feature of Jewish prayer is its regulation by the *Halakhah. There are laws of prayer: when prayer is to be offered, how it is to be offered, even the mood in which it is to be offered. Judaism knows of the need for spontaneity in prayer but both the standard prayers themselves and the times at which they are to be said are matters of law. Undoubtedly this stress on the legal aspects tends to be in opposition to the devotional mood. This is why a number of Hasidic groups, although otherwise strictly observant of the law, disregarded the Halakhic rules with regard to the times of prayer, reciting, for instance, the afternoon prayer after nightfall.

An interesting example of the introduction of legal norms into prayer is in the matter of the night prayer. After a discussion, the Talmud concludes that this prayer, unlike the morning and afternoon prayers, is optional. Yet since Jews everywhere took it upon themselves to recite this prayer, it became obligatory through the consensus of the Jewish community.

A Talmudic comment (*Taanit* 2a) on the verse: 'And serve Him with all your heart' (Deuteronomy 11: 13) states: 'What is service of the heart? This is prayer.' Maimonides, at the beginning of the section of his Code which deals with prayer, understands this to mean that, while the actual times and forms of the prayers are Rabbinic, there is a biblical injunction for every man and woman to pray daily. Others see the whole obligation to pray to be of Rabbinic origin but no less binding for that reason. The Orthodox authority Rabbi Moshe *Feinstein discusses whether a Gentile has this obligation to pray to God since it is not one of the seven *Noahide laws. He replies that there is no actual obligation but it is considered meritorious (a *mitzvah) if a Gentile does pray. Feinstein quotes the verse: 'For My house shall be called a house of prayer for all the peoples' (Isaiah 56: 7). Behind all the rules and regulations stands the doctrine of *Kavvanah, inwardness, in which the worshipper is expected to concentrate on what he is saying and not recite his prayers mechanically. A saying in Ethics of the Fathers (2. 213) is relevant in this connection: 'When you pray do not make your prayer a fixed form but [a plea for] mercies and supplications before God.'

*The Philosophy of Prayer*

It is somewhat surprising that there are only a very few discussions among Jewish thinkers on the philosophy of prayer. This comparative silence is probably due to Jewish teachers devoting their energies to the Halakhic niceties which demanded severe application, to the exclusion of matters held to be peripheral. The obvious question with regard to petitionary prayer, of whether God needs to be told what man needs, is addressed by *Albo (*Ikkarim* 4: 18). Albo endeavours to cope with the problem by suggesting that the act of turning to God in prayer is itself one of the conditions upon which God's help depends, just as it depends on other forms of human effort. Moses ben Joseph of Trani (1505–85), in his treatise on prayer (*Bet Elohim*, Pt. I, ch. 1), defines prayer as: '*The act in which man asks God for something he needs which he cannot achieve by his own efforts.*' This is explained as: *Man* and not an angel. Angels have no need to pray since all their needs are satisfied by God without them having to ask. *Asks* and not demands. Prayer is an appeal to God to exercise His mercy. It is not by right but by God's grace that prayer is answered. *Of God* and not of the angels. It is forbidden to pray to any creature. *For something he needs* and not for luxuries. *Which he cannot achieve by his own efforts*—man should only pray when his own efforts are futile. He should not rely on prayer to earn him a living, for example, since here God helps those who help themselves. With regard to prayers of adoration, the usual Jewish attitude is that these are offered because it is in the nature of human beings to praise the Highest, not because God needs to be told how wonderful He is.

In the Kabbalah, prayer is an exercise in promoting harmony on high, of assisting the unification of the *Sefirot. Prayer, like all other forms of worship, is for the sake of God, as the Kabblists put it, not for the sake of man. In Hasidism, too, petitionary prayer is 'for the sake of the *Shekhinah', that is, man prays for his needs to be satisfied not with any self-seeking motivation but because God's ultimate purpose remains unfulfilled when His creatures suffer deprivation. The Hasidic master Rabbi Judah Laib Alter, known as the Sefat Emet (1847–1905), gives expression to this idea in a comment to Psalm 18: 7:

'Although it appears obvious that a man should pray when he is in need, yet the truth is that prayer's chief value is when the mind of the worshipper is on the prayer itself, not on the request to be granted. For even when a man entreats God to grant his desire, yet when he engages in prayer he should forget his needs and be affected solely by the praise of God. It may then happen that his request will be granted because it resulted in his turning to God in prayer.'

In similar fashion, various Hasidic teachings seek to preserve both the traditional forms of petitionary prayer and the typical Hasidic doctrine of *annihilation of selfhood. In the act of prayer, even though it is the self that offers the petition, the self is transcended and lost to God.

For religious naturalists like Mordecai *Kaplan, God is not a Person who can answer prayer but the force that makes for righteousness. Prayer is directed to the highest in the universe and in oneself. Traditional theists obviously reject all such theories and try to cope with the problem of petitionary prayer in

the other ways mentioned above. Other Jewish modernists, not prepared to go as far as Kaplan, still move away from the idea of petitionary prayer as a means of influencing God, towards seeing the function of prayer as a way to affect man's attitudes. Prayer becomes a matter of severe self-scrutiny. For example: if I pray for wisdom, am I doing all I can to attain wisdom? If I pray for mercy, do I try to show compassion for the needs of others? But while this element is present in prayer, to reduce prayer entirely to an exercise in moral self-examination is illogical. The worshipper who prays for wisdom may well have in mind, and should ideally have in mind, that he must himself make the effort to attain wisdom but he is, after all, praying to God to grant him the wisdom he seeks. It is tautologous to say that prayer is self-scrutiny if prayer is said to mean self-scrutiny.

Friedrich Hecler, *Prayer* (Oxford, 1932).
Louis Jacobs, 'Prayer', in his *What Does Judaism Say About . . .?* (Jerusalem, 1973), 248–52.
—— *Hasidic Prayer*, with a new introduction (The Littman Library of Jewish Civilization; London and Washington, 1993).
Kaufmann K. Kohler, 'The Nature and Purpose of Prayer', in his *Jewish Theology* (New York, 1968), 271–7.
Isaiah Tishby, 'Prayer and Devotion', in his *The Wisdom of the Zohar*, trans. David Goldstein (The Littman Library Jewish Civilization; Oxford, 1989), 941–1075.

**Prayer Book** Heb. *Siddur* ('Arrangement'), a book containing the daily and Sabbath prayers. The book containing prayers for the festivals is known as a Mahzor (from a root meaning 'to come round', i.e. for use when the festivals arrive). All prayer books have the same basic features (see LITURGY) but each rite has its own additions and version, for example, the Ashkenazi Siddur, the Sephardi Siddur, the Italian Siddur, in modern times the Reform and Conservative Siddurim (plural of Siddur), and others, each in conformity with the ideological stance of the compilers and users.

In Talmudic times the prayers were recited by heart and there were no written orders of service at all. The first Prayer Book was compiled in the ninth century by Amram Gaon (see GEONIM), and is known as the Seder Rav Amram Gaon. This was followed in the tenth century by the Siddur of *Saadiah Gaon. Since then, especially after the invention of printing, numerous prayer books have been published. The Kabbalists have their own Prayer Book, of which there are a number of different versions. In these the special 'intentions', *kavvanot* (see KAVVANAH) of the Kabbalah are given to allow the worshipper to concentrate on them in his prayers. There are also a number of Hasidic prayer books, usually with comments offering guidance to the particular branch of Hasidism for which they are intended. Material was added to the Prayer Book from time to time, often at the mere whim of the printers.

Commentaries to the Prayer Book are printed together with the text in many editions. A feature of most traditional prayer books is the inclusion of notes on prayer in general and on the laws of prayer, the festivals, and fasts. Prayer books in Western lands usually have a translation of the text in the vernacular on opposite pages to the Hebrew.

> Israel Abrahams, *A Companion to the Authorized Daily Prayerbook* (New York, 1966).
> Stefan C. Reif, *Judaism and Hebrew Prayer* (Cambridge, 1993).

**Precepts, 613** A precept of the Torah, a *\*mitzvah*, is a divine command contained in the \*Pentateuch and can be either a positive precept—a command to do something—or a negative precept—a command to refrain from doing something. The command to give charity, for example, is a positive precept. The command not to steal is a negative precept. The idea that there are 613 precepts is first found in a homily delivered, according to the Talmud (*Makkot* 23b), by the third-century Palestinian preacher, Rabbi Simlai. This teacher states that there are 613 precepts: 365 negative precepts, corresponding to the days of the solar year and 248 positive precepts, corresponding to the 'limbs' of the body. 'Limbs' here denotes parts of the body, such as the joints of the fingers, and the concept of 248 parts in this sense is ancient and found in the Mishnah (*Ohalot* 1: 8). It is as clear as can be that all this belongs to the \*Aggadah. It is an instance of sermonizing in which the preacher used concepts that predated his observation, applying them to convey a moral lesson, as preachers do. The homiletical nature is apparent in the Midrashic comment that each 'limb' says to man: 'Perform a *mitzvah* with me' and each day of the solar year says: 'Do not commit a sin on me.' Louis Ginzberg has noted that in the ancient Aggadah, referred

to by \*Philo among others, the \*Decalogue is said to contain 613 letters. It was only at a later date that these 'letters' become 'precepts'.

The whole notion of the 613 precepts is thus artificial. Even a superficial glance at the commands in the Torah shows that there are more negative precepts than positive precepts and this forms the basis of Rabbi Simlai's homily. Availing himself of the two sets of numbers, 365 and 248, Rabbi Simlai develops his sermon without taking too seriously the actual numbers. In the whole of the Talmudic literature no attempt is made at listing the 613. But in the Middle Ages the great codifiers did try to make a list of them. When the attempt was made it was discovered that there are, in fact, far more than this number of commands, so that Maimonides and \*Nahmanides go to great lengths to discover which of the commands in the Torah are basic, and hence counted in the 613, and which secondary, and hence not counted directly. In later Jewish thought, a Jew who obeys all the laws of the Torah is said to be a Jew who keeps the 613 precepts. In point of fact, no single person can possibly keep all 613; some apply only to the \*priests, for example, and others are limited to particular and rare circumstances such as the precept of \*levirate marriage. One of the precepts, to give a further illustration, is for a thief to restore his ill-gotten gains to the rightful owner. A man who has never stolen anything cannot observe this precept. The thief, on the other hand, who can carry out this precept, has offended against the negative precept not to steal. Acknowledgement of its Aggadic nature must be retained even after the concept has passed into Halakhah.

> Louis Jacobs, *A Tree of Life* (Oxford, 1984), 16–17.

**Preaching** That sermons were delivered in the synagogue, especially on Sabbaths and the festivals, from early Rabbinic times, is attested in numerous Midrashim (see MIDRASH). It would seem that the later Midrashim had their origin in sermons, although the Midrashim themselves bear all the marks of literary productions in their own right. The usual preaching method, until the modern period, was to take scriptural verses out of context and to apply them to the religious and ethical questions of the preacher's time. This method of scriptural application became known as *derush* (from a root meaning 'to search' or 'to enquire') and the sermon became known as a *derashah* (from the same root, as is the word Midrash itself). Preachers were known as Darshanim or Maggidim ('Speakers' or 'Tellers'). Again until modern times, the function of preaching belonged not to the *Rabbi of a town but to the special class of preachers, usually learned men but not necessarily well versed in the practical *Halakah. In Eastern Europe, Maggidim would wander from town to town to preach in the synagogue, attracting the masses by their popular, homely expositions liberally sprinkled with proverbs, folk-tales, and illustrations from the daily life of their audiences. Collections were published of the sermons of the more renowned preachers and these were used as guides for preachers everywhere.

*Preaching in Modern Times*

Although the historian Leopold *Zunz, in his famous work, *Gottesdienstliche Vortraeger der Juden*, published in 1832, sought to demonstrate, when challenged by the Prussian government (under the influence of Orthodox groups who saw sermons in the vernacular as the beginnings of Reform), that preaching is an ancient Jewish institution, the traditional *derashah* took, in Germany, the new form of the *Predigt*, as it was called. The new type of sermon was more formal and in the vernacular, and it became a regular part of the service. The modern sermon is also based on a scriptural verse, usually taken from the portion of the weekly Torah reading, but treats a particular theme in systematic fashion and its aim is more one of edification rather than instruction. Alexander Altmann has shown how the early German preachers consciously modelled their sermons on the patterns of Christian homiletics and how they would even use the famous Christian preachers as guides to sermon-construction. At a later stage, opposition to this reliance on Gentile forms led preachers such as Isaac Noah Mannheimer and Adolf Jellinek to use much more Rabbinic material in their sermons. The modern type of sermon became the norm in England and in the USA. Even in Eastern Europe in the nineteenth century, where the art of the old Maggidim still flourished, the sermons in Yiddish were often more sophisticated than in the past and more relevant to the burning social and political issues of the day.

In modern Rabbinical seminaries, Orthodox, Reform and Conservative, homiletics is an important subject in the curriculum. For the modern Rabbi, preaching is an important part, perhaps the most important part, of his Rabbinic activity. Certain fashions in preaching have become the norm. On the festivals, for instance, every Rabbi would see himself as having failed in his duty if he did not devote his sermon to the particular theme of the festival—freedom for Passover, trust in God for *Tabernacles, the importance of Jewish survival for *Hanukkah, and so forth. The modern sermon is often polemical. The Reform sermon might attack Orthodoxy as being too reactionary. The Orthodox sermon might attack Reform for being heretical or disloyal to Jewish values. Conservative sermons often seek to encourage the advantages of the middle-of-the-road approach. Among the more general themes to which the modern pulpit addresses itself are: the alleged conflict between religion and science; the role of the State of Israel; the permissive society; intermarriage; Jewish education; war and peace; social justice; racial discrimination; the use and abuse of wealth; and Judaism in relation to other religions.

Israel Bettan, *Studies in Jewish Preaching* (Cincinnati, 1937).

A. Cohen, *Jewish Homiletics* (London, 1937).

Marc Saperstein, *Jewish Preaching 1200–1800* (New Haven, 1989).

**Priestly Blessing** The blessing recited by the *priests (see KOHEN) in ancient times in the Temple and nowadays in the synagogue. The biblical source is Numbers 6: 22–7: 'The Lord spoke to Moses: Speak to Aaron and his sons: Thus shall you bless the people of Israel. Say to them: The Lord bless you and protect you! The Lord deal kindly and graciously with you! The Lord bestow His favour upon you and grant you peace! Thus they shall link My name with the people of Israel, and I will bless them.' The blessing is in three parts and is called 'the threefold blessing'. In the Hebrew the first section consists of three words, the second of five, and the third of seven. In the Temple the priests recited the blessing twice daily, in the morning and afternoon, while they stood on a special platform, known as the *dukhan* ('platform'). In the synagogue the blessing is recited by the priests while standing in front of the *Ark. To this day, the recital of the priestly blessing is called in Yiddish *dukhenen*, literally, 'platforming', after the Temple procedures. In the majority of synagogues outside Israel the priestly blessing is only recited on festivals during the Additional service. This limitation is because the blessing can only be recited when the priests are in a joyous frame of mind which, it is believed, is possible in the Diaspora only on the festivals. In Israel the blessing is recited on the Sabbath as well and in Jerusalem it is recited daily. A reference is made by the Reader to the priestly blessing during his repetition of the *Amidah in the daily morning service.

The procedure in the synagogue is as follows. The Kohanim remove their shoes and have their hands ritually washed by *Levites. If there is no Levite in the congregation the washing of the hands of the Kohanim is done by a first-born and, failing that, by the Kohanim themselves. The Kohanim then stand before the Ark and the Reader calls out the word: 'Kohanim' as a signal for the priests to begin. The Kohanim then cover their heads with the prayer shawl, the *tallit, and recite an introductory benediction: 'Blessed art Thou O Lord our God, King of the universe, who hast hallowed us with the sanctity of Aaron and commanded us to bless His people Israel in love.' The Kohanim then raise their hands and arrange the fingers so as to form 'windows'. The idea behind this is that the blessing proceeds from God as if He is sending it through the apertures of the hands—a symbolic way of expressing the idea that God's blessing is present even when He hides Himself, so to speak. The Reader then recites the blessing word by word, the Kohanim chanting each word after the Reader. Reform and many Conservative congregations have dispensed with the priestly blessing. The blessing is also recited by parents in the home before the Sabbath meal but this is simply a pious custom. The priestly blessing proper in the synagogue can only be carried out by Kohanim.

The medieval thinkers discuss the obvious question of why God needs to bless the people through the Kohanim. Replies differ. Some believe that the Kohanim, the ancient teachers of the Torah, represent the blessings that stem from observance of God's law. Others see the Kohanim as the instruments by means of which God's blessings are transmitted. Human co-operation with the divine is required if blessings are to follow. In all interpretations a determined effort is made to play down any magical elements. It is God alone who blesses His people. The Kohanim are, at the most, the vehicles He uses to transmit His blessings.

Nehama Leibowitz, 'The Priestly Blessing', in her *Studies in Bamidbar (Numbers)*, (Jerusalem, 1980), 60–7.

Jacob Milgrom, 'The Priestly Blessing', in Nahum M. Sarna (ed.), *The JPS Torah Commentary: Numbers* (Philadelphia and New York, 1990), 360–2.

**Priests** In Temple times the chief function of the priesthood was to offer the sacrifices in the Temple. The priestly families served in a weekly rotation. The priests received no fees for officiating in the Temple but they were given generous portions of meat from the sacrificial animals and a proportion of all wheat, wine, and oil. The priest (see KOHEN) is described as holy. The people of Israel were to be 'a kingdom of priests and a holy nation' (Exodus 19: 6), but the special sanctity of the priest depended on his having been born as a descendant of *Aaron. Althrough a priest was not intrinsically holy or spiritually superior to ordinary Israelites, there is no doubt that priests in ancient times saw themselves as the aristocrats of the Jewish people. The Mishnah takes it for granted that if a Levite or an Israelite has become betrothed to a maiden and has led her to believe that he is a priest, the betrothal is rendered invalid when the deception is discovered, on the grounds of misrepresentation, since she thought she was marrying a person belonging to the upper classes. While the minimum amount for the marriage settlement, the *ketubah*, was 200 *zuz*, the priests would not allow their daughters to marry anyone not prepared to fix the minimum at 400 *zuz*. Only the males of the priestly families could officiate in the Temple. There were no female priests, but this has no relevance to the question of women *Rabbis: a Rabbi is not a priest but, basically, a teacher of the Torah.

Since the destruction of the Temple, those believed to be Kohanim because of a family tradition have the privilege of being called first to the Torah, of delivering the priestly *blessing and of being invited to say *grace after meals. A Kohen may not come into contact with the dead except for his near relatives and he may not marry a divorcee. Reform accepts neither the privileges nor the restrictions of priesthood because it sees the whole institution as having lapsed with the destruction of the

Temple. Still to maintain it, the Reformers hold, is to perpetuate a caste system. Orthodoxy retorts that it is absurd to see the very few laws concerning the Kohanim as perpetuating any kind of caste system.

**Pride**   Pride is, in the Jewish tradition, among the most serious of the vices, as *humility is among the highest of the virtues. The Talmudic Rabbis, perhaps because of their awareness that scholars are easily tempted to lord it over the ignorant, denigrate pride in the most caustic terms. God and the proud man, a Talmudic saying has it, cannot reside together in the same world. Pride is an abomination akin to idolatry and the self-sufficiently proud deny the basic principle of Judaism that God is the Lord of creation. In another Rabbinic homily, *Sinai is said to be the lowest of the mountains, which is why God gave the Torah on this mountain rather than on a loftier one. For the same reason, when God revealed Himself to Moses He did so out of a lowly bush (Exodus 3: 2). The Torah, say the Rabbis, is compared to water which flows only downwards, never upwards. The proud man can never truly assimilate the teachings of the Torah. Yet one Rabbi declared (*Sotah* 5a) that a scholar should have an 'eighth of an eighth' of pride out of respect for his own learning. His colleague remonstrated: 'He should not possess it [pride] or part of it,' quoting the verse: 'Every one that is proud in heart is an abomination to the Lord' (Proverbs 16: 5).

The Jewish moralists stress that avoidance of pride is not to be confused with self-deception. If a man has a good mind and worthy qualities he is not expected to try to ignore them, only not to take credit for them. Whatever talents a man possesses should be seen as God's gifts to him, undeserving though he is of them. Moses Hayyim *Luzzatto in his *Path of the Upright* exposes the various masquerades the proud man adopts:

'Another imagines that he is so great and so deserving of honour that no one can deprive him of the usual signs of respect. And to prove this, he behaves as though he were humble and goes to extremes in displaying boundless modesty and infinite humility. But in his heart he is proud, saying to himself, "I am so exalted, and so deserving of honour, that I need not have any one do me honour. I can well afford to forgo marks of respect." Another is the coxcomb, who wants to be noted for his superior qualities

and to be singled out for his behaviour. He is not satisfied with having everyone praise him for the superior traits which he thinks he possesses, but he wants them also to include in their praises that he is the most humble of men. He thus takes pride in his humility, and wishes to be honoured because he pretends to flee from honour. Such a prig usually goes so far as to put himself below those who are much inferior to him, even below the meanest, thinking that in this way he displays the utmost humility. He refuses all titles of greatness and declines promotion in rank, but in his heart he thinks, "There is no one in all the world as wise and as humble as I." Conceited people of this type, though they pretend mightily to be humble, cannot escape some mishap which causes their pride to burst forth, like a flame out of a heap of litter. Such a man has been compared to a house filled with straw. The house being full of holes, the straw keeps on escaping through them, so that after a while every one knows what is within the house. The humility of his behaviour is soon known to be insincere, and his meekness nothing but pretence.' (*Mesillat Yesharim*, trans. Mordecai M. Kaplan (Philadelphia, 1936), 104–5).

This whole question of pride is extremely delicate. Would Judaism frown on a man taking pride in his work or on a Jew taking pride in his Jewishness? And it can be argued that in some circumstances pride is the driving force for worthwhile activities. There must obviously be severe tensions over this problem. A Hasidic master put it this way. Every person must have two slips of paper in his pockets. On one he should inscribe the words uttered by Abraham: 'I am dust and ashes.' On the other he should inscribe the words taken from the Mishnah: 'For my sake the whole world was created.' In moments when the danger lurks of excessive pride he should take out the slip reminding him that he is dust and ashes. But when his self-doubt threatens to be completely stultifying, he must take out the other slip to reaffirm that the whole world was created for his sake.

**Principles of Faith**   The essential beliefs on which the Jewish religion is founded; the basic Jewish *dogmas from which all else in the religion follows. *Philo of Alexandria, the first Jewish thinker known to have compiled a list of articles of faith, observes that from the creation narrative in Genesis five such articles can be derived.

1. The eternal existence of God, aimed against *atheism.

2. The unity of God, aimed against polytheism.

3. The world has been created by God, aimed against the theory that the world is eternal.

4. The world, like its Maker, is one, aimed against the notion that there are many worlds.

5. God extends His providential care over the whole world, aimed against those who deny divine *providence.

It is obvious that Philo is responding to the pagan beliefs of his day rather than actually drawing up precise articles of faith. His fourth principle is otherwise inexplicable. In later Jewish thought the notion that God created other worlds as well as this one is found not too infrequently and was only denied by Philo in reaction to the philosophies of his day which he considered to be detrimental to belief in the One God. This was to happen repeatedly in the history of Jewish creedal formulations. The thinkers who drew up articles of faith called attention especially to those aspects of Judaism which had come under attack in their time, while ignoring other principles of equal importance that were not under attack.

In Rabbinic thought, the basic beliefs of Judaism are generally taken for granted. The Rabbinic emphasis is on practice. Even in the Mishnah (*Sanhedrin* 10: 1), in which there is found the nearest thing to a statement of principles of faith, there is a blend of theory and practical application. The Mishnah reads: 'And these have no share in the *World to Come; one who says that there is no *resurrection of the dead; and one who says that the Torah is not from Heaven; and the *epikoros. Rabbi Akiba says: Also one who reads the external books or who utters a charm over a wound and recites: "I will put none of the diseases upon thee which I have put upon the Egyptians: for I am the Lord that healeth thee" [Exodus 15: 26]. Abba Saul says: Also one who pronounces the Name [the *Tetragrammaton] with its proper letters.'

Clearly, the Mishnah is not an early Rabbinic attempt at drawing up a creed but is rather a warning against entertaining certain false opinions and carrying out religiously harmful practices stemming from such beliefs. Possibly, importance has to be attached to the expression 'One who *says*' in the Mishnah, perhaps implying that the Mishnaic opposition is directed not so much against private reservations on the part of individual Jews as against sectarian *declarations* of unbelief.

The real impetus to creed-formulation in Judaism was given in the Middle Ages when Jewish theologians had to face the challenges presented by Greek philosophical thought, and by Christianity and Islam. It then became necessary to define Judaism and to dwell on the unique features of the Jewish religion as a religious philosophy. It is noteworthy that the first Jews, after Philo, to draw up creedal formulations were the *Karaites, themselves sectarians and rebels against Rabbinic Judaism. The Karaites were the first, in the Middle Ages, to come into close contact with non-Jewish systems. Later formulations by thinkers in the Rabbinic tradition had the additional motive of combating Karaite beliefs and defending Rabbinism.

Maimonides' formulation, in his commentary to the Mishnah mentioned above, is the best known and the most influential attempt to define the basic principles of the Jewish religion, but Maimonides, too, is reacting to the beliefs prevalent in the non-Jewish world in his day. The thirteen principles of the faith as laid down by Maimonides are implied attacks on ideas the sage believed were foreign to Judaism. It is these thirteen that are significant for Maimonides because it was in the areas covered by them that the struggle between Judaism and rival faiths took place.

Maimonides thirteen principles are:

1. Belief in the existence of God.
2. Belief in God's unity.
3. Belief in God's incorporeality.
4. Belief in God's eternity.
5. Belief that God alone is to be worshipped.
6. Belief in *prophecy.
7. Belief in Moses as the greatest of the prophets.
8. Belief that the Torah was given by God to Moses.
9. Belief that the Torah is immutable.
10. Belief that God knows the thoughts and deeds of human beings.
11. Belief that God rewards and punishes.
12. Belief in the coming of the *Messiah.
13. Belief in the resurrection of the dead.

Maimonides adds a very dogmatic note. Even a complete transgressor, though he will be punished for his sins, has a share in the World to

Come if he believes in these principles. But anyone who denies one of these principles is an unbeliever and no longer belongs to the community of Israel. Maimonides here makes correct belief the supreme value. The believing sinner is included in the 'general body of Israel'. The unbeliever, even though he is not guilty of serious sin, is excluded from 'the general body of Israel' and, Maimonides continues, 'we are obliged to hate him and cause him to perish'. (This final statement may be sheer hyperbole but is indicative of Maimonides' severely dogmatic cast of mind.) For Maimonides a Jew is defined not by what he does but by what he believes.

The thirteen principles of Maimonides eventually became authoritative for the majority of traditionalist Jews, even though various subsequent thinkers challenged Maimonides' formulation. An indication of their significance is that they are found in most traditional prayer books in two forms; in the *Yigdal hymn and in the Ani Maamin ('I believe') catechism. The latter, of unknown authorship, first appeared in the year 1517. Before that time a catechism of the 'I believe with perfect faith' type was unknown in Judaism and almost certainly owes much to non-Jewish influences. But the very fact that Maimonides' principles appeared in the Prayer Book endowed them with far greater significance than they might otherwise have had.

Theologians such as *Crescas and *Albo discussed the question of how to determine which beliefs were so basic to Judaism that they could be considered to be principles of the faith and which, though significant, could not be considered principles since Judaism could be conceived of even without them. *Abravanel, in his *Rosh Amanah* ('Pinnacle of Faith') is unhappy about the whole attempt to draw up principles of the faith, since to do this appears to suggest that some aspects of the Torah are more important than others. Abravanel writes:

'Therefore I am convinced that it is improper to postulate principles or foundations with regard to God's Torah. For we are obliged to believe everything recorded in the Torah and we are not permitted to doubt the smallest matter therein that it should be necessary to prove its truth by reference to principles or root ideas. For whoever denies or doubts any matter, small or great, of the beliefs or narratives contained in the Torah is a heretic and an unbeliever. Since the Torah is true no single belief or narrative in it can be superior to any other.'

The renowned Halakhist David Ibn Abi *Zimra (d. 1589) cites Abravanel in a Responsum (no. 344) and agrees with him entirely.

*Modern Attitudes*

Maimonides' principles have to be seen against his medieval background and this is acknowledged even by Jews who still subscribe to them in broad outline. Although Orthodox Jews still accept all the thirteen as the definition of what it is that a Jew has to believe, a certain degree of flexibility is allowed in the matter of interpretation: with regard, for instance, to the eschatological beliefs (see ESCHATOLOGY). Moreover, the belief that Israel is the *Chosen People is held by all Orthodox Jews even though Maimonides does not state this as one of his principles. Conservative Judaism still grapples with the problems raised by *biblical criticism in connection with Maimonides' principle that the Torah is from Heaven and the principle regarding the truth of prophecy. In various 'Platforms', Reform Judaism has tried to issue new creedal formulations in the light of modern thought. Thinkers of all three groups accept Maimonides' first five principles, that God exists, that He is One, that He is incorporeal, that He is eternal, and that He alone is to be worshipped, although religious naturalists (see KAPLAN) reinterpret these five in accordance with their conception of God not as a Person but as the power that makes for righteousness.

Among many of the ultra-Orthodox (see ORTHODOXY) there is little interest in creedal formulations, partly because these Jews follow Abravanel and Ibn Abi Zimra that the whole Torah is a single great principle, and partly because of the central role of Talmudic and Halakhic studies in their scheme, which leaves no room for theological speculation. The attitude of such Jews is to affirm belief in everything handed down by the tradition but to concentrate on the performance of the precepts.

Louis Jacobs, *Principles of the Jewish Faith* (Northvale, NJ, and London, 1988).

**Printing** The invention of printing had an enormous influence on Jewish religious life, in which the study of the Torah is paramount. In the Middle Ages few were able to afford to have a good library, even when enough patrons of learning were found to pay skilful copyists to *produce books for the use of scholars. In the Geonic period, there were so few copies of the Talmud in Jewish communities that the *Geonim were often consulted not about the meaning of the texts but about what the texts actually said. With printing all this changed. Books of all kinds were published and widely disseminated. Editions of the Talmud, the Midrashim, the Codes, the commentaries, the works of the philosophers and the Kabbalists, and, of course, the Bible and the Prayer Book, placed all the sacred Jewish classics within the reach of everyone, if not in private homes at least in synagogue and communal libraries. The first complete edition of the Babylonian Talmud was printed by the non-Jewish publisher, Daniel Bomberg, in Venice in the years 1500–23. Not only did Bomberg's pagination become universally accepted, thus facilitating easy reference, but the placing in this edition of the *Tosafot together with Rashi's Commentary beside the text caused scholars to look upon these commentaries as part of the text itself, as it were, widening immensely the scope of Jewish learning. In the area of practical law, a major reason why the *Shulḥan Arukh attained the status it did as the standard Halakhic work is that this Code was produced after printing had been invented, so that Rabbis had easy access to the rulings of their predecessors.

The Halakhic authorities discuss whether a printed book has the sanctity of a written book. Does a printed sacred book which is torn or which otherwise cannot be used, have to be buried reverentially or can it be simply discarded? The consensus is that printed books do not have the same degree of sanctity as handwritten works but should still be treated with respect. The custom is to bury printed books that are no longer usable.

Another much-discussed question is whether a *Sefer Torah, a *mezuzah, and tefillin have to be handwritten. The Italian Halakhist and Kabbalist, Menahem Azariah da Fano (1548–1620), who flourished a century after printing had been invented in Germany (at a time when Italy was the main home of Jewish printing), considers the question in a Responsum (no. 93). Da Fano here remarks that he himself had engaged in printing and was thoroughly familiar with printing techniques. He permits a bill of divorce, a *get, to be printed even though the Talmud states that it must be 'written'. But,

writing at the end of the seventeenth century, Jair Hayyim Bacharach holds that da Fano would not permit ritual objects like a Sefer Torah and a mezuzah to be printed, especially if the printer is a non-Jew. Bacharach introduces a mystical idea:

'The sanctity of a Sefer Torah derives from it having been written by a human being in whom there is the spirit of God and a portion of the divine from on high. Through the intentions of such a man and his forming of the letters, these acquire sanctity. Every Israelite can be presumed to be of this status for they are attached by their souls to the Lord our God. It is as a result of this that the sanctity is drawn down to the Sefer Torah, tefillin, mezuzot and other books.'

On the basis of this distinction between the written and the printed word, Bacharach seeks to find a dispensation for a poor scholar with no other bedroom than his study in which to make love to his wife, since the printed books around the walls do not have complete sanctity. Mystical ideas such as that of Bacharach were responsible for the universal decision that, whatever the position in theory, a printed Sefer Torah is invalid. Sacred books written by the hand of a dedicated human being can never be replaced by the products of a soulless machine.

Louis Jacobs, *A Tree of Life: Diversity, Flexibility, and Creativity in Jewish Law* (Oxford, 1984), 166–9.

**Procreation** According to the Rabbis, the first *mitzvah* of the Torah is the command to engage in procreation (Genesis 1: 28; 9: 1). Procreation is, in addition to companionship, the aim of *marriage. Opposition to *birthcontrol is partly based on the duty to have children. According to the majority, and accepted, Rabbinic opinion this duty does not devolve upon women, no doubt because it was unreasonable in ancient society to demand that a woman should be obliged to attract a man to marry her.

**Prophecy** The *inspiration of certain individuals by the divine power, which enables them to gaze into the future and bring to other human beings a message from God. Maimonides' sixth *principle of faith defines prophecy in terms of his general intellectual approach:

'Prophecy. This implies that it should be known that among the human species there exist persons of very intellectual natures and possessing much perfection. Their souls are predisposed for receiving the form of the intellect. Then this human intellect joins itself with the active intellect, and an exalted emanation is shed upon them. These are the prophets. This is prophecy, and this is its meaning. The complete elucidation of this principle of faith would be very long, and it is not our purpose to bring proofs for every principle or to elucidate the means of comprehending them, for this affair includes the totality of the sciences. We shall give them a passing mention only. The verses of the Torah which testify concerning the prophecy of prophets are many.'

Maimonides here calls attention to the biblical prophets, those whose prophecies are recorded in the second section of the Hebrew *Bible, the literary prophets, as they are called. But it appears from Maimonides' discussion of prophecy in his other works that prophecy is possible even after all the biblical books had been compiled. True, in the Jewish tradition prophecy came to an end in Israel after the last of the biblical prophets, *Haggai, *Zechariah, and *Malachi, but there was an equally widely held view that prophecy would be restored, to usher in the Messianic age, during the thirteenth century, that is, possibly during Maimonides' lifetime. *Heschel has tried to show that Maimonides believed that he himself had attained to at least the lower stages of prophecy at occasional periods in his life.

In the section of his *Guide of the Perplexed* devoted to the theme of prophecy (2. 32–48), Maimonides sides with the Arabic philosophers who hold that anyone who attains intellectual and moral perfection automatically becomes a prophet. It is not a matter of divine grace but of human capacity and attainment. Maimonides has only one qualification to make. His reading of Scripture convinces him that only certain persons are chosen to be prophets. Maimonides therefore concludes that God may withhold prophecy from one suited to attain it by means of a miracle. Judah *Halevi, in his *Kuzari*, on the other hand, denies that prophecy is a natural process and sees it as entirely a divine gift. Nor does he believe that intellectual perfection is essential to the attainment of the prophetic vision. Furthermore, Halevi believes that prophecy is limited to the Jewish race so that a convert to Judaism, no matter how worthy, can never become a prophet (see CHOSEN

PEOPLE). And for Halevi geographical as well as biological considerations are involved. The prophet must belong in the line of prophets, reaching from Adam through Seth, Enosh, Noah, Shem, Abraham, Isaac, and Jacob down to the members of the Jewish race, and he must reside in the Holy Land. *Crescas occupies a position midway between Maimonides and Halevi. He disagrees with Maimonides that prophecy is a natural faculty and believes that in the main it is a matter of training. But while he agrees with Halevi in limiting prophecy to Jews, Crescas does not agree with him that this is because of a mystic, semi-biological faculty possessed by Jews. It is only that the rigorous training required before a man can become a prophet can only be provided by the Torah, the exclusive possession of the Jews.

*Modern Biblical Scholarship*

Like their medieval predecessors, modern biblical scholars have tried to explore the nature of prophecy as it appears from the biblical records. The term *navi* occurs as a noun, with the meaning of a prophet, over 400 times in the Bible, as well as more than 110 times in verbal form. The older view in biblical scholarship, that the word comes from a root meaning 'to bubble forth' and was held to refer to the prophet pouring out his words in an ecstatic frenzy or even to his foaming at the mouth in a kind of fit, has now generally been abandoned. Many modern scholars prefer the etymology given by some of the medieval Jewish commentators that the root meaning of the word is 'to call'. There is, in fact, an Akkadian root *nabu* meaning 'to call'. The meaning of *navi* according to this would be 'one who calls', a man with a message to deliver. There has also been a good deal of discussion in recent years on the role of the 'cultic prophets'. Abandoning the older view of a severe conflict between prophet and priest, modern scholars, on the analogy of Near Eastern patterns as revealed in cultic texts and hints in the Bible itself (e.g. 1 Kings 1: 34—Nathan the prophet and Zadok the priest; 2 Kings 23: 2; Isaiah 28: 7; Lamentations 2: 20), have argued convincingly for the existence of cultic prophets in ancient Israel.

The picture which emerges from the biblical accounts of conditions before the rise of the great literary prophets is that of bands of *neviim*, probably grouped in some way around the shrines, who were the spokesmen of God.

Some of these were 'true' prophets, serving as the conscience of the nation, others were 'false' prophets, failing to remind the people of God's demands on them. All of them seem to have cultivated something resembling the ecstatic state. The literary prophets were undoubtedly different from the earlier *neviim* but shared some of the latter's features.

Perhaps the most remarkable thing to be observed of the literary prophets is the assurance with which they speak of their message as coming directly from God. 'The lion hath roared,' declares *Amos, 'who will not fear? The Lord God hath spoken who can but prophesy?' (Amos 3: 8). *Isaiah tells of the Lord speaking to him 'with a strong hand' (Isaiah 8: 11). *Jeremiah tells how the Lord put words into his mouth (Jeremiah 1: 9) and how God imparted to him words of fire (Jeremiah 23: 29). The message which comes to the prophet is, in the first instance, to his contemporaries and it frequently has to do with future events. It is consequently too glib to make the common distinction between 'forthtellers' and 'foretellers' and to claim that the classical prophets belonged only to the former group. There is an element of prediction in the work of the classical prophets, too, though the predictions are of a future arising out of the present rather than a distant, unrelated future, notwithstanding the views of *Fundamentalism, whether Jewish or Christian.

*Jewish Theology and the Prophets*

The position taken in classical Reform Judaism, that the prophets are more significant than the Torah—Reform has sometimes described itself as 'Prophetic Judaism'—is untraditional, as the Reformers admitted. In the Rabbinic tradition the Torah contains God's complete revelation for Jewish practice so that the Rabbis could say that if Israel had not sinned, no further revelation through prophets and the sacred writings would have been required (*Nedarim* 22b). No prophet was able to make any innovations, once the revelation to Moses was complete (*Shabbat* 104a; *Megillah* 2b). This traditional attitude accounts for the fact that some ultra-Orthodox Jews (see ORTHODOXY) devote very little time to the study of the prophets and are even somewhat easygoing in chanting the *Haftarah, the prophetic readings in the synagogue. Yet no Jew, whether Reform or Orthodox, fails to acknowledge the tremendous significance for Judaism of the prophetic books of the Bible.

It has also to be said that views on the nature of the prophetic experience are irrelevant to the theological question of what is involved in the acceptance of Maimonides' sixth principle of faith. Many Jews today would be prepared to argue, with plausibility, that not being prophets ourselves we cannot hope to comprehend the exact nature of the prophetic experience. What matters is that however the prophets received their revelation, their message concerning the God who demands holiness, justice, and mercy in human affairs contains the highest demands made upon man, and this is so whether the classical prophets are understood as ecstatics or, as *Heschel sees them, as men who shared the divine pathos, or on any other understanding of the phenomenon of prophecy. As Otto Eissfeldt puts it:

'With regard to the psychology of the prophets, opinions still differ widely whether, and in what degree, supernormal—or to give the usual adjective "ecstatic"—qualities, experiences and acts are to be thought of. Yet all are at one in the view that the religious and ethical value of these figures does not depend on the answer given to this question, but that they have an enduring meaning for mankind in any case, and that here lies their true significance.'

Otto Eissfeldt, 'The Prophetic Literature', in H. H. Rowley (ed.), *The Old Testament and Modern Study* (Oxford, 1956), 115–161.

Abraham J. Heschel, *The Prophets* (Philadelphia, 1962).

Louis Jacobs, 'The Sixth Principle: Prophecy', in his *Principles of the Jewish Faith* (Northvale, NJ, and London, 1988), 184–205.

**Prostitution** Prostitution, 'the oldest profession', is naturally referred to frequently in the Bible (e.g. Genesis 38: 14; Joshua 2: 1). In the famous judgement of *Solomon (1 Kings 3: 16–27) the claim to be the true mother of the infant was made by two prostitutes. A *priest was forbidden to marry a woman who had been a prostitute (Leviticus 21: 7). The book of *Proverbs (ch. 7) warns against the loose woman who entices young men to sin with her. Israel is described metaphorically as a prostitute when unfaithful to God (Numbers 25: 1–2; Jeremiah 3: 6; Hosea 4: 12). In the ancient Near East, temple prostitutes (men as well as women) offered the gain of their bodies to the gods. It appears that this practice was at times copied by the Israelites from their pagan neighbours, hence the injunctions: 'No Israelite women shall be a cult prostitute, nor shall any Israelite man be a cult prostitute. You shall not bring the fee of a whore or the pay of a dog [usually understood to refer to a male prostitute] into the house of the Lord your God in fulfilment of any vow, for both are abhorrent to the Lord your God' (Deuteronomy 23: 18–19). The practice persisted until King Josiah suppressed it as part of his reforms (2 Kings 23: 7).

The Talmudic Rabbis not only condemned professional prostitution but also referred to any sexual contact between a man and a woman who were not married to one another as harlotry (*zenut*). When a Palestinian Rabbi waxed eloquent in describing the social improvements resulting from the Roman conquest, his colleague retorted that the Romans did build market-places but only so that they will be frequented by harlots (*Shabbat* 33b). Condemnation of harlotry persisted throughout Jewish history, although there is sufficient evidence that it was known in every period. In some medieval communities special regulations were drawn up against prostitutes and those who availed themselves of their services. The Galician Rabbi, Abraham Menaham Steinberg (1847–1928) was asked whether a former brothel can be used as a synagogue. Steinberg remarks that he was unable to find anywhere in the Talmud or the Codes that such a thing is forbidden. Yet, he states, it should not be permitted, since the average person will find it extremely odd that a brothel can be converted into a synagogue. Even things permitted by law must be rejected if they seem extremely offensive to the moral sense and cause the masses to view aspects of Judaism with distaste. The Rabbi of Moscow, Jacob Mazeh (1857–1924), relates in his autobiography that he refused to allow a costly curtain, donated by a notorious prostitute, to be placed in front of the Ark in the synagogue.

Louis M. Epstein, 'Harlotry', in his *Sex Laws and Customs in Judaism* (New York, 1948), 152–78.

**Proverbs, Book of** The second book in the third section of the *Bible, the *Ketuvim*, the Sacred Writings. This book of thirty-one chapters consists of collections of proverbs and wise sayings and belongs to what scholars refer to as the wisdom literature, a type of literature that flourished over many centuries in the ancient Near East and which had a marked influence on Proverbs, *Job, and *Ecclesiastes. Wisdom in this context refers to prudent counselling for the conduct of daily life, praise of learning, and warnings against sloth, profligacy, and the like. Hence the book of Proverbs has a strong universalistic tone but with a specific Israelite and religious thrust. Although a few sayings in the book are reminiscent of popular saws, the book contains literary forms produced by skilful writers and cannot be seen as a simple collection of examples of folk wisdom.

The book opens with the words: 'The proverbs of Solomon, the son of David, king of Israel' and Solomon is referred to in two other passages (10: 1 and 25: 1). Since it is said of Solomon that 'he spoke three thousand proverbs' (2 Kings 5: 12), the traditional view is that King Solomon is the author of the book of Proverbs. However, in a Talmudic passage (*Bava Batra* 15a), the book is said to have been 'written', that is, finally edited, or, possibly, committed to writing, by King Hezekiah and his associates, on the basis of the verse: 'These also are proverbs of Solomon, which the men of Hezekiah king of Judah copied out' (Proverbs 25: 1). The verdict of modern scholarship is that the book consists of a number of collections from different periods in Israel's history but all belonging to the wisdom type. There is no real reason, however, for rejecting the view that some of the material may have come from King Solomon himself or from members of his courtly circle.

In the Rabbinic literature, the 'wisdom' referred to repeatedly in the book of Proverbs is made to refer to divine wisdom, the wisdom of the Torah. The verse, for example, in praise of wisdom: 'Length of days is in her right hand; in her left hand are riches and honour' (Proverbs 3: 16) is interpreted to mean that even 'left-handed' study of the Torah, that is, study with insincere motivation, still brings blessings in its wake. The verse: 'The Lord by wisdom founded the earth' (Proverbs 3: 19) formed the basis for the idea that God used the pre-existing Torah as a blueprint for the creation of the world. The verse: 'She is a tree of life to them that lay hold upon her, and happy is every one that holdeth her fast' (Proverbs 3: 18) is recited in the synagogue when the *Sefer Torah is returned to the *Ark after the public reading. A well-known Rabbinic homily to the verse: 'Hear my son, the instruction of thy father, and forsake not the teaching of thy mother' (Proverbs 1: 7) understands 'father' in the verse to refer to God, whose 'instruction' is given in the Torah, and 'mother' in the verse to refer to the community of Israel. This interpretation became the basis for following established Jewish customs, the 'teaching of thy mother' enjoying authority together with the Torah, 'the instruction of thy father'. Under the influence of the sixteenth-century Kabbalists in Safed, the final verses of the book of Proverbs (31: 10–31) in praise of the woman of worth are recited by the master of the house in praise of his wife on the eve of the Sabbath, although originally the Kabbalists understood the 'woman of worth' to be the *Shekhinah.

Abraham Cohen, *Proverbs* (London, 1952).

R. N. Whybray, *The Book of Proverbs* (Cambridge, 1972).

**Providence** The Hebrew term for divine providence, *hashgaḥah*, was first used by the medieval Jewish theologians who, under the influence of Greek philosophy, preferred abstract terms to denote ideas found in concrete form in the Bible and the Rabbinic literature. But the idea that God controls and guides the world He has created permeates the Bible and the post-biblical literature. The very term *hashgaḥah* is based on the verse in Psalms (34: 14): 'From the place of His habitation He looketh intently [*hishgiaḥ*] upon all the inhabitants of the earth.' The abstract discussions of the medievals were largely around the scope of divine providence. Two types of providence are considered: 1. *hashgaḥah kelalit*, 'general providence', God's care for the world in general and for species in general; and 2. *hashgaḥah peratit*, 'special providence', God's care for each individual.

Maimonides, in his *Guide of the Perplexed* (3. 17–18), defends both types of providence but limits special providence to human beings and even then believes that it is only extended to individuals who lead intellectual and pious lives. *Gersonides, in his *Wars of the Lord* (Part IV), discusses the question at length and arrives at a similar conclusion. This means that, for instance, God takes care, so to speak, that the species of spiders and flies are preserved but He does not ordain that a particular spider catches a particular fly. That happens purely by chance. These thinkers thus allow the recognition that there is a random element in *nature. Only

man, when he rises in moral stature and intelligence, becomes linked, as it were, to the divine and so comes under the divine care for him as an individual. *Crescas, in his *Light of the Lord* (Part II, 2. 4), takes issue with this view. God created man because of His love for him and love is not dependent on conditions such as the intellectual or moral capacity of its recipients. All men, argues Crescas, not only saints and philosophers, enjoy God's special providence. All three thinkers do not accept the view of the Islamic Ashariyah that God decides which leaf should fall at which time from each tree: a view of divine providence rare in this stark form in Jewish thought until it became prominent in *Hasidism. The medieval thinkers were also profoundly concerned with the question of how human freedom can come into operation if everything happens as a result of divine providence (see FREE WILL).

The Talmudic Rabbis did not explore the question of divine providence as a philosophical problem and, generally speaking, prefer to affirm that God's care extends over all without dwelling too much on how providence operates. The result is that, as on other theological topics, a wide variety of opinions are expressed without any attempt at systematic treatment. The famous Talmudic statement regarding God's providence extending to all His creatures is the saying that God 'feeds the whole world from the horned buffalo to the brood of vermin' (*Avodah Zarah* 3b). The late second-century teacher Rabbi Hanina gave expression to the extreme view of divine providence over human beings when he said: 'No man bruises his finger here on earth unless it was so decreed against him from on high' (*Ḥullin* 7b).

The Italian Kabbalist Joseph Ergas (1685–1730), in his *Shomer Emunim*, 'Preserving Beliefs' (ii. 81), summarizes what he considers to be the Kabbalistic views on the subject: 'Nothing occurs by accident, without intention and divine providence, as it is written [Leviticus 21: 24]: "Then will I also walk with you in chance [*be-keri*]." You see that even the state of "chance" is attributed to God, for everything proceeds from Him by reason of special providence.' For all that, Ergas follows Maimonides, without mentioning the sage by name, in limiting special providence to the human species:

'However, the guardian angel has no power to provide for the special providence of non-human species; for example, whether this ox will live or die, whether this ant will be trodden on or be spared, whether this spider will catch this fly and so forth. There is no special providence of this kind for animals, to say nothing of plants and minerals, since the purpose for which they were created is attained by the species alone, and there is no need for providence to be extended to individuals of the species. Consequently, all events that happen to individuals of these species are by pure chance and not by divine decree, except, as we shall presently explain, where it is relevant for the divine providence concerning mankind.'

The Hasidim, otherwise admirers of Ergas, were scandalized by these remarks. For Hasidism, as for the Ashariyah centuries before, divine providence extends over everything; nothing moves without direct divine control, no stone lies where it does unless God wills it so. The early Hasidic master Phineas of Koretz remarks: 'A man should believe that even a piece of straw that lies on the ground does so at the decree of God. He decrees that it should lie there with one end facing this way and the other end the other way.' The later master, Hayyim Halberstam, similarly states: 'It is impossible for any creature to enjoy existence without the Creator of all worlds sustaining it and keeping it in being, and it is all through divine providence. Although the Rambam [Maimonides] has a different opinion in this matter, the truth is that not even a bird is snared without providence from above.' There are tales of Hasidic masters rebuking disciples who idly plucked grass as they walked along, since each blade of grass has its own particular place in the divine scheme.

Contemporary theologians, Jewish and non-Jewish, have grappled with the problem for divine providence posed by the greater realization, through scientific research, that everything proceeds by cause and effect. If God's providence extends to particulars, what precisely is the relationship of this type of providence to the perceived (and predictable) natural processes? Some have argued that scientific explanation employs probabilities in place of certainties. There is still a random element, acknowledged by the Jewish thinkers mentioned earlier, even in the picture of nature provided by scientific theories and it is in this area of 'chance', as Ergas has said, that divine providence comes into operation. Others have approached the subject from the point of view

of *existentialism. For the religious existentialist, God's providence does not consist in affecting the outcome of natural processes but in the way we relate to them (see MIRACLES). The problem is acute but then so is the problem, of which it is a part, of how God can be both transcendent and immanent (see PANENTHEISM).

Isaac Husik, *A History of Mediaeval Jewish Philosophy* (New York, 1958); see index: 'Providence'.

Louis Jacobs, 'Providence', in his *A Jewish Theology* (New York, 1973), 114–24.

**Psalms, Book of** Heb. *Tehillim* ('Praises'), the first book of the third section of the *Bible, the *Ketuvim*, Sacred Writings, comprising 150 psalms. Many of the psalms have superscriptions, describing their contents, their author, and, it is generally assumed, in some cases, the melodies to which they were sung in the Temple. In the Jewish tradition, but not in the King James Version, these superscriptions are counted as separate verses. (The New English Bible translation omits the superscriptions altogether: an extremely odd procedure, since, even if the superscriptions are later additions, they became part of the book at a very early period and one would have thought that the aim of any translation should be to convey the book as it has come down though the ages.) Many of the psalms are obviously liturgical compositions. The Levites sang a psalm for each day of the week and on the Sabbaths and festivals, accompanying the song with instrumental music.

It has long been noted that the first Psalm appears to be an introduction to the book as a whole, as Psalm 150 appears to be an epilogue. There is a concluding note at the end of Psalms 41, 72, 89, and 106, which suggests that the book is in five separate sections. The Rabbinic *Midrash to Psalms states that *David composed his Psalms in five books just as Moses wrote the five books of the *Pentateuch. In this Midrash, and very frequently in the Rabbinic literature, David is assumed to be the author of the book of Psalms. But in the famous Talmudic passage (*Bava Batra* 14b) on the authorship of the biblical books it is said that David included in his book psalms written by some who preceded him. The superscription to Psalm 90, for instance, is: 'A prayer of Moses, the man of God.' In fact, while seventy-two of the psalms are attributed to David, this one is attributed to Moses, and some to other authors. Some of the psalms are attributed to no particular author and are known, in the tradition, as 'orphan psalms'. It is incorrect, therefore, to say that on the traditional view David is the author of all the psalms in the book. Nevertheless, the tradition still sees David as the final author of the book, although he is said to have included the works of others in his final composition. In 2 Samuel 23: 1 David is described as 'the sweet singer in Israel'. This view of Davidic authorship was not left unquestioned in the Middle Ages and is rejected by all modern biblical scholars (see BIBLICAL CRITICISM and FUNDAMENTALISM) as anachronistic. Psalms 137, for instance, speaks of the period, hundreds of years after David's death, when the Temple had been destroyed and the Jews were in exile in Babylon. The book of Psalms is now seen rather as a collection or anthology of psalms compiled at different periods, though there is no real reason to deny that some of them may go back to David himself, with psalms or groups of psalms added later to the collection. There is no agreement on the dating of the various psalms. The older view that the whole book dates from as late as the period of the *Maccabees is now rejected by the majority of scholars, some holding, on the analogy of ancient Near Eastern texts unearthed fairly recently, that psalm-making, even with the employment of the same terms and language-patterns, was a feature of the surrounding culture long before Israel came on to the scene. Needless to say, the question of dating and authorship is totally irrelevant to the value of the book of Psalms as religious outpourings of the highest order, recognized as such by the millions of worshippers, Jews, Christians, and others, who have used the Psalms to express the deepest emotions of their own religion heart.

*Psalms in the Liturgy*

It is interesting that in the Talmudic period no Psalms were recited as part of the service except for the *Hallel psalms on the festival. As the post-Talmudic *liturgy developed, a large number of further psalms were incorporated into the *Prayer Book, not all at once but gradually over the centuries. To the daily morning service were added: Psalms 100 and 145–150. To the Sabbath and festival services were added Psalms 19, 34, 90, 91, 135, 136, 33, 92, 93 in this order, since on these days people, not having to go out to work, did not have to hurry from the synagogue. At the end of the morning service, a special psalm for each day is recited, prefaced with the words: 'This is the first [second, third, and so on] day of the week, on which the Levites in the Temple used to say . . .'. Psalm 24 is recited when the *Sefer Torah is returned to the *Ark after the reading on weekdays, and Psalm 29 on the Sabbath. The penitential Psalm 27 is recited at the end of the morning and evening service during the penitential season from the beginning of the month of *Elul until *Hoshanah Rabbah. Before the evening service at the termination of the Sabbath Psalms 144 and 67 are read. Psalm 104 is read during the morning service on *Rosh Hodesh, the New Moon, and during the afternoon service on winter Sabbaths. As part of their ritual for welcoming the Sabbath, the Safed Kabbalists in the sixteenth century introduced the recital of Psalms 95–9 and 29, corresponding to the six days of creation, on the eve of the Sabbath and this is now the universal custom at the Friday-night service. Verses from Psalms are scattered through other parts of the Prayer Book.

In addition to their recital as part of the standard service, the Psalms have been recited by individuals whenever the mood took them. Some pious Jews would recite the whole book of Psalms each week, some even each day. 'Saying Psalms' (*Zoggen Tillim*, in Yiddish), as it is called, is often practised as a prayer for a sick person or when other calamities threaten. In some communities there is a custom to recite on a *Yahrzeit verses of the eightfold alphabetical acrostic, Psalm 119, the initial letters of which are those of the letters of the name of the deceased. There are various chants in which the Psalms are recited and the Hebrew Bible even has notes for *cantillation of the Psalms but the musical system these represent is no longer known. The Lithuanian tradition has a particularly yearning and plaintive melody for 'saying Psalms'.

Abraham Cohen, *The Psalms* (London, 1950).
J. W. Rogerson and J. W. McKay, *Psalms*, 3 vols. (Cambridge, 1977).

**Psychology** The study of psychological states is prominent throughout Jewish thought even though there is nothing like a systematic treatment of the subject in the classical sources. The

Talmudic literature is especially rich in psychological observation. In the Rabbinic doctrine of the *yetzer ha-tov and the yetzer ha-ra, the good and evil inclinations, the Rabbis, like Freud, see man's internal struggle in terms of a tripartite division—the man himself, the good inclination, and the evil inclination. Man, in this doctrine, *has* the two inclinations, each pulling him in a different direction. The Jewish moralists, too, often probe human psychology. Bahya, *Ibn Pakudah's *Duties of the Heart*, as its name implies, is a call to the Jew to purify his inner thoughts and refuse to be satisfied with mere outward observances, the 'duties of the limbs'. While the demands of the moralists are severe, often too severe for a healthy approach to the moral life, they are usually tempered by a realism in which the individual is encouraged not to aim too high. The *Musar movement is based firmly on severe introspection, too much so according to opponents of the movement.

Many of the laws found in the Talmud, in addition to those regarding mental instability (see INSANITY) are based on psychological observation, on how human beings normally respond rationally and emotionally in given circumstances. With regard to contracts, the psychology of vendor and vendee is taken into account in determining whether or not there is a definite intention on the part of the one to sell and the other to buy. There is the case, for example, of a man who sold his estate because he wished to emigrate from Babylon to reside in the land of Israel, but at the time of the sale made no actual stipulation that the sale was conditional on his emigration (*Kiddushin* 49b). The man was unable to leave for the land of Israel because of circumstances beyond his control and he now wishes to revoke the sale. The fourth-century teacher, Rava, rules that this is a case of *devarim she-be-lev* ('matters in the heart'), that is, in the absence of an express verbal stipulation, the sale is treated as an unconditional one and cannot therefore be revoked. The point here is not that there is really any doubt that the man only sold his property because he wished to emigrate. There is no such doubt since everyone knew that his desire to emigrate was the sole intention of his wish to dispose of his property in Babylon. But, in the absence of an explicit verbal condition at the actual time of the sale, it is assumed that the mental reservation, albeit known to the two

parties concerned, is too weak to qualify the act of selling. Psychological analysis is also resorted to in order to determine the intention of a man who makes a documentary gift on his deathbed and then recovers (*Bava Batra* 146b). The question is whether the gift was made unconditionally or whether it was intended to be conditional on the man dying of that illness; that is, can he revoke the gift if he recovers? A distinction is made between the gift of the whole of his estate and a gift of only part of the estate. Where the man gave away the whole of his estate it can be assumed that it was only because he thought he would die and under these circumstances he can revoke the gift when he recovers. But where he gave away only part of his estate the very fact that he left some of it for himself shows he did not have in mind that he would die but gave the part he had stipulated as an unconditional gift. The Talmud and the Codes are full of rules based on this kind of psychological assessment of the human character, it being assumed that all normal human beings have the same basic mental attitudes and responses in everyday circumstances. Where a law is based on an assessment of normal human psychology, the law is operative even for a man who appears to have a psychological stance different from the norm. Thus the full *grace after meals cannot be recited after drinking wine because this form of grace must only be recited after a 'meal'. But what of the man who 'makes a meal' of his wine? The reply is that his attitude is ignored because it is contrary to the norm (*Berakhot* 35b).

*Religious Psychology*

Jewish ideas about the nature of the *soul, of which there many, have to be considered on their own. Here only a few ideas of the Jewish teachers on religious psychology in its practical manifestation can be discussed Although the *love and fear of God are often expressed purely in terms of practical observance of the precepts and study of the Torah, these are also seen as psychological states, especially in Jewish *mysticism and in the devotional literature. The ideal is for the deed to be sincerely motivated, hence all the emphasis on *Kavvanah, 'intention'. Numerous are the appeals for Jews who wish to tread the road towards perfection not to have ulterior motives and to carry out their religious duties 'for their own sake'; even though the advice of the early third-century teacher, Rav, is often quoted that a man should persist in performing the precepts even if his motivation is not completely pure, since the pure motivation will arise out of the less than pure. In some works of piety the avoidance of impure motivation is carried to extremes, in the doctrine of *disinterestedness and in the Hasidic ideal of *annihilation of selfhood. The *Tract on Ecstasy* by *Dov Baer of Lubavitch is an acute analysis of the true ecstatic state and how it can be distinguished from the sham and spurious. All the religious thinkers stress that self-delusion is to be avoided.

### Freud and Judaism

Any discussion of Judaism and psychology is bound to take into account the views of Freud, both because Freud himself was a Jew and because of the impact which psychoanalytic theory has had on modern thought. The parallel between the Rabbinic doctrine of the good and evil inclination has been noted above, though it is purely coincidental. Despite claims to the contrary, Freud was not familiar with Rabbinic or Kabbalistic literature and they certainly had no influence on his work. For all that, it is interesting to note that a close approximation to the Freudian idea of sublimation occurs in the Talmudic saying (*Kiddushin* 30b): 'My son, if this repulsive wretch [the evil inclination] attacks you, pull him into the House of Learning. If he is stone, he will dissolve. If he is iron, he will shatter into fragments.' Freud's idea that religion is a 'collective neurosis' is hardly acceptable to any branch of Judaism. Among religious Jews there are neurotic personalities who are constantly in fear that they have not carried out the rituals properly. This is not the fault of the rituals. Non-observant neurotics find their own means of catering to their neurosis. The Freudian critique of religion as wishful thinking does hit home, since religion is sometimes based on irrational desires and needs. But antireligious attitudes can similarly be the fruit of irrational desires and this applies to Freudian views as well. When the Jewish religion declares itself true, this does not necessarily mean that the truth is always arrived at by rational investigation and reflection. Religious Jews will acknowledge that they believe because they have a need for God but would go on to say that the

need is generated by the truth, not the truth by the need. If human beings have a hunger for God, Judaism affirms, this is because there is a God to satisfy that hunger, just as hunger for food arises because there really is food to satisfy the hunger.

Mortimer Ostow, *Judaism and Psychoanalysis* (New York, 1982).

Moshe Halevi Spero, *Judaism and Psychology: Halakhic Perspectives* (New York, 1980).

**Purim** The minor festival (on which it is permitted to work, unlike on the major festivals) which falls on 14 Adar. Purim is celebrated in commemoration of the deliverance of the Jews from the designs of Haman who cast lots in order to determine the date of their destruction, as related in the book of *Esther: 'For Haman son of Hammedatha the Agagite, the foe of all the Jews, had plotted to destroy the Jews, and had cast *pur*—that is, the lot—with intent to crush and exterminate them. . . . For that reason these days were called Purim, after *pur*' (Esther 9: 24–6). Modern biblical scholars (see BIBLICAL CRITICISM) have questioned the historicity of the events told in the book of Esther and have tried to discover the origins of Purim in a Babylonian festival, later adapted by Jews. But there is evidence that Jews celebrated Purim as early as the first century BCE. Classical Reform Judaism tended to look askance at the festival of Purim both because of the lack of evidence that the events really happened and because the festival was seen as too nationalistic and vindictive for Western taste. Orthodox, Conservative, and now some Reform Jews do celebrate Purim, as representing God's deliverances through the ages. The note sounded in the Middle Ages was that the festival of Purim is a reminder that God works behind the scenes, so to speak, when all seems lost, and, for this reason, the book of Esther is the only book in the Bible in which the name of God is not mentioned directly but only hinted at obliquely.

The central feature of Purim is the reading of the Megillah ('Scroll'), as the book of Esther is called, on the night of Purim and on the next morning. Although the Megillah is normally read on these two occasions during the synagogue service, where synagogue attendance is not possible it can be read in the home. During the morning service in the synagogue the reading of the Torah is from the passage which tells of the blotting-out of the memory of Amalek (Exodus 17: 8–16) because Haman was a descendant of Amalek. It has long been the custom for the members of the congregation, especially the children, to 'blot out' Haman's name by making loud noises with rattles and the like, whenever the name is mentioned during the reading of the Megillah. The more staid Rabbis, some would say Rabbinic spoilsports, objected to this practice on the grounds that it interrupts the reading and that the practice is unsuitable for a house of worship, but they were unsuccessful in getting the custom abolished.

Since the book of Esther speaks of sending portions to friends and gifts to the poor on Purim (Esther 9: 22), the rule, as stated in the Talmud (tractate *Megillah* is devoted to the laws of Purim), is that each person must send a gift of at least two items of food to a friend (some, today, prefer to send books instead) and give at least one donation to two poor men. From the reference to 'days of feasting and joy' (Esther 9: 17) the Talmudic Rabbis ordained that a special Purim meal be partaken of in the home, at which much wine is imbibed. The Talmudic statement in this connection (*Megillah* 7b) that a man is obliged to become so drunk on Purim that he is no longer aware whether he is blessing *Mordecai or cursing Haman, is still taken literally by some ultra-Orthodox Jews, although many Rabbis understand it as hyperbole and advise against taking drinking to the extreme of drunkenness, even on Purim.

Undoubtedly influenced by the Italian carnival, people dress up, and, children especially, perform Purim plays in which they take on the characters mentioned in the Megillah. In learned circles, it is often the practice to give fanciful interpretations of the Bible and Talmud and frivolously manipulate sacred texts. Scholars have seen in this 'Purim Torah', as it is called, a means of obtaining psychological relief, on one day in the year, from what otherwise might have become a burden too hard to bear.

According to the book of Esther (9: 18) the Jews of Shushan celebrated Purim on 15 Adar, unlike the other Jews whose Purim was on 14 Adar. According to the Talmud, honour was paid to the city of Jerusalem, rather than Shushan, so that any city, like Jerusalem, whose walls had stood in the days of Joshua, should celebrate Shushan Purim. Consequently, Purim is celebrated and the Megillah read in Jerusalem to this day on 15 Adar. For all Jews 'Shushan Purim' is celebrated as a minor, minor festival, as it were. Jews do not fast, for example, on this day.

That Purim is not to be taken too seriously is expressed in the popular Yiddish saying: 'A high temperature is not an illness and Purim is not a festival.'

N. S. Doniach, *Purim or the Feast of Esther: An Historical Study*, (Philadelphia, 1933).

# Q

**Quest** Although the Torah is traditionally conceived of as a 'given', conveyed by God to Moses in all its fullness, Jews are expected to enquire into its meaning and, in the process, receive new insights that have been left opaque—intentionally so, many Jewish theologians have held. The *Maharal of Prague (*Tiferet Yisrael*, ch. 2) goes so far as to say that just as God created an unfinished world for human beings to bring to perfection, He created' an incomplete Torah to be brought to completion through diligent application on the part of its students over the ages. Moses Hayyim *Luzzatto (*Path of the Upright*, introduction), in his contention that piety and saintliness are not easily attained but have to be won through enquiry, quotes the verse: 'If thou seekest for her as silver and searchest for her as for hidden treasures, then shalt thou understand the fear of the Lord' (Proverbs 2: 4–5). *Elijah, Gaon of Vilna is reported to have refused the offer of an angel to teach him the Torah since he felt obliged, as a Jew, to discover the truth for himself by unaided effort.

It has to be appreciated, however, that the quest referred to in these and similar traditional sources is for truths already there, so to speak, in the Torah but which can be discovered only if there is a search for them. The problem for the modernist Jew is that if he is a follower of the Torah, there are whole areas in which the quest must be in response to the challenges presented by modern thought. The modernist quest, in these areas, is a quest for the Torah itself (see FUNDAMENTALISM). Nevertheless, it is not too difficult for the modernist to base his particular quest on the idea stressed by the Maharal and others. The quest for the Torah is itself part of what is meant by Torah, so that it is not so much a question of seeking in order to find as one of finding in the very quest.

**Questions** Jews have been fond of asking questions, even of answering a question with a question (see HUMOUR). The Talmud is full of questions being raised in discussions on the Torah. Nothing is taken for granted. Even when answers are propounded, these too are questioned in turn as the argument proceeds. The *Responsa literature consists entirely of questions and answers. The Zohar (i. 1b–2a) states that there is a stage in the divine unfolding (see EN SOF and SEFIROT) of which one can ask the question: 'What is it?' without expecting any answer to be forthcoming, so elevated is that stage beyond human comprehension. It is permitted to ask but futile to expect an answer. The Zohar calls this stage 'Who' and ingeniously interprets the verse: 'Lift up your eyes and see who created these' (Isaiah 40: 20) to mean that 'Who' created, that is, brought into manifestation, the lower stages, called 'These' because they can be perceived by human thought. It is possible to point to them: God's mercy and compassion, for instance. The Zohar adds that of an even higher stage of the divine unfolding one cannot ask the question, so elevated is this above all human thought. Even to ask of this stage—what it is—is an absurd attempt to extend thought beyond its legitimate boundaries. Behind all this is the idea that the tremendous truths about God and His relationship to the universe cannot be delivered in a neat package and that in making the attempt to probe, deeper and unanswerable questions are bound to arise. *Nahman of Bratslav went so far as to say that the man who has no questions about God is not a believer in God at all: a far cry from the notion of some pietists that for the unbeliever there are no answers while for the believer there are no questions. In the world of the *Yeshivah the story is often wrily told of the student who remarked that he had found a wonderful answer if only he could discover the question to which the answer could be addressed.

**Quietism** The doctrine, found in some versions of Christian thought, that men of faith should sit back and leave everything to God. Quietism is rarely found in Jewish thought, which believes in human co-operation with the divine (see TRUST). *Saadiah Gaon (*Beliefs and Opinions*, x. 15), while admiring those who say that the highest endeavour of the servant of God in this world ought to be to dedicate himself exclusively to the service of his Lord, believes that it is contrary to Jewish teaching to take this to the extreme that a person ought not to take care of himself and make the effort for his affairs to prosper.

'So far as their assertion that a person must rely upon the Creator in the matter of the welfare of the body and the provision of food is concerned, what they say is correct. They have left out only one consideration: namely, that God has established for everything a special means and manner by which it is to be sought. If they had, indeed, been right in their assumption that reliance on God is to be universally applied, they should also have exercised it in the realm of worship, so that they would depend on Him to cause them to attain the reward of the Hereafter without worshipping Him. Therefore, just as this is inconceivable because worship has been established by God as a means for the attainment of the reward of the Hereafter, so, too, it is impossible to dispense with the effort to earn a livelihood and marriage and other occupations that have been designed by God as means conducive to the welfare of mankind.'

To be sure the *manna, given to the Israelites in the wilderness without their having to engage in any effort except to gather it in daily, introduces a quietistic note, and this was at times held up as an ideal, even though one impossible to reach by ordinary mortals (see MIRACLES and PROVIDENCE). Yet Saadiah's view is not only the one accepted by the philosophers but is the prevailing opinion among Jewish teachers. As the Midrash (Leviticus Rabbah 25: 5) puts it:

'During the forty years that Israel were in the wilderness, the manna fell, and the well came up for them, the quails were at hand for them, the clouds of glory encircled them, and the pillar of cloud led the way before them. When Israel were about to enter the Land, Moses said to them: "Let every one of you take his spade and go out and plant trees." Hence it is written [Leviticus 19: 23]: "When ye shall come into the Land, ye shall plant."'

The difference between trust in God and quietism is that trust involves the belief that God helps human effort, while quietism believes that no human effort is required at all and everything can be left to God.

**Qumran** The site on the north-west shore of the Dead Sea at which the *Dead Sea Scrolls were discovered. Ruined buildings, the Khirbet Qumran, had been discovered much earlier. At Khirbet Qumran there is much evidence of more than one occupation from Roman times. It is generally seen by scholars as most plausible to assume that the people of the Scrolls discovered in the nearby caves had their community at Khirbet Qumran.

# R

**Rabbi** Teacher of Judaism qualified to render decisions in Jewish law. The term is derived from *rav*, meaning 'great man' or 'teacher'; Moses is called Moshe Rabbenu ('Moses our teacher'). The suffix 'i', meaning 'my', is somewhat strange. Why '*my* teacher'? It has been suggested that the letters RBI should be vocalized, as they are among Sephardi Jews, as 'Ribbi', 'great one', and that the 'i' is not, in fact, a suffix at all. It has also been conjectured that the term Ribbi originally denoted a fully ordained teacher, one who received the *ordination reaching back to Joshua on whom Moses laid his hands. When full ordination came to an end (in the fourth century CE) the title Rabbi was given to every teacher of the Torah and was a purely honorific one. Even when full ordination was still in vogue, it was limited to Palestinian teachers who alone were called Rabbi. The Babylonian teachers appear in the Babylonian Talmud simply as 'Rav'. In the period of the *Geonim the distinction between the various Rabbinic titles was described as: 'Greater than Rav is Rabbi; greater than Rabbi is Rabban ['our teacher'; reserved for the Princes as in Rabban *Gamaliel]; greater than Rabban is the name [itself, e.g. *Hillel or *Shammai].' Historically considered, Rabbi as a title is not found before the beginning of the present era. There is a Rabbi Hillel in the Talmud but the title is never used for the famous *Hillel.

In post-Talmudic times, the conventional title among Sephardi Jews was Hakham, 'sage', and this title is still used by the Sephardim. The Ashkenazim preferred the term 'Rabbi' and developed a new form of ordination in which a prominent scholar subjected a candidate for the Rabbinate to an examination in order to determine his proficiency in Jewish law. The successful candidate was then given what came to be called Heter Horaah, 'Permission to Render Decisions'. *Abravanel (commentary to Ethics of the Fathers, ch. 6) suggested that the Ashkenazim adopted this new type of Rabbinic ordination and the granting of a diploma, under the influence of the Gentile universities which awarded doctorates to their graduates. The Hebrew form of 'Rabbi' is Ha-Rav. On the analogy of the Geonim, certain especially distinguished Rabbis were given the title Gaon, for example *Elijah, Gaon of Vilna. Eventually, the title Gaon was given to practically every Orthodox Rabbi. Nowadays, the title Ha-Rav Ha-Gaon is used so extensively as to be meaningless, When everyone is a 'Gaon', no one is.

The professional Rabbi was unknown before the fourteenth century. Scholars capable of rendering decisions in Jewish law performed this function without receiving any salary, following the Talmudic injunction against obtaining financial gain from the Torah, except that scholars were exempted from communal taxation and had the right to be served first when buying in the market-place, so as to enable them to devote more time to their studies. Many medieval sages, for example Maimonides and *Nahmanides, earned their living by practising medicine and gave their services to the Torah voluntarily. As late as the sixteenth century, scholars were to be found who prided themselves on serving as communal Rabbis without receiving any remuneration. But when economic conditions worsened, especially after the expulsion from Spain at the end of the fifteenth century, there was no way in which the average scholar could adopt the Rabbinic role unless he was supported by the community. The position of town Rabbi became established and the Rabbi received emoluments from the townsfolk. Once the Rabbinate became a profession, proper contracts of service were drawn up and these are discussed in the later Codes under the heading of general financial undertakings. This pattern was preserved among the Ashkenazim in Eastern European communities, as was the institution of the Hakham among the Sephardi and Oriental communities, and it is still the norm in the State of Israel and in the *Diaspora communities of the older Orthodox type. In communities that conform to this pattern, there are no special schools for the training of Rabbis. Students in the *Yeshivah do not study in order to become Rabbis, in obedience to the Yeshivah ideal of studying the Torah 'for its own sake'. When a student wishes to become a Rabbi he studies on his own the Codes and other sources of practical *Halakhah and then presents himself for examination. Strictly speaking, the granting of the Rabbinical diploma does not in itself entitle its holder to be called Rabbi. The diploma testifies only that he is capable of serving as a Rabbi. He actually becomes a Rabbi only when appointed by a community to serve as such. Nevertheless, the convention is to refer to anyone who holds the Rabbinical diploma as Rabbi. He is called to the Torah, for instance, as Morenu Ha-Rav, 'Our Teacher, Rabbi X son of Y'.

In the traditional pattern, the Rabbi is a scholar-saint, devoting himself entirely to learning (the study of the Torah is a never-ending occupation from which no one ever graduates), to guiding the community in spiritual affairs, and, especially, to acting as judge in civil cases and rendering decisions in matters of religious law. Some Rabbis were more powerful and more autocratic than others. There are many recorded instances of Rabbis at loggerheads with the lay leaders of the community. Although in modern times the English expression 'laymen' is often used, the term is basically inappropriate. The Rabbi is also a 'layman', occupying no sacerdotal role. It is consequently quite erroneous, as is often done by non-Jews, to describe the Rabbi as a Jewish *priest.

*Other Religious Functionaries*

There were other religious functionaries in addition to the town Rabbi and these were also usually given the title Ha-Rav. The town Rabbi, with a few exceptions, only preached sermons on rare occasions, normally on the Sabbath before Passover and the Sabbath before *Yom Kippur. *Preaching was the prerogative of the Maggid. The Maggid was usually a wandering preacher who visited various towns where the congregation would give him a remuneration for his services. But the larger towns, like Vilna, had, in addition to the town Rabbi, a permanent town Maggid, who received a regular stipend from the community chest. Following

the founding of the great Yeshivah in *Volozhyn in the early nineteenth century, Yeshivot were established in some Lithuanian and Russian towns and villages. In former times, the Yeshivah was under the control of the town Rabbi; students would come to the town to study at the feet of a renowned Rabbi who would then have the dual function of Rabbi and Rosh Yeshivah ('Yeshivah head'). With the proliferation of Yeshivot, the office of Rosh Yeshivah was detached from that of town Rabbi. The position of Rosh Yeshivah was held by a scholar whose particular skills and expertise lay in the field of purely theoretical study rather than practical law. After the *Holocaust, an unparalleled number of Yeshivot sprang up and a degree of rivalry emerged between the official Rabbis and the Yeshivah principals. Increasingly, in the Orthodox world, former students of a Yeshivah, while they will turn to the local Orthodox Rabbi for practical decisions, tend to look upon their Rosh Yeshivah as their true spiritual guide. Conflicts erupt sporadically between the practical Rabbis, who know the community and which demands they can and cannot make, and the Yeshivah heads, secure in their ivory towers.

*Hasidism developed a new type of leader, the Hasidic *Zaddik. To distinguish the Zaddik from the Rabbi proper, the former is usually called a 'Rebbe', though a few Rebbes also served as town Rabbis. The Rebbe of *Belz, for example, served as the Rabbi of this Galician town and was thus the Belzer Rav (or Rov in the Ashkenazi pronunciation) so far as his town was concerned, but the Belzer Rebbe so far as his widespread Hasidic fraternity was concerned. A Hasid owed his ultimate allegiance to his Rebbe but in matters of practical religious law would usually follow the decisions of the Rabbi of his town. Rebbes often had a good deal of influence on the appointment of a town Rabbi through the votes of their particular Hasidim. It was not unknown for the Hasidim in a town to be so divided on the choice of a Rabbi that, in order to avoid contention, they would vote for a Rabbi to be appointed who was not a Hasid at all. Belonging to no Hasidic group, the Rabbi was acceptable to all the groups in that he did not belong, at least, to a rival group.

*The Modern Rabbinate*

After the *Emancipation and the emergence of the Jew in Western society, the need was increasingly felt for a new type of Rabbi, one able to guide his congregation in the new situation in which they had to face challenges hitherto unknown. Even Orthodox congregations, in Germany for instance, required their Rabbi to be proficient in general learning, to be a cultured man able to represent his people to the non-Jewish world, and, where possible, to have a university degree. Seminaries were founded for the training of modern Rabbis, in which such subjects as homiletics, philosophy, ethics, history, and psychology were included in the curriculum as well as pure Rabbinics. So many roles are demanded of the modern Rabbi that it is impossible for even the most gifted to fill them all successfully. He has to be preacher, pastor, counsellor, fund-raiser, politician, and popular after-dinner speaker, so that he has little time and energy left for what used to be the Rabbi's main occupation, the study of the Torah. The old-fashioned Rabbi was also called upon from time to time to defend Judaism against attack but the modern Rabbi, Orthodox, Reform, or Conservative, has to defend his own group's understanding of what Judaism means. The problems of the modern Rabbinate are regularly discussed in the various Rabbinic and general Jewish journals.

In France and England the new office of Chief Rabbi was instituted. While the older communities sometimes had district Rabbis with jurisdiction over a whole province, these were usually governmental appointments and had little significance for Jews. According to the tradition, no Rabbi has authority over his colleagues, no matter how learned he happens to be. The British Chief Rabbinate was instituted after the patterns of the Anglican Church, with the Chief Rabbi being the Jewish equivalent of the Archbishop of Canterbury, with similar or even greater power over his colleagues. Until fairly recently, the British Chief Rabbi was, in fact, the only Rabbi in the Orthodox community. The spiritual leaders of the congregations under the Chief Rabbi's jurisdiction were known as Ministers and the majority, like earlier Chief Rabbis, but not the last two incumbents of the office, wore clerical collars. Under the British Mandate over Palestine, the British pattern had an influence there. To this day in the State of Israel there are two Chief Rabbis, one for the Sephardim and one for the Ashkenazim, 'the Heavenly Twins' as they are sometimes irreverently called. There is

little objection in Jewish law to the appointment of a woman as a Rabbi (see FEMINISM and WOMEN) and, in any event, the modern Rabbinate itself is an innovation not envisioned in the traditional sources. The voice of tradition is somewhat muted since the office of modern Rabbi is itself untraditional. To date there are no women Rabbis in Orthodox Judaism. Reform and Conservative Judaism decided years ago to ordain women as Rabbis and women serve in this capacity in Reform and Conservative congregations. Nevertheless, a considerable minority of Conservative Rabbis in the USA are opposed to the ordination of women as Rabbis and some have broken away from the main Conservative Rabbinic movement in protest.

Salo W. Baron, *The Jewish Community* (Philadelphia, 1942), ii. 66–94; iii. 118–42.

Robert Bonfil, *Rabbis and Jewish Communities in Renaissance Italy* (Oxford, 1990).

Robert Gordis, 'The Rabbinate: The History of Jewish Spiritual Leadership', in Harry Schniderman (ed.), *Two Generations in Perspective* (New York, 1957), 236–56.

**Rabbis, the Talmudic** The Rabbis who flourished in Palestine and Babylon in the first five centuries CE, the Tannaim and Amoraim, the sages who produced and appear in the Talmud and the *Midrash. These ancient teachers are usually referred to simply as 'the Rabbis' *par excellence*. In the Talmudic and Midrashic literature each of the Rabbis is depicted as an individual with virtues and faults, his own pattern of life, and his own personal opinions. There is nothing like an organized group of teachers with monolithic views even though all the Rabbis occupied the same universe of discourse. The Talmud nowhere speaks of itself as *the* Talmud nor does the Midrash as *the* Midrash. In the Talmud and the Midrash everything is in a state of flux. Opinions are discussed and debated, conflicts abound, and final decisions are often left in abeyance.

All this changed once the Talmud had been closed and became the final *authority for traditional Jews, especially after it had come under attack by the *Karaites. The Talmudic Rabbis (this term embraces the Rabbis of the Midrash as well) came to be seen as a corporate body of teachers. The actual date is uncertain but around the time of the Karaite rejection of the Talmud, the Rabbis began to be called *Ḥazal*, after the initial letters of *Ḥakhamenu Zikhronam Livrakhah*, 'Our Sages of Blessed

Memory'. Increasingly, the medieval thinkers tended to treat the Rabbis as mere cyphers in a single document of tremendous sanctity. They spoke not of Rabbi *A* saying this and Rabbi *B* saying that, but lumped together all the material in the Talmud and Midrash as if it came from a single source and spoke rather of *Ḥazal* saying this or that. It was not until the rise of modern historical scholarship (see JÜDISCHE WISSENSCHAFT) that the Rabbis began to reappear as individuals. *Ḥazal* came to be seen as superhumans never to be criticized. The saying in the Talmud (*Shabbat* 112b) is often applied to *Ḥazal*: 'If the early ones were the sons of angels [in parallel texts, 'like angels'], we are the sons of men. But if the early ones were [only] the sons of men we are like donkeys.' This eventually came to mean: those who declare that the Rabbis were ordinary human beings are stupid donkeys.

### Rabbinic Infallibility

From the writings of Maimonides it would appear he holds that the Babylonian Talmud enjoys its authority in *Halakhah because the community of Israel, as he puts it, had accepted that authority by a kind of consensus. For Maimonides, it is the Talmud as accepted by the Jewish people that is the final arbiter in matters of law, not the sages who appear in the Talmud. The Rabbis themselves are not seen as infallible teachers on all matters. Maimonides takes issue, for example, with the Rabbinic belief in *astrology and, when challenged with his disagreement with the Rabbis, replies in a letter that man was created with eyes in the front of his head not at the back. In scientific matters, Maimonides believes that the Rabbis only had the scientific knowledge of their day, and their astronomy was 'now' outdated (*Guide of the Perplexed*, 3. 14–end). The *Geonim similarly state (*Otzar Ha-Geonim* to *Gittin* 68) that no one should rely on the cures for various ailments found in the Talmud unless approved of by contemporary physicians since the Rabbis, when recording these remedies, based themselves on no firm tradition but only sought to convey the *medicine of their day. All Jews accept this opinion of the Geonim. It is unknown for Jews to go to the Talmudic passage for a remedy when they are ill, though the more pious would say that this is because we are unable to understand the words of the passage which are in an obscure Aramaic, not because

the Rabbis could have been mistaken. In the sixteenth century, Azariah de *Rossi maintained that the Rabbis were not historians and the devout Jew is not bound to accept all the historical statements by the Rabbis as factually correct. Joseph *Karo, on the other hand, wished to ban Rossi's book for this heresy, as he saw it.

### Modern Attitudes

In many Orthodox circles to this day the Karo attitude prevails, The Rabbis are seen as spiritual supermen, bearers not only of the tradition, the *Oral Torah, but of truths revealed to them by divine inspiration through the '*Holy Spirit'. Orthodox thinkers are prepared to say, on occasion, that some of the views of the Rabbis are difficult to accept in their plain meaning and require to be reinterpreted Some would follow the line of the *Tosafot in mediaeval France that *nature has changed so that, in scientific matters, the Rabbis were speaking of the nature that obtained in their day. And modern scholarship, even when engaged in by the Orthodox, tries to study the lives of the Rabbis as objectively as any other biographies. No Orthodox scholar today would fail to applaud David Hoffmann's attempt in the nineteenth century to write a biography of the third-century teacher Samuel (see RAV AND SAMUEL), and would totally disregard Hoffmann's Orthodox critics who contended that such an enterprise is heretical in its implication that a Talmudic sage can have a 'biography' compiled about him, as if he were an ordinary human being. For all that, on the theological level, no Orthodox thinker will ever allow himself to say that the Rabbis were wrong, any more than he would dare to say that the Bible was wrong. Even Reform theologians are usually hesitant in using expressions like right and wrong when speaking of the Rabbis since, after all, Rabbinic teachings belong to the evolution of Jewish thought. Even for Reform Judaism, the Rabbis are 'our' Rabbis, and the radical Reformer *Holdheim expressed himself circumspectly when he declared: 'The Talmud was right in its day and I am right in mine.'

C. G. Montefiore and H. Loewe, *A Rabbinic Anthology* (London, 1938). Solomon Schechter, *Aspects of Rabbinic Theology* (New York, 1961).

**Rachel** The biblical heroine, one of the four *matriarchs, wife of *Jacob and mother of

*Joseph and *Benjamin, whose story is told in the book of *Genesis (chs. 29–50). Rachel died as she gave birth to Benjamin, and she was buried 'on the road to Ephrath—now Bethlehem' (Genesis 35: 19). The prophet Jeremiah (31: 15) speaks of Rachel weeping for her children in exile. This passage from Jeremiah is read as the *Haftarah on the second day of *Rosh Ha-Shanah. When Boaz married Ruth the people blessed him that Ruth would be like Rachel and Leah, 'both of whom built up the House of Israel' (Ruth 4: 11). When parents bless their daughters on the eve of the Sabbath, the form of the blessing is: 'May God make you like Sarah, Rebecca, Rachel and Leah.' From as early as the tenth century CE the tomb of Rachel was identified as existing on its present site just outside Bethlehem. The tomb is a place of pilgrimage for the pious, who pray to God to help them in the merit of 'mother Rachel'. In the Kabbalah Rachel represents one of the aspects of the *Shekhinah and a section of the *midnight vigil is named after her.

**Racial Discrimination** A major source for the Jewish view on racial discrimination is the prosaic account of the family of nations (Genesis 10), where all the peoples then believed to be on earth are described as one huge family descended from the three sons of *Noah, the father of mankind after the *Flood. It is irrelevant to the issue that few believe nowadays that all men are descended from Noah and that races such as the Chinese are not mentioned at all, since the Jewish view is based on the passage as it stands in the Bible and its moral and religious truth does not depend on the account being factual. No people is declared to be in any way subhuman because of its colour or race. However the doctrine of Israel as the *Chosen People is understood, Israel's superiority is not seen seen to be established on racial grounds, except by a very few theologians. Any human being, if he so wishes, can be admitted as a convert (see CONVERSION) to Judaism and, in any event, the notion of a 'pure' Jewish race has long been exploded by biological science.

The Dutch Reformed Church in South Africa used to rely on the story of Ham in the book of Genesis (9: 20–7) to support its view that it is the divine intention for the black peoples to be subordinate to the white. Quite apart from the fact that the identification of Ham with the black peoples is extremely questionable, modern biblical scholarship (see BIBLICAL CRITICISM), rejecting *fundamentalism on good grounds, has succeeded in uncovering the real meaning of the story. It is to be noted that it is Ham's son, Canaan, not Ham himself, who is cursed to be a 'servant of servants to his brethren'. Obviously, the story was told to justify the conquest of Canaan by the Israelites. The truth is, so far as Jewish interpretation is concerned, that nowhere in the whole literature is there the slightest suggestion that it is the destiny of black peoples to be slaves or subservient. The figures mentioned in the Bible as illustrations of dark-coloured people are never Ham or Canaan but the Cushim, generally translated as the Ethiopians (see FALASHAS), though in Genesis 10: 6 Cush is also a son of Ham. In the famous verse in Jeremiah (12: 23) the prophet declares: 'Can the Ethiopian [Cushi] change his skin, or the leopard his spots?' The prophet Amos declares: '"Are ye not as the children of the Ethiopians [Cushim] unto Me, O children of Israel?" saith the Lord. "Have I not brought up Israel out of the land of Egypt, and the Philistines from Caphtor and Aram from Kir?" (Amos 9: 7).' For Amos, God is responsible for the movements of all peoples, and if Israel has been singled out as His covenant people this involves Israel in greater responsibility: 'For you only have I known of all the families of the earth, therefore I will visit upon you all your iniquities' (Amos 3: 2).

Very revealing in this connection is the ruling in the Talmud (*Berakhot* 58b) that if one sees a black-skinned person (Cushi), or a redskin or an albino, a hunchback, a giant or a dwarf or a dropsical person, one recites the *benediction: 'Blessed is He who makes strange creatures.' The blackskin, the redskin, the giant, and the dwarf were unusual in the time and place of the Talmudic Rabbis. The response of the Jew to the unusual sight was to be an acknowledgement that God in His wisdom has created many different kinds of people and thanks are to be given to Him for the rich variety of creatures. It is significant that in the same Talmudic passsage it is said that when one sees a person with an amputated limb or a blind or lame person one recites the benediction: 'Blessed be the true Judge.' Here the Jew acknowledges that while he cannot see why God should allow people to have amputated limbs, he does not question God's justice even though he cannot see how it operates. It follows that the colour of the skin or the unusual size of giants and dwarfs are not seen as deformities but as evidence that God has room in the world He has created for the unusual as well as the usual. Of course, black people would say that 'black is beautiful' and dwarfs that 'small is beautiful' and they would presumably have to thank God for creating the unusual white pigmentation of tall people, as He 'makes strange creatures'.

An important biblical passage in this connection is the account of *Miriam and *Aaron's complaint against Moses for taking in marriage a Cushite woman (Numbers 12). The Rabbis, commenting on the narrative, found it hard to discover what it was they were objecting to, but a plain reading suggests that they were objecting to the colour of her skin. The point of the narrative is that Miriam and Aaron were severely rebuked by God for their presumption. Incidentally, we learn from the narrative that Moses himself married a black woman. Of course, in Jewish teaching, marriage with someone of another faith is wrong (see INTERMARRIAGE), but that is because of religious differences and would apply whatever the colour of the skin of the spouse. Once conversion to Judaism has taken place there is no bar whatsoever on grounds of race.

> Robert Gordis, 'Race and the Religious Tradition', in his *The Root and the Branch* (Chicago, 1962), 115–36.

**Rainbow** After the *Flood and the deliverance of *Noah and his family, God shows Noah the rainbow in the clouds as a sign of His covenant with mankind that He will never again bring a deluge to destroy them (Genesis 9: 8–17). Nahmanides observes that the rainbow is a natural phenomenon, so that the narrative does not mean that God created the rainbow after the Flood, only that He declared that the already existing phenomenon would serve as the sign of His covenant from now on. The rainbow, pointing upwards, denotes, according to Nahmanides, that God's arrows would no longer shoot downwards to destroy the human race. The Talmud (*Berakhot* 59a) states that a special benediction should be recited when beholding a rainbow. The exact form of this benediction is elaborated on and now appears in the *Prayer Book as: 'Blessed art Thou, O Lord our God, King of the universe, Who remembers the covenant, is faithful to His Covenant, and keeps His word.'

The rainbow is mentioned again in the Bible in Ezekiel's vision of the *Chariot: 'Like the appearance of the bow which shines in the clouds on a day of rain, such was the surrounding radiance. That was the appearance of the semblance of the Presence of the Lord. When I beheld it, I flung myself down on my face. And I heard a voice speaking' (Ezekiel 1: 29). To be noted is the circumspect manner in which the prophet describes his vision of the glory—'the appearance of the semblance'. *Rashi, in a comment to verse 26, referring to the appearance of the glory, follows the Talmudic Rabbis: 'No permission has been given to reflect on the meaning of this verse.' The Talmud (*Ḥagigah* 16a) states that one who gazes too intently at the rainbow will suffer a diminution of his eyesight. In the Kabbalah, the colours of the rainbow represent the various shades of the *Sefirot. The rainbow has thus become in Jewish thought the symbol of both God's glory as manifest in the universe and God's faithfulness to His covenant to mankind and to the people of Israel. The word *berit* ('covenant') is used both in connection with the rainbow and with *circumcision, the covenant with Abraham.

**Rain, Prayers for** Failure of the rains to come in their proper season was the most serious calamity that could befall the Jewish community in ancient Palestine, an agricultural society which depended for its very life on a good harvest. Prayers for rain were therefore a prominent feature of congregational worship, a whole tractate of the Mishnah, tractate *Taanit*, being devoted in large measure to prayers for rain. In the *Gemara to this tractate there are tales of miracle-workers whose prayers for rain were heeded because of their saintly lives. Some of these tales, though legendary, express not only the attitude of trust in God but also the idea that the *saints have the power to coerce God to bring the rains. In the tale of Honi the Circle-Drawer, Honi draws a circle and threatens not to move from within it until God sends rain. The theological question of how prayers for rain can be effective did not seem to present much of a problem in the Talmudic Rabbis and was not considered in any detail until the Middle Ages, when it was discussed under the general heading of how *prayer could influence the natural order and how *miracles were possible. According to the Mishnah, the court ordained a series of daytime fasts increasing in severity if the rains had not come by the first day of Kislev (late in November). During the last seven days of the series, the *Ark (in those days a portable ark was used) was brought out into the open space of the town. Ashes were put on the Ark itself and on the heads of the notables and then everyone took ashes and put them on his head. The eldest among them uttered words of admonition, urging them to repent (Mishnah, *Taanit* 2: 1).

In addition to the practice mentioned above, prayers for rain were introduced into the daily liturgy. During the winter season (in Israel from 7 Heshvan until Passover, in the *Diaspora from 4 or 5 December until Passover) the request: 'Grant us dew and rain for a blessing over the face of the soil' is inserted in the ninth benediction of the Amidah, the *Eighteen Benedictions', the blessing for sustenance. During the summer months months, only: 'Grant us a blessing over the face of the soil' is said. During the winter months, the phrase: 'Who makes the wind to blow and the rain to fall' is inserted in the second benediction of the Amidah. This is not, however, a prayer for rain but a form of praise.

On the basis of the statement in the Mishnah (*Rosh Ha-Shanah* 1: 2) that on the festival of Sukkot ('*Tabernacles') the world is judged for rain, it is the universal custom, during the Additional Service on *Shemini Atzeret*, at the end of this Tabernacles festival, for the *Cantor to wear white robes as a symbol of purity and mercy and the *Geshem* ('Rain') prayer is chanted, in which God is entreated to send rain in the merits of biblical heroes about whom there are accounts concerning 'water'. On the seventh day of Tabernacles, *Hoshanah Rabbah*, there is now a more elaborate service of petition for rain. A similar service to *Geshem* takes place on the first day of Passover. This is called *Tal* ('Dew') and consists of a petition for God to grant the more gentle dew now that the rainy season is over.

Isaac Klein, *A Guide to Jewish Religious Practice* (New York, 1979); see index: 'Rain, prayer for'. *The Treatise Ta'anit of the Babylonian Talmud*, ed. and trans. Henry Malter (Philadelphia, 1928).

**Rape** The Jewish law on rape, as it was developed in the Talmud, is based on the biblical passages (Deuteronomy 22: 22–8) but with certain qualifications. For instance, the question of *capital punishment for a man who

raped a married woman was never applied since capital punishment for any crime was not carried out in Rabbinic times. A married woman who had been raped is not forbidden to her husband (unless he is a *Kohen) but where she consented to have sex with a man she is forbidden to her husband. But even here the final ruling is that her consent once the rape had begun is not treated as consent for the purpose and she is permitted to her husband on the grounds that in such circumstances it is assumed that she cannot be said to have been able to control the urge once the sex act had been initiated by the rapist. The Rabbis further limited the application of the law that where a man rapes a virgin he is obliged to marry her in the case of a girl under the age of 12 years and 6 months. Nevertheless, in all cases of rape the rapist must compensate his victim for her ordeal and the amount is assessed by the court. Each community has the right to fix its own penalties for rape. Thus in the State of Israel rape is treated under the general laws governing physical assault. The statement in Deuteronomy: 'But you shall do nothing to the girl. The girl did not incur the death penalty, for this case is like that of a man attacking another and murdering him' (Deuteronomy 22: 26), served the Rabbis as a test case for all offences for which no penalty was to be imposed on a person forced to commit the forbidden act. No one is ever culpable for an act performed under duress.

Louis M. Epstein, 'Rape and Seduction', in his *Sex Laws and Customs in Judaism* (New York, 1948), 179–93.

**Rapoport, Solomon Judah** Galician Rabbi and scholar (1790–1867), one of the pioneers of the *Jüdische Wissenschaft movement. Rapoport held no official Rabbinic position until his appointment in 1837 as Rabbi of Tarnopol. Before that time he was supported by his father and father-in-law or engaged in business, devoting most of his time to Talmudic learning and, under the influence of *Krochmal, to the study of science and Western languages. In 1840 Rapoport was appointed Rabbi of the prestigious community of Prague where the *Haskalah had made inroads and the community felt the need for a more or less modernist Rabbi.

Rapoport acquired fame as a result of his biographies of some of the *Geonim and *Rashi in which, for the first time, the lives of spiritual giants of the past were approached critically and historically. With astonishing erudition Rapoport supplied copious notes to his articles, his keen analysis helping to pave the way for all later scholars who wished to employ the historical-critical methodology in the investigation of the Jewish past. It was Rapoport's ambition to compile a lexicon, entitled *Erekh Millin* (*Words of Value*), to cover the whole of Jewish thought, but only a very small portion of this work, under the letter *Alef*, was completed.

Rapoport had his critics from the ranks of the Orthodox and the Hasidim on the right and from the more radical scholars on the left. These critics sensed a certain ambiguity in Rapoport's religious attitude. On the one hand, he served as the Rabbi of two Orthodox congregations and in his published portrait he looks with his long beard and *\*peot*, every inch an Orthodox Rabbi of the old school. He was strongly opposed to Reform, though he had friends among the early Reformers. On the other hand, he was a modern, critical scholar, less committed than his Orthodox colleagues in the Rabbinate to total veneration for the Jewish past. Perhaps inner conflict was inevitable in the breast of a scholar who tried to live in two, often contradictory, worlds. For all that, Rapoport was seen by most of his contemporaries as sincere in his Orthodox protestations. His father-in-law was the outstanding Talmudist Aryeh Laib Heller (d. 1813), one of whose works Rapoport published with his own introduction in quite the old style. The British Chief Rabbi, Nathan Marcus Adler, sent his son, Hermann, later to be his successor, to study with Rapoport in Prague. From Hermann's letters to his mother it appears that the youth was not too impressed with Rapoport's character but admired him, nonetheless, for his scholarship. It may be because Rapoport was prepared to compromise to a degree that Reform made no headway in Prague despite the city's proximity to Germany, where the winds of Haskalah and *\*assimilation* were blowing strongly.

Nathan Stern, 'Solomon Judah (Loeb) Rapoport', in his *The Jewish Historico-Critical School of the Nineteenth Century* (New York, 1973), 12–23.

**Rashbam** French commentator to the Bible and the Talmud (d. *c*.1174), called Rashbam after the initial letters of his name, *Ra*bbi *Sh*emuel *b*en *M*eir. Rashbam's father, Rabbi Meir, married Yochebed, daughter of *\*Rashi. Rashbam studied with his grandfather in Troyes, France. Rashbam's commentary to the Torah has become one of the standard commentaries, taking its place beside those of Rashi and *\*Nahmanides. Rashbam observes that Rashi had told him that if he could have had his time over again he would have put more emphasis on the plain meaning (*peshat*) of the text. Rashbam's aim is to explain the text in its plain meaning, though not without reference to the Rabbinic *\*Midrash. Rashbam, on occasion, gives the plain meaning of a verse even when it contradicts the *\*Halakah, the law which the Rabbis consider to be derived from the verse by their *\*hermeneutics. There has been much discussion around this question but it would seem that Rashbam held that the Torah has two levels of meaning, the plain and the Midrashic, so that the Halakhah, while not necessarily in accordance with the plain meaning, is still based on what the Torah really means on the other level. Rashbam's commentary to tractate *Bava Batra* of the Babylonian Talmud supplements that of Rashi who only commented on the first two chapters of the tractate and a small section of the third chapter. While Rashbam is more prolix than his grandfather, his commentary gains in its astonishing clarity. Every aspect of the topic under discussion is carefully weighed and analysed, so that many students of the Talmud find it a special delight to study this tractate with Rashbam as a guide.

Benjamin J. Gelles, 'Samuel ben Meir—Rashbam', in his *Peshat and Derash in the Exegesis of Rashi* (Leiden, 1981), 123–7.

**Rashi** Foremost French commentator, called Rashi after the initial letters of his name, *Ra*bbi *Sh*lomo *Yi*tzhaki (1040–1105). Rashi was born in Troyes in northern France and spent most of his life in this city. In his youth Rashi studied for a number of years at the great centre of Jewish learning, Mayyence in Germany, where his teachers, to whom he refers repeatedly in his commentaries, were the disciples of Rabbenu *\*Gershom of Mayyence, the spiritual father of Ashkenazi Jewry. Returning to his native city, Rashi taught without fee a number of chosen disciples, earning his living by means of the vineyards he owned. The Rabbinic injunction not to receive payment for teaching the Torah was rigorously adhered to in the Middle Ages (see RABBIS). Rashi's daughters married scholars, members of whose family established the school of the *Tosafot glosses to the Talmud. Rashi's two most famous grandsons were *Rashbam and his younger brother, Rabbenu *Tam.

*The Commentaries*

Rashi's undying fame rests on his commentaries to the Bible and the Babylonian Talmud, printed together with the text in practically all editions. Rashi's commentary to the Humash (the *Pentateuch) was first printed in Reggio, Italy, in 1475 and seems to have been the first Hebrew book ever printed. Over the generations this commentary has been used as the prime guide, so that the term 'Humash and Rashi' became part of the universal Jewish vocabulary. Rashi was jocularly called the 'brother' of the Humash. Rashi's method is to state what he considers to be the plain meaning (*peshat*) of the text and also homiletical comments (*derash*) culled from the *Midrash. For instance, in Rashi's comment on the first word of Genesis, *bereshit*, 'In the beginning', he notes that on the plain meaning this word, in the construct state (Rashi was a gifted grammarian), should be rendered as: 'In the beginning *of* ', that is, the word is connected with what follows in the verse: 'In the beginning of God's creation of the heaven and the earth, the earth was . . .'. But he also quotes a Midrashic comment according to which *bereshit* means 'because of the beginning', both the Torah and Israel being referred to in Scripture as 'The beginning', so that the verse states, homiletically, that 'God created the world because of the Torah and because of Israel'; in other words, God's ultimate purpose in creation was for Israel to receive the Torah. Unlike Maimonides and the Spanish School generally, Rashi, like the Rabbis of the Midrash, was not bothered by the philosophical question of what it can mean to say that God has a 'purpose', or of why his purpose should be so particularistic. The French and German School, to which Rashi belonged, was not interested in philosophical niceties. In Solomon Schechter's felicitous phrase, they 'neither understood nor misunderstood Aristotle'. Rashi lived in the time of the First Crusade (1095) which created havoc among the Jewish communities of the Rhineland where he had studied in his youth. It is not therefore surprising that his commentary to Psalms contains veiled attacks on Christian dogmas and the Christian interpretation of Scripture.

Rashi's great genius as a commentator is particularly evident in his massive running commentary to the Talmud. Rashi here rarely raises questions of his own but, with uncanny anticipation of the difficulties the student will find, supplies the required solution in a few well-chosen words. He also records variant texts he had discovered in his travels and, where necessary, suggests a plausible emendation of the text. The Tosafot and other commentators often take issue with Rashi's explanation but all students agree that without Rashi the Talmud would have remained a closed book. Rashi often explains Talmudic terms by giving the French equivalent. These *laazim* ('foreign words') have become a major source for scholars of Old French.

In all Rashi's writings there is evidence of his close familiarity with the world around him. This most lovable of all the medieval teachers was interested in buildings, food and drink, politics, economics, and many other topics, all of which he uses for the elucidation of the biblical and Talmudic texts. From the *Responsa he wrote, Rashi emerges as a very kind and gentle scholar sensitive to human needs. As his biographer, Liber, has observed, there is an effervescence in Rashi reminiscent of the Champagne country in which he lived for most of his life.

Maurice Liber, *Rashi* (Philadelphia, 1938).

Rashi, *Pentateuch and Rashi's Commentary*, ed. and trans. M. Rosenbaum and A. M. Silberman (London, 1929).

**Rationalism** The attitude in which religious faith has to justify itself at the bar of reason before it can be accepted. There is much reasoned appeal in the Bible. The Hebrew prophets seek to persuade by rational argument. The translation, in the Jewish Publication Society version, of the verse in Isaiah (1: 28): 'Come let reach an understanding says the Lord', may not be an accurate rendering. A footnote to the translation says: 'Meaning of Hebrew uncertain.' Yet the implication that the prophets do employ reason becomes apparent from even the most casual reading of the prophetic books, even though terms like 'reason' in the abstract sense are unknown in biblical Hebrew. The Talmud consists almost entirely of reasoned arguments, although the Talmud, like the Bible, does not normally rely on human reason to support *faith. Indeed, the problem of the relationship between belief in God (and the truth of the Torah) and human reasoning did not surface until the Middle Ages, when the Jewish thinkers, under the influence of Greek *philosophy in its Arabic garb, sought to prove the existence of God and to advance reasons for those laws in the Torah that seem opaque to reason (see MITZVAH). Abraham *Ibn Ezra's contention that reason is the angel mediating between God and man finds many an echo in the writings of the medieval thinkers. *Bahya, Ibn Pakudah (*Duties of the Heart*, I. 2) quotes with approval a 'philosopher' who maintained that the only persons who really worshipped God were the prophet, with his intuitive awareness of the Deity, and the philosopher, with his reasoned account of God and His nature. All other men, even though they believed they were worshipping God, were really worshipping something other than God, a mere figment of the imagination. In the *Haskalah ('Enlightenment') movement, which arose in the eighteenth century, the 'Age of Reason', there is the strongest emphasis on the ability of the human mind to arrive at the basic truths of religion by unaided human reason. This rationalistic tendency in Jewish thought has been heavily assailed by the religious existentialists (see EXISTENTIALISM) in modern times. The religious existentialists argue that God must be encountered as a 'given', not reached as the end of an argument, though even the existentialists are bound to rely on reason to support their very case. The mystics, too, are suspicious of philosophical enquiry in religious matters. God, the mystics affirm, is to be known through experience. Unlike the medieval philosophers, who hold that to 'know' God is to prove by reason that He exists and that belief means only that one takes it all on trust, the mystics declare that, on the contrary, reason can only tell a little about God, but to know God means to experience His nearness. The mystics declare that there are things *higher* than reason.

There are inevitable tensions between the surrender to faith and the employment of reason. Many thinkers have argued that a God who can easily be contained in the human mind is not the God whom Jews worship. Chesterton put it neatly: 'The philosopher tries to get the heavens into his head. The poet tries to get his head into the heavens.' There is some truth in Dr Isidore Epstein's remarks (*The Faith of Judaism* (London, 1954)) regarding the Tertullian paradox in relation to Judaism, but they are too sweeping, as will be noted later. Epstein writes (p. 117):

'Applied to the doctrines of Judaism, we can say that though they are not all in accord with understanding they are all in accord alike with reason and the established truths of scientific teaching. Contrast this with the Tertullian dicta: *"Credo quia absurdum"*, *"Credibile quia ineptum"*, *"Certum est quia impossibile est"* ("I believe because it is absurd", "To be believed because it is foolish", "It is certain because it is impossible"), making incredibility the test of credibility; see Tertullian, *On the Flesh of Christ*, v. Judaism, on the other hand, whilst having too much respect for human intelligence to subscribe to any proposition involving the total surrender of human reason, nevertheless rightly recognises the limitations of the human faculties and senses and may well proclaim as an act of revealed faith, *"Credibile quia non intellectum est"* ("To be believed because it is beyond the understanding")—quite a tenable and rational proposition which would be unscientific to assail or deny *a priori*.'

The same applies to Milton Steinberg's attack (*Anatomy of Faith* (New York, 1960)) on Kierkegaard's view that faith and reason are mutually exclusive, an attack which is too total in its rejection on behalf of Judaism. Steinberg remarks (p. 146): 'No Jewish thinker is on record as advancing Kierkegaard's contention of the radical incompatibility of religious truth and reason.'

*Antirationalism*

To declare, as Epstein implies and Steinberg says, that no Jewish thinker has ever gloried in a Jewish version of the Tertullian and Kierkegaardian paradox, is to ignore Jewish thinkers (few indeed, it must be admitted), who do come very close to affirming the paradox. One might argue that these men are not thinkers, but they are certainly Jewish and were possessed of high intellectual ability. It might well be argued, and very convincingly, that in the mainstream of Jewish thought there is nothing to suggest any acceptance of the paradox and that it is, in any event, logically absurd to use reason to reject reason. It is still not true to say that no Jewish thinker can ever be an antirationalist in his religious approach. *Shneur Zalman of Liady, for example, the founder of the *Habad movement in *Hasidism, can write (*Tanya*, ch. 18):

'Faith is higher than knowledge and comprehension for: "The simpleton believeth every word" [Psalms 14: 15]. In relation to God, who is higher than reason and knowledge and whom no thought can grasp at all, everyone is a simpleton, as it is said: "But I was brutish and ignorant; I was as a beast before Thee: Thou holdest my right hand" [Psalms 73: 22–3]. This means: Because I am brutish and as a beast I am continually with Thee.'

Shneur Zalman appears to be saying that only the 'simpleton' can always be with God, since faith is God's gift to man and faith is contrary to reason. It is not in spite of his brutishness that man can always be with God but because of his brutishness.

Another renowned Hasidic thinker, *Nahman of Bratslav, holds that man can never discover God through his reasoning powers and goes so far as to say that man is bound to have religious doubts (*Likkutey Moharan*, second series no. 52): 'It is entirely proper that objections can be found to God. It is right and suitable that this should be so because of God's greatness and exaltedness. Since in His exaltedness He is so elevated above our minds there are bound to be objections to Him.' A God who raises no problems for human thought would not be God for the very reason that the Infinite is bound to offend the finite mind. Since God cannot be grasped by the human mind, human reason in itself must not only fail to bring man to God but must be in contradiction to God.

Nahman of Bratslav, according to a disciple, is reported to have taken issue with the medieval Jewish philosophers who argue that, while God can do that which seems impossible, even He cannot do the absolutely impossible such as make a square triangle: 'They write in their books: "Is it possible for God to make a triangle into a square?" But our master [Nahman of Bratslav] said: I believe that God can make a square triangle. For God's ways are concealed from us. He is omnipotent and nothing is impossible for him.' Obviously, Nahman is involved in logical contradiction when he implies that the rules of logic apply only to humans. It is not that God cannot make a square triangle but that, by definition, there cannot be any such thing as a square triangle for God to create. A square means not a triangle and a triangle not a square. The question: 'Can God make a square triangle?' is simply to ask: 'Can God . . .?' without completing the question. As Aquinas puts it—and many of the Jewish thinkers, *Saadiah for instance, say the same thing—contradiction does not fall under the scope of omnipotence (See GOD).

It remains to be said that for Tertullian, as a Christian, the paradox at the heart of faith is due to the doctrine of the Incarnation. It is impossible for God to become man and yet the Christian must believe this 'impossible' thing. No Jewish thinker is moved by this because Judaism rejects the doctrine of the Incarnation. While Shneur Zalman, Nahman of Bratslav, and a few other Jewish thinkers have seen a similar 'absurdity' in all theistic faith, which is bound to remove faith entirely from the realm of conceptual thought, their views, and here Epstein and Steinberg are correct, remain on the periphery of Jewish thought. That Judaism contains a non-rational element, as religion is bound to do, does not mean that Judaism is essentially irrational.

Louis Jacobs, 'The Way of Reason', and 'Jewish Parallels to the Tertullian Paradox', in his *Faith* (London, 1968), 41–64, 201–9.

**Rav and Samuel** The two foremost teachers of the early third century CE in Babylon, belonging to the first generation of Amoraim (see TANNAIM AND AMORAIM). Both Rav (whose personal name was Abba but who was called 'Rav' [Rabbi *par excellence*] in respect for his great learning) and Samuel were born in Babylon but studied in the land of Israel under Rabbi *Judah the Prince. On Rav's return to Babylon he settled in the town of Sura where he served as teacher of the law and spiritual guide. Samuel settled in the town of Nehardea where a centre of learning had existed from much earlier times and in which he took the leading role on his return. After Samuel's death, his pupil Rabbi Judah ben Ezekiel settled in Pumbedita. Thus the colleges of Sura and Pumbedita in the period of the *Geonim traced their descent from the early third century.

The two teachers were very different in outlook but always treated one another with respect. From the Talmudic accounts (not always factual and including much that is reported second- or third-hand and therefore to be treated with caution) it appears that Rav was especially learned in religious law and ritual. To Rav is attributed the majestic prayer for the establishment of God's kingdom on earth which now forms part of the liturgy on *Rosh Ha-Shanah and *Yom Kippur. Samuel, skilled in civil law, was renowned as a judge. He was also an astronomer, once declaring: 'The pathways of the heavens are as familiar to me as the pathways of Nehardea.' The Talmud records and discusses the many debates between Rav and Samuel. Occasionally they are in agreement in given cases and the Talmud records this as: 'Rav and Samuel both say' (i.e., though usually they disagree with one another). It was eventually decided that wherever Rav and Samuel disagree the law (the *Halakhah) follows the opinions of Rav in purely religious matters and the opinions of Samuel in civil law. The two Amoraim were placed together in this way because the debates between them were frequent and well known. This does not necessarily mean that the debates always took place face to face. Two other teachers who are often mentioned together in the same way are *Abbaye and Rava. The Talmud refers to both series of debates as examples of the keenest argumentation.

**Reading of the Torah**    The practice of reading the Torah from a Scroll (*Sefer Torah) in the synagogue is mentioned in sources dating from the first century CE and it is evident that it had been long established. The Talmud even suggests that the reading of the Torah on Monday, Thursday, and Sabbath afternoon was introduced by *Moses so that the Israelites should not allow three days to go by without Torah. *Ezra is said to have introduced the weekly Sabbath reading on Sabbath morning. It is obvious, in any event, that the custom is ancient. To this day the custom is to read a lengthy portion of the Torah on Sabbath morning and a smaller portion of the next Sabbath reading on Sabbath afternoon and on Monday and Thursday morning. On festivals a suitable portion dealing with the particular festival is read. Although it is conventional to speak of the reading of the Torah, the Torah is, in fact, chanted (see CANTILLATION). In the land of Israel it was the custom to read the Torah in comparatively small weekly portions so that it took three years to complete the reading from the beginning of Genesis to the end of Deuteronomy. This was still the practice in some communities until well into the Middle Ages. But all communities today adopt the old Babylonian custom of dividing the Torah into longer portions so that the reading is completed each year (see *Simhat Torah).

*The Reading of the Torah as Practised Today*

The *Ark is opened and the Scroll from which the reading is to be done is taken in procession around the synagogue. Many people bow to the Scroll as it passes, although some Rabbis in the Middle Ages objected to this because it might seem that the Torah was being treated as an object to be worshipped. The Scroll is then placed on the reading-desk and a number of people are called up to the reading of a portion. The term for this privilege is *aliyah* ('ascent') and the usual expression is 'given an *aliyah*' (plural *aliyot*). In Talmudic times those called to the reading chanted the portion themselves but, since not everyone is capable of reading the unvowelled texts, the universal custom is now for the chanting to be done by a special competent reader; those called up recite a benediction before and after the reading of their portion in which they thank God for having given the Torah to Israel.

On the Sabbath there are seven *aliyot*; on Yom Kippur six; on the festivals five; on *Rosh Hodesh four; on Monday, Thursday, and Sabbath afternoon three. The first *aliyah* is given to a *Kohen, the second to a *Levite, and the third and the others to *Israelites*. Some members of the congregation are specially entitled to be given an *aliyah*: a boy celebrating his *Bar Mitzvah; a groom on the Sabbath before the wedding; the father of a new-born child; and a person on the anniversary of the death of a parent (on the *Yahrzeit). On Sabbaths and festivals a small portion of the reading is repeated as the Maftir ('Conclusion') and the person called up for this reads the prophetic portion for the day (the *Haftarah), not from the Scroll but from a printed vocalized book from which it requires no great expertise to read. It is considered a special honour to be given Maftir and to read the Haftarah. It is also considered a special honour to be called up for the reading of the third portion, the first given to an Israelite, and to the *Decalogue on the occasions when this is read. In many congregations there is much competition for the privilege of being given an *aliyah*, often paid for by a donation to the synagogue or to charity. In some congregations there is even an 'auction' of *aliyot* but this is frowned on in more staid congregations.

After the readings, the Scroll is lifted on high while the congregation chant (based on Deuteronomy 4: 44): 'And this is the Torah which Moses set before the children of Israel, according to the commandment of the Lord by the hand of Moses.' The Scroll is then rolled together and dressed with its mantle and ornaments. The Haftarah is read and the Scroll taken in procession around the synagogue and returned to the Ark.

Hyman E. Goldin, 'The Torah Reading on Sabbath and Festival', in his *Code of Jewish Law* (New York, 1961), ii. 84–7.

J. H. Hertz, 'Reading of Torah and Prophets', in his *The Authorised Daily Prayer Book* (London, 1947), 470–1.

**Rebbe, Hasidic**   The Hasidic master also called the *Zaddik. Unlike the formal *Rabbi, whose main function was to teach the Torah and render decisions in Jewish law, the Zaddik served his followers as a spiritual guide and mentor and offered prayers on their behalf. The term Rebbe is simply a variation of Rabbi and is used to distinguish between the two types of leader.

**Rebecca**   Wife of Isaac and mother of Jacob and Esau; the second of the four *matriarchs, whose story is told in the book of Genesis (22: 23–28: 5). Rebecca was buried beside her husband in the Cave of *Machpelah (Genesis 49: 31). The blessing given to Rebecca by her father and brother as she set out to meet her future husband (Genesis 24: 60) is recited in traditional communities before the wedding ceremony, when the groom places the veil over the bride's face as Rebecca veiled herself when she first saw her husband to be (Genesis 24: 65).

**Rebuke**   The source for the obligation to offer reproof to a neighbour is the verse: 'Thou shalt not hate thy brother in thine heart: thou shalt surely rebuke thy neighbour and not suffer sin because of him' (Leviticus 19: 17). The plain meaning of the verse is: if you believe that your neighbour has wronged you, do not keep silent and hate him in your heart but rebuke him for his offence and have done with it. It is as if the verse is saying: if you bear a grudge against someone get it off your chest and then forget about it, instead of bottling it up inside you and going about with hatred seething in your heart. But the Rabbis extend the obligation to offer

rebuke whenever a neighbour has committed or intends to commit any offence, whether ethical or religious, as the prophets rebuked the people for their shortcomings. This is based on the principle that all Jews are responsible for one another so that to fail to offer rebuke, when it is needed, is to participate in the offence. The conclusion of the verse is understood to mean: if you rebuke him for his sins all well and good but if you fail to do so, you share in his guilt.

From the intensive form: 'thou shalt surely rebuke' the Rabbis deduce that the obligation to reprove sinners is to be carried out over and over again until the sinner repents, unless the sinner becomes aggressive and resorts to violence. Rabbis and preachers, especially, were called upon to offer constant rebuke to their people, although *Hasidism was unhappy about the severe castigations indulged in by the preachers. The Rabbis were realistic enough to appreciate that a rebuke can all too easily encourage defiance, hence the Rabbinic saying: 'Just as it is meritorious to offer reproof when it is known that it will be heeded, it is meritorious not to rebuke when it is known it will not be heeded' (*Yevamot* 65b). In this connection the verse is quoted: 'Reprove not a scorner lest he hate thee; reprove a wise man and he will love thee' (Proverbs 9: 8). It cannot be denied that conscience-counsellors abounded in Jewish communities—prigs and busybodies who were only too ready to demonstrate their superiority by adopting a holier-than-thou attitude. This is probably why, even in Talmudic times, one Rabbi could say (*Arakhin* 16b): 'I doubt whether anyone in this generation is worthy to offer rebuke.'

**Reconstructionism**   The American movement, with branches elsewhere, founded by Mordecai *Kaplan with a view to revitalizing Judaism in the modern world. The central idea of Reconstructionism is that Judaism is more than a religion in the narrow sense but is a religious civilization, with its own art, music, literature, culture, and folk-ways. Although Reconstructionists like Milton Steinberg were believers in the Personal God of traditional Judaism, the movement generally follows Kaplan's naturalistic interpretation in which God is 'the power that makes for salvation'. Moreover, 'salvation' in this context does not mean of the soul in the Hereafter but of the Jewish people on earth through the enrichment of Jewish life that is the result of an acceptance of Jewish values and their dynamic adaptation to the new conditions in which Jews now find themselves. Reconstructionism has always been Zionistic in thrust. It sees the State of Israel as playing a central but not an exclusive role. The *Diaspora, too, has its part to play in the reconstruction. Because of its naturalistic understanding, Reconstructionism sees Judaism as existing to serve the Jewish people, not the other way round. Critics of the new movement have not been slow to point out that such a view involves a radical departure from the tradition in which only God is to be worshipped and Judaism is the way to God. True to its aim, Reconstructionism encouraged the establishment of synagogue centres, that is synagogues in which facilities are provided to foster all kinds of cultural activities in addition to prayer. At first Kaplan thought of the movement as one cutting across the usual divisions in Jewish life between Orthodoxy, Conservative, and Reform Judaism. But, while all three branches have been greatly influenced by Kaplan's ideas, their followers preferred to develop their own philosophies of Judaism. Kaplan's religious naturalism was far from being to everyone's religious taste. Reconstructionism has now developed as a fourth movement with its own seminary for the training of Reconstructionist Rabbis, the Rabbinical College in Wyncote, Pennsylvania, founded in 1957. A small number of Reconstructionist synagogues have also been established but Reconstructionist Rabbis serve in Reform and Conservative congregations as well. Founded in 1935, the journal *The Reconstructionist* is devoted to the philosophy of Reconstructionism.

Mordecai M. Kaplan, *Judaism as a Civilization* (New York 1934).

—— *Questions Jews Ask: Reconstructionist Answers* (New York, 1956).

**Redemption** Heb. *geulah*. In Judaism redemption usually denotes the saving of the Jewish people from exile and oppression. The Exodus from Egypt, for example, is called the Egyptian redemption. The final redemption will take place with the advent of the *Messiah. It is not, however, quite correct to say that Judaism, unlike Christianity, knows nothing of the idea of the redemption of the individual soul from sin. Psalm 130 certainly uses redemption in the sense of deliverance from iniquity. The difference between Judaism and Christianity

with regard to personal redemption is that, in Judaism, the soul is redeemed from sin by sincere repentance and the power of the Torah to influence human conduct, and God and no other is the Saviour. Redemption, in the sense of salvation of the people as a whole, is generally discussed in Judaism under the heading of the coming of the Messiah who will bring Israel's exile to an end and establish the Kingdom of God upon earth. In the Messianic age, all mankind will be saved from war, enmity, and hatred. In the Kabbalah, God Himself is redeemed, so to speak, when the *Shekhinah is restored from exile and all the *holy sparks have been rescued from the demonic forces. In modern times, Reform Judaism interpreted the redemption as the advance of modern society towards greater freedom, tolerance, and social justice. For *Zionism, redemption meant the return of the Jewish people to its homeland.

In the traditional understanding there is both a severely practical and a numinous approach to redemption. It is God who redeems Israel and the result of the final redemption is the emergence of a new and higher type of humanity. The *Mizrachi, the party of religious Zionists, wishing to preserve both the practical and numinous aspects in the emergence of the State of Israel, coined the expression *athalta degeulah*, 'beginning of the redemption', as if to say, the State of Israel is a state like any other, with normal political, economic, and social concerns, and with the inevitable faults and shortcomings of any political state. But, for the Mizrachi thinkers, the final Messianic dream is yet to be realized and this dream is on the way, at least, to its fulfilment now that the State of Israel has been established. This is an attempt to have one's cake and eat it. Traditionally, and logically, the final redemption can be said either to have come or not to have come. There is no such concept as a semi-final, final redemption.

**Red Heifer** Heb. *parah adumah*, the cow the ashes of which were used in the purification rites for one who had been contaminated through having come into contact with a corpse. As described in the book of Numbers (19: 1–22), the cow had to be slaughtered outside the Israelite camp and its blood sprinkled in the direction of the holy of holies in the *Tabernacle (in *Temple times, the holy of holies in the Temple). The cow was then burned whole together with cedar wood, a crimson thread, and hyssop. The ashes were mixed in a vessel containing spring water. The person contaminated was sprinkled on the third and seventh day of his defilement and he was then allowed to enter the sanctuary. This rite was followed in the Temple. The Talmud states that the red heifer was a rarity since it had to be completely red. But Milgrom has suggested that the word *adumah*, translated as 'red', really means 'brown' and the rarity consisted in it having to be completely brown without any white or black streaks or spots. There is some evidence that ashes of a a *parah adumah* were preserved for centuries after the destruction of the Temple. These ashes are no longer available and since, according to Maimonides, the site of the Temple still enjoys its sanctity and since everyone has come into contact with a corpse or with one who has, Orthodox Jews, nowadays, do not enter the Temple site and a notice appears at the entrance to warn them off.

The great paradox of the whole rite is that the priests who performed the purification became themselves defiled. This mystery, that the *parah adumah* purified the defiled and yet defiled the pure was, for the Rabbis, the supreme example of the unfathomable in connection with some of the divine commands, which the devout were obliged to accept unquestioningly. Even the wise King Solomon, say the Rabbis, was unable to explain the rite. Rabban *Johanan ben Zakkai is reported as saying, when a heathen accused the Jews of practising sorcery in observing this rite: 'The corpse does not have the power by itself to defile, nor does the mixture of ash and water have the power by itself to cleanse. It is a decree of the Holy One, blessed be He, who declared: I have set it down as a statute, I have issued it as a decree which you are not to question.' Nevertheless, preachers throughout the ages have read a number of ideas into this rite of purification. *Rashi quotes Rabbi Moses the Preacher who connected the *parah adumah* with the *golden calf. If Israel had not worshipped the golden calf the people would have been immune from death. When a person suffers corpse contamination, a cow with a gold-like colour is the means of purification. Modern preachers have used the paradox that those engaged in purification become themselves defiled to point out that often those who work for a good cause justify even ignoble means to achieve their purpose and become spiritually defiled in the process. The section of the Torah dealing with the *parah adumah* is read on the Sabbath before the month of Nisan as a reminder of Temple times when this portion was read to warn those contaminated to purify themselves in readiness for the offering of the Paschal lamb on the festival of Passover. This Sabbath is called: 'the Sabbath of Parah'.

Jacob Milgrom, 'The Paradox of the Red Cow', in Nahum M. Sarna (ed.), *The JPS Torah Commentary: Numbers* (Philadelphia and New York, 1990), 438–43.

**Reform Judaism** The religious movement which arose in early nineteenth-century Germany with the aim of reinterpreting (or 'reforming') Judaism in the light of Western thought, values, and culture where such a reinterpretation does not come into conflict with Judaism's basic principles. (Orthodox Judaism maintains that the very principle of Reform is in conflict with the basic *principle of faith that the Torah is immutable.) After the *Emancipation and the emergence of the Jew into Western society, the need for a degree of adaptation of the traditional faith to the new conditions of life was keenly felt. The *Haskalah movement of Enlightenment, of which Moses *Mendelssohn was the leading figure, grappled with this very problem but tended to leave traditional norms more or less intact. It was left to Reform to introduce various innovations in the synagogue service and in other areas of Jewish religious life. Reform, however, did not, at first, become organized as a separate movement. A number of cultured laymen in various German cities tried their hand at creating a liturgy and form of service which they believed was more in keeping with Western ideas. The first Reform congregation was established in Hamburg in 1818, in the Hamburg Temple. Reform generally came to prefer the term Temple rather than synagogue for its house of prayer in the belief that the Messianic doctrine could no longer be interpreted in terms of a personal *Messiah who would rebuild the *Temple. The new opportunities presented in the West for greater social and educational advancement and for the spirit of freedom to flourish were themselves seen as the realization of the Messianic dream and it was felt that the synagogue, standing in place of the Temple, should be known as such. The Prayer Book of the Hamburg Temple omitted most of the references in the traditional *Prayer Book to the return to Zion and the restoration of the Temple service. Prayers and sermons in the German language were introduced and an *organ was played to accompany the prayers.

The Hamburg Rabbis enlisted a number of prominent Orthodox Rabbis to publish a stern prohibition against these reforms. Not very long afterwards, a number of Rabbis educated in German universities met in conferences in the years 1844–6; Reform ideas were put forward and a fully fledged Reform movement became established. The leaders of Reform in Germany, Abraham *Geiger and Samuel *Holdheim, tried to develop a Reform theology in which Jewish particularism, while never entirely rejected, yielded to a far greater degree of *universalism than was envisaged at any time in the Jewish past. The European Reform movement was centred on Germany, but Reform congregations were also established in Vienna, Hungary, Holland, and Denmark. In England the Reform congregation, the West London Synagogue of British Jews, was established as early as 1840. At the beginning of the twentieth century a more radical type of Reform was established in England under the influence of Claude *Montefiore. This took the name Liberal Judaism. In Germany itself, however, the movement known as Liberal Judaism was more to the right than German Reform.

Reform spread to America where, at first, the guiding lights were German-born and German-speaking Rabbis, prominent among whom was the real organizer of Reform in America, Isaac Mayer Wise (1819–1900). In 1875, thanks to Wise's efforts, the Hebrew Union College was established in Cincinnati for the training of Reform Rabbis. At the banquet held to celebrate the ordination of the Hebrew Union College's first graduates, shellfish, forbidden by the *dietary laws*, was served. This '*terefah banquet', as it came to be dubbed, at the ordination of Rabbis, no less, caused traditional Rabbis and laymen to recoil in horror and led indirectly to the development of *Conservative Judaism and the establishment of the Jewish Theological Seminary for the training of Conservative Rabbis.

*Reform Theology*

In view of the many shades of opinion among Reform theologians it is preferable to speak of general Reform tendencies rather than of a specific Reform theology. From the outset the thrust of Reform was in the direction of universalism. Judaism, in the Reform view, is a universal religion, though centred on a particular people. The task of the Jew in the universalistic scheme is to be, in the language of the prophets, a 'light unto the nations'. Reform dwells on the idea of the 'Jewish mission' to mankind. Following this universalistic thrust, Reform was uneasy about such particularistic elements in traditional Judaism as the dietary laws, prayers for the restoration of the sacrificial system in the rebuilt Temple in Jerusalem, and the emphasis on ritual in general. For classical Reform, the essence of Judaism lies in the prophetic message that God requires of man that he practise justice, love mercy, and walk humbly with God (Micah 6: 8), hence Reform is often called by its adherents, 'Prophetic Judaism'. Reform was also influenced by *Biblical Criticism and the *Jüdische Wissenschaft movement to see Judaism as a developing religion. The *Written Torah*, and the *Oral Torah*, were seen as human creations in which the Jewish people sought to find God. Reform was at first opposed to *Zionism but eventually many Reform Rabbis became themselves leading Zionists. Once the State of Israel was established, Reform's uneasiness with the central role of the land of Israel in Jewish life and thought became a thing of the past. There is now a Reform movement and a Reform Rabbinical College in the State of Israel. Reformers do not see themselves as being unprincipled in the change from opposition to acceptance of Zionism and Zionism's implications, since, on the Reform view, it has always been in the nature of Judaism to adapt itself to new ideas and new conditions of Jewish life. In this and in other matters there has been a definite move to the right, toward greater regard for the tradition. There has even emerged a Reform *Halakhah, with Reform Rabbis discussing, if not the total application of the Halakhah in present-day Jewish life, at least the way the Halakhah can offer guidance in those areas where its demands can be realized without the sacrifice of Reform principles.

A useful way of noting the development of Reform in new directions is to compare the position adopted in the Pittsburgh Platform in 1885 with that adopted in the Columbus Platform in 1937. Among other statements the Reform Rabbis responsible for drawing up the Pittsburgh Platform declared:

'We recognise in the Mosaic legislation a system of training the Jewish people for its mission during its national life in Palestine, and today we accept as binding only its moral laws and such ceremonies as elevate and sanctify our lives, and reject all such as are not adapted to the views and habits of modern civilization. We hold that all such Mosaic and rabbinical laws as regulate diet, priestly purity and dress originated in ages and under the influence of ideas entirely foreign to our present mental and spiritual state. They fail to impress the modern Jew with a spirit of priestly holiness; their observance in our days is apt rather to obstruct than to further modern spiritual elevation.'

This condescending attitude yielded to a much more positive approach to the tradition in the Columbus Platform:

'The Torah, both written and oral, enshrines Israel's ever-growing consciousness of God and the moral law. It preserves the historical precedents, sanctions and norms of Jewish life, and seeks to mould it in the patterns of goodness and of holiness. Being products of historical processes, certain of its laws have lost their binding force with the passing of the conditions that called them forth. But as a depository of permanent spiritual ideals, the Torah remains the dynamic source of the life of Israel. Each age has the obligation to adapt the teachings of the Torah to its basic needs in consonance with the genius of Judaism.'

Particularly to be noted is the use of the term 'Torah' in the Columbus Platform instead of the insipid 'Mosaic legislation' in the Pittsburgh Platform.

Essentially, Reform departs from Orthodoxy in its understanding of *revelation. For Orthodoxy the Torah is the revealed will of God and the Jew is required to observe the commands of the Torah not because they enrich his spiritual life (though Orthodoxy believes that they do have this effect) but because this is God's will. Reform, with its doctrine of 'progressive revelation' believes that in successive generations God allows for different appreciations of the truth of the Torah. Critics of Reform have accused the movement of being too much influenced by the Zeitgeist in its departure from tradition. It is in the area of revelation that Conservative Judaism seeks to understand the concept in a way that acknowledges the human element in the Torah while recognizing, at the same time, that the practical observances, as laid down in the

Halakhah, are the will of God, albeit given *through* Israel not, as in Orthodoxy, simply *to* Israel. The three basic ideas on which Judaism is based are God, the Torah, and Israel. There is much truth in the generalization that, of the three, Reform places the stress particularly on God, Orthodoxy on the Torah, Conservative Judaism on the peoplehood of Israel.

Michael A. Meyer, *Response to Modernity: A History of the Reform Movement in Judaism* (Oxford, 1988).
David Philipson, *The Reform Movement in Judaism* (New York, 1967).
W. Gunther Plaut, *The Rise of Reform Judaism* (New York, 1963).
—— *The Growth of Reform Judaism* (New York, 1965).

**Reincarnation** The idea that a soul now residing in a particular body may have resided in the body of another person in an earlier period of time. Theories of reincarnation or metempsychosis are found in many religions and cultures, ancient and modern, but there are no references to the idea in the Bible or the Talmud and it was unknown in Judaism until the eighth century CE, when it began to be adopted by the *Karaites (possibly, it has been suggested, under the influence of Islamic mysticism). The usual Hebrew term for reincarnation is *gilgul*, 'rolling', that is, the soul 'rolls' through time from one body to a different body. The earliest reference to the doctrine is that of *Saadiah (*Beliefs and Opinions*, vi. 8). Saadiah writes:

'Yet I must say that I have found certain people, who call themselves Jews, professing the doctrine of metempsychosis, which is designated by them as the theory of the "transmigration" of souls. What they mean thereby is that the spirit of Reuben is transferred to Simeon and afterwards to Levi and after that to Judah. Many of them would even go so far as to assert that the spirit of a human being might enter into the body of a beast or that of a beast into the body of a human being, and other such nonsense and stupidities.'

We learn incidentally from Saadiah's discussion that one of the reasons these people believed in reincarnation (this reason resurfaces in the Kabbalah) was because of the theological difficulties in God allowing little children to suffer. That they do, it was argued, is because of sins they had committed in a previous existence. Among the other medieval thinkers, neither Judah *Halevi nor Maimonides makes any mention of the doctrine. Albo (*Ikkarim*, vi. 29) refers to the doctrine only to refute it. He argues that the whole purpose for which the soul enters the body is to become a free agent, but once a soul has become a free agent why should it return to occupy another body? It is even more unlikely, says Albo, that human souls transmigrate into the bodies of animals.

The Kabbalists, on the other hand, do believe in reincarnation. The Zohar refers to the doctrine in a number of passages (e.g. ii. 94a, 99b). *Nahmanides, in his commentary to the book of Job (to Job 33: 30), speaks of reincarnation as a great mystery and the key to an understanding of many biblical passages. The later Kabbalah is full of the belief in the transmigration of souls. Various sins are punished by particular transmigrations; for example, the soul of an excessively proud man enters the body of a bee or a worm until atonement is attained. The heroes of the Bible and later Jewish histories are said to be the reincarnation of earlier heroes. Thus the soul of Cain (Genesis 4: 1–16) entered the body of Jethro and the soul of Abel the body of Moses. When Moses and Jethro met in friendship they rectified the sin caused by the estrangement of the two brothers. (Exodus 18: 1–12). Manasseh ben Israel (d. 1657) devotes a large portion of his *Nishmat Ḥayyim* ('The Soul of Life') to a defence of reincarnation. In chapter 21 Manasseh observes that the doctrine was originally taught to Adam but was later forgotten. It was revived by Pythagoras, who was a Jew (!), and he was taught the doctrine by the prophet Ezekiel. The Hasidim believe explicitly in the doctrine and tales are told of Hasidic masters who remembered their activities in a previous incarnation.

In the Kabbalistic literature three types of reincarnation are mentioned:

1. *gilgul*, transmigration proper, in which a soul that had previously inhabited one body is sent back to earth to inhabit another body.

2. *ibbur*, 'impregnation', in which a soul descends from heaven in order to assist another soul in the body (this notion is not found before the Lurianic Kabbalah in the sixteenth century).

3. *dybbuk*, a generally late concept, in which a guilt-laden soul pursued by devils enters a human body in order to find rest and has to be exorcised (see EXORCISM).

The philosophical difficulty in the whole doctrine of reincarnation lies in the problem of what possible meaning can be given to the identity of the soul that has been reincarnated, since the experiences of the body determine the character of the soul. How can the soul that has been in two or more bodies be the 'same' soul? Scholem has suggested that it was this difficulty which led the Zohar to postulate the existence of the *tzelem* ('image'), a kind of 'astral body' which does not migrate from body to body and which therefore preserves individual identity. We are here in the realm of the occult, as, indeed, we are in the whole area of reincarnation. Some modern Jews are attracted to the occult and believe in reincarnation. Otherwise the doctrine has had its day and is believed in by very few modern Jews, although hardly any Orthodox Jew today will positively denounce the doctrine. This doctrine of reincarnation shows how precarious it is to attempt to see Judaism in monolithic terms. Here is a doctrine rejected as a foreign importation by a notable thinker such as Saadiah and upon which other thinkers, including Maimonides, are silent, and yet, for the Kabbalists, it is revealed truth (see DOGMAS).

Gershom Scholem, 'Gilgul' in his *Kabbalah* (Jerusalem, 1974), 344–50.

**Religion** As an abstract term the word religion is found in neither the Bible nor the Talmud, both of which use concrete language. *Zangwill once said that the Rabbis, the most religious of men, had no word for religion; perhaps, one might add, precisely because they were the most religious of men they could not contain their religious attitudes in a single word or in any kind of formula. For the Rabbis, the all-embracing term, Torah, stood for what we call religion. Moreover, the Rabbis, and the biblical authors, did not see their faith as one religion among many. People who believed in many gods and worshipped them were all lumped together as idolaters (see IDOLATRY). It was not until the Middle Ages, when *Christianity and *Islam had emerged, that Jewish theologians were obliged to consider Judaism as a religion, different from these two religions but resembling them in certain respects. For purposes of discussion and debate a term for religion had to be coined. The term the medieval thinkers used, *dat*, derived from a Persian word found in late passages in the Bible, originally meant law, in the very concrete sense of a particular way of conduct, but now came to denote religion in the abstract. The *dat* of Israel came to mean the religion of Israel and the plural, *datot*, the other religions. *Albo, for example, in his *Sefer Ha-Ikkarim*, contrasts the Jewish *dat* with other *datot*, meaning Christianity and Islam. For the first time, the medieval Jewish thinkers see Judaism as a religion with many of the same characteristics as other religions, albeit that, for these thinkers, Judaism is, of course, the only true religion revealed by God (see REVELATION).

### Judaism and Other Religions

The general argument of the medieval thinkers, especially pronounced in the *Kuzari* of *Judah Halevi, was that, since both Christianity and Islam acknowledged that Judaism was once the true religion, although now superseded, it was up to them to prove that this was so, not for Judaism to have to prove that it was true. The onus of proof was on them, and it was not forthcoming. The Far Eastern religions, incidentally, were completely unknown. This does not mean that the medieval thinkers saw no value at all in the rival religions. *Bahya, Ibn Pakudah, for example, often quotes in his work the Sufi teachers and even refers to them as 'saints'. Maimonides (*Melakhim* 9: 3–4) can say that both Christianity and Islam, though false, have a role to play in the divine scheme by acquainting mankind with truths about God it would not otherwise have had and thus paving the way for the coming of the *Messiah.

There is no uniform attitude among contemporary Jews on the relationship between Judaism and other religions. Many Jews adopt the attitude of the medieval thinkers that, while it is possible to learn some things of value from other religions, basically they are false and only Judaism true. Others adopt the relativistic attitude, often expressed as: it does not matter which religion you profess as long as you profess a religion or as long as your religion inspires you to lead a good life. But the fallacy here is obvious. To say that all religions are equally true is to say that all religions are equally false. Every believer in a particular religion, no matter how broad-minded he is and no matter how strong is his avoidance of triumphalism, cannot ignore the truth-claims

his religion makes. For all the things they have in common, the great religions of the world affirm as basic principles ideas that are simply not compatible with one another. If certain forms of atheistic Buddhism are true, then Hinduism with its many gods and Judaism, Christianity, and Islam with their one God must be false. When Judaism denies that God can ever assume human flesh it thereby rejects the basic Christian dogma. If the 'way' of the Buddha is alone 'true' for all men, then the way of the Torah cannot be true for Jews. For all that, it is exceedingly difficult to dub all the great religions of the world simply as idolatrous faiths of which Jews can and should be tolerant but which they should declare to be totally false. The increased knowledge of the rich vein of spirituality in all the world religions militates against such the notion of total rejection. Many modern Jews, eager to avoid undue dogmatism and, at the same time, uneasy with the vagaries of relativism, prefer to adopt the attitude that, while there is truth in all religions, there is more truth in Judaism. It is obvious that such an attitude leaves many questions unanswered but for all its vagueness many modern Jews see it as the only reasonable approach to the great mystery of the God whom Judaism brought to the world and who allows other religions apart from Judaism to exist.

Louis Jacobs, 'Judaism and Other Religions', in his *A Jewish Theology* (New York, 1973), 284–91.

**Responsa** The answers given by authorities in Jewish law to questions put to them; Heb. *sheelot u-teshuvot*, 'questions and answers'. There are occasional references in the Talmud to letters sent by one Rabbi to another asking for information in matters of law but the Responsa activity proper dates from the period of the *Geonim, when the practice developed of scholars addressing questions to the heads of the great Babylonian communities at Sura and Pumbedita in Babylonia, the foremost authorities in this period. Collections were made of the Geonic Responsa, especially those of *Sherira Gaon and his son *Hai Gaon, but while these collections were known to the medieval authorities they did not appear in print until as late as the nineteenth century. Essentially, the questions in the Responsa concern problems which arose out of new conditions, for which no direct answers could be found in the Talmud, the final *authority for Jewish *law. The leading

Respondents through the ages, faced with new questions, tried to discover analogies in the Talmud and the later Codes (see CODIFICATION) and from time to time the replies in the Responsa served as sources for new Codes.

Two examples, among many, can be given of how the process works. When *printing was invented, the question arose of whether it should be considered as writing for the purposes of Jewish law. Was a printed bill of divorce (*get*) valid, since the Talmud speaks of a written document? Do printed copies of the Bible enjoy the same sanctity as a handwritten text? Since printing was unknown in Talmudic times, no direct guidance on these questions could be forthcoming from the Talmud. The Respondents had to arrive at their rulings by careful study of the Talmudic definition of 'writing'. Similarly, when *electricity was discovered and harnessed to human needs, the question arose of whether switching on an electric light constitutes making fire and is therefore forbidden on the Sabbath. This, too, was considered by the Respondents by an examination of the Talmudic definition of making fire.

In addition to their importance for Jewish law, the Responsa collections (of which around two thousand have now been published) are not only important for Jewish law but serve historians as a rich source for the study of the social life of Jews reflected in them—a particularly reliable source since the details are mentioned in an incidental manner.

Among questions to which contemporary Respondents address themselves are: *artificial insemination; riding in an automobile on the Sabbath; *autopsies; heart transplants; and switching off a life-supporting machine (see EUTHANASIA).

It has to be appreciated that Respondents were not appointed by any kind of official body. A Rabbi was qualified to act as a Respondent simply because his peers looked upon him as a reliable authority. Needless to say, Respondents often differed in their decisions, so that there are to be found debates between Respondents, often conducted with vehemence: for example, on the question of whether machine manufactured *matzah* can be used for Passover or whether it must it be baked by hand. Responsa have been published not only by Orthodox Rabbis but also by Conservative and Reform Rabbis whose Responsa reflect their particular philosophy or *Halakhah.

Solomon B. Freehof, *The Responsa Literature and a Treasury of Responsa* (2 vols. in one; New York, 1973).

—— Reform Responsa and Recent Reform Responsa, 2 vols. in one (New York, 1973).

**Responsibility** Only a person who acts of his own *free will and in full knowledge of what he is doing is held responsible in Jewish law. A person of unsound mind is not held responsible for any injuries he inflicts on others nor has he any obligation to keep the precepts of the Torah. The degree of *insanity required is discussed in the Talmud and the Codes. A minor is similarly held unaccountable because his state of mind is considered to be defective. A boy loses his minor status to become fully responsible for his actions at the age of 13, a girl at the age of 12, hence *Bar Mitzvah and *Bat Mitzvah. Some sources indicate, though this is far from being generally accepted, that while a boy and girl, once they have reached the age of 13 and 12 respectively, are held responsible in civil and criminal law for acts they commit, so far as purely religious offences are concerned they do not have majority status until they have reached the age of 20. A person is not held responsible, even if he knows what he is doing, where he is forced by others to commit an offence (see RAPE). The Talmud states that if a man is threatened with death if he does not kill someone, it is his duty to allow himself to be killed rather than kill. Nevertheless, Maimonides and other codifiers rule that if he did kill in order to avoid his own death, his act is not treated as an act of murder since he did, after all, perform it under duress. While a father is not held responsible in law for acts carried out by his children, he has a responsibility to train them to lead an honourable and useful life and he has a responsibility for their education.

**Resurrection** The doctrine that in a future age the dead will rise from their graves to live again. This doctrine appears frequently in Jewish *eschatology, where it is associated with the doctrine of the *Messiah and the immortality of the *soul. There are only two biblical references to the resurrection of the dead, in passages generally held by biblical scholars to be of late date, so that it has been conjectured that the doctrine owes something to Persian influence. The first is: 'Thy dead shall live, my dead bodies shall arise, awake and sing, ye that dwell in the dust, for thy dew is as the dew of light, and the earth shall bring to life the shades' (Isaiah 26: 19); and the second: 'And many of them that sleep in the dust of the earth shall awake, some to everlasting life, and some to reproaches and everlasting abhorrence' (Daniel 12: 2).

There is no systematic treatment in the Rabbinic literature of the doctrine of the resurrection, any more than there is of any other theological topic. The ancient Rabbis were organic rather than systematic thinkers. Nevertheless, the picture which emerges from the numerous eschatological thoughts in this literature is of a three-staged series of events. The first of these is the state of the soul in *heaven after the death of the body. The second stage is the Messianic age here on earth 'at the end of days'. The third stage is that of the resurrection of the dead. Unlike the doctrine of the immortality of the soul, the belief in the resurrection was nationalistic rather than individualistic. It was the hope of national revival that came to the fore and this embraced the resurrection. After the restoration of the Jewish people to its homeland in the days of the Messiah, it was believed, the resurrection of the dead would take place. While there is no necessary contradiction between belief in the immortality of the soul and belief in the resurrection, there is some incompatibility between the idea of a great judgement day to take place after the resurrection of the dead and the judgement of each individual soul after the death of the body. When, as eventually happened, the two beliefs were fused together, there was bound to be some confusion on this matter and a large variety of views on how the two beliefs could both be true. This helps to explain the many details, sometimes of a contradictory nature, in the Rabbinic literature with regard to the final judgement. The *Pharisees seem to have held that both doctrines were basic to Judaism; the resurrection afforded hope for national survival, together with the idea of the Messiah, while the belief in the immortality of the soul appealed to the individual's need to be assured that he survives death. The *Sadducees appear to have rejected both beliefs, although some scholars claim that the frequent references to Sadducean denial apply only to the doctrine of the resurrection, not to that of the immortality of the soul. The Christian dogma of the Resurrection and the general eschatological picture presented in the *New Testament has thus to be seen against the background of Pharisaic beliefs in the early first century CE.

## Medieval Views

Although Maimonides lists belief in the resurrection as a basic *principle of faith (the thirteenth) he refers to it in a very off-hand manner. In Maimonides' *Guide of the Perplexed* there is no reference at all to the doctrine. There are one or two stray references to the resurrection in Maimonides' Code but, on the whole, he seems to identify the Rabbinic *World to Come not with the resurrection but with the immortality of the soul, or, rather, he seems to believe that the resurrection itself is of the soul, not the body. Maimonides' critics accused him, in fact, of denying the doctrine of the resurrection. These critics point out that his virtual silence on the fate of the body in the Hereafter certainly contradicts Rabbinic teachings on the subject. There are found in the Rabbinic literatures such statements as that the dead will be resurrected wearing their clothes (*Ketubot* 111b) and that the righteous whom God will resurrect will not return to their dust (*Sanhedrin* 72a), obviously pointing to a belief in bodily resurrection. Towards the end of his life, Maimonides wrote his *Essay on the Resurrection* (the view that this is not Maimonides' but a clever forgery is not now accepted by Maimonidean scholars) to defend himself. In this essay Maimonides protests that he had never denied the doctrine of a physical resurrection but advances a novel theory (though hinted at by a few other medieval Jewish thinkers) that the resurrected dead will not live for ever but will eventually die again. Maimonides could not conceive of the idea of a body inhabiting eternity. Only the soul is immortal.

On this subject the great debate took place between Maimonides and *Nahmanides. Writing after Maimonides' death, Nahmanides, in *The Gate of Recompense* devoted to the subject, takes strong issue with Maimonides' view that the bodies of the resurrected dead will also die eventually, although he does believe that these bodies will be exceedingly refined and ethereal. Crescas in *The Light of the Lord* (iii. 4) agrees with Nahmanides and discusses how the decomposed body will be reconstituted. It is not necessarily the case, say Crescas, that the same body the soul inhabited during its lifetime on earth will be given to it at the resurrection, but one that will have the same purpose. The identity of the individual will not be affected by this, since even during a person's life in this world the body suffers changes all the time. *Albo (*Ikkarim*, iv. 35) also agrees with Nahmanides and offers his speculations on how the new bodies will take form and shape. But Albo discourages too much speculation on what is by all accounts a miracle and a mystery. He quotes with approval the Talmudic saying: 'We will consider the matter when they come to life again' (*Niddah* 70b). As one might have expected, no perfectly coherent doctrine of the resurrection emerges from the medieval thinkers any more than it does from the Rabbinic literature.

### Modern Views

The tendency among some of the medieval thinkers to play down the doctrine of the resurrection is evident in the modern period in even greater measure. *Mendelssohn believed in the immortality of the soul and wrote his treatise, *Phaedon*, on the topic but did not seem to believe in a physical resurrection. Among many contemporary Jewish theologians there is a marked tendency to leave the whole question of eschatology without discussion, either because they do not believe in the Hereafter at all or because they believe that the finite mind of man is incapable of piercing the veil and it is best to leave the subject severely alone. Orthodox theologians still maintain the belief in the resurrection and refer to it, as did their forebears, in their daily prayers and at funerals. In the special Kaddish recited by a son at the funeral of a parent there are explicit references to the resurrection of the dead. At the same time, memorial prayers recited by the Orthodox contain references to the soul of the departed being at rest 'beneath the wings of the *Shekhinah'. Some Orthodox thinkers—very few, it must be said—develop further the idea that the resurrection means of the soul not of the body. One of the Orthodox objections to *cremation is on the grounds that it involves a denial of the doctrine of the resurrection. Reform Judaism in the nineteenth century went the whole way in rejecting the doctrine of the resurrection in favour of that of the immortality of the soul. In Reform prayer books passages in the traditional Prayer Book to the resurrection have either been deleted or interpreted as referring to immortality of the roul.

Isidore Epstein, 'Additional Note on the Resurrection of the Dead', in his *The Faith of Judaism* (London, 1954), 383–6.
George Foot More, 'The Hereafter', in his *Judaism in the First Centuries of the Christian Era: The Age of the Tannaim* (Cambridge, Mass., 1958), ii. 279–395.

**Revelation** The appearance of God to the prophets and, especially at *Sinai, to the people as a whole. The account of God's revelation to *Moses (Exodus 33: 18–23) posed a problem to the Rabbis and the medieval thinkers because of the extreme anthropomorphism in its wording. Moses requests God to show him His glory. God replies that He cannot show Moses His face, for no man can see God and live. God tells Moses to stand in a cleft of the rock while His glory passes by, covering Moses with His hand. After God's glory has passed, He removes His hand and Moses allowed to see God's back. In the Talmud (*Yevamot* 49b) the statement: 'No man can see Me and live' is contrasted with the prophet Isaiah's declaration: 'I saw the Lord sitting on a throne, high and lifted up' (Isaiah 6: 1). The contradiction is resolved by saying that Moses saw through a clear glass while Isaiah saw through a dim glass. The great French commentator, *Rashi, gives a novel interpretation to this Talmudic passage. Moses' vision of God was always through a clear glass and he, therefore, arrived, through his clear sight, at the conclusion that no man can see God. Isaiah, on the other hand, saw his vision through a dim glass and, in his clouded sight, imagined that he did see God. *Saadiah Gaon (*Beliefs and Opinions*, ii. 12), softening still more the anthropomorphism, understands God's glory seen by Moses to be a special light by means of which God appears to the prophets. Even this light could not be seen directly by Moses who was only allowed to see its 'back' as it passed by him. All the Jewish teachers are similarly circumspect when trying to explore the mystery of divine revelation, whether of God's manifestation or of the manner in which He communicates His word (see BAT KOL, ELIJAH, HOLY SPIRIT, and INSPIRATION).

### Revelation of the Torah

The form of revelation most discussed in Judaism is that of God's will as revealed in the Torah. In the Rabbinic formulation this is always referred to as the doctrine: 'Torah from Heaven.' While the manner of revelation in this sense is also seen as beyond the human mind to grasp there is no ambiguity about the content of the revelation. This traditional view, still adhered to in Orthodoxy, is based on the theophany at Sinai (Exodus 19, 20) but the scope of revelation is widened to include the whole of the Torah, both the *Written Torah and the *Oral Torah, together conceived as the complete communication of God's will. On this view God conveyed the *Pentateuch, the five books of Moses, directly and in its entirety to Moses (with the possible exception of the final verses in Deuteronomy, which speak of Moses' death) during the forty years in which the Israelites journeyed through the wilderness. The Torah is the very word of God—the teachings, laws, doctrines, and rules for the conduct of life as revealed by the Author of life. To study the Torah is to think God's thoughts after Him. To practise the precepts, the *mitzvot* (see MITZVAH), of the Torah is to obey God's revealed will. And this Torah has remained unchanged throughout the ages, conveyed, through the chain of tradition, from Moses to Joshua, from Joshua to the Elders, from the Elders to the prophets and from the prophets to the Men of the *Great Synagogue, as stated in the opening passage of Ethics of the Fathers, and then by father to son, teacher to disciple, through 3,000 years of Jewish history. While a few Jewish thinkers in the Middle Ages seemed to have held that only the laws of the Torah were revealed by God and they stopped short of affirming that every word of the Pentateuch was 'dictated' by God, the majority of the medieval thinkers seem to have agreed with Maimonides' categorical statement in his list of *principles of faith. Here the doctrine of 'Torah from Heaven' is formulated as:

'The eighth principle of faith. That the Torah has been revealed from Heaven. This implies our belief that the whole of this Torah found in our hands this day is the Torah that was handed down to Moses and that it is all of divine origin. By this I mean that the whole of the Torah came unto him from before God which is metaphorically called "speaking", but the real nature of that communication is unknown to everyone except Moses to whom it came . . . The interpretation of traditional law [i.e. the Oral Torah] is in like manner of divine origin. And that which we know today of the nature of *Sukkah, Lulav, *Shofar, *Tzitzit and *Tefillin is essentially the same as that which God commanded Moses and which the latter told us.'

In such a view there is no room for any notion of development in the Jewish religion; the Torah is a static body of truth revealed by God and handed down intact from generation to generation. Even the *Karaites held fast to the doctrine that every word of the Pentateuch was 'dictated' by God. Like the *Sadducees in an earlier period, the Karaites only took issue with the doctrine of the Oral Torah, which they held to be Rabbinic invention.

The traditional view of 'Torah from Heaven' undoubtedly has grandeur and power. The Infinite has revealed to the people of Israel, and through them, albeit in a less demanding way, to all mankind, how life should be lived. Every *mitzvah* is not only a means to an end but is itself the glorious end—none could be more sublime—of doing God's revealed will.

This view of 'Torah from Heaven' has been heavily assailed in modern times. *Biblical criticism has shown, satisfactorily to most students of the Bible, that the Pentateuch is a composite work produced at different periods in Israel's history. That the Pentateuch is the revealed word of God and hence infallible met with other difficulties in the nineteenth century when geologists demonstrated the immense age of the earth, astronomers that the universe is not geocentric, and anthropologists that human beings have been on earth far longer by hundreds of thousands of years than Genesis seems to suggest—all making it hard to believe that the Pentateuchal picture is the result of a divine revelation, a source of accurate information on all matters. Furthermore, the *Jüdische Wissenschaft movement applied the newly developed methods of historical investigation to the Oral Torah, asking, for example, how, why, and when the whole doctrine originated and why it was not accepted by the Sadducees and Karaites. The whole of the Talmudic literature, held to contain the Oral Torah, was subjected to intense scrutiny in order to determine how Rabbinic Judaism developed. The Rabbinic doctrine of 'Torah from Heaven' was itself seen to have had a history and to have come at the end of a long process of development.

## Modern Attitudes

How do contemporary Jews cope with the problem of revelation in the light of modern biblical and Rabbinic scholarship? Secularists hold that the new picture has succeeded in demolishing completely the whole idea of the Torah as God's revelation. For them the Torah has now to be seen as a series of purely human documents or traditions and for the secularist there is, in any event, no Revealer. *Fundamentalism, on the other hand, preserves the traditional picture intact and either rejects all modern thought or interprets the Bible in such a way that it is in accord with the scientific picture—a 'day' in the creation narrative in Genesis, for example, meaning a vast period of time. While many Orthodox Jews accept the critical method when applied to the prophetic books and the Rabbinic literature and rightly resent being dubbed fundamentalists, there is still a definite recoil from any acknowledgement of a human element in the Pentateuch itself. Reform Judaism accepts the findings of modern criticism and generally shifts the idea of divine revelation from the Torah to the prophets. Moreover, Reform believes in the doctrine of 'progressive revelation' according to which revelation was not a once and for all event of the remote past but an ongoing process. Conservative Judaism (although there are differing emphases in the movement on this topic) accepts the idea of revelation of the whole of the Torah but sees this in dynamic terms and recognizes a human element in the process. God revealed the Torah, on this view, not only *to* the people of Israel but *through* them. (See CONSERVATIVE JUDAISM, ORTHODOXY, and REFORM JUDAISM.)

Samuel S. Cohon, 'Revelation: Traditional View' and 'A Modern View', in his *Jewish Theology* (Assen, 1971), 128–34.
Isidore Epstein, 'The Relation of Revelation to Reason' and 'Revelation and Prophecy', in his *The Faith of Judaism* (London, 1954), 99–133.
Louis Jacobs, 'Torah as Divine Revelation', in his *God Torah Israel*, (Cincinnati, 1990), 21–54.

**Revenge** The biblical verse in which it is stated that it is wrong to take revenge is the same verse in which 'love thy neighbour' occurs: 'Thou shalt not take vengeance, nor bear any grudge against the children of thy people, but thou shalt love thy neighbour as thyself: I am the Lord' (Leviticus 19: 18). The plain meaning of the verse is that *love of the neighbour is to be expressed by refusing to take revenge because the neighbour is like the self. The Jerusalem Talmud (*Nedarim* 9: 4) gives the illustration, in this connection, of the man who cuts his hand while cutting meat. He will not be

so foolish as to cut out of spite the hand which did the damage. Evidently, the Jerusalem Talmud is stressing that man and his neighbour are one. To harm the neighbour is to harm the self. In the English version of the saying, it is cutting off the nose to spite the face.

A famous Rabbinic comment on the verse (*Yoma* 23a) draws a distinction between taking revenge and bearing a grudge. If a man asks his fellow to lend him his sickle and he refuses and on the next day the second asks the first to lend him his axe and he replies: 'I will not lend it to you, just as you would not lend me your sickle'—that is revenge. But if a man asks his fellow to lend him his sickle and he refuses and on the next day the second asks the first to lend him his robe (i.e. even his robe, let alone his axe) and he replies: 'Here it is, I am not like you'—that is bearing a grudge. Maimonides (*Deot* 7: 7–8) adds that the wise will refuse to take revenge because worldly things are simply not worth making a fuss about. To feel a sense of outrage because one has been refused the loan of a sickle is to magnify the importance of a sickle. Maimonides also understands the prohibition against bearing a grudge to be a means of avoiding the more serious offence of taking revenge. All this, concludes Maimonides, is the proper attitude to be cultivated if society is to be well established and social life possible.

*Nahmanides, in his comment to the verse, remarks that it is obvious, none the less, that where a man has a legitimate case against his neighbour it does not constitute revenge to summon him to a court of law. In the examples given in the Talmud of the sickle and the axe no redress is available in the courts. But one is certainly allowed to claim compensation for wrongs done, otherwise the prohibition of taking revenge would be an open invitation to the unscrupulous. It is wrong to be vengeful but this does not mean that one has to be a doormat.

In the same Talmudic passage it is stated, in fact, that taking revenge is only forbidden when the concern is with the use of objects, as in the case of the sickle and the axe. But when a man is insulted personally the prohibition does not apply. Nevertheless, even here, the ideal is expressed: 'Concerning those who are insulted but do not insult others, who hear themselves reproached without replying; who perform good deeds out of love and rejoice in their sufferings, Scripture says; "But they that love Him be as the sun when he goeth forth in his might" [Judges 5: 31].' Obviously, the pursuit of this ideal does not mean that one is bound to act in this saintly way always. That it is an ideal and one exceedingly difficult to realize is admitted by the famous moralist Moses Hayyim *Luzzatto in his *Path of the Upright* (ch. 11). Luzzatto urges his readers to avoid in all circumstances any semblance of revenge and bearing a grudge. Yet he can write:

'Hatred and revenge. These the human heart in its perversity finds it hard to escape. A man is very sensitive to disgrace, and suffers keenly when subjected to it. Revenge is sweeter to him than honey; he cannot rest until he has taken his revenge. If, therefore, he has the power to relinquish that to which his nature impels him; if he can forgive; if he will forbear hating anyone who provokes him to hatred; if he will neither exact vengeance when he has the opportunity to do so, nor bear a grudge against anyone; if he can forget and obliterate from his mind a wrong done to him as though it had never been committed; then he is, indeed, strong and mighty.'

Luzzatto suffered all his days from persecution, during a life in which he made many enemies because of his religious views. He seems to be addressing himself.

Louis Jacobs, 'Revenge', in his *What Does Judaism Say About . . .?* (Jerusalem, 1973), 271–3.

**Reward and Punishment** The idea that God rewards those who keep His commandments and punishes those who transgress them is one that runs through the whole of the Bible. The book of Deuteronomy speaks of God's love for Israel and the corollary that He wishes to reward them for keeping His laws but that He will not fail to punish them if they fall short of His demands on them: 'Know, therefore, that only the Lord your God is God, the steadfast God who keeps His gracious covenant to the thousandth generation of those who love Him and keep His commandments, but who instantly requites with destruction those who reject Him—never slow with those who reject Him, but requiting them instantly' (Deuteronomy 7: 9–10). This theme runs throughout the biblical record. The biblical writers are not unaware of the difficulties inherent in the doctrine of reward and punishment. The righteous often suffer and the wicked prosper. These difficulties are faced fearlessly in the

*Psalms, *Ecclesiastes, *Job (the whole book being devoted to the problem), and in other parts of Scripture, but while this certainly implies that the question was far from simple for the biblical writers, their basic belief in recompense and retribution was not really affected. And while the majority of the biblical passages speak of national reward and punishment, there are sufficient references to reward and punishment for the *individual as well. The prophet Ezekiel (Ezekiel 18) not only dwells on individual recompense and retribution but rejects the idea that an individual is punished for the deeds of his ancestors. The Talmudic Rabbis recognized that in this Deuteronomy and Ezekiel are in conflict and they tried to resolve the contradiction.

The biblical references are all to divine recompense and retribution in this world, in terms of material prosperity and suffering here on earth. But a remarkable shift of emphasis took place, it is generally held, at the time of the *Maccabees, when righteous men and women were being slaughtered because of their loyalty to their faith. In the face of such direct contradiction to the notion of reward and punishment in the here and now, faith could only be maintained by affirming that recompense and retribution were to be the fate of humans in the Hereafter, in the *World to Come, as it is called by the Rabbis. In the Rabbinic literature, while this-worldly formulations are not unknown, it is in the World to Come that the doctrine is made to receive its chief application (see GARDEN OF EDEN and GEHINNOM).

By the time Maimonides listed the doctrine of reward and punishment as a *principle of faith, the whole emphasis had long been on these taking place in the next world. Moreover, in Maimonides' formulation at least, the doctrine applies chiefly to the fate of the individual soul. This is clearly stated in Maimonides' eleventh principle of faith, although, obviously, Maimonides believed in the biblical application of the doctrine to national well-being and catastrophe as well. Maimonides' eleventh principle reads: 'The eleventh principle of faith. That He, the exalted one, rewards him who obeys the commands of the Torah and punishes him who transgresses its prohibitions. That God's greatest reward to man is the World to Come and that His strongest punishment is *karet' (understood by Maimonides, here and elsewhere in his writings, as the 'cutting-off' of the soul from eternal bliss in the Hereafter)'.

## Medieval Views

The question of reward and punishment exercised the minds of the medieval thinkers. Joseph *Albo has a full-scale treatment of the subject in his *Sefer Ha-Ikkarim* (Book IV, ch. 29 onwards). The numerous sayings of the Rabbis regarding the idea of virtue for its own sake, observes Albo, were not intended to suggest that there is no reward and punishment but to emphasize that the man who truly loves God is indifferent to considerations of rewards other than the greatest reward of all, the privilege of serving the Creator. Surveying the opinions held in this matter, Albo notes that there are four different views. Some thinkers reject the whole doctrine of reward and punishment. Others believe that there is both corporeal and spiritual reward and punishment, physical reward and punishment in this world and spiritual reward and punishment in the next. Others again believe in corporeal reward and punishment but not in spiritual reward and punishment. Finally, there are those who believe in spiritual reward and punishment in the next world but not in corporeal reward and punishment in this world. Albo rejects the first view as contrary to the opinions of both the Torah and the philosophers. The total rejection of reward and punishment implies that human beings are no different from animals, without freedom to pursue the good and reject evil. And those who hold that there is no spiritual reward and punishment in the Hereafter really reject the whole belief in the Hereafter. For them human beings have no soul that can live on to be rewarded or punished after the death of the body. The third opinion, that reward and punishment is confined to the Hereafter, is adopted by many Jewish thinkers because they conceive of true perfection and happiness only in spiritual terms. One of the Talmudic Rabbis remarked (*Kiddushin* 39b) that there is no reward in this world for the performance of the precepts. Albo's own opinion, which he considers to be the true doctrine of Judaism, is that there is reward and punishment both in this world and in the next, that reward and punishment is both corporeal and spiritual.

The picture which emerges from the writings of the medieval teachers on reward and punishment is that these principles operate by inexorable laws, even though their full workings cannot be grasped by humans. God is merciful and loves His creatures but in spite of this love (the medieval thinkers would say rather because of it) He does not fail to chastise sinners as He does not fail to reward the virtuous. All these teachers know of the higher type of religion in which the good is pursued for its own sake and out of the love of God (see DISINTERESTEDNESS), but this is never interpreted as a denial of God's strict justice and His goodness in rewarding His creatures for the good they do.

## Modern Attitudes

Over and above the difficulties faced by ancients and medieval thinkers, modern Jews have to face difficulties of their own, which are partly the result of the fresh interest in penal reform during the past century. Punishment as retaliation in a vindictive sense has been largely abandoned. The value of punishment as a deterrent and for the protection of society is widely recognized. But all the stress today is on the reformatory aspects of punishment. Against such a background, the whole question of reward and punishment in the theological sphere is approached in a more questioning spirit. It is true that many of the ancients refuse to allow that God is vindictive but it cannot be denied that in some of the literature of Jewish piety the impression is gained that punishment is retaliatory, a view moderns reject in that it suggests an inferior conception of the Deity. Furthermore, most Jewish thinkers today would be far more reticent than those of the Middle Ages in even attempting to describe the *scheme* by which God allots rewards and punishments (see *Providence). Not does it seem compatible with God's justice that little children should suffer or die because of the sins of their parents and few would accept the Kabbalistic 'explanation' (see *Reincarnation) that little children suffer because they had sinned as adults in a previous incarnation. Because of all these factors the doctrine of reward and punishment is frequently interpreted by modern Jews in terms of natural progress rather than in terms of tit-for-tat. Unless religion is to become a mere sentimental feeling for the divine it must teach that evil is evil and hateful in God's eyes. As C. S. Lewis has put it, some people want not so much a Father in Heaven as a Grandfather in Heaven, a senile Deity who says at the end of the day that a good time was had by one and all. A God who tolerates a Hitler would be as little deserving of worship and as little capable of being worshipped as a God who wantonly inflicts cruelty on His creatures. The emphasis among contemporary religious thought is on wickedness as carrying the seeds of its own destruction. The details can be left to God, while humans so conduct themselves that all the ancient teachings on reward and punishment are relevant to their lives. The doctrine as interpreted by moderns means that it is *ultimately* better to live the good life and reject an evil life.

> Louis Jacobs, 'Reward and Punishment', in his *Principles of the Jewish Faith* (Northvale, NJ, and London, 1988), 350–67.
> Kaufmann Kohler, 'Divine Retribution: Reward and Punishment', in his *Jewish Theology* (New York, 1968), 298–309.
> Solomon Schechter, 'The Doctrine of Divine Retribution in Rabbinical Literature', in his *Studies of Judaism*, first series (Philadelphia, 1945), 213–32.

**Righteousness** The carrying-out of religious and especially ethical obligation. The usual Hebrew word for 'righteousness', *tzedek* or *tzedakah*, has the root meaning of 'straightness', as in the English expression 'straight as a die' and is often used in the Bible in apposition to the word *mishpat*, '*justice', from a root meaning 'to judge'. Of Abraham the verse says: 'For I have known him, to the end that he may command his children and his household after him; that they may keep the way of the Lord, to do righteousness and justice' (Genesis 18: 19). The two terms are expressed as synonyms in the verse: 'Zion shall be redeemed with justice and they that return of her with righteousness' (Isaiah 1: 27). But righteousness often has a somewhat wider connotation than justice in that the practice of righteousness is advocated even beyond the claims of strict justice. The righteous man is called the *tzaddik*. In the Bible generally the *tzaddik* is not a saintly individual, a man of extraordinary piety and moral worth, but simply the ordinary good man and this is the meaning of the term in the Rabbinic literature, except for a few passages in which the term *tzaddik* is used of the saint, as in the famous statement (*Sukkah* 45b) that there are never less than thirty-six *tzaddikim* who welcome the countenance of the *Shekhinah daily (see LAMEDVOVNIKS). *In Hasidism the term *tzaddik* is used in the latter sense to denote the

Hasidic master, the *Zaddik (as the term is usually spelled in this connection in English). Interestingly enough, in the Rabbinic literature *tzadakah* is the term used for *charity, presumably implying that it is only right and just that the poor receive relief.

**Rituals** See MITZVAH and PRECEPTS, 613.

**Rome** That Palestine was a Roman colony; that the Jews fought against Roman dominion (see BAR KOCHBA and JOSEPHUS); that the Romans destroyed the Temple in 70 CE; that the emperor Hadrian persecuted the Jews for adherence to their religion; and that, on the other hand, Jews were bound to acknowledge that the Roman occupation had brought considerable benefits in its wake; all these factors help to explain the love–hate relationship between the Jews and the Romans. In a revealing Talmudic tale (*Shabbat* 33b) the late second-century teachers, Rabbi Judah, Rabbi Jose, and Rabbi *Simeon ben Yohai, were sitting discussing the Roman occupation. Rabbi Judah said: 'How fine are the works of this people! They have made streets, they have built bridges, they have erected baths.' Rabbi Jose remained silent but Rabbi Simeon protested: 'All that they made they made for themselves; they built market-places, to set harlots in them, baths, to rejuvenate themselves, bridges to levy tolls for them.' When the conversation was reported to the Roman authorities, it was decreed that Rabbi Judah should be honoured, Rabbi Jose exiled to Sepphoris, and Rabbi Simeon executed. Even if, as is probable, this tale contains legendary elements, it certainly reflects the ambivalent attitudes among the Rabbis. The Roman Empire is frequently referred to in Rabbinic literature as 'the wicked government' and yet Rome was identified with *Esau, the twin brother of the patriarch Jacob, the ancestor of the Jews. While Rabbi *Akiba is said to have been tortured to death by the Romans for teaching the Torah in public, tales are told of Rabbi *Judah the Prince being on the friendliest terms with the emperor Antoninus.

Roman influence is pervasive in the Rabbinic literature. The Mishnah and the Jerusalem Talmud were compiled when the Jews were under Roman rule and expressions taken from Roman life and culture abound in these works. Even the Babylonian Talmud, compiled by Jews under Persian rule, has numerous references to the Romans, reflecting not only conditions in Palestine but the impact of Roman civilization on Babylonian Jewry. In a remarkable Talmudic *Aggadah (*Avodh Zarah* 2a–3b), the nations are judged in the Messianic age, each nation appearing before God in turn to justify its dealings with the Jews. Of all the nations, Rome enters first because it is the most important, after which Persia enters as next in importance. Tractate *Avodah Zarah* in the Mishnah deals entirely with the religious attitudes Jews were to adopt towards the Romans and their gods. The Mishnah rules that it is forbidden for Jews to have dealings with *Gentiles (largely but not exclusively Romans) three days before pagan festivals such as (the Mishnah gives the actual name) Saturnalia. In the Middle Ages these rules were applied to Christians but with a definite tendency to soften their impact on the grounds that rules originally formulated in connection with the pagan Romans could not possibly be applied in all their severity to Christians, who believe in God.

An addition to the Mishnah (*Sotah*, end) states that in the days before the advent of the Messiah 'the empire shall fall into heresy', obviously referring to the establishment of the Christian Church as the official religion of the Empire. From this time, Edom, the Rabbinic name for Rome (because Esau was the father of Edom and, possibly, because of the similarity of sound between Edom and Rome), became the name for the Christian Empire and for Christianity in general, as *Ishmael became the name for the Islamic peoples (see ISLAM). The Roman government, while not permitting Jews to win proselytes, took no steps to ban them from doing so. We learn from Jewish and Roman sources that Jews were engaged in missionary activity and this continued, albeit with a far lesser degree of approval, under the Christian emperors (see CONVERSION). The much-discussed verse in Matthew affords clear enough evidence for the pre-Christian period: 'Alas for you, Scribes and Pharisees, you hypocrites! You who travel over sea and land to make a single proselyte, and when you have him you make him twice as fit for hell as you are' (Matthew 23: 15).

Generally on the question of Roman influence on Jewish religious life, it has to be noted that the ubiquitous references in the Rabbinic literature to God as King of the universe owe much to the Roman background. Numerous are the Rabbinic comparisons between the conduct of earthly kings (i.e. the Roman emperors) and the King of the universe. The Rabbis introduced a special *benediction to be recited when beholding a 'Gentile king': 'Blessed art Thou, who hath imparted of Thy glory to Thy creatures.' Nevertheless, the Rabbis warned against attempts to curry favour with the Roman officials. Two statement in Ethics of the Fathers are relevant. The first (1. 10) reads: 'Love work, hate lordship, and seek no intimacy with the ruling power.' The other (2. 3) say: 'Be on your guard against the ruling power; for they who exercise it draw no man near to them except for their own interests; appearing as friends when it is to their own advantage, they stand not by a man in the hour of his need.'

It has to be added, that statements about Jewish attitudes to Roman rule in the Rabbinic literature come from different periods so that it is not historically permissible to speak of any official Jewish attitude. Yet running through all the Rabbinic sources is the ambivalence mentioned above. The Romans are both hated conquerors and brothers; both foes of the Jewish religion and helpful in making Jewish life easier; both immoral idolaters and people of noble bearing from whom Jews could profitably learn regarding the conduct of life. A Midrashic comment (Lamentations Rabbah 2: 13) on the verse (Obadiah 8) which speaks of 'the wise men of Edom' observes: 'Should a person tell you there is wisdom among the nations, believe it. But if he tells you that there is Torah among the nations, do not believe it.'

Gerson D. Cohen, 'Esau as Symbol in Early Medieval Thought', in Alexander Actmann (ed.), *Jewish Medieval and Renaissance Studies* (Cambridge, Mass., 1967), 19–48.

Marcel Simon; *Verus Israel: A Study of the Relations between Christians and Jews in the Roman Empire* (the Littman Library of Jewish Civilization; Oxford, 1968).

**Rosenzweig, Franz**  Influential German Jewish existentialist thinker (1886–1929). Rosenzweig's parents belonged to an assimilated Jewish family with little attachment to Judaism or Jewish life. He himself, although extremely well educated in general German culture and especially proficient in the classics and philosophy, had, at first, hardly any Jewish knowledge. A cousin who had become a Christian urged Rosenzweig to take the same step. The story has often been told of how Rosenzweig felt that if he was to be converted to Christianity he ought to do so as a Jew, moving, as he saw it at the time, from a lower to a higher form of religion. While contemplating his conversion, he attended an Orthodox synagogue in Berlin on *Yom Kippur. There he was so profoundly overcome by the devotion of the worshippers as they sought forgiveness from the God of their fathers that he realized there was no need for him to find his salvation outside his ancestral faith. As he was later to put it, the Christian claim that no man can come to the Father except through Jesus was true for all others but not for the Jew, since Jews, being already with the Father, had no need to Him. Rosenzweig came to adopt the novel view that both Christianity and Judaism were true religions, Christianity for all others, Judaism for the Jews. The critique of this position has often been advanced. If there is room in God's world for these two religions to exist side by side, both as true religions, why should the same not be said of Islam, which is closer to pure monotheism than Christianity? The answer so far as an existentialist (see EXIST-ENTIALISM) like Rosenzweig is concerned, was that Islam was not, for him, in William James's famous phrase, a 'live option'. Rosenzweig's approach was subjective also in connection with the *mitzvot* (see MITZVAH), Jewish observances. He did think that he would one day become a fully observant Jew, but believed in the gradual approach in which the observances slowly made their impact by 'ringing a bell' for him. Typical of this approach is Rosenzweig's answer to someone who asked him whether he wore *tefillin:* 'Not yet,' he replied.

After his awakening, Rosenzweig devoted himself to Jewish studies and in 1920 established in Berlin the Lehrhaus where Jewish teachers of high renown lectured on many aspects of Jewish life and thought. This remarkable institution provided German Jews with opportunities to follow Rosenzweig in the *quest for a Judaism that spoke to their condition and would be authentic for them. Towards the end of his life, Rosenzweig was afflicted with a severe form of paralysis but he continued working and writing heroically; he used a specially constructed typewriter, pointing to its letters with one finger or with his eyes, for his devoted wife to type out. Freud used Rosenzweig's heroic life towards its end as an illustration of the power of the human will to triumph over all the odds.

Rosenzweig's major work, *The Star of Redemption*, was written, in part, on postcards he sent home from the trenches when he was serving in the German army at the end of World War I. In this work, God, the World, and Man are described as interrelated through a process of Creation, Revelation, and Redemption. God created the world and revealed His will for man to find redemption. This theme is represented by two interlocking triangles. At the three points of one triangle, pointing downwards, are Creation, Revelation, and Redemption. At the three points of the other triangle, pointing upwards, are Man, the World, and God. Man relates to the world and through the world to God. God relates to the world through creation and after creation from revelation through to redemption. The two interlocking triangles form the Star of Redemption (see MAGEN DAVID). Rosenzweig claimed to be giving expression to a new (i.e. existentialist) type of thinking. His work therefore, as he himself states, is heavy-going in parts. It is nevertheless seminal for twentieth-century Jews, though hardly to everyone's literary and philosophical taste.

Unlike in the general Jewish tradition, where *redemption is of the Jewish people as a whole, for Rosenzweig redemption means that the individual achieves the purpose for which he has been created. *Revelation, too, is given fresh emphasis by Rosenzweig in accordance with his existentialist philosophy. The Torah is, for Rosenzweig, not a once-and-for-all disclosure of the divine but will but an ongoing process in which the individual Jew finds his meaning in the Torah. Rosenzweig detects this process of discovery and rediscovery in the Torah itself, which is the record of the people of Israel's series of encounters with the divine. Hence Rosenzweig's remark that he is not perturbed by *biblical criticism. Even if the critics are correct that the *Pentateuch is a composite work, stemming from different periods, it was, on any account, finally edited by the Redactor, for whom the critics use the symbol 'R' (Redactor), but which stands, for Rosenzweig, for 'Rabbenu', 'Our Teacher'. The Torah which speaks to the Jewish soul is the Torah which is now in our hands and this is so even if the Masoretic Text (see MASORAH) is not accurate in all its parts and even if the *Samaritans, for example, had the better text. The person or persons who were finally responsible, those who sifted the older material and presented it to us as the Torah in its present form, are our teachers of the living Torah. In this spirit, Rosenzweig made the bold comment that the story of *Balaam's talking donkey is only a fairy-tale during the rest of the year, yet, when it is read as part of the Torah in the synagogue, it is no fairy-tale but the living word of God speaking to His people. This approach to revelation has commended itself to many Jews, anxious to adopt both the critical and the traditional picture of revelation, although Rosenzweig is less than clear on how the transition from Redactor to Rabbenu and from the documentary hypothesis to the living Torah, can successfully be made.

Nahum N. Glatzer, *Franz Rosenzweig: His Life and Thought* (New York, 1953).

Franz Rosenzweig, *The Star of Redemption*, trans. William W. Hallo (London, 1971).

**Rosh Ha-Shanah** 'Head of the year', the New Year festival. This festival is mentioned in the Bible as falling on the first day of the seventh month (counting from the spring month, the month of the Exodus, see CALENDAR) and is described as a day of blowing the horn (Leviticus 23: 23–5; Numbers 19: 1–6), The name Rosh Ha-Shanah stems from Talmudic teachings that on this day all mankind is judged for its fate in the coming year. For this reason the festival is also called: Yom Ha-Din, 'Judgement Day'. The theory has been advanced by some critics (see BIBLICAL CRITICISM) that the festival owes something to ancient Near Eastern agricultural festivals celebrated in the autumn, but this remains conjectural. In the book of *Nehemiah there is a vivid description of the dramatic occasion when the Jews who had returned from the Babylonian captivity renewed their covenant with God (Nehemiah 8: 1–8). Ezra read from the Torah on this first day of the seventh month; the people, conscious of their shortcomings, were distressed at hearing the demands of the law, but Nehemiah reassured them: 'Go your way, eat the fat, and drink the sweet and send portions unto him for whom nothing is prepared; for this day is holy unto our Lord; neither be you grieved for the joy of the Lord is your strength' (Nehemiah 8: 10). Owing to the fact that this festival falls at the beginning of the month and hence depends on the sighting of the moon, there was uncertainty about which day was the day of the festival and Rosh Ha-Shanah is now celebrated on both the first and second days of Tishri, the seventh month. Reform Jews, however, celebrate the festival only on the first day of Tishri. Rosh Ha-Shanah is also called Yom Ha-Zikkaron, 'Remembrance Day', because on this day God remembers His creatures. It is this name by which the festival is called in the liturgy.

Rosh Ha-Shanah is associated with *Yom Kippur which falls on 10 Tishri. Rosh Ha-Shanah and Yom Kippur, because of the judgement theme and the numinous quality of these days, are called 'Days of Awe'. The ten days from Rosh Ha-Shanah to Yom Kippur are the *Ten Days of Penitence, the special penitential season of the year. Rosh Ha-Shanah itself is thus a day of both joy and solemnity, joy in that it is a festival, solemnity in that it is the day of judgement. The themes of God as King and Judge feature prominently in the Rosh Ha-Shanah liturgy. The Musaf ('Additional Prayer') on Rosh Ha-Shanah consists of three groups of scriptural verses and prayers: 1. Malkhuyot ('Sovereignties'), in which God is hailed as King; 2. Zikhronot ('Remembrances') , in which God is said to remember His creatures; 3. Shofarot ('Trumpets'), referring to the blowing of the horn. Among the many interpretations that have been given to these three groups, is that they represent the three basic *principles of the Jewish faith: belief in God, belief in *reward and punishment (God remembers man's deeds), and belief in *revelation (the horn was sounded when the Torah was given at *Sinai; Exodus 19: 16). Another prayer of the day looks forward to the Messianic age (see MESSIAH) when the *Kingdom of Heaven will be established and all wickedness will vanish from the earth. At various stages in the liturgy there are prayers with the entreaty: 'Inscribe us in the Book of Life.' This is based on a Talmudic passage stating that the average person whose fate is in the balance has the opportunity to 'avert the evil decree' by repentance, prayer, and charity. Among the more sophisticated, this is interpreted in terms of self-criticism and the resolve to lead a better life in the year ahead rather than in terms of pleading before an undecided God. Many a Jewish thinker, especially in modern times, has said that the Jew should inscribe *himself* in the Book of Life.

The central feature of Rosh Ha-Shanah is the blowing of the horn, the *shofar*. The nature of the *shofar*, the elaborate rituals, and the numerous interpretations of the rite are discussed at length in the Talmud and the Codes.

It is the custom at the festive meal of Rosh Ha-Shanah to dip bread in honey and to eat other sweet things while praying for 'a good and sweet year'. In many communities the ancient custom of *tashlikh is observed, people going to the seaside or riverside to cast away their sins.

Philip Goodman, *The Rosh Hashanah Anthology* (Philadelphia, 1973).
Louis Jacobs, *A Guide to Rosh Ha-Shanah* (London, 1957).

**Rosh Hodesh** 'Head of month', the first day of the month (see CALENDAR). In Bible times Rosh Hodesh was an important festival, being compared to the Sabbath in a number of passages (2 Kings 4: 23; Isaiah 1: 13; Amos 8: 5), but it is now only a minor festival (see FESTIVALS) on which it is forbidden to fast but on which work is permitted. There is an ancient tradition, however, that women do not work on Rosh Hodesh, perhaps an echo from the biblical period. There is an old Midrashic idea that because women refused to paricipate in the making and worshipping of the *golden calf they were given Rosh Hodesh as a reward for their steadfastness.

**Rossi, Azariah de** Italian scholar, physician, and historian (*c.* 1511–*c.* 1578). Rossi is chiefly renowned for his *Meor Eynayim*, a study of aspects of Jewish *history in which the author, a typical Renaissance man, used Greek and Latin sources in his research. In addition to his numerous references to traditional Jewish literature, Rossi quotes extensively from *Philo, *Josephus, Plato, Cicero, Aquinas, and even the Church Fathers. The work is rightly seen, therefore, as the first attempt by a Jewish scholar to study the Jewish past 'scientifically' by using comparative critical methods, a pioneering effort to write real Jewish *history as distinct from the mere chronologies compiled before Rossi's time. It is no accident that scholars of the *Jüdische Wissenschaft school, such as *Zunz, utilized the *Meor Eynayim* extensively in their objective studies of the Jewish past. Among other original contributions, the work offers a correction of errors in Jewish chronology. Included in the work is a translation into Hebrew of the Latin version of the *Letter of Aristeas*, which tells how the *Septuagint came to be written.

Rossi was also the first Jewish scholar to point out that some statements in the Talmud about historical personages cannot be accepted as factual since they contradict known historical records. For instance, the Talmud (*Gittin* 56b) says that the emperor Titus who destroyed the Temple was punished by a gnat which entered his nose and grew in his head into a bird of brass with claws of iron. We know, Rossi observes, that Titus died a normal death. What the Talmud is saying is that a tiny gnat of remorse pecked away at Titus' conscience because he had destroyed the Temple, growing ever stronger until he could no longer live with his guilt. Rossi, in other words, recognizes that Talmudic and Midrashic legends are just that, legends told not as sober history but as pious tales intended to convey moral lessons. But Rossi goes further, following some earlier teachers who held that while the Talmudic Rabbis are to be accepted as authorities in matters of law and tradition, in scientific and historical matters they had only the scientific and historical knowledge of their day and could have been mistaken in these areas (see AUTHORITY and RABBIS, TALMUDIC). Although Rossi was a strictly observant Jew, his work aroused the ire of the traditionalist Rabbis, who saw his questioning of Talmudic statements as sheer *heresy. The attempt to impose a ban on Rossi's book failed but the result was that the work was largely ignored by learned Jews until the rise of *Jüdische Wissenschaft in the nineteenth century.

Meyer Waxman, 'Azarya De Rossi's Meor Enayim', in his *A History of Jewish Literature* (South Brunswick, NJ, New York, and London, 1960), ii. 516–22.

**Roth, Aaron** Mystical teacher and Hasidic master (1894–1944). Roth was born in Ungvar, Hungary. He studied the Talmud under Rabbi Isaiah Silverstein and Moses Forhand and came under the influence of various Hasidic masters, especially Rabbi Issachar Dov of *Belz and Rabbi Zevi Elimelech of Blazowa. The latter urged Roth to become a Hasidic master himself. A group of young followers gathered around Roth in the town of Beregszasz (Beregovo) and towards the end of his life a similar group was formed around him in Jerusalem. This was a departure in *Hasidism from the principle of hereditary succession. When Roth died the principle was restablished. He was succeeded by his son and son-in-law who were rival candidates for the succession each inherited his own group of Roth's Hasidim. Roth was known as Reb Arele, a diminutive of Aaron, and the followers of this branch are known as Reb Arelich Hasidim, noted for their wild piety and extreme opposition to *Zionism.

Roth's major work, *Shomer Emunim* (*Guardian of Faith*) stresses the supreme value of simple, uncomplicated faith. His *Shulḥan Ha-Tahor* (*The Pure Table*) advises on eating as an act of divine worship. In other works, Roth encourages his followers to engage in ascetic practices, though he stresses that these must not be overdone. Roth also stressed ecstatic prayer in the manner of some of the early Hasidic masters. His *Agitation of the Soul* (printed as a section of the *Shomer Emunim*), is a rare example in Jewish literature of a personal mystical testimony.

Louis Jacobs, 'Aaron Roth's Essay "Agitation of the Soul"' in his *Jewish Mystical Testimonies* (New York, 1977), 245–59.

**Ruth** Biblical heroine whose story is told in the book that bears her name. Ruth's marriage to Boaz, the kinsman of her first husband, is the central theme of the book of Ruth, at the end which King *David's ancestry is traced back to the child born to Ruth and Boaz. In the famous passage in the Talmud on the authorship of the biblical books (*Bava Batra*, 14b) the author of the book of Ruth is said to be the prophet *Samuel. Modern scholarship is generally uncertain about the authorship and the date of the book, some scholars postulating a date as early as the time of David, others as late as the time of *Ezra and *Nehemiah. On this latter theory, the book of Ruth is a gentle protest against Ezra's opposition to intermarriage, Ruth being a Moabite woman. There is no evidence, however, to enable a clear answer to be given on the question of date and authorship. The Rabbis too were puzzled by Ruth's marriage to Boaz. The usual reply is that Ruth was first converted to Judaism and, in fact, Ruth serves in the Rabbinic tradition as the supreme example of the sincere proselyte (see CONVERSION).

Judah J. Slotki, *Ruth*, in A. Cohen (ed.), *The Five Megilloth*, (London, 1952), 35–65.

# S

**Saadiah Gaon** Foremost medieval spiritual leader, Talmudist, biblical exegete, and philosopher (882–942). Saadiah was born in Egypt, and lived for a time in Tiberias, after which he was appointed by the *exilarch, David ben Zakkai, to be the head of the college at Sura in Babylon, hence the title Saadiah Gaon (see *Geonim). But rulers seem to have a habit of falling out with their protégés and David soon deposed Saadiah. The quarrel between the two lasted for seven years, remaining unresolved until Saadiah was reinstated. Saadiah, responding to the *Karaite interest in the Bible, wrote a translation of the Bible into Arabic, in which he displays his virtuosity as a grammarian and philologist as well as his vast knowledge of the Jewish traditional sources. His *Prayer Book was one of the earliest to be compiled and is more comprehensive than those of his very few predecessors. But Saadiah's fame rests on his philosophical work, *Emunot Ve-Deot*, (*Beliefs and Opinions*), written in Arabic and translated into Hebrew by Judah Ibn Tibbon. This work is the first systematic Jewish theology. It has a special significance as a philosophical defence of Rabbinic Judaism by the leading representative of that Judaism of his day.

The 'beliefs' in the title are the postulates of the Jewish religion, while 'opinions' are the truths arrived at by empirical investigation and rational reflection. Saadiah takes issue with those who see philosophy as harmful to faith. On the contrary, faith is strengthened when supported by reason. Influenced strongly by the thought of the Arabic thinkers who sought in similar fashion to reconcile Islam with philosophical enquiry, Saadiah holds that there are two ways to religious truth, reason (see RATIONALISM) and *revelation (of the Torah, for Saadiah). Both ways are essential: reason because without it superstitious ideas will proliferate; revelation because not everyone can arrive at the truth by speculation. Saadiah's famous

illustration is of the man who is told that a heap of coins contains a certain number of coins. He may not have the time to count them and will then have to rely on those who have told him the number of the coins. But, if he counts the coins, he will know how many they are with a certainty he would not otherwise have had. Saadiah thus proceeds to prove by reason the existence of God, relying chiefly on the cosmological proof. The world could not have created itself since it is a logical absurdity for anything to cause itself. God is the uncaused Cause of the universe but His nature is beyond human comprehension. When the Bible speaks of Moses seeing God's glory as it passed by (Exodus 33: 18–23) the reference is not to God Himself but to a special light that became manifest. Even this could be seen by Moses only indirectly so that he could see its 'back', not its 'face' (see REVELATION). God's omnipotence does not embrace the absolutely impossible. Even God cannot cause the world to pass through a signet ring without making either the world smaller or the ring larger. This is not because God's power is in any way limited but because there is no meaning to the statement about a world small enough to pass through a small ring while that world is as large as the world really is. This is akin to asking: 'Can God make a world that is very small and very large at the same time?', which is nonsense.

Among the many ideas of Saadiah discussed at length by later Jewish thinkers are: his rejection of the doctrine of *reincarnation as foreign to Judaism; his belief that the world was created for human benefit (here Maimonides disagrees and holds that God's will and purposes are unknown); and his belief that *animals will be rewarded in the Hereafter (see HEAVEN AND HELL and REWARD AND PUNISHMENT) for having been killed by man in order to obtain his food.

For all his acute reasoning powers, Saadiah is

more of an apologist for traditional Judaism than a pure philosopher starting from scratch. This is true, though to a lesser degree, of Maimonides. Neither Saadiah nor Maimonides entertained any doubts about the complete truth of God's revelation of the Torah, although they both believed that philosophy has an important role to play in so interpreting the Torah that its truths do not run counter to reason.

Henry Malter, *Saadia Gaon: His Life and Works* (Philadelphia, 1942).

Saadiah Gaon, *The Book of Beliefs and Opinions*, trans. Samuel Rosenblatt (New Haven, 1948).

**Sabbath**  The weekly day of rest, Heb. *Shabbat* (from the root *shavat*, 'to rest'), which begins on Friday at sunset and lasts until nightfall on Saturday (in the Jewish *calendar day follows night). The Sabbath is connected with God's creation of the world: 'On the seventh day God finished the work which He had been doing, and He rested on the seventh day from all the work which He had done. and God blessed the seventh day and declared it holy because on it God ceased from all the work of creation which He had done' (Genesis 2: 2–3). Although the actual word *Shabbat* is not used in this narrative the verbal form *shavat* is used to describe God's resting or ceasing from work. The Hebrew text can mean that God created also on the seventh day, which leads to the beautiful Rabbinic idea that rest from work is itself a creation. The command to keep the Sabbath is stated, as the fourth commandment, in both versions of the *Decalogue (Exodus 20: 8–11; Deuteronomy 5: 14–15). In the Exodus version the reason of the creation is given. In the Deuteronomic version a social reason is given, that the purpose of the Sabbath is to provide rest for all, including slaves, who are also entitled to a day of rest. The Israelites who were slaves in Egypt should know how rest from labour is needed both for themselves and for their slaves. In the Sabbath liturgy the Sabbath is said to be both 'a remembrance of the work of creation' and 'a remembrance of the Exodus from Egypt'.

The central theme of the Sabbath is God as the Creator. Man, it is implied, has been given the talent to improve the world which God has created in an unfinished state. The Sabbath provides the Jew with a weekly reminder that his power to control and shape the world is not

his by right but by permission. He is God's steward in the world of which God alone is the Creator who will demand of him an account of his stewardship. That is why, according to thinkers like Samson Raphael *Hirsch, the Rabbis define forbidden 'work' on the Sabbath in terms not of physical effort but of creative activity. To write on the Sabbath, for example, is not forbidden because it involves any severe effort but because writing is a creative act. *Nahmanides, in his commentary to the Decalogue, adds that there is a positive aspect to the Sabbath rest. The command to rest adds an extra dimension to the Sabbath over and above the command to refrain from 'work'. There is a positive demand to keep the day holy, the need to cultivate an atmosphere of spiritual ease and tranquillity. The Sabbath is a day when all human effort comes to a standstill and the Jew, his concerns set aside, basks in the radiance of the divine presence. The Talmudic Rabbis say (*Berakhot* 57b) that the Sabbath bliss is a sixtieth part of the bliss reserved for the righteous in the *World to Come. The Talmud (*Betzah* 16a) also speaks of an additional soul that is given to the Jew for the duration of the Sabbath. While *Rashi understands this, in a down-to-earth manner, as an extra capacity to enjoy good food and wine, the mystics understand it literally, that the Jew has an additional soul by means of which he attains to a deeper awareness of the spiritual side of existence. A Hasidic legend tells of a Hasidic master that he would grow a head taller on the Sabbath. Throughout the history of Jewish thought, the dual aspects of the Sabbath are stressed. On the one hand, there is the idea of the Sabbath as a day of spiritual refreshment and the acknowledgement of God as the Creator but, on the other hand, there is the idea of Sabbath delight (based on Isaiah 58: 13), understood by the Rabbis to mean wearing fine clothes and enjoying the choice fare provided at the Sabbath table. The needs of the body have to be satisfied, not only those of the soul. While the pseudepigraphic book of Jubilees (50: 8), compiled at the end of the Second Temple period, prohibits marital relations on the Sabbath (as a creative act), the Rabbis not only permit this but consider it especially meritorious on the sacred day. The Sabbath is also a day when there is leisure for the study of the Torah and for prayer and worship. Synagogue services are lengthier than on other occasions, though the mood of these services is one of praise and thanksgiving rather than of supplication.

## Sabbath Laws and Rituals

At least two candles are kindled before the advent of the Sabbath. Originally the Rabbinic rules of the Sabbath lamp were intended for the purpose of having a well-lit home in order to further what the Rabbis call: 'peace in the home', that is, the avoidance of the strife and contention in the family that might easily result from meals being partaken of in a dark room. Probably in reaction to the *Karaites, who forbade the burning of lamps on the Sabbath even if kindled before the Sabbath, the Rabbinic authorities in the Middle Ages introduced this practice of kindling two special lights even if the room is otherwise well lit. The kindling of the Sabbath candles is usually performed by the mother of the family, who offers a silent prayer for the well-being of her husband and children. The practice of waving the hands to and fro in front of the candles probably represents the summoning of the spiritual light of the Sabbath into the home.

Before the Sabbath meal on Friday night and Saturday morning, the *Kiddush is recited over a cup of wine, in which God is praised and thanked for giving the Sabbath to His people. At the termination of the Sabbath, the *Havdalah is recited over a cup of wine and God is praised for distinguishing between the Sabbath and the weekdays. According to the Rabbis, three meals have to be partaken of on the Sabbath, one more than the usual two meals a day in Rabbinic times. At these meals special songs (*Zemirot) are sung to joyous melodies. The *reading of the Torah on the Sabbath is from the portion of the week together with special readings on particular Sabbaths. The liturgy has a number of special references to the Sabbath. Indicative of attitudes to the Sabbath and of the fact that it was observed even as early as the *patriarchs is the passage in the Sabbath afternoon service:

'Thou art One and thy name is One, and who is like thy people Israel, an unique nation on the earth? Glorious greatness and a crown of salvation, even the day of rest and holiness, thou hast given unto thy people:—Abraham was glad, Isaac rejoiced, Jacob and his sons rested thereon:—a rest granted in generous love, a true and faithful rest, a rest in peace and tranquillity, in quietude and safety, a perfect rest wherein thou delightest. Let thy children perceive and know that this their rest is from thee, and by their rest may they hallow thy name.'

According to the *Halakhah, Jews are not permitted to discuss their business affairs on the Sabbath; they must not handle money; they must not carry anything in the street (but see ERUV); they must not ride in an automobile, even if driven by a non-Jew, and they do not switch on electric lights or use any electrical appliances (see ELECTRICITY). Since cooking food is forbidden on the Sabbath, food is cooked before the Sabbath and kept hot on the stove until it is required. Similarly, it is permitted to have a time-switch fixed to the electric lights before the Sabbath so that they go on and off when required. All these rules have been seen as bothersome to critics of Orthodoxy but, for the Orthodox Jew, they are not seen as a burden at all but as providing welcome opportunities of doing God's will and cultivating the special Sabbath atmosphere through which their lives are elevated far above the mundane. Reform Jews seek to preserve the Sabbath as the holy day while remaining largely indifferent to the precise rules and regulations. Conservative Jews accept the provisions of the Halakhah with regard to the Sabbath, as they do with regard to the Halakhah generally. But many, perhaps the majority, of Conservative Rabbis favour a more lenient interpretation of the Sabbath laws so as to permit, for example, the switching-on of electric lights and riding in a car to the synagogue where this is not within walking distance of home.

## The Sabbath in the Kabbalah

The Sabbath represents in the Kabbalah the male and female principles in the Godhead which are united on this day as on no other other (see SEFIROT). As a result of this union on high, lofty souls descend to occupy the bodies of children conceived on the holy day, which is why, for the Kabbalists, there is an additional reason for husband and wife to make love on Friday night. The Talmud (*Shabbat* 119a) tells of a Rabbi who would go out to welcome the Sabbath, saying: 'Come O Bride; come O Bride', the Sabbath being described as Israel's 'bride' in the Talmud and the Midrash. But in the Kabbalah, the 'Bride' is the *Shekhinah, the female principle, represented by the Sabbath, who is the 'bride' of the male principle.

The mystics of Safed in the sixteenth century used to dress all in white and go out into the fields to welcome Bride Sabbath. The hymn *'Lekhah Dodi', composed for this purpose, is now universally recited at the beginning of the Friday-night service. The 'woman of worth' of Proverbs (31: 10–31) is identified by the Kabbalists with the Shekhinah and this passage is now recited by the man of the house when he comes home from the synagogue, quite unaware of the original application and thinking of his own wife as the woman of worth. Also derived from the influence of the Safed Kabbalists is the recitation at each of the three meals of a hymn in Aramaic referring to the particular aspect of the Godhead which presides, so to speak, over that meal. In Hasidism the Sabbath meal is often partaken of by the Hasidim in the presence of the *Zaddik, who distributes to his followers portions of the various dishes from which he has tasted. The mystic mood is especially pervasive at the third meal on Sabbath afternoon. The Hasidim sit in the semi-gloom to listen intently to the 'Torah' of the Zaddik, his original thoughts on the Torah believed to be communicated to him by the *Shekhinah. Although the Mishnah forbids dancing and clapping the hands on the Sabbath, the Hasidim rely on those medieval authorities who hold that this law no longer applies and the sacred dance is a regular feature of Hasidic life on the Sabbath. Hasidim immerse themselves in a *mikveh before the Sabbath to purify themselves from all mundane thoughts. Hasidim also have a special meal, referred to in a Talmudic passage, after the Sabbath has ended, to escort the Sabbath on its departure. It is the practice at this meal for the Hasidim to relate tales of the great Hasidic masters of former times.

Elliot K. Ginsburg, *The Sabbath in the Classical Kabbalah* (Albany, NY, 1989).

Solomon Goldman, *Guide to the Sabbath* (London, 1961).

Abraham E. Millgram, *Sabbath: The Day of Delight* (Philadelphia, 1944).

Chaim Raphael, *The Sabbath Evening Service* (New York, 1985).

**Sabbatical Year** The seventh year, during which the fields were to be left fallow (Leviticus 25: 1–7) and debts released (Deuteronomy 15: 1–11); Heb. *Shemittah* ('Release'). The seven years are counted in the cycle of fifty culminating in the *Jubilee and are known by tradition. The year 2000/1, for instance, will be a Sabbatical year. In order to avoid the cancellation of all debts, a serious hardship in our commercial society, the device was introduced even in Talmudic times of handing the debts over before the end of the Sabbatical year, to a temporary court consisting of three persons, the debts then being considered to have been paid to the court beforehand. The problem of agricultural work in the Sabbatical year did not arise in modern times until, under the impact of *Zionism, colonies were established in Palestine; it is a severe difficulty now that the State of Israel has been established. The more Orthodox do observe the laws of the Sabbatical year, using only agricultural products bought from Arabs. But other Orthodox Rabbis have tried to find a dispensation by noting that according to many authorities the Sabbatical year is, like the Jubilee year, binding by biblical law only when the majority of Jews live in the land of Israel. (These laws do not apply to Jewish-owned farms outside Israel.) The laws are now Rabbinic, so that it is easier to find a dispensation. Moreover, there is considerable doubt whether the present identification of Sabbatical years is correct and whether the count begins again on the Jubilee year, the fiftieth, or on the next year, the fifty-first after the previous cycle. Because of all this and the great difficulty in keeping the law, the official Rabbinate in Israel adopts the legal fiction of selling the land to a Gentile on the analogy of the sale of leaven before Passover (see HAMETZ). Many have felt, however, that, while legal fictions have their place in Jewish law, it seems more than a little absurd to effect a merely formal sale of all Jewish land to a Gentile. Some religious kibbutzim resort to the new scientific method of hydroponics to avoid the prohibition and they donate a share of their proceeds during the Sabbatical year to charity. In any event, non-agricultural work is allowed in the Sabbatical year, which is called 'the Sabbath of the land'.

**Sacrifices** Animal sacrifices are described in detail in the book of Leviticus and were offered throughout the period of the First and Second Temples. That Gentiles as well as Jews brought sacrifices to the Temple is implied in the prayer of Solomon when he dedicated the Temple (1 Kings 8: 41–3) and in the declaration by the prophet that the Temple will be a house of prayer for all peoples (Isaiah 56: 7). The Rabbis say (*Ḥullin* 13b): 'Sacrifices are to be accepted from Gentiles as they are from Jews', although this saying dates from after the destruction of the Temple. The significance of the role of the sacrifice in the Temple period is expressed in the saying in Ethics of the Fathers (1. 3) that the world stands on three things, the Torah, the service in the Temple, and benevolence. That occasionally the prophets seem to decry the offering of sacrifices (e.g. Amos 5: 21–4; Isaiah 1: 11–13) is explained in the Jewish tradition, and this might well be the case, that the prophets only object to sacrifices used as an attempt to buy off God while practising iniquities. The ancients did not have the scruples of many moderns about offering up 'poor defenceless animals'. People did and still do kill animals for food and, apart from the wholly consumed burnt-offering, the meat of all the other sacrifices was eaten either by the priests or by those who brought the sacrifices. The whole of the Order Kodashim in the Mishnah is devoted almost entirely to the details of how the sacrifices were to be offered. This order was compiled in its present form after the destruction of the Temple but a good deal of the material undoubtedly stems from traditions in Temple times. The order was studied, even though the laws of sacrifices had fallen into abeyance, in the belief that these were all part of the divinely revealed Torah and that the sacrificial system would one day be restored.

Various explanations have been advanced in medieval and modern times for why God commanded that sacrifices be offered to Him. This kind of thinking was unknown to the Talmudic Rabbis. For them it was enough that God had ordained that sacrifices should be offered and they saw no need to ask why. But from the Middle Ages onwards, attempts were made to provide what seemed to be to those who made them plausible reasons for the sacrificial cult. According to Maimonides, in his *Guide of the Perplexed*, the sacrifices were ordained in order to wean the people of Israel away from idolatry, as if God were to say: if the idea of offering sacrifices has taken too strong a hold on you to be totally eradicated, at least offer the sacrifices in a central place and observe the rules in order to avoid the excesses practised by the idolaters when they sacrifice to their gods. *Nahmanides cannot accept such a facile view and Maimonides himself, in his Code, records all the laws of sacrifices and prayers for their restoration, which

hardly suggests that the sacrifices were, for him, no more than an emergency measure. For *Ibn Ezra and Nahmanides the sacrifices are symbolic. When a man offered a guilt-offering, for example, the killing of the animal and the offering of its blood and fat on the altar were a symbolic way of saying that this should have been the fate of the sinner were it not for God's mercy. A further reason advanced for the system is that the meat of the sacrifices was to be eaten in a holy place, the Temple for some sacrifices, anywhere in Jerusalem for others, and this turned the very act of eating into a sacred act by which man is brought nearer to God. In the Kabbalah, animal sacrifices provided the link between the animal world and human beings and between the world of human beings and the higher realms of the *Sefirot as the smoke on the altar ascended.

Although, in the nineteenth century, suggestions were put forward for the Temple to be rebuilt and sacrifices offered there once again, these were not taken seriously since, among other objections, the actual site of the altar is now unknown; corpse contamination cannot now be removed in the absence of the *red heifer; and there are no means of establishing the claim of the *priests that they really are such (see KOHEN). Thus the restoration of the sacrificial system was left to the *Messiah. There was even an opinion in the Middle Ages, quoted by *Rashi, that the Third Temple would drop ready-made from heaven. The Orthodox position today is that the offering of sacrifices will be carried out only when the Messianic age dawns and their restoration is not a matter of practical concern in the here and now, although there is a *Yeshivah in Jerusalem in which the Order of Kodashim is studied assiduously so that scholars will be able to advise on how the sacrifices are to be offered when the Messiah does come.

*Prayers for the Restoration of Sacrifices*

After the destruction of the Temple the verse 'we will render the bullocks of our lips' (Hosea 14: 3) was understood to mean that the repetition of the details of the sacrificial cult in prayer and the prayers for its restoration are accounted as if the sacrifices were actually offered in the Temple. But the prayers were not seen as a mere formality to make up for the loss. The belief remains strong in Orthodoxy that these prayers will be answered by God and the sacrifices restored. Prayers for the restoration of the sacrifices are scattered through the traditional liturgy. Especially in the Additional service, Musaf, on Sabbaths and festivals, the prayer is recited for Israel to be restored to its homeland, the Temple to be rebuilt, and the sacrifices offered. Reform Judaism, in the last century, reinterpreted the Messianic hope in universalistic terms and rejected not only prayers for the restoration of sacrifices but the whole idea of Israel's return to its homeland. While Reform Judaism today has a much more positive attitude to the return, the Reform attitude is still too universalistic to permit references to the old sacrificial system in prayer. Sacrifices were, indeed, once highly significant but they have now been superseded under divine guidance. Conservative Judaism, on the other hand, believes that to delete from the *Prayer Book all references to the sacrifices is to ignore the significant role the sacrifices played in Jewish history. And yet, since many Jews do not believe that the sacrificial system will one day be restored, to pray for its restoration is to engage in double-think. To cope with this problem, the Conservative Prayer Book retains the references to the system but substitutes for the words 'and there we will offer' the words: 'and there our forefathers offered'.

J. H. Hertz, 'The Sacrificial Cult', in his *The Pentateuch and Haftorahs* (London, 1960).

Baruch A. Levine, 'Leviticus in the Ongoing Jewish Tradition', in Nahum M. Sarna (ed.), *The JPS Torah Commentary: Leviticus* (Philadelphia, New York, and Jerusalem, 1989), 215–38.

**Sadducees** Heb. *Tzaddukim*, one of three main parties in the late Second Temple period, the others being the *Pharisees and the *Essenes. The Mishnah and *Josephus record the differences between the Sadducees and the Pharisees. From all accounts it would appear that the members of the Sadducean party were the aristocratic priests and the wealthy landowners. The meaning of the word *Tzaddukim* is uncertain. In the Talmud the Sadducees are said to be followers of a certain Zadok who rejected, as did the Sadducees according to both the Mishnah and Josephus, belief in the *World to Come. Modern scholarship suggests that the Sadducees were descended from Zadok, the priest who lived in the time of King David (1 Kings 1). The prophet Ezekiel declares that only the priests who are the sons of Zadok will be worthy to serve in the Temple (Ezekiel 44:

15–16) and it is plausible to suggest that the Sadducees identified themselves with this family of priests. With the victory of the Pharisees the Sadducean party vanished from the Jewish scene but some of their ideas enjoyed a subterranean existence until they resurfaced among the *Karaites.

**Safed** City in Upper Galilee. The economic life of Safed was strengthened by the influx of Jewish immigrants after the expulsion from Spain in 1492. Perhaps because of its elevation, nearly 3,000 feet above sea-level, its wide panoramic views, and its pure air, Safed was considered to be one of the four holy cities in the land of Israel, the others being Jerusalem, Hebron, and Tiberias. In the sixteenth century Safed was the home of some of the great luminaries in Jewish spiritual history, among them Joseph *Karo, Moses *Cordovero, and Isaac *Luria. All three are buried in Safed and their graves are still visited in *pilgrimage. The circle of Kabbalists in Safed pursued a mystic and ascetic way of life that became a model for later Jewish pietists. In modern Israel an artists' colony has been established in Safed.

Solomon Schechter, 'Safed in the Sixteenth Century: A City of Legalists and Mystics', in his *Studies in Judaism* (second series; Philadelphia, 1965), ii. 202–306.

**Saints** Like other religions, Judaism knows of individuals noted for their extraordinary piety and goodness. The usual term for this kind of individual is *hasid*, probably from a root meaning of 'abundance', that is, the *love of God and humanity of such intensity that it is almost about to burst its bonds. The Hasid is perceived as an identifiable type in the Bible, the Rabbinic literature and through to the *hasidey Ashkenaz*, 'the *Saints of Germany' and the followers of the *Baal Shem Tov, known as the Hasidim (see HASIDISM). The term *tzaddik* is often used in the earlier literature to denote simply a good man (see RIGHTEOUSNESS) but is also used to denote the especially saintly individual (see LAMEDVOVNIKS). This is not to say that there is anything in Judaism like the Catholic idea of official acknowledgement of people as 'saints' and there is nothing like the Catholic process of canonization. What happens in Judaism is that certain persons renowned for their holy life are afforded the title Hasid by a kind of consensus of the faithful.

The abstract noun *hasidut* is used, from

Rabbinic times onwards, for the quality of saintliness. In the Talmudic path to perfection, for example, attributed to the second-century teacher, Rabbi Phinehas ben Yair (*Avodah Zarah* 20b), the steps on the path are stated: 'Knowledge of the Torah leads to watchfulness, watchfulness to zeal, zeal to cleanness, cleanness to abstinence, abstinence to purity, purity to holiness, holiness to humility, humility to the fear of sin, the fear of sin to saintliness [*hasidut*], saintliness to the [attainment of] the *holy spirit, and the holy spirit to the *resurrection of the dead.' The Talmud adds that saintliness is greater than any of these since Scripture says: 'Then Thou didst speak in vision to Thy saintly ones' (Psalms 99: 20).

Yet admiration for the saint is often qualified when the saintly ideal comes into conflict with the obligation to *study the Torah. The saying attributed to *Hillel in Ethics of the Fathers (2. 9) that an ignorant man, *am ha-aretz, cannot be a Hasid may reflect the tension that existed in all periods between the scholarly and the saintly personality. The charisma of the saint was not to be a substitute for profound knowledge of the Torah. This is put almost aggressively in the Rabbinic saying (*Shabbat* 63a): 'Even if a scholar is vengeful and bears malice like a serpent, gird him on thy loins; whereas even if an ignorant man [*am ha-aretz*] is a saint, do not dwell in his vicinity.' There are many references in the Rabbinic literature to men of extreme piety, such as Honi the Circle-Drawer, Haninah ben Dosa, Abba Hilkia, and Amram Hasida, who were renowned for their saintliness but not for their learning and never as teachers of the *Halakhah. It is clear beyond doubt that while such men were held in high esteem, the scholar was held to be superior to them. In a Talmudic anecdote (*Berakhot* 34b) when Rabban *Johanan ben Zakkai's son was sick, the sage sent to Rabbi Haninah ben Dosa for him to pray for the son's recovery. When Rabban Johanan ben Zakkai's wife asked him: 'Is Haninah greater than you?' the sage replied: 'No he is not. But I am like a prince in the presence of the king, while Haninah is like a slave in the presence of the king.' A prince can only enter into the king's presence when protocol permits it, whereas the slave can enter to perform his duties whenever it is necessary. Part of the opposition to Hasidism by the *Mitnaggedim was caused by what the latter saw as a neglect of learning by the Hasidim in

favour of the Hasidic ideal of attachment to God, *devekut. Of course, too categorical a distinction between scholar and saint was avoided. A number of distinguished scholars were renowned as saints, *Cordovero and *Elijah, Gaon of Vilna to name only two, and the saintliness of many tended to obscure their considerable scholarship.

Generally speaking, Judaism discourages overt attempts to achieve sainthood. For one thing, it is appreciated that any conscious striving for the saintly ideal is self-defeating since humility is an essential ingredient of the saintly life. For all that, a number of works were composed with the express intention of mapping out the saintly path, among them: *Bahya Ibn Pakudah's *Duties of the Heart*, the Sefer *Ḥasidim*; *Cordovero's *Palm Tree of Deborah; Reshit Ḥokhmah (Beginning of Wisdom)* by Cordovero's disciple, Eijah de Vidas; Hayyim *Vital's *Shaarey Kedushah (Gates of Holiness)*; and Luzzatto's *Path of the Upright*. The majority of the Hasidic classics, while addressed to the ordinary Hasid as well, in their higher reaches were obviously intended as manuals of direction for the would-be saint. A number of the Hasidic masters drew up for themselves and their followers lists of saintly rules, making far more severe demands than those found in the standard works of Jewish law and ritual.

William James, in the chapters on 'Saintliness' in his *The Varieties of Religious Experience*, gives examples of the extravagant behaviour of some of the Christian saints. It is a gross error to view Judaism as too rational to tolerate such excesses, too 'sane' to permit its adherents to be 'fools of God'. In the literature of Jewish piety there are enough examples of extreme, not to say bizarre, conduct on the part of the saints. The Saints of Germany would engage in severe mortification of the flesh, rolling naked in snow and ice in winter and smeared with honey to be stung by the bees in summer. A number of the Jewish saints were fond of meditating, whenever they recited the Shema, on the theme of *martyrdom, allowing their minds to dwell on the tortures they would suffer rather than be faithless to God and His Torah. They would reflect in gruesome detail on the cruel fate that awaited them. The Hasidic master Aaron *Roth practised and urged his followers to practise various forms of self-torment including flagellation (albeit with a 'small strap') and refraining from ever scratching an itch.

In short, practically everything said of the saints of Christianity and Islam can be paralleled in Judaism. Miracle tales about the saints abound; there are descriptions of saintly rapture, levitation, and visitations after death; and *pilgrimages take place to the graves of the saints. The major difference between attitudes in Judaism and those of other religions is in the matter of saintliness versus learning, mentioned above. Prayers to the saints are naturally frowned upon in Judaism but the majority of the Rabbis did not object to requesting a dead saint to pray on one's behalf.

Louis Jacobs, *Holy Living: Saints and Saintliness in Judaism* (Northvale, NJ, and London, 1990).

## Saints of Germany

**Saints of Germany** Heb. *Ḥasidey Ashkenaz*, a group of pietists in twelfth- and thirteenth-century Germany. The German Saints were not organized as a movement but 'flourished as individual followers of a particular saintly path in the towns of Regensburg, Speyer, Worms, and Mayyence. The main leaders of this tendency were Samuel He-Hasid (second half of the twelfth century); his son, Judah He-Hasid (d. 1217); and Judah's disciple, Eleazar of Worms (d. *c.*1230). The major works produced in this circle are the *Sefer Ḥasidim* and the *Rokeaḥ.* of Eleazar of Worms. In these works the novel ideas of the group, influenced to some extent by the Christian monasticism of the period, are given expression. Naturally in the period of the Crusades, there is particular emphasis on *martyrdom for the sanctification of God's name. The Hasidim were ready at all times to suffer martyrdom if need be (see HASIDISM). Repentance for these Saints was not reserved for extreme sinners but was an essential ingredient in the life of piety. The Saints were ever conscious of their sinfulness and engaged in self-mortification both as a penance and as a means of overcoming the temptations of the flesh. The Hasid was expected to be exceedingly generous in relieving the fate of the poor. *Confession of sin, usually in Judaism a purely private matter between the individual and his God, was made to a spiritual mentor who advised the 'sinner' on how to rectify his faults. The tension between saintliness and learning (see SAINTS) is particularly evident among the *Ḥasidey Ashkenaz*. Many of these men were learned in the Torah but the ideal of saintliness in the circle was quite independent of learning. It was possible for a simple Jew,

with only a bare knowledge of the Bible, let alone the Talmud, to become a Hasid. The influence of the Christian background on the Hasidim is evident too in the superstitions (see MAGIC AND SUPERSTITION) referred to in the works of the *Ḥasidey Ashkenaz*. In their whole activity there is to be observed a remarkable blend of popular religion and mystical thought of the highest order.

Gershom G. Scholem, 'Hasidism in Mediaeval Germany', in his *Major Trends in Jewish Mysticism* (London, 1955), 80–118.

**Salanter, Israel** Lithuanian Talmudist and religious thinker (1810–83), founder of the *Musar movement. Israel's family name was Lipkin, but he is known as Israel Salanter after the town of Salant in which he grew up and where he studied to become an outstanding Talmudic scholar (although he sought, wherever possible, to conceal his great learning). A gifted teacher, he encouraged his disciples not to rely on him but to work things out for themselves. He once said that both the Hasidim and the *Mitnaggedim are in error: the Mitnaggedim in that they believe they have no need for a Rebbe, the Hasidim in that they believe they have a *Rebbe. He was admired by the Hasidim, who used to say that the Mitnaggedim had a Rebbe in Israel Salanter but failed to make the most of him. The picture that emerges from the accounts of Salanter's life is one of a severely introspective personality, torn between a realization of his unworthiness and the compelling need to teach others how to strive for self-improvement. Rabbi E. E. *Dessler, Salanter's great-grandson, reported that Salanter took literally the Talmudic injunction that a man has to get drunk on *Purim. In his cups Salanter could be heard saying to himself: 'If you have a mind capable of turning its thoughts this way and that, consider how tremendous is your responsibility.'

In his youth, Salanter came under the influence of Reb Zundel of Salant, from whom he obtained his particular stance, according to which mere mechanical performance of the precepts was totally inadequate to promote the good life as required by the Torah. Anticipating to some extent Freud's ideas about the unconscious mind, Salanter believed that the only way to self-improvement was to penetrate the deeper recesses of the personality by which human beings are motivated. Salanter stressed particularly the ethical demands of the Torah. A favourite saying of his was that one must not be frum ('pious') by standing on another's shoulders (i.e. by overriding the feelings of other people in the pursuit of godliness). It is said that he once met a pious Jew during the penitential period. This man was so engrossed in sombre reflection that he failed to greet Salanter, whereupon Salanter protested: 'Because you are so pious does this give you the right to deny me my "Good morning"?'

Salanter occupied no official Rabbinic position but served as Rosh *Yeshivah ('Head of a Yeshivah') in a number of places, including the town of Kovno where he established a Yeshivah in the spirit of Musar. It appears that Salanter did not originally intend that his Musar approach should be élitist but that it should promote greater inwardness in the lives of Jewish artisans and businessmen. However, eventually Salanter's ideas were appreciated only by Yeshivah students, and Salanter's disciples, encouraged by him, established Musar Yeshivot of their own. At first there was determined opposition by traditional Rabbis to the introduction of Musar into the Yeshivah curriculum. The Torah itself, these Rabbis argued, was balm for the soul and there was no need to supplement study of the Torah with Musar. But Salanter's ideas prevailed, so that the majority of the Lithuanian-type Yeshivot became Musar Yeshivot.

Salanter travelled to Germany and to Paris in order to increase awareness of traditional Judaism among German and French Jews. At one time he had the novel idea of translating the Talmud into German and wished to see the Talmud occupying an honoured place in Semitic studies at European universities. Towards the end of his life Salanter resided in Königsberg. Typical of his approach is the story told of his last moments in Königsberg. The community had arranged for a retainer to stay with him and Salanter, realizing that his death was nigh and that the retainer was terrified at the prospect of being left alone with a dead body, instead of spending the precious moments left to him in reflection on his end, devoted himself to reassuring the man that there is nothing to fear from a lifeless corpse. Salanter's biographers have noted that he had a morbid fear of fire. It is said that in order to remind himself of the terrors of *Gehinnom he would put his little finger into the flame of a candle and say: 'You see it hurts to be burned.' As Salanter himself would have said, every man has a darker side to his personality. Salanter remains one of the great spiritual figures of Lithuanian, and world, Jewry.

Hillel Goldberg, *Israel Salanter: Text Studies Ideas. The Ethics and Theology of an Early Psychologist of the Unconscious* (New York, 1982).

**Samaritans** The descendants of the people settled in Samaria, in the Northern Kingdom, after the ten tribes had been deported by the king of Assyria in 722 BCE. The verse in the book of 2 Kings (17: 24) states: 'The king of Assyria brought [people] from Babylon, Cuthah, Avva, Hamath and Sepharvim, and he settled them in the towns of Samaria in place of the Israelites; they took possession of Samaria and dwelt in its towns.' The passage continues that these foreign peoples worshipped their own gods but God let loose lions among them, as result of which the king of Assyria ordered a priest to be sent to teach them the worship of the true God. After the name Cuthah, one of the places from which these people came, the Samaritans are called Cuthim (*Kutim*) in the Rabbinic sources. The Rabbis understood the story in the book of Kings to mean that the Cuthim were eventually converted to Judaism, the only question being whether they were true converts or only 'lion converts', that is, never really converted to the true faith but only pretending to have been converted out of their fear of the lions. The conclusion in the Talmud is that their descendants are fully Jewish even though they do not keep all the precepts. Nevertheless, according to the Talmud (*Hullin* 6a), Rabbi Meir, hearing that some Samaritans had worshipped a dove on Mount Gerizim, declared that all Samaritans must henceforth be treated as if they were idolaters. The story of the dove is, of course, legendary. The Samaritans were monotheists and worshipped God on Mount Gerizim. Behind all this are echoes of the conflict in ancient times between the Samaritans and the Jews, the Samaritans claiming, in fact, that they were the descendants of the ancient Israelites and that the story in the book of Kings is a false account of their origins. The book of Nehemiah (ch. 4) relates how the Samaritans sought to prevent the Jews rebuilding Jerusalem after the return from the Babylonian exile.

For the Samaritans the central holy place is

not Jerusalem but Mount Gerizim in Samaria. For them, too, only the *Pentateuch, of which they have their own version, is sacred and they reject the prophetic and the other books of the Bible. The Samaritan Pentateuch differs considerably in some matters from the Masoretic Text (see MASORAH). For instance, the Samaritan *Decalogue has, as the tenth commandment, to locate the altar to God on Mount Gerizim. Modern biblical scholars use the Samaritan Pentateuch with caution to help establish the correct text (see BIBLICAL CRITICISM). The Samaritan calendar differs from the Jewish calendar with regard to the dates of the festivals.

There are at the time of writing around 500 Samaritans in the State of Israel. The Samaritans still offer the Paschal lamb on Mount Gerizim and this is now a tourist attraction. The Israeli Rabbinate is opposed to marriages between Jews and Samaritans. The Samaritans do recognize the validity of a marriages between a Samaritan man and a Jewish woman provided that she agrees to follow the Samaritan traditions. The marriage certificate issued for this purpose by the Samaritan priest is recognized by the Israeli minister of the interior.

James B. Montgomery, *The Samaritans, The Earliest Jewish Sect: Their History, Theology and Literature* (New York, 1968).

**Samuel** Prophet in the eleventh century BCE who anointed Saul as king and, when God rejected Saul, anointed *David. According to the famous Talmudic passage (*Bava Batra* 14b) on the authorship of the biblical books, the book of Samuel was written by Samuel himself up to the account of his death, and was completed by others. Modern scholarship views the book as a later work in which the author used oral traditions and written chronicles. In the Jewish tradition there is only a single book of Samuel. The division into two books, 1 and 2 Samuel is based on Christian versions of the *Bible, though it has come to be accepted by Jews when quoting the Bible. Legend locates the burial place of the prophet in the Arab village, near Jerusalem, called Nebi Samwil.

S. R. Driver, *Notes on the Hebrew Text of the Books of Samuel* (Oxford, 1890).
Solomon Goldman, *Samuel* (London, 1951).

**Sanhedrin** From the Greek *sunedrion* ('sitting in counsel'), the supreme court composed of seventy (or seventy-one) members which sat in the 'chamber of hewn stone' in Jerusalem until the destruction of the Temple in 70 CE, after which it was located in various other cities. Such is the picture of the Sanhedrin which emerges from the Mishnah, tractate *Sanhedrin*, and other Rabbinic sources. The references to the Sanhedrin in the *New Testament present a different picture. Here the High Priest, in his palace, presides over the Sanhedrin (e.g. in the trial of Jesus (Matthew 26: 57–68)), rather than a Nasi ('Prince') as in the Rabbinic sources. The older view among Christian scholars was that the New Testament account is correct and that of the Mishnah incorrect. Among Jewish scholars the opposite was said to be true: the Mishnaic account is the reliable one, the Christian account has bees altered for doctrinal purposes. Some later Jewish scholars suggested that there were two Sanhedrins: one a political body, a kind of parliament, the other a body to decide matters of Jewish law. This suggestion is now seen to be untenable. Both sources no doubt preserve ancient traditions of a supreme legislative assembly that existed in former times but each has read ideas of its own into the ancient institution. When the Roman government abolished the office of Nasi, the Sanhedrin came to an end. There was no longer any central *authority for Jews, although the Babylonian *Geonim did enjoy a measure of authority for Jews in other parts of the world. In any event, the Sanhedrin plays no role in later Jewish life. The attempt, soon after the establishment of the State of Israel, to revive the Sanhedrin for the purpose of introducing new legislation was doomed from the outset. There were those who held that Jewish law changes automatically whenever the need arises and those who denied that Jewish law can be changed even by a Sanhedrin. Both succeeded in quashing the idea that the Sanhedrin be revived. Nowadays, it was seen, a Sanhedrin would either be superfluous or ineffective.

Sidney B. Hoenig, *The Great Sanhedrin* (New York, 1953).
Hugo Mantel, *Studies in the History of the Sanhedrin* (Cambridge, Mass., 1961).

**Sarah** Wife of Abraham and mother of Isaac, the first of the four *matriarchs. In Rabbinic legend, Sarah was one of the most beautiful women who ever lived and she had a greater degree of prophetic insight even than her husband. The story of Sarah is told in the book of

Genesis (11: 29–23: 20). Abraham purchased the *Cave of Machpelah from Ephron the Hittite as a burial place for Sarah (Genesis 23) and Abraham himself was buried there by his sons.

**Satan**  The Devil, the prosecuting angel. The word Satan simply means an 'adversary' and is used in the Bible of any opponent or enemy, the root meaning of the word being 'to oppose', with no supernatural overtones. In the opening chapters of the book of Job, however, 'the Satan' (with the definite article, so the meaning is 'the Adversary' and Satan here is not a proper name) is an angel who appears in the council of the angels in order to challenge God to put Job to the test. Similarly, in the book of Zechariah (3: 1–2) the angel whom God rebukes for his evil designs upon Jerusalem is 'the Satan'. In the book of 1 Chronicles (21: 1) 'Satan' (without the definite article) is used as a proper name. Interestingly, in the parallel story in the book of Samuel (2 Samuel 24: 1) it is God, not Satan, who entices David to count the people. The later book of Chronicles, reluctant to ascribe the temptation to God, substitutes Satan. In subsequent Jewish literature Satan is the personification of both a demonic power outside man and the urge to do evil in the human psyche. Very revealing of the demythologizing tendency in Rabbinic thought is the saying (*Bava Batra* 16a) that Satan, the *yetzer ha-ra* ('evil inclination', see YETZER HA-TOV AND YETZER HA-RA) and the Angel of Death are one and the same. Maimonides (*Guide of the perplexed*, 3. 22) praises highly this saying as indicative of what he considers to be the only possible way of understanding the figure of Satan. Maimonides is hardly correct in this, so far as the Rabbis are concerned, since many other passages in Rabbinic literature do conceive of Satan as a supernatural figure who hates the Jews and brings their faults before the heavenly throne. This is certainly how Satan is depicted in Jewish folklore in which numerous superstitious practices are based on belief in Satan and his demonic hosts bent on doing harm (see LILITH and MAGIC AND SUPERSTITION). On the whole, it can be said that the figure of Satan does not occupy any prominent role in Jewish theology, though it would be incorrect to say that Satan is entirely ignored. In modern Jewish theology, even among the Orthodox, Satan, as a baneful force outside man, is relegated to the background if he is considered at all.

Joshua Trachtenberg, *The Devil and the Jews* (Philadelphia, 1961); see index, 'Devil' and 'Satan'.

**Schechter, Solomon**  Scholar, theologian, leading thinker of Conservative Judaism (1847–1915). Schechter was born in Fascani, Romania. His father, a *Habad Hasid, was a *shohet* (see ..SHEHITAH), hence the family name, Schechter. Schechter received a thorough grounding in traditional Jewish learning but, in his early twenties, went to Vienna to study at the Rabbinical College, where his main tutor was Meir Friedmann, a renowned Talmudist in the modern idiom. Later Schechter took courses at the University of Berlin and the Berlin Hochschule, where a fellow-student was Claude *Montefiore. Montefiore brought Schechter to England to be his private tutor. In England, Schechter cultivated the exquisite English style of writing (by reading numerous English novels, it is reported) which has made his *Studies in Judaism* and his *Aspects of Rabbinic Theology* classics of English literature as well as of modern Jewish thought, though, to his dying day, he spoke English with a strong foreign accent. In 1892 Schechter was appointed reader in Rabbinics at Cambridge University and in 1899 also Professor of Hebrew at University College, London.

Schechter's reputation in the scholarly world rests securely on his critical edition of *Avot, According to Rabbi Nathan* (1887) and his discovery of the Cairo *genizah, of which he was instrumental in bringing to Cambridge over 100,000 fragments, including the original Hebrew version of *Ben Sira. Schechter was appointed president of the Jewish Theological Seminary in New York, a position he occupied until his death. There Schechter, together with a number of distinguished Jewish scholars, was responsible for the training of the new type of Conservative Rabbis and for the establishment, together with sympathetic laymen, of the Conservative body of congregations, the United Synagogue of America.

Schechter's philosophy of Judaism is based on the ideas of Zechariah *Frankel. Both Reform and Orthodoxy fail, in this view, to understand 'positive hishtorical' Judaism. Reform, according to Schechter, fails to appreciate the positive elements in traditional Judaism, while Orthodoxy fails to grasp the dynamic aspects of the tradition itself. Schechter thus sought to encourage a marriage between the old learning and the critical methodology adopted in the *Jüdische Wissenschaft school. Schechter also stressed what he called 'Catholic Israel'. This means that the ultimate source of *authority in Judaism is the Jewish people as whole, in which a consensus emerges as to which aspects of the tradition are permanently binding and which are time-conditioned. Where is Catholic Israel to be located? Schechter's somewhat unhelpful reply is that all three movements, Orthodoxy, Reform, and Conservative Judaism, have their role to play, Based on his experience of the British parliamentary system, Schechter once described Orthodoxy as 'His Majesty's Government' and Reform as 'His Majesty's Opposition', both part of the same historical body and each with its own insights, the one in the direction of loyalty to the past, the other in the need for progress. The great question that can be put to Schechter's understanding, and to that of Conservative Judaism, is how contradictory ideas about the very nature of Judaism can be reconciled. This problem still awaits its solution. It is revealing that, in his famous essay on the *dogmas of Judaism, Schechter refuses to consider which of the dogmas can be accepted by the modern Jew. It should be added that Schechter's theological writings have won the admiration of Christian scholars, contributing to a far better appreciation than ever before in the non-Jewish world of the riches of traditional Judaism.

Norman Bentwich, *Solomon Schechter* (Philadelphia, 1948).

**Scholem, Gershom** World-renowned German Jewish scholar of Jewish mysticism (1897–1982). Scholem was born in Berlin, in an assimilated Jewish family, but became attracted to Jewish studies, eventually specializing in the study of Jewish mysticism. From 1925 until his retirement in 1965 Scholem taught as lecturer and later as Professor of Jewish Mysticism at the Hebrew University in Jerusalem. There he founded a school and succeeded in creating an entirely new scholarly discipline. It is not true to say that no scholarly work had been done in the field of Jewish mysticism prior to Scholem and his school, but the subject had been relegated to a remote corner of scholarly interest. Scholem examined the mystical texts by the best methods of modern critical and historical scholarship, demonstrating in the process that Judaism had not infrequently expressed itself in terms of the non-rational and the mythical.

Scholem's pioneering work, *Major Trends in Jewish Mysticism*, examines Jewish mystical tendencies from the Merkavah (*Chariot) mystics down to the latest manifestation in *Hasidism. His study of the false Messiah *Shabbetai Zevi uncovered the irrational forces, latent in the Jewish soul, which erupted when the time was ripe. This is not to say that Scholem approved of the bizarre events connected with Shabbetai Zevi. Scholem has described the reticence of the Jewish mystics in describing their own experiences, which is why, according to Scholem, there are so few personal Jewish mystical testimonies available. The same reticence can be observed in Scholem himself. He worked as an objective scholar and was usually very reserved about his own personal attitude to mysticism. He was certainly no mystic himself but seems to have been a religious, though not an Orthodox, Jew. There was an element of antinomianism in Scholem, an element he detected in some Jewish mystical texts, although in his scholarly work he showed that the Kabbalah, which invested every detail of the precepts with cosmic significance, saved Judaism as a religion of law.

David Biale, *Gershom Scholem: Kabbalah and Counter History* (Cambridge, Mass., 1982).

**Science and Religion** The struggle between science and religion in the nineteenth century, although largely engaged in, on the religious side, by Christians, was naturally of equal concern to religious Jews. With regard to the basic problem of the scientific approach to the discovery of truth versus religious faith, Jewish thinkers, believing that all truth comes from the One God, generally refused to adopt the 'two-truth' theory, according to which religion is in conflict with science but each is 'true' in its own sphere. Relying on the medieval discussions of faith versus reason (see RATIONALISM), the majority of Jewish thinkers who grappled with the problem held that religion has to do with life's values and with a reaching-out to the transcendent and is therefore fully compatible with scientific views about the composition and workings of the world perceived by the senses. While Judaism views with favour investigation into the nature of the physical universe—from the religious point of view this increases human perception of the glory of God as manifest in His *creation—such investigations are irrelevant to the question of religious faith. As C. S.

Lewis puts it, the scientist, in his field, knows, whereas the religious person believes. In other words, scientific explanation is of the way in which the universe works as it does, while religion seeks to explain the purpose of the universe and man's place within it. The one is a matter of knowledge, the other a matter of belief. Very few Jewish thinkers, for instance, felt themselves compelled by their religious faith to hold fast, despite all the new evidence, to the geocentric view of the universe. Far from the new picture of the immense size of the universe (with our whole solar system a mere speck in the vastness of space) destroying faith, it helps to increase man's sense of wonder at the divine wisdom.

The problem for religious Jews is not, therefore, science *per se* but the apparent conflict between particular scientific theories and the biblical record: for instance, between the Genesis narrative of spontaneous creation in six days and the theory of *evolution, or between the great age of the universe revealed by science and the biblical chronology according to which the world is no more than 5,500 years old. Some Orthodox thinkers here fall back on the idea that scientific theories are only 'guesswork' which it is folly to accept in the face of contradiction by the divinely revealed Torah. But others, like Rabbi *Kook, have maintained that the creation narrative has always been held by the tradition to belong to the 'mysteries of the Torah' and is therefore open to interpretation. It was not intended to be a literal description of how everything came into being, but to stress that it was God who called it all into being, and there is no reason why it should not be postulated that he used an evolutionary process to achieve His purpose.

Where science does come into conflict with the tradition is when scientific method is employed to examine the documents of the Jewish religion and to discover how religion itself came to be. *Biblical Criticism, and sociological and psychological theories about the nature of society and the human personality, do present a challenge to the doctrine of divine *revelation. Some Jewish thinkers have argued that biblical criticism is only conjectural, and sociology and psychology are not exact sciences to reject which is to reject reason. Orthodox thinkers still pursue this line, at least so far as criticism applied to the *Pentateuch, the very word of God, is concerned. Reform and Conservative thinkers hold that, indeed, the application of scientific method in these areas has to be accepted even if the conclusions reached demand a new approach to the whole question of revelation.

In connection with the science of *medicine all Orthodox thinkers welcome wholeheartedly the tremendous advances in this sphere. Already in the period of the *Geonim the view was held that the Talmudic Rabbis only had the medical knowledge of their day, so that one must not rely on remedies found in the Talmud, for all the *authority the Talmud possesses in matters of religion and law. In matters of Jewish law such as whether a person who is sick should eat on *Yom Kippur it is for the doctor not the Rabbi to decide and the doctor's knowledge is based on the advance of modern medicine. Scientific advances have, indeed, posed new problems for Jewish law and ethics— organ transplants and *artificial insemination are obvious examples—but no Jewish thinker has expressed the view that, because of the problems to which it gives rise, the advance of science should be halted.

The two items in the bibliography below are discussions of the relationship between science and religion from, respectively, the Reform point of view and the Orthodox point of view. As in many other areas, Reform and Orthodoxy have their differences, Reform allowing greater weight to modern thought when this is in conflict with the tradition than Orthodoxy is willing to do. Yet Orthodoxy, too, seeks an accommodation with science wherever possible—by a new interpretation of the tradition, for example.

Aryeh Carmell and Cyril Domb (eds.), *Challenge: Torah Views on Science and its Problems* (Jerusalem and New York, 1978).
Samuel S. Cohon, 'Theology and the Other Sciences', in his *Jewish Theology* (Assen, 1971), 15–42.

**Secularism** Although Judaism makes a distinction, as in the *Havdalah benediction, between the sacred and profane, it acknowledges that secular life is good in itself, for which God is to be thanked; hence the various benedictions over food, drink, and other physical and material pleasures. To be sure there have been Jewish societies in the past whose members avoided the temptations of the flesh and urban life by fleeing to the wilderness, as did, apparently, the people of *Qumran. But these were the exception. Usually the Jew is encouraged by his religion to live firmly in the 'secular city', provided life's spiritual side is also given its due. The Jew is not presented with the stark choice of either gaining the world and losing his soul or gaining his soul and losing the world. He can have both. Or, as William Temple has said, God is interested in many things apart from religion. Obviously, it is difficult to preserve the correct balance between the spiritual and the material aspects of life. A major portion of the Jewish moralistic literature is devoted explicitly to the way in which this balance is to be achieved.

In modern times, some Jews, who have lost their belief in God and the Jewish religion while still attached to what is called 'the Jewish way of life', have tried to develop a form of 'secular Judaism', in which Jewish observances and even prayer are cultivated not in obedience to the will of God but as colourful Jewish folkways. A good case can. be made for a non-believing Jew to follow the Jewish way of life as a means, perhaps the only means, for the enrichment of life. From the religious point of view it might even be said that such a Jew is doing God's will without knowing it. Yet, when all is said and done, 'secular Judaism' is a contradiction in terms since Judaism is a religion not a secular philosophy. Solomon *Schechter's remarks (*Studies in Judaism*, i. 150–1) are perhaps a little unfair when applied to the sincere secular Jew who really sees great value in the Jewish way, but his critique, written over a hundred years ago, is still relevant:

'Judaism, divested of every higher religious motive, is in danger of falling into gross materialism, or what else is the meaning of such declarations as: "Believe what you like, but conform to this or that mode of life", what else does it mean but: "We cannot expect you to believe that the things you are bidden to do are commanded by a higher authority; there is not such a thing as belief but you ought to do them for conventionalism or for your own convenience." But both these motives—the good opinion of our neighbours, as well as our bodily health—have nothing to do with our noble and higher sentiments, and degrade Judaism to a matter of expediency or diplomacy. Indeed, things have advanced so far that well-meaning but ill-advised writers even think to render a service to Judaism by declaring it to be a kind of enlightened Hedonism or rather a moderate Epicureanism.'

Judaism does embrace secularism but cannot possibly be identified with it. The secular Jew can follow *Micah's demand (Micah 6: 8) that he practise justice and mercy and walk humbly. It is arrogant of the believer and untrue to experience to declare that he cannot. But the believer adds the dimension of the sacred and when he tries falteringly to walk humbly it is with his God that he is trying to walk.

Louis Jacobs, 'Secularism', in his *What Does Judaism Say About . . .?* (Jerusalem, 1973), 274–5.

**Seder** 'Order', the festive meal and service held in the home on the first night of *Passover (and on the second night as well in the *Diaspora) at which various rituals commemorating the *Exodus are carried out and the *Haggadah recited, all in obedience to the injunction to parents to tell their children of God's mighty deeds in delivering the people of Israel from Egyptian bondage (Exodus 13: 8). The Seder is a re-enactment of the lives of the slaves and their joy when given their freedom. The keynote is sounded in the statement in the Haggadah that everyone is obliged to imagine that he or she has personally been delivered from Egypt. The essential features of the order (Seder) of procedure on this night are described in the Mishnah (final chapter of tractate *Pesaḥim*) but many additions have been made through the ages. The following is a brief description of what happens at the Seder in Jewish homes today.

*The Seder Ritual*

The table is covered with a white tablecloth upon which the festival candles are placed. A decorative plate (exquisite Seder plates have been produced by Jewish craftsmen) is placed on the Seder table upon which rest the symbolic foods required for the rituals. These are: three *matzot* (plural of *matzah*, unleavened bread); *maror*, 'bitter herbs', serving as a reminder of the embitterment of the lives of the Hebrew slaves by their Egyptian taskmasters (Exodus 1: 14); *ḥaroset*, a paste made of almonds, apples, and wine, symbolic both of the mortar used by the slaves in building and of the sweetness of *redemption; a bowl of salt water, symbolizing the tears of the oppressed; parsley for a symbolic dipping in the salt water; a roasted bone as a reminder of the Paschal lamb;

and a roasted egg as a reminder of the festival offering brought in Temple times in addition to the Paschal lamb. These last two are not eaten during the meal but left on the plate. During the Seder all the participants drink four cups of wine, representing the four different expressions for redemption found in the Exodus narrative. Since in ancient times the aristocratic custom was to eat and drink while reclining, the food and drink are partaken of in this way as a symbol of the mode of eating and drinking of free men. The view is ignored of some medieval authorities that the custom of reclining at the Seder has no meaning in an age when people do not normally eat in this fashion. Custom is all in such matters and reclining at the Seder is still the norm. Reclining does not, however, mean actually lying with the feet on a couch. The practice is simply to have a cushion or pillow at the left side of the chair upon which one reclines slightly.

The Seder begins with the *Kiddush, the festival benediction over the first cup of wine. The middle *matzah* is then broken in two, one piece being set aside to be eaten later as the *afikoman* ('dessert'), the last thing eaten before *grace after meals is recited, so that the taste of the *matzah* of freedom might linger in the mouth. It is customary for the grown-ups to hide the *afikoman*, rewarding the lucky child who finds it with a present. A cheeky child might bargain for the size of the present before handing over the *afikoman*. Some frown on this practice because it might encourage mendacity on the part of the children but most Jews ignore these spoilsports and see it as a harmless bit of fun that succeeds in holding the interest of the children. The parsley is dipped in the salt water and eaten. The youngest child present then asks the Four Questions, a standard formula beginning with the words: 'Why is this night different from all other nights?' The four differences are remarked upon by the child, one of which is: 'On all other nights we eat either leaven or unleaven, whereas on this night we eat only leaven.' The other three differences between this night and other nights are the bitter herbs, the reclining, and the dipping. The head of the house and the other adults present at the Seder then proceed to reply to the child's questions by reciting (more usually by chanting) the Haggadah, in which the answers are given in terms of God's deliverances. When they reach the passage in the Haggadah which tells of the ten plagues, a small amount of the wine is poured out from the second cup to denote that it is inappropriate to drink a full cup of joy in the deliverance, since, in the process, the Egyptians lost their lives. The pouring-out of a little of the wine is a symbolic way of saying: do not gloat over the downfall of your enemies even if they richly deserved their fate. This section of the Haggadah concludes with a benediction in which God is thanked for His mercies and the second cup of wine is drunk in the reclining position.

The celebrants then proceed to partake of the festive meal. Grace before meals is recited over two of the three *matzot* and, in addition to the benediction over bread (unleavened bread is still bread), the benediction is recited: 'Blessed art Thou, O Lord our God, King of the universe, who hath sanctified us with thy commandments and hath commanded us to eat *matzah*.' The bitter herbs (usually horseradish) are then dipped in the *ḥaroset* and eaten. Tradition has it that in Temple times the great sage *Hillel would eat *matzah*, bitter herbs, and the meat of the Paschal lamb together. As a reminder of Hillel's procedure, a sandwich (naturally called by the children a 'Hillel') is made of the third *matzah* and the bitter herbs. In many communities it is the custom to eat, as the first dish, hard-boiled eggs in salt water, symbolic of the tears of the slaves and their hard bondage.

At the end of the meal the *afikoman* is 'found', surrendered, and eaten and grace after meals is recited over the third cup of wine. The *Hallel (Psalms 113–18) and other hymns of thanksgiving are recited over the fourth cup of wine. Before the recital of the Hallel, a cup is filled for the prophet *Elijah, the herald of the *Messiah, who, legend states, visits every Jewish home on this night. The door of the house is opened to let Elijah in and the children watch eagerly to see if they can notice any diminution in Elijah's cup as the prophet quickly sips the wine and speeds on his way to visit all the other homes. From medieval times it was the custom to recite at this stage of the proceedings a number of imprecations against those who oppressed the Jews and laid waste the Temple. Many Jews no longer recite these imprecations, substituting for them a prayer for peace and freedom for all mankind. Some sing in English the famous spiritual, 'Let My People Go'. The Seder concludes with the cheerful singing of table songs, ending with 'Had Gadya', the tale of the kid, the cat, and the dog. Some pious Jews recite the *Song of Songs after the Seder before retiring to bed.

Practically all Jews with any association with Jewish life have a Seder but not necessarily in the home. It is now the practice in many synagogues and in many Jewish hotels to have a communal Seder but many feel that the full flavour of the Seder can only be tasted when it is a home celebration. It is the custom, however, to invite guests to the Seder, especially those who would not otherwise have one. Some invite non-Jewish guests and this custom is attested to in the writings of the eighteenth-century Rabbi Jacob *Emden. The Rabbinic authorities advise that the meaning of the rituals of the Seder and the Haggadah as a whole should be explained in the vernacular for the benefit of participants unfamiliar with Hebrew. Fuller descriptions of the Seder are to be found in the numerous editions of the Passover Haggadah.

**Sefer Ḥasidim** 'Book of Saints', the major work produced in the circle of the *Saints of Germany. Although Judah the Saint of Regensburg (d. 1217) is considered to be the author of *Sefer Ḥasidim* there are a number of passages which come from other hands. The book in its present form also contains the Ethical Will of Judah the Saint. The *Sefer Ḥasidim* is not a systematic work of religion and ethics but consists of moral tales, ethical maxims, short treatises on various religious themes, all describing the ideal life of the *Hasid, not necessarily a scholar, who strives to lead a life of extraordinary piety.

The ideal of *charity is particularly stressed. Reading between the lines, it becomes clear that the saintly demands were not always to the taste of the community heads responsible for the administration of charity funds. The following passage (No. 870) speaks for itself:

'The community leaders noticed that a good Jew in the town offered hospitality to visitors. He was once a rich man who made guests so welcome that they would always visit him. After a time the man lost his wealth but the guests continued to come to him. The members of the town council were then obliged to say to the man: "We know that you are unable to spend so much on your guests, but since they still come to you please accept this charity money so that you can continue to supply your guests with food and drink." It is in order for the man to inform his guests that the money with which he supplies their needs is charity money so that they should not think they owe him a personal debt of gratitude. If, however, the guests do think that the money is his own, and if they knew it was charity money they would be ashamed to accept it, then it is better not to tell them the truth. Even though they will think it is his own money that he is spending on them, this is not to be compared to misrepresentation since he has not misled them; they have misled themselves. Furthermore, even if the host, a God-fearing man who has lost his money, is ashamed to admit to his guests that he is using charity money, it is no worse than the man who says to the charity overseers: "Give me charity for myself" and then gives the money to the poor. Concerning such a case it is said: "Happy is he that considereth the poor" [Psalms 41: 2].'

What the community leaders had to say we are not told but can easily guess.

The *Sefer Ḥasidim* is insistent that Jews must be completely honest in their dealings with Gentiles and this against the background of the Crusades when Christian–Jewish relations were strained, to say the least. 'If a Gentile cheats himself in accounts, the Jew must return the additional amount, and if a Jew is poor, it is better for him that he beg than cheat a Gentile' (no. 661). It appears that, even in this period, it was not unknown for Christians to become converts to Judaism. The *Sefer Ḥasidim* says: 'If a Jew who is kind-hearted marries a kind-hearted proselyte woman, it is better for other Jews to marry their descendants rather than the descendants of pure Jews who lack their virtue' (no. 377).

Together with the lofty maxims, the *Sefer Ḥasidim* contains many medieval superstitions (see MAGIC AND SUPERSTITION), the common property of both Jews and Christians of the time. There are ghost stories, tales of werewolves and vampires who prowl at night, and advice on how to forestall the evil designs of witches. Some of these ideas, under the influence of the *Sefer Ḥasidim*, reappear in later Jewish works. But it is for its piety and sincere love of humanity that the book is admired as a classic of Jewish moralistic literature.

Meyer Waxman, 'The Book of the Pious', in his *A History of Jewish Literature* (South Brunswick, NJ, 1960), i. 360–4.

**Sefer Torah** 'Scroll of the Torah', the \*Pentateuch, written by hand on parchment, from which the reading of the \*Torah is carried out in the synagogue. The parchment on which the Sefer Torah is written must come from a \*kosher animal. There are detailed rules on how the Sefer Torah has to be written by the *sofer* ('scribe'), the expert skilled in the rules and in writing. The writing is done with a quill pen and black ink. Before the *sofer* writes he uses a ruler and stylus to make forty-two lines underneath which the letters are to be written and two vertical lines at the sides, so that the written text will have wide margins and be straight and uniform. The writing is done on strips of parchment, four columns of writing to each strip. The strips are then sewn together to form the complete Scroll. The sewing-together of the sections is done with material from the tendons of a kosher animal. A space is left between the letters and the words and at the end of the paragraphs. A space equal to four lines of text is left between the books of Genesis, Exodus, Leviticus, and Numbers. There is a tradition that some letters have to be written larger than the others and some smaller. The seven letters *shin, ayin, tet, nun, zayin, gimmel*, and *tzaddi* have little crown-like designs on the left-hand corner. Before writing, the *sofer* declares that he is doing it for the sake of the sanctification of the Sefer Torah. Some pious scribes immerse themselves in the \*mikveh before they begin to write.

In order to avoid touching the sacred Scroll with the bare hand, the Sefer Torah is mounted on wooden handles by which it is held when reciting the benediction over the Torah and when elevating the Scroll. Sephardim do not have these handles but instead have the Scroll wrapped in silk and placed in a kind of open box. The Sefer Torah, when it is not in use, is covered with an embroidered mantle over which are placed silver adornments consisting of two bells, a breastplate, and a pointer. The last is for the use of the Reader, who points to the words as he reads so as not to miss out any. Some Scrolls have a crown at the top of the handles instead of the bells. The breastplate is based on the breastplate worn by the \*High Priest which contained twelve precious stones on which the names of the twelve tribes were engraved (Exodus 28: 15–21). Some breastplates of the Sefer Torah have a representation of these stones. The bells are called *rimmonim*,

'pomegranates', after the bells and pomegranates attached to the coat of the High Priest (Exodus 28: 33–4). Most *rimmonim* today are in the shape of a tower. This has no significance and was introduced by eighteenth-century silversmiths who used the towers in Amsterdam for their model.

The Sefer Torah is the most sacred of all Jewish ritual objects. Nothing must be placed on top of it and even when the writing has faded so that the Scroll can no longer be used, it is not burned but buried reverentially, where possible in the grave of a scholar or exceedingly pious man. According to some authorities, if the Sefer Torah falls to the ground, all who are witnesses to the fall must undertake to fast for a whole day. The same applies when a Scroll is destroyed by fire. When a person is called up to the reading of the Torah he kisses the Sefer Torah by placing his \*tallit on the parchment and then putting the tallit to his lips. When the Sefer Torah is taken in procession around the synagogue, the whole congregation rises to its feet in honour of the sacred text. According to the Talmud, every Jew is obliged to write a Sefer Torah or have one written for him by a *sofer*. The difficulties in carrying out this obligation are obvious. Instead, it is the custom to leave some letters of the Sefer Torah in outline and the *sofer* guides people to fill in a letter each. Since the Sefer Torah is incomplete even if a single letter is missing, to fill in a letter is considered to be equivalent to writing the whole Sefer Torah. Yet for all the veneration Jews have for the Sefer Torah, it is never treated as an object of worship. Only God is to be worshipped. In fact some authorities object even to people bowing to the Sefer Torah. Their view is not followed but the idea behind it still holds good, that the Torah, represented by the Sefer, is not an end in itself but the means to the true end of religion, the worship of God.

Hyman E. Goldin, 'The Scroll and Other Holy Books', in his *Code of Jewish Law* (New York, 1961), i. 89–91.

**Sefer Yetzirah** 'Book of Creation', mystical work in Hebrew, containing less than 2,000 words, probably compiled between the third and sixth centuries CE. As its name implies, the *Sefer Yetzirah* consists of brief speculations on the creation. According to this work, God created the world by means of the twenty-two letters of the Hebrew alphabet and the numbers one to ten, that is to say, by the spiritual forces represented by these letters and numbers. The total of the numbers and the letters are called 'the thirty-two paths of wisdom'. The numbers (Sefirot) in the *Sefer Yetzirah* may simply have meant the numbers one to ten, though it is probable that the idea of cosmic entities is also implied. In any event, the work was understood by the Kabbalists as referring to their doctrine of the *Sefirot, the powers or potencies in the Godhead. The Kabbalists often quote the passage in the *Sefer Yetzirah* (1. 4): 'Ten intangible numbers [Sefirot]. Ten and not nine; ten and not eleven. Understand with wisdom and be wise with understanding.' The Talmud (*Sanhedrin* 65b) tells of third- and fourth-century teachers who created a 'man' and a calf by means of the *Sefer Yetzirah*, though it is uncertain whether this refers to our *Sefer Yetzirah*. Implied in the book itself is the notion that man, as a microcosm, can repeat, if he knows the secret, the creative processes by means of which God brought the world, the macrocosm, into being (see GOLEM). The *Sefer Yetzirah* concludes with a paean of praise to the patriarch Abraham who 'looked, and saw, and understood, and explored, and engraved, and hewed out, and succeeded at creation, as it is said: "And the creatures they had made in Haran" [Genesis 12: 5]'. On the basis of this passage and other references to Abraham in the book, the *Sefer Yetzirah* was ascribed in the Middle Ages to Abraham.

Isidor Kalisch, *Sepher Yezirah* (New York, 1877). Gershom Scholem, 'The Sefer Yezirah', in his *Kabbalah* (Jerusalem, 1974), 23–30.

**Sefirot** The powers or potencies in the Godhead as taught by the Kabbalah. The doctrine features prominently in the Zohar, although the Zohar does not actually use the word Sefirot, preferring terms such as 'stages' or 'crowns', probably because the Zohar is a pseudepigraphic work set in the second century CE and it would have given the game away to use a near-contemporary term like Sefirot. The doctrine runs that the *En Sof, the unfathomable Ground of Being, produces, by a process of emanation, ten powers in which It (En Sof is sometimes referred to in impersonal terms) becomes manifest. These ten Sefirot are the source of all cosmic energy and vitality. Ethics of the Fathers (5. 1) speaks of ten words by means of

which God created the world. In the context these are the ten 'sayings' mentioned in the creation narrative at the beginning of Genesis but are identified by the Kabbalists with the Sefirot. Similarly, the Ten Sefirot in the *Sefer Yetzirah* are, for the Kabbalists, 'their' Sefirot. The Kabbalists were aware of the radical nature of the whole concept. They were accused of believing, like the Christians but even more so, in multiplicity in the Deity (see CORDOVERO and KABBALAH). Their defence was that the doctrine is not really dualistic. En Sof is *in* the Sefirot, which can be compared to bottles of various hues into which clear water is poured. The water, while in the bottles, partakes of their colours. The central problem, to which the doctrine of the Sefirot addresses itself, is how the finite universe can have emerged from the Infinite. The En Sof brings about the emanation of the Sefirot in order to produce the various degrees of the finite, the limitations of the divine power required for the world to come into being.

### The Names of the Sefirot

The ten Sefirot, in the usual Kabbalistic terminology, are:

1. *Keter* ('Crown').
2. *Hokhmah* ('Wisdom').
3. *Binah* ('Understanding').
4. *Hesed* ('Loving-kindness').
5. *Gevurah* ('Power' or 'Judgement').
6. *Tiferet* ('Beauty').
7. *Netzah* ('Victory').
8. *Hod* ('Splendour').
9. *Yesod* ('Foundation').
10. *Malkhut* ('Sovereignty').

*Keter* is the first impulse in En Sof. It is also called the Will, not, as yet, the will to create but the will to will, the emergence of a will in that which is beyond 'willing' or any other constricting emotion or activity. *Keter* is the first stage of the limiting process and as such is the link between En Sof and the other Sefirot. From this will to will emerges *Hokhmah*, the will to create. This is called 'Wisdom' because at this stage all creative processes are contained *in potentia* in the divine Mind. In the next stage, *Binah*, all the potential aspects of *Hokhmah* are 'understood' in detail in the divine Mind. These three Sefirot, belonging as they do to the processes of the divine Mind, are too remote to allow the finite, human mind to comprehend them. They are the three higher Sefirot on which the human mind is forbidden to dwell. Less incomprehensible are the seven lower Sefirot which represent the divine emotions, so to speak. *Ḥesed* is the full flow of the divine love. If its powers were left unrestrained it would engulf the world in its abundant embrace. *Gevurah*, the power of judgement, provides the control needed for *Ḥesed* just as *Ḥesed* softens the stern judgement of *Gevurah*. *Tiferet* is the harmonizing principle, preserving the correct balance between *Ḥesed* and *Gevurah*. *Tiferet* is supported by *Netzaḥ* and *Hod* and all the eight Sefirot merge in *Yesod*, 'Foundation', so called because it is the foundation of all creation in bringing the power of the Sefirot to *Malkhut*, 'Sovereignty', the power that receives from the other Sefirot for the purpose of governing the lower worlds.

*Symbolism of the Sefirot*

A rich array of symbols for the Sefirot is found in the Zohar and the writings of the other early Kabbalists. Using colour symbolism, these sources make white the colour of *Ḥesed* and red the colour of *Gevurah*. Yellow, as a colour supposedly midway between white and red, is the colour of *Tiferet* but it is in *Malkhut*, into which the light of all the Sefirot streams, that there is a true blending of red and white. The opening passage in current editions of the Zohar sees the pink rose as the symbol on earth of the blend of white and red in *Malkhut*. *Keter* has various colour symbols. It is described either in terms of pure white—the whiteness of white—or of black (because it is opaque). At times *Keter* is described as colourless since, at this stage, there is as yet no differentiation of colour.

The three *patriarchs, Abraham, Isaac, and Jacob, represent, respectively, *Ḥesed*, *Gevurah*, and *Tiferet*. Abraham is the 'pillar of love'; Isaac, the 'pillar of justice'; Jacob, the 'pillar of truth'—truth consisting of a proper blend of justice and mercy. The biblical narratives about the lives of the patriarchs are read as describing the Sefirotic processes. Abraham, for instance, has to offer his son Isaac, at the *Akedah, in order to stiffen, so to speak, the principle of love through the principle of power. Only after such a blend of the two principles has been achieved, can Jacob, the harmonizing principle, be born. Evil stems from *Gevurah*. When the power of stern judgement is dissociated from

the other Sefirot it becomes a force of naked evil, which is why Isaac 'loves' Esau (Genesis 25: 28). *Malkhut*, the female principle, the *Shekhinah, is represented by the *matriarchs, *Rachel and *Leah, the wives of Jacob, the male principle. The biblical heroine, *Esther, also represents *Malkhut*. But while *Malkhut* is thought of as the female principle in relation to the other Sefirot, from which it receives, as the female receives from the male, with regard to the divine control of the lower worlds, *Malkhut* is a 'giver' and is thought of as a male principle of its own, hence the representation of *Malkhut* also as King *David.

The various *names of God in the Bible represent the Sefirot. The name Ehyeh, for instance, from *hayah*, 'to be', represents the pure being of *Keter*. The *Tetragrammaton represents *Tiferet*, while the name *Adonai* (from *adon*, 'lord') represents the sovereignty principle, *Malkhut*. The name *Elohim* (used also in the Bible for a judge) represents *Gevurah*.

Since the Kabbalists understand the *image of God in which man has been created (Genesis 1: 27) to mean that the human body is a representation on earth of the Sefirot, anthropomorphic symbolism is frequently used. *Keter* is the crown worn above the body. *Hokhmah* is the brain and *Binah* the heart. *Ḥesed* is the right arm, *Gevurah* the left arm. *Tiferet* is the torso and *Netzaḥ* and *Hod* the right and left legs. *Yesod* is the organ of generation, in which the 'covenant' of *circumcision is located. *Malkhut* is the mouth. The processes of human communication also represent the processes of divine communication, that is, the divine creation of the universe. A human being first has an idea in mind. His voice produces the sounds he utters when speaking in order to communicate the idea to others. Thus *Hokhmah* and *Binah* represent the divine thoughts, *Tiferet* the voice, and *Malkhut* speech, hence the references in the Genesis narrative to God 'speaking' as He creates the world. In similar fashion, *Tiferet* is the *Written Torah which has to be interpreted by *Malkhut*, the *Oral Torah.

Other symbols, too, are found. Gold, reddish in colour, represents *Gevurah*. Silver, whitish in colour, represents *Ḥesed*. Of the four directions of the compass, north represents *Gevurah*, south, *Ḥesed*, east, *Tiferet*, and west, *Malkhut*, which is why the Holy of Holies, the special abode of the Shekhinah, is located at the west side of the Temple.

It is obvious that the doctrine of the Sefirot introduces a radical, some have said a heretical, understanding of Deity. For the One God of the Bible and the simple Uncaused Cause of the philosophers, the Kabbalists have substituted the dynamic God of the Sefirot. There is an ever-present danger to Jewish monotheism that the whole doctrine will degenerate into polytheism. Some scholars have detected, in the Sefirotic doctrine, traces of such pagan notions as the birth of the gods, the existence of goddesses, and, in *Yesod*, a phallic symbol. The Kabbalists retort, as above, that the Sefirot are never seen as detached from En Sof. En Sof and the Sefirot are two different aspects of the One God: En Sof, God as He is in Himself, the Sefirot God in manifestation.

Isaiah Tishby, 'Sefirot', in his *The Wisdom of the Zohar*, trans. David Goldstein (The Lithman Library of Jewish Civilization; Oxford, 1989), 269–370.

**Selihot** Prayers for pardon, from the root *salaḥ*, 'to forgive'. These supplications, composed during the Middle Ages, are recited a few days before *Rosh Ha-Shanah and during the days between Rosh Ha-Shanah and *Yom Kippur. God is described as 'good and ready to pardon' (Psalms 86: 5) and the Psalmist prays: 'Pardon my iniquity for it is great' (Psalms 25: 11), making the Selihot prayers especially appropriate for the penitential season. Selihot are recited on Yom Kippur itself at every service, on the other days only during the morning service. The *confession of sin on Yom Kippur is recited privately but also by the whole congregation during the Selihot. In many communities on the first day of the week in which Rosh Ha-Shanah falls, Selihot are recited at midnight. The *Sephardim recite Selihot from 1 *Elul, the month before Rosh Ha-Shanah, with which the fuller penitential season begins. In addition to these days, Selihot are recited on all fast days and on Mondays and Thursdays throughout the year (except on festive occasions) since these days are seen as judgement days on the analogy of the human courts which sat, in Talmudic times, on Mondays and Thursdays. The central feature of every Selihot service is the recital of the verse containing, in the Rabbinic expression, the thirteen attributes of mercy: 'The Lord, the Lord, merciful and gracious, long-suffering, and abundant in goodness and truth; keeping mercy unto the thousandth generation, forgiving iniquity' (Exodus 34: 6–7, but with the omission of the words 'but that will by no means clear the guilty'). The Talmud (*Rosh Ha-Shanah* 17b) states: 'A covenant has been established that whenever the thirteen attributes are invoked in prayer, that prayer will not be in vain.'

Max Arzt, 'Selihot', in his *Justice and Mercy* (New York, and 1963), 205–21.

**Sephardim** The descendants of Spanish Jewry, as distinct from the *Ashkenazim, who are descended from German Jewry. The names Sepharad and Ashkenaz are found in the Bible but were used in the Middle Ages to denote, respectively, Spain and Germany. Spain was the land in which Jewry reached its Golden Age, as this has been called; an age which saw the flowering of Jewish culture and produced such eminent figures as *Maimonides, *Nahmanides, *Judah Halevi, *Ibn Gabirol, *Abravanel, and many others. After the expulsion from Spain in 1492, Spanish Jews resettled themselves in the land of Israel (see SAFED), the Ottoman Empire, and North Africa and later in America, in Amsterdam, and in other European cities. Sephardim and Ashkenazim are not divided on doctrinal lines and should not be considered as two distinct Jewish sects. The differences, of which there are many, between the two groups are the result of different cultural conditions, local customs, and, especially, the different Halakhic authorities favoured by each group. For instance, the *Shulḥan Arukh became the standard Code for both Sephardim and Ashkenazim but for the Sephardim, Joseph *Karo's rulings in this work are authoritative, while for the Ashkenazim the glosses of *Isserles to the work are authoritative, Karo generally following earlier Sephardi authorities, Isserles earlier Ashkenazi authorities. The rivalry between the two groups was often intense in former times, but is, less so, nowadays. Located, in the nineteenth century, outside Germany, the Sephardim were far less influenced by the *Haskalah than the Ashkenazim, which partly accounts for the absence of any organized Reform movement among the Sephardim, except for the comparatively mild form that emerged in London. The popular language of Sephardi Jews is *Ladino, as *Yiddish is of the Ashenazi Jews. Because of the differences in law, custom, and ritual between the two groups, Sephardi Rabbis lead Sephardi communities and Ashkenazi Rabbis Ashkenazi communities. There are, for instance, two Chief Rabbis in the State of Israel, one Sephardi, the other Ashkenazi, each holding sway over his own flock.

Lucien Gubbay and Abraham Levy, *The Sephardim* (London, 1992).

**Septuagint** The ancient Greek translation of the Pentateuch produced, according to the second-century BCE *Letter of Aristeas* (see ROSSI), in Alexandria in the reign of Ptolemy II (third century BCE). The name, Septuagint, is based on the story, in this letter, that the translation was made, at the request of the king, by seventy-two scholars (seventy being the nearest round number). The Talmud (*Megillah* 9a) has a different version of the story, according to which the translation was made by seventy sages, sitting in different rooms, each being inspired to make the same alterations to the text where the original might prove offensive to the king. The Talmud states that it was a dark day for Israel when the translation into Greek was made, whereas the Greek-speaking Jews of Alexandria, we learn from *Philo, hailed the translation as a great event. Many scholars now hold that the translation, first of the Pentateuch, later of the whole of the Bible, was made at different times by the Alexandrian Jews themselves and that later additions were made to the text from time to time.

In biblical scholarship the Septuagint (designated as LXX) is widely used, though with caution, for the establishment of the biblical text (see BIBLICAL CRITICISM). For instance, the verse states: 'On the seventh day God finished the work He had made' (Genesis 2: 2). But, according to the creation narrative, God rested on the seventh day, as, indeed, the verse goes on to say. The Septuagint version reads: 'On the *sixth* day God finished the work He had made.' This seems to make more sense, yet caution is required before taking it for granted that the Septuagint has preserved a better text, since it is possible that the Greek translators, puzzled by the discrepancy, simply altered the text without warrant and the verse might mean that God had finished His work by the seventh day. It is now held that the Septuagint translation of the word *almah*, meaning simply a 'maiden', in Isaiah 7: 14, as a 'virgin', is possibly a later addition by a Christian so as to make the prophet refer to the dogma of the virgin birth.

Sidney Jellicoe, *Studies into the Septuagint: Origins, Recensions, and Interpretations* (New York, 1974).

**Sex** Naturally, with regard to such a complex topic that effects human life so powerfully, there are to be found differing attitudes among religious Jews. On the one hand, the Bible has a positive attitude to marriage (see CELIBACY) and to sex within marriage, witness the fact that the patriarchs and Moses were married, and the Rabbis declare that it is a religious obligation for a husband to satisfy his wife's needs in this respect. On the other hand, it is urged that the sex drive be severely controlled and there is a definite tendency in Rabbinic thought to curtail too much sexual indulgence even in the marital bed, as when the Rabbis warn: 'There is a small organ in man's body which when hungry is sated but when sated is hungry.' Another Rabbinic saying has it that on judgement day a man will be told the frivolous conversations he has had with his wife. Maimonides (*Guide of the Perplexed*, 2. 36), though his view is Jewishly atypical, approves of Aristotle's remark that the sense of touch is 'shameful'. Risking a generalization, it might be said that the Jewish teachers welcome the sex drive as a divine gift to human beings while acknowledging, at the same time, that of all human instincts, sex is the most likely to lead people astray.

Claude *Montefiore (*A Rabbinic Anthology*, written in collaboration with Herbert Loewe (London, 1938)) remarks (p. xix) on the Talmudic Rabbis:

'Social intercourse with women was usually taboo. They were the source of moral danger. They were the incitements to depravity and lust. The evil impulse—the Yezer Ha-Ra—is especially and mainly the impulse which leads to sexual impurity. The result was not entirely healthy. The Rabbis were prevailingly chaste; there was probably *much* less adultery and fornication among the Rabbis than among us, but this chastity was obtained at a certain cost. The lack of healthy, simple companionship and friendship caused a constant dwelling upon sexual relations and details. In the Rabbinic literature sexual allusions are very frequent. Immense are the Halachic discussions about the details of sex life, and sexual phenomena. "Repel nature and it recurs." Repress it, and it grows up again, and not always in a healthy form. Where we would not dream of thinking that any sexual desire could be evoked, the Rabbis were always on the watch for it, dwelling on it, suggesting it. Though they were almost invariably married men, they seem to have often been oddly tormented by sexual desires, perhaps, too, the very absence of natural and healthy social intercourse between men and women drove them to dwell theoretically with double frequency upon every sort of sexual details and minutiae.'

Montefiore's critique of the Rabbis is too condemnatory and too sweeping to be true, to say nothing of his curious repetition of the word 'healthy'. Loewe, in a footnote, seeks to defend the Rabbis by pointing out that this tendency was characteristic of the age. Patristic literature is similarly marked. On the other hand, remarks Loewe, the Rabbinic writings do not eulogize virginity and monasticism. It is always precarious to attempt to psychoanalyse people of the past, to assume that what was considered 'unhealthy' in England in the 1930s was necessarily so over 1,500 years ago in Palestine and Babylon. The Rabbinic interest in sex was not prurient. The numerous Halakhic discussions, for instance, to which Montefiore alludes, are clinical in the extreme. One might just as well accuse a gynaecologist of a morbid interest in sex. Sex is an important part of life. The Torah has laws concerning sex. And the Rabbis, as teachers of the Torah, had to deal with this subject as they did with all other matters treated in the Torah. A closer look at what the Rabbis actually said about sex shows that their approach to this topic was as free, 'healthy', and lacking in frustration as is to be found in any work of religious literature, ancient or modern.

One of the most striking features of the Rabbis' attitude to sex is their acknowledgement that a woman has sexual desires as well as a man. Unlike the supposedly 'Victorian' attitude that it was unladylike for a wife to enjoy sex and that she should submit to her husband while 'thinking of England', the Rabbinic view, as mentioned above, is that it is the husband's duty to satisfy his wife's sexual needs. When she desires her husband, say the Rabbis, she should make it obvious to him, though she should express this by hints and not verbally (*Eruvin* 100b). The Mishnah (*Ketubot* 5: 6) gives a list of the times a wife can expect her husband to make love to her as an essential part of her *ketubah*, the marriage contract: 'The

duty of conjugal rights as enjoined in the Torah is: every day for those who have no occupation; twice a week for labourers; once a week for ass-drivers; once every thirty days for camel-drivers; and once every six months for sailors.' In the Talmudic discussion on this Mishnah it is argued that a husband cannot change his occupation without his wife's consent if this will affect her conjugal rights—from an ass-driver to a camel-driver, for example—since it can be assumed that a wife will prefer to have her needs satisfied even if, as a result, her husband's earnings will be less. Very strikingly in this connection, the Talmud (*Ketubot* 48a) states that a wife can demand that the sex act be performed while they are both naked and if the husband insists on the 'Persian' custom of both being covered she can petition for a divorce.

The Rabbis, of course, sternly disapprove of extramarital sex. Adultery is among the most serious of sins, forbidden by the seventh commandment (see *Decalogue). There is the strongest disapproval of male *homosexuality but hardly any condemnation is to be found of lesbianism (see also BIRTH-CONTROL, MASTURBATION, and PROSTITUTION). But in marriage unorthodox conduct was permitted. The third-century Babylonian teacher, Rabbi Huna, is said (*Shabbat* 140b) to have advised his daughters how to practise sex techniques with the object of arousing their husband's desire. While one Rabbi taught that children are born blind because the husband 'gazes at that place', are born dumb because he 'kisses that place', and are born lame because he 'inverts the table', the final ruling given is that all these are permitted (*Nedarim* 20a–b). The Talmud goes on to say, however, that it is forbidden for a husband to have another woman in mind during intercourse with his wife, nor must he have sex with her if it is his intention to divorce her. Following the Talmudic ruling, albeit with certain reservations, *Isserles remarks in his glosses to the *Shulḥan Arukh (Even Ha-Ezer, 25. 2):

'He can do as he pleases when he is with his wife: he can have intercourse at any time he pleases; he can kiss any part of her body; and he can have intercourse both in the usual way and in an unusual way or on her limbs, provided that he does not spill his seed. Some are more lenient and rule that unnatural intercourse is permitted even if it involves spilling of seed, provided it is only done occasionally, and he does not make a habit of it. Although all these are permitted, whoever sanctifies himself in that which is permitted to him is called holy.'

There is no doubt that among some of the medieval thinkers a less positive attitude to sex is adopted, although others, like *Nahmanides, saw in any suggestion that sex is unworthy a trace of the heretical view that matter is eternal and that there is therefore permanent warfare between body and spirit. Maimonides' acceptance of the view that the sense of touch is shameful has already been noted. *Saadiah Gaon (*Beliefs and Opinions* x. 6) takes issue with those who hold that sexual intercourse yields the most remarkable of pleasures, increases gladness of the soul, and drives out gloomy thoughts from the mind. Saadiah believes such a view to be too one-sided. A man, says Saadiah, should give his impulse free rein when in the estimation of reason it seems necessary, and check it when that need has been fulfilled.

For the Kabbalists, the sex act is especially significant in that it mirrors forth the union on high between the *Sefirot of *Tiferet*, the male principle, and *Malkhut*, the female principle, though the Kabbalists of *Safed in the sixteenth century insisted that the act be performed purely 'for the sake of heaven' and without either passion or pleasure. Some of the Hasidic masters believed that such an attitude, in their day at least, was unrealistic. It is impossible, these masters argued, for a man to perform the sex act without enjoying it and he should have in mind afterwards to thank God for this pleasure as he does for other pleasures of the body, even though he should try, before the act, to intend it as a religious obligation. Other Hasidic masters had a less welcoming attitude. Rabbi Elimelech of Lyzansk (1717–85) comments on the verse: 'And Adam knew Eve his wife; and she conceived and bore Cain' (Genesis 4: 1) that ideally, a man's thoughts at the time of intercourse should be on the divine alone, so much so that he should be unconscious that he is engaging in the act. When Adam became conscious (taking 'knew' literally) of being with his wife they gave birth to Cain, the first murderer. A young Hasid, it is reported, in former times, would be ashamed to show his face in the synagogue soon after his wife had given birth since his companions then knew that he had had intercourse with her. Such an attitude was certainly odd even among the very reserved Hasidim.

In modern Jewish thought until very recently, there have been no discussions of Jewish attitudes to sex. The reason is no doubt because of nineteenth century prudery, reflected in Jewish works of the time. Indeed, from the works of Jewish thinkers writing in European languages in the nineteenth century, one would imagine that they had no sex life at all or, if they did, they kept it very secret. It is only recently, when sex has been more frankly and openly discussed, that Jewish thinkers have begun to consider Jewish points of view. There is, in fact, no single Jewish attitude to sex, as noted earlier, except that a completely negative view of sex is not possible for thinkers in the authentic Jewish tradition.

Louis Jacobs, 'Sex', in his *What Does Judaism Say About . . .?* (Jerusalem, 1973), 281–8.

Robert Gordis, *Love and Sex: A Modern Jewish Perspective* (New York, 1978).

**Shaatnez** A mixed garment of wool and linen. The prohibition against wearing this kind of garment is stated in Leviticus (19: 19): 'neither shall come upon thee a garment of two kinds of stuff [*shaatnez*] mingled together'. The word *shaatnez* occurs in the Bible only here and in the parallel verse in Deuteronomy and its etymology is uncertain. According to the Rabbis the meaning is explained in the verse in Deuteronomy (22: 11): 'Thou shalt not wear a mingled stuff [*shaatnez*], wool and linen together.' It is curious to find that the priests wore garments that contained *shaatnez* (Exodus 28: 6, 8, 15; 39: 29), which the Rabbis explain as a special dispensation so that the priests were only allowed to wear the priestly garments while officiating in the Temple. Some modern scholars have suggested that this is precisely why *shaatnez* is forbidden. For a non-priest to wear such a garment is for him to encroach on the sacred. Maimonides (*Guide of the Perplexed*, 3. 37), on the other hand, suggests that the prohibition stems from the fact that the idolatrous priests wore garments of mingled stuff as sympathetic magic, to encourage the growth of produce in the fields. In the Leviticus verse the prohibition is mentioned together with those against cross-breeding animals and mixing plants, from which it appears that the idea behind it is to keep species separate as God has made them. Another interpretation, given in the Middle Ages, is that Cain brought his offering from the fruit of the soil and Abel from the choicest of his flock (Genesis 4: 3). Cain murdered his brother Abel, so that the prohibition of wearing a garment containing both the fruit of the soil and wool from sheep is a protest against murder. This seems very far-fetched, as does a recent suggestion that wool is obtained from the living sheep whereas flax is 'dead' once it has been detached from the soil; hence the prohibition is seen as forbidding any mingling of the dead with the living. Orthodox Jews still observe the law of *shaatnez* as a divinely given ordinance, whatever its reason. Reform and many Conservative Jews no longer keep this law since, according to them, it has no meaning for the modern Jew.

> Hyman E. Goldin, 'Laws Concerning Shatnez', in his *Code of Jewish Law* (New York, 1961), iv. 58–9.

**Shabbetai Zevi** Turkish scholar and mystic (1626–76) who claimed to be the *Messiah. The horrific Chmielnicki massacres (1648–9), in which many thousands of Polish Jews were murdered, brought about a revival in the Jewish world of the hope that God would send at last the promised Messiah to redeem His people from oppression and bring them back to the land of Israel. On the theological level, the Kabbalistic system developed by Isaac *Luria taught that the Messiah would come when all the *holy sparks had been rescued from their imprisonment by the demonic forces and that most of the sparks had already been reclaimed. Messianism was thus in the air, paving the way for the emergence of one of the strangest figures in Jewish history, Shabbetai Zevi, the man who succeeded in persuading large sections of the Jewish people that that he was the awaited Messiah.

Shabbetai Zevi was born in the city of Smyrna, where he received a sound grounding in the Talmud. He was ordained as a Rabbi at the early age of 18. He later acquired too, a comprehensive knowledge of the Kabbalah. Shabbetai was born on 9 *Av, the anniversary of the destruction of the Temple but also, according to tradition, the day on which the Messiah will be born. To prepare himself for his Messianic role Shabbetai consciously carried out a number of illegal acts, in the belief that in the redeemed world some of the laws of the Torah will no longer be required. He ate forbidden fat, pronouncing over it the benediction: 'Blessed art Thou who has permitted that which was formerly forbidden.' He aroused the

ire of the Smyrna Rabbis by pronouncing the *Tetra-grammaton as it is written (a heinous offence for Jews), so that he was compelled to move to Salonika where he formally declared himself to be the Messiah, winning the masses to his cause. In 1665 Shabbetai journeyed to the land of Israel where he was hailed as the Messiah by the young visionary Nathan of Gaza (1643–80) who claimed to be his *Elijah, the herald of the Messiah. When Shabbetai returned to Turkey his claim to be the Messiah became widely acknowledged.

The news spread rapidly throughout the Jewish world. There was even talk of Shabbetai assembling a Jewish army to reconquer the Holy Land. Jewish communities everywhere were captivated by these events which gave many their first taste of real religious enthusiasm. Even in distant England, as Pepys records in his *Diary* for 19 February 1665, a Jew in London offered a wager of ten to one to anyone prepared to take it that 'a certain person now in Smyrna' will, in less than two years time, be 'the grand Signor as the King of the world'. Encouraged by his excited followers and truly believing in his Messianic role, Shabbetai went to Constantinople in 1666 to depose the Sultan. Although he was arrested and confined to the fortress of Gallipoli, he was allowed to hold court and was visited by Jews from all over the world. The great Rabbinic scholar, David Halevi, sent his son and stepson from Poland to find out whether the rumours were true. But then Shabbetai was given the choice of either converting to Islam or being executed. Shabbetai became a Muslim, though he continued to practise the Jewish religion. Later Shabbetai was banished to Albania where he died still venerated by his loyal followers.

Shabbetai's followers denied that his mission had failed. To justify Shabbetai's apostasy, his followers developed a new theology of redemption, based on passages in the Zohar and the Kabbalah, according to which the Messiah had to descend into the domain of impurity in order to reclaim the holy sparks residing there, since all the other holy sparks had already been reclaimed. As these followers put it, if the only way to enter the king's palace is through he latrines, that is the way the king's son must go. After Shabbetai's death his followers still believed in him but kept quiet about it. These crypto-Shabbeteans behaved outwardly as learned and pious Jews but, in secret, carried out 'holy sins', sins committed for the express purpose of bringing to completion the task begun by Shabbetai. In one version of Shabbeteanism there was a belief in Shabbetai's 'second coming', when he would return to earth in all his glory to usher in the Messianic age. Shabbeteans were active in Prague until the beginning of the nineteenth century. In the eighteenth century the *Frankist sect, the followers of Jacob Frank, who claimed to be a reincarnation of Shabbetai Zevi, carried out bizarre rituals which included sexual excesses such as incest. Eventually the Frankists became converted to Christianity. In the aftermath of these startling events, the Rabbis banned the study of the Kabbalah for men before the age of 40 and became suspicious of groups such as the Hasidim, who were influenced by the Kabbalah. In the Rabbinic polemics against the Hasidim the complaint is voiced again and again that they are either Shabbateans or are, at least, influenced by Shabbatean heretical ideas. *Scholem was convinced that there was some truth in this contention but more recent scholarship is less confident that a link can be found between Shabbateanism and Hasidism. Similarly, the view has not been substantiated that the antinomian tendencies in Shabbeteanism had an influence on the early Reform movement.

Gershom Scholem, *Sabbatai Sevi: The Mystical Messiah*, trans. R. J. Zwi Werblowsky (London, 1973).

**Shammai** Prominent teacher, together with *Hillel, of the first century BCE. In the famous story of the two proselytes (*Shabbat* 31a) the Talmud advises: 'Let a man always be as humble as Hillel and never as cantankerous as Shammai.' It is curious, therefore, that the saying is attributed to Shammai in Ethics of the Fathers (1. 15): 'Welcome every man with a cheerful countenance.' There were probably different traditions regarding Shammai's character. The numerous debates between the House of Shammai and the House of Hillel are referred to frequently in the Mishnah and the Talmud. It is also somewhat strange that only a very few debates are recorded between Shammai and Hillel themselves, compared with the many between the two houses.

**Shavuot** The Feast of Weeks, Pentecost, the festival celebrated on 6 Sivan (and the 7 Sivan in the *Diaspora). In the book of Exodus (34:

22) the festival is called the Festival of Weeks (Shavuot means 'weeks') as it is in the book of Deuteronomy (16: 16), where it is one of the three pilgrim festivals when the people visited the Temple, the others being *Passover and *Tabernacles. The name Shavuot is derived from the statement in the book of Leviticus (23: 15–16) that the festival falls after seven weeks have been counted from the day after the *Omer is brought, hence also the name Pentecost ('fifty'), though this name is not used in the Jewish sources. The Rabbinic name for the festival is Atzeret, a name used for other festivals (Leviticus 23: 26; Numbers 29: 35). The original meaning of Atzeret is not clear (the word is usually translated as 'Solemn Assembly') but the Rabbis seem to understand it as meaning 'completion' or 'adjunct' and it is used of Shavuot in the sense that it is a complement to the festival of Passover. According to the Leviticus passage, the fifty days are to be counted 'from the morrow of the Sabbath'. The *Sadducees in Temple times, took this to mean the Sabbath during Passover, while according to the *Pharisees the 'Sabbath' ('day of rest') means the first day of Passover. Thus for the Sadducees Shavuot always falls on a Sunday. We are told that, as on other matters, there was a firece debate between Sadducees and Pharisees on this question.

A remarkable transformation of this festival took place in Rabbinic times. In the Bible Shavuot is obviously a harvest festival. But, based on the verse in Exodus (19: 1) that the children of Israel came to *Sinai on the third month (the month later called Sivan), the Rabbinic understanding of the real significance of the festival is that it commemorates the giving of the Torah and Shavuot is referred to in the liturgy as: 'The season of the giving of our Torah.' Since the whole idea of Shavuot as a celebration of the Torah is a later development, there are no rituals on the day to express this event. Later Jewish teachers have put forward the view that there cannot be any rituals, since the festival does not celebrate any particular aspect of the Torah but the Torah as a whole, which is beyond any specific ritual.

However, over the centuries, a number of Shavuot *customs were introduced. It is the custom to eat dairy products on Shavuot. This might have been simply because Shavuot falls in the hot season when milk dishes are more acceptable fare. But various further ideas have been read into the custom: for instance, that the Torah is compared to milk since it nourishes both the very young and the very old and because, if kept in golden vessels, milk turns sour—a warning to the Torah scholar not to give in to *pride. It is the custom to adorn the synagogue with plants and flowers on Shavuot. One reason given is that this denotes the fragrance and beauty of the Torah. In a Midrashic legend, when the Torah was given at Sinai, the barren mountain became covered with luxuriant foliage. A few later Rabbinic authorities, however, objected to this custom on the grounds that to follow it is to copy Christian celebrations of the harvest festival. Under the influence of the mystics of *Safed, many communities observe an all-night vigil on the first night of Shavuot, during which an anthology of passages taken from all the branches of Torah learning is read.

The Torah *reading for the first day of Shavuot is the account of the theophany at Sinai (Exodus 19: 1–20: 26). The *Haftarah is the account of the prophet Ezekiel's vision of the '*Chariot', appropriate to the theme of the festival as a revelation to the individual prophet similar to the *revelation at Sinai to the people as a whole. The Torah reading for the second day in the Diaspora is from Deuteronomy 16: 1–17 and the Haftarah is the third chapter of the book of *Habakkuk in which there is a reference to a theophany. It is customary to read the book of Ruth on Shavuot because *Ruth is the supreme example of a woman who accepted the way of the Torah of her own free will and because the book has an agricultural background. According to the tradition King David, descended from Ruth, died on Shavuot, another reason for reading this book on the festival.

Chaim Pearl, *Guide to Shavuoth* (London, 1959).

**Sheḥitah** 'Slaughtering', from the root *shahat*, 'to kill'; the manner in which animals and fowl have to be killed for food if their meat is to be eaten (see DIETARY LAWS, KOSHER, and TEREFAH). There is no explicit reference in the Pentateuch to the need for *sheḥitah* for animals not offered as sacrifices in the Temple nor are there any indications as to how *sheḥitah* is to be carried out. In the Rabbinic tradition the laws of *sheḥitah* were conveyed by God to Moses at *Sinai. *Sheḥitah* is performed by a specially trained person, the *shoḥet*, who has to use a

finely honed knife free from the slightest notch. For an animal *sheḥitah* involves the cutting of the major portion of both the windpipe and the foodpipe, for a bird the major portion of either of these. Further rules are described in great detail in the sources; it is stated, for instance, that there must be no pause in the act from beginning to end. Maimonides (*Guide of the Perplexed*, 3. 48) understands the reason for the *sheḥitah* laws to be the avoidance of unnecessary cruelty to animals. It is permitted to kill animals and birds for food but forbidden to do this in a cruel manner. In modern times animal-welfare groups have tried to have *sheḥitah* banned on the grounds that it is a cruel method. Jews reply that, on the contrary, *sheḥitah* is the most painless method available, especially since it has to be carried out by a learned and pious man. No Jewish woman, it has been pointed out, will ever take a chicken and wring its neck. Since some defects in the lungs of an animal render the animal unfit to be eaten, the *shoḥet* is expected, after *sheḥitah*, to examine the lungs to see if they are free from these defects. Orthodox and Conservative Jews still keep the laws of *sheḥitah* and consider meat that comes from an animal which has not had *sheḥitah* to be non-kosher, as do some Reform Jews, although classical Reform saw no need to be particular about the *sheḥitah* laws since these are not found in the Torah.

Isaac Klein, 'Shehitah', in his *A Guide to Jewish Religious Practice* (New York, 1979), 307–12.

**Sheitel** 'Wig', worn by married women to avoid the offence of going about with uncovered head. It was considered immodest for Jewish married women to go out into a public place with the head bare (see BARE HEAD). The usual practice was to have a head-covering, often richly embroidered. But when, in the eighteenth century, wigs came into fashion, many Jewesses preferred to wear a *sheitel* as a head-covering, despite the opposition of some Rabbis who claimed that the *sheitel* gives the appearance that the head is uncovered and hence defeats the whole purpose of the law. Some exceedingly pious women still prefer a proper head-covering but the majority of Orthodox women do wear the *sheitel*. Reform and Conservative Jews and even some Orthodox Jews do not consider the wearing of a head-covering to be necessary nowadays since women today do not insist on having their heads covered, so that failure to do so is no longer any indication of immodesty.

**Shekhinah** The in-dwelling presence of God, from the root *shakhan*, 'to dwell'. The verbal form is found in Scripture, for example, in the verse: 'And let them make Me a sanctuary, that I may dwell [*ve-shakhanti*] among them' (Exodus 25: 8) but Shekhinah as a noun is a Rabbinic coinage, used in the Talmudic literature and the *Targum both for the abiding of God in a particular spot (see *HOLY PLACES) and as a divine *name irrespective of spatial location. Abelson, in his fine study of the immanence of God in the Rabbinic literature, identifies the idea of the Shekhinah with that of divine immanence; though it is doubtful whether such a reading of abstract philosophical thought into the very concrete Rabbinic literature can be justified. In an oft-quoted Talmudic passage (*Megillah* 29a) it is said: 'Come and see how beloved Israel is before the Omnipresent; for wherever they went in exile the Shekhinah went with them. When they were exiled to Egypt, the Shekhinah went with them; in Babylon the Shekhinah was with them; and in the future, when Israel will be redeemed, the Shekhinah will be with them.' The emphasis here, and in many passages of like nature, is on God's presence not being withdrawn, however Israel seems to have been forsaken by Him. The idea of God at work in and through the processes of the universe is expressed in the Bible and in the Rabbinic literature but is implied rather than stated explicitly. The pseudo-physical nature of the Shekhinah's manifestations could hardly have been expressed in more downright fashion than in the continuation of the above-mentioned Talmudic passage: 'Where [is the Shekhinah] in Babylon? Abayye said: In the synagogue of Huzal and in the synagogue of Shaf-ve-yativ. Do not, however, imagine that it is here and there, but it is sometimes in one and sometimes in the other. Said Abbaye: May I be rewarded because whenever I am within a parasang I go in and pray there. The father of Samuel and Levi were sitting in the synagogue of Shaf-ve-yativ in Nehardea. The Shekhinah came and they heard a sound of tumult and they rose and went out. Rabbi Sheshet was once sitting in the synagogue of Shaf ve-yativ in Nehardea, when the Shekhinah came. He did not go out and the ministering angels came and threatened him.

He turned and said: Sovereign of the universe, if one is afflicted [Rabbi Sheshet was blind] and one is not afflicted, who gives way to whom? So God said to them: Leave him alone.'

As in other highly speculative topics it is impossible to speak of *the* Rabbinic view. Rabbinic thought is neither abstract nor systematic so that the most that can be done is to note a few typical passages while appreciating that they are direct responses to particular situations rather than a systematic theology of the Shekhinah. A favourite Rabbinic metaphor is the *light or 'shining' (*ziv*) of the Shekhinah. A Midrashic paraphrase of the verse: 'May the Lord cause the light of His countenance to shine upon thee' (Numbers 6: 25) is: 'May He give thee of the light of the Shekhinah' (Sifre to the verse). A Midrashic homily (Numbers Rabbah 12: 4) compares the shining of the Shekhinah in the tent of meeting (Exodus 40: 35) to a cave by the sea. The sea rushes in to fill the cave, but the sea suffers no diminution of its waters. Similarly, the Shekhinah filled the tent of meeting, but it filled the world just the same. The shining of the Shekhinah is referred to in the famous statement about life in the *World to Come by the third century teacher *Rav (*Berakhot* 17a): 'In the World to Come there is no eating nor drinking nor propagation nor business nor jealousy nor hatred nor competition, but the righteous sit with their crowns on their heads and bask in the radiance [*ziv*] of the Shekhinah.'

### The Shekhinah in Jewish Philosophy

The medieval Jewish philosophers generally seek to understand the doctrine of the Shekhinah in a way that avoids both anthropomorphism and dualism. *Saadiah Gaon understands the Shekhinah to be a special light or 'created glory' by which God appears to His prophets. Maimonides (*Guide of the Perplexed*, i. 25) similarly understands the Shekhinah as God's created light and also notes that the expression 'dwelling' need not have a spatial connotation but can be used in the sense of permanent attachment. *Judah Halevi (*Kuzari*, ii. 62) understands the Shekhinah to be the Divine Influence which occupies in Israel the same place as the soul within the body. 'It granted them a divine life, and allowed them to find lustre, beauty and light in their souls, bodies, dispositions and houses. When it was absent from them, their intelligence waned, their bodies deteriorated, and their beauty failed.' Elsewhere (v. 23) Halevi makes a distinction between the visible Shekhinah, which appears to the prophets, and the invisible and spiritual Shekhinah which is 'with every born Israelite of virtuous life, pure heart, and upright mind before the Lord of Israel'. A popular *Yiddish expression for a person with a 'numinous' look is: 'the Shekhinah rests on his face'.

*The Shekhinah in the Kabbalah*

However the idea of the Shekhinah was understood in the Rabbinic tradition and by the medieval philosophers, it was never personalized in the way it is in the Kabbalah. According to the Kabbalistic doctrine of the *Sefirot, the Shekhinah is the Sefirah *Malkhut* ('Sovereignty'), a female element in the Godhead, as the Sefirah *Tiferet* ('Beauty') is the male principle, known as 'the Holy One, Blessed be He'. In highly charged mythological terms, the Kabbalists speak of the harmony of the Sefirot, the powers in the Godhead, as the 'union' of the Shekhinah and the Holy One, Blessed be He. In the Kabbalistic scheme, the *sex act between husband and wife becomes a mirror of the divine processes on high. Moreover, the Rabbinic idea of the exile of the Shekhinah means for the Kabbalists that in an unredeemed world part of God is exiled, so to speak, from God. To be sure, the Kabbalists are fully aware how offensive such a conception is if understood literally and in a grossly anthropomorphic manner. The Kabbalists never tire of stressing that it is the *En Sof that operates constantly in the Sefirotic processes and that to detach the Sefirot from one another and from the En Sof is mystical heresy. According to the Zohar, Adam's sin consisted precisely in this, that he detached, in his thought, the Shekhinah from the other Sefirot. In other words, the use of terms like male and female of the Sefirot must never be taken to mean that there are in the doctrine echoes of pagan notions such as the independent existence of a goddess and any kind of sexual activity on high. The Kabbalists sternly warn would-be students of the hidden science against entertaining notions of what they call *hagshamah*, 'corporeality', in the higher realms. For all that, opponents of the Kabbalah, medieval and modern, have been scandalized by what they see as an attempt at introducing pagan ideas into Judaism.

A source of particular offence was the mystical formula, introduced by the *Safed Kabbalists, before the performance of a precept (see MITZVAH) in which the mystical adept declares that he intends the act he performs to be 'for the sake of the unification of the Holy One, blessed be He, and His Shekhinah'. In his famous Responsum (no. 210) on the Kabbalah, the great German Halakhist, Yair Hayyim Bacharach (1638–1702), tells of a man who asked him to explain the meaning of this formula. Bacharach replied that it refers to a great mystery incapable of being understood by all but the greatest sages. When the man persisted, Bacharach admitted that he himself did not understand the meaning of these cryptic words. Bacharach insists that his reply was not an exercise in false modesty or a mere subterfuge in order to rid himself of the man's importunities. He really does not know the meaning of the formula and doubts whether any contemporary Kabbalist really understands it. In the eighteenth century, Rabbi Ezekiel *Landau (Responsum no. 93 of the *Yoreh Deah* section of his Responsa collection) made a fierce attack on the Hasidim who use this formula but the Hasidic master, Hayyim of Czernowitz (d. 1813) sprang to the defence of the practice. Nowadays the formula is often used by Orthodox Jews who are neither Hasidim nor Kabbalists and it is printed in many traditional prayer books, but it is uttered without any real attempt at probing its meaning. Jewish feminists (see FEMINISM) have naturally welcomed the doctrine of the Shekhinah in its Kabbalistic understanding as providing powerful support, from one branch of Jewish thought at least, to their refusal to describe God solely in male terms.

J. Abelson, *The Immanence of God in Rabbinical Literature* (London, 1912).
Gershom Scholem, '*Shekhinah*: The Feminine Element in Divinity', in his *On the Mystical Shape of the Godhead* (New York, 1991), 140–96.

**Shema** The Jewish declaration of faith: 'Hear [*shema*] O Israel, the Lord our God, the Lord is One' (Deuteronomy 6: 4). To this basic verse of the Shema are added the whole paragraph containing the verse (Deuteronomy 6: 4–9); the paragraph beginning: 'And it shall come to pass' (Deuteronomy 11: 13–21); and the paragraph containing the law of *tzitzit (Numbers 15: 37–41). The two paragraphs in Deuteronomy state that 'these words should be spoken of when lying down and when rising up'. The Rabbis understand 'these words' to mean the words of the Shema and 'when lying down and rising up' to mean that the Shema must be recited in the evening and in the morning, so that it must be recited each night and morning, at the exact times described in detail in the Talmud and the Codes. The Mishnah in the first tractate of the Talmud, tractate *Berakhot*, rules, for instance, that the night Shema should ideally be recited before midnight but can be recited any time during the night until daybreak. The morning Shema should not be recited before daybreak or after the time when about a quarter of the day has gone by. The Mishnah also records a debate between the House of *Shammai and the House of *Hillel. The former took 'lying down and rising up' literally so that, in their view, the night Shema should be recited in a reclining posture, the morning Shema in an upright posture. The Hillelites, on the other hand, understood 'lying down and rising up' as referring to the times when the Shema is to be recited and, in their view, no particular posture need be adopted when reciting the Shema. The paragraph from Numbers was added because of the reference in it to the Exodus from Egypt, since the verse states: 'that thou mayest remember the day when thou camest forth out of the land of Egypt all the days of thy life' (Deuteronomy 16: 3). The two passages from Deuteronomy are written in the *mezuzah and are two of the four in the *tefillin.

After the first verse of the Shema, the words: 'Blessed be the name of His glorious Kingdom for ever and ever' are recited softly, unlike the Shema itself which is recited in a loud voice. The Talmud says that this has to be recited in an undertone because it is not in Scripture. Some modern scholars hold that, under Roman dominion, it was hazardous for Jews to recite this declaration in a loud voice since it might be understood by the Roman authorities as a challenge to their rule. The original implication of the declaration may, indeed, have been that it is as if to say: 'God is our King and not the Romans now ruling over us.' These two declarations are recited by the whole congregation in unison at the solemn Neilah ('Closing') service on *Yom Kippur, the Shema once, 'Blessed be the name' three times. Contrary to the practice during the rest of the year, 'Blessed be the name' is recited in the evening and morning on

Yom Kippur in a loud voice, as if to say: 'On the great Day of Atonement we fear no one in hoping for the Kingdom of Heaven to be established and we say these words aloud.'

Where physically possible, the first verse of the Shema is recited by a dying person when he senses that his soul is ready to leave the body. It is the custom to teach children to say the first verse of the Shema as soon as they begin to talk. There are records of Jewish *martyrs reciting the Shema as they went to their death. The Rabbis introduced a number of *benedictions to be recited before and after the reading of the Shema: two before and two after the evening Shema, two before and one after the morning Shema. A Talmudic statement that the Shema should be recited 'on the bed' is still followed by devout Jews who, in addition to the evening Shema, recite the Shema again before going to sleep. The Talmudic reason, that this is to ward off the *demons, is interpreted by Menahem *Meiri as meaning that it is to prevent heretical thoughts, the 'demons' of unbelief, entering the mind when it is less than alert as a man is about to go to sleep.

*Interpretations of the Shema*

Naturally, since it is a declaration of Jewish belief of the highest significance the Shema, especially the first verse, the Shema proper, has received numerous interpretations throughout the history of Jewish thought. One of the questions discussed is, who is the 'Israel' to whom the Jew refers when he says 'Hear O Israel'? Moses used the word 'Israel' because he was addressing the people of Israel as a whole, but who is being addressed as 'Israel' by the Jew who now recites the Shema? One interpretation is that when reciting the Shema, each Jew is addressing his fellow Jew, calling on him to 'hear' the declaration of faith. A beautiful Midrashic interpretation is that the 'Hear O Israel' refers to the patriarch *Jacob, given the name of Israel. The Jew declares to his ancestor, Israel, that he has kept faith with his teachings. A mystical interpretation is that the Jew is addressing the 'Israel' part of his own soul, reminding himself of his higher nature. He is saying to himself: 'Hear O Israel.'

The word *eḥad* in the Shema, usually translated as 'one', may originally have had the meaning of 'alone', so that the verse should be rendered: 'Hear O Israel, the Lord is our God, the Lord alone', this being intended to affirm the unity of God and to declare that there are no other gods. God alone is God. The medieval thinkers generally understood *eḥad* to mean 'unique'. For these thinkers, the Shema does not only declare polytheism to be false—that there is only one God, not many gods—but states that God is wholly other. His being is a unique being to which no creature can in any way be compared. According to the Zohar the divine names mentioned in the Shema hint at the *Sefirot, the powers in the Godhead, which must not be detached in thought from one another or from the *En Sof but must be seen as a unity. When a man recites the Shema and declares this unity, he assists in promoting the harmony of the Sefirot so that the divine grace can flow unimpeded throughout all creation. The recital of the Shema, like other ritual acts for the Kabbalists, has cosmic significance in that it exerts an influence on the higher realms. In some versions of Hasidic thought, *eḥad* means that, from the point of view of ultimate reality, there is only God. On this reading of the Shema, it declares that God is the One, the sole Being. Not only are there no gods, there are, from the divine point of view, no creatures. While creatures enjoy existence, from their point of view, from the divine point of view, so to speak, there is none else (see HABAD, HASIDISM, and PANENTHEISM).

The recital of the Shema is called in the Mishnah (*Berakhot*, 2. 2) 'the taking-on of the yoke of the *Kingdom of Heaven', that is, the acceptance of God as Creator and Lord of the universe with the implications of this belief for the conduct of human life. Devout Jews cover their eyes when reciting the first verse of the Shema as an aid to concentration on this tremendous theme of God's sovereignty. The theme of kingship is further expressed in the Shema, in the fact that of the three letters of the word *eḥad*, *alef* has the numerical value of 1; *ḥet* of 8, and *dalet* of 4. Thus, it is said, when the word *eḥad* is recited the thought should be in the mind that God, the One, is declared King in the seven heavens and the earth and in the four directions, north, south, east, and west. One of the Jewish moralists remarked that it is easy enough to declare that God reigns in the seven heavens, the earth, and in all four directions. The difficult thing is to accept His dominion over the individual self. The Kingdom of Heaven, for traditional Judaism, is not only a hope for the future but is realized for the

individual Jew when he accepts it on reading the Shema. Yet Rabbinic theology also knows of the establishment of the Kingdom of Heaven for all men in the Messianic age (see *Messiah) when all mankind will acknowledge the truth. The ancient Rabbinic Midrash known as the *Sifre to the first verse of the Shema understands the verse to mean that the Lord is our God in this world, where He is only hailed as God by Israel, but He will be acknowledged by all in the *World to Come, the Sifre understanding the end of the verse to mean: 'He *will* be One.' The Sifre quotes in this connection the verse in Zechariah (14: 9): 'In that day shall the Lord be One and His name One.' In another Midrashic interpretation, the two divine names in the Shema, the *Tetragrammaton ('the Lord') and Elohim ('our God') denote, respectively, God's quality of mercy and His quality of judgement; yielding the thought that it is all one to the righteous whether God shows Himself to them in the quality of mercy or of judgement. The legions of a human king, says the Midrash, only do battle on his behalf if he provides them with their rations but Israel fights the battles of the Lord even when He allows the people to go hungry. Clearly behind this kind of Midrashic comment is the ever-present temptation, in Rabbinic times, for Jews to entertain a dualistic philosophy of religion, of which there were many such in the Hellenistic world. Especially in Babylon, where Persian dualism was the official religion, the Rabbis warn constantly against believing in 'two powers', Ormuzd and Ahriman, the good god responsible for life's bounties, the evil god for life's woes. A fourth-century teacher (*Berakhot* 33b) went so far as to rule that it is forbidden to repeat the first verse of the Shema itself, since this may suggest that the repetition refers to two deities. It is ironic that the Shema, the declaration of pure monotheism, was used by Christian theologians in the Middle Ages to refer to the Trinity, since there are three divine names. The Jewish thinkers retorted that, on the contrary, the Shema is directed against precisely such doctrines as that of the triune God. 'The Lord is One,' they said, means that there is no multiplicity in His Being.

Eugene B. Borowitz (ed.), *Eḥad: The Many Meanings of God is One* (New York, 1988).
Louis Jacobs, 'God's Unity', in his *Principles of the Jewish Faith* (Northvale, NJ, and London, 1988), 95–117.

**Shemini Atzeret** The festival that falls on 22 Tishri and is the eighth day of the festival of *Tabernacles. Shemini means 'eighth' and Atzeret is usually translated as 'Solemn Assembly', thus 'the Eighth Day of Solemn Assembly', although Atzeret may mean 'adjunct'; so that this festival is understood to be a complement to Tabernacles as *Shavuot is to *Passover. According to the Rabbis, Shemini Atzeret is also a festival in its own right in some respects. It is mentioned as a separate festival in the book of Leviticus (23: 36) and in the book of Numbers (29: 35) in the list of festivals. There are no special rituals for Shemini Atzeret except that on it the special prayer for *rain called *Geshem* ('Rain') is recited during the Musaf ('Additional Service') of the day. In Israel Shemini Atzeret is also the festival of *Simhat Tórah but in the *Diaspora Simhat Torah is celebrated on the next day, though it is still referred to as Shemini Atzeret. As the culmination of the penitential season from *Rosh Ha-Shanah to *Yom Kippur and of the festive season of Tabernacles, Shemini Atzeret is the most joyous festival in the Jewish *calendar, though the joy is expressed in a less boisterous manner than on *Purim.

**Sherira Gaon** Head of the college in Pumbedita (see GEONIM). Reliable reports have it that Sherira lived for 100 years, the date of his death being given as around the year 1000. Sherira did not assume office as Gaon of Pumbedita until he was almost 70 years of age, after the Gaonite had suffered an eclipse. Thanks to Sherira's efforts, the Gaonite of Pumbedita became a central authority for Jews in other parts of the Jewish world. Because of Sherira's great age he was assisted towards the end of his life by his son, *Hai, who was officially appointed Gaon of Pumbedita when Sherira died. Sherira and Hai feature very prominently in the *Responsa of the Geonim, of which various collections have been made. Questions were addressed to these two Geonim from many parts of the Jewish world and their replies became authoritative in subsequent codifications of Jewish law.

Sherira's chief claim to fame rests on the letter he wrote in in the year 987 to Jacob ben Nissim of Kairowan in North Africa, Jacob having requested Sherira to explain in detail how the Mishnah and the Talmud had been compiled. Sherira's reply, in Aramaic, known as *The Letter of Rav Sherira Gaon*, is a major source for the history of the Talmudic period, based as it is not only on Sherira's erudition but also on the traditions preserved in the Babylonian schools. For the first time we have in the *Letter* a comprehensive account of how Rabbi *Judah the Prince compiled the Mishnah and how the Babylonian teachers compiled the Talmud. Sherira's *Letter* is, however, used by modern historians of the Talmudic period with a degree of caution since, after all, it was written hundreds of years after the events of which it tells and occasionally Sherira reads back into the Talmudic period the conditions in the Babylonian schools of his and recent ages.

**Shneur Zalman of Liady** Hasidic master (1745–1813), founder of the *Habad school in *Hasidism. Shneur Zalman (the name Shneur probably comes from 'Señor', suggesting that the family came originally from Spain) was born in the Belorussian town of Liozno, near Vitebsk. He married at an early age and, with the approval of his young wife but against the wishes of both his father and father-in-law who were suspicious of the new trends, he resolved to journey to *Dov Baer of Mezhirech, disciple of the *Baal Shem Tov and organizer of the Hasidic movement, in order to learn, as he said, how to pray. In this he was typical of those learned young men who required a more inward and mystical approach. Dov Baer arranged for his son, 'Abraham the Angel', as he was called because of his ascetic life, to introduce Shneur Zalman into the mysteries of the Kabbalah while Shneur Zalman would teach the Talmud to Abraham. From all accounts and from his own testimony, Shneur Zalman's Hasidic philosophy owes much to the ideas of Dov Baer as mediated through the 'Angel'. Dov Baer encouraged Shneur Zalman to compile a new *Shulḥan Arukh*, a code of Jewish law that would take into account the latest opinions. This work, published in 1814, is known as *Shulḥan Arukh Ha-Rav*, 'The Rabbi's Shulḥan Arukh,' and, written with great clarity in a fine Hebrew style, is now a major source for practical decisions even among Rabbis remote from Hasidism.

When Dov Baer died in 1772, Shneur Zalman became a Hasidic master in his own right. He and an older colleague, Menahem Mendel of Vitbesk, awakened the suspicions of the *Mitnaggedim led by *Elijah, Gaon of Vilna.

The two Hasidic leaders sought an audience with the Gaon of Vilna to persuade him that Hasidic views were in no way heretical but the Gaon refused to see them. Shneur Zalman's teachings and activity were brought, by the Mitnaggedim, to the attention of the Russian government, alert to any movement smacking of rebellion, and in 1798 he was arrested, on a trumped-up charge, and imprisoned in the fortress at St Petersburg. All charges were eventually dropped and Shneur Zalman was released on 19 Kislev. Habad Hasidim, and other Hasidic groups, saw Shneur Zalman's release as the divinely sanctioned victory of Hasidism over its opponents. To this day Habad Hasidim celebrate 19 Kislev as a minor festival. After his release Shneur Zalman settled in Liady. Shneur Zalman, unlike some other Hasidic masters, wished to see the Czarist forces prevail over Napoleon's army. In a letter to one of his followers, Shneur Zalman expressed his fears that if Napoleon were to be victorious the spiritual conditions of Russian Jewry would deteriorate, even though they would enjoy considerable material benefits. When Napoleon's army advanced on Moscow, Shneur Zalman fled to the Ukraine but died on the way. Shneur Zalman was succeeded by his son, *Dov Baer of Lubavitch. Habad Hasidim refer to Shneur Zalman as the Alter Rebbe ('the Old Rebbe'). An often reproduced portrait of Shneur Zalman (painted, it is said, during his imprisonment) shows him to have been, if such can be assessed from a painting, a profound thinker and holy man, a picture amply supported by his writings.

Shneur Zalman's *Tanya* (so-called after its opening word in Aramaic, *Tanya*, 'It was taught') is a systematic treatment of Kabbalistic and Hasidic themes in the Habad interpretation. The work, in its complete form, was published in Shklov in 1814 since when it has gone into numerous editions. Lubavitch Hasidim often place their copy of the *Tanya* in the bag in which they keep their *tallit and treat the work with a veneration that appears to the non-Hasid to be bordering on the bizarre. The first section of the *Tanya* deals with the psychology of the religious life. Here the Talmudic division of persons into the righteous, the wicked, and those in between is given a novel interpretation. The righteous man (*tzaddik*) has 'killed' his evil inclination, *yetzer ha-ra* (see YETZER HA-TOV AND YETZER HA-RA). He belongs in the ranks of the *saints who are no longer tempted by earthly desires. The 'in-between' (*benoni*) is not simply an average person, neither overrighteous nor very wicked, but is the man who does not wittingly commit any sin yet is engaged throughout his life in the struggle between his good and evil inclination. The reason why such struggle is unavoidable for every Jew other than the *tzaddik* is because a Jew has two souls: the 'animal soul', the basic life-force which sustains the body, and the 'divine soul', conceived of as a mystical divine spark in the Jewish soul, a portion of the *En Sof hidden deep in the recesses of the psyche. The animal soul drags a man down, the divine soul pulls him upwards towards God. Only Jews, the descendants of the righteous *patriarchs, have a divine soul. This and other features of Shneur Zalman's particularism have been attacked by modern writers but his followers have defended his views, presenting them in a less stark and offensive manner (see CHOSEN PEOPLE and GENTILES).

The second section of the *Tanya* deals with mystical theology. Here Shneur Zalman puts forward his acosmic philosophy (see PANENTHEISM), according to which the whole universe is 'in' God and creatures only appear to enjoy independent existence, just as, Shneur Zalman says, the rays of the sun can be seen and experienced as real on earth but in the sun itself the rays vanish into nothingness. According to Shneur Zalman, improvement of the character cannot be achieved by any direct onslaught on the emotions but only by reflection on the tremendous idea that all is in God. It is when the Jew reflects on the Kabbalistic teaching that the whole universe and man within it are part of a great chain of being reaching back to and included in the En Sof, that his emotions are bestirred and the character refined. As Shneur Zalman puts it, it is the intellect that influences the emotions, not the other way round. Because of the emphasis it places on intellectual perception, Habad is often referred to as the intellectual branch of Hasidism. In fact, Habad is, in a sense, a separate movement, differing in important respects from the highly emotionally charged thoughts and practices of other Hasidic groupings. Yet all Hasidim, to whichever *Rebbe they owe their allegiance, accept Shneur Zalman as one of Hasidism's pioneering spirits.

Nisson Mindel, *Rabbi Schneur Zalman of Liadi*, (New York, 1969).
Shneur Zalman, *Tanya*, bilingual ed. (New York and London, 1973).

**Shofar** The horn sounded on the New Year festival, *Rosh Ha-Shanah. This festival is described in the *Pentateuch as a day of blowing the horn (Leviticus 23: 23–25; Numbers 19: 1–6). According to the Talmudic Rabbis, the horn of any clean animal (i.e. any *kosher animal; see DIETARY LAWS), sheep, goat, or antelope, is fit to be used on Rosh Ha-Shanah but preference is given to the ram's horn because of the substitution of a ram for Isaac at the *Akedah (Genesis 22: 13). The only exception made by the Rabbis was the horn of a cow, because Israel had once worshipped the *golden calf and it is unfitting for Israel to appear before God on the great day of judgement with something which would recall this lapse. As the Rabbis put it: 'A prosecutor cannot act as a defender.' For the same reason the *Sefer Hasidim advises strongly against a quarrelsome man, notorious for fault-finding, being appointed to blow the shofar on Rosh Ha-Shanah.

*Reasons for the* Shofar

The Torah gives no reason for the command to blow the shofar on Rosh Ha-Shanah. This is one of the precepts referred to by the Rabbis as divine decrees which have to be obeyed even if the reason for them is unknown. When the Talmud (*Rosh Ha-Shanah*, 16a) asks: 'Why do we sound the shofar on Rosh Ha-Shanah?' the immediate retort is: 'Why do we blow [you ask]? We blow because the All-Merciful has told us to blow.' For all that, the strange, fascinating ritual has encouraged later teachers to suggest reasons of their own. Well known are Maimonides' remarks in this connection (in the section of his Code which deals with repentance):

'Although it is a divine decree that we blow the Shofar on Rosh Ha-Shanah, a hint of the following idea is contained in the command. It is as if.to say: "Awake from your slumbers, you who have fallen asleep in life, and reflect on your deeds. Remember your Creator. Be not of those who miss reality in the pursuit of shadows, and waste their years in seeking after vain things which do not profit or deliver. Look well to your souls, and let there be betterment in your acts. Forsake each of you your evil ways and thoughts.'"

Other Jewish thinkers have advanced their own reasons for blowing the shofar on Rosh Ha-Shanah or, at least, have read their ideas into the rite. David *Abudarham states that *Saadiah Gaon advanced no less than ten different 'reasons', of which the following have been particularly noted in later discussions of the rite. On Rosh Ha-Shanah God is hailed as King and trumpets are sounded at the coronation of a king. The sound of the shofar was heard at *Sinai (Exodus 19: 16, 19; 20: 18), so that on Rosh Ha-Shanah Jews reaffirm their loyalty to the Torah by re-enacting the theophany at Sinai. This theme is, in fact, found in the Rabbinic rule of the Shofarot, the scriptural verses recited during the Musaf service on Rosh Ha-Shanah in which the Sinai verses are quoted. On Rosh Ha-Shanah the merits of Abraham, ready to sacrifice Isaac, are invoked and the ram's horn is a reminder, as above, of Abraham's trial. The eschatalogical motif is also introduced. The prophet speaks of the great shofar that will be blown to herald the advent of the *Messiah (Isaiah 27: 13). Centuries before Saadiah, *Philo of Alexandria noted the connection between the blowing of the shofar and the theophany at Sinai. Philo also suggests that since trumpets are sounded when armies go into battle, the shofar is a reminder of the horrors of warfare, a prayer to God to help establish peace on earth, and an expression of gratitude to Him when the precious gift of peace is given to mankind. Jewish mystical writers note that the shofar is a wind instrument and the Hebrew word for 'wind', ruah, can also mean 'spirit'. The blowing of the shofar reminds the Jew to allow a greater degree of *spirituality to enter his life. The mystics also see the blowing of the shofar as a prayer without words, the world of the spirit being beyond any expression that can be given to it in words. The American thinker, Milton *Steinberg, noting that the shofar produces weeping sounds, sees the sounding of the shofar on Rosh Ha-Shanah as a reminder of weeping humanity, the unspeakable pain of the world which decent human beings have to seek to remove, so far as this lies in their power. All this is a good example of how Jewish thinkers have read significant ideas into an apparently meaningless rite, although it is only fair to say that the average Jew follows the rule that the shofar be blown on Rosh Ha-Shanah simply because this is the way of divine worship on the day as hallowed by tradition, and he does not bother to look for reasons.

## The Laws of the Shofar

As the rite of blowing the *shofar* was developed by the Rabbis in the Talmud, there are three distinct *shofar* sounds: the *tekiah*, a long drawn-out single blast; the *shevarim*, a series of three broken sounds (from the root *shavar*, 'to break'); and the *teruah*, sound of lament, a series of nine very short blasts. The *tekiah* is sounded both before and after the other sounds so that, at the least, there are thirty *shofar* sounds. When T is made to stand for *tekiah*, Te for *teruah* and S for *shevarim*, the scheme can be represented as:

TSTeT TSTeT TSTeT
TST TST TST
TTeT TTeT TTeT

The final *tekiah* is a very long drawn-out blast called *tekiah gedolah*, 'the great *tekiah*'. These sounds, like the *shofar* itself, have been given many interpretations. A popular one is that when a man makes his resolve to do better in the year ahead, he is at first confident that he will see it through. This is represented by the *tekiah*. But then his resolve weakens and there is a struggle in his soul, represented by the broken notes of *shevarim* and *teruah*. Yet, if he perseveres he will regain his confidence and win out, as represented by the second *tekiah*. In all congregations this set of thirty blasts is sounded after the reading of the Torah but there are varying customs regarding the blowing of the *shofar* at other parts of the service. Before the *shofar* is sounded the benediction is recited by the one who blows (any member of the congregation, provided he is skilful in producing the notes): 'Blessed art Thou, O Lord our God, King of the universe, who has sanctified us with Thy commandments and has commanded us to hear the sound of the *shofar*.' The congregation stands while the *shofar* is sounded. In order to prevent any mistakes being made by the one who blows, a member of the congregation calls out to him each note before he sounds it. The *shofar* should be held facing towards the right with its wider end facing upwards. The *shofar* should be curved, not straight, symbolic of man's readiness to bow in submission to God. The *shofar* is not sounded in Orthodox and Conservative congregations when the first day of Rosh Ha-Shanah falls on the Sabbath and it is then sounded only on the second day. Since Reform keeps only one day of Rosh Ha-Shanah, Reform congregations sound the *shofar* even when the festival falls on the Sabbath.

Max Arzt, 'The Sounding of the *Shofar*', in *Justice and Mercy* (New York, 1963), 149–55.

**Shulḥan Arukh** 'Arranged Table', the standard Code of Jewish law compiled by Joseph *Karo in the sixteenth century with glosses by Moses *Isserles. The *Shulḥan Arukh* is based on Karo's analysis of the decisions of earlier codifiers in his *Bet Yosef* to the Tur, the Code compiled by the German authority, *Jacob ben Asher. Karo's method is to examine all the opinions of his predecessors, weigh them up, and then arrive at a definite ruling in every case (see CODIFICATION). For the benefit of students, as he remarks, Karo presented his final rulings (but not the acute reasoning behind them) in the *Shulḥan Arukh*. Since Karo generally follows Sephardi authorities (in the *Shulḥan Arukh* he often simply quotes Maimonides verbatim) Isserles felt it necessary to add his glosses in which, among other matters, the Ashkenazi practices and customs would be recorded. There are thus two authors of the *Shulḥan Arukh*, Karo and Isserles, and the *Shulḥan Arukh* is a kind of double Code, Karo's rulings being the standard for *Sephardim those of Isserles for the *Ashkenazim. The *Shulḥan Arukh* follows the Tur in its arrangement of the laws in four parts: 1. *Oraḥ Ḥayyim* ('Path of Life'), dealing with prayer, the Sabbath and festivals, and general religious duties; 2. *Yoreh Deah* ('Teaching Knowledge'), dealing with more complex issues requiring Rabbinic decisions; 3. *Even Ha-Ezer* ('Stone of Help'), dealing with the laws of marriage and divorce; 4. *Ḥoshen Mishpat* ('Breastplate of Judgement'), dealing with civil law and general jurisprudence. The *Shulḥan Arukh* also follows the arrangement of the Tur with regard to the numbered sections in each part, but subdivides each section into paragraphs. The *Shulḥan Arukh* is, consequently, quoted by stating the part, the section, and the paragraph, for example, *Oraḥ Ḥayyim*, 141. 2.

A number of commentaries to the *Shulḥan Arukh* were published in the seventeenth century and these are usually printed in editions of the work at the side of the text. In these commentaries the arguments for the rulings of Karo and Isserles are examined, defended, and often criticized. The whole work then became authoritative, although, in fact, it is the Talmud, not the *Shulḥan Arukh*, which is the final *authority in Jewish law; the *Shulḥan Arukh* is the record of the Talmudic rulings after these had undergone the process of debate, discussion, and final acceptance for practical law. Legal authorities who lived before the *Shulḥan Arukh* are known as *Rishonim* ('Early Ones'), those after the *Shulḥan Arukh* as *Aḥaronim* ('Later Ones'). Rabbis, when deciding on matters not stated explicitly in the *Shulḥan Arukh* or when trying, for various reasons, to go beyond the rulings of the *Shulḥan Arukh*, will consult the works of both but will give greater weight to the opinions of the *Rishonim*.

As an illustration of how the process works, the opening paragraph of the *Shulḥan Arukh* (*Oraḥ Ḥayyim*, 1. 1) can be given. Karo's formulation, based on the Tur's lengthy introduction and a statement in the Talmud, is: 'He should be as strong as a lion to rise up in the morning for the service of his Creator so as to wake before the dawn.' Isserles adds a gloss, also based on the Tur, to the effect that, at least, he should not get up too late to pray together with the congregation in the synagogue. Isserles, a keen student of philosophy, adds further a paraphrase of the remarks by Maimonides, in the *Guide of the Perplexed* (3. 52), in which it is stated that people behave differently when in the presence of a king than when in their own home. How much more must a man conduct himself in awe and humility in the presence of the King of kings who is a constant witness of all his deeds. Passages like this, of which there are many, based on spiritual and ethical ideals, only belong to Jewish law because they have been recorded in the *Shulḥan Arukh* by Karo and Isserles. Except for the most saintly, they do not have the same binding force as, say, the *dietary laws or the laws of *marriage.

### Attitudes to the Shulḥan Arukh

Orthodox Judaism accepts the *Shulḥan Arukh* as binding, although this does not mean that Orthodox Jews follow all the bare rulings of the work. The standard commentaries and later authorities are often relied on where a ruling is required which departs from that of the *Shulḥan Arukh*, especially when new conditions demand fresh rulings. Many Hasidic masters, while generally accepting the authority of the *Shulḥan Arukh*, felt themselves free to offer their prayers at different times from those laid down in the *Shulḥan Arukh*. A Hasidic saying has it that the difference between the Hasidim and the

*Mitnaggedim is that the Hasidim stand in awe of God while the Mitnaggedim stand in awe of the *Shulḥan Arukh*. But generally, a strictly Orthodox Jew is known as 'a *Shulḥan Arukh* Jew'. Reform Judaism in the nineteenth century had a negative attitude to the *Halakhah generally, to say nothing of the codification of the Halakhah in the *Shulḥan Arukh*. At the Reform Synod in Augsburg in 1871 a debate took place on the suggestion that a new, thoroughly revised *Shulḥan Arukh*, more in line with Reform philosophy, should be produced. Against this it was argued that any revision would imply recognition that the *Shulḥan Arukh* is an authority, which it is not for Reform, that such a *Shulḥan Arukh* would stifle further development in Judaism, and that so little would be left when the obsolete elements (from the Reform point of view) had been removed that a revision was pointless. This remains the Reform position, though there is evident, in contemporary versions of Reform, a greater awareness of the values enshrined in some, at least, of the rulings of the *Shulḥan Arukh* (see REFORM).

Conservative Judaism, with its stress on the developing nature of Judaism in general and Jewish law in particular, has a far more positive attitude to the *Shulḥan Arukh* as a stage in this development but feels free to employ the Halakhic machinery in order to develop the law further even though, as a result, changes may be introduced contrary to the rulings of the *Shulḥan Arukh*: for instance, on the question of riding in an automobile to the synagogue on the Sabbath. It is also true that for all three groups the actual practice of Jews has a decisive voice, whether or not this is officially acknowledged. Even among Orthodox Rabbis, the saying is popular that there is a fifth, unwritten part of the *Shulḥan Arukh* by which the other four parts are to be interpreted. This is the part of common sense.

Boaz Cohen, 'The Shulḥan Aruk as a Guide to Religious Practice Today', in his: *Law and Tradition in Judaism* (New York, 1959), 62–99.
Isadore Twersky, 'The Shulḥan 'Aruk: Enduring Code of Jewish Law', in his *Studies in Jewish Law and Philosophy* (New York, 1982), 130–47.

**Siddur**  See Prayer Book.

**Simeon Ben Yohai**  Famous Rabbi of the second century CE, disciple of Rabbi *Akiba and colleague of Rabbi *Meir, Rabbi Judah, and Rabbi Jose. Rabbi Simeon ben Yohai's opinions in Halakhah are referred to frequently in the Talmudic records of the debates and discussions among the *Tannaim. He was also renowned as an exponent of Scripture and a miracle-worker. In the Talmudic legend, Rabbi Simeon made some adverse remarks about the Roman occupation of Judaea (see ROME) and when this was reported to the government authorities he was obliged to flee for his life. Together with his son, Eleazar, he lived in a cave for thirteen years. According to the Kabbalists, Rabbi Simeon ben Yohai is the author of the *Zohar, a work composed in the main during his forced stay in the cave and the bulk of which consists of mystical interpretations of Scripture by Rabbi Simeon and his chosen companions. Recent Zoharic scholarship has demonstrated that the true author of the major part of the Zohar was Moses de *Leon, who made Rabbi Simeon the hero of his pseudepigraphic work. An annual pilgrimage is still made on *Lag Ba-Omer, the anniversary of Rabbi Simeon's death, to his supposed tomb in Meron, near *Safed.

**Simhat Torah** 'Rejoicing of the Law', the festival at the end of *Tabernacles, on the eighth day (22 Tishri) in Israel, coinciding with *Shemini Atzeret; the ninth day (23 Tishri) in the *Diaspora, the second day of Shemini Atzeret. Reform Jews do not observe the second days of the festivals and, since they only have one day of Shemini Atzeret, Simhat Torah is celebrated on this day as it is in Israel. The celebration of Simhat Torah dates from the ninth century (in the liturgy the ninth day is referred to as Shemini Atzeret, not Simhat Torah) and is based on the Babylonian custom (now universally followed) of *reading the Torah in an annual cycle, unlike the triennial cycle in which the Torah was read by Palestinian Jewry in Talmudic times. The weekly portions are so arranged that the final portion of the Torah (Deuteronomy 33 and 34) is left to be completed on this day. On the same day the cycle begins again with the reading of the first portion of Genesis. The person who has the honour of being called up to the final reading from Deuteronomy is called the Hatan Torah, 'the Bridegroom of the Torah', while the one called to the reading of the first portion of Genesis is called Hatan Bereshit 'the Bridegroom of Bereshit' ('In the beginning', the first word of Genesis and of the whole Torah). On the eve of Simhat Torah and during the day all

the Scrolls (see SEFER TORAH) are taken from the *Ark and carried in procession seven times around the synagogue, accompanied by singing and dancing and general merriment. In many synagogues it is the custom to call up for the reading every member of the congregation, the portions being repeated for as many times as required for the purpose, though otherwise a portion is not read more than once on the same day. All the children in the synagogue are called up together to a portion of the Torah and they are blessed by the congregation and given sweets, apples, and other treats. The children also walk in the procession holding flags on which there is a symbol of the Torah. It is customary for the two 'Bridegrooms' to give a party, or at least, provide drinks and cakes, for the congregation. In some Reform congregations women are given these honours and are called: 'the Bride of the Torah' and 'the Bride of Genesis'—surely a little odd, since the Torah is a 'female'.

**Sin and Repentance** The usual word for sin, *averah*, is from the root *avar*, 'to pass over', hence 'transgression', overriding God's will. The usual word for repentance is *teshuvah*, meaning 'turning', that is, from sin to God. In Rabbinic theology sin is caused by the evil inclination, which tempts man to disobey God's laws (see YETZER HA-TOV AND YETZER HA-RA). No human being is free from temptation but is assured that sincere repentance is always accepted. In the Jerusalem Talmud (*Makkot* 2: 6) there occurs this remarkable and oft-quoted passage on the efficacy of repentance in removing the taint of sin (and see ORIGINAL SIN): 'They asked of Wisdom: What is the punishment of the sinner? Wisdom replied: "Evil pursueth sinners" [Proverbs 13: 21]. They asked of Prophecy: What is the punishment of the sinner? Prophecy replied: "The soul that sinneth it shall die" [Ezekiel 18: 4]. They asked of the Holy One, blessed be He: What is the punishment of the sinner? He replied: "Let him repent and he will be pardoned."' For the philosopher repentance is an irrational concept. Wrongdoing contains the germs of its own dissolution. Inexorable laws of cause and effect operate in the universe and the doom of the sinner is pronounced by the sinner himself when he sins. 'Wisdom' must declare that 'evil pursueth sinners'. The prophet sees things in the starkest terms of good and evil, right and wrong. The prophet can in no way compromise with falsehood. 'Prophecy' can only warn against the severe consequences of sin: 'The soul that sinneth it shall die.' But God, 'in his infinite mercy, so the passage implies, forgives the repentant sinner, disregarding, as it were, the ruthless logic of the philosopher and the moral condemnation of the prophet: 'Let him repent and he will be pardoned.'

Repentance is acceptable, the Rabbis teach, at any time but the special time for repentance is the the season from *Rosh Ha-Shanah to *Yom Kippur, the *Ten Days of Penitence. In all the Rabbinic sources repentance involves two things: remorse at having sinned and *confession of the sin. The numerous Rabbinic statements regarding sin and repentance are scattered through the Talmudic literature and are not presented in any systematic form. A useful summary is given by Maimonides (*Teshuvah*, ch. 1 and 2), although the very attempt at systemization departs, to some extent, from the openness and fluidity of Rabbinic thought. Maimonides writes:

'If a man transgresses, wittingly or unwittingly, any precept of the Torah, whether a positive precept or a negative, and repents and turns away from his wrongdoing, he is obliged to confess his sins to God, blessed be He. How does a man confess his sins? He says: "O God! I have sinned, I have committed iniquity, I have transgressed before Thee by doing such-and-such. Behold now I am sorry for what I have done and am ashamed and I shall never do it again." What constitutes true repentance? If the sinner has the opportunity of committing once again the sinful act and it is quite possible for him to repeat it and yet he refrains from so doing because he has repented—for example, a man cohabited unlawfully with a woman and after a time found himself alone with her again and he still loves her and is still as healthy as ever and it takes place in the same province in which he had previously sinned with her and yet he refrains from repeating the transgression—he is a true penitent. . . . Repentance or Yom Kippur can only win pardon for offences against God such as eating forbidden food or illegal cohabitation and so forth, but there is no forgiveness for offences against one's neighbour such as assault or injury or theft and so forth until the wrong done is put right. Even after a man has paid the restitution due to the victim he must beg his forgiveness. Even if all he did was to taunt his neighbour [i.e. and the question of restitution does not arise] he must

appease him and beg his forgiveness. If the victim does not wish to forgive him he should go to him in the company of three friends and they should beg him to grant his pardon. If their efforts were of no avail he should repeat the procedure with a second and a third group but if the victim still persists in his attitude he should be left alone and the victim is then sinful in refusing his pardon.'

Maimonides states here the Rabbinic view, albeit in a legalistic tone somewhat at variance with the broader outlook of the Rabbinic sources themselves (Maimonides, after all, records all this in his Code), that repentance is effected by a sincere resolve to give up the sin and by confession and restitution. There is no mention of physical mortification in order to win pardon. Nevertheless, the need for such mortification is found in later Jewish sources, chiefly under the influence of the *Saints of Germany. A prominent member of this circle, Eleazar of Worms, in his *Rokeah*, records detailed penances suitable for various sins, the principle being that pardon can only be obtained when the sinner's degree of pain is equal to the degree of pleasure that was his when he committed the sin. But, while Rabbis to this day will impose penances on sinners who consult them, they are rarely too rigorous in their demands. The general view was expressed by Ezekiel *Landau, Rabbi of Prague in the eighteenth century, who replied to a sinner who had requested him to impose a penance (Responsa, *Orah Hayyim*, no, 35):

'You have asked me a hard question since it is not my habit to reply to questions put to me unless I can find the principles discussed in the Talmud and the Codes. It is only in the moralistic literature that one finds references to these matters and most of what they have to say comes from theories that are from the belly [a "gut reaction"] and have no foundation, each work relying on the others without any basis whatsoever. It is not my practice to peruse these works but I recall them from the days of my youth. Hence I say that all this would be relevant only if repentance cannot be achieved except through fasting. But the truth of the matter is that fasting is only secondary and basically repentance consists of relinquishing the sin, confessing with a broken heart, and sincere remorse.'

Landau does not, however, reject entirely physical mortification such as fasting, but sees this as no more than the means of expressing true remorse and not as an end in itself. He does advise the sinner to fast but stresses that the giving of *charity has greater saving power. Charity as an aid to repentance is advocated in all the Jewish sources. One of the most popular hymns recited on Rosh Ha-Shanah and Yom Kippur on the theme of divine judgement concludes that the 'evil decree' is averted through repentance, prayer, and charity.

*Attitudes to Repentance*

The third-century teachers, Rabbi Johanan and Rabbi Abbahu, debate who is the greater, the man who has never sinned or the sinner who has repented (*Berakhot* 34b). Their contemporary, Rabbi Simeon ben Lakish, says in one version that when the sinner repents his intentional sons are accounted as if he had committed them unintentionally; but in another version, his sins are accounted as virtues! The Talmudic reconciliation (*Yoma* 86b) of the two versions is that one refers to repentance out of fear, the other to repentance out of love.

One of the very few philosophical discussions of the problem of repentance is that of Joseph *Albo (*Ikkarim*, iv. 25–8). How can the Talmudic statement, that when a man repents out of love his sins are converted into virtues, be understood? Where is the justice in this? Surely it is enough that they are not counted as sins; why should they be turned into merit? Albo replies that if justice were to be the determinative factor there would be no room for repentance at all. Justice demands that once the wrong has been done it can never be put right and, as 'Wisdom' declares in the passage from the Jerusalem Talmud quoted above, the sinner should receive his deserts. But repentance is effective as a result of God's grace, and this is infinite. When the sinner repents out of love he responds to God in love and so God's grace can flow in love to him, even to the extent of converting his sins into merits. Yet Albo is still bothered by the whole idea of repentance. The sin has been committed by an act, whereas repentance involves only regret and verbal confession. Is repentance not like a man who has demolished a house seeking to rebuild it by simply declaring that it is rebuilt? Albo's reply, anticipating Kant, is that only voluntary acts are deserving of moral praise and blame. It is notoriously difficult to define a voluntary act but for an act to be classed as voluntary rather than compulsory it is necessary for the one who

performs the act to wish it to stand afterwards. Sincere repentance demonstrates that the sin was not committed voluntarily but in error. If he could, the sinner would erase his act and he thereby demonstrates that he did not really wish it to be done. The same principle must necessarily apply to good deeds as well. If a man performs a good deed but later regrets having done it, the deed is considered to have been done involuntarily and no merit accrues to the one who has carried it out.

As in other matters, contemporary Jews interpret the classical sources on sin and repentance in accordance with their particular philosophy of Judaism and will take into account, too, modern psychological, sociological, and medical theories about the causes of criminal behaviour. Not everything considered to be a sin in the traditional sources is so considered by all Jews today. Reform Jews will hardly be moved to 'repent' for carrying out acts that, for Reform Judaism, are not sins at all. Yet no Jewish thinker has ever wished to be rid of the whole idea of sin and repentance. It can be seen from an examination of the sources quoted above that the teachings on these subjects strike on the whole a balance between childish irresponsibility and softness, for which saying 'sorry' is enough, and the kind of morbid guilt for which nothing done to repair the wrong is ever enough. The need to find peace in one's soul; to shed the guilt load by constructive means, namely, by making good the harm that has been done; the renewal of one's personal life; reconciliation with God and with other human beings; all these would be accepted by all religious Jews, whatever their particular stance, as tests of a mature religious personality. There is no Judaism, whether ancient or modern, without teachings about the evil of sin, as there is no Judaism without teachings about the high value of repentance. Both sin and repentance are religious concepts. It is before God that one sins and it is God who pardons.

Abraham Cohen, 'Sin' and 'Repentance and Atonement', in his *Everyman's Talmud* (London, 1949), 95–110.
Louis Jacobs, 'Sin and Repentance', in his *A Jewish Theology* (New York 1973), 243–59.

**Sinai** The mountain on which God appeared to the people of Israel (Exodus 19, 20). It is further stated (Exodus 34: 27–32) that Moses ascended the mountain and stayed there for

471 ..................................................................................................................................................... **Slander**

forty days and forty nights and then came down, with the *tablets of stone on which the *Decalogue was inscribed, to teach the people the instructions he had received there. This is the basis for the Rabbinic doctrine that at Sinai Moses received the *Oral Torah, the explanations of the laws conveyed to him during his stay on the mount. Hence, in the Rabbinic tradition, laws not stated explicitly in the *Written Torah but which have the status of biblical law are called 'laws given to Moses at Sinai'. Ethics of the Fathers opens with the statement: 'Moses received Torah from Sinai and he gave it over to Joshua.' The current expression 'Torah from Sinai' (*Torah mi-Sinai*) as synonymous with 'Torah from Heaven' (*Torah min Ha-Shamayyim*) is consequently very imprecise in describing the Rabbinic view. The latter doctrine refers to the whole of the *Pentateuch as well as to the laws given at Sinai and the Pentateuch itself records laws that were given and events that took place after the theophany at Sinai during Israel's sojourn in the wilderness. There is no warrant in the Rabbinic sources for the obviously anachronistic view that the whole of the Pentateuch was given to Moses at Sinai (and see BIBLICAL CRITICISM, CONSERVATIVE JUDAISM, and REVELATION). Christians, in the early Middle Ages, identified Mount Sinai with Jebel Musa ('the Mount of Moses') in southern Sinai, which is still known as Mount Sinai, and tourists visit the monastery of St Catherine built there by the Roman emperor Justinian. Interestingly enough, the Jewish tradition does not see Mount Sinai, even if its site were known, as a sacred spot (see HOLY PLACES), probably because the Divine Presence is said to have rested on the mountain only during the theophany. A Rabbinic homily has it that Sinai is the lowest of the mountains, to teach that the Torah can only find a secure place in the heart and mind of a humble scholar. Another Midrash has it that Sinai is a barren mountain but when God descended on it to give the Decalogue the mountain became luxuriant in its plants and flowers (see SHAVUOT).

**Slander** The strongest moral disapproval is expressed in Jewish teachings of slander in all its forms. The prohibition against going around as a tale-bearer is stated in the Holiness Code in Leviticus (Leviticus 19: 16). The prophet Jeremiah castigates those 'who go about with slanders and who speak iniquity' (Jeremiah 9:

2–4). The Psalmist declares: 'Who is the man that desireth life, and loveth days, that he may see good therein? Keep thy tongue from evil, and thy lips from speaking guile. Depart from evil and do good, seek peace and pursue it' (Psalms 34: 13–15). It is somewhat odd that Jewish law, as distinct from moral preachment, is less clear on slander as a crime punishable in the courts. There is the case mentioned in the Bible (Deuteronomy 22: 13–18) of a man who slanderously casts doubts on the chastity of his wife. He is to be punished with a fine and with chastisement. Yet, according to strict Talmudic law, there is no legal redress for slanderous statements, apart from this particular case. The reason is that, in Talmudic law, there is redress only for injuries inflicted directly on another person, not, as in slander, where the harm, though it can be excessive, is done indirectly. Obviously a situation where slanderers could get away with it could not be tolerated. In the Middle Ages the authorities did legislate against slander, relying on the Talmudic ruling (*Sanhedrin* 46a) that the courts can assume powers not normally given to them by the law where it is for the benefit of society. Because the whole development of the law of slander is based on the emergency powers granted to the courts, various penalties were introduced in different places and at different times. But in the sixteenth century it became possible for the *Shulhan Arukh* (*Hoshen Mishpat*, 420. 38) to formulate the laws about slander, though these are still not categorical and a good deal is left to the discretion of the court.

The *Shulhan Arukh* formulates the law of slander as follows:

'If a man spits on his neighbour, he is liable to pay damages but he should not pay if he only spits on his neighbour's garments or if he shames him verbally. But the courts everywhere and at all times should introduce legislation for this matter as they see fit. Some say that he is to be placed under the ban until he pacifies the victim of his insult, and some say that he is to be flogged. One who slanders his neighbour is to be treated as one who puts him to shame verbally. If a man taunts his neighbour by saying: "I am not an apostate", "I am not a criminal", even if he did not add "like you" it is as if he added "like you". If he said: "You behave like a bastard" or "you are like a bastard" it is nothing. But some authorities disagree, holding that if he said "You are like a bastard" it is as if he had said: "You are a bastard". . . . If a man slanders those who sleep in the dust, he must take upon himself to fast and to repent, and he should be fined by the courts as they see fit. If they are buried nearby he should go to their graves to ask their pardon . . . If a man calls his neighbour a slave or a bastard and it is true he is not culpable. But if the matter cannot be determined, even though he heard others speak in this way, he cannot be exonerated.'

The above is from the legal point of view. Morally, the slanderer meets with the strictest condemnation. A Rabbinic saying has it that a habitual slanderer is unworthy of 'receiving the divine countenance' in the *World to Come. Whoever makes a habit of speaking slander, say the Rabbis, acts as though he denies the existence of God (*Arakhin* 15b).

The scholar who, more than anyone else in the past few hundred years, devoted his life to combating *lashon ha-ra*, 'the evil tongue', as slander is called, was Israel Meir Kagan, the *Hafetz Hayyim. Among other matters mentioned by the Hafetz Hayyim in his comprehensive works on the subject is that Jewish law makes no distinction between libel and slander, between written and verbal calumny. He demonstrates that the prohibition of 'evil talk' includes: listening to it; making libellous remarks about a competitor's merchandise; and praising a person to his enemies, who will react by speaking ill of him. According to the Hafetz Hayyim defamation of a whole group, not only of an individual, is forbidden.

> Louis Jacobs, 'Slander', in his *What Does Judaism Say About . . .?* (Jerusalem, 1973), 289–92.

**Slavery** Civilized societies have abolished slavery. The problem is that while campaigners against slavery, such as Wilberforce, drew their inspiration from the biblical narrative of the redemption of the Hebrew slaves from Egyptian bondage and from the biblical teaching that all men are created in the image of God, the Bible and, for that matter, the Rabbinic literature, do tolerate the institution even though they do not positively advocate it. During the great struggle over the slavery issue in America in the nineteenth century, there were Jews as well as Christians on both sides of the debate. Rabbi David Einhorn, who risked his life to oppose slavery, declared it to be 'the greatest possible crime against God'. Rabbi Morris J.

Raphael, on the opposite side, pointed to the biblical law in support of the institution. Rabbi Raphael must have known that even in the biblical law a marked tendency can be observed to limit slavery and to demand that slaves be treated humanely. The Deuteronomic law states (Deuteronomy 23: 15–16): 'Thou shalt not deliver unto his master the slave who escapes from his master unto thee; he shall dwell with thee, even among you, in that place which he shall choose in one of thy gates, where it liketh him best; thou shalt not oppress him.' But, while Rabbi Raphael and those who shared his views hardly thought highly of slavery, they felt unable honestly to condemn outright an institution that was sanctioned by Moses speaking in the name of God.

All Jews today accept that the abolition of slavery was a great step forward for mankind. Many would say that the Bible and the Rabbinic literature have to be seen against the background of the times when they were compiled, when both slavery and polygamy were part of the very fabric of ancient society. In some periods of human history society would have collapsed without these two institutions. Jews accept that there are ideas of the utmost value that could not be realized until a different form of society had emerged. The abolition of slavery in the nineteenth century, many Jews would say, was the fuller realization of principles taught by the Torah.

**Sofer, Moses** Foremost Hungarian Rabbi, Halakhic authority, and champion of Orthodoxy (1762–1839), known, after the title of his Responsa collection, as Hatam Sofer ('Seal of the Scribe'). Sofer was born in Frankfurt where he studied under Rabbi Phineas Horowitz, the Rabbi of the town, and Rabbi Nathan Adler, a Talmudist and Kabbalist whose esoteric leanings were not to the taste of the staid Frankfurt community, which he was forced to leave, taking his disciple, Sofer, with him. After occupying Rabbinic positions in Dresnitz and Mattersdof, Sofer was appointed Rabbi of Pressburg (Bratislava) where he served until his death. He was succeeded in this position by his son, Abraham Samuel Benjamin Wolf (1815–71), known as the Ketav Sofer ('Writing of the Scribe'), who, in turn, was succeeded by his son, Simhah Bunem (1842–1906), known as the Shevet Sofer ('Pen of the Scribe'). It is a curious fact that each of the three Sofers served as Rabbi of Pressburg for thirty-three years and both the last two were appointed at the age of 29. Simhah Bunen's son, Akiba Sofer (1878–1959), known as the Daat Sofer ('Opinion of the Scribe'), succeeded his father in the Rabbinate of Pressburg but in 1940 he settled in Jerusalem and established there the 'Pressburg' *Yeshivah. The original Pressburg Yeshivah was founded by the Hatam Sofer, who, like his successors, was Dean of the Yeshivah as well as Rabbi of the town. This combination of the two roles, Rabbi and Rosh Yeshivah, in one person was traditional but was not generally followed in the great Lithuanian Yeshivot of the nineteenth century, where the post of Rosh Yeshivah was independent of the Rabbinate of the town. This is the main reason why in the Pressburg Yeshivah and its many offshoots in Hungary the emphasis was on practical law, while in the Lithuanian Yeshivot it was on pure theory and keen analysis of legal concepts. Out of the Pressburg Yeshivah and those influenced by it there issued generations of Orthodox Rabbis in the strict Hungarian mould.

Sofer saw danger to traditional Judaism in the *Haskalah movement and he had a largely negative attitude towards Moses *Mendelssohn and his followers. Yet it is a mistake to see him as obscurantist in his attitude. It has to be appreciated that the Jewish communities in central Europe were attracted to the Reform movement, then growing in influence, in nearby Germany. In Pressburg itself there were strong Reformist tendencies which Sofer successfully overcame in his belief that Reform threatened the very foundations of Judaism. When the Hamburg Reform Temple was established, the Hamburg Rabbinate issued, in 1818, the document *Eleh Divre Ha-Berit* ('These are the Words of the Covenant'), attacking Reform innovations. Sofer and his father-in-law, the famed Talmudist, Rabbi Akiba Eger, contributed to this protest well-reasoned essays in defence of total adherence to traditional forms.

Sofer's application of a Talmudic ruling became the slogan of Hungarian Orthodoxy. The Talmud, discussing the law of Hadash ('New'), the corn harvested before the *Omer (Leviticus 23: 14), rules that 'Hadash is forbidden by the Torah', meaning, it is a biblical, not only a Rabbinic, law that the prohibition of Hadash stands even after the destruction of the Temple and even outside the land of Israel. Sofer's pun on this ruling is that anything new

(*hadash*), any innovation in Jewish life, is forbidden by the Torah. It is ironic that this slogan itself, in the way it was understood in the Sofer-Hungarian school, is an innovation. Orthodox Rabbis, including Sofer himself, have always been ready to take into account in their decisions new conditions requiring fresh legislation. Sofer held, for instance, that improved communications made it easier for a wife whose husband was lost at sea (see AGUNAH) to be released from her married status on the grounds that it can nowadays be assumed that if he were alive he would have got in touch with her, even though it was not so assumed in Talmudic times. Also Sofer, more than any other authority of his day, placed the Rabbinate on a proper professional footing, giving details of Rabbinic contracts and saying that these should be drawn up to be as binding as any other business contract, even though the Talmud frowns on a scholar receiving any payment for his services (see RABBIS). Sofer writes (Responsa, *Yoreh Deah*, no, 230): 'Nowadays, where a Rabbi is appointed and he moves residence to settle in the town and they fix his salary, just like any other employee, and included in his stipend are the fees for officiating at weddings and divorces and so forth, he does not act in any way unlawfully by receiving his salary.'

Sofer's strong opposition to the Reform movement was continued by his son and grandson and their disciples. Every practice that seemed to have been influenced by Reform or by Christian practices was declared taboo, for instance, to have the *bimah at the end of the synagogue near the *Ark, or to have weddings in the synagogue with an address by the preacher to bride and bridegroom, or for the Rabbi and Cantor to wear canonicals. To this day Hungarian Orthodoxy, influenced by the Sofer school, is separatist in tendency, though few, nowadays, would go so far as Sofer's foremost disciple, Moses Schick (1807–59), Rabbi of Huszt, who asked his Rabbinic colleagues to declare openly that if the imposition of a *herem were permitted in Hungarian law, it would be essential to impose the ban on the Reformers. In any event, declares Schick, we must make it clear that the Reformers are not Jews (*sic*); that it is forbidden to intermarry with them; and that it is forbidden to pray in their Temples. This separatist attitude was adopted by Samson Raphael *Hirsch in Frankfurt.

M. J. Burak, *The Hatam Sofer* (Toronto, 1967).

**Solomon** King of Israel, tenth century BCE, son of *David; his story is told in the book of Kings (1 Kings 1–12). Solomon built the *Temple in Jerusalem, offering at its dedication his famous prayer (1 Kings 8). The two episodes in Solomon's reign that have become famous in world literature are the visit to him of the queen of Sheba (1 Kings 10: 1–13) and his famous judgement (1 Kings 3: 16–28). In the Rabbinic tradition Solomon is the author of the *Song of Songs, *Proverbs, and *Ecclesiastes and he is called, after the scriptural verse: 'the wisest of all men' (1 Kings 5: 11). Legends abound of Solomon's skill in interpreting the speech of animals and birds, of his power over the spirits, and of the way the demon *Ashmedai usurped Solomon's throne. When the Rabbis wish to describe how impenetrable is the mysterious rite of the *red heifer, they say that even the wise King Solomon tried to understand it without success.

**Soloveitchik Family** Lithuanian Rabbinic family of which the four most influential members were: Joseph Baer (1820–92); his son Hayyim (1853–1918); Hayyim's son, Isaac Zeev (1886–1960); and Hayyim's grandson, Joseph Baer (1903–93). The first Joseph Baer served as one of the heads of the famed Yeshivah of *Volozhyn and then as Rabbi of Brest-Litovsk (Brisk). Hayyim also served as a teacher in Volozhyn and then succeeded his father as Rabbi of Brisk, becoming known as Reb Hayyim Brisker. Isaac (Reb Velvel) succeeded his father as Rabbi of Brisk but settled in Israel in 1941, where he became the acknowledged leader of the ultra-Orthodox party. The second Joseph Baer studied philosophy at Berlin University and, in 1941, became head of the Talmud faculty at Yeshivah University in New York, where he influenced generations of modern Orthodox Rabbis. Unlike his forebears and his uncle, Reb Velvel, who were strongly anti-Zionist, the second Joseph Baer was identified with the *Mizrachi, the religious Zionist movement. Obviously reflecting his own torment at his departure from the family tradition in both his *Zionism and his espousal of secular learning, Joseph Baer pointed to the struggle between Joseph and his brethren (Genesis 37). Joseph had a 'dream' of a new way of life, different from that of his brethren and his father, Jacob, without denying that their way had been sufficient and valuable for their time.

New conditions in Jewish life demand that different challenges be met in a new way. Joseph Baer, a profound religious thinker, thoroughly at home in Western thought, tried to demonstrate that loyalty to the past, including strict Jewish observance, is compatible with a modern outlook. In his essay *The Lonely Man of Faith*, Joseph Baer adopts an existentialist approach, but in his equally famous essay *Halakhic Man* he depicts this eponymous figure in terms of the unemotional, objective approach of his family in which intellectual ability in Talmudic studies is prized above all. Because of his expertise in Talmudic learning and because of his ancestry, Joseph Baer was acknowledged as a teacher even by the ultra-Orthodox but in recent years, especially after his death, his views and those of his school have come under fire from the extreme right wing.

Reb Hayyim and Reb Velvel introduced a new and revolutionary method in the study of the Talmud, the Brisker Derekh, 'the Way of of Brisk', as it is called. Instead of *pilpul, the casuistic, far-fetched manipulation of the texts, the Brisker way placed the emphasis on keen analysis of Talmudic concepts. A favourite expression of Reb Hayiim is: 'There are two laws', meaning that an analysis of legal concepts often shows that a given law, to be fully understood, has to be approached from two different angles. For instance, when a family complained that the burial society had attended to the burial of a rich member of the community before attending to a member of their family who had died first, Reb Hayyim declared that, as the Rabbi of the town, he would offer a rebuke to the burial society but that this was not the concern of the complaining family. His reason was that Maimonides does not record the law that priority be given to the one who died first under the laws of burial. The rule of precedence for burial is therefore a law about priorities the observance of which is a matter of concern for the burial society, not any particular family. Similarly, when Reb Hayyim was lenient in allowing people whom the doctors had ordered to eat on *Yom Kippur to eat in the normal way, rather than, as was then the practice, to eat small quantities of food at intervals, he remarked that he was not being lenient with regard to the laws of Yom Kippur but strict with regard to the laws regarding the preservation of life. The Brisker way succeeded in capturing the Lithuanian Yeshivot and is today the staple fare of all Yeshivot in the old style. The exponents of this method of study have no use for modern historical investigation (see JÜDISCHE WISSENSCHAFT). The Brisker way has had its opponents even among traditional students of the Talmud, who view the new methods as often too tortuous, as a new kind of pilpul in fact. It must be admitted, nevertheless, that many an obscure passage in the Talmud becomes illuminated by the application of the Brisker way.

Hillel Goldberg, 'Rabbi Joseph Baer Soloveitchik', in his *Between Berlin and Slobodka: Jewish Transition Figures from Eastern Europe* (Hoboken, NJ, 1989).
Joseph B. Soloveitchik, *Halakhic Man*, trans. Lawrence Kaplan (Philadelphia, 1983).

**Song of Songs** Heb. *Shir Ha-Shirim*, the book of eight chapters in the third section of the *Bible, the *Ketuvim*, first of the five Megillot, 'Scrolls' (the others are: *Ruth, *Lamentations, *Ecclesiastes, and *Esther). According to the Rabbinic tradition generally, the author of the book is King *Solomon (based on the heading: 'The Song of Songs by Solomon', though this can also mean 'about Solomon') but in the famous Talmudic passage (*Bava Batra* 15a) on the authorship of the biblical books it is stated that the book was actually written down by King Hezekiah and his associates (based on Proverbs 25: 1). Modern scholarship is unanimous in fixing a much later date for the book than the time of Solomon, though opinions vary regarding the actual date. On the surface, the book is a secular love-poem or a collection of such poems and is considered so to be by the majority of modern biblical scholars. No doubt because of this surface meaning, the ancient Rabbis, while accepting the Solomonic authorship, debated whether the book should be considered part of the sacred Scriptures. The Mishnah (*Yadaim* 3: 5), after recording this debate, gives the view of Rabbi *Akiba, eventually adopted by all the Rabbis, that no one ever debated that the Song of Songs is sacred: 'for all the ages are not worth the day on which the Song of Songs was given to Israel; for all the *Ketuvim* are holy, but the Song of Songs is the Holy of Holies'. In the liturgy of the synagogue, Song of Songs is recited during the morning service on the intermediate Sabbath of *Passover. Under the influence of the Kabbalah the custom arose in some circles, especially in *Hasidism, of reciting the Song of Songs on the eve of the Sabbath.

*Interpretations of Song of Songs*

That the Rabbis in the second century CE could debate whether Song of Songs belongs to sacred Scripture is evidence enough that in this period there were some who took it all literally as a dialogue of love between a man and and a woman, sexual desire expressed exquisitely but with the utmost frankness. One or two Orthodox Jews in the twentieth century did try to suggest that even on the literal level the book can be seen as sacred literature, since love between husband and wife is holy and divinely ordained. But, while there is no explicit rejection of such a literal interpretation in Rabbinic literature, the standard Rabbinic view, and the reason why Rabbi Akiba declared the book to be 'the Holy of Holies', is that the Rabbis saw the 'lover' as God and the 'beloved' as the community of Israel. (The Christian Church took over this allegorical interpretation and saw the book as a dialogue between Jesus and the Church.) The Rabbis also understood the opening verse as 'Song of Songs *about* Shelomo' and took the name as referring not to King Solomon but to God, *she-ha shalom shelo*, 'to whom peace belongs'. Revealing in this connection is a passage in the Talmud (*Sanhedrin*, 101a) dating from the second century: 'He who recites a verse of the Song of Songs and treats it as a song and one who recites a verse at a banquet [this usually denotes a wedding feast], unseasonably, brings evil upon the world', from which it would seem that it was only the profane and frivolous use of the book in its plain meaning to which the Rabbis objected. Nevertheless, throughout Rabbinic literature it is the allegorical meaning that is followed. The Midrash Rabbah to the book interprets the whole book in this vein. For example, the verse (1: 2): 'Let him kiss me with the kisses of his mouth' is interpreted as referring to the *revelation at *Sinai when Israel took upon itself to keep the Torah and an angel was sent by God to kiss each Israelite. The verse (1: 5); 'I am black but comely' is given the interpretation that the community of Israel says to God: 'I am black through my own deeds, but comely through the deeds of of my ancestors', or 'I am black in my own eyes, but comely in the sight of God', or 'I am black during the rest of the year, but comely on Yom Kippur'. The verse:

'Like a lily among thorns, so is my darling among the maidens' (2: 2) is interpreted as referring to Israel's oppression by the secular powers: 'Just as a rose, if situated between thorns, when the north wind blows is bent towards the south and is pricked by the thorns, and nevertheless its heart is still turned upwards, so with Israel, although taxes are exacted from them, nevertheless their hearts are fixed upon their Father in Haeven.'

In the Zohar and the early Kabbalah the dialogue of love is between the two *Sefirot, *Tiferet*, the male principle in the Godhead, and *Malkhut*, the *Shekhinah, the female principle. In the opening passage of the Zohar, in current editions, the lily among the thorns is *Malkhut* attacked by the demonic forces but strengthened against these evil forces by the five strong leaves surrounding the lily, the other lower Sefirot.

The sixteenth-century mystic, Moses *Cordovero, interprets the book as a dialogue between the individual soul and God. Even in an earlier period, Maimonides (*Teshuvah* 10: 3) writes in the same vein, when discussing the *love of God:

'What is the proper form of the love [of God]? It is that he should love the Lord with great, overpowering, fierce love to the extent that his soul is bound to the love of God and he dwells on it constantly, as if he were love-sick for a woman and dwells on this constantly, whether he is sitting or standing, eating and drinking. Even more than this should be the love of God in the heart of those who love him, dwelling on it constantly, as it is said: "with all thy heart and with all thy soul" [Deuteronomy 6: 5]. And it is to this that Solomon refers allegorically when he says: "For I am love-sick" [Song of Songs 2: 5] and the whole of Song of Songs is a parable on this topic.'

Wesley J. Fuerst, *The Books of Ruth, Esther, Ecclesiastes, The Song of Songs, Lamentations* (Cambridge, 1975), 159–200.

S. M. Lehrman, 'The Song of Songs', in A. Cohen (ed.), *The Five Megilloth*, (London, 1952), pp. x–32.

**Soul, Immortality of The** The doctrine that the soul lives on for ever after the death of the body. There is no unambiguous reference to this doctrine anywhere in the Bible (see KARET). The verse in Ecclesiastes (12: 7): 'Then the dust shall return to the earth as it was: and the spirit shall return unto God who gave it', may

not mean that the human spirit is immortal but simply that man's individuality is absorbed back into God, with an obvious reference to Genesis 2: 7: 'Then the Lord formed man of the dust of the ground, and breathed into his nostrils the breath of life.' *Ecclesiastes is, however, a later book and it is just possible that the doctrine of the immortality of the soul had come into Judaism at that time. The verses: 'Many of those that sleep in the dust of the earth will awake, some to eternal life, others to reproaches, to everlasting abhorrence. And the knowledgeable will be radiant like the bright expanse of the sky, and those who lead the many to righteousness will be like the stars for ever and ever' (Daniel 12: 2–3), belong to a late stage in the history of Jewish *eschatology and probably refer to the different doctrine of the *resurrection of the dead. But the expression used of the patriarch Jacob: 'when I sleep with my fathers' (Genesis 47: 30) might mean that Jacob would be with his fathers after his death. It cannot refer to his burial in the vault in which his fathers were buried since a similar expression is used of Abraham (Genesis 25: 8) who was buried in the Cave of *Machpelah, not in the ancestral vault. In the book of Jeremiah (31: 14–15), the matriarch, *Rachel, weeps and is comforted by God. She is still aware of the sufferings of her children. Rachel is described as being near to her grave in Ramah, although this might all be purely poetic. The verses: 'The righteous man perishes, and no one considers, pious men are taken away, and no one gives thought that because of the evil the righteous are taken away. Yet he shall come to peace, they shall have rest on their couches, who walketh straightforward' (Isaiah 57: 1–2), do seem to imply that there is a Hereafter in which the righteous are rewarded but this, too, is not very definite.

The biblical references, then, to the Hereafter, are, at most, only implications and it is generally held that the full doctrine of the Hereafter only came into prominence during the period of the *Maccabees, when many good men were dying for their faith and the older view of *reward and punishment in this life became untenable. From this period, at least, there are to be found three connected eschatological ideas: 1. the immortality of the soul; 2. the doctrine of the *Messiah; 3. the resurrection of the dead. Basically there is a contradiction between the two doctrines of the immortality of the soul and the resurrection of the dead. According to the latter doctrine, in its original meaning, when the individual died he was truly dead and there was no separate soul to live on in *heaven after the death of the body. The resurrection of the dead was explicitly what that name implies. Later in Judaism, however, the two doctrines were combined and this helps to explain the tensions in this matter in the Rabbinic literature and the ambiguities in the Rabbinic term 'the *World to Come'. Once the two doctrines were combined, the three beliefs contributed to the Jewish eschatological scheme. In this, the individual does not lose his soul at death. The soul lives on in heaven. Some time after the coming of the Messiah the body is resurrected and the soul returns to it here on earth. Obviously, this bald description can serve as no more than an extremely abbreviated picture of a very complicated scheme.

*Josephus writes that the *Sadducees did not believe in the immortality of the soul and in the Talmudic literature it is said that the Sadducees did not believe in the existence of the World to Come, although, in that literature, this term usually, but not always, denotes the world after the resurrection of the dead. The apocryphal book 'Wisdom of Solomon', compiled in the first century CE, on the other hand, has a clear expression (3: 1–4) of belief in the immortality of the soul: 'The souls of the righteous are in the hand of God, and there shall no torment touch them. In the sight of the unwise they seemed to die; and their departure was taken to be their hurt, and their journeying away from us to be their ruin; but they are in peace. For though they be punished in the sight of men, yet is their hope full of immortality.' Philo seems to know nothing of the doctrine of the physical resurrection of the dead but believes strongly in the immortality of the soul, understanding the doctrine of the resurrection as referring to this.

The most powerful influence on subsequent Jewish thought on this topic is obviously the Talmudic literature and here both ideas, that of the resurrection and that of immortality of the soul, are found, but with most of the emphasis on the former. As noted, the World to Come usually refers to the resurrection. The usual Talmudic term for the immortality of the soul is the *Garden of Eden (and see GEHINNOM). Yet, on occasion, the World to Come also refers

to the immortality of the soul, as, for instance, in the following passage (*Kiddushin* 40b):

'Rabbi Eleazar ben Rabbi Zadok said: To what can the righteous in this world be compared, to a tree, the trunk of which stands in a place of purity with its branches inclining towards a place of impurity. Once the branches have been cut off the whole tree stands in a place of purity. In the same way, the Holy One, blessed be He, brings sufferings upon the righteous in this world in order for them to inherit the World to Come.'

It is just possible to interpret this passage, too, in terms of the resurrection but the many statements about the Garden of Eden certainly refer to the fate of the soul after the death of the body. In a famous Talmudic passage (*Berakhot* 18a–19a) there is a debate on whether the dead know what is happening on earth, implying that their souls are in 'heaven' and the same applies to the references to the dead scholars studying the Torah in the Yeshivah on High. Another passage (*Pesahim* 50a) tells of Rabbi Joseph, son of Rabbi Joshua ben Levi, who became ill and fell into a trance (according to some commentators the meaning is that he actually died). On his return to earth his father asked him: 'What did you see?' He replied: 'I saw a topsy-turvy world, those who are here elevated are there brought low and those who are low here are there elevated.' Yet, compared with references to the resurrection, the references to the soul 'up there' are astonishingly few. It is almost as if the Rabbis did not wish to dwell too much on the great mystery of immortality. Rabbinic thought is, in any event, organic rather than systematic. It was not until the age of the medieval thinkers that the whole question of the Hereafter was treated in systematic fashion and these thinkers were hampered by their reliance on the very unsystematic Talmudic literature.

### Medieval Views

*Saadiah Gaon devotes the whole of Part VI of his *Beliefs and Opinions* to belief in the immortality of the soul. Saadiah does not believe in pre-existent souls. The soul is created simultaneously with the body. When the body dies the soul remains in a state of separation until the number of souls to be created has been reached, when the soul is reunited with the body and both body and soul are rewarded or punished according to their conduct while they were united on earth. The purpose of God placing the soul in the body is for the soul to acquire greater luminosity through obedience to God's commandments despite the hindrances here on earth. *Sin, on the other hand, has the effect of making the soul's substance turbid. The sojourn of the soul on earth raises it to be tested and refined. Only such a refined soul is capable of attaining to eternal life and the body is the instrument the soul uses to achieve its lofty aim. When a man is about to die, the angel of death appears to him, at which dreaded appearance he shudders and his soul departs. All souls, after the death of the body, are stored up to await their reunification with the body at the time of the resurrection and the retribution. Pure souls are kept on high under the Throne of Glory. Turbid souls are fated to wander aimlessly below. Until the decomposition of the body the soul has no fixed abode and it suffers from the contemplation of the body's fate just as former inhabitants of a house now in ruins are aggrieved at seeing what has become of the house they had loved. Saadiah explicitly rejects belief in *reincarnation, considering this to be a foreign importation into Judaism.

Maimonides, in his Code (*Teshuvah* 8: 3–8) identifies the 'World to Come' with the immortality of the soul, arguing, surely unhistorically, that all the references to the World to Come in the Rabbinic literature are to the immortality of the soul. This world is only referred to as 'coming' because this state cannot be attained while the soul is in the body. In his *Essay on the Resurrection* Maimonides writes that, while he believes in the physical resurrection of the dead on earth, this will only be temporal. Eventually the resurrected dead will die again and only the soul will enjoy immortality. Moreover, Maimonides holds, following the Aristotelian view in its Arabic garb, that man's natural soul, that which keeps him alive and enables him to exist in the body, belongs, as in animals, to the body and ceases to function with the death of the body. Only that part of man's intellect that he has acquired through the contemplation of metaphysical truths is immortal. The ultimate purpose of human existence is, according to Maimonides, for the individual to gain the 'acquired soul' and with it his immortality. Leon Roth once said that it almost seems, according to Maimonides, that you can only get to heaven if you have a good degree in philosophy. Obedient to his philosophy, Maimonides comments on the saying of the third-century

teacher, *Rav (*Berakhot* 17b): 'In the World to Come there is no eating nor drinking nor propagation nor business nor jealousy nor hatred nor competition, but the righteous sit with their crowns on their heads basking in the radiance of the *Shekhinah', that it all has to be taken figuratively. When Rav says that the righteous 'sit', the meaning is that their souls are at rest, in a state of repose and tranquillity. The 'crowns' are the knowledge they had acquired during their lifetime on earth, which now becomes fully revealed and actualized.

The Zohar may have been influenced by Maimonides. In one Zoharic passage (i. 135b) it is said that while there is no physical eating and drinking in the Hereafter the righteous do enjoy the spiritual food and drink of ever-greater comprehension of divine truth, hence the references to the great banquet prepared for the righteous at which they will imbibe the wine stored in the vat from the six days of creation. According to the Zohar (i. 235a), without its probationary period on earth the soul is like a cistern, into which water is poured from outside. After the soul has acquitted itself well on earth, it ascends on high to become a fountain with water of its own. This passage and the Zoharic saying (i. 4a): 'Happy is he who enters here without shame' seem to be the source for an idea developed by the eighteenth-century Kabbalist, Moses Hayyim *Luzzatto. Luzzatto holds that God could have given man of His goodness without sending the soul down to inhabit the body. But then that goodness would be an unearned goodness, like the poor man who eats 'bread of shame' at the table of a rich man. The *Musar teacher, Rabbi E. E. *Dessler, devotes a major part of his works to an exploration of Luzzatto's doctrine of 'bread of shame'. In chapter 1 of his *Path of the Upright*, Luzzatto observes that man was created only to take delight in God and to bask in the radiance of His Shekhinah, the true delight and the greatest of all pleasures beside which all others fade into insignificance. The soul is sent down to earth in order for it to become perfect by overcoming the obstacles it has to face there:

'Tempted both by prosperity and adversity, man is engaged in a severe battle. But if he is valorous and achieves the complete victory, he becomes the perfect man worthy to enjoy communion with his Creator. Then he will pass from the vestibule of this world into the palace to enjoy the light of life. To the extent that a man subdues his evil inclination, keeps aloof from the things that prevent him from attaining the good, and endeavours to commune with God, to that extent is he certain to achieve the true life and rejoice in it.'

The medieval thinkers all anticipate the English poet Keats's description of this world not as a vale of tears but as a vale of soul-making.

From the above it can be seen how much of the whole question of the Hereafter and its nature is speculative; naturally so, since the Jewish thinkers make no claim to have 'been there' and, while they remain uncertain about the details, they base their opinions on the tradition, itself vague and opaque in many respects, and, especially, on their belief in the goodness of God who, they affirm, would not have created the human personality only to destroy it after the brief sojourn on earth.

*Modern Attitudes*

Orthodox Jews accept the whole traditional, eschatological scheme, believing in the coming of the Messiah, the resurrection of the dead, and the immortality of the soul, though most would admit that the details cannot be grasped by the finite mind of man and must be left to God. The Orthodox often quote Maimonides' saying that to seek, while in the body, to grasp the nature of pure spiritual bliss in the Hereafter is as impossible as for a man born blind to grasp the nature of colour. The rites attending *death and burial are all based on belief in the resurrection but in the *memorial prayers reference is made to the soul 'resting under the wings of the Shekhinah'. Hasidim, when commemorating a parent's death at the *Yahrzeit, invite their companions to a drink and the toast is: 'May the soul ascend higher.' Reform Judaism in the nineteenth century abandoned the belief in a personal Messiah and in the resurrection of the dead but Reform retained prayers for the dead and believed in the immortality of the soul. This return to Philo and, in a sense, also to Maimonides, can be observed among some of the Orthodox as well, who, similarly, prefer to stress the immortality of the soul rather than the resurrection of the dead, even while continuing to use the traditional vocabulary in their prayer books. In this connection it is interesting to find Dr J. H. *Hertz, the British Chief Rabbi, a man of unimpeachable Orthodoxy, writing in his Prayer Book (*The Authorised Daily Prayer Book* (London, 1947), 133) on the reference in the Prayer Book to the revival of the dead: 'He awakes the dead to new life.

This emphatic statement concerning the resurrection was directed especially against the worldlings, who disputed the deathlessness of the soul, its return to God, and its continued separate existence after its reunion with the Divine Source of being.' Hertz (p. 255) remarks further: 'Maimonides and Halevi make the doctrine of *teḥiat ha-metim*, lit. "revival of the dead", identical with that of the immortality of the soul, and explain the Talmudic sayings to the contrary as figurative language.' There are, however, a number, perhaps a large number, of contemporary religious Jews, and not only among Reform, who, under the impact of scientism, see Judaism as a completely this-worldly religion and entertain no belief in the immortality of the soul, or rather say that immortality is achieved through a person's works or his offspring or the lives he has made better. This is really sleight of hand. It is not the person who lives on in this way but the works or the offspring or the others who will in turn influence others. As Woody Allen says in one of his films when he realizes that one day he will die: 'I do not want to be immortal through my works. I want to be immortal by not dying.' And it is an odd sort of religious attitude in which God is believed in but not His power to guarantee immortality, unless the word 'God' represent not the Personal God of traditional Judaism but the 'power that makes for righteousness' (see KAPLAN). The majority of religious Jews continue to affirm that their religion is both this-worldly and other-worldly, seeing this life as good in itself but yet receiving its real and ultimate significance in the preparation it affords the soul to enjoy God for ever.

W. Hirsch, *Rabbinic Psychology: Beliefs about the Soul in Rabbinic Literature of the Talmudic Period* (London, 1947; repr. edn., New York, 1973).
Louis Jacobs, 'Immortality', in his *Religion and the Individual: A Jewish Perspective* (Cambridge, 1992), 94–112.
J. Ross, *The Jewish Conception of Immortality and the Life Hereafter* (Belfast, 1948).

**Space** Spatial *symbolism for the spiritual abounds in classical Jewish sources. One of the *names of God in the Rabbinic literature is Ha-Makom, 'the Place', explained as: 'He is the place of the universe but the universe is not His place', meaning God is both transcendent and immanent (see GOD and HOLY PLACES), although such abstract terms are unknown in this literature. The *angels are referred to as 'those on high' in contradistinction to human beings, 'those who are beneath', although, originally, this kind of terminology may well have been used literally, to vindicate that the angelic hosts are somehow 'up there' around the heavenly throne. The medieval thinkers certainly understood all this as purely symbolic. Maimonides (*Guide of the Perplexed*, 1. 8), for example, understands the verse: 'Blessed be the Lord from His place' (Ezekiel 3: 12) to refer to the distinguished degree and exalted nature of His existence, as when it is said of a dispute in law to which no conclusion is reached that 'it stands in its place' or when it is said that a man occupies the place of his ancestors in wisdom and piety. Often an originally spatial expression is adapted for a spiritual purpose. An example of this is the interpretation given in many moralistic works to the verses: 'Who may ascend the mountain of the Lord? And who may stand in his holy place? He that hath clean hands and a pure heart; who hath not set his desire upon vanity and hath not sworn deceitfully' (Psalms 24: 3–4). The Psalmist in all probability was thinking of an ascent to the Temple built on a hill. But 'ascending the mountain of the Lord' is frequently understood in terms of ascent in stages towards spiritual perfection (see HEIGHT). The Psalmist's plea: 'Out of the depths have I cried unto thee. O Lord' (Psalms 130: 1) seems to mean out of the psychological depths of sin and distress, as the Psalm continues (v. 3): 'If Thou, Lord, shouldst mark iniquities, O Lord, who could stand?' In Hebrew, as in English, a deep subject is one that is difficult to comprehend and a wide knowledge of a subject denotes a comprehensive acquaintance with it. This whole matter is extremely complicated by the fact that Hebrew is a very concrete language, so that abstractions are bound to be expressed in language that is normally reserved for things perceived by the senses.

**Spinoza, Benedict** One of the most significant figures in the history of general philosophy (1632–77). Spinoza was born in Amsterdam to Mikael and Hanna Deborah, Mikael's second wife who died when Spinoza was a little boy of 6. The family were *Marranos who had fled from Portugal in order to return to Judaism. The details of Spinoza's Jewish education are still unclear but he seems to have been taught by Rabbi Saul Morteira, teacher of Talmud at the Etz Hayyim school, and later taught himself, becoming especially proficient in medieval Jewish philosophy and general philosophy and science. He seems to have also acquired a knowledge of the Kabbalah, and the philosophical system he developed in his own original way owes something to the *Safed Kabbalist, Moses *Cordovero. There are echoes in Spinoza's thought of Cordovero's summary of the relationship of the universe to God: 'God is the all but the all is not God', although, according to the majority of his interpreters, Spinoza's pantheism goes much beyond Cordovero in actually identifying the universe with God, as in his famous maxim: *Deus sive natura* ('God or nature'), that is, God is the name given to the universe as a whole, monotheism becoming, for Spinoza, monism. Spinoza's approach and his general independent attitude to religion awakened the suspicions of both the Calvinists and the Jewish community in Amsterdam. On 27 July 1656, Spinoza was placed under the ban (*herem*) by the Amsterdam community. The ban, written in Portuguese, is still preserved in the archives of the Amsterdam community. The pronouncement preceding the ban reads:

'The chiefs of the council make known to you that having long known of evil opinions and acts of Baruch de Spinoza, they have endeavoured by various means and promises to turn him from evil ways. Not being able to find any remedy, but on the contrary receiving every day more information about the abominable heresies practised and taught by him, and about the monstrous acts committed by him, having this from many trustworthy witnesses who have deposed and borne witness on all this in the presence of said Spinoza, who has been convicted; all this having been examined in the presence of the Rabbis, the council decided, with the advice of the Rabbi, that the said Spinoza should be excommunicated and cut off from the Nation of Israel.'

It has often been noted that, in view of Christian opposition to Spinoza's opinions, the Jewish community had little option in dissociating itself from Spinoza's 'heresies'. After he had been placed under the ban, Spinoza settled in various other Dutch cities, ending his days in The Hague where he lived an independent life earning his living by polishing lenses.

### Spinoza and the Jewish Religion

Spinoza, in his *Tractatus Theologico-politicus*, published in Hamburg in 1670, relies on Abraham

*Ibn Ezra's cryptic remarks regarding passages in the *Pentateuch that must have been added after Moses, to put forward his view that the Pentateuch was not compiled by Moses but by Ezra. In his commentary to the Torah, Ibn Ezra is puzzled by the words of the opening verse of Deuteronomy: 'These are the words which Moses spoke unto all Israel beyond the Jordan.' In Moses' day the Israelites had not yet entered the land of Israel and the term 'beyond the Jordan' would not have been used for the side of the Jordan on which they were encamped. Ibn Ezra remarks: 'If you know the secret of the twelve, and of "And Moses wrote", and of "And the Canaanite was then in the land", and of "In the mount where the Lord was seen", and of "Behold his bedstead was a bedstead of iron", you will discover the truth.' Spinoza, and in this he was anticipated by the fourteenth-century commentator Joseph Bonfils, deciphers Ibn Ezra's remarks as follows. 'The secret of the twelve' refers to the last twelve verses of the Pentateuch which deal with the death of Moses and which could not have been written by Moses himself. Similarly, the words 'And Moses wrote' (Exodus 24: 4; Numbers 33: 2; Deuteronomy 31: 9) presuppose another author. 'And the Canaanite was *then* in the land' (Genesis 12: 6) is hard to explain if this verse was written by Moses since in his day the Canaanites were still in the land. 'In the mount where the Lord is seen' (Genesis 22: 14) is understood as referring to the Temple, which, of course, did not exist in Moses' day. 'Behold his bedstead was a bedstead of iron' (Deuteronomy 3: 11) speaks of the bedstead of Og, king of Bashan, who was slain by Moses towards the end of Moses' life, while the words seem to imply that the bedstead was pointed out as a landmark, or as an exhibit in the equivalent of the local museum, many years after Og had been slain. Ibn Ezra himself was only hinting that a few verses were added after Moses and he would certainly not have denied the Mosaic authorship of the Pentateuch as a whole. The belief that Moses wrote the Pentateuch at the 'dictation' of God was shared by Christians as well as Jews in the seventeenth century. Small wonder, then, that Spinoza's views were seen at that time as rank heresy of the greatest danger to faith. *Biblical criticism in the nineteenth century relied on Spinoza to develop the whole subject further. Many Jews today accept the general principles of biblical criticism and reinterpret their faith accordingly, so that, for them, Spinoza's view that Ezra is the true author of the Pentateuch is unacceptable on scholarly grounds but the question of heresy does not enter into the picture.

It is quite otherwise with Spinoza's ideas about God as developed in his *Ethics*, published posthumously. Here Spinoza's views, which, it must be admitted, are admittedly difficult fully to comprehend, seem to suggest that there is no God as the Supreme Being, only as a philosophical idea, God corresponding to the universe in totality. Spinoza's tight and carefully worked-out scheme is deterministic with no apparent room for the doctrine of free will and, for him, there is no longer any need for Jews to remain a separate people who worship God in a special way. For Spinoza God did not create *nature but is nature and neither intellect nor will can be ascribed to God. This, at least, is the usual understanding of Spinoza's pantheism, although a few scholars have interpreted his thought as rather more in accordance with traditional theism. In his lifetime Spinoza was accused of being an atheist. In a letter to Jacob Ostens (1625–78), Lambert Van Velthuysen (1622–85) openly states that in his view Spinoza's opinions are nothing more than a disguised form of *atheism:

'He [Spinoza] acknowledges God and confesses Him to be the maker and founder of the universe. But he declares that the form, appearance, and order of the world are evidently as necessary as the Nature of God, and the eternal truths, which he holds are established apart from the decision of God. Therefore he also expressly declares that all things come to pass by invincible necessity and inevitable fate . . . He does this in accordance with his principles. For what room can there be for a last judgement? Or what expectation of reward or of punishment, when all things are declared to emanate from God with inevitable necessity, or rather, when he declares that this whole universe is God? For I fear that our author is not very far removed from this opinion; at least there is not much difference between declaring that all things emanate necessarily from the nature of God and that the Universe Itself is God . . . I think, therefore, that I have not strayed far from the truth, or done any injury to the author, if I denounce him as teaching pure Atheism with hidden and disguised arguments.'

Ostens sent Spinoza Velthuysen's letter for

comment. Spinoza, in his reply, rejects vehemently the accusation that he is an atheist and that he teaches atheism: 'For Atheists are wont to desire inordinately honours and riches, which I have always despised, as all those who know me are aware.' It appears that in Spinoza's day the atheist was viewed with the strongest reprobation. Certainly the charge of practical atheism, with its association of a loose and reprehensible life, cannot be levelled against Spinoza, whose personal life was devoted to what he calls 'the intellectual love of God'. But on the theoretical level. Spinoza's identification of God with the universe does seem to amount to atheism.

All this obtains if Spinoza really teaches pantheism, as he seems to do, though some scholars prefer to think of Spinoza's philosophy as *panentheism, the doctrine that all is *in* God, a philosophy held particularly by *Shneur Zalman of Liady and the *Habad movement in *Hasidism which he founded (and see NATURE). The Habad philosophy was indeed seen by the *Mitnaggedim as heresy but there are a number of differences between pantheism and panentheism, so that while the former is undoubtedly false according to Jewish teaching the latter is not necessarily so. Moses Teitelbaum, Shneur Zalman's biographer, lists the following differences between the views of Spinoza and those of Shneur Zalman. For Spinoza God and nature are one and the same but for Shneur Zalman God is transcendent as well as immanent. For Spinoza there is no creation of the world by God but for Shneur Zalman the traditional doctrine of *creatio ex nihilo* still stands. For Spinoza the universe is eternal but for Shneur Zalman the world is temporal and God alone eternal, although individuals share in God's eternity in some way. For Spinoza it is impossible to ascribe will to God but for Shneur Zalman it is God's will which has created the world or, rather, which endows the world with the appearance of a reality apart from God. For Spinoza God does not work *through* nature but *is* nature; for Shneur Zalman God is revealed *through* nature.

From time to time attempts have been made to reclaim Spinoza for Judaism. If this means that Spinoza was a Jew and an admirable person who did not deserve to have been placed under the ban, many Jews would go along with it. But if it means that Spinoza's philosophy is compatible with Judaism, Spinoza himself would have rejected totally any such claim. Spinoza is generally seen by Jews as outside the religion and as therefore posing no threat to the religion. That is why nowadays religious Jews usually view the whole Spinoza question in a detached way and even feel proud of Spinoza's influence on world philosophy—one of 'us' extending such a great influence on 'them'. In a Hasidic tale, a Rebbe was told by one of his followers that, in Spinoza's view, there is no basic difference between humans and animals. The Rebbe replied: in that case, why have animals never produced a Spinoza?

Stuart Hampshire, *Spinoza* (Baltimore, 1951). Harry A. Wolfson, *The Philosophy of Spinoza* (Cambridge, Mass., 1934).

**Spiritualism** The attempt to get in touch with the spirits of the dead. Spiritualism as a modern religion, with its own doctrines, hymns, Christian references, and the like, is obviously at variance with Judaism and no Jew can, at one and the same time, be a Spiritualist in this religious sense any more than he can be a Christian, a Muslim, or a Buddhist (see RELIGIONS). But what of attending seances and other attempts at contacting the dead, and what of psychical research?

On the face of it there is a clear biblical injunction against any attempt at contacting the dead: 'There shall not be found among you any one that maketh his son or his daughter to pass through the fire, one that useth divination, a soothsayer, or an enchanter, or a sorcerer, or a charmer, or one that consulteth a ghost or a familiar spirit, or a necromancer. For whosoever doeth these things is an abomination unto the Lord' (Deuteronomy 18: 10–12). The story of the *Witch of Endor (1 Samuel, 28) is also relevant. Some of the medieval Jewish commentators, puzzled by the ability of the woman to raise the spirit of Samuel, held that she did not really do so but engaged in fraud pure and simple, as many mediums do in seeking to persuade the gullible.

The Halakhic position is, however, rather ambiguous. The Talmudic interpretation of the passage in Deuteronomy is that enquiring of the dead is only forbidden when the wizard does this by starving himself and spending the night in the cemetery that an 'unclean spirit might rest upon him' (*Sanhedrin* 65b). A further complication arises from the curious Talmudic tale (*Berakhot* 18b) of a 'saint' (Hasid) who spent the night in the cemetery where he overheard the spirits of the dead conversing with one another. In this tale there is not the slightest suggestion that the saint acted illegally or sinfully. The commentators try to resolve the contradiction by pointing out that the saint did not starve himself nor did he go to the cemetery in order for an unclean spirit to rest upon him. In fact, the tale begins with the statement that the saint's wife virtually threw him out of the house after a quarrel. It cannot have been easy for her to be the wife of a saint. Be that as it may, Maimonides, in his Code (*Akum* 11: 13) states categorically:

'What is the meaning of necromancy? It refers to one who starves himself and then stays overnight in the cemetery in order that a dead person should visit him in a dream to give him some information he requires. Some say that they [the necromancers] put on special garments, utter incantations, burn a special kind of incense, and then sleep alone—in order that a certain dead person should visit them and converse with them in a dream. The principle is as follows: whoever carries out any act the purpose of which is for a dead person to visit him and impart information, is to be flogged, as it is said: "There shall not be found among you . . . or a necromancer."'

True to his general attitude towards *magic, Maimonides does not say that it is possible for the necromancer to converse with the dead even in a dream, but the Torah, on Maimonides' understanding forbids the very attempt to contact the dead by the use of magical methods such as starving and staying overnight in the cemetery. Maimonides makes no reference to the unclean spirit referred to in the Talmud, evidently understanding the desire to perform the act as itself the resting of an unclean spirit.

The work *Hagahot Maimoni*, by a pupil of Rabbi Meir of Rothenburg (d. 1293), is a commentary to Maimonides' Code which often records German attitudes different from those of the more rationalistic Maimonides. This work, commenting on Maimonides' statement, quotes a strange distinction made by Rabbi Eleazar of Metz (d. 1198). This is that a prohibition applies only when the enquiry is addressed to the corpse itself; that is, the magical attempt at using the corpse as an instrument to contact the spirits is not permitted, but no offence is involved in trying to get in touch with the spirits of the dead. In this view it is permitted for two friends to make a pact to the effect that the one who dies first will return in spirit to the one who remains alive. The *Shulḥan Arukh* (*Yoreh Deah*, 179. 14) states the position in this way: 'It is permitted to make a dying person swear to return after his death in order to convey some information he will be asked. And some permit an attempt to do this even after the person has died provided that he does not conjure the actual corpse but only the ghost of the dead man.' The point here is that in the first instance there is no offence, since when the promise is made the man is still alive. The second opinion goes further and understands the whole prohibition as referring only to an attempt somehow to conjure up the actual corpse (like the zombi of horror films and fiction) and not the spirit or ghost of the dead. Rabbi Zevi Hirsch Spira of Munkacs (d. 1913), in his work on this section of the *Shulḥan Arukh*, quotes recent authorities who have considered the question of table-rapping and holds that this is strictly forbidden under the heading of magical practices.

The question of whether spiritualistic activities are permitted was asked of Rabbi A. I. *Kook in a letter dated 1912. His reply is included in his collection of Responsa, *Daat Kohen* (no. 69). The questioner was evidently of the opinion that if attempts to contact the spirits of the dead were shown to be successful it would deal a blow to any materialistic philosophy and would be a cause of strengthening religious faith. After quoting the views mentioned above, Rabbi Kook concludes:

'In my humble opinion it does not seem worth while to strengthen faith by means of such dubious methods which can easily lead to forbidden practices. It is far better to obey the injunction: "Thou shalt be whole-hearted with the Lord thy God" [Deuteronomy 18: 13] . . . In this I see fit to reply to you in brief as it appears to me. But it is obvious that it is impossible for me to express any *definite* opinion before I know certain details of this deep and mysterious business.' (Kook's emphasis.)

In a postscript, Kook adds: 'It is proper for the holy nation to cleave only to the Lord God of life.'

It would appear, then, that nowhere is there a clearly stated Halakhic ruling that attendance at a seance or staying in a house reputed to be haunted for purposes of psychical research or even out of sheer curiosity is forbidden. But, as

Rabbi Kook implies, more general considerations are involved.

> Louis Jacobs, 'Spiritualism', in his *What Does Judaism Say About . . .?* (Jerusalem, 1973), 299–301.

**Spirituality** The attitude in which the emphasis in life is placed on spiritual rather than material things. In the Bible and Talmud, while the idea behind spirituality is found throughout, it is never expressed in abstract terms. In the Middle Ages, under the impact of Greek thought, the term *ruḥaniyut* (from *ruaḥ*, 'spirit') was coined to denote spirituality and the term *gashmiyut* (from *geshem*, 'a bodily substance') to denote its opposite. For instance, concern with the religious life of prayer, worship, and the study of the Torah is said to be a concern with *ruḥaniyut* while a concern with eating, drinking, and the other needs of the body is said to be a concern with *gashmiyut*. But the two ideas are never kept in two separate compartments. It is possible, when engaging in *ruḥaniyut*, to have the mind on the material advantages that will result from the engagement—studying the Torah, for instance, in order to win wealth and fame—and then *ruḥaniyut* is converted into *gashmiyut*. Conversely, *Hasidism stresses the idea of *avodah be-gashmiyut*, 'worship through corporeality', and there is the Rabbinic saying in Ethics of the Fathers (2. 12), attributed to Rabbi Jose the Priest who is described as a Hasid 'saint': 'Let all your deeds be for the sake of Heaven.' In this *gashmiyut* is converted into *ruḥaniyut*. Furthermore, with regard to conduct towards the neighbour, the general principle is to have more concern with the neighbour's material well-being than with the state of his soul. As the nineteenth-century moralist, Israel *Salanter, once put it: 'Concern for the other's *gashmiyut* is *ruḥaniyut*.' Jewish saintliness (see SAINTS) does not normally involve living in an ivory tower of spirituality remote from the daily life of normal human beings with physical and material needs, hence the stress on *charity as an essential ingredient in the life of piety and the numerous tales of saintly men who prayed for rain, and for the health and sustenance, if not for themselves, for others who were in distress.

The question of *asceticism in Judaism is complicated. There have been any number of Jewish ascetics, contrary to the popular opinion that Judaism is too 'sane' a religion to have room for such spiritual excesses (see FASTING and SAINTS OF GERMANY). But those spiritually minded persons for whom asceticism was not the way to God, and who may even have seen asceticism to be a hindrance to the spiritual life, still tried to meet their Creator when engaged in normal living. Naturally opinions differ in this matter, as can be seen from a comparison of the views of Maimonides (in his introduction to Ethics of the Fathers, ch. 5) with those of Rabbenu Jonah Gerondi (d.1263) on the passage in Ethics of the Fathers regarding deeds for the sake of Heaven.

For Maimonides, the ideal of 'for the sake of Heaven' means that man's ultimate purpose should be the apprehension of God to the utmost of his intellectual capacity. In Maimonides' scheme even the performance of the precepts of the Torah is subordinate to the contemplative ideal. For this ideal to be realized or even pursued, man must have a healthy body and, consequently, as a means towards the achievement of his ultimate aim, he must have the secondary aim of keeping healthy (Maimonides was a physician and is always strong in his advocacy of bodily *health). His bodily appetites, far from being unworthy, are essential and must not be denied. But they should not be indulged in such a way as to thwart his ultimate aim. None of man's acts should be carried out without purpose. They should all be directed in the first instance to the improvement of his bodily health, which in turn will help endow him with the capacity to engage in contemplation of God. Physical fitness is thus the means to the fulfilment of the ultimate goal of contemplation. Physical pleasure is frequently associated with these means but where it is in conflict with them, such as where a pleasurable act is detrimental to health, it must be rejected. Food beneficial to the body should be eaten whether it is enjoyed or not and food that is tasty but unhealthy must not be eaten. The enjoyment of tasty food when ordered by the doctor for the purpose of increasing the appetite is similarly good since this, too, is conducive to health. Similarly, recreational pursuits have their place in life but never as an end in themselves, always as a means to physical fitness and ultimately to serve the aim of contemplation. Maimonides, here and elsewhere in his writings, advocates the living of a balanced life, not for the sake of balance and harmony as aesthetic ideals, as they were for the Greeks from whom he obtained the ideal of the golden mean, but as means to the only true end of life, the contemplation of God's majesty and glory.

Maimonides has a realistic, though very austere, understanding of the doctrine 'for the sake of Heaven'. It does not mean that physical pleasures are outlawed or that man should engage in pleasurable acts without enjoying them, if such a thing is possible. Maimonides is realistic, too, in his appreciation of how very difficult it is to live by this doctrine. He writes: 'Know that this stage is an exceedingly elevated and difficult one, only to be attained by the very few and then only after great training. If a man does manage to reach this stage I would not say that he is inferior to the prophets. The stage I am thinking of is that all man's psychological motivation and all his final aim is only for the knowledge of God. Such a man performs no act, whether great or small, and speaks no word, unless it brings him directly or indirectly to his ideal. He examines every one of his acts to see whether it leads him towards his aim or away from it . . . Our Sages of blessed memory have summed up this whole topic in a few short words which describe adequately the whole idea, and they have done it so effectively that if you note the way they have formulated this tremendous idea—one about which whole books have been written without exhausting the topic—you will appreciate that their words were undoubtedly uttered under the influence of the divine power. I refer to their injunction: "Let all your deeds be done for the sake of Heaven." This is the idea we have developed in this chapter.'

Jonah Gerondi goes much further than Maimonides. For Maimonides the ideal is for the deed to be done for the sake of Heaven and not *solely* for pleasure. But for Gerondi the deed should be done ideally for the sake of Heaven and *not* for pleasure, although Gerondi is commenting on Rabbi Jose's statement and does not necessarily advocate the ideal for all, only for those, like Rabbi Jose and Gerondi himself, who aspire to the saintly life. The *Shulḥan Arukh (Oraḥ Ḥayyim*, 231), however, contains a paragraph headed: 'That all man's deeds should be for the sake of Heaven.' It is astonishing to find, in this standard Code, as a matter of law and for every Jew, what can, for Maimonides, only be fully realized by the greatest of saints. Moreover, the ideal is stated in the more austere form of Gerondi, whom the *Shulḥan Arukh* quotes verbatim: 'Even permitted things such as eating, drinking, sitting, rising, walking, lying down, sexual intercourse, speech and all the needs of your body should be all for the worship of God or for that which brings about His worship, so that even if he was thirsty and hungry if he ate and drank for his pleasure it is not praiseworthy but he should have the intention of eating what he needs to preserve his vitality so that he can serve his Creator.' 'The *sex act,' the *Shulḥan Arukh* continues, 'is disgraceful if it is carried out in order to satisfy his lust or for his pleasure and even if his intention is to have sons who will serve him it is still not praiseworthy but he should intend it for the purpose of having sons who will serve God or to do his duty to his wife, like a man who pays his debts [i.e. the debtor pays his debts because he is so obliged but hardly enjoys the repayment itself].' The *Shulḥan Arukh* concludes: 'One who conducts himself in this manner serves his Creator all the time.' This is spirituality with a vengeance, surely beyond the reach of the average pious Jew for which it is intended. Interestingly enough, a few of the Hasidic masters, for example, Zevi Elimelech Spira of Dinov (d.1841), in his *Derekh Pikkudekha* (i. 5), are recorded as saying that all this only applies before the act but it is impossible for there to be no pleasure in the sex act itself and a man should give thanks to God, in the mind at least, for this pleasure as he gives thanks to God for other pleasures that are divine gifts.

The tendency among modern religious Jews is to feel themselves less bound to the medieval notion of the powerful dichotomy that exists between body and soul, a dichotomy expressed in the medieval maxim: the construction of the soul is in direct proportion to the destruction of the body. They will admit, naturally, that there is great spiritual power in the doctrine of 'for the sake of "Heaven"' but will interpret the doctrine in less stark terms than did the medieval thinkers. Dr J. H. *Hertz (*The Authorised Daily Prayer Book* (London, 1947), 641) interprets the saying in Ethics of the Fathers in a considerably softer and less self-deluding manner: 'Even the common actions of daily life should be consecrated to the service of God, and be hallowed by Religion. Thus, Hillel told his disciples that to keep the body clean by bathing, was a religious duty.' Dr Hertz quotes in this connection the lines of the hymn by the English poet, George Herbert: 'A servant with this clause makes drudgery divine; who sweeps a room as for Thy laws, makes that and the action fine.'

Another very wide-ranging idea in connection with spirituality is the doctrine of *Kavvanah, that mere behaviourism is not enough, for all the stress Judaism places on the deed, and that inwardness is to be cultivated when offering prayers and performing the precepts of the Torah, as in the doctrine of Lishmah ('for its own sake'). Kavvanah refers to the need for awareness and concentration when carrying out a precept. Lishmah refers to the proper motive for performing that deed, that it be done because it is a religious duty and in obedience to God's will not for any other ulterior, self-seeking motive.

*The Various Forms of Jewish Spirituality*

In addition to the spiritual ideals mentioned above, there are other aspects of Jewish spirituality, such as: contemplation and contemplative prayer, prominent among the medieval thinkers and in Habad; the performance of *yihudim* ('unifications') by the Kabbalists, acts intended to assist the unification of the *Sefirot; the recital of Psalms in order to capture for oneself the yearning for God of the Psalmist; the working on the self in the *Musar movement, severe self-scrutiny for the sake of inner integrity; the sacred table on the Sabbath and the festivals, in which good food and drink become the vehicles of holy living; and the cultivation of solitude among some of the medieval Jewish mystics and in the circle of *Nahman of Bratslav. Above all, Jewish spirituality has been expressed throughout the ages in the *study of the Torah, the approach to the divine presence through the investigation of God's word, the thinking of God's thoughts after Him, the Jewish version of the beatific vision, as Alexander Altmann has called it. In all these, as Arthur Green states in his introduction to the volumes he edited on Jewish spirituality, the aim was always to follow the Psalmist in seeking God's presence.

Arthur Green (ed.), *Jewish Spirituality*, 2 vol. (New York, 1986–7).
Solomon Schechter, 'Saints and Saintliness', in his *Studies in Judaism* (Philadelphia, 1945), 148–81.

**Sport** There are not many references to sport in the classical Jewish sources but this does not necessarily denote any lack of interest in the subject. Archery was practised as a sport as well as in warfare, as seems evident from the story of David and Jonathan (1 Samuel 20: 21–2). Jeremiah's reference to 'contending with horses' (Jeremiah 12: 5) has been understood to mean a kind of athletic contest, but this is very uncertain. The Psalmist's reference to the strong man running his course (Psalms 19: 6) is much clearer, though here, too, the reference is not necessarily to sport. The Mishnah (*Sukkah* 5. 4) and the Talmudic comments on it refer to the pious men ('Hasidim and men of good deeds') in Temple times on the festival of *Tabernacles dancing and juggling lighted torches. Ball games were played in Talmudic times. The Midrash (Lamentations Rabbah 2: 4) gives as one of the reasons for the destruction of Jerusalem that ball games were played on the Sabbath. However, the *Tosafot (*Betzah* 12a) state that ball games were permitted on the Sabbath in medieval France in private, though not in the public domain. The *Shulhan Arukh (Orah Hayyim, 308. 45) records two opinions on the permissibility of playing ball games on the Sabbath. Israel Abrahams provides many examples of Jewish sports and pastimes among medieval Jews. In more recent times in Eastern Europe horseback riding was enjoyed by many Jews. There are even tales of some of the Hasidic masters being fond of this sport.

The values promoted by sporting activities—health, the team spirit, refreshment of mind and body—are acceptable to Judaism. But it can be argued that sports such as boxing and wrestling, in which violence is consciously done to the person (unlike football and cricket, where any injury to the players is incidental and not intended) are hardly in keeping with the spirit of Judaism, although it might be going too far to suggest that these sports are forbidden by Jewish law. A Talmudic Rabbi (*Sanhedrin* 58b) declared that whoever lifts up his hand against his neighbour is called 'wicked' and he quotes in support the verse: 'And he said to the wicked one [in the context, "wicked" in the sense of guilty of starting the fight, but interpreted homiletically as really "wicked"]: "Wherefore smitest thou thy fellow?"' (Exodus 2: 13). Against this it can be argued that, while a man is not normally allowed to injure himself or to give permission to others to harm him, in a boxing match both participants engage in the fight for financial gain and know full well the risks they are taking so that, as in other instances of people taking risks in dangerous jobs, the contract to fight does not offend against the strict law. But it is doubtful whether sports involving conscious cruelty are in the spirit of the law, no matter what the letter of the law states. In a famous Responsum, Rabbi Ezekiel *Landau forbids *hunting animals for sport on the grounds of cruelty. It is obvious that Judaism would frown on the practice of 'throwing' games for financial and other gain, on the grounds of the general strong disapproval of dishonest practices.

Israel Abrahams, 'Medieval Pastimes and Indoor Amusements', in his *Jewish Life in the Middle Ages* (1932), 397–411.

**Steinberg, Milton** American Conservative Rabbi and theologian (1903–50). Steinberg studied philosophy at City College in New York and took the Rabbinical course at the Jewish Theological Seminary, where he was ordained in 1928. Steinberg first served as a Rabbi in Indianopolis but in 1933 he became Rabbi of the prestigious Park Avenue Synagogue in New York, in which capacity he served until his death at the early age of 47. At the Park Avenue Synagogue Steinberg became renowned for his thought-provoking sermons, some of which have been published in the form of sermon notes (*From the Sermons of Milton Steinberg*, ed. Bernard Mandelbaum (New York, 1954)). Steinberg's preaching methods have become models for modern Rabbis in their apt quotations from world literature and in their application of philosophical ideas to the traditional Jewish texts without distorting either the philosophical ideas or the texts themselves. Steinberg was greatly influenced by his teacher at the Seminary, Mordecai *Kaplan, whom he joined in Kaplan's Reconstructionist movement, contributing many articles to *The Reconstructionist*, the journal of the movement (see RECONSTRUCTIONISM). Later, however, Steinberg took issue with the religious naturalism of the movement, seeing no reason why the admirable aim of reconstructing Jewish life should be tied to a reinterpretation of the God idea in naturalistic terms.

Steinberg's novel *As a Driven Leaf* (Indianopolis, 1939, and frequently republished) has as its hero the tragic figure, Elisha ben Abuyah, the second-century Rabbi, colleague of Rabbi *Akiba and teacher of Rabbi *Meir, who became an apostate, torn as he was between his loyalty to Judaism and the allure of Roman life and civilization. As a powerful novel of ideas,

this work had a considerable influence on questing Jews obliged to grapple with problems similar to those faced by Elisha, albeit against a different cultural background. Steinberg was also a leading Zionist; his positive attitude to *Zionism can be observed in the posthumously published essays: *A Believing Jew* (ed. Maurice Samuel (New York, 1951)).

Steinberg's mature thoughts on religion are presented in the posthumously published *Anatomy of Faith* (ed. Arthur A. Cohen (New York, 1960)). Steinberg here presents Judaism as a religion which, while, like any other religion, based on faith, is supported by reason. To be sure, the medieval thinkers who sought to prove the existence of God were swayed too much by logic and failed to appreciate that 'reason can always argue against reason', yet an anti-intellectual approach to religion is similarly misguided. Steinberg sets out to answer the question: 'Does believing in God make sense? Or is religious faith something for the ignorant, the muddleheaded, those too wishful, lazy, or cowardly to think the matter through?' His reply is that belief in God should be seen as a hypothesis capable of being tested like any other hypothesis. The way of testing the religious hypothesis is to note the telling reasons for maintaining that Deity rather than Nullity moves behind and through the universe. For Steinberg the traditional arguments for the existence of God should not be seen as proofs or knock-down arguments but as pointers to the Reality, making better sense of human experience than any rival theory. As Steinberg puts it in formal philosophical language: 'Religious faith is a hypothesis interpreting reality and posited on the same grounds as any valid hypothesis, viz., superior congruity with the facts, greater practicality, and maximal conceptual economy.' The problem of evil is, indeed, a severe obstacle to belief in a benevolent Creator but attempts have been made by religious thinkers to show how the existence of evil can be compatible with the existence of God. There is, indeed, no completely satisfying solution to the problem but, then, the atheist has more questions to answer than the theist. How would the atheist account, asks Steinberg, for the existence of natural law, the instinctual cunning of the insect, the brain of the genius and the heart of the prophet?

Steinberg disagrees profoundly with Kierkegaard's 'leap of faith' and his idea of the 'paradox', believing the ideas of religious *existentialism to be largely of Christian rather than Jewish interest, since, as Christians themselves proudly declare, the basic Christian dogma is beyond the power of reason to penetrate. Judaism is a religion that does not glorify the unintelligible. At the same time, Steinberg does not believe Judaism to be a religion of reason after the fashion of a Maimonides or a Hermann *Cohen. Judaism has its mysteries and non-rationalities and it has even had its quota of antirationalists (see RATIONALISM).

Oddly enough, in the light of his general discussion of traditional Jewish ideas regarding the nature of God, there is only a single and casual reference to the Kabbalistic doctrine of *En Sof and the *Sefirot and very little about the general mystical approach to religion. Jewish belief in the Hereafter is hardly touched upon in Steinberg's writings. There is also very little about the meaning of religious language and the challenge presented to religious faith by modern linguistic analysis.

Simon Noveck, *Milton Steinberg: Portrait of a Rabbi* (New York, 1978).

**Sterilization** The use of artificial means to render persons or animals incapable of producing offspring. According to biblical law (Leviticus 21: 20) a priest who 'has his stones crushed' may not serve in the Sanctuary because he has a 'blemish'. He is compared in the verse to other persons with blemishes such as a hunchback or a dwarf. There is a further biblical law (Deuteronomy 23: 2) that one who is 'crushed or maimed in his privy parts' may not enter into the assembly of the Lord, understood by the Rabbis to mean that he must not marry. The prohibition against castrating *animals is stated, according to the Rabbis, in the verse (Leviticus 22: 24): 'That which hath its stones bruised or crushed, or torn, or cut, ye shall not offer unto the Lord; neither shall ye do thus in your land', the last clause being understood by the Rabbis to mean that it is prohibited to castrate human beings and animals. Does all this mean that sterilization is categorically forbidden in all circumstances? The Mishnah (*Shabbat* 14: 3) rules that since it is forbidden to take medicine on the Sabbath (provided there is no danger if it is not taken) it is forbidden to drink a 'cup of roots', evidently a certain herbal compound possessing healing powers. Commenting on this Mishnah, the Talmud notes that the 'cup of roots', while efficacious in curing jaundice, causes the

sufferer to become impotent so that it is forbidden for a man to drink this since it is a form of self-castration. With regard to a woman the matter is rather more complicated since, in the Rabbinic ruling, the duty of *procreation devolves only on men, not on women, although it is religiously meritorious, but not a full obligation, for a woman, too, to marry and have children. Elsewhere in the Talmud (*Yevamot* 85b) the conclusion is that since a woman has no actual obligation to have children she may drink the potion. In fact, the Talmud states that the wife of Rabbi Hiyya, who had had severe pain in giving birth to two sets of twins, resolved to drink the 'cup of roots' in order to prevent further pregnancies. On the basis of all this the ruling is that any interference with the organs of generation by a direct act is forbidden but that a woman may drink the 'cup of roots', since this is indirect. According to some authorities she may only drink it where, like the wife of Rabbi Hiyya, she has severe pains in childbirth but other authorities permit it in any event for a woman. These are the principles as laid down in the Talmud and the Codes. We no longer know what exactly is meant by the 'cup of roots' and modern medicine does not know of any sterilizing agent taken by mouth, but this does not affect the *principles*.

The final ruling given in the *Shulḥan Arukh* (*Even Ha-Ezer*, 5: 11–12) is that any act which prevents the organs of generation from functioning is forbidden, whether performed on a man or a woman or even on an animal. A woman is, however, permitted to sterilize herself by drinking the 'cup of roots'. This ruling is adopted by all Orthodox Rabbis, so as to forbid a sterilization operation. This is why, incidentally, some Orthodox authorities allow a woman to be on the pill (see BIRTH-CONTROL), the pill being a modern form of the 'cup of roots' and even better since it appears that the 'cup of roots' was irreversible. Since operations on the prostate gland almost inevitably result in sterilization, Rabbis have discussed whether it is permitted to have this operation. In most circumstances the tendency is to permit it.

Immanuel Jakobovits, 'Sterilization', in his *Essays Presented to Chief Rabbi Israel Brodie on the Occasion of his Seventieth Birthday* (London, 1967), 193–4.

**Streimel** The fur hat worn by Hasidic Jews on the Sabbath, festivals, and other festive occasions. This kind of fur hat was worn by the

Polish aristocracy when the Hasidic movement grew in the eighteenth century, as can be seen from prints of Polish noblemen, and was adopted by the Hasidim as a dignified head-covering suitable for wear on special occasions. Eventually the *streimel* became the specific Hasidic form of head-gear and various mystical ideas were read into it, for example, that the thirteen tails of which it is composed represent the thirteen attributes of divine mercy. There are variations in the form of the *streimel* among Hasidim of different groups. *Habad Hasidim do not wear the *streimel*, though it is reported that in the early days of Habad a *streimel* was kept in the synagogue to be worn by those who were called to the *reading of the Torah. Fierce battles were sometimes fought by the Hasidim against attempts by the government authorities to ban the wearing of the *streimel*, which as a result became the sign of strong Hasidic and Jewish identification. The majority of the Hasidim do not don the *streimel* until their marriage, when the father-in-law gives it as a present to the young bridegroom, but among some groups even small boys wear it. Some groups wear the *spodek*, a high fur hat, instead of the *streimel*.

**Strikes** It cannot be expected that there should be references to strikes in the classical Jewish sources since, before the industrial age, the economic forms of society were quite different from those obtaining today. Among other differences, in biblical and Rabbinic times workmen did not hire themselves out as more or less permanent employees of a particular employer, nor was there much organized labour in those days. Nevertheless, important principles are laid down governing the rights of workmen and these can be applied to the contemporary situation. Attempts have been made by Rabbis in the State of Israel to find some guidance in the ancient sources on the question of strikes in the modern sense.

In biblical law (Leviticus 19: 13; Deuteronomy 24: 14–15) there are stern injunctions against keeping back the wages of a workman. The Rabbinic Midrash, the Sifre, comments on this: 'Why does this workman ascend the highest scaffolding and risk his life if you do not pay him his wages as soon as they are due?' Among other Rabbinic rulings regarding the rights of workmen is the rule that a workman hired for a day can break the contract in the middle of the day if he so wishes (*Bava Metzia* 10a), though in the Talmudic discussion this right is some-

what qualified. Following Talmudic statements Maimonides records (*Shekalim* 4: 7):

'Those who kept the scrolls in order in Jerusalem and the judges who decided in cases of robbery in Jerusalem received their wages from the Temple treasury. How much did they receive? Ninety *manehs* a month. If this amount was insufficient, the wages should be increased, even if they objected to the increase, so as to be adequate for their own provisions and for those of their wives and families.'

The Talmud (*Sukkah* 51b; *Bava Kama* 116b) speaks with approval of craftsmen organizing themselves in guilds for their own protection. Similarly, the Talmud (*Bava Batra* 8b–9a) rules that the people of each locality are entitled to determine democratically such matters as prices and wages.

The following Talmudic passage (*Yoma* 38a) is also relevant:

'Our Rabbis taught: the house of Garmu was expert in preparing the shewbread, but would not teach it. The Sages sent for specialists from Alexandria of Egypt, who knew how to bake as well as they, but did not know how to take the loaves down from the oven as well.... The Sages then said: let the house of Garmu return to their office. The Sages sent for them but they would not come. So they doubled their wages and they came. Before this they used to get 12 *manehs* for the day; after this, *24 manehs*.'

None of this amounts to a clear statement about strikes in the modern sense and in any event Jews do not simply consult the Talmud with regard to social and economic problems but rely on their social conscience, knowledge of the conditions, and sheer common sense in trying to work them out. Yet there can be no doubt that the sentiments expressed in the Talmudic sources would justify, if such justification were needed, the organization of workers into trade unions with the perfectly legitimate right to strike. Naturally, Judaism encourages its adherents to avoid industrial as well as other forms of strife wherever possible. The ideal social order is one where fair wages and conditions of employment can be negotiated favourably without recourse to strikes and lock-outs.

Louis Jacobs, 'Strikes', in his *What Does Judaism Say About . . .?* (Jerusalem, 1973), 308–10.

**Study** From early Rabbinic times the study of the Torah was seen as a supreme religious obligation. In the opening passage of Ethics of the Fathers the Men of the *Great Synagogue are quoted as advocating the raising of many disciples. The opening Mishnah of tractate *Peah* states that the 'things which have no fixed measure' are deeds of loving-kindness and the study of the Torah (*talmud torah*). The Mishnah continues: 'These are the things whose fruit a man enjoys in this world while the capital is laid up for him in the *World to Come: honouring father and mother, deeds of living-kindness, making peace between a man and his fellow; and the study of the Torah is equal to them all.' *Elijah, Gaon of Vilna, in his commentary to the Mishnah, remarks that since the study of the Torah has no fixed measure, then one word of Torah falls under the definition of study of the Torah and this single word is 'equal to them all', more precious in God's eyes than all the other good deeds a man does. The Gaon of Vilna engages here in hyperbole. It is never as simple as that. In fact, according to the Talmud, if a good deed presents itself to a student of the Torah he must put his learning aside to carry it out, unless the deed can be performed by others just as effectively. The Talmud denigrates the scholar who declares: 'I shall have nothing but Torah' and states that such a scholar does not even have Torah. But in the school of the Gaon, the Lithuanian school of learning, as followed, for instance, in the Yeshivah of *Volozhyn and the other Lithuanian Yeshivot, everything was made subordinate to the ideal of Torah study. In a sense *Hasidism is a protest against the one-sidedness of the attitude of the *Mitnaggedim in placing study above all else and there is, in the history of Judaism, considerable tension between learning and piety (see SAINTS). However, Hasidism saw the study of the Hasidic devotional texts as the study of the Torah, an ideal they accepted with the same fervour as their opponents. A number of Hasidic masters were great scholars in the conventional sense as well. The Kabbalists, too, saw the study of the Zohar and the other writings of the Kabbalah as the study of the Torah, treating this, indeed, as the highest form of study.

Significantly, in this connection, the followers of the Gaon, himself a student of the Kabbalah, were fond of quoting the Zoharic statements about the supreme value of Torah study in the sense of mystical studies and applied these to the study of the Talmud. For instance, Abraham, brother of the Vilna Gaon, compiled a little treatise, entitled *Maalot Ha-Torah* ('The Lofty Advantages of [study of] the

Torah'), in which he quotes passages from many sources on the subject, including the following passage from the Zohar (i. 4b):

'How greatly is it incumbent on a man to study the Torah day and night! For the Holy One, blessed be He, is attentive to the voice of those who occupy themselves with the Torah, and through each fresh discovery made by them in the Torah a new heaven is created. Our teachers have told us that at the moment when a man expounds something new in the Torah, his utterance ascends before the Holy One, blessed be He, and He takes it up and kisses it and crowns it with seventy crowns of graven and inscribed letters.'

The Zohar refers to 'fresh discoveries' in mystic lore but the idea, found also in the Talmud, of finding new ideas in the Torah, was the ideal of every student throughout the ages in the plain sense of discovering some new idea or solution to a problem that no one had ever thought of before. The study of the Torah was never conceived of as a mere repetition of sacred texts. The student was expected to immerse himself in his studies and not allow himself to be fobbed off by conclusions reached by faulty logic, even if such conclusions were found in the works of great scholars. The mind was to be engaged in the study with full rigour and far from originality being despised, it was admired as evidence that the study was worthy of the name.

### Dedication to Study

In the addition to the chapter of Ethics of the Fathers (now ch. 6) entitled *Kinyan Torah* ('The Acquisition of Torah') the qualifications for study are carefully mapped out, forty-eight 'excellences' by which the Torah is acquired being listed (Ethics of the Fathers, 6. 6):

'By the hearing of the ear, by the ordering of the lips, by the understanding of the heart, by the discernment of the heart, by awe, by reverence, by humility, by cheerfulness; by attendance on the Sages, by consorting with fellow-students, by close argument *[pilpul] with disciples; by assiduity, by knowledge of Scripture and Mishnah; by moderation in business, in wordly occupation, pleasure, sleep, conversation, and eating; by long-suffering, by a good heart, by faith in the Sages, by submission to sorrows; by being one that recognizes his place and that rejoices in his lot and that makes a fence around his words and claims no merit for himself; by being one that is beloved, that loves God, that loves mankind, that loves well-doing, that loves rectitude, that loves reproof, that shuns honour and boasts not of his learning and delights not in rendering decisions; that helps his fellow to bear his yoke, and that judges him favourably, and that establishes him in the truth and establishes him in peace; and that occupies himself assiduously in his study; by being one that asks and makes answer, that hearkens and adds thereto; that learns in order to teach and that learns in order to practise; that makes his teacher wiser; that retells exactly what he has heard, and reports a thing in the name of him that said it.'

In the same treatise (Ethics of the Fathers, 6. 4) this advice is given to the student of the Torah: 'This is the way of the Torah: a morsel of bread with salt to eat, water by measure to drink; thou shalt sleep on the ground, and live a life of hardship, while thou toilest in the Torah. If thou doest thus, happy shalt thou be, and it shall be well with thee; happy shalt thou be—in this world, and it shall be well with thee—in the world to come.' It has to be appreciated that study in Talmudic times was not out of books. The student rehearsed the texts (of the Mishnah and other Tannaitic works for the Amoraim, the earlier material for the Tannaim) by heart, which explains the saying of the second-century Tanna, Rabbi Jacob (Ethics of the Fathers, 3. 7): 'If a man was walking by the way and studying and ceased his study to declare: "How fine is this tree!" or "How fine is this ploughed field!" Scripture reckons it to him as though he were guilty against his own soul.' This total dedication to the study of the Torah can be observed throughout the history of Jewish learning. There were, of course, rich students but the majority of students who journeyed long distances to sit at the feet of a master were poor and denied themselves for many years the luxuries, and often even the necessities of life, going hungry and thirsty in order to 'toil in the Torah'. The ideal scholar was one who was totally absorbed in his studies so that it was said (*Berakhot* 24b) that a scholar is forbidden to remain in unclean alleyways, where the Torah must not be studied, since a scholar would be incapable of diverting his mind from his studies. Of the fourth-century Amora, Rava (see ABBAYE AND RAVA) it was said (*Shabbat* 88a) that he was once so engrossed in his studies that he was unaware that his fingers were spurting blood.

This kind of devotion was not limited to the Talmudic period. Indeed, after the close of the Talmud, this work itself became the sacred text most studied and in the process even heavier demands were made on the student. To 'know Shas [the Talmud]' was the ideal. Numerous scholars were found who knew the whole Talmud by heart. But the ideal of Torah study was not only for scholars. Following Talmudic statements Maimonides (*Talmud Torah*, 1. 8) rules:

'Every man in Israel is obliged to study the Torah, whether he is firm of body or a sufferer from ill-health, whether a young man or of advanced age with his strength abated. Even a poor man who is supported by charity and who is obliged to beg at doors and even one with a wife and children is obliged to set aside a period for Torah study by day and by night, as it is said: "Thou shalt meditate therein day and night" [Joshua 1: 8].'

Maimonides refers here to a 'man' and there is no doubt that while a few women did win renown as scholars, the obligation to study the Torah devolved only on men and very few women, until modern times, studied the Torah (see FEMINISM and WOMEN). Except among the ultra-Orthodox women today do study the Torah and refuse to be excluded from one of the greatest privileges in Jewish life.

To be sure, all the passages quoted present an idealistic picture and the temptation to idolize or idealize the past has to be resisted. Not all Jews engaged so assiduously in their studies and the mental horizons of many who did, were at times, exceedingly narrow. *Schechter was being unfair when he spoke of the Eastern European scholars of his day as mere 'study machines' but the phenomenon of students merely getting through huge chunks of texts without any serious reflection is certainly not unknown. The numerous references in the literature of Jewish piety about the importance of studying so many hours a day and of the sin of wasting a moment that could be spent in study of the Torah do sometimes suggest an attitude of mind where the act of sitting before the open book and piously mouthing its words mattered more than the assimilation of its contents. But the ideal of Torah study, like any other ideal, has to be seen in the light of its best representatives.

### The Scope of Studies

While in the majority of the medieval schools practically all the emphasis was placed on the study of the Talmud and the *Halakhah, for many scholars the scope was much wider. In the 'ages of man' described in Ethics of the Fathers (5. 21) it is said, probably reflecting the actual educational conditions at that time, that the age of 5 is for the study of Scripture, 10 for the study of the Mishnah, 15 for the study of Talmud (meaning here the type of learning later presented in the Talmud, otherwise such an expression in the Mishnah is anachronistic). There is also a Talmudic saying (*Kiddushin* 30a) that a man should divide his study time so that a third is devoted to Scripture, a third to Mishnah, and a third to Talmud. Yet, especially in medieval France and Germany, most of the students' efforts were directed to the study of the Babylonian Talmud, particularly to the difficult, Halakhic sections of the work. Very revealing is the observation of the *Tosafot to the passage, in the name of Rabbenu *Tam, that the Babylonian Talmud is full of material from Scripture and contains the Mishnah, so that by studying the Talmud one studies the other two at the same time. Yet even the French school produced biblical scholars such as *Rashi and *Rashbam and the other renowned biblical scholars such as *Saadiah Gaon, Abraham *Ibn Exra, and *Nahmanides show that the ideal of Torah study was conceived of by many in far wider terms. The medieval philosophers did not only accept the need for philosophical studies in order to produce a rounded personality but they saw philosophy itself, as the pursuit of truth, to be part of Torah studies. Maimonides (*Yesodey Ha-Torah*, 4. 13), to the scandal of some of his contemporaries, went so far as to identify the esoteric disciplines, mentioned in the Talmud, known as the 'Work of Creation' and the 'Work of the *Chariot', with, respectively, Aristotelian physics and metaphysics, and ranked them higher in the Jewish scale of studies than Talmudic dialectics. Similarly, the Kabbalists regarded their subject—the 'soul of the Torah' (Zohar, iii. 152a)—as the highest pursuit. Hasidism, as noted above, included the study of Hasidic works under the heading of Torah study as the followers of the *Musar movement included the Musar literature under this heading.

The *Jüdische Wissenschaft movement posed problems of its own for the traditional ideal of Torah study. In a sense the modern historical-critical methodology of this school, which is, for that matter, followed today in departments of Jewish studies at universities and in Rabbinical colleges, is opposed to study as a devotional exercise, if only because it is far more difficult to treat as sacred texts that are examined objectively and critically in a 'scientific' manner. Conversely, acknowledging the sanctity of a text tends to lead to prejudgement of critical questions regarding its background and authorship. On the contemporary scene this conflict has resulted in two vastly different worlds of Jewish studies: the world of the Yeshivot, indifferent or even hostile to critical scholarship, and the world of modern learning with no formal interest in study as an act of religious worship. Voices are raised occasionally for religious Jews to allow the religious ideal of Torah study to embrace the new critical methods, much as Maimonides allowed it to embrace philosophy. But whereas for Maimonides it was only a question of admitting another discipline, for modern scholarship it is the more basic question of whether the Torah itself can be understood in a way totally different from the way it has been interpreted in the past. There are a few signs of it happening eventually, but to date there has been little meeting between the two worlds.

Abraham Cohen, 'Study of the Torah', in his *Everyman's Talmud* (London, 1949), 135–41.

George Foot Moore, 'Study', in his *Judaism in the First Centuries of the Christian Era* (Cambridge, Mass., 1958), 239–47.

**Subjectivity** The theological attitude, especially prevalent in *mysticism and in religious *existentialism, according to which the experiences of the person rather than *history or *revelation determine the truths of religion. Naturally there are different emphases in this matter among religious thinkers, ranging from very rare complete subjectivity to acceptance of revelation in enabling the person to make subjective judgements. The actual term 'subjectivity' is not found in Jewish religious thought, nor is the idea behind it found very frequently. The medieval Jewish philosophers, for example, all believed that they were investigating truths already conveyed in the Torah, which truths they tried to understand and explicate in terms of the similarly objective truths they saw in the Greek–Arabic philosophy of their day. Yet the personal subjective element in the religious life seems to be recognized in the

Talmudic saying (*Yoma* 86b) that if a man commits a sin and repeats it, it becomes for him as if it were permitted. Israel *Salanter commented on this that if a man commits the sin not only twice but three times it not only seems permitted to him but it tends to become for him a religious duty (*mitzvah*).

An appreciation of the subjective element in religious faith, that not all men have the same capacity for faith and that apprehension of the divine is arrived at in many different ways, is expressed in a Midrashic passage (Exodus Rabbah 5: 9) on the theme of revelation. Psalm 29: 4 is translated as: 'The voice of the Lord is with power', taking 'power' as referring not to God but to the power of the individual to hear the divine voice. The voice of God, says the Midrash, was heard by the men according to their capacity, by the women according to theirs. Young men heard it differently from old men. Each individual heard it according to his own capacity. It is not a distortion of the meaning of this passage to paraphrase it as: human nature and individual temperament have a role to play if the divine voice is to be heard.

Some Jewish thinkers have argued that the truths of religion are so obvious to the human mind that they would be immediately acceptable to all were it not for the fact that a person's subjective desires act as a barrier to his acknowledgement of God and His Torah. In this connection there is a popular interpretation of the verse: 'Let the wicked forsake his way, and the unrighteous man his thoughts' (Isaiah 55: 7). If the wicked will only forsake his *way*, the life he has chosen to lead, his *thoughts* of unbelief will vanish of their own accord. In the same spirit, the *Hafetz Hayyim removed the whole question of unbelief from the intellectual to the moral plane when he said that for the believer there are no problems while for the unbeliever there are no solutions. This goes to the extreme of denying that there are any honest doubters and in effect begs the question. If humans are only capable of a subjective assessment of truth, then this statement itself is tainted by subjectivity There seems to be no satisfactory way of avoiding either objectivity or subjectivity in the matter of religious faith, which is bound to contain both elements.

On the ethical level, Judaism holds fast to the belief that the moral law is objectively grounded in the will of God and therefore takes issue with ethical theories such as hedonism and eudaemonism in which the good is defined in terms of subjective pleasure and happiness, whether of the individual or of the greatest number of persons. This is not to say that individual happiness does not result from obedience to God's law. It does, but only as a by-product; it is not the aim of the religious life, and is not necessarily promised in this life at any rate (see REWARD AND PUNISHMENT and SOUL, IMMORTALITY OF). The typical Jewish attitude is expressed in the verse: 'Observe and hear all these words which I command thee, that it may go well with thee, and with thy children after thee for ever, when thou doest that which is good and right in the eyes of the Lord' (Deuteronomy 12: 28). *Nahmanides understands the reference to doing that which is good and right in the eyes of the Lord as still leaving room for subjective, personal decisions over and above the demand to keep God's laws. According to Nahmanides, it is possible for a man to avoid any actual infringement of the law and yet lead a thoroughly dishonest and unethical life. The Torah expects each individual to weigh up the particular circumstances in which he finds himself and to ask not only whether what he intends doing is lawful but also whether it is 'good' and 'right'. The divine law is heteronomous by definition but a degree of autonomy also enters into the picture of the ideal Jewish life.

On the intellectual level, the methodology of modern scholarship, in which the classical Jewish sources are studied scientifically and objectively (see BIBLICAL CRITICISM, FUNDAMENTALISM, HISTORY, and JÜDISCHE WISSENSCHAFT), presents a problem of its own to the traditional approach, since many of the later readings of the sources are now seen as subjective, owing much to the background and even temperament of their authors. In matters of religion, completely objective assessment is hardly possible but the new methodology, in which the sources are examined without bias, so far as this is humanly possible, has undoubtedly acted as a check to hasty generalizations and claims that ideas arrived at ultimately on purely subjective grounds belong to objective and divinely revealed truth.

**Sublimation** The transmutation of less worthy or unworthy instincts and thoughts into something more elevated; in psychoanalysis (see PSYCHOLOGY), the direction of energy, especially sexual energy, into more socially acceptable channels. The actual term 'sublimation' is not found in Jewish sources but the idea is implied in a number of Talmudic passages as well in subsequent Jewish teaching. For instance, the Mishnah (*Berakhot* 9: 5) understands the injunction to love God with all the heart (Deuteronomy 6: 2) to mean with both impulses, the *yetzer ha-tov* and the *yetzer ha-ra*, the good and the evil inclination. Some of the classical commentaries understand this simply to mean that man should overcome the temptations of the evil impulse, but others take it to mean that evil traits of character can be used in the service of God. Anger, for example, is bad in itself but when used in righteous indignation at wrongdoing, becomes good. Similarly, envy is an unworthy trait but, in the language of the Talmud, 'the envy of scholars increases wisdom'. The Talmud (*Berakhot* 63a) records the saying of Bar Kappara: 'Which is a brief scriptural passage upon which all the principles of the Torah depend? "In all thy ways acknowledge Him, and He will direct thy path" [Proverbs 3: 6].' On this Rava comments: 'Even for a matter of transgression', which seems to mean even when sinning have God in mind and, in fact, some texts of the Talmud add here a popular proverb: 'The thief on the point of breaking into a house calls on God to help him.'

A clearer anticipation of the notion of sublimation is found in a passage (*Kiddushin* 30b) where it is said: 'My son if this repulsive [creature, i.e. the Evil Inclination] assails you, lead him into the House of Learning; if he is of stone, he will dissolve; if iron he will shiver [into fragments]', which seems to mean that when a man finds his passions getting the upper hand he should sublimate them by putting his drives into passionate study, although, in the conventional reading of this, the meaning is simply that study in the House of Learning will help the passionate man to distinguish between right and wrong. Another relevant passage is that (*Shabbat* 156a) in which it is stated: 'One born under Mars will be a shedder of blood.' On this Rav Ashi commented: 'Either a cupper, a thief, a butcher, or a circumciser.' It does not require too much imagination to understand this to mean that a man cursed with a congenital propensity to shed blood has the option of becoming a bloodthirsty robber or a person who uses that very propensity to benefit others as a cupper, a butcher, or a circumciser.

A striking example of sublimation is found in *Hasidism. The doctrine, popular among the early Hasidim in the eighteenth century but later abandoned as spiritually risky, runs that when 'strange thoughts' invade the mind during prayer they should not be rejected but elevated to their source in God. These 'strange thoughts' are those of 'strange love' (sexual imaginings or thoughts of sexual sin) or of 'pride' (self-congratulatory thoughts of how pious and fervent the worshipper is in his prayers) or of 'idolatry' (irreligious thoughts or, perhaps, thoughts about the attractiveness of Christianity). These thoughts, it was held, were not sent by God (from whom they have entered the mind, since everything comes from Him) to be rejected but they should rather be elevated, that is, traced in the mind to their source in God and thus deprived of their baneful power. For example, if the Hasid finds that his devotions are being distracted by thoughts about a pretty girl he has met, he should dwell on the fact that her beauty, the cause of her attraction, is only a very pale reflection of the source of all beauty on high and this will help him to sense the illusory nature of all physical beauty in comparison with the divine. Or if the Hasid finds that his thoughts are turning towards a sense of his own importance, he should dwell on pride as a manifestation here on earth of God's majesty, the ultimate source of all pride. Or if he finds himself entertaining idolatrous notions, he should remind himself that the lure of idolatry is occasioned by the desire in the human breast to worship and he will then be led to the only true Object of worship. The *Mitnaggedim were scandalized by this doctrine, based, in fact, on the Lurianic idea of elevating the '*holy sparks' inherent in all things. Eventually, however, the general tendency among the later Hasidic masters, was to argue that the doctrine was only intended for the great 'saints' of former times. These alone were capable of the extremely difficult task of elevating impure thoughts. Of them alone could it be said that the 'strange thoughts' were sent by God. For later generations the 'strange thoughts' are really strange in the sense that they come from the domain of the impure. The sole exception in this matter was the Hasidic master, Yitzhak Eisik of Komarno (d. 1874) who, as late as the second half of the nineteenth century, could still write in his *Otzar Ha-Ḥayyim* (Lvov, 1858, p. 167c):

'When some evil and strange thought comes into the mind of any Jew, whether he be great or small, whether he be of those of little worth of the great ones in Israel, it comes to him so that he can put it right and elevate it. This applies to every man, not, as some would have it, contrariwise. Such an opinion is nonsense for to God small and great are the same. For if a man does not believe in this he does not take upon himself the yoke of the kingdom of heaven.'

In later Hasidism, the doctrine has become no more than a memory.

Louis Jacobs, 'The Elevation of "Strange Thoughts", in his *Hasidic Prayer*' (New York, 1973), 104–20.

## Submission

**Submission** Surrender of the individual to the will of God or to teachers of the Torah. For all the significance it attaches to the *individual, Judaism demands that personal will and opinions be abandoned in certain circumstances. Submission is obviously required to the will of God and the laws of the Torah in which this will is reflected. The Rabbis describe the first paragraph of the *Shema as 'the acceptance of the yoke of the Kingdom of Heaven' and the second paragraph as 'the acceptance of the yoke of the commandments'. The simile of the 'yoke' appears to be based on the verse: 'The ox knoweth his owner, and the ass his master's crib, but Israel doth not know, My people doth not consider' (Isaiah 1: 3). The implication is that the Jew is not free to cast off the burden imposed on him by the Torah any more than the ox is free to dispense with the yoke its master has placed upon it to direct its steps. God, being God, demands total submission to His will. This does not necessarily mean that submission to the divine will must always be made without protest. Abraham, pleading for the righteous men in Sodom, challenges God's justice in the name of that very justice: 'That be far from Thee to do after this manner, to slay the righteous with the wicked, that so the righteous should be as the wicked; that be far from Thee; shall not the Judge of all the earth do justly?' (Genesis 18: 25). Similarly Moses pleads with God to pardon His people: 'And Moses besought the Lord his God and said: "Lord, why doth Thy wrath wax hot against Thy people, that Thou hast brought forth out of the land of Egypt with great power and with a mighty hand?"' (Exodus 32: 11). The Hasidic

master, *Levi Yitzhak of Berditchev, is renowned as the folk-hero who argues with God on behalf of the Jewish people. In these instances, however, the pleas are on behalf of others. The distinction is generally drawn between submission where the individual self is concerned and submission where others are concerned. The prototype of total submission to the will of God where only the individual person himself is concerned is Aaron of whom it is said when his sons had died: 'And Aaron held his peace' (Leviticus 10: 3). There are numerous instances in the history of Jewish thought of the total acceptance of personal *suffering without protest and without any questioning of God's justice. At the funeral service the words of Job are repeated by the mourners: 'The Lord gave, and the Lord hath taken away; blessed be the name of the Lord' (Job 1: 21).

Concerning acceptance of the discipline of the Torah there is the hard saying of the third-century teacher, Resh Lakish (*Berakhot* 63b): 'The words of the Torah become established only for one who kills himself for it.' Yet the oft-repeated claim that in the 'Old Testament' and in Rabbinic Judaism God is conceived of as a tyrannical king imposing His arbitrary will on unwilling subjects is a complete canard. Against the apparently harsher passages in the literature which dwell on submission there should be placed the many in which God is spoken of as a loving Father who desires only the good of His creatures and whose demands are never for more than lies in the capacity of His creatures to undertake. A typical Rabbinic saying is: 'The Holy One, blessed be He, does not deal imperiously with His creatures' (*Avodah Zarah* 3a). Another saying in the same vein is: 'The Torah was not given to the ministering angels' (*Berakhot* 25b).

There are a number of Talmudic discussions on how far submission should be made to a prophet. Does an established prophet have the right to demand of people that they should heed his message even when it is in conflict with the laws of the Torah? The general principle laid down is that the words of the prophet should be heeded even if they contradict a plain law of the Torah provided the suspension of the law is only a temporary measure, as when *Elijah offered up sacrifices on Mount Carmel contrary to the law that sacrifices are only to be offered in Jerusalem.

But this kind of question was academic even in Rabbinic times since, in the Rabbinic view, *prophecy ceased after the last of the biblical prophets.

The question of how far individual submission to human beings, apart from a prophet, should go is complicated. The Mishnah (Ethics of the Fathers, 3. 12) advises: 'Be suppliant to a superior' or, at any rate, this is the usual translation of the Hebrew which means literally: 'Be light to a head.' Some of the standard commentators understand the 'head' to be the chief officer of a city, so that the advice is to be diplomatic when dealing with the Gentile authorities. But, in any event, this is no more than a piece of useful advice with little or no theological import. The broader question concerns submission to a superior *authority in Jewish learning. It is clear that the Talmudic Rabbis engaged frequently in debates with their fathers and teachers and did not feel inhibited in taking issue with them (see DECALOGUE on the fifth commandment). A famous Talmudic statement (*Kiddushin* 30b) has it that even father and son, master and disciple, become enemies of one another during their debates in learning, yet they do not stir from the debate until they come to love one another. Surrender of a student's opinions is not demanded. In the history of Jewish learning the right of an inferior scholar to defend his views even if they differ from those of a superior scholar is safeguarded. There is, of course, a whole area where the law has been decided in favour of one opinion, otherwise there would be no meaning to Halakhic decisions (see HALAKHAH). But even in this area a degree of freedom is given to the individual Rabbi to take part in the Halakhic process which, to some extent he can develop in accordance with the particular problems he is called upon to face. In *Hasidism, on the other hand, the Hasid is usually required to surrender his own, individual opinions in all matters in deference to the wisdom of the *Zaddik. A curious development, under the influence of Hasidism, in the twentieth century, is the notion of *Daat Torah*, 'The Opinion of the Torah'. On this view, the Gedolim ('Great Scholars'), the acknowledged religious authorities, have a kind of built-in sensitivity which enables them to state categorically the Torah attitude, even in politics and other extra-Halakhic topics. The difficulty with this attitude is that even if the very dubious proposition

be granted that the views of the Gedolim are the views of the Torah, which scholars qualify as Gedolim in this respect and what is to be done where the Gedolim differ among themselves? Respect for learning is a high Jewish value but there is no substitute for the individual Jew thinking matters out for himself. Submission to God is one thing, submission to another human being, no matter how eminent, is quite another.

Moshe Z. Sokol, *Rabbinic Authority and Personal Autonomy* (Northvale, NJ and London, 1992).

**Substitution** The idea that one thing can be substituted for another is found especially in connection with objects dedicated to the Temple. The rules of substitution or *pidyon* ('redemption') are in brief as follows. If, for example, a man dedicates his house to the Temple, it becomes sacred from that moment and no profane use may be made of it. But since the Temple has no need for the house but does need money for the repairs and general upkeep of the sacred building, the Temple treasurer can sell the house and its sanctity is then transferred to the money for which it is purchased. The man who dedicated the house can redeem it himself but when he does he is obliged to add a fifth to the value of the house, the whole becoming sacred (Leviticus 27: 14–15). Maimonides explains the addition of a fifth of the value where the redemption is done by the man himself on the grounds that he may undervalue the house, so the additional fifth makes up for any undervaluation. An animal dedicated as an offering to the Temple can only be redeemed if the animal develops a blemish that disqualifies it as an offering. If a man, having dedicated an animal as an offering, seeks to exchange it for another animal, declaring that this animal is the substitute (*temurah*) of the animal that has been dedicated, the rule is that both animals become sacred. 'One may not exchange or substitute another for it, either good for bad or bad for good; if one does substitute one animal for another, the thing vowed and its substitute shall both be holy' (Leviticus 27: 10). Tractate *Temurah* in the Mishnah is devoted largely to the details of this law.

These laws of substitution were applied homiletically in other areas of Jewish life and thought. The *Yigdal hymn on the thirteen *principles of faith uses the language of substitution for the doctrine of the immutability of the Torah, that God will never substitute another religion for Judaism: 'God will not exchange nor substitute His Law to everlasting for another.' *Nahmanides explains the *sacrifices themselves largely on the principle of substitution. The animal offered is seen as a substitute, especially for a sinner, who deserves to die for his sins but God in His mercy substitutes the animal to be in his stead. The ceremony of *Kapparot on the eve of Yom Kippur is based on this idea: the cockerel that is killed stands in the stead of the person wishing to find atonement. Many of the medieval authorities frowned on this practice as pagan and superstitious. Another superstitious practice (see MAGIC AND SUPERSTITION) is for the name of a sick person to be changed and the declaration made that if it has been decreed that X should die, the person whose name has been changed is no longer X but Y and for Y there has been no decree. In *Hasidism, the Hasid, when he visits his Rebbe, offers a sum of money to the master for the upkeep of his court and for general charitable purposes, and this is called a *pidyon nefesh*, 'redemption of the soul'. In all this it is the human being who offers the substitute which God, in His mercy, accepts. The only instance of God Himself engaging in substitution is in the Midrashic statements that God allowed His Temple to be destroyed rather than His people. God, it is said, poured out His wrath on the stones of the Temple rather than on the people who deserved to die for their sins. All this is far removed from the Christian doctrine of the Atonement in which Jesus is the substitute provided by God. Judaism, needless to say, rejects totally the Christian doctrine.

**Success** In Jewish life success, Hebrew *hatzlahah*, whether in material or in spiritual matters, is seen as a blessing; a popular Jewish wish is: 'May you have blessing and success in your undertaking.' In the *Hallel the verse is repeated by the Reader and the congregation: 'O Lord, deliver us! O Lord, let us prosper!' (Psalms 118: 25). Of Joseph it is said: 'The Lord was with Joseph, and he was a successful man' (Genesis 39: 2). And of David: 'David was successful in all his undertakings, for the Lord was with him' (1 Samuel 18: 14). In these verses success is made to depend on God. Similarly, Moses warns the people not to say:

'My own power and the might of my own hand have won this wealth for me' (Deuteronomy 8: 17). The normal Jewish attitude is neither to see failure as a sign of virtue nor success as somehow unworthy. Success is a good, provided it is not seen as self-made but as God-made, and is not attained through disregard for the interests of others.

**Succession** The order of priority of near relatives to inherit the estate of a deceased person. (For the right or lack of it to inherit an office or a position, see DYNASTIC SUCCESSION). The order of succession as stated in the Pentateuch (Numbers 27: 8–11) is: son, daughter, brothers, father's brothers, kinsman (i.e. next nearest relative on the father's side). There is no mention here of a father inheriting his son's estate but the Mishnah (*Bava Batra* 8: 2) fills in the gap by ruling that a father takes precedence over all his offspring' (i.e. that the order is: son, daughter, father, brothers, father's brothers). Even if a son is born out of wedlock and even if he is a *mamzer, he inherits the estate of his natural father, so that the concept of an illegitimate child in this connection is unknown in Jewish law. The Mishnah (*Ketubot*, 13: 3) rules: 'If a man dies, leaving sons and daughters, and his estate is large, the sons inherit it and the daughters are maintained by it; but if the estate is small, the daughters are maintained by it and the sons have to go begging.' The first-century judge, Admon, is quoted as asking, however: 'Because I am a male do I have to lose?' and Rabban *Gamaliel agreed with Admon that the sons as well as the daughters should be maintained from the estate. A husband inherits the estate of his wife. A wife does not inherit the estate of her husband but she is entitled, of course, to claim her *ketubah out of the estate. A wife's *ketubah* has to include a clause that any daughters she bears to her husband will be maintained out of his estate when he dies. If a son dies before his father and leaves children, whether sons or daughters, they take precedence in inheriting their grandfather's estate over their aunt, their grandfather's daughter. On this matter, we are told, there was a fierce debate between the *Sadducees and the *Pharisees, the Sadducees arguing: 'If my son's daughter, who represents my son, inherits me, should not my daughter who represents me inherit me?', meaning that both daughter and granddaughter should have an equal share in the estate. The Pharisees rejected this argument in favour of their view that inheritance proceeds always through the male line.

A first-born son inherits a double portion of his father's estate (Deuteronomy 21: 17). As understood by the Rabbis, a 'double portion' means not two-thirds of the whole estate but a portion double that received by his brothers.

These are the laws of succession as they are developed in the Talmudic sources. Communities have the right, however, to introduce special enactments of their own. For instance, there was a communal enactment in some places that a mother should inherit the estate of her son. In the State of Israel the traditional rules are the norm but with certain qualifications. In lands outside Israel the law of the particular state is binding. According to the Rabbis a man, while alive, can dispose of his property as a gift as he sees fit so that it is not against Jewish law for a man to make a will which does not follow the order of precedence as laid down in the Torah but if he does this he should not use the word 'inherit' but refer to a 'gift', because he gives whatever he does while he is alive (see WILLS).

Jacob Milgrom, 'The Inheritance Rights of Daughters', in Naturn M. Sarna (ed.), *The JPS Torah Commentary: Numbers* (Philadelphia and New York, 1990), 482–4.

**Suffering** The biblical authors and the Talmudic Rabbis, unlike the later Jewish philosophers, do not consider the general problem of evil in the universe, of why the benevolent Creator should have brought evil into being (see GOD). The earlier writers seem to have accepted the existence of evil as a 'given', seeing this, in so far as they gave any thought to it, as belonging, like questions on the true nature of God, to an area which it is beyond the capacity of the human mind to grasp. Their difficulty was not with the problem of evil *per se* but rather with the apparently random way in which sufferings are visited on creatures. In a Talmudic passage (*Berakhot* 7a) Moses is said to have asked God why one righteous man enjoys prosperity while another righteous man is afflicted with adversity; why one wicked man enjoys prosperity and another wicked man is afflicted with adversity. If all righteous men suffered and all wicked men were prosperous some kind of pattern might have emerged, perhaps on the lines that the righteous suffer

for their sins here on earth while the wicked are rewarded here on earth so as to be punished by being deprived of bliss in the Hereafter. This notion of divine reward and retribution as accounting for suffering is found frequently in the Talmudic literature but, in the passage quoted, it is implied, that such solutions fall short of the truth because of the sheer arbitrariness evident in the way afflictions and prosperity are apportioned. The book of *Job is directed explicitly to the rejection of the idea that suffering can be easily explained on the grounds of *reward and punishment. Job is a good man and yet he suffers greatly and he cannot accept the 'comforts' of his friends that his sufferings are the result of his sins. He cannot believe that any sins he may have committed are commensurate with the torment inflicted on him. Similarly, in Ethics of the Fathers (4. 15) Rabbi Yannai says: 'It is not in our power to explain either the well-being of the wicked or the sufferings of the righteous.' Some commentators read Rabbi Yannai as saying: 'We do not have either the well-being of the wicked or the sufferings of the righteous', that is, the idea that the righteous suffer and the wicked prosper is true but 'our' prosperity and afflictions do not belong to this scheme since 'we' belong neither to those who prosper because they are wicked nor those who suffer because they are righteous. In the twentieth century, the unparalleled horrors of the *Holocaust have presented Jewish theologians with the most acute and agonizing problem of suffering Jews have ever had to contemplate, one which it seems to be obscene to attempt to explain in terms of reward and punishment. In any event, it is generally recognized that any tidy solution to the problem of suffering is a bogus solution. All that can be done is to consider some of the ways in which the Jewish teachers tried to obtain brief glimpses of light in the darkness, while remaining fully aware that nothing like a complete answer to the problem is possible in this life.

That some of the Rabbis believed that the problem of suffering does not bear discussion at all can be seen from the Talmudic legend (*Menahot* 29b) in which God transports Moses through time to witness Rabbi *Akiba teaching the Torah. Moses asks God to show him what Akiba's fate will be and God shows him Akiba being tortured to death for teaching the Torah and his flesh sold by weight. Moses is moved to cry out: 'Sovereign of the universe, such Torah and such a reward!' to which God replies: 'Be silent, for such is My decree.'

Typical of the various, sometimes contradictory, views on the subject is the Talmudic passage (*Berakhot* 5b) in which the problem of suffering is discussed and in which ideas are dismissed without any definite conclusion being reached. In the passage the second-century teacher, Rabbi *Simeon ben Yohai, remarks that three precious gifts were given by God to Israel and they were only given through sufferings. The three precious gifts are: the Torah, the land of Israel, and the *World to Come. There is here a constant weaving of ideas around the question of suffering in terms of reward and punishment. Three narratives are recorded, in each of which a Rabbi who suffers is asked by a colleague whether his sufferings are dear to him. In each instance the Rabbi replies that he desires neither them nor their reward, whereupon the colleague miraculously restores him to good health by giving him his hand to raise him from the bed of sickness. Another narrative concerns the third-century teacher, Rav Huna, who has 400 flasks of wine which have turned sour, involving him in severe financial loss. When the scholars visit Rav Huna, they urge him to look into his deeds, that is, they hint that he has been guilty of some dishonesty in connection with an employee of his engaged in the manufacture of wine. Rav Huna eventually admits that he has been guilty in the matter and no sooner does he agree to compensate his employee than the sour wine becomes sweet again. All this is in no way a theological exposition of the problem of suffering. There is obviously a legendary element in all these narratives and there is even a touch of humour. In another version of the same story the Talmud says that Rav Huna's wine did not miraculously revert to its former sweet state; the miracle was that while the wine remained sour, the price of vinegar shot up so that it was equal to the price of the wine!

In this passage the striking idea is introduced that there can be 'sufferings of love'. This section reads:

'If a man sees that sufferings have come upon him, let him scrutinize his deeds, as it is said: "Let us search and try our ways, and return unto the Lord" [Lamentations 3: 40]. If he did scrutinize his deeds without finding [any sin for which he would deserve to suffer] let

him attribute it [the suffering] to the sin of neglect of the Torah [i.e. there may be no sin of commission for which he deserves to be punished, but there may be, nevertheless, this serious sin of ommission], as it is said: "Happy is the man whom Thou chastenest, and teachest out of Thy Torah" [Psalms 94: 12; i.e. God chastises a man so that he should return to the study of the Torah]. If he did attribute his sufferings to his neglect of the Torah without finding [that he has been indolent in study of the Torah], it then becomes known that they are sufferings of love, as it is said: "For whom the Lord loveth He correcteth" [Proverbs 3: 12].'

Thus 'sufferings of love' are neither for sins of commission nor of omission, but are due solely to God's love and are not penal. The passage contains a further discussion as to how to know when sufferings are penal and when they are 'sufferings of love'.

*Rashi, obviously puzzled by the whole concept of 'sufferings of love', comments: 'The Holy One, blessed be He, chastises him in this world, though he is guiltless of any sin, for the purpose of increasing his reward in the World to Come to a degree greater than his merits would otherwise have deserved.' Maimonides, in his *Guide of the Perplexed* (3. 17), refers to this Talmudic passage in which the Rabbis speak of 'sufferings of love' and remarks that according to this opinion sometimes misfortunes befall an individual not because of his having sinned before, but in order for his reward to be the greater. Maimonides considers this to be a minority opinion, one which, in his view, is hard to reconcile with God's justice. Maimonides contrasts this with the other Rabbinic sayings: 'There is no death without sin, and no sufferings without transgression' (*Shabbat* 55a) and: 'A man is measured with the measure he himself uses' (Mishnah *Sotah* 1: 7). This latter saying, continues Maimonides, occurring as it does in the Mishnah, enjoys special authority.

Throughout the literature of Jewish piety, the idea is found of accepting suffering in love and faith in God. The Mekhilta (see MIDEASH) to the verse: 'Ye shall not make with Me gods of silver and gods of gold' (Exodus 20: 23) comments: 'Do not behave towards Me as heathens behave to their gods. When happiness come to them, they sing praises to their gods, but when retribution comes upon them they curse their gods. If I bring happiness upon you give thanks, and when I bring sufferings give thanks also.' On the same lines the Mishnah (*Berakhot* 9: 5) states: 'A man is duty-bound to utter a benediction for the bad even as he utters one for the good.' The benediction on receiving good tidings is: 'Blessed is He, the good and the doer of good.' On receiving bad tidings the benediction is: 'Blessed is He, the true judge.' The Talmud (*Berakhot* 60b) observes that the benediction over the bad should be recited with the same joyfulness as that over the good. A Hasidic tale tells it all. A man came to the great master, *Dov Baer of Mezhirech and asked him to explain how a man can possibly recite the benediction over the bad with the same joyfulness as he recites the benediction over the good. The master replied that he, too, did not know the answer to this question but the man should go to the saintly Reb Sussya, a man stricken with poverty, ill health and other severe sufferings. When the man asked the question of Reb Sussya, the saint replied: 'It is a good question but I cannot answer it since I have never experienced a day's suffering all my life'!

Abraham Cohen, 'Reward and Punishment', in his *Everyman's Talmud* (London, 1949), 110–20.
C. G. Montefiore and H. Loewe, 'On Sufferings', in their *A Rabbinic Anthology* (London, 1938), 541–55.
Solomon Schechter, 'The Doctrine of Divine Retribution in Rabbinical Literature', in his *Studies in Judaism* (first series; Philadelphia, 1945), 213–32.

**Suffering Servant** The servant of the Lord referred to in the second part of the book of *Isaiah (Deutero-Isaiah), especially in chapter 53 but also in chapters 42: 1–4; 49: 1–6; 52: 13–15. In Christian theology the 'suffering servant' used to be identified with Jesus but modern Christian scholarship no longer reads the prophetic books as foretelling events of the remote future. The Jewish commentators understand the 'servant' to be the God-fearing Jews who were in exile, the people of Israel in general, and so forth, although, occasionally, the passages are read as referring to the *Messiah. It is interesting that, while the Haftarot (see HAFTARAH) for the seven weeks of consolation between the Ninth of *Av and *Rosh Ha-Shanah are all taken from Deutero-Isaiah, they do not include any of the 'servant' passages, probably in conscious reaction to the Christo-logical interpretation. It can safely be said that the whole concept of the 'suffering servant' and, indeed, the detachment of the passages from the rest of the book, is a Christian invention of no relevance to Jewish theology and is only discussed by Jewish theologians in response to the Christian claim.

C. G. Montefiore and H. Loewe, *A Rabbinic Theology* (London, 1938); see index: 'Suffering Servant'.

**Sufism** The Islamic ascetic and mystical movement which, it has been conjectured, was partly influenced by the Jewish Midrashic literature but which certainly, in turn, exercised considerable influence on Jewish mystical and ethical literature. (The term Sufi is usually said to be derived from the Arabic word *suf*, 'wool', because the adherents of this school wore simple woollen garments in order to avoid ostentation.) There is enough evidence from the Cairo *genizah to show that a pietistic movement arose among Egyptian Jews, the members of which called themselves Hasidim (see HASIDISM), not to be confused with the Hasidim belonging to the *Saints of Germany, and these were indebted to Sufism. Abraham Maimonides, son of the famous philosopher, was an ardent follower of this pietistic movement. Abraham's son, Obadiah Maimonides (1228–65) in his *Treatise of the Pool*, only recently published from manuscript, provides guidance, in the Sufi spirit, to the wayfarer along the Path to God. But the most marked influence of Sufism on Jewish thought is found in *Bahya, Ibn Pakudah's *Duties of the Heart*, where the very title and the ideas behind it belong to Sufism. Bahya gives examples of Hasidim who are not Jews and are probably Sufi saints. The arrangement of the material in the form of Ten Gates in Bahya's work also owes much to Sufi treatises. Some of the titles of these 'Gates' to piety are the titles used in Sufic works. In Gate Nine, on the theme of abstinence, Bahya quotes sayings of the Sufis whom he calls Perushim ('Seperatists' or 'Abstainers') in the sense of ascetics, although he takes issue with the extreme *asceticism followed by the Sufis.

Through Bahya and the Kabbalist Isaac of Acre, Sufi ideas found their way into Jewish mystical literature. It is always difficult to trace influences on religious thought with exactitude. Nevertheless, it would seem that the ideal of *disinterestedness or equanimity, which first appears, among Jewish thinkers, in Bahya, has its origin in Sufism, which itself was influenced by Stoicism. The Hasidic doctrine of *annihilation of selfhood also seems to have had its origin in Sufi thought, whence it came through various channels to the latter-day Hasidim. And there are echoes of Sufi thought in the Hasidic idea, developed especially in *Habad, that from God's point of view there is no world at all, only God enjoying true existence. The attacks of the *Mitnaggedim on this doctrine, on the grounds that it tends to obliterate the distinctions between good and evil, are virtually the same as the attacks of Islamic Orthodoxy on the Sufis.

Paul Fenton, *The Treatise of the Pool by 'Obadyah Maimonides* (London, 1981).

**Suicide** In Jewish teaching the prohibition of suicide is not contained in the sixth commandment: 'Thou shalt not kill' (Exodus 20: 13 and Deuteronomy 5: 17). Obviously it does not follow from the fact that a man may not take the life of another that he may not take his own life. There is, in fact, no direct prohibition of suicide in the Bible. In the Talmud (*Bava Kama* 91b), however, the prohibition is arrived at by a process of exegesis on the verse: 'and surely your blood of your lives will I require' (Genesis 9: 5), interpreted as: 'I will require your blood if you yourselves shed it.' It is possible that there is no direct prohibition because very few people of sound mind would be inclined to commit suicide in any event.

It follows from this that suicide and murder are two separate offences in the Jewish tradition, as they are in most cultures. Suicide is not homicide and is not covered in the *Decalogue. In the usual Rabbinic classification of duties, homicide would be considered an offence both 'between man and God' and 'between man and man', whereas suicide would fall only under the former heading. Maimonides' statement (*Rotzeah*, 2. 2–3) that there is no 'death at the hand of the court' for the crime of suicide, only 'death by the hands of Heaven', is puzzling, since how could a suicide, no longer alive, be punished for the crime by the court? In all probability Maimonides formulates it in this way to distinguish between the two crimes of murder and suicide. Maimonides' statement that a suicide is punished by the 'hands of Heaven' no doubt refers to punishment in the Hereafter but the popular saying that a suicide has no share in the *World to Come, which

would cause a far more severe punishment to be visited on the suicide than on one guilty of murder, has no support in any of the classical sources. It has plausibly been suggested that the saying, though bogus, tended to be quoted as a warning to would-be suicides in stressful periods when there was a spate of suicides in the Jewish community.

*Attitudes to Suicide*

Suicide is considered to be a grave sin both because it is a denial that human life is a divine gift and because it constitutes a total defiance of God's will for the individual to live the life-span allotted to him. The suicide, more than any other offender, literally takes his life into his own hands. As it is put in Ethics of the Fathers (4. 21): 'Despite yourself you were fashioned, and despite yourself you were born, and despite yourself you live, and despite yourself you die, and despite yourself you will hereafter have account and reckoning before the King of kings, the Holy One, blessed be He.' Yet there are exceptional circumstances when a man is permitted to take his own life or allow it to be taken, of which martyrdom is the supreme example. The general tendency among the later authorities is to extend the idea of mitigating circumstances so that the law, recorded in the *Shulhan Arukh (*Yoreh Deah*, 345), that there are to be no rites of mourning over a suicide is usually set aside wherever it can reasonably be assessed that the act was committed while the suicide was 'of unsound mind'. Saul's suicide (1 Samuel 31: 4–5) is defended on the grounds that he feared torture if he were captured by the Philistines and would have died in any event as a result of the torture. Similarly, Samson's suicide (Judges 16: 30), in which he destroyed himself together with his Philistine tormentors, is defended on the grounds that it constituted an act of *Kiddush Ha–Shem, 'sanctification of the divine name', in the face of heathen mockery of the God of Israel. *Josephus (*Jewish War* 7. 8–9) tells how the garrison of Masada committed mass suicide. While this, too, is usually hailed as an example of martyrdom, some Halakhah authorities have questioned whether the act of these heroes was justified in the light of the later Halakhah, since the Romans may have spared their lives, albeit as slaves to the conquerors. Even the mass suicides of Jews in the Middle Ages in order to avoid forcible baptism was not defended by all the authorities, some of whom argued that while martyrdom was demanded it was wrong for the Jews themselves to take their own lives. From all this it can be seen that no hard and fast rules were given and ultimately the judgement of a suicide should be left to God.

The late Hasidic master, Mordecai Joseph of Izbica (d. 1854) in his commentary to the Torah, has an unusual discussion relevant to the theme of suicide. This author appears to have been the first to ask, from the theological point of view, whether a man, struggling for the truth against seemingly overwhelming odds, may give in mentally and entreat God to release him from the struggle by allowing him to die. For such a man actually to commit suicide is unthinkable, but is it impious for him to pray to God that he should die? The two biblical examples of this kind of prayer are the plea of *Jonah ( Jonah 4: 4) and the prayer of *Elijah (1 Kings 19: 4). Both prophets uttered their plea for death when their mission seemed to have failed. This Hasidic master reads the narratives of Jonah and Elijah as expressing disapproval of this kind of prayer. The good man, says Mordecai Joseph, should not take his distress at the wrongdoings of his contemporaries so much to heart as to wish that he were no longer alive to witness their sinful deeds.

Sidney Goldstein, *Suicide in Rabbinic Literature* (Hoboken, NJ, 1989).

**Sukkah** The booth in which Jews are commanded to dwell during the festival of *Tabernacles, as stated in the book of Leviticus (23: 42–5): 'You shall live in booths [*sukkot*] seven days; all citizens in Israel shall live in booths, in order that future generations may know that I made the Israelite people live in booths when I brought them out of the land of Egypt, I am the Lord your God.' According to the Talmudic Rabbis, a sukkah has to have at least three walls (though the third need not be a complete wall) and a covering. It has to be at least 4 square cubits in size, but this does not necessarily mean that it has to have a square or oblong shape A circular sukkah, for instance, is valid provided it covers an area of at least 4 square cubits (a cubit is approximately 18 inches). The covering must be of things that grow from the soil (e.g. straw or leaves of trees) but it must be detached from the soil, so that it is not valid to use the leaves of a tree still growing from the soil as a sukkah covering. The covering has to

have more shade than light, that is, there must be more covered than uncovered space. The covering can be quite thick, although it is customary to make the covering sufficiently sparse for the stars to be seen through it. The sukkah has to be outdoors. A sukkah under a roof is not a valid sukkah, nor is it valid to have a sukkah underneath, say, the overhang of a balcony.

All full meals should be eaten in the sukkah, that is, meals at which bread is partaken of, although some pious Jews do not eat or drink anything outside the sukkah. In Talmudic times people slept in the sukkah, treating it as their abode for the duration of the festival. In Western lands the majority of Jews do not sleep in the sukkah (some of the more pious still do, however). The rationale for this is that where to stay in the sukkah is uncomfortable, the obligation is set aside and in colder climes it is certainly uncomfortable in autumn to sleep outside in the sukkah. For the same reason there is no obligation to eat in the sukkah when it is raining and the rain comes through the covering. According to the authorities, it is undesirable for a man to stay in the sukkah even when the rain comes in, on the grounds that to persist in carrying out a religious precept when the law does not demand it suggests an attitude of religious superiority, of trying to be more pious than the Torah demands. Nevertheless, it is the custom of the majority of Hasidim (see HASIDISM) to stay in the sukkah even when it is raining. The Hasidic rationale is that the reason there is no obligation to stay in the sukkah when it rains is because of discomfort and a true Hasid will never find discomfort in staying in the sukkah, no matter how severe the weather. Nowadays, many sukkahs are built with a roof on pulleys so that, after the meal, the roof can be lowered so as to prevent rain coming into the sukkah during the times it is not used. When the time comes to use the sukkah the roof is raised and the sukkah is once again open to the sky. The raising and lowering of the roof does not constitute forbidden 'work' and can, therefore, be done on the Sabbath and the festival days. Synagogues often have an adjacent sukkah to which the congregation repairs for *Kiddush after the service. In some Reform congregations the Sukkah is erected in the synagogue itself but, according to the Orthodox law, such a sukkah is invalid since it is covered by the roof of the synagogue.

On the principle of adorning the precepts (i.e. carrying out the precepts of the Torah in as beautiful and elegant a manner as possible), it is the practice to decorate the sukkah and to hang fruit and fragrant plants from the covering. These must be left in place until the festival has come to an end.

*Interpretations of the Sukkah*

Modern biblical scholarship sees Tabernacles originally as a harvest festival, the booths being erected as temporary dwellings for the farmers at harvest times. Following the general tendency to connect the ancient seasonal festivals with events in the history of Israel, the reason for the sukkah as stated in Leviticus is to remind Jews of the booths in which the children of Israel dwelt during their journey through the wilderness. The usual understanding of these 'booths' is that they are the tents in which the Israelites dwelt. Rabbi *Akiba, however, translates the word *sukkot*, not as 'booths'; but as 'coverings', the reference being, according to him, to the 'clouds of glory' which accompanied the Israelites in order to provide them with divine protection from all hostile forces. The sukkah is called a 'temporal dwelling' as distinct from the 'permanent dwelling' in which people normally live. On the basis of this the idea has been read into the sukkah of a symbolic surrender of too close an attachment to material things. The Jew leaves his house to stay in the sukkah where he enjoys divine protection. Judaism does not frown on material possessions, if these are honestly acquired, but, by leaving his home to stay in the sukkah, the Jew declares that it is the spiritual side of human existence that brings true joy into life. Tabernacles is the festival of religious joy. In the Kabbalah to dwell in the sukkah is to be under the 'shadow of faith'. A Hasidic master has said that the sukkah is unique in that while the other precepts are carried out by only one part of the body, in the sukkah the whole body enters into the precept, so to speak.

> Hyman E. Goldin, 'The Sukkah (Tabernacle)' and 'Dwelling in the Sukkah', in his *Code of Jewish Law* (New York, 1961), iii. 93–101.
> Isaac Klein, 'The Building of a Sukkah', in his *A Guide to Jewish Religious Practice* (New York, 1979), 160–2.

**Sun** The sun and the *moon are compared with one another in Jewish symbolism. The nations of the world, say the Rabbis, have a solar *calendar but Israel has a lunar calendar because the fortunes of Israel, unlike those of other nations, wax and wane like the moon. The face of Moses is said to have been like that of the sun with its own light while the face of Joshua, Moses' disciple, was like the face of the moon, enjoying only reflected light. In the Kabblistic doctrine of the *Sefirot, the sun represents the male principle, *Tiferet*, while the moon represents the female principle, *Malkhut* or the *Shekhinah. In opposition to the sun-worshippers the Bible throughout speaks of the sun itself as worshipping its Creator, bowing to Him as its moves joyfully from east to west, in the words of the Psalmist, like a groom coming forth from his chamber (Psalms 19: 6). Once every twenty-eight years, Orthodox Jews recite a special benediction praising God for the order of the universe of which the sun in its course is a supreme example.

**Sun, Moon, and Stars** The worship of the heavenly bodies, so prevalent in ancient religions, is severely condemned throughout the Bible, which demonstrates incidentally that the Israelites, too, were prone to idolatrous worship. In the creation narrative at the beginning of the book of Genesis, God creates 'the two great lights, the greater light to dominate the day and the lesser light to dominate the night, and the stars' (Genesis 1: 16). The Deuteronomist declares: 'And when you look up to the sky and behold the sun and the moon and the stars, the whole heavenly host, you must not be lured into bowing down to them or serving them' (Deuteronomy 4: 19). The Mishnah (*Avodah Zarah* 4: 7) records that the Jewish elders on a visit to Rome were asked why God, if he had no pleasure in idols, did not make an end of them? The elders replied that, for the sake of fools, God does not wish to destroy the sun, moon and stars of which the world has benefit. The Romans said: 'If so, let Him destroy that which the world does not need and leave that which the world needs.' The elders replied: 'We should but confirm them that worship them, for they would say: Know that these are gods, for they have not been brought to an end.'

Maimonides has the science of his day, according to which the sun, moon, and stars are fixed to transparent spheres which sing to their Creator as they revolve around the earth:

'All the stars and spheres are intelligent

beings, endowed with life and permanence and they recognise the One who said and the world came into being. And all of them, each in accordance with its stage, praise and glorify their Creator like the angels. And just as they recognise the Holy One, blessed be He, so do they recognise themselves and recognise the angels that are superior to them. The degree of knowledge possessed by the stars and the spheres is less than that of the angels but greater than that of human beings.' (*Yesodey Ha-Torah*, 3. 10).

This is the ancient notion of the music of the spheres as expressed in Shakespeare's *The Merchant of Venice*: 'There's not the smallest orb which thou behold'st | But in his motion like an angel sings | Still quiring to the young-eyed cherubins.'

**Supernatural** The ancients had no word for the supernatural any more than they had for *nature. All events proceeded from God; some of these events were so contrary to the perceived order of things that they were seen as *miracles. In modern Jewish thought, however, the distinction is often made between the natural order as perceived by the senses and the supernatural invasion of that order by spiritual forces (see KAPLAN, SPINOZA, and SPIRITUALISM).

**Supplication** The offering of petitionary prayers in the mood of entreaty. The attitude to supplication is summarized in a saying attributed to the second-century teacher, Rabbi *Simeon ben Yohai, in Ethics of the Fathers (2. 13): 'When you pray do not make your *prayer a fixed form but supplications before God.' Similarly, the earlier teacher, Rabbi Eliezer, is recorded in the Mishnah (*Berakhot* 4: 4) as saying: 'He who makes his prayer a fixed task, his prayer is no supplication.' In the Jewish literature of prayer there is a constant demand that prayer should be expressed from the heart and not as a mere fixed duty. The majority of the prayers of supplication in the traditional Prayer Book are in the plural: 'Grant us', 'Help us', and so forth. This form of request was evidently considered to be less self-serving than prayers for the individual solely on his own behalf. There is, of course, no objection to an individual offering up his own private supplications and the special prayer for protection against suffering known as Tahanun ('Supplication') consists entirely of individual

supplications taken from the book of Psalms. In the Psalms it is often difficult to know whether the first person is used of the Psalmist or of the people as a whole conceived of as an individual person. A distinction is drawn in the Mishnah (*Berakhot* 2: 4) between the recital of the *Shema and prayer. Workmen at the top of a tree or scaffolding may recite the Shema where they are but for their prayers they must descend. The Shema involves a bare recital, whereas prayer requires a supplicatory mood impossible to sustain while precariously balanced high up in the air. Some Jewish teachers say that in prayers of supplication a man should see himself as a beggar asking humbly for his needs out of the bitterness of his heart.

**Sura and Pumbedita** The two great seats of learning in Babylonia which enjoyed, with few interruptions, a continuous existence from the third to the tenth century CE. In the period of the *Geonim the colleges of Sura and Pumbedita each had its own head, the Gaon of Sura enjoying a greater degree of authority than the Gaon of Pumbedita, which is why Sura is usually mentioned first in the literature. *Saadiah was Gaon of Sura, *Sherira and his son *Hai were Geonim in Pumbedita. Sura and Pumbedita were the prototypes of *Yeshivah learning throughout the ages.

**Surrogate Mother** The following question has recently been discussed in Jewish legal literature: where a naturally fertilized ovum has been removed from the womb of a pregnant woman and reimplanted in the uterus of another woman, which of the two is considered to be the 'mother' in Jewish law? To date the problem has not been solved; some authorities hold that the donor is the true mother, others that the woman who actually gives birth to the child is the true mother, and others again that the child will have two 'mothers'. There has also been a discussion on whether the practice would be approved of according to the Jewish tradition. The whole problem is too recent to allow any kind of consensus to emerge but for a helpful summary of the issues involved, see 'Host-Mothers' in J. David Bleich, *Judaism and Healing* (New York, 1981), 92–5.

**Suspicion** The general attitude in the Jewish ethical sources is that people should be encouraged to give those whose conduct is not above suspicion the benefit of the doubt. The earliest saying in this connection in the Rabbinic literature is: 'Judge every man in the scale of merit' (Ethics of the Fathers, 1. 7). A hyperbolic statement in the Talmud (*Shabbat* 97a) has it that whoever entertains a suspicion about a worthy man will be bodily afflicted, as was Moses when he suspected that the children of Israel would not believe him (Exodus 4: 1–6). In another Talmudic saying (*Shabbat* 127b), whoever judges others in the scale of merit will himself be so judged. When Eli, who had imagined Hannah to be drunk, discovered his error, he apologized and blessed her (1 Samuel 1: 12–17), from which the Rabbis conclude (*Berakhot* 31b) that such is the proper form when a person has been unjustly suspected of wrongdoing. Those guilty of the suspicion should apologize and offer a blessing.

All this was not taken to mean, however, that a man should be gullible, allowing himself to become the victim of every confidence-trickster because of his refusal to suspect anyone of wishing to take advantage of him. The post-Talmudic treatise *Derekh Eretz* (ch. 5) gives the realistic advice: 'Let people be in your eyes as robbers but respect them as if they were Rabban *Gamaliel.*' Or, as the pungent popular proverb has it: 'Respect him but suspect him.'

A further teaching on suspicion is that a man should not behave in such a manner as to awake suspicion, even if he knows that he is doing nothing wrong. Charity collectors, for example, in Talmudic times, always went about soliciting donations in pairs. A single collector might be suspected of pocketing for himself some of the money he receives. The principle here is that of *marit ayyin* (lit. 'appearance of the eyes') meaning that an act innocent in itself should not be carried out in circumstances where other people may think that a wrong is being committed. For instance, the Talmud (*Berakhot* 3a) states that a man should not enter a ruined building on his own since people might imagine that he has an assignation there with a harlot. Similarly, if a man knows that someone has stolen a valuable object belonging to him he should summon the thief to court but should not take the law into his own hands by entering the thief's house to recover his property, since this might lead people who witness it to think that he is a thief (*Bava Kama* 27b).

For all the many references to the sin of suspecting the innocent and of allowing oneself to be suspected, it is obvious that hard and fast rules cannot be laid down and, ultimately, individual discretion and conscience must be the guiding principles.

**Swastika** The cross consisting of four L shapes placed at right angles to one another and used as a magic symbol in many ancient civilizations. Archaeological discoveries of swastikas on ancient synagogues show that these were used by Jews, too, albeit only as decorations. The swastika had as little significance in Judaism as any other form of decoration. It was neither favoured nor denigrated and there was no mention of the swastika in Jewish literature until the Nazis adopted it as their emblem, when it became the most abhorrent symbol for Jews as well as for many others as a reminder of the *Holocaust and the other atrocities of Nazism. Jews today recoil with horror from any use of the swastika. To the consternation of decent people everywhere, vandals have been known to daub swastikas on Jewish tombstones.

**Swaying** The movement of the body during prayer and the study of the Torah, still practised by many Jews (see GESTURES). The earliest references to swaying in Jewish literature are in connection with the study of the Torah. Judah *Halevi, in his *Kuzari* (ii. 79–80), gives a rational explanation for the custom of swaying to and fro when studying the Torah. It often happened that ten or more people read from a single volume so that each was obliged to bend down in turn to read a passage and then turn back again. Thus swaying became a habit through constant seeing, observing, and imitating, which is human nature. The Zohar (iii. 218b–219a) gives a mystical reason for why Jews sway when they study the Torah. The souls of Israel, says the Zohar, have been hewn from the Holy Lamp, as it is written: 'The spirit of man is the lamp of the Lord' (Proverbs 20: 27). 'Now once this lamp has been kindled from the supernal Torah, the light upon it never ceases for an instant, like the flame of a wick which is never still for an instant. So when an Israelite has uttered a single word of the Torah, a light is kindled and he cannot keep still but sways to and fro like the flame of a wick.' Evidently, some time during the late Middle Ages, the custom arose of swaying during prayer as well as during study.

*Isserles, in his gloss to the *Shulḥan Arukh*

(*Oraḥ Ḥayyim*, 48: 1), quotes earlier authorities who advocate swaying during prayer on the basis of the verse: 'All my bones shall say, Lord who is like unto Thee?' (Psalms 35: 10), the verse being taken literally to mean that all the bones should be involved in prayer by a swaying motion of the body. On the other hand the Kabbalist Isaiah *Horowitz remarks in his famous compendium of the Jewish religion:

'One who sways during his prayers causes his powers of concentration to be destroyed while to stand perfectly still without any movement at all assists concentration. As for the verse: "All my bones shall say", this applies to the recitation of the songs of praise, to the benedictions of the *Shema, and to the study of the Torah, but not to prayer. If any authority has declared that it applies to prayer as well it seems to me that his view should be ignored since experience proves that to stand perfectly still during prayer is an aid to concentration. Just see for yourself! Would a man dare to offer *supplication to a king of flesh and blood when his body moves as the trees of the forest in the wind?'

In his note to the passage in the *Shulḥan Arukh*, Abraham Gumbiner, a standard commentator to the work, after quoting authorities who favour swaying during prayer and others who denigrate it, concludes: 'It is correct to prefer either of these opinions provided that it assists concentration' (see KAVVANAH).

In *Hasidism swaying in prayer is generally the norm, some Hasidim making violent side movements of the head as well as moving the body to and fro. In a book published in Altona as early as 1768, only eight years after the death of the *Baal Shem Tov, founder of the Hasidic movement, Rabbi Jacob *Emden could write about 'a new sect of foolish Hasidim which has arisen in Volhynia and Podolia', who 'clap their hands and shake sideways with their head turned backwards and their face and eyes turned upwards'. To the scandal of the *Mitnaggedim and the Maskilim, the followers of the *Haskalah, in an early Hasidic text the need to sway in prayer is described in grossly erotic terms:

'Prayer is copulation with the *Shekhinah. Just as there is swaying when copulation begins, so, too, a man must sway at first and then he can remain immobile and attached to the Shekhinah with great attachment. As a result of his swaying man is able to attain a powerful stage of arousal. For he will ask himself: Why do I sway my body? Presumably it is

because the Shekhinah stands over against me. And as a result he will attain to a stage of great enthusiasm.'

This kind of erotic imagery soon fell into disuse among the Hasidim, whatever its original mystical meaning. Obviously in reaction to the Hasidic practice, Hayyim of *Volozhyn, disciple of *Elijah, Gaon of Vilna, a strong opponent of Hasidism, laconically observed that swaying in prayer has one purpose only, to keep the worshipper alert. Consciously to sway has little point, this author remarks, but if the swaying comes automatically out of powerful longing and purity of heart, it is praiseworthy. The Hasidim themselves decried swaying in prayer with the aim of making an impression of extraordinary piety or as a mere conditional reflex. A Hasidic saying in this connection gives an interesting turn to the verse: 'And when the people saw, they swayed, and stood afar off' (Exodus 20: 15). 'If a man sways in prayer in order that people might see him [and admire him for his piety] it is a sign that he is afar off, remote from God.' A variant of this is: 'A man can pray and sway in his prayers and still be afar off, remote from God.'

The writer Jiri Langer, a friend of Kafka who became a Belzer Hasid, describes vividly his first encounter with prayer at the court of *Belz on a Friday evening in the second decade of the twentieth century. The old Rabbi of Belz had advanced to the reading-desk in order to lead the Hasidim in the recital of the Psalms to welcome the Sabbath.

'It is as though an electric spark has suddenly entered those present. The crowd which till now has been completely quiet, almost cowed, suddenly bursts forth in a wild shout. None stays in his place. The tall dark figures run hither and thither round the synagogue, flashing past the lights of the Sabbath candles. Gesticulating wildly, and throwing their whole bodies about, they shout out the words of the Psalms. They knock into each other unconcernedly, for all their cares have been set aside, everything has ceased to exist for them. They are seized by an indescribable ecstasy . . . The old man throws himself about as though seized by convulsions. Each shudder of his powerful body, each contraction of his muscles is permeated with the glory of the Most High. Every so often he claps the palms of his hands together symbolically.'

This kind of swaying and violent movement can still be observed in many a Hasidic conventicle, though there are also tales of Hasidic masters who remained completely immobile during their prayers, in awe of the Creator.

Reform Judaism generally frowns on swaying in prayer as falling short of Western standards of decorum and this attitude is often shared by the Orthodox in Western lands. But at least a gentle swaying is often the norm among many non-Hasidic Jews when praying or when studying the Torah.

Louis Jacobs, *Hasidic Prayer* (New York, 1972), 54–67.

Jiri Langer, *Nine Gates* (London, 1961), 6–8.

**Swedenborg, Emanuel** Swedish author, scientist, and mystic (1688–1772). Some of Swedenborg's ideas have certain affinities with Jewish *mysticism. There is some evidence that Swedenborg was influenced by the Zohar but none, however, of any influence of Swedenborg on later Jewish mystical ideas. The most striking resemblance is between Swedenborg's idea that God alone enjoys ultimate existence and Hasidic *panentheism (and see HABAD). The anti-Hasidic author Joseph Perl (1773–1839), in his *Uiber Das Wesen Der Sekte Chassidim* (ed. A. Rubinstein (Jerusalem, 1977), 81) does refer to *Hasidism as bearing strong resemblances to Swedenborg's thought, but only with reference to Swedenborg's visionary notions about the three heavens and the world of the spirits; he says nothing about Swedenborg's theosophical opinions and their resemblance to Hasidic thought.

Moshe Idel, *Kabbalah: New Perspectives* (New Haven and London, 1988); see index: 'Swedenborg, Emanuel'.

**Swimming** Among the duties of a father to his children listed in the Talmud (*Kiddushin* 29a) is teaching them how to swim, because their lives may depend on it. The verse: 'neither shalt thou stand idly by the blood of thy neighbour' (Leviticus 19: 16) is interpreted by the Rabbis to mean that if a man is in danger of drowning, a man who can swim is obliged to save him. An example of a 'foolish pietist' is given as a man who can swim but refuses to save a woman in danger of drowning because he does not wish to touch a female. Swimming was adopted as a metaphor for immersion in the 'sea of the Talmud' and skilful Talmudists were given the title of 'great swimmers'. Of the scholar who adduces a proof that leads nowhere it was said (*Bava Kama* 91a) that he has dived into deep waters only to bring up an oyster shell without the pearl. The Talmud (*Rosh Ha-Shanah* 23a) incidentally has a vivid description of divers bringing up coral in the Persian Gulf. Swimming in the river was a favourite pastime among *Yeshivah students in Eastern Europe.

**Sword** Although *warfare is not banned entirely in the Bible, hatred is often expressed of the sword as the symbol of warfare (see PEACE). That 'no sword shall cross your land' is stated as a supreme blessing (Leviticus 26: 6), just as the unsheathing of the sword is the worst of curses (Leviticus 26: 33). Esau, later identified with *Rome, was 'blessed' that he would live by the sword (Genesis 27: 40). However, there are plenty of examples in the Bible in which killing by the sword is justified. Psalm 149 speaks of the battling saints who sing the high praises of the Lord while holding a two-edged sword in their hands. Execution by the sword for certain offences, was, according to the Mishnah (*Sanhedrin* 7: 1–3), one of the four methods of execution meted out by the *Sanhedrin, although this statement is purely theoretical as, in the time of the Mishnah, there was no *capital punishment. From Rabbinic times onwards Jews thought of the sword as, at the most, a necessary evil. In the older illustrated editions of the Passover *Haggadah the wicked son is depicted holding a sword in his hand. In an oft-quoted Midrash, the sword and the book came down from heaven bound together, God declaring: 'You can choose which to have but you cannot have both.' All weapons of destruction came to be designated as the 'sword'. In a very revealing passage in the Mishnah (*Shabbat* 6: 4) it is said that Rabbi Eliezer permitted a man to go out on the Sabbath wearing a sword, since this could be seen not as carrying in the public domain (forbidden on the Sabbath) but as simply having an item of dress, an adornment. But the sages retorted that a sword can never be considered to be anything but a reproach and they quoted the verse: 'And they shall beat their swords into plowshares' (Isaiah 2: 4).

**Symbolism** The use of concrete things to denote abstract ideas. Judaism does not tolerate the making of plastic images of God (see GOLDEN CALF, IDOLATRY, and IMAGE OF GOD). The idea behind the prohibition of image-making appears to be that while an image of God is bound to be present in the mind, otherwise it would be impossible to think about God, to give this any kind of permanence in a concrete and lasting image is to attempt to perceive as the reality that which is beyond all human perception. Symbolism for the divine is either purely verbal, calling attention to natural phenomena, as when the prophet *Ezekiel uses the *rainbow in his vision of the *Chariot: 'Like the appearance of the bow which shines in the clouds on a day of rain, such was the appearance of the surrounding radiance' (Ezekiel 1: 28). It is noteworthy that in the whole of this account the prophet speaks of 'what looked like', as if to distance the symbol from the Reality.

In the Bible generally, terms such as height, light, and spirit (the Hebrew *ruah* can also mean 'wind') are used in symbolic representation of the divine and the divine influence. The biblical prophets use the marriage relationship as a symbol of the relationship between God and Israel (Jeremiah 2: 2; Hosea 3: 21–2). In Rabbinic literature the whole book of *Song of Songs is read as symbolizing the relationship between God and His people, as the 'lover' of the song woos his 'beloved'. The prophetic visions are full of symbols. Isaiah compares sin to crimson which can, in repentance, turn to the colour of white fleece (Isaiah 1: 18) and sees God as a king on a high and lofty throne (Isaiah 6: 1). Jeremiah (ch. 1) uses the symbols of the almond tree and the steaming pot to convey the message that God's judgement is soon to come. Amos speaks of the sinful women as 'cows of Bashan' (Amos 4: 1) and compares Israel to a fallen maiden (Amos 5: 2). In the best-known Psalm (23) God is a Shepherd. The book of Proverbs advises the binding of words of wisdom about the throat like a necklace (Proverbs 3: 3) and compares the embracing of wisdom to the hugging of a beloved woman (Proverbs 4: 8). In Proverbs, too, a phrase well turned is like golden apples on silver settings and a wise man's reproof like a ring of gold (Proverbs 25: 11–12). These are only a few instances of the ubiquitous use of symbols in the Bible. Biblical, and for that matter Rabbinic, language is very concrete and has to rely on symbolism for the expression of abstract ideas.

### The precepts as symbols

In the Bible the Sabbath is a 'sign', that is, a symbol, of God's covenant with Israel (Exodus 31: 16–17). The fringes (*tzitzit) at the corners

of the garment are reminders of God's commandments (Numbers 15: 38–40). The *tefillin* are described in the *Shema as a 'sign' as, it is implied, is the mezuzah (Deuteronomy 6: 8–9). The *sukkah is a symbol of the 'booths' in which the children of Israel lived during their journey through the wilderness (Leviticus 23: 42–3). The *shofar* sounded on *Rosh Ha-Shanah has received many symbolic interpretations, for example that it is a call to alertness to God's will, or symbolic of the crowning of God as King since trumpets are sounded at a coronation. The four species of *Tabernacles (Leviticus 23: 40) have been given various symbolic interpretations, for example, the upright palm branch represents the human spine; the heart-shaped citron, the etrog, the heart; the willows of the brook, the mouth; and the myrtle the eye, all of which are called upon to play their part in the worship of God. From early times Judaism itself was symbolized by the *menorah, itself the symbol of spiritual light, and by the *tablets of stone. The symbol of the *Magen David is, however, very late and was not used as a symbol for Judaism until the nineteenth century.

### Symbolism in the Rabbinic Literature

In the Rabbinic literature symbols are often taken from the natural world. Water is the symbol of the Torah because it is essential to life and because just as water only flows downwards, never upwards, the Torah cannot find its place among haughty and arrogant scholars. The Torah is also compared to fire because it burns away the evil traits in the human character and because it provides spiritual warmth and illumination. Scholars are compared to builders, craftsmen, carpenters, weavers, and other such useful and creative workers. Following Jacob's use of animal symbolism when blessing his sons (Exodus 49), Rabbinic literature is full of such comparisons. The second-century teacher, Rabbi Judah ben Tema, says (Ethics of the Fathers, 5. 20): 'Be strong as the leopard and swift as the eagle, fleet as the gazelle and brave as the lion to do the will of thy Father in Heaven.' In the later literature scholars are often referred to as 'the great lion' or 'the great eagle'. Some of the medieval writers interpreted the *sacrifices symbolically as a representation of what ought to have happened to the sinner were it not for the divine mercy which allowed the animal as a substitute. The relationship between this world and the *World to Come is described symbolically as the relationship between the eve of the Sabbath and the Sabbath itself. Only those who make provisions on the eve of the Sabbath are able to enjoy the Sabbath bliss. Similarly, this world of error and darkness is compared to the night while the World to Come is compared to day.

Living as they did in an agricultural society, the Rabbis used the products of the soil as symbols for the life of Torah. The tree is used as a metaphor for the Torah on the basis of the verse: 'It is a tree of life to them that hold fast to it' (Proverbs 3: 18). The value of a tree consists chiefly in the fruit it produces and so, too, the student of the Torah should be fruitful in the performance of good deeds. And just as a small tree sets fire to a larger tree, young scholars can set on fire the minds of more mature scholars by providing them with keen questioning of their opinions. The vine, too, is the symbol of the Torah. One who learns from the young is like one who eats unripe grapes but one who learns from the old is like one who eats ripe grapes. Israel is compared to the olive, based on the verse: 'The Lord called thy name, a green olive tree, fair, with goodly fruit' (Jeremiah 11: 16). The olive, while still on the tree, is first marked out and then taken down and beaten; after which it is transferred to the vat, put into the mill, and ground. Only after a long process can the oil be produced. And so, too, Israel is buffeted from place to place by the heathen nations but when Israel repents God answers. And just as oil does not mix with other liquids, Israel does not mingle with other nations so as to lose its identity. There is no need to refer to further examples. The Midrashic literature, in particular, is full of this kind of symbolism.

*Symbolism in the Kabbalah*

The Kabbalah is especially rich in symbolism of the *Sefirot. The symbol of *light is frequent in the Zohar, the Sefirot being described in terms of illuminations flashing forth and reflecting one another, and various colours are allotted to particular Sefirot. The *patriarchs, Abraham, Isaac, and Jacob, represent, respectively, the Sefirot of Loving-kindness, Power, and Harmony. In the opening passage of the Zohar (in current editions) the Sefirah of Sovereignty is symbolized by the pink rose, in which

there is a blend of the Sefirot of Power, represented by the colour red, and Loving-kindness, represented by the colour white. The right arm represents Loving-kindness and the left arm Power, and other parts of the body are made to represent other aspects of the Sefirot. The union of the Sefirot is often depicted symbolically as the union of male and female. It has to be appreciated, however, that in all this the Kabbalists themselves think of the various representations as something more than mere symbols. For the Kabbalists, for example, the human arms are the form assumed on earth by the spiritual entities on high. Light, for the Kabbalists, is the physical form of spiritual light on high, and so forth. In the later Kabbalah the spiritual forces that inhere in matter are called '*holy sparks'.

Edwyn Bevan, *Symbolism and Belief* (London, 1962).

Asher Feldman, *The Parables and Similes of the Rabbis Agricultural and Pastoral* (Cambridge, 1927).

Isaiah Tishby, 'An Array of Symbols', in his *The Wisdom of the Zohar*, trans. David Goldstein (The Littman Library of Jewish Civilization; Oxford, 1989), 290–307.

**Symmachus** Translator of the Bible into Greek. Symmachus lived towards the end of the second century CE. Some have suggested that Symmachus was a *Samaritan converted to the Judaism of the Rabbis and there was even an ancient report that he was not a Jew but a Christian. These are pure conjectures, since no details of his life are available. It is curious that the Talmud speaks of a teacher called Symmachus who was a a disciple of Rabbi *Meir, and he, too, lived at the end of the second century. *Geiger's suggestion that the two are one and the same is not generally accepted, because the Symmachus mentioned in the Talmud is renowned for his acumen in Halakhic debate and decision, and there is no mention of him being a translator.

**Sympathy** The need for fellow-feeling with those who suffer is a constant theme in Judaism, finding its expression in practical acts of benevolence and *charity. The many biblical injunctions to care for and show *compassion to widows, orphans, and strangers and not to oppress them, all imply that the key to such care and consideration is sympathy with their lot. With regard to widows and orphans this is stated in the starkest terms: 'Ye shall not afflict any widow, or fatherless child. If thou afflict them in any wise—for if they cry at all unto Me, I will surely hear their cry—My wrath shall wax hot, and I will kill you with the sword; and your wives shall be widows, and your children fatherless' (Exodus 22: 21–3). In the previous verse, the Israelite is reminded to feel for the stranger because Israel knows what it is for an alien to suffer: 'And a stranger shalt thou not wrong, neither shalt thou oppress him; for ye were strangers in the land of Egypt.' This idea of putting oneself into the shoes of the unfortunate was expressed by the great French commentator, *Rashi, in his comment to the verse: 'If thou lend money to any of My people, even to the poor with thee' (Exodus 22: 24). The words 'with thee' mean, says Rashi, that the way to avoid hard-heartedness is to imagine yourself to be a poor man begging for help. The poor man is to be 'with thee', as if you were he. Think how you would like it if someone refused to lend you money in your desperate need. The book of Job gives expression to the same theme. *Job, accused by his friends of deserving the calamities that had befallen him, protests: 'For I saved the poor man who cried out, the orphan who had none to help him. I received the blessing of the lost; I gladdened the heart of the widow. I clothed myself in righteousness and it robed me; justice was my cloak and turban. I was eyes to the blind and feet to the lame. I was a father to the needy, and I looked into the case of the stranger' (Job 29: 12–16). In the same vein is the account in the Talmud (*Kiddushin* 33a) of the third-century teacher, Rabbi Johanan, rising in respect before old Arameans, even though they were heathens. Rabbi Johanan would say: 'How many troubles have passed over these', meaning, they deserve that tokens of respect be paid to them because they have had to cope, during their long lives, with so much adversity.

God is said to have sympathy with the sufferings of Israel in the verse: 'In all their affliction He was afflicted' (Isaiah 63: 9). Actually, this rendering of the verse is questionable. According to one reading the verse should be rendered: 'In all their affliction He was not afflicted' and, in any event, the *Septuagint has a completely different arrangement of the words. Yet in Jewish thought the verse is often quoted with the meaning that God suffers in sympathy with His children when they are in pain and distress. In *Hasidism, when a man prays for

his needs, his motivation should be not for his own needs to be satisfied but for the lack in the *Shekhinah to be made good, since the divine presence is affected whenever creatures are in want. This idea goes back, in fact, to the Mishnah (*Sanhedrin* 6: 5) in a saying attributed to Rabbi *Meir.

Rabbi Meir comments that God suffers in sympathy even with the criminal who is executed for his crimes: 'When a man is sore troubled, what does the Shekhinah say? My head is ill at ease, my arm is ill at ease [some texts add here the words, "if it is permitted to say this"]. If God is sore troubled at the blood of the wicked that is shed, how much more at the blood of the righteous?'

*Heschel's well-known study of the Hebrew prophets depicts the prophet as a person who sees the world with the eyes of God and who suffers with God when human beings suffer. According to Heschel's understanding, the consciousness of the prophet is in such sympathetic union with the *pathos* of God that he can bring that union to bear in any given set of circumstances. In Heschel's powerful summary of the prophetic character: 'The prophet is a man who feels fiercely. God has thrust a burden upon his soul, and he is bowed and stunned at man's fierce greed. Frightful is the agony of man; no human voice can convey its full terror. Prophecy is the voice that God has lent to the silent agony, a voice to the plundered poor, to the profaned rules of the world. It is a form of living, a crossing point of God and man. God is raging in the prophet's words.'

Abraham J. Heschel, *The Prophets* (Philadelphia, 1962).

**Synagogue** The building in which Jews worship and offer their prayers. The word synagogue, from the Greek word meaning assembly, corresponds to the Hebrew name *bet ha-keneset*, 'house of assembly', that is, the place in which Jews come together. (Solomon Zeitlin's suggestion that originally the 'assembly' was a gathering of the worthies in the local town hall for secular purposes but where the sessions opened with prayer, this later being transformed into the synagogue, has not been widely accepted by other scholars.) It is only in European languages that the term synagogue is used and this is obviously not the normal Jewish term for the institution. It is true that in the Zohar the word *esnoga* (the Portuguese word for the institution) is interpreted as *esh nogah* ('fire and light'), as if the term was of Jewish origin, but this is one of the many indications that the Zohar was composed much later than the traditional date of the second century CE. The Zohar is, in fact, giving a Hebrew meaning to a Portuguese word. But this does show that the word synagogue or *esnoga* was used by Jews for the *bet hakeneset* in the thirteenth century when the Zohar was compiled. Nor is it any way authentic to use the term Synagogue as a synonym of Judaism; to say, for instance, this or that is the view of the Synagogue, as if there is an entity known by this name. This usage is simply an adaptation of the term 'the Church' in Christian literature. In Jewish usage the synagogue is the building in which Jews worship, and nothing else.

From the Talmudic period and throughout subsequent Jewish literature there are numerous references to a similar institution, the Bet Ha-Midrash ('house of study'), the place in which the Torah was studied (see STUDY). It would seem that in Talmudic times the two institutions were quite separate from one another. There was one building, the synagogue, in which Jews congregated for prayer, and another building, the 'house of study', in which they came together in order to study the Torah. The study, incidentally, was largely by heart, with the only books handwritten copies of Scripture, so that it is somewhat hard to imagine how the 'house of study' actually functioned. Especially after the invention of printing, the 'house of study' is thought of by Jews as a room full of books but that was obviously not the case in the Talmudic period. Wherever possible the synagogue was situated in the town at its highest point, whereas the house of study was usually situated in the fields outside the town, perhaps in order to avoid distractions and, possibly, in order to preserve study as an élitist activity. Eventually, however, the 'house of study' was combined with the synagogue, either as an adjunct to the synagogue building or as an additional, important function of the synagogue itself. The Yiddish term *Schul* was used in medieval Germany for the synagogue. The synagogue was called a 'school' rather than a house of prayer which might have been viewed with disfavour by the Christian rulers as a rival to the church. In reality, although the term *Schul* was adopted for reasons of prudence, the synagogue did

have the function of a school in that it embraced the 'house of study'. Yiddish-speaking Jews usually refer to the synagogue to this day as the *Schul*. A '*Schul* Yid' is a Jew who regularly attends all the synagogue services.

Reform Jews often call the synagogue a Temple, Reform Judaism rejecting the belief that the *Temple in Jerusalem will be rebuilt in the Messianic age (see MESSIAH) and sacrifices offered there as in days of old. The idea that prayer in the synagogue now takes the place of the sacrifices is found in the classical sources but Reform holds that the synagogue is not only a substitute for the Temple but is the Temple, wherever it is located, a view which Orthodoxy rejects because it hopes for the rebuilding of the Temple itself. Some Orthodox Rabbis have objected to the use of 'the house of God' for the synagogue both because this is the term used by Christians for a church and because the term refers to the Temple proper in Solomon's prayer (1 Kings 8: 11) and in the book of Ezra (Ezra 9: 9). Despite the fact that in the Talmud (*Shabbat* 11a) the verse in Ezra is applied to the synagogue as well as to the Temple, Jews, for the reasons stated, do not normally refer to the synagogue as 'the house of God'.

*History*

For all its importance in Jewish life, little is known of the origins of the synagogue. There are no explicit references to anything like a synagogue anywhere in the Bible. Many scholars have suggested that the synagogue originated in the period of the Babylonian exile, which followed the destruction of the first Temple in 586 BCE. On this theory the earliest synagogues were small meeting-places in which the exiles gathered together for prayer. The prophet *Ezekiel, in Babylon, states in one of his addresses: 'Thus saith the Lord God. Although I have cast them afar off among the heathen, and although I have scattered them among the countries, yet will I be to them a small sanctuary in the countries where they shall come' (Ezekiel 11: 16). What the prophet means by God becoming for them a small sanctuary is unclear, but the Talmud (*Megillah* 29a) identifies the 'small sanctuary' with the synagogue. The reference in the book of Psalms to the enemy destroying 'all the meeting-places of God in the land' (Psalms 74: 8) has also been understood as applying to the synagogues.

However, if synagogues did exist in this early period it is astonishing that there is no explicit reference to them. All that can be stated with certainty on the question of origins is that by the first century CE the synagogue had long been an established institution. The Mishnah (*Tamid* 5: 1; *Yoma* 7: 1) refers to a synagogue in the Temple itself. Philo refers to a synagogue in Rome and, as evidence from the Talmud and the *Septuagint shows, there were synagogues in ancient Alexandria. In the New Testament, Jesus is said to have preached in the synagogues of Galilee (Matthew 4: 23) and, according to Acts, Paul preached in synagogues in Damascus, Asia Minor, and Cyprus. Archaeologists have uncovered the remains of synagogues in Palestine and elsewhere dating from this early period. The institution of the synagogue had become so much part of Jewish life everywhere by the second century CE that the Mishnah takes this for granted. The many references in the Mishnah to the reading of the Torah in the synagogues and to prayers in the synagogue, as well as to laws about such matters as the sale of synagogues, are made (*Megillah* ch. 3) in such a way as to imply that it was extremely rare for a Jewish community of any size not to have a synagogue in which the citizens gathered for worship.

In the post-Mishnaic period a teacher declared that a man's prayers are only heard in the synagogue (*Berakhot* 6a) and another teacher that anyone who has a synagogue in his city and does not attend services there is called a 'bad neighbour' (*Berakhot* 8a). Another saying in similar vein is that if a person who regularly attends synagogue misses a day, God enquires after him (*Berakhot* 6a). Sayings of this kind show that while it was considered extremely meritorious for people to frequent the synagogue, not everyone did so on a regular basis, otherwise the preachments would not have been necessary. The fact that Rabbis down to the present day have had to urge Jews to go to the synagogue shows that the problem has persisted throughout the ages. That Jews enthusiastically built synagogues wherever they lived is beyond doubt. That they were not always scrupulous in attending the synagogue is also beyond doubt. A prayer for the congregation still recited in synagogues refers to 'those who build synagogues for prayer and those who enter there to pray'—the two were by no means always identical.

From Talmudic times onwards the preference was for one large synagogue rather than a number of smaller ones. The verse quoted in this connection (*Megillah* 27b) is: 'In the multitude of people is the king's glory' (Proverbs 14: 28), understood to mean that the more worshippers present in a given synagogue, the greater the glory of God. But naturally, in the larger towns, there was more than one synagogue. Following the breach between the Hasidim (see HASIDISM) and the official leaders of the communities, the Hasidim worshipped in small conventicles, each owing allegiance to a particular *Zaddik. Owing to theological and ideological differences, Reform and Conservative Jews established their own synagogues in which their particular preferences were given suitable expression. Unique in Jewish life is the United Synagogue in Greater London, consisting of a body of synagogues all belonging to the same central organization under the jurisdiction of the Chief Rabbi; otherwise synagogues conduct their affairs quite independently of one another. There are, however, a number of synagogue bodies to which individual synagogues are loosely attached, such as the World Union of Progressive Synagogues (Reform) and the United Synagogue of America (Conservative). In the *Diaspora the synagogue is, in many ways, the focal point of communal life, with social and charitable activities all organized under the aegis of the synagogue. In the State of Israel, on the other hand, the numerous synagogues function solely as places of prayer and study, the social aspects being taken care of by the other institutions of the State.

### Form, Structure, and Furnishing of the Synagogue

There are no rules in Judaism regarding the architectural form of the synagogue building. Jews have adopted the styles of the countries in which they lived (see ARCHITECTURE). The famous Altneu synagogue in Prague, for instance, is in the Gothic style in which churches were built at the time. On the other hand, in Western lands during the nineteenth century, it was far from unusual to build synagogues in the oriental style, in the belief that this best represented the 'oriental' origins of Judaism: a romantic lapse from the Westernization that was proceeding apace. But many synagogues in the West were also influenced by church buildings, although, of course, the cruciform mode was never adopted. Orthodox Rabbis were opposed, too, to a synagogue having a spire like a church, and their advice was generally followed by the non-Orthodox as well.

On the question of synagogue architecture, there is a representative Responsum by Rabbi Ezekiel *Landau of Prague (Responsa *Noda Biyhudah*, second series, *Oraḥ Ḥayyim*, no. 18). Dated Tishri, 5548 ( = 1787), this Responsum was in reply to a query from Trieste, in which the questioner asked Rabbi Landau whether it was permitted to build a synagogue in an octagonal shape, or whether the synagogue had to have four walls only, that is, to be in the form of a square or an oblong. Rabbi Landau replies, on the principle that Jewish law permits innovations where there is no reason to forbid them, that a synagogue can have any form the architect and the congregation that employs him wishes, even if the form is unusual and untraditional. There is nothing, he says, in any of the classical sources about a particular form that a synagogue has to have. He does feel obliged to add that motivation is important here and if the motivation is to display Jewish wealth and the like, such ostentation should be avoided. Conscious of the new winds that were beginning to blow in Western Europe, which moved many Jews, Rabbi Landau concludes his Responsum with this warning:

'All this I have said in accordance with the strict letter of the law. But I wonder why they should want to do this and I thought that perhaps they saw something like this in the palaces of princes or in some other houses and they wished to copy it. But the truth is that it is not proper for us in our exile to copy princes and to be envious of them. I recite for this the verse: "And Israel hath forgotten his Maker, and builded palaces" [Hosea 8: 14]. It is better, therefore, not to change any of the old customs, especially in this generation. But if the reason was that there would be more room if the synagogue were built according to these specifications there is not the slightest fear of anything wrong.'

Rabbi Landau's ruling became authoritative. Any architectural form is suitable for a synagogue and architectural innovations are allowed. But his advice, nevertheless, to keep the building simple was rarely heeded, Jews evidently believing that whatever moral objections there are to ostentation in general, these cannot apply to the erection of a splendid synagogue to the glory of God.

The Talmud (*Berakhot* 34b), citing the example of Daniel of whom it is said that his windows were open toward Jerusalem (Daniel 6: 11), states that a man should only offer his prayers in a house with windows open to the sky. *Rashi explains this on the grounds that openness to the sky increases reverence for God. The Talmud does not refer to a synagogue but to a private house, and some synagogues were built with very few windows, either on grounds of expediency or because the synagogue building itself promotes feelings of reverence. The *Shulḥan Arukh* (*Oraḥ Ḥayyim*, 90: 4) does apply the Talmudic rule to the synagogue which should have 'doors and windows facing Jerusalem'. This rule, based on the Zohar, was not always observed since it presented, at times, difficulties in the construction of the building. Nor was it always possible to have the doors of the synagogue facing the direction of Jerusalem (see MIZRAH). Under the influence of the later Kabbalah, the *Shulḥan Arukh*, in the same passage, states that ideally a synagogue should have twelve windows corresponding to the twelve tribes of Israel, each with its own window to heaven, so to speak. In some modern synagogues in the USA, this is taken a stage further and glass is used for the walls in order to make the sanctuary open to the sky and a place in which light rather than the conventional gloom predominates.

One or two later authorities held that there should be no trees in the grounds of the synagogue, on the basis of the verse: 'Thou shalt not plant thee an Asherah of any kind of tree beside the altar of the Lord thy God, which thou shalt make thee' (Deuteronomy 16: 21). But this opinion is rejected since the verse speaks only of a sacred tree planted beside the altar, which is taken to mean that trees were only forbidden in the Temple in ancient times because of their association with idolatrous worship, not in the synagogue where there is not the slightest suspicion of the congregation associating trees with idolatry.

There is no mixed seating in the traditional synagogue nowadays. Women sit separately from the men either in a ladies' gallery or behind a *meḥitzah* ('partition'), high or low depending on the degree of punctiliousness of the congregation in this matter. In ultra-Orthodox synagogues the women have a separate room at the back of the synagogue, where the men cannot see them but where they can see what is going on in the synagogue, with some difficulty, through small windows in the joining wall or through a grill in the wall. The reason for this insistence on separate seating is usually given that it is to prevent the men being distracted in their worship by the proximity of the women. Women, evidently, on this view, are not so easily distracted by being able to see the men, an interesting psychological postulate. This question of separate seating in the synagogue has been a bone of contention from the time of the rise of the Reform movement. The Reformers held that to separate the sexes in prayer is contrary to Western egalitarian standards. The Orthodox retorted that to depart from the tradition is an offence against 'the sanctity of the synagogue', the title of a well-known book compiled in defence of the tradition. The evidence from archaeology seems to point to the absence of such separate seating arrangements in ancient synagogues, since no traces have been found of a separate compartment for women in any of the ancient synagogues that have been uncovered. From one or two passages in the Talmud it also appears that men and women were seated together in the synagogue in Talmudic times. It has consequently been argued that separate seating in the synagogue came into medieval Jewish life under the influence of Islam. Nevertheless, separate seating is the norm in Orthodox synagogues with very few exceptions but in practically all Reform and Conservative synagogues the sexes do sit together (see FEMINISM and WOMEN).

Every synagogue has an *Ark in which the Scrolls of the Torah are kept (see SEFER TORAH); a *bimah, the platform from which the Torah is read; and a perpetual *light over the Ark. On the analogy of the *parokhet* ('curtain') in the *Tabernacle (Exodus 26: 31–4), a richly embroidered curtain is hung in front of the Ark in Ashkenazi synagogues. In Sephardi synagogues the *parokhet* is placed behind the door of the Ark. The seating is either in the form of built-in pews or of movable chairs or benches. The more prized seats are those nearer to the Ark in the eastern wall of the synagogue. In obedience to egalitarian principles many synagogues have a first-come, first-served arrangement, all the members of the congregation being entitled to sit wherever they choose. But the custom of purchasing the choice seats is still the norm in many other synagogues. In the older, traditional synagogues, the leader of the prayers (see CANTOR) stood not on the bimah, as is often the practice today, but at a special low reading-desk in front of the Ark to suggest humbleness in the presence of God. Again in the older synagogues, there was no special pulpit, preaching being carried out from the bimah. But, under Western, not to say church, influence it is customary in most modern synagogues, Orthodox as well as Reform and Conservative, to have a special pulpit from which the Rabbi delivers his sermons. In the majority of Reform and Conservative synagogues the pulpit, the bimah, and the Reader's desk are situated on a raised platform adjacent to the Ark, with the Cantor facing the congregation. The Orthodox object to this arrangement as an attempt to copy the Christian practice of siting the altar at the end of the church and because it is unfitting to have the Cantor face the congregation on whose behalf he prays to God. He should, the Orthodox argue, face his Maker, that is, have his face to the Ark, not to the congregation. In this whole area there is constant tension between the need to avoid copying Christian forms and the need to adorn the synagogue in as fitting a manner as that which obtains among Christians—'anything you can do we can do better'. The medieval synagogue in Cologne, for instance, had stained-glass windows.

With regard to synagogue decoration in general it is certainly unusual, but not entirely unknown, to have depicted human beings and animals (see ART). In the ancient synagogue discovered at Dura-Europos in Syria there are mosaics depicting the heroes of the Bible and even in contemporary Orthodox synagogues this type of decoration can sometimes be seen, at least in the stained-glass windows. A fierce debate took place between the Orthodox and the Reformers in the nineteenth century on whether it is permitted to have an *organ in the synagogue to accompany the prayers, the Orthodox objecting strongly to the use of the organ as an example of an undignified aping of Christian modes. Reform and Conservative synagogues, today, do use the organ but only very few have a built-in organ in the style of a church.

*Respect for the Synagogue*

Jewish teachers, legalists and moralists, never tired of stressing that strict decorum and reverence are to be observed by worshippers in the synagogue. There must be no idle conversation in the synagogue and the worshippers must always be aware of the fact that they are in the presence of God. These constant appeals for decorum in the synagogue demonstrate that the problem was acute, naturally so since for many Jews the synagogue was the main place for social intercourse, often serving, whether or not the Rabbis approved, as a kind of club. The Mishnaic rule (*Berakhot* 9: 1) that one must not use the Temple Mount as a short-cut is applied in the Talmud (*Berakhot* 62b) to the synagogue as well. This together with other rules is recorded in the *Shulḥan Arukh* (*Oraḥ Ḥayyim* 151) under the heading: 'The Laws With Regard to the Sanctity of the Synagogue'. This section of the *Shulḥan Arukh* reads in part:

'One should not behave in a frivolous manner in a synagogue or house of study, by cracking jokes there, for instance, or by indulging in humorous or pointless gossip. One should not eat or drink there nor should one adorn oneself there or walk about there. One should not enter there in summer to cool off or in winter to seek shelter from the rain. In an emergency scholars and their disciples are permitted to eat and drink there. [Isserles adds:] Some say that in a house of study this is permitted even where there is no emergency. No monetary calculations should be made there unless they are for religious purposes, collecting money for charity, for example, or for the redemption of captives. No funeral orations should be delivered there unless it is for one of the leading citizens of the city when all assemble there for the purpose. If a man finds it necessary to enter there for his own needs, to call someone, for instance, he should read or study something and then call him so that it should not appear as if he has entered for his own needs. . . . It is forbidden to have even a short nap in a synagogue but this is permitted in a house of study. It is permitted to eat and sleep in the synagogue if it is for religious purposes. For this reason [of religious purpose overriding the prohibition] one may sleep in the synagogue on *Yom Kippur.'

The reason why the *Shulḥan Arukh* treats the 'house of study' more leniently than the synagogue is because scholars spend a good deal of their time in the former, so that a dispensation is required in order to enable them to study without interruption. Otherwise, in the

Rabbinic view, the 'house of study' possesses a greater degree of sanctity than the synagogue, a typical illustration of the high significance the Rabbis attached to the study of the Torah above all other religious obligations.

Curiously enough, the *Shulḥan Arukh* rules that it is permitted to spit in the synagogue provided the saliva is erased with the foot or where there is an absorbent material there so that the saliva is not seen. This ruling obviously has to be seen against the social background of the times. In these matters it is generally held, nowadays, that Western standards of decorum should be preserved on the grounds that Jews should not behave less decorously than Christians do in church. For this reason (see GENTILES) Orthodox Rabbis forbid smoking in the synagogue (but not in the 'house of study'). While there is no actual prohibition against smoking in the synagogue, the sources being compiled before *tobacco had been brought to Europe, since Christians do not smoke in church for Jews to do so would suggest that they have less respect than Christians for the place in which they worship.

It was the common practice in the Middle Ages for pious folk to donate candles to the synagogue, not as votive offerings, of which Judaism knows nothing, but in order to keep the building well lit. Nowadays, when illumination is provided by electric lights, this practice is no longer in vogue, although in some synagogues tallow candles are still used in front of the Reader's desk.

The question of selling a synagogue that is no longer used has been much discussed. As stated above, the question is discussed in the Mishnah (*Megillah* 3) and in the Talmudic elaboration of the Mishnah. The final ruling is that when a synagogue can no longer be used it may be sold on the grounds that synagogues are sanctified on condition that they are used as such, so that once the synagogue is no longer used it loses its sanctity and may be sold. The Talmud does make a distinction between a synagogue in a village and one in a large city. A synagogue in a village belongs to the villagers and can be sold by them. But a synagogue in a large city does not belong solely to the citizens, since the frequent visitors from other towns have presumably contributed to the building and are thus part-owners, so that the town council has no right to dispose of their share. Later authorities, however, hold that since, nowadays, each synagogue has its own members who contribute to its upkeep these members are the sole owners and the synagogue may be sold when it is no longer used as such even where it is in a large town. For this reason a synagogue may be sold to be used as a church or a mosque, although here it is common practice to sell the synagogue indirectly through a third party. The accepted opinion among the authorities is that, conversely, it is permitted to buy a mosque or a church to be used as a synagogue, though, in the case of the church, the building must not contain any symbols of the Christian faith, built-in crosses for example.

The main function of the synagogue is for public worship but there is, of course, no objection to a person entering the synagogue for private meditation at other times than those of public worship. The advice is given in the sources to proceed hurriedly when going to the synagogue but to depart from the synagogue with unhurried steps, to indicate eagerness to be there and reluctance to leave. The verse is homiletically interpreted in this connection is: 'We shall run to know the Lord' (Hosea 6: 3). The verse does not, of course, refer to the synagogue but is made to yield the meaning that it is right 'to run' to know God and to go to the synagogue is to proceed to a greater knowledge of the divine.

*The Synagogue in Jewish Mysticism*

In the Zohar the synagogue is said to be the representation on earth of the *Shekhinah, the divine presence. According to the doctrine of the *Sefirot, the Sefirah, *Malkhut*, 'Sovereignty', the Shekhinah, is called the 'assembly of Israel' because in it, so to speak, all the Sefirot come together as the worshippers congregate in the synagogue. As the Zohar (ii. 59b–60a) puts it:

'The Tabernacle that Moses made in the wilderness was entirely modelled on the one above. The Temple that King Solomon built was a house of repose on the celestial pattern, with all its adornments, so that there might be in the restored world above a house and repose and rest [for the Shekhinah]. Similarly, the synagogue should be on the celestial pattern with every kind of beautiful adornment, so that it might be a house of prayer for affecting restoration [of the Shekhinah, the female principle, to *Tiferet*, the male principle] through prayer . . . You might say in the field as well so

that the spirit can ascend [i.e. when one prays in the open air the spirit can ascend more easily]. But this is not right. A house is essential, so that a house can exist below on the model of the house above [i.e. the Shekhinah is the "house" of the Sefirot on high].'

The Zohar seems to admit here that inspirational prayer can more effectively be achieved outside the synagogue in the open air. Nevertheless, prayer in the synagogue is essential because a 'house' of prayer alone can represent the Shekhinah and have a theurgic effect on the Sefirotic realm. It would seem certain that this Zoharic passage is an elaboration, in Kabbalistic terms, of the Talmudic account (*Megillah* 29a) that the Shekhinah appeared in the synagogue of Shaf-ve-yativ in Nehardea accompanied by a sound of tumult which struck terror into the hearts of the Rabbis praying there so that they were obliged to rush out of the building.

The sixteenth-century Kabbalist Elijah de Vidas, in his work *Reshit Ḥokhmah* ('The Beginning of Wisdom'; 'The Gate of Fear', ch. 12) has an elaboration of the Zoharic theme of the glory of God manifested in the synagogue. In de Vidas's understanding of the idea of *holy places, an objective reality is present in the sacred spot. De Vidas writes:

'Now although the whole earth is full of His glory yet because of His love for us He concentrates His Divine Presence among us as He used to do between the staves of the Ark and the place of the Holy of Holies in the Temple. Of the Tent of Meeting we also find that once it had been finished Scripture says: "And Moses was not able to enter into the tent of meeting, because the cloud abode thereon, and the glory of the Lord filled the tabernacle" [Exodus 40: 35]. Similarly, of the Temple, when Solomon brought the Ark into the Holy of Holies, Scripture says: "The priests could not stand to minister by reason of the cloud; for the glory of the Lord filled the house of the Lord" [1 Kings 8: 11]. The Synagogue, too, is filled with the light of the glory of the Lord. Even though we see nothing it is essential to believe this with perfect faith.'

*Attitudes to the Synagogue*

While all Jews have a reverential attitude towards the synagogue, some no doubt finding much significance even in the mystical understanding of the synagogue as the abode of the

Shekhinah, a degree of resistance has come about in modern times, as it did in former times, to the idea that Judaism is synagogue-oriented. Rabbis are fond of preaching that Judaism demands far more than regular worship in the synagogue and that, for example, many of the highest ideals of the Jewish religion are realized in the Jewish home rather than in the synagogue. Worship in the synagogue is a sublime end in itself but it is also a means of inspiring Jews to lead a full Jewish life and much of life has its place outside the synagogue. There is a Torah for the synagogue, detailed rules, regulations, and attitudes to be adopted in the synagogue, but this is only part, albeit a significant part, of the Torah as a whole. The Torah is always described as 'the Torah of Life', that is of life as a whole. For all that, the majority of Jews, nowadays, still view the synagogue as the best means of retaining loyalty to Judaism and preserving Jewish identity. As with regard to other particular aspects of Judaism, synagogal life is both an end in itself and a means to the ultimate end of Jewish life, the worship of God in every one of life's situations: 'In all thy ways acknowledge Him, and He will direct thy paths' (Proverbs 3: 6). Contemporary Rabbis thus find themselves in a dilemma. On the one hand they feel obliged to urge Jews to attend synagogue services regularly but, on the other hand, they cannot countenance the view that synagogue attendance is the be-all and end-all of Judaism. It is hard to determine how many Jews are regular attenders at the synagogue during the rest of the year, but a majority of Jews are found there on *Yom Kippur, which exercises a powerful fascination over Jews as the great day of reconciliation with their God.

This has been the problem of the synagogue, to make it a place apart in which the Jew communes with God together with his fellow-worshippers and, at the same time, to make it a place wide open to the daily concerns of its members. A complete division between the sacred and the secular was never attempted. Appeals for charity were regularly made in the synagogue, hospitality to visitors, offered there and mourners comforted there. It was not unknown for services in the medieval synagogue to be interrupted by someone with a complaint in financial matters that was not being adequately addressed, the complainant refusing to allow the services to proceed until he had obtained an assurance that his case would be considered. Against these attempts at comparative 'secularization', some Ashkenazi Rabbis refused to allow parents to kiss their children in the synagogue where, they argued, love should be expressed only to God. Orthodox Rabbis, especially in Hungary, refused to allow marriages to be celebrated in the synagogue, as was the Sephardi practice. To have the *huppah in the synagogue with an address by the Rabbi to the bride and bridegroom, was, they held, an obvious attempt at copying the practices of the Church, apart from the fact that the huppah should ideally be in the open air. Nowadays it is the norm, however, even among the Orthodox, to have the huppah in the synagogue.

Israel Abrahams, 'Life in the Synagogue', in his *Jewish Life in the Middle Ages* (London, 1932), 29–48.
Hyman E. Goldin, 'The Sanctity of the Synagogue and the House of Study', in his *Code of Jewish Law* (New York, 1961), i. 43–4.
Isaac Levy, *The Synagogue: Its History and Function* (London, 1963).
Lee Levine (ed.), *Ancient Synagogues Revealed* (Jerusalem, 1981).

**Syncretism** The assimilation by Judaism of elements stemming from other religions and civilizations. The process of syncretism in Judaism is rarely conscious or intentional, but as Jews came into contact with the ideas and institutions of the various peoples among whom they resided, their language and thought-patterns were naturally and automatically affected, so that Judaism itself came to absorb these ideas into its own theology. This does not mean that Jews simply adopted uncritically the beliefs and practices of their neighbours. A kind of consensus has been at work in the history of the Jewish religion by virtue of which those elements that could be adapted to Judaism without in any way coming into conflict with essential Jewish beliefs (see DOGMAS) were not totally rejected but given a Jewish interpretation. Where ideas from without were seen to be incompatible with the Jewish religion they were rejected without any attempt at compromise. Naturally, considerable tensions arose in these matters. The prohibition against copying the practices of the *Gentiles militated against too easy an acceptance of the forms of a faith different from Judaism, and opinions among Jews were often divided on the legitimacy or otherwise of adaptation in this or that instance.

Biblical scholars (see BIBLICAL CRITICISM) have called attention to syncretic elements in the Bible itself. The creation narrative at the beginning of the book of Genesis, for example, speaks of the 'deep' (Genesis 1: 2), the Hebrew for which is *tehom*. This word has been connected with the Babylonian creation-myth in which the primal chaos is personified under the name Tiamat. The resemblance is very striking, yet the biblical narrative is totally non-mythological in nature and when it is appreciated that in Babylonian usage *tiamatu* became a generic term for 'ocean' it can be seen how precarious it is to read the Genesis narrative in such mythological terms. Similarly, the account of the 'great sea-monsters' of Genesis (1: 21) may bear traces of ancient, Babylonian mythology, but only traces. God creates the 'sea-monsters' and these are in no way divine. The story of *Noah and the *Flood provides a particularly striking illustration of how the biblical authors used ancient mythological material, but used it in support of monotheism. The resemblances between the story of Noah and the Babylonian myths are strong even in some of the details, yet in the Genesis narrative there is sounded the most powerful monotheistic and ethical note, one that is totally absent in the Babylonian myth. The same applies to the list of the *antediluvians in Genesis (ch. 5). As Cassuto has suggested, in the biblical record the mythical notion that some men in remote antiquity lived for exceedingly long periods until they became gods has been adapted to monotheistic belief. None of the antediluvians managed to live for a thousand years, and they procreate as humans do, as if to say: these ancients did live for a very long time but they were otherwise ordinary human beings with ordinary human lives and were in no sense divine. The *dietary laws and the *Sabbath have similarly been seen as having their origin in the practices of the Babylonians and other ancient civilizations but even if this is accepted (it is by no means certain that such theories are warranted by the evidence), what matters for Judaism is that the dietary laws are laid down in the *Pentateuch as the means to holy living and the Sabbath as the day in which the One God is hailed as the Creator and all this is true whatever the actual origin of the dietary laws and the Sabbath.

This dual process of adaptation and rejection can be observed throughout the history of Judaism. Judaism has been compared to a sponge, which both absorbs and exudes moisture. In the first two centuries CE the supreme court, the *Sanhedrin, had a Greek name; the *Sefer Torah could be, and in Alexandria was, written in Greek; some Jews, including Rabbis, had Greek names; and Rabban *Gamaliel could bathe in a bath-house in which there was a statue of Aphrodite; yet the strongest opposition was expressed to any association, no matter how indirect, with the worship of the pagan gods. In the Babylonian Talmud, ideas taken from the Persians, like the belief in *demons and the way in which these operate, are recorded and evidently accepted, yet, precisely because the Zoroastrian religion was the Persian religion, the Talmudic Rabbis constantly spare no effort in opposing Zoroastrian dualism (see ZOROASTRIANISM).

Syncretism in Judaism can be observed in the attempt of the medieval Jewish philosophers to cope with the problems raised by Greek philosophy in its Arabic garb. The whole of Maimonides' *Guide of the Perplexed* is devoted to the consideration of how much of Greek philosophy can be accepted as true and hence as part of Judaism and how much is to be rejected in the name of the Jewish religion. With regard to the religions of Christianity and Islam there was, of course, total rejection of the truth-claims of these two faiths yet, at the same time, both religions exerted an influence on the development of Judaism. The influence of *Sufism is clearly evident in Bahya *Ibn Pakudah. Rabbenu *Gershom's ban on polygamy for Ashkenazi Jews obviously owes much to Christian practice. The severe *asceticism of the *Saints of Germany was influenced by Christian monasticism. Maimonides, under the influence of Islam, ruled that a Jew must bathe his feet before the daily prayers whereas the Talmud speaks only of washing the hands.

When Western civilization posed a threat to the survival of Judaism, the diverse ways in which Jews responded to the challenge resulted in a degree of syncretism. The *Haskalah, Reform and Conservative Judaism, and Samson Raphael *Hirsch's neo-Orthodoxy are all examples of adaptation of the old to the new. In the area of scientific theory, many Jewish thinkers accepted the view that the universe is not geocentric, that life has been on earth for a vast period of time and that human beings have evolved from lower forms (see EVOLUTION) and they reinterpreted the biblical record so that it could be understood in accordance with the new picture of the universe. Thus, while the actual term 'syncretism' is not found in any of the Jewish sources, and while Jewish fundamentalists (see FUNDAMENTALISM) deny that any form of syncretism ever took place in Judaism, the idea denoted by this term is clearly evident to Jews with any sense of history, although this recognition does not interfere with their belief in the basic truths of the religion. On the contrary, the evidence for syncretism is evidence of the Jewish genius that has made Judaism an undying faith.

**Synods, Rabbinical** Assemblies or conferences of Rabbinic leaders at which rulings were given governing the social life of Jews under their jurisdiction. In the Middle Ages the synod was known as the *asifah* (*'assembly'*). The Rabbinical synods differed in two respects from the synods of the Church. First, the Christian synods were convened largely for the purpose of defining complicated issues of dogma, whereas the Rabbinical synods were chiefly concerned with practical legislation. Secondly, the Christian synods enjoyed an international authority, whereas the Rabbinical synods in the Middle Ages were confined to particular communities or districts. Once the period of the *Geonim has come to an end there was no central *authority for Jews. The main activity of the Rabbinical synods was to establish *takkanot* ('enactments'). A *takkanah* (a 'putting right') consists of new legislation to cover situations for which the standard laws are inadequate or on which they are silent. The principle behind the *takkanah* is that locally accepted authorities have power, granted to them by the community itself, just as members of Parliament act on behalf of the country. A synod had the power to issue new financial and social regulations, at first binding only on those under the particular Rabbinic jurisdiction but often finding their way into the Codes of law, when they thus became binding on Jews outside the original communities in which the *takkanot* were promulgated. For instance, the famous ban (*herem*) on polygamy, attributed to the Synod of Rabbenu *Gershom of Mayence, became binding eventually not only on Jews living in Germany but on all Ashkenazi Jews. This extension of the ban did not apply however, to Sephardi Jews, who, nevertheless, introduced

certain restrictions of their own against a man taking more than one wife, for instance by encouraging the drawing up of a *ketubah* (marriage settlement) in which it was stated that the consent of the first wife is required before her husband can take another wife. Such Sephardi regulations were also limited in that they applied only to the particular community in which they were promulgated. Similarly, the ban against the study of science and philosophy by youths under the age of 20, promulgated by the Synod of Barcelona on 26 July 1305, under the leadership of Solomon Ibn *Adret, was binding only on the Jews of Barcelona, although attempts were made to extend the ban to other communities. The idea behind it all is that the synod enjoyed its powers by the consensus of the community, so that any legislation that emerged was binding by the community's acceptance, not in any way because of the dictate of the Rabbis themselves. No synod had the right to introduce legislation to change religious law, except through the normal Halakhic channels.

A number of *takkanot* are attributed in the Talmud to the synod of Usha, a town in Lower Galilee in the middle of the second century CE. This synod had the aim of re-establishing the *Sanhedrin after its exile from Jerusalem when the Temple was destroyed. Among the *takkanot* of Usha are: that a man must support his young children and that a man must not give away to the poor more than a fifth of his capital, resolutions which are both understandable against the background of the time, when poverty was rife as a result of the severe decline of the economy that followed the wars against Rome.

Around the year 1150 the famous French teachers, Rabbenu *Tam and his brother the *Rashbam, convened a synod to discuss the conditions of Jewish life following the Crusades. In Germany soon afterwards synods were convened by the three communities of Speyer, Worms, and Mayence. The regulations issued at these synods are known in the literature of Jewish law as the *takkanot* of Shum (after the initial letters in Hebrew of the three towns). Synods were often convened at the great fairs to which the merchants would bring their Rabbis to adjudicate in disputes between them and where the Rabbis of important communities had the opportunity to meet. The Council of the Four Lands (Major Poland,

Minor Poland, Red Russia, and Lithuania) met regularly from the middle of the sixteenth century, their enactments being known as the *takkanot* of *vaad arba aratzot* ('Council of Four Lands').

In modern times the various Rabbinical conferences took the place of the synods. Nowadays, Orthodox, Conservative, and Reform Rabbis have their usually annual conferences to discuss questions of general and Jewish concern in the light of the particular movement. These conferences are much wider in scope than the medieval synods and while Halakhic issues are discussed, their thrust is largely in the direction of social justice, theology, and the wider teachings of Judaism. To what degree the proposals put forward and accepted at these conferences are binding on the members of the organization depends on the constitution of the organization.

> Salo W. Baron, *The Jewish Community* (Philadelphia, 1945); see index: 'Councils', 'synods'.
> David Menahem Shohet, *The Jewish Court in the Middle Ages* (New York, 1931); see index: 'Synods'.

**Synonymous Parallelism**  The feature of biblical poetry, described by modern scholars, who were anticipated by Abraham *Ibn Ezra and *Kimhi in the Middle Ages, in which the same idea is repeated for effect in different words. For example: 'For fire went out from Heshbon, flame from the city of Sihon' (Numbers 21: 28). Sihon was the king of Heshbon, so that the second clause simply repeats in different words the statement in the first clause. 'My doctrine shall drip as the rain, my speech shall distill as the dew; as the small rain upon the tender grass, and as the showers upon the herb' (Deuteronomy 32: 2). In Psalm 23, in which the Lord is described as the Shepherd, the Psalmist declares: 'He maketh me to lie down in green pastures; he leadeth me beside the still waters' (v. 2); the second clause, although referring to a different form of pastoral care from the first, is a parallel to the first in that both are examples of that care. Many biblical commentators try to discover subtle differences between the two clauses wherever this phenomenon occurs but, while their comments can be valuable as homiletics, they are far removed from the plain meaning of the verses. Other forms of poetic parallelism in the Bible are antithetic and synthetic, that is, the second

clause is contrasted with the first and elaborates on it. All this provides an excellent illustration of how the Bible can be understood at the level of its plain meaning without detriment to the homiletical insights (see MIDRASH). On the plain meaning biblical poetry is just poetry plain and simple, the poet expressing his thoughts in the form of parallelism to produce an effect.

**Syriac**  A dialect of eastern *Aramaic. The Talmud (*Bava Kama* 83a–b) implies that Syriac was used by Palestinian Jews while Aramaic was used by Babylonian Jews. Rabbi *Judah the Prince is reported as saying: 'Why use the Syriac language in the Land of Israel where either the Holy Tongue [Hebrew] or the Greek language could be used?' Rabbi Jose is reported as saying: 'Why use the Aramaic language in Babylon where the Holy Tongue or the Persian language could be used?' In point of fact scholars have noted that the Aramaic of the Babylonian Talmud is a Jewish modification of Syriac. Syriac is so called because it was the Aramaic dialect of the people who lived in Syria and has no special connection with that country any more than Babylonian Aramaic had any special connection, other than that of dialect, to the country of Babylon. The written documents in Syriac, in a script different from that of Hebrew and Aramaic, come from the Christians in Syria in the early centuries CE.

Syriac is important for comparative purposes in the study of biblical philology but is especially significant because of the Syriac translation of then Bible known as the Peshitta ('The Simple', i.e. the simple translation of the Bible), made by the Syriac Church of Edessa probably at the beginning or middle of the second century CE. The Peshitta, like the *Septuagint and other ancient versions, is used by biblical scholars for their investigations into the original biblical text, but they warn that great caution has to be exercised in relying on the Peshitta to emend the Masoretic Text (see MASORAH), since it is far from evident that the Syriac translation is necessarily based on an authentic version of the text. Nevertheless, where a text different from the Masoretic is found also in other versions, it is less precarious to use the Peshitta for a suggested emendation (and see BIBLICAL CRITICISM).

**Systematic Thinking**  The type of thinking in which diverse ideas and concepts are brought together to form a coherent whole. It is obvious to even the most casual reader that biblical thought is not of this order. The Hebrew prophets, for example, urge their people, in the name of God, to practise *justice and show *compassion but Socratic analysis of the concepts of justice and compassion are completely foreign to the biblical way of thinking in which it is taken for granted that these and similar values are good without having to use any abstract term such as 'values' for them to be substantiated. Even in the book of Proverbs, which does form a unit and was intended as such, there is no attempt at systematization. The proverbs are precisely that, a series of dynamic responses to various situations and, since human life is full of variety, hope, and frustration, it is pointless to attempt to find consistency in the book. Contradictory advice is offered in Proverbs because what is called for in one situation is unhelpful in a different situation. The book of Job is a tremendous poem on the sufferings of a righteous man but one will look in vain there for an examination of why evil and suffering should exist at all.

The same absence of systematic thought is evident in Rabbinic literature. Even the Mishnah with its six orders is not presented systematically and is more of an anthology of Rabbinic laws and ideas than an ordered presentation. Isaac Heinemann and Max Kadushin have rightly described Rabbinic thought as 'organic'; that is to say, the thought of the Talmudic *Rabbis emerges from their experience of life and their belief in the Torah without their having to engage in any philosophical defence of Jewish living in the light of the Torah. As Solomon *Schechter (*Aspects of Rabbinic Theology* (New York, 1961), 11–12) puts it:

'A great English writer has remarked that "the true health of a man is to have a soul without being aware of it; to be disposed of by impulses which he does not criticise". In a similar way the old Rabbis seem to have thought that the true health of a religion is to have a theology without being aware of it; and thus they hardly ever made—nor could they make— any attempt towards working their theology into a formal system, or giving us a full exposition of it. With God as a reality, Revelation as a fact, the Torah as a rule of life, and the hope of Redemption as a most vivid expectation, they felt no need for formulating their dogmas into a creed, which, as was once remarked by a

great theologian, is repeated not because we believe but that we may believe. What they had of theology, they enunciated spasmodically or "by impulses". Sometimes it found its expression in prayer "when their heart cried unto God"; at others in sermons or exhortations, when they wanted to emphasize an endangered principle, or to protest against an intruding heresy.'

This did not deter Schechter from painting his picture of Rabbinic theology, aware though he was that there is no such thing in the form in which he presents it, since his thinking and ours is historically conditioned to be engaged in systematically.

It was under the influence of Greek *philosophy, which came to them in Arabic garb, that the medieval thinkers tried to present their thoughts systematically and, since a good deal of their thinking had to do with the teachings of the Bible and the Talmud, they were bound to cast the ideas found in these works into a form essentially alien to their nature. The very systematization of biblical and Rabbinic thought, even when that thought was conveyed accurately (this was not always the case), was a distortion. Nevertheless, once Jewish thinkers had become accustomed to systematic thinking, there could be no turning back. This kind of thinking had become endemic to the Jewish mind as it had to the human mind in general. Even in the area of Jewish law the need for systematic presentation became imperative, as is evidenced by the great Codes of Jewish law: Maimonides' *Mishneh Torah,* Jacob ben *Asher's *Tur,* *Karo and *Isserles' *Shulḥan Arukh,* and their successors.

From the Middle Ages onwards, great works of systematization were produced on the various aspects of Jewish thought. *Bahya, Ibn Pakudah's *Duties of the Heart* is such a presentation of the theme of its title. This work is far more than a simple anthology of ethical and religious ideas. It involves rather a construction of a complete system of thought in which various themes are all brought together to produce a complete scheme. Maimonides' *Guide of the Perplexed* offers systematic advice to the 'perplexed' of the title, even though, granted the nature of the difficult problems with which the sage deals, many readers have emerged from their reading of the work more perplexed than when they began. In the area of the Kabbalah, the Zohar is in the nature of a running commentary to the Pentateuch and is consequently unsystematic, but Joseph Gikatilla's *Shaarey Orah* is a systematic exposition of the doctrine of the Sefirot and Hayyim *Vital's *Etz Ḥayyim* a similar presentation of the Lurianic Kabbalah. In Isaiah *Horowitz's *Shelah*, virtually an encyclopaedia of the Jewish religion, there is also very comprehensive treatment of Kabbalistic themes. Moses Hayyim *Luzzatto, a genius of systematization, compiled a systematic treatise on Talmudic logic, a number of such treatments of Kabbalistic themes, and his *magnum opus*, *The Path of the Upright*, a manual of holy living in which each spiritual stage recorded is made to lead on to a higher stage. The various Talmudic methodologies were intended to guide the student through the labyrinth of Talmudic argumentation. Hasidic writings are usually unsystematic, with a few exceptions such as the *Tanya* of Rabbi *Shneur Zalman of Liady and the *Tract on Ecstasy* by his son, *Dov Baer of Lubavitch.

In modern times, the majority of works on the various aspects of the Jewish religion and Jewish thought, whether in Hebrew or in other languages, are, it goes without saying, systematic in nature, their fondness for system owing much both to the great systematizers of the Middle Ages and the general tendency of Western thought.

**Szold, Henrietta** American Zionist leader and philanthropist (1860–1945). Henrietta was born in Baltimore where her father Benjamin Szold served as the Rabbi of Congregation Oheb Shalom. She was educated by her father and in private schools, became a schoolteacher, and wrote articles for the Jewish Press. Under her father's influence and that of Russian refugees who had settled in Baltimore, she became a fervent Zionist. She was the co-founder of Hadassah, the Women's Zionist organization, served on the Executive of the Jewish Agency, and in her last years was active in Youth Aliyah, the movement engaged in saving young Jews from Nazi persecution. It is not strictly correct to describe Szold as a Jewish feminist. The Jewish feminist movement did not come into existence until many years after her death. But her active participation in Zionist affairs and her prominent role in founding Hadassah at a time when it was rare for women of her background to be anything like so active in communal affairs entitle her to be called one of the pioneers of *Feminism, and her example inspired the members of the movement.

# T

**Tabernacle** The portable structure erected by the Israelites at the command of God to accompany them in their journeys through the wilderness, as told in the book of Exodus (25: 1–31: 17; 35: 1–40: 38). The Tabernacle consisted of an outer courtyard, oblong in shape, 100 cubits by 50 cubits. This enclosure consisted of all-round hangings with an opening, the entrance, at the east side. These hangings were the means of separating the sacred spot from the profane realm outside it but did not form a cover to the area within it, which was open to the sky. The hangings of the courtyard were supported by upright pillars of acacia wood, overlain with gold, secured by sockets of copper. This oblong consisted of two squares, each 50 by 50 cubits. The western square contained the Holy Place, the Sanctuary proper, at the western end of which was situated the holy of holies, divided off from the Holy Place by a curtain. A screen was placed at the entrance to the Holy Place to divide it off from the rest of the courtyard and another screen at the entrance to the courtyard. There were thus three separate entrances, each leading to a more sacred spot: the entrance to the courtyard, with a screen in front, the entrance to the Holy Place, with a screen in front, and the entrance to the Holy of Holies, with the curtain in front. Only the *priests were allowed to enter the Holy Place and no one was allowed to enter the holy of holies, except the *High Priest on *Yom Kippur.

The *Ark was placed in the holy of holies behind the curtain. In the Holy Place there was a table in the north, the *menorah in the south, and a golden altar, the altar of incense, placed in front of the curtain in front of the Ark at the entrance to the holy of holies. The table and the altar were made of wood overlain with gold but the menorah was of solid gold. In the eastern square of the courtyard were placed the wooden altar covered with copper, upon which the sacrifices were burnt and their blood sprinkled, and a laver for the washing of the hands and feet of the priests. The Holy Place and the holy of holies were draped with hangings which completely covered the whole area. There were four separate layers of hangings, one on top of the other. The innermost hanging, the one that could be seen by whoever came into the Sanctuary, was made of fine linen decorated with figures of *cherubim, as was the curtain in front of the Ark. Over the hanging of fine linen was placed a coarser hanging made of goat's hair and over this a hanging of tanned rams' skins and over this a hanging of the skins of *teḥashim*, a word of uncertain meaning, often translated as 'dolphins'. The outer hangings of leather seem to have been intended as a protection from the elements. These hangings were supported by gilded pillars of acacia wood set in silver sockets. On each of the three walls (the fourth, at the eastern side, had an opening to form the entrance) there were five gilded crossbars of acacia wood placed into ring-like holders in the uprights in order to secure the structure. The whole structure was designed to be dismantled whenever the Israelites journeyed onwards and to be set up again wherever they encamped.

There are difficulties to be faced throughout the narrative. Where, for example, did the Israelites in the wilderness find all the wood, gold, silver, and copper needed for the construction? Moreover, the measurements seem idealistic rather than practical, since it is hard to see how a real structure with these measurements could stand at all securely. Consequently, on the older critical view (see BIBLICAL CRITICISM), the Exodus account is unhistorical, an artificial reconstruction based on Solomon's Temple. But more recent scholarship has demonstrated that a number of ancient civilizations before the wilderness period did know of similar structures so that, while some of the details may well have been added at a later date, there is no reason to deny that the Israelites in the wilderness really did have a portable Tabernacle in which they offered sacrifices. Cassuto has noted that the pagan temple was the residence of the god, who was supplied with a throne, a table at which he ate, a candelabrum to give him light, a bed on which he slept, and a chest of drawers for his clothes. In the Israelite Tabernacle there was nothing so anthropomorphic as a bed and chest of drawers and the table was for the shewbread eaten by the priests. The menorah was not placed in the holy of holies since God, unlike the pagan deities, does not require any light. The Ark, containing the *tablets of stone, took the place of the throne upon which the divine presence rested. Thus the Tabernacle may indeed have owed something to the pagan temples but was transformed and adapted to monotheistic religion.

Other more recent scholars have noted that the Hebrew word used for the Tabernacle is *mishkan*, from a root meaning 'to dwell temporarily' (see SHEKHINAH, from the same root). Thus the Tabernacle, in which God resides temporally, so to speak, represents the two ideas which the philosophers refer to as as transcendence and immanence. God is beyond the universe but He comes down to 'tabernacle' there.

The Tabernacle lends itself easily to *symbolism of various kinds. The Rabbis of the Midrash noted the connection between the Tabernacle and the cosmos, and modern scholars have pointed out that words used in the account of the Tabernacle resemble closely the creation narrative at the beginning of the book of Genesis. The Tabernacle, on this view, was intended as symbolic of the cosmos: the innermost hanging with its decoration of cherubims representing the sky and the angels, God's messengers, and the structure itself the earth and all that is in it. In the account itself it is stated that the purpose of the Tabernacle was for God to take up His abode among the people: 'And let them make Me a sanctuary that I may dwell among them' (Exodus 25: 8). A later Rabbinic homily observes that the verse does not say: 'that I may dwell in it' but 'that I may dwell *among them*', to denote that the purpose of the Tabernacle was not for God to reside therein but to encourage the people to make room for God in their hearts. Throughout the history of Jewish thought, *holy places were seen either as containing somehow the

objective presence of the divine or as sacred by association.

U. Cassuto, 'The Tabernacle and its Service', in his *A Commentary on the Book of Exodus*, trans. Israel Abrahams (Jerusalem, 1967), 319–485.
Nahum M. Sarna, 'The Tabernacle', in his *The JPS Commentary: Exodus* (Philadelphia, New York, and Jerusalem, 1991), 155–237.

**Tabernacles** The autumn festival which begins on 15 Tishri and lasts for seven days, followed by the festival of *Shemini Atzeret on the eighth day in Israel (and on the ninth in the *Diaspora). The ninth day in the Diaspora is called *Simhat Torah but in Israel Simhat Torah and Shemini Atzeret are celebrated on the same day, the eighth. Thus, the Rabbis say, there are really two festivals, one following on the other, Tabernacles and Shemini Atzeret, but both came to be named as Tabernacles. The Hebrew name for Tabernacles is sukkot, and is so called after the command to dwell for seven days in the *sukkah (singular of sukkot), as a reminder of the 'booths' or 'tabernacles' in which the Israelites dwelt during their forty years' journey through the wilderness (Leviticus 23: 32–44). Since Tabernacles falls at harvest time and is also the last of the three pilgrim festivals, it is the especially joyous festival (Deuteronomy 16: 13–17). In the liturgy Tabernacles is referred to as 'the season of our joy'.

In addition to the sukkah, the precept of the 'four species' is carried out on Tabernacles (i.e. on the seven days of Tabernacles proper but not on Shemini Atzeret.) This command is given as: 'And ye shall take you on the first day the fruit of goodly trees, branches of palm-trees, and boughs of thick trees, and willows of the brook, and ye shall rejoice before the Lord your God seven days' (Leviticus 23: 40). The Rabbinic understanding of the verse, still followed universally by Jews, is that 'ye shall take' means to hold in the hand these four species. From early times the 'fruit of goodly trees' was understood to mean the etrog (citron), the 'boughs of thick trees' the myrtle. The other two species are, as stated explicitly in the verse, the palm branch (the lulav) and the willow. These four species are held in the hands, the lulav, together with three sprigs of myrtle and two of willow in the right hand and the etrog in the left hand. These four are waved upwards and downwards and in the four directions of the compass during the recital of the *Hallel.

One reason given for this waving is that it is for the purpose of dispelling harmful winds. Another reason is that it is to acknowledge God as Lord of all that is above and below and on all sides. The four species are also taken in a circuit around the synagogue while the petition Hoshanah ('Save now') is recited for a good harvest. On the seventh day seven circuits are made and hence this day is called *Hoshanah Rabbah, the 'Great Hoshnanah'.

In the Rabbinic Midrash the four species are given various symbolic interpretations. Two of the best known are the following: the straight lulav resembles the human backbone, the myrtle the eye, the willow the mouth, and the etrog the heart, all of which should combine in the worship of God. Alternatively, the lulav, which has taste (the dates) but no fragrance represents the Jew who has learning but few good deeds; the myrtle which has fragrance but no taste the Jew who has good deeds to his credit but little learning; the willow the Jew with neither taste nor fragrance; and the etrog the learned Jew rich also in good deeds. All four are combined to denote that it takes all sorts to make a Jewish community, the more learned and generous helping the others. Maimonides, in his *Guide of the Perplexed* (3. 45) treats these Midrashic interpretations as pure homiletics, valuable in themselves but far removed from the plain understanding of the rite, that it is in celebration of the harvest. This harvest motif is found in the Hoshanah prayers and in the prayer for rain on Shemini Atzeret. In the Kabbalah the four species represent various combinations of the *Sefirot.

A minor celebration is held in the evenings of the intermediate days of Tabernacles in commemoration of the *Water-Drawing ceremony in Temple times. This takes the form of gatherings in the sukkah where songs are sung and good food and drink enjoyed. In addition to the Torah and *Haftarah readings, which deal with the theme of sukkot, the four species and other matters connected with the festival (see READING OF THE TORAH). The book of *Ecclesiastes is read in many synagogues on the intermediate Sabbath of Tabernacles or on Shemini Atzeret when there is no intermediate Sabbath.

Isaac N. Fabricant, *A Guide to Sukkoth*, London, 1952.
Isaac Klein, 'Sukkot', in his *A Guide to Jewish Religious Practice* (New York, 1979), 155–73.

**Tablets of Stone** The two tablets upon which the Ten Commandments were inscribed. The book of Exodus (31: 18; 32: 15–16) tells of Moses receiving from God the 'tablets of the testimony' inscribed by 'the finger of God'. When Moses came down from the mount and saw his people worshipping the *golden calf he cast the tablets from his hands and broke them (Exodus 32: 19). Moses pleads with God to pardon the people and God tells him to hew out two further tablets upon which God will write the words that were on the first tablets (Exodus 34: 1). In an interesting homily the Rabbis observe that the theophany at *Sinai which resulted in the inscribing of the first tablets was attended by thunder and lightning (Exodus 20: 15), whereas the inscribing of the second tablets was a quiet affair, from which they conclude that the Torah, symbolized by the tablets, is more likely to find lodgement in an atmosphere of quietude and serenity than among the more spectacular events of human life. The tablets as a symbol of the Torah is also found in Ethics of the Fathers (6. 2) in a comment on the verse: 'And the tablets were the work of God,' and the writing was the writing of God, graven [*harut*] upon the tablets' (Exodus 32: 16). The word *harut* is read as if it were written *herut*, meaning 'freedom' and the conclusion is that the Torah is no unpleasant burden but provides humans with true freedom. Nevertheless, the tablets of stone do not appear in Jewish *art as a symbol of the Torah until the Middle Ages. Moreover, the conventional picture of the two tablets as joined together with a copula at the top is not a traditional Jewish picture but was adopted from representations in Christian illuminated manuscripts (see DECALOGUE).

**Tallit** The robe with which the worshipper is wrapped during prayer and hence often referred to as a 'prayer shawl', though this is not the traditional Jewish name for the garment, which was not originally associated particularly with prayer. In the book of Numbers (15: 37–40), the Israelites are commanded to put *tzitzit ('fringes') on their garments in order to remind them of God's laws. But in the book of Deuteronomy (22: 12) it is stated that these fringes have to be placed on the four corners of the garment, from which the Rabbis conclude that only four-cornered garments have to have tzitzit affixed to them. In Talmudic times people wore four-cornered garments and to these tzitzit were attached. In fact, the word tallit, of uncertain etymology, simply means a robe or a cloak (some connect the word with the Latin *stola*). The sole significance of the tallit was in the tzitzit. The tallit itself had no religious significance. The result was that in Europe in the Middle Ages, where people did not wear four-cornered garments, the precept of tzitzit was in danger of being forgotten. To prevent this Jews took it upon themselves to wear a four-cornered garment to which they would be obliged to attach the tzitzit and thus restore a precept that was in danger of vanishing from Jewish life. This special four-cornered garment was given the name tallit on the analogy of the four-cornered garments worn in ancient times. Strictly speaking, the precept of tzitzit has to be carried out for the whole of the day but since Jews could hardly go about wearing such an unusual garment as the tallit all day, the wearing of the tallit was limited to the time of the morning prayers.

In the Rabbinic tradition the precept of tzitzit applies only during the day. Consequently, the tallit is only worn during the morning prayers except on *Yom Kippur when it is worn, as a token of special reverence for the holy day, during the night service of *Kol Nidre.

Another device similar to the tallit has also been adopted by pious Jews. This is to wear under the outer garments a kind of vest with four corners to which the tzitzit are attached. This garment is worn all day and is known as the *tallit katan* ('small tallit') or the *arba kanfot* ('four corners').

According to the *Halakhah *women are exempt from the obligation to carry out those precepts that depend for their performance on a given time. Since the precept of tzitzit is binding only during the day and not during the night it follows that this is a precept from which they are exempt. Thus women have no obligation to wear the tallit and until recent years it was extremely unusual for women to wear it for prayer. Nowadays, even among some Orthodox women (see FEMINISM), there has been a strong desire to wear the tallit for prayer and many women now do so, often having a special coloured or decorated tallit in the latest fashion. Orthodox Rabbis generally disapprove of women wearing the tallit, chiefly because it is untraditional for women to do so, but others see no objection to it. In some Ashkenazi

communities unmarried men do not wear the tallit. The reason given is that the Deuteronomic verse about the wearing of a garment with fringes is followed by the verse (Deuteronomy 22: 13): 'If a man marries a women', indicating that a tallit is not to be worn until one is married. It has been remarked that the real reason is to enable the young ladies in the women's section of the synagogue to observe which young men are eligible for marriage.

The tallit is usually of wool or silk and should ideally be long enough to cover most of the body. Although many Jews in modern times wear a silk tallit that is really little more than a scarf around the neck, in more recent years the older form of a woollen tallit covering most of the body has again become the norm.

Before putting on the tallit the benediction is recited: 'Blessed art Thou, O Lord our God, King of the universe, who hast hallowed us by Thy commandments, and hast commanded us to enwrap ourselves in the fringed garment.' In the traditional *Prayer Book the following meditation before putting on the tallit is found, based on the Kabbalah: 'I am here enwrapping myself in this fringed robe, in fulfilment of the command of my Creator, as it is written in the Torah, they shall make them a fringe upon the corners of their garments throughout their generations. And even as I cover myself with the tallit in this world, so may my soul deserve to be clothed with a beauteous spiritual robe in the World to Come, in the garden of Eden.'

The ultra-Orthodox wear the tallit over the head when they recite the more important prayers. The earlier authorities are divided on the question of covering the head. Some are none too happy with a practice that might be seen as showing off, since the essential idea of covering the head in this way is for the worshipper to be lost in concentration, on his own before God, as it were. Religious one-upmanship is generally frowned upon. Some hold that only a *Talmid Ḥakham*, a man learned in the Torah, should cover his head with the tallit. The final ruling is that one should follow whatever is the local custom.

J. H. Hertz, 'Tallith', in his *The Authorised Daily Prayer Book* (London, 1947), 44–5.

**Talmid Ḥakham** 'Disciple of the wise', the name given to the scholar, especially one proficient in Talmudic and Halakhic studies since these were the main subjects of Torah *study in the traditional scheme. There is no clear evidence as to when the term *Talmid Ḥakham* was first used. The suggestion that Jewish sages, in their humility, have always spoken of themselves as 'disciples' is no doubt homiletically inspiring but it is historically unsound. The facts are that the term is not met before the second century CE. Before that time scholars were called *Ḥakhamin*, 'sages', not disciples, a term reserved for the students who had not as yet attained to great learning. But from around the second century the term is applied to the mature scholar. It has been suggested that the original term was *Talmid Ḥakhamim*, 'disciple of the sages', that is, a follower of Rabbinic Judaism who walks in the paths of the sages of old, but this is purely a conjecture. In later Jewish life the mature scholar is referred to as a *Talmid Ḥakham* (the term is in the singular, although, oddly enough, the plural form is *Talmedey Ḥakhamim*, 'disciples of sages').

The *Talmid Ḥakham* is not necessarily a Rabbi (see RABBIS). Many a *Talmid Ḥakham* throughout the ages did not occupy any Rabbinic office. He may even have shunned such an office. The *Talmid Ḥakham* owed his status to his acknowledgement as such by his peers. In Jewish life the *Talmid Ḥakham* is often contrasted with the *am ha-aretz, the man ignorant of learning. It is not unknown for a scholar to hurl the insult of *am ha-aretz* at another scholar with whom he disagrees and it is also true that some claimed the title *Talmid Ḥakham* without possessing the learning required to justify it. The ideal was retained nevertheless. Even if the numerous descriptions in the Talmud of how a *Talmid Ḥakham* was to behave are exaggerated, these set the standards for followers of the Rabbis throughout the Middle Ages and beyond.

The *Talmid Ḥakham* was expected to be scrupulous in his religious observances and to lead a high moral and ethical life. The *Shulḥan Arukh* (*Yoreh Deah*, 243: 3) rules that a *Talmid Ḥakham* who is lax in his religious observance has no greater claim to respect than 'the meanest member of the community'. The reputation of the *Talmid Ḥakham* was sufficiently high for a Talmudic teacher to say (*Berakhot* 19a): 'If you see a *Talmid Ḥakham* commit a sin by night, entertain no condemnatory thoughts about him next day, for he has certainly repented.'

The rise of the *Jüdische Wissenschaft movement and the development of modern Jewish scholarship from the nineteenth century brought about a complete reassessment of the role of the *Talmid Ḥakham*. Even those modern scholars who have acquired expertise in Talmudic studies adopt a 'scientific' approach to their studies—a critical stance towards the sources, one that is at variance with the attitude of total acceptance typical of the traditional *Talmid Ḥakham*. The modern Talmudist is generally known as a 'scholar' rather than a *Talmid Ḥakham*, though some modern scholars refuse to give up the traditional title and, of course, the traditional attitude is still preserved in the world of the *Yeshivah, where every student has the ambition to become a *Talmid Ḥakham* in the old sense.

**Talmud** The work containing the teachings of the Amoraim (see TANNAIM AND AMORAIM) of Palestine and Babylon, presented in the form of a running commentary to the Mishnah. The term Talmud is from the root *limmed,* 'to learn', and means 'teaching' or 'study'. In the Middle Ages the substitute term *Gemara was used for Talmud. There are, in reality, two Talmuds: the Palestinian and the Babylonian. The former is often called the Yerushalmi or Jerusalem Talmud, although there were no schools in Jerusalem itself. The Babylonian Talmud is referred to as the Bavli ('of Babylon').

As noted under *Mishnah, this digest of Tannaitic teachings, edited by Rabbi *Judah the Prince at the end of the second and beginning of the third century CE, is divided into six orders. These are:

1. *Zeraim*, 'Seeds' (agricultural laws).
2. *Moed*, 'Appointed Time' (Sabbath and festival laws).
3. *Nashim*, 'Women' (laws of marriage and divorce).
4. *Nezikin*, 'Damages' (torts, buying and selling, jurisprudence in general).
5. *Kodashim*, 'Sanctities' (laws of the sacrificial system in the *Temple).
6. *Tohorot*, 'Purities' (the laws of ritual contamination and the means of purification).

In addition to the Mishnah, other works containing Tannaitic teachings are quoted extensively in the two Talmuds. These works are: the *Tosefta ('Supplement' to the Mishnah); the Mekhilta ('Measure'), on the biblical book of Exodus; Sifra ('The Book'), on Leviticus, also called Torat Kohanim ('The Law of the

Priests'); and Sifre ('The Books') in Numbers and Deuteronomy. The last three are known as the Halakhic Midrashim or the Tannaitic Midrashim (see MIDRASH). There are also other Tannaitic teachings quoted in the Talmud and these, as well as the aforementioned, are all known as Baraitot (singular: Baraita; the word means 'outside', i.e. teachings not found in the Mishnah but which come from without).

Once the Mishnah had won acceptance as a canonical text, the teachers in both Palestine and Babylon devoted much of their efforts to its elucidation; hence the name Amoraim, 'Expounders' of the Mishnah and the other Tannaitic texts. The scholarly debates and discussion of the Amoraim were largely conducted in *Aramaic, although, naturally, many of the legal maxims and quotes from earlier sources were in Hebrew. The Palestinian Amoraim used the western Aramaic dialect, the Babylonians the eastern dialect, and these are the two dialects used in the Yerushalmi and the Bavli respectively.

*The Editing of the Talmud*

Around the year 400 CE the teachings, debates, and discussions that took place among the Palestinian Amoraim were drawn on to form the Palestinian Talmud, the Yerushalmi. There has been much discussion on the question of who the editors of the Yerushalmi were. There is evidence, stylistic and historical, that some sections of the Yerushalmi were edited earlier, and in a different centre, from others. The style of the Yerushalmi is, in any event, terse, even 'choppy', so that some scholars have suggested that the work never received any final redaction at all and is an incomplete, unfinished work.

A similar process is to be observed in the Babylonian Talmud, the Bavli, compiled some time around the year 500 CE (the date is very approximate). The style of the Bavli is, however, much more elaborate than that of the Yerushalmi. Apart from five tractates, the style of the Bavli is uniform, suggesting that the same editors were responsible for the whole work, with the exception of these tractates. Yet even these five tractates differ only slightly from the rest in style and vocabulary, so the impression is gained of a co-ordinated editorial activity, though one carried out in at least two different Babylonian centres. Although Palestinian Amoraim are frequently mentioned in the Bavli and Babylonian Amoraim in the Yerushalmi

(naturally so, since some of the sages of each country visited the other from time to time, carrying the teachings with them), the weight of scholarly opinion is that the editors of the Bavli did not have before them the actual text of the Yerushalmi, nor did the Palestinian editors have anything like a proto-Bavli. If the editors of either had had access to an actual text of the other, it is inconceivable that they would not have mentioned this. Here the argument from silence is very convincing.

The material in the Talmud is of two kinds: *Halakhah and *Aggadah. The Aggadah embraces everything not included in the Halakhah, the latter dealing with the laws, the rules and regulations of Jewish religious life in all its manifestations. It has been estimated that the Halakhic material comprises about two-thirds of the Bavli. This does not mean that there are two clearly delineated sections, one of Halakhah, another of Aggadah. The editors, usually by association or similarity of theme, often introduce a piece of Aggadah into a Halakhic debate and vice versa. For instance, the Bavli in tractate *Berakhot* opens with a Halakhic discussion on the times when the evening *Shema may be recited. One of the times mentioned is 'the end of the first watch'. This leads to an Aggadic statement that just as there are watches on earth there are watches in heaven at which times God deplores the fact of Israel's exile, and further Aggadic material is introduced by association until the original Halakhic theme is taken up again.

The actual term 'editors' is found neither in the Yerushalmi nor in the Bavli. Indeed, both Talmuds are completely silent on how they were put together. A few scholars have even suggested that, as with the Yerushalmi, there was no editorial process at all in the Bavli: that the material simply grew as additions were made from time to time. While the unfinished state of the Yerushalmi might just lend support to the view that this Talmud simply grew (though some editorial work is evident here as well) such an opinion is untenable for the Bavli. There is a uniform framework in the Bavli into which the words of the Amoraim are inserted and this framework is obviously the work of anonymous editors. Our major source of information for the editing of the Talmud is the famous letter of *Sherira Gaon. But this was compiled centuries after the 'close' of the Talmud so that, while containing reliable traditions, the work does not solve all the problems and, at times, reads later conditions into the Talmudic sources. A close examination of the Bavli succeeds in detecting four stages in the construction of this massive edifice. First there are the bare opinions of the Amoraim, usually quoted in Hebrew. Secondly, these opinions were used by the anonymous editors in their creation of the framework to form the Talmud. Thirdly, a number of additions can be detected, introduced after the framework was complete, and according to Sherira and all subsequent scholars, these are attributed to the Saboraim (a word of uncertain derivation but obviously connected to the Talmudic term *sevara*, 'theory', and hence the Saboraim were probably so called because they made some things clearer). Fourthly, scholars have detected a very few additions from the period of the early *Geonim.

Yet problems remain. For instance, there is no clear indication whether the Talmud was originally produced in written form or whether it was at first transmitted by word of mouth and was originally not a literary work at all. The French school in the Middle Ages, the leading exponent of which was *Rashi, held that the Mishnah was originally a purely oral composition as was the Talmud, the whole being committed to writing as late as the eighth century. Maimonides and the Spanish school generally held that the Mishnah was a written work and that the Talmud, too, was originally produced as a literary composition. The fact that there are numerous literary devices used in the framework, that it is beyond comprehension that such a gigantic, complex work could have been transmitted intact by word of mouth, and the fact that it was eventually written down on any showing, all lend the most powerful support to the view that the Bavli, at least, if not the Mishnah and the Yerushalmi, was originally a literary composition, though much of the argument would apply to the Mishnah and the Yerushalmi as well. This is not to deny that earlier strata are to be found in the Bavli in the form of units complete in themselves. Such strata can be detected in the work, but the whole seems to have been refashioned to provide a complete literary unit. The debate on this and similar matters still goes on among modern Talmudic scholars.

Another problem is why it was decided to put all the material together at the particular time when this was done. What was the reason for 'the close of the Talmud' as this was referred to in the Middle Ages, suggesting that at a certain date in the history of Jewish learning a halt was called to a continuing process which now had to be finalized? Sherira Gaon, and he is followed by all subsequent scholars, gives as the reason the persecutions to which Jews were subjected which could have resulted in them forgetting the Talmud, or rather the actual debates and so forth, unless these were compiled and recast in a complete, accessible form.

The Yerushalmi in all current editions consists of the Mishnah and the Gemara of the Yerushalmi, and the Bavli of the Mishnah and the Gemara of the Bavli. But properly speaking the Talmud Yerushalmi consists of the Gemara alone and the Talmud Bavli of the Gemara alone. (The Mishnah, of course, is a work of its own, compiled long before the Gemara.) Nevertheless, the whole is now referred to as the Talmud. Since the Mishnah is now part of the complete Talmud, and there are six orders of the Mishnah, the Talmud is often referred to as Shas (an abbreviation formed from the initial letters of Shishah Sedarim, 'Six Orders'). Thus a scholar with profound knowledge of the Talmud is spoken of as a 'baki ['expert'] in Shas'.

### Contents of the Talmud

The following list is of the tractates of the Mishnah. The letter 'J' (for Jerusalem) denotes that there is a Yerushalmi Gemara to the tractate, the letter 'B' that there is a Bavli Gemara. Where neither letter appears this denotes that there is no Gemara at all to the tractate. The name usually explains the contents of each tractate.

*Zeraim*
*Berakhot* ('Benedictions', prayers and blessings) JB.
*Peah* ('Corners' of the field, gleanings; Leviticus 19: 9–10) J.
*Demai* ('Uncertain', doubtfully tithed produce) J.
*Kilayim* ('Mixed Kinds'; Deuteronomy 22: 9–11) J.
*Sheviit* ('Sabbatical Year'; Exodus 23: 10–11) J.
*Terumot* ('Offerings', to the priests, Leviticus 22: 10–14) J.
*Maaserot* ('Tithes', Numbers 18–21) J.
*Maaser Sheni* ('Second Tithe', Deuteronomy 14: 22–6) J.
*Hallah* ('Dough Offering', Numbers 15: 17–21) J.

*Orlah* ('Uncircumcised', fruit of trees in the first three years; Leviticus 19: 23–6) J.
*Bikkurim* ('First Ripe Fruits'; Deuteronomy 26: 1–11) J.

*Moed*
*Shabbat* ('The Sabbath') JB.
*Eruvin* ('Boundaries', 'Sabbath Limits') JB.
*Pesahim* ('Passovers') JB.
*Shekalim* ('Shekels'; Exodus 30: 11–16) J only, but a version of this J in B.
*Yoma* ('The Day' of Atonement) JB.
*Sukkah* ('Tabernacles') JB.
*Betzah* ('Egg', laid on the festival and other festival laws) JB.
*Rosh Ha-Shanah* ('New Year') JB.
*Taanit* ('Fast', the laws of fasting) JB.
*Megillah* ('Scroll' of Esther, read on Purim, and other Purim laws) JB.
*Moed Katan* ('Minor Festival', the intermediate days of the festivals) JB.
*Hagigah* ('Festival Offering'; Deuteronomy 16: 16–17) JB.

*Nashim*
*Yevamot* ('Levirate Marriage; Deuteronomy 25: 5–10) JB.
*Ketubot* ('Marriage Documents') JB.
*Nedarim* ('Vows') JB.
*Nazir* ('Nazirite') JB.
*Sotah* ('Wife Suspected of Adultery'; Numbers 5: 11–31) JB.
*Gittin* ('Divorces') JB.
*Kiddushin* ('Marriages') JB.

*Nezikin*
*Bava Kama* ('First Gate', of jurisprudence) JB.
*Bava Metzia* ('Middle Gate' of same) JB.
*Bava Batra* ('Last Gate' of same) JB.
*Sanhedrin* ('Laws of Judges') JB.
*Makkot* ('Stripes', flogging as a penalty) JB.
*Shevuot* ('Oaths') JB.
*Eduyyot* ('Testimonies' of the Rabbis).
*Avodah Zarah* ('Idolatry') JB.
*Avot* ('Fathers', 'Ethics of the Fathers').
*Horayot* ('Wrong Decisions'; Leviticus 4) JB.

*Kodashim*
*Zevahim* ('Animal Sacrifices') B.
*Menahot* ('Meal Offerings') B.
*Hullin* ('Profane' meat, i.e. the dietary laws) B.
*Bekhorot* ('Firstlings'; Deuteronomy 15: 19–23) B.
*Arakhin* ('Valuations'; Leviticus 27: 1–8) B.
*Temurah* ('Substitute' offering; Leviticus 27:10) B.

*Keritut* ('Extirpations'; Leviticus 18: 29) B.
*Meilah* ('Trespass Offering'; Leviticus 5: 15–16) B.
*Tamid* ('Permanent' offering, daily offering; Numbers 28: 3–4) B.
Middot ('Measurements' of the Temple).
*Kinnim* ('Birds' Nests'; Leviticus 5: 7).

*Tohorot*
*Kelim* ('Vessels', contamination of).
*Ohalot* ('Tents', in which there is a corpse; Numbers 19).
*Negaim* ('Plagues'; Numbers 13, 14).
*Parah* ('Cow', the red heifer; Numbers 19).
*Tohorot* ('Purifications').
*Mikvaot* ('Ritual Baths', to remove contamination).
*Niddah* ('Menstruant') JB.
*Makhshirin* ('Preparing', rendering of food for contamination; Leviticus 11: 37–8).
*Zavim* ('Men with Running Issue'; Leviticus 15).
*Tevul Yom* ('Immersion on the Day'; Leviticus 22: 6–7).
*Yadayim* ('Hands', contamination of).
*Uktzin* ('Stalks' of plants, in relation to contamination).

From the table of contents it can be seen that there is no Bavli to Zeraim (except for tractate *Berakhot*) and none to Tohorot (except for *Niddah*). There is no Yerushalmi to Kodashim and none to *Tohorot* (except for a small portion of *Niddah*). There is no Bavli to *Shekalim* but, in the printed editions, a version of the Yerushalmi to this tractate is added. It is understandable that there is no Bavli to Zeraim, since the agricultural laws with which this order deals applied only in the Holy Land. *Berakhot* is the exception because this tractate deals with payers and benedictions, obviously applicable in Babylon as well. For a similar reason there is no Bavli and no Yerushalmi to Tohorot since these laws, unlike the agricultural laws, no longer applied after the destruction of the Temple, even in the Holy Land. *Niddah* is the exception, since the laws of separation of a *menstruant from her husband are of practical application even after the destruction of the Temple. It is something of a puzzle why there is a Bavli (but no Yerushalmi) to Kodashim, the bulk of which (*Hullin* is the exception) was also inapplicable after the destruction of the Temple. The reason is probably because of the Rabbinic belief that to study the laws of the sacrifices is a substitute for the sacrifices themselves offered in the Temple, but, in that case, why is there no Yerushalmi to this order? It has been argued that in the Middle Ages there did exist a Yerushalmi to Kodashim, which was later lost, but this seems extremely unlikely. (Parts of the 'lost' Yerushalmi to Kodashim appeared in print at the beginning of the twentieth century but it has now been established that these were nothing more than a clever forgery.)

*Editions*

The first complete edition of the Babylonian Talmud was printed by Daniel Bomberg (a non-Jew) in Venice between 1520 and 1523, but a number of individual tractates were printed earlier in other places, soon after the invention of printing. The pagination used in the Bomberg edition is now used in practically all subsequent editions. The best printed edition is that of the Romm publishing house in Vilna, photocopies of which are now published regularly. (A copy of the original *Vilna Shas* is now a rarity and a collector's item.) The first edition of the Yerushalmi is also that of Bomberg, dated 1523–4. The pagination of this Venice Yerushalmi is followed in the Krotoschin edition of 1866. The Romm publishing house produced a fine edition of the Yerushalmi as well as of the Bavli. The printed editions of the Bavli are in the form of opposite sides of each folio, *a* and *b*, beginning not with page 1 but with page 2 (page 1 is the title page). The printed editions of the Yerushalmi have two columns to each side. As in the printed editions of the Bavli, the Gemara is arranged to correspond to the section of the Mishnah on which it is a comment. The pagination of the Yerushalmi in the Venice and Krotoschin editions is in accordance with sections of the work as a whole, rather than the particular tractate as in the Bavli. Thus the usual way of quoting the Bavli is, for example: '*Bava Kama* 36a.' The usual method of quoting the Yerushalmi is '*Bava Kama* 4: 1', with the page and column of the Venice, Krotoschin edition in parenthesis (e.g. 4a).

The Bomberg edition of the Bavli relies on the only extant manuscript of the work, the Munich Codex dating from 1334. The Bomberg Yerushalmi relies on the Leiden manuscript written in the year 1289. There are naturally many copying errors in these manuscripts and the Bomberg printers often made printing errors, to say nothing of the fact that variant readings are found in other manuscripts and printed copies. A major activity in modern Talmudic scholarship is to try to establish a correct text on the basis of further investigation of these and other manuscripts and early printed editions but the task is fraught with difficulty and it is generally acknowledged that, at this late date, the recovery of the original texts in their entirety is impossible, which, of course, does not mean that the exercise is futile. As Rashi and other great commentators realized, many of the difficulties the student of the Talmud faces are the result of faulty texts.

There are a number of so-called minor tractates of the Talmud which now appear in printed editions of the Babylonian Talmud at the end of the order of Nezikin. These tractates were composed in the Geonic period, though the actual names and dates of the compilers are unknown. A good deal of the material in the minor tractates is found in the earlier sources but there is also much material stemming from post-Talmudic sources. The following is a list of the minor tractates with brief explanations of their contents.

*Avot de-Rabbi Nathan* is a lengthy commentary to tractate *Avot* ('Ethics of the Fathers') in which there are many elaborations of the sayings recorded in the latter work. There has been much discussion of why this treatise should have been attributed to the second-century teacher, Rabbi Nathan. Some scholars hold that the name is given to the work simply because a saying of Rabbi Nathan is recorded at the beginning of the book. But even if Rabbi Nathan is not the author, some of the material in this treatise does date from the period of the Tannaim.

*Soferim* ('Scribes'), as the name implies, deals with the laws of writing a *Sefer Torah, a *mezuzah, and *tefillin, and with kindred topics.

*Semahot* ('Joys', a euphemism for 'sorrows') deals with the laws of mourning.

*Kallah* ('Bride') deals with marriage laws and sexual conduct in general. This treatise is in two parts: the *Greater Kallah* and the *Lesser Kallah*.

*Derekh Eretz* ('The Way of the Earth', i.e. sound ethical conduct). This, too, is in two parts: the *Greater Derekh Eretz* and the *Lesser Derekh Eretz*.

The following seven minor tractates are really collections of laws found in the Talmudic sources but arranged in the form of a Code of law, that is, with the material presented in an ordered fashion: *Gerim* ('Proselytes'); *Kutim* ('Samaritans'); *Avadim* ('Slaves'); *Sefer Torah*; *Tefillin*; *Tzitzit*; and *Mezuzah*.

## Commentaries to the Talmud

Throughout the ages commentaries were written on the Bavli and, to a much lesser extent, on the Yerushalmi. Here are mentioned only the main, standard commentaries which appear side by side with the text in the Romm editions of the Bavli and the Yerushalmi. (The Venice, Krotoschin edition of the Yerushalmi has only the bare text without commentaries.) Rashi's running commentary to the majority of the tractates of the Bavli is printed on the inside of the page. The comments of the *Tosafot are printed on the outside of the page. These two commentaries became so much part of the Talmud that students of the Bavli called themselves students of Gefat, an abbreviation, after the initial letters, of *Ge*mara, *Pi*rush ('Commentary', of Rashi) and *To*sefot. To these are added in the Romm edition other commentaries and super-commentaries. The two standard commentaries printed together with the text of the Yerushalmi are the *Korban Ha-Edah* of David Fraenkel of Berlin (1704–62; Fraenkel was, incidentally, the teacher of Moses *Mendelssohn) and the *Peney Moshe* of Moses Margolies of Kaidan in Lithuania (d. 1780). There is a host of commentaries on individual tractates of the Talmud and even on individual sections of certain tractates. These are printed as separate works. Students have come to know which commentator is especially helpful as an aid to the study of a particular tractate. There are a number of works on Talmudic methodology which seek to explain the technical terms used in the Talmud, the Talmudic forms of argument, and other such matters.

## Attitudes to the Talmud

Christian denunciations of the Talmud in the Middle Ages were based on the supposedly adverse comments found in the work on Christianity and Christians. In Paris in the year 1242, it is reliably reported, twenty-four wagon-loads of books, among them many copies of the Talmud, were confiscated and later destroyed and there were burnings of the Talmud in other places, which explains why only a single manuscript of the complete Bavli, the Munich Codex, is extant. In point of fact the references to Christianity in the Talmud are scanty and pure fancy, since the Babylonian Jews had no contacts with Christians and they obtained their information only at second and third hand and even then in vague form. But Christian accusations, justified or not, caused Jewish copyists and later printers to exercise their own *censorship of the Talmud, omitting the few references to Christianity (these were later collected and published as a separate small volume) and substituting such 'innocent' terms as 'Egyptian' or 'Sadducee' for the original goy, 'Gentile'.

The *Karaites rejected the Talmud as they did the doctrine of the *Oral Torah on which it is based. The Geonim were much concerned with refuting the accusations of the Karaites that, for instance, the Talmud contains grossly anthropomorphic and other inferior conceptions of God. Reform Judaism, in the early days of the movement, had a similar negative attitude towards the Talmud, one that was softened to a considerable degree in the later history of Reform. It was not that the Talmud was considered to be valueless in itself, only that the Reformers no longer saw the Talmud as the source of authority for Jewish practice. *Holdheim summarized the classical Reform attitude when he said: 'The Talmud was right in its day and I am right in mine.'

Within the Rabbinic camp the Talmud was the main subject of *study, the supreme religious duty to study the Torah being expressed by scholars without number in the mastery of the Talmudic texts. Probably in reaction to the Karaite rejection of the Talmud, the Talmudic *Rabbis came to be designated as Ḥazal (an abbreviation of the Hebrew for 'Our Sages of blessed memory') and, in many circles, came to be regarded as infallible authorities on every topic which they considered. Maimonides' statement was accepted that the Babylonian Talmud has been adopted by the whole of Jewry as the supreme *authority in Jewish law so that 'to it [the Talmud] one must not add and from it one must not diminish'. For all that, many teachers in the Middle Ages, while accepting that the Talmud is the final court of appeal in Jewish law, did not feel themselves bound by every statement in the Talmud on such matters as medicine, astronomy, and even on Jewish history (see ROSSI). Maimonides' categorical statement only applied to the laws of the Talmud and he rejected the *magic and superstition found there as well as the belief in *astrology. Some Jewish commentators to the Bible like Abraham *Ibn Ezra often preferred what they considered the plain meaning of the text over the Midrashic interpretations found in the Talmud and the Midrash except where issues of Jewish practice were involved.

In Jewish law the opinions of the Bavli came to be accepted over those of the Yerushalmi. The main reason for this preference is that the Geonim in Babylon saw themselves as the successors of the Babylonian Amoraim, so that the Bavli became 'our Talmud'. As a result of the Geonic preference this became the normal attitude among the later codifiers, although reliance on the Yerushalmi in certain circumstances is certainly not unknown. This is the reason why the study of the Yerushalmi was engaged in to a much lesser extent than that of the Bavli.

The Talmud has been studied by modern scholars, Jewish and non-Jewish, for the light it throws on the customs, dress, architecture, languages, philosophy, religion, and ethics of the Hellenistic world. As Marcus Jastrow remarks in the preface to his great dictionary of the Talmud and kindred literature:

'The subjects of this literature are as unlimited as are the interests of the human mind. Religion and ethics, exegesis and homiletics, jurisprudence and ceremonial laws, ritual and liturgy, philosophy and science, medicine and magic, astronomy and astrology, history and geography, commerce and trade, politics and social problems, all are represented there, and reflect the mental condition of the Jewish world in its seclusion from the outer world, as well as in its contact with the same whether in agreement or in opposition.'

Louis Jacobs, *Structure and Form in the Babylonian Talmud* (Cambridge, 1991).
Moses Mielziner, *Introduction to the Talmud* (New York, 1968).
Adin Steinsaltz, *The Talmud* (New York, 1989).
H. L. Strack and G. Stemberger, *Introduction to the Talmud and Midrash*, trans. Markus Bockmuehl (Edinburgh, 1991).

**Tam, Rabbenu** The name given to Jacob ben Meir (1100–71), the foremost French authority of the Middle Ages. The name is based on Genesis 25: 27: 'Jacob was a mild man [*ish tam*],

dwelling in tents', interpreted in the Rabbinic tradition to mean that Jacob was a 'perfect' man, dwelling in the tents of the Torah; hence this famous teacher is known universally as Rabbenu Tam, 'Our Teacher the Perfect One'. A daughter of the great French sage, *Rashi, married Rabbi Meir of Ramerupt and Tam was the youngest of their three sons; the other two were Rabbi Samuel ben Meir (*Rashbam) and Rabbi Isaac ben Meir (Ribam). Tam studied under his father, his much older brother Rashbam, and Jacob ben Samson, a pupil of Rashi, eventually to become the acknowledged spiritual leader of French Jewry and the most outstanding contributor to the *Tosafot glossses to the Talmud.

Tam was born in Ramerupt, northern France, and lived there for the greater part of his life. As a financier and wine-merchant, Tam acquired much wealth and had close, often strained, relations with the Christian noblemen of his day. During the Second Crusade, the mob invaded his home, stabbed him in the head, and would have killed him if not for the intervention of a Christian nobleman who promised the attackers that he would arrange for the Rabbi to be converted to Christianity, a promise he had, of course, no intention of keeping. Tam's experiences are reflected in his opinions, found in the Tosafot, on the correct attitude Jews ought to adopt with regard to Christianity and Christians. There is no doubt that Tam, like the other French scholars, thought Christianity to be an idolatrous faith, but he tried to promote better relations with Christians, demonstrating, for instance, that some of the Talmudic regulations against social intercourse with pagans did not apply to Christians.

Tam established a *Yeshivah in Ramerupt, teaching the Torah to scores of distinguished Talmudists. (The report that each of Tam's students was a particular expert in a chosen tractate of the Talmud is now seen to be legendary.) Tam's fame spread beyond France. Questions were addressed to him from other parts of the Jewish world and he was known as far as Spain as a great Halakhist, teacher, and liturgical poet, corresponding with Abraham *Ibn Ezra, who visited Tam during his stay in France. Tam's main work is the *Sefer Ha-Yashar*, an influential compendium of Jewish law and Talmudic notes, often confused with a different *Sefer Ha-Yashar*, a moralistic work erroneously fathered on him.

There is no doubt that Tam had an autocratic nature, imposing his authority on the communities under his guidance and brooking no opposition. He saw his role as in some ways the leader of his generation and said so, issuing such ordinances (see SYNODS) as that once a bill of divorce has been given it is forbidden for anyone to cast doubts on its validity. Although he had no use for some popular customs that had crept into Jewish life he defended others with all the force of his powerful personality. The attempt by some nineteenth-century scholars to see Tam as a forerunner of the liberal approach to Rabbinic Judaism is purely apologetic and misguided, as Urbach, in his book on the Tosafot, has demonstrated.

Commenting on the relevant Talmudic passage, Tam took issue with his grandfather, Rashi, on the correct order of the paragraphs in the *tefillin. As a result, some Jews today wear two pairs of *tefillin*, those of Rashi and those of Rabbenu Tam. The *Shulḥan Arukh* rules that only a man renowned for his saintliness is allowed to wear the *tefillin* of Rabbenu Tam; otherwise it is simply a parade of piety that should be discouraged. Nevertheless, the custom took root and nowadays all Hasidim and many other strictly Orthodox Jews do wear the *tefillin* of Rabbenu Tam in addition to those of Rashi. That Rabbenu Tam could have disagreed with his grandfather Rashi in this and in other matters shows, as many authorities have noted, that the obligation to honour a parent or a grandparent does not include the duty to bow to their opinions in matters of Torah learning.

Hersh Goldwurm, '"R' Yaakov ben Meir', in his *The Rishonim* (New York, 1982), 127–9.

**Tammuz, fast of** The public fast on 17 Tammuz. The Mishnah (*Taanit* 4: 6) lists five calamities which took place on this date as a result of which the fast was ordained. On this day Moses broke the *tablets of stone; the daily offering ceased; the wall of Jerusalem were breached; a general named Apostomus (exact identity unknown) burnt the Torah; and an idol was set up in the Sanctuary. There is considerable doubt about the meaning of these events, but clearly most of them have to do with the destruction of the Temple. The three weeks from the Fast of Tammuz to the Ninth of *Av (Tisha Be-Av) are weeks of mourning during which no marriages are celebrated and observant Jews do not listen to music. According to the sources, the Fast of Tammuz (see FAST DAYS) lasts only from early morning until sunset, unlike the fasts of Tisha Be-Av and *Yom Kippur which last from sunset to sunset. With the establishment of the State of Israel some (even Orthodox) Jews do not observe the Fast of Tammuz, but many Orthodox Jews retain the tradition.

Chaim Pearl, *Minor Festivals and Fasts* (London, 1963).

**Tannaim and Amoraim** The Talmudic *Rabbis, the teachers whose views are recorded in the Talmudic literature. Both these terms are also found in the Talmud in connection with learning activity. In this context, a Tanna ('rehearser' or 'teacher') was a functionary who rehearsed opinions and statements of the teachers of the first two centuries CE; an Amora ('expounder') was a different functionary, whose job it was to explain to the assembly the words of a contemporary sage, the latter making only a series of brief rulings which the Amora would then explain in detail. But, in the later passages of the Talmud, both these names were adopted for the two sets of teachers mentioned in the first sense above. The name Tanna was given to the teachers who flourished in Palestine in the first two centuries CE and whose views appear in the Mishnah and other literature from this period. The name Amora was given to the expounders of the Tannaitic teachings. The Amoraim belong both to Palestine and Babylon down to the end of the fifth century CE. Thus, in the most common usage, the Tannaim are the Palestinian teachers of the first two centuries and the Amoraim the Palestinian and Babylonian teachers from the third to the fifth centuries CE. In the discussions of the Babylonian Talmud, for example, where two different teachers are referred to in the Mishnah, the first is called the Tanna Kama ('the first Tanna').

The general principle followed in the Talmudic arguments is that an Amora is not at liberty to disagree in matters of law with a Tanna unless he can quote another Tanna in support. This principle was no doubt established after the Mishnah had acquired canonical status, so that teachers belonging to the Mishnaic period, whether or not their opinions were actually recorded in the Mishnah, came to enjoy a much greater degree of *authority. Thus one finds frequently in the Talmud an objection of the sort: how can Amora *A* say such-and-such, since a Tanna has said otherwise? The reply is either that the Tanna said no such thing, his statement being reinterpreted, or that the Amora can produce the opinion of another Tanna who takes issue with the first.

Although the Tannaim enjoy greater authority than the Amoraim, the actual decisions in Jewish law are not rendered on the basis of Tannaitic statement in themselves but on these statements as expounded by the Amoraim.

Of the many Tannaim and Amoraim it is possible here to list only some of the more prominent, those whose names occur very frequently in the literature.

*Tannaim*

The members of the schools of *Hillel and *Shammai; Rabban Johanan ben *Zakkai; Rabban *Gamaliel I and II; Rabbi *Eliezer; Rabbi *Joshua; Rabbi *Ishmael; Rabbi *Akiba and his disciples: Rabbi *Meir, Rabbi Judah, Rabbi Jose, and Rabbi *Simeon ben Yohai; Rabbi *Judah the Prince, editor of the Mishnah, and his disciples: Rabbi Hiyya, Rabbi Hoshayah, and Rabbi Hanina.

*Palestinian Amoraim*

Rabbi Joshua ben Levi; Rabbi Johanan; Rabbi Simeon ben Lakish (usually referred to as Resh Lakish); Rabbi Eleazar ben Pedat; Rabbi Simlai; Rabbi Abbahu; Rabbi Ammi; Rabbi Assi; Rabbi Zera; Rabbi Jeremiah.

*Babylonian Amoraim*

*Rav and Samuel; Rav Huna (the Babylonians did not have the full title 'Rabbi'); Rav Hisda; Rav Judah ben Ezekiel; Rav Nahman; Rav Sheshet; *Abbaye and Rava; Rav Pappa; Rav Ashi and Ravina. The last two are said (in the *Letter* of *Sherira Gaon) to have been the editors of the Babylonian Talmud but this cannot be taken too literally since both feature as 'heroes' of the work and are mentioned in the third person, apart from the fact that there are clearly to be detected Talmudic passages that obviously derive from a later period.

The problem of dating the various Tannaim and Amoraim is notoriously difficult, given the paucity of biographical detail and the legendary nature of some of the details that are given.

H. L. Strack and G. Stemberger, 'The Most Important Rabbis,' in their *Introduction to the Talmud and Midrash*, trans. Markus Bockmuehl, (Edinburgh, 1991), 69–110.

**Targum** 'Translation', of the Bible from the Hebrew into other languages, especially *Aramaic. In the ancient synagogue during the *reading of the Torah, there was a verse-by-verse translation into Aramaic by a Meturgeman ('dragoman', 'interpreter'). From the warnings that the Meturgeman had to keep to the text and not introduce into it meanings of his own, it would seem that, at first, the Meturgeman supplied his own translation. Eventually, however, standard, official Targumim came to be used. One of these, the Targum Onkelos, was considered to be the most authentic and is now printed together with the original Hebrew text in most editions of the *Pentateuch. (Two other Targumim, that of Pseudo-Jonathan and Targum Yerushalmi (of Jerusalem) are also printed in the better editions, as are Targumim to the rest of the Bible.)

A problem regarding the Targum Onkelos has been much discussed in modern scholarship. According to the Babylonian Talmud (*Megillah* 3a) this Targum was made in the second century CE, by Onkelos, a convert to Judaism, under the guidance of Rabbi *Eliezer and Rabbi *Joshua. But in the parallel passage in the Jerusalem Talmud, it is stated that the convert Aquilas made the translation under the guidance of Rabbi Eliezer and Rabbi Joshua. Moreover, the translation by Aquilas is in Greek. The problem is usually solved by postulating that the Babylonian Talmud has applied the details regarding the Greek translation by Aquila to the Aramaic translation by Onkelos. In any event, the present text of Onkelos is a later compilation with many additions. Targum Onkelos is largely a literal translation of the text, although its tendency is to paraphrase anthropomorphic statements so as to make them more acceptable, for example, by using expressions like 'the word of God' instead of 'God'. For instance, the verse: 'the God of thy father, who shall help thee' (Genesis 29: 25) is rendered by Onkelos: 'the word of the God of thy father, shall be thy help'. The verse: 'And the Lord came down to see the city' (Genesis 11: 5) is rendered by Onkelos as: 'The Lord revealed Himself to punish those who built the city.' Similarly, the verse: 'I will go down now and see' (Genesis 18: 21) is rendered: 'I will reveal Myself and judge.' Occasionally, Onkelos gives a Midrashic explanation to the text. For instance in the verse: 'the voice of thy brother's blood crieth unto Me' (Genesis 4: 10) the word for 'blood' is in the plural, literally 'bloods'. This leads Onkelos to paraphrase the verse as: 'the voice of the blood of the seed that would have come from thy brother crieth unto Me'. Rashi, in the commentary to the verse, quotes a Rabbinic Midrash to the same effect. *Rashi often quotes the Targum Onkelos in his commentary to the Torah.

Once Jews in Western lands had little or no knowledge of Aramaic the institution of the Meturgeman came to an end. Nowadays, everywhere in the Jewish world, the reading of the Torah consists of the Hebrew text alone. Yet the Targum Onkelos has acquired a great sanctity of its own. On the basis of a Talmudic statement (*Berakhot* 8a–b) that a man is obliged to read for himself twice during the week together with the Targum the weekly portion read in the synagogue, it is still the practice of pious Jews to read twice in their homes each week the sidra ('portion') of the week, together with Targum Onkelos.

In modern biblical scholarship, the Targumim are used for the purpose of establishing the correct text. But it is generally acknowledged that where the Targum differs from the Masoretic Text (the current text of the Bible, see MASORAH), this does not necessarily mean that the Targumim really preserve a better text. They might simply be paraphrasing the text. But, when used in conjunction with other ancient versions such as the *Septuagint, the Targumim can he helpful for the purpose of textual emendations. Where, as happens occasionally, Targumic interpretations differ from those found in the Rabbinic literature, attempts are made by Rabbinic scholars to discover whether there are really different traditions. Needless to say, both traditional and modern scholars have used the Targumim in their attempts to elucidate the meaning of Scripture.

Otto Eissfeldt, 'The Targums', in *The Old Testament: An Introduction*, trans. Peter R. Ackroyd (Oxford, 1966), 696–8.

**Tashlikh** The ceremony in which sins are symbolically cast into water, after the verse: 'Thou wilt cast [*ve-tashlikh*] their sins into the depths of the sea' (Micah 7: 19). The *tashlikh* ceremony, apart from its intrinsic interest, has been much discussed in connection with the observance of *customs in general where these appear to have originated in *magic and superstition. *Tashlikh* is observed on the first day of

*Rosh Ha-Shanah (the second if the first day falls on the Sabbath). Jews repair to a river or the sea to cast therein their sins, while reciting scriptural verses (Micah 7: 18–20; Psalms 118: 5–8 and 130; Isaiah 11: 9). In some rites Kabbalistic passages and prayers are also recited. A further custom is for the garments to be shaken as a token of total cleansing by casting away every vestige of sin.

The *tashlikh* ceremony is not found in any of the ancient sources, although *Isserles (*Shulḥan Arukh, Oraḥ Ḥayyim*, 584: 2) records it as a custom to be followed. The earliest reference is by Jacob Moellin, the Maharil (d. 1425), in his compendium of customs observed by German Jews. Moellin, obviously seeking to provide a reason for a custom that had been established before his day, states, in addition to the plain idea behind the ceremony, that, according to a Rabbinic Midrash, when Abraham was on his way to the *Akedah, *Satan assumed the form of a river to prevent him from carrying out the terrible deed. Abraham was undeterred, and his descendants go to a river on the first day of the New Year in order to remind themselves of his spirit of self-sacrifice which they are determined to follow in their own lives. The river, it is said, should ideally contain fish, either to demonstrate that we are like fish caught in the nets or because fish always have open eyes so that they are a reminder that the Guardian of Israel never sleeps and constantly cares for His people. In a city where there is no access to a river or the sea the ceremony is carried out, as in Jerusalem, at a well. In another work of Isserles, repairing to the water is said to be a reminder of the waters in the creation narrative in Genesis, appropriate for the day on which the Jew hails God as Creator.

Since the sources for *tashlikh* are all very late, a number of scholars have seen the ceremony as a late superstition which has entered Judaism. Lauterbach, on the other hand, in his lengthy treatment of the subject, sees in *tashlikh* very early echoes of ancient beliefs, as in Greek mythology, that divinity is especially present in streams and rivers. Whatever its origin, *tashlikh*, like many an original pagan custom, has been adopted by giving it a Jewish interpretation. Nevertheless, a number of Rabbis have been uneasy about the observance of *tashlikh*. It is widely reported that Elijah, *Gaon of Vilna did not go to the river for *tashlikh* and this has remained the attitude of many of his followers.

*Tashlikh*, an Ashkenazi custom, was not observed by the earlier Sephardim but, nowadays, the Sephardim in most places have adopted the custom. Some Reform Jews, too, now observe *tashlikh* as a colourful ceremony, although classical Reform was opposed to *tashlikh* and similar customs with an apparently superstitious origin.

Avrohom Chaim Feuer, *Tashlich* (New York, 1989).

Jacob Z. Lauterbach, 'Tashlik', in his *Rabbinic Essays* (Cincinnati, 1961), 299–433.

**Tattoo** The prohibition of tattooing is stated in the verse: 'You shall not make gashes in your flesh for the dead, or incise any marks on yourselves, I am the Lord' (Leviticus 19: 28). Commentators explain the prohibition on the grounds that it was an idolatrous practice of the ancient pagans to incise in the skin the name of their god. In the Hebrew of the verse a tattoo is called *ketovet kaaka*, literally, 'writing of kaaka'. The last word is not found anywhere else in the Bible but clearly some kind of tattoo is meant. Since the verse speaks of 'writing', the Mishnah (*Makkot* 3: 6) states that the law only applies when words or letters are incised. Another opinion in the Mishnah is that the prohibition refers only to the tattooing of the name of a pagan god. Nevertheless, according to Rabbinic law, every form of tattooing is forbidden and very few Jews have tattoos of any description.

**Tefillin** The cube-shaped black leather boxes, containing four scriptural passages, attached to the head and arm and worn during the morning prayers. It is purely coincidental that the word *tefillin* so closely resembles the word for prayer, *tefillah*, since, although eventually the *tefillin* were only worn for the morning prayer, in Talmudic times they were worn all day and had no special association with prayer. As Maimonides (*Tefillin*, 4. 25–6) puts it: 'Great is the sanctity of *tefillin* for as long as the *tefillin* are upon man's head and arm, he is humble and God-fearing and is not drawn after frivolity and idle talk, and does not have evil thoughts, but directs his heart to words of truth and righteousness. Therefore a man should try to have them on him all day . . . Even though they should be worn all day it is the greater obligation to wear them during prayer.' In point of fact some few extremely pious individuals, even in post-Talmudic times, did wear *tefillin* all day and this seems to have been Maimonides' own

practice. But the vast majority of Jews only wear *tefillin* during the morning prayer.

The etymology of *tefillin* is uncertain but possibly is connected either with a Hebrew root meaning 'to attach' or with a root meaning 'to distinguish'. If this is correct, *tefillin* mean either 'attachments' to the body or else the means whereby the Jew is distinguished from *Gentiles. *Tefillin* is usually translated in English as 'phylacteries'. This is based on the New Testament Greek: 'But all their works they do to be seen of men; they make broad their phylacteries' (Matthew 23: 5). This passage, hostile to the *Pharisees, uses the Greek word, from which the English is derived, meaning 'things which guard'; in other words, the *tefillin* are a kind of amulet to offer protection against the demonic powers; whereas in all the Jewish sources the *tefillin* serve, like the *tzitzit, as a reminder of God's laws.

*What are the* Tefillin?

In four Pentateuchal passages it is stated that certain words should be on the hand and between the eyes. Many commentators, including *Rashbam, hold that the plain meaning of these passages is that the words of the Torah should be constantly in mind, as in the verses: 'Set them as a seal upon thy heart, as a seal upon thine arm' (Song of Songs 8: 6) and 'Let not kindness and truth forsake thee; bind them about thy neck, write them on the table of thy heart' (Proverbs 3: 3). The *Karaites understood the passages in this figurative way and did not wear *tefillin*. But very early on, as can be seen from the reference in the New Testament, Jews understood the passages in a literal sense and wore these four sections on the head and the arm, the words being those in the sections themselves. These are the *tefillin*, although, undoubtedly, they have developed over the years to assume the form they now have. The following is a brief description of what *tefillin* are now and how they are worn.

The *tefillin* consist of two cube-shaped leather boxes, one worn on the head, the other on the arm, with leather straps fixed to them for attaching them to the head and the arm. Into these boxes, known as *batim*, 'houses', the four passages, written by hand, are inserted. The hand *tefillin* (in the Rabbinic tradition the 'hand' here means the arm) contains all four sections written on a single strip of parchment. In the head *tefillin* there are four separate compartments, one for each of the four. The four sections are: 1. Exodus 13: 1–10; 2. Exodus 13: 11–16; 3. Deuteronomy 6: 4–9; 4. Deuteronomy 11: 12–21. Although the box (*bayit*, 'house', singular of *batim*) of the head *tefillin* has to be in the form of an exact square (in the part into which the sections are inserted; this part rests on a larger base), it is divided into four compartments for the insertion of the sections, care being taken that these should not be separated from one another in such a way as to interfere with the square shape. The box of the hand *tefillin* consists a single compartment into which all four sections, written on a single strip, are inserted. The boxes have to be completely black as well as square-shaped. Black straps are inserted into each of the *batim*. The straps of the head *tefillin* are made to form a knot that will be at the back of the neck when the *tefillin* are worn. This knot is in the shape of the letter *dalet*. The strap of the hand *tefillin* is attached to the *bayit* to form another knot shaped in the form of the letter *yod*. The letter *shin* is worked into the leather of the head *tefillin*, a three-pronged *shin* on the right side of the wearer and a four-pronged *shin* on the left (this is probably because of uncertainties as to how this letter should be formed). We now have the three letters *shin*, *dalet*, *yod*, in the *tefillin*, forming the word *Shaddai*, one of the divine names. (Some have the letter *mem* instead of the *dalet* as the shape of the knot and the three letters then form the word *shemi*, 'My name'.) All these matters are attended to by the manufacturers of the *tefillin*, who arrange for the writing to be done by a competent scribe and for the sections to be inserted into the *batim*, which are then sewn up and the straps inserted. Naturally, pious Jews will only buy a set of *tefillin* from a reliable, trustworthy merchant. *Tefillin* often come with a guarantee from a Rabbi that they have been properly prepared.

The procedure for putting on the *tefillin* is as follows. The hand *tefillin* is taken out of the bag in which the *tefillin* are reverentially kept, and placed on the upper part of the left arm, and the benediction recited: 'Blessed art Thou, O Lord our God, King of the universe, who hast hallowed us by Thy commandments, and hast commanded us to put on the *tefillin*.' The knot is then tightened and the strap wound seven times around the arm. The head *tefillin* is then taken out of the bag, placed loosely on the head, and the further benediction recited: 'Blessed art

Thou, O Lord our God, King of the universe, who hast hallowed us by Thy commandments and hast given us command concerning the precept of *tefillin*.' The head *tefillin* are then tightened round the head so that the *bayit* rest in the middle of the head above the forehead and where the hair begins. The strap of the hand *tefillin* is then wound thrice around the middle finger while the verses (from Hosea 2: 21–2) are recited: 'And I will betroth thee unto me for ever; yea, I will betroth thee unto me in righteousness, and in judgement, and in loving-kindness, and in mercy: I will even betroth thee unto me in faithfulness: and thou shalt know the Lord.'

In the Rabbinic tradition, the *tefillin* are to be worn on 'the weaker hand' (perhaps the idea here is to symbolize that it is the weaker side of human nature that requires to be strengthened by observing the precept). For this reason a left-handed man wears the *tefillin* on his right arm. The *tefillin* are not worn on the Sabbath and festivals. The reason given is that these are described as a 'sign', and so are *tefillin*. When these 'signs' are present there is no need for *tefillin* to be worn. *Tefillin* are worn only during the day, not at night. Consequently, *tefillin* is one of those precepts dependent on time from which \*women are exempt. There are one or two references to women wearing *tefillin* even though they are exempt, but this is extremely rare. Even women who nowadays do wear a \*tallit do not normally wear *tefillin*. A minor is not obliged to wear *tefillin* and the usual practice is for a boy to begin to wear them just before his \*Bar Mitzvah.

### Rashi and Rabbenu Tam

In the Middle Ages, there was a famous debate on the order in which the sections are to be inserted in the *tefillin* between \*Rashi and his grandson, Rabbenu \*Tam. According to Rashi the order is, starting from the right of the one facing the wearer, that in which the sections appear in the Torah, namely, as above: (1), (2), (3), and (4). But according to Rabbenu Tam our section (3) is placed after our (4) so that (3), which contains the \*Shema, is on the outside, namely, the extreme left of the one facing the wearer. Since the *tefillin* have to be written in the order in which the sections are in the Torah, then according to Rabbenu Tam, the scribe, when writing the hand *tefillin*, writes (3) first at the end of the script, leaving a space in which he then writes (4). All this is extremely complicated but, according to the Talmud, where the sections are inserted in the wrong order the *tefillin* are invalid. Thus 'Rashi's' *tefillin* are invalid according to Rabbenu Tam and 'Rabbenu Tam's' invalid according to Rashi. In practice Rashi's order is followed. (Maimonides' order is the same as Rashi's.) But pious Jews, including all Hasidim, wear two pairs of *tefillin*, those in accordance with Rashi and those in accordance with Rabbenu Tam. Some wear the sets together at the same time but the usual practice among the pious is to wear Rashi's *tefillin* first and Rabbenu Tam's at the end of the service. It is of interest that at *Qumran, *tefillin* were found which seem to have followed both systems, showing that the debate goes back to ancient times. The whole episode is worthy of mention as an illustration of the principle that, normally, where there is a doubt in matters of Jewish ritual, the actual law follows current practice.

*The Significance of* Tefillin *and Observance*

The Talmudic Rabbis wax eloquent on the value of *tefillin*. The Talmud (*Rosh Ha-Shanah* 17a) defines a 'sinner in Israel with his body' as 'a skull that does not wear *tefillin*'. Yet, even in the Geonic period, there was a certain laxity in the observance of *tefillin*. Some of the *Geonim, and they were followed by the *Tosafot (to the passage) observed that the Talmudic denunciation applies only to those who refuse to wear *tefillin* out of irreligious reasons, but if a man does not wear *tefillin* because he believes he has not attained to the purity of body and mind required for them to be worn, he is no sinner at all. It is known that Rabbi Moses of Coucy travelled through Spain and France in the year 1237 on a preaching mission in which he urged the Jews of these lands to wear *tefillin*, arguing that sinners require all the more this 'sign' of allegiance to the divine law. The result has been that Orthodox Jews, although they no longer wear *tefillin* all day, since they do not believe they have the degree of purity so to do, do wear them for prayer, and *tefillin* have become one of the indications of Orthodoxy. The majority of Reform Jews, however, do not wear *tefillin*, interpreting, as did the Karaites, the references to binding on the arm and head as purely figurative. Conservative Jews do wear *tefillin*, like the Orthodox.

Over the ages, the *tefillin* were given various symbolic interpretations. For instance, the head *tefillin*, the hand *tefillin*, and the wearing of the latter opposite the heart was all taken to suggest that head, heart, and hand must all be brought into play in the service of God. That there are four sections on the head *tefillin* and only one in the hand *tefillin* has been understood to convey the idea that opinions may differ but Jewish practice should be uniform. That the hand *tefillin* have to be covered with the shirt-sleeve while the head *tefillin* are uncovered has been understood as suggesting that a man's religious emotions and his benevolent deeds should be private to him and not paraded in order to demonstrate his piety and generosity. In the Kabbalah various mystical ideas are read into the *tefillin*: that, for example, they represent on earth details of the *Sefirot on high.

Under the influence of the Kabbalah the following meditation appears in many prayer books for recital before putting on the *tefillin* (*Hertz Prayer Book, p. 46):

'I am now intent upon the act of putting on the Tefillin, in fulfilment of the command of my Creator, who hath commanded us to lay the Tefillin, as it is written in the Torah, And thou shalt bind them for a sign upon thine hand, and they shall be for frontlets between thine eyes. Within these Tefillin are placed four sections of the Torah, that declare the absolute unity of God, and remind us of the miracles and wonders which He wrought for us when He brought us forth from Egypt, even He who has power over the highest and the lowest to deal with them according to His will. He hath commanded us to lay the Tefillin upon the hand as a memorial of His outstretched arm; opposite the heart, to indicate the duty of subjecting the longings and designs of our heart to His service, blessed be He; and upon the head over against the brain, thereby teaching that the mind, whose seat is in the brain, together with all senses and faculties, is to be subjected to His service, blessed be He. May the effect of the precept thus observed to be to extend to me long life with sacred influences and holy thoughts, free from every approach, even in imagination, to sin and iniquity. May the evil inclination not mislead or entice us, but may we be led to serve the Lord as it is in our hearts to do. Amen.'

Samuel S. Cohon, 'Tefillin', in his *Essays in Jewish Theology* (Cincinnati, 1987), 335–54.
Hyman E. Goldin, 'The Tefillin', in his *Code of Jewish Law* (New York, 1961), i. 26–34.

**Teitelbaum Family** Hungarian family, the members of which served as town Rabbis as well as Hasidic masters. The founder of this Hasidic dynasty, Moses Teitelbaum (1750–1841), Rabbi of Ujhely and author of Halakhic *Responsa, although distant from *Hasidism at first, became a disciple of the Hasidic master known as the 'Seer' of Lublin. His work in the Hasidic vein, *Yismaḥ Moshe* ('Let Moses Rejoice') is acknowledged by all Hasidic groups as a classical work in the *genre*, but as a late-comer to Hasidism, Teitelbaum displays all the confidence, not to say aggression, of the convert. For instance, in his comment to the verse: 'If you do well, lift your head up' (Genesis 4: 7) he remarks that, for all the value of humility, there are times when a man is required to be self-assertive, otherwise he will despair of his ability to achieve anything worth while in God's service. He understands the verse to mean: 'If you want to do well, lift your head up.' In a sense this attitude departs from the earlier Hasidic stress on *annihilation of selfhood; generally the members of this dynasty pursue an independent line.

Moses Teitelbaum's grandson, Jekutiel Judah Teitelbaum (1808–83), was Rabbi of Sziget, also writing Responsa and a number of works in the Hasidic vein. He was succeeded in the Rabbinate of Sziget by his son Hananiah Yom Tov Lipa Teitelbaum (d. 1904). These two Rabbis were influential in setting the tone of fiery opposition in Hungary to anything that smacks of Reform, following the stand taken by Rabbi Moses *Sofer. Their zeal was inherited by Hananiah Yom Tov Lipa's son, Joel Teitelbaum (1888–1979), Rabbi of Sotmar. After Rabbi Joel's arrival in the USA, he established his 'court' in Williamsburg, New York, and became the Zaddik of virtually a new dynasty, his followers being known as the Sotmarer Hasidim. Joel Teitelbaum, a fierce opponent of *Zionism, poured forth a stream of books and pamphlets urging Jews to wait patiently for the coming of the Messiah and forbidding them to participate in any way in the redemption of the land of Israel by human means. While his extremism was not to the taste of the majority of even the ultra-Orthodox, Rabbi Joel was admired for his great learning, his benevolent activities, and the educational institutions for which he was responsible. Sotmar also engaged in a continuous battle with the rival Hasidic group of *Lubavitch. One of the points at issue

in the struggle was Sotmar's rejection of the Lubavitch campaign to persuade non-observant Jews to put on *tefillin; Sotmar argued that non-observant Jews are lacking in the conditions of holy living that are the requisite for wearing the *tefillin*.

Herman Dicker, 'The Sziget Community and the Teitelbaum Dynasty', in his *Piety and Perseverance* (New York, 1981), 60–5.

Solomon Poll, *The Hasidic Community of Williamsburg* (New York, 1969).

**Telz Yeshivah** The world famous *Yeshivah that flourished in the town of Telz in Lithuania from 1875 to 1941. The first principal of the Yeshivah was the Rabbi of Telz, Eliezer Gordon, a disciple of Israel *Salanter, founder of the *Musar movement. Gordon's efforts to introduce Musar into the curriculum of the Yeshivah met with opposition on the part of the students. Eventually, a somewhat different and more philosophical form of Musar was introduced under Gordon's son-in-law, Joseph Laib Bloch (d. 1930). This variant was called Daat ('Knowledge') rather than Musar. In Bloch's published *Lectures on Knowledge* (*Sheurey Daat*) such philosophical issues are discussed as the old problem of how divine foreknowledge can be reconciled with human freedom of choice. After World War II, Joseph Laib's son, Elijah Meir Bloch, and his son-in-law, Hayyim Katz, re-established the Telz Yeshivah in Cleveland, Ohio, where it became one of the outstanding Yeshivot in the world. Bloch and Katz were succeeded in the principalship of the Yeshivah by the American-born Rabbi Mordecai Gifter, who had studied as a young man in Telz in Lithuania. A branch of the Yeshivah was established in Telstone, near Jerusalem.

Under Bloch and the other renowned scholars, Simeon Shkop and Hayyim Rabinowitz, the special approach to Talmudic studies was developed. The 'Telzer Derekh' ('the methodology of Telz') consists of a keen analysis of legal concepts found in the Talmud and the *Halakhah. Basically, the method involves an examination of a particular concept in terms of its positive and negative aspects, for example: is $X$ true of $A$ because it is $X$ or because it is not $Y$? There is no doubt that this methodology has shed light on many an obscure Talmudic passage but it has been criticized as hairsplitting. A skit on the Telzer Derekh has a student trying to discover what makes the tea sweet, the stirring or the sugar. If the stirring what need is there for the sugar, and if the sugar what need for the stirring? The conclusion reached is that it is the stirring, the purpose of the sugar being so that the tea-drinker will know for how long he has to stir the tea for it to become sweet!

**Temple** The great building on Mount Moriah in Jerusalem, the place in which sacrifices were offered to God by the people of Israel. The First Temple, built by King Solomon, as told in the first book of Kings, was destroyed by the the armies of Nebuchadnezzar in 586 BCE. When the Babylonian exiles returned, the building of the Second Temple began around the year 515 BCE. This Second Temple was reconstructed by Herod from the year 20 BCE and stood until it was destroyed by the Romans in the year 70 CE. These are the bare bones of the history. For the full details the standard encyclopaedias should be consulted. The main sources for the way in which the Second Temple functioned are: *Josephus, the *New Testament, and the *Mishnah, but there are discrepancies between these sources which cannot adequately be resolved at this late date. It has also to be appreciated that the Mishnah was compiled some 150 years after the destruction of the Temple so that, while the Mishnah undoubtedly contains some reliable traditions, the picture that emerges is to a large extent academic and idealized, in part factual and in part legendary. The statement in Ethics of the Fathers (5. 5) that 'ten miracles were wrought for our fathers in the Temple', among them that no fly ever appeared near the meat of the sacrifices and that the pillar of smoke on the altar always went straight up and was never prevailed over by the wind, is obviously a nostalgic dwelling on departed glories rather than a tradition handed down from the past. Nevertheless, from the point of view of the Jewish religion, it was the Mishnaic picture of Temple life, of which the following is a very brief description, that was preserved in the folk-memory.

*Structure*

According to the Mishnah tractate *Middot* ('Measures'), the Temple stood on an area 500 cubits square known as the Temple Mount (a cubit measures approximately 18 inches). Within the northern part of this square and bearing to the west there was a rectangle of 135 cubits on its east and west sides and 322 cubits on its north and south sides. The space in the main square of the Temple Mount that was outside the rectangle was known as the 'Court of the Gentiles' since Gentiles were allowed to enter this area. At the eastern end of the rectangle there was a square of 135 cubits known as the 'Court of the Women', divided from the Court of the Gentiles by the *Ḥel*, a rampart, which ran right round the whole large rectangle. There remained in the larger rectangle a smaller rectangle (187 cubits east to west and 135 cubits north to south) and this was known as the Temple Court, the *Azarah* ('courtyard'). The easternmost strip of the Temple Court, measuring 11 cubits east to west, was known as Court of the Israelites. West of this was a strip of equal length known as the Court of the Priests. Fifteen semicircular steps led into the middle, from the Court of the Women to the Court of the Israelites, and opposite these steps between the Court of the Israelites and the Court of the Priests there was a platform upon which the *Levites stood. To the west of the Court of the Priests stood, to the south, the altar with the ramp leading up to it. West of the Altar stood the *Hekhal*, the Sanctuary, the actual Temple building. Twelve steps led from the Inner Court, the *Azarah*, into the porch which led into the *Hekhal* proper. The Holy of Holies was situated at the western end of the *Hekhal*, hence the Rabbinic saying: 'The *Shekhinah was in the west.' Around the court there were chambers for special purposes, among them the Chamber of Hewn Stones, where the *Sanhedrin sat in judgement.

The Mishnah (*Kelim* 1: 6–9) gives a list of ten sanctities in ascending order (see HOLY PLACES*). The land of Israel is holier than any other land. The walled cities in the land of Israel are still more holy in that lepers must be sent forth from their midst. Within the wall of Jerusalem is still more holy. Only therein may the meat of those sacrifices possessing a lower degree of sanctity be eaten. The Temple Mount is still more holy, for no man or woman who has a flux, no menstruant, and no woman after childbirth may enter therein. The rampart is still more holy, for no Gentile may enter therein and none that has contracted contamination from a corpse. The Court of the Women is still more holy, for none that has immersed himself that day may enter therein. The Court of the Israelites is still more holy, for none whose atonement is incomplete may enter therein. The Court of the Priests is still more holy, for Israelites may not enter therein except when bringing their sacrifices. The area between the porch and the altar is still more holy, for no priest who has a blemish or whose hair is unloosed may enter therein. The *Hekhal* is still more holy, for no priest may enter therein without first washing his hands and feet. The holy of holies is still more holy, for none may enter there at all save the *High Priest on *Yom Kippur. The Mishnah states, incidentally, that when the walls of the Holy of Holies had to be repaired, the workmen were lowered down from the roof in enclosed cages so that their eyes should not feast on other parts of the sacred section.

As in the *Tabernacle in the wilderness, there was a golden altar of incense near the entrance in the *Hekhal* and the *menorah in the south and the table for the shewbread (the twelve loaves for the priests set there each week) to the north. To the west of the ramp which led to the altar stood the laver from which the priests washed their hands and feet. In the First Temple the Holy of Holies contained the *Ark, but the Ark was lost and in the Second Temple the Holy of Holies was completely empty, except, according to the Mishnah, for the jutting stone upon which the Ark rested in the First Temple. This stone was known as 'the foundation stone' in the belief that it was from this stone that the creation of the world began.

*The Temple Service*

The Mishnah treats in great detail the various kinds of *sacrifices, public and private, that were brought to the Temple. These were carefully regulated, each stage having to be carried out in the correct manner, in the correct place, and by the correct person. All the rules and regulations are set out in the Mishnah and Talmud of the order of Kodashim, where they can be studied. Here are mentioned in broad outline only the procedure adopted for the morning offering, described in full in tractate *Tamid* ('The Daily Offering').

Before daybreak, the Temple officer ordered the assembled priests to cast lots to decide which of them should slaughter the daily offering of the morning, which should sprinkle the blood on the altar, and so forth. The officer then instructed them to see if it was dawn and he then ordered them to bring a lamb from the Chamber of Lambs. The priest upon whom the lot had fallen to slaughter the lamb took it to the place of the slaughtering. The priest then slaughtered the animal and another priest, the one whose lot had entitled him to sprinkle the blood, took over, receiving the blood in a consecrated bowl and taking it to be sprinkled on the altar. The first priest then flayed the animal and gave its various parts to the priests whose lot had entitled them to place the parts on the ramp. These priests first salted the parts and then went to the Chamber of Hewn Stones to recite the *Shema, the Ten Commandments, and a number of *benedictions. This was the only *liturgy in the Temple, the chief function of which was the offering of the sacrifices.

The whole procedure is elaborated on in the Mishnah, including the pouring-out of the drink-offering of wine at which a signal was given with a towel for the cymbal to be sounded and for the Levites to break forth into singing. The Mishnah concludes (*Tamid* 7: 3): 'When they reached a break in the singing they blew upon the trumpets and the people prostrated themselves; at every break there was a blowing of the trumpet and at every blowing of the trumpet a prostration. This was the rite of the Daily Whole-Offering in the service of the House of our God. May it be His will that it shall be built up again, speedily, in our days. Amen.'

In this fashion the procedures adopted in connection with the other sacrifices are detailed throughout the Mishnah and received their elaboration in the Talmud. As the prayer at the end of tractate *Tamid* and numerous other passages shows, there was a longing for the Temple to be rebuilt and the whole sacrificial system reintroduced. Together with this the idea took root that the study of the laws was in itself a substitute for the original form of worship. As the Rabbis put it: 'Whoever studies the law of the burnt-offering it is considered as if he had offered a burnt-offering; whoever studies the law of the sin-offering it is considered as if he had offered a sin-offering.'

The law that a person who has contracted corpse-contamination may not enter even the rampart, to say nothing of the more sacred spots in the Temple, gave rise to the question of whether this prohibition continues even after the destruction of the Temple; in other words, is it permitted to enter the site of the Temple since, in the absence of the purification rites of the *red heifer, all persons are in a state of corpse-contamination in that they have either come into contact with a corpse or with one who has had such contact. The Talmudic sources are ambiguous on the question and some medieval authorities held that once the Temple had been destroyed the site itself no longer possessed its original sanctity for this purpose. Maimonides, however, rules that the law applies even to the site of the Temple. In Jerusalem, today, a notice can be seen attached to the entrance to the Temple site warning observant Jews not to proceed beyond the *Western Wall, the wall that surrounded the whole area in Temple times, in case they encroach on the areas it is forbidden to enter.

*The Third Temple*

In addition to the mourning rites of the Ninth of *Av, Tisha Be-Av, the anniversary of the destruction of the Temple, other practices were introduced in remembrance of the destruction. Although not widely observed, there is the rule that a portion of the house near the door should be left undecorated. One of the reasons for the breaking of a glass by the bridegroom under the *huppah* is that it is a reminder of the destruction of the Temple. A few pious bridegrooms still follow the Talmudic rule that a groom should have ashes on his head during the marriage ceremony. They do this by placing a little cigarette ash in tissue paper which they wear under the hat. Pious Jews, too, still follow the Talmudic rule of rending the garments when first seeing the site of the Temple, although only a token tear of a garment is made.

Throughout the ages the hope was kept alive that with the advent of the *Messiah the ancient glories would be restored through the building of the Third Temple that would never be destroyed. This hope was expressed in hymns and prayers. Typical is the prayer recited as part of the Additional Service on the three pilgrim festivals (see PILGRIMAGES) of Passover, Shavuot, and Tabernacles:

'Our God and God of our fathers, merciful King, have mercy upon us, O Thou who art good and beneficent be Thou entreated of us; return unto us in Thy yearning compassion for the fathers' sake who did Thy will; rebuild Thy house as at the beginning, and establish Thy Sanctuary upon this site; grant that we may see it in its rebuilding, and make us rejoice in its re-establishment; restore the priests to their service, the Levites to their song and psalmody, and Israel to their habitations; and there we will go up to appear and worship Thee at the three periods of our festivals, according as it is written in Thy Torah.'

Given the conditions that existed in the Middle Ages, it is hardly surprising that no attempt to rebuild the Temple in anticipation of the Messianic age was ever thought of. Now that such a project has become feasible with the establishment of the State of Israel, only a tiny fringe group has tried to plan the rebuilding of the Temple. The vast majority of the Orthodox find insuperable Halakhic obstacles to such a plan. The site of the sacred places is not known with anything like certainty, for example, and the status of people who claim to be Kohanim ('priests') is in doubt, so that a prophet is awaited who will show what has to be done. The whole matter is left to the Messiah. An ancient tradition, recorded by *Rashi, has it that the Third Temple will not be built at all by human hands but will drop ready-formed from heaven. This has not prevented some of the Orthodox from making a diligent study of the laws of the Temple and the sacrificial system in order to be prepared when the hoped-for event takes place. Reform Judaism has long reinterpreted the Messianic hope in terms of a Messianic age of universal peace and does not believe that one day the Third Temple will be built. Conservative Judaism is similarly very uneasy abut the belief in the restoration of the Temple. However, Conservative Jews, unlike the Reformers, still retain the references to the sacrifices in the Prayer Book but change the words so as to read: 'and there our fathers offered the sacrifices' instead of: 'and there we will offer the sacrifices'.

Menahem Haran, *Temples and Temple-Service in Ancient Israel* (Oxford, 1978).
Baruch A. Levine, *In the Presence of the Lord* (Leiden, 1974).
*The Mishnah*, trans. Herbert Danby (Oxford, 1954), Order Kodashim, pp. 457–602.

**Ten Days of Penitence** The ten days from *Rosh Ha-Shanah to *Yom Kippur during which repentance is especially acceptable to

God. The Rabbis comment on the verse: 'Seek the Lord while He can be found' (Isaiah 55: 6) that these ten days are the time referred to by the prophet, the special period in which God can be found. In an oft-quoted passage in the Babylonian Talmud (*Rosh Ha-Shanah* 16b) a saying of the third-century Palestinian teacher, Rabbi Johanan, is quoted. Three books are open on Rosh Ha-Shanah, the beginning of the new year and the day of judgement. One is the book of the righteous, another the book of the wicked, and the third the book of the average persons, those who are neither completely righteous nor completely wicked. The righteous are recorded at once in the book of life, the wicked in the book of death. The fate of the average is left in abeyance during the days until Yom Kippur (the actual expression 'The Ten Days of Penitence' is found in the parallel passage in the Jerusalem Talmud). If they repent of their misdeeds they are written and sealed in the book of the righteous, otherwise they are written and sealed in the book of the wicked.

Rabbi Johanan's homily is far removed, of course, from anything like a precise theological statement. Wicked people do live on during the coming year and righteous people die during the year. But the Jewish theologians treat the saying as factual, explaining it on such grounds as that when the wicked live on it is because they have significant good deeds to their credit and the righteous die because they have some evil deeds which require expiation. As a result of the discussion and the insertion of prayers in the liturgy to be recorded in the book of life, it was all taken very seriously as demanding a special effort to repent during these ten days. Jews otherwise not particularly observant of the precepts try to mend their ways and be more scrupulous in these days in their religious and ethical conduct. Many modern Jews understand the whole matter more as a reminder to do better in the year ahead rather than as an attempt to persuade an undecided God to decide in their favour.

**Ten Martyrs** The ten teachers, among them Rabbi *Akiba, Rabbi *Ishmael, and Rabban Simeon ben *Gamaliel, who suffered a *martyr's death at the hands of the Romans. The story of the ten martyrs is told in a late Midrash and poetic versions of it are part of the *liturgy for the Ninth of *Av, Tisha Be-Av, and *Yom Kippur. According to this legend, the Roman emperor wished to put to death ten of the foremost scholars in expiation of the sin of Joseph's brethren who had sold him (Genesis 37,) since the Torah states: 'He that stealeth a man and selleth him . . . shall be put to death' (Exodus 21: 16). These ten were selected to atone for the sin of their ancestors. Rabbi Ishmael purified himself and ascended on high, where he was informed that the decree of death had indeed been pronounced, and the ten submitted to their fate. Scholars have found the whole legend puzzling on a number of counts. While there are references in the Talmud to Rabbi Akiba and one or two of the others suffering a martyr's death, they could not all have been executed, as in the legend, on the same day, since they did not all live at the same time. And it is certainly contrary to Jewish theological thought that innocent men should die for a sin committed by their forebears, to say nothing of the fact that it is the emperor who is determined to obey the laws of the Torah. Some scholars have suggested that the whole legend consists of a veiled attack on the Church, which persecuted the Jews who remained faithful to their religion for the sin of their ancestors who supposedly were responsible for the death of *Jesus. In any event, Jews have read the legend as a tribute to Jewish martyrdom throughout the ages.

**Terefah** Food which it is forbidden for the Jew to eat, so termed after the verse: 'And ye shall not eat any flesh that is torn [*terefah*] of beasts in the field; ye shall cast it to the dogs' (Exodus 27: 30). The Rabbis understand terefah as applying to any animal or fowl with a serious defect in one of its vital organs. Although the term was originally used in this sense only, it came to be used for anything forbidden by the *dietary laws, the opposite, in fact, of the term *kosher. The term is often shortened to *treif.*

**Tetragrammaton** The four-letter name of God formed from the letters *yod, hey, vav,* and *hey,* hence YHVH in the usual English rendering. The older form JHVH is based on the rendering of *yod* as *jod.* This name is usually translated in English as 'the Lord', following the Greek translation as *kyrios.* All this goes back to the Jewish practice of never pronouncing the name as it is written but as Adonai, 'the Lord'. In printed texts the vowels of this word are placed under the letters of the Tetragrammaton. (Hence the name was read erroneously by Christians as 'Jehovah', a name completely unknown in the Jewish tradition.) The original pronunciation of the Tetragrammaton has been lost, owing to the strong Jewish disapproval of pronouncing the name. The pronunciation Yahveh or Yahweh is based on that used by some of the Church Fathers but there is no certainty at all in this matter. Most biblical scholars, nowadays, prefer to render it simply as YHWH or JHVH without the vowels. This name occurs 6,823 times in the present text of the Hebrew Bible.

What does the name mean? In Exodus 3: 14–15 the name is associated with the idea of 'being', and hence some have understood the original meaning to be 'He-Who-Is', or 'He who brings being into being'. Generally, as Cassuto and others have noted, the name Elohim ('God', see *Names of God) is used in the Bible of God in His universalistic aspect, the God of the whole universe, while the Tetragrammaton is used of God in His special relationship with the people of Israel.

*The Tetragrammaton in Post-Biblical Literature*

The Tetragrammaton is known in the Rabbinic literature as Ha-Shem ('the Name') or *Shem Ha-Meforash*, meaning either the 'special' name or the name uttered explicitly, that is, by the *High Priest in the *Temple. The Rabbis also refer to it as *Shem Ha-Meyuḥad* ('the Unique Name') or as 'the Four Letter Name'. There is evidence that even after the change-over (between the fourth and second centuries BCE) from the old Hebrew writing to the so-called 'square' script now used, the Tetragrammaton was sometimes written in the Scrolls in the old script. Although the Rabbis rejected this procedure, it is attested to as late as the fifth century CE in a fragment of Aquila's Greek translation (see TARGUM) and is mentioned by Origen as well as being found in some of the *Qumran texts.

The data regarding the prohibition of pronouncing the Tetragrammaton as it is written are complicated but the following are the main details. *Philo (*Life of Moses*, ii. 11) observes that on the front of the High Priest's mitre were incised the four letters of the divine name which it is lawful only for the priests to utter in the Temple (in the *priestly blessing) and for no one else to utter anywhere. The Sifre

(Numbers 43) similarly states that in the Temple the priestly blessing was given with the pronunciation of the special name (*Shem Ha-Meforash*) but outside the Temple with the substitute name (Adonai). The Mishnah (*Sotah* 7: 6; *Tamid* 7: 2) also states that that in the Temple the name was uttered as written but outside the Temple by its substitute. In another Mishnah (*Yoma* 6: 2) it is stated that on *Yom Kippur when the High Priest uttered the *Shem Ha-Meforash* the people fell on their faces and proclaimed: 'Blessed be the name of His glorious kingdom for ever and ever.' Even in the Temple, it was later said (*Kiddushin* 71a), when there was an increase of unworthy persons, the name was spoken softly, the High Priest uttering it in such a way as to be drowned by the singing of the other priests.

The most relevant text for the prohibition against uttering the Tetragrammaton as it is written is the Mishnah (*Sanhedrin* 10: 1) in which Abba Saul declares that one who pronounces the divine name with its letters (i.e. as it is spelled) has no share in the *World to Come. On the other hand, another Mishnah (*Berakhot* 9: 5) states that in order for the faithful to recognize one another as a guard against the intrusion of the heretics it was ordained, as a special dispensation, that the divine name be used for greeting. The conclusion to be drawn from all these sources, though they are in part contradictory, seems to be that at an early period the Tetragrammaton was not uttered as spelled. The reason why Jews were reluctant to utter the Tetragrammaton is not too clear, but appears to be based on the idea that this name is so descriptive of God that it was considered to be gross irreverence to use it. It is also possible that the use of this name in some circles for magical purposes was a further reason why its pronunciation was forbidden. In the Babylonian Talmud (*Pesaḥim* 50a) there is a homily on the verse: 'In that day shall the Lord be One, and His name One' (Zechariah 14: 9). This is understood to mean that in this world the Tetragrammaton is read as Adonai but in the Messianic age the name will once again be pronounced as it is written.

Generally in the Rabbinic literature, the Tetragrammaton is interpreted as referring to God in His attribute of mercy and Elohim to God in His attribute of judgement. Thus a Midrash explains why the Tetragrammaton is used together with Elohim in the second chapter of Genesis while Elohim on its own is used in the first chapter, on the grounds that God created the world with His attribute of strict justice but added the attribute of mercy so that the world could endure. Similarly, the verse: 'God [Elohim] is gone up amidst shouting, The Lord [the Tetragrammaton] amidst the sound of the horn' (Psalms 47: 6) is interpreted to mean that when the *shofar* is sounded on *Rosh Ha-Shanah God rises from His throne of judgement to sit on His throne of mercy.

### The Tetragrammaton in Medieval Philosophy and the Kabbalah

*Judah Halevi in his *Kuzari* (iv. 1–17) has a lengthy excursus on the distinction between Elohim and the Tetragrammaton. Elohim represents divinity but does not necessarily refer to God. Sometimes in Scripture this name refers to the gods of polytheistic religion. The Tetragrammaton, on the other hand, is God's personal name. Man can know Elohim by means of his unaided reason—he can know that there is a God—but this God, the result of ratiocination, is cold and remote, the distant God of the philosophers who issues no commands and cannot be worshipped. The people of Israel alone have the intuitive knowledge of God represented by the Tetragrammaton because He has revealed Himself to them through the *prophets. The substitute for the Tetragrammaton, Adonai, also implies something which stands at such an immeasurable distance that a real designation is impossible. We can only know those things created by Him by means of which He becomes manifest. The meaning of Elohim can be grasped by speculation since reason postulates that the world has a Governor. The meaning of Adonai cannot be grasped by speculation, only by the special kind of prophetic vision by means of which certain men are, as it were, separated from other human beings and brought into contact with angelic beings. Man yearns for Adonai as a matter of love, taste, and conviction; while attachment to Elohim is the result of speculation. A feeling of the former kind invites those who possess it to give their very lives for God's sake. Speculation makes for veneration only as long as this entails no suffering.

For Maimonides (*Guide of the Perplexed*, I. 61) all the divine names are simply descriptions of God's actions. This includes the name Adonai, which simply expresses the lordship of God

and lordship is applicable, too, to human beings. The sole exception is the Tetragrammaton, which, unlike the other names, gives a clear, unequivocal indication of God's essence. This name has no derivation. The prohibition against pronouncing the Tetragrammaton exists because this name is indicative of the divine essence in a way that no created thing is associated with Him. When the Rabbis say that before the world was created there was only God and His name they call attention to the special nature of this name and how it differs from all the other names for God. The other names are derived from God's acts in the world and therefore could only have come into being *after* the world had been created. But the Tetragrammaton indicates God's essence and was therefore in being *before* the world was created. Maimonides takes strong issue with the doctrine, popular in his day, that the Tetragrammaton has magical power or that there are a number of divine names by which magical influences can be brought to bear on the world. The Tetragrammaton is nothing else than the four-letter name, distinguished from all others solely because it is indicative of God's essence.

In the Kabbalah all creation is by means of the letters of the Tetragrammaton in various combinations. This name contains all the *Sefirot and has innumerable combinations, each representing an aspect of divine manifestation. These, contrary to Maimonides, do have magical power and those who know how to draw on this power can work miracles, hence the name Baal Shem ('Master of the Name') for this practitioner of 'white' magic. In the Lurianic Kabbalah there are four ways of spelling out (see GEMATRIA) the letters of the Tetragrammaton, which yield four different totals—72, 63, 45, and 52—each representing an aspect of God in His relation to the world in which He is manifested. Unlike for Maimonides, the Tetragrammaton does not represent God's essence but His manifestations in the Sefirot. God's essence is denoted by the term *En Sof. In another Kabbalistic understanding the Tetragrammaton represents the Sefirah *Tiferet*, the male principle on high, while Adonai represents *Malkhut*, the *Shekhinah, the female principle. The combination of these two in the mind of the Kabbalist assists in the unification of these principles on high and promotes harmony in the Sefirotic realm. For this reason

Kabbalistic prayer books depict the divine name in the form of an interweaving of the letters of the Tetragrammaton with those of Adonai.

George Foot Moore, *Judaism in the First Centuries of the Christian Era* (Cambridge, Mass., 1958); see index: 'Name of God'.
Louis Jacobs, *A Jewish Theology* (New York, 1973), 136–51.

**Tevet, Fast of** One of the public *fast days, falling on the tenth day of the month of Tevet. This fast is in commemoration of the day on which the siege of Jerusalem by the armies of Nebuchadnezzar began (1 Kings 25: 1), an event which led to the destruction of the *Temple in 586 BCE. Like the other minor fasts, this one lasts only from dawn to dusk and does not begin on the previous night like Tisha Be-av (see AV, NINTH OF) and *Yom Kippur.

**Thanksgiving** In Temple times, in order to express his gratitude to God for having dealt bountifully with him, a man would bring a thanksgiving offering (*todah*), the details of which are found in the book of Leviticus (7: 12–15). To this day, 'Thank you' in modern Hebrew is '*Todah*' and 'Many thanks', '*Todah Rabbah*'. It is a general principle in Judaism that gratitude is to be shown not alone to God but to human beings who have been gracious and bountiful, and ingratitude is held to be a serious defect. From Talmudic times onwards a special benediction of thanksgiving was introduced based on Psalm 107. In this Psalm deliverances from severe danger to life are mentioned: 1. travellers who reach their destination after a hazardous journey (vv. 4–9.); 2. prisoners who regain their freedom (vv. 10–16); 3. sick persons who have been restored to health (vv. 17–22); 4. sailors who reach land in safety (vv. 23–32). After each of these the Psalmist concludes: 'Let them give thanks unto the Lord for His goodness, and for His wonderful works to the children of men.' Thus in the Talmud (*Berakhot* 54b) it is stated: 'Four types of person must offer thanksgiving: those who go down to the sea, who journey in the desert, the invalid who recovers and the prisoner who has been set free.' The Talmud supplies the details of this *benediction, and further details and later *customs are supplied in the *Shulḥan Arukh* (*Oraḥ Ḥayyim*, 219). The general tendency is not to restrict the benediction to the instances recorded in the Talmud but to extend it to all cases of deliverance from danger, after an escape from a bombing or a mugging, for example. Nowadays, when air travel is much safer than it used to be, there is some doubt whether the benediction should be recited after a safe return from travel in a plane. The benediction is not recited after a journey in a car or a train unless there has been a serious accident.

The custom, nowadays, is for the benediction to be recited after the person has been called to the *reading of the Torah. The benediction is : 'Blessed art Thou, O Lord our God, King of the universe, who bestoweth [*ha-gomel*] good to the undeserving, and who hast dealt kindly with me.' The members of the congregation respond: 'He who hath shown thee kindness, may He deal kindly with thee for ever.' After the word *ha-gomel*, the recital of this benediction is known in Yiddish as *gomel bentchen*, 'reciting the benediction of gomel'. It is not customary in Orthodox circles for women to recite the gomel benediction, probably because the benediction is now recited after being called to the reading of the Torah and, in Orthodox congregations, women are not called to the reading. There is, of course, no reason why a woman should not thank God in private for her escape from danger. It is only the public declaration from which women are exempt. In some communities there is a special service of thanksgiving for a woman who has given birth. This takes place after the statutory service in the synagogue.

In addition to the formal gomel benediction in public, the Jewish tradition has it that a man should give thanks to God in private for whatever extraordinary event happens to him, in the belief that, though it might seem to be to his disadvantage, it is ultimately to his advantage, since God desires only good for His creatures. A Rabbinic saying has it: 'Let a man accustom himself to say always: "Whatever the All-merciful does is for the good."' In some sources it is said that if a person has had a *miracle wrought for him, that is, if his deliverance seems quite beyond what is expected from the natural order, he should set aside a sum of money for *charity and say: 'Behold I give this money to charity and may it be the Divine Will to count it as if I had brought a thanksgiving offering.'

J. H. Hertz, *The Authorised Daily Prayer Book* (London, 1947), 486–8.

**Theft** According to the Talmudic Rabbis, the eighth commandment (see *Decalogue): 'Thou shalt not steal' (Exodus 20: 15) refers to kidnapping, a capital offence (like that of murder in the sixth commandment), though it is sometimes made to include other types of theft. The prohibition of theft in general, that is, theft of property, is derived from the verse: 'Ye shall not steal' (Leviticus 19: 11). In the book of Exodus two different penalties are recorded for theft. In one verse (Exodus 21: 37) it is stated that if a man steals an ox or a sheep, and then kills it or sells it, he is obliged to pay (to the victim) five oxen for an ox and four sheep for a sheep. But in another verse (Exodus 22: 3) the penalty is stated that the thief must pay double (i.e. only twice as much) to the victim. These verses are understood to mean that one who steals any object has to pay double to the victim, whereas in the case of the ox or the sheep he is obliged to pay four or five times over, but only if, after he has stolen it, he either kills the animal or sells it. This law applies only to the theft of an ox or a sheep, not of any other animal. A distinction is also drawn between a thief, who steals by stealth, and a robber, who takes something directly from his victim despite the victim's protest. The laws of paying double or four or five times over only apply to the thief. The robber has simply to make restitution by either giving back that which he has stolen, if the object is still in his hands, or compensating the victim to the value of the stolen object. The payment of double or four or five times over is held to be in the nature of a fine, and admission to an offence involving a fine exonerates the perpetrator from payment of that fine. Thus if the thief admits to the court, before he has been charged, that he is guilty he pays only the object he has stolen or its value.

The Talmud (*Bava Kama* 79b) offers this rationale for the distinction between the thief and the robber. At first glance, the thief's offence is less than that of the robber and yet the thief has to pay double and the robber only has to compensate his victim to the value of that which he has stolen. But the thief, unlike the robber, hides from people when he steals and yet disregards the fact that God sees him, whereas the robber has regard neither for God nor man and simply does not care who sees him. The illustration is given of two people in a town who make a banquet. One invites the townspeople but fails to invite the members of the royal family while the other invites neither the townspeople nor the royal family. The former commits a greater offence in that he offers a slight to the royal family.

In the same passage a rationale is given for why there is a payment of five oxen for an ox and only four sheep for a sheep. Two reasons are given. The first is that in the case of the ox the thief has deprived the owner of the labour of his ox, whereas a sheep does not work for its owner. The second reason is that one who steals an ox simply leads it away, whereas the thief has to suffer the indignity of carrying the sheep away on his shoulder. The first reason offers a homily on the value of productive labour, the second a homily on human dignity.

There are further homilies on theft in the sources. It is forbidden to steal ideas so that, in the wider sense, the prohibition of theft embraces plagiarism. Again, in the wider sense, all trickery is included in the prohibition of theft. This is called 'stealing the mind of people', by misleading them or cheating them. Thus, to overcharge is a type of theft as is, to give another example, to offer lavish hospitality to a neighbour while knowing full well that he will not accept. Some moralists extend the prohibition against tricking another so as to embrace fooling oneself into believing that one is more pious or more learned than is really the case. A Hasidic tale tells of the Hasid who said he journeyed to his *Rebbe to hear the Decalogue bring recited. You can hear that at home, it was objected, to which the Hasid replied: 'At the court of the Rebbe I hear the commandments in a different, deeper way.' 'Thou shalt not steal' includes, as the Rebbe teaches it, the command not to engage in self-delusion.

In the Rabbinic tradition, the prohibition of theft is one of the seven *Noahide laws and therefore applies to *Gentiles as well as to Jews. It is also forbidden to steal from a Gentile just as it is forbidden to steal from a Jew. The Talmud (*Gittin* 55a) records a debate between the houses of *Hillel and *Shammai. According to the House of Shammai, if a man stole a beam and built it into his house, the victim has the right to demand that the thief return to him the beam even if this means that the thief has to demolish the whole building. But the House of Hillel ruled that the victim can only claim the value of the beam. This rule is said to have been introduced in order not to place obstacles in the way of *repentance: if the strict law is enforced in such circumstances the thief will refuse to own up rather than have his whole house demolished.

Boaz Cohen, *Jewish and Roman Law* (New York, 1966); see index: 'Theft'.

Bernard S. Jackson, *Theft in Early Jewish Law* (Oxford, 1972).

**Theology** Theology, as defined by Richard Hooker, the Renaissance theologian, is 'the science of things divine'. Theology (from the Greek *theos*, 'God', and *logos*, 'word', 'doctrine') involves the systematic treatment of what belief in God entails and Jewish theology can therefore be defined as an attempt to think through consistently the implications of the Jewish religion as the way to God. Jewish theology differs from the study of Jewish *history in that it involves personal commitment on the part of its practitioners. To be sure, the theologian must avail himself of the accurate findings of the historians, otherwise his speculations will belong to fantasy. But while the historian of the Jewish religion asks what happened in the Jewish past, the theologian asks what in the traditional religion should shape the life of the Jew in the here and now. The historian uses his skills to demonstrate what Jews have believed. The theologian is embarked on the more difficult, but, if realized, more relevant task of discovering what it is that a Jew can believe in the present. There is no need for the historian of Judaism to be a believer in the truth of the texts and ideas he investigates. He does not even have to be Jewish; some of the best work in the field has been done by non-Jews. But a Jewish theologian who lacks any belief in the truth of Judaism, no matter how he may interpret the religion, is as much an oddity as a present-day physicist who believes that the earth is flat.

The kind of questions the theologian asks and seeks to answer are chiefly concerned, by definition, with *God. The Jewish theologian deals with questions such as: what is the Jewish concept of God? *Is* there a Jewish concept of God? What does Judaism teach about the nature of God? Does God reveal Himself to mankind and if so how? How is God to be worshipped? But as soon as questions of this nature are raised the element of absurdity in the whole theological enterprise becomes overwhelming. The best religious thinkers have

been unanimous in declaring that God is unknowable. As Maimonides writes (*Guide of the Perplexed*, 1. 59):

'All men, those of the past and those of the future, affirm clearly that God, may He be exalted, cannot be apprehended by the intellects, and that none but He Himself can apprehend what He is, and that apprehension of Him consists in the inability to attain the ultimate term in apprehending Him. Thus all the philosophers say: we are dazzled by His beauty, and He is hidden from us because of the intensity with which He becomes manifest, just as the sun is hidden to eyes that are too weak to apprehend it.'

Judging by the experience of the most subtle of religious thinkers, the more one reflects on the tremendous theme the more one is inclined to reject all faltering human attempts to grasp the divine. The question has consequently been put with regard to both general and Jewish theology, does all this not mean that the whole exercise is futile? The theologian replies that he follows respectable antecedents when he draws a distinction between God as He is in Himself, which indeed cannot be discussed at all, and God in manifestation, that is, in relationship with mankind. The latter can be discussed unless theistic faith is itself ruled out of court.

If, for example, *prayer is engaged in, it becomes quite legitimate to ask what it is people are doing when they pray and which kinds of prayer are valid, which invalid. Furthermore, the doctrine that God is unknowable is itself a matter of human perception, arrived at by those who hold it after rigorous and sustained thought, and is therefore itself a thesis within the scope of theology. Bahya, *Ibn Pakubah, in his *Duties of the Heart* (i. c. 2) goes so far as to quote with approval the saying of a 'philosopher' that only the prophet, who knows God intuitively, and the philosopher, whose ideas about God have been refined in the crucible of his thought, worship God. All others worship something other than God. To discuss whether Bahya is right or wrong in this contention is in itself to do theology.

*Is there a Jewish Theology?*

It has been argued that the whole notion of a Jewish theology is a contradiction in terms and that there is no warrant for theology in the Jewish tradition. This position has been advanced on two grounds. The first of these is that Jewish thinking in its classical and formative periods—those of the Bible and the Rabbinic literature—was 'organic' rather than systematic, a response to particular concrete situations rather than a comprehensive account of what religious belief entails (see SYSTEMATIC THINKING). Secondly, the emphasis in Judaism is on the *Halakhah, on action, on doing the will of God, not on defining it.

While there is some truth in both these contentions, it is far from the whole truth. A concern with systematic thinking about Judaism did not emerge until Greek modes had made their impact on the Jewish teachers. Once this happened, however, sustained reflection on the nature of the Jewish faith was seen as an imperative, at least in those circles which experienced the full force of the collision.

Unless *Philo of Alexandria, *Saadiah, *Bahya Ibn Pakudah, *Maimonides, *Gersonides, *Crescas, and *Albo among the ancient and medieval thinkers; *Cordovero, Isaac *Luria, *Shneur Zalman of Liady among the Kabbalists; and, in modern times, Moses *Mendelssohn, *Krochmal, *Schechter, *Kook, *Rosenzweig, and *Baeck; are to be read out of Judaism, theology is a legitimate pursuit for Jews.

It is understandable when a secular Jewish nationalist pronounces on the un-Jewish nature of theological thinking, since his interest is in the Jewish culture and ethics and he has no need for the God hypothesis. The secularist objects to the *theos* not to the *logos* of theology. What is extremely puzzling is the fact that some Jewish religious teachers roundly object not to the *theos* but to the *logos* of theology. Some of these first say that Judaism has no theology and then proceed to state in detail what it is that Judaism would have Jews believe—generally, the acceptance as infallible truth of every traditional view. A good case can be made out for reliance on tradition or experience rather than on reason for the basic issues of belief in God but if such a position is argued for, it is theology that is being done. If, however, all that is implied in the rejection of Jewish theology is that the medieval thinkers were too much influenced by Greek and Arabic thought, this might be conceded. The modern period in Judaism has seen new insights emerging as well as the recapturing of some old ones (the biblical, for instance) and room has to be found for these in any contemporary Jewish theology.

A quote from the Midrash (Lamentations Rabbah, introduction, 2) is often heard among those who declare theology to be un-Jewish. The Midrash comments on the verse: 'They have forsaken Me and have not kept My Torah' (Jeremiah 16: 11). The Midrash is puzzled by this statement of the prophet. If the people have gone so far as to forsake God, it is obvious that they have not kept God's Torah. The Midrash therefore imagines God to be saying: 'Would that they had forsaken Me if only they had kept My Torah.' This Midrash is said to mean that God does not want Jews to think about Him (i.e. to be theologically minded) but to concentrate instead on keeping the Torah. In point of fact, the Midrash can hardly mean that God does not want people to think about Him. The meaning is rather that God is prepared, as it were, to settle for uninformed, self-seeking observance of the Torah because such is the spiritual power of the Torah even where the motivation is unworthy, that its study and practice will eventually lead Israel to Him. As the Midrash concludes 'since by occupying themselves with the Torah, the light which it contains would have led them back to the right path'. In the very next passage of the Midrash the saying is quoted: 'Study the Torah even if it be not for its own sake, since even if not for its own sake at first it will eventually be for its own sake.' This Midrash consists of a homily on the spiritual power inherent in the Torah and has nothing to do with the question of whether or not Jewish theological thinking is advisable. The Midrash and the Rabbinic literature in general is full of thoughts about God, though these are expressed, as above, in an organic rather than systematic way.

Apart from its intrinsic worth, theology is relevant for Jewish practice since, unless a purely behaviourist attitude is acceptable, Jewish religious practice depends on its theological basis. The idea that all that matters in Judaism is observance of the Halakhah, pan-Halakhism, as Heschel calls it, can only be defended on extra-Halakhic, that is, on theological grounds, otherwise the statement is tautologous—all that matters is the Halakhah because all that matters is the Halakhah. The most determined pan-Halakhist is obliged, somewhere along the line, to invoke extra-Halakhic arguments as to why the Halakhah should have this supreme significance. All the divisions among religious Jews on the scope and obligation of Jewish observances, on the role of the Halakhah in Jewish religious life, depend ultimately on differing views regarding a basic theological question, the meaning of divine *revelation.

## Contemporary Jewish Theology

There is evidence on the contemporary scene of a renewed interest in Jewish theology. At the height of the 'God is Dead' controversy in the early 1960s, occasioned by the publication of the Bishop of Woolwich's book *Honest to God*, the magazine *Commentary* submitted to Rabbis and other Jewish thinkers a series of theological questions to which they replied each from his own theological standpoint, Orthodox, Conservative, Reform, or Reconstructionist. This symposium has now been published in book form as: Milton Himmelfarb (ed.), *The Conditions of Jewish Belief* (Northvale, NJ, and London, 1988). The editor's remarks quoted on the jacket blurb hit the nail on the head:

'Historically, some Jewries were more theological than others. The more advanced the culture they lived in and the more vigorous its philosophical life, the more they had to theologize. Mediaeval Spanish Judaism was more theological than Franco-German Judaism, Maimonides more than Rashi. In those terms, we live in Spanish and not Franco-German conditions, and we too need theology, How much? More, I would say, than we are getting.'

The questions to which the symposium addresses itself are in essence these: 1. In what sense do you believe the Torah to be divine revelation? 2. In what sense do you believe that the Jews are the chosen people of God? 3. Is Judaism the one true religion? 4. Does Judaism as a religion entail any particular political viewpoint? 5. Does the 'God is dead' question have any relevance to Judaism? It is somewhat surprising that there was no question regarding belief in the Hereafter and question (4) only borders on theology. Yet this symposium showed that theology was once again on the move and the variety of views presented provided some indication of the state of theological thinking among American Jews.

A more comprehensive series of original essays on aspects of Jewish belief is Arthur A. Cohen and Paul Mendes-Flohr (eds.), *Contemporary Jewish Religious Thought* (New York, 1987). But this valuable collection seeks to achieve a balance among the intellectual, theological, and philosophical modes of thinking

and is hence not a work limited to theology. Orthodox thinkers have participated in this and in the *Commentary* symposium but the Orthodox have not been as prominent in theological thinking as the members of other groups, no doubt because of the greater emphasis Orthodoxy places on the practical rather than the theoretical aspects of Judaism. The opposition to Jewish theology referred to above comes largely from the ranks of the Orthodox. An exception is the collections of essays by Orthodox scientists: Aryeh Carmell and Cyril Domb (eds.), *Challenge Torah Views on Science and its Problems* (Jerusalem and New York, 1978). More recently a series of essays was published, edited by Dan Cohn-Sherbok, under the title *Problems in Contemporary Jewish Theology* (Lampeter, 1991), in which particular theological problems are addressed.

From the Conservative point of view, two works can be mentioned. These are: a series of essays by Conservative thinkers: Seymour Siegel and Elliot Gertel (eds.), *God in the Teachings of Conservative Judaism* (New York, 1985) and *Sacred Fragments: Recovering Theology for the Modern Jew* by Neil Gillman (Philadelphia and New York, 1990). It is surprising that there are only three works (those in the Bibliography below) devoted entirely to the subject of Jewish theology. Of these the first two are from the Reform standpoint, the third from the right-wing Conservative standpoint. Kohler's work, the first of the three, was a pioneering one. No other Jewish thinker in modern times had thought of devoting a whole work to theology, although, of course, theological discussions did feature in works compiled in the late eighteenth century and onwards. No work dealing explicitly with theology has been compiled in Hebrew, despite the vast output of Hebrew works covering every other branch of Jewish scholarship.

The main topics considered in Jewish theology are: the Jewish approach to God and how this differs from the approaches of other religions (see RELIGION); the relationship between God and man; the meaning and significance of worship; the doctrine of *reward and punishment; the doctrines of the *Messiah and *heaven and hell; the idea of the *Chosen People and the theological implications of the State of *Israel; the problem of evil; the question of divine *providence and *miracles; in short, all those topics which have to do with Jewish belief in contradistinction to Jewish practice. Obviously an important topic for Jewish theology is the question of *dogmas in Judaism. Questions raised by modern thought will also obviously feature in any treatment of Jewish theology today, especially the challenges presented by the scientific picture of the universe, *psychology, comparative religion, linguistic analysis, and *existentialism.

Samuel S. Cohon, *Jewish Theology* (Assen, 1971). Kaufmann Kohler, *Jewish Theology Systematically and Historically Considered* (New York, 1968). Louis Jacobs, *A Jewish Theology* (New York, 1973).

**Therapeutae** The order of contemplatives who settled in the first century CE on the shores of a lake called Mareotis near Alexandria in Egypt and were described by *Philo in his *On the Contemplative Life*. Philo understands the name Therapeutae either as 'Healers' (of the soul) or as 'Worshippers'. Philo's is the only contemporary account of this group . Although some scholars have questioned the ascription of the work to Philo and have argued that it was fathered on him by a Christian writer who wished to describe Christian monasticism as existing in that early period, the scholarly consensus is not only that the account is Philo's own but that there really existed such a Jewish sect since Philo, who lived in Alexandria, would hardly have invented the circumstantial details he supplies, although it is probable that he does present an over-idealized picture in accordance with his own philosophical leanings. According to Philo's account, the Therapeutae differed from the *Essenes in that the latter engaged in physical work while the former were pure contemplatives, although we are not told how they earned their living and managed to survive.

Philo has a vivid description of the ascetic practices of the Therapeutae. Their houses are built near to each other so that they can commune together in worship. Each house has a place of seclusion called the sanctuary where they gather to study the Scriptures and offer their prayers. Philo writes:

'Twice daily they pray, at dawn and at eventide; at sunrise they pray for a joyful day, joyful in the true sense, that their minds may be filled with celestial light. At sunset they pray that the soul may be fully relieved from the disturbance of the senses and the objects of sense, and that retired to its own consistory and council chamber it may search out the truth. The entire interval between early morning and

evening is devoted to spiritual exercise. They read the Holy Scriptures and apply themselves to their ancestral philosophy by means of allegory, since they believe that the words of the literal text are symbols of a hidden nature, revealed through its underlying meanings.'

There are no references to the Therapeutae anywhere else in Jewish literature. Their sole importance for the history of the Jewish religion lies in the evidence they provide that there existed a group of ascetic contemplatives in this early period. (See ASCETICISM and CONTEMPLATION.)

Samuel Sandmel, *Philo of Alexandria* (Oxford, 1979), 34–9.

**Thirteen** The number thirteen, far from being 'unlucky', features in the Jewish tradition as a highly significant number. There are thirteen attributes (Heb. *middot*, lit. 'measures') of divine mercy. These thirteen attributes are found by the Talmudic Rabbis (*Rosh Ha-Shanah* 17b) in the verses in the book of Exodus (34: 6–7) in which God assures Moses that He will pardon the people for worshipping the *golden calf. In the Talmudic passage it is said that whenever Jews are in trouble they should recite these verses and God will have mercy on them; following which these thirteen are recited from time to time during the *Yom Kippur services, on other *fast days, and as part of the *Selihot prayers. They are also recited as part of the special prayer offered when the *Ark is opened on *festival before the *reading of the Torah. The verses read: 'The Lord! the Lord! A God compassionate and gracious, slow to anger, abounding in loving-kindness and faithfulness, extending kindness to the thousandth generation, forgiving iniquity, transgression, and sin. . . .' Actually, the verse states: 'yet He does not remit all punishment', but this is reinterpreted, by a transposition of the Hebrew words, to read: 'and He remits', thus making the thirteenth attribute the remission of sin. The commentators are at variance over how exactly these verses are to be divided so as to contain the thirteen attributes: are the two references to 'the Lord' counted as two separate attributes? In practice the two are counted separately but there are differences of opinion regarding the exact identity of some of the others.

The prayer recited on Yom Kippur and Selihot before the recital of the thirteen attributes reads:

'Almighty King, who sittest upon a throne of mercy, and governest the world with loving-kindness, who pardonest the sins of Thy people, causing them to pass away one by one, freely extending pardon to sinners, and forgiveness to transgressors, doing charity to the spirit of all flesh, and not requiting them according to their evil; O God Thou hast taught us to recite Thy thirteen attributes. Remember then unto us this day, the covenant of the thirteen attributes.'

According to the Kabbalah (Zohar iii. 131a) there are, in addition, thirteen higher attributes of mercy stemming from the Supernal Crown (see SEFIROT), the stage of the divine unfolding at which there is no judgement. These thirteen higher attributes are found in the verses (Micah 7: 18-20):

'Who is a God like unto Thee, that beareth iniquity, and passeth by the transgression of the remnant of His heritage? He retaineth not His anger for ever, because He delighteth in mercy. He will again have compassion upon us; He will subdue our iniquities: and Thou wilt cast all their sins into the depths of the sea. Thou wilt show faithfulness to Jacob, mercy to Abraham, as Thou hast sworn unto our fathers from the days of old.'

*Cordovero's work on *Imitatio Dei, The Palm Tree of Deborah*, describes in detail, in the first chapter, how man can resemble these thirteen higher attributes in his daily life. Behind the whole concept, as understood by the commentators, is the idea that the recital of the thirteen attributes affords a reminder to the worshippers that if they are to receive God's mercies they must make themselves worthy by themselves showing mercy and compassion.

The number thirteen also features in the thirteen principles (also called *middot* in Hebrew) by means of which the Torah is expounded. These principles of *hermeneutics, attributed to Rabbi *Ishmael, are now incorporated into the daily liturgy and have become part of the mental furniture of ordinary Jews, far removed from any real understanding of these intricate rules. Since the same word, *middot*, is used for both the thirteen attributes of mercy and the hermeneutical principles, the Zohar (iii. 227b) refers to the hermeneutical principles themselves as principles of mercy. It is possible that the number thirteen for the attributes of mercy is taken from the earlier number of the hermeneutical principles. If this

is correct, it would explain the difficulty of finding the number in the Exodus verses, since it has been arrived at arbitrarily on the analogy of the other thirteen.

Still another famous instance of the number thirteen occurs in the thirteen *principles of faith laid down by Maimonides. There has been much discussion around the question of why Maimonides should have laid down thirteen principles in particular, but he may have chosen this number on the analogy of the other two thirteens.

Other examples in the Rabbinic literature of classification by the number thirteen are: the thirteen years spent by Rabbi *Simeon ben Yohai and his son in the cave hiding from the Romans (*Shabbat* 33b); the thirteen siftings of the *Omer (*Menaḥot* 76b); the thirteen main categories of damage (*Bava Kama* 4b); the total of thirteen fasts when the rains failed to come as recorded in the Mishnah (*Taanit* 1: 4-6); and the three different fines in cases of assault: three, five, and thirteen (*Bava Kama* 27b).

Max Arzt: 'The Thirteen Attributes', in his *Justice and Mercy* (New York, 1963), 126, 206-7. Moses Cordovero, *The Palm Tree of Deborah*, trans. Louis Jacobs (London, 1960).

**Three Weeks** The weeks of mourning between 17 *Tammuz and the Ninth of *Av. These three weeks correspond to the three-week siege of Jerusalem before it was destroyed. During this period marriages are not celebrated and observant Jews do not listen to music or have their hair cut. There is a curious custom according to which this period is particularly open to risk of harm so that schoolteachers must not beat their charges even when they are unruly. *Corporal punishment in Jewish schools is in any event rare nowadays. With the establishment of the State of Israel even many Orthodox Jews favour a degree of relaxation of the laws of mourning over the destruction of the *Temple, but no marriages are celebrated during the three weeks in Orthodox synagogues.

**Throne of God** The great throne upon which God is seated, seen by the prophet Isaiah: 'I saw the Lord seated on a high and lofty throne' (Isaiah 6: 1). In the vision of the prophet *Ezekiel, who, unlike Isaiah, lived outside the Holy Land, the throne is carried to him on a chariot (Ezekiel 1). Ezekiel's vision is the subject of contemplation by the mystics described as Riders of the *Chariot. The book of Kings (1 Kings 22: 19) tells of the vision of the prophet Micaiah (not to be confused with the prophet *Micah) who spoke of God seated upon His throne, with all the host of heaven standing in attendance to the right and left of Him. A particularly anthropomorphic description of the throne is found in the late book of *Daniel (Daniel 7: 9): 'Thrones were set in place, and the Ancient of Days took His seat, His garment was like white snow, and the hair of His head was like clean wool. His throne was tongues of flame; its wheels were blazing fire.' Against these visions, in which God is located on a special throne, the prophet of exile declares: 'Thus saith the Lord, The heaven is My throne, and the earth My footstool' (Isaiah 66: 1). The Talmudic Rabbis often speak of God leaving His throne of judgement to sit on His throne of mercy, when, for example, the *shofar is sounded on *Rosh Ha-Shanah.

In all the biblical instances the throne is seen in a vision so that, with the exception of the thirteenth-century German Talmudist, Moses of Tachau, the medieval thinkers interpret the throne as a metaphor. Moses of Tachau really believes that God is seated on a throne on high surrounded by the heavenly hosts, or, rather, that God occasionally assumes this form. *Saadiah Gaon (*Beliefs and Opinions*, ii. 10) holds that the throne was created by God out of fire for the purpose of assuring His prophet that it was He and no other that had revealed His word to him. For Maimonides (*Guide of the Perplexed*, 1. 9) the throne is a metaphor for God's greatness and sublimity. In the Kabblah the Throne represents an aspect of the *Sefirot. In one version the throne is the Sefirah *Malkhut*, Sovereignty, and God seated on the throne represents the unification of the male and female principles on high, *Tiferet* and *Malkhut*. In another version, *Tiferet* is the throne because on it there rest the higher influences. In still another version, the throne of Mercy is *Binah* because on this Sefirah there rest the complete mercies of *Keter*. The throne of glory is a constant theme in liturgical poetry. Throughout, the throne of God represents the idea of God as King (see KINGDOM OF HEAVEN).

**Time and eternity**   Maimonides' fourth *principle of faith, that God is eternal, having neither beginning nor end, is no more than a restatement of that which is axiomatic in every version of Judaism. Maimonides gives as the proof-text, if such were needed, the verse: 'The eternal God is a refuge' (Deuteronomy 33: 27). The Hebrew of this verse means 'the ancient God' or 'the God [existing] from before'. In a number of other biblical verses there is a particular stress on the eternity of God, 'Before the mountains were brought forth, or ever Thou hadst formed the earth and the world, even from everlasting to everlasting Thou art God' (Psalms 90: 2). 'Thus saith the Lord, the King of Israel, and his Redeemer the Lord of hosts: I am the first, and I am the last, and beside Me there is no God' (Isaiah 44: 6). The Psalmist states that when all else has perished God will still be: 'They shall perish, but Thou shalt endure: Yes, all of them shall wax old like a garment; as a vesture shalt Thou change them, and they shall pass away; But Thou art the selfsame, and Thy years shall have no end' (Psalms 102: 27–8). The creation narrative, with which the book of Genesis opens, is silent, unlike the pagan mythologies, on the whole question of the divine before the creation process begins: 'In the beginning God created the heaven and the earth' (Genesis 1: 1). It is completely at variance with biblical modes of thought to apply terms like 'birth' and 'death' to God. The philosophical *'Adon Olam' hymn opens with the words (in *Zangwill's translation):

Lord of the world, He reigned alone,
While yet the universe was naught,
When by His will all things were wrought
Then first His sov'ran name was known.
And when the All shall cease to be,
In dread lone splendour He shall reign,
He was, He is, He shall remain
In glorious eternity.

In medieval thought the *Tetragrammaton is spelled out as: *hayah*, 'He was'; *hoveh*, 'He is'; and *yiheyeh*, 'He will be', to denote that God is the Lord of eternity; past, present and future are all the same to Him.

The word most frequently used in the Bible to denote eternity is *olam* (possibly from a root meaning 'to be concealed'). This word is used in some biblical contexts to denote simply an extremely long duration of time, particularly ancient time, that is, the days of old. But when used of God, the word (usually translated as 'for ever') does refer to God's eternity, though such an abstract term as 'eternity' is foreign to the concrete nature of biblical language and thought-patterns. Another biblical word suggesting the concept of eternity is *netzaḥ* (from a root meaning 'to be bright', 'to shine', and hence 'unfading' or 'everlastingness'). The Psalmist (Psalms 16: 11) declares that at God's right hand is bliss for evermore (*netzaḥ*) and the prophet Isaiah (Isaiah 25: 8) declares that God will make death to vanish for ever (*la-netzaḥ*). It is possible, however, that the standard English translations have been influenced by medieval abstractions and that, in the Bible, while God is certainly different from man, the full concept of eternity is left unexplored.

In Rabbinic thought the contrast between God and man is often drawn: 'Come and see! The measure of the Holy One, blessed be He, is unlike the measure of flesh and blood. The things fashioned by a creature of flesh and blood outlast him but the Holy One, blessed be He, outlasts the things He has fashioned' (*Berakhot* 9a). Inevitably, considering the dependence of Jews in Rabbinic times on the frequently arbitrary goodwill of powerful rulers, the contrast between God and man is often drawn in terms of the eternal, reliable God and the mortal, unreliable king or emperor. Constantinople outlasts by far Constantine, Antioch outlasts Antiochus, Alexandria outlasts Alexander, but the Lord lives for ever and will rebuild Zion and Jerusalem and the cities of Judah (Midrash Psalms 9: 8).

The Talmudic Rabbis has quite literally a down-to-earth attitude in this matter. God is eternal but it is not given to man to explore the full meaning of this idea. Aimed at contemporary attempts to pierce the veil is the famous statement in the Mishnah (*Ḥagigah* 2: 1): 'Whoever reflects on four things it were better for him that he had not come into the world: What is above? What is beneath? What is before? And what is after?' No doubt there are echoes here of Gnostic ideas about *creation and it is even possible that 'before' and 'after' do not refer to time at all but to space, that is, what is in one direction beyond the earth and what in another direction. One cannot therefore expect to find in the Rabbinic literature anything like a detailed examination of what is involved in the doctrine of divine eternity. The medieval thinkers, on the other hand, were much concerned with philosophical questions regarding time and eternity and their relationship to God.

Maimonides (*Guide*, 2. 13) believes that time itself is created, so that expressions such as that God *was before* He created the world (suggesting a time-span 'before' time was created) are to be understood as a supposition regarding time or an imagining of time and are not to be understood as referring to the true reality of time. However, Maimonides (*Guide*, 2. 27–9) also argues for the indestructability of the universe, which implies endless duration in time. Maimonides' view would seem, therefore to be that 'once' time has been created it endures for ever. Ideas such as these go back to Plato's *Timaeus*, in which time is distinguished from what is in time, though the difficulty has often been noted in the idea of time as a kind of box into which is placed that which is in time. *Albo (*Ikkarim*, ii. 18–19) observes that the concepts of priority and perpetuity can only be applied to God in a negative sense. When, in speaking of God, terms are used such as 'before' or 'after' some period, this means no more than that He was not non-existent before or after that period but, in reality, terms life 'before' or 'after', indicating a time-span, cannot be applied to the Eternal One. Albo, following Maimonides, makes a distinction between two kinds of time. The first is measured time, which depends on motion and to which the terms prior and posterior can be applied. The second is not measured or numbered but is a duration existing prior to the 'sphere' (in the medieval view the entity into which the planets are fixed). This time in the abstract is possibly eternal. Consequently, the difficulty of whether or not time originates in time is avoided. The second kind of time has no origin. It is only the 'order of time', the first kind, that originates in time in the other sense. It is, indeed, difficult, if not impossible, to conceive of a 'duration' before the creation of the world, but, says Albo, it is similarly difficult to think of God as 'outside' space. This is why, Albo concludes, the Rabbis of the Mishnah (mentioned above) declare that one must not ask what is above, what is below, what is before, and what is behind. (Albo obviously understands these terms as applying to space and time.)

In all this the medieval thinkers are grappling with the insurmountable problem of the relationship between the eternity of God and time as humans perceive it. The Jewish mystics draw in this connection on the Neoplatonic idea of the 'Eternal Now', though they do not attribute this idea to non-Jewish sources. They rely on this idea to solve the age-old problem of how God's foreknowledge can be reconciled with human *free will. In his commentary to the Pentateuch, Bahya, *Ibn Asher comments on the verse: 'The Lord will reign for ever and ever' (Exodus 15: 18): 'All times, past and future, are in the present so far as God is concerned, for He was before time and is not encompassed by it.' Rabbi Moses Almosnino (1510–89) comments on: 'For now I know' (Genesis 22: 12), a verse that seems to imply that God did not know it beforehand, that 'now' in the verse is the 'Eternal Now'. This notion of God being beyond time or, as the mystics put it, 'higher than time', is repeated in many a mystical text. The Hasidic master *Nahman of Bratslav, has this to say on the subject:

'God, as is well known, is above time. This is a truly marvellous notion, utterly incomprehensible, impossible for the human mind to grasp. You must appreciate, however, that essentially time is the product of ignorance, that is to say, time only appears real to us because our intellect is so puny. The greater the mind the smaller and less significant does time become for it. Take a dream, for instance, in which the mind is dormant and the imaginative faculty takes over. In a dream it is possible for a seventy-year span to pass by in a quarter of an hour. In a dream it seems as if a great span of time has elapsed but in reality only a very short space of time has been traversed. On awakening, the dreamer realises that the whole seventy-year period of the dream occupied in reality only a fraction of time. This is because the dreamer's intellectual capacity has been restored to him in his waking life and so far as his mind is concerned the whole seventy-year period of the dream is no more than a quarter of an hour . . . There is a Mind so elevated that for It the whole of time is counted as naught, for so great is that Mind that for It the whole time-span is as nothing whatever. Just as, so far as we are concerned, the seventy years which pass by in a dream are no more than a quarter of an hour in reality, as we have seen, so it is with regard to that Mind which is so far above anything we know as mind that for It time has no existence at all.'

Present-day philosophical discussion of eternity as timelessness are concerned with the question of whether this notion can be 'cashed' (as linguistic philosophers would put it): does the notion have any meaning? Yet the Jewish discussions still try to say something on the subject. The twentieth-century *Musar teacher, Rabbi E. E. *Dessler, reflects on the idea of spiritual progress in the Hereafter since the *World to Come is beyond time and progress implies a time-sequence. His solution is that the soul is endowed with the capacity to experience time when it has left the material world behind. This capacity, as well as that of comprehension, both of which prevent the soul from becoming absorbed in the divine (see UNIO MYSTICA) and hence incapable of spiritual progress, belong to the 'bodily element' of the soul, the *guf* ('body') which the soul inhabits even in eternal life.

The problem of time is one of the great mysteries. The mind reels at the thought of time flowing endlessly along. The notion of eternity has been understood by many religious thinkers as conveying the thought of existence beyond or outside time. An illustration sometimes given is of fictitious two-dimensional creatures who may be able with difficulty to imagine a third dimension but who would be obliged to think of it in terms of the two dimensions they know and would be incapable of grasping the nature of the third dimension. In whatever way time is thought of, the only recourse is to fall back on the insoluble. Even if time is thought of as duration alone, the human mind is presented with the alternatives of either postulating that time will eventually come to an end or that it will last for ever. As Kant has noted, whenever we think of time as coming to an end we find ourselves asking: and what will happen *then*? Endless duration in time is similarly quite beyond our imagination. The attitude of religious Jews to the whole question of time and eternity is that to try to gain knowledge in this area is as futile as to try to grasp the nature of God. Jews generally prefer to speak of God as the 'Timeless' or 'Eternal' and leave it at that.

Louis Jacobs, 'Eternity', in his *A Jewish Theology* (New York, 1973), 81–92.

**Tisha be-av**  See AV, NINTH OF.

**Tithing**  The main biblical passages regarding the tithing of produce are: Numbers 18: 21–32 and Deuteronomy 14: 22–7 and 26: 12. Biblical scholars (see BIBLICAL CRITICISM) have seen the differences in these sources concerning the recipients of the tithe as due to the social background of two separate sources, each having its own applications. Throughout the Rabbinic literature, however, the sources are harmonized and the following system emerges. The tithes have to be given from corn, wine, and oil by biblical law and from fruit and vegetables by Rabbinic law. The farmer first separates from the yield a portion (a sixtieth, fiftieth, or fortieth at the farmer's discretion), known as *terumah* ('heave offering' or 'gift'). This is given to a *Kohen (*priest) and is treated as sacred food in that it must not be eaten when the priest is in a state of ritual contamination or when the *terumah* itself has suffered contamination. Nor may it be eaten by a non-Kohen. A tenth of the remainder of the yield, known as *maaser rishon*, 'the first tithe', is then separated and given to a *Levite. The Levite, in turn, separates a tenth of his tithe and this, known as *terumat maaser*, is given to a Kohen to be treated with the same degree of sanctity as the original *terumah*. The portion given to the Levite has no sanctity and may be eaten by an ordinary Israelite. The farmer separates a tenth of the reminder of his yield, known as *maaser sheni*, 'the second tithe'. This has to be taken to Jerusalem and consumed there in a spirit of sanctity. If it is too difficult to take the second tithe to Jerusalem, it can be redeemed by substituting for it a sum of money which is then taken to Jerusalem and food and drink purchased with it to be consumed there. However, every third and sixth year of the cycle culminating in the *Sabbatical year, the second tithe is given to the poor and is known as *maaser ani*, 'poor man's tithe'. After the destruction of the *Temple, *maaser sheni* was redeemed for a small amount and this tithe could then be consumed by the farmer wherever he happened to live. Produce from which the tithes had not been separated was strictly forbidden but once the tithes had been separated their actual distribution could be postponed. The farmer could please himself as to which Kohen or Levite he gave his tithes. Not everyone was scrupulous in separating the tithes. A whole tractate of the Mishnah, tractate *Demai* ('Doubtful Produce') is devoted to the need for tithing produce bought from an *am ha-aretz* suspected of laxity in the matter.

According to the Rabbis, the laws of tithing only apply to the land of Israel, and farmers in the *Diaspora have no obligation to give tithes, although there is some evidence of communities outside Israel, in Egypt for example, having a system of tithing. Again according to the Rabbis, the full tithing laws apply only when the majority of Jews live in the land of Israel and since, in the absence of the purification rites of the *red heifer, everyone today suffers from corpse-contamination, the *terumah* is inoperative in any event. Moreover the purpose of tithing, for the upkeep of the priests and Levites, has no meaning nowadays. The present practice in the State of Israel is to have only a token separation of the tithes.

Some Rabbinic sources make reference to a tithe of money as well as of produce, although it is not too clear whether this was seen as a voluntary contribution rather than an obligation. Nevertheless, many observant Jews today do donate a tenth of their annual income to *charity. This is known as *maaser kesafim*, 'the money tithe' or 'wealth tax'.

**Titles** In the Rabbinic tradition each of the more famous biblical characters is given a title suitable to his or her life's work. The *patriarchs are known as the 'fathers' and the *matriarchs as the 'mothers', for example: 'Abraham our father', 'Sarah our mother'. A passage in the Talmud (*Berakhot* 16b) states that only the three patriarchs are to be called 'fathers' and only the four matriarchs 'mothers'. The early teachers, whose doctrines and sayings are recorded in the Mishnah are known collectively, though not individually, as 'the Fathers' as in Ethics of the Fathers. But the individual title 'Father' is reserved for the patriarchs. Moses (except for one reference in the Mishnah) is always called 'Moshe Rabbenu' ('Moses our Teacher'), although, obviously under the influence of Islam, the medieval thinkers sometimes refer to Moses as 'the Prophet'. Joseph is usually called 'Joseph the Righteous' (Ha-Taaddik), because he resisted the advances of the wife of Potiphar (Genesis 39). Miriam is known as 'Miriam the Prophetess' (Ha-Neviah), after Exodus 15: 20; David is 'David Ha-Melekh' (King David) and his descendant, the *Messiah, as 'Ha-Melekh Ha-Mashiah'. The *High Priest is naturally given this title to distinguish him from the ordinary *priests. The Vice-High Priest was called 'the Segan' ('Deputy'). The President of the *Sanhedrin is known as the Nasi ('Prince') and the Vice-President of this body as 'Av Bet Din' ('Father of the Court'). The head of the Jewish community in the land of Israel is also known as the Nasi, as in *Judah the Prince. The bearer of this office is also called 'the Parnas' (literally: 'the Sustainer', in the sense of the person responsible for the government of the community).

Among the *Tannaim and Amoraim, the Talmudic *Rabbis, the title Rabbi was reserved for the Tannaim and the Palestinian Amoraim. The Babylonian Amoraim, who did not have full *ordination, were called simply Rav. The earliest teachers had no title at all; they were simply *Hillel and *Shammai, not Rabbi Hillel and Rabbi Shammai. The Nasi, from the time of *Johanan ben Zakkai and *Gamaliel, was known as Rabban ('Our Teacher'). As it is put in the *Letter* of *Sherira Gaon: 'Greater than Rav is Rabbi. Greater than Rabbi is Rabban. Greater than Rabban is the name [on its own without any title].' Mar, meaning Sir or Master, is a common appellation for scholars in the Talmud but it is also found as a proper name. The lay head of the Babylonian community, corresponding to the Nasi in the land of Israel, and often in conflict with the Rabbis, was known as the Resh Galuta, the *exilarch.

The general titles for the medieval and later authors are, depending on their particular bent: the Meforashim ('Commentators') and Posekim ('Those Who Decide' (questions of Jewish law)). *Karo and *Isserles are known as 'the Authors of the *Shulhan Arukh*'. The legal authorities who flourished before the *Shulhan Arukh* are known as the Rishonim ('Early Ones') and those who flourished after this work had been compiled as the Aharonim ('the Later Ones'). The Rishonim generally enjoy greater *authority in Jewish law than the Aharonim.

With the development of the Rabbinic office (see RABBIS), the Rabbi is called Ha-Rav or Av Bet Din. A judge is known as a Dayan (the word means a judge). A preacher is called a Darshan (from *darash*, 'to expound') or a Maggid (lit. 'a teller'). The title Gaon was at first given only to the heads of the colleges of *Sura and Pumbedita in the period of the *Geonim but was later given to any Rabbi distinguished for his great learning as in *Elijah, Gaon of Vilna. Later still it became so customary to call practically every scholar Ha-Rav Ha-Gaon that it was considered an insult not to address a Rabbi as a Gaon. The more pompous title 'the True Gaon' or 'the Gaon of Geonim', adopted for some Rabbis, only tended to invite ridicule. Sephardi Rabbis usually have the title Hakham ('Sage')

rather than Rabbi. A title given to a learned layman is Haver ('Associate'), a title that goes back to the early Talmudic period, or Morenu ('Our Teacher'). Scholars belonging to the modern historical-critical school are generally given the name Hakham or Hoker ('Investigator'). A Kabbalist is a Mekubbal ('One who is versed in the *Kabbalah'). One who has attained a high degree of piety and sanctity is known as a Baal Madregah ('A Master of [Spiritual] Stages'). A miracle-worker is known as a Baal Mofet ('Master of Miracle') or as a Baal Shem ('Master of the [Divine] Name'), as in Israel *Baal Shem Tov, the founder of *Hasidism.

Among scholars, especially in *Yeshivah circles, a particularly diligent student, one who spends most of his time in his studies, is known as a Matmid (from *tamid*, 'continuously', i.e. an unceasing student). A scholar with a vast amount of knowledge (see STUDY) is known as a Baki ('Expert'), while one noted for his keen intellect is known as a Harif ('Sharp One'). A scholarly genius is known as an Illui ('Superior One') and a bit of a genius as a Hatzi-Illui ('Half-Genius'). The old gibe has it that an Illui is crazy and a Hazti-Illui is only half-crazy. A thinker in the philosophical vein is called a Baal Mahashavah ('Master of Thought') or a Filosof ('Philosopher'), the latter often used pejoratively, as in the story of the Hasidic master who asked: 'Why is the world like a glass of tea?' and when his followers asked: 'Why, indeed?' replied: 'Am I then a Filosof?'

In Hasidism there is an abundance of titles. The Hasidic Master himself is known as a *Zaddik or *Rebbe (to distinguish him from the 'Rabbi') or Admur (abbreviation of Adonenu, Morenu Ve-Rabbenu—'Our Master, Teacher, and Rabbi') and his followers are called Hasidim. Flowery titles, based on Talmudic and Kabbalistic texts, are given to the Zaddik, such as 'the Bright Candelabrum'; 'the Holy Rabbi'; 'the Glory of his Generation'; 'the Mighty Hammer' or 'the Right Pillar of the Temple'. The publishers of *Levi Yitzhak of Berditchev's *Kedushat Levi* describe the author, on the title-page, as: 'Admur, Excellence of Our Strength, Ha-Rav, the True Gaon, Man of God, Teacher of all the Sons of the Diaspora, Renowned in every corner of the earth, His Holy Honour, Our Teacher Rabbi Levi Yitzhak, May His Memory be a Blessing.' While the followers of the *Musar movement were normally very sparing in their praises, even they seem to have come under the influence of Hasidism in the matter of titles. The publishers of Israel *Salanter's *Or Yisrael*, on the title-page, describe this founder of the movement as: 'Admur, the Great Rabbi and Gaon, Head of all the Sons of the Diaspora, Saint and Humble Man, Light of the World, Renowned in every corner of the earth'—a case of anything you can do, we can do better.

A severe reaction eventually set in against the use of grandiose titles, even among the Orthodox who had long been accustomed to them without taking them too seriously. Orthodox Rabbis today generally scorn such titles and prefer to be called simply 'Rabbi' (Ha-Rav). Rabbis with a doctorate from a university often prefer to be called 'Dr *X*'. In the Orthodox Press, Reform and Conservative Rabbis are sometimes dubbed Ra Banim ('Bad Children') in a play on words on Rabbanim, plural of Rabbi.

For the names given to Jewish books, see BOOKS.

**Tobacco** When tobacco first began to be used in Europe there was considerable objection to it on the part of the Church. Rabbis, on the whole, saw no objection to tobacco *per se*, but its use has been widely discussed by Jewish teachers from various other aspects of the law.

One of the questions discussed was whether a benediction has to be recited over the use of tobacco. The Talmudic Rabbis coined *benedictions for eating and drinking in obedience to the principle that God should be praised and thanked for His gifts. The Rabbis had no knowledge of tobacco but once this new means of enjoyment became available the question of a benediction arose. An early discussion is that of Abraham Gombiner (d. 1683) in his *Magen Avraham*, a commentary to the *Shulḥan Arukh* (*Oraḥ Ḥayyim*, 210. n. 9). Gombiner remarks: 'Further thought has to be given to the question of those who place the herb known as tobacco into a pipe which they light and inhale the smoke and then exhale it. The problem is whether this is to be compared to one who tastes food but does not swallow it, in which case no benediction is required. Or whether it should rather be compared to smelling sweet spices over which a benediction is required, and this would apply here *a fortiori* since there is physical pleasure in that some people are as

sated from smoking as if they had enjoyed food and drink. Further thought is required.'

Since there is a doubt, the principle that no benediction is required in doubtful cases applies, and it is the universal custom not to recite a benediction over tobacco.

Mordecai Ha-Levi (d. 1684), judge and Halakhic authority in Cairo for over forty years, discusses whether it is permitted to smoke on a *fast day and on a *festival. On the face of it, to smoke on both these days is to be involved in contradiction. On a festival it is permitted to light fire only in the preparation of food. If, therefore, smoking is treated as food and is permitted on a festival, it ought to be forbidden on a fast day when no food is allowed to enter the mouth. But the author comes to the conclusion that it is permitted to smoke on both these days, his argument being that smoking cannot be considered to be food and is hence permitted on a fast day; however, the definition of preparation of 'food' has to be understood as embracing every form of physical pleasure, including smoking. In an interesting aside, Ha-Levi remarks that Jews should not smoke in public on a fast day since Muslims do not smoke on their fast days and Jews must not give the wrong impression that they are less scrupulous in their religious observances than their Gentile neighbours are in theirs. Ha-Levi frowns, however, on smoking on Tisha Be-Av (see AV, NINTH OF) when even the study of the Torah is forbidden because it is a joyful experience. In practice, Orthodox Jews do smoke on Yom Tov and on Tisha Be-Av after midday. It is also a widespread custom to take snuff on *Yom Kippur, since this does not fall under the heading of any of the 'afflictions' forbidden on the day, such as food and drink. On the same lines as Mordecai Ha-Levi, the famed German authority, David Hoffman (1843–1921) holds that while, strictly speaking, it is permitted to smoke in a *synagogue (not, of course, during the services) it should not be done since Christians would not dream of smoking in a church and it would constitute a profanation of the divine Name if Jews behaved with less reverence in their houses of worship than Christians do in theirs.

In early *Hasidism tobacco occupied an important role. Some of the Hasidic masters looked upon tobacco as the modern equivalent of *incense in *Temple times and many of them used to smoke a meditative pipe before they offered their prayers. A further idea found among the early Hasidim is that there are subtle '*holy sparks' in tobacco which, under divine providence, was brought to Europe so that the masters could elevate these sparks in order to complete the full restoration that would result in the coming of the *Messiah. A later Hasidic master said that tobacco was used by pagan savages before it was brought to Europe. Its use by the Hasidim raises the weed from the profane to the sacred in that no one is ashamed to accept from another a peck of snuff or a pipeful of tobacco and so acts of *benevolence are carried out through it all the time. The smoking of a pipe by the Hasidim must have been a prevalent practice in early Hasidism since, in the polemics against them, there are repeated accusations that they waste hours in smoking. The *lulke* (churchwarden's pipe) of the *Baal Shem Tov features frequently in Hasidic legend. Some sources report that the Baal Shem Tov used to recite a benediction before smoking his pipe. The suggestion that the Baal Shem Tov's pipe contained a substance other than tobacco is completely unwarranted.

Rabbi S. Sevin, in his biographies of famous Halakhists, reports a curious episode about smoking in his life of the famous *Yeshivah principal, Baruch Bear Leibovitz (1866–1939). Rabbi Leibovitz had an original way of 'smoking' cigarettes. He would place the cigarette in his mouth and chew and suck it without ever lighting it, deriving a certain amount of satisfaction in the process. The reason for his strange behaviour was that his father once gave him a cigarette but when his teacher saw him smoking, the teacher said: 'Why do you have to smoke?' Anxious to satisfy the dictates of both his father and teacher, he decided that he would take cigarettes into his mouth without actually smoking them.

In more recent years, when medical research has demonstrated that there is a causal relationship between smoking cigarettes and lung cancer (and heart disease), a number of Rabbis, especially Conservative Rabbis, have suggested that the *Halakhah now be invoked to forbid smoking as injurious to health. Undoubtedly, the Jewish tradition is emphatic that *health should be preserved but it is somewhat questionable whether the Halakhah can be invoked in this area. There is a risk as well as advantages in smoking, as there is in imbibing alcohol and in failing to have a sensible diet,

and, indeed, in driving a motor car. Each individual should at his own discretion balance the risks against the advantages. To be sure most people will probably decide that the risk is not worth taking and this outweighs any advantages, but such decisions cannot be made a matter of Jewish law. Or, in any event, this seems to be the attitude of law-abiding Jews who do smoke.

Elliot N. Dorf and Arthur Rosett, *A Living Tree: The Roots and Growth of Jewish Law* (Albany, NY, 1988), 345–62 (examines the different attitudes to smoking by the various religious groupings).

**Tolerance** Religious tolerance is, in the main, a modern idea advanced by thinkers such as *Spinoza, John Locke, and John Stuart Mill, who broke consciously with tradition in this matter. Pre-modern Judaism, like pre-modern Christianity and Islam, held that there could be no toleration of religious viewpoints other than its own. Jews with a historical sense appreciate that certain ideas acceptable in a pluralistic society are simply not found in the classical sources but are none the worse for that. Taking this for granted, it is still possible to extrapolate from the tradition ideas about religious tolerance, even though these do not receive there anything like full explication.

The most striking fact which emerges from the biblical writings in the matter of tolerance is that the prophets of ancient Israel were totally uncompromising with apostasy and *idolatry among their own people but tolerant of the idolatry of their pagan neighbours who had no opportunity to know the God of Israel. The prophets do castigate the neighbouring peoples for the atrocities they commit in the furtherance of their cult—*Molech-worship is a case in point—but nowhere is there found in the Bible the idea that the worship of the pagan gods by the nations is to be condemned in itself. So far as the internal life of the people was concerned, the Hebrew prophets had to be ruthless if the long struggle against idolatry was to be successful. The cry of *Elijah (1 Kings 18: 21) was echoed by all the prophets: 'How long halt ye between two opinions? If the Lord be God, follow Him: but if Baal, follow him.' Similarly, while the Deuteronomist declares that the gods of the nations were 'allotted' to them by God Himself (Deuteronomy 4: 19), he is altogether ruthless when it comes to Israel worshipping strange gods. In the book of

Deuteronomy (13: 13–19), the doom of the city that has gone astray to worship strange gods is pronounced in the most virulent terms: 'Thou shalt surely smite the inhabitants of that city with the edge of the sword, destroying it utterly, and all that is therein and the cattle thereof, with the edge of the sword.' It should none the less be noted that, as the Talmudic Rabbis remark, this passage is academic. There is no record of this kind of procedure ever having been carried out.

Among the Talmudic Rabbis, too, there appears the distinction between tolerance to those outside and those within. The Rabbis teach everywhere that converts to Judaism can only be accepted if they come of their own free will. But so far as Jews are concerned there are numerous instances in Rabbinic literature of coercion in matters of belief and practice; the *herem is only one example of religious coercion of Jews by Jews. According to Maimonides (*Edut*, 11. 10) the *epikoros has to be destroyed (this, too, is academic, since Jews in Maimonides' day did not have any such powers) and has no share in the *World to Come. For all that, two outstanding twentieth-century Orthodox authorities declare that these ancient regulations are no longer operative. Rabbi A. I. *Kook argued that present-day unbelievers are quite different from the defiant *epikoros* of whom the Rabbis speak, while Rabbi Abraham Isaiah Karelitz (1878–1953), known as the 'Hazon Ish', declared that nowadays we must try so far as we can to bring them back to the truth by means of the cords of love and to help them see the light.

Many of the Orthodox still follow this distinction between tolerance towards those without and those within the Jewish camp. *Dialogue with Christians, for example, receives no condemnation, quite the opposite, in most Orthodox circles, while there is no toleration of Reform and Conservative viewpoints, although individual Reform and Conservative Jews are never read out of Judaism. As the British Chief Rabbi, Jonathan Sacks, has written, non-Orthodox Jews are to be seen, from the Orthodox standpoint, as, in a Talmudic phrase, 'children brought up among Gentiles' who are not held blameworthy for their rejection of an Orthodoxy they have never had a real chance to know. Naturally, the non-Orthodox see such an attitude as patronizing.

Louis Jacobs, 'Tolerance', in his: *What Does Judaism Say About . . .?* (Jerusalem, 1973), 317–18.

Jonathan Sacks, *One People? Tradition, Modernity, and Jewish Unity* (The Littman Library of Jewish Civilization; London, 1993).

**Tombstone** Heb. *matzevah* (from a root meaning 'to stand', hence 'pillar'). When his wife died the patriarch Jacob marked her grave: 'And Jacob set up a pillar [*matzevah*] upon her grave; the same is the pillar of Rachel's grave unto this day' (Genesis 35: 20). Historically speaking, Jews in ancient times did have tombstones, as the archaeological evidence shows, but in the Jerusalem Talmud (*Shekalim* 2: 5) there is a saying that tombstones should not be erected over the graves of the righteous, since their deeds are their memorial. This saying has puzzled the commentators in view of the verse regarding Rachel. In any event, it is now the universal custom to erect a tombstone, especially under the influence of the Kabbalah in which great importance is attached to the custom. In Hasidic practice it is even the custom to erect a mausoleum over the grave of a *Zaddik, to which *pilgrimages are made. Among the *Sephardim the tombstone is placed horizontally on the grave but the *Ashkenazim have a vertical stone. In these matters all depends on local *custom, as does the time for the 'tombstone setting', as it is called. The usual practice in the State of Israel nowadays is to set the stone thirty days after the burial but in other communities it is set either during the eleven months after the burial or after twelve months (see DEATH AND BURIAL).

The inscription on the tombstone, in which the praises of the departed are often sung, was always in Hebrew but in many communities there is also an inscription in the vernacular. It is also customary to depict two hands raised in blessing on the tombstone of a *Kohen (see PRIESTLY BLESSING). An abbreviation of the Hebrew for 'May his/her soul be bound in the bundle of life' is usually inscribed on the stone. In many modern Jewish communities there is a special order of service for the setting of the tombstone, with psalms and prayers for the repose of the soul of the departed. The custom of placing small stones on the tombstone is intended to show that the grave has been visited and that the departed has not been forgotten.

Harry Rabinowicz, 'The Tombstone (Matzevah)', in his *A Guide to Life: Jewish Laws and Customs of Mourning* (New York, 1967), 114–20.

**Torah** 'The Teaching.' In the *Pentateuch the word *torah* is used frequently to denote a particular law or ritual, for example, the *torah* of the burnt-offering (Leviticus 6: 2). But once the Pentateuch itself was seen as the revealed will of God in its entirety (see REVELATION) it became known as : 'the Torah of Moses' or 'the Torah' without qualification, so that the Hebrew *Bible is divided into the three sections of Torah ( = the Pentateuch), the Prophets, and the Hagiographa. All three came to be subsumed under the heading of the *Written Torah. In addition, the expositions and derivations from Scripture found in the Rabbinic literature were also thought of as revealed, that is, as given verbally in the first instance to Moses and then handed down from generation to generation, with provision for various additions and adaptations to new circumstances as they arose. This whole process is called by the Rabbis the *Oral Torah. Both these *torot* are thought of as one complete *torah* so that, in the tradition, the term Torah denotes: 1. the Pentateuch; 2. the whole of Jewish teaching as revealed by God in the Written and the Oral Torah; 3. the later applications and deeper understanding of these down to the present day, so that the Torah is synonymous with the Jewish religion. The English translation of the Torah as 'the Law' goes back to the *Septuagint, in which the word *torah* is rendered in Greek as *nomos*. This term has come to stay, although traditionally the Torah is far more than law in its narrow sense. It rather embraces, as above, the whole of the Jewish religion, and the Pentateuch itself contains much material that is in no way purely legal.

This is the traditional view, in which the Torah is the same always. It is the will of God for the Jewish people and in a wider sense for all mankind (see *Noahide Laws). The Jew is obliged to *study the Torah and to observe the *precepts, the *mitzvot* (see MITZVAH). This static view of Torah has been challenged in modern times and attempts have been made to interpret the doctrine: 'The Torah is from Heaven', in the Rabbinic formulation, in a manner that takes into account the findings of historical research into the origins of Judaism (see BIBLICAL CRITICISM; CONSERVATIVE JUDAISM; FUNDAMENTALISM; HISTORY; and JÜDISCHE WISSENSCHAFT).

The central idea in the tradition is that the Torah does mean the Pentateuch, as in the term *Sefer Torah ('Scroll of the Torah') from which the *reading of the Torah takes place, but, by implication, the Pentateuch embraces the whole of Jewish teaching. This idea is expressed, no doubt with a degree of hyperbole, in a typical Talmudic comment (*Berakhot* 5a) on the verse: 'And I will give thee the tablets of stone, and the Torah and the commandment, which I have written that thou mayest teach them' (Exodus 24: 12). Each clause of this verse is made to refer to a part of the Torah as a whole. Thus 'the tablets of stone' are said to refer to the *Decalogue; 'the Torah' to the Pentateuch; 'the commandment' to the *Mishnah; 'which I have written' to the Prophets and the Hagiographa; and 'that thou mayest teach them' to the Talmud. This teaches, the passage concludes, that all these were given on *Sinai. The meaning seems to be that all later developments were implicit in the Torah given to Moses. Solomon *Schechter has put the all-embracing, traditional view succinctly:

'When certain Jewish Boswells apologised for observing the private lives of their masters too closely, they said: "It is a Torah, which we are desired of learning" (*Berakhot* 62a). In this sense it is used by another Rabbi, who maintained that even the everyday talk of the people in the Holy Land is a Torah (that is, conveys an object lesson). For the poor man in Palestine, when applying to his neighbour for relief, was wont to say, "Acquire for thyself merit, or strengthen and purify thyself" (by helping me, Leviticus Rabbah 34: 7), thus implying the adage—that the man in want is just as much performing an act of charity in receiving as his benefactor in giving. In the east of Europe we can, even today, hear a member of the congregation addressing his minister, "Pray, tell me some Torah". The Rabbi would never answer him by reciting verses from the Bible, but would feel it incumbent upon him to give some spiritual or allegorical explanation of a verse from the Scriptures, or would treat him to some general remarks bearing upon morals and conduct.'

When the Sefer Torah is elevated in the synagogue after the reading of the Torah, the congregation sings the verse: 'And this is the Torah which Moses set before the children of Israel' (Deuteronomy 4: 44). In the context the verse refers to the particular laws recorded in the passage, but it now refers to the Torah as recorded in the Scroll and, by implication, to the Torah in its widest sense.

## The Significance of the Torah

Throughout Jewish history the Torah has been hailed as Israel's supreme and most precious gift, given by God as His own special benefaction to His people. In the Midrash the Torah is said to have been created before the creation of the world, God using the Torah as the architect uses his blueprint. When God wished to give the Torah to Israel, the Midrash observes, the angels objected, wishing to retain the Torah for themselves. Moses managed to convince the angels that the Torah, containing as it does such teachings as: 'Thou shalt not steal'; 'Thou shalt not commit adultery'; 'Thou shalt not kill', could only have meaning for creatures of flesh and blood who are sorely tempted by envy, lust, and hatred. In this vein, the Talmudic Rabbis declare that the Torah does not make too heavy demands on humans since: 'The Torah was not given to the ministering angels.' In many a psalm the praises of the Torah are sung. The first Psalm praises the man who avoids the counsel of the wicked for whom the Torah is his delight. In Psalm 19 (v. 8) the Torah of the Lord is said to be perfect, renewing life. The whole of Psalm 119, the Pharisaic Psalm, as this has been called by Christian scholars, utilizes each letter of the alphabet eight times in praise of the Torah: 'Oh, how I love Thy Torah! All day long it is my study' (v. 97).

The love of the Torah is given expression in the benediction recited before the reading of the *Shema: 'O our Father, merciful Father, ever compassionate, have mercy upon us; O put into our hearts to understand and to discern, to mark, learn and teach, to heed, to do and to fulfil in love all the words of instruction in Thy Torah. Enlighten our eyes in Thy Torah, and let our hearts cling to Thy commandments, and make us single-hearted to love and fear Thy name, so that we may never be put to shame.' In this benediction the giving of the Torah to Israel is an act of divine compassion and mercy. When the Babylonian Talmud quotes a scriptural verse it uses the expression: 'The All-merciful says.' A prayer found in the Zohar is recited in many congregations when the *Ark is opened in order to take out the Sefer Torah for the reading:

'I am the servant of the Holy One, blessed be

He, before whom and before whose glorious Torah I prostrate myself at all times; not in man do I put my trust, not upon any angel do I rely, but upon the God of Heaven, who is the God of truth, and whose Torah is truth, and whose prophets are prophets of truth, and who aboundeth in deeds of goodness and truth. In Him do I put my trust, and unto His holy and glorious Name I utter praises. May it be Thy will to open my heart unto Thy Torah, and to fulfil the wishes of my heart and of the hearts of all Thy people Israel for good, for life, and for peace.'

Yet for all the supreme significance of the Torah it is never an object of worship. God alone is to be worshipped, the Torah being the means of coming to God. The usual expression in Jewish piety is: 'love of the Torah and the fear of Heaven'. The term 'fear', denoting worship, is never applied to the Torah. Some authorities even object to bowing to the Torah since this might suggest that the Torah is being worshipped. The custom, however, is to bow to the Torah just as one bows to a person one wishes to honour without the slightest suggestion that he is being worshipped. The reference to prostration before the Torah in the Zoharic prayer may similarly be metaphorical, although in the Kabbalistic scheme the 'Supernal Torah' or the 'Soul of the Torah' in the celestial realms is an aspect of the *Sefirot, a doctrine that certainly comes close to the apotheosis of this celestial Torah, the source of the Torah below.

In the Kabblistic vein, *Nahmanides, in his introduction to his commentary to the Pentateuch, states that, on one level, the Torah is really a combination of divine names (see NAMES OF GOD), meaning that the Torah represents the cosmic forces after which the material world is fashioned. In the Zohar, as well as in the Lurianic Kabbalah, the narratives of the Torah, while referring on the mundane level to the events of which they tell, also have this inner meaning relating to the various powers in the Sefirotic realm. In the Zoharic scheme the pre-existent Torah is the Sefirah of *Hokhmah* ('Wisdom'), from which stem the Sefirah *Tiferet* ('Beauty', the male principle), identified with the Written Torah, and the Sefirah *Malkhut* ('Sovereignty', the female principle), identified with the Oral Torah. *Elijah, Gaon of Vilna, in his commentary to the section of the Zohar known as *Sifra De-Tzeniuta* ('Book of Concealment'), goes so far as to state that everything is hinted at in the Torah. Every human being, every animal and plant is found therein for one who has eyes to see. An oft-quoted passage in the Zohar (iii. 152a) states:

'Woe to the man who says that the Torah merely tells us tales in general and speaks of ordinary matters. If this were so we could make up even nowadays a Torah dealing with ordinary matters and an even better one at that. If all the Torah does is to tell us about worldly matters there are far superior things told in worldly books so let us copy them and make up a Torah of them. But the truth is that all the words of the Torah have to do with lofty themes and high mysteries.'

For the Zohar, as this passage continues, the Torah on the mundane level is only the garment of the Supernal Torah.

'The angels are spirits but when they come down to earth they have to be clothed with the garments of this world. If they are not clothed in something like the garments of this world they cannot remain in the world and the world cannot contain them. Now if this is true of the angels how much more is it true of the Torah, which created them and created all the worlds, all of which only survive because of the Torah. The Torah could not be contained in the world were she not clothed in the garments of this world. Consequently, the stories in the Torah are only the garments of the Torah.'

This mystical view of the Torah reappears in subsequent Jewish thought but there is a definite tendency among non-practising Kabbalists, even if they accept the notion of 'secrets of the Torah', to leave the understanding of these mysteries to the soul in the Hereafter. In this world, it is the duty of man to study and practise the Torah in its revealed, that is, in its plain, sense.

### The Immutability of the Torah

It is axiomatic in Judaism that the Torah is immutable. God does not change His mind and no other religion can ever take the place of Judaism. On this all religious Jews are agreed. But the doctrine of the immutability of the Torah has also been taken to mean that its laws are binding for all eternity, although the view is to be found that in the Messianic age the precepts of the Torah will be abrogated as no longer essential to the new, perfected world that will emerge. Maimonides' ninth *principle of faith puts the matter in this way: 'The ninth

principle of faith. The abrogation of the Torah. This implies that this Torah of Moses will not be abrogated and that no other Torah will come from before God. Nothing is to be added to it nor taken away from it, neither in the Written Torah nor in the Oral Torah, as it is said: "Thou shalt not add to it nor diminish from it" [Deuteronomy 13: 1].' Thus Maimonides, by quoting the Deuteronomic verse, adds to the doctrine that the Torah cannot be abrogated the idea that its laws can never be changed.

Among the many medieval discussions on this doctrine, the most comprehensive is that of *Albo in his *Sefer Ha-Ikkarim* (iii. 13–23). Albo begins by giving three reasons why it seems to many that there can be no change in the Torah. The first is that God who gave the Torah does not change and it should follow that the Torah which stems from God does not change. Secondly, the Torah was given to the whole people of Israel and, unlike an individual, a people does not change. Thirdly, since the Torah is truth it cannot suffer change, for truth is eternal. If it is true, for instance, that there is only One God it is inconceivable that there should come a time when this will no longer be true and there will be many gods. For all that, Albo believes that there is no a priori reason why a divine law should not change, since it is directed to recipients whose conditions in life are not always the same and who require, therefore, different rules of conduct for their different situations. A physician may prescribe a certain regimen for one period and a different one at a later stage of his patient's cure. It is not that the physician has changed his mind but that there are stages in the patient's restoration to health. Moreover there are examples in the Torah itself of a divine law being changed. Adam was only permitted vegetable food (Genesis 1: 29), Noah was permitted animal food (Genesis 9: 3). Abraham was given the additional precept of *circumcision and many new precepts were revealed to Moses. But from Moses onwards there have been no changes in the divine law. According to Maimonides, then, the Torah of Moses will never change and since, as Albo has demonstrated, a divine law can change, this must mean that the Torah of Moses is the sole exception to the rule.

After showing that changes in practice did take place after the time of Moses—*Ezra, for example, introduced the square Hebrew script in which the Torah is written in place of older cursive script—Albo concludes, contra Maimonides, that a law can be changed by a *prophet who orders this at the command of God, but the change will only be temporary so far as the last eight laws of the Decalogue are concerned. (The first two, that there is one God and that no other gods are to be worshipped, cannot be abrogated by a prophet even for a time.) As for other laws of the Torah, these can be changed even permanently provided that the change is made by a prophet speaking in God's name, just as Ezra arranged for the introduction of the square script.

From the whole medieval discussion of the doctrine, it emerges that the question of the Torah's immutability has to do with the question of whether a law promulgated by God will ever be repealed and from Albo's further discussion it emerges that Maimonides' ninth principle stands only in connection with the claims of Christianity and Islam that a new religion has superseded the Jewish religion. That modern historical studies have demonstrated conclusively that the *Halakhah has developed over the ages in response to changed conditions does not therefore really pose a challenge to the doctrine of the immutability of the Torah. Many modern Jews, accepting that Judaism has developed historically, have found refuge in the distinction between the abrogation of the Torah as a whole and the element of change evident in the Halakhic system.

While it is true that some statements in the Rabbinic literature do suggest that, as in the passage quoted above, everything was given by God to Moses at Sinai so that there can be no change at all in the Halakhah, and while some Orthodox authorities have roundly declared that, in the famous saying of Rabbi Moses *Sofer, 'Anything new is forbidden by the Torah', it is extremely doubtful whether such views were really taken too seriously even in the pre-modern era. Yom Tov Lippmann Heller (1579–1654), in the introduction to his commentary to the Mishnah, gives a profound and original interpretation of the ancient Rabbinic saying that God showed to Moses all the interpretations of later generations of scholars. This should not be taken to mean, says Heller, that the ancient Rabbis believed that each generation received a complete Halakhic tradition from its predecessors. He writes:

'Although there existed a complete interpretation of the Torah and its commands there is no generation in which something new is not added and which is without its own legal problems. Do not contradict me by pointing to the Rabbinic saying that God showed Moses the minutiae of the Torah and the minutiae of the Scribes and the innovations that would be introduced by the Scribes, for I say that this was not handed down by Moses to anyone else. A careful examination of the Rabbinic saying shows that they spoke of God "showing" Moses, not "teaching" or "handing down" . . . By using the word "showing" they meant that these teachings were revealed to Moses but not "given" to him, like a man who "shows" his friend an object but does not give it to him.'

Modern Jews, more aware than Heller could have been of development in the Halakhah, would no doubt word it differently but the basic principle is there in Heller. Internal changes in the Halakhah have taken place in the past and are taking place in the present and this is acknowledged by the Orthodox, although the Orthodox generally make a distinction between the Halakhah itself, which is unchanging, and the changing conditions to which the Halakhah addresses itself. The extent to which changes from within are allowed is the essential feature of the ongoing debate between Orthodoxy and Reform (and Conservative Judaism). Each of these movements understands the Torah in its own way. Yet all agree that the Torah, however conceived of in that movement, will never be abrogated by God. Except for purposes of reference, no Jew, no matter to which denomination he belongs, will speak of the Hebrew Bible as 'Old Testament' since he does not believe that there has been a 'New Testament'.

Louis Jacobs, 'Torah as Divine Revelation' in his *God, Torah, Israel* (Cincinnati, 1990), 23–54.
Solomon Schechter, *Some Aspects of Rabbinic Theology* (New York, 1961), 116–69.
Isaiah Tishby, 'Torah', in his *The Wisdom of the Zohar*, trans. David Goldstein (The Littman Library of Jewish Civilization; Oxford, 1989), 1077–1154.

**Tosafot** 'Additions' to the Babylonian Talmud; the glosses, now printed together with the text in practically all editions, produced by the French and German scholars during the twelfth to the fourteenth centuries. The Tosafot activity, in which the Talmud was examined minutely and in such a manner as to further the debates and discussions found in that work, began among the members of the family and pupils of *Rashi. The Tosafists flourished in northern France, England, and Germany, the two best-known of the three hundred or so practitioners being Rashi's grandson, Rabbenu *Tam and the latter's nephew, Isaac of Dampierre. There are various collections of Tosafot, the printers of the Talmud selecting from those they had to hand in order to incorporate these into the published work. There is also a collection of Tosafot to the Pentateuch, known as *Daat Zekenim (Opinion of The Elders)* but this work is far less influential than the glosses to the Talmud.

Unlike Rashi's, which is a running commentary to the Talmud, the Tosafot consist of glosses to particular topics on which the authors have something to add. Very frequently, the Tosafot take issue with Rashi's understanding of a particular passage. They often point out apparent contradictions between Talmudic passages which they then either resolve by casuistry or else admit that the passages are in conflict. Time and again the whole of the Babylonian Talmud relevant to a particular discussion is surveyed by the Tosafot, hence the saying that the Tosafot treat the Talmud as a ball thrown from hand to hand. No responsible student of the Talmud can afford to ignore the difficult Tosafot. It was these that gave zest to the study of the Talmud, which became known as the study of Gefat, an abbreviation of *Gemara, Pirush ('Commentary' of Rashi), and Tosafot. Although the Tosafot are in the nature of pure commentary, they naturally refer to the practical conclusions to be drawn. These were later collected under the heading of *Piskey Tosafot* ('Decisions of the Tosafot') and have had an influence on the *codification of Jewish law.

Meyer Waxman, 'The Tosafists' and 'Composers of Tosafot', in his *A History of Jewish Literature* (South Brunswick, NJ, 1960), i. 269–75.

**Tosefta** 'Addition' to the Mishnah. The Tosefta contains the rulings, sayings, and debates of the *Tannaim and is arranged on the same pattern as the Mishnah in six orders and with the same tractates within the orders. The name Tosefta would seem to suggest that the work is a supplement to the Mishnah but the problem of the relationship between the two works is far more complicated in that the Tosefta contains material not found in the Mishnah at all and it

gives throughout the impression that it is a separate work standing on its own. The problem is further complicated by the fact that while the Babylonian Talmud frequently quotes Baraitot (Tannaitic teachings not found in the Mishnah) from the Tosefta it only has one reference to a Tosefta and it is by no means certain that this is to our present Tosefta, which, scholars have suggested, is a post-Tannaitic compilation, although it undoubtedly is of Tannaitic origin. Passages found in our Tosefta are often quoted in the Talmud in a paraphrased form for the purpose of the Talmudic discussion. The Tosefta is printed in sections in many editions of the Babylonian Talmud at the back of each tractate. M. S. Zuckermandel published what is now the standard edition of the Tosefta (Pasewalk, 1880). Saul Lieberman has published an edition comprising three orders of the Tosefta, *Zeraim, Moed,* and *Nashim* (New York, 1955–73). The study of the Tosefta was engaged in far less than that of the Mishnah and the Talmud, receiving only very few commentaries. But modern scholars have utilized the Tosefta to shed much light on the whole Talmudic period.

H. L. Strack and G. Stemberger, 'The Tosefta', in their *Introduction to the Talmud and Midrash*, trans. Markus Bockmuehl (Edinburgh, 1991), 167–181.

**Tower of Babel** The great tower built by 'the children of men', with its top reaching to the heavens, as told in Genesis 11: 1–9. God was displeased with the attempt to build the tower as a result of which He confounded human language so that each nation would have its own language, unintelligible to the others, and He 'scattered them abroad upon the face of all he earth'. The generation which built the tower is called in the Rabbinic literature: 'the Generation of the Dispersion'. The Mishnah (*Bava Metzia* 4: 2) states that of a man who had given his word to a contract not legally enforceable the sages have said: 'He that exacted punishment from the Generation of the *Flood and the Generation of the Dispersion will exact punishment from him that does not abide by his spoken word.' While there are no parallels to the narrative in ancient Mesopotamian literature, biblical scholars have noted the resemblance of the great tower to the Assyrian and Babylonian ziggurats. The building of the tower is said to have taken place in Babylon, Bavel or

Babel in Hebrew, hence the name 'the Tower of Babel'. By a pun on the word the verse renders this as *balal*, 'to confuse', a reference to the confounding of human language, hence the English expression 'babbling' or 'a babble of voices'. The Jewish commentators offer various explanations for the offence of the tower-builders. In a Rabbinic Midrash their offence is said to have been that they wished to storm the heavens in order to wage war with God, possibly an echo of the practice of climbing to the top of the highest stage of the ziggurat in which there was a shrine of the god. In another Rabbinic legend the offence was the complete disregard of human life. If a man fell down in the course of the construction and met his death, no one paid heed to it but if a brick fell down and broke into fragments, they were grieved. *Ibn Ezra and *Gersonides do not see the whole episode as a sin at all. On the contrary, the intention of the builders was to keep their society intact. When God scattered them it was for their own good, either in order for the whole earth to be populated, or to prevent them from being overtaken by an earthquake or a great fire had they have continued to live in one central place. *Abravanel, on the other hand, sees the sin of the tower-builders to have been their longing for an urban life more sophisticated than the simple, agricultural life, God had originally ordered for them. This does not mean, however, that God does not now want men to live in cities. A rural life was indeed the ideal but once men had chosen this way it would have been contrary to human nature for God to have forbidden it. Consequently, the narrative contains a warning to mankind that if they have to live in cities, they should make sure that they practise justice in these cities. Abravanel lived in the late Renaissance when the problems of urban living exercised the minds of thoughtful men. As with other biblical narratives there is no official Jewish interpretation, each commentator seeking to provide his own understanding of the meaning.

Nahum M. Sarna, 'The Tower of Babel', in his *The JPS Torah Commentary: Genesis* (Philadelphia, New York, and Jerusalem, 1989), 80–4.

**Trees, New Year for**  The minor festival that falls on 15 Shevat, known as Tu Bi-Shevat (from the letters *tet* (9) and *vav* (6) = 15). In the Mishnah (*Rosh Ha-Shanah* 1: 1), 15 Shevat is said to be, according to the House of *Hillel,

the New Year for Trees. This means that the *tithes for fruit of the tree had to be given from each year's growth separately and it was consequently necessary to determine when the new year begins for this purpose. Most of the rains had fallen before this date so that fruit that blossomed after the date belonged to the next year for tithing purposes. In the Mishnah the New Year for Trees is not a festival at all, but it became a minor festival chiefly under the influence of the mystics of Safed in the sixteenth century. In the State of Israel, especially in the kibbutzim, Tu Bi-Shevat is celebrated as an agricultural festival. Generally, nowadays, the festival is taken as an opportunity for encouraging children to give thanks to God for the growth of trees and flowers.

Chaim Pearl, *Guide to the Minor Festivals and Fasts* (London, 1961), 23–33.

**Tribes, Lost Ten**  The tribes of Reuben, Simeon, Dan, Naphtali, Gad, Asher, Issachar, Zebulan, Ephraim, and the half-tribe of Manasseh, who belonged to the Northern Kingdom in ancient Israel and who were exiled when the Northern Kingdom fell to the Assyrians in 722 BCE, as told in the book of Kings (2 Kings 17, 18). Many legends circulated according to which the lost ten tribes established a new kingdom, across the mysterious River Sambation in some versions, and one day they will be returned. Travellers' tales in the Middle Ages told of people who had managed to reach the lost tribes, returning with reports of their military prowess. As early as the Mishnah (*Sanhedrin* 10: 3) a debate is recorded between Rabbi *Eliezer and Rabbi *Akiba, the former holding that the ten tribes will be restored (i.e. in the Messianic age), the latter holding that they are lost, never to return.

In the nineteenth century various attempts were made at identification of the lost tribes with contemporary peoples. Among the candidates suggested were: the Japanese, the American Indians, and the African tribes. The British Israelites sought to identify the British people with the lost ten tribes. Among the fanciful etymologies to support this theory are the name British as meaning Berit Ish ('Covenant of Man') and London as meaning Le-Dan ('belonging to the tribe of Dan'). Of these theories it was said that those who advanced them were more 'lost' than the tribes themselves. So far as the Jewish religion is concerned the whole fascinating affair of the lost ten tribes has little if any significance, though it still seems to be of interest among some small groups in relation to the doctrine of the *Messiah.

Allen H. Godbey, *The Lost Ten Tribes: A Myth*, with a prolegomenon by Morris Epstein (New York, 1974).

**Truth**  Generally speaking, while Judaism obviously attaches great significance to intellectual honesty, as evidenced, for example, in the constant quest for the truth in the Talmudic debates and among the medieval philosophers, the main thrust in the appeals for Jews to be truthful is in the direction of moral truth and integrity. An oft-quoted Rabbinic saying (*Shabbat* 55a) is: 'Truth is the seal of the Holy One, blessed be He.' In *Rashi's explanation this saying refers to the Hebrew word for truth, *emet*, formed from the first letter of the *alphabet, *alef*, the middle letter, *mem*, and the final letter, *tav*. The God of truth is found wherever there is truth and His absence felt where there is falsehood. The prophet similarly declares: 'The Lord God is truth' (Jeremiah 10: 10) and the Psalmist declares: 'Thy Torah is truth' (Psalms 119: 142). Of the verse in Psalms: 'And speaketh the truth in his heart' (Psalms 15: 2) one explanation by the Jewish moralists is that the God-fearing man should keep his promise even if he only made it in his heart, even if it was no more than a promise he had kept to himself without revealing it to the one to whom he made it. This based on the Talmudic tale of Rav Safra (*Makkot* 24a). Rav Safra was approached to sell something he had and was offered a price which suited him, but he was unable at the time to signify his consent because he was reciting his prayers and was unable to interrupt them. The prospective buyer, under the impression that the Rabbi had rejected his bid, kept on increasing the price but the Rabbi insisted on selling for the original price to which he had consented 'in his heart'. Naturally, this kind of exemplary conduct was not intended for all, otherwise it would not have been recorded for a saintly man like Rav Safra. But the stern injunctions throughout Jewish literature against cheating and dishonesty in business affairs and in other areas of life are directed towards every Jew, as when the prophet says of his people: 'They have taught their tongue to speak lies, they weary themselves to commit iniquity' (Jeremiah 9: 4).

Among the many rules regarding honesty in commercial transactions the following can be quoted as illustrations. The Mishnah (*Bava Batra* 5: 10) rules: 'The shopkeeper must wipe his measures twice a week, his weights once a week, and his scales after every weighing.' On the verse: 'Ye shall do no unrighteousness in judgement, in meteyard, in weight, or in measure' (Leviticus 19: 35). The Talmud (*Bava Metzia* 61b) comments: ' "In meteyard" refers to the measurement of land, that he may not measure for one in summer [when the measuring line is contracted through the heat] and for another in winter; "in weight", he may not keep his weights in salt [to make them heavier]; "in measure", he may not make the liquid produce a foam.' Deceiving others is strictly forbidden: 'The Holy One, blessed be He, hates a person which says one thing with his mouth and another in his heart' (*Pesaḥim* 113b). Defrauding by the seller overcharging or the buyer undercharging is condemned and the Mishnah (*Bava Metzia* 4: 10) states: 'As there is wronging in buying and selling there is wronging with words. A man must not ask: "How much is this thing?" if he has no intention of buying it.'

The fourteenth-century moralist, Isaac Aboab, in his *Menorat Ha-Maor* ('Candelabrum of Light') gives what is no doubt in part a counsel of perfection; yet many Jews, aware of the severe demands he makes, did try to live up to them, judging by the frequency with which the work is referred to in the literature of Jewish piety. Aboab writes:

'There are other matters which fall under the heading of falsehood; for example, when a man praises himself for having virtues he does not really possess. It sometimes happens that a man may persuade his friend into believing that he has spoken well of him or done him a good turn when, in fact, he has done nothing of the kind. In this connection our Rabbis teach that it is forbidden to mislead others even if they are heathens. Another example is one who promises to do something for his neighbour and fails to carry out his promise. All this is to fulfil the verse: "The remnant of Israel shall not do iniquity, nor speak lies, neither shall a deceitful tongue be found in their mouth" [Zechariah 3: 13]. The meaning is that even where nothing iniquitous is involved, they shall not have a deceitful tongue in their mouth but all their words should be truthful. Some liars mislead their neighbours into believing that they are friends, who have their welfare at heart, but their real purpose is only to win their neighbour's confidence so as to be able to harm him. Of those it is said: "One speaketh peaceably to his neighbour with his mouth, but in his heart he layeth his wait for him" [Jeremiah 9: 8]. The verse goes on to say: "Shall I not punish them for these things? saith the Lord; shall not My soul be avenged on such a nation as this?" Other liars have their eyes on future benefits and tell lies in order to persuade their neighbours to give them gifts. Other liars mislead their neighbours by telling lies so as to obtain something of value from them or from others so that they can steal it for themselves. The Rabbis compare this to idolatry for this is precisely what the idolaters do when they pretend that their gods have power.'

Yet, for all the high value it attaches to truthfulness, the Jewish tradition is sufficiently realistic to acknowledge that there are occasions when the telling of a 'white lie' can be in order; for instance, where the intention is to promote peace and harmony (*Yevamot* 85b). The Talmud (*Bava Metzia* 23b–24a) observes that a scholar will never tell a lie except in the three instances of 'tractate', *purya*, and 'hospitality'. The commentators explain 'tractate' to mean that a modest scholar is allowed to declare that he is unfamiliar with a tractate of the Mishnah in order not to parade his learning. Rashi translates *purya* as 'bed' and understands it to mean that if a scholar is asked intimate questions regarding his marital life he need not answer truthfully. The *Tosafot find it hard to believe that such questions would be addressed to the scholar or to anyone else and they understand *purya* to be connected with the festival of *Purim. If the scholar is asked whether he was drunk on Purim he is allowed to tell a lie about it. 'Hospitality' is understood to mean that a man who has been treated generously by his host may decide not to tell the truth about his reception if he fears that as a result the host will be embarrassed by unwelcome guests.

A. Cohen, 'Honesty', in his *Everyman's Talmud* (London, 1949), 227–8.
Louis Jacobs, 'Truth', in his *What Does Judaism Say About . . . ?* (Jerusalem, 1973), 324–6.

**Tzitzit** The fringes the Israelites were commanded to put in the corners of their garments: 'Speak unto the children of Israel, and bid them that they make throughout their generations fringes [*tzitzit*] in the corners of their garments' (Numbers 15: 38). The tzitzit are now placed in the special *tallit worn during prayer. The insertion of the tzitzit in the tallit is as follows. Four threads, one longer than the other three, are inserted in a hole at the corner of the tallit and then doubled over to form seven threads of equal length and one longer one at the right-hand side. The threads of the two sides are tied in a double knot. The longer thread is then wound around the others seven times and a further double knot is made. The longer thread is then wound around eight times and another double knot is made. A third winding is then made eleven times and a double knot is made, and then there is a winding of thirteen and the last of the double knots is made. It is desirable that after the windings and the knots have been made, all eight threads are of equal length. (The manufacturers of the tzitzit make the longer thread of a length sufficient for this to be done.)

The symbolism of all this has been variously interpreted, Thus, on one view, the Hebrew word *tzitzit* has the numerical value (see GEMATRIA) of 600 (*tzaddi* = 90; *yod* = 10; *tzaddi* = 90; *yod* = 10; *tav* = 400; = 600 in total). When the eight threads and the five knots are added there is a total of 613, corresponding to the 613 *precepts of the Torah. In another version, the eight threads correspond to the eight days that elapsed from the Israelites leaving Egypt until they sang the song of deliverance at the sea (Exodus 15). The five knots correspond to the five books of Moses (the *Pentateuch). The numerical value of the Hebrew for 'the Lord is One' in the *Shema is 39 and this is represented by the total of the windings (7 + 8 + 11 + 13 = 39). Since the tzitzit are on all four corners of the tallit they act as a reminder to Jews to acknowledge God and His Torah at every turn.

Hyman E. Goldin, 'The Tzitzit (Fringes)', in his *Code of Jewish Law* (New York, 1961), i. 19–26.

# U

**Unio Mystica** The union of the mystic's soul with God. In many religious traditions the ultimate aim of man is for his soul to be absorbed in the transcendent—in theistic religious traditions, in God—and not only in the Hereafter but in this life as well, in rare moments of religious *ecstasy. The actual term *unio mystica* is not found in Jewish *mysticism, such abstract expressions being foreign to Jewish thought in general. The question, therefore, is rather whether the phenomenon itself is found there under different headings. It has been suggested that, while the Jewish mystics do speak of communion with God, they draw back from any idea that there can be a complete union of the *soul with God, in view of the strongest Jewish emphasis on the utter transcendence of the Deity.

The nearest thing to the *union mystica* in Jewish mysticism is the ideal of *devukut*, 'attachment' to God, but the great authority on Jewish mysticism, Gershom Scholem, has argued that *devekut* falls short of union with the divine. As *Scholem puts it (*Kabbalah* (Jerusalem, 1974), 176): '*Devekut* results in a sense of beatitude and intimate union, yet it does not entirely eliminate the distance between the creature and its Creator, a distinction that most kabbalists, like most Hasidim, were careful not to obscure by claiming that there could be a complete unification of the soul and God.' In view of the nature of the mystical experience generally, which the mystics themselves find it virtually impossible to describe to others, it is difficult to know how Scholem's distinction is to be drawn and Scholem himself seems to admit that for some of the Jewish mystics, at least, the *unio mystica* was thought of as possible. The doctrine of *disinterestedness in some of its formulations does appear to come very close to the *unio mystica*, as does the Hasidic doctrine of *annihilation of selfhood.

Moshe Idel, 'Unio Mystica in Jewish Mysticism', in his *Kabbalah: New Perspectives* (New Haven, 1988), 59–73.

**Universalism** The question of universalism in Judaism is, and is bound to be, an extremely complicated one. The God Jews worship is the Creator of the whole world and of all peoples yet Jews believe that they are the *Chosen People, however the latter concept is understood. The balance between universalism and particularism has always been difficult for Jews to achieve. In point of fact, terms such as these are never found in Judaism, which does not usually go in for abstractions. What is found in Jewish religious literature are statements about God's watchful care for all His creatures side by side with statements expressing the supreme significance of the Jewish people, who have freely accepted the Torah and have the desire to live in obedience to the divine word. No Jew, no matter how particularistic his attitude, can dare ignore the universalistic aspects of his religion. And no Jew, no matter how universalistic his stance, can dare ignore the simple fact that there can be no Judaism without the Jews. In the very affirmation of God's choice of Israel the universalistic idea is implied. A tribal god cannot choose one tribe from all the others since such a god is identified with his tribe alone. Conversely, a universal God, in the sense of one who has *equal* concern for all peoples on earth, does not choose a particular people to achieve part of His purpose in creating the nations of the world, unless it be held that He has a special purpose for each of the peoples of the world. This latter view has been held among Jews.

It is all really a matter of where the emphasis is to be placed and there have been varying emphases in this matter throughout the history of Judaism. Some Jews have spoken as if God's chief, if not total, interest, so to speak, is with 'His' people. Others, especially in modern times, have gone to the opposite extreme, preferring to stress universalism to the extent of watering down the doctrine of particularism to render it a vague notion of loyalty to a tradition in which universalism had first emerged. Few Jews will fail to admit that there are tensions between the two doctrines.

Some biblical passages, frequently quoted by Jewish universalists, do provide pointers to universalism but these passages must not be taken out of context. In a fine study of the topic, Harry Orlinsky has shown that ideas that have been read into these passages by both Jews and Christians are not really there; not, at least, in the form in which they have been understood by later generations. Take, for instance, the verse in *Malachi (2: 10): 'Have we not all one father? Has not one God created us?' This verse is often taken to mean that the prophet is declaring that God is the Father of all the nations He has created, with the implication that they are all of equal concern to Him. In point of fact, as can be seen from the whole passage in which the verse occurs, the prophet is not referring at all to non-Israelites. He is denouncing the priestly caste in ancient Israel who believed that they enjoyed special favour in the eyes of God. There is no reference to what Orlinsky calls 'internationalism' anywhere in the book of Malachi. Similarly, the famous injunction: 'Love thy neighbour as thyself' (Leviticus 19: 8) has been taken out of context and misinterpreted to mean the impossible, that all human beings are obliged to love all other human beings as much as they love themselves (see LOVE OF NEIGHBOUR).

Another biblical verse often quoted as teaching complete universalism is: 'You are to Me the same as the children of the Ethiopians, O children of Israel, declares the Lord. I brought up Israel from the land of Egypt, and the Philistines from Caphtor, and the Arameans from Kir' (Amos 9: 7). This verse has been read as advocating internationalism on the highest level, that Ethiopians, Israelites, Philistines, Arameans, are all equally regarded by the God of Israel. But this verse only means that God has directed the historical course of the peoples mentioned not, as is clear from the book of Amos itself, that God has 'chosen' these nations as He has chosen Israel. It is true that for Amos the choice of Israel imposes a tremendous and special responsibility: 'You alone have I singled out of all the families of the earth— that is why I will call you to account for all your iniquities' (Amos 3: 2). But that special responsibility is the result of God singling out the children of Israel. Orlinsky summarizes the biblical idea as follows: 'The God of Israel is at the same time the sole God and Master of the universe without being the God of any nation but Israel, the *national* God of biblical Israel is a *universal* God, but not an *international* God' (Orlinsky's Italics).

So much for the biblical sources. In speaking of the Jewish attitude, however, it is essential to ask not alone what the biblical record in itself has to say but how the Bible has made its impact on Jewish thought. Here there is no doubt that at a very early period in post-biblical history Jews did come to interpret the Bible as teaching universalism in its highest form. For example, reference must be made to the verses in Isaiah (19: 24–5): 'In that day, Israel shall be a third partner with Egypt and Assyria as a blessing on earth, for the Lord of Hosts will bless them, saying: "Blessed be My people Egypt, My handiwork Assyria, and My very own Israel."' Even if Orlinsky is right in seeing these verses as a later addition to the book of Isaiah, the addition is now found in the Bible, as are the books of *Ruth and *Jonah, both late according to the majority of scholars. In the book of Ruth a Moabite woman marries Boaz and became the ancestress of King David. In the book of Jonah God sends the prophet to urge the people of Nineveh, the enemies of Israel, to repent. All of this serves to demonstrate the correctness of the view that complete universalism did eventually emerge among Jews early in the post-exilic period.

The Talmudic Rabbis coped with the problem by postulating that God did not give the Torah only to Israel but to the nations of the world as well in the form of the *Noahide laws. And while Rabbi *Eliezer held that only Israelites have a share in the World to Come, the view followed in Judaism is that of Rabbi *Joshua, who taught that all the righteous of the nations of the world have a share in the World to Come (see GENTILES). In Rabbinic thought, too, the hope is repeatedly expressed that in the Messianic age God will be hailed as King by all peoples. A section of the kingship prayers on *Rosh Ha-Shanah is now recited by Jews as the Alenu prayer at the end of every service:

'We therefore hope in Thee, O Lord our God, that we may speedily behold the glory of Thy might, when Thou wilt remove the abominations from the earth, and the idols will be utterly cut off, when the world will be perfected under the kingdom of the Almighty, and all the children of flesh will call upon Thy name, when Thou wilt turn unto Thyself all the wicked of the earth. Let all the inhabitants of the world perceive and know that unto Thee every knee must bow, every tongue must swear. Before Thee, O Lord our God, let them bow and fall; and unto Thy glorious name let them give honour; let them all accept the yoke of Thy kingdom, and do Thou reign over them speedily, and for ever and ever.'

And no discussion of Jewish universalism can afford to neglect the hymn 'And all the world shall come', of unknown authorship, for long part of the liturgy on Rosh Ha-Shanah and *Yom Kippur, the first stanza of which reads in *Zangwill's translation:

All the world shall come to serve Thee
And bless Thy glorious name,
And Thy righteousness triumphant
The islands shall proclaim
And the peoples shall go seeking
Who knew Thee not before,
And the ends of earth shall praise Thee,
And tell Thy greatness o'er.

The tensions persist among modern Jews, as they did in the age of the medieval Jewish philosophers and in the eighteenth-century *Haskalah but in every variety of the Jewish religion today there is the most powerful affirmation that every human being is created in the *image of God.

Raphael Loewe (ed.), '*Studies in Rationalism Judaism and Universalism in Memory of Leon Roth* (London, 1966).

Harry M. Orlinsky, 'Nationalism—Universalism and Internationalism', in his *Essays in Biblical Culture and Bible Translation* (New York, 1974), 78–116.

**Urim Ve-Thummim**　The oracles in the breastplate of the *High Priest: 'And thou shalt put in the breastplate of judgement the Urim and the Thummim [etymology uncertain but could mean "Lights and Perfections"]; and they shall be upon Aaron's heart, when he goeth in before the Lord; and Aaron shall bear the judgement of the children of Israel upon his heart continually' (Exodus 28: 30). That the Urim and Thummim were oracles can be seen from other biblical passages, for instance from: 'And he shall stand before Eleazar the priest, who shall inquire for him by the judgement of the Urim before the Lord; at this word shall they go out, and at his word they shall come in, both he, and

all the children of Israel with him, even all the congregation' (Numbers 27: 21). A Talmudic passage (*Berakhot* 3b) states that King David, before deciding whether or not to go to war, would consult the *Sanhedrin on whether it was permitted and the Urim Ve-Thummim to discover whether he would win the battle if he did go.

The nature of these oracles has eluded scholars, ancient and modern. Some commentators believe that the Urim Ve-Thummim were two lots placed in the breastplate but others identify them with the breastplate itself. The Talmudic Rabbis understood the oracle to work by certain letters of the precious stones on the breastplate, upon which were inscribed the names of the twelve tribes, becoming miraculously illumined. For instance, if the answer to a query was in the negative the letters forming the world *lo* ('No') would shine forth. In a Talmudic passage (*Yoma* 73b) it is stated that the Urim Ve-Thummim are so called because they illumine (from *or*, 'light') and are complete (from *tam*, 'perfect'). The problem of the Urim Ve-Thummim still awaits its solution.

Jacob Milgrom, 'The Urim and Thummim', in Nahum M. Sarna (ed.), *The JPS Commentary: Numbers* (Philadelphia and New York, 1990), 484–6.

**Ushpizin**　'Guests', the seven celestials who visit the *sukkah on the festival of *Tabernacles. The seven Ushpizin are first mentioned in the Zohar (iii. 103b) in which it is stated that Abraham and five others, together with David, visit the sukkah. These seven correspond to the seven lower *Sefirot. The portion of the Ushpizin is to be given to the poor who have to be invited to sit in the sukkah, otherwise the Ushpizin depart. The seven Ushpizin are: Abraham, Isaac, Jacob, Moses, Aaron, Joseph, and David. As the custom developed, it became the practice to welcome Abraham (the counterpart of the Sefirah Ḥesed ('Loving-kindess') on the first day of Tabernacles and the others with him; Isaac on the second day, and so on. The custom of inviting the Ushpizin is still observed by many pious Jews, especially by the Hasidim, with special emphasis on the injunction to care for the needy when rejoicing on the festival.

**Usury**　The payment of interest on a loan by borrower to lender. The two biblical passages which forbid the taking of interest are: 'If thou lend money to any of My people, even to the poor with thee, thou shalt not be to him as a creditor; neither shalt thou lay upon him interest' (Exodus 22: 24). 'Thou shalt not lend upon interest to thy brother: interest of money, interest of victuals, interest of any thing that is lent upon interest. Unto a foreigner thou mayest lend upon interest; but unto thy brother thou shalt not lend upon interest; that the Lord thy God may bless thee in all that thou puttest thy hand unto, in the land whither thou goest in to possess it' (Deuteronomy 23: 20–1). The meaning of these verses is clear. In an agrarian society a loan to a poor man to tide him over, for instance, until the harvest or to help him buy farming instruments, was a basic act of human kindness which should be done freely without demanding any return. For the lender to take interest on the loan would be to impoverish the borrower still further. But the 'foreigner', the man who is on a visit to the land of Israel, is not bound by this law. He will take interest on any loans he makes to Israelites so that there can be no obligation for the Israelite not to reciprocate and take interest when lending to him. The Christian Church in the Middle Ages adapted the law as it stands in the Pentateuch but understood 'thy brother' as referring to other Christians and the 'foreigner' to non-Christians, hence Jews were allowed to become money-lenders, with many a sorry consequence, as Jewish history shows.

The Talmudic Rabbis held that the terms 'usury' and 'interest' are synonymous and they extended the biblical laws so as to prohibit any benefit the borrower bestows on the lender, even to greet him if it was not his usual practice to greet him, or even to thank him for the loan. According to the Rabbis the prohibition applies to the borrower as well as to the lender; that is, it is not only forbidden to lend on interest but also to borrow on interest. The witnesses to the transaction also offend against the law, as does the scribe who draws up the bond of indebtedness. The laws against usury are treated in detail in chapter 5 of tractate *Bava Metzia*. Here are discussed questions regarding business transactions, some of which may fall under the heading of usury by Rabbinic law. The general principle laid down in this connection is 'any reward for waiting is forbidden', meaning, it is forbidden for a lender to be rewarded by the borrower for 'waiting' for the return of his money.

The spirit of the law against usury would not seem to be violated when money is invested in business in our advanced economy, since the money is being used to increase profits and there is no reason why $A$ should invest his money in $B$'s business as a sleeping partner unless he hopes to gain as $B$ hopes to gain. Nevertheless, the letter of the law was held to be violated even where the loans were of a commercial nature. From the sixteenth century, a device, known as the *hetter iska* ('dispensation for commerce'), was introduced in which money invested in a commercial arrangement is treated as 'half loan and half deposit'. Even though the principle presumably behind the original prohibition of usury, that of helping the needy, hardly applies to business investment, many observant Jews still arrange for the *hetter iska* document to be drawn up when investing money in a business.

J. David Bleich, 'Hetter Iska', in his *Contemporary Halakhic Problems* (New York, 1983), ii. 376–84.

# V

**Values** The thought of the biblical authors and the Talmudic Rabbis—comprising the classical sources of Judaism—is of a concrete nature. Nowhere in these sources is there to be found an abstract term like 'value'. When modern Jews speak of such ideals (this abstract term, too, is never found in the classical sources) as *compassion, *truth, *holiness, *humility, *love, and *peace as Jewish values, they are really spelling out what is implicit but never explicit in the tradition. This is not a mere semantic quibble. Even if the classical sources had known of the idea of value, it is doubtful whether they would have seen it as 'valuable', since the whole notion of value implies selectivity. Ideals such as those mentioned are ends in themselves not to be evaluated against higher or more comprehensive ends. It was for a similar reason that some Jewish thinkers objected to the drawing-up of *principles of the Jewish religion. To speak of principles implies that these are in some way more significant than all the other *precepts of the Torah, whereas all are to be observed as the command of God. The word for 'value', *erekh* in Hebrew, is found in the Bible but only in the narrow sense of evaluation or assessment. In the book of Leviticus (27: 1–8) the law is stated that if a man vows to give the value of a human being to the Sanctuary, this is not assessed by the market value (of a slave in the market-place) but in accordance with the person's age, fixed sums being stated for each age-group. It is almost as if the law is implying that any real evaluation of the worth of a human being is not possible for humans and this applies *a fortiori* to the evaluation of the will of God. For all that, modern Jews do speak of Jewish values and the term is not entirely devoid of meaning.

Religious as well as ethical ideals are described as Jewish values: the *study of the Torah; the *love and fear of God; *Kiddush Ha-Shem ('sanctification of the divine name');

and *holiness. The use of the adjective 'Jewish' in Jewish values is not intended to suggest that these values are the invention, or the exclusive preserve, of Jews; still less that they are not found among non-Jews and in faiths other than Judaism. Basic to all the higher religions are ideals corresponding closely to those described as Jewish. Non-religious, as well as religious, ethical thinkers have expounded the worth of humility, truth, love, and compassion. If the adjective 'Jewish' is used the intention is to suggest: (*a*) that these values receive a special kind of emphasis in the Jewish tradition, a Jewish way of looking at them, and (*b*) that they are no remote ideals but are a real, vital force in the lives of Jews. Hardly any Socratic-type discussion of the nature of *justice is found among the Jewish thinkers but all Jews are urged to practise justice. Furthermore, these values are upheld by all Jews, whether Orthodox, Reform, or Conservative. Reform Jews may, for example, question whether this or that aspect of the *dietary laws is nowadays conducive to holiness, but no Reform Jew will ever reject holiness itself as a supreme value.

Louis Jacobs, *Jewish Values* (London, 1960).

**Vashti** Persian queen, wife of King Ahasuerus. The story of Vashti, as told in the book of *Esther (1: 9–22), relates how the king, while in his cups, orders Vashti to appear before the assembled nobles wearing her royal crown in order to display her charms to them. (The Talmudic Rabbis embellish the tale by understanding the king's order to mean wearing her royal crown and nothing else.) Vashti refuses to obey the king's command, accusing him, according to the Rabbis, of not being able to hold his liquor, after which his counsellors advise him to depose her, otherwise all women will take her as an example to defy their husbands. The king deposes Vashti, thus paving the way for the eventual appointment of Esther as queen. Henceforth, the verse states, every man will be 'lord in his house'. In the Jewish tradition, Vashti is portrayed largely as a figure of fun but in Jewish *feminism she is the heroine of the feminists because of her refusal to submit to the extraordinary and obscene demands of her drunken husband.

**Vegetarianism** Vegetarians often quote two biblical passages in support of their view that it is morally wrong for human beings to kill *animals for food. In the creation narrative (Genesis 29: 30) both man and animals were given the herbs of the field for their food and they were not permitted to prey on one another. In Isaiah's vision (Isaiah 11: 7) 'the lion shall eat straw like an ox'. The first passage, however, only expresses the ideal that obtained at the beginning of creation and the second an ideal for 'the end of days', later understood as referring to the Messianic age. It is nowhere stated in the Bible that in the here and now vegetarianism is an ideal. On the contrary, when Noah and his sons emerge from the *ark the animals are given to them as food. In any event, in Judaism attitudes are not formed simply on the basis of biblical verses culled from here and there but on the way the teachers of Judaism have interpreted the religion throughout the ages.

To be sure, Judaism is firmly opposed to cruelty to animals but it does allow man to use animals for his needs—to work for him and provide him with wool, skins, and milk for instance—and even permits him to kill them for food, though insisting that the pain caused to animals in the process be reduced to a minimum (see SHEḤITAH). The Talmud (*Pesaḥim* 109a) states that meat and wine are the means by which man 'rejoices' and it is on this basis that it has long been customary for Jews to eat meat and drink wine on the *festivals. In he Kabbalah the further idea is introduced that when man eats the meat of animals and then worships his Maker with renewed strength he 'elevates' the animal by using the strength it has given him in the service of God. This is the Kabbalistic explanation for why the Talmud (*Pesaḥim* 49b) states that an *am ha-aretz*, the man who does not study the Torah, may not eat meat.

There is, of course, no actual obligation for a man to eat meat and there are even a number of Jewish vegetarian societies. But it can be argued that for a Jew to adopt vegetarianism on the grounds that it is wrong to kill animals for food is to introduce a moral and theological idea which implies that Judaism has, in fact, been wrong all the time in not advocating vegetarianism. For this reason many traditional Jews look askance at the advocacy of vegetarianism as a way of life superior to the traditional Jewish way. Some pious Jews in the past did not eat meat but this was either as a penance or in order to control the appetites, not as an idealistic stance in which the killing of animals for food is in itself morally wrong. A further point worthy of mention is that the suggestion made by some vegetarians that it is wrong to use animals because they have *equal* rights to humans is risky, in that it tends to obliterate the distinction between animals and human beings created in the *image of God.

Elijah Judah Schochet, 'Jewish Vegetarianism', in his *Animal Life in Jewish Tradition* (New York, 1984), 288–98.

**Venice** There was an influx of Jews into Venice after the expulsion from Spain, among them Don Isaac *Abravanel who, in his commentary to the Pentateuch, is eloquent on the advantages of the oligarchical system of government in the Venetian Republic over the monarchical system to which he had been accustomed in Spain. It has been estimated that Venice had around 900 Jews in 1552. Shakespeare's *Merchant of Venice* is therefore a not inaccurate reflection of Jewish–Christian relationships in Venice, although the picture of Shylock who demands his 'pound of flesh' is, of course, pure invention. It was in Venice that the Jews were confined in the 'foundry' known as the *ghetto and were obliged to wear the special badge or hat to distinguish them from Christians. The old Jewish ghetto in Venice, with its high-rise buildings and beautiful synagogues, is now a tourist attraction. Venice is renowned as the great nursery of Hebrew *printing. The house of Daniel Bomberg, a non-Jew, poured forth Hebrew books, printed with fine type on paper of excellent quality, which won the widest acceptance—among them the famous Rabbinic Bible, known as *Mikraot Gedolot*, and the first edition of the complete Babylonian Talmud, the form and pagination of which became the model for practically all subsequent editions.

Cecil Roth, *Venice* (Philadelphia, 1930).

**Via Negativa** 'The Negative Way', of speaking of God. The proponents of this way believe that God is so beyond all human comprehension that it is only possible for humans to describe what He is not, never to attempt to speak of His true nature. Prominent among the medieval Jewish philosophers who prefer the way of negation are Bahya, *Ibn Pakudah and *Maimonides, both of whom develop the theory of negative attributes. For Maimonides the attributes which are of God's essence—existence, unity, and wisdom—have to be understood solely as negating their opposites. With regard to the attributes which refer to God's activity, these can be applied to God even in positive form but that is because they are not of God's nature but only of His actions. When, for example, God is spoken of as good this is meant in a positive sense but denotes only that such action would be attributed to goodness if a human being had carried it out. The Kabbalists go further in not permitting even negative attributes of God as He is in Himself. This aspect of God is called by the Kabbalists *En Sof or Ayin ('Nothing') because nothing can be said or even thought of It. Only of God as manifest in the *Sefirot is it permitted to speak, but then one can speak in a positive sense.

The Bible and the Rabbinic literature are not bothered at all by the question of anthropomorphism and repeatedly speak of God in positive terms. In these sources Pascal's famous distinction obtains between the 'God of the philosophers' and the 'God of Abraham, Isaac and Jacob'. Yet here and there in the Rabbinic literature passages are to be found in which silence is preferred to speech where God is concerned. There is, for example, the interpretation of the verse: 'Praise is silence for Thee O God' (Psalms 65: 2) in the Jerusalem Talmud (*Berakhot* 9: 1) according to which the verse means that the ultimate praise of God is silence. 'It can be compared to a jewel without price: however high you appraise it, you still undervaluate it.' The parallel passage in the Babylonian Talmud (*Megillah* 18a) adds the popular proverb: 'A word is worth a *sela*, silence two.' In another Talmudic passage (*Berakhot* 33b), so helpful to Maimonides that he comments on it at length (*Guide of the Perplexed*, I., 59), the story is told of a prayer-leader who was rebuked by the second-century teacher, Rabbi Haninah. This man is said to have praised God by listing His attributes at length. When he had finished, Rabbi Haninah rebuked him by asking if he had now exhausted the praise of God. The parable is given of a king who possesses millions of gold pieces but who is praised for possessing silver pieces. This is not to praise him but to dispraise him. Maimonides' comment is to the effect that in the parable the king is praised for possessing silver pieces when, in reality, he possesses gold. The parable does not say that the king is praised for possessing thousands of gold pieces when, in reality, he possesses millions, for that would suggest that the difference is one of degree not of kind. Whatever is said of God in praise is so remote from reality that the parable can only use the simile of gold and silver pieces. The very coin of praise is different.

While the *via negativa* is certainly Jewishly unconventional it still has, as the above examples show, a respectable history in Jewish thought.

**Vienna** The city of Vienna, capital of Austria, came to occupy an important place in the history of Jewish learning from the fourteenth century, when many German Jews emigrated to Austria. Prominent among the 'Sages of Vienna' were the renowned Isaac Or Zarua (so-called after the title of his work on Jewish law) and his son Hayyim. But it was in the nineteenth century that the Jewish community in Vienna became a centre where the new trends in Jewish life after the emergence of the Jews from the *ghetto were given a unique expression. Here European culture flourished and here the *Haskalah movement, originating in Berlin, found many advocates. In Vienna, as in Germany, the struggle over Reform was acute. Later still, it was in Vienna, the home of Theodor *Herzl and Sigmund *Freud, that both *Zionism and psychoanalysis (see PSYCHO-LOGY) began to exercise a powerful influence on Jewish, as well as on general, life. The three notable preachers in Vienna, Isaac Noah Mannheimer, Adolf Jellinek, and Moritz Gudemann, all three belonging to the moderate Reform tendency, set, to a large extent, the standards for modern Jewish *preaching. The Bet Ha-Midrash in Vienna had among its teachers Isaac Hirsch Weiss and Meir Friedmann, notable Talmudists, and the Bet Ha-Midrash was highly influential in spreading the approach and the methodology of the *Jüdische Wissenschaft movement. It is not true, of course, that all the outstanding thinkers, writers, and composers of Vienna were all loyal Jews. Many of them had no more than a Jewish background. Yet it is true that what has been called 'the spirit of Vienna' acquired a special vigour when it met, albeit at second hand, with the spirit of Judaism. Robert Wistrich rightly remarks: 'Can one conceive of twentieth-century culture without the contributions of Freud, Wittgenstein, Mahler, Schoenberg, Karl Kraus, or Theodor Herzl? Whether they were full-blooded Jews, half-Jews, self-haters, converts, or Zionists, this secularized Jewish intelligentzia changed the face of Vienna and, indeed, of the modern world.'

Max Grunwald, *Vienna* (Philadelphia, 1936).
Robert S. Wistrich, *The Jews of Vienna in the Age of Franz Joseph* (Oxford, 1990).

**Vilna** Lithuanian city renowned for its contribution to Jewish learning and piety and hence known as 'the Jerusalem of Lithuania'. the Jewish community of Vilna flourished from the seventeenth century until its destruction in the *Holocaust. Vilna was the home of many prominent Rabbis and preachers, the most notable being *Elijah, Gaon of Vilna, who occupied no official Rabbinic post but whose influence extends to this day over all Orthodox Jews. The famous printing-house of Romm in Vilna published works in every branch of Jewish learning. The splendid Romm editions of the Babylonian and Jerusalem Talmuds are highly prized and are now the current editions in photocopy. Although Vilna in the eighteenth century did not tolerate the slightest deviation from the traditional view (there was even a pillory into which 'heretics' were exposed to public derision), eventually the city became a centre of the *Haskalah movement in Lithuania. There was a *Karaite community in and around Vilna but, as in Lithuania generally, the Reform movement never gained any hold there.

Israel Cohen, *Vilna* (Philadelphia, 1943).

**Violence** In Jewish law, as in other legal systems, the victim of an assault is entitled to receive adequate compensation (see DAMAGES) but, in addition, Jewish teaching is emphatic that any attack on another's person is strictly forbidden. The Hebrew word for 'violence', *hamas*, denotes especially robbery with violence —'grievous bodily harm' in English legal phraseology—as in the verse (Genesis 6: 11): 'And the earth was corrupt before God, and the earth was filled with violence [*hamas*].' In the Babylonian Talmud (*Sanhedrin* 58b) there is a list of sayings directed against physical violence in itself, even where there is no attempt at robbery. The third-century teacher, Resh Lakish, is reported as saying: 'He who only lifts his hand against his neighbour, even if he did not actually smite him, is called a wicked man.' The third-century Babylonian teacher, Rav Huna, is reported to have said: 'His hand should be cut off', quoting the verse: 'Let the uplifted arm be broken' (Job 38: 15). Some scholars understand Rav Huna to mean that the court actually applied this punishment, illegal in the Jewish system, possibly under the influence of Persian practice at the time. But other commentators, refusing to believe that Rav Hùna would have imposed an illegal punishment, understand the saying as pure hyperbole, as in the saying of Rabbi Eleazar, quoted in the passage: 'The only thing to be done with him is to bury him', obviously not intended to be taken literally. *Rashi, however, does take Rav Huna's saying literally but holds that the reference is to a man who habitually raises his hand against others. Still others hold that the cutting-off of the hand means that a very heavy fine was to to be imposed so as to 'cut off the hand', to prevent the man acting in this way in the future. *Isserles, in his gloss to the *Shulhan Arukh* (*Hoshen Mishpat* 388: 7), quotes an opinion that the victim of a violent attack is permitted to take his case to the Gentile courts even though this may cause the attacker to suffer a heavy loss. In all this a good deal is left to the discretion of the court and the particular circumstances. In any event, the seriousness of the offence is stated without qualification in all the sources. Although violent punishments were meted out by the medieval courts, this is now unknown in Jewish life.

**Visions** The Bible contains accounts of prophetic visions of various kinds. Both the prophet Isaiah (Isaiah 6: 1–7) and the prophet Ezekiel (Ezekiel 1) see a vision of the *throne of God, the latter as coming to him on a *chariot. The Talmud (*Hagigah* 13b), seeking to explain Ezekiel's prolixity in comparison with Isaiah's brevity, observes that Isaiah, accustomed to seeing this kind of vision, can be compared to a townsman who sees the king while Ezekiel can be compared to a villager who sees the king and on whom the sight makes a greater impression. In another Talmudic passage (*Yevamot* 49b) it is said that King Manasseh had Isaiah slain because he claimed to have seen God whereas his teacher, Moses, had said: 'For man shall not see Me and live' (Exodus 33: 20). The Talmud seeks to resolve the contradiction by making a distinction between seeing through a clear glass and seeing through a dim glass. As *Rashi understands this distinction, Moses, whose visions generally were through clear glass, had the insight that God cannot be seen, whereas Isaiah, whose general visions were through a dim glass, imagined that his vision of God reflected the true Reality. Another explanation of the passage is that when Moses declared that no man can see God, he referred to seeing through a clear glass, implying that He could be seen through a dim glass as Isaiah in fact saw Him. In any event the use of the glass simile suggests that it is impossible to see God directly, even in the most intense prophetic vision. This remained the Rabbinic and medieval attitude, that the true 'beatific vision' is only possible after death: 'For man shall not see Me *and live.*'

The Jewish mystics known as the Riders of the Chariot, whose activities extended over the first thousand years of the present era, believed that by using certain techniques they could have an ascent of the soul into the heavenly halls, the Hekhalot. The Hekhalot literature abounds in vivid description of these halls but, as Rav *Hai Gaon states, the ascent is made in the recesses of the mystic's psyche.

There are numerous accounts in the Bible of people seeing *angels. In Maimonides' view, all the biblical accounts of angels appearing to humans in the guise of men do not refer to a real vision but to seeing the angels in a dream, since angels are spiritual forces and it is impossible for them actually to appear on earth. The Zohar states that the angels adopt the form of this world when they appear to human beings, otherwise the world could not contain them. *Nahmanides, in his commentary to the Pentateuch (to Genesis 18: 1), takes strong issue with Maimonides. The circumstantial material in the biblical accounts, observes Nahmanides, can only be understood as referring to an actual appearance of the angels on earth.

There are frequent references in the Talmudic literature and later works to scholars having a vision of the prophet *Elijah who, it was believed, returns to earth from time to time to impart wisdom to pious scholars. The more rationalistic commentators tend to see these accounts as referring to a psychic experience rather than an actual vision of Elijah. The famed Kabbalist, Isaac *Luria and his disciple, Hayyim *Vital are reported to have claimed to have been visionaries, the latter keeping a mystic diary in which his visions were recorded. In *Hasidism, there are numerous legends of the masters seeing visions of Elijah and other saints no longer alive on earth. The eighteenth-century master known as the 'Seer of Lublin' was believed to be a clairvoyant, as his name implies. In the famous *Letter* of the *Baal Shem Tov, the founder of the Hasidic movement, there is an account of his mystical ascent of soul in which he saw a vision of the Messiah who assured him that his teachings will spread abroad.

The late Hasidic master, Yitzhak Eizik Safran of Komarno (1806–74) kept a secret diary, *Megillat Setarim*, in which he recorded his visions. An astonishing entry in this diary reads:

'I was in the town of Dukla. I arrived there in the middle of the night and there was none to offer me hospitality until a certain tanner invited me to his home. I wanted to recite the night prayers and count the *Omer but was unable to do so in the home of the tanner [because of the unpleasant smell] so I went to the Bet Ha-Midrash of the town to pray there. I came to realise the meaning of the descent of the *Shekhinah and Her anguish as She stood in the street of the tanners. I wept sorely in the presence of the Lord of all because of the anguish of the Shekhinah. In my distress I fainted and slept for a while. I saw a vision of light, a powerful radiance in the form of a virgin all adorned from whose person there came a dazzling light but I was not worthy to see the face. No more of this can be recorded in writing. Her light was brighter than the sun at noonday.'

Of course, Rabbi Safran had no truck with any Christian beliefs but, if the account is authentic, it tells a great deal about the religious *psychology of Jewish visionaries, who saw whatever they saw in terms of the world around them. Biblical scholars have tried to explain some of the visions recorded in the Bible similarly in terms of the social background of the authors. It might also be noted that, according to some scholars, some of the biblical authors may have used the vision purely as a literary device, a means of conveying the particular message it was theirs to deliver.

Louis Jacobs, *Jewish Mystical Testimonies* (New York, 1976).

Gershom Scholem, *Kabbalah* (Jerusalem, 1974); see index: 'Visions'.

**Visiting the Sick** Among the acts of benevolence enjoined by the Torah, visiting the sick is especially significant. The Rabbis depict God Himself as a visitor of the sick when He appeared to Abraham just after he was recovering from his *circumcision (Genesis 18: 1), and they give this as an example of man pursuing the ideal of *Imitatio Dei. For the Rabbis and in subsequent Jewish teaching it is not the simple visit that counts, though this is also important. The main purpose of the visit is to see if the sick person's needs have been attended to and to help him obtain whatever extra help he requires over and above his medical requirements to which his doctor attends. Among the instructions for visiting the sick are that people who do not belong to the sick person's immediate family should wait a while before visiting him in order not to call attention to the fact that he is sick; that the sick person should be visited often but not where this imposes a burden on him and his family; that a sick enemy should not be visited because it may appear as gloating over his discomfiture. A sick visitor should be tactful, neither giving the impression that the sick person is beyond human help nor giving false hopes of recovery. The general principle in the sources is that it is not necessary to inform a seriously ill person that his illness is incurable; some hold that, unless there is a real need for it, he should not, in fact, be told that the doctors have given him up. Prayers for the sick are recited during the synagogue services and at other times. In Hasidic and many other circles it is customary when praying for the sick to use the patient's mother's name rather than the father's, for example: Moses son of Sarah not Moses son of Abraham. Every Jewish community of any size has a special society devoted to visiting the sick.

Hyman E. Goldin, 'Visiting the Sick', in his *Code of Jewish Law* (New York, 1961), iv. 87–9.

**Vital, Hayyim** *Safed Kabbalist (1542–1620), chief disciple of Isaac *Luria, the Ari, whose teachings Vital propagated through his voluminous writings. In his youth Vital studied Talmud and Codes under the guidance of Moses Alsheikh who ordained him as a Rabbi. Vital began to study Kabbalah in 1562. At first Vital followed the Kabbalistic system of Moses *Cordovero but when Luria arrived in Safed he studied the Lurianic system with Luria until the latter's death in 1572. Vital wrote his *Sefer Ha-Ḥezyonot* ('Book of Visions') while he was in Damascus between the years 1609 and 1612. As its name implies, the work contains his dreams and *visions and those of others about him. A typical entry in this work is the account of a vision seen by a clairvoyant:

'The year 5338 [ = 1578]. On Sabbath morning I was preaching to the congregation in Jerusalem. Rachel, the sister of Rabbi Judah Mishan, was present. She told me that during the whole of my sermon there was a pillar of fire above my head and *Elijah of blessed memory was there at my right hand to support me and that when I finished they both departed. Also in Damascus in the year 5362 [ = 1602] she saw a pillar of fire above my head when I conducted the Musaf service in the Sicilian community on *Yom Kippur. This woman was wont to see visions, demons, spirits and angels and she has been accurate in most of her statements from the time she was a little girl until now that she has grown to womanhood.'

In this and the other entries in the work Vital appears as a visionary among visionaries, groups of whom were certainly not unknown in the mystic circles of the time. Vital's *Shaarey Kedushah* ('Gates of Holiness') is a guide to holy living, the last chapter of which (unpublished and still in manuscript) contains guidance for one who wishes to attain to the *Holy Spirit.

Vital's major work, *Etz Ḥayyim* ('Tree of Life', a pun on his name Hayyim) is a huge compendium in which he presents the Lurianic teachings or, rather, his own understanding of them. A number of versions of this work exist. The two editions of the *Etz Ḥayyim* most used today are those of Menahem Heilperin (Warsaw,

1890) and Y. Z. Brandwein (Tel Aviv, 1960). Heilperin claims to have discovered the key to the study of the work, that the student should at first skip, the passages he indicates, but his views have not won wide acceptance.

Vital's methodology can be gauged from his description, at the beginning of the *Etz Ḥayyim*, of the manner in which the *En Sof emerges from concealment in order to initiate the cosmic processes:

'Know that before there was any emanation and before any creatures were created a simple higher light filled everything. There was no empty space in the form of a vacuum but all was filled with that simple infinite light. This infinite light had nothing in it of beginning or end but was all one simple, equally distributed light. This is known as "the light of En Sof". There arose in His simple will the will to create worlds and produce emanations in order to realise His perfect acts, His names and His attributes. This was the purpose for which the worlds were created. En Sof then concentrated His being in the middle point, which was at the very centre, and He withdrew that light, removing it in every direction away from that centre point. There then remained around the very centre point an empty space, a vacuum. This withdrawal was equidistant around that central empty point so that the space left empty was completely circular. It was not in the form of a square with right angles. For En Sof withdrew Himself in circular fashion, equidistant in all directions.'

Vital then proceeds to describe the whole process of divine emanation.

Gershom Scholem, 'Hayyim Vital', in his *Kabbalah* (Jerusalem, 1974), 443–8.

**Volozhyn** Russian town famed for its Rabbi, Hayyim of Volozhyn (1749–1821) and for the *Yeshivah he established there in 1803. Hayyim of Volozhyn was the foremost disciple of *Elijah, Gaon of Vilna. Like his master, Hayyim preferred the analytical approach to Talmudic studies in which excessive casuistry (*pilpul) is avoided and an attempt is made to discover what the Talmudic texts are actually saying rather than what ingenious but far-fetched exegesis makes them say. Moreover, the *Codes should not be relied on in themselves but only the Codes as based on the Talmud. A saying of Hayyim recorded by his disciples is: 'People say that the study of the Codes without the Talmud resembles eating fish without pepper [the word for pepper is pilpul] but in my opinion it is like eating pepper without fish.' Again like his master but with considerable less vehemence, Hayyim was opposed to *Hasidism, both because of the movement's theology and because of its implied and often overt denigration of Talmudic scholars.

Hayyim of Volozhyn's *Nefesh Ha-Ḥayyim* (*The Soul of Life*, a pun on his name Hayyim) was published posthumously. In this work he takes issue with the Hasidic doctrine of *panentheism, that all is in God. Hayyim does not reject the doctrine entirely. There are rare occasions, he remarks, when the soul can be set on fire through reflection that all is in God. But to dwell on this idea is dangerous in that it can easily result in a blurring of the distinctions between the sacred and the profane. If everything is ultimately in God the impure is also in God and to have this in mind will lead, in Hayyim's colourful phraseology (based on the Talmud), 'to thinking on words of Torah in unclean places', because, on the panentheistic view, there are no unclean places since there is only God. Hayyim also rejects the Hasidic notion that the Rabbinic ideal of 'the *study of the Torah for its own sake' means that study should be engaged in as a devotional exercise with God in the mind during the studies, in obedience to the Hasidic ideal of *devekut, 'attachment', to God at all times. According to Hayyim it is impossible to master the difficult Talmudic texts if God, instead of the subject-matter, is in the mind. The Rabbinic doctrine, according to Hayyim, means what it says: study for the sake of the Torah, that is, the study of the Torah is in itself the supreme good, an end not a means to devotion. Hayyim here summarizes the intellectual approach typical of the *Mitnaggedim and the Yeshivah he founded was intended to further this approach.

Despite attempts by the Russian authorities to interfere with the curriculum of the Yeshivah and despite its complete closure in 1892 (to be reopened surreptitiously), it functioned, albeit in severe decline, until the *Holocaust. The Yeshivah reached its zenith in the nineteenth century under Naftali Zvi Judah Berlin, known, after the initial letters of his name, as the Netziv. Hundreds of keen students flocked to the Yeshivah, some even from America. Contributions to the upkeep of the Yeshivah, which had a building of its own, were solicited from

Jews in all the European communities. Emissaries, Meshulahim, went out to elicit support which was usually given willingly. A joke in the Yeshivah was that there cannot be men on Mars, for if there were, our Meshulahim would have laid them under tribute to support the Yeshivah. It was arranged that some students would study in the Yeshivah during the whole of the day and others for the whole of the night. It was the Yeshivah's boast that the voice of the Torah was heard unceasingly there by day and by night. Before Rabbi Hayyim *Soloveitchik succeeded his father as Rabbi of Brisk, he taught at the Yeshivah of Volozhyn, where he introduced his special methodology of logical analysis which, through his students at Volozhyn, set the pattern for the Lithuanian-type approach in all the major Yeshivot that arose after the decline of Volozhyn.

Yet while on the surface traditional faith was unchallenged at Volozhyn, the *Haskalah and secular philosophies found their way into the Yeshivah. A number of the students read Haskalah and scientific works hidden between the pages of the Talmud they were supposed to be studying. The official teachers at the Yeshivah were either unaware of these trends or turned a blind eye to them. But even those students who later deserted traditional Judaism still retained their admiration of this 'factory in which the soul of the people is manufactured', as the Hebrew poet Bialik, a former student at the Yeshivah, described it.

**Vows** The basic text regarding the taking of vows is: 'When a man voweth a vow unto the Lord, or sweareth an oath to bind his soul with a bond, he shall not break his word; he shall do according to all that proceedeth out of his mouth' (Numbers 30: 3). In the traditional understanding of this verse the reference is to a vow or an oath to refrain from some enjoyment as a kind of sacrifice to God. (The term 'oath' is also used to refer to *oaths taken in a court of law, but both vows and oaths in this text denote only personal declarations of a religious nature.) According to the Rabbis, the vow refers to the object, the oath to the person. For instance, a man may place a ban on wine for a given period, perhaps as a means of controlling his drinking habits that seem to be getting out of control. This ban on the object, the wine, is said to constitute a vow. If, on the other hand, he swears that he will not drink wine, this constitutes an oath. In both instances for the man to break his word is a religious rather than an ethical offence. The idea behind it all is that the man has given to God his word, which he must not break. It is only a verbal declaration that constitutes a vow. A vow 'taken in the heart', as the Rabbis call it, a mental resolve, has no binding force.

The Talmudic Rabbis are divided on whether the taking of vows and oaths is desirable; some of them see no harm in the practice, others frown on it even when the promise is in a good cause, a promise to give to *charity for example. The general tendency is to frown in principle on vow-taking but to leave room for a personal decision as to whether the circumstances demand it. For instance, if a man promises to study a portion of the Torah in order not to surrender to indolence in his studies this, while not ideal, would be tolerated and perhaps even advocated. A whole tractate of the Talmud, tractate *Nedarim*, is devoted to the subject of vows.

The Rabbis further ruled that vows can be nullified by a sage. The procedure is for the sage to ask the man who made the vow whether he would have made it had he known that circumstances would arise which would have prevented him from keeping the vow. An instance given is of a man who placed a ban on wine but at a later date wished to take wine with the guests at his son's wedding. If the sage ascertains that had the man known that the vow would cause him this embarrassment he would not have made it, the vow is then treated as one made in error or unwittingly and the sage can declare it to be null and void. The *Kol Nidre formula is a means of nullifying unwitting vows. Some pious Jews, when making any promise, declare that they do it *bli neder*, 'without a vow', that is, they are declaring that they do not wish the promise to have the status of a vow, to break which is a serious offence. In some synagogues it is still the custom for a man called to the *reading of the Torah to promise to give a gift to the synagogue or to charity in return for the honour paid to him. The formula for this, recited by the Reader, is: 'Bless $A$ son of $B$ because he has vowed to donate sum $X$'. The Hebrew for 'because he has vowed' is *baavur she-nadar*, and this kind of promise is called in Yiddish *shnoderren* or, in English-Yiddish, 'shnoderring'. In many congregations the wording is altered to 'because he offers a voluntary gift', so as to avoid the actual taking of a vow.

The sources also speak of vows made out of spite and enmity, for instance, where $A$ takes a vow that he will not enjoy any benefit from anything that belongs to $B$ or where $A$ bans his property against $B$'s enjoyment of it. This kind of vow is treated as more unworthy than any other for obvious reasons.

Jacob Milgrom, 'Oaths, Vows, and Dedications', in Naturn M. Sarna (ed.), *The JPS Torah Commentary: Numbers* (Philadelphia and New York, 1990), 488–90.

# W

**Warfare** Although Judaism sets the highest store on *peace, it does not adopt the completely pacifist stand according to which warfare can never be justified, no matter what the circumstances. At the most, Judaism treats warfare, when it has to be engaged in, as a necessary evil but an evil none the less, or at any rate this has been the way Jewish teaching on the subject has developed. There are numerous references to the biblical heroes including King David, engaging in warfare. But the Chronicler (1 Chronicles 22: 8) implies that, even if his wars were justified, David's plan to build the *Temple had to be frustrated because a warrior is not a suitable person to build a House of God: 'But the word of the Lord came to me saying, Thou hast shed blood abundantly, and thou hast made great wars: thou shalt not build an house unto My name, because thou hast shed much blood upon the earth in my sight.' It is possible, indeed, that the Chronicler, reflecting on David's career, denies that all David's wars were justified. In the Rabbinic literature there is a definite tendency to downgrade David's prowess as a warrior and anachronistically to turn him into a scholar whose fights were in the battles of the Torah, as the Rabbis call debates among scholars. Nothing could be more indicative of the Rabbinic attitude towards peace than the Midrash quoted in part by *Rashi, on the verse: 'And if thou wilt make Me an altar of stone, thou shalt not build it of hewn stone; for if thou wave thy iron tool over it, thou hast profaned it' (Exodus 20: 22). The altar, observes the Midrash, makes peace between Israel and their Father in heaven, and therefore it is not fitting that there should come upon it that which cuts and destroys. 'If of stones,' the Midrash concludes, 'which cannot see nor hear nor speak, yet because they promote peace no iron tool may be raised against them, it follows that all the more no punishment will come to the man

who makes peace between a man and his neighbour, between husband and wife, between city and city, between nation and nation, between kingdom and kingdom, between family and family.'

The truth of the matter is that, as in other extremely complicated matters of great moral concern, there is no single, official view in Judaism on the legitimacy of warfare. The fact is that in the post-biblical period Jews did not have any opportunity to engage in warfare, since, until the establishment of the State of Israel, no Jewish State existed to which the terrible question could be addressed. Every Jewish discussion on what Christian theology calls the 'just war' could only have been purely academic. The general principle laid down in the Talmud (*Sanhedrin* 72a) is: 'If someone intends to kill you, get in first and kill him' (i.e. to kill another in self-defence does not constitute an act of murder). Even then the rule is stated that if you can save your life by only maiming the attacker, to kill him does constitute murder. It is obviously difficult to extrapolate from this principle (which refers to an individual would-be murderer and an individual defender of his life) rules about a whole people engaging in warfare where the issue is always far from clear-cut. For that matter, it is rarely clear-cut even with regard to individuals. Once a whole nation has resolved to make war in self-defence the result is bound to be the killing of innocents, and yet for a nation simply to sit back and let an attacking nation take over can also result in great suffering and severe loss of life. A further question is whether a preemptive strike comes under the heading of self-defence.

The Mishnah (*Sotah* 8: 7 and *Sanhedrin* 1: 5) makes a distinction between a 'commanded war' (*milḥemet mitzvah*) and an 'optional war' (*milḥemet reshut*). The latter, defined as a war engaged in by the king to secure his borders or to obtain glory (the reference to the king clearly demonstrates the academic nature of the discussion on the 'optional war'), can only be engaged in with the approval of the *Sanhedrin, which has to decide whether the proposed war possesses some element at least of legality. This qualification, too, makes the whole question of an 'optional war' completely beyond the bounds of practical life, since the Sanhedrin had ceased to function long before the Mishnah was compiled. While there is considerable discussion on the meaning of a 'commanded war', all agree that a war in self-defence comes under this heading and is not only permitted but advocated; no distinction is in fact made between individual and national self-defence. The prohibition of murder is one of seven *Noahide laws which apply to *Gentiles as well as to Jews. Consequently, the Jewish authorities who discuss the question concur that any nation is entitled, according to the Torah, to defend itself against attack, even if this aim can only be achieved by a declaration of war. Whether an 'optional war' is permitted to Gentiles according to the Torah is a moot point. It is unheard of, of course, for Gentiles to ask Rabbinic authorities whether or not they are allowed to wage war, but, if they did, the authorities are divided on whether an 'optional war' is permitted to Gentiles. Some hold that if Jews are not allowed to engage in such a war in the absence of the Sanhedrin, it is *a fortiori* forbidden to Gentile nations. Others, however, hold that Gentiles are not bound by the decisions of a Sanhedrin, so that while murder is forbidden to Gentiles, it is permitted, according to the Torah, for Gentiles to engage in warfare even where there is no question of self-defence.

It can be seen from the above how little help is found in the sources with regard to the legitimacy or otherwise of the wars the State of Israel has been obliged to fight. There are all sorts of questions which arise in modern warfare that are unenvisaged in the classical sources of Judaism—the use of highly developed technical weapons, for instance, which bring about mass destruction and which can surely only be contemplated as a last resort. Moreover, the question of war and defence in the State of Israel is decided not by Rabbis, who have no voice in the matter, but, as among other nations, by generals and politicians, and the whole question of diplomacy arises, to say nothing of the authority or otherwise of the United nations. Nevertheless,

Rabbis have not been inhibited from stating what appears to them to be the attitude the Torah would have Jews adopt. With hardly any exceptions, Jewish teachers have held that the wars engaged in by Israel when attacked or threatened by attack by the Arab nations were completely justified as wars of self-defence. On the war in Lebanon alone opinion was divided.

J. David Bleich, 'Pre-emptive War in Jewish Law', in his *Contemporary Halakhic Problems* (New York, 1989), iii. 251–92.

**Wasserman, Elhanan** Foremost Lithuanian Talmudist (1875–1941). Wasserman studied in his youth in the Yeshivah of *Telz and for several years in the house of his father-in-law, Rabbi Meir Atlas. He later spent some years in the town of Radin, the home of the famous *Hafetz Hayyim, whom Wasserman considered to be his chief mentor in his religious approach to the Jewish problems of the day. His main official position was as principal of the Yeshivah in the town of Baranowitz in Poland, to which students flocked from many parts of the Jewish world. Wasserman was active in the ultra-Orthodox Aggudat Israel movement. Essentially a kind and gentle man, Wasserman was none the less fearless and outspoken in his struggle against Reform, Zionism, and secularism, all of which, he believed, were preventing the coming of the *Messiah by attempting to take Jewish destiny into their own hands instead of relying on God to save His people. He was greatly admired for his sincerity, piety, and learning by the Hasidic masters, some of whom encouraged Hasidic youngsters to study with him. In 1941 he and other Rabbis were arrested in Kovno by the Nazis and condemned to be shot. It is reported that while awaiting his arrest and the fate he knew was in store for him he studied the Talmud with the others as if nothing was to happen, secure in his faith in God. He declared to his colleagues: 'It seems that for all our unworthiness we are looked upon in Heaven as righteous men whose death, the Rabbis say, is a sacrifice that atones for the sins of the generation.' He is therefore called Ha-Kadosh, 'Holy Man', the title given to a *martyr.

Wasserman was one of the chief exponents of the Lithuanian type of study, in which the method is used of analysing methods, legal concepts, and pilpul is avoided. This method is displayed in the collections of his lectures and notes to the Talmud that have been published as excellent guides to the intricacies of the Talmudic debates. He also wrote letters and essays on theological topics, some of them very controversial, as when, for example, he suggested that Jews have suffered from the *blood libel because their ancestors, Joseph's brothers, dipped his tunic in blood (Genesis 37: 31). In an oft-quoted letter to a German Jewish student he remarked that secular studies are only permitted as a means to an end, in order to be equipped to earn a living, but are never to be engaged in as good in themselves. Only the Torah is to be studied for its own sake. Wasserman is now one of the heroes in the revival of ultra-Orthodoxy. Tales are told of him as if he were a Hasidic *Zaddik. It is said, for instance, that during a visit to the USA he was taken in a taxi whose windows were blackened past 43rd Street in Manhattan; when the taxi passed near strip-shows and shops selling pornography, he suddenly remarked that he sensed a spirit of impurity pervading the area.

**Water-Drawing Ceremony** The ceremony that took place in the *Temple during the seven days of the festival of *Tabernacles. The usual libation on the altar was of wine but after the Tamid, the perpetual offering, had been offered in the morning of each of these seven days there was a libation of water, the festival of Tabernacles being the season when prayers for *rain were offered. The whole ceremony was rejected by the *Sadducees as having no basis in the Bible. But the *Pharisees declared it to be a 'law given to Moses at *Sinai' and they set the greatest store by it. A verse quoted in this connection was: 'Joyfully shall you draw water from the fountains of triumph' (Isaiah 12: 3). The Mishnah (*Sukkah* 5: 1–5) describes the great celebration that took place in honour of the water-drawing from the night after the first day of Tabernacles and on the subsequent nights of the festival. The Mishnah states: 'He that has never seen the joy of the Bet Ha-Shoevah ['the joy of the House of the Drawing'] has never in his life seen joy.' Some pious Jews today still have a minor celebration on each night of Tabernacles, in commemoration of the ancient festivities and called by the ancient name 'the joy of the Bet Ha-Shoevah', but this is no more than a pious custom.

**Wayfarer's Prayer** The prayer recited before setting out on a journey. The source for this prayer is in the Talmud (*Berakhot* 29b), where the prayer for the journey (*tefillat ha-derekh*) is referred to as taking counsel with the Creator before setting out. The Talmud gives the following version of this prayer: 'May it be Thy will, O Lord my God, to conduct me in peace, to direct my steps in peace, to uphold me in peace and to deliver me from every enemy and ambush by the way. Send a blessing upon the work of my hands and let me obtain grace, loving-kindness and mercy in Thine eyes and in the eyes of all who behold me. Blessed art Thou, O Lord, Who hearkeneth unto prayer.' However, *Abbaye says in the passage that prayers should be offered in the plural in order for the individual to associate himself with the community, so that the wording should be: 'May it be Thy will, O Lord *our* God, to conduct *us* in peace', and so on. The practice, therefore, is to follow Abbaye and in most versions of the prayer the plural is used. In the *Hertz *Siddur*, for some reason, the prayer is in the singular and a number of scriptural verses have been added, based on earlier prayer books. It is customary nowadays to recite the wayfarer's prayer before travelling in a plane, even though the hazards are far less than they would have been when journeying in a caravan in Talmudic times.

J. H. Hertz, 'Prayer to be Said When Going on a Journey or Voyage', in his *The Authorised Daily Prayer Book* (London, 1947), 1044–5.

**Western Wall** Part of the wall around the *Temple Mount built by Herod in the first century BCE. Five rows of the original huge stones, each weighing many tons, are now seen above ground; the lower, original stones are below ground. The smaller stones that can now be seen were added at various periods. This wall, called Ha-Kotel ('the wall') is not the actual wall of the Temple, as some imagine, but of the Temple Mount. The reference in the Midrash to the 'Western Wall from which the *Shekhinah will never depart' may originally have been to the actual western wall of the Temple, since the holy of holies was situated in the west. But pilgrims to Jerusalem increasingly understood the Midrash as referring to this wall with the result that, at least from the sixteenth century, the wall was held to be a specially sacred spot from which prayers offered there ascended directly to heaven. Some pious Jews still insert written petitions in the crevices of the wall. Because Jews have mourned there over the destruction of the Temple, the wall came to be known, by non-Jews, as the 'Wailing Wall', but this name is unknown in the Jewish tradition.

After the Six Day War, when east Jerusalem came into Jewish hands once again, a large space was cleared in front of the wall to form a plaza and, nowadays, constant services are held there, men and women being separated in accordance with the Orthodox view (see SYNAGOGUE). Some Jews, especially those of Oriental extraction, celebrate a boy's *Bar Mitzvah at the wall accompanied by singing and dancing (and see HOLY PLACES).

**Widows and Orphans** There are numerous injunctions in the Bible to care for widows and orphans and to avoid taking advantage of their situation of having husband or father to protect them. The underprivileged to whom the poor man's tithe (see TITHING) was to be given include 'the orphan, and the widow' (Deuteronomy 26: 12). The warning not to oppress a widow or an orphan is stated with full rigour: 'You shall not ill-treat any widow or orphan. If you do mistreat them, I will heed their cry as soon as they cry out to Me, and My anger shall blaze forth and I will put you to the sword, and your own wives shall become widows and your children orphans' (Exodus 22: 21-3). The Midrash stresses the word 'any' in the verse to include 'the widow of a king' and in the Jewish tradition generally concern for the feelings of the widow and orphan applies even to wealthy widows and orphans, not only to the poor and disadvantaged. From Talmudic times onwards the courts appointed a guardian for orphans, a trustworthy man who would administer faithfully and voluntarily the estate they had inherited from their father. The prophet Isaiah urges his people: 'Uphold the rights of the orphan; defend the cause of the widow' (Isaiah 1: 17). Similarly, the prophet Jeremiah declares: 'No, if you really mend your ways and your actions; if you execute justice between one man and another; if you do not oppress the stranger, the orphan and the widow' (Jeremiah 7: 5-6). Job, protesting his innocence, says: 'For I saved the poor man who cried out, the orphan who had none to help him. I received the blessing of the lost, I gladdened the heart of the widow' (Job 29: 12-13).

In Jewish law as developed by the Rabbis,

while orphans inherit their father's estate, a widow does not inherit her husband's estate. But the *ketubah consists of a settlement on the estate from which the widow is entitled to maintenance until she remarries. Many Jewish communities had an orphanage in which the young charges were cared for, not always as kindly as they should have been judging by the frequent complaints found in Jewish literature. A teacher was allowed to chastise an orphan 'for his own good' but orphans should otherwise be treated with special tenderness and consideration. Unfortunately, some teachers appear to have interpreted 'for his own good' in a less than generous way.

The *High Priest alone was forbidden to marry a widow (Leviticus 21: 14) from which and from other scriptural passages the Talmud (*Kiddushin* 13b) deduces that a widow is permitted to others than the High Priest. On the other hand, another Talmudic passage (*Pesaḥim* 111a-b) quotes the advice given by Rabbi *Akiba to Rabbi *Simeon ben Yohai: 'Do not cook in a pot in which your neighbour has cooked', explained, in one version in the Talmud, to mean that Rabbi Simeon was advised not to marry a widow because, as it is put euphemistically, 'not all fingers are alike', that is, she may compare, to his detriment, the performance of her second husband with that of her first. Although this certainly does not constitute advice for all Jews, a passage in the Zohar (ii. 102a-b) states that to marry a widow is dangerous because the spirit of her first husband can cause harm to her present husband. Here again the Zohar does not actually forbid a widow to remarry and, in any event, Jewish law does not normally take the Zohar into account where its teachings are in contradiction to clear rulings of the Talmud. While a few pious men in the past did refuse to marry a widow, the normal attitude throughout the ages is permissive and there are many instances of pious scholars marrying widows. In some medieval sources, however, it is stated that the widow of a *martyr should not remarry. Where a man dies without issue, the laws of *levirate marriage and Halitzah come into operation.

The Talmud (*Yevamot* 64b) observes that it is dangerous to marry a woman who has been widowed from two former husbands, either because she may have some malignant disease in her womb which caused their deaths or because it may be her fate not to have a husband to support her. The second view is applicable to cases where the woman was widowed from her first two husbands without having lived with them or where the death was due to an accident. The *Shulḥan Arukh* (*Even Ha-Ezer* 9: 1) rules that if her marriage to the third husband had already taken place there is no need for them to be divorced, and further qualifications are found among the codifiers.

**Wills** The chief religious problem with regard to a will, in which a person declares how his estate is to be distributed after his death, is that, on the face of it, any disposition that is not in accord with the laws of *succession, as stated in the Torah (Numbers 27: 8–11; Deuteronomy 21: 16–17), is contrary to the laws of the Torah. According to the Talmudic sources, however, the laws of succession only apply where the testator states that the deposition of his property in is the form of an inheritance. The laws of succession do not apply if the deposition is given as a gift, that is, if the estate is distributed while the man is still alive, with the stipulation taking place immediately but the distribution only when he dies, since a man is allowed to give away that which he owns to whomsoever he pleases. The key passage in this connection is the Mishnah (*Bava Batra* 8: 5) which states: 'If a person gives his estate, in writing, to strangers, and leaves out his children, his arrangements are legally valid [literally, what he has done is done], but the spirit of the Sages finds no delight in him. Rabban Simeon ben Gamaliel said: If his children did not conduct themselves in a proper manner he will be remembered for good.' Most authorities, consequently, see no harm in a man making a will in favour of whomsoever he wishes, provided it is in the form of a gift not an inheritance, since the will is precisely that— a gift given in his lifetime to come into operation 'from now until after his death', as this is formulated in the Mishnah in the same tractate. Nevertheless, he should leave a substantial amount to his children in order to satisfy the 'spirit of the Sages'.

Judah Dick, 'Halacha and the Conventional Last Will and Testament', in Alfred S. Cohen (ed.), *Halacha and Contemporary Society* (New York, 1983), 278–91.

**Wills, Ethical** Instructions given in writing by a father to his children in anticipation of his death. The term 'ethical will', now widely used to describe published works in this genre, seems to have originated with Israel Abrahams, who called his famous collection *Hebrew Ethical Wills*. But the term is very imprecise in that the concerns of the writers of these documents were religious as well as ethical and they often give instructions regarding such matters as the procedures to be followed at the writer's burial. The Hebrew term is simply *tzavaah* ('testament') the term used for *wills in general. Israel Abrahams himself gives the Hebrew title of his work as: *Tzavaaot Geoney Yisrael*, 'The Last Testaments of the Great Men of Israel'. Advice and admonition by fathers to their children is known from ancient times and in all cultures. David on his deathbed instructs his son Solomon to be faithful to his charge: 'I go the way of all the earth: be thou strong therefore, and show thyself a man; and keep the charge of the Lord thy God, to walk in his ways, to keep his statutes, and his commandments, and his judgments, and his testimonies' (1 Kings 2–3). Such instructions are found, too, in the Talmud, and examples of these are given by Abrahams at the beginning of his work. But these early instances are all in verbal form, delivered from person to person. It was not until the Middle Ages that Jewish scholars and pietists actually wrote down their religious and ethical instructions, which were later published. The nature and flavour of this kind of work can be gauged from the following brief extracts from Abrahams's work. *Nahmanides writes to his son:

'And now, my son! Understand clearly that he who prides himself in his heart over other men is a rebel against the Kingship of Heaven. Such a one presumes to adorn himself in the robe of the Omnipresent. For it is God, enthroned, who wears the majesty . . . Accordingly I will explain how thou must habituate thyself to the quality of humility in thy daily practice. Let thy voice be low, and thy head bowed; let thine eyes be turned earthwards and thy heart heavenwards. Gaze not in the face of him thou dost address. Every man should seem in thine eyes as one greater than thyself.'

*Elijah, Gaon of Vilna writes to his sons before his intended visit to the land of Israel:

'On Sabbaths and festivals speak not at all of matters which are not absolutely essential, and even in such cases be very brief. For the sanctity of the Sabbath is great indeed, and only with reluctance did the authorities allow even the exchange of greetings—so severe were they regarding even a single utterance. Honour then the Sabbath to the utmost, as was done when I was with you. Be in nowise niggardly, for though God determines how much a person shall have, this does not apply to Sabbaths and festivals.'

At the end of many Hasidic works, the *tzavaah* of the author is printed in which, in addition to giving instructions to his children, the *Zaddik urges his Hasidim to follow the particular Hasidic way he represents. This mode of instruction has continued until the present day, where it is followed by modern writers with no pretensions to be Rabbis and scholars.

> Israel Abrahams, *Hebrew Ethical Wills*, foreword by Judah Goldin, (Philadelphia, 1954).
> Jack Riemer and Nathaniel Stampfer (eds.), *Ethical Wills: A Modern Jewish Treasury* (New York, 1983).

**Wine** There are differing attitudes in the classical sources of Judaism towards the drinking of wine. The Psalmist declares that wine gladdens the heart of man (Psalms 104: 15) and the Rabbis introduced a special *benediction over wine as well as ruling that other important benedictions such as the *Kiddush and *Havdalah have to be recited over a cup of wine. At the *marriage ceremony the benedictions are recited over a cup of wine from which bride and bridegroom drink. Libations of wine were offered on the altar as an accompaniment to the *sacrifices. The practice developed of giving mourners wine to drink to assuage their grief on the basis of the verse which enjoins giving wine to 'the bitter in spirit' (Proverbs 31: 4). A Talmudic saying (*Eruvin* 65a) has it that wine was only created for the purpose of comforting mourners. On the other hand, according to one view in the Midrash, the fruit of the tree from which *Adam and Eve partook was the grape which 'brought a curse to mankind'. The *Nazirite, whose vow includes abstention from wine, is praised by one Rabbi in the Talmud as a 'holy man', although according to another opinion, the Nazirite is a sinner in that he rejects God's gift of wine (see ASCETICISM and HOLINESS). There is a biblical reference to a family which abstained from wine as well as from building houses and cultivating the soil. These men, the Rechabites (the descendants

of Jonadab son of Rechab) were held up as an example of loyalty and obedience by the prophet Jeremiah (Jeremiah 35) but there is no suggestion in the chapter that it was advisable for others to follow the ways of the Rechabites.

The general principle that emerges from all the debates and discussions on the subject is that the drinking of wine, and other intoxicating drinks, is harmless and can even be desirable except where it can lead to drunkenness. Only on the festival of *Purim is intoxication allowed. A Rabbi is forbidden to render decisions after he has partaken of wine since his mind will then be clouded, just as the *priests in the *Temple were forbidden to drink wine immediately before they carried out their services (Leviticus 10: 9–11). In *Hasidism the drinking of wine and alcoholic beverages in general was held to be conducive to the joy a Jew should experience as a worshipper of God, but the *Mitnaggedim were not slow to accuse Hasidim of drunkenness and frivolity because of their addiction to wine. Since wine was used in idolatrous worship the Talmudic Rabbis imposed a ban on all wine manufactured by *Gentiles. Orthodox Jews and some Conservative Jews still abstain from drinking 'Gentile wine'.

> Louis Jacobs, 'Alcohol', in his *What Does Judaism Say About . . .?* (Jerusalem, 1973), 14–18.

**Wisdom** The Hebrew word *ḥokhmah*, usually translated as 'wisdom', is used in Jewish literature, in a variety of ways, to denote mental processes and intellectual attitudes. In the Bible the word often means 'skill'. Bezalel, the architect of the *Tabernacle and his co-workers, are said (Exodus 36: 2) to have been gifted with *ḥokhmah*, meaning here the skills which enabled them to carry out their tasks successfully. Similarly, the Talmudic Rabbis say that to blow the *shofar on the Sabbath does not fall under the heading of 'work' but of *ḥokhmah*, that is, it is a skilled performance, for which one has to be trained, but cannot be construed as physical effort. In the books of the Bible belonging to what is known as the 'Wisdom Literature'—*Proverbs, *Job, and *Ecclesiastes —*ḥokhmah* acquires a more intellectual meaning. The sage, *ḥakham*, in this literature, and in some other late passages in the Bible, is the man who has acquired knowledge of the world and human nature, sharing his experience with others. As in the book of Proverbs, the *ḥakham* gives prudent advice and is the author of wise saws. Thus the prophet Jeremiah, referring to different types of people admired for their extraordinary attainments, declares: 'Let not the wise man [*hakham*] glory in his wisdom [*hokhmah*], neither let the mighty man glory in his might, let not the rich man glory in his riches' (Jeremiah 9: 23). In Rabbinic literature the 'wisdom' of the book of Proverbs is made to refer to the 'wisdom of the Torah' so that the *hakham* now becomes the scholar well versed in the Torah (see STUDY and TALMID ḤAKHAM). This identification of the Torah with wisdom goes back in fact to the book of Deuteronomy (4: 5–6): 'See, I have imparted to you laws and rules, as the Lord my God has commanded me, for you to abide by in the land which you are about to invade and occupy. Observe them faithfully, for that will be proof of your wisdom and discernment to other peoples, who on hearing of all these laws will say, "Surely, that great nation is a wise and discerning people."' Yet the Rabbis preserve the distinction between the wisdom of the Torah and universal human knowledge. As a Midrashic statement has it: 'If you are told that there is wisdom among the nations believe it but if you are told that there is Torah among the nations do not believe it.'

Among the medieval thinkers *hokhmah* usually refers to prowess in philosophical argument and there is a marked tendency to blur the distinction made by the Rabbis between the Torah and universal knowledge, the latter itself being considered to be part of the Torah, albeit a part of Torah knowledge arrived at by purely human reasoning, not through *revelation. In modern times, *hokhmah* often denotes the sciences as well as the scientific, objective study of the Jewish sources. The Hebrew name for *Jüdische Wissenschaft is: *Hokhmat Yisrael* (literally, 'The Wisdom of Israel' or 'Jewish Wisdom') referring to the employment of the historical-critical methodology.

The Kabbalists refer to their discipline as *Hokhmah Nistarah* ('Hidden Wisdom'), abbreviated to *Hen* ('Grace'), hence the Kabbalists become the *Yodei Hen* ('Those Who Know Grace'), those who have been initiated into the secret lore. In the Kabbalah, too, *Hokhmah* is one of the *Sefirot, representing the stage in the divine unfolding at which the idea of creation has emerged in the divine Mind. In the human psyche, on the analogy of the divine processes, *Hokhmah* represents a bare idea in the mind, an idea not as yet fully formed. This notion is elaborated on in the *Habad movement in *Hasidism, the name Habad being formed from the initial letters of *hokhmah*, *binah* ('understanding'), and *daat* ('knowledge').

In everyday Jewish use *hokhmah* denotes wisdom of a deeper quality than mere cleverness. The *hakham* is not a clever know-all but a man capable of penetrating into the depths of the human situation and of seeing things as a whole.

**Wise, Isaac Mayer** Reform Rabbi, pioneer of Reform Judaism in America (1819–1900). Although Wise received, in his native Bohemia, a good grounding in the traditional Jewish sources, he was largely self-educated in the more modern Jewish thought and the general culture of his day. In 1846 Wise left for America, serving, at first, as Rabbi to an Orthodox synagogue in Albany in which he attempted to introduce certain reforms contrary to the wishes of the congregation. Such was the opposition to Wise's reforms that the president of the congregation came to blows with him on *Yom Kippur. Wise left his post to found a synagogue on his own. In 1854 Wise became a Reform Rabbi in Cincinnati, which city, through his efforts and strong and stubborn personality, became the home of American Reform. It was the dream of Reform as suited to life in the New World that inspired Wise, unlike the Reformers in Germany whose aim it was to accommodate Judaism to Western life and civilization in general, rather than to a particular country. At one period in his career Wise became so convinced that a moderately reformed Judaism would prove attractive to all reasonable people that he forecast that in fifty years Judaism would overtake Christianity to become the religion of America as a whole—a nonsensical dream, of course, but indicative of Wise's reforming zeal and broad, though fanciful, vision.

Wise wished to establish what he called a Minhag America ('Custom of America'), a uniform ritual for all American Jews. He wrote extensively on his favourite topic, meeting, however, with opposition both from the Orthodox and from the more radical Reformers. The latter believed Wise to be too traditional in his approach and he was indeed averse, for example, to *biblical criticism being applied to the *Pentateuch. Wise was instrumental in forming the Union of American Hebrew Congregations and in 1875 the Hebrew Union College in Cincinnati, of which he became President. The College was intended to be a general school of learning in which Orthodox as well as Reform Rabbis would be trained but when, at the banquet to celebrate the ordination of the College's first Rabbis, non-*kosher food was served, the traditionalists would have nothing further to do with the College. This led eventually to the establishment of the Jewish Theological Seminary for the training of Conservative Rabbis and to the creation of the third denomination in American life, Conservative Judaism.

Sefton D. Temkin: *Isaac Mayer Wise Shaping American Judaism* (The Littman Library of Jewish Civilization; Oxford, 1992).

**Wise, Stephan S.** Prominent Reform Rabbi, social activist and Zionist leader (1874–1949). Wise was born in Budapest but, at the age of 2, was brought to America. He studied at Columbia University from which he later obtained a Ph.D. Wise pursued Rabbinic studies privately and was ordained as a Rabbi by the famous preacher, Adolf Jellineck of *Vienna. In 1907 Wise founded the Free Synagogue in New York—'free' both in the sense that no fees would be demanded of the congregation and in that Wise was allowed to express his views without any interference from the governing body of the synagogue. Wise was one of the first Reform Rabbis to break with the attitude of hostility Reform had shown to *Zionism, a cause he espoused with the great oratorical power for which he was renowned. Wise was also the founder of the Jewish Institute of Religion in New York. This institution originally had the aim of providing Jewish studies on an interdenominational basis but this goal was never fully realized and the Institute eventually merged with the Hebrew Union College in Cincinnati, the major college for the training of Reform Rabbis. After the rise of Nazism Wise worked unceasingly to alleviate the sufferings of the Jews in Europe, for which he was admired and respected even by the ultra-Orthodox whose views on Judaism were so different from his and who, not too unkindly, dubbed him 'one of the saints of the nations of the world'! His close friendship with the Christian minister, John Haynes Holmes, has been recorded by Voss.

Carl Hermann Voss, *Rabbi and Minister* (Cleveland and New York, 1964).

**Wissenschaft** See JÜDISCHE WISSENSCHAFT.

**Witchcraft** The key biblical verse on the subject of witchcraft: 'Thou shalt not suffer a witch to live' (Exodus 22: 17) was understood by the Talmudic Rabbis to mean that a witch had to be executed. It is important to appreciate, however, that when this view was put forward it was purely academic, since no court in Talmudic times was empowered to impose capital *punishment (and see *Sanhedrin). Although the Hebrew uses the feminine form, the Rabbis observe that this is only because women were especially addicted to witchcraft. A wizard is as culpable as a witch. As with regard to *magic in general, opinions were divided among the Jewish teachers over whether witchcraft can work so as really to do harm. Maimonides believes that there are no supernatural magical powers, and that the Torah injunction against magic is based on a false belief that it is efficacious. Although it was not unknown for some Jews to practise witchcraft in spite of its strong condemnation, the claim in the Middle Ages that the Jew was in league with the devil to harm Christians owes everything to overheated imagination and nothing to fact (and see BLOOD LIBEL).

Joshua Trachtenberg, 'The Jew as Sorcerer', in his *The Devil and the Jews* (Philadelphia, 1982).

**Witch of Endor** The woman who was consulted by King Saul and who brought up the prophet *Samuel from the dead, as told in the 1 Samuel 28. The problems connected with the story were discussed in the period of the *Geonim. Samuel ben Hophni, Gaon of Sura (d. 1013), father-in-law of *Hai Gaon, was asked whether the story was to be taken literally, and whether the witch actually succeeded in raising Samuel from the dead. Samuel ben Hophni replies that he finds it impossible to believe that God would have made a witch the instrument of raising Samuel. The true meaning of the story is that the witch, by trickery, persuaded Saul that she had succeeded in bringing up Samuel. The words attributed to Samuel in the narrative are the words the witch put into Samuel's mouth in order to convince Saul that she had succeeded. In that case, it can be asked, how is it that she forecast so accurately that Saul would die in battle? To this the Gaon replies that she either knew it because Samuel had so prophesied while he was still alive, or it was pure guesswork which by coincidence happened to come true. If God had really desired to inform Saul of his impending death in battle, He would have done so through a prophet, not through a witch. The Gaon adds that while he is aware that earlier teachers, namely the Talmudic Rabbis, did understand that story literally, we are in no obligation to follow them when what they say is contrary to reason.

Both *Saadiah Gaon and Hai Gaon, on the other hand, refuse to accept Samuel ben Hophni's rationalistic interpretation. According to both these Geonim, God really did bring Samuel up from the dead. The witch, not having enjoyed such miraculous powers hitherto, was consequently astonished, as Scripture implies, that she had been successful. The Talmudic Rabbis clearly understood the story to mean that it was Samuel who spoke to Saul, not the witch in Samuel's name. Scripture states that Samuel said: 'tomorrow shalt thou and thy sons be with me' (v. 19), upon which the Rabbis (*Berakhot* 12b) comment: ' "with me"—in my section in Paradise'. If it was the witch who said these words, how could she possibly have known such a mystery?

This whole debate is significant over and above the particular instance of the Witch of Endor. Reading between the lines, it becomes clear that important theological issues were at stake. The first concerns the *authority of the Talmudic *Rabbis. It is one thing to be guided by common sense where the Talmudic Rabbis disagree among themselves. Here, Hai states, he is prepared to favour what appears to be the most reasonable view. It is quite another to reject, in the name of reason, what appears to be the unanimous view of the Rabbis, even though the matter does not concern Jewish law. Samuel ben Hophni is prepared to go to the lengths of preferring his rationalistic interpretation to the unanimous view of the Rabbis. The other Geonim could not agree to go so far.

The second point at issue, and this is stated explicitly by Samuel ben Hophni and the other Geonim, is the attitude the Jew should adopt towards Scripture as a whole. What was at stake was not simply the correct interpretation of a single chapter. If, as Samuel ben Hophni has argued, the scriptural references to Samuel 'saying' this or that mean no more than that someone imagined him as saying it, what guarantee is there that other scriptural references to

someone 'saying' something are authentic; for example, when Moses 'said' something or when God 'spoke' to Moses?

In the whole debate problems emerge about which Jews agonized in later periods, such as the question of reason versus revelation (see RATIONALISM); the way in which Scripture is to be interpreted; whether *Aggadah is to be understood in as rigorous a fashion as *Halakhah; and the whole question of *biblical criticism.

**Witness** The general rule in Jewish law is that in criminal cases and in cases involving claims on property two witnesses are required in order to establish the facts of the case. The two key biblical texts in this connection are: 'One witness shall not rise up against a man for any iniquity, or for any sin, in any sin that he sinneth; at the mouth of two witnesses, or at the mouth of three witnesses, shall a matter be established' (Deuteronomy 19: 15). 'At the mouth of two witnesses, or three witnesses, shall he that is to die be put to death; at the mouth of one witness he shall not be put to death' (Deuteronomy 17: 6). The Rabbis explain the reference to 'three witnesses' to mean that if one of the witnesses is found to be disqualified, although two undisqualified witnesses remain, the case is dismissed since all three give a single testimony. In financial disputes, however, where one witness testifies on behalf of the plaintiff, his testimony, though it cannot disturb the defendant's possession, is sufficiently strong to compel the defendant to take an *oath. Witnesses must be perfectly reliable persons; robbers, for example, are disqualified from acting as witnesses. Witnesses must not be related to the contestants in a case nor must they be related to one another. The disqualification of a witness on the grounds of close relationship applies even where the witness testifies against his relative. A *marriage, too, is only valid if two proper witnesses are present. If a man betroths a woman and she accepts but no witnesses are present or the only witnesses are relatives of either bride or bridegroom, the marriage is invalid and no bill of divorce (*get) is required to dissolve it. In the above cases only males can act as witnesses. With regard to religious law, however, only one witness is required to declare that food, for example, is *kosher and here a woman can serve as a witness. A woman can also testify that a missing husband has died so that the wife can remarry. According to the Rabbis, the laws of witnesses are relaxed in this case, so that a single witness is sufficient. The reason for the relaxation is said to be in order to prevent the wife from having the status of an *agunah, a woman who remains bound to a missing husband and, unless he can be presumed to be dead, cannot remarry. Respectable witnesses are believed on their word alone. In Jewish law it is unknown for witnesses to have to take an oath before their testimony is accepted. Where the witnesses contradict one another or where one set of witnesses testify for the plaintiff and another set for the defendant, the case is dismissed. These are the essential laws regarding witnesses. They receive much elaboration in the Talmud and the *Codes.

The theological idea that the Jewish people are witnesses to the truth of monotheism is based on a number of biblical passages. The prophet declares: 'Ye are My witnesses, saith the Lord; and My servant whom I have chosen; that ye may know and believe Me, and understand that I am He; before Me, there was no God formed, neither shall any be after Me' (Isaiah 43: 10). A Rabbinic homily (Midrash Leviticus Rabbah 6: 5) reads the idea into a verse which speaks of testimony in general: 'He is a witness, whether he hath seen or hath known. If he do not utter it, then he shall bear his iniquity' (Leviticus 5: 1). The Midrash expounds the verse as follows. '*He is a witness* . . . the reference is to Israel; *Whether he hath seen* . . . "thou hast been brought to see and know that the Lord he is God, there is none else beside Him" [Deuteronomy 4: 35]. *Or hath known* . . . "And thou shalt know this day and lay it to thine heart that the Lord He is God, in heaven above and upon the earth beneath: there is none else" [Deuteronomy 4: 39]. *If he do not utter it, he shall bear his iniquity* . . . If you do not utter my divinity to the Gentile world, I exact punishment from you.'

The *Tabernacle erected in the wilderness is called 'the tabernacle of the testimony' (Exodus 38: 21) because it contained the *Ark in which rested the *tablets of stone upon which the *Decalogue was inscribed, the Ark being itself called the 'testimony': 'And thou shalt put therein the ark of the testimony' (Exodus 40: 3). Further on in the same chapter (Exodus 40: 20) it is stated: 'And he took and put the testimony into the ark.' The Psalmist (Psalms 19: 8) speaks of the Torah as being God's

testimony: 'The Torah of the Lord is perfect, restoring the soul; the testimony of the Lord is sure, making wise the simple.' The English word 'martyr' is derived from the Greek word meaning witness. Although the Hebrew for 'martyr' is a different word (*ha-kadosh*, 'the holy') the Jewish *martyrs believed that the supreme sacrifice they were making was part of the Jewish witness to God's truth.

Leon Roth, 'The First Witnesses', in his *Judaism: A Portrait* (London, 1960), 59–68.

**Wolfson, Harry Austryn** Historian of ideas, professor for many years at Harvard University, and author of important works on the history of Jewish and general philosophy (1887–1974). In his youth Wolfson studied at the famed *Yeshivah of Slabodka in Lithuania. Arriving in the USA in 1903, he at first earned a living as a Hebrew teacher and writer but later studied philosophy at Harvard. In 1925 he was appointed Professor of Hebrew Literature and Philosophy at Harvard where he was highly admired, becoming known as 'Wolfson of Harvard'. Wolfson's works on *Philo, *Crescas, *Spinoza, and the Church Fathers won great renown. Wolfson claimed to have based his methodology on the Talmudic dialectics (*pilpul) the knowledge of which he had acquired in Slabodka, and which he applied to the study of philosophical works. This methodology has been challenged by other scholars in the field but none deny the great significance of Wolfson's work. Though not very observant of Jewish law and ritual in his private life, Wolfson had little truck with Reform Judaism. He once described himself as 'a non-practising Orthodox Jew'.

Leo W. Schwarz, *Wolfson of Harvard: Portrait of a Scholar* (Philadelphia, 1978).

**Women** Any consideration of the role of women in Judaism has to reckon with the obvious: that the classical sources of the Jewish religion were all compiled by men. In the Bible, for example, while *Miriam, *Deborah, and Huldah are spoken of as prophetesses, demonstrating that in ancient Israel women, too, could enjoy the prophetic faculty, the literary prophets and those who recorded their prophetic utterances were male. Similarly, the Talmudic authors and editors and the great codifiers were all men, as were the medieval philosophers and the Kabbalists. Even when the tradition affirms that the biblical authors (and, albeit to a lesser degree, the others mentioned above) were inspired by the *Holy Spirit, the inspiration came through a male, not a female personality and this must have affected the way in which inspiration was expressed, unless the *fundamentalist view is adopted that it is God alone who 'speaks' through the inspired person in such a way as to override his personality entirely. Jewish *feminism has seized on all this to claim that there is evident in the sources a marked bias against women. Other Jews, females as well as males, do not believe that the clock of history can be turned backwards, although they, too, are naturally concerned to remove any injustices from which women suffer. In this entry the various statements in the sources about women are noted as objectively as such an emotion-laden topic will allow.

### Women in the Halakhah

According to the *Halakhah, there are no differences whatsoever between men and women in matters of Jewish belief, ethical obligations, and the criminal law. A Jewish woman, as well as a Jewish man, is expected to believe in the *principles of the faith, to love and care for others, to be generous and kindly, not to steal or cheat. With regard to religious law, however, women are exempt from the performance of any *precept, *mitzvah, which depends for its performance on a given time. Thus women are not obliged to wear *tzitzit (because these are not worn at night and are hence dependent on time) or to hear the *shofar on *Rosh Ha-Shanah. Nevertheless, it is customary for women to hear the shofar, to sit in the sukkah on *Tabernacles, and to take the four species of plant on this festival. In recent years some women have worn the *tallit with its tzitzit for prayer and even in former times there were reports here and there of especially pious women wearing *tefillin, though the Rabbis frowned on such exhibitions of extraordinary piety. The reason why women are exempt from the observance of positive precepts depending on time is not stated in the Talmud. One reason given in the late Middle Ages is that it would have been considered unreasonable to expect a woman to have to attend to these time-bound precepts since her time is not her own in view of her need to attend to her home and family. This seems to be a rationalization. In a late Midrash it is suggested that women are more

naturally refined and religious and they consequently do not require so many means of refinement as do men. Some modern scholars have tried to trace back the reason to the prominence of women in the ancient, pagan cults, the ceremonies of which took place at given seasons. Since the *Shema is dependent on time (the morning Shema can only be recited in the early morning and the night Shema only when night has fallen), women are exempt from the obligation, though women do, in fact, recite at least the first verse of the Shema twice daily. The *mezuzah is not a time-bound precept, so that a house in which women live has to have a mezuzah even if no men reside there. *Grace after meals and daily prayer are stated in the Mishnah (*Berakhot* 3: 3) to be obligations binding upon women but the usual custom is that, while women do recite the full grace, they do not recite the full statutory prayers but offer their own personal prayers each day.

A more curious exemption is the study of the Torah. Women have no obligation to study the Torah and a father has no obligation to teach his daughter the Torah. The Mishnah (*Sotah* 3: 4) quotes the opinion of Rabbi *Eliezer that 'whosoever teaches his daughter Torah teaches her lasciviousness'. This is a minority opinion, and in any event, has to be understood in the context of the unfaithful wife with which the Mishnah deals. Nevertheless, some authorities in the Middle Ages frowned on women studying the Talmud, though not the Bible and works of devotion. Very revealing in this connection is the Talmudic observation (*Berakhot* 17a) that women acquire the merit of studying the Torah by participating in this indirectly in that they send their sons to study and encourage their husbands to study. The practice of the wife being the breadwinner while the husband studies is still the norm in ultra-Orthodox circles. The result was that women were not at all well versed in Jewish learning, although some few women in the earlier period did become renowned as scholars and even as Talmudists. In modern times, all circles in Jewry, with the exception of the ultra-Orthodox, not only see no harm in the study of the Torah by women but advocate it as a positive good. So far as studying the sources of Judaism by the modern historical-critical method, in Hebrew departments of universities there are many women students and several women professors and there is no sexual discrimination in this area at all. Since women in the past did not normally study the Torah there were only a very few women competent to become Rabbis. But there is neither any Halakhic nor doctrinal reason why a learned woman should not serve as a Rabbi, although the Orthodox do not allow this on the grounds that, as they put it, 'it is against the Jewish spirit'. Reform and Conservative seminaries do ordain women as *Rabbis, and, for that matter, as *Cantors.

Women cannot serve as *witnesses in civil and criminal cases. Thus ruling is not based, as it is sometimes suggested, on the notion that women are unreliable, since in religious matters women are held to be completely reliable witnesses. The Talmud here, too, is silent on the reason why a woman cannot serve as a witness. Some of the later teachers have argued that the disqualification was intended to free women from having to attend court where unsavoury details are often related of the cases that come before it. Maimonides is alone among the earlier authorities to rule that a woman cannot hold any position of trust in the community. The Orthodox have now extended this to apply even to a woman serving on the board of management of the synagogue, and some still further, so that women have no vote in communal affairs. This disenfranchisement of women is contrary to modern susceptibilities and has given way to an attitude of complete equality between men and women in Reform and Conservative congregations. In these congregations men and women sit together, but there is no mixed seating in Orthodox synagogues (see SYNAGOGUE).

With regard to *marriage, in biblical and Talmudic law a woman is at a disadvantage in that a man can have more than one wife and a husband can *divorce his wife without her consent. On the Ashkenazi world, however, the ban of Rabbenu *Gershom against both these was upheld. The institution of the *ketubah, the marriage settlement, from early Talmudic times, militated, in any event, against hasty divorce. Yet in the final analysis a husband could exercise the power given to him by the law to refuse to deliver the bill of divorce (the *get) to his wife, resulting in her having the unfortunate status of an *agunah. Moreover, if the wife lived with another man without having obtained the get her children would be mamzerim (see MAMZER). While the Rabbinic

authorities throughout the ages have tried valiantly to solve the problem of the *agunah* and the mamzer and while much has been achieved in this area, a satisfactory solution acceptable to all has not yet emerged.

*Attitudes towards Women*

It is impossible to speak of a uniform attitude towards women in the Jewish sources, which, as mentioned above, were compiled by men and which depend on the social background as well as on individual temperament. In the Bible, polygamy is sanctioned (Deuteronomy 21: 15). Yet the biblical narrative of *Adam and Eve implies that the ideal state is that of one husband and one wife, even though there is no complete equality since the husband is said 'to rule over her' (Genesis 3: 16). Some biblical scholars (see BIBLICAL CRITICISM) have detected differing attitudes to women in the two versions of the *Decalogue (Exodus 20: 14 compared with Deuteronomy 5: 21). In the Deuteronomic version the neighbour's wife is mentioned in a separate verse, whereas in the Exodus verse she is mentioned together with his chattels. The oft-quoted section of Proverbs (31: 10–31) in praise of the capable wife is ambiguous since the wife, for all her significance to the family, is depicted as subordinate. The prophetic comparison of the love of God for Israel to the love of a husband for his wife suggests a cultural background in which women were highly respected and in which they occupied an important place, as does the existence of prophetesses as well as male prophets and the participation of women in the choral services in the *Temple (Ezra 2: 65) in one period at least. Although the masculine pronoun is used of God and He is described as a Father, in one prophetic simile God's comfort to mourners is compared to the comfort a mother affords her child (Isaiah 66: 13). Comparing this verse in Isaiah with the verse: 'Like as a father hath compassion upon his children, so hath the Lord compassion upon them that fear Him' (Psalms 103: 13), a Rabbinic homily observes that it is the nature of a father to show compassion but of a mother to afford comfort.

A variety of attitudes towards women is found in the Talmudic and Midrashic literature. Too much should not be read into the wording of the benediction, recited each day, in which a man thanks God for not having made him a woman (*Menaḥot* 43b), whereas a woman simply thanks God for having made her 'according to His will', since it is clear from the context that the thanks are for the greater opportunities a man has for carrying out the precepts, women being exempt, as above, from carrying out those precepts dependent on time. Claude *Montefiore (*A Rabbinic Anthology* (London, 1938), 507) states the Reform and Liberal opposition to this benediction in a particularly strong but one-sided manner:

'No amount of modern Jewish apologetics, endlessly poured forth, can alter the fact, that the Rabbinic attitude towards women was very different from our own. No amount of apologetics can get over the implications of the daily blessing, which orthodox Judaism has still lacked the courage to remove from its official prayer book, "Blessed art Thou, O Lord our God, who hast not made me a woman". At the same time it must be readily admitted that the Rabbis seemed to have loved their wives, that they all, apparently, had only one wife each, and that the position of the wife was one of much influence and importance.'

That the Rabbis themselves did not practise polygamy is fairly well established. Indeed, it has been convincingly argued that, while polygamy was legally sanctioned in Talmudic times, it was rarely practised by Jews. The Oriental Jews, who in the Middle Ages and later did have more than one wife, were influenced by Islamic practice rather than by Talmudic legislation.

In the Rabbinic Aggadah chivalrous statements about women alternate with sayings of a far less noble character. The reason for God creating Eve from Adam's rib is stated thus: 'God said: I will not create her from the head that she should not hold up her head too proudly; nor from the eye that she should not be a coquette, nor from the ear that she should not be an eavesdropper; nor from the mouth that she should not be too talkative; nor from the hand that she should not be too acquisitive, nor from the foot that she should not be a gadabout; but from a part of the body that is hidden, that she should be modest.' But, the Midrash ungallantly concludes, it was all to no effect (Midrash Genesis Rabbah 18: 2). In the list of tens given in a Talmudic passage (*Kiddushin* 49b) it is said that of the ten measures of speech that descended into the world, nine were taken by women.

Women were often feared by the Rabbis as a source of temptation. In Babylonia, perhaps because of the loose sexual standards in the general population, the Rabbis said that a woman's voice or her hair or her leg were sexual enticements, so that the Shema must not be read where they are seen (*Berakhot* 24a). One Babylonian teacher went so far as to declare that under no circumstances should a man be served at the table by a woman other than his wife (*Kiddushin* 70a). In all probability this is the reason for the extremely harsh, obscene description of a woman, paralleled in the Church Fathers, as 'a pitcher full of excrement with its mouth full of blood, yet all lust after her' (*Shabbat* 152a). As the ending implies, this coarse simile was used as a check to unbridled sexual lust.

Other passages in high praise of women have to be set against the above derogatory ones. A man without a wife lives without joy, blessing, and good, and a man should love his wife as himself and respect her more than himself (*Yevamot* 62b). When Rav Joseph heard his mother's footsteps he would say: 'Let me rise up before the approach of the *Shekhinah' (*Kiddushin* 31b). Israel was redeemed from Egypt by virtue of its righteous women (*Sotah* 11b). Women have greater powers of discernment than men (*Niddah* 45b). For this reason the age when a girl reachers her majority (*Bat Mitzvah) is at 12 while the age for a boy is 13 (*Bar Mitzvah). The Torah is personified as a woman. She is the daughter of God and Israel's bride. It is unnecessary to multiply examples of how different, and often contradictory, views persist among the Rabbis on the subject of women, as they do in all cultures.

Differing attitudes towards women can also be observed among the Jewish teachers in the Middle Ages. On the whole, the French and German teachers, living in a Christian society, tended to treat women more chivalrously than teachers in Islamic lands. Maimonides, in his writings, often lumps women together with children as people from whom one cannot expect too much intelligence. Maimonides (*Ishut*, 21. 3, 10) rules that if a wife persistently refuses to carry out her wifely duties such as washing her husband's hands and feet and serving him at table, the court can have her chastised with rods. Maimonides' critic, Abraham ben David, protests: 'I have never heard that it is permitted to raise a rod against a woman.' *Isserles (*Shulḥan Arukh, Even Ha-Ezer*, 154: 3) records the French, German, and Polish attitude according to which it is unheard of that a husband should ever be allowed to beat his wife.

## Women in the Kabbalah and Hasidism

The Kabbalistic attitude towards women was influenced by the doctrine of the *Sefirot, according to which *Binah* ('Understanding') is the mother and *Malkhut* ('Sovereignty') is the female principle in the Godhead. *Malkhut* is the Shekhinah, the bride of *Tiferet*, the male principle. These doctrines often resulted in a profound respect for womanhood among the Kabbalists. The famous Safed Kabbalist, Isaac *Luria, would kiss his mother's hands on the eve of the Sabbath. A Kabbalist was enjoined never to stay anywhere without his wife, the counterpart on earth of the Shekhinah, unless it was absolutely necessary. The Safed Kabbalists used to recite on Sabbath eve the verses in Proverbs in honour of the 'capable wife' which they referred also to the Shekhinah. On the other hand, the 'female' Sefirot are passive recipients of the light of the 'male' Sefirot and they are the source of sternness and judgement, with the result that the Kabbalists tend to see the female as in some ways inferior to the male and women as more cruel, less creative, and less capable of the higher reaches of thought than men. Gershom *Scholem advances this somewhat negative aspect of Kabbalistic thought on the role of the female as a reason for the virtual absence of female mystics in Judaism.

In *Hasidism the Kabbalistic attitude prevails to a large extent. The suggestion that in Hasidism women are equal to men is unfounded, despite the honour paid to such Hasidic women as the daughter of the *Baal Shem Tov and his granddaughter, the mother of *Nahman of Bratslav, and the very infrequent instances of women who served in some way as Hasidic *Rebbes.

Both the *Haskalah and Reform movements can claim with justice that they sought to improve the status of the Jewish woman and this tendency has been followed by Conservative Judaism and by many of the Orthodox.

Louis M. Epstein, *Sex Laws and Customs in Judaism* (New York, 1948).

Moshe Meiselman, *Jewish Woman in Jewish Law* (New York, 1978).

Judith Romney Wegner, *Chattel or Person? The Status of Women in the Mishnah* (Oxford, 1988).

Solomon Schechter, 'Woman in Temple and Synagogue', in his *Studies in Judaism* (Philadelphia, 1946), i. 313–25.

**Wonder** The biblical authors call attention to the marvellous features of the universe in order to awaken or increase man's sense of wonder at the works of God. The prophet declares: 'Lift up your eyes on high, and see: who hath created these? He that bringeth out their host by number, He calleth them all by name; by the greatness of His might, and for that He is strong in power, not one faileth' (Isaiah 40: 26), thus anticipating Kant's famous observation: 'Two things fill the mind with ever new and increasing admiration and awe, the more often and the more steadily one reflects on them; the starry heavens above and the moral law within.' The theme is repeated by the Psalmist: 'When I behold Thy heavens, the work of Thy fingers, the moon and the stars, which Thou hast established; what is man, that Thou art mindful of him? And the son of man, that Thou thinkest of him?' (Psalms 8: 4–5). The Psalmist hails God as the One 'who alone doeth great wonders' (Psalms 136: 4) and proclaims: 'I will give thanks unto Thee, for I am fearfully and wonderfully made; wonderful are thy works, and that my soul knoweth right well' (Psalms 139: 14). In the majestic passage in the book of *Job (Job 37), God 'thundereth marvellously with His voice, great things doeth He, which we cannot comprehend' (v. 3) and Job is urged: 'Hearken unto this, O Job; stand still, and consider the wondrous works of God' (v. 14). In Moses' great song of deliverance the verse occurs (Exodus 15: 11): 'Who is like unto Thee, O Lord, among the mighty? Who is like unto Thee, glorious in holiness, fearful in praises, doing wonders?'

These ideas were carried over into the Prayer Book. In the thanksgiving at the end of the Amidah (see LITURGY), thanks are offered to God for His 'wonders, which are wrought at all times' and the verse from the Song of Moses is recited during the benediction of the evening *Shema. The 'wonders' are not only the miracles which God performs but the marvellous way in which He has fashioned the human body and keeps human beings alive. The benediction recited after the performance of natural functions deserves to be quoted in this connection: 'Blessed art Thou, O Lord our God, King of the universe, who hast formed man in wisdom, and created in him many passages and vessels. It is well known before Thy glorious throne, that if but one of these be opened, or one of those be closed, it would be impossible to exist and stand before Thee. Blessed art Thou, O Lord, who art the wondrous healer of all flesh.'

According to Maimonides, reflection on the wonders in creation leads man to the *love and fear of God. Maimonides writes in his Code (*Yesodey Ha-Torah*, 2. 1–2):

'How does man come to love and fear God? No sooner does man reflect on His deeds and His great and marvellous creatures, seeing in them His incomparable and limitless wisdom, than he is moved to love and to praise and to glorify and he has an intense desire to know the great Name, as David said: "My soul thirsteth for God, for the living God" [Psalms 42: 3]. When man reflects on these very things he immediately recoils in fear and dread, aware that he is only a puny creature, dark and lowly, standing with his minute fraction of unstable thought, in the presence of the Perfect in Knowledge.'

*Habad thought takes it all a stage further. In the Habad view the natural order (see NATURE) is in itself the greatest source of wonder. Habad speaks of the sheer existence of the world and the creatures in it as a *pele* ('marvel') in that, from God's point of view, so to speak, there is no world at all apart from God Himself (see PANENTHEISM). The fact that the *En Sof, the Infinite, has withdrawn to allow the apparently independent universe to exist is the true wonder beyond all wonders. In modern Jewish though, *Heschel in particular has drawn on the idea of wonder as an essential ingredient in the life of religion.

Abraham J. Heschel, 'Wonder', in his *God in Search of Man: A Philosophy of Judaism* (London, 1956), 43–53.

**Word** In Jewish thought much is said about the power of the word, whether it be the creative word of God or the word in human speech. In *Philo the Logos represents the means by which God creates. The *Targum of Onkelos often uses the Aramaic *memra* ('word') as a means of softening the biblical anthropomorphisms so that instead of the Hebrew in which it is stated that God does this or that it is the *memra* from God that is active. Although the influence of Greek thought is evident in all this, the Hebrew prophets also trace their message to the word or oracle of God. It goes without saying that the identification of the Logos with Jesus in the Gospel of John (1: 14)

introduces a notion completely foreign to any version of the Jewish religion. On the contrary, Philo and the Targum are at pains to use the Word in order to distance man from the direct action of the Deity. In Judaism the 'Word' is never 'made flesh'.

Commenting on the statements in the creation narrative in Genesis chapter 1, Ethics of the Fathers (5. 1) observes that God created the world by means of ten sayings. Actually the expression: 'And God said' occurs only nine times in the creation narrative but, as the Talmudic Rabbis remark, the first verse: 'In the beginning God created' is also treated as a 'word'. The various commands in the Pentateuch are prefaced either by 'And God spoke' or by 'And God said'. The Rabbis understand the difference to be that God 'speaking' denotes a greater degree of sternness than God simply 'saying' and the same applies to other instances in which the terms are used. For example: 'These are the words which Moses spoke unto all Israel' (Deuteronomy 1: 1) means, according to the Rabbis, that Moses spoke sternly to the people, rebuking them for their shortcomings in the past. In Rabbinic teaching the *Oral Torah is the means by which the full meaning of the *Written Torah is communicated. In the Kabbalistic doctrine of the *Sefirot, the lowest of the Sefirot, *Malkhut* ('Sovereignty') represents the divine 'speech' through which the divine power is given expression for the creation and government of the world.

The power of speech is seen as God's precious gift to humanity. The Targum renders the words: 'and man became a living being' (Genesis 2: 7) as 'and man became a being that speaks'. The power to speak, to communicate, the Rabbis constantly stress, should be used only for good, never for evil. In the list of sins in the Al Het confession recited on *Yom Kippur the majority of the faults mentioned are sins of speech. In a Midrashic tale, Rabban *Gamaliel instructs his slave, Tabi, to bring him the choicest thing for sale in the market and Tabi brings back a tongue. When Rabban Gamaliel instructs Tabi to bring him the worst thing for sale he also brings him back a tongue, all to symbolize: 'Death and life are in the power of the tongue' (Proverbs 18: 21). The *study of the Torah is to be verbal, according to the Rabbis. The words have to be uttered and indeed chanted and not only dwelt upon in the mind. Prayers, too, have to be mouthed, even the 'silent prayer'. All this seems to based on the psychological principle: 'No impression without expression.' In Rabbinic teaching 'the *voice* of Jacob' (Genesis 27: 2) has to be heard in prayer and study. By the same token, while to think about business concerns is not forbidden on the Sabbath, these must not be actually expressed by word of mouth. The Jewish moralists note that man has two ears, two eyes, and two nostrils but only one mouth, to remind him to be circumspect in his speech. The moralist Israel *Salanter is reported to have advised: 'Not everything of which you think ought to be said. And not everything you say ought to be written down. And not everything you write down ought to be published.'

**Work** The verse that springs to mind in any discussion of the Jewish attitude to work is (in the King James' version): 'Six days shalt thou labour, and do all thy work; but the seventh day is the sabbath of the Lord thy God; in it thou shalt not do any work' (Exodus 20: 9–10). A superficial reading of the verse would suggest that 'six days shalt thou labour' and 'thou slalt not do any work [on the Sabbath]' are two separate injunctions; one forbidding work on the Sabbath, the other enjoining work on the six days of the week. Such an understanding might be implied in the Rabbinic comment (*Avot de-Rabbi Nathan*, ch. 21) on the verse: 'Just as Israel is commanded to keep the sabbath, Israel is commanded to work.' This statement occurs, however, in a panegyric on the high value of work and is more a homily than a precise theological doctrine. Nowhere do we find that it is a *mitzvah*, a religious obligation, in the formal sense, to work. The whole of this section constitutes the fourth commandment of the *Decalogue and deals, according to the tradition, solely with the Sabbath. There is no special *benediction to be recited before working, as there is for the other *precepts. Furthermore, *Nahmanides understands the verse as supplementary to the command to keep the Sabbath, as if to say: do whatever work is necessary for your maintenance during the six days only and refrain from work on the Sabbath. This, in fact, is the rendering of the New English Bible: 'You have six days to labour and do all your work. But the seventh day is a sabbath of the Lord your God, that day you shall not do any work.'

This textual excursus is far from irrelevant

to the theme of Jewish attitudes towards work. The verse does imply that it is part of the divine plan for man to work but it would be going beyond the evidence to affirm, on the basis of this verse (as is sometimes done in the Protestant ethic) that to be idle is an offence against the Ten Commandments; although, naturally, idleness is disapproved of by the Jewish moralists as by other moralists. (Incidentally, idleness need not receive unqualified condemnation. It can have its own value as an antidote to an irksome busyness.) In other words, work is a means to an end, not an end in itself. If it were an end in itself, and to work would be to carry out a *mitzvah*, the workaholic should be admired for his zeal in carrying out the divine will.

For all that, a high value is placed on work in the Jewish ethic. Human dignity is enhanced when man sustains himself by his own efforts. As the Psalmist says: 'When thou shalt eat the labour of thine hands, happy shalt thou be, and it shall be well with thee' (Psalms 128: 2). In a Talmudic passage (*Pesaḥim* 113a) it is said that the Babylonian teacher, Rav, urged his disciple, Rav Kahana: 'Rather skin a carcass for a fee than be supported by charity. Do not say: "I am a priest" or "I am a scholar" so that it is beneath your dignity.' It has often been noted that the Talmudic *Rabbis engaged in a variety of occupations ('work' was not necessarily construed by them to mean only manual labour, though some of them were artisans) in order to earn their living. A father is obliged to teach his son a trade or a craft that he be able to earn an honest living, advice being given on the occupations which the father, ideally, should *not* teach his son to follow because they are degrading or disruptive of character (*Kiddushin* 82a–b). Another revealing Talmudic homily (*Pesaḥim* 118a) is in the form of a comment on the verses: 'Cursed is the ground for thy sake; in toil shalt thou eat of it all the days of thy life. Thorns and thistles shall it bring forth to thee; and thou shalt eat the herb of the field. In the sweat of thy face shalt thou eat bread' (Genesis 3: 17–19). Adam is imagined as being terribly disturbed when he heard that he was to eat the herb of the field, for this would make him no different from his ass whose food is ready to hand. But when Adam heard that he was to toil for his daily bread his mind was set at rest. 'In the sweat of thy face shalt thou eat bread' is seen not as a curse but as a reassurance to man, that his dignity will not be compromised in his incessant quest for sustenance, because the human spirit remains discontented unless a man earns his keep.

In the Jewish tradition a man's work has to be beneficial to society. One who earns his living by following an occupation which makes no constructive contribution to the well-being of others is declared by the Rabbis (*Sanhedrin* 24b) to be so unreliable that he is disqualified from acting as a witness in a court of law. Well known is the Talmudic tale (*Taanit* 23a) of the saint who saw an old man planting trees. 'Why do you plant the trees since you will never enjoy the fruit?' the saint asked, to be given the unanswerable reply (from the Jewish point of view): 'I found trees planted by my ancestors from which I enjoyed the fruit. Surely, it is my duty to plant trees that those who come after me might enjoy their fruit.'

In addition to the need to earn a living and to make a contribution to society, man is advised to work for the therapeutic value of physical effort. In the passage quoted above on the verse: 'Six days shalt thou labour and do all thy work', the word 'all' is stressed, so as to refer also to the man who has no particular work to do. He should still find some work he can do. 'If he has a run-down yard or run-down field let him go and occupy himself with them', or, as we would say, let him do odd jobs about the house, help with the washing-up, take up carpentry, or grow flowers and vegetables. It is interesting that some form of bodily activity is advocated, not an intellectual pursuit, either because the Rabbis were also thinking of people for whom intellectual pursuits had no attraction or, more plausibly, because, in the absence in Rabbinic times of anything like present-day sporting activities, some physical effort was advocated even for the scholar. 'Idleness leads to dullness' is a popular saying quoted by the ancient Rabbis and subsequently by the Jewish moralists, though they would presumably agree with the saying that it is all work and no play that also leads to dullness. Recreational activities were engaged in by Jews throughout the ages.

Abraham Cohen, 'Labour' in his *Everyman's Talmud* (London, 1949), 191–6.

**Worlds, Four** In the later passages in the Zohar there are one or two references to four worlds, one beneath the other. The doctrine of the four worlds assumes special significance in the Lurianic Kabbalah (see *LURIA). The highest of these four worlds is known as 'the World of Emanation'—*Olam Ha-Atzilut* in Hebrew. The root of the word *Atzilut* is found in the biblical description of the spirit *spreading* from Moses to the elders (Numbers 11: 25). The names of the three lower worlds are taken from the verse: 'Every one that is called by My name, and whom I have *created* for My glory, I have *formed* him, yea I have *made* him' (Isaiah 43: 7). Thus the World of Emanation is the world of the *Sefirot. The World of Creation (*Olam Ha-Beriah*) evolves from the World of Emanation. Evolving from this is the World of Formation (*Olam Ha-Yetzirah*) and lower still and evolving from this is the World of Action (*Olam Ha-Asiyah*). The World of Creation contains the *throne of glory. The World of Formation is the abode of the heavenly hosts, the *angels. In some Kabbalistic schemes the World of Action is the material cosmos, but in others it is rather the spiritual counterpart and direct source of the material universe. The whole creative process is seen as a flow of the light of *En Sof into the World of Emanation which then descends from world to world until the material world emerges as the last stage in the great chain of being. Human beings have been given the tremendous task of upholding the four worlds by their deeds (see HOLY SPARKS). The four letters of the *Tetragrammaton, through which all creation is effected, represent the four worlds in the order of these four letters.

**World to Come** There is considerable ambiguity regarding the meaning of the Rabbinic doctrine of the World to Come (Heb. *Olam Ha-Ba*) and its relation to the *resurrection of the dead (see ESCHATOLOGY and HEAVEN AND HELL). In the Middle Ages Maimonides is alone in identifying the World to Come with the immortality of the *soul, while *Nahmanides is emphatic that it refers to this world, which will be renewed, after the resurrection. For instance, the Mishnah (*Sanhedrin* 10: 1) states that one who denies the resurrection will have no share in the World to Come, upon which the Talmud (*Sanhedrin* 90a) comments that this severe punishment is meted out to him on the principle of measure for measure; since he denies the resurrection it is only just that he does not rise at the resurrection. In this passage, at least, the World to Come is identified with the resurrection, though it is not absolutely certain that the Mishnah itself identifies the two so closely. In later Jewish thought the World to Come becomes a generic term for the Hereafter. The Mishnah quoted begins with the words: 'All Israel has a share in the World to Come' but then continues that some Israelites, for example, those who deny the resurrection or that the Torah is from Heaven, do not have a share in the World to Come. In the *Tosefta (*Sanhedrin* 13: 2) there is a debate between Rabbi *Eliezer and Rabbi *Joshua on whether the World to Come is reserved for Jews or whether this blissful state is the reward of *Gentiles as well. Rabbi Joshua holds that 'the righteous of all peoples have a share in the World to Come' and this became the official view of Judaism (see NOAHIDE LAWS).

The other-worldly thrust is evident in the whole of Jewish thought until the modern period. Of the numerous Rabbinic teachings about the World to Come, the following are typical of this thrust. The Mishnah (*Bava Metzia* 2: 11) rules that if a man's father and his teacher have lost something, he should first try to restore the article lost by his teacher, since a father brings his child into this world whereas a teacher of the Torah brings his students to the World to Come. In Ethics of the Fathers (4. 16) it is said that this world is like a vestibule before the World to Come. 'Prepare yourself in the vestibule, that you may enter into the hall of the palace.' Yet the statement of the second-century teacher, Rabbi Jacob, also in Ethics of the Fathers (4. 17) acts against a too-hasty claim that according to the Rabbis this world is only a preparation or school for the World to Come and has no intrinsic good. Rabbi Jacob's famous teaching reads: 'Better is one hour of repentance and good deeds in this world than the whole life of the World to Come; and better is one hour of blissfulness of spirit in the World to Come than the whole life of this world.' Significant in this connection is the saying of *Rav (relied on by Maimonides for his identification of the World to Come with spiritual bliss of the soul rather than the resurrection): 'In the World to Come there is no eating nor drinking nor propagation nor business nor jealousy nor hatred nor competition, but the righteous sit with their crowns on their heads feasting on the brightness of the *Shekhinah' (*Berakhot* 17a). Yet the Jerusalem Talmud (*Kiddushin* 4: 12)

quotes the same teacher, Rav, who is so eloquent on the purely spiritual nature of bliss in the Hereafter, as saying that in the World to Come a man will be obliged to give an account and a reckoning before the judgement seat of God for every legitimate pleasure he denied himself in this world. Very striking, too, is the saying (*Berakhot* 57b) that three things afford a foretaste in miniature of the bliss of the World to Come: the Sabbath, sexual intercourse, and a sunny day, although the Gemara is doubtful whether sexual intercourse should be included since it results in weakness of the body.

In the light of the above it is difficult to give an unqualified reply to the question of whether Judaism is a this-worldly or an other-worldly religion. Risking a generalization, it can be said that the other-worldly thrust predominates in times of oppression and the this-worldly in times of prosperity. Moses Hayyim *Luzzatto's *The Path of the Upright*, compiled in the eighteenth century, is typical of the other-worldly approach. Luzzatto begins his guide to holy living with these words:

'It is the foundation of saintliness and the perfect worship of God for a man to realise what constitutes his duty in his world and to which aim he is required to direct all his endeavours throughout his life. Now our Sages, of blessed memory, have taught us that man was created only to find delight in the Lord, and to bask in the radiance of His Shekhinah for this is the true happiness and the greatest of all possible delights. The real place in which such delight can be attained is the World to Come, for this has been prepared to this very purpose. But the way to attain to this desired goal is this world. This world, the Sages remark, is like a vestibule before the World to Come. The means by which man reaches this goal are the *precepts God, blessed be He, has commanded us and the place in which the precepts are to be carried out is only in this world. Man is put here in order to earn with the means at his command the place that has been prepared for him in the World to Come.'

Luzzatto concludes this section of his work by saying that man is tempted in this life both by prosperity and by adversity and adds: 'If he is valorous and wins the battle from every side, he becomes the perfect man who will have the merit of becoming attached to his Creator. Then he will emerge from the vestibule of this world to enjoy the Light of Life.' Luzzatto here seems to identify the World to Come, partly at least, with the fate of the soul after death, though it is clear from the work as a whole that Luzzatto believes in the final resurrection.

In *Hasidism and the *Musar movement, the World to Come is conceived of partly in terms of spiritual bliss of the soul after the death of the body. It is not that the doctrine of resurrection is denied in these movements, but it is treated as a mystery so far beyond human apprehension that speculation on it is futile. Rabbi *Shneur Zalman of Liady follows the intellectual thrust of the *Habad movement, of which he was the founder, when he writes (at the beginning of his *Likkutey Torah*):

'It is well known that the concept "the World to Come" means that souls enjoy the radiance of the Shekhinah and this delight that the soul enjoys is nothing other than comprehension of the divine. For we know from experience that there is no enjoyment and no delight whatsoever unless the thing enjoyed has been grasped in the mind. It follows that delight in the divine must first become substantial and have a separate identity in the process of the soul's enjoyment before the soul can enjoy it.'

The idea is also found in Hasidic works that the saints can enjoy the bliss of the World to Come even while on earth. The early Hasidic master, Elimelech of Lizansk, writes in his *Noam Elimelekh* (section *terumah*):

'A saint who serves God by carrying out the precepts and keeps himself far from transgressing even the lightest commandment, and is meticulous in carrying out his obligations in the best possible manner, yet has not attained to the stage in which his performance of the precepts brings him in attachment to the Creator, blessed be He, and to a great longing for Him, blessed be He; such a saint has to wait for his recompense to be given to him in the World to Come. But there is a saint who serves with great purity of thought and, through the precepts, attaches himself to the Creator, blessed be He, with great attachment and longing, seeing, at all times, how elevated is the Creator. Such a saint does not need to wait in anticipation for the delights of the World to Come since he enjoys the same delights in this world.'

The contemporary teacher of the Musar school, E. E. *Dessler, writes in the section of his work *Mikhtav Me-Eliyahu* entitled 'The World to Come':

'The man with potential for good from the beginning will always have that potential but this can never qualify as "the World to Come" since it has been actualised neither in his comprehension nor in his own being. On the other hand, even the smallest fragment, if it has been acquired through effort, is in itself the life of the World to Come. Concerning this it is said [Proverbs 16: 26]: "He that laboureth laboureth for himself." We must, therefore, be exceedingly strong in withstanding temptation and to acquire in ourselves states of being produced by the Torah. For it is only through these that we shall see light and joy for all eternity. Heaven forbid that we be satisfied with the virtues we already possess for it is not through these that we will attain to the great future. This is the principle from which we dare not depart: "He that laboureth laboureth for himself."' (See also INDIVIDUAL.)

Modern Jews entertain a variety of views on the World to Come. The religious naturalists, if they do not reject the whole concept, tend to see the World to Come as a metaphor for the emergence of a better world in the future here on earth. But. this is to remove from the concept all its spiritual power and all sense of transendence. Naturalistic interpretations of this kind are sadly lacking in numinous quality. Reform Judaism, following to some extent *Philo and Maimonides, does preserve the concept but identifies the World to Come with the immortality of the soul. Conservative Judaism, too, generally follows the Reform line, though both Reform and Conservative Judaism tend to veer towards the naturalistic understanding of the doctrine. This cannot be stated too categorically, however, and many Reform and Conservative Jews still accept the doctrine of the World to Come in its traditional formulation, at least in terms of the immortality of the soul. Some few of the Orthodox as well place the emphasis on the immortality of the soul but, if it is possible to speak of the official Orthodox position in these matters, it obviously includes the resurrection of the dead after the age of the *Messiah in its doctrine of the World to Come (and see DOGMAS and PRINCIPLES* OF FAITH).

Abraham Cohen, 'The World to Come', in his *Everyman's Talmud* (London, 1949), 364–78.

George Foot Moore, 'Eschatology', in his *Judaism in the First Centuries of the Christian Era* (Cambridge, Mass., 1958), ii. 377–95.

Samuel S. Cohon, 'Our Immortality', in his *Jewish Theology* (Assen, 1971), 426–46.

**Worrying** For the Jewish moralists, to worry over-much about the future betokens a lack of faith and trust in divine providence. For instance, after the laws which forbid recourse to magicians and necromancers (see MAGIC AND SUPERSTITION) the verse (Deuteronomy 18: 13) states: 'Thou shalt be perfect with the Lord thy God.' *Rashi comments on the verse: 'Walk before Him whole-heartedly, put thy hope in Him and do not attempt to investigate the future, but whatever it may be that come upon thee accept it whole-heartedly, and then thou shalt be with Him and become His portion.' For Rashi it is not only that recourse to foretellers is wrong because of idolatrous associations and the like; the very attempt to know what the future will bring is evidence of a lack of trust in God. A popular proverb in the Middle Ages was: 'The past has gone by, the future has still to reply, God's help comes in the blink of an eye, to worry why try?' In *Hasidism it is held to be wrong to worry over-much even about one's spiritual future, since this interferes with the joy the Jew should always experience at being a servant of God. Yet to worry about the future seems to be endemic to the human situation, hence the Talmud (*Yoma* 75a) advises the man who is in a state of anxiety either to put it out of his mind or to find relief by sharing his worries with sympathetic friends. Another moralist is quoted as saying that the only thing worth worrying about is why one worries.

**Writing** The author of the book of *Ecclesiastes may implicitly protest that there is no end to the making of many books (Ecclesiastes 12: 12) yet, from the earliest times, *books were produced; the sacred Scriptures are only one example. It is true that in Talmudic times the *study of the Torah was conducted solely by word of mouth and, with a few exceptions, the discussions were not committed to writing, but, eventually, the Talmud itself was presented as a literary work. Even in Talmudic times a scholar was advised to cultivate the art of writing for other purposes (*Hullin* 9a). The *Sefer Torah, *tefillin, and the *mezuzah had to be handwritten by a competent scribe. Such writing is called in the Talmud 'heavenly work'. With the invention of *printing there was some discussion as to whether a Sefer Torah and the others could be printed but the consensus emerged that printing does not qualify as writing for

these purposes. A *get has to be written by hand. Writing is one of the types of 'work' forbidden on the Sabbath. If the *name of God had been written, it is forbidden to erase it. A recent discussion in this connection is whether the name of God in a word-processor can be erased. The general opinion here is that the words on a word-processor are no more than electrical impulses, so that they are not treated as if they were in writing and the name of God appearing on the screen can be erased—a boon to authors of religious books who work by this method! In the Responsa of Rabbi Akiba Eger (1761–1837) the interesting question is discussed whether writing qualifies as the spoken word; for example, if a man writes a letter on which he states the day of the Omer, does this qualify as counting the *Omer? The testimony of *witnesses has to be presented by them verbally and in person and written testimony is not accepted. Nevertheless, a written bond of indebtedness, duly signed by the witnesses and authorized by the court, is accepted as evidence because of the attestation of the court. The general principle behind all this is that the written *word is more powerful and makes a more permanent impression than the spoken word. A key verse in this connection is: 'Let not kindness and truth forsake thee, bind them about thy neck, write them upon the table of thy heart' (Proverbs 3: 3). Similarly, verbal study is compared to writing in the Ethics of the Fathers (4. 20): 'He that learns as a child, to what is he like? To ink written on new paper. He that learns as an old man, to what is he like? To ink written on paper that has been blotted out.'

**Written Torah** The term Written Torah usually refers in the Talmudic literature to the *Pentateuch, the Torah of Moses, in contradistinction to the Oral Torah, the traditional explanation of the Written Torah. In a homily by the third-century teacher, Rabbi Johanan (*Gittin* 60b), a verse (Exodus 34: 27) is read so as to refer to both the Written and the Oral Torah: 'And the Lord said unto Moses, *Write* thou these words: for by the *mouth* of these words I have made a covenant with thee and with Israel.' Rabbi Johanan comments that God only made a covenant with Israel for the sake of the Oral Torah, meaning that Israel alone possess the true meaning of the Written Torah which is conveyed only in the Oral Torah.

Usually, in the Rabbinic literature, the term Written Torah refers only to the Pentateuch, not to the other books of the *Bible, as when the same Rabbi Johanan says (*Megillah* 31a) that a teaching is found in the Torah, in the Prophets, and in the Sacred Writings (the Hagiographa). Teachings found in the other sections of the Bible are sometimes referred to (e.g. in *Bava Kama* 2b) as 'words of tradition', meaning that although these teachings are also part of the Written Torah they are stated only in the later books, the authors of which know them by tradition. Occasionally, however, a verse from other parts of the Bible is also referred to as the Torah (e.g. in *Sanhedrin* 34a) In the Talmudic passage in which is discussed proof 'from the Torah' for the doctrine of the *resurrection of the dead (*Sanhedrin* 91b), texts are quoted from the Prophets and the Hagiographa. It can be said, therefore, that the term Written Torah, at first denoting the Pentateuch, was later extended to include the other biblical books and then both the Written and the Oral Torah were referred by the embracing term '*Torah' and this eventually came to include all the teachings of Judaism. The *Samaritans, on the other hand, accepted only the Pentateuch as the Torah and the *Karaites, while applying the Written Torah to the other books of the Bible as well as the Pentateuch, rejected the doctrine that there is an Oral Torah which explains the Written Torah.

Solomon Schechter, 'The "Law"', in his *Some Aspects of Rabbinic Theology* (New York, 1969), 116–26.

# Y

**Yad Vashem** The organization to commemorate the six million Jews who perished in the *Holocaust, the headquarters building of which is situated on Memorial Hill in Jerusalem. The word *yad* (lit. 'hand') means 'monument', *vashem* means 'and a memorial', following the verse: 'Even unto them will I give in My house and within My walls a monument and a memorial [*yad vashem*] better than sons and daughters; I will give them an everlasting memorial, that shall not be cut off' (Isaiah 56: 5). The Yad Vashem complex contains a Hall of Names (of those who perished); a synagogue; comprehensive archives; a museum of the Holocaust; and a commemoration of the 'righteous *Gentiles', non-Jews who risked their lives to save Jews from the fury of the Nazis.

**Yahrzeit** 'Time of the year' in Yiddish (from the German *Jahrzeit*), the anniversary of the death of a parent and other relatives for whom the rites of *mourning are carried out. The special observances of the Yahrzeit originated among the Ashkenazim, German Jews, in the fifteenth century, from where they spread to other Jewries. The *Sephardim generally use the term *nahalah* ('inheritance') for Yahrzeit. *Karo does not refer at all to the Yahrzeit but *Isserles (*Shulhan Arukh*, *Yoreh Deah*, 402. 12) records the Ashenazi practice and states that it is customary for people to fast on the Yahrzeit. As early as Talmudic times there is a reference to people abstaining from eating meat and drinking wine on the anniversary of the death of a parent (*Nedarim* 12a). Manasseh ben Israel (1604–57), in his treatise on the immortality of the *soul (*Nishmat Hayyim*, ii. 27) gives a mystical reason for observance of the Yarhrzeit. On each anniversary of the death the souls of the righteous depart from a lower world to a higher, so that each year there is a further departure, as it were, from their living relatives

on earth. On the Yahrzeit the son recites the *Kaddish in the synagogue, *memorial prayers are recited, the son is called up to the *reading of the Torah on the preceding Sabbath, and *charity is distributed to the poor. Originally the Yahrzeit was observed only for parents but it is now the general custom to observe it for the other relatives for whom there is a period of mourning, namely, husband, wife, brother, sister, son, and daughter. Another custom is to keep a Yahrzeit candle burning on the day of the Yahrzeit. This custom is based on the verse: 'The soul of man is a candle of the Lord' (Proverbs 20: 27). The observance of Yahrzeit has become very widespread. Even Jews not otherwise known for their strict observance of the rituals light a Yahrzeit candle and follow the other customs of the Yahrzeit.

In *Hasidism the Yahrzeit of a Hasidic *Zaddik is observed as a festive occasion, contrary to the tradition that it is a day of mourning. The idea behind the reversal is that although the Zaddik's soul departs further, as Manasseh ben Israel says, from his followers on earth, yet, precisely because of this, they rejoice in his further elevation on high year by year. The Hasidim do not recite the Tahanun (the supplicatory prayer) and they drink a Lehayyim ('For life') in honour of the departed saint. The *Mitnaggedim used to scoff at the Hasidic practice both because it was untraditional and because, as they saw it, it served an excuse for the Hasidic addiction to alcohol. A custom which seems to be peculiar to Anglo-Jewry, and is not known elsewhere, is for people to say to one observing a Yahrzeit: 'We wish you long life.' There is a basis for this in the Midrash (Esther Rabbah 8: 2): 'In ordinary cases when a man's son dies, people say to him, to comfort him, "May your other son who is left you live"; and if he has no other son they say: "We wish you long life".'

H. Rabinowicz, 'The Yahrzeit', in his *A Guide to Life: Jewish Laws and Customs of Mourning* (New York, 1964), 103–13.

**Yalkut** 'Collection', the name given to an anthology of Midrashic homilies. There are three such anthologies, the main one being the *Yalkut Shimeoni*, often called simply *The Yalkut*. This work was compiled by Simeon the Darshan ('Preacher') in the thirteenth century and consists of verse-by-verse homilies to the whole of the Bible, culled from the Midrashim and the Talmud. The *Yalkut Shimeoni* became for many preachers a substitute for all the other Midrashim, since it contains so much of these. It has proved valuable to modern scholars of Midrashic literature for the variant readings it contains of the Midrashim, and for Midrashim for which it is the only source. The *Yalkut Makhiri*, compiled by Makhir ben Abba Mari of France in the fourteenth century, is a less comprehensive work, covering only a few books of the Bible. The third Yalkut, *Yalkut Reuveni*, was compiled in the seventeenth century by Reuben Kohen of Prague. This work is really an anthology of Kabbalistic works arranged as a running Midrash to the Pentateuch.

H. L. Strack and G. Stemberger, *Introduction to the Talmud and Midrash*, trans. Markus Bockmuehl (Edinburgh, 1991), 383–6.

**Yarmulka** The skull-cap worn so as not to pray or study the Torah with *bare head. The etymology of this Yiddish word is unknown. The suggestion that it is derived from *yarey malka*, 'he fears the king' (by having his head covered) has nothing to commend it. In some communities the yarmulka is called a *cappel* (small cap) and in Hebrew a *kipah* with the same meaning. The modern Orthodox in Israel wear a small knitted yarmulka known as the *kipah serugah* ('knitted'). The ultra-Orthodox, with their large black yarmulkas covering the whole head, scoff at those poor folk who only cover a very small part with the *kipah serugah*. Orthodox Jews wear the yarmulka at all times, not only for prayer and study. In recent years the wearing of the yarmulka has been taken up by many Reform Jews as well. In the Orthodox tradition only men wear a yarmulka but, nowadays, in Reform and some Conservative circles women wear it too, and women Rabbis generally officiate in the synagogue wearing a yarmulka. The yarmulka is, however, simply a covenient head-covering and has no significance as a religious object in itself.

**Yemen** Country in south-west Arabia, *Teman* in Hebrew. The Jewish community of the Yemen claimed to be the oldest *Diaspora community in the world, going back, according to legend, to the dispersal after the destruction of the *Temple in 586 BCE. At all events, the ancient Yemenite community lived a distinctive life remote from other Jewish communities with its own liturgical rites, its own pronunciation of Hebrew (oddly enough, similar in some respects to that of Lithuanian Jews), and its own customs. The Yemenite Jews earned their living in a variety of occupations but were renowned especially as goldsmiths and silversmiths. Generally speaking, the Yemenite Jews were treated fairly well by the Islamic rulers, although they suffered periods of adversity and, at times, religious persecution. The community produced a number of scholars, among them the famed Kabbalist, Shalom Sharabi (1720–82), who established in Jerusalem the Bet El synagogue, still standing in the old city, in which the prayers were recited according to the Kabblistic *kavvanot* ('intentions', see KAVVANAH). The Yemenites were strongly influenced by the Kabbalah from the time when they became aware of the existence of this doctrine from visitors from other lands. It is reported that they would read the Zohar as a purely devotional exercise without necessarily understanding the abstruse teachings, in the belief that the mere mouthing of the words is balm to the soul. Some of the Yemenite scholars, however, after reading European works of *Haskalah, protested against the influence of the Kabbalah and, at the beginning of the twentieth century, established a Yemenite Haskalah movement known as the Darda (an abbreviation of Dor Deah, ('Generation of Knowledge')), with the aim of promoting general education in the community and the eradication of superstitions, all on the lines of the Haskalah. With the establishment of the State of Israel, the vast majority of the Yemenites emigrated to the new land in the mass exodus known as the Magic Carpet. Never having seen before an aeroplane, the Yemenites applied to the new means of transport taking them to the Promised Land the verse: 'I bore you on eagles' wings, and brought you unto Myself' (Exodus 19: 4).

In the thirteenth century there was a severe persecution of the Yemenite Jews, who were being threatened with forced mass conversion to Islam. A Jewish convert to Islam sought to persuade the Jews that Islam was the true faith and, at the same time, a pretender claimed that he was the long-awaited *Messiah who would redeem the Jews from their exile. Jacob al-Fayyumi addressed a letter to Maimonides in which he requested the sage to advise the Yemenite community on how they should respond to the threat hanging over them and how they should view the Messianic claims. Maimonides replied in 1172 in his *Iggeret Teman* ('Epistle to Yemen') in which he encouraged the Jewish community to avoid succumbing either to the oppressors or to Messianic delusions. Maimonides, who, in Egypt, also lived under Islamic rule, was fully aware that he might be putting his life in danger but he persisted in the belief that when a Jewish community is threatened with apostasy individual concerns for safety must be disregarded. The Yemenite Jews, grateful to Maimonides, introduced a reference to him in the *Kaddish and subsequently based their Jewish practices on the rulings found in Maimonides' Code.

Abraham Halkin and David Hartman, 'The Epistle to Yemen', in their *Crisis and Leadership: Epistles of Maimonides* (Philadelphia, New York, and Jerusalem, 1985), 91–207.

**Yeshivah** Institution of higher learning in which the *study of the Torah is pursued in an organized fashion to produce learned men (see TALMID ḤAKHAM). It would seem that·the term Yeshivah (from the root *yashav*, 'to sit') referred originally to a 'sitting' of the court but, at least in the later passages of the Talmud, the term also refers to a school or college in the above sense, and it is this sense that the term became universal in Judaism. The concept of the Yeshivah in which there are lectures and keen debates in matters of the Torah was projected both into the remote past and into the Hereafter. There are Talmudic and Rabbinic references, obviously anachronistic, to the patriarch *Jacob studying for several years in 'the Yeshivah of Shem and Ever'. The Talmud (*Bava Kama* 92a; *Bava Metzia* 86a) speaks of 'the Yeshivah on High' in which the souls of the departed scholars engage in debate and discuss the Torah with God Himself; in the latter passage the scholars are daringly said

even to take issue with Him in matters of Jewish law. All this reflects the actual conditions in the Talmudic Yeshivah, although it has to be said that full details are lacking about how Yeshivot functioned in Talmudic times.

In the Geonic period (see GEONIM) the two great Yeshivot of *Sura and Pumbedita functioned both as centres for decisions in Jewish law and practice and as academies in which lectures were given to advanced students. Yeshivot were found in Kairouan in North Africa, in Fez, Algeria, and in Cairo. Spain was the home of Yeshivot, including those of *Nahmanides in Gerona and Solomon Ibn *Adret in Barcelona. In France the Yeshivah of Rabbenu *Tam was especially renowned. The *Tosafot are based on the discussions in this and in other French Yeshivot. Rabbenu *Gershom established a Yeshivah in Mayyence and there were Yeshivot in other German cities. Isaiah *Horowitz refers in his *Shelah* to the types of problems set in the Yeshivot of Nuremberg and Regensberg, which problems he calls 'Nurembergers' and 'Regensbergers'. From the sixteenth century, famous Yeshivot were established in Poland. In these Yeshivot the art of dialectics, *pilpul, was heavily cultivated, although the method met with opposition on the part of some Rabbis. Ezekiel *Landau established a Yeshivah in Prague in the eighteenth century and Rabbi Moses *Sofer a Yeshivah in Pressburg in the nineteenth century, the latter setting the the pattern for the Hungarian Yeshivot in the nineteenth and twentieth centuries. It is important, however, to appreciate that, before the rise of the Lithuanian Yeshivot, the Yeshivah was not an independent institution. It was the local Rabbi of the town, such as Landau an Sofer, who headed a Yeshivah as part of his Rabbinic duties, the students who came from other parts to study under him being supported by the townsfolk. Rabbinic contracts often included stipulations to this effect. It was not until the development of *Volozhyn that the Yeshivah began to enjoy an existence independent of the town Rabbi with its own principal, the Rosh Yeshivah ('Head of the Yeshivah'), its own separate building, and its own administrative staff. Yeshivot were largely unknown in Hasidism. Hasidic young men were generally encouraged to study in the Bet Ha-Midrash in their home town without any formal organization or course of study. The two main exceptions were the

Yeshivah established in *Lubavitch, in which *Habad ideas were taught alongside the Talmud, and the Hasidic Yeshivah established in the Polish town of Lublin by Rabbi Meir Shapira (1887–1934).

*The Yeshivah Today*

After the Holocaust and the destruction of the great European Yeshivot, the few older Yeshivot were reorganised and new Yeshivot were established in the USA; the State of Israel; London, Manchester, and Gateshead in England; and in other European cities. On the contemporary scene there has been an unparalleled proliferation of Yeshivot, with far more students studying the Torah as a full-time occupation than ever before in the history of Jewish learning. The students, teachers, and graduates of the Yeshivot are today referred to as 'the Yeshivah World', which has its own particular stance in matters of learning and strict observance of the *precepts. Since the curriculum of the Yeshivot places the emphasis on theory and the students are often discouraged from taking up a career as a Rabbi, there is now evident a degree of rivalry between the Yeshivah World and the practical Rabbinate. In the ultra-Orthodox circles to which the Yeshivah World belongs, the supreme authorities are rarely Rabbis with a congregation or at the head of a community, but the Yeshivah heads and the Hasidic masters; these are both seen as spiritually superior to the Rabbi, who is said to be immersed in worldly concerns and, by virtue of his position, to be compromising the highest religious standards.

There are a few Yeshivot on the Sephardi and Hungarian pattern, in both of which the courses include the study of the ·Codes and practical decisions in Jewish law as well as the Talmud. There are also a very few Hasidic Yeshivot, in which the Hasidic classics are studied in addition to the Talmud, and there are one or two Yeshivot in which the Kabbalah is studied in addition to the Talmud. Mention must also be made of the Yeshivot which cater especially to the 'returners' (see BAAL TESHUVAH), young Jews from a non-Orthodox background who wish to become totally observant and who have spiritual needs of their own which the other Yeshivot cannot satisfy. But the majority of the Yeshivot today follow the Lithuanian pattern as this was set in the famous Yeshivot of Volozhyn, *Telz, Mir, Slabodka, Ponevezh, Kamenitz and many others. This Lithuanian type has several distinguishing features. The main subject of study, as in other Yeshivot, is the Talmud, but the Talmud is studied by the special methods developed by Rabbi Hayyim *Soloveitchik and his disciples—the method of keén analysis of legal concepts. The preference is to study only eight tractates of the Talmud (*Bava Kama, Bava Metzia, Bava Batra, Yevamot, Ketubot, Nedarim, Gittin,* and *Kiddushin*) which deal with complicated issues that lend themselves readily to such analysis. These tractates are studied over a four-year period, after which the Seder ('Order' or 'Course') begins again. In more recent years other tractates such as *Sanhedrin* have also been studied.

The students, of which there are several hundreds in the larger Yeshivot (the Yeshivah of Ponevezh in Bene Berak, near Tel Aviv, has a greater number of students than any other Yeshivah in all history), are seated in the large study-hall where they prepare, either on their own or, more usually, with a companion, the section of the tractate on which the Rosh Yeshivah will lecture, lectures usually taking place twice a week. In the majority of the larger Yeshivot both the lectures and the studies in general are conducted in Yiddish as in Lithuania. Attendance at the lectures is not usually compulsory and the general tendency is to rely on the students, as mature scholars (students are not admitted until they are capable of studying the Talmud and commentaries on their own), to pursue their studies without too much interference. Nevertheless, each Yeshivah has a Mashgiah, a kind of moral tutor, who will offer guidance and, where necessary, admonition, to the students for their religious and ethical conduct. The Mashgiah is an exponent of *Musar, the moralistic trend introduced by Israel *Salanter. Once or twice a week the Mashgiah will deliver a 'Musar talk' to the assembled students. For around half an hour each night the students sit on their own reciting the classical works of Musar in a mournful tune as an exercise in self-improvement—'working on the self', as this is called in Yeshivah circles.

The majority of the students come from out of town in obedience to the Talmudic injunction: 'Exile yourself to a place of Torah.' They are accommodated in dormitories in the Yeshivah and have their meals there. The wealthier students pay for the accommodation and tuition but there are scholarships for the poorer ones, especially if they are particularly bright. The normal age of admission into the Yeshivah is 18. Younger boys are prepared to enter the Yeshivah proper in a preparatory Yeshivah known as Yeshivah Ketanah ('Minor Yeshivah'). Students may study the Bible and other religious works but such studies, if not actually frowned upon, are not part of the curriculum. Secular learning is never allowed within the confines of the Yeshivah, although Yeshivah graduates may take courses in science or economics in order to earn a living. Talmudic learning is not normally pursued by the modern historical-critical methods used in departments of Jewish studies at universities and modern Rabbinical seminaries. The Yeshivah ideal is 'the study of the Torah for is own sake'. For this reason the students do not have a graduation ceremony at the end of the course. There is no end of the course, and the students stay for as long as their parents can support them. Some students will study for the Rabbinate but Rabbinic studies, too, are not normally part of the Yeshivah curriculum. Again on the Lithuanian pattern, however, the majority of the Yeshivot have a *kolel* (the word means 'all-embracing') in which married students and their families are supported while they study for the Rabbinate. Through the Yeshivot, ultra-Orthodoxy has acquired a powerful voice and a renewed confidence in its future.

Samuel Heilman, *Defenders of the Faith: Inside Orthodox Jewry* (New York, 1992).
William B. Helmreich, *The World of the Yeshiva* (New York, 1982).

**Yetzer Ha-Tov and Yetzer Ha-Ra** 'The good inclination and the evil inclination.' In the typical Rabbinic doctrine, with far-reaching consequences in Jewish religious thought, every human being has two inclinations or instincts, one pulling upwards, the other downwards. These are the 'good inclination'—*yetzer ha-tov*—and the 'evil inclination'—*yetzer ha-ra*. The 'evil inclination' is frequently identified in the Rabbinic literature and elsewhere with the sex instinct but the term also denotes physical appetites in general, aggressive emotions, and unbridled ambition. Although it is called the 'evil inclination', because it can easily lead to wrongdoing, it really denotes more the propensity towards evil rather than something evil in itself. Indeed, in the Rabbinic scheme, the 'evil inclination' provides human life with its driving power and as such is essential to human life. As a well-known Midrash (Genesis Rabbah 9: 7) puts it, were it not for the 'evil inclination' no one would build a house or have children or engage in commerce. This is why, according to the Midrash, Scripture says: 'And God saw everything that he had made and behold, it was very good' (Genesis 1: 31). 'Good' refers to the 'good inclination', 'very good' to the 'evil inclination'. It is not too far-fetched to read into this homily the idea that life without the driving force of the 'evil inclination' would no doubt still be good but it would be a colourless, uncreative, pallid kind of good. That which makes life *very* good is the human capacity to struggle against the environment and this is impossible without egotistic as well as altruistic, aggressive as well as peaceful, instincts. In similar vein is the curious Talmudic legend (*Yoma* 69b) that the Men of the *Great Synagogue wanted to kill the 'evil inclination', personified in the legend. The 'evil inclination' warned them that if they were to be successful in their attempt the 'world would collapse'. They therefore imprisoned him for three days, and searched all the land for a new-laid egg but could not find one. Instead of killing him, they put out his eyes so that he could no longer entice Jews to commit incest or worship idols.

Demythologizing this Talmudic passage, the interesting thought emerges that the Men of the Great Synagogue, despite their mighty efforts to further and establish Judaism, were not permitted to be so 'successful' in the fight against the 'evil inclination' as to destroy it completely; for if that were to happen, the world would die. However, they did succeed in containing the grosser forms of depravity. Israel is no longer tempted to commit incest or to worship idols, vices prevalent in the biblical period. This is possibly why the Rabbis refer to the 'evil inclination' as the 'leaven in the dough' (*Berakhot* 17a). Although the leaven can be responsible for overfermentation, without it the dough would be unpalatable.

The Rabbinic view is, then, realistic. Human beings are engaged in a constant struggle against their propensity for evil but if they so desire they can keep it under control. The means of control are provided by the Torah and the precepts. One of the most remarkable Rabbinic passages in this connection states that the Torah is the antidote to the poison of the 'evil inclination' (*Kiddushin* 30b). The meaning appears to be that when the Torah is studied and when there is submission to its discipline, morbid guilt-feelings are banished and life is no longer clouded by the fear that the 'evil inclination' will bring about one's ruination. The parable told in this passage is of a king who struck his son, later urging the son to keep a plaster on the wound. While the plaster remains on the wound the prince may eat and drink whatever he desires without coming to harm. Only if the plaster is removed will the wound fester when the prince indulges his appetites. God has 'wounded' man by creating him with the 'evil inclination'. But the Torah is the plaster on the wound, which prevents it from festering and enables him to embrace life without fear.

It follows that for the Rabbis the struggle against the 'evil inclination' is never-ending in this life. Nowhere in the Rabbinic literature is there the faintest suggestion that it is possible for humans permanently to destroy the 'evil inclination' in this life. (Eschatological references to the total destruction of the 'evil inclination', and its transformation into a 'good angel', are irrelevant. The *World to Come is not the world in which humans struggle in the here and now.) For the Rabbis, the true hero is, as stated in Ethics of the Fathers (4. 1), one who 'subdues' his 'evil inclination', one who exercises severe self-control, refusing to yield to temptation. It is not given to anyone actually to slay the 'evil inclination'. Nor are there are references in the Rabbinic literature to the idea, prevalent in the Jewish mystical and moralistic literatures, of 'breaking the evil inclination'.

The idea of 'breaking' is found, however, in a passage in the Zohar (i. 202a). Nothing can succeed in breaking the 'evil inclination', the Zohar observes, other than the Torah. In the same passage the Zohar states that if a man is unsuccessful in his struggle with the 'evil inclination', he should reflect on the day of his death in order to acquire a broken heart. The Zohar spells it out:

'For the evil inclination resides only in a place where there is the joy of wine and of pride so that where it finds such a broken heart it departs from man and no longer resides with him. Therefore he should remind himself of the day of death and he should break [i.e. mortify] his body and then the evil inclination will depart. Come and see! The good inclination wants the joy of the Torah but the evil inclination wants the joy of wine, fornication and pride. Consequently, a man should always be in dread of that great day, the day of judgement, the day of reckoning, when nothing can act as a shield for a man except the good deeds he performed in this world.'

*Shneur Zalman of Liady (*Tanya*, i, chs. 1–16) is a lone voice in stating that the perfect saint has no 'evil inclination' because 'he has killed it by his fasting'. But even this Hasidic master considers such a stage very extraordinary, attained by only a few of the greatest of saints.

The doctrine of the 'evil inclination' makes it precarious blithely to affirm, as is often done, that Judaism, unlike Christianity, knows nothing of the notion of original *sin. There is no doubt a difference in emphasis and, in Judaism, it is the Torah not a 'saviour' which counteracts the power of the 'evil inclination', but that human beings have a propensity for sin is not denied.

The Mishnah (*Berakhot* 9: 5) states that God is to be served by the 'evil inclination' as well as by the 'good inclination'. Some of the commentators understand this to mean only that the 'evil inclination' should be subdued for the sake of God's service but others develop the idea that it is possible to serve and love God even with the baser elements in human make-up, by using aggression against wrongdoers, for instance, or by using inordinate ambition in order to become extremely well versed in the Torah.

There are a number of passages about the 'evil inclination' in which there appears to be some anticipation of Freudian *psychology. It is tempting, for instance, to read the notion of the Id and the unconscious mind into the Talmudic passage (*Sukkah* 52a) that the 'evil inclination' is called the 'hidden one' because it is hidden within the heart of man. This whole passage contains acute psychological observations on the 'evil inclination'. In the world of the future God will bring the 'evil inclination' and slay it in the presence of the righteous and the wicked. To the righteous it will have the appearance of a towering hill; and to the wicked it will have the appearance of a mere thread of hair. Both the righteous and the wicked will weep; the righteous will say: 'How were we able to overcome such a towering hill?', and the wicked will say: 'How is it that we were unable to conquer such a thin thread?' God, the passage continues, will marvel with both. Furthermore it is said that scholars are especially prone to the blandishments of the 'evil inclination' since 'the greater the man the greater his evil inclination'. Yet something like the notion of sublimation is found in the same passage: 'If this repulsive wretch [the evil inclination] meets with you, drag him to the House of Study [i.e. apply yourself to the study of the Torah]. If he is of stone, he will dissolve, if of iron he will shatter into fragments.'

The idea that the study of the Torah is in itself sufficient to overcome the 'evil inclination' is prominent in traditional Rabbinic thought. The student of the Torah, it was held, has little need for devotional books, since the Torah he studies possesses the marvellous quality of automatically refining the character. Revealing in this connection is the story told of Hayyim of *Volozhyn, who overheard two students sitting in the study hall of the Yeshivah discussing how to combat the 'evil inclination'. The teacher said to them: 'The evil inclination is happy to see you discussing how to overcome him as long as talking about him interrupts your study of the the the Torah.' Yet both *Hasidism and the *Musar movement believed that other means are also required in addition to study—enthusiasm and the idea that the divine power pervades all for Hasidism, and sombre reflection on the vanities of the world for Musar. A saying of the Hasidic master, *Nahman of Bratslav, has it that the 'evil inclination' is like a man asking a high price for that which he holds in his closed first. When the price has been paid the fist is opened and it is seen to hold nothing at all. Israel *Salanter, founder of the Musar movement, is said to have tried to analyse the doctrine of the 'evil inclination'. Is it to be identified with the bodily instincts, or is it a spiritual force? He replied that it is both. For if it were only a spiritual force, it should tempt all men in the same way, whereas physical temptation varies from person to person. On the other hand, if it were only to be identified with physical appetites, why is it that it entices to non-physical faults and vices such as pride, anger, and hatred? In the Musar school generally, preoccupation with the 'evil inclination' often results in morbid introspection and a jaundiced view of human nature. Yet one of the most extreme of the Musar teachers, Rabbi Yoizel Horowitz of Navaradock, a man who, in his youth, lived the ascetic life of a hermit, could say that the doctrine of the *yetzer*

*ha-ra* is not intended to deny the value of human inclination as such. On the contrary, the doctrine implies that for a man to be absorbed in petty, worthless things is for him to have a 'bad' inclination, bad in the sense of narrow, one that actually frustrates his wider and true inclination to enjoy a decent, moral, and worthy life, not only in order to go to *heaven but in order to enjoy life to the full in the here and now. Hasidism is far less obsessive than the Musarists, believing that joy in the service of God and the influence of the *Zaddik are sufficient, together with the balm of the Torah, to enable the Hasid to free himself from the fetters of the 'evil inclination'. Modern Jewish thought usually prefers to discuss the human situation in the abstract and is far less inclined to speak of the good and evil inclinations. Yet it is still aware, as it must be, of the contradiction in the human psyche between what is and what ought to be, and some moderns see no reason to abandon the older, powerful terminology.

Louis Jacobs, 'Sin and Repentance', in his *A Jewish Theology* (New York, 1973), 243–59.

Solomon Schechter, 'The Evil Yezer: The Source of Rebellion', in his *Aspects of Rabbinic Theology* (New York, 1961), 242–92.

**Yiddish** From *Jüdisch* ('Jewish') and *Deutsch* ('German'), the language spoken by Jews whose ancestors came from Germany, the *Ashkenazim. Yiddish is an amalgam of Old German, Hebrew, and Aramaic, written with Hebrew characters and reading, as in Hebrew, from right to left. At a later date Slavonic elements were introduced and later still, elements of the languages of other lands in which Jews resided. Yiddish was used in writing, until modern times, chiefly for religious purposes, for example in translations of the Bible and *Prayer Book for the benefit of Jews, especially *women, with only a scanty knowledge of the original Hebrew. In ultra-Orthodox circles Yiddish is preferred to Hebrew for everyday, secular use; Hebrew is reserved for sacred activities. The traditional *Yeshivah uses Yiddish for the exposition of the Talmud, so much so that many *Sephardim who study in the Yeshivot have been obliged to master the language. In the Yeshivah World in the USA there has been such a strong assimilation of English into Yiddish that this form is sometimes spoken of as Yinglish. There are a number of different Yiddish dialects and different forms of pronunciation. For instance, the word Torah is pronounced by Lithuanian Jews as Tayreh and by Polish Jews as Toireh and with the accent on the first syllable, whereas in Hebrew the accent is on the last syllable. There exists now an abundance of Yiddish literature in the modern vein and a Yiddish Press still flourishes. Yiddish is also studied academically in university departments. The term Yiddishkeit ('Jewishness') is now often used as a synonym for Judaism but with a more popular and 'nationalistic' connotation. Yiddish is a homely, one might say voluptuous language and has come to be seen as the liveliest expression of the Jewish spirit, although with the rise of *Zionism and the establishment of the State of Israel a keen rivalry has developed between those who prefer Hebrew and those who prefer Yiddish; the former, naturally, win out for obvious reasons.

Lillian Mermin Feinsilver, *The Taste of Yiddish: A Warm and Humorous Guide to a Fascinating Language* (South Brunswick, NJ and New York, 1980).

**Yigdal** 'May He be magnified', the opening word of a hymn, after which it is named. The Yigdal hymn consists of Maimonides' thirteen *principles of faith in poetic form. In the Ashkenazi version, Yigdal has thirteen lines, one for each of the principles. The Sephardi version adds: 'These thirteen principles are the foundation of Moses' Torah and his prophecy.' Yigdal is written in rhyme and metre, the rhyme consisting of a repetition at the end of each line of the same sounds. The hymn was composed in Italy at the beginning of the fourteenth century, probably by Daniel ben Judah of Rome. Yigdal is printed in Ashkenazi prayer books at the beginning of the daily service but is normally chanted only at the end of the evening service on Sabbath and the festivals. There are a number of popular melodies for Yigdal. Some communities use a special melody for the Sabbath and a different one for each of the festivals. The famous Kabbalist, Isaac *Luria, did not approve of reciting the Yigdal hymn, probably because he did not believe that this and other late hymns reflected the Lurianic *kavvanot* (see KAVVANAH) and because he was not happy with the whole Maimonidean attempt at drawing up principles of the faith, an attempt which implies that some parts of the Torah are more significant than others. Following Luria, the Hasidim do not recite Yigdal. Modernists, who believe in the immortality of the *soul but not in a physical *resurrection of the dead, alter the line of Yigdal referring to the latter doctrine or recite it as it stands but only on the grounds that it represents a poetical manner of referring to belief in immortality.

The principles of the faith are given in more or less philosophical form in Yigdal. For instance, the first line reads in English translation: 'Magnified and praised be the living God: He is, and there is no limit in time unto His being.' The third line dealing with the principle of God's incorporeality, reads: 'He hath neither bodily form nor substance: we can compare nought unto Him in His holiness.'

Stefan C. Reif, *Judaism and Hebrew Prayer* (Cambridge, 1993), 211–14.

**Yiḥudim** 'Unifications', meditations on various combinations of the letters of the Tetragrammaton and on the various vocalizations of this name provided in the writings of Hayyim *Vital and other Kabbalists of the Lurianic school. Isaac *Luria, Vital's master, provided detailed *yiḥudim* to be performed at particular periods and in accordance with the special soulroot of each mystical adept. The *yiḥudim* were believed to be theurgic, affecting the upper worlds and the elevation of the mystic's soul. In post-Lurianic prayer books, the instruction is given to the worshipper to recite: 'For the sake of the unification of the Holy One, blessed be He, and His *Shekhinah' before carrying out a precept of the Torah. Rabbi Ezekiel *Landau took strong exception to the recital of this formula by the Hasidim, which resulted in a fierce polemic between Landau and some of the Hasidic masters. Another of the *yiḥudim*, printed in the Kabbalistic prayer books, is that in which the letters of the Tetragrammaton are mingled with the letters of the divine name, Adonai ('Lord'). The Kabbalists, however, sought to limit the practice of other, more esoteric, *yiḥudim* to initiates and, even for these, urged that it is all to be treated with great circumspection. In *Buber's mystical novel on the activities of certain Hasidic masters at the time of the Napoleonic wars, there is a vivid account of how the master known as the Yehudi, wishing to hasten Israel's redemption, performed a Unification that cost him his life (*For the Sake of Heaven* (New York, 1958), 285–6: 'Kalman said: "I am worried about the life of the

Yehudi. There is a secret Unification which may be accomplished on this day. But none can accomplish it and live, save in the land of Israel. And it seems to me as though the Yehudi was daring to accomplish it."' Except in a very perfunctory manner, the practice of *yiḥudim* is now virtually unknown among Kabbalists because of the risks it is believed to involve, although Aryeh Kaplan was not averse to encouraging the practice by recording *yiḥudim* in English.

Gershom Scholem, *Kabbalah* (Jerusalem, 1974); see index: '*Yiḥudim*'.

Aryeh Kaplan, 'Yichudim', in *Meditation and Kabbalah* (York Beach, Me., 1982), pp. 218–60.

**Yom Ha-Atzmaut** 'Independence Day', celebrating the proclamation of the Israeli Declaration of Independence on 5 Iyyar 5708 (corresponding to 14 May 1948). This day was declared a public holiday by law in Israel in 1949 and is a day of rejoicing for the majority of Jews except for the anti-Zionist group Neturey Karta, which observes it as a day of mourning and fasting. In order to avoid public desecration of the Sabbath, when the day falls on a Friday or a Sabbath, the celebrations are held on the previous Thursday. In addition to a torch-lighting ceremony at the tomb of *Herzl on Mount Herzl in Jerusalem, various cultural and sporting events take place. However, the earlier practice of a parade by the armed forces of Israel has been discontinued as being too militaristic to be in accord with the Jewish spirit.

The problem of religious services to mark the day was aggravated by the reluctance of Orthodox Rabbis to introduce a new religious festival for all Jews, even though the *Halakhah advocates prayers of thanksgiving for '*miracles' through which individual communities are saved from destruction. There was a similar reluctance to introduce prayers without direct sanction in the tradition on the grounds that we 'pygmies' have no right to emulate the spiritual 'giants' of the past who created the Jewish *liturgy. Eventually, however, the Israeli Rabbinate drew up an order of service acceptable to most traditionalists. As the famous Halakhist, Rabbi Meshullam Rath, puts it in a Responsum on the subject:

'It thus becomes self-evident in our case, which affects the community of Israel in its entirety, and is a case of deliverance from

slavery to freedom; for we have been redeemed from subjection to other powers, having become a free people and attained to independence; we have also been rescued from death, for we were delivered from the hands of our enemies who rose up against us to destroy us—that we are surely duty-bound to fix a festive day. And it is good timing to have fixed this very day on which the major part of the miracle occurred, when we became free from [political] subjection by the Declaration of Independence.'

The innovators won the day. The order of service for Yom Ha-Atzmaut drawn up by the Israeli Rabbinate includes the recital of the *Hallel; the recital of Psalms; the public reading of the Torah (Deuteronomy 7: 1–8: 18) and a *Haftarah (Isaiah 10: 32–11: 12); the recital of *Nishmat and other hymns usually recited only on the Sabbath and festivals; and the sounding of the *shofar*. Opinions still vary on whether the *benedictions before the Hallel, the Torah, and Haftarah should be recited and on whether the Shehehiyanu ('Who has kept us alive') benediction should be recited since it is forbidden to utter God's name in a benediction unless the benediction has been ordained by the Rabbis. Under the jurisdiction of the Chief Rabbi in the UK, a special Festival Prayer Book was published with the same format as the Routledge prayer books for the other festivals. Although Yom Ha-Atzmaut falls during the *Omer period, when marriages do not take place, it is the practice in the State of Israel for this rule to be set aside in honour of the celebration of independence and some Diaspora communities follow suit.

The theological tension behind the whole question of celebrating Yom Ha-Atzmaut as a religious festival with special prayers is severe. On the one hand innovations of such a far-reaching nature have been frowned upon even by those who would not go along with Rabbi Moses *Sofer's round declaration: 'Anything new is forbidden by the Torah.' On the other hand, there is the pressing need to be grateful to God and to thank Him for one of the most tremendous events in all Jewish history. The tension is partly resolved by trying to achieve a balance between too startling an innovation and a failure to give the day any religious significance at all by treating it as a purely secular holiday. This is only another way of saying that the full theological implications of the establishment of the State of Israel have not as yet been explored.

*Order of Service and Customs for the Synagogue and the Home with Notes and References for Israel Independence Day*, adapted for Diaspora Jewry, ed. and transl. Moses Friedlander, with the approval of the Very Rev. Israel Brodie, Chief Rabbi (London, 1964).

**Yom Kippur** 'Day of Atonement', the great fast on 10 Tishri. The Yom Kippur ritual in *Temple times was based on the vivid description in Leviticus 16. On this day, the *High Priest was to discard his garments of splendour and, wearing only the plain linen tunic, breeches, girdle, and turban of the common priest, he was to enter the Holy of Holies, the most sacred spot in the Sanctuary, there to atone for his own sins, those of his household, and those of the whole community of Israel. Two goats were to be taken, upon which lots were to be cast, one for the Lord and one for *Azazel. The goat chosen for the Lord was to be offered as a sacrifice. The other goat was to be taken to Azazel in the wilderness. The major part of the Talmudic tractate *Yoma* is devoted to the Temple rites on Yom Kippur, even though the Temple had long been destroyed when the tractate was finally compiled.

For the Talmudic Rabbis, Yom Kippur is the great and holy day when Israel meets its God. Yom Kippur is judgement day, the culmination of the *Ten Days of Penitence which begin with *Rosh Ha-Shanah. The verse: 'Seek the Lord while He can be found, call to Him while He is near' (Isaiah 55: 6) is applied by the Rabbis to these ten days, beginning on Rosh Ha-Shanah and ending on Yom Kippur, when God is very near. It was on Yom Kippur, say the Rabbis, that Moses came down from the mount with the second *tablets of stone, bringing his people the good tidings that God had shown mercy to them and had pardoned them for the sin of worshipping the *golden calf.

The Mishnah in tractate *Yoma* (8: 9) records the accepted teaching that Yom Kippur atones only for sins committed against God, for religious offences. But for offences against a neighbour there is no atonement on Yom Kippur until the neighbour has been pacified and the wrong done righted.

Although Yom Kippur is a day of fasting and self-denial it is, for the Rabbis, a day of joy on which sin is pardoned and reconciliation achieved with God. Another Mishnah (*Taanit*

4: 8) attributes to Rabban Simeon ben *Gamaliel the saying that Yom Kippur was one of the two happiest days in the year for Israel, when the daughters of Israel would go out in borrowed finery (borrowed, in order not to shame those who had no fine clothes of their own) and present themselves before the young men of their choice that they might propose marriage to them. The Rabbis saw no incongruity in having proposals of marriage take place on this holy day, since to marry and have a family is also a religious duty and Yom Kippur was a day of gladness in Temple times. It was not until the destruction of the Temple and the bitter persecutions to which many Jews were subjected in the Middle Ages, that the note of tragedy was heard in the Yom Kippur *liturgy and a more sombre mood came to prevail. By the Middle Ages, Yom Kippur had evolved as a day to be spent almost entirely in prayer and worship. Some Jews would not even return home on the night of Yom Kippur, preferring to spend it in the synagogue chanting hymns and singing psalms until daybreak. Although in the ordinary way it is forbidden to sleep in the synagogue, an exception was made on this day so as to enable those who spent the whole twenty-four hours in the synagogue to snatch some sleep. Most of the Rabbis, however, advised against the practice of an all-night vigil if as a result the worshipper would become drowsy during the prayers of the day.

Yom Kippur has retained its numinous appeal. Many Jews, otherwise not observant of the rites and ceremonies of the Jewish religion, make it a point of honour to be present in the synagogue on this day and to fast for the whole twenty-four hours. While Rabbis are fond of reminding their congregations that the observance of Yom Kippur is far from being the be-all and end-all of Judaism, this day seems to possess a unique appeal to Jews who are at all sensitive to the spiritual side of Jewish existence. As the Rabbis quaintly put it, *Satan has no power to present his pleas against Jews on Yom Kippur. The Satan of stubborn resistance in the Jewish heart yields to the Yom Kippur magic.

The name Yom Kippur is the Rabbinic version of the biblical (plural form) *Yom Ha-Kippurim*. *Yom* means 'day' and the root meaning of *kippur, kippurim,* and *kapparah* (the form most frequently found for 'atonement') is 'to scour', 'to cleanse thoroughly', 'to erase'. Sin is thought of as a stain to be removed if the soul is to appear pure before its Creator. Another possible meaning is 'to cover'. In atonement sin is covered; it is hidden out of sight. Yom Kippur is thus the day of cleansing from sin, the day on which Israel once again finds favour in God's eyes. Among the ancient Rabbis, only Rabbi *Judah the Prince taught that the day itself is endowed with the power of erasing sin and his view is not accepted as normative doctrine. Throughout Rabbinic and moralistic literature the view is propounded that there can be no forgiveness and no atonement without repentance (see SIN AND REPENTANCE). Repentance is the human approach to God; *kapparah* is the divine response.

*Fasting on Yom Kippur*

'In the seventh month, on the tenth day of the month, ye shall afflict your souls' (Leviticus 16: 29). From this verse is derived the obligation to fast on Yom Kippur. The word *nefesh*, usually translated as 'soul', means in this and other biblical passages something like the 'self', so that a more accurate translation would be: 'You shall afflict yourselves.' From the earliest times this 'affliction' was understood not in terms of positive self-torment such as flagellation, but in the negative sense of self-denial, that is, by abstaining from food and drink. It is of interest that when the prophet speaks of 'afflicting the soul' (in the portion read as the *Haftarah on Yom Kippur) he uses this expression as a synonym for fasting: 'Wherefore have we fasted, and Thou seest not? Wherefore have we afflicted our soul, and Thou takest no knowledge? Behold in the day of your fast ye pursue your business, and exact all your labours' (Isaiah 58: 3). *Fasting generally is associated with prayer and repentance (and see ASCETICISM). With regard to Yom Kippur in particular the obligation to fast is understood by the commentators as having four aims. Fasting is a penance, an exercise in self-discipline, a means of focusing the mind on the spiritual, and a means of awakening compassion. To know what it means to go hungry, even for a single day, encourages pity for the hungry, the oppressed, and the unfortunate who suffer far worse deprivations. This thought is expressed by Isaiah, which is one of the reasons why the passage above is read as the Haftarah on Yom Kippur. The prophet castigates his people for their neglect of the poor and needy. Fasting and a pretence of piety is not acceptable to God, the prophet declares, if it serves merely as a cloak for inhumanity: 'Is not this the fast that I have chosen? To loose the fetters of wickedness, to undo the bands of the yoke, and to let the oppressed go free, and that ye break every yoke? Is it not to deal thy bread to the hungry, and that thou bring the poor that are cast out to thy house? When thou seest the naked, that thou cover him, and that thou hide not thyself from thine own flesh?'

The Mishnah (*Yoma* 8: 1) lists certain other 'afflictions' to be practised on Yom Kippur in addition to fasting. 'On the Day of Atonement, eating, drinking, bathing, anointing [the body with oil, the normal practice in Mishnaic times], putting on sandals, and marital intercourse are forbidden.' 'Putting on sandals' refers to the wearing of leather shoes only, so that many pious Jews today wear rubber shoes or felt slippers during the whole of Yom Kippur. Another reason given for not wearing shoes of leather on Yom Kippur is that these can only be obtained after an animal has been killed and since God's mercy is over all His creatures, it is not fitting to wear leather on the day when God's mercy is sought.

*Laws and Customs of Yom Kippur*

Non-Jews sometimes refer to Yom Kippur as the 'Black Fast', a name more appropriate for Tisha Be-Av (see AV, NINTH OF). Yom Kippur should more correctly be seen as the 'White Fast'. The *Ark in the synagogue is draped in white, as are the Scrolls of the Torah and the reading-desk. Many Jews wear the white *kittel. The original reason for wearing white garments was as an indication of the divine mercy and because Israel on Yom Kippur resemble the *angels who are 'clad in white'. At a later date the white robe was identified with the shrouds worn by the dead, so that the kittel serves as a reminder of human mortality. White is also the colour of purity: 'Come now, and let us reason together, saith the Lord; though your sins be as scarlet, they shall be as white as snow; though they be red like crimson, they shall be as wool' (Isaiah 1: 18).

The rite of *Kapparot on the eve of Yom Kippur has been widely discussed, some authorities negating it as superstition, others advocating it as an established *custom in Israel. It is customary on this evening for people to beg one another for forgiveness for any wrongs done to them during the past year. The day of reconciliation with God must be preceded by reconciliation among human beings. It used to be the custom for men to undergo a token flogging in the synagogue on the eve of Yom Kippur, but this practice seems to have fallen into total disuse. It is also the custom to give or to set aside money for charity on the eve of Yom Kippur.

In an interesting ruling the Talmudic Rabbis declare that it is a religious duty, a *mitzvah*, to eat well on the eve of Yom Kippur. Only easily digested food should be eaten at the final meal of the day, the one just before the fast. At this meal a piece of the bread, over which grace before meals is said, is dipped in honey, while the prayer is recited: 'May God grant that the year ahead be a good and sweet one.' The obvious reason for eating well on the day before Yom Kippur is to gain strength for the fast, to prepare for the rigours of the day ahead. Another reason has also been given. Yom Kippur is a festival, a day of joy, because on this day Israel is reconciled with God. On all the other festivals the Jew is commanded to make merry, to eat and drink in honour of the occasion. Since this is impossible on Yom Kippur, the festive meals are partaken of on the preceding day. Before making their way to the synagogue for the Yom Kippur service, parents bless their children. The idea that only shabby clothes should be worn on Yom Kippur is perverse and results from a confusion of this day with the other fast of Tisha Be-Av (see AV, NINTH OF). On the contrary, Sabbath best clothes should be worn.

In addition to fasting and the other 'afflictions' it is forbidden to work on Yom Kippur as it is on the Sabbath. Some pious Jews do not even handle food on Yom Kippur, although the law certainly permits this, without fear that the food may be inadvertently eaten. Even the extremely pious make an exception to handle the food they give to their children. Children under the age of 9 should not be allowed to fast even for a few hours. From the age of 9 children are trained to fast by postponing their breakfast for an hour or two longer each year. When a boy reaches the age of *Bar Mitzvah and a girl the age of *Bat Mitzvah they are obliged to fast like everyone else. A sick person whose life will be endangered by fasting is not only allowed to eat on Yom Kippur but is obliged to do so, and when he eats he should recite the grace before and after meals. Although

food and drink are forbidden on Yom Kippur, there is no objection to smelling aromatic herbs or other perfumes and it is permitted to take snuff.

### The Yom Kippur Services

The service on Yom Kippur begins with the *Kol Nidre declaration chanted in the well-known melody in which expression is given to the emotions of uncertainty and remorse, then resolution, and finally triumphant hope. Throughout the day, at the end of each of the services, there is a *confession of sin. The hymns and liturgical poems recited during the services give expression to the ideas of human unworthiness and sinfulness and to the belief that God pardons those who sincerely repent. In many of the poems God is glorified for having given Yom Kippur to Israel, yet some of them are marvellously universalistic, looking forward to the day when all God's creatures will recognize their Creator and pay joyous homage to Him. The Torah reading for Yom Kippur morning is from Leviticus 16 (the account of Yom Kippur in the Sanctuary) and, from a second Scroll, the section dealing with the special sacrifices of the day that were offered in Temple times (Numbers 29: 7–11). The Haftarah, as mentioned earlier, is from the book of Isaiah (57: 4–58: 14). After the reading of the Torah, *memorial prayers are recited.

A major feature of the Musaf ('Additional Prayer') is the Avodah ('Temple service'), at which stage the Reader chants the order of worship in the Temple, telling of how the High Priest uttered the ineffable Name of God and all the people fell on their faces. In many Orthodox congregations it is the practice for all the assembled worshippers to kneel at this stage and to place their foreheads to the ground, although kneeling is not otherwise known in Jewish worship today. The Musaf service also contains a martyrology in which the fate of the *ten martyrs and other *martyrs is recounted.

The afternoon service begins with the reading from the Torah of the list of forbidden marriages in Leviticus 18. Various reasons have been put forward for the choice of this reading on Yom Kippur: for instance, that it is a reminder of the importance of adherence to the ideals and high standards of Jewish family life, or of the need to resist sexual temptation. The more probable reason is that, since the sixteenth chapter of Leviticus is read in the morning, the eighteenth chapter is a natural choice for the afternoon reading. (The seventeenth chapter is skipped because it is of no relevance to Jewish life after the Temple period.) The Haftarah of the afternoon is the complete book of *Jonah and three verses from the book of Micah (7: 18–20). The message of the book of Jonah—that God takes pity on all His creatures and that it is impossible for a prophet to flee from Him, that He is ready to accept true repentance even from the pagan Ninevites—make this book an obvious choice for a Yom Kippur reading.

Unlike on any other day of the year, there is a special, additional service, the Neilah ('Closing') service, on Yom Kippur, with which the long day of prayer ends. In Temple times deputations of laymen were delegated to be present each day when the priests offered up the *sacrifices. Towards the end of the day, when the Temple gates were about to be shut, these men would recite the Prayer of the Closing of the Gates. On public fast days, when the rains failed, this special concluding service was added to the prayers of the day, but in the course of time the Neilah service came to be reserved for Yom Kippur. At a later period it was natural to associate the idea of the closing gates with the gates of heaven open to prayer during the day of Yom Kippur. The note sounded at Neilah is one of hope. The sun is about to set, the prayers have ascended on high, Israel has become reconciled to its God. The traditional melodies of Neilah express the mood of longing, of yearning for a better life, of triumph over sin. The words of the prayer, recited during the Ten Days of Penitence, in which God is requested to 'inscribe us in the Book of Life', are changed, for the Neilah service, so that the request is to be 'sealed' in the Book of Life.

The climax of Yom Kippur is reached at the end of the Neilah service. The first verse of the *Shema—'Hear O Israel'—is recited aloud by the whole congregation. This is followed by the addition to the Shema: 'Blessed be the name of His glorious Kingdon for ever and ever', repeated three times by the whole congregation. There then follows the seven-times recital by the whole congregation of: 'The Lord, He is God.' This expression goes back to the confrontation by *Elijah of the prophets of Baal at Mount Carmel. When the people witnessed Elijah's victory over the heathen prophets they declared: 'The Lord, He is God; the Lord, He is God' (I Kings 18: 39). By these awesome declarations at the end of Yom Kippur, Jews proclaim their loyalty to the God of Israel and their determination to live by His laws.

The ordinary weekday Maariv ('Evening') service is then recited; this signifies the Jew's coming down to earth, so to speak, and implies that the observance of the Jewish religion is a day-to-day affair and is not confined to Yom Kippur. The *Havdalah rite is then carried out and finally a single *shofar blast is sounded. The night following Yom Kippur is treated as a minor festival. The Midrash states that after the day of fasting and repentance has come to a close, a heavenly voice (*Bat Kol) proclaims: 'Go thy way, eat thy bread with joy, and drink thy wine with a merry heart; for God hath already accepted thy works' (Ecclesiastes 9: 7).

Max Arzt, *Justice and Mercy: Commentary on the Liturgy of the New Year and the Day of Atonement* (New York, 1963).

Philip Goodman, *The Yom Kippur Anthology* (Philadelphia, 1971).

Louis Jacobs, A *Guide to Yom Kippur* (London, 1957).

**Yom Kippur Katan** 'Minor Yom Kippur', the name given to the day before *Rosh Hodesh ('New Moon') in that this day is treated as one of fasting, repentance, and supplication on the analogy of *Yom Kippur. Yom Kippur Katan originated among the *Safed Kabbalists in the sixteenth century and is referred to by a disciple of Moses *Cordovero, Abraham Galante, who states that it was a local custom in Safed for men, women, and schoolchildren to fast on this day and to spend the whole day in penitential prayer, confession of sin, and flagellation. There is no reference to Yom Kippur Katan in the standard Code of Jewish law, the *Shulḥan Arukh*, but a later Halakhist, Joel Sirkes, in his commentary to *Jacob ben Asher's Tur, mentions it and as a result the day acquired something of a Halakhic footing and came to be observed in communities with little connection to the Kabbalah. A number of small booklets were published containing the prayers and customs of the day. Nowadays, Yom Kippur Katan has largely fallen into disuse, yet the rite itself is of interest for its amalgam of Talmudic and Kabbalistic themes.

The Talmud (*Hullin* 60b) quotes an amazing comment of Rabbi Simeon ben Lakish that the he-goat offered on Rosh Hodesh is called 'a sin-offering unto the Lord' because it is an atonement for God Himself for having made the moon smaller than the sun. Arising out of this is the idea, expressed in the Rosh Hodesh liturgy, that Rosh Hodesh affords pardon for Israel's sins. There is a pre-Safed reference to people fasting on the eve of Rosh Hodesh, since Rosh Hodesh is a minor festival on which no fasting is allowed. The waning and waxing of the moon became associated with the fate of Israel which is compared in the Talmud to the moon. In the Kabbalah these ideas were interpreted so as to convey the mystery of the exile of the *Shekhinah, brought about by the sins of Israel. According to the doctrine of the *Sefirot, the sun represents *Tiferet* and the moon *Malkhut,* the Shekhinah, hence the mythically charged notion that the exile of the Shekhinah from Her Spouse, the disharmony in the Sefirotic realm, is caused by Israel's sinfulness, and harmony above will only be fully restored when Israel repents. Everything in the great cosmic drama is leading up to the coming of the *Messiah. With the advent of the Messiah the exile of the 'holy moon', the Shekhinah, will be ended. The new moon is welcomed as evidence of the future redemption of the Shekhinah from Her exile but, on the day before, Yom Kippur Katan, there has to be prayer, fasting, and supplication in order to find atonement for the sins committed during the previous month and thus hasten the redemption.

Gershom G. Scholem, *On the Kabbalah and its Symbolism,* trans. Ralph Manheim (London, 1965), 151–3.

**Yom Tov Ishbili** Spanish Talmudist and Halakhic authority (d. 1330), known as the Ritba, after the initial letters of his name, Rabbi Yom Tov ben Avraham Ishbili (Ishbili means 'of Seville'). The Ritba's teachers were Solomon Ibn *Adret and, especially, Aaron Ha-Levi of Barcelona. After Ibn Adret's death, the Ritba was acknowledged as the most prominent spiritual guide by the Jews of Spain and other lands. Ritba was a student of philosophy. His *Sefer Ha-Zikkaron* ('Book of Remembrance') defends Maimonides' *Guide of the Perplexed* against the strictures of *Nahmanides in the latter's Commentary to the Torah, although Ritba believed that Maimonides' approach was only valid from the philosophical point of view, while Nahmanides was also right from the

Kabbalistic point of view; the conflict between philosophy and the Kabbalah in the time of Ritba finds echoes in his works. Ritba left no works on the Kabbalah and it is doubtful whether he can actually be classed as a Kabbalist merely on the strength of the stray and veiled references to the Kabbalah in his works. For instance, on the Talmudic statement (*Eruvin* 13b) about the controversies between the houses of *Hillel and *Shammai that 'both these and these are the words of the living God', Ritba observes that the French scholars take the statement literally to mean that God delivered the two sets of opinions to Moses at Sinai, leaving it to the two houses to choose which set to follow. 'From their point of view,' Ritba writes, 'the understanding of the French scholars is correct. But according to the way of truth [the Kabbalah] there is a reason and a mystery in this matter'; meaning presumably that, according to the Kabbalah, the House of Shammai was governed in its decisions by the principle of *Gevurah* ('Power' and 'Judgement'), hence its strictness, while the House of Hillel was governed by the principle of *Hesed* ('Loving-kindness'), hence its leniencies. Questions in Jewish law were addressed to Ritba from a number of communities but his *Responsa were not published until the twentieth century.

Ritba's chief fame rests, however, on his great commentaries to the Talmud. It has to be noted that modern scholarship has detected that some works attributed to Ritba are not his, while some works attributed to other authors are really his. In recent years, many of Ritba's commentaries to the Talmud have been published by Mossad Harav Kook in Jerusalem in sumptuous, scholarly editions. Ritba's commentaries to the Talmud display his keen logical method in analysing legal concepts as well as his familiarity with the *Tosafot and other earlier commentaries, enabling the student easily to survey all the different opinions. In this respect Ritba resembles Menahem *Meiri, whose works have similarly been republished to become extremely popular as guides to the intricacies of the Talmudic debates.

Hersh Goldwurm, 'R` Yom Tov Asevilli (Ritba)', in his *The Rishonim* (New York, 1982), 99–100.

**York, Martyrs of** Less than a year after the coronation of King Richard I (Richard the Lion-heart) in September 1189, anti-Jewish rioting broke out in the city of York, despite the king's orders that the Jews were not to be molested. The sheriff allowed the Jews to take refuge in the royal castle, Clifford's Tower, where a tablet marks the spot. Suspecting the intentions of the sheriff, the Jews expelled him from the castle which was surrounded by a mob intent on killing the Jews and plundering their possessions. The Jews of York, among whom was the famous scholar Yom Tov of Joigny, one of the Tosafists (see *TOSAFOT), committed mass suicide on the Sabbath before Passover, corresponding to 6 March 1190. The few who did not give their lives pleaded that they be allowed to escape death by converting to Christianity. Being reassured, they left the castle and were massacred. In the later Halakhah the martyrdom of the Jews of York was used as proof that *suicide is permitted if it is in order to escape torture or conversion. Cecil Roth has published a poignant elegy on the massacre by a contemporary of the event, Joseph ben Asher of Chartres. One stanza of the elegy reads: 'In place of their herds they offered up their children, and they slaughtered their first strength before their eyes.' This sacrifice of children, which occurred in other places as well, was questioned by some of the Halakhists on the grounds that while martyrdom is enjoined for adults, children have no such obligation and the fathers were not justified in taking this dread step. Some years ago the attempt by builders of a supermarket to interfere with the bones believed to be those of the martyrs was abandoned under public pressure. The community of York was later re-established and continued until the expulsion of the Jews from England in 1290. The belief is unfounded that a *herem exists against Jews living in York, and a small community has existed there since the nineteenth century.

Albert M. Hyamson, 'The Massacre at York', in his *A History of the Jews in England* (London, 1928), 35–41.

Cecil Roth, 'A Hebrew Elegy on the York Martyrs of 1190', *Transactions of the Jewish Historical Society of England*, 16 (1952), 213–21.

**Yose, Rabbi** A number of Rabbis mentioned in the Talmud are called Yose, each with his father's name, but where the name Rabbi Yose occurs on its own the reference is to Rabbi Yose ben Halafta, a second-century Tanna (see TANNAIM AND AMORAIM). Together with Rabbi *Meir, Rabbi Judah, and Rabbi *Simeon ben Yohai, Rabbi Yose is numbered among the sages taught by Rabbi *Akiba in his old age. Rabbi Yose is quoted more than 300 times in the Mishnah and very frequently in the *Tosefta. Debates between Rabbi Yose and his colleagues are recorded, the Talmud (*Eruvin* 46b) stating that in such instances the opinion of Rabbi Yose is decisive. Rabbi *Judah the Prince, editor of the Mishnah, was a pupil of Rabbi Yose.

In addition to his prowess in the *Halakhah, Rabbi Yose was known for his theological observations. Attributed to him is the famous statement (Genesis Rabbah 68: 19) that God is called Ha-Makom ('the Place') because 'He is the place of the world but the world is not his place'. Another theological observation attributed to Rabbi Yose is that 'the *Shekhinah never descended to earth and Moses and *Elijah never ascended on high' (*Sukkah* 5a). A Talmudic legend (*Berakhot* 3a) tells of Rabbi Yose entering one of the ruins of Jerusalem to pray and Elijah greeting him as 'Rabbi'. When Elijah asks Rabbi Yose what sound he had heard in the ruin, Yose replies: 'I heard a *Bat Kol moaning like a dove, crying: "Alas for My children for whose iniquities I destroyed My house, burnt My Temple, and exiled them among the nations".'

The early chronological work *Seder Olam* is attributed in the Talmud (*Yevamot* 82b) to Rabbi Yose, although there are later additions to the work from a much later period. The *Seder Olam* is the first chronological work in which historical events are dated from 'the creation of the world'. This method of dating, however, was not adopted by Jews generally until the Middle Ages.

H. L. Strack and G. Stemberger, *Introduction to the Talmud and Midrash*, trans. Markus Bockmuehl (Edinburgh, 1991); see index: 'Yose (ben Halafta).'

**Zaddik** The charismatic leader in *Hasidism, also known as the *Rebbe in order to distinguish him from the *Rabbi in the conventional sense. This spelling of the word in English is now the usual form but a more correct transliteration would be *tzaddik,* meaning 'righteous man'. This type of spiritual guide, renowned not for his learning but for his saintliness and ability as a religious mentor, is not entirely unknown in traditional Judaism. The model for the Zaddik was found in Hasidism in the miracle-working prophets *Elisha and *Elijah, in some of the holy men of prayer in Talmudic times, and in various saintly figures (see SAINTS) in the Middle Ages. But only in Hasidism, from the earliest days of the movement, did the figure of the Zaddik come to occupy a supreme role, with total *submission to him being demanded of his followers. Later in the history of Hasidism, the Zaddik's son was believed to have acquired something of his charisma, based on the idea that the Zaddik's holy thoughts when he made love to his wife could succeed in bringing down an elevated soul into the child conceived at the time, so that the notion of dynasties of Zaddikim developed, each with its own loyal followers.

In the writings of *Jacob Joseph of Polonnoye and in other early Hasidic works the Zaddik is the 'channel' or 'conduit' through which the divine grace flows to bring blessings to his followers in particular but also to others. The prayers of the Zaddik can produce results that the prayers of his followers could never have produced unaided. Even the food which the Zaddik has tasted is charged with spiritual power, hence the Hasidic practice of 'snatching' pieces of the food over which the Zaddik had recited grace before meals. There even developed a system of relics in which such things as the *tefillin of the Zaddik or even his pipe and the clothes he had worn were capable of bringing blessings into the home of the

persons who had purchased them. The *Mitnaggedim seized on the doctrine of the Zaddik to attack Hasidism as a kind of idolatry, although it is only fair to note that, while the Zaddik is venerated, he is never an object of worship and the more refined Hasidim turn to the Zaddik for spiritual guidance rather than for him to work miracles on their behalf. Some of the Hasidic Zaddikim were especially known for the *miracles they were believed to be able to perform. Others were seen more as spiritual mentors than as miracle-workers. But in every branch of the movement the two roles of the Zaddik are accepted as beyond question. A false picture is presented when the occult aspects of Zaddikism are played down in such modern works as *Buber's *Tales of the Hasidim.*

Whenever Hasidim pay a visit to the 'court' of the Zaddik (the royal metaphor is applied throughout) they present him, through his *gabbai* ('retainer' or 'overseer') a *kvittel* ('scrap of paper') and a *pidyon nefesh* ('redemption of soul'). The *kvittel* is a written statement by the Hasid, containing his name and that of his mother, of his more pressing needs, material or spiritual. The *pidyon nefesh* is a sum of money which goes to the upkeep of the Zaddik. The usual rationale for the latter is that, while the Zaddik really needs nothing for himself, his Hasidim can only have real contact with him by contributing to his upkeep. In some versions of Hasidism the Zaddik must live in regal splendour in order for the channel of blessing which he represents to be broad and wide. Much of the money, it has also to be said, is distributed for charitable purposes. A basis for the whole practice was found in the biblical passage (1 Samuel 9: 6–8):

'And he said unto him, "Behold now, there is in the city a man of God, and he is a man that is held in honour; all that he saith cometh surely to pass; now let us go thither peradventure he can tell us concerning our journey whereon we go." Then said Saul to his servant, "But behold, if we go, what shall we bring the man? For the bread is spent in our vessels, and there is not a present to bring to the man of God; what have we?" And the servant answered Saul again, and said: "Behold, I have in my hand the fourth part of a shekel of silver, that will I give to the man of God, to tell us our way."'

In many Hasidic circles it is the practice for a Hasid to place a *kvittel* on the grave of his Zaddik so that the Zaddik in the upper worlds should pray there on his behalf. The Mitnaggedim poured scorn on the whole institution, maintaining that the Hasid is wasting money that could better be spent on alleviating his sufferings and those of his family. True, the Mitnaggedim argued, there are biblical parallels like the one quoted but the 'man of God' in the Bible is a true prophet while, for the Mitnaggedim, every Hasidic Zaddik is a false prophet.

The Hasidim were not unaware that in making the claims they did for the Zaddik they were implying that, in some measure, the Zaddik possesses powers akin to those of the biblical prophets. They defended this daring comparison of the Zaddik to the prophet or the holy men of earlier times on various grounds, one of the most popular being that in the generations before the advent of the *Messiah an abundance of new spiritual illumination has been released in anticipation of the tremendous event. As Solomon of Radomsk (d. 1866) puts it:

'This is why Scripture says: "And God made the two great lights" [Genesis 1: 16], hinting at the two types of Zaddikim, those of earlier times and those of later. "The greater light to rule the day", this refers to the Zaddikim of former generations who had the power to nullify all decrees against the children of Israel. "And the lesser light", referring to the Zaddik of this generation, "to rule the night", in the bitter exile which is like night. He, too, has the power of prayer as in former ages. God speaks well both of the early ones and the later ones, for He has eternal paths reaching from heaven by means of which He can be seen on earth.'

The famous prayer of *Levi Yitzhak of Berditchev is, in reality, an adaptation by this Zaddik of an old *Yiddish prayer. This prayer, rendered here in an English translation, is recited by many Hasidim at the departure of the Sabbath, when the Zaddik is said it have

recited it, and it is thus typical of Zaddikism in relation to prayer:

'God of Abraham, of Isaac, and of Jacob! Guard Thy people Israel from all evil for the sake of Thy praise. As the beloved, holy Sabbath departs, we pray that in the coming week we should attain to perfect faith, to faith in the sages, to love of our fellows, to attachment [*devekut*] to the Creator, blessed be He. May we believe in Thy thirteen *principles of the faith and in the redemption, may it come speedily in our day, and in the *resurrection of the dead, and in the prophecy of Moses our teacher, on whom be peace. Sovereign of the universe! Thou art He who gives the weary strength! Give, then, also to Thy dear Jewish children [*Kinderlech*, lit. 'toddlers', 'little children'] the strength to love Thee and to serve Thee alone. And may the week bring with it good health, good fortune, happiness, blessing, mercy, and children, life and sustenance, for us and for all Israel, and let us say, Amen.'

The prayer of the Zaddik for his followers to be blessed with 'children, life and sustenance' is found in many a Hasidic text. The basis in the Talmud is the saying (*Moed Katan* 28a): 'Life, children and sustenance depend not on merit but on *mazzal*.' In the context *mazzal* means 'luck'—it is not by a person's merits that he has good health, sustenance, and children but by sheer chance. But Hasidism, treating the word *mazzal* as if it came from a root meaning to flow, use the Talmudic passage for the doctrine of Zaddikism. Even if a man does not deserve to have good health, sustenance, and children on his own merits, he may be given them as a result of the special 'flow' of divine blessing through the 'channel' that is the Zaddik.

Samuel S. Dresner, *The Zaddik* (London, New York, and Toronto, n.d.).

Louis Jacobs, 'The Prayers of the Zaddik', in his *Hasidic Prayer*, with a new introduction (The Littman Library of Jewish Civilization; London and Washington, 1993), 126–39.

**Zangwill, Israel** English novelist and playwright (1864–1926). Zangwill's writings are relevant to Jewish religious trends in the contemporary world because they express, better than most, the tensions in his soul which were typical of those suffered thinking Jews torn between intense loyalty to the religious tradition and the allure of the wider world. Troubled, for instance, by the doctrine of the *Chosen

People, Zangwill countered with his famous epigram: 'The Chosen People is a choosing people', thus shifting imperceptibly the emphasis from God to the people. Jewish peoplehood was in the forefront of Zangwill's thought and activities. When *Herzl visited England in 1895, Zangwill introduced him to a number of influential Jews, and as a result the Zionist movement took root in Great Britain with Zangwill as an influential member. Later on Zangwill, still emphasizing the significance of Jewish peoplehood, took up the idea of Jewish territorialism as a substitute for *Zionism, founding the ITO, the Jewish Territorialist Organisation, in which what mattered was not the settlement of Jews in Palestine but having them settle somewhere, anywhere in the world —wherever they could build a home as an independent people.

Zangwill's agonizing over the problem of Jewish peoplehood is to be observed especially in his two most famous books, at least from the point of view of the Jewish religion. In his *Children of the Ghetto*, now in many editions and a classic of English literature, Zangwill wittily describes, mixing admiration with irony, the life of Russian immigrants to England in the *ghetto of the East End of London, where Zangwill was born. But in his series of sketches *Dreamers of the Ghetto*, he depicts mainly Jewish renegades (though the book does contain a study of the *Baal Shem Tov) such as Uriel Acasta, *Spinoza and *Shabbetai Zevi, for whom, for one reason or another, the burden of the Jewish religion became too hard to bear. The pull of Judaism is also evident in Zangwill's translations of some of Ibn *Gabirol's poems and of Jewish liturgical hymns. The latter, although far from representing Zangwill at his best, were admitted into the standard English Festival Prayer Book, the Routledge Mahzor. Zangwill can hardly be considered a profound Jewish thinker, but few have succeeded as well at giving expression in good English to the turmoil of the modern Jew trying to live in two worlds; this is not to say, however, that Zangwill provides anything remotely resembling a solution to the problem.

Joseph Leftwich, *Israel Zangwill* (London, 1957). M. Wohlgelernter: *Israel Zangwill: A Study* (New York, 1964).

**Zanz** Town in Galicia of which Hayyim Halberstam (1793–1876) was the Rabbi; he was also the founder of the Zanzer dynasty in *Hasidism. Halberstam, a profound Talmudist, was won over to Hasidism by Shalom Rokeah of *Belz. All eight of his sons became Hasidic masters, the most famous of them being Ezekiel Shraga of Sieniwa (1811–90). A grandson founded the dynasty of Bobov, and Bobover Hasidism still flourishes in the USA. Like Hayyim himself, his descendants were noted both for their learning and their zealotry. Hayyim Halberstam, unusually for a Hasidic master, was familiar with the works of the medieval Jewish philosophers. It is said that on *Kol Nidre night he would study Maimonides' *Guide of the Perplexed*, evidently believing that many of its ideas can be accommodated within Hasidic doctrine. His *Divrey Ḥayyim* on the Torah was published in Munkacs in 1877 and his *Responsa, with the same title, in Lvov in 1875. A mystical note is sounded even in Halberstam's Responsa, as when he defends (no. 105) the idea that the *Holy Spirit 'was still at work in the writing of such later authors as Hayyim *Ibn Atar and that anyone who denies this is a heretic.

Louis Jacobs, 'Hayyim Halberstam of Zanz', in his *Hasidic Thought* (New York, 1976), 210–15.

**Zealots** Jewish freedom-fighters in the War against Rome, 66–73 CE. *Josephus in *The Jewish War* refers to the Zealots together with other rebels against the Roman occupation. The Mishnah (*Sanhedrin* 9: 6) refers to the Zealots as *Kannaim*, a Hebrew word with the same connotation, and generally in the Rabbinic literature an ambivalent attitude emerges towards these rebels. Modern scholarship discusses at length the relationship between the Zealots, the Sicarii ('dagger men'), other rebels against Rome, and the *Qumran sectarians. The best summary of the whole question is provided by Menachem Stern (cited below). In later Jewish literature, the term *Kannaim* is applied to zealots of every description who use questionable means in their fight against those they consider to be enemies of God and the Jewish religion. Jacob *Emden, for example, was proud to call himself *kannai ben kannai* ('a zealot son of a zealot') in his struggle against the followers of *Shabbetai Zevi. (See also FANATICISM.)

Menachem Stern, 'Zealots', in C. Roth and G. Wigoder (eds.), *Encyclopedia Judaica Year Book* (Jerusalem, 1973), 135–52.

**Zechariah** Prophet whose first prophecy was made in the second year of the reign of Darius, 520 BCE. The prophets Zechariah, *Haggai, and *Malachi are often mentioned together in Jewish literature as the last of the biblical prophets, after whom, the Talmud (*Yoma* 9b) states, the *Holy Spirit ceased to function in Israel. Zechariah and Haggai sought to encourage the people to continue the task of rebuilding the *Temple, begun after the return from the Babylonian exile but discontinued because of its difficulty. The book of Zechariah is the eleventh in the Book of the Twelve Prophets and is in two parts. The first eight chapters deal with the life and activity of the prophet but in the last six chapters a strong eschatological note (see ESCHATOLOGY) is sounded and came to be understood as referring to the Messianic age (see MESSIAH). The majority of modern biblical scholars consider the author of these final chapters to be an unknown prophet. The book of Zechariah is particularly noted for the vivid descriptions of various prophetic *visions, especially of *angels. The verse (Zechariah 14: 9): 'And the Lord shall be King over all the earth; in that day shall the Lord be One, and His name one' forms the conclusion of the Alenu prayer and is seen to express the supreme hope of Jews for a future in which all mankind will hail God as King and obey His laws (see CHOSEN PEOPLE and UNIVERSALISM).

Eli Cashdan. 'Zechariah' in A. Cohen (ed.), *The Twelve Prophets* (London, 1970), 267–332.

**Zeitlin, Hillel** Religious thinker and exponent of Jewish *mysticism (1871–1942). Zeitlin belonged to a family of *Habad Hasidim, acquiring in his youth a sound knowledge in all branches of traditional Jewish learning. He was self-educated in European literature and thought and, attracted by these studies, he gave up to a large degree the practice of the Jewish religion. At a later period in his life, Zeitlin returned to his Jewish roots to become once again a strictly Orthodox Jew. Zeitlin contributed to Jewish journals essays in Hebrew and Yiddish on various themes. His writings on the Kabbalah and *Hasidism, include a key to the Zohar and an annotated translation of the introduction to the Zohar. These were collected and published in two volumes in Tel Aviv (1965 and 1975). In 1943 Zeitlin died a martyr's death when, wearing his *Tallit and *tefillin, he was shot by the Nazis on the way to the concentration camp of Treblinka to which they were taking him.

**Zelophehad, Daughters of** The book of Numbers (27: : 1–11) tells of Zelophehad dying in the wilderness without leaving any sons to inherit his portion in the land promised to the tribes. The five daughters of Zelophehad presented to Moses their claim to the inheritance. When Moses, uncertain of the law in such a case, presented the claim of the five daughters to God, Moses was informed that, in the absence of sons, daughters do inherit. When the heads of the clan later appealed to Moses that the decision in the case of the daughters might result in a diminution of their tribal lands, since the daughters might marry into another tribe so that the land given to them would then pass over to that tribe, Moses, at the command of God, decided that the daughters of Zelophehad might only marry into their own tribe (Numbers 36). According to the Rabbis this ruling, banning intermarriage between the tribes, was rescinded in a later generation (see SUCCESSION). Together with other biblical heroines, the daughters of Zelophehad have been praised by Jewish feminists (see FEMINISM) as pioneers in the struggle for women's rights.

**Zemirot** 'Songs', sung at the table on the Sabbath. The Zemirot, some of them composed as Sabbath-table hymns, others as independent liturgical hymns and adapted for the purpose, date from the Middle Ages down to the sixteenth century. Each community, and even individual families, often have their own special melodies for the Zemirot with different tunes for each. The idea behind the Zemirot is the need to celebrate the Sabbath as a day of joy and gladness with a combination of spiritual and material fare, a day which, in the words of the Rabbis, is a semblance of the *World to Come. One of the most popular of the Zemirot, 'Yah Ribbon', was composed by Israel Najara (1555–1628) in Aramaic. The opening stanza of this hymn (in Israel Abraham's translation) conveys the flavour of the Zemirot: 'God of the world, eternity's sole Lord! King over kings, be now Thy name adorned! Blessed are we to whom thou didst accord this gladsome time Thy wondrous ways to scan.'

Nosson Scherman (ed.), *Zemiroth: Sabbath Songs* (New York, 1981).

**Zephaniah** Prophet in Jerusalem during the reign of King Josiah (640–608 BCE). According to the Rabbis, Zephaniah was a contemporary of the prophet Jeremiah and the prophetess Huldah. Since he castigates the people of Jerusalem for worshipping idols it would seem that Zephaniah's oracles were delivered before the reforms of Josiah in 621 BCE, when the king suppressed idolatry. The only detail of Zephaniah's life is provided by the superscription to the book of Zephaniah (the ninth in the Book of the Twelve Prophets): 'The word of the Lord that came to Zephaniah son of Cushi son of Gedaliah son of Amariah son of Hezekiah, during the reign of King Josiah son of Amon of Judah.' Abraham *Ibn Ezra holds that the Hezekiah referred to is King Hezekiah, since otherwise there would be no reason for tracing Zephaniah's descent particularly to him, but this view is contested since this ancestor is not called King Hezekiah. The most prominent feature in Zephaniah's prophecies is his warning that the 'day of the Lord' will dawn in which the idolaters will be severely punished for their apostasy, yet this 'day' will also usher in a new era in which Jerusalem will be saved from her oppressors and God will dwell therein (Zephaniah 3: 14–29). This final section of the book of Zephaniah features prominently in later Jewish *eschatology.

S. M. Lehrman, *Zephaniah*, in A. Cohen (ed.), *The Twelve Prophets* (London, 1970), 231–51.

**Zerubbabel** Governor of Judah in the late sixth century BCE (the name means 'scion of Babylon'), to whom there are references in the books of *Ezra, *Haggai, and *Zechariah. Zerubbabel was a grandson of King Jehoiachim of Judah who was deposed by Nebuchadnezzar in 597 BCE. In Zechariah's vision (Zechariah 3 and 4), Zerubbabel and Joshua the High Priest are encouraged in their attempt to rebuild the Temple. In this section the words occur: 'This is the word of the Lord to Zerubbabel: Not by might, nor by power, but by My spirit' (Zechariah 4: 6), words that have served as an inspiration throughout Jewish history to practical leaders of the same type as Zerubbabel and as a reminder to them not to depend overmuch on their own abilities. Zerubbabel remains, however, a shadowy figure, and there is considerable uncertainty about the exact role he played after the return from the Babylonian exile. In one passage in the Talmud (*Sanhedrin*

38a) he is identified with *Nehemiah. In the *'Maoz Tzur' hymn sung on *Hanukkah, the name Zerubbabel is rhymed with *ketz bavel* ('the end of Babylon').

**Zevi Elimelech of Dynow** Hasidic *Zaddik, Rabbi, and author (1785–1841). Extremely learned in the Talmud, Codes, Kabbalah, and the literature of early *Hasidism, Zevi Elimelech objected to Jews studying secular subjects and was a fiery opponent of the *Haskalah. Once, it is reported, carried away by his zeal, he begged God that even if Moses *Mendelssohn was in heaven, since he was a pious Jew in practice, he should be brought down to the nethermost part of *Gehinnom for the part he played in causing Israel to sin. Zevi Elimelech, a very prolific author, is best known for his *Beney Yissakhar* (*Sons of Issaachar*), a classic of Hasidic literature abounding in original ideas, though based firmly in the tradition. The tile of the book is taken from the verse: 'And the sons of Issachar, men that had understanding of the times' (1 Chronicles 12: 33). This refers to the nature of the work as a detailed commentary to the 'sacred times' in the Jewish *calendar, the Sabbath and the *festivals.

Zevi Elimelech was strongly opposed to philosophical arguments to 'prove' the truths of religion. There is no solution capable of being grasped by the human mind of the old problem of how divine foreknowledge can be compatible with the *free will of humans to choose. Yet, precisely because Jews believe in faith even those matters beyond their capacity to understand, they are treated by God in His attribute of mercy which is higher than reason, so that He does not punish them even when it seems reasonable for Him to do so. 'God has concealed even from the wise how punishment can be justified, for sins committed due to a bad choice, since God knows it all beforehand. But the children of Israel believe in it by virtue of the Torah, the Torah of mercy, higher than reason. It follows automatically that even from the point of view of justice, it is only right for their sins to be pardoned and for mercy to be shown to them.' Thus Zevi Elimelech, for all his great knowledge and keen intellect, is to be classed among the few Jewish thinkers with an antirationalist stance (see RATIONALISM).

In his work *Derekh Pikkudekha* (*Way of Thy Commandments*), Zevi Elimelech points to the various ways in which the bare commands of the Torah can receive wider application. For instance, the fifth commandment (see DECALOGUE) embraces the need for a man to have respect for his own reasoning powers given to him by God since, according to the Kabbalah, 'Wisdom' is described as 'Father' and 'Understanding' as 'Mother'. Similarly, the sixth commandment includes the injunction for a man not to 'kill' his potential for study by wasting his words on trivialities. The ninth commandment, not to bear false witness, embraces the idea that one who recites the *Shema and simply mouths the words without concentrating on their meaning, bears false witness to God.

> Louis Jacobs, 'Zevi Elimelech Spira of Dynow', in his *Hasidic Thought* (New York, 1976), 185–90.

**Zimra, David Ben** Egyptian Halakhic authority and Kabbalist (1479–1573), known, after the initial letters of his name, as Radbaz (*R*abbi *D*avid *B*en *Z*imra). Radbaz, leaving Spain, where he was born, at the time of the expulsion of the Jews in 1492, studied in *Safed and then became a judge in Cairo and eventually both the spiritual and lay head of Egyptian Jewry. Towards the end of his long life he settled again in Safed, where he served as a member of Joseph *Karo's court. As a man of great wealth Radbaz was able to achieve a stern independence throughout his career. Radbaz is chiefly renowned for his collection of Responsa containing over 2,000 items. *Azulai writes of him: 'In the light of his keen reasoning walked those who had wandered in darkness and his Responsa went forth to every questioner from all over the world.'

In a famous Responsum (no. 344) on the *principles of the Jewish faith, Radbaz opposes the whole attempt at drawing up principles since this implies that some aspects of the Torah have greater significance than others. In the same Responsum, Radbaz sides with *Yom Tov Ishbili against Maimonides, in the belief that a Jew is obliged to suffer martyrdom (see MARTYRS) rather than embrace *Islam, even though Islam is not an idolatrous faith. In another Responsum (no. 352) Radbaz replies to a questioner who had asked why Scripture forbids a man to marry the mother of his mother-in-law but allows him to marry his own grandmother. Is it not an *a fortiori* argument? If he is forbidden to marry his wife's grandmother he should certainly be forbidden to

marry his own grandmother. Typical of Radbaz's attitude to the limited role of human reasoning in Judaism is his reply that the *a fortiori* argument is based on human reasoning, whereas the forbidden degrees of marriage are a divine decree, so that human reasoning is inoperative there. All we can say is that God has so ordained. One degree of relationship is forbidden, the other permitted. Nevertheless, if the questioner persists, Radbaz is prepared to offer a tentative solution. Those affinities are proscribed for which man in his lust has some inclination. But no man would ever want to marry his own grandmother, so there is no cause for Scripture to record a special law prohibiting this. On the other hand, it is not beyond the bounds of possibility that a man should wish to marry his wife's grandmother. If, for example, a man marries a young woman of 13 and he is 40 years of age, it is possible for his wife's grandmother to be younger than he, and so be attractive to him. Radbaz concludes that, in fact, this solution has been given by Menahem *Meiri.

Radbaz and other Jewish leaders were obliged to face the problems raised by Jews threatening to convert to another religion if the Jewish court insisted on punishing them for offences they had committed. Radbaz was asked (no. 187) whether a Jewish court should relax its demands in such circumstances. Radbaz, aware of the seriousness of the problem, writes: 'All my days I have been disturbed by the matter you have raised. The result of leniency will be a diminution of the Torah, and yet we have no power to coerce the wicked. Every day I offer the prayer that nothing untoward should happen through me, yet I shall share my thoughts with you.' He comes down on the side of a refusal to yield to threats. If the courts are to yield to blackmail, the wicked will be undeterred from robbery, plunder, rape, and other crimes. Throughout Jewish history the courts wielded their *authority and never desisted because of threats of apostasy. In any event, he remarks, a Jew who is prepared to make threats of this kind will sooner or later leave the Jewish fold whatever the court may or may not do. Nevertheless Radbaz is reluctant to provide a blanket ruling. Each case should be decided according to the particular circumstances.

Especially interesting from both the theological and psychological point of view is the Responsum (no. 985) dealing with a great scholar who lost a son but did not shed a single tear. Is such a Stoical attitude reprehensible or is it commendable? Radbaz replies:

'This is an evil trait demonstrating hard-heartedness and bad character. This cruel atti-tude is that of the philosophers who say that this world is vanity, a huge joke . . . But we who have received the Torah must believe and appreciate that this world is very precious to those who use it properly and who conduct themselves in a fitting manner. It is through the way he behaves in this life that man attains to the *World to Come and to immortality, for this world is called the world of deeds. Conse-quently, we must never treat it as vanity, attri-buting its sorrows to the poor way in which it is governed and complaining about the woes of temporal existence, as the majority of the poets have done.'

On the question of *asceticism Radbaz (no. 981) discusses the Talmudic saying (*Nedarim* 10a) that one who fasts is a sinner. How can this be, since many of the great *saints used to fast? Radbaz refers to a report that Rabbi Eliezer of Metz (in the twelfth century) argued that one who fasts is only a sinner if he does it out of bad temper or because he is disillusioned with the world, not if he fasts for the sake of heaven. This is incorrect, however, and is contradicted by Rabbi Eliezer of Metz's own comment to the Talmudic passage, where the Rabbi observes that the man is, indeed, a sinner but this sin is sometimes worthwhile. Another solution is that he is a sinner only when he fasts without following the advice of the prophet (Isaiah 58: 7) to deal out bread to the hungry on a true fast day. Radbaz himself fails to see any problem here. There are, in fact, two opinions on the matter in the Talmud, not one. We do not follow, he says, the view that one who fasts is a sinner but rather the view that he is a holy man. However, Radbaz concludes, this only applies if he has the strength to engage in fasting. Mortification of the flesh to an exces-sive degree is forbidden by all the authorities.

Louis Jacobs, *Theology in the Responsa* (London and Boston, 1975), 110–30.

**Zionism** The movement that arose at the end of the nineteenth century with the aim of establishing a homeland for Jews in Palestine, as it then was. The actual term 'Zionism' was coined by Nathan Birnbaum in 1891 to denote the political efforts to achieve this aim, although

the settlement of Jews in Palestine had begun earlier and was represented by the *Hovevey Tzion* ('Lovers of Zion'). Zion had been a synonym for *Jerusalem from biblical times. The Psalmist, for example, makes the exiles in Babylon say: 'By the rivers of Babylon, there we sat down, yea we wept, when we remem-bered Zion' (Psalms 137: 1). In the Middle Ages, Judah *Halevi wrote his 'Songs of Zion' in yearning for the resettlement of Jews in Palestine, of which Zion had become the su-preme symbol. Theodor *Herzl's Zionism was thus only new in that the opportunity was seized of attempting the settlement of Jews by political means. The full Zionist story has been told in numerous books and pamphlets. Here can only be considered the implications for the Jewish religion of Zionism, and its im-plementation in the establishment of the State of Israel.

Jewish peoplehood, from the destruction of the Temple until the nineteenth century, was understood by Jews in a religious, not in a nationalistic, sense. It could hardly have been otherwise. An ethnic group settled in many different lands, with neither a land of its own nor a common language except for prayer, could only find its cohesiveness in the religious faith professed by the majority of its members. It is equally true that in the earlier period the Jews were a nation—in the biblical idiom 'a holy nation', but a nation none the less. With the rise of modern Zionism the question was naturally posed: were the Jews a nation or were they the adherents of a religion?

Opposition to Zionism on the part of some Jews came from a number of different direc-tions. Many Reform leaders thought of Jewish nationalism as a betrayal of *universalism. It was a divine boon, they argued, not a calamity, that Jews had no land of their own and so were able to keep their religion unsullied by particularistic national ideas which tend to frustrate the wider hope of a mankind united in the service of God. Many Orthodox thinkers shared the Reform suspicion of a revival of Jewish nationalism and they added the fear that a return to the Holy Land by human effort in the pre-Messianic age amounts to a denial of the *Messiah for whose coming Jews are to wait patiently. According to the classical scheme, the Jews, exiled from their land because of their sins, had to wait until God sent the Messiah to redeem them from subservience to the nations and bring them back to the land of Israel. It was positively impious, on this view, to anticipate the divine intervention by human endeavour on the political level, although the religious duty of settling in the Holy Land was still binding on individual Jews who should, whenever possible, go to live in Palestine.

The whole question was further complicated by the fact that the Zionist movement was inspired by the rise of nationalistic movements of a secular nature in Europe and that many of the most prominent Zionist leaders were secularist in outlook. The fierce denunciations of Zionism were not always based on distrust of the new but on a real apprehension that Judaism itself was being redefined in secular, nationalistic terms. Jewish nationalism was sometimes seen as a kind of idolatry, the nation being accorded the place previously reserved for God.

A typical Reform statement in contained in the 'Pittsburgh Platform' in 1885:

'We recognise in the modern era of universal culture of heart and intellect the approach of the realisation of Israel's great Messianic hope for the establishment of the kingdom of truth, justice and peace among all men. We consider ourselves no longer a nation but a religious community, and therefore expect neither a return to Palestine, nor a sacrificial worship under the administration of the sons of Aaron, nor the restoration of any of the laws concerning the Jewish state.'

The Reform leader, Felix Goldman, observed in 1911:

'If Zionism frankly admits that in the sense of nationalism one can be a good Jew and at the same time an atheist who is contemptuous of religion, then in the same moment Zionism would be condemned to death in the eyes of all thinking Jews. The spread of Zionism under such conditions would mean death for Judaism. We non-Zionists frankly declare that we have no interest in a Judaism in which religion is not the first, highest and most important part. Therefore we have no interest in a mere nationalism, and not merely because of the purely theoretical reason that we believe the progress of civilised humanity will occur only by lessening nationalism and chauvinism. We therefore see no advantage for us or for anybody else if we add another nation to the world, a nation which in importance, capacity for cultural development and power would only be equal to the robber states of the Balkans.'

However, this opposition to Zionism on the part of Reform Judaism eventually yielded not only to a tolerant acceptance but to strong advocacy on the part of some of the most distinguished and influential Reform Rabbis who became, indeed, leaders of the Zionist movement.

From the Orthodox side the following statement by Rabbi Shalom Dov of *Lubavitch can be quoted as an illustration of how a large number of European Rabbis saw Zionism as a menace to the Jewish religion:

'From all these articles written by Zionists we can clearly see that their main aim and activity is to make—and unfortunately they do—the impression among the people of Israel that the whole purpose of the Torah and the commandments is merely to strengthen collective feeling. This theory can easily be adopted by young people who regard themselves as instruments prepared for the fulfilment of the Zionist ideal. They naturally regard themselves as completely liberated from the Torah and the commandments for now, they think, nationalism has replaced religion, and is the best means for the preservation of society.'

Many religious Jews, however, warmly embraced the Zionist philosophy, seeing it not as a foe of religion but as the greatest aid to religious loyalty on the part of the Jew tempted to abandon his faith. There are enough passages in the classical literature regarding the duty of populating the Holy Land to provide ammunition to religious Zionists who argue that Zionism in the contemporary world is a *religious* obligation. The *Mizrachi movement in particular advocated religious Zionism with its slogan: 'The land of Israel for the people of Israel according to the Torah of Israel.' There are also enough passages in the classical literature on the idea that God uses human effort in order to fulfil His purpose to make specious the argument that the return of the Jews to the Holy Land must be solely by supernatural means. Judaism does not advocate *quietism in such matters as earning a livelihood. Why, then the religious Zionists argued, should it be considered impious to engage in human effort on behalf of the alleviation of Jewish suffering that would result from the realization of the Zionist ideal?

Conservative Judaism, attaching great significance to Jewish peoplehood from its inception, naturally embraced Zionism. Solomon

*Schechter, pioneer of Conservative Judaism in the USA and Chancellor of the Jewish Theological Seminary, stated in one of his seminary addresses, published in 1909:

'The reproach that Zionism is unspiritual is meaningless. Indeed, there seems to be a notion abroad that spirituality is a negative quality . . . In general it is the antinominian who will tell you that he is the only heir to the rare quality of spirituality, whereas the real saint in all his actions is so spontaneous and so natural that he is entirely unconscious of possessing spirituality, and practically never mentions it. The Zionists are not saints, but they may fairly claim that few movements are more free from the considerations of convenience and comfort, and less tainted with worldliness and otherworldliness than the one they serve. Nothing was to be gained by joining it. All the powers that be, were and still are, opposed to it, whether in their capacity as individuals or as wealthy corporations. The Zionists are just beginning to be tolerated, but I remember distinctly the time when adhesion to the cause of Zionism might interfere with the prospects of a man's career, the cry being, "no Zionist need apply".'

Two factors have combined to make all this debate a dead letter. The *Holocaust, in which six million Jews perished, brought in its wake a fierce and completely justified resolve on the part of Jews everywhere to put an end to the kind of Jewish homelessness which had made such horror possible. The creation of the State of *Israel, a result of this resolve, made academic the whole Zionist question. The State of Israel is a reality. It has won by its achievements the goodwill of the majority of Jews everywhere. The existence of the State of Israel has so influenced Jewish thinking that it is now nonsensical to debate whether Jews are *only* the adherents of the Jewish religion. In Israel, at least, the Jews are a nation.

This is not to say that with the establishment of the State of Israel the problem of Jewish nationalism and its relationship to religion has disappeared. In many ways the success of the State of Israel has aggravated the problem. The new reality of Jewish nationalism poses in far more acute form than ever before the problem of how to reconcile Jewish nationalistic aspirations with universalism, the secular with the sacred, belief in divine providence with human endeavour, justice for the Jews with the rights of the Arabs, love for the Holy Land with the loyalty Jews outside Israel owe to the lands in which they reside. With hindsight, the majority of Jews today see that the Rabbis who opposed Zionism were misguided. But they were not wrong when they pointed out that an unbridled nationalism is a form of idolatry, that no State, however noble its aims, is to be worshipped, that the *individual counts because he is unique, possessing, as Judaism sees it, a fraction of the divine light which only he or she can reveal.

W. Gunther Plaut, 'Zion: The Great Debate', in his *The Growth of Reform Judaism* (New York, 1965), 144–58.
Arthur Hertzberg, *The Zionist Idea: A Historical Analysis and Reader* (New York, 1959).
Louis Jacobs, *A Jewish Theology* (New York, 1973); see index: 'Zionism'.

**Zodiac** An imaginary zone in the heavens determined by the twelve different positions of the full moon during the year. These twelve constellations were seen by the ancient astronomers as having the appearance of animals and other creatures, hence the name zodiac from the Greek, meaning 'little animals'. The constellations of the zodiac feature prominently in astrological calculations and are referred to by Jews who believe in *astrology, a belief rejected by Maimonides who only refers to the zodiac in an astronomical context (*Yesodey Ha-Torah*, 3. 6) without actually using the word zodiac. Nor is there any mention of the zodiac in the Talmud. In the Middle Ages, however, the constellations of the zodiac are referred to and are given in Hebrew as an exact equivalent of the Latin terms. The zodiac features in a number of late Midrashim, as, for instance, in the suggestion that they correspond to the twelve tribes of Israel. Libra, the zodiacal sign for the month of Tishri, was held to be entirely appropriate for the month during which *Rosh Ha-Shanah and *Yom Kippur fall, since these are judgement days when human fate is weighed in the balance. Similarly, a Midrashic comment notes that the month of Sivan, the month in which the festival of *Shavuot falls (the anniversary of the giving of the Torah), has the sign of Gemini, representing the twins, *Jacob and *Esau, to suggest that the teachings of the Torah regarding the seven *Noahide laws apply to Esau, identified with *Rome, as they do to Israel. Some of the older festival prayer books depict the zodiacal signs in the sections containing the prayers for *rain and dew on

*Tabernacles and *Passover respectively, but there was strong Rabbinic objection to the practice.

**Zohar** 'Illumination' or 'Brightness', the classical work of the Kabbalah, containing the record of revelations regarding the divine mysteries alleged to have been vouchsafed to the second-century teacher Rabbi *Simeon ben Yohai and his mystic circle. The name Zohar is based on the verse (Daniel 12: 3), commented on at the beginning of the work (as a comment on the first verse of Genesis): 'And the intelligent shall shine like the brightness [ke-zohar] of the firmament, and they that turn many to righteousness like the stars for ever and ever.' The Zohar first saw the light of day through the efforts of *Moses de Leon of Guadalajara in Spain, at the end of the thirteenth century. Modern scholarship concurs with the views of *Scholem that Moses de Leon was in fact the author of the work, which does not mean that Moses de Leon was engaged in pious fraud and that, as *Graetz puts it out of hostility to the Kabbalah, the Zohar is 'the book of lies'. The work bears all the marks of a pseudepigraphic production; that is to say, Moses de Leon used the figures of Rabbi Simeon and his associates as the vehicle for the transmission of his own ideas. It has also been noted that many of the Zoharic ideas go back to a much earlier period than that of de Leon. Strictly speaking the Zohar is not a single book but a complete body of literature united under an inclusive title. In the many printed editions the Zohar appears in five parts: (i)–(iii) the Zohar proper, a commentary to the Pentateuch in three volumes; (iv) *Tikkuney Ha-Zohar* ('Perfections of the Zohar'), also known as the *Tikkunim*, on the first verse of Genesis; (v) *Zohar Hadash* ('New Zohar'). These five are not usually printed as a set. (i)–(iii), (iv), and (v) are printed as three separate volumes. The *Zohar Hadash* consists of new Zoharic material published from manuscript and belongs to the Zoharic corpus of (i)–(iii). The *Tikkuney Ha-Zohar* is from the hands of a later author writing in the style of the Zohar. The matter is further complicated in that the Zohar to the Pentateuch consists, in itself, of a number of sections, not all of them from the same author. For the purpose of this entry, however, the Zohar is treated as a single work. For the various theories on the apportioning of the sections of the work, Scholem and Tishby

should be consulted (see the bibliography at the end of this entry).

*The Literary Problem*

Few works have presented a more fascinating literary problem than the Zohar. According to contemporary reports, Moses de Leon copied the Zohar from a manuscript in his possession which contained teachings from the circle of Rabbi Simeon ben Yohai who, in the Talmudic account, spent thirteen years in a cave together with Rabbi Eleazar his son. There, in the Kabbalstic elaboration, they were taught the secrets of the Torah by *Elijah. According to one report the work was sent to Spain by Nahmanides from the land of Israel, Nahmanides being presented with the manuscript by the King of Aragon to whom it had been brought but whose sages found it indecipherable. According to a different report, Moses de Leon wrote the work by means of a 'Holy Name', that is, through divine *inspiration.

From the sixteenth century onwards voices were raised to demonstrate that, whoever was the author of the Zohar, it could not have been Rabbi Simeon ben Yohai in the second century CE. For one thing the Aramaic in which the major part of the work is written is highly artificial in form, an amalgam of the Aramaic of the Babylonian Talmud, the Jerusalem Talmud, and the *Targum. Secondly, there is no reference to the Zohar in the Talmudic literature, in which Rabbi Simeon is mentioned very frequently. Most significantly, some of the heroes of the Zohar lived long after Rabbi Simeon ben Yohai. Jacob *Emden, in particular, though he believed in the sanctity of the Zohar, was appalled at the use of the work by the followers of *Shabbetai Zevi, the false Messiah. Emden called attention to the many anachronisms in the work in order to demonstrate that a major portion, at least, could not have been written by Rabbi Simeon. Emden's critique was followed by modern scholars who noted further anachronisms. In practically every case a solution has been attempted by defenders of the traditional authorship but when the evidence is put together it is as clear as can be that the Zohar was complied in the thirteenth not in the second century. Among the anachronisms are references to the Crusades and to Islam; the use of Hebrew philosophical terms unknown before the Middle Ages; mystical interpretation of the Portuguese word for synagogue, *esnoga*; and a reference to the two pairs of *tefillin, those of *Rashi and Rabbenu *Tam, though these are not actually mentioned by name. Furthermore, most calculations regarding the advent of the *Messiah put the date of his coming near to their own time. In the Zohar the beginning of the end is fixed in the years 1300–10. The Zohar also contains mystical interpretations of the names of the vowel-notes and the notes used in the *cantillation of the Torah, and yet it is the verdict of modern scholarship that these were not introduced until after the close of the Talmud. There are references to prayers that were not composed until much later, such as the *Kol Nidre, and to additions to the liturgy of prayers for life during the *Ten Days of Penitence which date from the period of the *Geonim. There are also barely concealed quotations from Talmudic and Midrashic passages, and from the works of Rashi, Maimonides, Abraham *Ibn Ezra, Nahmanides and *Kimhi, and from the poems of *Ibn Gabirol. The reply of the traditional Kabbalists is generally to admit that additions were made to the Zohar at a later date, but to maintain there are so many of these as to make it entirely implausible that the critique can be disposed of on these grounds. Needless to say, whether the Zohar was composed by Rabbi Simeon ben Yohai or by Moses de Leon, the value of the work does not stand on this question. Whoever its author, the Zohar remains the great depository of Kabbalistic doctrine, with many an insight into the mystical aspects of the Jewish religion.

## The Nature of the Zohar

Essentially, the Zohar consists of a running commentary to the Torah in which the doctrine of the *Sefirot is read into the narratives. The six days of creation in the first chapter of Genesis, for instance, are made to refer to the divine unfolding and the emanation of the six lower Sefirot, with the Sabbath day, the seventh, representing *Malkhut* ('Sovereignty'). The Zohar does not use the actual term Sefirot coined by the Kabbalists (presumably to have done so would be 'to give the game away'). The Zohar prefers instead such terms as 'crowns', 'measures', 'brilliances', and so forth. Nor is there any explicit reference to *En Sof, which is referred to only by hint and in a very circumspect manner. The Zohar is very rich in poetic formulations; the unfamiliar and resounding Aramaic itself provides an air of great

antiquity and mystery. In the narratives strange figures make an appearance from time to time in order to impart the mystical doctrines, such as the ghost of the Old Man and the Yanuka ('Babe'), a child of tender years who spouts wisdom. The famous, lengthy passage (Zohar, iii. 127b–145a) known as the Idra Rabbah ('Great Assembly') opens with the captivating account of how Rabbi Simeon assembled his disciples to initiate them into the most profound secrets:

'It is taught that Rabbi Simeon said to his companions: How long shall we sit by a column that has but a single base [i.e. studying only the revealed aspects of the Torah]? It is written: "It is time to do something for the Lord. They have frustrated Thy Torah" [Psalms 119: 126]. Time is short, and the creditor is impatient. A herald cries out every day. But the reapers in the field [the mystical adepts] are few, and they are on the edges of the vineyard. They do not look, nor do they know fully where they are going. Assemble, friends, at the Idra, garbed in mail, with swords and lances in your hands. Look to your equipment, counsel, wisdom, understanding, knowledge, sight, power of hands and legs. Appoint a king over you who has the power of life and death and who can utter words of truth, words that the holy ones above will heed, and that they will rejoice to hear and know.'

After this awesome preamble, Rabbi Simeon proceeds to give a detailed exposition of the *Sifra De-Tzeniuta* ('Book of Concealment') in which are described the various aspects of 'the Holy Ancient One'.

Another section to the Zohar, the 'Raya Mehemna' ('Faithful Shepherd' = Moses) gives a mystical interpretation of the precepts of the Torah. This section is not printed as a separate work but is inserted into the text wherever there is a reference to one of the precepts. This section seems to be from the same author or authors as the *Tikkuney Ha-Zohar*. Although the bulk of the Zohar is in Aramaic, a whole section, known as the 'Midrash Ha-Neelam' ('The Esoteric Midrash') is in a mixture of Hebrew and Aramaic.

## The Influence of the Zohar

The first two editions of the Zohar were published in Mantua (1558–1560) and Cremona (1559–60). A fierce debate took place on whether the Zohar should be printed at all, some Kabbalists arguing that it is forbidden to spread the

Kabbalistic doctrines among the masses, the inevitable result of its publication in print. With the printing and subsequent wide dissemination of the Zohar, the process, beginning after the expulsion from Spain, continued of treating the Zohar as a sacred book and not only for the Kabbalists. Moralistic works quoted extensively from the Zohar. Laws and customs based on the Zohar found their way into the standard Codes, although there was much discussion on how far Zoharic practices should have the status of law. The general principle that emerged was that where the rulings found in the Zohar (and the Kabbalah generally) are in conflict with those of the Talmud and the Codes, it is the latter rulings that are binding. But where there is no conflict, the rulings found in the Zohar should be followed. In the Christian Kabbalah and in the *Shabbetai Zevi movement the Zohar was set off against the Talmud, the former being held to be the true, secret meaning of religion. Naturally, this distinction was totally negated within Judaism where the idea was developed that the Zohar contains the secret meaning of the Torah and its teachings for the Kabbalists alone, while the Talmud and the Codes belong to the 'revealed Torah' binding upon all devout Jews, whether or not they are Kabbalists. The followers of the *Haskalah movement, on the other hand, denigrated the Zohar and the Kabbalah in general as a foreign shoot implanted into Judaism to encourage superstition and the irrational in religion. There are echoes of this conflict in the *Yemen, where followers of the Darda movement rejected the Zohar as a sacred work.

In *Hasidism the Zohar became a 'canonical' book together with the Bible and the Talmud. The early Hasidic master, Pinhas of Koretz, it is said, used to thank God that he had not been created before the appearance of the Zohar for it was the Zohar that had preserved him for Judaism (*gehalten bei Yiddishkeit*). Of the *Baal Shem Tov *it is related that he would carry a copy of the Zohar with him at all times and he would see the whole world in the Zohar. *Elijah, Gaon of *Vilna, the fierce opponent of Hasidism, also believed in the supreme sanctity of the Zohar and his attitude was shared by the majority of the *Mitnaggedim.

The Zohar, like other classical works of Judaism, has been the subject of applied study by modern scholars in the historical-critical mode. On the contemporary religious scene,

many Orthodox Jews, even if they have little or no knowledge of the Zohar, still revere the work as sacred literature. But it has never become a matter of *dogma to believe that the Zohar is a sacred work and, even among the Orthodox it is possible to be a good Jew and a true believer without accepting the Zohar as an inspired work. Reform and Conservative Judaism is normally critical of the Zohar and its influence while at the same time admiring the many beautiful ideas and numinous insights found in this remarkable work, unique in the history of religion for its mystical style and daring flights of the imagination. (See also CORDOVERO, EN SOF, KABBALAH, and SEFIROT.)

Gershom Scholem, 'The Zohar', in his *Kabbalah*, (Jerusalem, 1974) 213–43.

Daniel Chanan Matt, *Zohar: The Book of Enlightenment* (London, 1983).

Isaiah Tishby, *The Wisdom of the Zohar*, trans. David Goldstein (The Littman Library of Jewish Civilization; Oxford, 1989).

**Zoroastrianism** The religion founded by the Iranian prophet Zarathustra in the sixth century BCE. The third century CE, the period of stormy conflicts between Persia and Rome—between Graeco-Roman civilizations and the oriental traditions which were dominant in Persia—saw the collapse of the Parthian dynasty and the rise of the Sassanians. Ardeshir, the first of the Sassanian rulers, was crowned at Chorossan. He became the ruler of the Persian Empire, holding sway over forty million people. One of his first acts was to restore the religion of Zarathustra and give great power to its priests, the Magi. The followers of the religion of light and darkness, of Ormuzd, the god of light, and Ahriman, the god of darkness, destroyed the Greek temples, taught that redemption was possible only through the intercession of the Magi, and began to persecute the adherents of other religions. Bitter attacks on the Jewish religion are found in Pahlavi works (of the Middle Persian period) and this bitterness was not confined, at first, to verbal attacks. The Talmud refers to the destruction of synagogues by the Magi (*Yoma* 10a) and to harsh decrees issued against Judaism (*Yevamot* 63b). Since the Magi opposed the burial of the human corpse as polluting the sacred soil, they would, at times, resurrect the Jewish dead (*Bava Batra* 58a). On the Persian festivals no fire was to be kindled in the home (*Shabbat* 45a;

*Gittin* 17a) and fire for use in the Persian temples was taken forcibly from Jewish homes (*Sanhedrin* 74b). In one Talmudic passage (*Kiddushin* 72a) the Magi are compared to demons. The severity of this persecution, however, gradually waned and, under Shapur I (241–72), Jewish rights were restored. Shapur's edict of toleration reads: 'The Magus, the Manichaean, the Jew and the Christian, and what other sects there are, shall live in peace according to their religion.' On the whole the Jews fared far better in the Persian Empire than in Palestine under Roman rule. The *exilarch enjoyed almost the status of a Jewish king within the Persian state. The friendliest relations seem to have existed between the Jewish sages and some of the Persian rulers. Even if the Talmudic accounts of this friendship, such as that some of the Babylonian Amoraim held conversations with the Persian rulers, are legendary, the very fact that such stories were recorded in the Talmud is indicative of the situation. It was not only in Amoraic times in Babylon that Judaism came into contact with Zoroastrianism, but it was in this period that the tensions between the adherents of the two religions were particularly acute.

Zoroastrian dualism, with Ormuzd, struggling against Ahriman, presented a greater challenge to Jewish monotheism than did polytheism, since the Jewish religion also acknowledges the struggle between good and evil. It has been suggested that as long ago as Deutero-Isaiah the unknown prophet preaches against Persian dualism: 'That they may know from the rising of the sun, and from the west, that there is none beside Me; I am the Lord, and there is none else; I form the light, and create darkness; I make peace, and create evil; I am the Lord, that doeth all these things' (Isaiah 45: 6–7). It is probable that Persian dualism had, in fact, an influence on Jewish thought in the emergence of the doctrine of *Satan, although, in Rabbinic thought, Satan is completely subordinate to God and is in no way a rival to Him. It is not at all surprising, therefore, to find so many passages in the Rabbinic literature in which the dualistic challenge is squarely faced.

The Rabbinic term for dualism is *shetey reshuyot*, 'two powers' or 'two authorities, that is, two gods in control of the world. The Sifre to the verse: 'See now that I, even I, am He, and there is no god with Me' (Deuteronomy 32: 39) comments: 'If anyone says that there are

two powers in heaven the retort is given to him: "There is no god with Me."' The Mishnah (*Berakhot* 5: 3) rules that if a man says in his prayers: 'We acknowledge Thee, we acknowledge Thee' (repeating the expression found in the liturgy), he is to be silenced. While the Mishnah does not give the reason, the Talmudic explanation (*Berakhot* 33b) is that it appears as if he acknowledges 'two powers', each of which he addresses separately. In a curious passage (*Ḥagigah* 15a) it is said that Elisha ben Abuyah, who became a Jewish sectarian, was led into error when he saw the angel *Metatron having such high status in heaven that he came to believe in 'two powers'. George Foot Moore has summed it all up very cogently:

'The difficulty of reconciling the evils of the world with the goodness of God was so strongly felt in the early centuries of our era in the East and the West, and a dualistic solution of one kind or another was so widely accepted in philosophy and religion, that it is idle to attempt to identify the Jewish circles which accepted this solution. It must suffice that we know there were such circles; that they tried to fortify their position with texts of Scripture; and that the rabbis refuted them with their own weapons. It is certain also that whatever leanings there may have been in this direction, Judaism, with its inveterate monotheism, was not rent by dualistic heresies as Christianity was for centuries.'

Dualistic traces did, indeed, linger on in the doctrines of Satan and Metatron and in the Kabbalistic views on the *Sitra Aḥara* ('the Other Side'), the demonic realm. But as Jewish monotheistic thought developed, the complete subordination of the powers of evil to God became dominant in Judaism. Dualism has virtually vanished from the religious scene, partly for the sane reason that monotheism came to be seen as superior to polytheism. In a world divided up among the various gods it is hard to explain the the evidence of unity in the world. It has often been noted that modern science, based on the idea that there is such a unity, could not have arisen against a polytheistic background. *Saadiah Gaon devotes a section of his *Beliefs and Opinions* (ii. 2) to a refutation of dualism on philosophical grounds. If there are two gods, says Saadiah, neither of which could create without the help of the other, then neither would be a god, since his power would be limited. If, on the other hand, one can act without the other, how is it that their desires always coincide and why does it never happen that one wishes to keep a person alive while the other wishes to kill him? Furthermore, if the two powers are connected with one another, then they would really be one. If, on the other hand, they are distinct from each other, then the separation would have to be produced by a third principle which is neither one nor the other. *Bahya, Ibn Pakudah argues the same case in his *Duties of the Heart* (i. 7). If there are two gods, then either each one could create the world without the other's help or he could not do so. If one could have created the world without the other's help, then the other is superfluous. If, on the other hand, neither could have created the world without the other's help, then each is weak in himself and neither is omnipotent, and a god who lacks omnipotence is no god. Furthermore, the profound sense of unity which human beings have and which they see in the universe would be inexplicable if two conflicting powers are at work. This kind of argument was expressed in the Talmud (*Sanhedrin* 39a) in its own inimitable way against the Zoroastrian background. There it is said that a Magus (*amgushi*) said to Amemar: 'From the middle of your body upwards you belong to Ormuzd; from the middle downwards, to Ahriman.' Amemar replied: 'In that case why does Ahriman allow Ormuzd to send water through his territory'—how are the digestive and excretory processes possible, how can the human body function as a unit if it belongs to two contending forces?

Rabbinic attacks on the idea of 'two powers' apply to Christianity as well as to Zoroastrianism. There are no attacks in Rabbinic literature on the doctrine of the Trinity, which emerged later in Christianity, but on the dualism implied, as the Rabbis saw it, in the doctrine of the Incarnation. Thus the third-century teacher, Rabbi Abbahu, who lived in Caesarea, where he was in close contact with Christians, preached against both Christian and Persian dualism using the verse: 'I am the first, and I am the last, and beside Me there is no God' (Isaiah 44: 6). Rabbi Abbahu comments (Midrash Exodus Rabbah 29: 5): '"I am the first", for I have no father; "and I am the last", for I have no son; "and beside Me there is no God", for I have no brother.'

In the opinion of many scholars, Jewish *eschatology has such an unmistakable affinity

with that of Zoroastrianism, in the idea of the separation of the souls of the righteous and wicked at death and in the doctrine of the *resurrection, that it is reasonable to conclude that the whole system was appropriated, as Moore puts it, from the Zoroastrians; the same applies, to some extent, to Jewish demonology (see DEMONS), especially as it developed in Babylon.

George Foot Moore, *Judaism in the First Centuries of the Christian Era* (Cambridge, Mass., 1958); see index: 'Dualism' and 'Zoroastrianism'.

**Zugot** 'Pairs', the five sets of two teachers each, whose period preceded that of the *Tannaim. The Mishnah in Ethics of the Fathers (1. 4–12), in the chain of tradition from Moses down to the Tannaim, list five pairs of teachers and their particular doctrines, although, in this source, they are not actually referred to as the Zugot. The pairs are: 1. Yose ben Yoezer and Yose ben Johanan of Jerusalem; 2. Joshua ben Perahyah and Nittai the Arebelite; 3. Judah ben Tabbai and Simeon ben Shatah; 4. Shemaiah and Avtalion; 5. Hillel and Shammai. The two teachers of the last Zug ('pair', singular of Zugot) are the founders of the two houses, Bet Hillel and Bet Shammai, the first of the Tannaim. In another Mishnah (*Ḥagigah* 2: 2) it is stated (though here, too, the actual term Zugot is not used) that the first of each pair was the Nasi ('Prince') and the second the Av Bet Din ('Father of the Court'). Some modern scholars see this attribution as an anachronism on the grounds that these two offices were not known in the early period. The date of the first Zug appears to be in the Maccabean period (see MACCABEES), 174–164 BCE. In the *Ḥagigah* passage the five sets of Zugot are said to have debated whether a man may lay his hands on the sacrifice he brings on a festival. The puzzling feature here is that this dispute, of apparently only minor significance, should have engaged the teachers over five generations. Even more puzzling is the fact that very few debates among these early teachers are recorded elsewhere in the Tannaitic literature. Even Hillel and Shammai themselves debate only a very few matters, the great debates taking place only between the houses of Hillel and Shammai. Thus the whole question of the Zugot and their role is obscure. Their importance in the later literature of the Jewish religion lies in their role as the links in the transmission of the *Oral

Torah from the Men of the *Great Synagogue down to the period of the Tannaim.

> H. L. Strack and G. Stemberger, 'The Earlier Period and the Five "Pairs"', in their *Introduction to the Talmud and Midrash*, trans. Markus Bockmuehl (Edinburgh, 1991), 69–72.

**Zunz, Leopold** German historian of Judaism (1794–1886). Zunz is rightly considered to be the foremost figure, if not the founder, of the *Jüdische Wissenschaft movement, in which Judaism is studied by the historical-critical method (and see HISTORY, FRANKEL, KROCHMAL, and RAPOPORT). Zunz received his early education at the Samson School in Wolfenbuttel, where the principal of the school referred to the young boy of 11 as a 'genius'. He settled in Berlin in 1815, studying at the University of Berlin and obtaining a doctorate from the University of Halle. Together with other young men, among them the poet Heinrich Heine, Zunz founded in Berlin in 1819 the *Verein für Cultur und Wissenschaft der Juden*. In 1823 Zunz became the editor of the *Zeitschrift für die Wissenschaft des Judentums*, in which he published a biography of *Rashi in the new, scientific mode. Unfortunately, neither the *Verein* nor the *Zeitschrift* lasted very long.

In his personal life Zunz was possessed of a fiercely independent spirit because of which he either relinquished or refused to accept various lucrative positions that were offered him, preferring to eke out a meagre livelihood as a journalist and teacher. For a time he also received a stipend from the Berlin Jewish community. Towards the end of his long life his admirers provided the means to enable him to be financially completely secure. Zunz was hardly an Orthodox Jew—he was ordained as a Rabbi by the early Reformer, Aaron Chorin, served for two years as a preacher in the Reform New Synagogue in Berlin and, it is reported, he used to write on the Sabbath—but he had a great love for the tradition, writing, for example, an essay on the high value of wearing *tefillin*. There is an element of ambiguity in Zunz. He could write in 1855: 'If there are ranks in suffering, Israel takes precedence of all the nations; if the duration of sorrows and the patience with which they are borne enoble, the Jews can challenge the aristocracy of every land; if a literature is called rich in the possession of a few classic tragedies—what shall we say to a National Tragedy lasting for fifteen

hundred years, in which the poets and the actors were also the heroes?' Yet he seems to have had little use for the Talmud and the Kabbalah and, at one time, was uncertain whether Judaism itself had a future. These facts are worthy of mention because Zunz's religious struggles were typical of the angst of all the practitioners of the new movement, who had learned to see Judaism objectively and in the context of its historical development, so that, as someone has put it, their head was without but their heart within.

Zunz's major achievement, published in 1832, is his *Die gottesdienstlichen Vorträge der Juden historisch entwickelt*. The work is a completely objective study of Jewish preaching throughout the ages and is, in fact, a pioneering effort of lasting significance to describe the evolution of *Midrash as a whole. Yet, typical of Zunz's lifelong concern with politics, it had the aim of convincing the German authorities not to ban Jewish preaching in the vernacular as an innovation (these authorities were always suspicious of innovations which might lead to rebellion). Zunz demonstrated not only that preaching had been an art in Judaism from the Rabbinic period but that the sermon was not infrequently in the vernacular. Zunz's *Namen der Juden* was written, at the behest of the Jewish community, when a royal decree ordered that Jews should not use German first names. Zunz demonstrated, again in a completely objective study, that Jews had used foreign names from an early period. Critics of the Jüdische Wissenschaft movement have maintained that its practitioners, with one eye on the effect of their researches on the Gentile world, were never really objective. Zunz, at least, showed that it was possible for a great scholar to pursue his researches in a completely objective manner while frankly acknowledging that he had an axe to grind in the process. Zunz was objective, too, in his biblical studies. At first these were on the later books of the Bible, but later on he espoused the full critical methodology with regard to the *Pentateuch as well (see BIBLICAL CRITICISM).

> Nathan Stern, 'Leopold Zunz', in his *The Jewish Historico-Critical School of the Nineteenth Century* (New York, 1901) 37–50.
> L. Wallach, *Liberty and Letters; The Thought of Leopold Zunz* (London, 1959).

**Zusya of Hanipol** Hasidic master and hero of Hasidic folk-tales (d. 1800). Zusya was attracted to *Hasidism in his youth, becoming a disciple of *Dov Baer, the Maggid of Mezhirech, and encouraging his brother Elimelech to join him. Zusya was not noted for his learning, unlike his brother who became the famous *Zaddik of Lizansk and author of the Hasidic classic, *Noam Elimelekh*. Zusya's fame rests on his generous disposition and his charismatic personality. He was less of a leader (though he did have a small following of Hasidim) than a model of Hasidic piety, pursuing his quest in solitude and influencing others more by his example than by his teachings, of which very few are recorded in Hasidic books. The later Hasidic master, Israel of Ruzhyn, noted that of all the disciples of the Maggid, Zusya was unable to pass on what he had learned because as soon as the Maggid had begun to quote Scripture, Zusya would break out in such ecstatic shouting that he had to leave the room. Together with his brother, Zusya wandered from place to place both as a penance and in order to participate in the exile of the *Shekhinah. The Hasidim love to tell of the adventures which befell the two brothers in their journeys. Typical of Zusya's individualistic approach as a 'fool of God' is his reported saying that when he reached the judgement seat he would not be asked why he was not a Moses or a Rabbi *Akiba but why he was not a Zusya. In a Hasidic tale which illustrates Zusya's acceptance of *suffering in simple faith, the Maggid was asked how it is possible, as the Rabbis say, for a man to thank God for his sufferings with the same joy as when he thanks God for his good fortune. The Maggid directed his questioners to Zusya, a man whose days were full of pain and adversity but who replied: 'It is, indeed, a great difficulty but I am not the person you should consult since I have never known a day's suffering all my life.' Like the other Hasidic masters, Zusya, for all his constant communion with God, loved the Jewish people. It is said of him that whenever he met a Jewish boy he would bless him with the words: 'Be healthy and strong as a goy.'

Martin Buber, 'Zusya of Hanipol', in his *Tales of the Hasidim: The Early Masters* (New York, 1947), 235–52.

**Zweifel, Eliezer** Russian author (1815–88), representative of the moderate tendency in the *Haskalah. Zweifel was born in Mogilev into a family of *Habad Hasidim, acquiring in his youth a very sound knowledge not only of the Bible and Talmud but also of the Kabbalah; he educated himself too in Russian, German, and general secular learning. He wrote extensively in a good Hebrew style but all his work is vitiated by his extreme verbosity and lack of systematic arrangements of the topics with which he deals. His copious quotes from other authors display his tremendous erudition in all branches of Jewish thought, but they often hinder rather than advance his arguments. In this respect, however, Zweifel's works can still serve as anthologies of Jewish teachings on many important subjects. In 1853 Zweifel was appointed lecturer in the Talmud at the government-sponsored Rabbinical Seminary in Zhitomir, remaining there and influencing the students towards a greater appreciation of the tradition until the seminary was closed in 1873. Both by training and temperament Zweifel, as he rightly claimed, tended to see good in everything. Though a staunch defender of Judaism and the Jewish tradition he acknowledged the value of the Haskalah's critique of strict Orthodoxy and, though viewing some aspects of *Hasidism as irrational and superstitious, he warmly espoused the cause of the movement against its enemies. His opponents accused him of lacking the ability to make up his mind. His very name, Zweifel, meaning 'doubt', they said, suited him entirely.

The two main works of Zweifel are *Sanegor* ('Counsel for the Defence'), published in Warsaw in 1885, and *Shalom Al Yisrael* ('Peace upon Israel'), published in Zhitomir and Vilna between 1868 and 1873. The *Sanegor*, as its name applies, consists of a vigorous defence of the Talmud, Jewish law, and traditional Jewish opinions. The first part of the work is an introduction to the whole. Part 2 is a defence of the Talmud against its denigration by the English missionary, Alexander McCaul, whose book, *Old Paths*, had been translated into Hebrew by a Jewish convert to *Christianity (under the title *Netivot Olam*,) and had created a stir among Russia Jews. Part 3 has the aim of exposing the calumny that Jewish law discriminates against women. Parts 4 and 5 seek to demonstrate that the alleged hostility of Jews towards *Gentiles has no foundation and that Talmudic passages said to express such hostility have been misunderstood. Zweifel's defence partakes more of apologetics than sound scholarship. For all that, it contains material that has been effectively employed by subsequent defenders of Judaism.

*Shalom Al Yisrael* is concerned with what Zweifel considers to be the unfortunate rift between Hasidism and its opponents, especially the Maskilim. In Zweifel's view, Hasidism contains numerous elevated teachings on God and spirituality, many of which he quotes, without always giving the sources accurately. True to his compromising attitude, he acknowledges that there are less worthy ideas in Hasidism and he naïvely appeals to renowned Hasidic masters to rid Hasidism of these. The work pleased neither the Hasidim nor the Maskilim, the latter maintaining that Zweifel had sold out, betraying the Haskalah in favour of the irrational in religion. Here, too, Zweifel's work was unsatisfactory as scholarship but it succeeded in paving the way for a better appreciation of Hasidism and, in a sense, for sound scholarly work to be done on the movement in modern times. It is no accident that the work was republished in photostat (Jerusalem, 1970).

Meyer Waxman, 'Eliezer Zweifel', in his *A History of Jewish Literature* (South Brunswick, NJ, New York, and London, 1960), iii. 315–18.

# Reference Works

Articles on various aspects of the Jewish religion are found in the two general encyclopaedias: James Hastings (ed.), *Encyclopedia of Religion and Ethics*, 12 vols. and an Index vol. (Edinburgh, 1908) (abbreviation: *ERE*); and Mircea Eliade (ed.), *The Encyclopedia of Religion*, 16 vols. (New York, 1987) (abbreviation: *ER*). Both these have bibliographies at the end of the articles. *ERE* is well written by competent scholars and is still worth consulting, provided it is kept in mind that it has long been out of date and that religion is understood throughout in 'Occidental' terms. *ER* redresses the balance but is rather too 'Oriental' in its thrust and some of the articles on the Jewish religion are less comprehensive than those in *ERE*.

There are three encyclopaedias in English dealing solely with Jews and Judaism, all containing articles in which every aspect of the Jewish religion is treated thoroughly. Isidore Singer (ed.), *The Jewish Encyclopedia*, 12 vols. (New York, 1901 and various editions until 1926), has long been an indispensable work (abbreviation: *JE*) but is obviously dated. Isaac Landman (ed.), *The Universal Jewish Encyclopedia*, 10 vols. (New York, 1939) (abbreviation: *UJE*), was published before the Holocaust and the establishment of the State of Israel, and is now, on these grounds and others, also hopelessly out of date. The most up to date of the three is: Cecil Roth and Geoffrey Wigoder (eds. in Chief), *Encyclopedia Judaica*, 16 vols. with additional yearbooks from time to time (Jerusalem, 1972) (abbreviation: *EJ*). The student of the Jewish religion who consults these three works will notice the differences in both approach and the weight given to the various subjects. The articles on the Kabbalah in *JE* and *UJE* (where the English form 'Cabala' is preferred) rely almost entirely (as can be seen from the bibliographies appended to the articles) on nineteenth-century scholarship, while the article in *EJ* is by Gershom Scholem who revolutionized the study of the this subject; it constitutes a large book in itself and was later published as such. Perhaps naturally for the time when it was compiled, *UJE* is too apologetic in tone in the articles on Jewish–Gentile relations. The subject of Talmud in *UJE* and *EJ* is treated in far too perfunctory a manner for such an important subject compared with the rich detail on the subject in *JE*, although *UJE* and *EJ* are, naturally, more abreast of recent scholarship. The study of Hasidism has come into its own after World War II and this is reflected in the wide survey of the subject and the list of Hasidic dynasties and their relationship to one another in *EJ*, compared with the totally unsatisfactory treatment in *JE* and *UJE*. The student is well advised, therefore, when using these three reference works, to note the many points of difference and to try to achieve a balanced view of his or her own; this is no defect but rather a gain in serious study.

There are a number of single-volume works, without bibliographies, useful for quick reference: Cecil Roth (ed. in chief), *The Standard Jewish Encyclopedia* (New York, 1962); its successor: Geoffrey Wigoder (ed.), *The Encyclopedia of Judaism* (New York, 1989); Alan Unterman, *Dictionary of Jewish Lore and Legend* (London, 1991); and, dealing with general Jewish culture in modern times and not primarily with the Jewish religion: Glenda Abramson (ed.), *The Blackwell Companion to Jewish Culture* (Oxford, 1989) (this work does include up-to-date bibliographies).

Works on the Jewish religion are listed in: *The Study of Judaism: Bibliographical Essays*, published by the Anti-Defamation League of B'nai B'rith (New York, 1972) and in Barry Holtz (ed.), *The Schocken Guide to Jewish Books* (New York, 1992), containing sufficient bibliographical material in English to last more than a lifetime of application to study.

The following are among the most important works in English on Jewish history (naturally containing a good deal of material on the Jewish religion). Heinrich Graetz's

*History of the Jews*, translated by various hands, 6 vols. (Philadelphia, 1944), is now largely itself only of historical interest. Graetz's notes in the original German, for which the work is justly famed, have been omitted. The value has been widely acknowledged of the single volume: *A History of the Jewish People* by Max L. Margolis and Alexander Marks (Philadelphia, 1944), very dry and unexciting but making up for it in accuracy. The same applies to H. H. Ben-Sasson, *A History of the Jewish People* (Cambridge, Mass., 1976). More readable surveys are provided in Jeremy Silver and Bernard Martin, *A History of Judaism*, 2 vols., with useful bibliographies (New York, 1974); and in Robert M. Seltzer, *Jewish People, Jewish Thought: The Jewish Experience in History* (New York, 1981). The most erudite work on Jewish history in English is Salo Wittmayer Baron, *A Social and Religious History of the Jews*, 18 vols. (New York, 1952–83). Baron intended to bring his history down to the present but died after the completion of the eighteenth volume. Baron's copious notes and bibliographies still provide a mine of information for scholars—mine is the right metaphor, since much digging is needed to extract the gold in view of the odd arrangement of the material. Menahem Mansoor's *Jewish History and Thought: An Introduction* (Hoboken, NJ, 1991), is a valuable, concise survey, particluarly useful for dates.

Religious literature, personalities, and movements are fully examined in the two huge histories of Jewish literature in general: Meyer Waxman, *A History of Jewish Literature*, 6 vols. (South Brunswick, NJ, New York, and London, 1960); and Israel Zinberg, *A History of Jewish Literature*, trans. and ed. Bernard Martin, 12 vols. (Cleveland and London, 1972–8). Zinberg's captivating style and the sumptuous standard in which the volumes have been produced make him more easy to read than Waxman, but both works treat the subject in a scholarly manner and are the only wide-ranging works on the subject in English.

Religious thought is studied in the two works in English on Jewish philosophy: Isaac Husik, *A History of Mediaeval Jewish Philosophy* (New York, 1940); and Julius Guttmann, *Philosophies of Judaism*, trans. David W. Silverman (Philadelphia, 1964). Husik's work is confined to the medieval thinkers but treats these in great detail. Guttmann's work brings the story down to modern times.

## The Bible

It is unfortunate that, until recently, Jewish biblical scholarship has lagged behind non-Jewish scholarship with the result that the serious student of the Jewish religion cannot afford to ignore the work of the non-Jewish scholars who have explored the 'Old Testament' from every angle. Ideally there should be no such thing as Jewish or Christian scholarship but, human nature being what it is, the religious stance of each biblical scholar is bound to influence his attitude, for all his striving for complete objectivity. The very fact that Christians refer to the Hebrew Bible as the 'Old Testament' is in itself a cause for concern, from the scholarly point of view, in that it implies that there is a 'New Testament' to which the 'Old' is the prelude; which is not to imply that all Jewish biblical scholars are free from their own religious bias. Nevertheless, there has emerged a consensus among both Jewish and Christian biblical scholars (and among scholars who are adherents of neither the Jewish nor the Christian religion) that it is possible and desirable to study the Bible on its own terms. The vast majority of works in English on the Bible have been compiled by non-Jewish scholars. The student of the Jewish religion is bound to take these into account while, if he is religiously committed to Judaism, making his own theological adjustment, even if he is not prepared to go along the whole way with Solomon Schechter's one-time dubbing of the higher criticism as 'the higher anti-Semitism'.

Works in English on the Hebrew Bible by non-Jewish scholars are far too numerous to mention here but three works can be noted as typical, which the student can supplement from his or her own reading. These are: *Peake's Commentary on the Bible*, ed. Matthew Black and H. H. Rowley (London and Edinburgh, 1962); Martin Noth, *The Old Testament World* (London, 1966); and Otto Eissfeldt, *The Old Testament: An Introduction*, trans. Peter R. Ackroyd (Oxford, 1966). Two works on the Pentateuch by Jewish scholars are: J. H. Hertz, *The Pentateuch and Haftorahs* (London, 1960); and W. Gunther Plaut, *The Torah: A Modern Commentary* (New York, 1981). Dr Hertz was the British Chief Rabbi and his Orthodox bias shows in his many attacks, often unwarranted, on the documentary hypothesis and, indeed, on the whole modern critical enterprise. But Hertz's work is still very valuable as a good devotional commentary in which the full flavour of Jewish piety is evident throughout. Plaut, a distinguished Reform Rabbi, faces squarely the critical question and his work is one of sound scholarship, for which, however, he often pays with the absence of anything approaching the devotional character of Hertz's work. The 'Hertz Chumash' was published by the Soncino Press, responsible for many fine works of Jewish literature and religion. The Soncino Press also published, under the editorship of Dr A. Cohen, a commentary to all the books of the Hebrew Bible by serious authors, which has gone into many editions. The books of the Soncino Bible, although conservative in attitude, do take fully into account the findings of modern scholarship. Since the Soncino had already published the Hertz Chumash this Press published a separate Soncino commentary to the Pentateuch, also under the editorship of Dr Cohen: *The Soncino Chumash: The Five Books of Moses with Haphtaroth*, which has also gone into many editions. *The Soncino Chumash* avoids the problem of criticism in connection with the Pentateuch by providing a novel commentary which is really a digest of the standard medieval Jewish commentaries. More recently, the critical problem was faced head-on in the commentary to the Pentateuch published by the Jewish Publication Society of America: *The JPS Torah Commentary*, under the editorship of Nahum M. Sarna (Philadelphia, New York, and Jerusalem, 1989–94). In this commentary, with extensive scholarly notes, the books of Genesis and Exodus are by Sarna himself, the book of Leviticus by Baruch A. Levine, Numbers by Jacob Milgrom, and Deuteronomy by Jeffrey H. Tigay. The tone is set in the preface:

In the last century, a new way of looking at the Bible developed. Research into the ancient Near East and its texts recreated for us the civilizations out of which the Bible emerged. In this century, there has been a revival of Jewish biblical scholarship; Israeli and American scholars, in particular, concentrating in the fields of archaeology, biblical history, Semitic languages, and the religion of Israel, have opened exciting new vistas into the world of the Scriptures. For the first time in history, we have at our disposal information and methodological tools that enable us to explore the biblical text in a way that could never have been done before. This new world of knowledge, as seen through the eyes of contemporary Jewish scholars and utilizing at the same time the insights of over twenty centuries of traditional Jewish exegesis, is now available for the first time to a general audience in *The JPS Torah Commentary*.

It is for the reader to decide whether or not this attempt to wed the tradition with modern scholarship has been entirely successful. (Throughout, for example, the Mosaic authorship of the whole of the Pentateuch is denied implicitly but this is nowhere stated explicitly.) Yet the *JPS Commentary* will undoubtedly be acknowledged as the standard Jewish commentary to the 'Chumash', although the absence of the Haftarot prevent it being used for services in the synagogue.

For the 'intertestamental period' the standard work is R. H. Charles, *The Apocrypha and Pseudepigrapha of the Old Testament in English* (Oxford, 1913). The standard edition of Josephus is that of the Loeb Classical Library, with the English translation side by side with the original (Cambridge, Mass., 1978); of Philo, in the same Library (1929–67).

### Talmud and Midrash

Herbert Danby's translation of the Mishnah into English with a learned introduction and notes is justly a classic: *The Mishnah* (Oxford, 1933 and subsequent editions). This work is a remarkable achievement for a non-Jewish scholar, despite a number of errors. The Soncino Press published, under the editorship of Dr Isidore Epstein, its famous English translation of the Talmud: *The Babylonian Talmud*, 35 vols. including an Index vol. (London, 1948–52 and subsequent editions). Each of the Talmudic tractates is translated by a competent scholar who provides notes to clarify the text. In a work of such magnitude some mistakes are inevitable and the translation itself is sometimes unclear. The editor's notes (in square brackets) in particular, call attention to the historical background and the opinions of modern scholars on the subjects which the Talmud happens to be discussing. The Israeli scholar Adin Steinsaltz translated many Talmudic tractates into Hebrew in which a degree of modern Talmudic scholarship is drawn upon, but there could have been more. *The Talmud: The Steinsaltz Edition* (New York, 1989 onwards), consists of translations of some of these into English, including an introductory volume on the Talmud in general. In these expensive but beautifully produced works, the English translation is printed side by side with the original text. Some tractates of the Talmud were published with an English translation side by side with the original text, in the ArtScroll series: *Talmud Bavli*, ed. Hersh Goldwurm and Nosson Scherman (New York, 1990 onwards). The ArtScroll publishers have also published, under the same editors, a multi-volume translation of the whole of the Mishnah (1982 onwards). The ArtScroll series generally is hostile to modern, critical scholarship and many of the notes are unhistorical, yet, more than the other translations, the ArtScroll series manages very successfully to capture the flavour of Talmud study as this has been pursued in the traditional Yeshivot for centuries.

A number of Midrashim have been translated into English, among them: Jacob Z. Lauterbach, *Mekhilta de-Rabbi Ishmael* (Philadelphia, 1976); H. Freedman and Maurice Simon, *The Midrash Rabbah* (London, 1977); and William G. Braude's fine translations, published in the Yale Judaica Series: *The Midrash on Psalms* (New Haven, 1959) and *Pesikta Rabbati* (New Haven, 1968). Together with Israel J. Kapstein, Braude also translated *Tanna De Be Eliyahu* (Philadelphia, 1981). Still another translation by Braude, a giant in the field, is: *The Book of Legends Sefer Ha-Aggadah: Legends from the Talmud and Midrash*, ed. Hayim Nahman Bialik and Yehoshua Hana Ravnitzky (New York, 1992). This is an anthology culled by the Hebrew poet Bialik and is a treasury of Talmudic and Midrashic teachings and stories.

The religious thought of the Talmudic Rabbis is presented in *A Rabbinic Anthology*, selected by C. G. Montefiore and H. Loewe (London, 1938); George Foot Moore, *Judaism in the First Centuries of the Christian Era* (Cambridge, Mass., 1958); Solomon Schechter, *Aspects of Rabbinic Theology* (New York, 1901; paperback, 1961); and E. E. Urbach, *The Sages: Their Concepts and Beliefs*, trans. Israel Abrahams (Jerusalem, 1979). All four works are scholarly and objective but Montefiore, a Liberal Jew, and Loewe, an Orthodox Jew, use the occasion also to debate, in a highly polished English, the theological issue of Reform and Orthodoxy. Their work is less important for what it tells about the Rabbis than for what it has to say about Montefiore and Loewe.

Of introductions to the Talmud in English the earliest was that of Moses Mielziner, published in the fourth edition as *Intoduction to the Talmud*, with a new bibliography (1925–67), rather sketchy but still useful. The title of Jacob Shachter's *The Student's Guide through the Talmud* (London, 1952), is misleading. The work is, in fact, a translation, with notes, of a work by the nineteenth-century scholar Z. H. Chajes and really consists of a series of essays on the Talmud rather than a guide or an introduction. H. L. Strack's *Introduction to the Talmud and Midrash* (Philadelphia, 1945), contains a good deal of information from secondary sources (far too much) but is inadequate in its treatment of the Talmudic and Midrashic texts themselves. H. L. Strack and G. Stemberger, *Introduction to the Talmud and Midrash*, trans. Markus Bockmuehl (Edinburgh, 1991), although based on the original Strack, is in fact a fresh work by Stemberger and has fast become the standard guide to the Talmud and Midrash in any language. Nevertheless, the original Strack is still worth consulting for the material that Stemberger omits. Stemberger's bibliographies refer the reader to scholars writing in English on the Talmud such as Louis Ginzberg, Louis Finkelstein, Joseph Heinemann, Jacob Neusner, and others, whom the student can consult to his or her great advantage. (The awkward 'his or her' is used intentionally, since a new feature of Jewish intellectual life is the interest of women in studying the Talmud, some even teaching Talmud in higher institutions of learning.) A. Cohen's *Everyman's Talmud*

(London, 1940), consists of an anthology of Talmudic views on many subjects with Dr Cohen providing the links and the interpretation. The work is prized as English literature and has been published in the Everyman's Library series of classical works in English.

## Religious Belief and Practice

The three works in English in which Jewish theology is presented systematically are: Kaufmann Kohler, *Jewish Theology Systematically and Historically Considered* (New edn., Ktav and New York, 1968); Samuel S. Cohon, *Jewish Theology* (Assen, 1971); Louis Jacobs, *A Jewish Theology* (London, and New York, 1973). The first two approach the subject from the Reform point of view, the third from the moderately Conservative point of view. M. Friedlander, *The Jewish Religion* (2nd edn.; London, 1900), represents the view of right-wing Orthodoxy, and Morris Joseph, *Judaism as Creed and Life* (London, 1903), the view of moderate Reform as followed in Anglo-Jewry. These last two are now out of date but are worth consulting for some interesting material not found elsewhere. Nick Gillman's *Sacred Fragments: Recovering Theology for the Modern Jew* (Philadelphia, 1990), lives up to its subtitle.

The medieval Jewish thinkers have been well served by translators into English. Saadiah Gaon's major work has been translated from the Arabic by Samuel Rosenblatt: *Saadia Gaon: The Book of Beliefs and Opinions* (New Haven, 1948). There are two translations of Bahya, Ibn Pakudah: *Duties of the Heart*, trans. Moses Hyamson (Jerusalem and New York, 1970); *The Book of Directions of the Duties of the Heart*, translated from the original Arabic version by Menahem Mansoor (London, 1973). For Judah Halevi's *Kuzari* there is: *Kitab Al Khazari*, translated from the Arabic by Hartwig Hirschfeld (new revised edn.; London, 1931). A good deal, but not the whole, of Maimonides' great Code has been translated in the Yale Judaica Series: *Mishneh Torah* (New Haven, 1949–65). There are two editions of M. Friedlander's translation of Maimonides' *Guide: The Guide of the Perplexed*, 3 vols. (London, 1881); and *The Guide for the Perplexed*, 1 vol. (London, 1936). The first work has excellent notes by Friedlander but has long been out of print. Friedlander, in the earlier work, gives the title as *Guide of the Perplexed* but in the second as *Guide for the Perplexed*. The original lends itself to either form. The best translation is that of Shlomo Pines: *The Guide of the Perplexed*, 2 vols. (Chicago, 1974). Albo's work has been published in translation together with the original Hebrew text: *Sefer-'Ikkarim Book of Principles*, trans. Isaac Husik, 5 vols. (Philadelphia, 1946).

On Jewish practice, Hyman E. Goldin, *Code of Jewish Law*, revised edn. (New York, 1961), gives the strict Orthodox view; Isaac Klein, *A Guide to Jewish Religious Practice* (New York, 1979), the moderate Orthodox or, better, the right-wing Conservative view; and Samuel S. Cohon, *What We Jews Believe & A Guide to Jewish Practice* (Assen, 1971), the Reform point of view. The titles of the two popular illustrated books by Louis Jacobs describe the contents: *The Book of Jewish Belief* (New York, 1984) and *The Book of Jewish Practice* (New York, 1987).

## Mysticism

A comprehensive bibliography on Jewish mysticism is provided by Sheila A. Spector, *Jewish Mysticism: An Annotated Bibliography on the Kabbalah in English* (New York and London, 1984). Gershom G. Scholem, *Major Trends in Jewish Mysticism* (London, 1955), is the standard survey of the subject, although much work in this field has been done by Scholem and his school and by many others since then. The same applies to Hasidism for which, in addition to the many bibliographies provided in the encyclopaedias, there should be consulted: *Essential Papers on Hasidism*, ed. Gershon David Hundert (New York, 1991). The translation of the Zohar into English by the Soncino Press is still used extensively by students of the greatest treatise on the Kabbalah: *The Zohar*, trans. Harry Sperling and Maurice Simon, 5 vols. (London and Bournemouth, 1949). But some of the most important and most difficult sections of the Zohar have not been translated at all. Moreover, the translation, although in good English, is bound to leave the reader puzzled owing to the absence of notes. The Zohar is written in a kind of code and in such a work notes for the decoding are essential. More satisfactory in every way is Isaiah Tishby, *The Wisdom of the Zohar*, trans. David Goldstein (The Littman Library of Jewish Civilization; Oxford, 1989). In this work, in three large volumes, the major passages in the Zohar are translated and arranged according to subject, with excellent introductions and learned notes. Daniel Chanan Matt, *Zohar: The Book of Enlightenment* (London, 1983), provides a translation of a few sections of the Zohar presented as poetry. Matt's suggestion that the Zohar was intended to be read as poetry rather than prose is unsubstantiated but the work does convey the mystical flights of the original and has a useful introduction. Roy A. Rosenberg has translated, with an introduction and notes, the sections in the Zohar omitted in the Soncino translation: the Book of Concealment, the Great Holy Assembly and the Lesser Holy Assembly, and the Assembly of the Tabernacle, with the startling title: *The Anatomy of God* (Ktav, New York, 1973). An earlier translation of these sections, from the Latin version of Knorr von Rosenroth, is: *The Kabbalah Unveiled*, trans. S. L. Macgregor Mathers (London, 1968). This work must be treated with caution, as must the quirky work in an odd form of English: A. E. Waite, *The Holy Kabbalah* (New York, 1969). Both these last two works, though containing some important insights into the Kabbalah, have enjoyed popularity in circles more interested in the occult than in the serious study of the Kabbalah. As Kenneth Rexroth remarks in his introduction to the Waite book:

A. E. Waite was an odd fish out of an odder barrel. He was not only one of the few persons in modern times, Jew or Gentile, to write a sensible and sound book on Kabbalah. He was a genuine scholar of occultism who himself came out of the welter of occult sects and movements of the end of the last century. He lived in the world of Eliphas Levi, Stanislas de Guaita, 'Papus', Sar Peladan, Mme Blavatsky, A. P. Sinnett, Macgregor Mathers, Whynn Westcost, Annie Besant, and 'Archbishop' Leadbeater, and more American oddities and rascals than you could shake a stick at.

All this would have been totally out of place in a book on the Jewish religion were it not for the fact that 'occultists' and 'New Agers' tend to rely on the Kabbalah and interpret works such as the Zohar in a way the authors would never have recognized.

## Modern Jewish Thought

Practically every book on the Jewish religion refers to the problems and challenges to the tradition presented by modern thought. The works dealing with this subject are far too numerous to list. A few helpful introductions should, however, be noted. Two books by Jacob B. Agus analyse the problem: *Modern Philosophies of Judaism* (New York, 1941; paperback, 1970); *Guideposts in Modern Judaism: An Analysis of Current Trends in Jewish Thought* (New York, 1954). Other works on similar lines are: Samuel H. Bergman, *Faith and Reason: An Introduction to Modern Jewish Thought*, trans. Alfred Jospe (Washington, 1961; paperback, New York, 1963); Joseph L. Blau, *Modern Varieties of Judaism* (New York, 1966); Nathan Roternstreich, *Tradition and Reality: The Impact of History on Modern Jewish Thought* (New York, 1973). Two symposia should also be mentioned: Joseph Zeitlin, *Disciples of the Wise: The Religious and Social Opinions of American Rabbis* (New York, 1970); and: *The Conditions of Jewish Belief: A Symposium Compiled by the Editors of* Commentary *Magazine* (Northvale, NJ and London, 1989). A very interesting attempt at compiling a dictionary in which Jewish thinkers from different denominations as well as secularists discuss religious concepts in the light of their own understanding is Arthur P. Cohen and Paul Mender-Flohr (eds.), *Contemporary Jewish Religious Thought* (New York, 1987).